North by West

A History of the Crampin Steam Fishing Company and a Personal Life Story

Bill Crampin

First published in Great Britain in 2017 by

Bannister Publications Ltd
118 Saltergate
Chesterfield
Derbyshire S40 1NG

Copyright © Bill Crampin
ISBN 978-1-909813-35-9

Bill Crampin asserts the moral right to be identified
as the author of this work

A catalogue record for this book is available from the British Library

This book is sold subject to the condition that it shall not, by way of trade or otherwise, be lent, re-sold, hired out or otherwise circulated without the copyright holder's prior consent in any form of binding or cover other than that in which it is published and without a similar condition including this condition being imposed on the subsequent purchase.

All rights reserved. No part of this book may be reproduced or transmitted in any form or by any means, electronic or mechanical including photocopying, recording or by any information storage and retrieval system, without permission from the copyright holder, in writing.

Typeset in Palatino Linotype by Escritor Design, Bournemouth

Printed and bound by CMP UK Ltd, Great Britain

*This book is dedicated to my children,
Lucy, Thomas and Sophie,
and to my grandchildren,
Hamish, George, Rowan,
Charlie, Freddie, William, Archie,
Alice & …..?*

Contents

Preface v

Introduction vii

Origins 1

A Parallel History of the 19

Waltham 27

Harry's Inventions 33

Abbey Road, and Infant and Junior School 39

Senior School and the Holiday Bungalow 43

Working on the Docks and Going to Sea 49

Between the Docks and University 61

What to Do Next? 65

My Own Practice as an Architect 69

And so into Retirement 73

The Crampin Steam Fishing Company Photographs and Press Records 75

Appendix: My Most Memorable Trip to Sea 113

About the Author 123

Preface

WHEN THE WEATHER is bad it is often not possible for trawlers to transit the Pentland Firth (the Firth), that stretch of water that lies between North East Scotland and the Orkney Islands. Several tides meet at this point and in high winds the seas can be almost vertically sided and coming at you from all directions, added to which there could be adverse tides running.

I recall when I was on the Statham with Skipper Alan Whitelam in 1967; we were transiting the Firth and ploughing ahead at 13.5 knots. Alan took a bearing of the lighthouse, and another bearing a few minutes later. He demonstrated that our speed over the ground was, unbelievably, virtually zero and would remain so until there was a change in the tides.

Under these circumstances, trawlers would sometimes opt to leave the Orkneys to port and sail around Dennis Head, which was a greater distance but considerably more comfortable.

Should it be decided to run the gauntlet of the Firth, then a course of

North by West

will pretty much get you to Southeast Iceland, leaving the Faroes to starboard. The ultimate destination was usually the North Cape of Iceland, which lies at the north western point of Iceland. The magnetic variation here is approximately 29 degrees west, so there is a huge difference between magnetic and true north, caused by the magnetic volcanic anomalies in the area. Until about 1956 all trawlers used only magnetic compasses, so extreme care in navigation was essential.

Fishing was, therefore, carried out mostly above the Arctic Circle, which lies at 67.5 degrees north. Hence, the possibilities of appalling weather, together with dangerous icing conditions, were never far away.

Iceland was the most common fishing ground for deep water trawlers, but even in the 1920s and 1930s these sturdy vessels would fish grounds as far apart as the west coast of Greenland, Spitsbergen, Bear Island, the Barents (White) Sea and Murmansk.

Pride of the Crampin Steam Fishing Company Fleet, the steam trawler Statham arrives in Grimsby after her delivery trip from the builders, Rickmers Werft, in Bremerhaven, 1956.

Introduction

This is a project I have been meaning to undertake for some time. As we get older, how often do we wish we had learnt and recorded more about our roots and family history before our grandparents and relatives died off? In my case, very often, because I have a fascinating family background, involving, inter alia, the creation from nothing, by my grandfather, of a major, deep-sea trawling business, which became one of the largest in the UK between the First and Second World Wars. A wealth of interesting family personalities, talents and hang-ups, only serves to add interest to a complex picture. Good knowledge about my family goes back about a century, and my purpose in writing this for my family is to put an end to nature's habit of depriving them of information about their own backgrounds.

What a time to have lived! In the eternity of the millions of years of the human occupation of this planet, we have been privileged to see, within only two generations, the application of electric light, the telephone, the motor car, the aeroplane, the television, space travel, the mobile telephone and the computer, not to mention huge progress in medical and all other forms of science!

Evolution may become even more rapid as the power of technology grows exponentially. My hope is that each of my children, and theirs in turn, will extend this story through their own lifetimes in their own individual directions. Within a few generations, their descendants will have fascinating historical accounts, and will truly understand their own roots and where their genes came from, and will perhaps understand why they excel at certain things and may have difficulties with others.

The key thing is to start before one becomes too senile, before recollections fade and before sources of information disappear. It is now 2006, and I am 59. (It is now actually 2016 and I am 70, so I've been at this for ten years!) When I think that my paternal grandfather was born in 1872 and that his grandfather would, therefore, have been born in about 1820, it becomes clear just how many years one can go back in a few generations. My grandfather died aged 84 at 7.30pm on November 30th 1956, when I was aged 10. The fact that I remember the time and date so well may convey to you something of the greatness of this man, of which there will be more later. Had I been able to have a good conversation with him, I would have had direct knowledge, through him AND HIS grandfather, of the Georgian age! Similarly, I could have extracted more information from my father, mother, uncles and aunts, which would have contained a wealth of interest. I do not want this mistake to be perpetuated.

It is a sad fact that I know practically nothing of the history of my mother's side of the family. The personalities were not as strong, and everything seemed to get subsumed into my father's side.

What I would say to my children and others is that they should make a start sooner rather than later, and make at least some record of every stage of their lives. It is surprising how memories fade, chronologies become confused and how things that seemed unimportant at the time acquire a different perspective later in life.

1

Origins

Our family story centres around the town of Grimsby in North Lincolnshire, although I was only the third generation of my family to live there. I understand that on my father's side, way back, we were of Huguenot origin, that is to say French protestants, so we anticipated the European Union by a couple of centuries or so!

Although our family tree is now traced back to Samuel Crampin in 1788, the family that I knew well consisted of my grandfather, Herbert George Crampin, my grandmother, Betsy Ann (nee Robinson), and their four children, my uncle Herbert Walter, my aunts Betsy Emma ('Betty') and Sarah Abigail, and my father Harry. Two other children, who died very early on in life, were John Fitzroy and Alice May. Grandma and Grandpa lived at 385 Grimsby Road, Cleethorpes: a once-beautiful Victorian villa. My uncle, Herbert Walter, married Dorothy Culham, and produced my cousins, Norman and Margaret. A third child, Marjorie, died at a very young age in 1929. They lived on Vaughan Avenue, Cleethorpes. My aunt Betty never married; she lived partly at Harrogate, where my grandfather had bought a large house in case of war time evacuation from Grimsby, and partly at 'Silverdale', an elegant house on the edge of The Park in Grimsby. Sarah married Cedric Wilson, a keen motor enthusiast. My grandfather bought a garage for him to run, Bratleys, at Toll Bar, New Waltham, but I do not believe this was ever a great success. They produced my cousins, Janice and Lesley. My father Harry, married Dorothy Enid Buxton, and they produced my elder sister Gibby, me and my younger brothers, Leon and Tex. My strongest recollection is of the Christmases we spent at '385' with uncles, aunts and cousins – they were very special. Cedric was killed at Swallow crossroads, just south of Grimsby, when his racing car came off the road and overturned.

So these, then, are the personalities I knew well. Others referred to in what follows are relations we were told about, or read about in various articles or letters on family history. And so to the history...

***

My paternal grandfather, Herbert George Crampin, was born in Shelford, near Guildford, in 1872, and spent his early years in the village of Beaumont in Essex. He moved to London, probably aged about twelve, and secured an apprenticeship in the whip trade. I picked up the following information from his two daughters, my aunts Sarah and Betty, and I believe it to be accurate because they were still only middle aged at the time of our conversations, and were able to confer with each other at the time. Yes, it was a bit like the Maurice Chevalier song *Oh Yes, I Remember It Well*, but I think I managed to distil the essence.

He was very poor during his time in London, and one story goes that he would wait outside a café, until a slightly thicker sandwich seemed like the next to be sold, and then proffer the appropriate (old) penny. This was clearly not a question of greed, but was about the need to survive at a time when the only other option, entry to the workhouse, seemed somewhat less than attractive! A fierce sense of independence and self-sufficiency was, therefore, clearly built into this seemingly barbaric way of life. But its advantages, for him, were to manifest themselves later.

After, I imagine, a couple of years, my grandfather – let's call him HG – met with a well-to-do gentleman called Mr Towers. The circumstances of their meeting are not clear, but Mr Towers was obviously impressed by something about HG because he offered to take him into his service as a page, an offer that was accepted. I can only interpolate timescales here, but my best guess is that he stayed with Mr Towers for a year or two, after which he would have been aged about 15 or 16. During that time, HG would have been exposed to a totally different side of life, sophistication, probably the landed gentry, and would also have had Mr Towers taking a special interest in him and doing something about HG's basic educational skills. I can well imagine that this would have impressed HG, and may have been the root of his own aspirations to succeed in his own right. He would also have been influenced by the kindness of Mr Towers; HG turned out to be a very kind and considerate person. I learnt very early on from this that you don't need to be a 'head banger' to succeed in business – but you do need to have high standards and insist on them being applied.

The date, by then, would be about 1888, and the new rail network was being expanded throughout Lincolnshire, up to and including Grimsby. Fishing was already carried out from Grimsby, which is a natural port on the south bank of the River Humber. The extension of the rail network, however, brought with it the possibility of supplying fresh fish direct to Billingsgate, London and elsewhere, which had enormous potential for the port.

HG knew he had relations in Grimsby who carried out fishing in a small way: in wooden smacks and small line-fishing vessels on the North Sea. I believe HG first sailed with the trawler owners Moody and Kelly. HG also had an uncle, William

Wesney Crampin, who was probably the founder of the first Crampin Steam Fishing Company. Thanks to the research of my cousin Norman, we do know quite a bit about William Wesney, and it is timely to take a closer look at his life before returning to HG.

***

William Wesney, let's call him WW, was born in 1846 of humble parents in the little Essex village of Tendering. Again, thanks to Norman, our family tree has been traced back to Samuel Crampin, WW's grandfather, who was born in 1788. The following information comes from a *Grimsby Evening Telegraph* article of 1927 in the year of his death (he died on February 2nd 1927).

WW was apprenticed as a boy to a firm of smack owners in Harwich, Messrs Groom & Sons, and served on a small sailing craft that was engaged in running from Norway to Harwich carrying lobsters.

By the age of 20 he had come to Grimsby, which would be in 1866, and sailed in Mr Thomas Campbell's fishing smacks. Very soon, he was given command of a 35-tonner named the *Dido*. It was several months later that he actually acquired a Master's Certificate, so things must have been considerably more lax in those days than now.

He was a very successful skipper, and, after a further year with another firm, Messrs Meadows & Co, he had saved sufficient money to purchase his first ship, the *Ellen Campbell* – presumably one of Thomas Campbell's former vessels. This was followed by a further sailing smack, the *Coningsbro' Castle*, which he sailed very successfully, along with the Ellen Campbell, for around 20 years.

Around 1890, we find reference to the second *Coningsbro' Castle*, GY 533; this time a steel-hulled line-fishing vessel, with steam propulsion, possibly one of the first steam fishing vessels built. She also carried two large sails, a loose-footed triangular main from the foremast and a loose-footed gaff sail from the mizzen. Obviously, steam propulsion was not entirely trusted at that time. From a painting of 1899, I would judge her to be about 90ft overall (o/a) length, and probably capable of eight or nine knots under power, with dubious performance to windward without engines!

WW and these three ships were the foundation of the 'first' Crampin Steam Fishing Company. Extracts from the Crampin Steam Fishing Company's annual statements show that there was a board meeting at the Royal Hotel, Grimsby (which was near to the Dock Offices building) on October 31st 1898, so the actual formation of the company would have been in about 1890, when the second *Coningsbro' Castle* was built for the company. At the 1898 meeting, the directors were Mr GA White

(Chairman), WW, Mr Walter Crampin, Mr Morris Arthur Bruce (whose name appears within the family tree) Mr Martin Kirk and Mr George Middleton, with Mr Edwin Thomas Grantham as company secretary.

Clearly, between 1890 and the board meeting of 1898, WW had encouraged other investors to join him in forming a formal Crampin Steam Fishing Company, as opposed to it being an owner/operator organisation. This is borne out from the notes of that meeting, from which we see that the *Nellie Bruce* had been purchased (presumably from Morris Arthur Bruce). Also, a further vessel had been purchased since October 31st of the previous year, the name of which is not mentioned. The meeting note also records that an order had been placed for a fourth vessel, delivery of which was expected in February 1899. The fleet at that time therefore would have been the *Coningsbro' Castle*, the *Nellie Bruce*, the unnamed vessel purchased and the vessel ordered. By this time, therefore, the first *Coningsbro' Castle* and the *Ellen Campbell* would have been scrapped.

WW sailed as a successful skipper until 1907, when he retired from the sea and took up full time duties as a director of the company. His trawling career was colourful: in the course of which he rescued three crews, including that of a German trawler. In recognition of his gallantry and seamanship, the Kaiser of Germany himself presented WW with an ebony box containing a pair of Zeiss binoculars – their whereabouts is still unknown.

Several other remarkable salvage feats were due to WW's initiative. During the war he joined with a partner in a daring speculation when he purchased the wreck of a Government trawler, the *Fair Isle*, which had sunk in the Pentland Firth (see Introduction). The Government had given up all hope of salving the ship, but WW and his partner succeeded in raising her '… and on last information the Fair Isle was sailing out of Granton'

It appears that the first ship owned by the first properly formulated Crampin Steam Fishing Company was the line fisher *Nellie Bruce*, purchased second-hand from Morris Arthur Bruce. The first ship built specifically for the company was the second *Coningsbro' Castle*.

A footnote to the *Grimsby Evening Telegraph* article records that the first *Coningsbro' Castle*, on March 18th 1890, rescued the crew of a Norwegian square rigger in trouble in heavy seas (author, 1890). An oil painting of this event and a copy of the report in the local paper still exist.

The fourth annual general meeting (AGM) of the company was held at the Royal Hotel on December 12th 1901. The directors were unchanged, and the vessels then owned were the *Nellie Bruce, Coningsbro' Castle, Victoria* and *Belvoir Castle*.

The fifth AGM, held on December 18th 1902, shows the directors were again unchanged, but a fifth vessel, the *Sirdar*, had been added to the fleet.

The sixth AGM, held on October 31st 1903, indicates that the *Victoria* appears to have been either lost or sold.

There is then a gap in the record of formal meetings. The next reference to an AGM, held on February 29th 1912, shows the first reference to HG Crampin, my grandfather, as a director of the newly formed Bunch Steam Fishing Company – clearly some family deals had been done and different companies formed to reflect differing ownerships. His co-directors were Walter Crampin and I Bunch, with W Westoby as company secretary. The new company was incorporated on March 6th 1911, and owned the *Coningsbro' Castle*, presumably purchased from WW's company, and the *Huxley*.

The auditors for all of the above information were Hodgeson Harris & Co of Hull.

Things would have gone on like this until the advent of the First World War (1914–1918) when the ships would either have carried on fishing, or been requisitioned by the Royal Navy and converted to minesweepers. The main winches were normally removed and replaced with four-inch guns.

The second Crampin Steam Fishing Company, the one as we knew it, was formed in 1918 following the signature of the First World War Armistice. At this time, the *Ophir 3*, *Sea Lion* and *Swan 2* were all transferred from the ownership of WW Crampin, to the Crampin Steam Fishing Company Limited, of which HG was by then the leading light and the driver behind the formation of the new business. It can be assumed that other ships such as the *Huxley*, *Coningsbro' Castle*, *Nellie Bruce* and *Belvoir Castle* would have been either scrapped or subsumed into the new company.

***

And so back to HG, born in 1872, who came up from London to try his hand in the fishing industry around 1890, when WW was building the *Coningsbro' Castle*. He would have been 18 years old at the time.

HG worked his way up through the ranks, from deckhand to third hand, to mate, and then to skipper. He therefore knew every aspect of fishing in great detail. His period at sea consequently would have stretched from 1890 to 1918, the end of the First World War, and the time that the Crampin Steam Fishing Company 'proper' was formed between HG and WW.

One anecdote is that HG spent a few days in an Aberdeen jail for an alleged illegal fishing incident within the then three-mile limit off the Scottish coast! He was eventually discharged, but reported that he did not enjoy the experience, and that the door keys 'were like choppers!'

HG married my grandmother, Betsy Ann Robinson, who, so far as I recall, had been brought to his attention by one of his cousins. At the time she was in the employment of WW, having formerly been in the Caistor workhouse, and it proved to be a heart-warmingly successful relationship. I remember her as one of the kindest, warmest and most considerate people one could ever meet, and she was a great support to HG. They had the four children referred to previously, Herbert Walter, Sarah Abigail, Betsy Emma and my father Harry. In HG's speech at the celebration for his golden wedding anniversary in 1948, of which actual recordings still exist, he refers to first meeting Grandma Crampin, i.e. Betsy Ann Robinson, who was then working as a servant at WW's house. He found her a most congenial, attractive, kind and pleasant woman, and, as he says, "she must have been efficient otherwise she wouldn't be working there!" He invested 4d in a box of chocolates, and everything else followed.

Their lives would have witnessed their transformation from poverty to relative wealth, but extravagance never featured in the behaviour of any our family – the roots of economy went far too deep. Grandma Crampin, as we called her, was a great strength in HG's life, from the time they got together at about the turn of the century. I remember stories of grandma knitting and mending grandpa's 'abb' socks, rather rough, foul things that purportedly kept your feet warm at sea. A tin can was also discovered in her kitchen labelled 'pieces of string, too short to use'.

That, then, is how my family became established in Grimsby.

***

HG continued to grow the business that he and WW formed in 1918. He bought other vessels, second-hand and in a wide variety of conditions, as well as more steel vessels driven by steam engines. This was a profoundly significant move because the range of operation of the fishing fleet was extended from the North Sea and the Western Isles to Iceland, Greenland, the White Sea and Bear Island. Amazingly, fishing was still by line in those days, and remained so until after 1930. The depth of water off the North Cape of Iceland is about 50 fathoms, or 300 feet. The lines would have to be about five times the depth of the water, say about 1,500 feet long. Baited hooks had to be attached to the lines every ten feet or so, and the line could now only be hauled aboard using a steam-driven winch. The labour associated with this whole process can only be imagined, but it went on, including fishing for halibut off the west coast of Greenland, in even deeper water and in far worse conditions.

Vessels were built as line fishers up to about 1930, after which they were converted to, or built as, trawlers. This was a totally new technology, and involved fitting trawl winches instead of line winches and huge gallows brackets to handle the two massive cables that towed the trawl, together with a whole system of pulleys, blocks, yardarms, winches and fairleads to enable the whole system to work. In addition to this, the whole concept of the trawl itself had to be developed into a mechanism that would work in deep sea waters, as opposed to the relatively shallow waters in which smaller versions had already been tried.

The essentials of a trawl are as follows. It is about the size of two tennis courts, and is towed anything up to half a mile behind the trawler (three times the water's depth) at a speed of about three knots. The two towing cables, or 'warps' as they are known, are about 25mm diameter steel, and are wound aboard on a winch that has two huge receiving reels. The mouth of the trawl is its widest point, and is kept open by two huge 'trawl doors' that act like sub-aquatic kites; they are each about 4m by 2m and weigh about a ton each. The bottom of the mouth of the trawl is kept on the bottom with a string of 'bobbins', which are heavily built in steel, are about 600mm in diameter, and roll along the ocean floor. The top of the mouth of the trawl is opened by virtue of a string of aluminium floats fitted along the top of the mouth. The trawl narrows towards the 'cod-end', which is where the fish collect, and cow hides are attached to the net below the cod-end to prevent undue abrasion from the sea bed. The trawl is towed for two or three hours, depending on the amount of fish about, and the net is then hauled alongside the trawler. The later 'stern trawlers' would haul the net over a stern ramp as the name suggests. The majority of the trawl is left in the water, but the cod-end is hauled aboard, suspended over the fish pounds on the deck and a special knot is released to allow the fish to spill into the pounds. The fish are then gutted and thrown into a fish washer, after which they flow down a chute to a platform in the fishroom. Here, they are sorted and packed away in ice. They are either 'bulked', which means they are thrown randomly onto the ice and protected with a layer of fish boards every metre or so, or the better quality fish are 'shelved', which means that the fish are laid on their bellies, on ice, with a sprinkling of ice on top, and then a protective layer of boards to keep them in top condition.

The golden age of fishing began after the First World War and continued until the Second. HG had involved some of his cousins, who had been working for Moody and Kelly, in the new business, namely Alf and Walter. They were real characters, and one story has it that, during the trawler building boom after the war, Alf ordered a new ship without even telling HG! It must have been quite a cavalier operation at that time.

Perihelion, an early line fishing vessel, the picture was taken prior to her conversion to trawling.

HG continued to expand the business, and bought another trawling company by the name of the Malmata Steam Fishing Company, which gave him a number of additional vessels. At that time the company livery was adopted – the owner of each ship was identified by the graphics displayed on the ship's funnel. He chose a buff coloured stack, a blue band with a white 'C' on it, and a black top. The painting companies in Grimsby were not the most subtle of people, and often the stacks were painted yellow instead. My grandfather, who never used too many words, simply said to them, "it's not yellow, it's bloody buff!", and the stacks were duly repainted.

My first evidence of him building a new trawler was in 1926 when the *William Wesney* was launched, obviously named after his uncle. She was built by Cook, Welton & Gemmell at Beverley in Yorkshire. The hulls were constructed there, launched broadside on, and then floated down the River Hull to the city of Hull, on the north bank of the Humber, where they were fitted out. I still have the solid-silver cigar box that was presented to my Aunt Betty by the builders, as she officially launched the ship.

The trawler *Malmata* was launched from the same yard in 1930. She was built as a line fisher, and clearly no pattern for the naming of the trawlers had yet evolved. My family has a very beautiful half-model of the *Malmata*, which shows a lot of the constructional detail with complete accuracy, as it was made by Cook, Welton & Gemmell's own model maker.

Shortly after that, a decision was made by HG to name all his trawlers after famous cricketers – he must have been quite keen on the game! That tradition survived for the life of the company, and the ships were generally known as 'the Cricketers'. Each trawler's name had seven letters, as did his own surname.

The *Malmata* was renamed the *Gregory*, and there then followed a spate of intense shipbuilding activity. My grandfather was undoubtedly a 'grafter', but he was also in the right place at the right time; fish were landed in unprecedented quantities during this period, and the market fortunately expanded accordingly, presumably due to reduced imports.

It was one of those times during which, however many ships you built, they could be operated at a profit. They were mostly built at one of two yards in Yorkshire, those of Cook, Welton & Gemmell of Beverley, as mentioned above, and Cochranes of Selby.

Paynter, an early trawler prepares to leave the Fish Docks and put to sea for a twenty one day Voyage to Iceland.

Star of the Realm, a trawler purchased from another owner prior to a name change into the 'Cricketer' Class.

Many of the ships' names are lost to me in the depths of time, but, for the sake of record, the following ships were to my knowledge built during this period after the *William Wesney* and the *Malmata*:

Juliana
Beldock
Hassett
Larwood
Hendren
Paynter
Pataudi
Barnett
Wellard

These were followed after the Second World War by:
Bradman   1950
Yardley   1950
Statham   1956

Trueman   1960
Padgett   1960

There were many more. They fished very successfully until the outbreak of the Second World War. At that time, they were taken over by the Government and turned into minesweepers. I know there were many more because all of the above vessels, with the exception of the *Juliana*, survived the war, and yet I know that we lost as many as five vessels in one day at the Battle of Narvik off the Norwegian coast.

Each winter there were inevitable catastrophes in the Arctic. These were usually due to 'black ice'. This is a situation where temperatures fall so low, that spray falling on the superstructure of the trawlers instantly freezes. It would build up, sometimes at a rate quicker than it could be disposed of, and the ship would become top heavy and capsize. There were never any survivors from this situation. Attempts would be made to chip the ice away manually using fish-room choppers, and also by using steam hoses. When steam gave way to diesel propulsion in the late 1950s this steam facility was denied to later trawlers. These disasters continued into the 1960s. One has to remember that communications were very difficult in those days, relying entirely on the use of long wave Morse code via Wick Radio. When silences came, a cloud formed over the whole town of Grimsby whilst information on the fate of the ship and its crew was awaited. Wives and families would wait for days at the entrance to the fish dock – the 'lock pits' – in the hope that they would see the return of the vessel and their loved ones. Sometimes they were lucky, most often not.

Sometimes, ships simply disappeared, and the *Juliana* was one of these mysteries. She became overdue, communications had been lost, but the weather was not unduly adverse, except that widespread fog was in evidence. The wives and children again amassed at the lock pits, but on this occasion to no avail. Eventually a picture was put together that deduced her assumed fate. Other ships, as they returned to Grimsby gave reports of sightings of the *Juliana*, and so her position was fairly well established, which, together with the times of the sightings, would have been entered in each ship's log. It was clear that she had been fishing off Southeast Iceland in an area close to the Kidney Bank, so called because of its shape, which was a rich hunting ground for cod. In that area is a rock known as 'the Whaleback' because of its shape, which actually becomes exposed at very low water. It normally lurks just below the surface. Best evidence is that the *Juliana* struck the Whaleback in fog, was severely holed, and sank with all hands before any distress message could be sent.

The weather was a constant enemy for the trawler fleets of Grimsby and Hull, and, although not always so, sometimes it was diabolical. Weather forecasts were not sophisticated and sometimes ships were caught out with no time to run for

Wellard, originally named '*El Capitan*', she saw extensive service in World War 2 as a mine sweeper, having been commandeered by the Royal Navy.

shelter. Heavy North Atlantic seas were not a major problem as trawlers are incredibly seaworthy vessels, although such weather would stop them fishing because of the uneven pull on the gear, not to mention the possibility of losing men over the side. When the seas contained lumps of ice, or when seas became excessively steep, it was altogether a different matter. Alan Whitelam was a skipper with our firm for many years, a gentleman, a highly skilled seaman and one not prone to exaggeration. He took the *Yardley*, as skipper from new, which was one of our largest trawlers, and was caught out in very steep seas in the White Sea, north of Russia. He had no time to retrieve the trawl gear, and at one time this huge ship was laid on her side with the sea pouring down the funnel, putting out the boiler fires. Although the situation was recovered, he said after that trip that he really thought he had lost the ship!

It is worth noting at this point that during this era navigation was a very basic art – and I use the word 'art' advisedly. There was a great demand for skippers and mates due to the expansion of the industry, yet the prevailing standard of education was not high. It would not, therefore, have been possible to educate skippers to anything approaching present-day standards to meet the high demand. Learning was, therefore, largely empirical, but I did come across one amazing document from the 1920s, which was the syllabus for qualification as a trawler skipper. I could not believe what I read! Nothing about the ability to fix one's position by the use of sextants, running fixes or whatever.

These men had to memorise a set of courses that would get them out of the Humber, in fog if necessary, up the east coast of the UK, through the Pentland Firth (a treacherous piece of water between Scotland and the Orkneys), into the North Atlantic, past the Faroe Islands, and on to Iceland or destinations further afield. (Our trawler the *Bradman* once fished within 200 miles of New York harbour!) They were expected to take soundings using a lead line, and to know the quality of the sea bed in various locations so that they could further deduce their position by examining what material was stuck to the lead, which would have been coated in a sticky substance called 'tallow', together with the measured depth of water.

The magnetic compass was the primary instrument of navigation. It was mounted on a cylindrical binnacle on the bridge top, and was viewed in the wheelhouse via a circular mirror in front of the helmsman's eyes, angled upwards at 45 degrees. It saddens me to see the ability to 'box the compass' that is to say, to name all its points, becoming a lost art, although I realise that this is pure emotion. For the record, the points of the magnetic compass are as follows.

North
North by east
North north east
North east by north
North east
North east by east
East north east
East by north
East (90 degrees)
East by south
East south east
South east by east ... and so on in the same pattern.

Each 90 degrees of the compass is therefore divided into eight segments of 11.25 degrees each. Each segment is then subdivided into four 'points' which are just under 3 degrees each. This would suffice for general purposes because it would not be possible to steer a vessel to much greater accuracy. A typical order from the skipper to the helm might therefore be, "steer north by east a quarter east". This would equate to north by east, which is 11.25 degrees, plus a quarter point east of 3 degrees, giving an actual magnetic course of about 014 degrees.

The difference between magnetic north (where the compass points) and true north (the axis of the Earth's rotation) was very important to trawlers; this is because at the North Cape of Iceland the difference between the two (variation) is as much as 29 degrees west, due to the volcanic magnetic irregularities of the area.

Navigation was, therefore, less than precise. I remember well an embarrassing occasion that happened around 1953, when one of our largest trawlers the *Bradman*, under the command of one 'Shadow' Phillips was returning from the White Sea with full holds. At 185 feet long and 1,000 tons deadweight, she managed to miss Grimsby and finished up on the beach at Mablethorpe! Fortunately, without damage.

I also remember her sister ship, the *Yardley*, which was built with an aluminium bridge top in an attempt to reduce top weight and hence the effects of black ice. Little was known at the time about electrolytic action, and the combination of the brass compass binnacle, the aluminium bridge top and salt water, turned the whole paraphernalia into, effectively, a corrosive battery! The binnacle eventually fell through the bridge roof and landed in the wheelhouse!

One casualty of less than perfect navigation was our trawler, the *Beldock*, which ran onto rocks in the Western Isles. Several hands were lost in the attempt to get men ashore using the 'breeches buoy' system.

Another tragedy was the *Hassett*, lost off the Lofoten Isles, Norway, on her way to the White Sea (north of Russia). I have good photographs of her demise, taken from an aeroplane chartered by the *Grimsby Evening Telegraph*. This story was even more tragic, as its cause was a fight between the skipper and mate, whereby no one was watching where the ship was actually going. Drink was most likely a contributory factor; an eternal demon of the industry. Again, several hands were lost in similar circumstances to the *Beldock*.

Fishermen were a highly skilled and resourceful lot, and this impressed me greatly. They were a community of up to 21 men, away for trips that lasted up to 24 days. What you couldn't make, mend or adapt, you went without. There are some lovely stories about this.

One of our ships was fishing for halibut off Greenland when the connecting rod, or 'con-rod', of the steam generator broke, depriving the whole ship of light and secondary power. A steam trawler has four different steam-driven engines. One is the main propulsion unit, the second is the trawl winch engine, the third is the anchor windlass and the fourth is the steam-driven electrical generator; it was this latter unit that failed. The con-rod is the steel bar that connects the piston to the crank shaft in any reciprocating engine, and is fundamental to its function. The prospect of having to put into port for repairs was extremely unattractive. Time would be wasted, fish already caught would be getting older, and the trip would be a financial disaster for

Yardley, a sister ship to the Bradman, Yardley was built in 1950 by Cook Welton & Gemmell of Beverley. Bradman was built in the same year by Cochranes of Selby.

the skipper and crew, who were paid by 'poundage' on what the ship earned. The chief engineer made a new con-rod out of a large deck spanner, which worked sufficiently well for the ship to continue fishing and make it back to Grimsby. He was complimented on his efforts by the owners and insurers, who commented that it was a shame not to leave his repair intact for the next trip!

In similar circumstances, a deckhand broke his leg in heavy weather and a similar choice faced the skipper. Presumably by mutual consent, an anaesthetic was issued in the form of half a bottle of Harvey's Bristol Cream sherry, the leg was set more or less straight, and put in an oversized wellington boot that was split open and then filled with deck concrete. (Deck concrete is used to seal the hole in the foredeck where the anchor chain exits the deck. If this is not done, a plume of spray would cover the working deck every time the ship put its head into the sea). The whole thing was then bound with deck twine and the job was considered complete. It must have been very painful for the man concerned, but the story has it that the leg did not need

Yardley leaves for her next voyage to the White Sea.

re-setting when the ship reached port. Had he gone over the side, he would have disappeared very rapidly!

The working environment was undoubtedly dangerous. Surfaces were slippery, always moving; there were few, if any, safety lines; there were masts to be climbed in all weathers; and no trawlerman ever wore a life jacket! They simply became expert at what they did, were self-reliant and learnt to work as a team.

These things profoundly influenced me, and perhaps gave me an inbuilt reaction against excessive health and safety issues, the 'nanny state' and the idea that, whatever happened, you could always blame somebody else! It seems to me to disempower people, and rob them of inventiveness, resourcefulness and the belief that there would be a solution that they could find for themselves.

Many of our ships had been lost in the Second World War, with only the aforementioned seven ships surviving. We were compensated at pre-war values by the Government, which very nearly broke our firm. HG, however, with the same determination and courage that started the business in the first place, set about rebuilding it.

In 1953, our trawler *Yardley* was chosen to represent Grimsby at the Spithead Review near the Solent.

As I was born in 1946, I will shortly continue with my own life story, in which the Crampin Steam Fishing Company featured very prominently.

***

At this juncture, I will backtrack as I have other valuable information provided by my cousin Norman. He has put a great deal of time and effort into recording accurate facts, which are notoriously difficult to come by, and the family is very grateful to him.

This information parallels the history described above, which is derived from all the sources I could establish. Norman's information adds many more fascinating details, validates much of my own account, but also highlights areas of uncertainty, which is inevitable over a century later. I am recording the information verbatim so nothing further can be lost in the translation! Much material is included because it exists and it would be a shame to lose it. However, some readers might like to skip those parts that are simply a matter of historical record, but pages 24, 25 and 26 should not be missed out.

2

A Parallel History of the Crampin Steam Fishing Company

This chapter is based on information provided by Norman Crampin. Norman Crampin is my cousin, son of Herbert Walter Crampin, the eldest of the four of HG's children. Being several years older than me, Norman worked in the firm much longer than I; therefore, his recollections and access to information are extremely valuable. This is his report.

The following dates, etc. are from HG Crampin's certificates from the 1890s. (Much of the immediately following information will be of little interest to many, but is included simply because we have it).

Apprenticeship indenture (3-year) to Grimsby Steam Fishing Co.; fishing boat: *Gaelic*; undertaken on August 7th 1890, and signed and stamped as completed satisfactorily on August 17th 1893. Place of birth given as Shelford in Surrey.

Entry	Discharge	Ship	No	Age	Real Age	Capacity
08/08/1893	20/10/1894	*Swallow*	GY489	21	22	Deck hand
23/10/1894	23/05/1895	*Blackbird*	GY635	21	23	Deck hand
25/05/1895	25/10/1895	*Robin*	GY757	22	23	Deck hand
13/11/1895	13/08/1896	*Magnetic*	GY854	23	24	Deck hand
01/09/1896	06/02/1897	*Wren*	GY770	23	24	Third hand
02/1897	05/1897	*Jurassic*	GY259	24	25	Third hand

NB. All ships given as 'SS'.

Blackbird, *Robin* and *Magnetic* (consecutive) entry and discharge dates are for the same day of the month (coincidence or slapdash clerkmanship?).

All dates here presented as given on the certificates.

'Bird'-named ships: The Pioneer Steam Fishing Company Ltd.

'…ic'-named ships: The Grimsby Steam Fishing Company Ltd.

By 1890, both of the above companies had amalgamated and were operated as a single company, known as Moody and Kelly.

Berths as Mate:

Ship	From	To
Lyric	03/11/1897	10/06/1898
Starling	25/06/1898	30/03/1899
Gaelic	01/04/1899	02/06/1899

United Navigation Committee (Insurance) Fishing Skipper's Ticket: 20/06/1899.
Grimsby Board of Trade Fishing Skipper's Ticket: 21/6/1899.

NB. Herbert George Crampin (my grandfather) was the nephew of brothers Weston William and Walter Crampin. At this juncture, it should be noted that Weston William and William Wesney are one and the same person (William Wesney being the name given on his birth certificate). From the late 19th century onwards, Walter Crampin, who was and remained without issue, became his mentor and was later often mistakenly thought to be his father.

Extracts from the Steam Fishing Companies' annual statements

The Crampin Steam Fishing Company Limited Financial Statements and Directors' Report to 31st October 1898 (Crampin Steam Fishing Company, 1898).

'Directors: Mr G A White, Chairman, Mr Weston William Crampin, Mr Walter Crampin, Mr Morris Arthur Bruce, Mr Martin Kirk, Mr George Middleton, Mr Edwin Thomas Grantham, Secretary.'

'To be presented to the first Annual General Meeting of Shareholders to be held at the Royal Hotel Grimsby on Wednesday 30th November at 6.30pm.'

'... for the period from the incorporation of the Company, 4th June 1897, to 31st October 1898.'

'The *Nellie Bruce* has been at sea for 254 days and the *Coningsbro' Castle* for 227 days. A further vessel has been purchased since the 31st October and is now at sea, and a contract has been signed for a fourth vessel which is now in the course of construction, delivery of which is expected in 1899.'

NB. Both the *Nellie Bruce* and the *Coningsbro' Castle* were built in 1898 and first operated by the Crampin Steam Fishing Company Limited. The *Coningsbro' Castle* was named after the second sail-fishing vessel owned Weston William Crampin. The first sail-fishing vessel he owned was called the *Ellen Campbell*. A recently acquired document (copy 2012) suggests that at some time before the incorporation of the first Crampin Steam Fishing Company, William Weston Crampin had been operating a fleet of five fishing smacks (sailing vessels). It is not known why the *Nellie Bruce* was so named. Several possible explanations could be put forward; for example it may have been originally ordered by Morris Arthur Bruce (one of the directors, see above) and named after his wife or daughter; shortly afterwards, he decided to join forces with the newly formed Crampin company. In any event he does not seem to have lasted long as a fishing-company director, as in the next annual statement (1901) he is no longer a Crampin company director.

(Reports from 1899 and 1900 are not held.)

Crampin S.F. Co Ltd., 4th Annual Report 12/12 1901 at the Royal Hotel (Crampin Steam Fishing Company, 1901).
'Directors: Mr G A White, Chairman, Mr Weston William Crampin, Mr Walter Crampin, Mr George Middleton, Mr Martin Kirk, Mr Edwin Thomas Grantham, Secretary.'
'Vessels: *Nellie Bruce, Coningsbro' Castle, Victoria* (86 days), *Belvoir Castle*.'

Crampin S.F. Co Ltd., 5th Annual Report 18/12/1902 at the Royal Hotel.
'Directors: as 1901.'
'Vessels: *Nellie Bruce, Coningsbro' Castle, Victoria* (86 days), *Belvoir Castle, Sirdar* (46 days).'

Crampin S.F. Co Ltd., Auditor's Report for the year ending 31/10/1903.
'Vessels: *Nellie Bruce, Coningsbro' Castle, Belvoir Castle, Sirdar*.'

NB. In 1911, the Bunch Steam Fishing Company Ltd was formed by the amalgamation of the Crampin Steam Fishing Company with the ships of Isaac Bunch, who seems to have been an operator of older fishing vessels. Walter Crampin had married Emma Bunch, a relative of Isaac Bunch. Mr Herbert Walter Crampin (son of HG) once observed that there had been a falling out between the brothers Weston William and Walter Crampin for which he didn't know the reason, which was almost certainly that Weston William disapproved of what he regarded to be the infiltration of an outsider, Isaac Bunch. Herbert Walter took no part in the Bunch Steam Fishing

Company, and withdrew all but two ships and operated them independently under his own name.

Bunch S F Co Ltd. Financial Statements and Report 29/2 1912 (Bunch Steam Fishing Company, 1912).
'Directors : Walter Crampin, H G Crampin, I Bunch, W Westoby Secretary.
'… the incorporation of the Company viz 6th March 1911 …'
Vessels : *Coningsbro' Castle, Huxley.'*

NB. The *Nellie Bruce* was one of the ships taken in 1911 by Weston William Crampin. Documents recently acquired (in 2012) show that a certain George Whitbread had four spells as skipper of the *Nellie Bruce*, 24/01/1912 to 27/07/1912, 20/11/1912 to 09/01/1913, 18/11/1913 to 24/01/1914, and 27/11/1914 to 22/01/1915.

In September 1916, the *Nellie Bruce* was sold to the firm White and Willows, and herein is what happened next.
'At 9.30am on October 30th 1916, when line fishing off the S.E. coast of Iceland in 40 fathoms (240ft) of water under the command of Thomas Bell, a German U-boat was sighted approaching from the West in a position 64'30"N, 11'30"W about 3 miles distant. Without warning the submarine opened fire on the unarmed Nellie Bruce, with the first six shots falling wide of the vessel. Skipper Bell ordered the boat to be lowered over the side. With all 15 crew in the boat, they pulled away from their vessel as quickly as possible as the U-boat closed in. They counted up to 40 shots and when the firing ceased, their ship had disappeared. Skipper Bell set sail and headed for the land. At midnight he decided to anchor in 70 fathoms (420ft) of water using fishing line, but the wind began to freshen and it started raining heavily, so two hours later he decided to proceed towards land, which was sighted at daybreak. They ran the boat ashore and set off to seek help as they were all numb with cold and soaked through. They came to a farm house named Kross, where they stayed overnight and were warmly received by the Icelanders. The following day it was decided to take them to Stodvarfjord by motor boat. The weather was so bad it delayed them for another day. From here they were transferred to Faskrudsfjord before being returned home to Grimsby. The submarine responsible for the sinking was U-24 commanded by Walter Remy.'
This information is taken from a document provided by Mr Alan Shepherd, the grandson of George Whitbread, who is mentioned above.

***

The Second Crampin Steam Fishing Company

No early documents have been held, but, by the end of the First World War, Weston William and Walter seem to have made up their differences. Charles Cox's *The Steam Trawlers and Liners of Grimsby* shows that *Ophir 3*, *Sea Lion* and *Swan 2* were all transferred from the ownership of 'W Crampin' (it is unknown if this is Weston William or Walter, but it is probably the former) to the Crampin Steam Fishing Company, in February 1919. Isaac Bunch and his ships were no longer in evidence. The Second Crampin Steam Fishing Company was, therefore, probably formed in late 1918 after the signing of the First World War Armistice. By 1920, both brothers, Weston William and Walter had given up going to sea (Weston William probably in 1907), and their nephew Herbert George Crampin became managing director of the Crampin and Bunch Steam Fishing Companies. As was common in those days, most of the hands-on fishing vessel owners also engaged individually in fish merchanting, and both the brothers, at least initially, continued in this. Between 1920 and 1927, possibly earlier, the Perihelion Steam Fishing Company became part of the Crampin Group (the date and circumstances are not known). Throughout the 1920s, all ships in the Crampin Group were engaged in line fishing, as this had been the main occupation of the brothers in their sea-going time. The ships, however, were built so they could trawl, if required, by fitting an alternative winch. Weston William Crampin died in 1927 and Walter Crampin in 1929. After this the ships, and newly acquired or newly built ships, were quickly converted to trawling, as HG had served his apprenticeship in this type of fishing. The Malmata Steam Fishing Company is thought to have been formed circa 1929 by another Walter Crampin, the third son of Weston William, for the purpose of operating the ship of that name that he had had built. This company was later subsumed into the Crampin Group. At some time later the *Malmata* was renamed *Gregory*.

***

Dates from Walter Crampin's Certificates

Apprenticeship Indenture (5 year) to William Groom, Harwich, undertaken on July 16th 1867 'aged 16 years' (he was in fact 15) and signed as completed satisfactorily on February 16th 1872.

United Navigation Committee (insurance) Fishing Skipper's Ticket, March 8th 1881; and address of candidate: 94 Orwell Street, Grimsby. (Date of birth given as April 1851 but thought to be April 1852.) Name given as Walter 'Crampton', two entries of which were corrected, but not, apparently, officially.

Board of Trade Fishing Skipper's Ticket, December 7th 1889; address of candidate: Granby House, Beaconthorpe, Grimsby; and place of birth: Tendering, Essex. (Date of birth given erroneously as 1846.)

Weston William Crampin (birth certificate name William Wesney).

Weston William Crampin's sea certificates don't seem to have accessibly survived, but notice of his death (died 02/02/1927) in the *Grimsby Evening Telegraph* reads as follows:

'***A fishery pioneer – sudden death of Mr W W Crampin***. *From apprentice to ship owner.*'

'*Another of the "old standards" of the Grimsby fishing industry has passed away in Mr Weston William Crampin, whose death occurred suddenly yesterday evening. The news of his death came as a great shock to many people on Grimsby Fish Docks today, for Mr Crampin was on the docks yesterday and was apparently in good health. After lunch, he had motored to Wooton with his son, and on arriving at the house of a friend there, was taken ill and died within a few minutes. Mr Crampin was 73 years of age and together with his brother, Mr Walter Crampin, has played no small part in helping to build up the great industry of the port. Born of humble parents in the little Essex village of Tendering, he was apprenticed as a boy to a firm of smack owners at Harwich, Messrs Groom and Sons, and served on a small sailing craft that was engaged in running from Norway to Harwich with lobsters.*

'***Master at Twenty***

'*At the age of 20 he came to Grimsby (i.e. he came to Grimsby in 1873, or much more likely in 1874) and sailed in Mr Thomas Campbell's fishing smacks. Very soon he was given command of a smack, the Dido, a ship of 35 tons. The Board of Trade regulations were not enforced so rigorously in those days, for Mr Crampin did not secure his Master's Certificate until he had been in command of the Dido for some months. He was a very successful skipper, and after a year or so with Messrs. Meadows and Co., he had saved sufficient money to purchase his first ship, the Ellen Campbell.*

'*Later he purchased the Coningsbro' Castle (sailing vessel) from the Great Grimsby Coal Salt & Tanning Company, and gradually his fleet increased, as other fleets did. Some thirty years ago, Mr Crampin and his brother began to develop line fishing, and subsequently the Crampin Steam Fishing Company was formed to pursue this type of fishing.*

'A Pioneering Firm

'The Firm may indeed be regarded as the leaders of line fishing, and as recently as a year ago, they equipped a liner for an experimental voyage to the White Sea, where up to that time only trawlers had ventured. (The term 'White Sea' refers to the 'Barents Sea' this particular misnomer survived into the 1960's [sic] in the fishing industry.)

'Mr Crampin retired from the sea about twenty years ago after a distinguished career in the course of which he rescued three crews, including that of a German trawler. In recognition of his gallantry on that occasion the Kaiser presented him with an ebony box. (Containing a pair of binoculars, which together with the box are still extant.)

'Several rather remarkable salvage feats have been due to Mr Crampin's initiative. During the war he joined with a partner in a daring speculation, when he purchased the wreck of a Government trawler, the Fair Isle. The Government had abandoned all hope of salving the ship, but Mr Crampin and his partner, a salvage expert, succeeded in raising the wreck, and when last heard of, the Fair Isle was sailing out of Granton.

'Mr Crampin took a very keen and active interest in the affairs of the Crampin S. F. Company and the Perihelion Company up to the time of his death. He rarely missed his daily visits to the offices of the Company in Fish Dock Road. He lived at Clement Villa in Abbey Park Road, and he leaves a widow and several sons. The internment will take place at the Scarthoe Road cemetery on Saturday afternoon.'

NB. It was in the sailing vessel *Coningsbro' Castle* that, on March 18th 1890, WW Crampin rescued the crew of a Norwegian square rigger in trouble in heavy seas. An oil painting of this event and a copy of the report in the local paper still exist. This was in special edition of the *Grimsby Express* on Friday May 2nd 1890, and reads as follows:

'Rescued at Sea

'Sir, Kindly allow me through your valuable columns, to publicly offer on behalf of myself and crew, our most sincere and heartfelt thanks to Captain W W Crampin and crew of the smack Coningsbro' Castle, who so bravely, and at imminent risk of their lives, succeeded in rescuing us from our vessel, the brig Martin Luther of Drammen, Norway. These brave fellows, during a tremendous gale and with mountainous seas running, with the greatest possible risk and difficulty, in launching their boat, came to our rescue, landing us safely on their vessel, and for 11 days we were treated with the greatest kindness and attention. We feel we owe a deep debt of gratitude to those courageous Grimsby fishermen who saved us from a watery grave.

'Thank you for inserting this. Yours, etc., J C Hansen, late Master of the Martin Luther Rescued March 18th 1890.'

Note that, during the First World War, HG Crampin served mainly as a mate on various fishing vessels. For mutual protection, they fished in groups in sight of each other. On one occasion a German submarine surfaced close by. As was the pattern, they picked on one vessel, in this case the one in which HG Crampin was sailing, who ordered the crew to lower their boat and pull away from the ship, which was then sunk by gunfire. Before leaving, the submarine captain ordered the fishing crew to hand over their sea boots – presumably to incapacitate them – and gave them a bottle of German wine! The other ships in the group immediately returned and picked up their unfortunate fellow mariners.

***

Mr Herbert Walter Crampin

Herbert Walter Crampin was the eldest son of HG Crampin. He did not go to sea, probably owing to remembering the anxieties of his mother concerning her husband (HG), especially during the First World War. He became secretary of the Crampin Group in the year of his marriage, 1926. He remained in this position until the early 1950s when he became the managing director of the Crampin Group on the retirement of his father. At about the same time, he followed Sir Jack Croft Baker as president of the Grimsby Trawler Owners' Association, later called the Grimsby Exchange. After his own retirement in 1964, when the Crampin ships were sold to the much larger Ross Group, he was awarded an OBE. He had always felt uneasy concerning certain fishermen's charities, which never seemed to dispose of any money from their funds. For instance, Sir Alec Black had started a charity to provide clean sheets for any fishermen that were hospitalised. Mr Crampin took legal counsel, which he financed himself, and eventually managed to have most if not all of the funds of these charities transferred to active concerns such as the Fishermens' Dependents Fund and the Sailors' Children's Society. Although his OBE was awarded for 'Services to the Fishing Industry' it was thought that this retirement activity was the real reason. He died on January 2nd 1974.

***

This concludes Norman Crampin's record of events.

3

Waltham

I WAS BORN ON March 23rd 1946, at home, in a house in the village of Waltham, near Grimsby, where my parents lived at that time.

My father Harry was the fourth child of HG and his wonderful wife, my grandmother, Betsy Ann (nee Robinson). He had two older sisters, Betty and Sarah, and an elder brother, Herbert. Harry married my mother, Dorothy Enid (nee Buxton) in 1942.

We lived in a 'between the wars' house, which was detached, with a long back garden. The house can still be seen; if you stand with your back to the church where I was christened, it is the one immediately to the left of the house with a green, pantiled roof, where our physician, one Dr Chidlow, used to live. It had a bathroom half way up the stairs with a semi-circular window, which features prominently on the front elevation. It was undoubtedly a comfortable, middle-class home, which I recall as being huge. But when one revisits such places with an eye level of six feet rather than two feet six, proportions do look entirely different!

My elder sister Gibby was also born there, three years previously, but my two younger brothers, Leon and Tex were born in Grimsby, four and eight years after me, respectively, to which we moved in 1950.

I need to explain here that my father Harry was a highly intelligent but totally eccentric and unorthodox individual, and this eccentricity extended into the choice of names for his children. Logically, he did not see the point in using conventional names, when their very purpose was to differentiate between one person and another! My sister and two brothers rather think that the name 'Gibby' was taken from a close family friend, Alice Gibson, who had that as a nickname. When it came to my turn, William cropped up as a possibility, but, in his inimitable style, Father decreed that as it would get shortened to 'Bill' anyway they might as well start from there. So that was the name I was given and christened with. And what a bind it has been ever since! Thanks, Dad! The origin of the name was evidently a miscreant dog we once had, whose name was Billy Airedale. Billy preferred life at my grandparents' house at 385 Grimsby Road, Cleethorpes. This must have been at least five miles away, but

Billy was quite capable of getting there under his own steam, whereupon my grandmother would pick up the phone to Harry, saying, "that bloody dog's here again!", and Harry would have to get out the Austin 12 and go and retrieve him, suitably admonished!

My father was a very keen musician, although his appreciation of music exceeded his abilities as a performer in any sense. He was a reasonably competent pianist, but his real love was the classical guitar. He was a great fan of oboist Leon Goosens, and so 'Leon' was the name chosen for child number three, my younger brother, born in 1950. My Aunt Betty, one of Harry's two elder sisters, always insisted that it should be pronounced as though with an acute accent over the 'e', but this was far too posh for Dad, who would pronounce it something like "Lee-un". Dad always wanted to emphasise the working class nature of his heritage, whilst Betty was the direct opposite! When the fourth child came along, Harry realised that he had got the length of Christian names down from five to four letters, so to finish with a three would be a triumph. He was an ardent economiser, and considered that the amount of ink that would be saved in signatures over a lifetime would be significant! So Tex he became.

If one moves house at the age of four as happened to me, it puts down a marker in time that makes it easy to recall what events happened where. My recollections of Waltham are obviously limited, but I do recall a thing called a 'switch-back' in our back garden. This was, in effect, a linear, gravity-driven train set with a rail gauge of about a foot, which was about thirty yards long, with one hump in the middle. We kids sat on little trucks in an elevated position at one end of the track, pushed off, and were transported to the other end of the track under gravity. It was great fun, and I don't know why these things don't still exist – health and safety probably! It could well have been made as a one-off on the fish docks, where there were support industries to the trawlers that could make absolutely anything. Gibby had a red truck and I had a blue one, in accordance with the conventions of the time.

I also recall that, from the back garden, we could squeeze through the hedge and gain access to the adjacent housing estate. This was frowned upon for reasons I did not understand at all, but I do recall my mother telling my father of a meeting between Gibby and one Peter Eskham. The story as reported, went thus – Gibby to Mother.

"Peter Eskham can get his willy out, he can wee, and he can stop it and start it again all by himself!" (I note here that 'spell check' wanted a capital W so it clearly has no idea what I'm on about!)

I would have found this profoundly impressive because, at the age I would have then been, I was probably more efficient at 'starting it' than 'stopping it!'

I can remember the garden tool shed, which to me was like Aladdin's cave itself; my tricycle, with which I was evidently fairly reckless; and the general environment of Waltham, over which I had ridiculous freedom to roam at will. I chose to use this freedom, evidently, by purloining a book of stamps from the sideboard in the living room and sticking one on every gatepost in the High Street. Dad was seen later with a primus stove and a kettle, steaming them all off again! I would have thought the differential between the cost of the paraffin and the value of the stamps would be marginal to say the least, but perhaps there were important matters of principle at stake here.

I can also remember my introduction to music, as all four of us were made to take up the piano at the age of four or just under. I don't recall anything significant about this, but it was the start of a life-long relationship with music, which was to figure prominently in all our lives.

I also became aware of a close friendship between our family, the Crofts (Frank and Pat), who lived a few doors along the High Street towards Humberstone, and the Browns (Tom and Laura), who lived on the Brigsley Road. My sister was probably closer to the Crofts, as they had girls, Gail and Rae, whilst I was closer to the Browns with their boys, Stuart and Guy. Gail and Stuart were Gibby's age, and Rae and Guy were my age. (Actually Guy is a year older than I, which felt like a century at the time!) All three families had other children later, but we were the ones who were around at that time. These friendships were very special; they survived the whole period of our growing up, and they survive to this day. I know that Frank was a refrigeration engineer, and a lovely man, but died of cancer at quite a young age, but this was clearly something that was not to be discussed with we kids. His daughter Rae later took up the violin, as did I at the age of seven, and Rae and I came up against each other regularly at local music festivals. She usually won by a ratio of about three to one, much to my father's annoyance! Laura Brown was my godmother, and what a wonderful woman she was; she died sometime around 2002 in Louth, Lincolnshire. Tom her husband, founded the business of T H Brown Limited, and became a very successful haulage contractor. This business survives to this day, run by his third son, Martin.

I recall one day in 1954, Gibby and I were to go on our first holiday! She was going to stay with the Crofts for a week, and I was going to stay with the Browns. Although only eight, I had no reservations about this as the families were already close friends. Of course, what it was all about was the impending birth of my second brother, Tex. I have a few powerful memories of this holiday.

First, I was duly delivered at the Browns, and my father handed my music case to Laura, with strict instructions that I must be made to practise the piano for one hour every day. Laura, bless her, would have none of this, and the case was never opened. She was also instructed to give me a good clip round the ear if I misbehaved in any way. She never did that either – what a star! Unlike most people, Laura never had the slightest difficulty in standing up to Harry.

The Browns had a major asset of which I was very envious – a semi-derelict caravan in a field at the end of their huge garden. Guy and I, along with Stuart, had a fine time in this thing; the main game being for one to try and sneak up on the other two, who would be in the caravan, without being detected. After a while, when Guy and I were in the caravan, we got fed up and went in for lunch. About an hour later, Stuart arrived, extremely annoyed that we were not still in the caravan, and that he had spent the last hour on his stomach crawling through the field! Unfortunately, the caravan was later destroyed by a fire, which I think we may have lit.

I also remember a year or two later, Guy telling me that his father had just bought a Jaguar. I had no idea what this was, but the garage door was duly opened, and there was a beautiful, brand-new, gleaming, metallic-beige Jaguar Mark IX with the most sumptuous interior imaginable. It bore no relationship to our Austin 12, and I had simply never seen anything like it. Guy and I became very close friends, and remain so to this day, although he now lives abroad for much of the year. He was a resourceful and adventurous lad, and we always got on really well. One day, however, when I was not with him to offer advice – he would have been about six or seven at the time – Guy, quite reasonably, decided to take the Jaguar for a test run. He had managed to find the keys and start the engine, but had some initial difficulty with the gearbox. The net effect of this was that the Jaguar went forward, clean through the end of the wooden garage, causing some damage to both it and the car. This was perhaps the first of a series of incidents between Guy and mechanically propelled vehicles that did not go quite according to plan – I have to confess to being involved in some of the others, but more of that later.

I also recall dinghy sailing with Mum and Dad in a clinker-built boat, which was gaff rigged and about twelve feet long. It was known as a 'Lymington Scow'. We once sailed this thing from Grimsby all the way to Spurn Point at the mouth of the Humber, with myself and my sister also aboard. We were advised by the lifeboat crew not to attempt a return to Grimsby as the weather was deteriorating. Harry rather stupidly ignored this advice and we set off with the wind behind us, going like a rocket! Evidently, my sister clung to the mast for dear life and I went to sleep! Harry had rigged up a mast-head light in case it got dark before we returned, driven by a 12V lead-acid accumulator, which must have weighed a ton. Had we capsized, the dinghy would have sunk like a stone. As it happened, we must have got back to Grimsby in one piece.

Yet, all the time, even at the age of four or under, I was aware that life was controlled by the pulse of the fishing industry. It was a living, breathing way of life that affected the whole area, and it was impossible not to be aware of it. You knew when it was high tide, what ships were expected, which were due to sail, and you knew which ships had landed their catches by the fresh fish that was brought home by my father for distribution between friends and relatives. This feeling is one of the strongest I have ever experienced, and is doubtless common to other industries, but I have never experienced it before or since.

Such are my recollections of Waltham, but then life was to change quite significantly!

4

Harry's Inventions

Back to the plot. After Leon's birth in 1950, we moved house to 33 Abbey Road, Grimsby; an event I remember well! My father bought the house from his sister, my Aunt Sarah, who moved to 'Sunnydale', Princes Road, Cleethorpes. There was much about number 33 not entirely to Harry's liking, and he set about moulding it to his requirements with gusto! All light fittings were taken down and replaced with six-foot fluorescent tubes – because they were 'efficient'. My mother must have been devastated, but did not appear to have got much of a vote on the matter. The Aga was moved from Waltham and installed in Abbey Road. It was a coke-driven affair, so Harry had a huge, metal chute constructed on the docks (as ever), which lived in a single-storey extension at the back of the house, was top-filled by the coalmen from the flat roof of the extension, and had a hopper arrangement at the bottom whereby the coke hods could be filled from inside the house. I have to say it worked well, but I feel for the coalmen who had to lug the one-hundredweight (112lb, 50kg) sacks to the rear of the house and up a ladder, which was also built on the docks. It had the sort of steep gradient you only find on ships, where on the way up your toes will always catch on the tread immediately above the one on which you are standing, and on the way down your heel is scuffed by the tread immediately behind you. There were no hand rails. The health-and-safety people would have gone apoplectic, but, as it happened, there were never any accidents!

Harry's next project was to wire up his Grundig TK 24 tape recorder, with extensions to every room in the house – and I mean every room! He was passionate about Bach, and I grew up in an environment where this would be played around the clock. In fact we were not allowed to listen to anything written after 1750, as Dad considered it trivial. That was a major error on his part! Changing the seven-inch tape reels became burdensome, so Harry had made, again on the docks, outriggers to the TK24 so that he could play purpose-made, thirteen-inch reels, which would give greatly extended playing time. This was not as easy as you might think, as the gearing had to be modified as well to achieve the correct tape speed. The machine was, by now, acquiring awesome proportions, so a special cabinet was beautifully made for him by a joiner by the name of Mr Farrow – a superb job, and the family still has the cabinet. Not content with this, Dad decided that it would be useful if the tape reversed itself at the end of each track, thereby extending the playing time to sixteen hours! This he did by inserting a section of foil tape at the end of each reel, which effectively shorted out the circuit between the playing heads, and they then resumed operation in the opposite direction. He had, in fact, invented the reversing tape, and was on 'Inventors' Club' on BBC Television in 1953. I went to London with him and watched the programme from the hotel. He never made a bean out of the idea, but it was down to him that every tape cassette thereafter could reverse itself when it came to the end of the track!

His interest in recording progressed, and he decided to make a disc-cutting machine that could produce 33rpm long players (LPs) from a tape recording. Where all the bits came from I don't know, but much of it was again made on the docks. There was a thing called a 'swarf pump' that removed the waste material cut from the grooves to make the record. This had to be acoustically separate from the house for obvious reasons, so Harry put it against the outside wall of the house on next door's land. There ensued an argument about exactly where the boundary was, which went on for many years and I am not sure if it was ever resolved. He would often record groups or bands, and make records for them to help with their promotional activities. He once made a record for Norma Proctor, the internationally acclaimed contralto, who was a lovely woman that we got to know well; she lived in Cleethorpes at the time. I remember well the air of complete silence that had to be observed throughout the house whilst recording was taking place, and woe betide anyone who made the slightest squeak!

Harry was also passionate about photography. The bathroom was duly divided into two to create a dark room. As kids we spent many hours in there with him, and learnt about film processing, developing, enlarging and printing. He made his own enlarger, which included a wooden cam and an arrangement of levers that made it self-focussing at any distance of the enlarger from the print surface. He did all the mathematics himself, and I have to say it worked well. His exploits into colour photography, however, were a disaster, but I later found out he was colour blind.

Even then, it struck us as ironic that we would be made to split open empty toothpaste tubes to extract every last ounce of toothpaste as an economy measure, whilst father would think nothing of buying Leica, Rolleiflex and Hasselblad cameras until they were coming out of his ears!

The next project was to build a garage, which was duly accomplished by a charming, old chap by the name of Jack Dann. I spent many happy hours with Jack, assisting him – mainly in unhelpful ways. We had also brought the garden tool shed from Waltham, but Dad decided we needed more workshop space. It was decided, therefore, to build a second storey on top of the garage. Dad held no truck with things like planning and building regulation approvals, and there ensued months of argument with the authorities, for whom he had scant regard. He won in the end by obtaining his own copy of the Planning Acts and discovering that if the extension was designated as a 'boat loft', then it did not need planning approval. The building is there to this day, and that is why it has this huge door at first floor level, which does nothing and has never been used, and was, ostensibly, for admitting boats to the building!

Harry also brought with him from Waltham his electric bike. The history of this arose from fuel rationing during the war. He had already tried putting sails on motor cycles, but the law enforcement agencies did not take kindly to this, it was also a wind-dependent notion, and the project had to be abandoned. The electric bike, however, was quite a beast! He started with an old-fashioned butcher's bike, one of those things with a small wheel at the front and rather fat tyres. A Lucas car dynamo was mounted on the handlebars and connected up with reverse polarity so that it ran as a motor, and was driven from a huge lead-acid car battery slung beneath the crossbar. A length of bicycle chain connected the motor to a cog on the front wheel and control was via a Bakelite on-off switch. I tried this machine when it had not been used for many, many years, and it went perfectly first time, although the speed control 'on-off' switch was somewhat abrupt! Dad was quite a fine, if uneducated, engineer!

Being a bit of a technocrat, Harry was among the first to have a 405-line TV set – I know it predated the coronation in 1953 as we had quite an audience that day! Reception from the Holme Moss transmitter was not all it might have been, Grimsby being out on a bit of a limb, and the new Belmont transmitter had not then been built. Harry decided, therefore, that a taller aerial was required, and that 100 feet (30m) should just about do the trick. I well remember the day, involving about 15 people from the docks, when this construction started its skyward journey, in sections pushed up from below, with people heaving away from north, south, east and west in an attempt to keep the whole thing in some sort of equilibrium, and ending up with the fire brigade, ladder at absolute full stretch, lending a hand. Stability, by that stage, had turned into something of an emergency when one of the chimney-stack anchoring points became detached from the rest of the house.

Harry was in no way a natural gardener, but decided that a new lawn should be laid at the rear of the house. This task was undertaken in his usual fastidious way, and it was so level that you could have used it as a snooker table! He took great offence at the starlings eating the grass seed, and so purchased a 0.22 airgun! We were taught to shoot, and shot starlings and sparrows mercilessly. This is a part of my upbringing that I now very much regret, but we did have a lot of fun with the airgun and became fairly skilled in its use. I remember trying to demonstrate to my school friends that it was possible to shoot pellets into next door's stained glass window without breaking it. I had done this once, but the demonstration was a failure! There were ramifications. We consoled ourselves with shooting out the whole of a row of plant pots that our neighbour, Mr Peel, had lovingly aligned. We shot through each plant stem first, and then broke the pots. There was quite a row about that too! There was, much later, on the subject of airguns, an incident that I considered rather unfair. We were at our holiday bungalow in Humberstone, of which more later, and were indulging in some innocent target practice, shooting tins off a wooden trestle. I knew I had got the measure of the sights exactly right, and shot a tin out of a friend's hand, one Paddy Abbott, an explosives expert aged about twelve, of which much more later! Anyone who thoroughly understands airguns and sights will realise that this was in fact a fairly safe procedure, but my father, who happened to be watching, and who would forgive us any number of outrageous acts, took exception to this and hit me over the head with a plank. I can never be sure whether there was any long-term damage, but if, dear reader, you perceive that there is, then this is where it came from!

However, back to the lawn. The spring came, the grass grew and everything looked perfect. Harry's next project was to design and build his own electric lawnmower, which had a chain drive from the electric motor. The chain was lubricated by a drip-feed mechanism, using old engine oil from the new Austin 16. It had the habit of leaving long, black, perfectly aligned stripes down the lawn, which it did with regularity. When we kids were given the job of cutting the lawn, the cardinal sin was to run over the flex, which would then have to be renewed in its entirety! This, again, we did with regularity.

Having become attuned to petrol rationing and the shortages of the war, the fuel consumption of the new aforementioned Austin 16 caused Harry some consternation. He, therefore, decided to convert it to diesel, and imported a 1600cc Borgward diesel engine from Germany. (It was imported in one of the lifeboats of the Statham, a trawler we had built in Bremerhaven in 1956, ostensibly as a lifeboat engine, so no import duty was paid). This was about the most awful car to drive imaginable! But it was very economical. The economy was somewhat improved when he realised that he could run it on red diesel taken from the trawler generator tanks, which was free of tax. A Guinness label for a tax disc completed his economic strategy, and his motoring costs were, to all intents and purposes, nil. Always ahead of his time, he probably owned the first diesel car in the UK. My Dad was certainly no angel, but certain bits of his heart were in the right place! He later took to importing Mercedes diesel cars, again the first in the country, and more about that later too!

His inventiveness continued and he was never without a project. The tragedy of Dad, in my view and with the benefit of hindsight, is that he was incredibly intelligent, but was denied the advantage of a university education, which would have given him the discipline he so desperately needed to use to best advantage what he had. He won a scholarship from his school, De Aston in Market Rasen, to Cambridge, but HG would not let him go. My grandfather did not make many really bad decisions, but that was certainly one of them. His logic ran that there are three million unemployed, there is a job for you on the docks, so you get yourself down there!

So much for Dad's inventions! But this was the environment in which I had to grow up.

5

Abbey Road, and Infant and Junior School

SHORTLY AFTER WE moved to 33 Abbey Road, I acquired my first girlfriend at the age of four and a half. Her name was Louise Thomas, and she was the daughter of a couple that ran the chip shop around the corner on Wellowgate.

My initial overtures may be considered unsophisticated, but we had a bit of a session in the tool shed. We jointly took the lids off about ten tins of paint, and painted the whole of the shed floor and quite a lot of ourselves! It was altogether quite a good day, and I suppose I must have been too young to be chastised, but I do remember serious evening meetings between her parents and mine. I did not see Louise again, and decided it might be best to keep clear of women.

My first day at school was now not far away; only recently I drove past Nunsthorpe Primary School and looked at the gates where I was deposited by my mother on my first day at school. Nunsthorpe, it has to be said, was a rough area, but I loved that school and so many people I met there had hearts of gold. The next few years were spent in a rough-and-tumble environment, but I think I prospered fairly well. I don't remember a lot about it, but I do remember painting a red wall in art. It required a lot of paint and not a lot of imagination or ability! It was a mixed school, and when I was in Miss Frisby's top class, aged seven, I remember falling for Lynn Pulfrey and Celia Wright. Neither relationship progressed, however. They must have thought me a real twerp. I remember putting up my hand and saying, "please, Miss Frisby, I've lost my bus fare!" That would have been one (old) penny. She had the whole class scouring the floor for about 15 minutes, and then I had to say, "please, Miss, I've found it; it was in my hand!" It must have been my first bus fare; I was so terrified of losing it and had held it so tightly that my fingers must have gone numb!

There was a short period when my sister Gibby was persuaded to take me to school on the back of her bicycle, to which a small seat had been fitted. But this turned out to be a bit of a tall order as we lived about three miles from the school, so it did not survive as a long-term solution. Also, at about this time, still aged just over four, I had learnt to ride my own cycle, and persuaded Mum and Dad to let me take myself to school. This was great fun and involved crossing a small brook at the end of

Westward Ho, which was bridged with two planks and no handrail. My favourite stunt was to cross the brook riding 'no-handed', which I regularly did, without incident.

I progressed, aged about eight, to the adjacent junior school, which was sex segregated in two connected, adjacent buildings; my sister Gibby was already attending the girls' school. I had made no progress with Lynn or Celia at infant school, but really fell for Janet Mills, a prefect in the girls' school whose parents owned a grocery shop in Chelmsford Avenue.

She was, I thought, a pretty lass. We would pass notes to each other in the school corridors, and, eventually, we agreed to meet at her parents' shop on the following Saturday. I don't know what exactly I did wrong, but when I duly arrived, she was out!

A gang of us formed a strong friendship at Nunsthorpe; the names I remember well are Les Smith, Bobby Nutten, Norman Semple, Tony Mitchell, Ernie Green and Peter Linford. Les would, many years later, join me on my first trip to Iceland on the Statham, probably when we were about 15.

But, at Nunsthorpe, cricket became the primary passion, and we would play almost every lunchtime and every evening after school. Sometimes we would use the school playing fields, which were very extensive at that time, and sometimes the new lawn at Abbey Road, which my father had so kindly levelled for us! The main problem with this was that, at the time a second storey was put on the garage, it was also extended down the garden in order to accommodate two cars in tandem. This made the garage's end window far too close to our wickets, and the local glaziers had a field day before hard balls were banned. The other problem with cricket at Abbey Road was that, often, as Les Smith and I were getting into the swing of it, Dad's car would come rattling down the drive and his standard opening remark was, "Leslie go home, Bill do your piano practice." So we stuck to the school playing fields.

Our equipment was basic to say the least, but the best – and one of only two presents I ever got from Dad was a brand new cricket set bought from Gamages in London! Needless to say, the cricket bag was made on the docks out of sail cloth. The other present was a rather magnificent pedal car; as you might imagine, no ordinary machine. It was made entirely on the docks, had a proper chassis and steering, but was propelled with bicycle pedals so it could really get a move on! I recall Ernie Green and I took it to Immingham and back one day, a round trip distance of probably 20 miles, spoilt only by getting one of its pram-style wheels buckled in the tram tracks. The return journey took some time, but in those days no one was concerned about where we were!

By age seven, I had taken up the violin in addition to the piano, Gibby had already added the cello to her skill set and Leon was just starting with the piano. There then followed several years of a routine of weekly music lessons, piano with Miss Rushton in Farebrother Street and violin with Mrs Parkinson in Brighowgate.

This would have taken me to age eleven, when I had to sit the eleven-plus exam that would determine which secondary school we were to attend. The year would have been 1957. The brightest kids went to Wintringham Grammar School. The next level down either went to the technical college in Eleanor Street or to Havelock School in Cleethorpes. The least intelligent went to Chelmsford Secondary Modern School, not far from Nunsthorpe.

By some good fortune, Gibby and I got in to the grammar school. There was a boys' school and a girls' school, separated by a large playing field where the sexes intermingled at break and lunchtimes. Thus started the next phase in my life.

6

Senior School and the Holiday Bungalow at Humberstone

Life at Wintringham went ahead in a more serious vein, with sciences and languages introduced into the syllabus. I don't recall anything exceptional about my time at grammar school; all the interesting things happened outside school hours! However, the cricket had to take more of a back seat, although Gibby and I did find time to play in the school orchestra. I didn't much enjoy that as the standard was pretty ropey, but the operas we put on were quite good fun. *Trial by Jury*, a Gilbert and Sullivan farce, was one I particularly enjoyed.

Most days, after school finished at 4.15pm, I would get on my bike with a random collection of mates and we would hare down Hainton Avenue and Freeman Street to Grimsby Fish Docks. It would be unusual for us not to have one of our ships in port, so we would spend many happy hours exploring the ships, tampering with anything we felt like and generally being a complete bloody nuisance to the watchmen. On the positive side, we did learn a lot about trawlers, steam engines (as they all were at that time), winches, electronic equipment, ropes, knots, nets, windlasses and so forth.

The trawlers would be in one of about four locations on the docks. The first was Fish Dock No. 1. This is where the fish were landed and sold on the market. The following day they would take aboard about 100 tons of ice in preparation for the next trip. The filthy, old steam tugs would then tow the trawlers back through a narrow lock into the larger area of the fish docks. We always thought it was a great bonus if we could ride on the ships while they were being towed. The only snag was that it was then a long walk back to pick up our bikes!

The second area was where the crane jetties were. This was really a repair and provisioning area with massive cranes equipped for heavy lifting, which was frequently required on trawlers.

The third area was adjacent to the crane jetties; this was where the slipways were located. Trawlers could be pulled out of the water on cradles heaved by huge winches, in large, brick buildings, pulling on 75mm diameter steel cables. Here below-waterline repairs could be effected, hulls painted, propellers changed and so on. I well recall that the only access to the trawler was then via a vast ladder that reached from the ground to the ship's gunwale, which could be anything up to 60 feet in the air. A bit of slack rope formed the only handrail, and at mid span these ladders acquired a terrifying bouncing motion with which I never felt really comfortable. Health and safety would again have gone apoplectic, but I don't recall there being any accidents.

The fourth area was the 'North Wall'. This is where the ships took on their final provisions and prepared for sea. The ships were almost always moored 'bow on', so still more flimsy death traps called ladders were required to gain access.

There was a fifth area, the 'coaling jetty', where huge hammerhead cranes would be used to load coal into the holds of the trawlers. However, by this time all our ships were either built as oil burners or had been converted to burn oil, so we didn't need to use them.

So, clearly, the fish docks was an Aladdin's cave of intrigue and interest, which kept we schoolboys fascinated for many happy hours. Our bicycles were our essential transport and our only means of getting around. In the summer we would ride to the bathing pool on Cleethorpes sea front, always mob handed, and I remember these as very happy times. We would think nothing of cycling 30 or 40 miles in a day, and no one ever knew or even asked where we were; again, incredible by today's standards.

It would be about 1958 when the three families referred to earlier, namely the Crampins, the Browns and the Crofts, built holiday prefab bungalows next to each other in a place known as the 'Humberstone Fitties' (the Fitties). This was basically a shanty town of largely home-built holiday shacks, close to the sand dunes and the beach. The Fitties are located near the mouth of the River Humber opposite the Hailsand Fort that was part of a wartime submarine defence system. This was a fabulous area in which to grow up, and it is a real shame that it has now been ruined by the influx of hundreds of holiday caravans.

The fort was about a mile out to sea in the Humber Estuary, and there was a cast-iron boom defence that connected the fort to the shore. It consisted of two rows of large, iron columns about 2.5m apart, and a lattice of 100mm wide iron angles connecting the columns in the horizontal plane. There was one famous occasion when Guy Brown and I rather recklessly climbed onto the shore end of the boom at high tide, and walked on top of it all the way to the fort. It was low tide by the time we got there so it must have taken us several hours.

Gibby and I had a canoe each and we learnt our basic boat-handling skills in those treacherous waters, where the currents could run at five knots or more. As it happened, we never got into any difficulties. However, when a French pen-friend called Jacques, who was staying with the Browns, decided to have a go, he was not so lucky. Basically he was washed out to sea and the big, yellow Sikorsky helicopter had to be scrambled from RAF North Coates. We kept a low profile during this operation as we correctly assumed that our pocket money would not cover the costs of the rescue!

I well recall another hairy venture, this time involving inflatable lilos. Another family who were good friends with us also had a nearby holiday bungalow. They were the Abbotts, and young Paddy – the explosives expert – was a staunch member of our gang. One day he and I decided to experiment with the seagoing characteristics of lilos. I would sit up front, sculling with my hands, and Paddy would lie on his back with fins on to provide the major propulsion. This was so successful that we decided to attempt a trip around the Hailsand Fort. The air supply in the lilo had to be topped up a few times – no easy task in the water. We could so easily have been washed or blown out to sea, and it was only because we could achieve a fair turn of speed that we got away with it.

Paddy figured large in our escapades, and taught us to make two types of bomb. The first was made of 'crow scarers', which are basically a string of ten or so extra-large bangers twisted onto a paraffin-soaked rope. You lit one end, and every half an hour or so one of these things would go off. One evening, we put a string under Aunt Sarah's bungalow. She did not get her best night's sleep and we were not popular for a few days, to put it mildly. To obtain an even greater effect, the bangers were taken off the rope and tied together. This device was capable of doing quite a lot of damage.

The second type of device was the more elegant. Dry ice, which is solid carbon dioxide, was readily available on the docks. It is very cold, being about -20°C, and was used to keep fish cool during transit in delivery vans. It gradually evaporates, but if you put it in water it bubbles away merrily. In one scenario, you put a few chips into a strong lemonade bottle with an internal thread, half fill it with water, screw it up tight and keep well clear. The pressure gradually builds up until the whole thing goes up with considerable force, and a lot of glass is scattered all over the place.

In a second scenario, we did the same thing, but with a bottle with a soft, external, metal top. We stuck the bottle, suitably primed, top first into the ground. In this situation the top blows off before the bottle bursts. Some more friends, the Hudsons from Doncaster, had a car and caravan in the next field. When this thing went off it shot about 200 feet into the air, intact, and landed between the car and the caravan. That was a near thing that, fortunately, they did not need to know about.

John Hudson, the father, was a great guy and he taught us all to drive his Land Rover in that field, which was a terrific experience. He had very successfully flown Mosquitoes in the war as part of the Pathfinder reconnaissance squadron. Much later, he suffered a terrible accident at their holiday home in Spain. Basically, he had climbed a tree with a chainsaw, fallen and broken his neck. He died a few weeks later.

Then there was the saga of the sand yacht. I don't know quite how Dad got involved with these things, but I do recall going to Southport to meet a chap called Millet Denning, then the world speed champion, from whom Dad bought our bright-orange yacht. This was a somewhat lethal device with reverse wheel steering in the opposite sense to normal, i.e. you turned the wheel left to steer to the right. The plan of the yacht's structure was essentially like a cruciform. There were two widely spaced wheels at the front, on the ends of the arms, and two steering wheels close together at the rear, above which the driver would be seated. The mast, however, was stepped at the very front, forward of the two front wheels. Thus, during a strong gust of wind the machine would rotate around the front wheels, lifting the rear wheels clear of the ground. You would find yourself doing about 60 mph with no steering!

We all had a lot of fun with this machine and went many miles on it between Cleethorpes and North Coates. The normal arrangement was for Dad to tow us from the bungalow to a cut-through in the sand dunes, thereby giving us access to the beach. He would then meet us at a pre-arranged time to tow us back. I recall that one time Guy and I were waiting for Dad to give us a tow back, but he had failed to appear. So we thought we would sail the thing back down the road. This was no problem until we got to the bungalows. Without thinking I turned into the gap between our bungalow and the Browns. Unfortunately, it was down wind! The yacht accelerated alarmingly, and the gap was obstructed, on the left by Gibby's canoe and on the right by the Brown's brand-new Morris 1000 Traveller. I had to decide which one to hit and chose the brand-new car. Again, not popular with either family.

Dad was very good at providing larger than life toys! Another thing he bought was a kite about 2m tall, which we could probably get about 200 feet into the air. We would then attach a bag full of stones about half way up the kite string, with one corner torn off the bottom of the bag. Thus by jerking the line we could drop stones from a great height on to more or less any bungalow we chose.

About this time, Gibby reached the age of 16, and Dad bought her a motor cycle and sidecar. Not an ordinary example, but a 500cc 1930 Sunbeam with a hand gear change. This machine was an absolute beast with masses of low-end torque. Paddy requested a go on this thing, to which, of course, I readily agreed, assuming he knew roughly what he was doing. In this instance, I was disastrously wrong. He opened the throttle wide with his right hand and instantly let out the clutch with the other. The front wheel lurched into the air, such that the right-hand lock that he had desperately applied was ineffective, and the contraption gathered speed in a sort of bucking bronco straight line. Unfortunately, in his path, some poor chap was laboriously building a timber-framed bungalow. The frame was almost complete, but no cladding had been applied, so the whole thing was fairly fragile. Paddy tore into this structure, smashing the sidecar to smithereens, and, regrettably, knocking the whole bungalow frame out of square. Again, this was not one of our better days. Dad replaced the sidecar bodywork with a large wooden packing case. Poor Gibby would drive this thing to school each day with her cello in the packing case – quite a sight!

There were many families in the gang; in addition to Crampins, Browns and Crofts, there were the Abbotts, the Hudsons, the Fitzwilliams, the Picks and probably a few more. Aunt Sarah would sometimes arrive with our cousins, Janice and Lesley, who would all join in.

Against this background, there was always the annual barbecue, probably involving about 50 of us. The day would start with us trawling the beaches and dunes for firewood, and we would invariably produce a huge bonfire. These events were spectacular, involved everyone and were very much enjoyed by us all. Although my stories inevitably refer to our section of the gang, each sex and age group had its own opposite numbers who formed up and did different things. The barbecue was the one event where everyone was together. For fireworks Dad would bring home out-of-date distress flares from the trawlers, which would put more conventional incendiaries to shame!

Sometimes Guy's elder brother Stuart would join in our exploits, but he was about three years older, which is a lot at that age. That probably explains why Stuart took so much interest in the two beautiful, Faroese au pair girls hosted by the Browns, Lita and Vinnie. There was a bit of a sub culture going on here, also involving one or two of our maids and their friends, who were of a similar age and sex. I remember that our maid Meryl and her friend Wilma once walked out to the Hailsand Fort. There were a couple of soldiers on the fort at that time. Unfortunately, they were cut off by the incoming tide and were stuck there for another twelve hours!

When there was trouble, either Guy or Paddy was seldom far away. Guy and I pulled off a spectacular raid at Wonderland, an amusement centre in Cleethorpes. A key part of a functioning radar is the cavity magnetron. The core of this device is two immensely powerful magnets strapped back to back, and, obviously, we had access to these magnets from the trawlers. We set off on our bikes, and I remember I had a magnet stuffed up my jumper. The first snag was that, going around corners, the magnet would suddenly grab hold of the metal handlebars with predictable results.

The amusement hall had dozens of machines where you inserted an (old) penny and a metal ball appeared in front of a flicker. With the magnet we could guide the ball around the track and drop it into the winning holes. We collected buckets full of pennies before we were apprehended. Guy arranged for old George, the yard hand at T H Brown Haulage Ltd., to collect us. He pretended to be our father, promising the security man that we would be severely reprimanded when we got home. So we cleared off laughing at our good fortune. Strangely we kept the pennies. I can only assume this was because there was no notice to say that cavity magnetrons could not be used to enhance the performance of slot machines, so no one knew if it was actually illegal!

And so life went on during my time at Wintringham Grammar school: a mix of school, Humberstone and the fish docks. There were no other holidays unless Dad wanted to pick up a new car from Germany. Nevertheless, I feel we had a rich and privileged upbringing where we learnt a huge amount about lots of different things. We also had great friends.

My final days at Wintringham terminated after my O-level examinations. My results were not good enough for me to progress into the sixth form, although I did get a Grade A in woodwork!

My lack of progress at school is a great regret to me. It had two fundamental causes. First, I assumed I would walk into a job on the docks and therefore felt no need to make any effort. Second, because of this, I was put in the lower forms where I mixed with a fairly rough crowd whose ambitions did not include furthering their education. There is, I feel, a very important lesson to be learnt here, which I sincerely hope my grandchildren will heed.

7

Working on the Docks and Going to Sea

Fortunately, I was given a job on the docks; this would have been in 1962. I loved and was totally committed to the trawling industry, and never thought for a moment I would ever do anything else. I was paid £10 per week, but had to give half of this to my mother. I was, therefore, living on the breadline and I remember how difficult it was to keep up with my friends who always seemed to be so much better off.

That notwithstanding, this was, on reflection, one of the happiest times of my life, although I had to work twelve-hour days and be available around the clock to assist with trawlers either landing or putting to sea.

In the absence of those activities, my day would start at 8.00am. I was basically part of the 'heavy gang' whose function was to turn the trawlers around, and carry out the endless carting about of supplies and machinery for the ships. The offices of the Crampin Steam Fishing Company were an Aladdin's cave. First there were two general stores full of nets, shackles, twine, ropes, spare propeller shafts and the like. I loved the smell of sisal, which was so evocative of the ships themselves. Then there was the metalwork shop. 'Harry the Tinner' (Harry Pickard) would make all the metal cooking utensils and the H-shaped galley funnels for the ships. If it ever crops up in *Trivial Pursuit*, the 'H' shape at the top of the chimney is called the 'Charlie Noble' – origin unknown!

There was nothing luxurious about our stores and workshops; they had bare concrete floors and a rough, concrete staircase that led to the radio department where my father worked. His role was to procure and maintain all the electrical and electronic equipment on the ships, quite a big job with a departmental staff of only four. Nowadays this work would be farmed out to specialists, but that wasn't the company culture at the time. Bob Leach was my father's right-hand man, who also spent some considerable time working on our cars adding bits and pieces. The radio department was a fascinating place, with radars, transmitters and echo sounders lying around against a backcloth of yards of wooden shelving full of valves and other essential spares.

The main offices ran to linoleum flooring; the office staff sat on Dickensian high stools and worked on long benches. Arthur Rimmer was the company secretary, Don Burman the chief cashier and Eric Beighton the superintendent engineer. Bill Moss, a company director, and Norman Slater were chief fish salesmen and general clerical. My cousin Norman also worked alongside the team; he was a great organiser and I recall very good at graphs! I would man the telephone switchboard over lunchtime, and one of my jobs was to type out the crew lists for each new trip: name, rank and address. Hence, I learnt to type, and can to this day still type out the word 'Deckhand' faster than anyone else – there were quite a few of them on each list.

The 'Gaffer's Board Room', was just off the main office and equally spartan. This would have been originally occupied by HG Crampin, my grandfather, but, after his death, his eldest son, my uncle HW Crampin took over. The loos are worth a mention. Pretty basic, the loo paper was a recent *Financial Times* torn up into squares and hung up on a piece of twine. Bill Moss kept his own private loo roll, and woe betide anyone who tried to pinch it!

The fish docks at that time were a hive of activity with dozens of specialist firms carrying out highly skilled work. I remember with great affection many of these firms, and feel sadness when I go around the docks today and see that they all disappeared with the demise of the trawling industry around 1970, when Iceland's fishing limits were increased from 12 to 200 miles. Hence, there were few places of any consequence left to fish.

You were on the docks, or 'down dock' once you traversed the level crossing near Riby Square, and acknowledged the policeman in the small brick hut who monitored all comings and goings. Our offices were then on the right at the top of Fish Dock Road, now completely demolished. As you walked along, next was the ice manufacturing house, then, as I remember, the offices of the Grimsby Steam Fishing Vessels' Mutual Insurance Company, which was run by one marine surveyor, Bill Taylor. It was he to whom the skippers had to report and explain any damage to the ships. Other buildings were occupied by the Trawler Owners' Club (a fine lunchtime hostelry, I suspect), Olsen's the compass adjusters, and the Great Grimsby Coal Salt and Tanning Company or Cosalt as it is now known. Only this latter firm now survives, owing to its foresighted diversity into other activities. Originally, it was the main provider of provisions for the trawlers, including everything from food supplies to ropes, nets and shackles.

When we had a ship landing, we would wait at the lock gates – near the dock tower, with friends and family of the crew, waiting to meet and greet the ships coming home. The dock gates were only opened two hours either side of high water, so trawlers had to wait at anchor in the river until the height of tide was right. The ships would enter the docks and pass through the swing bridge and into Fish Dock One to land their catches. We would hurtle round from the dock gates to meet them and catch the heaving lines, which in turn were attached to the main mooring warps. There was quite an art to catching the heaving lines, which relied on the personnel at both ends performing with a degree of proficiency. If the catch failed and the heaving line went into the dock water, on the next attempt the line would, of course, be soaked, resulting in not the best of days for your attire. I would then go aboard to greet the skipper, along with relatives of the crew, and a couple of customs officers. These were convivial occasions with cans of Barclay's beer or glasses of Harvey's Bristol Cream sherry available all round. A few packets of cigarettes were handed around, left over from the bonded store in the skipper's cabin. These obviously had not had duty paid on them, and this practice was what the customs officers were supposed to prevent, but no one seemed to mind. And then home to bed, often arriving well past midnight.

I would arrive at 5.00am the following morning, with Bill Moss and Norman Slater, to sell the fish to the dozens of local fish merchants; the ships having been unloaded overnight by the 'lumpers', one of the toughest jobs on the docks. We wore quite-smart white coats and heavy, wooden-soled clogs with iron horse shoes nailed to their undersides. Although designed for safety, these things were quite lethal. The dockside quay sloped significantly towards the water and was always covered in fish slime. How more accidents were avoided, I will never know. At the end of the sale, following the mayhem of bidding for and labelling the fish boxes allocated to the merchants, it was off to Dobson's Café, or 'Dobbie's' as it was known, for tea out of huge pint mugs and a bread roll with some sort of fried potato mash inside. Absolutely delicious!

Then to the office, or, more correctly, to the store, where a quantity of fish was being filleted by Maurice Cutting, our store manager, for distribution to family and friends. There I would report to my immediate boss, Hector Butt, the company's outside manager to be briefed on the day's tasks. The ships, meanwhile, would be towed by scruffy, little tugs to the opposite side of Fish Dock One to receive ice for the next trip.

Next call for the ships would be the crane jetty, which catered for heavy lifting and major engineering works, located next to the slipways.

Bridges and Salmon, shipwrights, was run by Jack Salmon and his son Duncan. Duncan would supervise the hauling out of the trawlers onto the slips, when work below the water line was needed. This was a very tricky job as every ship had a different underwater profile and the supports had to be exactly right.

To support the general servicing of the ships, there were many other specialist firms that I remember well. Clark & Co Engineers, where two of their blacksmiths would pick up the back of my minivan and push it around like a wheel barrow, with me still in it. Then there were Bemrose the painters, Sleights the plate layers, Fenners the tank cleaners, Jack Vincent Outfitters, Kelvin Hughes Marine Electronics, Decca and so it went on; in all employing hundreds of skilled people.

The ships were then moved to the North Wall for final provisioning and preparation for sea. After the previous three-week trip, the crew usually had only three days' leave before setting off on the next trip. However, the annual fit out took about six weeks, so that gave the crews at least one decent break, although some elected to sail in other trawlers. Having landed, the crews picked up significant amounts of money from the office cashier. However, it was not unusual for some of them to return to the office the following morning for a £2 sub, having spent the £100 or so the night before.

The sailing time would then be announced. The early morning ones were incredibly atmospheric. Ship's lights shimmering in the dark; the smell of steam, oil and sisal; the hum of the generators as perhaps ten or fifteen ships prepared for sea; and the hive of activity as streams of taxis brought the crews to the ships. Finding some of the crew was not always easy, and this was the job of the ships' husband, Arthur Richardson. I spent many hours driving around Grimsby with him in the early hours collecting the latecomers. This was an art in itself as the addresses from which they were sometimes collected was not always the same as the one I had typed in the crew list! Sometimes, we might knock on the wrong door by mistake, not much appreciated at 3.00am. One response to this from a lady in rollers in an upstairs window was, and I quote, "if you don't f*** off I'll chuck this piss pot on your 'ed". So we learnt to be very careful. If the ship had an early mechanical problem and returned to Grimsby unexpectedly from the Humber, this was known to have caused a few marital problems!

Our fleet at that time comprised five trawlers, a vastly reduced fleet compared with pre-war times when we had up to 50 deep-water trawlers, so many having been lost in the war. Also quite a few had been scrapped due to being uneconomic coal-burners. These would be the *Wellard, Barnett, Paynter* and *Gregory*. The *Hassett* and *Beldock* had been lost at sea with some tragic loss of life.

So we had a fairly modern fleet consisting of the *Bradman* and the *Yardley*, both built in 1950; the *Statham*, built in 1956; and the *Trueman* and the *Padgett*, both built in 1960. Most of our ships were built by either Cochranes of Selby, or Cook, Welton and Gemmell of Beverley. The *Statham*, however, was the exception, being built in Bremerhaven by Rickmanswerft. She was one of six similar ships built for various owners, which were among the first to have welded hulls instead of riveted, the smoother profile giving them, perhaps, an extra knot of speed. The others were the *Royal Lincs*, *Coldstreamer*, *Black Watch*, *Northern Eagle* and the *Lord Beatty* out of Hull.

On her maiden voyage from Bremerhaven to Grimsby, the *Statham* averaged 15 knots, a huge improvement on the more usual 12.5 knots.

I recall most of the skippers of the time, Alan Whitelam (the *Yardley* followed by the *Statham*), Olley Emmons (the *Bradman* followed by the *Statham*), Alan Denison (the *Bradman* after Olley), Eric Tofton (the *Padgett*) and Mick Lynch (the *Trueman*). The biggest money earners were undoubtedly Olley Emmons and Alan Denison, although 'Deno' as he was known ran up costly repair bills with his rather cavalier ship handling, which tended to take the shine off his performance. He was, therefore, denied the superior, but costly, manganese bronze propellers and had to make do with cast iron because of excessive damage, and this would cost him perhaps half a knot of speed. I recall Deno bringing the *Bradman* through the lock gates at a fair rate of knots. He would claim he achieved better steering that way. The dock master, however, didn't see things in quite the same way, and yelled at Deno, "one of these days you'll finish up in Riby Square toilets" (language slightly modified for the purposes of this book). Riby Square is just off Fish Dock One, but you would have to plough through a fair number of roads, buildings and a railway line to get there!

Olley, I recall, made the *Grimsby Evening Telegraph* with a record catch of plaice from the North Cape of Iceland. Among other fish, he caught 1,200 kits of plaice, and 800 kits of cod and haddock – a kit being ten stones, or 64kg for younger readers. The trip grossed £14,700, when £8,000 would be more normal at that time for an average trip.

Eventually, the time came for me to further my experience by doing a few trips to sea. I had spent six months at the Grimsby Nautical College for Fishermen, so I wasn't completely useless, I could braid a net and do a decent splice. These trips were usually 21 days in duration, but could be anywhere between 18 and 24 depending on how prolific the fishing was.

I did six trips in all. Three were in the *Statham* with Alan Whitelam; two were in the *Bradman* with Olley Emmons and later Alan Denison; and the other in the *Trueman* with Mick Lynch. Mostly ships fished the North Cape of Iceland, but also the White (Barents) Sea, Greenland, Bear Island and the Faroes.

I was totally intoxicated with trawlers and the sea. It was a great privilege to have the opportunity to learn deck skills; seamanship and navigation; the operation of radars, echo sounders and radios, including learning the now redundant Morse code; and learning how to operate the huge steam engines. On one occasion, I did two trips

The launch of the *Statham* at the yard of Rickmers Werft in Bremerhaven in 1956.

back to back on the *Statham* with only a three-day break. This now surprises even me as I suffered badly from almost continuous sea sickness.

The memories blur somewhat after 50 years, but there were a few events that I still remember well.

We were heading for home in the *Statham* with Alan Whitelam, cruising southbound along the east coast of Iceland. We had a very mediocre catch of about 1,400 kits. Alan had the echo sounder on, and as we passed over the Kidney Bank, the ocean floor was suddenly covered in black echo reflections scribed into the paper readout. He immediately rang 'Stop' and put the nets over the side.

We only had about four hauls of about an hour each, and basically doubled our catch to 2,400 kits. The fish were all huge cod, each between three and four feet long. Having been caught at the end of the trip they were at their freshest and sold very well. We were abeam the Faroe Islands by the time we had finished gutting all the fish, not an easy job lifting a four-foot cod and then having to throw it into the fish washer.

Statham arrives in Grimsby from the builders in Bremerhaven, with the tug *Brenda Fisher*.

I did another North Cape trip in January, and will never forget the intense cold. Outbound we had passed through the Pentland Firth, a treacherous bit of water between the north east corner of Scotland and the Orkney Islands. Here seven tides meet, and in 'wind over tide' situations the faces of the huge waves were near vertical and crashed into the side of the ship like a fleet of tanks. Sometimes, even the largest trawlers would avoid this area and route via Dennis Head at the north end of the Orkneys. The strength of the tides in the Firth were unbelievable. The skipper demonstrated this by setting up a transit between two objects ashore. Our speed through the water was 13.5 knots, but the transit didn't change, showing that, in fact, we were going nowhere and would continue to do so until the tides changed – some tides!

Perhaps my favourite trip was in the *Bradman*. In fact, she was my favourite ship and had the enviable reputation of being 'lucky'. Although she was a bit older and slower than the *Statham*, she was an exceptionally good sea ship. This was probably because she had a superstructure that was two decks high, as opposed to the *Statham*'s three, and therefore had a lower centre of gravity. I also hated the *Statham*'s

Statham leaves Grimsby on her maiden voyage.

low-pressure turbine. The steam passed through this having been through the triple-expansion steam engine, and made one almighty din. I'm surprised it didn't scare the fish away, bearing in mind how easily sound travels through water. The *Bradman* had a beautiful, open-sided steam engine, which went about its business with a smooth hiss. She also had a lovely, big, old-fashioned helm driving a hydraulic steering system, rather than the small wheels of later ships that were simply electrical switches with no feel whatsoever, but linked to automatic pilots that took all the fun away.

The only compass on the *Bradman* was the magnetic one on the bridge top. The binnacle then passed through the deck head into the wheelhouse, where it sat at a high level in front of the helm and was read via an angled mirror. We had no true north reference on the *Bradman*, so great care was necessary with a variation up to 29 degrees west around Iceland's North Cape, caused by the volcanic magnetic anomalies in that area.

We transited the Firth safely, and I got myself on the helm and was given a course of north by west towards Iceland. This is one of my strongest memories, the sheer joy of powering that ship past the Faroes in a moderate Atlantic swell; I loved the experience so much I stayed on the helm for eight uninterrupted hours.

We arrived at the North Cape of Iceland and the sea was eerily mirror calm. But we were in a huge field of 'pancake ice', basically very flat sheets of ice ranging in size from a few feet across to the size of four tennis courts, none of which would do the ship a lot of good on contact. When the wind gets up, these things start to surf down the waves and you are then in real trouble. Your only option is to steer with the sea rather than against it so that you are moving at roughly the same speed as the ice. On one haul, the steel warps towing the net caught on a huge sheet of ice, so that the entire net, including the trawl doors, bobbins and floats, all finished up on top of the ice. We eventually dragged it clear, but this was the first time the skipper had ever seen a trawl in its full operational configuration.

We then decided to steam east to try a different fishing ground near Grimsey Island, just north of Akureyri. The Arctic Circle passes through this island at 67.5 degrees north. I took the helm, as I did at every possible opportunity, but we were still in the thick of the ice and doing about 12.5 knots. I thought this was a bit fast for the conditions, but assumed the skipper knew what he was doing. The next thing I noticed as I turned round was that the skipper had disappeared into his cabin, leaving me alone on the bridge at the age of 19, driving a 1,000-ton trawler through what I thought were very dangerous conditions. After about half an hour, still on my own, it was beginning to get very scary. The ice was thickening and I was running out of 'weaving' room so safe routes through were becoming difficult to find. Dare I ring the engine room telegraph to 'Stop', which of course was the obvious thing to do? At that age you are very unsure where the limits of your authority lie. Eventually, common sense prevailed and I did ring the telegraph to 'Stop', which brought the skipper out of his cabin at break-neck speed! He was very good about it. It was many years later in conversation with another of our skippers that I found out he was a little too fond of the bottle, which explained a lot.

I remember another trip in the *Statham*, this time with Olley Emmons. We were racing south just to the east of Spurn Point. Gradually overtaking us, just as we were about to turn west into the Humber, was a very fast, new, Icelandic trawler. The prime position at the fish market in Fish Dock One was determined by the order in which ships arrived at the anchorage, awaiting the opening of the lock gates. Olley wasn't having any of this and decided to take a short cut between the Binks banks and Spurn Point. The Binks is a very dangerous collection of shoal sand banks barely a mile from the coast. However, we got through and won our prime position at the fish market. On studying the charts later, I realised that we could only have had about a fathom of water below the keel! I never knew Olley to make mistakes or break

Trueman and *Padgett* were near identical middle water trawlers, both built by Cook Welton & Gemmell in 1960.

anything, he was a very fine seaman and obviously had an encyclopaedic knowledge of his charts.

The *Bradman* was coming home from the White Sea under the command of 'Shadow' Phillips. I was not aboard on this occasion. It was thick fog and he managed to miss the Humber altogether and finished up aground on Mablethorpe beach. At low tide, the ship was high and dry, which made for a very embarrassing photograph on the front page of the *Evening Telegraph*. Had she settled on uneven ground she could easily have fallen on her side, which would have been a much more serious problem. However, she remained upright and re-floated at high tide, the only damage being to the skipper's pride!

So that gives a flavour to how life was during my time with our firm, between 1962 and 1965. And then came disaster! We were all called into the main office, and informed that our firm was to be sold to the Ross Group for a consideration of £500,000, probably about £18m at today's prices. This was devastating news to me, and we were all immediately unemployed, having been given two week's wages for

Trueman leaves Grimsby for the Faroe Islands on her maiden voyage.
The main Faroes fishing ground is 'Faroe Bank' which lies about
20 miles due west of the islands.

each year of service. I think I got about £70. I had to sign on at the labour exchange, which I vowed I would never do again: an embarrassing and humiliating experience. We were then all interviewed by Ross Group in the person of one Dennis Roberts to establish if they had any suitable employment opportunities. I was offered a job as a petrol-pump assistant, which made me furious at the time, but in retrospect it was probably the biggest wake-up call of my life.

8

Between the Docks and University

So it transpired that the sale of the Crampin Steam Fishing Company in 1965 was a huge wake-up call for me. There I was, no job, no qualifications, experiencing the misery of being unemployed, and my market value seemed to be that of a pump attendant. How I now regretted so wasting my days at school, luxuriating in the complacency of thinking that my future was assured with the firm.

I think my parents hold a degree of responsibility here. First, they should have absolutely insisted that I received a decent education, whatever that might entail. Second, they should have instilled much more self-confidence into their children, we were constantly being told what idiots we were. Third, we should have been educated far better on the importance of consideration for other people. These three things I now see as crucial to success in life. However, I must blame myself most for living my early life so stupidly.

I do think I possess a degree of 'grit', and this was the time when it first came to the fore. "Right," I said to myself, "I'll show the lot of them." I wanted a career involved with the future rather than the past, which would provide reasonable job security, make use of such skills as I may have had and give me a respectable position in society. I am no great scientist or mathematician, and I am no great artist either, but my combination of reasonable skills across the board I considered to be a strength.

I believed that to become an architect would best reflect these thoughts, which I recall so vividly. My whole attitude to life changed at that moment, and I became totally focussed on my ambition. I would need to spend two years taking more O and A levels, and then, if I managed to get into university, seven more years prior to qualification. I decided to give it a go.

I attended the College of Further Education at Nuns Corner, Grimsby, which was able to provide the courses I needed. I thought this college to be a fantastic organisation, giving qualifications to anyone who was determined enough to get them. I started at the college in September 1965, and that Christmas, three months later, I passed seven further O levels and two A levels, the latter two being English and art. I then spent a further 18 months studying double maths A level.

It was very hard work, but I made some very good friends at that time, both within the college and in north Lincolnshire generally.

I was great friends with many of the farming families in the area, and these people became the nucleus of my circle of friends. We worked hard, played hard, and went into lots of pubs. I learnt to shoot – a passion that has always stayed with me. I remember Rod Dawson from Bishopsthorpe Farm had a clay pigeon trap bolted to the back of his Land Rover. He also took us rabbit shooting at night in the headlamps of his Hillman Hunter estate car. We would stand at the back on the tailgate whilst he hurtled around the farm. I sometimes thought the rabbits had the better of the bargain!

Rod and another farmer, James Walker, each bought Fireball dinghies at the same time. Sailing in strong Humber winds from Humber Mouth Yacht Club was an unforgettable experience. We later took all the boats, including my old Albacore dinghy, to Abersoch in North Wales for an amazing holiday.

Poor Rod died of cancer at a very young age; it was a huge loss to us all.

We also learnt to water ski on Fenwick's lake at Croxby in the north Lincolnshire Wolds, and, having mastered that, progressed to the Humber; all tremendous fun. To this day I still shoot at the excellent Fenwick's Estate, one of the best. Unfortunately, the shoot was discontinued fairly recently.

I did some labouring on some of the farms; I remember picking weeds out of a field at John Spilman's farm and picking potatoes just to earn some cash. That's when I learnt what back ache really was! I was always very short of money.

This was very evident and embarrassing at the time; John Spilman had his Sunbeam Alpine, Roger Clayton had his MGB, some of the wealthier fraternity (Tony Hallet and Dave Rodgers) had their E Type Jaguars and I had my minivan. My only consolation was that Mike Bacon only had a Morris Minor pick-up truck! Dave Rodgers, by the way, was the son of Norman Rodgers, one of our skippers, on the *Yardley* I think.

And, of course, at around this time we were getting interested in girls! If they remember me I would like them to know what a privilege it was to know them and what a huge amount they contributed to the quality of my life and those of our friends. All great people; I was very lucky.

I met Liz, probably my first girlfriend, at the Conservative Club, Bargate, in Grimsby, where a delightful lass, Sue Cobley, was also a member. I record here, with great sadness, that Sue was killed in her teens in a motor accident, caused as I recall by stupidly reckless driving on the part of the chap she was with, whom I will not name.

There was another death at about the same time. It is said that those of us of the right age will all remember where we were when John F Kennedy was assassinated. I was in the downstairs bar of that same Conservative Club, in 1968 I would assume.

About this time, simply through the pressure of my father and his insistence that we pursued music rigorously, I was accepted into the National Youth Orchestra (NYO).

This was, and still is, an amazing organisation with some of the best young musical talent in the country. It was easiest to get in, as I did, on the viola, as there weren't that many viola players around. We had three courses each year, lasting about ten days, but the summer course was longer and we frequently toured abroad. I remember the Poland–Switzerland tour, the Israel–Greece tour and the European tour.

The operation was run with an iron fist by a highly talented and capable lady, Ruth, later Dame Ruth Railton. She was an amazing personality and achieved even more amazing things; in fact, there was very little she could not achieve. She married Cecil King of the Harmsworth family, editor of the *Daily Mirror*. He paid for many of the chartered aircraft we used to travel abroad, and was doubtless able to pull many strings for Ruth.

I remember when we were in Israel, Ruth addressed the orchestra and said she was going to give us all a 'wonderful experience'. We were silently led out to the shores of Lake Galilee where the moon was rising, the water was flat calm and the reflections of the moonlight on the water were totally enchanting. We gathered at the water's edge. This evidently was to be the 'wonderful experience', but at the peak of the silence and wonder, Ian Miller, the double bass player with a voice like a news reader, whispered in a voice that could be heard by everyone, "she's going to walk on the lake!" It was just the most hilarious thing. I'm not sure if Ruth caught it or not.

Each section of the orchestra had a professional tutor, and these people were truly excellent. Leonard Hirsch for violins (with whom I had lessons in London); Fred Riddle for viola, leader of the violas in the Royal Philharmonic Orchestra (RPO); and Douglas Cameron for cello. My sister Gibby (now Imogen) had cello lessons with Douglas' wife Lilley in London at the same time as I was tutored by Leonard Hirsch. We used to drive down to London together in the family Austin 16, converted to diesel propulsion on the fish docks. It's a wonder that we ever got there! I think Gibby was too young to have a licence, and we would stop at Laceby crossroads just outside Grimsby for a packet of fags and a bottle of wine! We would stay at a bed and breakfast in Bedford Place in London.

Going back to the NYO, we were privileged to play under some of the best conductors of the time, Sir Malcolm Sargeant, Hugo Rignold, Rudolf Schwarz, Oivin

Fjeldstad to name but a few. We also played in some of the finest concert halls in the world, including the Royal Albert Hall and the Royal Festival Hall in the presence of the Queen Mother. There was an especially memorable concert abroad that we gave at the open-air amphitheatre in Caesarea, as the sun went down over the Mediterranean.

The then smokers amongst us would have a fag in the loos during the breaks. One confederate was Mark Elder, always smartly turned out in a maroon velvet jacket and now quite a famous conductor.

So, I experienced some hugely memorable and valuable times between leaving the fish docks in Grimsby and deciding what to do next.

9

What to Do Next?

My A-level results were in and I was thinking very seriously of becoming an architect.

I had also considered becoming an airline pilot and attended an interview at the College of Air Training in Hamble. On the architecture front, I applied to Nottingham and Bristol. There came a strategic day when I received acceptances from Nottingham, Bristol and Hamble in the same post! Talk about life-changing events – I don't think I fully grasped that my decision would affect every second of the rest of my life! I decided to go for Nottingham and architecture. My good friend Steve Lorraine went for interview at Hamble at the same time as I did, and that is where he decided to go and he became a pilot with British Airways. He rose to captain before he retired, and now spends most of his time on his boat in Falmouth. After a gap of many years, we got in touch with each other again and are still firm friends.

At Nottingham, I was in Lincoln Hall for the first couple of years, a fairly institutional existence, and no cars were allowed, which was mildly inconvenient.

I found the initial years quite difficult, and I put this down to my lack of confidence, resulting mainly from being told by my father, year after year, what an idiot I was! However, at the end of the second year, I won the James Edward Schimeld Prize for Architecture and this began to put things right.

I enjoyed my time at university, and took an active part in musical activities. The music department put on a performance of Wagner's *Das Liebsverbote* and it was during rehearsals for this that I met Jacky Reddaway, who was later to become my wife. We were married in 1970.

Architecture was a seven-year course, three years in, one year out, two years in and a final year out. During my first year out, Jacky and I moved to Norwich, where I worked for a fine firm by the name of Feilden & Mawson. They held a long lease on a beautiful, little cottage at 23 Cathedral Close, which we were able to rent for the year.

I remember my first cock-up as an architect! I was designing a scheme of apartments in an old warehouse building in Wells-next-the-Sea. I realised, fortunately before work started on a new extension at one end, that the site levels I had assumed were incorrect. A bulldozer was working on the site next door, so I slipped the driver £20 and got him to modify the site so that the levels fitted my drawings! Other interesting Norfolk projects were another residential conversion at Binham Priory, and a lot of work on a competition entry to design Robinson College on Grange Road in Cambridge. Unfortunately, we came second, but not a bad result all considered.

I started to do private work at this stage. Jacky and I did a lot of skiing at this time, and through this met David and Joan Parry, who became close, long-term friends. David and I had common interests in skiing, flying and boats, so we got on really well.

Before I was fully qualified, David asked me to design him an old-fashioned inglenook fireplace in his 17th-century house, a lovely edifice in Laindon, Essex. I took all the advice I could, and the fireplace and chimney were duly constructed. David and Joan redecorated the living room, and bought two new settees covered in an Aztec velvet material, really splendid pieces which must have cost a fortune. Then came the day for the lighting of the fire. It was a disaster.

Smoke poured into the room wrecking the decorations and ruining the two new settees. David and Joan were remarkably good about it, and that is how I learnt that the cross-sectional area of a fireplace flue must be between a sixth and a tenth of the area of the main front opening. I complained to my professor who had advised me on the project, and told him the saga of my mock mediaeval fireplace and how badly it smoked. To which he replied, "oh yes, they all did!" Rather disingenuous I thought. However, after some experiments and rebuilding of the entire chimney, it worked very well.

My private work continued through my time at university, and through David Parry I received a commission from the Tully family, to convert a large country house into ten apartments. This was in Essex in the village of North Stifford, and the mansion was called Coppid Hall. The job went very well, although I had to employ two members of staff and a couple of students to help me finish the job.

I went back to university after Norwich to complete the next two years, and sit my second degree. This was passed quite well, although I nearly failed one question: 'you are given a bottle of Scotch for Christmas by a building contractor, what do you do with it?' My answer, 'drink it quickly,' was evidently incorrect! I then had a final year out to do. So, Jacky and I went to London that year. I got a job with Derek Lovejoy & Partners near Victoria Station, ostensibly to learn about landscape architecture, but the job turned out to be redesigning filling stations for Esso! So I moved on. The second six months were very rewarding, spent working in Queen Anne's Gate for a firm called Brett & Pollen, which comprised Lionel Brett, otherwise known as Lord Esher, and Francis Pollen. I met some highly talented people, including Harry Teggin and David Taylor, and am hugely indebted for the vast amount I learnt from them in a relatively short time. I worked largely on the York Report, a Government sponsored report to prepare a master plan for the future development of the City of York.

And so it was back to Nottingham to take my professional practice exams, which I passed without difficulty. We then decided to stay in Nottingham as, by then, we had made many good friends, and Nottingham seemed well located to take on work anywhere in the country.

I got a job with Architects' Design Group (ADG), based at Lockington Hall near East Midlands Airport. I worked on the St Fergus Gas Terminal near Aberdeen, and the main generator building at Littlebrook D Power Station, which is the one near the Queen Elizabeth Bridge Thames River crossing. Having done big buildings with not a lot of architectural content, I moved on to W D Sterland, which was in an office just outside the park in Nottingham on Derby Terrace. This was a commercial housing practice, so not that inspiring, but I was broadening the base of my experience all the time.

Between Norwich and this time, Jacky and I had three wonderful children, Lucy (in 1975), Thomas (in 1977) and Sophie (in 1980). We were so lucky with these three, they have remained a constant joy to us both throughout our lives. They can tell you their stories when, I hope, they get around to continuing this family history.

It was around 1981 when my son Thomas started school at Greenholme, that we met the Wade family, Charles and Jemima with their children Daniel and Natasha. Thomas was contemporary with Daniel, and Sophie with Natasha. It was one of those highly fortuitous friendships which survives to this day, some 36 years later! It was simply that all of our family got on famously with all of theirs. We went on many holidays together, mainly skiing, and have all remained close friends ever since.

10

My Own Practice as an Architect

It was at W D Sterland's office that I met Mike Pring, and we set up our own practice, Crampin & Pring, on July 7th 1977 – the day of the Queen's Jubilee as it happened! The practice was set up on the basis that Mike had a commission to design a new squash complex in Keyworth, and I had a commission from David Parry to design some factory units in Braintree, Essex. Both jobs went very well, although I recall we didn't take any salary for the first twelve months, but in the second year took a princely monthly draw of £200 each!

We did discover that, when you take the initiative to set up on your own, people do tend to bend over backwards to help you, and new commissions rolled in very nicely. We did a lot of work for Nottingham Building Society and designed about 30 new branch offices for them. NBS was very supportive of Crampin & Pring, critically due to the trust put in us by the CEO, John Webster. This gave us continuity of work, without which survival would have been difficult.

It was in their hot air balloon that I broke my back in 1980. The balloon landed in the top of a large tree, and a branch broke as I was climbing down with still about 30 feet to go. I was then in Lodge Moor Hospital for 14 weeks, and although walking was a bit difficult thereafter, I was, in fact, very lucky.

Our practice continued to grow, and by 1982 we were employing about ten other people. Our big breakthrough came about then, when a London property developer wanted to redevelop the original Boots building to the rear of the Nottingham Council House. The developer was Clayform Properties of Charles Street, London, and we got on very well with them, carrying out many large retail developments and shopping centres. Our best known was White Lion Walk in Guildford, for which we won the British Council's Small Centres Award, which really put us on the map. One job often leads to another, and we did a lot more work in Guildford, including the new railway station and the office block next to it.

The years rolled by, and around 1990 we moved from our rented office space in St Peter's Church Walk to our own premises at 11–23 Warser Gate. These buildings have served us very well; we still have them in 2016 and are where we now employ just under 100 people. We have now also opened offices in China and London, which I hope will grow well in the future. We had previously opened offices in London and Sheffield, which were a complete failure and cost us a lot of money. The reason for this was simply not having the right people in charge, and not watching carefully enough what they were up to. We also got badly stung by the end-of-lease dilapidations clause – a good one to look out for. I wish I knew then what I know now!

It was in 1995 that Crampin & Pring agreed a merger with another very successful Nottingham practice, namely James McArtney. The directors (not partners as they were a limited company) were Tim McArtney and Jack Gant. Tim had started the business slightly before we started Crampin & Pring, and Jack joined him some time later, having been a director at Boots who was in charge of a very large architects department. The new practice was originally called Crampin Pring McArtney, but that didn't seem fair on Jack, as we were all equal directors. And so it changed to Crampin Pring McArtney Gant, which we then decided was a bit of a mouthful, and hence CPMG was born.

The merger was very successful; the practices were of comparable size, our sectors of work experience were highly complementary, and we were able to shed McArtney's building and a complete set of overheads. We were strong in retail and general commercial, and they were strong in health and public sector work.

Obviously, significant adjustments had to be made to facilitate the merger. We were a partnership and they were a limited company, but we agreed on a single limited company as the best vehicle for the new practice.

We flourished from the start having doubled our former size and reduced overheads at a stroke. We now had the clout to go for much larger projects and the combined expertise to win them. And the more we won, the better our track record became.

The industry then underwent a gradual change with the introduction of the 'Design and Build' form of contract. Rather than the architect being the team leader, the contractor became clients' first port of call. So, rather than the architect putting the work out to tender to contractors, the contractor put out the work to tender to architects. Eventually this worked very well for us.

Originally, the Design and Build contract was a disaster. We would prepare a design for the contractor, and he would then build it as cheaply as possible. It was when we realised, and persuaded our clients, that we should prepare a full set of detailed drawings and a complete specification as the 'Employer's Requirements' before involving the contractor that quality came back into the industry. There were many variations and hybrids of the format, but, eventually, we all arrived at a consensus, and different forms emerged for different jobs.

Each contractor dealing with large projects required us to have specialised and expensive computer-aided design (CAD) systems; we were now big and strong enough to procure these, and become experts in their use. Thus, for subsequent projects, there was a great incentive for the contractor to stick with the same architect, and this played into our hands very well in acquiring subsequent work.

We became successful and active in almost all major sectors, including such esoteric building types as waste recycling centres and air traffic control (ATC) towers. The latter arose from my love of flying, so I was able to interview with a passion, which evidently paid dividends. I recall I flew into East Midlands Airport in my twin-engine plane for our first interview, and parked it outside the M.D.'s office. He also loved flying – and we got the job. I didn't tell him I had only flown nine miles from Nottingham Tollerton!

We then found that once you had done one project in a highly specialised area you rapidly became a world expert, and to date we have built nine ATC towers, including two military ones. The plane was great for site visits, as projects were invariably at some distance: RNAS Yeovilton, Bristol, Liverpool, RAF Coningsby, Manchester and Isle of Man to name but a few. The Isle of Man project was particularly suited to my mode of transport. Getting there from Nottingham by any other means would be a full day's travel. I could do it door to door in two hours! I remember a taxi driver in the Isle of Man asking what time our flight left. It was lovely to be able to say, "I haven't decided yet!"

I recall a very amusing incident at RNAS Yeovilton. My brother Tex had his own human factors business, with the Ministry of Defence (MoD) being his main client. He was working on the ATC centre for the new aircraft carriers, and his boss, or point of contact, was one Lieutenant Commander Paul Clarke. Those two got on really well together, but then Paul was transferred to RNAS Yeovilton. That was where I first met him, at a meeting attended by a lot of the top brass to discuss the brief for their new ATC facility. The question of disabled access to the visual control room cropped up – that's the glass bit at the top. The installation of a lift would have obscured part of the required 360 degree visibility. Paul remarked that not many of his air traffic controllers were blind or deaf. As a flyer myself, I just couldn't resist saying that I thought they all were! Paul's memorable response was, "I've just got rid of one Crampin and now I get another bugger!" All was taken in good spirits, fortunately.

We went on to design the new command centre at Yeovilton; a highly secret establishment. It was very odd when designing the interior rooms to ask the question, "What is the function of this room?" to be given the answer, "Sorry, we can't tell you that!"

The practice continued to grow and flourish, and by the year 2000 we were a truly national practice, with Nottingham becoming a minority market for us, although not one to be neglected. Gradually, the drawing boards were replaced with computers. Currently, there are no drawing boards and everyone has at least two screens! Although there are many advantages to this change, I still maintain that a building designed on CAD is different from one designed starting with pencil sketches. The building seems to lose something of its soul because it is tempting to let the computers do what they are good at. I can design nothing on a computer, but I can design anything with nothing more than a ruler and pencil. I ended up as the only person in the office that could do this, but my skills were not in great demand!

Mike and Tim then retired, leaving myself and Jack at the helm for the next few years. We made a conscious effort to encourage four of the next generation and groom them for eventually taking over, which ultimately paid dividends. We had tried for some time to market the business, and came close to a deal with PM Group, a highly competent firm based in Dublin, but negotiations did not result in a sale.

We came close to disaster when a London firm, Archial, made a very attractive bid of several million pounds for CPMG. They wanted to pay us entirely in their own shares and take over our business in its entirety, including some half million pounds in the bank. It transpired that this was what they were really after. Fortunately, the deal didn't go ahead, and shortly after this Archial was bankrupt. Had we been paid in their shares we would have lost everything.

A year or two went by, and our turnover and profit were both increasing nicely. We then concentrated on handing over the business to the four people we had identified as most likely to be able to run the business successfully. The main problem was, where would they get the kind of cash we were looking for?

Our accountants finally came up with an ingenious solution. It was to be a combination of a management buy-out and a management earn-out. The deal was that Jack and I would get 50% of the agreed sum on day one. This was funded by our taking significant funds out of the business, which fortunately was cash rich, and with the 'new four', as they were known, making a reasonable capital contribution.

The remaining 50% was paid part monthly, part annually and part from dividends, as Jack and I still each owned 10% of the business, with our final 10% share-holding being paid at a pre-agreed price after the fourth year.

As CPMG had flourished very well indeed, this all went through with the firm's cash reserves never under threat. So it was a very successful outcome for all parties.

11

And so into Retirement

I HAVE BEEN EXCEPTIONALLY lucky to have enjoyed two fantastic careers, the trawling business followed by life as an architect.

Although I only worked on the docks and with the ships for three years, that time was a source of immense value and enjoyment. I had an absolute passion for it that no other experience could match. The ships themselves were fantastic, living, humming entities capable of sailing in the world's worst weather. The people I met, such characters, so highly skilled; the vast array of different businesses serving every requirement of the fishing fleet; and the atmosphere at 3.00am on the North Wall as ships prepared for sea, the ship's lights seen through the early morning mist, the smell of steam and trawl twine, and the hive of activity as last minute issues were resolved; all these things leave an indelible memory that I treasure so greatly.

Thus, when the business was sold to Ross Group, I was devastated, although with hindsight we were lucky as the whole industry later disintegrated thanks to the stupidity of our politicians.

As I wind down towards retirement I can reflect on much good fortune. I have been married to three fantastic women at different stages of my life, all on good terms. This has meant that my family unit has remained intact, which is very precious to me. I have been blessed with three wonderful children, all of whom are very successful in their own areas. And I currently have seven grandsons and a granddaughter, with more future possibilities!

The family name will continue.

12

The Crampin Steam Fishing Company Photographs and Press Records

THE FOLLOWING RECORDS are arranged in approximate date order, starting with the earliest and progressing to the latest. They have been collected over many years and I am grateful for the many contributions that have been sent to me by others in the knowledge that this book was in preparation.

The press cuttings contain a few errors that are worth pointing out.

First, they confuse, on more than one occasion, my father, Harry Crampin, with my grandfather, Herbert George Crampin. Harry died when he was 64. Herbert George died on November 30th 1956, aged 84.

Second, there is confusion between the *Statham* and the *Trueman*, which are portrayed as sister ships in one article. In fact, they were nothing like. The deep-water steam trawler *Statham* was built in Bremerhaven in 1956 by Rickmers. Sister ships *Trueman* and *Padgett*, which were middle water diesel trawlers, were built in 1960 by Cook, Welton and Gemmell of Beverley, Yorkshire.

The 185-foot steam trawler *Statham* was our fastest ship capable of 15 knots. The 140-foot M/Ts *Trueman* and *Padgett* were capable of twelve knots, speed being a function of waterline length amongst other things.

Regrettably, the quality of some of the pictures can be no better than that of the original documents, but my main objective is that the historical record should not be lost.

Various Crampin S F Co line fishers and trawlers. These vessels would date from the 1920s and 1930s. The precise identity of each ship is not known, but they all have the Crampin funnel. By the mid-1930s we had nearly 50 vessels similar to these.

S/T *Minerva*, a Crampin S/F Co vessel of the late 1930s.
As evidenced by the inverted 'U' shaped gallows, she had been converted from line fishing to trawling.

The S/T *Leyland*, GY 254, arrives home from Iceland. Seen here entering the lock pits to Grimsby docks, circa 1934.

Life on the Larwood

What a splendid bunch of fellas! The crew of the Larwood obviously more than delighted to have their photographs taken for posterity. The pose with the ship's lifeboat was a familiar one for the time. And as usual with such pictures it was turned into a postcard which no doubt found a host of collectors. The Larwood was one of the Crampin fleet of Grimsby trawlers named after famous cricketers. She was bombed while on war duty off Norway and eventually foundered in a fjord. However, she was later raised by the Germans and saw service with the Kriegsmarine.

The arrival of the *Larwood* in Grimsby. A new trawler was always a good excuse for a party, attended by owners, families and crew.

The *Larwood* on the slips for routine maintenance.

Note this is not the launch of a new ship, the railings would not have been in place, and she could not be launched stern-first at either Cook Welton & Gemmels, nor at Cochranes, due to the width of their respective launch rivers.

This would have been the arrival of a new Crampin trawler, as evidenced first by the apparent party going on, and second because the steel trawl warps have not been loaded onto the trawl winch.

When a new trawler was ordered, the ship builders usually presented the
owners with a beautifully crafted scale model of the vessel.
I believe this to be the *Hendron*, by Cook Welton & Gemmell.

The trawlers that didn't stand a chance

MENTION in our last bygones, Time and Tide, of the two famous Crampin trawlers, the Hammond and the Larwood brought back the saddest memories for former Cleethorpes cafe proprietor and one-time Royal Navy seaman William Jackson.

For he saw both ships shot to pieces and sunk by the Germans.

Mr. Jackson, who now lives at 12 Westport Road, Cleethorpes, served aboard the converted 1914-18 war cruiser Vindictive in the Norwegian fjords during the early part of the last war.

HMS Vindictive, a venerable old lady doing duty beyond her time as a fleet repair ship, was a soft and very vulnerable target for the Germans and had a hard time for years.

Mr. Jackson, who had worked since leaving school on the Fish Docks, had joined the navy in 1939 and, a year later, became involved in the Narvik operation.

By complete coincidence two trawlers from his home town, Hammond and Larwood, were on minesweeping service ahead of the British and allied warships.

One memorable day in the summer of 1940 the two trawlers were steaming ahead when German bombers, flying from their base only 19 miles away, took the pair by surprise.

Bombed and machine gunned, the Grimsby ships stood no chance.

Both were set on fire and sank.

Mr. Jackson, using a familiar camera, the box Brownie, took this picture of the last moments of one of them.

"Navy ships went alongside when it was possible and a few of the crew were rescued. But the Germans came in, releasing their bombs before we could see them, appearing for only moments. We could do nothing to hit them," he recalls.

Mr. Jackson, whose further war service took him to the Mediterranean among many other places, survived hostilities to return to work on the docks. Later in life he owned the Pop In Cafe at Cleethorpes for eight years.

The picture survives by fluke.

Mr. Jackson was a keen photographer. But his later war pictures were lost in enemy action. These sad reminders of the fate of so many Grimsby trawlers were left at home.

MR. JACKSON — "we could do nothing"

TEN
Grand Old Ladies
No. 16: The Wellard

She rode her luck on the high seas

THE WELLARD was, as one of her skippers described her, "a bit of a water novelty."

One crewman even went so far as to claim that the Wellard was where he learned to swim — in his sleep!

The vessel was to give at least one Grimsby skipper the fright of his life and to lead another to declare "If you had two years in the Wellard they said you deserved a medal."

She was built in Beverley in 1937 for Sir Alec Black

by Steve Richards

and originally named the El Capitan — one of a fleet of six such vessels which also included the Italia Caesar, the Fighter and Le Tiger.

Just a year after she was built, the vessel was sold to Crampin's. She was "called up" by the Navy in August 1939 and then joined the US Navy under the name El Capitan. She later changed her name to the Wellard following the company's policy to name the vessels after cricketers.

In 1946, she went back fishing.

After just a few trips, however, she was back in port. A hammer had been left in one of the engine cylinders after work was carried out. When letting go for sailing the hammer smashed the engine and the Wellard had to spend around six months in dock.

When she finally went back to sea it was not long before tragedy struck. Her skipper Albert Barratt died on board the 173ft. vessel.

Ice conditions

She was then taken by Skipper Alan Whitelam and others who followed included Jim Wright, George Peacock, Don Liste, Oily Emmons and Alan Denison.

It was Don Lister who claimed to have the worst experience of his career aboard her.

"I took her when I was 24. We had sailed late in December 31 years ago for Bear Island and were caught in a north-easterly storm.

"It was the first time I had expeienced really severe ice conditions," he recalled.

The weather was so bad that Skipper Lister could not get the crew down to chop away the ice.

"The coal slipped down the bunker. She went over. The water was up to the middle of the hatches in the middle of the deck.

"I got all the crew together up on the bridge and told them that if they wanted to live they better shift the coal. Everybody was there having a go. Even the cook was scrambling around using bare hands to move the coal back. We finally made it," said Mr. Lister.

And without hesitation he added:"It was an absolute nightmare. But it taught me an awful lot."

Skipper George Peacock who now lives in Brereton Avenue, Cleethorpes, had a similar experience. He took the Wellard between 1954 and 1956.

"We got knocked down off the North Cape. It was a full storm. We were going head to wind. I dared not stop," he remembered.

The trawler was hit by the sea and before she could recover she was hit again.

Mr. Peacock said the vessel had then spent more than 70 hours dodging the weather.

So severe was that assault from the sea that he actually remembered the trawl boards floating past the bridge.

"We used to keep all the trawl boards forward — but there they were drifting past," said Mr. Peacock.

But despite her shocking sea-going reputation, the Wellard still impressed as a good ship.

"She could certainly pull a trawl and get the fish," he said.

But he added: "If you had two years in the Wellard they said you deserved a medal."

Lost an eye

Mr. Snowy Burrell, who is still involved in the fish trade on the docks, has a painful memory of the Wellard. He was to lose his left

The Icelandic gunboat Thor about to warn on illegal fishing.

eye while working aboard her under Skipper Peacock.

"We were fishing off the coast of Russia and I was splicing some heavy wires when one flew up and hit me in the eye," he said.

But despite that unhappy incident Mr. Burrell had a kind word for that trawler. "She was a nice ship, but a bit of a naughty ship," he said.

Mr. Pete Costello who also had a spell aboard this cricketer-class vessel was even more light-hearted.

"She was where I learned to swim in my sleep," he said, making reference to her sea-going reputation.

He served as third hand for 5½ years.

"She took the water in solid big lumps," he quipped.

But he remembered she was a happy ship.

Cement box

And he recalled one incident which summed up the adaptability of trawlermen!

"We thought the mate, who was Alan Denison, had broken his ankle. We had to do something and so we cut a big seaboot down, put his foot in it and filled it up with concrete. He was the only man in Grimsby ever to have a cement box on his foot!" said Mr. Costello.

The Wellard's water problems were, he said, due to her weight.

And in an effort to ease matters a big steel veranda on the front of the bridge was removed. They did not stop there either. The Wellard was one of the first ships in Grimsby to be fitted with radar — a large ex-RAF set.

"That was taken off as well and replaced with, shall we say, a more civilised set," recalled Mr. Costello.

He had an affectionate tale too about Skipper Albert Barratt who died aboard the vessel.

"The Wellard used to have a port side bridge door which would open and close on its own. We used to say it was Albert going aft for his supper.

"Anyone new to the ship used to look at you gone-out," said Mr. Costello.

EVENING TELEGRAPH, Thursday, March 3, 1983

Above: Olly Emmons today, and right, as skipper of the Wellard.

Belgium, Skipper Emmons taking her on that last sad trip.

Seven blanks

It was Skipper Olly Emmons who described the Wellard as "a watery novelty."

"She was a bit awkward. We used to lose boats in the winter," he claimed.

But he remembered how the Wellard could give an Icelandic gunboat a run for its money.

"We had a bit of trouble inside Iceland's 12-mile limit. We were just off the coast when the gunboat came at us. We took off and he chased us about 17 miles. He fired about seven blanks. At least we thought they were blanks. Everytime he fired we ducked down," said Mr. Emmons.

Eventually, it all got a little hot and the Wellard gave itself up. The vessel was taken into Iceland where Skipper Emmons was fined around £3,000.

Heavy seas caused further problems for the trawler in 1956 when she sprung a leak. Skipper Emmons fished on undeterred but when he went below he found the vessel was rapidly filling with water.

"We radioed for help but nobody seemed interested in us," he said wryly.

The Wellard made it to Scrabster and beached stern-first on the beach. It was then that a hole as large as a teacup about three inches in diameter was found in the stern post.

"We put a cement block in it and came home," said Mr. Emmons.

A couple of years later, the Wellard managed to behave herself when she carried a VIP passenger, the then MP for Brigg and Scunthorpe, Sir Lance Mallalieu — although he did not get his knighthood until 1974.

The MP, now dead, sailed to Icelandic waters to look at Cod War activities and the Wellard, under Skipper Emmons, got the job of bringing him safely back to Grimsby.

It was during the fishermen's strike of 1961 that the trawler landed her last trip. She eventually went to be scrapped in Ghent,

Next week: The Northern Spray. A Grimsby trawler which ended her days wrecked off Iceland. I am anxious to hear from anyone with photographs or memories of the vessel. Anyone who can help should write to Steve Richards at the Evening Telegraph, 80 Cleethorpe Road, Grimsby, by Tuesday of next week.

A healthy catch of fish aboard taken off Iceland.

The Wellard pictured during her war service.

Former Brigg and Scunthorpe MP, Lance Mallalieu (centre) aboard the Wellard after a trip to Iceland.

Grimsby Fish Docks, with the Royal Dock for commercial shipping in the background. Note the sheer number of trawlers!

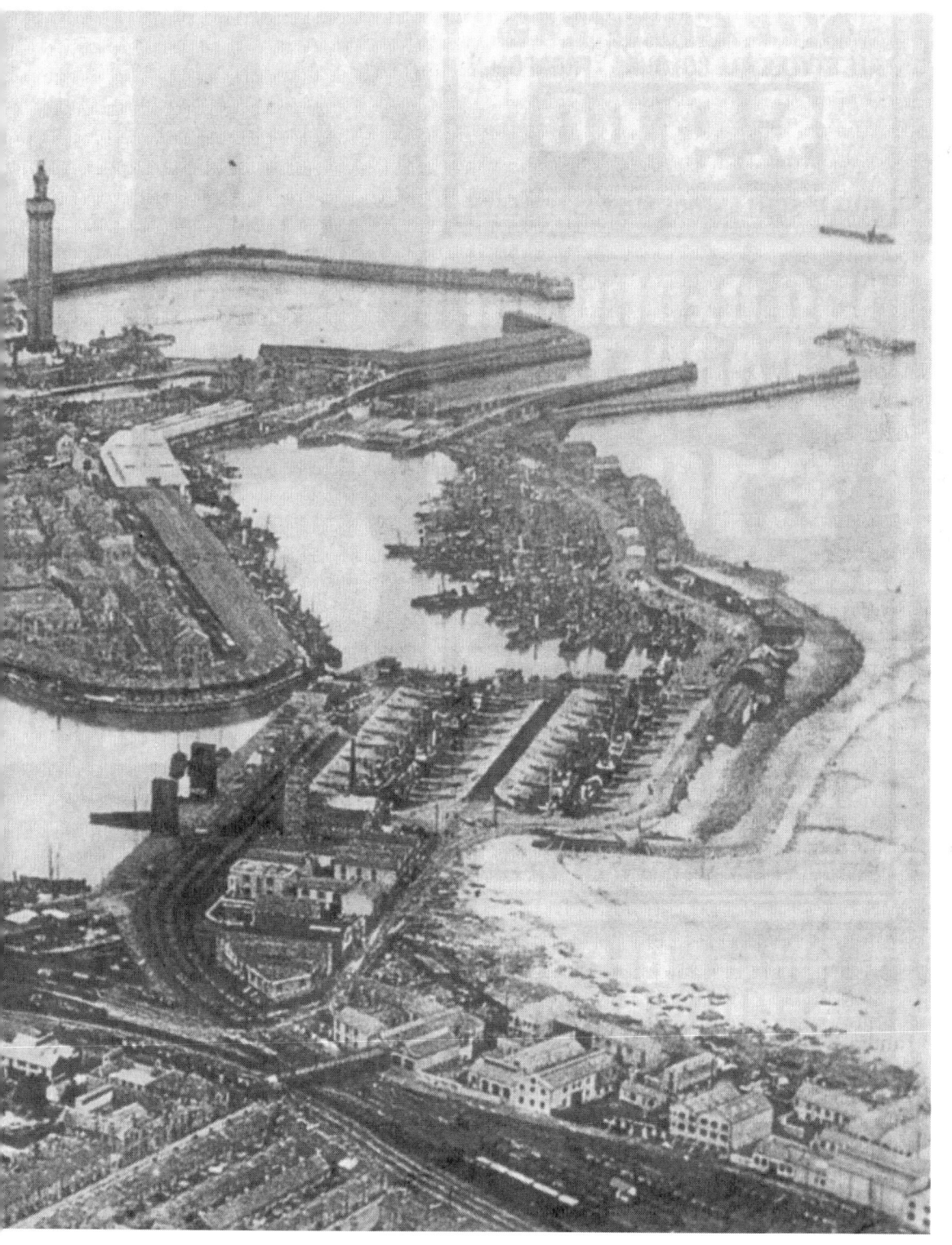

fine catch on the pontoon on Grimsby Fish Docks.

One of my jobs on the docks was assisting the fish salesmen. Every time a ship landed it was a 5.00am start, then tea and hash brown burger in Dobbie's Cafe at 8.30am.

Ice Hazards

The pictures on the following pages illustrate exactly what it was like when, at age 19, I was left alone on the bridge of the Bradman, doing 12 knots through the ice. The skipper was having a nap assisted by a large gin I suspect. Weaving a route through the pack ice was not easy, and eventually, as the ice thickened I plucked up the courage to ring 'stop' on the engine telegraph. The skipper reappeared extremely quickly, but all was well.

The pack ice doesn't look too threatening, but at any speed it can soon rip open the side of a ship.

Pack ice on a flat sea is one thing. Imagine the ice surfing down a 10ft swell towards you. The only way to survive that was to turn downwind and go with it at its own speed.

You would have thought that more modern trawlers would be better equipped to deal with ice hazards, but this was not the case.

First, they were often built as 'three deckers' instead of two as their size increased. Thus their centre of gravity was inevitably higher. Second, steam gave way to diesel between the mid to late 1950s and there was therefore no steam hose available, which was one of the best ways of disposing of the superstructure ice.

ICE!
Nightmare which faced the deep sea trawlers

FOR MEN who fished the northern waters, ice was a common hazard which could never be ignored.

Ice could threaten, ice could trap and ice could kill.

No one knows exactly how many trawlers have been lost because of ice but the number is large.

During the winter there was the ever-present danger of "icing up", of vessels becoming unstable when rigging, aerials, masts and the very superstructure became covered in frozen spray making the trawler dangerously top heavy and liable for collapse.

The only way of dealing with a situation like this was to physically remove the ice, with axes, knives or steam hoses. It was cruel work for the men involved but one they always tackled willingly. They knew their very lives depended on it.

Ice posed another danger in the spring when the thaw sent bergs drifting south into the fishing grounds.

The photographs on this page were all taken by Grimsby fishermen at sea and illustrate only too clearly what a danger ice could be.

The horrors of ice

Scenes like these were commonplace when Grimsby had a fleet of trawlers fishing the inhospitable Northern waters.
Crewmen had to work frantically in the sub-zero temperatures to chip away the ice before its sheer weight capsized the vessel. It's hard to believe that under this solid white blanket are thin ropes and a powerful winch.

The violent sea. The trawler's bows disappear as she plunges into a trough during a nasty gale.

Progress through heavy seas could be slow. In extreme cases we had to resort to 'dodging', which means steaming slow ahead, bow to weather.

How we lost the cod war

The Icelandic gunboat Ageir makes a close run on a Grimsby trawler in choppy seas off the coast of Iceland.

THE loss of the Icelandic fishing grounds to Grimsby trawlers after a series of "cod wars" was a bitter blow and hastened the demise of the port's distant water fleet.

Gradually fishermen saw their traditional grounds reduced in size as the Icelanders, anxious to safeguard their major industry, pushed their limits further and further out.

The trawlermen resisted and backed up by British warships attempted to operate in the disputed waters.

Clashes with Icelandic gunboats were inevitable and trawl warps were cut as vessels like the Thor and the Ageir protected their territory.

There were more serious incidents too with rammings and shells fired.

And all the while negotiations continued between the two sides. Eventually the Icelanders got their way and British trawlers were effectively thrown out of their waters.

The attitude of Iceland created tremendous bitterness — and some no doubt remains.

But it is clear now that if British fishermen had been willing to accept a quota settlement Grimsby could possibly have continued fishing those inhospitable northern waters.

The Royal Navy frigate HMS Cleopatra provides a close escort for a trawler attempting to fish in the disputed waters off Iceland.

The scene may appear tranquil but incident was never very far away in the Cod Wars with Iceland.

A famous name was reborn in Grimsby after the war when the trawler owners Crampins launched the Bradman, named after the great Australian cricketer Sir Donald.

Her earlier namesake was sunk by the Germans while on war service off Norway in 1940.

The launch is recalled clearly by Mrs. Eliza Butts now living on the Belvoir Estate at Cleethorpes, whose late husband, Mr. Hector Butts, was not only the nephew of the firm's founder, Mr. Herbert Crampin, but manager of the firm for 32 years.

Mrs. Butts' father, the late Mr. Ernest Buckingham, a one-time skipper for Consolidated, also joined the firm as ship's runner and was also at the launch.

The firm's ships, all named after cricketers, were mostly Beverley built. The Padgett, another in the fleet, stands at her berth for fitting out after launching in the early '60s.

ON THE PONTOON

● Another trip over. Five trawlers moored on the Pontoon early one morning in the early 60s at the end of another trip. Once their catches were discharged the trawlers would be moved, in most cases to the North Wall where they would be prepared for their next trip to the fishing grounds. The picture here shows the Crampins trawler Bradman, the second to carry the name, on the left. In November 1965, as part of the great shake-up amongst the trawling firms, she was to be renamed the Ross Anson. Next to her is the Vindora, a big post-war vessel then owned by the Atlas Steam Fishing Company. In 1966 she passed to Northern Trawlers and went to Belgium for scrap in 1968. In the centre is a Belgian trawler. Fourth in the line is an unidentified Consolidated Fisheries trawler which the fifth vessel is again unidentified but is a relatively new diesel. On the extreme right is the Longset, built for Lindsey Trawlers in 1959. In April 1966 she was renamed Locarno and left the port later in the same year for Aberdeen where she continued to fish for some years still carrying her Grimsby registration before starting a new career on oil rig standby work.

No 37. Bradman
Painting by Steve Farrow

THE Grimsby trawler Bradman was built for the Bunch Steam Fishing Company, (a subsidiary of Crampin's), at Cochrane's Shipyard in Selby, Yorkshire.

She was, like all of the company trawler's named after famous cricketers, in this case after Australia's, Don Bradman.

She was first registered in November, 1950 as GY 161, following closely behind the Yardley which arrived in April, from the builder's yard of Cook, Welton, and Gemmell. Although these two vessels were not exactly sister-ships in appearance, their layout and dimensions were the same, writes STEVE FARROW.

The Bradman was always considered a "lucky ship", except on the occasion when skipper "Shadow" Phillips once put her on the beach at Mablethorpe, having missed the Humber on the way home from the White Sea! Fortunately, there was no damage.

Perhaps, her most successful skippers were Olley Emmons, who later took the Statham, and Alan Denison (Deno). Olley had an incredibly successful run in the Bradman, so much so that he was at first reluctant to move to the newer and faster trawler Statham. He had one memorable trip fishing off the North West Cape of Iceland in 1961 where he caught 1,200 kit of plaice, and grossed £14,700, probably a record for any ship at that time.

Alan Denison also caught a lot of fish in his time, but was also remembered for his practice of coming through the lock pits at a rate of knots – he said it gave better steerage!

On one occasion the Dock Master shouted at him: "One of these days you'll end up in the Riby Square toilets!"

In November, 1965 the Bradman was sold to Ross Group and renamed Ross Anson. She was transferred to Hull in 1966 until 1967 when she returned to Grimsby.

In February, 1967, under the command of Skipper Harry Saunderson, she towed the Hull trawler Ross Procyon from Harstad in Norway to the Humber Lightship, 1,130 nautical miles.

She was scrapped in August, 1968.

- Steve Farrow can be contacted on (01472) 311994, by email at steve.farrow51@ntlworld.com or at www.trawlerart.com
- See also page 28.

Tonnage: 693 tonnes (gross), 252 tonnes (net).
Power: 1,075 horsepower, (oil-fired steam reciprocating engines).
Length: 180ft
Beam 31ft
Draught 16ft
Official builders' number: 182662

The launch of S/T *Yardley*, 1950, in Beverley. Launched by the wife of Skipper Alan Whitelam. H.G. Crampin on the left with hand on my shoulder, aged 4. My father on the right, with tripod.

HARRY CRAMPIN was one of the most influential figures in the Grimsby fishing industry in the 30's.

A man of great vision, he had a dream of a fleet of big, modern trawlers, equipped to handle the worst weather in the North Atlantic and still land the big catches.

Crampin was a cricket buff and decided to name his trawlers after heroes of the day... Bradman, Hammond, Larwood, Hendren and Leyland.

His company was eventually able to "field" a full team of 11 Cricket-class trawlers (plus several reserves), but war service and the rationalisation which followed was to ensure that they were to have no second innings.

The pride of the fleet was, in fact, wiped out in five vicious days, along the Norwegian coast in April, 1940.

The Bradman, Hammond, Larwood and Jardine were all in Admiralty service and were involved in the major Royal Navy operations in support of the Norwegian campaign.

The first to go was the Bradman, caught by Luftwaffe bombers off the Norwegian coast on April 25. Less than 24 hours her sister ship, the Hammond, was attacked and sunk by aircraft off Aandalsnes.

Three days later it was the turn of the Larwood. She was bombed while supporting action just off the Norwegian coast. She eventually foundered in a fjord, but was later recovered by the Germans and was re-fitted and saw service with the Kriegsmarine.

The fourth cricketer, Jardine, was badly damaged

The firm which fielded a full 'team' of trawlers

● Skipper Alan Whitelam pictured on board the Yardley, which was to represent the Grimsby fishing fleet at the Spithead Review in 1953, a momentous year for the trawler, her skipper and crew. On the wall is a signed photograph of Norman Yardley, whose name the trawler bore.

This is one example where they are actually referring to my grandfather, H.G. Crampin, not my father Harry. Note all the 'cricketer' trawlers' names had seven letters, as did the name 'Crampin', so '7' became a lucky number. The text continues on facing page.

by dive bombers on April 30. She was abandoned and finally sunk by a British destroyer.

A fifth cricketer, the Leyland, was sunk while serving with the Admiralty. She was on convoy escort duties and in November 1942, while shepherding a group of merchant ships off Gibraltar, was involved in a collision with one of the freighters she was protecting and sank.

New 'team'

The only cricketers still fishing after the war were the Barnett, the Paynter, the Wellard and Pataudi but they were to be joined by four others, the Yardley, a new Bradman, the Trueman and the Statham.

The Wellard had been built at Beverley for Sir Alec Black and first fished as the El Capitan before being acquired by Crampins. When the war began she, too, was pressed into Admiralty service and later transferred to the U.S. Navy, where she served as the USS El Capitan. She was returned to Crampins and in 1946 renamed the Wellard.

Her first skipper was Albert Barrett and others who were to command her over the next 15 years included Alan Whitelam, Jim Wright, George Peacock, Olly Emmons and Alan Denison. She was eventually scrapped in Belgium in 1961.

It was Alan Whitelam who was in command of the Barnett on November 28, 1946, when she smashed the landing record, her 2,000 kits of White Sea plaice selling for a new record of £13,000. What would 2,000 kits of prime plaice sell for today? Her chief engineer at the time was Bill Walker, OBE.

The Yardley, built after the war at Beverley, was to earn herself a place in the history books of Grimsby's trawling industry thanks to two incidents in 1953.

The first came in April when the trawler went to the rescue of a small Norwegian fishing vessel. It was heroic seamanship in any circumstances as

● **The Yardley enters port. She was to become one of Grimsby's outstanding trawlers of the 50s.**

the Yardley, again under the command of Alan Whitelam, lay broadside on to the storm to allow the crew of the Norwegian trawler to jump to safety.

Later that day the Yardley repeated the rescue, this time plucking a Norwegian father and his three sons from their sinking vessel. It was a remarkable achievement which earned the crew a celebration banquet when they landed the crews of the two ships at a Norwegian port.

When the Yardley returned to Grimsby she was spruced up to represent the port in that year's Royal Spithead Review when she took a party of fishing industry executives, including Mr. Crampin, Mr. Albert Butt, Mr. J. R. Cobley, Mr. Edwin Bacon and Mr. F. B. Robinson, to the Navy's royal day in the Solent.

Smashed record

In 1964 the Yardley was bought by Ross Group and she ended her days some years later in a braker's yard.

The second Bradman was built at Selby and launched in November, 1950 and 11 years later smashed the landing record for plaice at Grimsby when she caught 1,200 kits of flats off Iceland. Her skipper at the time was Olly Emmons.

The last pair of cricketers were, fittingly, the Statham and the Trueman. The Statham was built in Germany and arrived in Grimsby in September 1956. Harry Crampin was then 84 but insisted on being driven to the docks to see the arrival of his new trawler. Again the ubiquitous Alan Whitelam was in command.

The Trueman followed in 1960, built at Selby and launched by the wife of the England fast bowler. Freddie himself was there that day along with Herbert Sutcliffe. Crampin's proudly announced she was the fastest middle water trawler in the fleet . . . named after England's fastest bowler.

She was to be badly damaged in a fire within two years of her maiden voyage and had disappeared from the list of trawlers registered in Grimsby within 10 years.

The innings was over for Crampin Trawlers . . .

✱   This is where they get the *Statham* and the *Trueman* mixed up!

Statham, the pride of the Crampin fleet, arriving in Grimsby from Bremerhaven in 1956, averaging 15 knots for the whole crossing.

The Crampin Steam Fishing Company Limited
Record of Shore Staff Wages, circa 1965

NAME	DUTIES	AGE	WEEKLY WAGE £.
W. D. Moss	Director, Fish Salesman	57e	28a
A. Rimmer	Secretary	50	25a
H. Butts	Ships' Husband	60	22
Bill Crampin	Asst. "	19	12a
E.H.Beighton	Super Engineer	52	28a
D.C.Burman	Cashier	63	20
R. Leach	Radio Officer	50	22
P. Robinson	Asst. "	34	17.12.6
M. Cutting	Storeman	55	12
P. Allen	Asst Ship's Husband	57	13
A. Gilbert	Foreman Lumper	38e	13
T. Richardson	Runner	50e	12
Tradesmen			
H. Pickard	Tinsmith	55	14.15.-
J.W. Roberts	Electrician	45e	18. 5.-
P.J. Osborne	Electrician	32e	17.12.6

N.B. In Age column, e = estimated; others believed to be correct.

In wage column, a = approximate figure.

The day they launched the Trueman

THIS was the day they launched the Crampins' trawler Trueman at the yard of Cook, Welton and Gemmell at Beverley.

She was launched by the wife of England and Yorkshire fast bowler Freddy Trueman. But, true to form, the launch had to be delayed because of rain. So much of it fell on the day of her launch, December 22, 1960, that the river was three feet above normal at the scheduled time of launch.

Then there was another problem. The bottle of champagne failed to break on the bows of the 152ft trawler and it needed a second attempt. All this prompted a comment of "You're out for a duck!" from the great man himself.

Also there was the former Yorkshire and England batsman Herbert Sutcliffe.

At the time the Trueman was reckoned to be one of the fastest trawlers afloat but her debut was delayed. She arrived in Grimsby after completing her fitting out and trials just in time to find herself in the midst of a fishermen's strike.

The Trueman later sailed into tragedy. Two years later that Trueman caught fire while steaming off the Norwegian coast. Her skipper, Alan Whitelam, had to steam into a fjord looking for help and it was five hours later before the bodies of two crewmen who perished in the blaze had been recovered.

The Trueman and her partner the Statham were to have a relatively short innings in the port. By 1970 both had been sold as the name of Crampin Trawlers disappeared from Grimsby.

The Statham had been built for the company in Bremerhaven and was the last of his own trawlers that Harry Crampin was to see arrive in Grimsby.

That was in the autumn of 1956. Convalescing from an illness, Mr. Crampin, then 84, insisted on being driven to the lock pits to see the arrival of the Statham.

Freddie Trueman, left, my uncle Herbert (HW) second from the right. The vessel was a 140ft overall length, middle water trawler; not the 152ft as stated, and she was not as fast as the Statham, or any of the new deep water trawlers.

I attended this launch, aged 14, and stood right on the water's edge for a good view. Big mistake! The wash from the opposite bank drenched me to above the knee.

Above, Mrs. Enid Trueman prepares to launch the trawler under the careful gaze of her husband. RIGHT — The official party at the launch, Freddy Trueman, Herbert Sutcliffe, Mrs. Trueman, Mr. H. Wood and extreme right, Mr. Rowland Jackson, managing director of the builders, Cook, Welton and Gemmell Ltd. TOP, — The Trueman is launched into the River Hull.

My Grandparents' Golden Wedding party held at the Town Hall, Grimsby

Sir Jack Croft Baker proposes a toast to HG and his wife, Betsy Ann (nee Robinson). A proud moment for my grandfather, in his white tails, a far cry from the poverty of his early years in London.

Mr Harry Crampin dies at 64

ONE OF the best-known characters in the fishing industry before he retired in 1965, Mr. Harry Crampin, of 33 Abbey Road, Grimsby, died suddenly on Saturday. He was 64.

One of the well-known Grimsby trawling family, Mr. Crampin was a man with a lively and curious mind, inventive and unconventional.

As a director of the family firm, he took a particular interest in the electrical and radio side of trawling, and was a major innovator.

He was the first man ever to instal radar in a trawler, and thanks to him the Crampin trawlers were the first anywhere to operate with AC rather than DC current.

The second son of the late H. G. Crampin, who founded Crampin Steam Fishing Co. early this century, he spent his working life in the family firm, he and his older brother, the late Herbert Crampin, taking over on their father's death in the late 1940s.

He retired when the firm joined Ross Group in 1965, and since then had given much of his time to charitable work.

For years, he had maintained and repaired "talking books" for the blind; he actively helped the Spare-a-Mile organisation for the housebound; and he took an active interest in the Diamond Jubilee Provident Homes, with which there was an old family link.

Electronics and photography were his great interests, but he was also a keen musician, playing piano and guitar.

Mr. Crampin is survived by his two sisters, and leaves a wife, Enid, four children and five grandchildren. A service will be held at Grimsby Crematorium on Friday.

Mr. Herbert W. Crampin, of Woodside, Vaughan-avenue, Grimsby, pictured at Buckingham Palace yesterday after receiving the O.B.E. from the Queen at an investiture. With him are his wife (left) and sister, Miss B. E. Crampin. Mr. Crampin is a former chairman of the Grimsby Fishing Vessel Owners' Association.

Buckingham Palace, 13th November 1964. HW, my uncle Herbert, HG's eldest son, did a lot of charitable work to do with alms houses, and the Fishermen's Dependence Fund. Seen here with his wife Dorothy and his sister, my Aunt Betty.

The only picture that I can find of '385'. This was HG's home for many years and we had great family Christmas celebrations there.

It is a shame that, since it was sold, it has been rendered and mock-Tudor boarding applied.

An Account of the Best Trip to Sea that I Ever Did

I wanted to record the detail of one trip in the *Bradman* to Iceland's North Cape. It had a huge effect on my life and aged me in terms of experience by about ten years! There will be some repetition here with what has gone previously. I apologise for that, but wanted this story to be complete in its own right.

Sketch by the author, made in biro on a tablecloth.

Appendix

My Most Memorable Trip to Sea
Bradman to the North Cape

I WAS 18 YEARS old and working on the Grimsby Fish Docks at this time, in the cold winter of 1964. Our family-owned trawler business had operated as the Crampin Steam Fishing Company since it was formed by my grandfather in the early 1900s.

Having worked for the firm since leaving school, assisting the shore staff with turning around the ships at the end of each voyage, it was decided that it was high time I did a trip to sea, which was, in fact, the first of five. Each voyage lasted between 18 and 24 days; the deep-sea ships having a compliment of 21 souls.

I had some training under my belt; one learns a lot just being around ships, seeing them in, selling the fish on the early morning market, organising repairs, re-provisioning and seeing them off to sea again. I had also spent six months (part time) at the Grimsby Nautical College, a training school for fisherman, and learnt the basics of braiding nets, splicing and general seamanship.

I recall those early days, burning the candle at both ends (and probably in the middle as well). It was midnight with a cold mist in the air, and I well recall trekking 'down dock' on my somewhat temperamental NSU motorbike, freezing cold, to see in the *Bradman* on its return from the White Sea. I set to work catching the heaving lines, securing the warps and settling the ship into its berth. This was followed by gathering together the requisitions for the forthcoming trip and noting any repairs that were required. There was a great sense of urgency about all this because, notwithstanding major issues, the *Bradman* would be off to sea again in three days.

It was always good to climb aboard an incoming trawler with friends and families, in this case clambering over the ice-covered bulwarks and into the warmth of the skipper's cabin. The skipper on this occasion was Olley Emmons, one of the firm's most successful fishermen. Everyone was cheerful, the crew because they were home after three weeks at sea and everyone else content to see the safe return of one of our ships with a fine catch. Those early mornings were magical, with dawn a long way off; lights twinkling; the emotive smells of steam, sisal and the docks themselves; and the hive of activity that always accompanied an arrival. There was always Scotch and sherry on offer, which seemed to combat the cold, but probably didn't!

There was a particular sense of excitement for me as I was scheduled to join Olley in the *Bradman* on its next trip, which was to be 21 days to the North Cape of Iceland.

I arrived home at about 2.00am and set the alarm for 4.00am, as I was due to assist Bill Moss and Norman Slater with the fish sales, which usually commenced at about 6.00am. Onto the motorbike again, even colder now, with an old Gannex overcoat on, a pair of leather gloves with holes in most fingers and certainly no crash helmet in those days. Into the office store, a quick cup of tea if we were lucky, and a warm coke stove aglow if we were even luckier. Then on with the traditional white coats and the heavy clogs we had to wear. These, I suppose, were meant to be safe and practical, but in reality were dangerous instruments of torture. The leather had the consistency of sheet steel, and the two inch thick wooden soles were underclad with steel 'horseshoes' that skidded like ice skates on the slippery docksides. I remember acquiring my first pair of clogs. The first thing that had to be done was to half fill them with oil, which then soaked into the wood to ensure they were water tight. This they were, but for the next six months old sacking was worn over one's socks to prevent them being wrecked by the slowly drying oil.

And so we went on to the fish market, a short walk from our store on Fish Dock Road. By this time it was already a hive of activity as the dozens of fish merchants had already inspected the catches of perhaps ten or twelve trawlers to decide upon the lots for which they wanted to bid. The *Bradman* was in berth number one, pole position, as this is where the bidding starts. It then progressed in a clockwise direction around Fish Dock No. 1 . The position in the Fish Market was decided upon by the order in which the ships arrived in the River Humber. They would then anchor and await the opening of the lock gates, which were only accessible two hours either side of high water.

The auction commenced at breakneck speed in what seemed to all intents and purposes to be a completely foreign language, which I suppose it was. It takes a few months to get the hang of it. When the lots have been sold, the merchants clamber over the piles of aluminium boxes, each containing a 'kit' (10 stones) of fish, spreading their labels, seemingly randomly, to lay claim to their purchase. Their day would continue by filleting the fish, and packing and distributing it to their customers all over the country. Our day was totally committed to starting the turnaround process for the ship's next voyage.

A memorable and very welcome short break was a visit to Dobbie's Café for a pint mug of tea and an indefinable kind of hash brown burger in a white bread bun, with loads of HP brown sauce, which was totally delicious.

By 8.00am I was back in the store going over the *Bradman*'s requisitions, and writing the orders to the many firms who had work to do over the next 24 hours. There was an element of routine and repetition about this, and therefore Grimsby's immensely skilled workforce became efficient beyond belief in carrying out these tasks, completing in a matter of hours jobs that ought to take a week, including lifting out items of equipment weighing several tons, executing repairs and reinstating them before you'd noticed they were missing. However, the fish docks were well equipped with heavy lifting gear, and the blacksmiths were quite useful too. I later had a minivan, which two of them would pick up by the back end and trundle around the docks like a wheelbarrow, with me in it!

Then it was back to the *Bradman* and organising the tugs to move her to the other side of Fish Dock One. Here she would take aboard about one hundred tons of ice in preparation for the next voyage. The Ice House was in Fish Dock Road, and the ice was transported to the trawlers via overhead gantries, which can still be seen today (2017), and thence by sloping chutes down to the ship's foredeck and through the fish room hatches and into the fish pounds. The hatches were then firmly closed. This was at the part of Fish Dock One that was the nearest to the Ice House.

It was time for the tugs once more, and the *Bradman* was towed to the crane jetties where most of the ongoing repairs were carried out. Thus, for reasons of convenience, most of the specialist workshops were located in this area. Clarke & Co engineers, Bridges & Salmon shipwrights, Bemrose the painters, Sleights the platers, Fenners the tank cleaners and so on. The crane jetties were next to the slipways, which today are still functioning and capable of hauling the largest trawlers out of the water. This was done for repairs to propellers and steering gear, and for repainting the underwater parts of the hull. This would usually add a day to the shore time of the ship. Changing propellers was a fairly regular operation. Our trawlers were 'side winders'; that is, the trawl warps were towed over the side of the vessel, usually the starboard side. Thus, when the helm is put to port, the warps come very close to the propeller, which occasionally results in an unfortunate meeting. The later 'stern fishers' obviously did not have that problem, but I hated the fact that they had a huge ramp at the stern ready to accept a hostile following sea. It is believed that this is how the Hull trawler *Gaul* was swamped and lost. Propellers were very expensive, and if a particular skipper was very heavy on propellers, he was demoted from manganese bronze to cast iron, resulting in a half knot loss of speed.

Tugs were then used again, this time to tow the *Bradman* to the North Wall. This was the final stop before sailing and was where all final provisioning would take place. Ships were usually moored 'stem on' through pure pressure of dock space, and carting all provisions for a three-week trip for 21 people up a rickety ladder and over the bow was no joke.

During days two and three of the ship's stay in dock, my time was spent mostly outside with the 'heavy gang', assisting with provisioning. I also spent some time in the office, usually doing a lunchtime relief shift as I was deemed not to require lunch. Perhaps that is why I was earning the massive wage of £10 per week. On this particular occasion I was delighted to learn that the *Bradman* had grossed £10,000 for the previous trip, always a cause for celebration. My next job over lunch was to type out the crew list for the forthcoming voyage: name, rank and address. It was strange to type my own name with the title 'supernumerary' for the next trip. The most common rank is of course 'deckhand', and I am sure I can still type that word more quickly than anyone else!

I went home at about 6.00pm and my packing had to be done for the following morning; we were due to sail at 6.00am. And so it was done; it took about an hour, and then I went down to the pub to say a farewell to my mates. The packing was woefully inadequate as I possessed nothing like the appropriate gear, and finished up borrowing and begging waterproofs, sea boots, gutting knives and so forth from other obliging crew members. I do remember packing a lovely, green, woollen, polo-neck sweater, but this went over the side before we were out of the Humber – green is not a lucky colour to trawlermen, and they take no prisoners.

I duly arrived aboard in plenty of time for the sailing, but, as usual, only about half the crew had arrived. The ship's husband, Arthur Richardson, was charging around Grimsby fishing out the crew from where he knew from experience they would usually be. We had 20 men aboard, one deckhand short, and Olley was getting well fed up, an hour lost is an hour's lost fishing time, and so he decided to let go.

The warps were released and the *Bradman*'s beautiful 1000HP triple-expansion steam engine hissed slowly astern.

It is an awkward turn from the North Wall to the lock pits. Most propellers are manufactured to rotate clockwise ahead. There is a characteristic called 'prop walk', which is due to the sideways paddle-wheel effect of a slowly rotating propeller. This means that on reversing away from the North Wall, the stern actually goes to port, the opposite of what you want when you need a turn to port when going forwards. The trick is, very slow and brief astern, it doesn't make much difference where the helm is, then fairly smartly ahead with full port rudder. Obviously skippers became very adept at this, but there were still some difficult moments when the wind was against you.

Then came crawling slowly and quietly toward the lock gates, with a mist in the air and still not fully daylight. Sometimes a few trawlers would let go at the same time, rules of the road didn't seem to apply, and the eventual solution was a judgement based on the skipper's temperament and an assessment of probable damage.

I remember we squeezed perfectly through the lock gates, probably a foot of space on either side of the ship, and at this point we were fortunate in that the final crew member had turned up and, with a heroic jump, he landed safely aboard.

We increased to half speed, and the lights of the dock began to recede to the rhythmical hiss of the *Bradman*'s engine increasing in speed. Again, it was a magical moment, our navigation lights reflecting in the early morning mist and the glow of the red light on the Burcome buoy coming into view.

Our speed increased to 'full ahead' as dawn was breaking, and the familiar sight of the Bull Fort and Spurn Lighthouse at the mouth of the Humber came into view. The Bull Fort was left to starboard, by now we were doing our maximum speed of 12.5 knots, then we made a turn to port at the lighthouse, staying well clear of the Binks sandbanks. Then it was north up England's east coast, past the Tyne, the Forth, Peterhead (where you can just see the jail) and into the jaws of the Pentland Firth. This notorious stretch of water has been the graveyard for many ships, owing to its potentially appalling weather and cross-running tides. We were fairly lucky and made the transit without incident. Then we went north by west, passing the Orkneys and the Old Man of Hoy, a famous rock formation of the type called a stack, and on into the Atlantic.

It was now time for the preparation of the fishing trawl. If the same net was used as for the last haul, it would still be nicely alongside. If a new net was required, however, it was hauled out of the forward hold in pieces, which all had to be stitched together. The Gordian Knot has nothing on a trawl in pieces, but, then again, familiarity breeds a huge quality of adeptness.

As we settled on our course I took the helm for the first time, guided by the overhead magnetic compass. The *Bradman*'s helm was a good old-fashioned ship's wheel connected by cables and chains to the hydraulic steering gear that is located above the rudder. Later trawlers had small, car-like helms, which were in fact nothing more than electrical switches, with no feel or feedback whatsoever. They also had auto pilots, which to me cut all the fun out of it. With the *Bradman*'s helm it was a living thing, almost like wearing the ship, and I loved it. So much so that I remained on the helm, refusing to give it up for a full eight hours.

It was night when we passed the Faroes, leaving them to starboard. Again, it was mystically atmospheric: lights in the far distance, the efflorescence from our bow wave looking like a November 5th firework display, and *Johnny Remember Me* by Johnny Leyton playing away quietly in the background, picked up on the long-wave radio.

And so we progressed northwards until we picked up the coast of Southeast Iceland on the radar. This gave us an accurate fix, very important as we negotiated our way around the infamous 'Whaleback' rock, which lurks just below the surface at high water. Without the radar we would have relied on the Loran receiver, which would pick up directional signals from shore stations, with any two signals giving us a reasonable fix. However, shore stations were not always available, so it was then down to taking bearings from land-based objects, or, in their absence, dead reckoning. The echo sounder readings compared with the indicated depth on the chart was also useful.

We made good progress up the east coast of Iceland, averaging 12.8 knots for the previous six hours. We must have had a kindly tide behind us, and the flattish sea also helped. We were in the lea of the land as the prevailing wind was westerly at the time. And so we went on towards the Langanes peninsular, the horn of Iceland at its northeast extremity, jutting out arrogantly towards the Eastern Atlantic.

Helm was gently to port as we rounded Langanes onto our new westerly course. It was then like opening an air-tight door into a wind tunnel, and the change in weather hit us like a brick as we came out of the lea of the land. The ship was then bucking around like a cannon ball in a tumble dryer, not one part of the outside of the ship was free from either spray or solid water. I always suffered from sea sickness, so it was time for me to retire to my bunk, which offered some respite. Not the best bed I've ever slept in, squeezed into a small cabin next to the main winch engine, but at that moment a welcome sanctuary.

We were now on the final leg of our outbound journey towards the North Cape, which lies at Iceland's north western extremity. We passed just north of Grimsey Island, through which the Arctic Circle runs at 67.5 degrees north.

The weather abated a little, and we were partly in the lea of the North Cape as we commenced our first shooting of the nets. Each trawling session usually lasts for two hours, with the ship's speed reduced to around four knots. There were usually other trawlers close by, as the prime fishing bank north of Isafjord was one of the most prolific and popular. With each ship's gear towed about a quarter of a mile astern, great care was needed to avoid fouling the gear of another ship, which would be a very serious occurrence.

As night fell the temperature dropped as the wind veered to the northwest, and large flat pieces of ice started to appear as they drifted southeast from Greenland. This is called 'pancake ice' and is no immediate concern in a fairly flat sea, so we were able to continue fishing on a 24-hour basis. Our hauls, every two hours, were reasonable, and I well remember the rumble of the steam winch engine and the screeching of steel cables under enormous tension, all of which meant that continuous sleep was impossible.

The following morning the ship was covered in light icing, not enough to be of any concern, but every external surface was too cold to touch and no skin could be exposed to the elements at -25°C. It was now time for me to be initiated into the art of gutting fish. At the North Cape, the majority of fish caught is cod and haddock, with a few plaice and halibut, which were very welcome, and some coley, ling and rough red bream, which were not. The spines on the reds were poisonous, and if you encountered a large catfish, its jaws were strong enough to bite through your boot, including your foot, so some care was needed. I got the hang of gutting fish fairly readily. Most of the fish you buy at the fish and chip shop is, in fact, only a part of a much larger fillet. It is not unusual for a cod to be four feet long, and gutting one of those takes some lifting! There were the occasional giant halibuts, five or six feet long, which required special handling. I always felt some remorse at bringing such a life to an end as some of these fish would be about 60 years old.

I then spent a spell in the fish room stacking the catch away in the fish pounds. The main problem was that the 100 tons of nice, flaky ice taken aboard in Grimsby had now coagulated into a solid lump. So it was choppers at the ready, and keep chopping until there was enough loose ice to pack away the previous catch. To access the fish room one had to drop through the hatch onto a waist-high staging where the fish landed for sorting, and thence drop down onto the central gangway. However, through the same hatch came the fish, down a slide from the fish washer above. I remember just having landed myself on the staging when one of the crew above thought it would be really funny to throw down a four-foot catfish, which duly landed on the back of my neck. Humour was not my strong point at that moment.

When fishing was good, there were seldom any breaks between hauls and so work was continuous throughout the watch. No one seemed to mind this as good fishing meant good money. Some relief was offered when the skipper thought fit to offer a tot of Harvey's Bristol Cream sherry around the crew. Why this obscure drink I have no idea, but it certainly hit the spot in the freezing temperatures. Ironically, it was often warmer in the ice-filled fish room than it was on deck.

Olley was one of Grimsby's finest fishermen, and even had some fishing charts left to him by his father, which were not shown to anyone, ever! I am sure these helped him a lot. But when fishing got a bit thin he had other tricks up his sleeve. Each haul was measured in baskets, each basket being about five stones of fish. Twenty baskets was meagre, 50 quite good and 100 excellent. More than that was a bonus. There was great competition between the ships of different firms, and codes were often used in pre-arranged radio schedules in order to exchange information between one's own ships. Sometimes, however, Olley would go on the open radio purporting to call one of our ships, and report, "last haul 50 baskets". If other ships then came to him, he would know they were catching less than this. If they didn't then they were probably catching more, so he would go to them. You never knew, however, the extent to which double and treble bluffing took place in this dark art.

I spent a lot of time in the *Bradman*'s engine room. During hauling and shooting many changes of engine speed and direction were called for, and I spent many happy hours learning to control her magnificent main engine. The sides were completely open so you were in direct visual contact with the massive pistons and the crankshaft, quietly going about their business. In heavy seas it would have been fatally easy to fall into the machinery and I was surprised that more protection was not available. However, I never heard of an accident in this respect. Sound travels for miles under water, and I often wondered if the later, noisy, diesel trawlers suffered a disadvantage in that the noise might scare away the fish – I'll never know.

I was picking up new skills in every department on an almost daily basis, and loving it. I decided that I would like to do some serious chart work, and learn how to read and use charts properly: Looking at the chart date and establishing if the corrections were up to date. Are the depths measured in feet or fathoms (and, these days, maybe metres)? What is the variation in the local area, and what overall correction should be applied once deviation was applied? (Variation is error caused by variations in the earth's magnetic field. Deviation is compass error, which is defined on the compass card issued by the compass adjuster.) Do you add or subtract the variation from true north? I remember the mnemonic 'compass best, error west; compass least, error east'.

Plotting courses with the parallel rule was straightforward, except that the type with the roller system wouldn't stay in one place with the ship rolling all over the place. Distances were then taken from the scale at the edge of the chart, always at the same latitude as your position. This is because, on the Mercator projection chart, the latitude scale increases the further north you are. The distances are taken using the dividers, which can then be used to apply multiples of, say, ten nautical miles to the course line on the chart by rotating them end for end. I once watched Olley doing this. Instead of using the dividers he used his thumb and first finger, end over end! I think he always had an instinctive idea of exactly where he was.

At this stage the radio room was still a mystery, so I decided to spend some time there. Using the basic equipment was fairly straightforward, but Morse code was totally baffling. There were no satellites in those days, and communication with the UK could only be achieved by using Morse via Wick Radio on long wave for onward transmission. And so I set about learning Morse, now almost totally defunct. I had learnt the basic dots and dashes, but I never got anywhere near deciphering them at speed from an incoming message. Evidently, you have to assimilate the rhythm rather than listen to individual dots and dashes. I got so that I could tap out one word at proper speed, and that word was 'August' for reasons that are totally inexplicable. ._ .._ _ _. .._ ... _ was how it went.

We carried on fishing at the North Cape for nearly two weeks, in varying weather conditions, and finally it was time to head for home. The homeward journey calculation is extremely complicated. What day do you want the fish to be on the market? What other ships will be landing on the same day and how will that affect auction prices? What time must you enter the Humber to make that market, and what are the local tide times and thus availability to enter the fish docks? What will the overall weather be like and does contingency time need to be added? What are the Atlantic winds and current doing, and will this affect our speed? Which way will the tides be running in the Pentland Firth, which could cost several hours? How many total hours need to be allowed for the homeward trip? This is yet another skill I never mastered: a complete black art.

The homeward trip was uneventful and very enjoyable. We paused for a two-hour trawl on the Kidney Bank off Iceland's east coast as we thought we just about had the time in hand. We brought up a huge haul of giant cod, which really added lustre to the overall catch that now totalled 2,400 kits.

We entered the Humber on schedule and dropped anchor, awaiting the opening of the lock gates. As we were the first deep-water ship to arrive, the *Bradman* again would have the pole position on the fish quay. The shape signals were raised at the lock pits, a ball, a diamond and another ball, so the time had arrived to weigh anchor and head for the lock gates. The crew were all scrubbed up having had what was probably their first proper wash or bath, and shave, in three weeks. For some inexplicable reason the deck crew had a shore uniform consisting of a light-blue suit usually worn with a red tie. Not a good look! They would all be on deck hanging the rope fenders over the side as the tolerance between the side of the ship and the edge of the lock was very tight. Again, we went through without a touch, and on through the swing bridge and into Fish Dock No. 1.

We were safely moored alongside, and there was the usual happy meeting with family and friends, and the odd noggin of sherry or Scotch.

I left the *Bradman* and headed for home, exhausted but euphoric. If you have read thus far you will probably understand my passion for trawlers.

***

About the Author

Bill was born in 1946 and now lives in Bramcote, Nottingham. He very much values the two careers he has enjoyed, and still remains active as an architect, being involved in development and investment opportunities. His love of the sea has never wavered and he has never been without a boat of one sort or another. Sailing boats have featured prominently, several cross-Channel trips having been made. However, the onset of advancing years has led to a change to motor yachts, based in Salcombe, Devon. Other activities involve shooting, music, flying (until very recently), drawing, writing … and holidays !

About the Author

W Robert Griffiths KC, SC is a practising barrister. Born in Mumbles, Swansea, and brought up in Pembrokeshire, he attended Haverfordwest Grammar School from which he was awarded an Open Scholarship to St. Edmund Hall, Oxford. He was called to the Bar in 1974 and appointed a Junior Counsel to the Crown (Common Law) in 1989, a Special Advocate in 1990 and appointed a QC in 1993. He was appointed a Senior Counsel (SC) in New South Wales, Australia in 1999. He was The Times Lawyer of the Week (2007) for his representation of the Australian umpire Darrell Hair in his claim against the International Cricket Council in respect of the ball tampering affair at the Oval. He is a Senior Master of Middle Temple and a Fellow of the Erasmus Forum in recognition of his contribution to law, philosophy and sport. He was Chairman of the MCC Development Committee for four years Chairman of the Laws Sub-Committee for six years and a member of the MCC Committee for twenty years. He was a director of The London Chamber of Commerce and President of The London Chamber of Arbitration. He was formerly a trustee of The Lord's Taverners and a special adviser to The Prince's Regeneration Trust. He is a Vice President of Crawshays Rugby Club, President of Johnston (Pembrokeshire) Cricket Club and he is a Freeman of the City of London.

He was originally a member of Lamb Building Temple, where he did his pupillage with Gary Flather (later QC), subsequently joint Head of Chambers of 4-5 Grays Inn Square and Head of Mondial (Commonwealth Chambers) and is currently a member of Selborne Wentworth Chambers Sydney and 6 Pump Court, Temple, London. He has been described as 'one of the biggest names at the Bar' (Frances Gibb, legal editor of The Times), 'conspicuously able' and an 'outstanding advocate; his core strength is in dissecting the other side's case and seeking to deliver the client's case in the best light' (Legal 500). Previous publications include *Beyond the Concept of Sport* (2024, Austin Macauley).

To my late parents John and Megan for their love and encouragement always, and to my much-loved children, Anna, Helena and Charles, and to my younger brother Allen.

W Robert Griffiths

A LEGAL MIND

Meditations on the Philosophy of Law and Life

AUSTIN MACAULEY PUBLISHERS
LONDON * CAMBRIDGE * NEW YORK * SHARJAH

Copyright © W Robert Griffiths 2025

The right of W Robert Griffiths to be identified as author of this work has been asserted by the author in accordance with sections 77 and 78 of the Copyright, Designs and Patents Act 1988.

All rights reserved. No part of this publication may be reproduced, stored in a retrieval system, or transmitted in any form or by any means, electronic, mechanical, photocopying, recording, or otherwise, without the prior permission of the publishers.

Any person who commits any unauthorised act in relation to this publication may be liable to criminal prosecution and civil claims for damages.

The story, experiences, and words are the author's alone.

A CIP catalogue record for this title is available from the British Library.

ISBN 9781037103865 (Paperback)
ISBN 9781037103872 (Hardback)
ISBN 9781037103889 (ePub e-book)

www.austinmacauley.com

First Published 2025
Austin Macauley Publishers Ltd®
1 Canada Square
Canary Wharf
London
E14 5AA

Acknowledgements

To the many lawyers, judges, jurists and philosophers who have inspired me through their thoughts, words and wisdom. My sincere thanks and great appreciation to Lord Neuberger for writing the foreword. Many thanks to Rebecca Ramsey Owens for her friendship, assistance throughout and especially for composing the poem 'An Ode to Law' as set out in the epilogue.

Foreword

Throughout more than fifty years of studying, practising and dispensing law, I have always been much more comfortable dealing with specific legal problems (normally in the form of individual cases) rather than thinking about the broader and more abstract concepts raised by legal philosophy. I have tended to fight shy of reading books on legal thinking, and when I have tried, such books have seemed turgid in style and detached from reality in content.

I believe that this cast of mind is typical of many lawyers brought up and working in the common law. We common lawyers are like the great Francis Bacon's "men of experiment," who, he said are "like the ant, they only collect and use." By contrast, he said, legal philosophers are 'men of dogmas' or 'reasoners' who "resemble spiders, who make cobwebs of their own substance." Bacon went on to suggest that better than either was "the bee [which] takes a middle course: it gathers its material from the flowers… but transforms it and digests it by a power of its own." In terms of thinking, the bee, he said, combines the "two faculties, the experimental and the rational."

Robert Griffiths has written a book about legal thinking, but it is very much from the perception of a practising lawyer. Having read this book, I think it can be said he has shown himself to be a bee, in that he manages to straddle both the formic common law world and the arachnid world of legal philosophy. His impressive career as a practising barrister (leading counsel since 1993) in England for the past fifty years and in New South Wales for the past twenty-five years more than establishes his common law credentials. This book shows that a practising common lawyer can make legal thinking accessible and interesting to a reader who is not a lawyer and to a reader like myself who is not naturally attracted to reading about abstract legal thinking.

Robert Griffiths does this through a combination of engaging descriptions of many of his more interesting forensic experiences, memorable and apt references to, and quotations from, a wide-ranging collection of poets, authors, philosophers, statesmen and the occasional lawyer, and some more in-depth analyses of famous thinkers of the past.

To take a few examples: He makes the important point that there is a real difference between a lawyer's prose style when writing a legal opinion or a judgment as opposed to when he or she is performing in court. He describes (very open-mindedly for a common lawyer) 'the magnificence and the magistracy of the Napoleonic Code'. He reminds us of the usefulness of Occam's Razor when resolving factual disputes, and he summarises the seminal thinking of Immanuel Kant.

Despite the seriousness of the topics covered in this book, it is written simply, at no great length, and with a light touch.

David Neuberger, Lord Neuberger of Abbotsbury (2025)

Introduction

If you think that you can think about anything inextricably attached to something else without thinking of the thing which it is attached to you have a legal mind.
Thomas Reid Powell

An ordered mind and razor tongue.
Michael Atherton about the author (2007)

Thinking is the commitment of Being by and for Being.
Heidegger

The mind resorts to reason for want of training.
Henry Adams

The mind of man is more intuitive than logical and comprehends more than it can co-ordinate.
Vauvenargues

Minds differ still more than faces.
Voltaire

Lawyers, I suppose, were children once.
Charles Lamb

He makes his Christmas pies of lawyers tongues and clerk's fingers.
J. Florio

The state of a man's mind is as much a fact as the state of his digestion.
Lord Justice Charles Bowen in *Eddington v Fitzmaurice* (1878)

The law is a process of reality, which has stabilised itself in an idea of validity.
Alf Ross

Facts alone are wanted in life. Plant nothing else. You can only form the minds of reasoning animals upon facts; nothing else will be of any service to them
Charles Dickens, *Hard Times*. Spoken by the schoolmaster Thomas Gradgrind, "A man of realities. A man of facts and calculations"

The law is the last result of human wisdom acting upon human experience for the benefit of the public.
Samuel Johnson

The prophecies of what the courts will do in fact and nothing more pretentious are what I mean by law.
Oliver Wendell Holmes

Laws and institutions must go in hand with the progress of the human mind.
Thomas Jefferson

Natural law is an obscure phantom, which, in the imagination of those who go in chase of it points sometimes to manners, sometimes to laws, sometimes to what the law is, sometimes to what it ought to be.
Jeremy Bentham

The grand thing about the human mind is that it can turn its own tables and see meaningless as ultimate meaning.
John Cage

The essential precondition for the effectiveness of law, in its function is ideology, is that it shall display an independence from gross manipulation, shall seem to be just. It cannot seem to be so without upholding its own logic and criteria; indeed, on occasion, by actually being just.
E.P. Thompson

A revolt of the judiciary is more dangerous than any other even a military one.
De Tocqueville

I am not sure even after the efforts of so many illustrious writers that the concepts of law and justice have been made sufficiently clear.

Leibniz (1693)

And he said Woe unto you also, ye lawyers! For ye lade men with burdens grievous to be borne, and ye yourselves touch not the burdens with one of your fingers. Woe unto you, lawyers! For ye have taken away the key of knowledge: ye entered not in yourselves, and then that were entering in ye hindered.

St Luke

Preface

Drinks Before Dinner
I am always disappointed when a book lacks a preface: it is like arriving at someone's house for dinner, and being conducted straight into the dining-room. A preface is personal, the body of the book impersonal; the preface tells you the author's feelings about his book, or some of them. A reader who wishes to remain aloof can skip the preface without loss; but one who wants to be personally introduced has. I feel, the right to be.

Michael Dummett

The mind is the soul's eye, not its source of power; that lies in the heart, in other words, in the passions.

Vauvenargues (1746)

Order and reason, beauty and benevolence are characteristics and perceptions which we find solely associated with the mind of man.

Karl Pearson

The mind of men is a mystery; and like the plant each one of us naturally appropriates and assimilates that about him that responds to that which is within.

Joseph Roux

In *Unweaving the Rainbow*, having set out the disparaging remarks quoted above from the Gospel of Luke in a chapter titled 'Bar Codes at the Bar', presumably by way of approval, Richard Dawkins says:

On the face of it, the law may seem about as far as you can get from poetry or the wonder of science. Perhaps there is poetic beauty in the abstract ideas of justice or fairness but I doubt if many lawyers are moved by it.[1]

It is that sort of dogmatic statement that scientists such as Dawkins are prone to make on matters outside their domains of expertise including law and religion (see also Dawkins, The God Delusion).

This book, as I explain later, is not about the dogmatics of law, nor about its general jurisprudence or what Kant called the Science of Right. Those topics have historically been dealt with comprehensively and profoundly by the glitterati of the academic legal world, such as Hobbes, Austin, Bentham, Edmund Burke, Hume, A.V. Dicey, R.D. Laing, Hubert Hart, John Rawls, Lon Fuller, Roscoe Pound and Joseph Raz. The contributions of Wendell Holmes and Benjamin Cardozo as Judges of the United States Supreme Court, Lord Reid, Lord Wilberforce, Lord Diplock, Lord Upjohn, Lord Denning, Lord Scarman, Lord Devlin, Lord Woolf, Lord Simon Brown, Lord Justice Laws, Lord Bingham, Lord Hoffman, Dyson Heydon, (High Court of Australia) Lord Neuberger, Lord Sumption and Lord Lloyd-Jones; are also not to be ignored as distinguished judges. I am also hugely indebted to the writings of such outstanding general philosophers as Confucius, Demosthenes, Socrates, Plato, Aristotle, Rousseau, Immanuel Kant, Hegel, Fichte, Gottlob Frege and Ernst Cassirer, who spoke and wrote extensively about legal philosophy.

In 2019, I travelled to Seychelles, and on four other occasions over the next five years, with my junior, Nicola Strachan, to represent two clients, Gary Camille and Veronique Shaw, who had a legal claim under the Seychelles Civil Code in relation to the estate of their alleged natural father, Albert Reneé. He had been the President of the Seychelles for 27 years and was thereby the longest-serving leader of any country in history. I had previously advised on the merits of their case in London at my chambers and discovered that Seychelles law was based on the French Code Napoleon.

I had met Gary Camille in the oldest French wine bar in London, Le Beaujolais, whose owner and patron, Jean-Yves Darcel, had become so interested in the case that he subsequently travelled to Seychelles to attend the hearings. His attendance gave me insight into his appreciation of the theatre of the court, especially as the proceedings were conducted in Seychellois and French, albeit translated into English. He subsequently told me that they were a wonder and beauty to behold. Incidentally, I should add that the case was successful. Gary and Veronique were declared the natural children of Albert René.

My consideration of that case drew my attention to the magnificence and the magistracy of the Napoleonic Code. First published in 1804, it is still in force, helping distinguish the continental countries that fell under Napoleonic influence. As *The London Times* reported recently (see article 4 March 2025 by the appropriately named Adam Sage), Napoleon, after he was sent into exile by Britain to St Helena, said, "My real glory is not to have won forty battles. Waterloo will erase the memory of so many victories. What nothing will erase, which will live on forever, is my Civil Code."

Having immersed myself in the language of the Civil Code, in French and translated into English, I understand why Napoleon was so proud of it. The code combines the beauty of expression, exactitude and plenitude of meaning. It is a literary work of genius and belies any suggestion that legal documents cannot have outstanding aesthetic quality. Richard Dawkins should have read it! The Civil Code, written by four jurists in meetings often chaired by Napoleon himself, is widely viewed as a legal milestone. The Napoleon Foundation says it was 'a triumph of written law over custom'. The work served as a model for many other countries. The second edition, published in 1807 after Napoleon had himself declared Emperor, was officially named the Napoleonic Code.

This book is about lawyers and philosophers and the way they think. Both have had bad press historically, so for me, it is a daunting but enchanting topic. In Jonathan Swift's *Travels of Lemuel Gulliver* (1726), Gulliver explains our legal system as follows:

I said there was a society of men among us bred up from their youth in the art of proving by words multiplied for the purpose that white is black and black is white according as they are paid... It is likewise to be observed that this society hath a peculiar cant and jargon of their own that no other mortal can understand and wherein all their laws are written which they take special care to multiply whereby they have wholly confounded the essence of truth and falsehood of right and wrong.

Keats, one of my favourite poets, said in a letter in 1819, "I think we may class lawyers in the natural history of monsters." Erasmus in *The Praise of Folly*

(1509) was even more damning about philosophers when he said, "Next to these (logicians and sophisters) come the philosophers in their long beards and short cloaks, who esteem themselves the only favourites of wisdom, and look upon the rest of mankind as the dirt and rubbish of the creation: yet these men's happiness is only a frantic craziness of the brain; they build castles in the air, and infinite worlds in a vacuum." So there is a lot for me to deal with in what follows in this book about lawyers and philosophers.

However, as any good advocate will say, we have to put this in context. All professions and disciplines have their critics and, indeed, enemies. Borrow in Lavengro (1851) saw that "all people have their enemies, especially authors."

But if I may say so, the criticism I most enjoy is the damning indictment of politicians, which remains as pertinent today as it was when American senator Boies Penrose (1860–1921) said, "Public office is the last refuge of the incompetent."

Nothing changes! That is, unfortunately, why the people never get the government they deserve. Most politicians go into politics because they are not qualified or capable of doing anything else. Of course, I say that tongue-in-cheek, but it is empirically largely true. The intellectual quality of our politicians has, in my experience, radically deteriorated in the last twenty years. That is why so few lawyers, doctors and other professional people are to be found in parliament. That is a sad state of affairs.

The seed (some may say the germ!) for this book, which, although not in any way autobiographical, was sown by the aforementioned England captain, Test cricketer, now cricket correspondent for *The Times*, who wrote the above-quoted observation in *The Times* and later in his book *Glorious Summers*. He wrote about my performance in my representation of Darrell Hair, the Australian cricket umpire whom I represented in an industrial tribunal hearing concerning the ball-tampering affair in the summer of 2007, to which I have referred in more detail in my book *Beyond the Concept of Sport* published in 2024. It got me thinking about the nature of the legal mind and all its connotations.

My interest in that theme has lately been fuelled by the media and press' disparaging remarks about our Prime Minister Keir Starmer. We have been exposed to such comments as, "He's a lawyer, not a leader." Such glib, simplistic and dogmatic observations have irritated me. To devalue him as a leader because he has a legal mind is popular political journalism at its worst. In that regard, I note that his right-wing critics were conspicuously silent when he displayed this skill, emanating from his legal mind, in helping resolve the public fallout between President Trump and President Zelenskyy at the Oval Office on 28 February 2025. In those circumstances, it was his legal mind and skills that proved decisive in bringing people together over the push for peace in Ukraine.

Some of our greatest historical figures, including statesmen and literary giants, have been lawyers or had legal training. Witness: Justinian, Cicero, Thomas Jefferson, Theodore Roosevelt, Lloyd George, Robert Kennedy, Margaret Thatcher and Tony Blair, all had legal minds. There is also considerable evidence that the greatest Englishman in my view by far—not Churchill but William Shakespeare—had legal training. His plays are stuffed with fee simples and the like; the butcher's boy turned strolling player would scarcely have had such profound acquaintance with lawyers' technicalities. Why should a country lad, when he grew up to be a dramatist and sonneteer, so often draw his images from the seal and parchment of the lawyer's office? Being a magician in his own craft, Shakespeare could turn legal jargon to majestical purposes, and Romeo's heart breaks as he bids his lips:

Seal with a righteous kiss
A dateless bargain to engrossing Death.

'Engrossing death' is a strange epithet for one not legally minded. Even Shakespeare's women, and not only Portia, are strangely legalistic. Mistress Page has fee simple, fine and recovery at her lips ends, and Silvia thinks in terms of pawn and fealty. Very frequently, Shakespeare's mind, in quest of imagery, seems to draw on memories of work with a lawyer. Indeed, he could build a whole sonnet on the language of title and lease.

Wherever we turn, there is law; even Greeks and Trojans in Troilus and Cressida talk in terms of fee farm and fee simple. Fee farm means tenure without limit. Why should Shakespeare be so technical about enduring possession? And why should Hamlet, skull in hand amid the Danish sepulchres, be so extremely precise about the grim relic's possible owner and the details of his past conveyancing? It is almost as though Shakespeare visualised the very bones of some dead master (pupil master?) who had ruled his youth.

Every time I have dinner in Middle Temple Hall, where Shakespeare's *Twelfth Night* was frequently performed, I think of these matters and how our greatest bard used legal metaphors to convey his wondrous and imaginative ideas and philosophy. So much for Keir Starmer allegedly being not a leader but a boring lawyer! Shakespeare also understood the nature of the adversarial legal system and the legal mind. In *The Taming of the Shrew*, he wrote, "Do as adversaries do in law, Strive mightily but eat and drink as friends."

This book is about the legal mind and the way lawyers think about law and what they do. It is not a practical guide to advocacy. Here again, there are outstanding didactic works of instruction on the techniques of oratory and advocacy from Plato and Cicero onwards. However, I doubt whether great advocates such as F.E. Smith required such manuals. They just did it because they could. That is not to say that they did not think about such 'abstract ideals of justice or fairness' or were 'not moved by it'.

From my own personal acquaintance with such giants of the legal profession as Sydney Kentridge, Robert Alexander, George Carman, Michael Mansfield, Michael Beloff, Tony Grabiner, Charles Falconer and David Pannick although different in style and technique, all have an intuitive and instinctive feel for justice and fairness, and they have displayed, contrary to Dawkins's view, a poetic beauty in the execution of their craft.

William James, in his *Pragmatism—A New Way for Some Old Ways of Thinking* (1907), divided philosophers and men generally into tough- and tender-minded. He drew a distinction between tender-minded rationalists and tough-minded empiricists. In my view, depending on the circumstances, we are all a mixture of both especially lawyers.

I hope this book, in some small way, provides insight into the philosophy of legal thinking—not just abstract ideas of truth, justice, fairness and democracy—but how the legal mind has applied and treated those ideas in practice. Science does not have a monopoly on beauty and wonder. The legal mind has to grapple with matters that transcend science: the way we treat our fellow human beings and the way in which our society is governed. The protection of liberty, freedom, the rights of man and democracy is the noble cause to which it aspires. That is a beautiful and wondrous thing.

Wittgenstein, in his *Philosophical Investigations*, referred to a conversation he had with the philosopher F.P. Ramsey, who described logic as a 'normative science'. He said that he did not know exactly what Ramsey had in mind, but it was doubtless closely related to what only dawned on him later; namely, that in philosophy, we often compare the use of words with games and calculi that have fixed rules, but we cannot say that using language must be playing such a game.

I would say that the language of the law is logic, which involves 'the use of words with games and calculi that have fixed rules'. But the language and logic of the law are different concepts and are to be distinguished from the meaning of the law and its application. Furthermore, they do not provide a holistic insight into the true nature of the legal mind.

Wittgenstein said the question raised was, "In what sense is logic something sublime?"

"For there seemed to pertain to logic a peculiar depth—a universal significance." To me, law has that universal significance. It explores the nature of all things. It seeks to see the bottom of things and is not meant to concern itself with whether what actually happens is this or that. It takes its rise not from an interest in the facts of nature, nor from a need to grasp causal connections, but from an urge to understand the basis or essence of everything empirical. We want to understand something that is already in plain view. That is what I wish to explore and understand in what follows. What is the essence of the legal mind?

To me, the epitome of a legal mind is Immanuel Kant, who combined logic, reason and beauty of expression in his articulation of legal concepts. His penetrating insight into the nature of legal thinking belies the unjustified criticism of the law and legal thinking made by lesser thinkers such as Richard Dawkins and other contemporary thinkers who sadly lack that insight.

I commend to any of those interested in the legal mind Kant's works *The Philosophy of Law* and *the Science of Right* (1796). Some of it is difficult to construe, but it is worth trying.

Kant wrote about the reproach of obscurity levelled against his philosophical style of exposition. His response was to draw attention to the distinction between the sensible and what he called the 'supersensible' which is attained by reason and logic. Reason and logic, in this regard, he observed, can never be made popular, nor can any formal metaphysic, because we are here forced to use scholastic accuracy. Even though it should have to bear the reproach of troublesomeness, it is only by such technical language that the precipitancy of reason and logic can be arrested and brought to understand itself in the face of its dogmatic assertions. Precision and clarity of expression invariably require scholastic accuracy, which is a form of legal technique and, in my view, stylistic beauty and wonder in itself.

Kant's three immortal critiques: *The Pure Reason* (1781), *The Practical Reason* (1788) and *The Judgment* (1790), unfolded all the theoretical principles of his critical philosophy and established his claim to be recognised as both the most profound and the most original thinker of the modern world. As the experience of life deepened around and within him, his interest became more and more absorbed and concentrated in the practical.

For him, as for all great and comprehensive thinkers, philosophy only has its beginning in the theoretical explanation of things; its chief end is the rational organisation, animation and guidance of the higher life in which all things culminate. Kant had carried with him through all his struggle and toil of thought the cardinal faith in God, freedom and immortality, as an inalienable possession of reason, and he had beheld the human personality transfigured and glorified in the divine radiance of the primal ideas. But he has further to contemplate the common life of humanity in its varied on-goings and activities, rising with the innate right of mastery from the bosom of nature and asserting its lordship in the arena of the mighty world that it incessantly struggles to appropriate and subdue to itself.

Kant considered the chaos and conflict of the social life of man. He searched out the principles of order and form to vindicate the rationality of the human being. His penetrating vision saw a new world suddenly born before him. He realised that it was only the pure and practical reason in its utmost union which constitutes the birthright of man and his freedom. He embodied the cardinal principle of this thinking in his Science of Right as the philosophical Magna Carta of the age of political reason and the permanent foundation of all true philosophy and law. Kant's Science of Right constituted an epoch in jural speculation, and it has commanded the homage of the greatest legal thinkers since.

Chapter 1

"When I use a word, it means just what I choose it to mean- neither more nor less".
Words spoken by Humpty Dumpty in Lewis Carroll's Through the Looking Glass.

The meaning of a word depends on its application.
Wittgenstein, *Philosophical Investigations* (1953)

Words and language are not wrappings in which things are packed for the commerce of those who write and speak. It is in words and language that things first come into being and are.
Heidegger (1920)

We must think things not words, or at least we must constantly translate our words into the facts for which they stand, if we are to keep them real and true.
Oliver Wendell Holmes, in his address to the New York State Bar Association (17 January 1889)

Words, in their primary or immediate signification, stand for nothing but the ideas in the mind of him who uses them.
John Locke, *An Essay concerning Human Understanding* (1690)

Words, like glass, obscure when they do not aid vision.
Joseph Joubert, *Pensées* (1842)

Man does not live by words alone, despite the fact that sometimes he has to eat them.
Adlai Stevenson (1952)

Words should be an intense pleasure, just as leather should be to a shoemaker.
Evelyn Waugh, *New York Times* (19 November 1950)

Words should be weighed and not counted.
Yiddish proverb (1949)

Those things for which we find words are things we have already overcome.
Nietzsche Skirmishes, 'War with Age', *Twilight of the Idols* (1888)

A word is not the same with one writer as with another. One tears it from the guts. The other pulls it out of his overcoat pocket.
Charles Péguy, 'The Honest People', *Basic Verities* (1943)

Words are the small change of thought.
Jules Renard, Journal (November 1888)

Words are like Leaves, and where they most abound, much fruit of sense beneath is rarely found.
Alexander Pope, *An Essay on Criticism* (1711)

Words are lawyers' tools, and how they use them reflects a lawyer's mind. Clarity and intelligibility are at the essence of legal drafting and court advocacy. As to the latter, G.M. Young put it neatly when he commented:

> *The final cause of speech is to get an idea as exactly as possible out of one mind into another. Its formal cause, therefore, is such choice and disposition of words as will achieve this end most economically.*

Cervantes, in the preface to Don Quixote, put it more poetically. His advice was:

> *Do but take care to express yourself in a plain, easy Manner, in well-chosen, significant and decent Terms, and to give a harmonious and pleasing experience, Turn to your periods, Study to explain your thoughts, and set them in the truest light, labouring as much as possible, not to leave them dark nor intricate, but clear and intelligible.*

The legal mind focuses on clarity and certainty of meaning in the expression of its concepts and ideas. The reason why certainty of meaning is so paramount is that the documents lawyers are required to draft impose obligations and confer rights, and neither the parties to them nor the draftsmen of them have the last word in deciding exactly what those rights and obligations are. They can only be settled in a court of law based on the words of the documents. If anyone is to be held irrevocably to meaning what he says, he must be very careful to say what he means.

Stephen in his *Commentaries on the Laws of England* (1841–1845) noted:

Even where the Counsel in Chambers is merely advising on a case or drawing up a conveyance of property, he is really thinking of what view the court and the judges will take of his advice or his draftsmanship if any dispute arises on them. The supreme test in every case is:

Will this stand the scrutiny of the court?

In my view, language disguises thought, and the real forms of thought only become apparent when the language in which they are expressed has been analysed and broken down into its ultimate components, which are elementary propositions. The ability to do that is the hallmark of a great legal mind. It is necessary to understand that there is a class of factual and conceptual propositions that are logically independent of one another. The truth of an elementary proposition never implies the truth or falsity of any other proposition. It is necessary to prove, as a deduction, that all factual propositions are analysable into minute factual propositions that are logically independent of one another. The same is true of conceptual ideas.

Words are an imperfect instrument for expressing complicated concepts; arguably only mathematics and physics can be sure of doing that. Glanville Williams, an outstanding legal academic, pointed out in 'Language and the Law', *Law Quarterly Review* (April 1945):

Words have a penumbra of uncertainty.

Therein, he wrote:

The ordinary man is not usually troubled with these perplexities. It does not matter to the seaman whether an anchor is or is not called part of the vessel. A chemist does not need to answer the question, yes or no, does a rolled gold watch come within the description gold. Biologists may find difficulty with their classification but nothing turns on the question whether they classify a creature under one head or another; it is simply a question of verbal expediency. With the lawyer it is different. The lawyer, like the theologian, is faced with a number of texts that he regards as authoritative and that are supposed to settle any question that could conceivably arise. Each text was once drawn up by someone who presumably meant something by it; but once the document has left its author's hands it is the document that matters, that still remains in the author's mind. For the lawyer the words of the document are authoritative, as words and there is no possibility of obtaining further information from the author, either because the author is dead or because the rules of evidence preventing reference to him.

It is therefore the duty of a draftsman of these authoritative texts to try to imagine every possible combination of circumstances to which his words may apply and every possible misinterpretation that might be put on them and to take precautions accordingly. All the time, he must keep his eye on the rules of legal interpretation and the case law on the meaning of particular words and choose the phraseology to fit them.

Legal language in drafting documents cannot always be elegant or luminous. But that is not the case with advocacy. The best advocates deploy legal language in an elegant, luminous and appealing way. That is the true art of advocacy. It is truly an art form of wonder and beauty. For the advocate, it is a highly pleasurable and enjoyable experience when words effortlessly, almost without thought, flow in one's own style.

Boswell says of Johnson, "He seemed to take pleasure in speaking in his own style; for when he had carelessly missed it, he would repeat the thought translated into it."

It was Swift who said, "Proper words in proper places make the true definition of style."

Similarly, Shakespeare in his *Sonnets* (1609) said, "Nimble thought can jump both sea and land."

When that happens for the advocate, it is an ecstatic experience. However, as Confucius identified, "If language is not correct, then what is said is not what is meant; if what is said is not what is meant, then what ought to be done remains undone." It is then, for the advocate, a hugely deflating experience.

I now turn to what I regard as another vital tool (suitably modified for the lawyer's, especially the advocate's, armoury and way of thinking—Ockham's Razor; French spelling: Occam). I have referred earlier to Michael Atherton's description of my having 'an ordered mind and razor tongue'. I do not know whether Michael knew about the concept of Occam's Razor, but whether he did or not does not matter. In that description of my approach, he touched on something that reminded me then and now of the case of Occam's Razor, which many advocates consciously or unconsciously deploy in their legal arguments.

William Ockham (1285–1347) was an Englishman and one of the three most important European philosophers of the late Middle Ages. He was very original, provocative and admirable in his approach to knowledge, reason and philosophy. However, much one may agree or disagree with his views they are extremely interesting. As with any important intellectual figure, it remains controversial who Ockham was philosophical, what he really thought and how he influenced subsequent philosophers. Some people claim, not without reason, that Ockham invented the Western idea of church and state separation. Some style him as an analytical philosopher ahead of his time or as the man who brought the harmonious medieval union of faith and reason to an end in Europe. Some think of him as the champion of the scientific approach to life.

He was an excellent logician. His philosophical centre of gravity was the proper use of language in thinking and reasoning through philosophical arguments. His skill with logic led him to ideas that are fixed points in all our thinking.

- Many philosophers are too simplistic when they argue about the function of language.
- Philosophers overstate the power of human reason.

Ockham was a formidable debater. He took part in a philosophical debate called 'Quodlibet'.

Nearly everyone has heard of Occam's Razor: "Do not multiply entities beyond necessity." However, few people understand the principle in any great depth, and it is often used to support the reasoning that Ockham might have found a suspect; therefore, it is not surprising that Ockham was excommunicated by the Pope. All of his philosophy has an Aristotelian cast to it. He recognised that some things we rightly believe come not from direct experience but by reasoning (say in mathematics) or by revelation (intuition). He was an empiricist who privileged the role of sensory experience above all else in the production of what is properly called 'knowledge'.

Ockham believed that we must be very careful to distinguish certain situations where we are talking about language, as opposed to situations where we are talking about non-language, and similarly to distinguish when we are talking about mental things as opposed to non-mental things. In particular, he emphasised that we must be careful to distinguish cases where we are really talking about concepts in subtle ways—cases where we are using terms of first imposition and second intention.

Occam's Razor is a philosophy often applied by lawyers in their thinking especially the view that a plurality ought not to be accepted without necessity.

Ockham never uses the term 'razor' or any similar form of it. He expressed the concept in a number of forms. My preferred expression of it is as follows:

No plurality should be assumed unless it can be proved.

a) *by reason*
b) *by experiencer*
c) *by some infallible authority*

Ockham assumed that the world is maximally simple.

That is the way lawyers invariably try to portray their arguments. The answer is obvious: the simple explanation is the truth. Do not overcomplicate things. In my experience, that approach invariably works. Concepts and truth are self-evident. There is one conceptual answer to the most complex of issues, and the most obvious, most factual answer provides the truth. We all know that this does not necessarily represent reality, but that is the perception the lawyer, especially the advocate, seeks to establish in his submissions and arguments. That is usually correct. When it is not, that is when miscarriages of justice take place and when things go wrong. Occam's Razor usually provides the right answer, but it can produce the wrong one and can be too simple by half.

Nonetheless, Occam's Razor is a good guiding principle readily adapted by the legal mind, but in some instances, it needs to be modified. That ability, in my view, is the hallmark of a creative and innovative legal mind beyond the norm. Great advocates and legal thinkers possess the ability to see beyond the obvious.

A famous story recounts that the great French scientist Pierre-Simon Laplace (died 1827) was once asked by Napoleon why his book on celestial mechanics contained no reference to God. Laplace's response was, "I have no need of that hypothesis." This is a good example of Occam's Razor in action. It is the trimming of needless hypotheses. That is essentially how lawyers approach a case: get to the essence and merits of the issue. Trim the unessential. Only in exceptional circumstances, there is a need to go beyond that. It is often said that usually, one point decides a case. It is just a case of finding it, but it can backfire as I can illustrate from my own career.

I was doing a case for a factory owner who was being sued for damages for personal injuries as a result of an employee losing two fingers while using a cutting machine. It seemed to me that the obvious point to be made was whether the employee wrongly misplaced his hand on a certain unprotected part of the machine. Therefore, in my first question in cross-examination, I asked him, "At the time of the accident, where was your hand?"

The witness immediately responded, "At the time of the accident, my hand was at the end of my arm."

The Judge immediately intervened and, to my embarrassment, said, "Try again, Mr Griffiths!"

I cannot remember now whether I won that case, but I vividly recall the judge's reaction to my attempt to deploy Occam's Razor. Notwithstanding that experience, Occam's Razor is a valuable guide to focused and penetrative advocacy. Parsimony and pragmatism are vital tools for both the philosopher and the lawyer. Philosophers have discussed this idea both before and after Ockham. These include Aristotle who said, "God and nature do nothing that is pointless." Furthermore, more recently, John Duns Scotus, Immanuel Kant and W.V. Quine have all advanced versions of their own.

Modern interest in this principle continues unabated; philosophers, mathematicians, scientists and lawyers are still fascinated by the meaning and limits of this principle. All parsimony principles have in common that they come down favourably on the question of reduction and the point of view that it is bad to have too much.

All other things being equal, we should prefer the simpler theory.

This is a fine rule of thumb, and it is clearly a principle of parsimony since it extols reduction. But it does not attempt to make a claim about the nature of reality; all it states is that simpler theories are to be preferred. It does not attempt to tell us anything about the world and what it is actually like, only which theories of the world are the best. By itself, Occam's Razor is not committed to the view that the simplest theory is not necessarily accurate or that reality itself is simple, but only that when choosing between theories that are otherwise equal, preferring the simpler one is rational.

An erudite philosophical example of Occam's Razor in practice is to be found in Sir Isaiah Berlin's brilliant essay 'Two Concepts of Freedom' published in 1958, in which in Ockhamist mode, he refers to freedom from external constraints and coercion. It is defined as the freedom of an individual to act without interference from others.

In other words, a person is negatively free if no one prevents him from acting as he sees fit. For example, if the government does not impose unreasonable prohibitions and restrictions, then the individual has negative liberty. However, Berlin also noted that negative liberty is not absolute and may conflict with other societal goods, such as security or equality.

The opposite of negative liberty is positive liberty, which refers to the individual's ability to self-determine and control his own life. Most recently in my view, COVID restrictions have been a classic illustration of unreasonable constraints on our freedom. I agree with Lord Sumption who in *The Challenge of Democracy* (2025) describes the situation as an illustration of the fact, "We are entering a Hobbesian world, the enormity of which has not yet dawned on our people."

Finally, to conclude this chapter on a political note related to Occam's Razor, Larry Bartell in *Democracy Erodes* (2023) noted that when there are scandals, politicians often respond with complicated explanations to increase transparency, but it does not work. It does not create trust. The public unwittingly applies Ockham's reasoning. They are looking for a simple explanation of reality. Remy De Gourmont saw this when he said, "Thinking is hard work. One cannot bear burdens and ideas at the same time." Personally, I would add, "A fortiori with legal thinking. It is hard work but, gladly, not a burden." Or perhaps only sometimes!

Chapter 2

Two things fill the mind with ever new and increasing wonder and awe, the more often and the more seriously reflection concentrates upon them: the starry heaven above me and the moral law within me.

Immanuel Kant

Wonder is the basis of worship.

Thomas Carlyle

Moral good is a practical stimulus; it is no sooner seen than it inspires an impulse to practise it.

Plutarch

Diogenes said "When Thales was asked what was difficult" he said "to know oneself" and when asked what was easy he said "to advise another".

Analysis kills spontaneity.

Henri Frédéric Amiel

The law is a sort of hocus-pocus science, that smiles in your face while it picks your pocket; and the glorious uncertainty of it is of more use to the professors than the justice of it.

C. Macklin, *Love À La Mode*

Old father antic the law.

Shakespeare, *King Henry IV*, Part I

In law, what plea so tainted and corrupt,
but, but, being seasoned with a gracious voice,
Obscures the show of evil?

Shakespeare, *Merchant of Venice*

Plato, Schopenhauer and many other philosophers have said that the origin of philosophy is a kind of wonder or refusal to take things for granted. Archimedes said that he could move the world if he could find a point in space that would serve as the fulcrum for a sufficiently long lever. His idea can be used as an image to illustrate the origin of philosophy.

Philosophy originates in the desire to transcend the world of human thought and experience to find some vantage point from which it can be seen as a whole. The understanding sought by philosophers goes beyond that sought by scientists. But though this is true, it is vague, and however positive it may sound, it really only gives a negative characterisation of philosophy since it does not tell us where a thinker who ventured beyond the limits of science would go.

The world of human thought and experience must not only be seen but appreciated and described, and that creates two needs: the need for a set of ideas that could be applied universally and the need for a master language to express those ideas. The ultimate purpose is not merely to describe but also to explain and understand. The understanding that is sought is higher. The desired understanding is more synoptic. What is always the case is that philosophy seeks a wider view and an understanding that goes beyond what counts as understanding in any other discipline.

This is very evidently true of metaphysical philosophy, but it is also true, in a different and less obvious way, of legal philosophy. For example, a detailed analysis of legal judgements, however narrowly focused it may seem to be, will really be comparative because it will try to place legal judgements in relation to other types of judgement, and in so doing, it will raise questions beyond the limits of law.

Philosophy, in the traditional sense of the word, attempts, by means of pure thinking, to find the answers to the most general problems of existence, such as the relation between the psychic and the physical, the question of freedom of will or determination, the foundations or limitations of human understanding, as well as the object and the meaning of human life; in short, the problems of valuation.

As a theoretical philosophy, it tries to gain a deeper comprehension of that which *is*.

In recent times, it is first and foremost the theory of understanding that has captivated the interest of philosophers in this respect. As a practical philosophy, it is the direction for human activity, i.e., the ethical problems, with which philosophy occupies itself. These ethical problems may be studied generally and formally by examining the possibility, in principle, of valid statements with normative content and the possibility of drawing logical conclusions from such statements. Ethical problems may also be treated, especially materially, by trying, through free thinking, to find a valid standard for all kinds of human activity.

Philosophical thought thus comprises extremely diverse problems. It encompasses a wide field, from the most fundamental questions of the limits of knowledge and the very possibility of objectively valid appreciation to the practical questions of how it is 'right' to act in the innumerable factual or possible situations of life.

Philosophy even extends to the world of humour. G.K. Chesterton was of the view that every good joke has a philosophical idea somewhere inside. Woody Allen said, "You know what my philosophy of life is? That it is important to have some laughs no question about it, but you have to suffer a little too otherwise you miss the whole point of life."

Again, and again thinkers have worked on these questions, and yet one cannot point to definite results that are generally recognised as correct. But no feeling of the overwhelming immenseness, perhaps even the impossibility, of the task can bring philosophical thinking to a standstill. Each generation needs to orient itself afresh in the main problems of life with which philosophy occupies itself.

The problems which philosophy sets itself are different from those which occur in any of the specialised sciences. What philosophy gives is not generalisations of the results of the natural science;[2] however, general may be the law of nature which one believes to have been ascertained. The problems of a fundamental view of life are not solved even by the most magnificent survey of the historical life of human beings that historical science can provide.

Theoretical philosophy examines the foundations of research in natural science but does not itself represent such research. Practical philosophy examines the logical character of dogmatic thought but is not itself dogmatics.

Practical philosophy may use the teachings of history as a means in its work with the problems of morality and of the meaning of life. But history itself says nothing about the object and meaning of human life.

The branch of philosophy which the philosophy of law constitutes, is not concerned with generalisations or scientific results, either. Legal philosophy is not general sociology of law, nor is it general legal dogmatics. Examinations of the most common terms under which positive law may be comprised, terms such as 'legal subject', 'legal relation', 'subjective rights' etc. are not the concern of legal philosophy but of 'general jurisprudence'.

The philosophy of law, which may be regarded as a branch of ethics in the widest sense of the word, thus wishes neither to interpret dogmatically nor to explain causally the phenomena of law. Its object is to try to understand law as a spiritual phenomenon—to determine the notion of law and examine the logical character of legal thought and the logical possibility of an objectively valid valuation of the contents of the law. This is what I call the problems of the general philosophy of law.

Secondarily, it may also be regarded as a task of the philosophy of law to try to determine the contents of what is right law. This part of the philosophy of law, which it is most natural to designate as the policy of law, finds its supporters among numerous juridical authors, who are distant from the problems of the general philosophy of law, but who thus nevertheless—more or less expertly employing the empirical material of sociology—contribute to solving the problems of practical philosophy. Granted that the legal-political reflections of the lawyers may be equally marked by interest and just as ideologically and subjectively coloured as the deliberations on social questions of the so-called laymen; but at the same time, they are very often marked by the intention of their originators to give information as to the objectively right settlement in the field of law they are commenting upon. To find the objectively right law—that is precisely one of the eternal, but never quite attainable aims of practical philosophy.

I shall explain some of the problems attached to the determination of the notion of law itself. A central question is whether, in principle, the notion of law may be determined on an empirical basis, or whether the acceptance of certain points of departure must be postulated a priori. But above all, it is a question of whether the legal rule quite logically may be understood as an idea which has a normative content and is 'valid'. The 'validity' of the legal norm corresponds to the 'legal duties' of the subjects of the law. The question as to the notion of 'legal duty' is of a legal-philosophical nature, while the problems related to the notion of legal rights are dogmatical. The notion of legal duty is indissolubly bound up with the very idea of the law, while 'right' or 'subjective right' are terms for juridical situations which positive law indeed constantly knows, but does not necessarily need to know.

After treating, the problems of normativity and legal validity, I pass on to the basic questions of legal thinking. First and foremost, this concerns the question of the possibility of drawing logically binding conclusions from legal statements. The object is not the psychological one of describing and explaining actually occurring juridical thinking, but the logical one of examining the forms of correct mental operations in legal thinking.

In the most intimate connection with this problem, stands the question: to what extent is it possible at all to reach objectively valid results in juridical thinking? The question is whether, by the application of positive legal norms in a special case (i.e., by legal dogmatic thinking), one may reach binding objective results from the given points of departure; or whether every application of 'existing law' necessarily implies an element of free option. This is in itself not a legal dogmatic, but a legal-philosophical question. It lies at the very heart of this book.

I shall then consider certain of the main problems of the valuation of law. It is not the legal-political questions—not the question of what would be the ideal of right law in a given place and time—that I shall not deal with. What I shall examine is, on the contrary, the theoretical question of whether there be certain necessary metaphysical postulates for our valuations of existing law, and of whether it be possible in these valuations of ours to reach results which have objective validity. All laws must serve certain purposes. Does not our valuation of the purposefulness of legal rules assume that there are certain fundamental values in social life that we accept as objectively valid?

The law has to be just. Does not the demand for justice stipulate certain assumptions of a metaphysical nature with regard to human volition and its freedom? Is all valuation of the law from legal ideals merely a psychological phenomenon? Or does something objectively valid, which is accessible to human understanding, apply here?

It is these problems, or rather problem-complexes, which are the objects of examination of the legal mind.

The nature of law that is applied in legal dogmatics, and that legal philosophy makes the object of examination, comprises all existing law, irrespective of its contents. This has nothing to do with a generalisation of the contents of the manifold provisions to be found in historically given, positive legal orders, but concerns the logical form of the law. Not what, but how, is the question that legal philosophy must answer, when it expounds the nature of law.

Legal philosophy tries to find a common nature for all existing laws. Does this concern a nature, the contents of which are given *a priori*? In other words, does it concern a nature which we have not formed by observing outer reality, but which we have created in our minds, independently of experience, and with which we ourselves meet the material of experience?

Kant's theory of understanding operates, as is well-known, with certain *a priori* forms of understanding, that is to say, ideas, which human beings have not obtained by the observation of reality, but which serve to give form and sense to the experience of reality. Space and time are such forms of understanding. Is not the nature of law, too, such a form of understanding? Is not the nature of law given *a priori*, in the same way as the natures of space and time?

It is this which is the doctrine of the Neo-Kantian school in legal philosophy. The German legal philosopher, Rudolf Stammler, speaks of the 'pure forms of thinking' of juridical understanding, which is not subject to the vicissitudes of history, and of the nature of law as the formal species and manner in which what is changeable and variable is determined as right.[3] The Italian *Girgio Del Vecchio* also characterises the nature of law as a 'logical form'; all understanding of law presupposes, according to Del Vecchio, common nature of law; and this nature of law cannot be attained by a historical-comparative method.[4]

If this Neo-Kantian doctrine of the nature of law is really to be understood as declaring that the nature of law is exclusively an *a priori* form,[5] we must take our point of departure in psycho-physical phenomena, which indubitably belong to legal life. Such a decision is, for instance, a decision by the legislature, and is called 'Law'. The content of ideas it expresses is existing law. Such and such acts are manifestations of a convention of law. This convention of law is at the centre undoubtedly in accordance with a rule of customary law.

When in the determination of the nature of law, we take our point of departure in individual phenomena, which we can establish for certain as legal, this no more implies a circular argument than when the same procedure is employed in the determination of nature of reality. Ross, who, in his *Theorie der*

Rechtsquellen, disputes the possibility of proceeding in this way in determining the nature of law, nevertheless admits that by reasoning thus one does not reason in a circle, any more than when one, for instance, defines the nature of 'horse' by starting from a series of individual specimens, which undoubtedly are horses.[6] But he thinks that this procedure cannot be justified here, where the nature which is to be defined itself determines the whole system that the nature is referred to.[7]

To this, it must be added that the nature of law, even if the point of departure be taken in the phenomena of factual legal life, nevertheless itself comprises norms, that is to say, contents of ideas, and may be defined as a particular species of such norms, different from other contents of ideas. In other words: in our determination of the nature of law we certainly do not refer to this nature as the 'system of understanding' of reality, even if we have taken our point of departure in an immediate psycho-physical reality. We refer to the nature of law as the world of ideas where it belongs.

In order to reach an understanding of the nature of law, we must consequently first ascertain that such and such contents of ideas—norms with a foundation in reality—without doubt may be regarded as 'law'. The determination of the nature of law first demands a generalising survey of these special spiritual phenomena. But the very jump from the observation of the psycho-physical realities—the statutes, legal conventions, acts of observance—to the acceptation of a 'binding rule of law' implies *a priori* element. That the norm is 'binding'— that it has 'validity'—is not something we can observe in the world of reality. Thus, we must admit that the Neo-Kantians are partly right, in so far as we cannot get past a certain *a priori* element in the nature of law.

The law cannot be understood except by means of the postulates of validity which are at the base of the validity of each individual legal rule. It is from the *a priori* assumption that the fundamental rules of the legal system are 'binding'— from the assumption of the 'validity' of the constitution, of customary law and of a series of ordinary legal principles, that we can ascribe validity to the individual legal rule, and determine whether the contents of a norm, in a case of doubt, are to be regarded as valid, existing law or not. The idea of validity is the *a priori* element of the nature of law.

The 'validity' of the law is equivalent to its obliging force. This is not necessarily to be called a metaphysical conception. Even if one would call the conceptions of the validity of morality, and of moral duty, metaphysical ideas, it does not follow that the ideas of legal validity and of legal duty are metaphysical.

The nature of legal duty cannot be regarded as a subordinate nature to the nature of moral duty.

In my opinion, the conception of the 'validity' of law and of the 'duty' to observe the dictates of law are purely formal natures—*a priori* conceptions, which are necessary to the understanding of the meaning of the law, but which are independent of the moral (or if one prefers, metaphysical) conception of a true duty to act in accordance with the dictates of the law. It is therefore no logical contradiction to regard a rule as binding law, but at the same time to judge oneself morally obliged to break it.

There are a number of crackpot ideas about the legal mind. Perhaps, the most notorious is known as the 'Judge for Breakfast' theory. This was an idea to be found in the work of Karl Llewellyn and Jerome Frank. An outstanding judge Charles Bowen encapsulated it when he said, "The state of a man's mind is as much a fact as the state of his digestion."

This was an exaggeration of the legal realist's approach to legal thinking. It led to a professor of law, Walter Kennedy, jokingly saying in mockery of the legal realists, that they should become stomach specialists and that advocates should take a sly glance at the judge's breakfast menu. It is doubtful whether realists claimed anything of the sort. Whether they did or not is in my view errant nonsense. It is the kind of thinking that Ernst Cassirer would have characterised as mythical thinking. The core of legal thinking is how you apply concepts to empirical facts.

Concepts are multifaceted and variegated. In that regard, one should consider the concept of the Rule of Law. The Rule of Law is the starting point for dealing with any alleged breach of law. As such if the Rule of Law is not followed, the validity of any alleged or decided breach comes into question. The seminal work on the Rule of Law's meaning is A.V. Dicey's Introduction to the Study of the Law of the Constitution (1897). It is a maxim that underpins the honesty and integrity of the justice system and ensures a state's dealings with all its citizens are permissible and fair under the law. Lord Bingham, elucidating on Dicey's famous exposition described its core as follows:

All persons and authorities within the state, whether public or private, should be bound by and entitled to the benefit of laws publicly made, taking effect (generally) in the future and publicly administered in the courts. That is to say that a certainty in the law is ensured so that a person knows what the law is, laws are not made arbitrarily, and that they will be tried in a fair, open and just manner.

Tom Bingham and Allen Lane, *The Rule of Law* (2010)

In my book *Beyond the Concept of Sport* (2024), I wrote about the philosophical significance of seeing beyond the surface of sport in order to understand the concept of sport, the same is true of law and legal thinking.

Chapter 3

It ain't no sin if you crack a few laws, just as long as you don't break any.
Mae West

Men of most renowned virtue have sometimes by transgressing most boldly kept the law.
Milton

Human law is law only by virtue of its accordance with right-reason and by this means it is clear that it flows from Eternal Law. Insofar as it deviates from right-reason it is called an Unjust Law; and in such a case, it is no law at all, but rather an assertion of violence.
Saint Thomas Aquinas

Since it is Reason which shapes and regulates all other things, it ought not be left in disorder.
Epictetus

There is a higher law than the constitution.
W.H. Seward, Speech (11 March 1850)

Reason is the life of the law, nay, the common law is nothing else but reason… The law is the perfection of reason.
Sir Edward Coke

Logicians have but ill-defined
As rational the human mind
Reason, they say, belongs to man,
But let 'em prove it if they can …

I must in spite of 'em maintain,
That man and all his ways are vain,
And that this boasted Lord of Nature
Is both a weak and erring creature
That instinct is a truer guide
Than reason-boasting mortals' pride;
And that brute beasts are far before 'em,
Deus est anima brutorum.

      Thomas Hardy, *The Logicians Refuted, In Imitation of Dean Swift*

The Swedish thinker, Axel Hägerström, and his supporters tried to demonstrate that the idea of duty is an irrational conception. When one expresses one's opinion that something is a 'duty', this is, according to *Hägerström*, a hopeless attempt to formulate as a rational statement something which in reality is only an emotional experience. *Tegen* expresses the matter thus: "The sense of duty itself is only an association between an idea and an emotion, even though it be expressed in a proposition formed as a judgement."[8]

Now this standpoint assumes in the first place that one does not recognise the idea of something objectively valid in the field of morality. If, on the contrary, one does so, the conception of the moral norm and the moral duty acquires the meaning that a certain mode of action shall or ought to take place—irrespective of whether the individual himself feels this or not. This standpoint on the question of objective morality may be called metaphysical.

But even if one is only willing to recognise a 'subjective morality', in the sense that moral views cannot in any way be otherwise than subjective, and thus can never have any objective validity, it is logically possible to distinguish between the experience itself and the idea that it is conceived through the experience. In other words: in morality, it is possible and necessary to distinguish between, on the one hand, the psychic phenomenon itself that a person experiences the urge to action implied by the feeling of duty, and, on the other hand, the idea of right which corresponds to such an experience. The psychological experience is one thing, the corresponding spiritual contents, the moral idea or conception of duty, is another. The whole of human activity is based on the idea of norm and duty and on the possibility of drawing logical conclusions in this field.

The conception that a certain way of acting is duty, may refer both to an individually determined and to a generally determined situation. Rules of law are general, normative propositions, i.e., general propositions about duty. When the rules of law are 'applied' in individual cases, we are still concerned with normative statements, i.e., statements saying that something is or is not duty. For example: this contract between A and B must be kept. (Application of the legal command stating that contracts must be kept.)—X. is entitled to a driving licence. (Application of the legal command stating that persons who fulfil such and such conditions are entitled to driving licences.)

The normative proposition is never a proposition about a real connection. It does not say that something *is*, but that something *ought to be*. Nor is it possible to change the very character of the normative proposition by altering its form so that the contents become a proposition about real connection.

Husserl,[9] it is true, maintains that any normative proposition that says 'an A has to be B' encloses the purely theoretical proposition 'Only an A, which is also B, has the quality C'. 'C' is then used to denote the quality to which the value is attributed. To take an illustrating example: the proposition 'A soldier has to be brave' says the same as the proposition 'Only a brave soldier is a good soldier'.

According to Husserl's logical system, this last proposition should be a theoretical one. In my opinion, however, this is not correct. In reality, this proposition, too, has a practical character. It expresses a valuation and does not set forth a real connection. The fact that purely linguistically it does not contain words like 'has to', 'ought to' or 'may', has no importance for the real contents of the proposition.[10]

In the domain of moral life, the ideas which correspond to the experience of duty as a psychic phenomenon will often be conceptions of valid 'values' and not binding 'norms'. A person who realises, without great inner struggles, a dignified life by the force of the natural aptitude of his own character, will not have a feeling of living his life under the domination of moral norms which command him to do what is right.[11] In relation to ethics of norms, ethics of value represent a standpoint which is freer, more harmonious and also, presumably, more comprehensive. In any case, it will be easier for it to incorporate such values of life as art and science, whose fate it has been to fall between two stools in many a strictly normatively formed system of moral ideas!

However, it is precisely morality as a system of normative ideas with which it is most natural to compare the law. A positive legal order constitutes a system of norms. Its authority is based on a postulate of the validity of this system of norms. But the postulate of validity is established also in view of the social fact that the system is on the whole accepted by public opinion and maintained by organised force.

Against the conception of law as a system of 'binding norms', many voices of criticism have been raised historically within legal philosophy and legal science, in Scandinavian countries.

With penetrating sharpness, *Axel Hägerström* examined the fundamental notions of juridical thinking and tried to demonstrate that the traditional conception of law as a system of norms, which are logically applied to factual occurrences, involves hopeless logical contradictions. He took issue with the conception of a positive law, "Which is supposed at once to be an objective reality and yet contain obliging rules also."[12]

The notion of a legal order, which obliges the judge, is, "Only a chimaera, as is the whole of the refined extract of old superstition which is embodied in the idea of law as determining rights and duties."[13] Jurists have here bound up in "mystic notions remote from reality."[14]

In his comment on Hans Kelsen's strictly normativistic doctrine of law, Hägerström says that the import of this doctrine is really to regard knowledge (i.e., juridical theory) and the object of knowledge (the law) as one and the same thing.[15]

A.V. Lundstedt, whose writings for many years had been marked by his adherence to Hägerströmian philosophy, considered the legal rule as expressing that a certain factual course of events will probably ensue if such and such acts are carried out or refrained from. According to Lundstedt, legal rules cannot be understood otherwise than as expressions denoting that organs of state act in a certain way in situations of a certain kind, which again depends on a series of psychologically operative factors, and which in turn influence the acts of individuals in different ways.[16]

In the same way, a 'right' only denotes the factual circumstances that one person in relation to another under certain conditions may have 'forcible state measures' effected against the other, or that the latter, for his part, loses a possibility he would otherwise have had of getting such forcible measures effected.[17] "The statement that 'such and such a rule is binding', is something which by its words has no contents that can be realised in the mind."[18] The notions of 'accordance with law' and 'illegality' are both of 'an equally chimerical nature'.[19]

In American jurisprudence, where the so-called sociological tendency has played an important part over the years, a pronouncement by the former distinguished judge of the Supreme Court, *Holmes*, is not infrequently cited. It runs thus: "The prophecies of what the courts will do in fact and nothing more pretentious are what I mean by law."[20] As far as I can see, this is a pertinent summary reproduction of the doctrine which is also the main contents of the legal philosophy of Lundstedt.

Another of Hägerström's Swedish supporters, too, *K. Olivecrona*, attacked, in a work published in 1939,[21] the normativistic conception of law. But Olivecrona nevertheless approaches this conception. For him, law consists of 'independent commands'[22] which function as 'patterns of conduct'.[23] The purpose of law is 'to direct people's actions',[24] and to this end the legislature makes use of the idea of duty as an excellent means.[25] Yet Olivecrona wished to ban the idea of the 'binding force' of the law—an idea which he regarded as superstition.

The Norwegian jurist *G Astrup Hoel* had—independently of Hägerström and his pupils—given an interesting criticism of the normativistic conception of law.[26] But it is to the Danish jurist and philosopher, *Alf Ross* that we owe the most penetrating and philosophically best-founded criticism that after Hägerström has been directed against the conception of law as a 'binding norm'.

Already in his first larger work, Theorie der Rechtsquellen, where in his main points he followed the Austrian champion of normativistic legal philosophy, *Hans Kelsen*, there was a hint that the rules of law may be understood as statements of a real sequence of events. For he maintained that the proposition 'A soll sein' may be understood as synonymous with the two following propositions: 'Wenn nicht A, dann S' and 'Wenn A, dann nicht S'.[27] 'S' here clearly meant the social sanction which attaches itself to the breach of law. Therefore, the substance of Ross's assertion was here that the contents of the legal rule are that sanctions take effect if one acts against the rule, but not otherwise. But not till his two works published in 1933 and 1934 did Ross fully develop his antinormativistic doctrine of law.[28]

Like Hägerström, Ross, too, regarded the statements of the so-called practical understanding as 'urteilsmässig camouflierte Ausdrücke emotionaler Erlebnisse'.[29] The proposition 'this is duty' has the form of a judgment, but it is still nothing else than the rationalised expression of an irrational experience. As expressions without truth value, the normative statements cannot be the objects of logical treatment. The traditional theories of law represent the law, as "a metaphysical revelation of the valid in the world of reality."[30] The insurmountable difficulty caused by these theories, is that the law is supposed to be both a fact in the world of reality and at the same time a 'validity'.[31]

In all this, one may say that Ross's criticism of the normativistic view concurs with that of Hägerström and Lundstedt. But Ross, more clearly than anyone before him, had seen (and had been willing to accept) that the idea of the validity of positive law—even if this idea is of a metaphysical nature and is represented as a superstition—is still a social reality, and moreover a reality of the very greatest importance. "The law is a process of reality, which has stabilised itself in an idea of validity."[32]

It is common ground of the above-mentioned opponents of the normativistic conception of law that they all choose to regard the law quite realistically. They understand the law partly as an expression of probability, based on the factual regularity in social life, partly as a psycho-physical fact characterised, among other things, by an irrational experience of an idea of validity.

If one seriously tries to carry through the conception of law as the expression of a sociological probability (Lundstedt), it turns out that precisely what is typical of law and of legal thinking disappears. The rule of law—the legal proposition—is not a proposition stating that a certain future course of events is probable. It is not that which is its characteristic feature. Neither the judge nor the juridical theoretician can confine himself to ascertaining the ideas of validity that attach themselves to the rule, and the probability of its being enforced. Practical legal life, especially, is unthinkable without the conception of law as a binding norm.

A layman, who in a certain situation, asks the question of what is existing law, may perhaps content himself with trying to foresee the probable social reactions that his actions—whether he acts one way or another—will produce. But the judge can scarcely do that. He cannot confine himself to trying to calculate the consequence for himself of his deciding the case in such or such a way. At most, it is conceivable that a calculation of the chances for a judgment to be affirmed in a higher instance, be made the basis of a decision in the lower instance. But in any case, a court that itself passes judgment in the last instance cannot resort to such a calculation.

In reality, of course, one does not reason in that way at all, when legal questions are to be decided. Legal thinking does not consist of an examination of more or less probable motivation processes on the part of the persons acting in the judicial machinery. But it consists of more or less certain conclusions from ideas with normative contents. In order to comprehend these ideas—the legal norms—we certainly take our point of departure in psycho-physical realities, such as statutes, regular modes of action in connection with ideas of validity, etc.

But the norms are not identical with any single psychic or physical reality of this kind. Solely by means of mental operations which have the character of logical inferences from norms, can the 'science of law' answer the question that society necessarily must put to it, namely: what is right and what is wrong in the endless number of conflicts which are provoked by all social life?

One may call this view of the law and of legal thinking metaphysical. I doubt if that is correct. But even if it were—if the notions of 'norm', 'legal duty' and 'validity' really must be regarded as metaphysical notions, it would be a mistaken 'realism' to try to eliminate these notions from juridical thinking. Without these notions, all juridical thinking is impossible. That is something which the legal and philosophical examination of the notions cannot avoid ascertaining.

When *Ross*, on his side, so strongly adopts the view that legal statements are emotional expressions, without any logical meaning, it quite accordingly turns out that this standpoint cannot be consistently maintained. That is natural enough. It is a view which is at fault in the logical point of departure itself: that no other statements can have a logical meaning and be the objects of logical treatment than those which can be either true or false.

A normative statement cannot be true or untrue (false). But it can be correct or incorrect. Then such statements must also be able to form the foundations for logical operations, the conclusions of which can likewise be correct or incorrect. This is a necessary condition for all juridical (legal dogmatic) thinking. Ross himself must accept the necessity of legal dogmatic thinking.[33]

The fact that normative statements can be correct or incorrect and form the foundations for logical operations is a necessary assumption for all the cultural life of human beings. This assumption is here just as fundamentally necessary as is, in theoretical understanding, the assumption that our statements about reality can be true or false and that they can form the foundation for inferences according to the laws of logic.

Chapter 4

Laws that only threaten, and are not kept, become like the log that was given to the frogs to be their king, which they feared at first, but soon scorned and trampled on.

Cervantes

If we are to extend the law it must be by the development and application of fundamental principles. We cannot introduce arbitrary conditions or limitations: that must be left to legislation.

Lord Reid in *Myers v. D.P.P.* (1965)

The law is simply and solely made for the exploitation of those who do not understand it or of those who, for naked need, cannot obey it.

Bertolt Brecht

No lawgiver inner or outer, gives laws in a vacuum; he always has real or supposed facts in mind which influences his rulings about what ought to be.

C.S. Lewis

Justice is conscience; not a personal conscience but the conscience of the whole of humanity.

Alexander Solzhenitsyn, 'The Struggle Intensifies' (1970)

When will our conscience grow so tender that we will act to prevent human misery rather than avenge it?

Eleanor Roosevelt, on the Universal Declaration of Human Rights (1998)

In the preceding chapter, I have attempted to demonstrate that law must be conceived as a system of binding norms, with its peculiar foundation in social reality.

But one must then further ask what this system of norms really is—what kind of 'existence' it has? Must we assume a kind of ideal existence of legal norms a sort of world of notions? Or is it, on the contrary, a question of the contents of certain factual acts of consciousness?

With regard to the latter hypothesis, it may be immediately rejected. Every factual content of consciousness is necessarily attached to a single individual. But law does not consist of norms which are characterised by the fact that they live, or at any time have lived, in the minds of definite individuals. The fact that all positive legal systems have their point of departure in factual acts of consciousness—decisions and convictions—is not the same as saying that all legal norms constitute the contents of one or more such definite acts of consciousness.

A legal norm may be conceived to follow of compelling necessity as the consequence of a legal provision, without this consequence as yet being discovered by anyone. It is then a 'valid' or 'existing' norm, even before it has been alive in the consciousness of any human being. A rule of customary law may have legal validity in a positive system of law, even if those who observe it have never attempted to formulate it in any statement, and even if it has not been discovered in theory.[34]

That enacted law is not identical with the contents of what individuals with legislative functions quite factually have thought, most modern jurists will easily realise. If one assumed an identity here, the consequence would be, among other things that all interpretation of the law must have for its object to seek enlightenment as to what the legislators had actually meant. In other words, one would end up in the most rigorous, 'subjective' method of interpretation of the law. This result for the theory of interpretation is directly opposed to what modern jurists think and practise.

In earlier writings on legal philosophy, the law was often represented as the expression of some sort of will. In this way, people wished to make the law the contents of actual consciousness. Certainly, the 'will of the state' a concept which has been widely used in philosophical and juridical literature, is at times a purely metaphysical notion. In such cases, the state is conceived as a supersensible being, a kind of god, which in a mystical way rules its subjects. Or the (will of the state) is only a compendious expression of the social forces, which support the legal system.

If the 'will of the state' is a metaphysical notion, or if it is simply a construction, the 'will theory' in reality gives no explanation of the phenomena. The theory is inane. But the conception of law as being identical with the contents of the actual will of the state organs is also untenable. To think that the law as a whole is 'willed' at all times by the highest organs of state naturally implies a quite arbitrary fiction. Besides, many of the legal norms which 'exist' in society have never formed the contents of any act of volition at all.

Above all, this applies to the unenacted customary law. Only that part of the law which is laid down by the decisions of the public organs of authority might perhaps be characterised as identical with historically given contents of the will. But even here this view does not lead anywhere. The law as a binding norm does not necessarily coincide with what the wills of such and such legislators have comprised. Indeed, even if the legislator should have factually carried out the act of legislation without any will in any direction, i.e., if he had only co-operated in the purely external expression of will, it is conceivable that the law has come into being in a valid way according to the existing constitutional order, and must be regarded as binding law.[35]

As we have seen, the legal norms cannot be identified with the contents of a series of factual acts of consciousness. They do not constitute the ideal contents of what is meant or what is willed by a series of individuals in a community.

Must we then attribute a kind of independent, spiritual 'existence' to law? Is it, in reality, a perfectly adequate way of expressing oneself to say, as so many lawyers do in their everyday work—without any philosophical reflection whatever—that such and such a rule of law cannot be 'found', does not 'exist', or that 'one has' a rule, 'there is' a provision of such and such a purport, etc., etc.?

In all other fields of our knowledge, there is something which completely corresponds to the problem of this spiritual or ideal 'existence' of law.

With legal and other norms, logic and mathematics have in common the fact that their propositions do not contain anything about the connection of reality. Logic deals with the connection, necessary to thought, between abstract contents of thought—it does not pronounce laws of nature concerning the facts of spiritual life.[36] And mathematics is a science of numbers—not of things.

It is obvious that the propositions contained by logic and mathematics have validity irrespective of whether they are known in any human brain or not. For that matter, one may well speak of a kind of 'existence' of the propositions both of logic and of mathematics.[37]

Logic covers everything that can be said in advance of experience, everything that is *a priori*, Experience can only give us a world of facts but this floats in a space of possibilities which is given *a priori*. When logic discloses the structure of factual discourse, it also discloses the structure of reality which factual discourse reveals. These two structures which are really one, may be regarded as a framework of coordinates spreading through the whole space of possibilities in which the world of facts floats. The limit of this space which is reflected in the limit of factual discourse is determined by logic. Logic reveals the essential structure of reality.

Something similar applies also in the field of the knowledge of reality itself. All our understanding of nature rests on the assumption that what is true, is true independently of whether we succeed in knowing the truth. A regular connection in nature between certain phenomena is the same before and after the scientist has discovered it. The law of nature, however, is not identical to the proposition that tries to give it expression.

The regular connection in nature consists of an absolute necessity and regularity. But no statement of the regular connection in nature can be credited with more than perhaps an extremely high degree of probability. The connection in reality determined by the laws of nature is one thing. Propositions about this connection are another. The propositions can only have a higher or lower probability value. But the connection of reality itself has 'existence' in the sense that it remains, independently of our understanding.

Incidentally, one may speak of a truth, independent of our understanding, also where the statements of the language are concerned. Any expression, formed in any language, has an ideal content of thought, which is determined by the rules of the language, and which cannot be directly identified with what some single individual actually has thought when using the expression. A literary work of art is not identical with the actual spiritual experience of those who read it. But it is a work of the mind which has a kind of independent, ideal existence. That literary work has an existence which is different from the psychic and physical realities to which it is attached, has been more or less clearly expressed in the legislation of all civilised countries.[38]

The 'existence' of normative relations.

Propositions with normative contents—like the propositions of logic and mathematics—do not express anything about a connection to reality. But they are akin to our statements about reality in the fact that they do not have the absolute validity of the mathematical or logical proposition. If we say that such and such a law of nature applies in such and such real relationships, our statement of this can never express more than a—perhaps very high—degree of probability. The actual regularity certainly subsists, and it subsists independently of our understanding. But a statement of it can never attain the absolute certainty which distinguishes mathematical and logical propositions.

It is similar to law. There is an 'existing law', which is not identical to the contents of factual acts of consciousness.[39] And in a number of legal conflicts, we may assume that a definite solution to the legal questions is the correct one according to a definite legal system, regardless of whether we find it out. Thus, as far as that goes, the law may be said to 'exist' independently of our knowledge of it. But it is not the formulated statements in the laws or in legal dogmatics that we conceive as existing ideally when we speak of the 'existence' of law.

The certainty with which we may assume that a legal statement expresses what is legally existing may be great or little—these are questions that I shall deal with in the next chapter. Here, it suffices to ascertain the necessary logical distinction: What is legally existing is one thing; another thing, and one which differs from it in principle, is the contents of the legal statements which attempt to give linguistic expression to what is legally existing. It is, for instance, possible to imagine different linguistic formulations of the legal norm that one may regard as legally existing on the grounds of a certain custom. Even the linguistic expression employed by the law itself may have a meaning that is different from what we must legally regard as existing law, by virtue of this linguistic expression.[40]

Legal Validity

It is not the question of the moral, 'true' duty to obey the commands of the law that we are here concerned with. The question of such a duty may, if one likes, be called a metaphysical one. Here is another question that occupies us, namely this: how are we to give logical grounds for and explain the 'validity' that we attribute to the norms of positive law? What does this 'validity' mean? What is the criterion of the legally valid norm?

The typical legal norm—the rule which is determined by law—exists, because it has come into expression in a way which is regulated by other norms, namely the provisions of constitutional law for the competence of the legislating organs. As the last resort, it becomes a logical postulate of law that the constitution itself exists. The 'fundamental norm' itself here exactly imports that norms which have come into existence as this constitution are legally valid, and from this we then further conclude that norms which directly or indirectly can deduce their validity from the constitution, are also legally valid.

This doctrine of the fundamental norm has found its most pure form in the works of *Hans Kelsen* on the philosophy of law. In his 'Allgemeine Staatslehre',[41] Kelsen has set forth the doctrine as follows: As the fundamental norm first institutes a law-producing organ, it forms the constitution in the legalo-logical sense. As the legislature thus created fixes norms which regulate the legislating authority itself there arises—in the second stage—the constitution in the positive legal sense. But it is the original fundamental norm, i.e., the postulated norm of the competence of the original legislator of the constitution which, according to Kelsen, is the 'constitution' in the legalo-logical sense of the word.

When the individually enacted norm has validity as law, it is thus a logical consequence of our postulate that the act whereby the constitution of the state came into being created a valid constitution. Or, to state it more simply: The law is valid because the constitution is valid, and that the constitution is valid follows from a postulate of legal thinking.[42]

But however, correct this point of law may be in itself, it does not provide a complete explanation. Legal reality itself is too complicated for this view to be sufficient to solve the problem of legal validity. If the courts apply the law, the matter is clear so far. But supposing the courts simply override the law, although it has been created in accordance with the rules of the constitution? Are not the decisions of the courts just as much legal reality as the decisions of the legislator? Why may one not just as well take one's point of departure in the decisions of the courts and formulate the fundamental norm of legal logic in accordance with these, as take one's point of departure in the validity of the construction and consequently have to regard the court decisions as contrary to law?

It is *Ross's* merit that he has posed this problem with special penetration and tried to solve it within the bounds of the doctrine of the fundamental norm and the construction of the law in steps.[43] According to Ross's exposition of these questions in 'Theorie der Rechtsquellen', there certainly exists logically a possibility of either concluding deductively and downwards from the postulated fundamental norm, or inductively and upwards from the judgments and to another fundamental norm. In the former case, the irregular judgments will become—if not invalid—at least contrary to law. In the latter case, the postulated fundamental norm must be subjected to revision.[44]

Which road one should choose is dependent on what will create the greatest 'correlation' between the different social acts. This must probably mean that the decisive question is what postulate of validity answers best to social reality, i.e., agrees with the greatest number of acts by individuals, with the most widespread and strongest conviction of law and with the existing social distribution of power.

Again one must say, as one did with regard to the main contents of Kelsen's doctrine of the fundamental norm that the theory is correct but incomplete. It is admittedly the case that legal reality decides how we are to set up our fundamental norms. We do not regard as valid a constitution, which after the definitive victory of a revolution is no longer maintained in factual public life. But if we say that the postulate of validity must answer to reality as well as possible—that it must give the greatest possible 'correlation' between the social acts, we still remain without an answer to a number of questions concerning borderline cases. When are we to regard a whole system of law as being overthrown by a revolution, and when has a new system acquired such stability that a new fundamental norm must be postulated as valid? How is one to solve a question that arises from a collision between legal practice and the norms that are fixed in the existing constitution?

There seems to be a shortcoming in the Vienna theory of the fundamental norm. It does not explain the problems of customary law. The norms that determine the conditions of the validity of customary law, cannot themselves be of the nature of customary law. In this field of law, too, we must stop at norms and the validity of which we postulate. The written constitution is usually silent on this point. Above all, even a fundamental norm which in the most perfect way covers the reality of legal life, will not be able to answer such questions of law as cannot be solved with certainty from the positively determined norms. In all application of existing law, one must necessarily operate with the supposition of valid ends, independently of all that is positively and directly determined. Here, too, we have postulates of validity that supplement the postulate of the validity of the constitution.

We may, if we like, also use the term 'fundamental norms' for those norms that determine conditions for the creation of customary law, solutions of conflicts between different kinds of norms and guiding principles for the decision of legal questions in the legal vacuum. In any case, it is certain that the validity of the law is not explained by the postulate of a single fundamental norm that gives validity to the constitution.

I would like to conclude this chapter with a related digression from the concept of consciousness, to the concept of conscience. A man might be defined as a reflexive animal. It is conscience that makes us human; it is our personal lawgiver. A person cannot help thinking and speaking of himself as and even feeling for certain purposes, as two people, one of whom can act upon and observe the other. He is privy to his own acts as his own accomplice. The murderer in Richard 111 says that conscience makes a man a coward. Seneca said, "All wish to hide their sins but a good conscience loves the light. In Bunyan, we find I am conscious to myself of many failings."

Conscience is an inner witness who gives evidence about matters of fact, the criminality or the innocence of the fact has been fixed by the legislature and will be declared by the judge. Conscience issues no commands or permissions, but my conscience tells me this is wrong. Those can come from the law or the bench but not from the witness box.

Aquinas said conscience is the application of our knowledge of good and evil to our own acts. Our conscience is the general repository of our own moral principles. It can be called the inner lawgiver who tells us what we should or should not do. Deguileville, in his *Pilgrimage of Man*, defines it as the higher part of reason. Tatian says, "Conscience is God." Origen says, "God rules in us by his substitute our conscience." Milton, I will place within them as a guide, my umpire conscience.

Some have suggested conscience is directly or vicariously a divine lawgiver. Some have inconveniently claimed exemption from the laws of the state on the grounds that their own conscience forbids them to obey them. Famously, Thomas More refused to take Oath of Supremacy urged by the Lord Chancellor to observe that all the bishops, universities and scholars in England had agreed to the Act. More replied that he did not see "why that thing in my conscience should make any change, it will not alter my conception of my duty or will alter my view."

The Hart Devlin debate which I deal with later in the book, considers the extent to which the law should reflect morality and could be adapted to consider the extent to which the law should reflect a man's conscience as can the right to die debate and assisted dying, which again is specifically addressed in this book.

Chapter 5

One precedent creates another. They soon accumulate and constitute law. What yesterday was fact, today is doctrine.
The Letters of Junius (1769–1771)

All bad precedents begin as justifiable measures.
Julius Caesar

In all usages and precedents, the times be considered wherein they first began, which if they were weak or ignorant, it derogateth from the authority of the usage, and leaveth it for suspect.
Francis Bacon.

Everywhere the basis of principle is tradition.
Oliver Wendell Holmes, Speech (8 January 1897)

General principles are not the less true or important because from their nature they allude immediate observation; they are like the air, which is not the less necessary because we neither see nor feel it.
   William Hazltt 'Edmund Burke', The Eloquence of the British Senate (1807)

Norms set out how people are to behave. A norm amounts to an ought; it specifies what should not, what must or what will always happen in a particular situation. So ought cannot be derived from only other norms. According to Kelsen's Pure Theory of Law (1934), a legal system should be understood as a system of positive norms within a hierarchical structure. This system is that of a dynamic hierarchy; all the norms are inter-related because they belong to the same system and new norms will continue to be created through the same system.

The creation of laws can therefore be explained by reference to this chain of validity.

The first great problem that is raised by legal thinking, concerns all normative thinking. The question is this: can binding conclusions be drawn from statements with normative contents? Let us imagine a normative statement of general contents. We imagine a statement which connects a notion of a certain duty of action to a notion of factual situations of a certain kind. Can one thence draw the conclusion that a concrete factual situation, which is comprised in the fact-notion of the norm, entails a concrete duty which is the application of the notion of duty of the norm?

In other words, is the syllogism justified in normative thinking also? When A (a generally determined fact) entails the duty B (a generally determined duty), and 'a' is comprised by the notion A—can one then conclude that fact 'a' entails concrete duty of action 'b'? As an example, one may take the normative statement that promises must be kept. Can one, when such a norm is valid, conclude from this that such and such a concrete promise must be fulfilled in accordance with its special contents?—This also embraces the question of the logical justification of the so-called 'subsumption'.

Whatever opinion one may hold of the logical validity of the subsumption and of the norm-syllogism, it cannot in any case be disputed that people actually reason in this way in every society, and that this is a social reality of the greatest importance. In all education for joint social life, general statements of normative contents are necessities employed with regard to both children and adults. The intention is, of course, that the mode of action in the concrete situation shall be determined by the logical inference from the norm to the situation. No well-ordered life in common is possible unless certain valuations are more or less clearly formulated in normative statements, which are 'observed', i.e., made concrete by logical conclusions (subsumptions), and carried out in concrete situations.

The conclusion from a rule of law to a concrete legal duty is not a conclusion from an expression of will. From the fact that a person expresses his will to realise a generally determined purpose, one cannot conclude that his will actually comprises the special purposes that are included under the general expression. Nor can one conclude that he wills that which is the necessary means to realise the purpose. One obviously cannot assume that persons have the logical consistency in their volitional lives that this would demand.[45] But the fact that it is impossible to conclude from the general will to special, is without importance to the question of the logical justification of concluding from the general norm to its application in the special case. The norm is not an expression of the volitional impulses of one or more persons, but a statement of duty, of what must or may be performed or refrained from.[46]

The norm-syllogism—the application of the general command to the special or quite concrete case—is the logically necessary form of normative thinking. It is not only a common psychological phenomenon that we are confronted with.[47] But it is the only possible form of rationality in our moral and legal life. In our understanding of nature, we must necessarily assume the principle that everything has a cause. In the understanding of moral or legal duty, we must necessarily assume that everything must have a reason.[48] The reason cannot be anything other than a norm which is more general than the one which is to be established. Thus, we find an explanation by deducing the special from the general—in the same way as our explanation of reality consists in seeing the special phenomena as applications of laws of nature, of as comprehensive a character as possible.

Besides, it is not only the fundamental principle of our understanding that demands that a juridical point of view should be capable of being deductively established. It is also the principle of justice. It is not possible to satisfy the fundamental human need for justice unless the juridical decisions in society are applications of rules which attach uniform legal consequences to uniform premises.

Max Weber was certainly right in stating that jurisdiction has by no means always manifested itself in history as an understood application of legal norms to concrete facts. On the contrary, the case is probably that 'irrational Rechtsfindung' comes first in the history of human communities.[49] But that does not prevent the need for a rational foundation being laid down in human nature, nor does it alter the fact that the rational foundation of a concrete decision is quite unthinkable without a conclusion from the norm to the individual case.

According to a doctrine of moral philosophy set forth by *Georg Simmel* in penetrating writings dating from his later years,[50] it is completely erroneous to conceive moral life as determined by general commands, i.e., moral laws. The sense of what is morally right accompanies the whole of our lives with greater or less clearness, not as a formulated law or one that may be formulated, but as an indefinite, emotional appeal. It is only Kant's artificial 'Moral-Homunkulus' that constantly appeals to the moral law.[51] Every person carries in himself the ideal of his own life, the individual law which he is to follow. This does not mean that the only law which applies to him is that by which he himself acknowledges himself to be bound.[52] The moral norm is objective. But it is not produced as the result of a logical conclusion from a rule.

Simmel has indubitably brought out certain features of our moral experience which are essential. We feel what is right rather than reason it out. The normal relation, so to speak, of the normal human being to the moral demand, is an indefinite sense of ideals, duties and demands—not a logical argumentation with logical operations of the mind from general moral commands that are formulated in sharply defined notions. Neither can anyone who has occupied himself with moral problems be a stranger to the idea that the moral demand must be marked by the particular aptitudes and the situation in the life of each individual personality.

Nevertheless, Simmel's opposition to the general moral law does not give a full understanding of our comprehension of morality. Our comprehension of what is morally right does not absolutely always arise as an irrational sense of a concrete impulse. We will often be in doubt as to the right way of acting. In that case, we do not only need our instinct or intuition but also our reason. Our deliberations cannot go on except as a seeking after the ends we should work for and the principles we are to follow. However individually determined our duty of action may be in the concrete situation, the fact remains that it can only be intellectually established by logical deductions from the general to the special.

Thus, norm-syllogism has its logical justification in the domain of moral understanding, even if one starts from the conviction of the individual determination of all morality.

The legal norm can never, like the oral one, take into consideration all the peculiarities of the individual person and the individual case. The demand for a rational foundation of every standpoint that is taken to ethical questions, makes itself felt in quite a different way in the field of law than it does in the field of morality. One is here concerned with views which are not only decisive and one's own acts, but which one wishes to have recognised or enforced as law of the society. The objections against the norm-syllogism have here no foundation whatever. This applies even if one were to reject the norm-syllogism as a means of attaining an understanding of the moral, individual law.

There is an essential difference between the syllogism by which we argue from the general to the special in our understanding of reality and the norm-logic syllogism. In the syllogism of the understanding of reality, all propositions are statements of reality. In the norm-syllogism, the major premise is a normative statement. The minor premise (the subsumption) lays down a real notional connection. But then the conclusion again has a normative character. (E.g. Contracts must be kept according to their contents. This is a contract. Therefore, it must be kept according to its contents.)

The fact which, in the minor premise, we have characterised as a contract, entails the legal effect that the contract must be kept according to its contents. Thus, by the conclusion we have attached to the fact a legal consequence, which is a specialisation of the generally determined legal consequence of the major premise.—If the general normative statement attaches its legal consequence directly to a notion of right, such as right of ownership, right of lien, right of citizenship etc., the legal consequence of the conclusion will here, too, have the nature of a specialisation of the general legal consequence that is set forth in the general statement.

This specialisation of the legal consequence by the very fact of the logical conclusion from the norm-statement, raises new problems. Often it will be clear that the subsumption is appropriate. It may, for instance, be indubitable that there is a contract in the legal sense. It will then be clear that the contract must be kept according to its contents. But the question may arise as to what it means to fulfil this contract according to its contents.

Thus, there may be a disaccord between the words used in the contract, and the understanding of the words that one of the parties has had. Is it the words or is it what the party means by them that shall be decisive for the question of what are his duties under the contract? In this, as in other similar cases, a conflict may thus be fought out concerning the further determination of the specialised legal consequence laid down by the conclusion. The question can only be solved by one or more new logical conclusions.

We argue, for instance, thus: It is a common basic principle of law that one must try to attain solutions that agree with the need of security in commercial life. It agrees with this need for security that decisive importance should be attributed to the words. Therefore, this solution is to be chosen. Further: the intention of a party should only take precedence of the letter of his declaration when this intention of his was visible to the other party. Here the intention was not visible. Therefore, the letter should be decisive.

Special questions arise in the determination of the legal consequence in the conclusion of the syllogism when the major premise comprises a sliding scale of facts. As an example, we may take a penal command, which to certain 'contents of action' attaches the legal consequence of punishment within a certain 'frame of punishment'.[53]

Just as the logical conclusion is the necessary means of proceeding from the general, normative statement to the individual judicial decision, it is also a necessary means of knowing the contents of the general legal norms themselves.

As has been mentioned,[54] the whole of that part of the law that is laid down in statutes has its validity by virtue of the provisions of the—written or unwritten—constitution concerning the legislative power. The norms of customary law are valid by virtue of the fundamental norms that determine the conditions on which valid customary law may come into being. Thus, we recognise the individual provision of law and the individual rule of customary law as existing law by the logical conclusion of the following type: "decisions made by such and such an assembly in such and such forms assented to by such and such an executive organ of state, have, according to the constitution, the effect of law."

This individual decision has been made in this way. Therefore, it has the effect of law. Further: rules which are observed in such and such a way, are, according to our postulate of customary law, to be regarded as valid customary law. This individual rule is observed in this way. Therefore, it is a valid rule of customary law.

This scheme of legal thinking, commonplace in itself, precisely shows that the logical conclusion from general to special is also necessary as a means of ascertaining what norms we are to regard as valid law.[55]

The deductive operations of the mind—the conclusions from general to special—are, for the rest, not the only way of gaining an understanding of the norms that are to be regarded as expressions of existing law. We also apply in our legal thinking norms that we have found by a more or less conscious generalisation of positively determined rules of law. We argue—by a kind of induction—from the validity of certain special norms to the validity of a more general norm, of which these special norms may be regarded as applications. Or we skip this conclusion from the special to the general norm and argue by analogy directly from the special norm to another special norm concerning a 'nearly related' circumstance. This so-called analogical conclusion is, as is known, a constantly recurring figure of thought in juridical arguments.

In many cases, the justification of such an analogical conclusion is evident.[56] From a regulation that prohibits the bringing of dogs into railway trains, one may, for instance, conclude with certainty that the bringing of bears is also prohibited! In other cases, it is just as obvious that one must argue antithetically and not analogically. The analogical conclusion may be forbidden by a valid, positive, legal norm, as is the case in certain legal systems in the field of penal law. Its use may also in many cases be out of the question, even if it is not positively forbidden. From a rule stating that lectures are suspended on Sundays, one cannot analogically conclude that they are also suspended on weekdays. Here, on the contrary, the antithetical conclusion is indubitable.

Thus, logic has its necessary position in all understanding and application of existing law. It would have no sensible meaning at all to have a legal order if the legal norms that the legal order consists of could not form points of departure for conclusions as to what is to be regarded as binding in special and individual cases. Human beings take for granted that norm-syllogism is a justified form of logical argument. The fact that they take this for granted and arrange themselves accordingly, is the condition of all regulated social life.

Logic has its place in legal thinking. But it has no undivided power. It is far from being the case that all legal questions may be solved by logical conclusions alone.

Chapter 6

A case is only an authority for what it actually decides. I entirely deny that it can be quoted for a proposition that may seem to follow logically from it. Such a mode of reasoning assumes that the law is necessarily a logical code, whereas every lawyer may acknowledge that the law is not always logical at all.
Oliver Wendell Holmes, The Common Law (1881), cited by Lord Macmillan in *Read v. J. Lyons* (1947)

Courts determine issues of fact and law. In a dispute between two parties (either both private or in a criminal case between citizen and state), courts create individual norms by drawing on the law and principles contained in general norms. Kelsen in his General Theory of Law and State, stressed that general norms which take the form of statutes and customary laws are only semi-manufactured products which are finished only through the judicial decision and its execution and the process of steadily increasing individualisation and concretisation.

Judicial decisions represent the last stage of law creation. Courts also have the power to create general norms in the form of judicial precedents. Kelsen's view was that decisions have the character of a precedent only if it is not the application of a pre-existing general norm of substantive law if the court acts as a legislator. They occur when a court is required to adjudicate on an individual case and there are no general norms (of substantive or customary law) present to help determine the court's decision in such a case in order to find a resolution, they must determine the issue without the presence of a general norm.

The notions of which general, legal statements are composed are always more or less indefinite. In life, there are no sharp transitions. But legal notions impose limitations in view of the needs of human society. Thus, in law, a limit is drawn between acts that are inadvertent and acts which are not, between the use of property which is customary and that which is not. The limit becomes decisive in the question of right and duty, for instance, the question of whether damages are to be paid or not. But the need for notional limitation in law does not prevent the fact that doubt often must prevail as to where the limit is really drawn. Even if the law defines the notions it uses, new doubts will present themselves in the limitation of the notions employed by the definition.

Thus, the logical subsumption under the statements of the law is not in all cases self-evident.[57] And this does not only apply to such normative statements that in their applications explicitly assume a valuation. As an example, may be mentioned a prohibition of 'undue' competition or a rule stating that certain agreements are invalid because it would be contrary to 'integrity or good faith' to appeal to them. That the field of operation of such rules is indefinite and not automatically given, needs no further proof. But rules which do not straightforwardly refer to a concrete valuation in this way will also raise numerous questions concerning the limitation of the notions and consequently of the field of operation of the rules. A law regulates, for instance, the sale of milk. Does the notion of milk here comprise cream as well?

It may thus be established that the notions employed in general normative statements, always have fluid limits. One must go still further. The immediate conclusion from the general legal statement to a statement of a special case never gives more than a more or less strong presumption that the conclusion is the correct one according to the system of law to which the general statement belongs.

There exists here a certain parallelism between the syllogism of our understanding of reality and the norm-logic syllogism. It has long since been generally acknowledged that the syllogism we use in our understanding of reality cannot give us certain information about anything we do not know before. This syllogism has the following form: When $B = C$ and $A = B$, then $A = C$. (All birds are vertebrates. This is a bird. Therefore, this is a vertebrate.) Here we cannot really establish the major premise with certainty without previously having made sure that it also comprises the subject of the minor premise. (We cannot establish with absolute certainty that all birds are vertebrates, without having really examined all birds, i.e., also this bird.)

Nevertheless, the syllogistic conclusion is an important instrument of thought in the investigation of reality. We generalise our observation in a common statement long before we have observed all the individual phenomena comprised by the statement. In this way, we form a hypothesis. Any new instance that turns up we bring under our common statement, thus drawing a conclusion, and we must afterwards ascertain by verification whether the conclusion led us to a result that agrees with our experience of reality. (We examine whether the bird really was a vertebrate, in accordance with what we concluded.)

The case of the norm-logic syllogism is similar. We take our point of departure in a general, normative statement, and subsume the special case under the general statement; the result we arrive at in this way, we subject to a subsequent test, where, incidentally, new norm-logic arguments are brought to application. These operations of the mind may present themselves more or less clearly to the reasoning person. As usual, one forms one's opinion much more by instinct than by circumstantial, clearly formulated mental operations of this kind. Nevertheless, it is according to this schema that legal arguments are carried out.

The test of the result of the subsumption that corresponds to the verification of a hypothesis, is quite different from the examination of an actual circumstance.[58] It is not here a question of ascertaining that an event takes place or that a factual quality is present. But the result of the norm-conclusion must be accepted or rejected as it harmonises or disagrees with other valid statements of normative contents. The verification is carried out by new logical subsumptions. A certain interpretation of a rule of law is, for instance, rejected because it definitely disagrees with certain interests, which the rules of the law are designed to further and which must be regarded as guides to the interpretation.

Even if the wording of the law linguistically leads to a certain result, it is not therefore certain that precisely this subsumption is the correct one. It is a well-known phenomenon that the lawyer at times has to set aside the letter of the law in favour of its 'reasonable' meaning. The conclusion at which one arrives by an automatic subsumption under the words of the law is tested, in other words, by means of guiding propositions, which serve as bases of logical deductions.

A result which follows from the commands of the law and the existing principles of interpretation of the law is immediately binding. The position, however, is different when one has to draw conclusions from legal propositions, which are based on a generalisation of existing rules, or when one bases oneself on general principles of law, which one regards, without further ceremony, as valid in the community in question. Very often in such cases 'not determined by law', several solutions will present themselves as logically possible, according as one lays decisive stress on one or the other element of the case and consequently subsumes it under one general proposition of law or the other. For example, is the person who has paid a sum of money in the erroneous belief that he owed the sum, to be able to demand that the sum be returned, even if the recipient was in good faith?

C.J. Arnbholm, in the discussion of this question, states among other things: "Usually, of course, it is only the visible faults that may be charged on the other party, when he is in good faith.—but, as opposed to this argument, one may, on the other hand, stress the peculiarity of the act of fulfilment."[59] Here he has exactly indicated two possibilities of subsumption, both of them logically indisputable. Examples of such alternative possibilities of solutions abound in legal thinking.

We have seen that the notions with which the general, normative statements operate, have fluid limits. The subsumption under a general notion often gives occasion for doubt. The rules of law are to govern the life of the future. In the incessant flow of life, which the law is to regulate, there will constantly emerge cases which make the subsumption under the given rule problematical. One or the other element of the case may create a logically possible connection with another rule. As *Astrup Hoel* has emphasised, the subsumption of the special case under the general rule implies, from a psychological point of view, a decision.[60] And in many cases, there is necessarily an element of arbitrariness about it.

Must one not then regard the whole of the apparatus of legal logic as resting on an illusion, or perhaps even on a social fraud on a large scale? When the legal decisions of the courts in a civilised community appear as conclusions, evolved from binding rules, by means of logically necessary subsumptions, then this is—one might say—only a means of giving these decisions a kind of moral authority. In reality—according to this view—one has to do with nothing else than a social mechanism, whereby a series of factors of power produce certain decisions and effects of these decisions, in the interest of ruling groups and classes.

The powerful class of professional lawyers is then not least tied by the whole of its existence to the fallacy that law is a system of norms which are to be interpreted and applied; for the lawyer, more than anyone else, becomes 'der Erhalter, Verkünder and Deuter der Schrift'.[61] Legal logic would thus be a fiction of legal dogmatics, which is maintained from extremely varied motives, of unequal social value.

In my opinion, this view is not correct. As has been mentioned, the foundation which we, as rational beings, demand for every solution to a legal conflict, cannot be made other than by a logical conclusion from a normative proposition, to which we attribute validity. It is certainly true that it is not necessarily given what norm we are to subsume the special case under. Every subsumption has in common with a theoretical hypothesis the fact that it must be tested—although the subsumption is tested by new subsumptions and not simply by the establishment of facts. These features of legal thinking create particular problems, which are all connected with its normative character.

But this does not prevent many of the operations of the mind in legal thinking from appearing just as certain to us as our most certain conclusions concerning the relation between facts. An example: X has promised me to supply a quantity of goods at such and such a price. He has the goods. The price is not unusual. He is not in a position of distress, and he has made his promise with a full knowledge of all the circumstances that might interest him in this connection.

Nor have the public authorities any interest in asserting against this bargain. Is there any doubt whatsoever that this promise comprises the legal norm that declares the promise to be binding? Is not the subsumption here indubitable? Is there any element of arbitrariness in the subsumption decisions that the legally thinking individual—whether a private person or a public organ—has made? It is still more obvious that one can with absolute certainty give negative answers in a number of cases to legal questions of subsumption. One may, for instance, establish with absolute certainty that such and such an act is not affected by such and such a provision in the penal law. Altogether the relation to the law is indubitable with regard to by far the greater number of human acts and abstentions. The fact that doubt, disagreement and controversy about legal questions arise, is, after all, an exceptional phenomenon.[62]

Thus, in innumerable cases, the subsumption appears evident. Presumably, this feeling of evidence is really, in the last instance, the basis we have to build upon.

It applies to all laws whose its social function is to serve certain purposes. Therefore one must demand of every juridical method that it shall take this subservience of the law to its purpose into consideration.

All the acts by which the contents of the law are determined, and the acts by which the law is observed, are links in the causal connection in the community. The passing of a new law has a series of social effects. I will conclude this chapter by referring to Kant's observation in his Philosophy of Law, the Science of Right as to the operation of the three powers—legislative, the executive and the judicial. In his view, it was by the cooperation of these powers the state realised its autonomy which consisted of "organising, forming and maintaining itself in accordance with the Laws of Freedom and it was in their union that the welfare of the state is realised." By this, he stressed this is not to be understood merely as the well-being and happiness of the citizens but as the welfare of the state.

Chapter 7

For we both alike know that into the discussion of human affairs the question of justice enters only where the pressure of necessity is equal, and the weak grant what they must.

Thucydides (fifth century BC)

Rigorous law is often rigorous injustice.

Terence

Peace is more important than all justice; and peace was not made for the sake of justice, but justice for the sake of peace.

Martin Luther

The Sword of justice has no scabbard.

Joseph de Maistre

This is a court of law, young man, not a court of justice.

Oliver Wendell Holmes

The demand for justice is axiomatically inherent in all law and the application of the law. As formal justice, one may designate the decision of a special case in accordance with the existing general norm. The demand for formal justice is to this extent synonymous with the demand that the special case shall be decided by norm-logic conclusions from general norm-propositions. What material justice consists of at all times been a subject of discussion. Aristotle's formula that similar things are to be treated similarly and dissimilar things dissimilarly, does not tell us much.

The question immediately suggests itself: in what does the similarity or dissimilarity consist which is to be decisive for the judgment? Quite generally I suppose one may say that it is an essential feature of material justice that the benefits and evils which the law allows be distributed according to the degree of ethical merit and guilt.[63] Certainly the notions of 'merit' and 'guilt' raise new problems, partly of a metaphysical nature.[64] But if the notion of material justice is conceived in this way, it at least escapes the charge of inanity that has been brought against the idea of justice.[65]

The demand that the law shall be just, does not coincide with the demand that it shall be adapted to its purpose.[66] Formal justice only consists in giving the solution of legal questions a norm-logic foundation from existing rules of law. Material justice is a quality of the law, which sometimes coincides with, and sometimes does not coincide with, the adequacy of the law to its purpose. A legal arrangement by which the wages of an individual are determined by his ethical merit is, one may imagine, inadequate from the point of view of production techniques. It may be that the machinery of production of modern society cannot be efficacious without a system of distribution which also has regard for factors quite different from ethical merit.

In the same way, the demand that punishment shall be fixed in regard to guilt may collide with the demand that punishment shall be fixed in regard to the need of society for security—as a last example, one may adduce what *Knoph* says about the rights of patent and pattern and the rights of authors. "For the boundary of the rights is determined by a weighing of the interests where the consideration of the just reward of the author has conflicted with the desire of the public that all spiritual values should be free."[67]

The demand that the law shall serve certain purposes is a determinant for legal thinking. The same applies to the demand that the law shall be just. A subsumption may have to be rejected if it leads to a result that conflicts with the demand for adaption to guilt and merit. We think it unjust, for instance, that an injury should be recumbent on the injured person, and not come home to the person who has caused the injury. It is possible that this principle may be decisive to our solution to a question of compensation which otherwise may raise doubt.

The purpose of the law and the demand for justice give lines of direction to legal thinking. But these lines of direction may cross, and it is far from being the case that they give us an unequivocal answer to all the difficulties of subsumption.

The different juridical theories of method indicate different courses that juridical thinking may follow, in order to attain the correct results. We will now glance at the two main directions to be noticed in the juridical theory of method.

The sliding scale from certain to uncertain understanding of the law.

One may imagine an infinite series of legal statements, where the extremities are the undoubtedly correct and the undoubtedly incorrect statements, and where the intermediate statements represent all degrees of certainty. There will then be statements the correctness of which is indubitable, and statements the incorrectness of which is indubitable. There will be statements the correctness or incorrectness of which is doubtful to a higher and a lower degree. In the central point of the series, there will be such statements as cannot be asserted to be either correct or incorrect; in other words, there are equally strong arguments for one solution as for the other.

This idea may also be expressed thus: our statements of legal relationship represent a sliding scale from the certainty of correctness to complete uncertainty and further to the certainty of incorrectness. We are not here concerned with degrees of correctness. One can no more speak of degrees of correctness in connection with normative statements than one can speak of degrees of truth in the understanding of reality. But one may speak of degrees in the certainty with which a normative statement may be set forth as correct. One may speak of degrees in the probability with which a statement of reality agrees with reality.[68]

In legal thinking itself, one is familiar with the idea of a sliding scale. The conception of the continuity of reality[69] and of imperceptible transitions from greater to lesser interests[70] are conceptions with which lawyers are quite familiar. Thus, the law accords certain claims to a buyer if goods are supplied that have 'essential' defects. All the possible defects of an article, however, represent a scale from undoubtedly essential to undoubtedly unessential ones. Somewhere the lawyer must draw the line. But in the borderline cases, the subsumption will be doubtful.

The current conception of a sliding scale in subsumption questions of this kind has an application in all legal thinking. Even the most precise formulation of a provision of law cannot prevent a case arising one day in which the subsumption must give occasion to doubt. The standing one takes to subsumption questions in such a doubtful case has a lower degree of certainty than the stand one may take to the normal questions of subsumption, so to speak, in the application of such clearly defined provisions of law create relatively few subsumption doubts, which—from the point of view of legal security—gives these provisions their superiority to legal 'standards', 'general clauses', in short: indefinite commands of the law.

But it thus applies to all conceivable legal statements that they may be imagined to be arranged in a sliding scale according to the degree of certitude with which they may be regarded as correct or incorrect.[71] Even statements about a general legal proposition as being valid law also represent every degree of certainty and uncertainty. About a proposition in a law that has been recently passed, we decide with a high degree of certainty that it expresses existing law. About a proposition in an old and rarely applied decree, the same assertion is perhaps very doubtful. Of a proposition in a law that has been newly repealed, we may lay down with certainty that it gives no adequate expression for what is existing law today.

In every domain, the logic of legal thinking is ruled by the principle of the sliding scale.

There is a certain parallelism between the sliding scale in the certainty of legal statements and the sliding scale in the probability of statements about the future, in our knowledge of reality. One may be of the opinion that everything that happens, happens by necessity—under the domination of the law of cause and effect—or one may believe in a certain indefiniteness, first and foremost in a certain scope for the freedom of the human will. But whichever standpoint to the problem of determinism is true, it is in any case certain that no statement about the future on the basis of our knowledge of the regularity of nature can attain more than a higher or a lower degree of probability.[72] In relation to the regularity and necessity that govern the events of the future, our statements about these future events represent a sliding scale of probability.

It is in the same way with our historical insight. Our historical knowledge consists of statements of all degrees of certainty and uncertainty—from the statements that rest on our own direct observation, to the statements that represent the boldest guesses of the historian and the archaeologist.

Legal statements may thus represent all degrees of certainty, and it must be the task of legal science to achieve results that represent the highest possible degree of certitude. The generalising, 'constructive' science of law seeks the logical connection between the legal norms, as it tries to attain propositions of law that are as comprehensive as possible and under which newly arising cases may be subsumed. The sociologico-telelogically directed science of law aims at understanding the social functions of the law and at drawing conclusions from statements about the ends of the law. No juridical method can disregard the demand that the law shall function justly.

A comprehensive exposition of all these circumstances may in many cases lead to results that may be characterised as undoubtedly correct. Even if no generalisation is logically necessary—even if the values that the law is to further may be found to be unmeasurable, and though the notion of justice may raise problems even of a metaphysical nature, the result of the juridical operations of the mind may nevertheless at times have such a character that there is no reasonable cause for doubt.

Even the most comprehensive juridical investigation, however, cannot—as it has been demonstrated—lead to certain results in all cases. Often the results we arrive at must give rise to stronger or weaker doubts. There are cases in which the rational thing may be that legal science merely indicates the different possibilities of solution, without making any choice itself. It may point to the fact that such and such solutions are out of the question for such and such reasons. It may show the logical foundation and the social consequences of one or the other of the possible solutions. But if one of the proposed solutions gives no greater security for its correctness than the other, then legal science should only ascertain this fact. Theory need not, like the courts, make decisions in every question that is propounded.

The knowledge of the varying degrees of certainty of legal statements has still another consequence. In light of this knowledge, it is not easy to maintain any blind faith in the infallibility of every point of view one thinks one should adopt to questions of existing law. A certain scepticism with regard to legal dogmatic thinking and its results becomes unavoidable.

Chapter 8

"It is odd, that there are people in the world who, having renounced all the laws of God and nature, have themselves made laws which they rigorously obey". –
Blaise Pascal, Pensées.

The law, as I see it, has two great objects: to preserve order and to do justice, and the two do not always coincide. Those whose training lies towards order, put certainty before justice, whereas those whose training lies towards the redress of grievances, put justice before certainty. The right solution lies in keeping the balance between the two.
Lord Denning

The only liberty I mean, is a liberty connected with order, that not only exists along with order and virtue, but which cannot exist at all without them.
Edmund Burke

All law is determined by its purpose. Its contents are determined by the fact that it intends to further certain ends. The purpose of the law is a guide to its application.

If we examine most closely the purposes that the creation of a legal norm aims at furthering, we see at once that these special purposes stand, in turn, in the service of other purposes. A law which is to promote the security of commercial life is by this means to promote the prosperity of the community. Even prosperity is not an end in itself, but a means of furthering the cultural values which are recognised in the community. Other rules of law aim at furthering spiritual values directly. This does not only apply to the large parts of the administrative law of the modern state which are directed at furthering the artistic and the scientific, the moral and the religious life of the nation.

But it applies also to many rules of private law, e.g. rules concerning the legal relations of the family and spiritual ownership. The legal order of a society is marked by the ideal of personality that is predominant. In a civilised society, many provisions of the law will also testify that the life of the individual human being itself is accorded a specific value, which is victorious in the collision with many social 'regards of utility'.

Life is supported and protected—even the life that only means a burden and an annoyance to society as a whole. The lunatic or the socially useless person is allowed to live, even if no one else in the society has any interest in the continuation of this life even though, on the contrary, many interests would be served by its cessation. The law declares life to be sacred, cutting across all calculations of utility. Purely disinterested cultural values are also among the ultimate aims served by the law. The truth has value in itself; that is a thought to which the law is not a stranger either.[73]

Now it is not necessary in itself, in order to be able to think legally, that one personally believes in the values that the positive system of law is to further in the last instance. I have previously tried to show that the conception of the validity of the law does not imply that one regards oneself or others as being obliged—i.e., 'really', ethically obliged—to observe the commands of the law.[74]

I have therefore called the idea of legal validity, not a metaphysical idea, but an *a priori* one: it is an element of the notion of law that we do not derive from the world of experience. In the same way, the idea of the ultimate purposes of the law does not mean that our legal thinking presupposes belief in the value of these purposes. We can understand and apply the rules of existing law, as long as we act *as if* these values had validity. In other words, we draw our conclusions from normative postulates stating that the furthering of these values is the ultimate purpose of the law.

This then applies to legal thinking in the sense of legal dogmatic thinking—i.e., thinking the purpose of which is to find an answer to the question of what is existing law.

It is different, however, if we propose to ourselves the aim of attaining a valid valuation of existing, positive law. We cannot then avoid metaphysical problems. We are then forced to make up our minds ourselves about such problems as these: which values are the highest ones? How is a conflict between the values to be solved? No investigation of nature can give us any objectively valid answer to these questions. One may hold as many natural scientists do—that nature itself shows human beings what is the meaning of their lives.[75]

Or one may hold—as, for instance, many Marxists do—that tendencies in the development of society show us what it is we ought to fight for. But faith in this respect will always involve a leap into the metaphysical. There is no binding conclusion from the knowledge of reality to the belief in objectively valid values.[76] And if we wish to value existing law, we cannot, as in legal dogmatic thinking, be content with a quite formal assumption of validity and values as the point of departure of our thinking. It is certainly logically possible to make a valuation of the law starting from arbitrarily chosen validities and values.

We may value the law from a number of such assumptions to which we ourselves are indifferent. But I doubt whether such a purely 'dogmatic' valuation, which would thus in principle be independent of the personal view of the valuer, is psychologically possible. In any case, it is not to such a mental activity one refers, to when one speaks of a valuation of the law. Likewise, one may study sociologically the valuation of existing law which is actually carried out in society, and which is determined to such a great extent by class interests and other interests of the valuing persons. But the valuation of law is different in principle also from this sociological study.

One cannot make a valuation of existing law without taking a stand to metaphysical problems.[77] And not only must one take a stand to the question of the order of precedence of values. One is also confronted with the question of the freedom of the human will.

Our ideals of law are not something that only comes to us from without, by influences from our environment in the community in which we live. They are also determined by the whole structure of our minds. The demand for justice in the community is rooted in our spiritual nature just as strongly as the need for logical connection in our thinking. In art, we must recognise that there are, in spite of all, valuations that are raised above subjective arbitrariness and changing directions.

It is in the same way with legal valuation as well, in so far as it is not an arbitrary matter. It is bound by norms, which are as *a priori* and eternal as the laws of thinking and of art. This does not mean that legal ideals necessarily have to be invariable in their contents. But the principles themselves that govern our valuation of law eternal and *a priori* are: the demand for justice and for logical connection, the demand that the law shall be a serviceable means of furthering the highest purposes.

As has been previously stated,[78] it is a matter of belief whether we are to assume that every question of what is existing law according to a definite system of law has a solution and only one which is the right one. It is likewise a matter of belief whether we are to assume that there is one and only one system of legal norms that is the objectively right one for a definite community at a definite time. But, to my mind, we are at least justified in assuming that certain statements about right and wrong at a given time and a given place are obviously correct and that certain other statements about right and wrong are obviously incorrect. The evidently correct and the evidently incorrect statements form the extremities of a sliding scale of legal valuations, concerning the correctness of which we may have a higher or a lower degree of certainty.

We are far from being able to make a certain judgment of the correctness of all contents of the law. On the contrary, we are often forced to acknowledge that we are unable to make any objectively valid judgment of what would be the right legal arrangement in certain circumstances of life. Insight and a comprehensive view will necessarily lead to carefulness in every judgment of what is right law and will make tolerance with regard to the opinions of others quite matter-of-course. But tolerance does not assume that conflicting views are always and necessarily equally right or equally wrong. In many cases, our knowledge is certainly so incomplete that we cannot be more sure that one view is right than that the other is so. In other cases, however, we may, with a higher or a lower degree of certainty, characterise one view as right, and the other as wrong.

The belief in a 'natural law' in the sense of a complete, integral system of law, which should be the ideal one for all nations and for all times, is certainly a very naive conception. Nor was it probably thus that the leading theoreticians of natural law in the eighteenth century imagined the matter.[79]

But what one may imagine is a 'natural law' in the sense of rules of ideal law, which are adapted to the constantly changing conditions of life, i.e., a 'droit naturel au contenu variable'.[80] This is an idea that the Scandinavian jurists of the twentieth century, in spite of all their sharp polemics against the doctrine of natural law, themselves act upon, giving broad space in their works to discussions of questions of what will be right law. That they do so is well and good. But one may perhaps miss a certain critical attitude with regard to personal valuations—a clearer understanding of the greater or lesser uncertainty that necessarily adheres to all our valuations of law.

I would like to conclude this chapter by considering the concept of natural law, that is of a system of laws of universal validity. That system was embodied and transmitted to posterity in the law books of Justinian.

It is no exaggeration to say that next to the Bible, no book has left a deeper mark upon the history of mankind than the Corpus Iuris Civilis. Much has been written about the impact of Rome upon Western civilisation. Much has been disputed about 'The Ghost of the Roman Empire' That still lurks far beyond the shores of the Mediterranean. In my opinion the heritage of Roman law is not a ghost but a living reality. It is present not only in the court but also in the market place. It certainly inspired me as a young law student at Oxford to pursue a career as a barrister. It lives on not only in the institutions but in the language of our country and all civilised nations.

In my opinion our greatest debt to the Roman inheritance is the notion that law is the common patrimony of men, a bond that can overcome their differences and reduce them to unity.

The great compilation and codification of legal material which is commonly known by the name of the Corpus Iuris Civilis, was completed in the year 534AD, by a body of Byzantine lawyers who had been ordered to undertake that task by the Emperor Justinian. In the eyes of posterity, it was Justinian's greatness to have given the laws symmetry and simplicity. In my Preface I commented on the fact that Napoleon was of the view that his contribution to civilisation was not the battles that he had won, but his Napoleonic Code. It appears that Emperor Justinian's view was similar to what his greatest contribution was as Emperor. Dante reserved a special place in Paradise for the Byzantine Caesar with the following couplet in his Paradiso:

"Who by the will of Primal Love possessed,

Pruned from the Laws the unneeded and the vain".

What impressed later generations, besides the admirable construction of Justinian Law-Books, was their claim to Universal validity. It was through her law that Rome re-conquered the provinces that he had lost on the battlefield. That claim to validity was not based on force, but on reason. It was an appeal to the intrinsic dignity of the law, rather than to its power of compulsion. In a resounding proclamation, Justinian declared that it had been his purpose to erect a temple to Justice, a citadel of law.

"Of all subjects none is more worthy of study than the authorities of law, which happily disposes things divine and human, and puts an end to iniquity".

Roman jurists saw law as an art and a science all in one. As a science, it is a knowledge of human and divine things, a theory of right and wrong. As an art, it is the furtherance of what is good and equitable. To the Roman legal mind the mission of the jurist might rightly be compared with that of a priest. He is a minister of justice, for justice and law are correlative.

Laws are of different sorts. There is the law of the State, which expresses the interest of one particular community. There is a law of Nations which men had devised for their mutual intercourse. But there is also a law which expresses higher and more permanent standard. It is the law of nature (ius naturale), which corresponds to "That which is always good and equitable" (bonum et aequum).

Thucydides said "history is philosophy teaching by example". In my view law is philosophy teaching by decree and precedent.

In my view, it is an undeniable fact that the greatest periods of history have coincided with the progressive development of law. Witness the legislation of Edward I in England, the Justinian Code in Rome, the Napoleonic Code in France, the Declaration of Independence in America (1776) and even the laws of Hywel Dda in Wales, whose reign was from 942 to 950, is traditionally credited with codifying these laws, which were passed down from generation to generation by word of mouth. What in each case was cause or effect, was debatable.

The lesson of natural law is to remind the jurist of his own limitations. Jurisprudence is unable to say the final word about law. No philological effort will ever be able to explain a work of art. Nor can jurisprudence reach the ultimate core of law and account for its existence. The lesson of natural law is that the logical character of law does not necessarily imply a denial that law is part of ethics. What language is to ideas, norms are to values. Ultimately it is on the basis of these, that man makes his choice and determines his action. The transformation of a norm into a command is essentially a matter of subjective appreciation. Surely there is no command where there is no obedience. We cannot ignore that the certainty for which conscience craves is not that of transient laws but that of absolute values. If he be the man of truth he will provide such grounds for obedience as are capable of carrying conviction. But he will also take into account the unrelenting quest of man to rise above the letter of the law to the realm of the spirit. Natural law theorists were the first to explore the ambiguous borderland between law and morals They were the first to secure the comparative independence of the lawgiver as well as the inviolable rights of the individual conscience. They were the first to analyse the complex interplay of legal and moral obligation, the mysterious process by which the truly honest man abides by the law and yet is free from its bondage. We must be careful before we reject the eloquent plea that law is a part of ethics. We must ask ourselves whether there is not a permanent element of truth in their contention that law and morals are closely intertwined and yet fundamentally different. It is from the idea of good that all normative judgments proceed and yet that the essence of moral experience is freedom.

Kant in a famous passage which I would like to quote had a clear grasp of the incommensurable difference between legality and morality "A perfectly good will cannot be conceived as necessitated to act in conformity with law since of itself in accordance with its subjective constitution it can be determined only by the concept of good". See Kant's Moral Law in Groundwork of the Metaphysics of Morals (1785).In my view the point where values and norms coincide is the ultimate origin of law and at the same time the beginning of moral life. However, the sad fact is that although the legal process is a bonafide attempt to identify truth and apply justice as it is a system administered by imperfect man, it can only ever result in partial truth and approximate justice.

In the film A Few Good Men Jack Nicholson's character, after being challenged for the truth by a defence attorney played by Tom Cruise shouts "You want the truth. You can't handle the truth!" I adapt and adopt that saying in relation to our legal system, but no one and nothing is perfect!

Chapter 9

Abstract speculation has been the salvation of the world... To set limits to speculation is treason to the future.
Alfred North Whitehead, The Function of Reason

The common problem, yours, mine, everyone's
Is not to fancy what were fair in life
Provided it could be—but, finding first
What may be, then find how to make it fair
Up to our means: a very different thing!
Robert Browning, Bishop Blougram's Apology

...what is the real foundation of English liberty...is not where search has been made for it, in political institutions, which have been copied to no purpose, but rather in the conception of law.
Bertrand De Jouvenei, On Power

Borders are scratched across the heart's of men
By strangers with a calm, judicial pen
And when the borders we watch bleed with red
The lines of ink along the map turn red.
Mrya Mannes, 'Gaza Strip' Subversive Rhymes for Our Times (1959)

An explosion in the nuclear laboratories of the state of Utopia sends up a lethal radioactive cloud of dust. Strong winds carry the cloud across the American prairies, damaging persons, livestock, and crops.[81]

Is Utopia legally responsible for the effect beyond its borders of an explosion that occurred entirely in its own territory? Does it matter whether the explosion was a 'test' or an accident? Is it an answer to Americans' claims for damages that the nuclear cloud, which would ordinarily have risen upward to be neutralised in the far reaches of outer space, was on this occasion carried horizontally forward by unexpectedly strong air currents: a fluke, an unexpected 'act of God'? Are the claims of American citizens for compensation valid, even though many of them, inured to the too-familiar wail, contributed to the disaster by ignoring the sirens' warnings to take shelter?

It is the distinction, the hallmark of a highly organised society it is argued to have laws, and these emanate from a government of leaders aided by a professional system of enforcement which ensures the obedience of the community. The trouble with this theory is that we now know that even a much less organised society may nevertheless govern much of its conduct by laws. Indeed, if this were not so, it is difficult to see how any community of men could traverse the landscape of history from savagery to political sophistication.

In so-called primitive societies, it is often the case that government, police, and the community as a whole are one and the same thing. The specialisation and separation of two elites, one to *rule* and another to *enforce*, may await a later stage when the growth of the law, centralisation, and the increasing complexity of life make it nearly impossible for one person, or one group of persons, to have the special skills, not to mention the time, to do everything equally well.

However, there are social philosophies that do not see as a continuous inevitable upward line of human evolution this movement from disorganised to highly organised; from little, undifferentiated government to burgeoning government with a separation of powers and an aggregation of power to the separate parts. Paradoxically, anarchist and Marxian and even some Christian and non-Christian political philosophies, all visualise social progress as a path leading full circle back to a community related to the isonomic stage of the Greek city state, which Hannah Arendt described as "a form of political organisation in which the citizens lived together under conditions of no-rule, without a division between rulers and ruled."[82]

These divergent lines of philosophical extrapolation, each in its own way of grouping data and applying insight, happen to have arrived at the postulation of a society in which law and its enforcement are natural concomitants of the voluntary, socially conditioned and socially motivated conduct of each individual member of the community as a whole, and in which government and indeed, law as we know it become anachronisms, which wither away as each individual comes to assume more true responsibility for *himself.*

Teilhard de Chardin, the Catholic social historian and philosopher, saw our society inexorably evolving toward a closely-knit form of organisation wherein human love, understanding, and faith, rather than political organisation and creative coercion, form the framework: "men awakening at last, under the influence of the ever-tightening planetary embrace, to a sense of universal solidarity based on their profound community, evolutionary in its nature and purpose."[83]

Approaching it psychologically rather than theologically, but meeting across the same ontological backyard fence, was R.D. Laing, who conjectured that man must retrieve his true psychic nature:

To Laing, the source of valid law and constructive power must originate in individual introspection, a trip into inner space.[84]

In essence, there are three systems of problem-solving known to the law. They may operate independently, or successively, or they may be integrated into a single process.

The first system is distinguished by its *power* syndrome, and it operates where the community permits (or cannot prevent) the imposition, by force, of the will of one party on another. It is this Hegel-Fichte-oriented approach to law, with the asserted triumphant will, or historical necessity, as a sufficient moral justification in itself.

In relations between states, unfortunately, the unilateral use of power remains a much more common source of law. Military conquest, annexation, imposed treaties, economic boycott. These have all been more or less tolerated by the international community as legitimate ways of making law. Such recognition is, of course, little more than a realistic acceptance by that community of the consequence of its weakness and lack of cohesion, and the equally indisputable phenomenon of *force* creating *order*, and of the will behind force justifying itself by reference to certain standards by which it is exercised and thus made 'lawful'. Witness the current situation in Hong Kong, mainland China's dominant position in relation to its governance and legal system, and most recently Russia's invasion of Ukraine and the Hamas and Israeli conflict.

The dispute, in 1962, between the United States, Russia, and Cuba over the placing of nuclear missiles in the Caribbean helps further to illustrate this proposition. According to the United States, Russia's action in putting missiles on Cuban soil was an international wrong because it was done in secrecy and deceit because it forcefully upset the world balance of power, and because it violated the integrity of the Western Hemisphere as declared in the Monroe Doctrine. Russia, on the other hand, contended that the United States could not have it both ways: either all overseas bases are wrongful, aggressive threats to the peace—in which case the United States should dismantle its bases in Western Europe, Turkey, the Philippines, Formosa etc.—or else all bases are legal, in which case Russia was perfectly within its rights in setting up shop in Cuba.

By its 'peaceful blockade', the United States persuaded Russia to withdraw its missiles from the Caribbean. Such an exercise in the use of unilateral force, accompanied by an extensive polemic, exchanges of notes, debates in the UN, and formal negotiations ought, presumably, to have had some law-making effect. But what law did it yield? Since Russia and the United States never agreed on what the dispute was about, there could not, of course, be agreement as to what the successful use of force actually decided. Those who side with the American view, for example, can assert that the emerging rule is that the Monroe Doctrine remains in effect and all foreign bases in the Western Hemisphere constitute aggression against the collective hemisphere. Those who sided with the Russians can allege that the emerging rule is that all overseas nuclear missile bases are hostile, aggressive and illegal and should therefore be dismantled; that America's continued refusal to apply this rule reciprocally to itself proves Washington's disdain for international law and equity.

Still others, more cynically, and the entire polemic as nothing but propaganda window dressing, sound and fury signifying nothing, an exercise in *pure power*. The same is true it seems to me in public opinion as to the Chinese approach to Hong Kong. The meaning of this term we will shortly examine. For the present, however, it is sufficient to note that when a problem is resolved by recourse to *power*, to one-party law-making, the solution one party imposes on another does not yield a clear-cut rule of law, when as often happens in a *power*-oriented solution, the various members of the international community and the parties, in particular, retain their different views of *what the issues were* and therefore will continue to disagree as to *what was decided*. The world will only know *who won*, but not what *principle* the victory established, for they will not have a definitive statement of the issues on which it was decided.

For the long-range prospects of peace, it is less important to know who won than what principle was established. This is a hypothesis many will not share, but it marks the dividing line between an orderly community and the jungle. A system of decision-making which does not yield an agreed principle is like a rifle without a sight: lacking not in effect but in *predictable* effect. Without these principles of decision, there can be no prediction and thus, perhaps, no future.

Neither two-party law-making, employing the *compromise* syndrome, nor third-party law-making, employing the *impartiality* syndrome, suffers from this important defect. A court of law, for example, will attempt to have the parties agree as to the facts and issues on which the case is to be decided. But failing that, the court will itself decide which facts and what issues are relevant to its decision. In this way, the judicial settlement of a dispute generally yields not only a *decision* but a *rule of law*.

The two-party system is marked by a *compromise* syndrome. This operates in disputes where the law sanctions the reconciliation of contending claims in a mutually acceptable agreement devised by the parties themselves. The parties, so to speak, write their own law. Our ordinary everyday business contracts are laws made by compromise, as are the wage agreements negotiated by trade unions and conciliation boards. Most international agreements, treaties and their genus are laws made by mutual accommodation and consent.

The system of compromise may simply involve two-party negotiation, or it may call for complex mechanical devices as well as reference to other systems of decision-making.

The *compromise* syndrome manifests two-party law. The parties to the dispute themselves may make laws to suit their own needs through a process of negotiation. This is in contrast to the *power* syndrome, which manifests one-party law, and in which the stronger makes the law both for himself and for the weaker party.

Two-party law, unlike one-party law, continues to occupy an important role in the development of even sophisticated legal systems; especially in the continuing and ever-growing use of the adaptable idea of contract. It can also be located closer to the soul of our complex modern national societies, for it is readily apparent that *all* law can only operate within a general framework of applied consensus or compromise. This fundamental community consensus, which H.L.A. Hart called a 'rule of recognition', generally originates in a confluence of popular opinion or will, although it may also be the product of revolutionary charisma. Without either an imposed or agreed basic norm or group of such norms, however, and in the absence of a new socially conditioned breed of men who act invariably and voluntarily according to harmonious social principles that are natural to them, law would remain in a state of opinion where each man, and therefore *no* man, is king.

Charles Manning and Lon L. Fuller demonstrated by reference to *games* that communities of children and adults tend to develop imaginatively within their community those agreed guidelines necessary to allow their chosen activity to proceed. Underlying these guidelines of the game is a remarkably seldom-challenged common assumption or set of assumptions which may be unenunciated, but of which the 'rules of the game' are symptomatic.[85]

Manning has called this human flair for games 'an association on the basis of make-believe' and this may, indeed, also be both a happier and more accurate definition of the phenomenon underlying law than is 'social contract'. It must be remembered here, however, that 'make-believe' is used to denote not a sham, for the phenomenon of the game-in-progress, or of the community, is real enough. Rather it means an exercise of the creative imagination by which a disordered group calls itself into being as a working society made possible by the belief that certain rules of its own creation are superior even to those who were its originators.

One of the agreed 'rules of the game', in particular, merits further attention, for it is basic to the third category of decision-making, which operates by using the *impartiality* syndrome, as well as to law-making that uses the *power* and *compromise* syndromes. If this rule is ignored, neither the *power* nor the *impartiality* syndrome can yield what is generally acceptable to the community at law. This agreed rule of the game is thus obviously one of great importance. It may be described as the rule of philosophical consistency, linear reasoning, or logical deduction, and we shall consider its operation in detail later. Plato's dialogues are its fountainhead, and its impact on the West has never diminished in 2,300 years, despite repeated efforts by the early Christian dogmatists to turn it upside down by substitution of the illogical paradox (life through death, joy through suffering, wisdom through simpleness, and even conception through virginity), or the effort of Hegel and Marx to substitute 'thesis-antithesis-synthesis' as a way of thinking.

Philosophical consistency is the triumph of the intellect, of 'pure' reason, and it provides the bridge between arbitrary, selfish, and isolated decision-making and promotes the emergence of a set of knowable and predictable rules for the exercise (and restraint) of authority: In other words, it facilitates *law*. It is not the sole component of good law for which there must also be mercy, feeling-perception, and an awareness of public policy, but it is the indispensable prerequisite to the existence of a legal system.

Suppose the caveman, Ug, has begun his autumnal hunt by killing a dinosaur. Having left his lethal flint-axe in its heart, he continues on his hunt, intending later to return with his family to gather the carcass. Two days afterwards, his neighbour, Og, stumbles across the dead animal. With the aid of his wife and ten children and the expenditure of two days' work, Og succeeds in dragging the cadaver to his cave. Once Ug has returned from his hunt, he traces the missing carcass to Og's cave and demands its return.

Depending upon the degree of sophistication Ug and Og have achieved, this story can have various climaxes:

1. Ug and Og could simply clout each other with the jaw bones of asses in that familiarly primitive manner of problem-solving and decision-making first attributed to Abel and Cain or Romulus and Remus. Such a contest involves no thought for either past or future conduct. The parties are concerned neither with laying down principles for solving future disputes nor with applying to a present dispute the lessons of comparable disputes in the past. They are concerned only with one immediate—and no doubt to them vital—question: Who gets the dinosaur? This, then, is the use of *pure* power to reach a decision, and it yields no law, unless some future disputants, by benevolent induction, read a reasonable principle into Ug and Og's seemingly mindless contest of strength and apply it to solve their own predicament.

    It is just conceivable that the battle between Ug and Og might in this way gradually come to be accepted as a law stating that dinosaurs killed and left behind on autumnal hunts may be taken by any person strong enough to defend his title. That such a rule of law sanctioning and regulating a contest of pure or mindless power is not entirely fanciful will be seen by recalling the extensive role of trial by combat and its refinement, the duel, in medieval European and also Oriental systems. The role of the law in associating itself with a contest of pure power in order to impart to it a trace of its grace and order is like that of the church in blessing dictators, senselessly warring armies, and the shrines of pagan cults.

2. On the other hand, Ug might reason: "This dinosaur is mine because I killed it and impressed on it my mark of conquest. To allow you, Og, to take this carcass from me merely because I left it to continue my hunt would be to admit a principle that would make the whole business of organised autumnal hunts impossible."

In reply, Og might contend that the abandonment of carcasses during a hunt is a socially undesirable, wasteful practice, that it leaves them exposed to the ravages of other beasts, that oft-times carcasses go unclaimed for weeks while they rot in the sun, that moreover, by dragging the carcass home, Og did far more than Ug of the actual work necessary to reduce it to a commodity capable of ownership and use.

After that, Ug and Og, if they are deadlocked, may still rely on asses' jawbones to club each other to a violent verdict. *But in this case, the outcome would yield a solution based on power as a law-making device.* The difference is a simple one. Suppose Ug is the winner. Suppose that, the following autumn, the same events recur but with the roles reversed. It would be difficult for Ug now to contend that a newly killed dinosaur, temporarily abandoned during a hunt, becomes the property of a finder who drags it home.

His sense of honour and consistency would probably shame him into obeying the 'law' he made by force of arms only a year earlier. If it does not, Og's neighbours, outraged by Ug's shameless inconsistency, would probably rally to his aid. Ug and Og would have discovered that not only judges and lawyers but the public as a whole, even in primitive societies, have an extraordinary, seemingly innate preference for action that is consistent, and at a more sophisticated state, can be *seen and expressed* to be consistent with what has gone before. This preference, which appears as a universal social instinct, is an essential ingredient in the emergence of a rule of law, and it means little more than that men do not simply do whatever they feel like doing, or whatever they think they can get away with, but only that which they can 'justify'. Power relationships, as we have noticed, often fail to yield such neutral principles, but sometimes, fortunately, they do—either because the contest of power took place between champions of two explicit principles, or because historical forces conspire to pretend that it did.

3. Ug and Og might not fight at all. Instead, they might haggle in the presence of flowing jugs of clover wine. They might, in a soggy euphoria of good fellowship, together set out to kill another dinosaur so the needs of each might be satisfied. Or they might, to the same end, pillage the larder of Hugh, the arch enemy of Ug, taking from its sufficient booty that the needs of both are sated. Or they and their kinfolk might tug and pull at the carcass until it came apart near the middle, whereupon they might simply resign themselves each to their portion and stalk away.

   Or Og might take one of Ug's ugly daughters as wife, whereupon the grateful father of the bride might bestow the dinosaur upon the groom as dowry. *All of these solutions represent the triumph of pure compromise.* As between Ug and Og, they may be *ad hoc* 'political' solutions, but they yield no, or very little, law unless others, later, choose to adopt this purely 'one-shot' procedure as a model or principle applicable to themselves in a similar dispute, or again, unless historical forces conspire to 'find' a logical principle where, in fact, there had been none.

4. Ug and Og might themselves decide to emulate prior conduct. They might sit down to their clover wine and remember that a similar incident once arose between two fellow villagers, T'Bo and Hun, who could reveal that the earlier quarrel had been happily resolved by an agreement of the parties to divide the carcass: the bulk of it going to the hunter, but the prime hindquarter fittingly being bestowed upon the one who provided the transportation. This would be a solution by reference to the law-making compromise syndrome. Rational principles are here set out, applied, and reapplied to obtain solutions, which, as to both form and substance, are philosophically consistent with each other and generate a tendency toward logical progression and analogy in problem-solving.

Let us now look again at the Cuban missile crisis of 1962.

The difference between *power* and *compromise* as a description of action arising out of pure *will*, and as law-making syndromes generating law through the development of enunciated, logical principles capable of being deductively extrapolated was dramatically illustrated at that time by the important debate that took place within the United States Government over how to explain to the world America's unprecedented action in imposing a peacetime quarantine on Cuba.

Some government lawyers argued that these actions—this exercise in power—should be formulated in terms of legal principles.

It was suggested, for example, that the United States should have taken the position that the prohibition in the United Nations Charter against the use of force against another state except in the event of an armed attack had become obsolete in an age of missile-delivered nuclear weapons; that no nation could be expected to wait until *after* an armed attack before striking back; and that existing law should be reinterpreted to permit the use of force against anticipated, and not merely *actual* aggression.[86] Had this advice been accepted as the official American position, and had the Russians and Cubans joined issue on this basis, the success of the power gambit might have *made law* and thus effected a *de facto* amendment of the United Nations Charter. The State Department, however, shied away from committing itself to a rule that might be taken to authorise any state to respond with force to any alleged *threat* of aggression (and what war has ever been launched without some such allegation?).

Moreover, the international court had already spoken on the matter since the advent of the Atomic Era. In rejecting the British argument that a violation of Albanian sovereignty by Royal Navy minesweepers was a use of force justified as "a new and special application of the theory of intervention," the necessity of which was the failure of international organisation to provide a speedy, effective remedy, the majority of judges firmly held the traditional line, saying: "The court can only regard the alleged right of intervention as the manifestation of a policy of force, such as has, in the past, given rise to most serious abuses and such as cannot, whatever be the present defect in international organisation, find a place in international law."[87]

Then, too, some efforts were made to base the Cuban blockade on other principles, such as a conveniently abridged version of the Monroe Doctrine, omitting the doctrine's other side of the coin, which precludes America from all intervention in Europe. None of these doctrinal approaches carried the day within the United States Government, which followed, instead, the lead of those advisers who urged the position that America owed the world no philosophical explanation other than the self-evident enunciation of national *will*, particularly the will to survive and be omnipotent. This position was best stated by Dean Acheson, who said, "The Cuban quarantine is not a legal issue. The power, position and prestige of the United States had been challenged by another state, and law simply does not deal with such questions of ultimate power—power that comes close to the sources of sovereignty. I cannot believe that there are principles of law that say we must accept destruction as our way of life."[88]

How a Russian missile base in Cuba guaranteed the destruction of the United States any more than a United States missile base in Turkey guaranteed the same fate to the USSR is not immediately apparent to the naked eye. Be that as it may, Acheson saw the Cuban quarantine as an exercise in *pure power*, yielding eventually a solution by pure power with perhaps a touch of compromise. He neither claimed nor would have accepted even in victory that the action proceeded on an established principle of law or that it created a new legal norm; one which, for example, would have allowed Russia to impose a quarantine on Turkey and obliged them to remove their missiles.

Such *ad hoc* use of power need not be cynical. Indeed, it may proceed from an ethical as well as from a cruder motive—but its reasons will be special to the parties and the occasion, rather than generally applicable and capable of reasoned development by comparison and analogy. Neither the victim nor the victimiser will acknowledge that he has established a pattern for general behaviour advancing the good order of society. An unemployed, starving beggar may steal an apple or a loaf of bread to stay alive. He may even vigorously defend him of the means of honest gain. But he is unlikely to believe, unless he is mad or an anarchist, that the law condones theft or even that the law *ought* to permit every person who feels himself underprivileged just to take whatever he can carry away.

The element, then, that must be added to the mere event of conduct in order to constitute *law-making* conduct is an expressed or impliable *consciousness of the action being not a mere expression of will, but rather of defined obligation*, whether the sense of obligation be induced by consciousness of moral duty, preference for consistency, for a system of practical reasoning, respect for reciprocal benefits, or fear of a coercive power.

Chapter 10

The search for a static security—in the law or elsewhere—is misguided. The fact is that security can only be achieved through constant change, through the wise discarding of old ideas that have outlived their purpose, and through the adapting of others to current facts.
Judge William O. Douglas-Stare Decisis

If we never do anything which has not been done before, we shall never get anywhere. The law will stand still while the rest of the world goes on; and that will be bad for both.
Lord Justice Denning, Packer v. Packer (1954)

Common law was weaned on the consistent application of patterns of applied practical power and compromise by the parties to disputes. The very term 'common' reflects the origin of the law in the consciously and repeatedly applied and widely extrapolated customs of the people, the customs that commonly or consistently prevailed among the people in their relations with each other, and that found their content in a balance of popular convenience and consistency. This common agreement to resolve disputes, whether by one-, two-, or three-party methods, in accordance with the principled application of practical reasoned consistency is history's social response to the challenge of chaos.

Ug and Og's problem, for example, continued for a few years to be reflected in the whaling industry. Whaling, like some other technologies, had recently become more efficiently lethal. Previously, however, a harpooned whale might continue the fight for a very long time, eventually breaking from, or even towing away, his would-be captors. At what point could such an animal be captured by someone else?

This issue first came before the courts of England in 1788, at the York Assizes. An action was launched by one captain against another, in "trover for a whale, which had been struck first by a harpooner of the plaintiff's ship, and afterwards by a harpooner of the defendant's." The counsel on both sides, and all the parties concerned, agreed the law to be, both by the custom of Greenland and as settled by former determinations at Guildhall, London, as follows:

While the harpoon remains in the fish, and the line continues attached to it, and also continues in the power and management of the striker, the whale is a fast fish: and though during that time struck by a harpooner of another ship, and though she afterwards breaks from the first harpoon, but continues fast to the second, the second harpoon is called a friendly harpoon, and the fish is the property of the first striker, and of him alone. But if the first harpoon or line breaks, or the line attached to the harpoon is not in the power of the striker, the fish is a loose fish, and will become the property of any person who strikes and obtains it.[89]

With the parties agreed—*compromised*—to the extent of accepting both the binding force of prior solutions and also as to the practical principle emerging from these prior solutions, the work of the court was to apply this past practice taken from the experience of previous disputes to the present one. The word 'compromise' is here used in the special legal sense. A compromise *egume* is, technically, an agreement between the parties to a dispute delimiting the area of concepts within which they or a court may search for a solution to their dispute. Thus, a Belgian and a Frenchman may agree that the law of France shall govern their relations. In a large sense, all persons engaged in a whaling industry at a particular time and place agree, implicitly, to be governed by its necessary norms—international treaty, long-standing custom, and tradition.

Some of these norms are compulsory and thus *legal*, others etiquette that is merely convenient. But beneath all efforts to maintain orderly relationships through law lies a compromis, an agreement between the parties that they shall argue their cause, and that the cause shall be decided within a certain circumference of admissible kinds of argument, and not outside it. Thus, the use of evidence of past practice is everywhere in the common-law world even at the very centre of—that circle, while the fact that one of the disputants is ugly, is usually clearly outside the agreed circle.

Most disputes are not quite so easily resolved as our example, the whaling case. While there is usually agreement that prior solutions should be consistently applied, the calculations that go into the extrapolation of one or several precedents to new facts are usually more complex and far less self-evident in humans than in mathematical calculations. It is for this reason that an agreement—a compromise—to apply precedent, essential as it is to an organised society, is often not enough *by itself* to resolve a dispute. There are still likely to be disagreements as to *which* of several possible precedents, several arguments all within the agreed circle, is to be applied, and even if there is only one applicable line of precedent, whether differences in circumstances that distinguish the earlier disputes from the present one do not justify modifications in the precedent. Such disputes generally cannot be settled by an agreement between the parties themselves, but require the help of an impartial third party.

This brings us to the third category of law-making. Some years after the *York Assizes* case, in 1808, the House of Lords was asked to consider a whaling case seemingly 'similar' to the one raised at the 1788 Assizes. One Luce, captain of the whaler *William Fenning*, harpooned a whale near Greenland. While still fighting it, he hit another whale. Being unequipped to fight on two fronts, he tied the second harpoon line to a buoy or 'droug'. By the time the first whale was secured, the second had dragged line and buoy far out to sea. According to the House of Lords:

...the wound produced the usual effect of this weapon, it retarded the progress of the fish, by causing it to struggle with the harpoon for a considerable time...and the droug floating on the water marked its course, so that it was with the more certainty pursued by Anthony, the master of the Caerwent, who, in consequence of a signal made to him by Luce, followed the fish, and killed it. He extracted from it the oil and other valuable matter, but rendered no part of it to the Plaintiffs. Numerous witnesses deposed, that a custom had universally prevailed in these seas, from the origin of the fishery, until within a few years past, that the party who first struck the fish with the droug would receive one half of it from the party who killed it. But it appeared by the testimony of the defendant's witnesses, that for a few years past, since 1792, many captains of the ships employed among the Galapagos islands, among others, one American, had usually agreed that the striking a fish with a droug should not entitle the striker to a share. In the year 1805, Anthony, with five or six English captains, of whom Luce was not one, had, upon their arrival at the fishing station, acceded to these terms. The defendant's counsel contended that the Plaintiff must be

nonsuited, because, according to his own claim, he was tenant in common with the defendant: but on account of the testimony of one witness, who stated that the person who first struck the fish was entitled to the whole, rendering half to the party who killed it, the Chief Justice left the case to the jury, who found that by the custom the plaintiff was entitled to half the fish, and gave him in damages the value of a moiety.[90]

So must courts choose between contending principles and a multitude of fact-data, similar but not identical to that found in earlier cases, to determine the relevant integers to be taken into account in calculating a logical deduction.[91] Such a process of logical calculus requires an impartial mind.

In the international, as in the national, community *power* and *compromise*, the one- and two-party law-making syndromes, may simply be *used*, or they may be *used to make law*. Hitler's bombing of undefended 'open' cities was a use of power bereft of legal intent, and of course, yielding no law. The Anglo-French invasion of Suez and the Indian invasion of Goa, on the other hand, constituted uses of force in support of strongly urged legal principles, and the outcome in each case has had law-making significance. Not only substantive but also procedural practice, whether derived by power or by compromise, is capable of making law, if it proceeds with an enunciated concept capable of being applied to other than this one instance, and if it works.

We have noted how fundamental is the use of agreement of compromise in the conscious development of law; but also, that it is an insufficient ingredient in a sophisticated system of problem-solving because the calculations involved in the application of pre-existent principles to new events involve dilemmas of choice not presented by purely mathematical calculations. Let us illustrate this further. A man drives into an intersection while the traffic light is green. An oncoming car ignores the light. Thinking himself the victim of a bluff, or in blind fury, our man fails to yield, insists on his right of way, and collides with the other car.

Later, it is learned that the driver of the car proceeding against the light had lost control of its braking system. Who is at fault? "Not I," says our man, "I had the green light." "Not I," says the other. "Through no fault of mine, I couldn't stop. The other driver saw me coming and had the last clear chance to avert the accident." Who is right? As it happens, both drivers have some precedent on their side, since some courts apply a simple test of 'fault', while others follow the 'last clear chance' doctrine to attach responsibility to the man—be he at 'fault' or not—who had the last opportunity to prevent the accident.

Then too, a fragment of principled reasoning can often be spun out to put a patch of respectability on the exercise of what would otherwise be pure power. If the parties to this dispute are not always able to settle it alone, then an impartial third party is needed if there is to be a settlement without violence. How this third party is to choose between two precedents, both being commonly accepted reasons for the solution of comparable motor vehicle problems. Suffice it here to point out that the third party is needed, and that his chief qualification is not that he is an expert, or particularly wise—although both may be desirable—but only that he is genuinely a *third* party and not one of the *interested* parties.

Whatever the efficacy of *power* and *compromise* syndromes in the development of national and international law, and it must not be minimised, one- and two-party law-making cannot suffice to guarantee a community against chaos. In the modern state, third-party law has assumed this ultimate law-making function. We return, therefore, to consideration of this third system of law-making. It is identifiable and can be distinguished from the other two systems by its impartiality syndrome—that is, submission to the binding determination of a neutral third party, being the judge in a court of law, arbitrator, administrative civil servant, mutual friend of the disputants, or tax official passing on the validity of exemptions.

Examples of the impartiality syndrome should also include such mechanical devices as that which formed a part of the Timken compromise—that is, the flipping of a coin. The two men flipping a coin are referring their dispute to the mechanical impartiality of fate. They do so because it is one sure, simple way to get a speedy decision and because they have determined that any decision is better than none. The decision's the thing. Unlike other appeals to the third-party judgment of God, this reference to impartial non-theistic fate is not expected to yield 'justice' or 'truth' but only a decision—albeit one arrived at with perfect impartiality.

Understanding the concept of impartiality requires an initial appreciation of the historical and religious ethos that surrounds it.

The search for a quality of human impartiality comparable to that of God or fate has conditioned the progress of societies toward third-party law-making. In Western, as distinguished from Oriental, religions God is judged and eschatology is concerned with judgment. To the Jew, this is the specific judgment of *Yom*

Kippur, the holiest of days, on which God reads each man's record of the previous year and decides his fate: "who shall live and who shall die, who shall be raised up and who cast down." To the Christian, it is the judgment of the communion in which a kindlier God, made beneficent by Christ's suffering as a surrogate for all men, judges by "not weighing our merits but pardoning our offences." He shall "come again with glory to judge both the quick and the dead"!

In Western, unlike Eastern, religions God is always judging man and man is always judging God. As a society, we are dedicated to judgment. Moreover, man in his grace relates ontologically and epistemologically to the world, the universe, and God through a process of impartial, rational, philosophically consistent decisions, which are facilitated by the divinely given power of right-reason. In this way, man also 'judges' God and all his works.

Impartiality thus is a fundamental and religiously related virtue, however secular its manifestation. This is apparent in the Bible, where practical instructions to judges naturally reflect this lively religious concern of the ancient Hebrews with the subject of judicial impartiality, even though the matter being decided is a secular one: "Thou shalt not respect persons, neither take any gift: for a gift doth blind the eyes of the wise…" "Ye shall hear the small as well as the great; ye shall not be afraid of the face of man…"[92] "Ye shall do no unrighteousness in judgment; thou shall not scorn the person of the poor nor honour the person of the mighty; but in righteousness shalt thou judge they neighbour."[93]

The Book of Common Prayer reflects the universal desire for impartiality by requiring Anglicans to pray for all those "who truly and indifferently minister justice." The religious origins of impartiality continue to be relevant to the role of courts to this very day. In 1966, Justice Kenneth Keating of New York noted, apparently with satisfaction, that a survey had shown a majority of New Yorkers to believe that judges perform their functions under divine guidance. (A trial lawyer commented that "Keating must have meant that Christ only knows what they're doing"!) The problems for impartiality raised by such supernatural associations, and by its disestablishment and demythologisation, will be examined later.

So highly was judicial impartiality prized in Roman courts that it was required then, as it is in most legal systems today, that the judges' fairness not only be *but appear to the litigants to be*, unimputable. The *Codex* of Justinian[94] provides: "Although a judge has been appointed by imperial power, yet because it is our pleasure that all litigation should proceed without suspicion let it be permitted to him who thinks the judge under suspicion to recuse him before the issue is joined so that the cause go to another."[95]

The equally universal concern that judges be protected against biasing pressures is underlined by the Declaration of Independence, in which the American settlers charged that the British king "has made judges dependent on his Will alone, for the tenure of their offices, and the amount and payment of their salaries."

An appreciation of the deep historic-religious roots of the idea of impartiality is essential to an understanding of the law. So basic to our thinking about courts and other decision-makers is this historical and religious ethos that no breakthrough in the direction of peaceful third-party law-making can be expected in the international community until the problem of the impartiality of decision-makers is satisfactorily resolved. In a world divided by politics, economics, race and geography, this is no small challenge.

Nevertheless, it comes to this: *Whether the struggle to create a climate of human impartiality succeeds will determine the scope, if any, given by society to a system of third-party law-making.* That there is a direct relationship between the impartiality of third-party impartial decision-makers and the extent to which the community utilises the third-party decision-making process would appear to be axiomatic, and is the underlying hypothesis of this paradigm. Put conversely, it is assumed that no administrative or judicial decision-making system, except in a dictatorship, can expect to be widely accepted and routinely resorted to until it has established its essential credential of impartiality.

It has already been said that third-party law-making is not a substitute for, but a supplement to, one- and two-party methods of settling disputes. To place the purpose of this study into perspective, this point might well be sharpened further, now that the three methods of law-making have been introduced. It is not at all intended, by focussing on third-party law-making, to diminish the importance of, in particular, the two-party system for which there continues to be ample scope.

Indeed, paradoxically, the growing intervention of the state in private economic and social relations has, by increasing the real equality of the individual, and therefore, his capacity to bargain effectively, placed him in a better position to participate equally with other individuals in private or two-party law-making. The same is true of the growing power-equality among states. Since the chips are more widely distributed than ever before, the poker game of direct negotiation has more players than before, and they tend to stay in the game longer. The parties to a dispute must always be given every opportunity to 'work things out for themselves' before an outsider is justified in imposing a solution. Hence the recent emphasis on mediation and dispute resolution in the procedural rules of many legal systems.

There has, of course, long been *ad hoc* third-party decision-making in international relations. It appears to have been used in disputes between ancient Greek city states, Roman provinces, and thirteenth-century Swiss cantons, to have risen and fallen with the medieval papacy, and to have revived in modern times with the Jay Treaty of 1794 and the Alabama Awards of 1872.[96] As long ago as 117 BC, it has been discovered, two Romans, sons of Quintus Minucius Rufus, were sent to investigate and decide a territorial controversy between the cities of Genoa and Vituria, which they did by fixing and demarcating the boundary and by decreeing a settlement, which is engraved on a bronze tablet discovered near Genoa 450 years ago.[97]

It is only in the last century, however, that an effort has been made to create *permanent* machinery for the resolution of international disputes by impartial third parties. The stirrings in this direction could be detected in the British-French Treaty of Arbitration of 1903 and the Hague Convention for the Pacific Settlement of International Disputes of 1899,[98] which set up the Permanent Court of International Arbitration.[99] It has been said that the Permanent Court of Arbitration is not permanent, is not a court and does not engage in arbitration. In any event, its relatively long, somnolent life has been disturbed by fewer than two dozen actual calls to service. A very much larger step forward was taken by the creation, in 1921, of the Permanent Court of International Justice, but even it currently handles an average of fewer than three cases a year.[100]

It is surprising that so many of the most intellectually voracious international legal minds are still willing to be put out to pasture where the grazing is so thin. But in the last two or three decades both international and domestic arbitration have grown immensely and now, especially in the commercial field are much more popular choices for third-party dispute resolution than third-party litigation.

Chapter 11

One of the greatest delusions in the world is the hope that the evils of the world can be cured by legislation.

Thomas B. Reed

Every law is an evil, for every law is an infraction of liberty. It is with government as with medicine, its only business is the choice of evils.

Jeremy Bentham

The assumption that statute is a superior source of law because common law rules may be abrogated by statute, neglects the role and power of judicial interpretation. Dicey recognised the limitations to statutes when he wrote:

Powers, however extraordinary, which are conferred or sanctioned by statute are never really unlimited because they are confined by the words of the Act itself and what is more by the interpretation put upon the statute by judges. It is not the case that judges only ever interpret the law because in interpreting the law they also create the law.

In that context, the courts can be seen to have a substantive, independent role from that of parliament and judges have the power to limit indirectly or possibly extend the operation of statute. In this context, they have the power to legislate. What then, is the nature of the legislative process in terms of the three decision-making syndromes?

Legislatures do, of course, differ significantly from courts in the decision-making tools which they generally employ. In legislating, they lay out the broad, long-term direction of the law, whereas courts, applying this blueprint, build the actual path from one solved dispute to the next. The broad general direction is embodied in legislation that is the product of a political process, usually utilising the tools of *power* and *compromise*, while the application of general legislation to specific persons and disputes is the prerogative of courts usually acting *impartially*. But it is also possible, and it not infrequently occurs, that courts, in deciding a specific case, must make a decision, the importance of which is so broad and general as to be 'legislative'. This is particularly true if courts are acting in a dispute for which no prior blueprint has been drawn. Much of the United States Constitution, although a legislative blueprint of sorts, is only sketched in, using deliberately faint and fuzzy demarcations like 'due process'.

Consequently, courts giving specific meaning to the constitution are placed in the role of a legislature. The desegregation decisions in the United States and the decisions on the right to strike in Britain are among classic historical examples of courts having to act in a legislative or blueprint-drafting capacity. When courts legislate, they ought to be sensitive to *power*; to the prevailing political standards and mores of the community, and to the need for *compromise* and agreement between the various interests and factions of that community. They must, in such cases, act at least in part as a legislature. When they fail to do so, they meet, and deserve, the fate of the Supreme Court of the United States in the period 1933–1937, when it irresponsibly chose to block the broad social policies of the Roosevelt New Deal and to substitute, instead, its own political preferences.

Conversely, there are occasions when a legislature does not generate broad and general, but narrow and specific, laws. This kind of legislation is exemplified by laws 'for the relief of' a particular person—to grant residence or citizenship or exemption from a more general law to one or several persons. In Canada, the federal parliament even enacts 'relief' laws granting divorce to residents of the two provinces that do not have divorce laws. These specific acts are generally passed on the recommendation of a respected member of the legislative body who indicates to his colleagues how impartial justice and fairness will be advanced by the enactment of this 'judicial' legislation.

In the United States, Congress can try citizens for contempt and obstruction of the legislative process and can imprison them until the end of the legislative session. The British parliament has similar powers. Members of the legislature are in these circumstances expected to vote on the matter impartially, without reference to their political affiliation. In British Commonwealth countries where rigid political discipline is usually enforced in the legislature, a small but important number of decisions on legislation of a 'judicial' type, calling for impartial determination of the merits, are usually held on a free vote—that is, with political discipline expressly lifted. Sometimes even broad general determinations of social policy are made by political bodies with quasi-judicial impartiality.

The abolition of the death penalty in Britain in 1965 and criminal sanctions against homosexual acts committed in private between consenting adults, in 1967, were enacted in a free or nonpartisan vote after a debate in which only the merits were discussed and partisan political lines were irrelevant. The British parliament often enacts important social change only after it has heard from an impartial Royal Commission appointed by it to investigate and make recommendations. The question of reforming laws pertaining to certain homosexual practices has in Britain had the benefit of both an impartial commission and a nonpartisan parliamentary debate. Foreign policy, in the Congress of the United States, has at least since 1941 tended to be treated as a bi-partisan matter as to which differences of opinion may arise, but only the merits impartially determined by the members of Congress and not partisan political passions aroused in the community will be the determining factors in decision-making.

Even when an issue before a legislative body like Congress or the General Assembly is intensely political, a substantial and perhaps controlling number of representatives may have no political interest in, or commitment to, either side and are thus free to bring to the decision-making process an attitude of impartiality. 'Neutralism', 'nonalignment', or bipartisanship are terms preferred by the jargon of international and domestic politics. But, whatever the name, a third-party status of impartiality is not reserved to judges, any more than political responsiveness is solely the prerogative of the legislature.

In general, the broad political direction of society's progress should be charted by politicians, acting in a manner responsive to the demands of the community's power structure, and allowing for the need to compromise in the name of national unity. The specific application of laws to particular instances of human or national conduct should be made by judges acting in a manner responsive to their sense of impartial justice, and allowing for the need to compromise the ideal by reference to the possible. But it would be quite misleading to consider this an exhaustive description of government anywhere, whether at the local, national, or international level. Judges are, in the nature of things, called upon to make decisions that broadly chart the political direction of society's progress.

In this respect, they do exercise political judgement and make quasi-political decisions not within a historic and consistent denial that they do not. When they are, they must be responsive to the demands of the community's power structure and to the need for compromise in the name of national unity. Political representatives are not infrequently called upon to apply an agreed principle or precedent to a particular instance of choice. When this happens, they ought to act in a manner responsive to their sense of impartial justice, tempered by compromise between the ideal and the possible.

The jaggedness of the line between impartial and political decision-making also makes difficult any facile classification of the nature of law-making through instruments of public administration. Here again, it is the opinion of most lawyers in constitutional democracies that some kinds of administrative decisions are appropriately made by reference to the *power* structure or politico-social *compromise*, while others should be made neutrally and *impartially*.

The clear distinction constitutional democracies make between the two types of administrators—those primarily engaged in politics and those making mostly impartial, decisions—is manifest in the differing methods by which they are appointed and by which they may be discharged by the government. The Conseil d'Etat of France represents perhaps the most remarkable instance of administration concerned with specific disputes rather than the setting of general policy or the conduct of policy experimentation. Its procedures and the tenure of its decision-makers have commensurately been raised to ensure a level of impartiality virtually indistinguishable from that of a court. The Judicial Committee of the Privy Council and the House of Lords (now the Supreme Court), Britain's two highest courts, are historical examples of a gradual institutional transition from partisan political to impartial judicial decision-making.

As the functions of these two institutions have become more in the nature of third-party decision-making, the method and quality of appointment have undergone a subtle but almost total transition to ensure their independence and impartiality. So, too, in the international community: administrators, when making broad policy decisions, must be responsive to the popular will as ascertained by reference to *power* and *compromise*. When making specific impartial decisions these considerations should be at most secondary. Ordinarily, the two kinds of decisions should be made by two differently conceived administrations.

Chapter 12

Laws are like spider's webs which if anything small falls into them they ensnare it, but large things break through and escape.

Solon

On many occasions I have argued that for the purpose of today our picture should be one, not of a God-given order laid down once for all on the lives of a society of the past, not of a reflection of the divine reason governing the whole universe and photographed once for all in the last century, nor of a body of unchallengeable deductions from ultimate metaphysical-given data at which men arrived a century ago in seeking to rationalise the social phenomena of that time—that our picture should be none of these things but rather a picture of a process of social engineering.

Dean Roscoe Pound, *The Theory of Judicial Process*, an address to the Bar Association of the City of New York (23 January 1923)

Was there ever a profession such as ours, anyway? We speak of ourselves as practising law, as teaching it, as deciding it; and not one of us can say what law means.

Justice Benjamin N. Cardozo, *Jurisprudence*, an address to the New York State Bar Association (22 January 1932)

...in the great stream of absolute truth, man's knowledge of the concrete process at each given stage of development is only relatively true. The sum total of innumerable relative truths is the absolute truth.

Mao Tse-Tung, *On Practice*

Law, like religion, science, and politics, is a way of resolving conflicts between those two familiar essentials of existence: *order and change*. One just aptly refers to "the perpetual antimony between stability and change which every legal system which has escaped the danger of petrification at some particular stage of its development represents a continuing attempt to resolve."[101]

Order, in the social community, manifests and vests itself in property, precedent, process and pattern. *Change* attacks order and then, like a successful social climber, itself becomes part of the established order. The cycle never ceases: Title is subject to trespass and to transfer, procedures are revised, and precedents overruled.

Left unregulated, this cyclical, never-ending struggle between *order* and *change* can devastate the social landscape, transforming it into the "darkling plain…where ignorant armies clash by night," which Matthew Arnold saw in his vision on 'Dover Beach'.

As Jackson Pollock has demonstrated in his revolutionary visions on canvas: Form, dimension, sequence—these are things which *we*, the beholder, impose on a world of atomic fragments. They are the containers in which we try to capture in an existential moment the continuum of motion that Einsteinian physics indicates to be the essence of all matter. They are also those patterned or 'programmed' dimensions of contingency the intelligence perceives when it searches beyond the necessary, rudimentary state or condition of things apparent on the surface as to a camera. But photography, or statistical analysis, of course, does not begin to reveal the whole state of being either of a man or even of a sunset.

Human relations, too, are a continuum of motion in which each person moves according to certain harmonious and conflicting, changing and static, principles of interest and in which this motion is perceived first on a superficial level evident to the naked eye and later on many deeper levels of contingency apparent to the trained artist, the skilled psychoanalyst, and the competent 'social engineer'.

Seen in its 'raw' state, the human landscape emerges much as a Jackson Pollock composition. Law, in the hands of the social engineer, seeks to impose upon it a framework of form, dimension, and sequence, not so as to make it static, not to establish fixed classifications and stultifying norms, not to pin the moments, struggling, to the page, but as cognitive preconditions of *orderly change*. Law does this first by introducing a socially reciprocal factor to the coordinates of individual self-interest. It says to each citizen: It is *in your interest* to act within a legal framework because it is in your interest to be part of a society under law. It does it, second, by establishing a system not so much of rules or decisions as of procedures for making decisions, of applying rationally consistent principles to bring the existential moment through a crisis in the order-change progression.

Law is not, however, the only such framework. Man tries in various ways to regulate and reconcile the order-change struggle. Just as numbers may be 'systematised' in their relation to one another by being arranged in harmonic or geometric progressions, or alternating series; just as musical sounds can be arranged along seven- or twelve-tone scales, in diatonic or chromatic; so, too, there are many ways of systematising human relations for the management of the conflict between order and change. There are many such systems, all of them more or less operative, and in a free society, different systems are allowed to coexist. Man is tolerably free to choose from among them, to reject them altogether and exist in relative formlessness of conduct and perception, or to adhere to more than one, so long as the system or systems he chooses do not bring him into violent or strident collision with the adherents of other systems.

As Kipling said:

There are nine and sixty ways of constructing tribal laws
And-every-single-one-of-them-is right.

Religions, for example, try to regulate the conflict between order and change by imposing on their adherents various codes of ethical conduct. The sonnet constitutes a way of managing words and images, with its own uniform code of standards. Science has reference to a system of quantum physics of chemical, nuclear, or physical norms. The study of politics and economics has created competing systems under such titles as 'economic determinism', 'capitalism', 'Marxism' and 'socialism'.

Each system or framework is in a sense based upon 'laws'—'laws' of God, 'laws' of economics, 'laws' of human behaviour, 'laws' of onomatopoeia, 'laws' of science and nature. They could, perhaps, be called 'ways of looking at things' or ways of giving form and meaning to what are otherwise mere random phenomena. For our purposes, however, it would be helpful to call them *rules* and to reserve the term *law* for the thing properly so called.

It is useful to begin with this definition because we are about to make an important substantive distinction between these various systems of rules on the one hand, and on the other, that system which is the law, or more exactly, *third-party, law*.

We have already noted that although the various systems of rules may conflict with one another—those of religion and economics, for example, may clash over the implications of the population explosion or climate change—they have in common the essential quality that they *purport to derive their validity from something more than the purely subjective preference of man*. The substance of the rules may be humanly *perceived*; but they also claim to have a reality of their own, outside and therefore above human perception. Water would freeze at 32° Fahrenheit whether man agreed or not, *pace* Bishop Berkeley.

The church, through its sacraments, maintains that it saves souls whether Paul Blanshard thinks so or not; or, more pointedly, the church, as Graham Greene never tired of telling us, ordains priests whose sacramental powers are independently operative no matter how depraved or degenerate the priest himself may become. A worker generally works harder, according to the capitalist economic creed, when applying himself for private gain rather than in a so-called public interest. Those who adhere to these systems of order—physics, Christianity, Islam, capitalism—generally believe that their systems of rules are *perceived* by them but that they were *conceived* in some possibly higher but certainly external and therefore objective reality. Even the lowly rhyme, in a poem, is a phenomenon the writer can be said to have achieved or not, according to the standards that are verifiably true and not mere subjective conjecture. 'Cat' rhymes with 'hat' but does not rhyme with 'house' as anyone can plainly hear.

The use of the term *law* to describe these systems of rules produces confusion because a modern lawyer means something very different when he talks about *third-party law*. To him, particularly if he is Anglo-American in his training, *third-party law* is a purely subjective pragmatic phenomenon, as much a phenomenon indeed as the events giving rise to the dispute to which the law is applied. The law applied is only the law *shaped in the mind of its perceivers and existing only insofar as, and only because, it has been perceived*. We shall later see how radically this contemporary realist definition of law departs from the classical unified field or *natural* theory of law, which has shaped Western thought since the time of Plato and Aristotle, but particularly since St Thomas Aquinas.

Suffice it for the moment to note that Roscoe Pound could write, only half a century or so ago, that the American lawyer "as a rule still believes that the principles of law are absolute, eternal, and of universal validity and that the law is found, not made."[102] This is in large part because of the religious-historic ethos of the idea of impartiality to which we alluded earlier.

To regard law as a pragmatic human process, albeit one using tools of logical principles of consistency, rather than as an ordained natural or divine code of necessarily evident truth is not, of course, to say that law is whatever anyone says it is. We know by the parking tickets we have collected from our windshields that this is not so. Nor could it be. In order to avoid the total chaos that would follow if each man were free to perceive and thus give existence to his own laws, our order-creating syndrome has devised the role of 'Order Perceiver'—impartial persons officially charged with perceiving and relating to the rest of us the content of the law. Judge Cardozo used the colourful but perhaps misleading term 'appointed searches of the juristic heavens'—misleading only because it suggests that law is a series of celestially fixed points.[103]

Perhaps 'sifters of the juristic sands' would be more appropriate. These 'perceivers', be they judges or administrators generally function in response to a *particular* demand for law arising from a *particular* problem or dispute requiring immediate legal settlement. They do not perceive the law capriciously, for they must earn their right to be the community's 'law perceivers' by following certain decent procedural rites: giving a full, fair, and adversarial hearing to the properly trained representatives of both sides, for example. They apply to the particular facts of a particular dispute in a particular moment a process of logical deduction employing principles intellectually perceivable in earlier decisions or verbalised in legislative enactments. They tend, on the whole, to use principled methods of judgment, that is, they weigh and develop their decision with "arguments that, by consensus of the participants in the system, are regarded as legitimately useable in the business of building up a structure of persuasion."[104]

Moreover, while the function of perceiving the law is delegated to these men, their perception of the law ought not generally to differ too radically from that of the community—lest they be, in one way or another, replaced, or worse, ignored. (Unlike most other modern authors, judges, in their decisions, make a deliberate effort *not* to shock the community).

Law, as lawyers know it, is therefore, at least in common-law countries, understood to be a patchwork quilt of existential, man-made, *ad hoc* decisions: what De Jouvenel calls a system "which drew its inspiration not at all from the specific needs of Power but responded only to those of the body of society"[105]

Frenchmen, from Montesquieu to De Jouvenel, appear to have had a somewhat rosy view across the English Channel—a pleasant ophthalmological defect from which they now are fully recovered. But De Jouvenel's words should be read in the light of Dean Roscoe Pound's observation that even when law ceases to serve an absolute and begins to serve people, there remains the danger that the old absolutes will be replaced by a new one: judicial caprice. So there continues to be a struggle, familiar to Aquinas, Kant, and Pound, between the *law as will* and the *law as reason*.[106]

The law of most states-in-being is therefore more (or less) than a set of rules: It is primarily a process—a process for resolving conflict between *order* and *change* by the application of impartial third-party decision-making.

However, since this process exists only insofar as it is perceived by man, it (or, if one prefers, its perception by men) is therefore forever fallible, incomplete, mutable, existential.

The difference between *rules* on the one hand, and *process* on the other is, admittedly, one of degree. Nevertheless, it is an essential distinction. It can be dramatically illustrated by the classic case of *Regina v. Dudley and Stephens*.[107]

Dudley and Stephens, members of the crew of a sinking vessel, and a cabin boy, Parker, were cast adrift during a storm in an open lifeboat. They found themselves without food or water more than a thousand miles from the American coast. On the twentieth day, Dudley and Stephens killed the cabin boy, who being extremely weak, did not resist. They fed on him for four days, being thereafter rescued by another ship.

Dudley and Stephens were, of course, charged with murdering the cabin boy. A British court heard their plea of necessity—that they were obeying the 'law' of survival. "To preserve one's life is generally speaking a duty," the judge replied, "but it may be the plainest and highest duty to sacrifice it."[108] "Who is to be the judge of this sort of necessity? By what measure is the comparative value of lives to be measured: Is it to be strength, or intellect, or what? It is plain that the principle leaves to him who is to profit by it to determine the necessity which will justify him in deliberately taking another man's life to save his own. In this case, the weakest, the youngest, the most unresisting was chosen."[109]

The court's objection, here, was not so much to the fact of eating the cabin boy as to the fact that the defendants were urging the right of every Englishman to decide or perceive for himself how and when he might save himself by killing another. Indeed, the court was more than sympathetic to Dudley and Stephens' consumption of Parker under the circumstances, and freely conceded that "if the men had not fed upon the body of the body they would probably not have survived" and that "the boy being in a much weaker condition was likely to have died before them."[110] "It is not suggested," said Lord Coleridge, the Chief Justice, "that in this particular case, the deeds were 'devilish', but it is quite plain that such a principle, once admitted, might be made the legal cloak for unbridled passion and atrocious crime."[111]

What Principle?

A Christian applying his religious system of rules to the case might say that the principle to be applied to this order-change conflict must be one which is responsive to the question of whether a man can ever justify the taking of the life of another to save his own. The Holy Scripture and the perceived word of God provide a Christian with a definitive, negative answer, an answer that depends for its verification on divine revelation or edict, not on the opinion or reason of man. Hear again the 'comfortable words' of St Thomas: "Because, by reason of the uncertainty of human judgment, especially on contingent and particular matters, different people from different judgments on human acts; whence also different and contrary laws result...therefore, that many may know without any doubt what he ought to do and what he ought to avoid, it was necessary for man to be directed in his proper acts by a law given by God, for it is certain that such a law cannot err."[112] What God-given law can be clearer than that 'thou shalt not kill'? And what greater comfort than the assurance that this law is incapable of error?

A Darwinian social scientist might see the issue in other terms: "Can the physical survival of the fitter be justification for a deliberate policy of eliminating the weaker?" An anthropologist might answer the issue as he saw it by evidence that cannibalism under such circumstances is 'normal', while a dietician, seeing and answering the issue within his frame of reference would presumably decide that Parker was 'digestible' and 'nutritious'. Each answer would reflect the preoccupation of a system of order with applying its objective data and the rules derived therefrom, its 'laws', to the dilemma posed by Dudley's and Stephens' conduct. In each of these instances, the answer would be provided by some system of order, which at least to its exponents, rests upon objectively or scientifically verifiable (or divinely revealed) data. Whatever the answer, it would claim to be more than a matter of opinion. Can third-party law in Dudley and Stephens' case make such a claim?

Some societies, particularly those of the civil law system, do make special definitive provisions in their criminal codes which exempt from punishment persons who injure or kill another to save their own life.[113] Such a code cannot claim the authority of scientific verification, but it does somewhat restrict the judges in the exercise of their discretion. But not very much. The codes still leave wide open such key questions as whether, in a given circumstance, the decision to kill another was reasonably taken to save one's own. Suppose, for example, you were adrift for three weeks and thought you could hold out no longer.

But no sooner had you killed the cabin boy than a rescue ship loomed over the horizon. Should have waited a bit longer? Would you then have risked being too weak to act? Could you be expected to have gauged exactly how long you could hold out? Should the impairment of your judgment by hunger be taken into account? Questions like these still require answers perceivable only subjectively, and in the circumstances of each particular case. They require, in other words, the employment of the third-party decision-making system.

The English court, however, was even more on its own. Being part of the common-law system, it had the benefit of no pre-existing statutes or codes comparable to those in Greece, China, Germany, or Japan. The judges did not, subjectively, *feel* particularly repelled by the defendants' conduct; but they did fear the effect on the legal *process* of deciding the case as in the British common-law system the judges were free to decide it) in such a way as to legalise the defendants' act. To do so, they suspected, would establish each man as judge and executioner of those of his fellows who happened to be in the same boat.

Typically, the court solved its dilemma pragmatically. It set in motion a process involving judges, the attorney general, and the Queen. First, the judges reaffirmed the general rule that necessity does not excuse murder, and proceeded to pass a sentence of death upon the prisoners.[114] This did more than provide technical compliance with Mr Justice Cardozo's rule "that there shall be no breach of the legal order in the house of its custodians."

It made clear that each man could not with finality judge or perceive the law for himself, particularly in such a way as to affect the lives of others. In this sense, law—a principle of general applicability—was made. At the same time, the court subtly recommended that the Sovereign (i.e., the law officers of the government) might exercise "that prerogative of mercy which the constitution has entrusted to the hands fittest to dispense it."[115]

The sentence of hanging was promptly commuted to six months' imprisonment, these having already been served. The legal principle must thus be seen both within and without the context of its specific instance of application. Given somewhat different facts, the application of logically consistent reasoning, applying the same principle, could conceivably hang a defendant.

It is in this sense impossible to state precisely what emerged as the 'law' in *Regina v. Stephens* so long as we persist in trying to think of the law as a table of consequences guiding us unambiguously to clear knowledge of the legal implications of everything we do nor might conceivably contemplate. The law is both more and less, but it is not this. We do know from *Stephens* that the British, like the Greek or Chinese, the legal system does not fail to sympathise with men who commit murder in the struggle for survival, that murder under the pressure of necessity is not necessarily treated like ordinary murder, but that the law reserved strictly for its official and impartial law perceivers the right to decide whether, in any particular case and taking into account all the circumstances, the drastic act and its method of execution were excusable. The result is only a shade different from that of the Greek or Chinese codes.

In both, there is a final impartial determination of whether the survival-killing was 'reasonable' and 'necessary' in the circumstances. The British process creates a sort of presumption against reasonableness and necessity while the codes apply the general presumption in favour of the defendant. But both say to him: If you kill to survive, the law neither simply excuses nor condemns your act but leaves you to convince impartial judges (or jurors) of its verifiable reason and necessity. Inevitably, the first judgment is passed by the men in the boat who must decide whether to sacrifice the cabin boy. The court acknowledges this as a logistic fact placing the crew on notice that their actions must be very clearly *justifiable* according to the lights, the subjective values, and opinions of their society as perceived by its judiciary.

This litigation has its American counterpart in *U.S. v. Holmes*,[116] where the result was much the same. Both cases illustrate the crucial role of third-party decision-making in bringing the legal system to bear on the lives of individuals caught up in the potential chaos of the order-change dilemma. But they also tell us something of great importance about the third-party system itself, something that explains both its great strength and its concomitant weakness. Both cases hadtwo factors that give third-party law its special character as a system of order creation:

1. Third-party decisions are to a very important extent determined by specific events which give rise to them (viz, it is existential and phenomenological).
2. Third-party decisions, although they strive to establish principles of general applicability, are fallible and changeable, subject always to interpretation, and often, in time, to reversal and revision.

Third-party law is born of a specific conflict. This is not to say that third-party law affords no generalised answers outside the context of particular disputes. We have already noted that a reservoir of reasoned, consistent principles is essential to a legal system. Landmark judgments make *any* producer of ginger beer responsible for snails found at the bottom of his bottles by a startled consumer, and make *any* touching of another in anger an assault. Relatively little, however, is that clear, and even these landmark judgments are not closed doors to future reconsideration or reinterpretation in the light of changing perceptions of order. Specifically, until all the facts, mitigations, public policy, and equities had been argued, rebutted, and weighed in the *Regina v. Stephens* litigation, who could have known with complete certainty how the law would resolve that particular conflict?

True, *Regina v. Stephens* poses unusual, even bizarre facts, which complicate the task of predicting the law. But most litigation proceeds on 'unusual' facts—on conflicts just sufficiently different from those resolved by the limited or ambiguous terms of a code, a statute, or another judicial decision to make men ready once more to join issue with gown and periwig.

Chapter 13

No man can point to any law in the US by which slavery was established. Men first make slaves and then made laws.
Frederick Douglass, alias Frederick Augustus Washington Bailey, former slave (1817–95) in a speech in Washington (1889)

By its very nature, litigation counterposes two parties, mostly acting in good faith and out of pocket, who have made opposite plausible predictions as to how the application of a statute, a code, or one or more principles will resolve their particular *order-change* conflict. Since few cases ever incorporate identically all the elements of an earlier case, and since there is often more than one plausible principle that could be applied to yield opposite solutions to a dispute, new disputes frequently call for new appeals to a third-party process that alone can quickly and relevantly find new answers to new issues, adapt old ones to changing social circumstances, or choose reasonably between competing solutions.

In this sense, the third party is the translator in a dialogue between general principles and mores on the one hand and specific legal effects on the other. But the courts as translators offer a peculiarly crucial service, for they do not merely repeat, but *add creatively to* the dialogue.

The school segregation cases demonstrate this clearly. In *Brown v. Board of Education of Topeka*,[117] four cases from various states dealing with the same issue were joined. The Supreme Court of the United States had to decide whether Negro children were being denied the right assured them, under the Fourteenth Amendment to the constitution, to 'equal protection under the laws' by state legislation assigning them to public school facilities separate and segregated from those provided for white children.

The issue of segregation was not new to the United States Supreme Court. Fifty-eight years earlier, in *Plessy v. Ferguson*,[118] it had been asked to decide the validity of a Louisiana statute requiring equal but separate accommodations for black and white train passengers. Supreme Court Justice Brown wrote in 1896 that such a law was constitutional and did not deny the Negro 'equal protection of the laws'.

The object of the Fourteenth Amendment, he said, was undoubtedly to enforce the absolute equality of the two races before the law, but in the nature of things it could not have been intended to abolish distinctions based upon colour or to enforce social as distinguished from political equality, or a commingling of the two races upon terms unsatisfactory to either. Laws permitting, and even requiring, their separation in places where they are liable to be brought into contact do not necessarily imply the inferiority of either race to the other…[119]

We consider the underlying fallacy of the plaintiff's argument to consist in the assumption that the enforced separation of the two races stamps the coloured race with a badge of inferiority. If this be so, it is…solely because the coloured race chooses to put that construction upon it.[120]

Plessy v. Ferguson continued to control United States judicial decisions until, in 1954, the Supreme Court at last decided that 'separate but equal' facilities no longer provided 'equal protection'.

What had changed? The constitution had not. The issues had not. But times had. At the time of *Plessy v. Ferguson*, the southern Negro had just been emancipated from slavery. Economically, socially, and intellectually, the horizon he was able to see was one still limited by his imposed past, as were his aspirations. It could be argued that integration was not a real objective for the southern Negro of the 1890s and that its denial therefore constituted no hardship—merely the recognition of social, economic, or intellectual facts, rather like poverty or ignorance, which also operate to segregate persons.

Since then, and despite all the handicaps society and economics could devise, the black man has pushed aside many of the artificially constructed barriers of poverty and ignorance that limited his horizon. By 1954, if not in fact much earlier, the separation of the black man could no longer be defended on the basis of his shortcomings, but only because of those of prejudiced whites. 'Today', Chief Justice Warren said in the *Brown* case, "many black men have achieved outstanding success in the arts and sciences as well as in the business and professional world."[121] It does not matter to these people that these separate facilities they 'enjoy' are in every way equal to those provided by whites. "We must look instead to the effect of segregation itself...upon the Negro."[122] Speaking of black schoolchildren, the Chief Justice said:

To separate them from others of similar age... [is to imply] inferiority as to their status in the community that may affect their hearts and minds in a way unlikely ever to be undone... Whatever may have been the extent of psychological knowledge at the time of Plessy v. Ferguson, this finding is amply supported by modern authority.[123]

What changed between 1896 and 1954 was the status of the American Negro, and the knowledge available to man. Therefore, a new result, appropriate to the specific circumstances of this conflict between *order* and *change* in 1954, was obtained. "The old order changeth, yielding place to new," Tennyson said. The old opinion had to yield to the new opinion. "How long so ever it hath continued," a right-minded if somewhat too optimistic sixteenth-century British Lord Chancellor remarked of the judicial precedent, "if it be against reason, it is of no force in law."[124]

Yet, in continuing its consideration of the problem a year later, the Supreme Court[125] again emphasised the existential, process-oriented nature of third-party law. The objective, the legal principle, was defined clearly enough: "All provisions of federal, state or local law requiring or permitting discrimination must yield..."[126]

But even so, what the judges were declaring was a legal principle subject to further judicial editing in the specific instance. Indeed, the decision specifically invites such editing by proclaiming that "While...the courts will require that the [states] make a prompt and reasonable start towards full compliance...once such a start has been made, the courts may find that additional time is necessary to carry out the rulings in an effective manner."[127] The law as to integration thus remains a *process*, to which the third-party law beyond the moment of decision is never the decision itself but only the fact of the human process by which it is made.

Third-party law, unlike the other order-creating systems, can only be understood as a process—and a fallible, existential human process at that—rather than a compendium of rules that are certain and immutable. Principles, concepts and evidences, there are, but certainty is impossible, even if it were desirable, and immutability is undesirable, even if it were possible.

How does the process of the *law* differ from the process of other order-creating systems such as religion or science? Surely their *rules* also evolve to take into account new revelations and new discoveries? Of course, they do. But it is in the *source* of change that the law differs from the rules of other systems of social order. Religions have traditionally claimed to receive new revelation from a source of ultimate truth. Each revelation of religion is, of course, new to man, but since it—its ultimate validity—resides outside the time-space continuum, it cannot be 'new' but only newly revealed to man. Neither can it be mistaken or wrong, for what exists, exists not only temporally in space, but eternally in God.

St Thomas was forced to the conclusion that "even an unjust law, in so far as it retains some appearance of law, through being framed by one who is in power, is derived from the eternal law; for all power is from the Lord God…"[128] Science, too, like religion, *discovers* data, new to the discoverer, but that has always lain like a shell on the beach, waiting for someone with a trained eye to come along and pick it up. This data both pre-existed discovery by man and owes its validity to something more than mortal perception of it. The rules of science are claimed by traditional scientists to be purely descriptive of what *is*. What is true *is*, and what is, is *true*.

But the law made by a court, on the other hand, is *new* in that it neither had nor claimed to have, any existence—except in the human, contingent condition of reason applying principle to social data—before being proclaimed by a judge. A law so made, unlike a rule of science or religion, cannot be objectively verified but can be amended or repealed. In that sense, the law never can aspire to such a pure state of being as permits the scientist with certainty to fix a rule describing for all time the boiling point of water at sea level. The 'is' is of the law at any given moment, like the man himself, consists of a historic past, an existential present, and an aspirational future—and all three of these ingredients are in constant development and motion defying the legal 'scientist' to fix them to the page in immutable rules.

Law is more a *process* than it is a system of *rules*. This distinguishes third-party law from other systems of order creation. What a momentous difference! Almost alone in the ordering systems, law neither seeks nor claims validity outside the fact of its existential being. Law is thus, literally, humanised: bound to man in a common awareness that its validity is always limited to a specific, self-determined, or free act in a given moment of time and relevant to a single point in the continuum of change. This is not to say that the law, any more than the human self, must be seen as nothing but a series of *actes gratuits*.

As Dr Bronowski said of the human self, so of the law: "A self must have some consistency: its actions tomorrow must be recognisably a piece with the actions it carried out yesterday."[129] Man, in his freedom, tends to act with a broadly characteristic consistency, which is why, among other things, he invented law and why it continues to be a generally workable process, one making as much use as possible of generally acceptable, mutually affirming principles.

The law, as a process, treats primarily the *currently possible*: that which reasonable men may reasonably be expected to do in good faith at *this* moment in *these* circumstances. It is attributed to the *currently possible* no inferiority in relation to an abstract perfection or truth. Most religions, in contrast, regard what is, the imperfect, conditional present state of being as something that, while falling short of the dogmatically or naturally revealed normative absolute—'the way things ought to be'—can be brought into closer harmony with the absolute through expiation, contrition, good works, faith, or right-reason.

In medical science, a universally *True* measure of human 'normalcy' is the measure of us all. Those who fall short can often be 'normalised' through therapy or surgery. Religion abhors apostasy, and medicine, abnormalcy; the role of the priest and the doctor is to discover universally valid norms, and to bring their flocks toward them, meanwhile teaching them through expiation or therapy to alleviate the temporising limitations and imperfections of the debased *currently possible*.

The adjudicative process, on the other hand, embraces imperfection insofar as it embodies the existential *currently possible*. The *Brown* case sets up no creed. Integration is an objective, but it is not invested with eternal or infinite validity or specific certainty. It does create a principle, but one that suggests mutable probabilities, not fixed certainties.

It is not possible, and certainly not prudent, to speak of judge-made law in the terms of religious revelation or scientific verification: as Truth, which "was in the beginning, is now, and shall ever be."

The uniqueness of existential relativism in the order-creating system of judge-made law must not, of course, be overstressed. No art, no system of problem-solving is ever entirely creedal. All involve an element of the process, of interpreting the general rules in the light of specific facts. Every religion, every science, every political creed has its human, pragmatic element. Theologians, operating under a system of divine law and eternal revelation nevertheless differ bitterly as to its meaning in specific situations of *order-change* conflict.

Marxists, armed with a complete and infallible blueprint for development, find themselves in open schism over its application to military argocommunes, peaceful coexistence, consumer industry, and managerial decentralisation. Doctors, operating within spheres of scientifically verifiable data, disagree as to its meaning and relevance in resolving such scientific problems as the merits of live *versus* dead virus serums, the connection between smoking and cancer or cholesterol and heart disease, or the value and role of outpatient therapy.

Unlike the law, however, the processes of religion, politics, and sometimes even science and the arts tend to obscure to the outsider their pragmatic aspect when stress is laid on the *rule* as an absolute rather than on the *process* as a relativist experiment. Illustratively, John Ruskin, in *The Stones of Venice*, begins a chapter entitled 'The Virtues of Architecture' with these words:

We address ourselves, then, first to the task of determining some law of right, which we may apply to the architecture of all the world and of all time; and by help of which, we may as easily pronounce whether a building is good or noble, as, by applying a plumb-line, whether it be perpendicular.[130]

Ruskin really believed that such a rule both exists and can be perceived by man. Change, the *ex post facto* and human 'third-party' element, is no doubt accepted as necessary by every system, but to many, it also is embarrassing, for it involves either an admission of a change in the things perceived—a change that by definition is impossible for the system's authors to admit without admitting that its components are not absolutes—or an admission of prior error in their *perception* of the true order.

An admission of such error, or of the possibility of error, tends to shock us and detract from the prestige of the system. Most of us would not like our doctors to speak of our upcoming operation as an experiment, or of a prescription as an informed hunch, even if this were a more honest description of what doctors in fact do. We *want* a rule that is scientific, divine and eternal to be objectively valid, not merely the reasonable, practical, principled opinion of a man in an instant situation.

Consumer research into the merchandising of ideas would show that 'Truth' outsells 'reason' ten to one; for one thing, it can be packaged so much more neatly, without a lot of modifying, temporising clauses to clutter its appearance. For another, once purchased, it lasts forever, whereas the products of reason are forever wearing things, breaking down, going out of fashion or having to be replaced because they prove no longer to fit.[131]

Most Western and some Eastern religions are based on principles they witness to be *divine* and *eternal*. Often their claim to divinity and eternity looms far more important than the actual substantive content of their beliefs. Without the seal of divinity, the creed is no creed at all. The Churches themselves draw the issue: Either Christ was God, or he was a liar, or mad. His validity cannot be saved by the temporal reasonableness of his teachings.

The Church of England, for example, defends to the last drop of candlewax and grain of incense its status as part of the one true Apostolic Catholic church; for who would bow to a creed, however 'workable', born by the lust of a king? Protestantism, too, thrives on the certainty that it alone is rooted in the transcendental, transcribed words of Christ and his apostles; that its faith is purified in a stream flowing from the scriptural Godhead. In its certainty that each man can learn the Truth through the direct inspiration of Christ and scripture, Protestantism, at least in its more fundamental forms, postulates the infallibility of *everybody*. Roman Catholicism, for its part, is somewhat more elite, but scarcely less certain. Since the right-reason is not equally at the disposal of all, but varies according to learning and intellectual capacity, there are some in society who will know more of the natural law and understand its application in particular conflicts better than the masses.

Medical science, political theory and religion, do undergo change and do have a process of conflict resolution, but their pragmatic element is still for the moment less apparent to the eye of the laity than that of the law has become. This is not entirely their fault. Attempts have been made by scientists themselves, Roger Penrose, Daniel Dennett and Dr Bronowski, to take the public into the scientists' confidence.

The latter said that scientific truth, like legal truth, "is not there to be found, once for all, like a lost umbrella," and that science too, is a process whose values "are generated by the search and not by the findings, that the nature of life is to be found in ambiguity and change," but that we "get rid of ambiguity in science by decision. We make provisional assertions that the world is organised in such a way and not in a more complex way, and we give to these inductions a status which we cannot justify but which justifies itself by success—so long as the success continues."

Bronowski could have well been speaking of the law (or any other branch of human knowledge looking at itself honestly). The reason his insights can be generalised in this way is that their ability lies not within any particular discipline but in the nature of the human condition. As he says:

It is plain that it is not possible for the brain to arrive at certain knowledge. All those formal systems, in mathematics and physics and the philosophy of science, which claim to give foundations for certain truth are surely mistaken. I am tempted to say that we do not look for truth but for knowledge. But I dislike this form of words for two reasons. First of all, we do look for truth, however we define it; it is what we find that is knowledge. And second, what we fail to find is not truth but certainty; the nature of truth is exactly the knowledge that we do not find.[132]

Although the vocabulary is different, the message here is exactly the same as ours, and it comes as a fresh breeze blowing through the heavy, musty drapes of our ignorance.

Some scientific truths, at least, are absolutes in the sense that they are readily and continuously discoverable and verifiable by man. The pot of water at sea level boils at the same temperature today as in Cleopatra's day, regardless of the opinions, culture, or status of the beholder. But much scientific and political theory is of a different cast—a man-made hypothesis, not an eternal absolute *discovered* by man. These formulated 'truths' must yield to change under exactly the same pressures as the 'separate but equal' doctrine of *Plessy v. Ferguson*—the movement of time, knowledge and the human condition. Yet science and religion do not undergo change nearly so visibly as does the law—and when change comes to them, it is not because the former 'Truth', but merely its perception by scientists and priests, was faulty—something the perceivers do not particularly like to admit to the world.

Paul Valéry, in *Socrates and His Physician*, has the dying Socrates say to his doctor, who is assuring him of his imminent recovery:

I marvel at what you must be, you and your medicine, in order to obtain from my nature that blessed oracle and to have a presentiment of its propensity for the better. This body, which is mine, confides and entrusts itself to you and not to myself; to which it only addresses itself in the form of troubles, fatigues and which it can utter when it is displeased... While it tells you clearly what it wishes and does not wish and know its state. It is strange that you should know a thousand times more than I do about myself, and that I should be as it were transparent to the light of your knowledge, while I am for myself quite obscure and opaque. Nay more: you even see that which I not yet am, and you assign to my body a certain good, to which it must make its way, as though on your orders and at such and such a moment fixed by you.

This classically remains the illusion most of us harbour about our doctors and scientists and which many of them are not too modest to confirm.

But law as we know it in Britain and the United States and as it is understood in most of the world has, on the other hand, become undisguisedly a pragmatic human process. It is made by men, and it lays no claim to divine origin or eternal validity. In history, law-making has clearly and unashamedly laid its process bare before the public. Judges are constantly reversed on appeal by other judges, which is to say they are held to be wrong—but only in a non-absolute sense. Courts frequently refuse to follow prior decisions because, for one reason or another, they are no longer immediately valid, which is to say they are not, and never were meant to be, eternal.

When judge-made law is changed or reversed by another judge, it is not because the first judge wrongly perceived a right principle, but because the principle either was unsatisfactory even at the time the judge proclaimed it or more likely, because changes within the time-space continuum make it unsatisfactory today. The same principle, even, or particularly, when applied with reasoned consistency, can frequently be seen to lead to different results in different existential moments of decision.

The frankness with which the human and fallible element is admitted and dramatisedin decision-making is unique among the problem-solving arts. It is the strength of the system, for it makes for a certain vigorous flexibility, and it places the emphasis on the only part of the system that can hope for stability: its process. Judges whose decisions are changed, reversed, overruled, or distinguished by other judges, do not stand accused of propounding an Untruth or of misperceiving a Truth. Their opinion has simply been supplanted by another opinion. Under the circumstances, it is not surprising that a judge reversed does not generally rally armies, lead schisms, or try to disbar his brothers.

Lawyers and professors who disagree with a court are not burned, exiled, or excluded from their profession when they continue to advocate their disagreement in the pages of the learned journals or the rallies in the marketplace. Their day may well come, and when it does, 'the past', to quote Jacob Bronowski, again, will be 'respected in the present' because it is accepted as part of the emphasis on *process* that "the process of discovery is more important than any discovery."[133] The relationship between process and discovery was cryptically put by Wittgenstein in his *Philosophical Investigations* as follows:

The results of philosophy are the uncovering of one or another piece of plain nonsense and bumps that the understanding has got by running its head up against the limits of language. These bumps make us see the value of discovery.

The development of the law is not infrequently a 'bumpy ride'. It is to be hoped that we get there in the end!

Chapter 14

Four things belong to a judge: to hear courteously, to answer wisely, to consider soberly, and to decide impartially.

Socrates

Judges must be aware of hard constructions and strained inferences; for there is no worse torture than the torture of laws.

Francis Bacon

I have always said that advocacy is like a battle. You plan at best you can in advance, when the battle takes place, nobody can quite foresee which way the tide will flow.

George Carman QC, BBC Radio 4 (8 June 1999)

Lawyers and judges may disagree, and vociferously. But if they are talking about the law, the statement of their disagreements, perforce, customarily proceeds with the weapons of hypothesis or preference rather than truth and certainty, which is a most significant form of rhetorical de-escalation.

On the other hand, that no judicial decision is ever 'final', that the law both follows the event (is not eternal or certain) and is made by man (is not divine or True) cannot be so publicly, frankly, and continuously revealed to the profession and to the general public except at some cost. That cost is a certain cynicism, intellectually classified as 'legal realism', which is handsomely shaped by Judge Holmes' dictum, probably the most famous quotation in the history of the law that "The prophecies of what the courts will do in fact, and nothing more pretentious, are what I mean by, the law."[134]

The legal realists, like the social realist painters, believe that maximum public exposure of frailties and shortcomings is right in itself, but is also a step in the direction of adjustment and progress. Theirs is a subtle blend of morality touched with exhibitionism, and they have succeeded in laying bare for all to see, the imperfections, the temporisations, in short: the essentially human quality of the judicial process. Some of them have done so to the exclusion of all the higher rational and intuitive human qualities of the third-party process.

The more extreme cultists seem sometimes to be saying that "the law is what the judges had for breakfast"—a judicial whim. They deny both the claim of codes and statutes to be considered *law* and the existence of any element of consistency in judicial logic and social policy. These they abjure as vigorously as they deny divine inspiration or eternal truth. They do not admit that statutes, codes, prior decisions of courts, and the principles of cultural morality and reciprocity do appeal to a judicial instinct for philosophical consistency (or, at its least, for professional conformity). Neither do they admit the existence of a creative philosophical framework both concerned with looking forward to the objectives, the meaning and ends of man and society, and over its shoulder at past judicial behaviour; at patterns of conduct, at statutory language, and at other sources of norms.

The extreme realists are, of course, wrong. Judges do generally operate within a creative philosophical framework and use reasonable, mutually re-enforcing concepts. They are not merely reacting to each conflict before them as an electric eel does to danger. Rational man's judgments are not whims, not purely organic reactions to viscerally sensed stimuli.

More important than that the extremists are wrong that they are defeatists. Any definition of the third-party law-making system that excludes the creative role of the judge as a social philosopher is a poor route map for society's progress. In throwing out the divine element in the law and bringing it down to the level of man, at least some legal realists have set their measure of man too low. The alternative to God-made legal theory is not necessarily man-made legal whim. Man, whether or not actually made in the image of God, is able to formulate and pursue enunciated ends with ethical, principled reason, and man's pursuit of a philosophical constant only varies from God's in that it is, *and should be seen to be*, his working hypothesis and not an ultimate or absolute truth. Thus, man is both more limited and more free than God, for man is free to judge both God and himself, while God can judge only man.

Meanwhile, let us reaffirm that while we do not adopt the extreme 'realist' posture, we nevertheless walk part of the way with realism, agreeing that third-party law is, and should candidly be, presented to the public as a human process and not an inspired system of rules or scientific 'fact'. Having taken this stand, the lawyer must not be surprised that his system is more open to challenge, and less likely to inspire unquestioning mass loyalty than other less candidly process-centred order-creating systems. The central figure in our system is the decision-maker, a man who is neither as infallible as God nor, usually, quite as democratically responsive to the will and whim of the public as a legislator. His extraordinarily powerful role in a sophisticated legal system can therefore only be understood by an extraordinarily sophisticated community.

It is for this reason that the law itself so long hesitated before publicly admitting the public to look at its core of fallible human process, preferring to clothe itself in an aura of metaphysical certainty. To understand fully the impact of legal realism on the third-party law-making system, it is necessary to look back to an earlier period, when the law was less candid in revealing its temporal origins, and when its place in the community was propped up by pretensions to divine origin and sanction.

Judge Cardozo reminded us that in a debate between a lawyer and a doctor in thirteenth-century Florence the lawyer maintained that medicine is not a science at all, for it "keeps growing not merely by the use of man's noble reason, but by magic inventions and by daily experiments," that it is, in short, mutable, while the law, by contrast, is a science, because "it proceeds by definitions and divisions and since it has its universals which cannot be otherwise." To this Cardozo remarks: "The tables have been turned with a vengeance since those days."[135] They have, indeed! They began to turn when the law broke away from religion and certainty.

In Europe and early feudal England, the origins of modern judicial systems were likewise swaddled in the divine mystique. The swearing of oaths, not only by the parties to litigation but also by their kinsmen, constituted a direct appeal to a higher judge. Up until the Lateran Council of 1215 the clergy performed a vital part in the trials by ordeal, where supernatural 'proof' was obtained by observing parties subjected to submersion in water or boiling oil.

Trial by combat was another early means by which disputes could seem to be referred to divine judgment. Its theory is described by Thayer as follows:

The plaintiff offers battle and puts forward a champion who is a complaint-witness, and who speaks as of his personal knowledge...and stands ready to fight for his testimony. Before the battle the two champions swear to the truth of what they say.

In the mother-country, Normandy, one might hire his champion; but in England, theoretically, it was not allowed. In 220 one Elias Piggun was convicted of being a hired champion, and lost his foot... What was thus forbidden seems, however, to have been much practiced...[136]

It is surprising how long this particular pursuit of the ephemeral shadow of legal certainty continued. As late as 1819, the English Court of King's Bench in the case of *Ashford v. Thornton*[137] had occasion to engage in a full discussion of the practice of judicial battle, and *approved* it! Not until 22 June 1819, was the custom ended by a statute which concluded that "trial by battle in any suit is a mode of trial unfit to be used; and it is expedient that the same should be wholly abolished."[138]

Men have never ceased to nominate God for the job of society's Law Perceiver. The craving among men for the certainty a theory of natural or divinely-inspired law affords is a phenomenon an understanding of which is absolutely fundamental to any realistic appreciation of the trouble that ordinary, humanistic judge-made law faces in being accepted by world society.

The question of a divine imprimatur on law has traditionally proceeded from two related motives: the need for certainty and the need for sanction. Both motives, but particularly the latter, found expression in the doctrine of the Divine Right of Kings, so prevalent in the period of the Middle Ages that saw national monarchs vying on the one hand with bishops in the service of a Roman empire and on the other with parochial feudal barons.

Kings maintained that they, rather than the bishops or the barons, held a warrant from God and that the ultimate source of legality was, therefore, their royal command. King Charles I, in his final dramatic bid to escape the death sentence of Cromwell's court, argued fervently that "this day's proceedings cannot be warranted by God's laws; for, on the contrary, the authority of obedience unto Kings is clearly warranted and strictly commanded in both the Old and New Testament."[139]

Unhappily for Charles I, his vision of himself as the jurisprudential fountainhead was not shared by the judges at his trial. That same abrasive scepticism with which the English judges regarded the royal pretensions to divine legal sanction, they were not, however, nearly so ready to use on themselves. Under the title of natural law and in the very thick of the Age of Reason, jurists continued lovingly to nurture what Roscoe Pound has characterised as the "conception of a set of fundamental legal principles of universal validity for all men, in all places, in all times..."[140] They did not, of course, escape vociferous criticism any more than did the kings before them or the bishops before the kings.

Natural law—human law divinely valid—is defined by a cynical Jeremy Bentham as the device "for prevailing upon the reader to accept of the author's sentiment or opinion as a reason for itself."[141] It is, he said, "an obscure phantom, which, in the imagination of those who go in chase of it, points sometimes to manners, sometimes to laws, sometimes to what the law is, sometimes to what it ought to be."

Is the comment unfair?

In the beginning, one must carefully distinguish between the *natural* law of which we now speak and the *divine* law. Divine law, which is properly within the system of religion, can be defined as a system which is with clarity and certainty given by God to man through revelation and faith because it transcends the power of man to attain it through reason. Natural law, which is properly within the system we call law, is defined by St Thomas Aquinas in his essay 'On the Various Kinds of Law' as the product of "the light of natural reason, whereby we discern what is good and what is evil... [It] is nothing else than an imprint on us of the divine light. It is therefore evident that the natural law is nothing else than the rational creature's participation of the eternal law."

This emphasis on the rational discernibility of natural law through right-reason is important because it extends the ambit of the True far beyond the relatively narrow range of scriptural and other theological revelation and into the area of law, which appears to us in the form of human reason. Not only these great mysteries of God's relation with man to which divine law provides an answer are resolvable by reference to external verity, but even the ordinary everyday conflicts between men and men, which yield to right-reason. For, according to the natural law system, right-reason also perceives eternal verities.

St Thomas Aquinas does not try to evade this paradox, but this explanation is not entirely satisfying. "The human reason," he said, "cannot have a full participation of the dictates of the Divine Reason, but according to its own mode, and imperfectly... Man has a natural participation in the eternal law, according to certain general principles, but not as regards the particular determination of individual cases, which are, however, contained in the eternal law."[142] Therefore, St Thomas concludes:

> *We must say that the natural law, as to general principles, is the same for all, both as to rectitude and as to knowledge. But as to certain matters of detail, which are conclusive, as it were, of those general principles, although it is the same for all...yet in some few cases it may fail...since in some the reason is perverted by passion, or evil habit, or an evil disposition of nature. Thus formerly, theft, although it is expressly contrary to the natural law, was not considered wrong among the Germans...*[143]

Today, this explanation would run into heavy weather; a majority of people and states now favour the taking of property under certain circumstances without necessarily paying full compensation (the progressive tax, nationalisation of industries, etc.). On the other hand, a fundamental form of 'theft'—the taking of man's freedom through enslavement—was not thought to violate the law perceived by the common right-reason of mankind in St Thomas' day, but is certainly popularly so regarded today. There are other examples given by Aquinas which are scarcely more successful.

In his essay 'On the Natural Law', the Fourth Article, he declares that it is a fundamental natural law that goods held in trust for an owner must always be restored to him, except in the event that they would be used in fighting against one's country. This chauvinism and the rigid insistence on indefeasible property title sound strangely obsolete for a principle that is supposed to be eternal. All the more so does his definition of the 'just war', which is hopelessly archaic if not downright immoral in the age of the United Nations Charter.

One can, of course, say that Aquinas was mistaken in his examples of natural law without thereby having proved that natural law does not exist. The most and least that can be said is this: The proponents of natural law have yet to produce a single example of a law that is accepted by all reasoning societies, everywhere, at all times, and in all places. So long as the examples are of laws subject to being overtaken by change, just as human law changes, those laws show themselves not to be immutable and therefore *not* eternal. The dilemma of the natural lawyer thus remains unresolved, although the craving for eternal certainty and sanction still sends great jurisprudential explorers forth, lemming-like, in search of the law's equivalent of the lost continent Atlantis.

But what's the harm in that? The alleged uncertainty of the content of natural law is not, after all, demonstrably much greater than that of judicial third-party law. Indeed, it differs from 'rational' legal deduction only in attributing its validity to divine logic rather than to human reason. Even if natural law and human law are both prone to inconsistency, vagueness, confusion of the 'is' and the 'ought', and a tendency to fuse morality, manners, and law, what does it matter if it is called one thing by some and another by others? But it is just because natural law suffers from the same defects as human law that doubt is cast upon the claim of 'natural lawyers' that men can, by 'right-reason', perceive a higher system of legality. An ugly duckling only becomes the homelier for insisting it is a beautiful swan.

And, unfortunately, the illusion of certainty in 'natural law', when resorted to, as it frequently was and sometimes still is, serves the judges in the way it did the kings and bishops, as 'a sufficient reason for itself'—an opinion that needs no further justification. Take, for example, the English High Court decision in the case of *Lepre v. Lepre*.[144] In this case, the British court was faced with a request to give effect to the decision of a Malta court in a matrimonial matter.

Since the Malta court had jurisdiction, the British judges would ordinarily not hesitate to implement the decree of a fellow judge in another part of the British Commonwealth. In this instance, however, it was decided to ignore the Malta decision and award a conflicting judgment of alimony—which is based on the existence of a valid marriage—to the plaintiff, even though her marriage had earlier been annulled by the Maltese court. Why did the English bench refuse in this exceptional instance to honour the earlier Maltese decision? Because, the judge said as if this were a self-evident and sufficient explanation, "The Maltese decree offends our notions of *natural justice*…"

What was this dreadful, self-evidently offensive thing the Maltese court had done? It followed canonic or church law, which is part of the law of Malta, in holding that a civil marriage in Malta, without clergy or sacrament, is invalid. This the church holds to be the law of God; Malta accordingly accepts it as the law of the state, since the law of man must conform to the natural law.

The English judges, being of a different inclination, considered that Malta's rule offends against *natural justice*—which is natural law by another name! And so, we find the natural law as manifest in Malta to be violative of the natural law as it is manifest in England! Is God speaking with two voices? The very question raises another: Was all this judicial talk about 'natural law' or 'natural justice' not a waste of time for all concerned, time which might better be spent facing openly such issues as the happiness of the parties and the social policy toward family and marriage? Was it not an escape from reason to false certainty?

But, it is said, if we do not, in fact, have access to a natural or certain, eternal, True system of law, we must at least pretend that we do, otherwise society would disintegrate. In the best of all possible worlds, men may reason their way forward toward greater happiness for the greater number with tentative opinions and experimental hypotheses. This may work in a free, pragmatic, liberal society. But what happens when liberal pragmatism meets positivistic, dogmatic evil?

Nazi Germany, with its lawfully enacted, constitutionally sanctions system of evil was just such a situation. In that aberrational society, the waging of aggressive war, the bombing of open cities, execution of prisoners and extermination of six million Jews was carried out under the aegis of positive law. Faced with such repulsive man-made law, humanity turns, historically, to a higher 'natural' law to void the effect and punish the promulgators and executors of the evil decrees.

The Nuremberg trials, which sentenced Nazi leaders to prison and execution for carrying out the law of the land, is often cited as an example of the need for an eternal natural law to take precedence over positivistic man-enacted evil. Only if there is a higher law, it is argued, a natural law, can the citizen have the right to disobey evil laws and punish evil lawmakers.

It is this that Sophocles caused Antigone to debate with Creone after she had violated his law by giving burial to her brother:

Nor did I deem thy edicts strong enough
Coming from mortal man, to set at nought
The unwritten laws of God that know not change.
They are not of today nor yesterday,
But live forever, nor can man assign
When first they sprang to being.

Again, in the words of St Thomas, "Every human law has just as much in the nature of law, as it is derived from the law of nature. But if in any point it deflects from the law of nature, it is no longer a law but a perversion of law."[145]

At the Nuremberg trials, the judges were faced with the defence that Nazi atrocities were, at the time of their commission, legal in Germany. Did the tribunal at Nuremberg afford the natural lawyer an unanswerable case for resorting to a higher, objective law?

It did not. The judges at Nuremberg made no pretence to reach out for justification through natural law. True, there must have been a great temptation to bolster the work of the International Military Tribunal with a natural law warrant to save it from a 'weakness' that has a special meaning to natural lawyers: the matter of *ex post facto*. Admittedly, the substantive laws, the humanitarian principles of Nuremberg, were enunciated *after* the occurrence of the events these principles made into crimes. But, as we have seen, the nature of adjudication, inevitably, is to some degree *ex post facto*.

Judgment always follows the specific event. Yet Hitler's cohorts had a palpably good opportunity to predict their punishment by the application of developing principles of international law, as evidenced by the Geneva Conventions and the custom of the community, which clearly condemned aggression, genocide, the shooting of prisoners, and the bombing of open cities. On the basis of this evidence, the Nazis had at least as good an opportunity to predict their fate at the hands of an international court unfettered by Nazi law as segregationist school boards and cannibalistic sailors had to predict the legal consequences of *their* acts in a court whose horizons extended beyond those of the defendants, beyond the lifeboat or the Deep South.

All things being equal, we shy from *ex post facto* law, from the punishment of men for crimes that were not clearly designated as crimes when—and in the legal system in which—they were committed. But we cannot guarantee that a court will not draw its law from a wider community than that which appeared to sanction the act in question. The cannibalistic sailors could hope their British judge would imagine himself in their predicament, but they must also have known that he would keep in mind the wider constituency whose interests he serves.

There are, perhaps even less onerous circumstances in which the individual may feel compelled to refuse, in conscience, to obey the national law. But if he rejects the notion of law as True, eternal, or anything more than a temporal opinion of constituted authority, then the prospect of breaking the law becomes far less awesome. Of course, the law ought generally to be obeyed, such a person would think, but not because it is sinful or evil to break the law, but merely because violating it diminishes the orderly human process of government, which is necessary for social progress and individual safety. But what if the government no longer appears to be using the law to promote either social progress or individual safety?

If the ordinary citizen regards law, with healthy realist-scepticism, as the opinions of other mortal, fallible men, then it is not necessarily either unthinkable or unjustified for him to set his personal opinion against the collective opinion of his society and its appointed law perceivers. As the court in *Regina v. Dudley and Stephens* pointed out, the breaking of a human law (unlike the divine one) may not be 'devilish' but merely illegal. He who breaks it takes a calculated gamble. To set his personal judgment or will against that of the community's designated perceivers of law may result in punishment; but it may also result in forgiveness—as in the case of Messrs. Dudley and Stephens—or even vindication, changes in the law and sometimes honours for the 'criminal'.

Chapter 15

The injustice done to an individual is sometimes of service to the public.
Letters of Junius (1769–1771)

There is no crueller tyranny than that which is perpetrated under the shield of law and in the time of justice.
Charles Montesquieu

The law begins by reflecting the public conscience and the public conscience ends by reflecting the law!
Anon

A man who breaks the law out of personal conviction and can advance a very good reason for doing so may render an important service by starting the community toward a rethinking of the very basis and social utility of the law he has broken. There is a role for this kind of rational, principles law-breaking in a thoughtful society. Historical evolution may sometimes sanction the deliberate act of rebellion motivated by human reason, but only chaos can result from a system of laws that acknowledges a citizen's right to divide his allegiance between a superior law of God and an inferior law of man.

Yet it cannot be denied: The unanswered call for a divine and eternal legal absolute continues to find an echo in the hearts of men. This may explain, in part, the ritualistic semi deification with which England and France, in particular, continue to surround their courts. 'Living oracles', the great Blackstone called judges.[146] 'M'Lord', scarlet and ermine gowns, maces and periwigs suggest a euphemistic analogy to 'Mon Pere', capes, orbs and mitres, all in response to the lingering popular demand for a pseudo-religious mystique in the law-making process.

It also explains why the British courts, in particular, still strive so mightily and hypocritically to make a new judicial decision, no matter how much more suitable to the time and occasion than its predecessor, appear somehow, arm-wrenchingly, to be consistent with the very case it is overruling. This is, at most, judicial ancestor worship. It is, at least, as if the judge feels compelled to display toward prior decisions the diffidence with which Othello strangled Desdemona in her sleep: "I kiss'd thee ere I kill'd thee."

On the whole, however, a gradual (and not entirely complete) transition of government from deified to humanised legislative and judicial processes in England and America has taken place against a background of growing social unity and maturity. As the stature of our national courts has grown, judges have increasingly abandoned their pretence at discovering 'truth' and have instead raised the standard of human reason—even as governments have lifted the legislative process off the back of God and put it squarely onto the conscience of political man, where Aristotle had long ago known it to belong. The judges and the political leaders have ceased their ritualistic pretence at 'declaring' and 'discovering' law and now frankly admit *making* it. In so doing, they have had the help of sociological, psychological, and economic data, which has become more useful a guide to judges and legislators than mystical ritual.

Thus, two gradual changes have been occurring simultaneously. We have already observed that, as a society becomes more complex, one- and two-party law-making must increasingly (although not necessarily altogether) yield ground to third-party law-making. Now we must add the observation that in a maturing society, the third-party process sheds its pretence at certainty and Truth and allows itself to be humanised, and made existential.

This transition to a humanised, existential third-party law, however, is harmful to the social prestige and viability of the process, unless there develops, concurrently, a mature identification, a growing social unity, between the judges and the parties; that is, as Hegel said, "the confidence which the parties feel in the subjectivity of those who give the verdict."[147]

When there is such subjective identification between the parties to the legal process—Hegel suggests a similarity between the judges and the parties in respect of 'their peculiarity', which is to say their social position, way of life, and values—then the community feels less need to be reassured with fairy tales about the judges as purveyors of an eternal or objective Truth. The client does not so much mind having a mere human as his law perceiver, instead of God or

God's agent, so long as the mere man so invested with the openly creative third-party role is the client's trusted and responsive fellow and equal.

How this trust is nurtured is the story of the structuring of judicial impartiality. A happy and successful judge, to paraphrase Aristotle, is a good judge, and a good judge is one who performs his profession well and virtuously, and is seen by the community to perform it so. The state of character that is the author of the judge's natural goodness and virtue is *impartiality*. Judges have, by and large, achieved this state of virtue.

The individual confronting a judge is asked to commit himself not to the infinite or verifiable truths of God or Science but simply to another individual, probably a lawyer seated on a bench and wearing a gown, claiming the client's allegiance to nothing more than his personal qualities of 'fairness', 'experience', and 'rationality' in applying principles devised by himself or by other equally fallible men. Naturally, the citizen, and in the international community, the state, is inclined to be dubious about the claim to special qualities of 'fairness' and 'rationality' of a judge who is the minister of a system—the law—that reveals to the judge neither eternal nor even scientifically verifiable absolutes.

The litigant observing the judge and wondering whether to patronise his services may well ask: "If you do not believe in absolute right and wrong, black and white, beginning and end, true and false, how can you be 'fair'?" Aristotle equates the 'unfair' with the 'unequal', in a geometric sense,[148] and the *just* to him, is a matter of fair proportion.[149] But this sounds better to a philosopher in his chamber than to a judge in his. How is a judge to measure the midpoint in a line that has no absolutely fixed points of reference?

The pragmatist's answer, of course, is that the lawyer like the mathematician, must become experienced in hypothesis. Like the mathematician, he must work with hypotheses not because he believes or knows them to be true in any ultimate sense, but in order to construct a workable pattern of relations, which at least has *internal* validity. A 'foot' is a hypothesis, manifested and preserved in the form of a metallic bar kept at Greenwich, England. Having adopted the hypothesis that this bar demonstrates, it becomes logically possible for us to say that, truly, two feet are twice as long as one, and that it is not true that three feet are less than two—it is always remembered that these 'truths' (as distinguished from Truths) are valid only for internal travel, within the jurisdiction of that particular hypothesis. They are 'intruths'.

On the other hand, it is obviously impossible to say that a foot is a *true* distance while a metre is *false*. Both are, equally, working hypotheses incapable of objective verification. *Neither* is externally true or false. It is merely possible to say that the foot *applies* (or 'works') in England while it does not apply in France. It is also possible to say that the metre is digitally simpler than the foot.

Social scientists too, must work with hypothesis. Just as it is permissible for a mathematician to say so, a social scientist may state that a particular social hypothesis better answers the dominant needs of a given community at a given time and insofar as these needs are manifestly ascertainable, but to say this is still to state no more than an 'intruth', not an 'extruth'. The validity of the conclusion rests entirely upon the observation made by one fallible social scientist of the prevailing value—hypotheses of a particular community of fallible men. There are in Africa, for example, certain countries in which it is considered more convenient to have large doughnut-shaped coins with holes in their middles.

In the United States and the United Kingdom, such coins would clearly *not* be regarded as 'more convenient'. But in those African societies in which most persons wear few clothes, and there are consequently few pockets, it may be a great boon to have a basic currency that can be worn as a necklace. Big, heavy, doughnut-shaped coins *work* in such a community. They would scarcely 'work' in London, New York or Chicago.

Similarly, the 'fairness' and 'logic' of a judge is at best only internally true to the system of legal hypotheses within which he works or other systems that operate on similar hypotheses. Change the venue to a society with different hypotheses, alter the values of the same society or perceive those values differently, and the same judgment becomes unfair and illogical within its self-created rational contest. In South Africa, the law was that a black man who left his job before the expiration of his work contract could be sent to jail and released only when he agreed to complete his term of work.

The prevailing legal hypothesis is that an employer purchases a proprietary right in the labour of his employees. From this, it followed that at one time for the employee to deprive his employer deliberately of that labour was a sort of criminal theft, for which prison and compulsory restitution are an appropriate remedy. In the United Kingdom and United States, this hypothesis was rejected in favour of another: that man will not be compelled to work for gain against his own will and that a man's labour is and always remains his own property. It therefore follows that a man who refuses to carry out a service contract has not committed theft but simple breach of contract, for which he may not be jailed. *Neither* hypothesis is an 'extruth'. An American judge who sentenced a labourer to jail for quitting his job could be said to be unfair, illogical, and wrong, but this is purely to state an 'intruth', a limited conclusion relevant only within the system of the legal hypothesis of the society in which this particular judge operates or in others which have a similar hypothesis.

One possible 'extruth' which could be stated regarding the then South African hypothesis was that the South African system did not accurately reflect the values of South African society but was imposed by a white minority for its own exclusive benefit on a black majority, thereby creating potential revolutionary conditions in the context of rising contingent-wide human rights. Social science may be unable to tell us things that are more than relatively true, but it can tell us things that are absolutely false. Another possible extruth is that the South African law did *not work*. That is, it could not in most instances, be enforced even in South Africa and did not in that country create the stable working force which is its objective; while, perhaps, the English system did.

Even such a judgment is difficult to make, however, without recourse to other purely subjective, hypothetical assumptions and can usefully be made only if these further (secondary) subjective hypotheses really *are* those of the society whose legal system is under consideration, and not those of some other society or of the observer. Then telling a South African that the existing system may lead to revolution is not a useful comment if, as a South African prime minister once said he has made up his mind he would rather die than change his system.

The 'fairness' of a judge is really his ability to locate the midpoint of a line that has no existence except as an assumption perceived by designated members of the community on its behalf. Hopefully, in a democratic society the community will share in authoring or at least approve of the assumption. The impartiality of the judge is his ability to perceive, and then work with, hypotheses that, like sets of numbers, have no provable external validity but are the hypothetical shorthand of group communication used to communicate group values. Moreover, he must be able to sense when the hypotheses have shifted, and if the shift is clear and nonaberrational, he should be able and willing to find the midpoint of a new line or work with a new set of figures.

It is difficult for any judge to solicit an 'act of faith' in favour of a process so epistemologically subjective and temporal. This is essentially true of the judge who must seek a commitment from various societies operating within *differing* systems of legal hypothesis.

Chapter 16

And always the loud angry crowd
Very angry and very loud
Law is We,
And always the soft idiot softly Me.

W.H. Auden, *Law Like Love*

The lawyer's truth is not truth but consistent expediency.

Thoreau

But the mediating Ego, the 'impartial spectator' (uninteressierer Zuschauer) do not rediscover an already given rationality, they 'establish themselves' and establish it, by an act of initiative which has no guarantee in being, its justification resting entirely on the effective power which it confers on us of taking our own history upon ourselves.

M. Merleau Ponty, *Phenomenology of Perception*

There is no truth, only perception.

Gustave Flaubert

Fairness and impartiality are essential ingredients in law-making. This statement, however, encompasses a vast assumption that is not universally shared. Those who do not share it come to a quite different conclusion about these concepts.

Suppose, for example, that Ug and Og were arguing about the length of time it takes to walk up to the edge of the earth. "It takes three weeks," says Ug.

"No," Og replies, "it requires three whole months."

Ug, wishing to avoid an argument, suggests that the matter be submitted to their local headman, who is known to be both wise, impartial and fair-minded.

Og, however, refuses, "Why should I ask our headman," he says, "when I already know the answer, for I have walked to the edge of the earth? I am not interested in impartiality or fairness but in the truth. In the face of known truth, impartiality and fairness is at best irrelevant."

The unconscious assumption on which Ug proceeds and Og does not, is that the truth is relative to the perceiver rather than perceivable absolutely, that it can be *decided*, but it cannot be *known*, that it is *existent* rather than *valid*, in the words of Merleau Ponty.[150] Ug, therefore is *detached* by experience, while Og is *committed* by his experience.

Fairness and impartiality, it would seem, are relevant only in disputes in which both sides concede the *possibility that they could be wrong* and are not committed to the inevitable, objective rightness of their positions.

The ability to be strongly inclined toward one's preferences and trustful of one's perceptions while yet knowing that they are not necessarily True, is a special condition of the human intellect not given but acquired, a kind of self-discipline, which is closely related to the total personality or what we now call our 'lifestyle'.

In his historic series of lectures on 'Pragmatism', William James begins with a classification of thinking persons into two categories: the 'tender-minded' and the 'tough-minded'. Modestly, he himself called this classification a 'barbaric disjunction', one which is 'monstrously oversimplified and rude'. But James succeeds in reminding us of the oft-forgotten fact, well enough known to Plato, that man is a creature of *temperament* and that when we speak of a person as a 'type', we generally refer not to that composite that is his skin and bone structure, but to the image traced on our eyes and ears by his personality as each of us perceives it.

The best way to describe the moral quality a disputant must bring to the third-party process if it is to be relevant, is in terms of two temperaments: *detachment* and *commitment*. The former is conducive to, and the latter destructive of, the third-party process.

To describe the two antithetical temperaments let us adopt another technique of James's and list certain characteristics of each:

Commitment	Detachment
given to generalisation	given to particularisation
bipolar	pluralistic
garrulous	cautious
active, excitable	calm, patient
formulative	descriptive
verbalistic	introspective
given to proselytising	nonproselytising
certain	doubting
secure	insecure
very religious or very antireligious	agnostic or nominally church-affiliated
perfectionist	temporising
speaks of 'truth' and 'good'	speaks of 'taste' and 'preference'

Corporate presidents, generals, professional politicians, lawyers, and sportsmen would generally appear to tend toward the *commitment* temperament, and teachers, doctors, actors, diplomats, and stock-market analysts toward *detachment*—but the temperaments are not, of course, allocated by professions. Certainly, too, most persons have some of the characteristics of each list. But we also know that in most persons one or the other temperament appears to predominate. Yet it would be quite misleading to suppose that we can tell a person temperamentally *committed* from temperamentally *detached* by the cut of his clothes or his casual conversation.

Indeed, it is generally, at first, difficult to tell them apart even from their expressed opinions. Only the profoundest but often most imperceptible difference distinguishes the man who *believes* in a thing as a matter of *taste or preference*, as perceived by the interaction of senses, reason, values—all of these being grounded in experimental subjectivity—and the thing perceived as object, which brings its own existence as object (its *objectivity*) to the experience of being *subjectively* perceived; from the man who is certain that the thing perceived, as perceived by him, is *true* and *good*, or *bad* in the sense not merely of its objective existence but also of objective perception of the thing perceived.

Yet the former is *detached* and the latter is *committed*. Although they may both happen to choose the same food, the same clothes, the same political party, the same newspaper, and the same church, the difference in their temperamental reasons for choosing them is fundamental.

Let us try to illustrate the difference, which is basic not only to law-making but to all human relations.

In religious terms, Buddha may be said to represent *detachment*, and Christ, *commitment* (so also Karl Marx). It is Buddha who said that his teachings would be taken up by twelve sects of Buddhas and that "these schools will be the repositories of the twelve diversified fruits of my scriptures without priority or inferiority—just as the taste of sea-water is everywhere the same—or as the twelve sons of one man, all honest and true, so will be the exposition of my doctrine advocated by these schools."[151] Not only were these words spoken, but they have been practised: with monks of different sects sharing the same monasteries and monarchs supporting each sect equally.[152]

There is no suggestion in Buddhism that sectarianism is the work of the devil, any more than we would say that Bach lovers are blessed but Beethoven lovers damned. On the contrary, Coomaraswamy says:

The only true missionary is he who brings to the support of the scriptures of others, that which he finds in his own books. The more one knows of various beliefs, the more impossible it becomes to distinguish one another; and indeed, no religion could be true which did not imply the same which every other religion implies.[153]

The Mahayana added to this an external tolerance, as well, "Perceiving an incarnation of the Dharmakaya in every spiritual leader regardless of nationality and professed creed, Mahayanists recognise a Buddha in Socrates, Mohammed, Jesus, Francis of Assisi, Confucius, Laotze, and many others."[154]

No doubt, in practice, this eclecticism has not been uniformly applied by followers of the Buddha, and heresy, excommunication, and exclusive salvation are all to be found within at least some manifestations of the Buddhist religion. But a quick reference to our checklist of characteristics would place the 'typical' Buddhist Bodhisattva preponderantly in the 'detached' column, as it places the Catholic saint into the 'committed' one. Temperamentally, as its saints go, so goes the nation.

Among Christian nations, especially those most temperamentally inclined first to cause and then to adore sainthood, *commitment* is next to godliness. But in Buddhist society *sunya*, 'void' or disengagement—not to avoid, but to be better able to perceive the world—is the path to ultimate reality. (Confucianism too, praises the state of voidness as the key to enlightenment through learning.)

Of course, the Buddhist, like the Christian, seeks passionately for an ultimate reality. But whereas the Christian reality is a substantive, intellectually apprehended reality—Christ came into the world to save sinners—the reality of Buddhism is intellectually unknowable and substantively inexpressible. Mahayana teaches that there are two different forms of knowledge: *conditional* and *relative* truth on the one hand, and *transcendental* or *absolute* truth on the other.

Of course, all good Buddhists strive for the latter, which is higher enlightenment. But they also concede, and this is the crux of the difference, "that we cannot know absolute truth in our practical everyday life, and therefore that relative truth is sufficient for the field of human experience. It is conditional, empirical, pragmatic, and serves for ordinary life."[155]

The higher truth in Buddhism is restricted to the subjectively, intuitively perceived sense of void, or essence, in which all matter, the 'suchness' of all being, becomes united. But it is readily conceded that this enlightenment is *purely* perceptive—it cannot be communicated. "All that can be said of it fails to give any correct idea of it. In fact, it is no idea at all, as it is to be intuitively grasped and not logically represented."[156]

This being the case, there could never be in Buddhism an Inquisition, or a Dictatorship of the Proletariat, the justification for which is the conversion of recalcitrant individuals to one irresistibly pervasive Great Idea. The Buddhist religion provides some *procedural* or methodological devices for individual enlightenment, but it cannot express, let alone force others to accept, a substantive higher truth because the Buddhist objective truth is only to be apprehended in the senses of the perceiver, which in terms of theological policies means that it cannot be learned from, and certainly cannot be compelled by, another. This *procedural* approach to higher spiritual truth, together with an acceptance of the relativity of temporal truth, makes even—or especially—the most enlightened Buddhist a tolerant and temperamentally *detached* being.

With illumination (*prabjakari*), the Buddhist "reflects upon the nature of things and practises patience, which really means *forbearance toward people and things as they are*. The patience of forbearance is one of the chief Buddhist virtues."[157] Indeed, high among those Buddhist virtues, the practice of which is procedurally conducive to enlightenment (the six *paramitas*), is patience (*kshanti*), which "is a kind of forbearance. The aspirant to Buddhahood never grows angry, impatient or excited over what is done by ignorant persons, for he must ever keep in mind that all trouble is due to causes."[158]

It is impossible to conceive of Gautama flailing money-lenders in the temple. Whereas Christianity and Western political philosophies like capitalism and Marxism have substantive creeds, Buddhism has a procedural approach to truth, a series of recommended steps or aids to the achieving of individual dharma, which if objectively true, is nevertheless subjectively perceived. Whereas Western philosophy tends, in the words of Merleau Ponty, to escape from existence (sense-experience) into the universe of things said, Buddhism, and the school of existential phenomenology that is gaining favour in the West looks for 'a harmony without concept', which allows man to experience his own nature "as spontaneously in harmony with the law of understanding."

According to this *weltanschauung*, "the world is not what I think but what I live through." Thus, "our relationship to the world, as it is untiringly enunciated within us, is not a thing which can be any further clarified by analysis".[159] In the West, phenomenological philosophy, like Buddhism, has built into its very fibre a kind of knowledge of every man's fallibility, which is the essential precondition to a successful third-party decision-making system.

It is necessary to reiterate that both the *committed* person (as exemplified by the traditional devout Christian or Marxist) and the *detached* person (as represented by the Bodhisattva) believe in certain ultimate truths, and would, under certain circumstances, disobey a command or lay down their lives. But the committed person acts as he does because of an intellectual commitment to a *course of action* that is the *One True Way*, whereas the detached person acts as he does because of a *subjective, intuitive belief* or *preference*. The committed person must strive to reorganise the society of man in accordance with the one correct master plan. The detached person concentrates on seeking to improve his ability to perceive and feel, to sensitise himself to the world.

The committed person sees all substantive deviation from his social master plan as an error. Such error in others is abominable and intolerable to him, both because he has a positively imposed duty to propagate the Truth and because the errors of others make impossible the realisation of one's own perfection, which is ultimately dependent upon total social perfection. The *detached* person has no social master plan to which others must conform, is pragmatically open to the use of relatively true evidence to enlist his support for relatively true social objectives, and sees no threat to his spiritual master plan in the conduct of any other person if it does not positively prevent his efforts to enlighten himself. He understands that man perceives other men and God through his senses and his perceptive imagination. He realises that his mind, his eyes, his touch, approach all phenomena with a subjectivity which is experientially deduced. This does not make the subjective perceptions of the perceiver entirely haphazard: "one damn thing after another."

But the rationality of subjective perception is confined to its own boundaries, the circle of reasonably possible dispositions, like the *truth* discussed earlier. Within those boundaries, the subjective perceptions may or may not blend with each other in accordance with a meaningful theory, and may or may not confirm each other. A man looking at the Lever Building in New York may see beauty, utility, ugliness or real estate. To admit this is not to admit that he may reasonably see a cow, not because we know with objective certainty that the Lever Building is not a cow but because, for most utilitarian purposes—although not, for example, for purposes of surrealist painting—our society cannot confirm the perception as possible.

But 'reality' even when thus confirmed, still is not an objective truth, is not, in Merleau Ponty's phrase 'pure being', but rather is the form traced by the conjunctive and coordinates of subjective experiences, where the paths of my various experiences intersect, and also where my own and other people's intersect and engage each other like gears. It is thus inseparable from subjectivity and intersubjectivity, which find their unity when I take up either my past experiences in those of the present or other people's in my own.[160]

Or, in the case of the judge, his subjectivity finds its confirmation if it seems 'just' to him and to the community and if it 'works' in the sense of advancing the shared value-oriented expectations of the society. Like fairness and impartiality, this confirmation is defined only in the limited sense of being a generally shared rule of exclusion by putting certain perceptions 'beyond the pale'.

Chapter 17

Justice is truth in action.

Benjamin Disraeli, Speech (1851)

The law is not a rigid animal or a rigid profession but a constant search for the truth… Justices of the Supreme Court should grow constitutionally during their terms.

Henry Andrew Blackman

The submission of disputes to an impartial third-party decision-making process, if it is to be a way of life and not merely an occasional expedient, requires of the disputants an acceptance of this way of seeing reality, this *temperamental detachment*. By this, we mean that both disputants renounce the possibility of being *objectively* right. They will then enter the court or bureau with a *preference* for winning but a *willingness* to lose.

The detached disputant, like the Thomistic God, is both within and outside the event. He is a partisan for his cause, but he is also clear that the only transcendent 'given' in the dispute is the third-party procedure itself, by which he, to preserve an orderly society, has agreed to settle it. He does not believe that there is a single True answer to a dispute between human beings, but that there is only a preferred and an abhorred perception, that there is only *my* way of seeing it and *your* way.

Fortunately, the Western philosophies have spun off a very large number of persons who are who, *although having a genuine, reasoned preference* for their social system, do not confuse that personal, temporal, relative preference with eternal, absolute and universal truth. Such persons, while retaining and even cherishing their personal perceptions as reasonable, are prepared to scrutinise them in the light of new scientific discoveries and social needs, and of an overriding personal preference for the rule of law, by which they, like the

Bodhisattva in search of truth, mean no more than a series of steps in a fixed procedure designed to advance the cause of good order in accordance with the hypothetical *intruths* of the community.

Law is primarily a pragmatic process of problem-solving, rather than a system of revealed truth. The truths pronounced by judges are valid or invalid, effective or ineffective, 'true' and 'good', or 'false' and 'bad' only within the context of a given value system. We referred to these value-oriented hypotheses as *intruths*. Where a system of third-party decision-making operates in a community in which the relevant values are *not* commonly shared, the judges are in effect being asked to do the impossible: invent a decision that is universally valid—an *extruth*.

Although the search for natural law in human history has yielded pride of place only to the search for a fountain of youth and the alchemists' formula, no such *extruth* has so far been discovered. Only mechanical justice, the flipping of a coin or the taking of a poll, could be totally impartial. All decisions made by human judges embrace the subjectivity of human perception. Judges therefore cannot be expected to transcend their subjectivity to arrive at *extruths*.

It is important to emphasise this aspect of the impartial third-party decision-maker's role. The claim he makes cannot be based on objectivity of judgment, which he does not have. Like the parties to a dispute, his perceptions are grounded in the senses and are thus subjective. Where he differs from the parties, and the only unique quality he brings to a dispute, is that *his* subjectivity is *not that of a disputant*. His detachment gives him an opportunity to make a subjective determination on the basis of the greatest possible openness, sensitivity, and receptivity.

Merleau Ponty uses the term 'impartial spectator' (or *uninteressierter Zuschauer*) to describe the maximal human condition for perception, although even the best observational process still only yields the most thorough subjective observation of truth, not Truth itself. This is no more than to say what science is also slowly coming to accept: The observations of the scientist are conditioned by the fact that the sensed data is perceived through, and affected by, each man's eyes, mind, and the mere fact of his relativity in the time-space continuum, although a scientist—who is well trained, intelligent, imaginative, sensitive, and uses good laboratory equipment—can produce more thorough data than one less well trained and endowed.

I have emphasised the subjectiveness of the judicial decision in order to explain the difficulty of third-party law—and particularly international third-party law—might face in gaining the confidence of its consumers. Now we see the reciprocal of this. It is not *only* judges who cannot know objective truth. Neither, *ipso facto*, can the consumers. *Unless* the peoples and nations of the international community accept the subjectivity of legal truth—both the law as they advocate it in disputes and as it is finally pronounced by a judge—the third-party system *cannot work*.

Only insofar as it is generally accepted that in any international dispute *no* view—not that of America, or Russia, or Nigeria—is *True*, but all are only opinions of what the law *ought to be* (or ought to do), can we bear to submit the dispute to an impartial decision-maker, whose view is also subjective but differs from the subjectivity of the parties in its non-national, international perspective, in its absence of bias and openness to reason, and in certain procedures he follows in an effort to maximise fairness.

On the other hand, if disputants take their predictive preferences to be the *Truth*, then third-party decision-making, however excellent its process, becomes little more than irrelevant meddling. Impartiality has no place in an inexorable contest between Good and Evil, Right and Wrong, Truth and Error.

In both communist and non-communist states, international relations have tended to be seen in this absolutist way, as a struggle between Right (us) and Wrong (them), or in Marxian terms, between the Correct and Inevitable way (theirs) and the Reactionary and Doomed way (ours). Such a frame of reference for international relations excludes the possibility of third-party decision-making as a means to the settlement of international disputes even if the existence of a neutral were to be conceded by the parties.

But such primitive faith in the absolute correctness of ideological creeds is fast receding, giving way to ideological pragmatism and indeterminacy. If this observation is correct, it is of the greatest theoretical and practical importance to human evolution and the possibilities of a peaceful world community under law. Even in China, Russia and the United States there is arising a new, younger generation, which, while it is no less interested in resolving the problems of the country and system than the parents, is far less concerned about the 'threat of the international communist conspiracy' or 'capitalist-militarist imperialism'. A generation may at last be upon us that is more interested in mastering the challenge of its own traditional being than in conquering other persons and lands.

Such persons would seek liberty, justice, and peace by seeking first to influence their personal perception and conduct and that of their own country.

In the third world of Asia and Africa, this has, of course, been the prevailing theme since the awakening of those continents. The weakness of most new nations compels them to abjure some of the bristling ideological certitudes and pretensions of the more powerful, more 'civilised' states. But this is not the whole story. Throughout the world, the real class struggle increasingly appears to be not between the bourgeoisie and the workers but between a younger class of pragmatists and an older class of ideologists.

Pragmatism, detachment and subjectivism can, of course, also be an ideology, but they differ from traditional ideology in exactly the way Buddhism differs from Christianity. Both show the way to truth, but the former sees that way as many parallel paths vanishing into a 'cloud of knowing', while the latter has tended to see many ways converging on a single fixed pinnacle that stands out clearly against the flat surroundingbadlands.

Ideological pragmatism, a national *temperament of detachment* coupled with a pluralistic view of international relations, alone makes international third-party decision-making possible: not in every dispute, and not as a substitute for negotiated two-party law-making, but as the normal, ultimate alternative to chaos. It requires us to accept that man cannot know truth in the objective sense, and that this applies not only to judges but also to disputants. In the absence of a way to know objective Truth, the next best thing is to have a method by which subjective experience can be applied in a peaceful process by a detached decision-maker using the best procedural 'equipment'.

The structure of the process is therefore important, but it is not the precondition. The precondition is a temperament, a way of being, and as such, is a matter of individual and, derivatively, national moral philosophy. It may well be that the most important work currently being done toward the structuring of impartial third-party decision-making is not in the realm of institution or system building but in the struggle of writers, artists, philosophers, poets, scientists, and even lawyers and politicians to win acceptance for a pluralist international community in which a multitude of opinions and values freely and peaceably contend, and none are regarded by those holding them as ultimate, inevitable, or indispensable.

Neutral principles, the idea of *reciprocity*, is a procedural concept which helps to assuage the subjectivity of third-party law-making. When earlier we encountered two primordial hunters, Ug and Og, they were disputing title to a dinosaur Ug had killed but abandoned and Og had dragged home to this cave. We noted that there were various ways in which the parties, even without recourse to a judicial system, could settle the dispute—by the exercise of:

1. Pure power
2. Pure compromise
3. Law-making power
4. Law-making compromise.

We also noted that the difference between (1) and (2) on the one hand and (3) and (4) on the other is that the latter methods of settlement do not merely effect a solution to this particular instance of disagreement, but they also proceed to define a *general principle* by reference to which the specific dispute is decided. They also elaborate on the reasons for that principle.

We noted that in settling a future comparable dispute this enunciated rule and its reason would probably be of great importance. We noted that not only judges and lawyers, but the public as a whole, even in primitive societies, have an extraordinary, seemingly innate preference for action which is consistent, and at a more sophisticated state, can be seen and expressed to be consistent with what has gone before.

Such a preference for judicial and administrative action that appears to be consistent with the substance, direction, or purpose of prior action is easy to understand. By confirming itself, the law promotes a certain public confidence in its *reality*, just as a person's subjective feelings—horror at an act of cruelty, for example—take on a greater reality for the individual if his response is confirmed by a similar reaction on the part of others, and his perception that the Lever Building is not a cow is confirmed by what others see, or more exactly, do not see. Consistency is a form of self-confirmation.

Secondly, legal consistency, by seeming to confirm the reality of the law despite the subjectivity of its process of perception, gives a public ruled by the law a sense of legal *fixity*. It promotes the idea that the content of the law is knowable, and that, for example, I can be reasonably certain as to whether my day-to-day conduct will land me in jail or get me fined by looking at case law made in respect of others, as well as at the statutes which apply equally to everyone. This is what we mean when we say that the law is principled—that it proceeds by principles of general application which permit us to make reasoned guesses as to how the law will, or again more accurately, will *not* affect us. Without some element of fixity, the law becomes totally capricious in its effect on each of us—a dictatorship of whim which most citizens would not long tolerate.

Finally, there is the moral feeling that whatever the law does to Ug it ought, under comparable circumstances, to do to Og. This is what is meant by *reciprocity*, and as an elementary principle of justice, it is central not only to the law but to religion. In the Judeo-Christian world, it is enshrined in the Golden Rule. In Confucianism, it is called the principle of *Shu*, the doing to others what one likes oneself,[161] or the not inflicting on others what one does not want done to oneself.[162] Reciprocity is closely linked to the virtue of fixity or consistency. Confucius said 'when' a ruler speaks, his "acts must be consequent" like the steady fall of "water-on-stone, water on-stone."[163]

This preference for consistency, for reciprocal principles is given as a lawyer's creed by Mr Justice Cardozo in his famous essay, *The Nature of the Judicial Process*:

It will not do to decide the same question one way between one set of litigants and the opposite way between others. "If a group of cases involves the same point, the parties expect the same decision. It would be a gross injustice to decide alternate cases on opposite principles. If a case was decided against me yesterday when I was the defendant, I shall look for the same judgment today if I am the plaintiff. To decide differently would raise a feeling of resentment and wrong in my breast; it would be an infringement, material and moral, of my rights." Everyone feels the force of this sentiment when two cases are the same. Adherence to precedent must then be the rule rather than the exception if litigants are to have faith in the even-handed administration of justice in the courts.[164]

This search for neutral principles was alluded to either as the instinctive demand for reasonable principles applied and reapplied to obtain solutions, which, as to both form and substance, are confirmatory of each other and generate a tendency toward the definition of agreed outer limits to judicial discretion.

We have also noted that the rubbery element of human subjectivity in the third-party decision-making process was nevertheless given a sort of spine by what Herbert Wechsler called "criteria that can be framed and tested as an exercise of reason and not merely as an act of wilfulness or will."[165] This is what is meant by "a government of laws, not of men."

Let us take an example.

I quoted a part of Judge Koretsky's opinion in the *Certain Expenses* case.[166] In that instance, the court was asked to decide whether special expenditures incurred by the Security Council and the General Assembly in organising the United Nations Emergency Force following the Suez crisis and the United Nations Congo Operation constituted 'expenses of the Organisation' within the meaning of Article 17(2) of the United Nations Charter. Behind this legalistic formulation, much was at stake.

If the question were answered in the affirmative, the General Assembly could compel each United Nations member to pay his fair share of the cost of the two peacekeeping operations. Nations that refused could be denied their voting rights in the assembly. On the other hand, if the question were answered negatively, future peacekeeping operations would be severely handicapped by uncertainty about financing.

Judge Koretsky's position was that his important question was one the court should refuse to answer because "financial policy in peacekeeping matters" is "first and foremost…a political question."[167]

It is axiomatic—and the point has been stressed that a court ought not to refuse to decide an issue except for extremely convincing reasons. What reasons did Judge Koretsky advance for his refusal? Only that, first, "a question of the powers and responsibilities of the principal organs" is inherent in any decision on peacekeeping operations and that therefore "the political aspect of the question…is the prevailing one…" and, second, that a decision, if one were given by the court, "may be used as an instrument for political struggle."

As a neutral principle of general application, this totally fails the expositional test. It does not establish a standard that, being applicable to this particular case, also gives meaningful, reasoned guidance to courts faced with similar problems in the future. Nor does it refer to a principle to be derived from past experience. *Why* is a question about the scope of a political organ's power itself primarily a political question? These particular political powers happen to be defined in a contrast between states: The United Nations Charter.

If a term of that contrast is ambiguous, what instrument is better suited than a court to clarify its meaning? And does Judge Koretsky really intend that no decision should ever be rendered if its application is likely to lead to a 'political struggle'? If he were right, why did the authors of the United Nations Charter specifically lay down a procedure for enforcing decisions of the court by political means, including, if necessary, the use of force—the ultimate weapon in 'political struggle'?[168] On this, see later my next chapter on judicial review and democracy.

The gist of Wechsler's argument came to this: The judicial process "must be genuinely principled," which means that every step along the judge's discursive road to his decision must proceed by "analysis and reason quite transcending the immediate result achieved." The great qualities of judicial decisions, and those that distinguish them from a commissar's whim or a politician's decree, are "their generality and their neutrality."[169]

This introduces a further aspect of the subject of neutral principles which relates back to our earlier discussion, of the necessity, if there is to be fairness and impartiality, for a certain *detachment* of temperament not only on the part of the judge but also of the disputing parties. In a court of law, the role of the advocate is not simply to say everything that can accrue to the benefit of his client. It is, rather, to stand both in and above the specific dispute and to propose to the judge a rule that would work rationally *in the general application* and, almost incidentally, to the advantage of his client.

The rival advocates in litigation, if they are competent, will, in effect, present the judge with a choice between two ready-made judgments, both incorporating neutral principles, both taking fully into account past history and future contingency. A good advocate must aspire to be not only a social engineer but also a historian and contingency planner. It is a poor lawyer who argues only in terms of benefit to his client. The better counsel strives for a kind of detachment from his client's specific self-interest sufficient to allow him to argue with neutral principles.

Fairness and impartiality thus turn out to be not only an indispensable quality of the judge or of the quasi-legislative body but a necessary intellectual discipline of the advocate. Not that the advocate *is* impartial, but if he hopes to persuade the decision-maker, he must be prepared to establish an identity between the specific interest of his clients and the general well-being and good ordering of the community.

Lon Fuller defines the essence of law in these terms: "What the Golden Rule seeks to convey," he says, "is…that Society…is held together by a pervasive bond of reciprocity."[170] And society is rapidly thrown into darkness by the necessary converse of this fundamental social norm: "So soon as it becomes perfectly clear that you have no intention whatever of treating me as you yourself would wish to be treated, then I shall consider myself as relieved from the obligation to treat you as I would wish to be treated."[171] In short, the alternative is chaos.

Chapter 18[172]

Government can easily exist without law, but law cannot exist without Government.

Bertrand Russell

Government, like a dress, is the badge of lost innocence; the palaces of kings are built on the ruins of the bowers of paradise. For were the impulses of conscience clear, uniform, and irresistibly obeyed; man would need no other law givers; but that not being the case, he finds it necessary to surrender up a part of his property to furnish means for the protection of the rest which in every case advises him out of two evils to choose the least.

Thomas Paine

No democracy can long survive which does not accept as fundamental to its very existence the interest of minorities.

Franklyn. D. Roosevelt (Letter to the National Association for the Advancement of Coloured People 1850)

Representative democracy is not about just counting heads and leaving it to parliament. The courts are a fundamental democratic component of our unwritten constitution. The Rule of Law and the Separation of Powers are hallmarks of our democracy. They are not antithetical to it. The resolution of moral, social and even 'political' issues is not the exclusive prerogative of parliament. The courts too have a fundamental role in resolving these matters.

Frank Underwood in *House of Cards* said, "democracy is so overrated." This may have come from his reading of Plato and Aristotle who, speaking from the home of democracy thousands of years earlier had expressed their serious reservations about the Athenian constitution. There is a view that a democratic constitution is in itself undemocratic if it gives all power to the elected government. This has been referred to as the 'tyranny of the majority'. De Tocqueville, when commenting on the newly formed United States Constitution said,

I am trying to imagine under what novel features despotism may appear in the world. In the first place I see an innumerable multitude of men, alike and equal, constantly circling around in pursuit of the petty and banal pleasure with which they glut their souls...over this kind of men stands an immense, protective power which is alone responsible for securing their enjoyment and watching over their fate.

He was referring to democracy.

John Dryden in in the seventeenth century in *Absalom and Achitophel* said:

Nor is the people's judgment always true; the most may err as grossly as the few.

The justification for democracy is not, therefore, that a majority is likely to be right, but that majority voting is fair since it treats everyone equally. But even here there is a problem, because logically unless there is a confined choice between only two options, majority voting cannot guarantee a majority preference. The second problem comes from human nature that a majority may oppress unpopular minorities or create repressive laws as a response to an emergency or be used as a tool by a ruling cabal.

Modern democracy, which revolves around an idea of popular sovereignty has no necessary connection to liberalism and is alien to the thinking of the ancient Greeks. In classical Athens, democracy presupposed shared norms, a shared religious horizon and a shared protection of egalitarian ideals; it revolved around periodic public assemblies in which all the citizens met as one, and had, as its characteristic procedure, the random selection of citizens to fill almost all the key offices of justice, administration and government. As Socrates discovered at his trial for impiety and corrupting the youth in 399 BC, the ordinary citizens of ancient Athens found no truck for non-conformists. Their collective freedom to wield their power was perfectly compatible with the complete subjugation of the individual to the community.

Rousseau was characteristically blunt in conceding that his views had also no connection with any concept of natural rights in the Social Contract, his 1762 treatise on political rights; he argued strenuously that slavery was unnatural and illegitimate but speculated that it was perhaps a prerequisite of democracy in Athens. He wrote:

There are some unfortunate situations when one cannot preserve one's freedom except at the expense of others, and when the citizen can only be perfectly free if the slave is enslaved.

It is to be noted that this was the case in the first decade of the American experiment in democracy.

Hans Kelsen made a similar observation about modern conceptions of democracy in his 1920 monograph, The Essence and Value of Democracy:

Even with the limitless expansion of state power and, consequently, the complete loss of individual freedom and the negation of the liberal ideal, democracy is still possible as long as this state power is constituted by its subjects. Indeed, history demonstrates that democratic state power tends toward expansion no less than its autocratic counterpart.

This point is illustrated by James Miller in Can Democracy Work?[173] He suggests that a majority of voters in a modern representative democracy may very well support policies that are explicitly illiberal, as some Americans fear had happened after the election in 2016 of Donald J. Trump as the forty-fifth President of the United States. His opinion is that democracy does not entail liberalism, and vice versa—even if the two ideas sometimes became intertwined, as most notably occurred in America in the course of the twentieth century.

This country claims to be a liberal democracy, as do most European states and the United States. We have a constitution which has resulted from a compromise between individual freedom and the public good. Our elected government can restrict our freedom by enacting legislation which prioritises one way of life above another but does not tie the hands of change. The doctrine of the separation of powers has as its principal objective, the prevention of the tyranny of the majority by dividing up power. It is in that context that judicial review should be seen as a fundamental check on the downside of majority rule.

In so doing, the application of the remedy will disclose the essential characteristics of a representative democracy. This means a system of governance which emanates not simply from the will of the people but from the application of the normative values which we as individuals hold intrinsic. That involves keeping an equilibrium between the general interests of our society and our individual rights. The distinction between general interests and individual rights is at the heart of judicial review and our legal system. It is getting that balance right which is the problem.

Lord Hoffman, in *R (Alconbury Ltd) v Environment Secretary* [2003] 2 AC 295 on page 325 said:

In a democratic country, decisions as to what the general interests requires, are made by democratically elected bodies or persons accountable to them.

He observed that sometimes the subject matter is such that parliament can itself lay down general rules for enforcement by the courts and cited taxation as an example in that parliament decides on grounds of general interests what taxation is required, and the rules according to which it should be levied. The application of those rules to determine the liability of a particular person is then a matter for independent and impartial tribunals such as the General or Special Commissioners or the Courts.

However, often one cannot formulate general rules and the question of what the general interests require has to be determined on an empirical basis. Town and country planning, in which every decision is in some respects different, is an archetypal example. In such cases, parliament may delegate the decision-making power to local democratically elected bodies, or to the Ministers of the Crown responsible to parliament. Lord Hoffman's view was that in that way the democratic principle is preserved.

Professor Jeffrey Jowell has stated, "It is the prerogative of parliament to undermine democracy by overriding constitutional principle, however fundamental." He argues, "We have moved significantly towards a model of democracy that is based upon limited government rather than majority rule alone." This he says is a 'fundamental shift' which has been accelerated by the operation of the Human Rights Act 1998.

However, Lord Hoffman's approach is that there is no conflict between Human Rights and the democratic principle as he argues, "respect for human rights requires that certain basic rights of individuals should not be capable in any circumstances of being overridden by the majority even if they think that the public interest so requires." It has been suggested that the familiar refrain in which almost all public lawyers still happily join that parliament can exclude any and every right, "by express language or by necessary implication" is really a fudge designed to obscure some awkward questions of constitutional authority.

The key issue is if it were to be accepted that the courts now properly enforce a higher order of rights inherent in our constitutional democracy and recognise that such rights emanate not from any implied parliamentary intent, but from the framework of modern democracy within which parliament legislates it may seem that we have repudiated unqualified majority rule. Both Professor Jowell and Sir John Laws have stated that fundamental rights are not a consequence of the democratic process, they are logically prior to it. They, therefore, cannot be abrogated by a simple parliamentary majority.

In those circumstances, it is argued that ultimate sovereignty rests in every civilised constitution, not with those who wield governmental power, but in the conditions under which they are permitted to do so. It follows that parliament's sovereignty cannot be a creature of statute but rests on the judicial interpretation of an unwritten constitution. If a higher order law confers it, it must of necessity limit it.

To return to the example of Human Rights given by Lord Hoffman in *Alconbury*, even rights which are not stricto senso human rights should, "be capable of being overridden in very restricted circumstances" (page 325 D). He describes those rights as rights "which belong to individuals simply by virtue of their humanity, independently of any utilitarian calculation." In his judgment, the protection of these basic rights from majority decision is for the courts.

They should have the power to decide whether legislation infringes them and either (as in the United States to declare such legislation invalid or as in the United Kingdom) to declare that it is incompatible with the governing Human Rights instrument. But he emphasises outside these basic rights there are many decisions which have to be made every day, "for example about the allocation of resources" in which the only fair method of decision is by some person or body accountable to the electorate.

All democratic societies recognise that while there are some basic rights which attach to the ownership of property, they are heavily qualified by the considerations of the public interest. This can be seen in Article 1 of the Protocol of the Convention:

Every natural or legal person is entitled to the peaceful enjoyment of his possessions. No one shall be deprived of his possessions except in the public interest and subject to the conditions provided for by law and by the general principles of international law.

The preceding provisions shall not, however, in any way impair the right of a state to enforce such laws as it deems necessary to control the use of property in accordance with the general interest or to secure the payment of taxes or other contributions or penalties.

The first paragraph of the Protocol provides that property may be taken by the state on payment of compensation if the public interest so requires. Under the second paragraph, the use of property may be restricted without compensation on similar grounds. In Lord Hoffman's view, "importantly, the question of what the public interest requires for the purpose of Article 1 of the first Protocol can and should be determined according to the democratic principle—by elected local or central bodies or by ministers accountable to them." He maintained, "there is no principle of human rights which requires such decisions to be made by independent and impartial tribunals."

The other fundamental principle which must exist in a democratic society is the Rule of Law. Where ministers or officials make decisions affecting the rights of individuals, they must do so in accordance with the law. The legality of what they do must be subject to review by independent and impartial tribunals. The principles of judicial review give effect to the Rule of Law. They ensure that administrative decisions will be taken rationally in accordance with a fair procedure and within the powers conferred by parliament.

Democracy does not mean whatever the people may decide at a given moment. It means a set of rules and procedures for securing their control over decision-making or decision-makers on an ongoing basis. The Rule of Law is the means for ensuring such control and making it effective. There are a number of constituent parts. There must first be institutional arrangements in place to affect such control, a democratic electoral system and limits to the powers of judges, ministers and legislators.

There should be a high degree of openness, transparency and accountability on the part of those in power. There should be an independent and impartial judicial system in place to provide remedies for individuals against illegal state action or maladministration. There should be a set of guaranteed liberties such as freedom of speech so that the people have the opportunity to express their views and influence the government in policymaking.

What I have described above can be characterised as popular control which in my view is a fundamental principle of democracy. The second fundamental principle is political equality. This is essentially a moral principle that all people should be equal in the exercise of popular control. We all have the right to express views on what might affect our lives and we all have an equal capacity for self-determination. It is this principle which ensures that citizens are treated equally before the law and share equal rights of citizenship.

The argument that the United Kingdom has what was described as a 'democratic deficit' emerged in the 1980s. The question is, does it still have that deficit in 2025? Are there effective institutional arrangements in place to ensure a distribution of power between people and government and between different levels of government?

Is there an arguable democratic deficit in the UK in that central government has gained total dominance over local government so that the latter has become just the means whereby central policy is executed at a local level? On the other hand has the central government at Westminster seen power over many issues passed to the European Community? It is arguable that for the democratic deficit to be addressed, there needs to be a clearer division of power between the various levels at which government can operate—local, regional, national and in the case of the EEC, supranational.

Is there not an argument that policy should be determined at that level of government most able to implement it, and that should be the lowest level practicable? Effective local government is in this view essential to the overall democratic vitality of society. There is also an argument relating to devolution in Scotland, Wales and Northern Island that regional government should be a feature of a truly democratic system to reflect the legitimate aspirations of people in particular areas of the nation.

The individual today is overregulated, which encourages conflicts between the individual and the state. The purpose of administrative law is to provide legal rules, institutions and machinery which try to guarantee that governmental functions are exercised efficiently to produce beneficial effects for the individual. Government policies should be operated in such a way as far as possible not to produce conflict. Power should be exercised openly, fairly and impartially and individuals aggrieved by administrative action should have recourse to independent dispute resolution machinery and expert advice.

But legal rules, institutions and machinery cannot by themselves create a Utopia. Many disputes between individuals and the state fall beyond the range of law. Complaints about the personal style of administrators and the ways in which they behave towards those lives they affect and the manifold range of conflicts that arise merely from the fact of being governed are unlikely to receive adequate redress in court.

Often issues of democracy come down to who should decide—parliament, or the Courts? It is an aspect of the doctrine of the Separation of Powers which is an intrinsic part of our constitution. Let's take then a relatively recent example of democracy in action in the case of *R (Nickleson) v DPP* [2014] UKSC 38. This involved the consideration of the right to assisted suicide. Mr Nickleson applied to the High Court for a declaration that:

a) It would be lawful for a doctor to kill him or to assist him in terminating his life, or if that was refused.
b) A declaration that the current state of the law was incompatible with Article 8 of the European Convention on Human Rights.

Lord Sumption's judgment is of some relevance in that it considers whether an issue of this kind requires a democratic mandate. He and the other members of the court took the view that the question of relaxing or qualifying the current absolute prohibition on assisted suicide was a classic example of the kind of issue which should be decided by parliament. The first reason he gave was that the issue involved a choice between two fundamental but mutually inconsistent moral values upon which there is, "at present no consensus in our society" (see page 85). Such choices, he said are, "inherently legislative in nature." The decision he said, cannot fail to be strongly influenced by the decision-maker's personal opinion about the moral case for assisted suicide. On this point, he concluded:

this is entirely appropriate if the decision-makers are those who represent the community at large. It is not appropriate for professional Judges. The imposition of their personal opinions on matters of this kind would lack all constitutional legitimacy.

A second reason was that parliament had already made the relevant choice in that it had passed the Suicide Act in 1961 and as recently as 2009, amended Section 2 of the Act without altering the principle. He said that in recent years there have been a number of Bills to decriminalise assistance to suicide, at least in part, but none have been passed into law. (I note that at the time of writing this book, this still remains the case as there is a Bill but no act). On this basis, he observed that there simply has not been enough parliamentary support for a change in the law and that represented the current position of the representative body in our constitution. He cited Lord Bingham's observations in *R (Countryside Alliance) v Attorney General* [2008] AC 719 at paragraph 45:

The democratic process is liable to be subverted if on a question of moral and political judgement, opponents of the Act achieve through the courts what they could not achieve in Parliament.

Thirdly, he considered that the parliamentary process is a better way of resolving issues involving controversial and complicated questions of fact arising out of moral and social dilemmas. He stated in paragraph 232:

The legislature has access to a fuller range of expert judgement than forensic legislation can possibly provide. It is better able to take account of the interests of groups not represented or not sufficiently represented before the court in resolving what it surely a classic polycentric problem.

Critical to his analysis on this issue was that where firm factual conclusions are elusive, parliament can legitimately act on an instinctive judgement about what the facts are likely to be in a case where the evidence is inconclusive or slight. He concluded that it was for parliament to act, "where the truth is inherently unknowable."

Although the above reasoning is that of Lord Sumption, it largely reflects the majority of the Judgments of the Supreme Court in its consideration of the democratic principles which apply to the demarcation between what is for the legislature and what is for the courts. Lord Neuberger (who wrote the foreword to this book) in *Nickleson* on the issue of assisted suicide on page 27 in paragraph 84 said, "any question of decriminalisation should be left to parliament as it is a controversial, difficult and sensitive moral and politico-social issue which requires the assessment of many types of risk and the imposition of potentially complex regulations and it is not a matter on which judges are particularly well informed or experienced."

In *Nickleson*, the Supreme Court was, it seems to me, saying essentially that the issue before them was not justiciable. A number of reasons are given for this, none of which in my view are individually or collectively supportive of that ruling. Lord Neuberger's list was as follows; firstly, the question was controversial. That cannot be a reason for not deciding an issue. Nearly all cases raise controversial questions, especially at the appellate level.

Secondly, he said the question was difficult. That again cannot result in the conclusion that it is, therefore, not justiciable. The third reason was, "it was a sensitive moral and politico-social issue." Again, the fact that a question is a sensitive one and raises moral and politico-social issues does not mean that the court's jurisdiction to decide it is excluded. There are many cases decided in the common law which are of such a kind.

Notwithstanding my differences of opinion with that great judge, a former Master of the Rolls and President of the Supreme Court, you will have noticed that he has written a very flattering foreword to this book. That is because we both understand that differences of opinion are very common at the Bar and the Bench, but we remain learned friends. Some more learned than others as in the case with he learned Lord Neuberger. The above just shows that great minds do not necessarily think alike, especially legal minds!

If I may at this point slightly digress on a related matter, dissenting judgements. The concept of a dissenting judgement is one of the cornerstones of our court system at appellate levels. Maybe it is a case of to err is human but to dissent is divine! Dissenting judgements often contain the most interesting and perceptive analyses of legal issues. Some would say that they often represent pearls of judicial wisdom and creativity.

Morality and the extent to which the law should enforce morals is a major jurisprudential issue as exemplified by the Hart/Devlin debate in the 1960s. Of course, law, in its essence, enforces normative values including morality. The right to assisted suicide is much more than a moral issue. It also raises issues which can properly be characterised as legal—namely the existence or otherwise of a fundamental right. For the same reason, the fact that it is a politico-social issue (whatever that means) does not make it non-justiciable. All issues of law could be characterised as having a political-social aspect to them.

Lord Sumption took the view that the view was 'inherently legislative in nature'. Again, I do not accept that as a good reason for ousting the jurisdiction of the courts. The development of the common law meant and meant that the judges make law. True, not through Acts of Parliament but because of the powers vested in them as the judiciary. The purpose of the common law is in large part to supplement legislation and judges have the power to do that and have historically done that for centuries.

Although law is an emanation of the state it should be remembered that the courts too are part of the state. The doctrine of the Separation of Powers and the Rule of Law vests in the court the power to determine issues which are not expressly covered by legislation. The courts are concerned with the administration of justice and the protection of the rights of the individual and society generally.

The right to assisted suicide is arguably a right vested in an individual in the same way as other rights of a fundamental nature such as the right to liberty, freedom of speech, equality of opportunity and access to justice. If the right to die is a correlative right to the right to live then how can the courts conclude that it is not a matter for them to consider because of the controversial and difficult nature of the question?

Of course, it raises difficult issues which I would more properly characterise as legal and philosophical. But for the courts to refuse to entertain the argument is, in my view, an abrogation of their responsibilities as judges to administer justice. In fact, it is denying access to the courts on an issue of fundamental significance as to the rights of man and a matter of public interest relating to the public good.

The common law has historically prided itself on the development of the law in the interests of the public good, as well as the resolution of private disputes between the parties before the court. There is a difference between law and justice. Parliament can enact unjust laws, but the courts are there to ensure that justice should prevail where the strict application of the law will result in an injustice to an individual or society generally. Interpreting a statute in such a way as to reach a fair and just decision is a proper canon of statutory construction.

Lord Sumption also refused to consider the issue because at present there is 'no consensus in our society' and the issue raised matters of 'personal opinion'. Again, the reason why judges are called upon to decide issues is invariably because there is no consensus as to a matter and the fact that there may be differences of opinion in different persons is precisely why courts are invariably asked to choose between differences of opinion. He further went on to say that if the courts went on to consider this matter, "it would lack all constitutional legitimacy."

With respect, I disagree. It is entirely legitimate for the courts and consistent with their obligation to individuals and to society generally to determine matters which, although difficult and controversial, should be determined by the courts. There is nothing in the principles of democracy which would preclude such consideration. The courts are a fundamental part of the democratic process.

Judges, in my view, would be more informed and experienced in the task of resolving jurisprudential issues of this kind than lay Members of Parliament. A judicial ruling on whether there is a right to assisted suicide is to the extent that the issue is does that right exists in law and whether should relief be granted by way of declaration are pre-eminently matters for the judges. There would be nothing inconsistent with the principles of democracy in their so doing. On the contrary, it would be supportive of the two fundamental planks of our democracy—the Separation of Powers and the Rule of Law.

Chapter 19

I at least think it better that my lyre be out of tune and discordant or a chorus I might equip be disharmonious, or that most men might disagree with me and say the opposite of what I say than that I—just one man be discordant with myself and say opposite things within myself.

Socrates

When Demosthenes was asked what was the first part of oratory, he answered 'action' and which was the second he replied 'action' and which was the third 'action'.

Plutarch

Eloquence is the depiction of thought.

Pascall

Plato's *Gorgias*[174] is about the 'ethics' of argument in the literal sense of that term (which in Greek means both 'habit' and 'character') for the main issue to which it returns again and again is the kind of character a person defines for himself and offers to others—the kind of life and community he makes—when he chooses to think and talk in one way rather than in another.[175] This is Plato's concern from the very beginning when Socrates gives Chaerephon the seemingly innocuous, but in fact deeply threatening text, direction to ask Gorgias 'who he is' (447c), and it runs through to Socrates' defence of his own way of life, despite its terrible costs, at the end (521a-27e).

In the *Gorgias*, Plato focuses upon two contrasting ways of speaking, of being, and of establishing a community with others, both of which can be described as forms of argument: 'rhetoric', which he attacks, and 'dialectic', which he defends and intends to exemplify. Of rhetoric, there are three representatives: Gorgias, the Sicilian visitor to Athens and one of the first teachers of rhetoric; Polus (which means the 'colt'), his brash young student; and Callicles, a mature practitioner of the rhetorician's art. Opposed to them are two exemplars of dialectic: Socrates, in relation to these interlocutors, and Plato, in relation to the reader.

Gorgias of Leontini was born in Sicily early in the fifth century BC and lived to be over one hundred years old. He came to Athens for the first time in 427 BC, making a great impression with his oratory. He was a contemporary of Protagoras, the sophist about whom Plato wrote a dialogue of that name, and is sometimes said to have been a sophist, too. But Gorgias' interest was less in the sophisticated devices of reasoning by which the weaker case could be made to appear the stronger than in the emotional power of rhythmic and musical speech.

For our purposes, it is best to take both Gorgias himself and the 'rhetoric' of which he was the master as they are defined for us by the present text, rather than engaging in an independent historical inquiry about them. Of Callicles and Polus, almost nothing is known beyond what Plato tells us here, except that Polus became a teacher of rhetoric.[176]

The dramatic date of the dialogue is impossible to determine since evidence within it supports dates ranging from 429 to 405 BC.[177] [178]

Citations to the *Gorgias* will be made in this chapter by parenthetical references to the uniform Stephanus page numbers and letters.

The *Gorgias* is a dialogue, not a treatise, and it is important to ask at the outset why Plato chooses to write this way, instead of simply telling us what he believes in some straightforward fashion. Is it his idea to make philosophy entertaining, to put a sugar coating on the dull pill of truth, or does this form have purposes of another sort? In particular, why do we have three interlocutors of such different capacities and characters talking with Socrates on the same subject?

This will mean that some arguments are brought up in different terms and contexts all over again and that some arguments raised early are later dropped and never answered. Indeed, the very topic of the dialogue seems never to stay fixed: now it is rhetoric, now pleasure, now what we mean by the shameful or the admirable, now whether it is important to be able to protect oneself against harm, and so on. Nor are the methods of argument all of a piece: sometimes Socrates engages in a logical refutation.

The most important Greek terms of value used in the *Gorgias* are *agathon* ('good') and its opposite *kakon* ('bad'), and *kalon* ('noble') and its opposite *aischron* ('shameful'). These words are the most powerful terms of praise and blame in the Greek of the time, operating as terms of final conclusion in an argument: if it is *kakon* or *aischron*, no one could want it; if it is *agathon* or *kalon*, everyone will want it, for that is what the terms mean. Not surprisingly, then, they have a very wide range of uses and associations, not wholly reproducible in English even by lengthy disquisition, let alone by bland substitutions such as the traditional ones given above. As one would expect of such terms, within their ranges of meaning there are deep conflicts and contradictions that reflect tensions basic to the culture as a whole.

The *Gorgias* is in an important sense about these words and others related to them: about what they should be taken to mean, how they should be defined or redefined; about the ways in which the contradictions they entail might be resolved; and about the patterns of meaning in which they should be arranged. Its object is to construct a coherent language of value out of the naturally complex and inconsistent materials of its time and, in so doing, to define new possibilities for the life of the self and of the community.

There are in Greek other uses of the words *agathon*, *kakon*, *kalon*, and *aischron* that commend the presence or decry the absence of what we would be more inclined to call moral virtues: lawfulness, mercy, a sense of community and equality, and the like. These can for our purposes be summed up, as Plato and Socrates do, under the headings of justice and temperance. The tension between these two kinds of usage creates a problem deep in the Greek language and culture, which is a central purpose of the *Gorgias* to address and elaborate on.

The dialogue goes in outline something like this. When asked 'who he is', as defined by what he does in the world, Gorgias says that he is a rhetorician and a teacher of rhetoric (449a). In response to a series of questions by Socrates, he defines rhetoric as the art of persuading others, especially those with power in the state, primarily about questions of justice and injustice; rhetoric itself is thus an enormous power, which can be used for good or ill (449d-54b). It works not by imparting knowledge about such things as justice and injustice, but by giving rise to the desired opinions about them (454e-55a).

When Socrates asks whether the individual who is to practise this art must himself nonetheless know about the just and the unjust, the humiliating (*aischron*) and the admirable (*kalon*), the advantageous and the good (*agathon*), and the worthless and the bad (*kakon*), about which he is to persuade others, Gorgias says that of course, a rhetorician must know these things and that if a student comes to him who does not know them, Gorgias will teach him (459d-60a).

It is to be noted that Socrates does not now pursue the line of questioning obviously left open by Gorgias' response: what is the nature of 'justice', how is it known, and how is it taught? That is because this dialogue is not about the nature of justice—for that see the *Republic*—but is about a prior question, the proper standing of talk about justice in the first place. When Gorgias concedes the importance of the question he concedes Socrates' essential point.

Young Polus, eager to tangle with Socrates, now breaks in and rejects the concession that Gorgias has just made. He says that Gorgias is simply ashamed (*aischunomai*) to admit the truth, which is that a rhetorician need have no special knowledge of justice, injustice, and the rest, in order to practise the art of persuading people about them (460b-60c). Socrates welcomes his participation, so long as Polus agrees to engage in the process of refutation by question and answer, as he chooses (461d-62b). Polus elects to do the questioning, but quickly reveals that he has no idea at all how to do it; he ends up simply asking Socrates what kind of art he thinks rhetoric is (462b-62e). In response, Socrates makes a brief speech in which he says that it is not an art at all, but merely a knack, which has as its object the production of pleasure—in fact, it is merely a form of flattery (463a-63c), as cosmetics and cookery are.

Socrates is now asked an amusingly confused series of questions by Polus, at the heart of which is the assertion that it must be a great thing to be a rhetorician, for they have so much power in the city that they are practically dictators (466b-66c). Socrates responds by asserting a set of paradoxical propositions, which Polus at first denies, but then is forced to concede. The first of these is that the rhetorician and the dictator have the least power in the cities of which they seem to be masters (466d-68e), "for they do virtually nothing that they want to do, but only whatever they think best" (466e).[179] (That is, they can do whatever they wish but still be mistaken about whether it will advance what they really want.)

In a similar fashion, Polus is led to conceding that it is worse (more *kakon*) to do injustice than to suffer it and that although the unjust man cannot be happy, he will be less wretched if he is punished than if he is not (469a-79e).[180] These statements are paradoxical because the words for 'doing injustice' and 'punishing' have a substantial element that means 'injure', without regard to what we would call right and wrong. In the competitive sense of '*agathon*', it cannot possibly be 'better' to suffer an injury—a diminution of autonomy and power—than to inflict one.

Socrates compels these concessions in his usual manner: first by eliciting acquiescence in certain propositions that the interlocutor cannot deny, and then by showing that they lead to conclusions very different from what he had imagined. In this conversation, the key admission is that although it is in Polus's view worse (more *kakon*) to suffer injustice, it is more ugly and humiliating (more *aischron*) to do injustice (474c). Socrates shows that this is not a possible set of positions, because what is more *aischron* must also be more *kakon* (474c-75d).

At this point, Callicles intervenes. He rejects this concession, saying that Polus, like Gorgias, is ashamed (*aischunomai*) to admit what he really thinks, which is that it is obviously better both to do wrong rather than suffer wrong and to avoid punishment rather than endure it (482d-82e). The defect in Socrates' refutation, he says, is that it confuses the categories of nature and convention: it is by nature *kakon* to suffer injustice; only by convention is it *aischron* to inflict it. If one looks to nature rather than to convention it is both more *kakon* and more *aischron* to suffer than to do injustice (483a). That is the position Polus was ashamed to admit.

As Socrates earlier claimed that whatever is *aischron* is *kakon*, Callicles here reverses the equation: what is *kakon* is *aischron*. The conventions that establish the sense of *aischron* used by Socrates and accepted by Polus, says Callicles, are the work of weak people who seek to protect themselves from their natural masters (483b-83c). Being inferior, they are happy enough to settle for general equality. But nature itself declares that it is just for the better (the more *agathos*) to have more than the worse (the more *kakos*), for the more powerful to have more than the less powerful (483d). This is natural as opposed to conventional justice (484a-84c).

Callicles in this way rejects the very language of morality upon which Socrates' refutation depends. He seeks to avoid the traps and limits of the language of his culture by standing outside it, claiming the power to remake his language to coincide with reality as he sees it.

Callicles' substantive position is one of radical hedonism: according to what he calls natural justice and excellence, one who wants to live correctly should allow his desires to be as great as possible, satisfying them as they arise, without attempting to restrain them (*kolazein*), but rather serving them with all his manliness and intelligence (491e-92a). Of course, this is not possible for most people, so out of shame (*aischune*) for their own weakness, the majority blame such a man and treat lack of restraint or licentiousness (*akolasia*) as shameful and ugly and humiliating (*aischron*). It is because of their own lack of manliness that they praise temperance and justice (492a-92b). In the natural scheme of things, wantonness and licentiousness (*akolasia*) and liberty, if supported by force, are virtue and happiness (492c).

When asked whether or not some pleasures are better than others—how high does the pleasure of scratching an itch rank with him, for example? (494c-94e)—Callicles at first persists in refusing to acknowledge distinctions among them and asserts that the good and the pleasant are the same (494c-95b). But he is then made to admit, among other things, that the coward feels as much pleasure at the retreat of the enemy as the brave man does, perhaps even more, and that the foolish man is as capable of pleasure as the intelligent man: will Callicles, therefore, call the pleasures of such people good (*agathon*)? (497e-98c). If all pleasures are equally good (*agathon*), he must do so.

As a consequence, however, the man called *kakos* because of his cowardice or stupidity becomes as *agathos* as the *agathos* man, an absolutely impossible position for Callicles, for whom the *agathos* man is above all manly, brave, and successful (499b). But to accept the alternative, and admit that some pleasures are better than others, would be to accede to a standard of judgment of exactly the sort he has been at such pains to deny (499b-99c). This in turn opens up the question of what art that standard is to be discovered and defined, which returns us to the subject of rhetoric and dialectic (500a-00d). Callicles thus begins as one who boldly claims to remake his language to accord with moral reality as he sees it but quickly finds that he cannot escape his commitment to its central terms after all. He retreats into a sullen pretence of acquiescence (501c).

The alternative to such ingratiation, which makes one like the object of one's flattery, is to have the aim not of pleasing the people but of making them as good as possible (most *agathos*) (513e). This, in fact, is the aim of Socrates, and of dialectic, which means that he is one of the few, if not the only one, who practises the true art of statesmanship (521d-21e). This also means that, as the world is, Socrates could not put up much of a defence if someone were to use the law unjustly against him (521e-22c); but he does not think that this is humiliating or shameful (*aischron*), as it plainly would be if he were unable to protect himself against the far greater evil of saying or doing unjust things (522d-22e). Socrates then tells a story of the afterlife, in which a person's soul is judged naked, just as it is, for what it is; he says that this is the real trial for which he wishes to prepare himself, not some proceeding brought against him by his enemies at Athens (523a-26d). He concludes by saying this:

Among the many arguments we have made, while the rest were being refuted (elenchomai), this alone stood firm: that one should avoid doing injustice more than suffering it and that more than anything it should be a man's object to be, not to seem, good (agathos), in public and in private; and if one becomes bad (kakos) in some respect, one must be punished or corrected (kolazesthai); and that the second good (agathon) after being just is to become so, and to be corrected (kolazesthai) by paying the penalty; and that one should shun all flattery of oneself or others, of the few or the many; and that rhetoric should always be used towards the end of justice as should every other activity (527b-27c).

Throughout the dialogue, Socrates is at pains to define what he calls 'dialectic' as a way of thinking and living, and to oppose it to rhetoric. For example, he says at the beginning that he does not want to hear an oratorical display by Gorgias, but instead wishes to engage in conversation with him (447c). When Gorgias subsequently makes great claims for the power of rhetoric, Socrates rather gently makes great claims for the power of dialectic.

Socrates rather gently says that he would like to take issue with what Gorgias has said, for it does not seem consistent, but also that he does not want to be offensive. He adds that he himself welcomes being refuted (*elenchomai*) when he says something untrue and welcomes refuting others when they fail to speak the truth; if Gorgias is of the same mind they can proceed; otherwise, they should let the conversation drop (457c-58b). Only when Gorgias agrees to these conditions does Socrates begin his questioning (458b).

Dialectic thus proceeds by question and answer, we learn, and its object is something called 'refutation' or 'correction'. We discover something more about it when Polus seeks to establish that a man can be both unjust and happy by citing the instance of Archelaus, the tyrant of Macedonia (470d). Socrates first speaks to Polus not about the merits of his claim, but about the method by which Polus is proceeding, saying that this sort of argument may be persuasive rhetorically because perhaps most people would agree with it, but that it is no demonstration whatever in dialectic, because he, Socrates, does not agree with it, and a dialectical refutation (*elenchus*) requires that one make the other agree with what one says (471e-72c).

What matters between us is not the other witnesses who can be brought forward to support your view or mine, but whether you can make me your witness, or I can make you mine. For dialectic to exert its full force upon the individual mind, complete frankness is essential; it requires a kind of shamelessness in saying what one really thinks. Thus, Gorgias and Polus perhaps avoid the full force of Socrates' mind by agreeing with him too readily, and Socrates welcomes Callicles' bluntness of speech (487d), for his candour may make possible a real engagement of mind with mind.

The aim of dialectic is to expose contradictions in one's thought, which to Socrates are contradictions in one's very self. He tells Callicles, for example, that he must refute (*exelencho*) the argument that doing injustice is the worst of evils.

> or, Callicles himself will not agree with you, Callicles, but you will be in discord all your life; and yet I at least think it better that my lyre be out of tune and discordant, or a chorus I might equip be disharmonious, or that most men might disagree with me and say the opposite of what I say, than that I—just one man—be discordant with myself and say opposite things within myself (482b).

Still, as I suggested above, the most important definitions of dialectic are actually to be found not in such statements as these, but in the activities presented in the text, those activities by which Socrates engages the minds of his interlocutors, and Plato the mind of his reader. What can be said of these?[181] What is the life exemplified here and how does the peculiar form of the dialogue work to express it? What kind of attention does this text invite, and what kind of meaning does it yield?

Mind and Language: Dialectical Culture

We can start with the paragraph quoted at the close of the summary given above.[182] Here, we have a set of propositions, each of which has been repeated over and over during the course of the dialogue; upon them, Socrates now says that he confidently rests, however erroneous his other statements may have been (527b). This paragraph is thus explicitly offered as the central statement of the text as a whole. But the statement is a strange one because all of the propositions it collects, as their earlier reception in the dialogue has made plain, are what is called, in Greek as well as in English, 'paradoxical', that is, preposterous, 'out of place', what no one would ever say.

How can it possibly be more *agathon* (advantageous) and *kalon* (befitting to the powerful) and less *aischron* (humiliating) and *kakon* (worthless) to suffer wrong than to inflict it? It seems that the words cannot bear the meanings given to them. If the rest of the dialogue did not exist and these statements stood alone, they would seem crazy or meaningless. They could certainly not be taken seriously, for they arrange the materials of the culture in ways that are, in the first instance at least, simply impossible.

But this very fact suggests a way of understanding the aim of the dialogue as a whole: it is to offer the reader a set of experiences that so change his sense of things, including his sense of his language and himself, that when at the end these statements occur together as a kind of summary of what has been said over and over in various ways in the rest of the dialogue, they no longer seem paradoxical, but natural and coherent and powerful and clear. In this rather literal sense, it can be said that the object of the dialogue is the making of a new language.

But what kind of language is this and how is it put together? It is important to see that this is for the most part not an artificial or theoretical language, based upon stipulative definitions that are then combined into propositions connected by the laws of logic, but is instead what might be called a natural or poetic language, in which terms have overlapping and inconsistent meanings, internal complexities and lacunae. Accordingly, in establishing this language the dialogue proceeds not by logical progression from premise to conclusion but in an associative fashion, with many repetitions of question, idea, and term, often leaving a subject only to return to it later, perhaps in a surprising way. It is full of play and paradox and has a structure less of a formal argument (as we usually think of it) than of a poem, drama or musical composition. The recurrences of terms and statements are not really repetitions after all, for they acquire new meaning from what else is said, as a metaphor or image or melody may do: at the end, they make sense in a new way.

This view of the dialogue helps explain how Socrates can speak in the closing paragraphs so dismissively of the other statements he has made when he suggests that they can perhaps be refuted (527b).[183] The reason is that the relationship between those statements and what he says now is not one of logical proof (if it were, the validity of his conclusions would depend absolutely upon the validity of the earlier statements) but is both looser and more complex than that. Some of the 'proofs' Socrates offered in the conversation were plainly specious;[184] others we suspected to be so; and much was plainly motivated, in emphasis at least, by the nature of the social or dramatic moment.[185]

Here, Socrates is saying that he knows all this and that it does not matter. Not that we could not go back to those arguments and straighten them out, or at least arrive at a common view of them. But we cannot do everything at once, and the things he says now are those that matter most and that we know most clearly.

Socrates here also tells us that he does not put the same weight on everything he says, as he would have to do if the form of the discourse were that of a mathematical or scientific proof; rather, he recognises that we live in a world in which there are many things to say, of which some are jokes, some seem right but we are unsure, some seem dubious, and some are statements upon which one rests. It is the last that we are given in the final paragraph.

How is this language of paradox made? The most obvious method is the overt definition of terms. Consider, for example, the definition of rhetoric that Socrates leads Gorgias to make at the very beginning. He starts with the question: with what is the art of rhetoric concerned (449c-49d)? With words (or speech)? But so, in a way are many other arts; medicine, for example, uses words for diseases and for medicines.

Might rhetoric be concerned with words abstracted from the material universe, with words alone, so to speak? But so is arithmetic. Gorgias then says that what rhetoric offers is the power to persuade (*peitho*) (452e). But rhetoric is not the only art of persuasion, Socrates responds; in fact, every art that has a subject persuades with respect to that subject, as medicine does with respect to sickness and health (453b). With respect to what subject does rhetoric persuade? Gorgias answers: with respect to what is just and unjust (454b). And so on. This is a process of conceptual clarification that seems to be not threatening but helpful, a way of asking how we can accurately describe this part of our social and intellectual universe. The fact that the definitions are not stipulated, but cooperatively arrived at, means that it is not merely a clarification but an instruction in the processes of making things clear.

By contrast, in his definition of rhetoric as flattery[186] Socrates is not drawing distinctions his interlocutors already make (perhaps without knowing it) so much as offering a new set of distinctions for shared use, and doing so argumentatively, for he knows that the others will not see things in this way. Socrates similarly creates a new system of meaning when, in his engagement with Polus, he draws a distinction, not present in ordinary Greek, between doing 'whatever one thinks best' and doing 'what one wants' (467b).

At times, the language of Socrates is overtly poetic rather than logical, for example, in the fable he seeks to show Callicles that the orderly (*kosmios*) are happier than the licentious (*akolastos*). Imagine two men, he says, each with a number of jars to be filled with milk, honey, wine, and the like. The jars of the one are sound and full, and he wants nothing; those of the other are leaky, and he must constantly struggle to keep them full. Does this image not portray the difference between the life of one who wants nothing and the life of one who is constantly scurrying after pleasures? (493d-94a).

This fable is addressed not to the intellectual part of Callicles, but to the part of his mind that thinks and feels in images. It asks him to imagine, almost as if he were dreaming, what it would really be like to be a leaky jar, constantly running out and being refilled, and to be an owner, in frantic motion, constantly filling, or to be sound and full and at rest. As in a dream, the image of the self takes more than one form, here both jar and owner, and the story is about deep feelings of the self: anxiety and loss versus security and gain.

Or consider Socrates' discussion of Archelaus as an example of felicity (470d-72d): to ask a person to imagine himself as someone else, and to see how he would like it, is very different indeed from asking an abstract question. It invites a response of feeling and taste, as well as of intellect. Likewise, the imagined trial in the afterlife should be read not as a religious statement (especially not as an expression of a proto-Christianity) but as a way of conceiving the self as an entity, naked and isolated.

The social implications of these poetic modes of discourse are different from those of the logical refutations; they are less competitive and combative. While the logical proofs and refutations have a kind of forcefulness that the myths, stories and speeches lack, their very form means that they can also be refuted, as the more poetic parts cannot be, or at least not in the same logical way.

The ethical premise in the dialogue is the central importance of motive or intention in determining the condition of the self. The difference between rhetoric and dialectic is at heart one not of method but of aim. It is for this reason that Socrates is satisfied when Gorgias says that the good rhetorician must know and be able to teach justice (459c-60a) for once that is granted all else that Socrates cares about will follow.

As we have seen, the social character of rhetoric is directly contrasted with that of dialectic at every point. The goal of rhetoric, for example, is the power to persuade (*peitho*) others, to reduce them to one's will. The goal of dialectic is the opposite of persuasion: to be instructed by being refuted (*elenchomai*), humiliated and corrected. This means that rhetoric naturally treats others as means to an end, while dialectic treats others as ends in themselves. Rhetoric persuades another not by refuting but by flattering him, by appealing to what pleases, rather than to what is best for him.

If successful, it injures him. It injures the persuader as well, for the flatterer, in the nature of things, becomes like the object of his flattery: he praises what the other praises, blames what he blames; in the fullest sense he comes to speak the other's language, and unless the other is a model of excellence, one becomes what one would not be, in one's very self, and that is the worse (the most *kakon* and *aischron*) thing of all.

Dialectic is wholly different both in method and in object. It proceeds not by making lengthy statements or exhibitions, but by questioning and answering in a one-to-one conversation. Its object is to engage each person at the deepest level, and for this, it requires utter frankness of speech on each side, a kind of shamelessness in saying what one really thinks. One's concern is not with what people generally think but with what one thinks oneself and what the other thinks. This is not a competition to see who can reduce the other to his will, but a process of mutual discovery by mutual refutation.

One accepts refutation gladly, for it reduces the divisions and disharmonies within the self, which Socrates tells Callicles are so much worse than those in a discordant orchestra or those between oneself and other people (482b-82c). The object of it all is truth, and its method is friendship, the full recognition of the value of self and the other in a universe of two. One can see why the language of sexuality seems natural to describe these two relations: dialectic is a recognition of self and other and rhetoric is a reification and seduction.

In the world presented in the *Gorgias*, the ideal of dialectic is never achieved. Socrates' attempts to establish relations of this kind all end in failure. Gorgias concedes a central point, but without really understanding it.[187] Polus is refuted, but only in the limited sense that he is beaten and cannot go on (478c-81b); he has not been brought to the position of independent understanding that dialectic requires.[188]

And Callicles, having begun by boasting of his total frankness, at the end simply refuses to talk with Socrates in any honest way and leaves him alone, without an interlocutor, to make the speech in which he defends the way of life that may bring him death.[189] In this sense, the *Gorgias* is the story of a failure of community, not of its success.

This failure suggests a way to define the object of Plato's text: to create in the real world with the reader the kind of dialectical relationship that Socrates is unable to establish with others in the world of the text. Observe how this textual community works: it has as its only object the education of the reader, making him in the Socratic sense more *agathos*, and it works only by his free cooperation and engagement. Its proofs and paradoxes operate, as I have suggested, to loosen the moorings that connect the reader to his language and culture: they break down his language so that he can say neither what he used to say, nor what Socrates offers him to say.

He becomes a self outside his culture, faced with the fact of his own responsibility for making sense of what he hears and says, for becoming his own centre of meaning and of language. The reader is led to see that what is at stake when he decides how to speak and what to say—whether to practice 'rhetoric' or 'dialectic'—is nothing less than 'who he is' and what kind of community he will have with others.

Chapter 20

The utmost abstractions are the weapons with which to control our true thought of concrete fact.

Alfred North Whitehead

Logic turns out to be a good way to verify truth, but this is not the same as convincing others of truth. Verifying truth and conveying truth are two different things

Eugenia Cheng, *The Art of Logic*

The greater part of mankind may be divided into two classes; that of shallow thinkers, who fall short of the truth; and that of abstruse thinkers, who go beyond it. The latter class are by far the most rare; and I may add, by far the most useful and valuable.

David Hume

In law what plea so tainted and corrupt; But being seasoned is the gracious voice which obscures the show of evil.

Shakespeare, *The Merchant of Venice*

The function of law is to maintain a language that keeps alive this very tension between fact and ideal, expediency and justice, self and other; this tension is in fact essential in the practice of talking about what justice requires.

Euphemes

To the modern lawyer, the *Gorgias* presents both a puzzle and a threat. On the one hand, the description of dialectic I have given may remind the lawyer of his or her own legal education, making it seem more truly Socratic than it is sometimes given credit for being. Certainly, the sense that one's relation with one's language is broken down, as one response after another is disproved, is familiar to the law student, as probably also is the sense that these 'proofs' are sometimes deeply fallacious. On the other hand, the object of legal education sometimes seems to be not the establishment of a new shared ground from which questions of justice and injustice can be talked about in a truer way, but mere rhetorical training, the mastery of the means of persuasion available in our legal culture.

Indeed, if what Socrates says about ancient rhetoric and its practitioners is true, how can it not be equally true of modern law and modern lawyers? It is the function of the lawyer, like the rhetorician, to persuade about the just and the unjust, about the expedient and inexpedient, and to do so not among people generally but among those who have power—in the courts, legislatures, and assemblies. Moreover, the lawyer always speaks in the service of someone else whose interests he represents and he accordingly says not what he believes to be true or right about an issue he addresses, but whatever will persuade his audience to act in furtherance of those interests. He is, it seems the modern rhetorician in its purest form, and the law professor is his teacher—a modern Gorgias.

To ask how *Gorgias* speaks to the modern lawyer, and how he might respond, will thus shed light in two directions: forward upon the ethical character of the modern practice of law, which I think is often misperceived, and backwards upon the *Gorgias* itself, as we discover or invent responses on behalf of the modern lawyer to the challenge it presents him.

We do not have a real Socrates with real lawyers, and we must therefore imagine how their argument would go. The exercise is not wholly impossible, however, for the outline of the Socratic case is plain enough from what we have read, and one knows something of lawyers oneself! In what follows, I will present such an imagined conversation, in which I try to show how two lawyers, of somewhat different types, might respond to the case made against rhetoric in the *Gorgias*. These two men, Euerges and Euphemes (Euerges means 'good doer'; Euphemes means 'good speaker'). They have agreed to talk with Socrates as they walk back and forth through a large city park on a spring afternoon.

Socrates: *What I really want to know is who you are and what you do. I know you are called a 'lawyer', but what I want to know is this: what do you do in the world that makes you what you are?*

Euerges: I would put it this way: I give advice to people who seek it from me about their legal rights and duties, and I represent them in legal proceedings.

Socrates: In whose interests are you acting when you do these things?

Euerges: In the interests of my clients, of course. In the interest of the law as well, for in my work I help see to it that the law is obeyed and adhered to and that legal institutions function as they are intended to.

Socrates: Let us take the client first. How does what you do serve his interests?

Euerges: By increasing what can be called his power over the world: his range of choices for action, his liberty, and his wealth. Those are all good things and my clients show by their appreciation that they know this is true. I use the law to help them get what they want. I am their friend in the law.

Socrates: But is it always in someone's interest to increase what you call his 'power'? I suppose you would agree that people sometimes use their 'power' in ways that are self-destructive, and in such cases to increase their power is not a help, but an injury.

Euerges: That is a theoretical possibility, I suppose, but, as the world goes, not a real one. My clients are intelligent, practical people who know what they want and are satisfied by my efforts to help them get it. If what you mean is that it might in some way be better for one of my clients to do something else with his time, energy and money, to become a South Seas missionary, for example, or to write the novel he has always talked about, that is, I suppose, possibly so, though I do not often think about such things. I am not even sure what it would mean to say that such a course was 'better' for one of my clients, since everyone is entitled to his own views on such personal matters. Anyway, who am I to make such a judgment about someone else, especially when I know so few of the relevant facts?

Socrates: But it remains true that you do not after all serve your client's interests, as you originally said, but instead what appear to him to be his interests, that is, his wants and desires. Isn't that right? And in what you have just said you do not deny this but seek to explain or justify it, by pointing to the supposed competence of your clients (and your own supposed incompetence) at deciding what is good for them, and to the allegedly uncertain character of that judgment, whoever makes it. Strictly speaking, then, it is true that you serve not your client's interests but his wishes or his wants.

Euerges: Strictly speaking, that is true.

Socrates: *If so, you are in this respect no different from the keeper of one of those Pleasure Ranches they have out West, who sells its customers whatever they desire, however bad for them it might be: too much food and liquor and drugs, and every kind of sex. In both cases, it is not the client's interests that are catered to but his desires, and in the case of the law, the desire in question is more dangerous than any other, for it is the desire for power.*

Euerges: *This is nonsense! Don't you know that an important part of the practice of law is talking with one's client about the wisdom of one course of action over another, in a mutual attempt to determine what his true interests require? We are constantly teaching our clients that they cannot have everything they want and advise them to pursue what is more important to them and to forgo what is less important. We help them to discover their true interests and to shape their wants to suit those interests.*

Socrates: *If that is so, the present conversation can come to an end, for I have no differences with you, and we should begin on another subject: how do you do what you have just described? Nothing could be more wonderful than to discover a person who knows not only what is best for himself and for others but also how to teach others what their true interests really are. But I imagine that not every lawyer would make such a claim and that many of those who did would mean it by nothing more than this: that they advised their clients how they could gratify their desires the most—as a really expert keeper of a Pleasure Ranch might do, telling his customers not to drink to incapacitation, or not to combine drug A and drug B, and so on—but having no concern at all for their true interests. Shall I tell you what I would say to such a lawyer? If you permit me, I will make a speech to him, and you can tell me when I am done whether you and I are wrong, or he is.*

Here is what I would say: by reason of your training and natural capacities you have what is commonly called a great power, the power of persuading those who have power of a different kind, political and economic power, to do what you wish them to do. Of course, your power is not absolute, for there are limits to what even you can achieve. Properly speaking, this is not a true power unless it is exercised in your true interests, but it is a real force, as your record of success and the fees you receive demonstrate, and we can speak as others do and call it a 'power' too, though putting it in quotation marks.

Your professional aim is to present your case, whatever its merits so that those with control over economic and political forces will decide for your client, and you must succeed when you most prevail. You use your mind, as we used to say of the sophists, to make the weaker argument appear the stronger. Your goal in all of this is to get the most, first for your client, but ultimately for yourself, for what you do with your 'power' of persuasion is to sell it, getting in exchange another 'power', that of money. Of course, neither the power of money nor the power of persuasion is a good thing in itself; that depends upon whether they are used to advance or injure one's interests, and that is no concern of yours, with respect to your client or apparently to yourself.

You say you are your client's friend, but you do not serve his interests; in truth, you are not his friend, but his flatterer, which is to be his enemy. Your concern is not with his real interests but with assisting him to attain whatever it is he may desire. If it should happen that what you do does advance his true interests and thus tends to make him happy rather than unhappy, that still does not make you his friend, because for you that result is accidental, of no interest or consequence. Not having been your object it can be no ground for your satisfaction. Likewise, you are no friend to the law, for you will always say that justice requires whatever it is that your client wishes, and you use all your skill and art to make it seem that this is so.

In all of this, you are least of all friends to yourself, for in return for money that you cannot take the time to learn how to spend, you give yourself the mind and character of one who does these things. You never ask yourself in a serious way what fairness and justice require in a particular case to do that would not leave time for what you do. In fact, you incapacitate yourself for the pursuit of such a question by giving yourself the mind of the case-maker and brief-writer, of one who looks ceaselessly for the characterisation, the turn of phrase, or the line of argument, that will make your client's case, however weak, seem the stronger. To persuade those whom you must persuade you devote yourself with the attention of a lover to the ways in which they can be pleased, to the tricks of voice and manner and tone, to the kinds of argument, that will persuade this jury or that judge, this tax official or that fellow lawyer.

The art of rhetoric is in fact the art of ministration to the pleasures of another, really a species of prostitution. As the sexual responses and energies of a prostitute are debased and debasing by the way they are employed, so also are your intellectual energies and responses, your ways of seeing things and describing them, your ways of making appeals and claims and arguments, the very workings of your mind and the feelings of your heart.

When you represent an unjust client you are in the position of actually wanting an unjust result. What do you get in return? A prostitute's pay. Like other flatterers, you tend to become like the object of your flattery, but since you have so many and various objects of attention what you really give yourself is the character of none but that of the chameleon, who appears to be whatever suits the moment. In your trade, you lose yourself.

Well, **Euerges***, what do you say of my speech? Is it fair or not? I speak not of you, of course, but of those lawyers who serve a client's wants rather than his interests.*

Euerges*: Of course, it is not fair, Socrates, but idiotic. What you do not understand is that the lawyer does not operate alone, but as a part of a community of lawyers and judges, as one component in a larger system. Since the aim of that system is to do justice, it is justice that the lawyer ultimately serves, even such a one as you describe. Of course, he wants to make a good living, and of course, he wants his client to prevail—that is part of his function in the system—but above these wants is a larger intention, that of serving justice itself. Our adversarial, individualistic, and pluralistic system, although undoubtedly imperfect, has been shown by experience to be the best system for achieving justice yet devised in our imperfect world.*

Socrates*: I am full of questions about the remarkable claim you have just made—How do you know that this system produces justice? What kind of justice is it? What kind of experience teaches you this? And so on—but I will put these questions aside for the moment to continue with what we were talking about. For even if it were agreed that the 'system' does what you claim, that would only justify the sacrifice of character made by the lawyer, not deny it. He would still subject himself to the same deformities of mind and feeling; the only difference would be that he could say that it was all in a good cause, as a soldier might say who died a horrible death for his country. But the self-inflicted deformity would still be there.*

Suppose, for example, that you represented a white man in dispute with a black man, that your client was in the right, and that the judge and jury who were to hear the case were white racists. Your appeals to their bigotry, whether explicit or implicit, whether expressed in words of silence or shrugs or looks or tones of voice, would be in the 'cause of justice' in the sense that you mean, but they would still deform both you and your audience, polluting both the process and the community.

Argument of this kind can never be truly in the cause of justice, as an argument based on falsity can never be in the cause of truth, yet your duty, as you call it, requires you to make arguments that are unjust and false, at least in the sense that they do not represent what you believe justice and truth to require. You must do this not merely where your client is right, as in the example I have given, but where he is wrong as well.

Euerges: *Socrates, you are speaking as if we had made no progress at all since the fifth century, as if the modern lawyer really were like the ancient rhetorician and subject to no constraints of law and custom, indeed, as if there were no substance to the rules he applies and follows and argues about. Actually, doing a lawyer's work is a discipline in responsibility and truth. In the first place, there are ethical limits upon the way he can argue: he may not misrepresent either the facts of the case or the law, and he may make only those appeals legitimised by our system. Appeals to bigotry and the like, then, are out.*

And while there is of course some leeway in the interpretation of legal doctrines, they are by no means infinitely pliable—indeed much of our time is spent applying plain rules with plain effects. This is one way the law is made real in the world. Although the rules that we apply are, like everything else in the world, imperfect, they are rooted in a democratic form of government; having the assent of the people, they are more likely to be just than any other rules. There is a sense, indeed, in which they are by definition just, for they are the product of the most just of all constitutions.

Socrates: *But all this, even if I accept it, merely confines and limits the evil, it does not deny it. Your claim essentially is that you are a rhetorician in a good cause, or with good effects, but you remain a rhetorician, with all that that means. Suppose a similar claim were made, for example, by a historian, who said that he did not try to write what he thought was true, but what would most favour a particular person or group or party: every statement of fact, every term of evaluation, was chosen and placed to serve such ends.*

Suppose further that he was to justify this practice by saying that it was what everyone does, and that experience has shown that what he calls 'advocate's history'—and what you and I would call propaganda—produces a completer and more accurate version of the truth than any other kind. Would you have respect for such a historian, and for such history or contempt? Would you want to be such a historian or want your child to become one? And it would not matter much if there were some ethical limits on the degree to which one could shade things, for the historian would still be a shader of truth, a propagandist, not a historian.

One cannot be a propagandist in the service of truth or an advocate in the service of justice, for the character and the motives are wrong. Character and motive are for these purposes everything, for 'truth' and 'justice' are not abstract absolutes, to be attained or not in materially measurable ways; these are words that define shared motives out of which a community and a culture can be built and a character made for the individual and his world. They express an attitude, imply a process, and promise a community.

The true historian, who tells the truth as well as he can, exposes himself to refutation: if he is shown to be wrong, it is he who is wrong and it is he who learns from the refutation. He has a self in the world that can teach and can learn. But the lawyer, or such a rhetorical historian as I describe, can never be refuted, but only beaten. He has no self in a world of others.

And is not something like this true even of you, Euerges, when you move from working out with your clients what their true interests require to representing their interests at law? Then you, too, must speak the legal language according to legal conventions: you become an accomplished shader of the truth, and give yourself the facile and shifting mind of the lawyer. Or do you simply say to other lawyers and judges what you honestly believe that justice requires?

Euphemes: Of course, he doesn't do that, Socrates, and neither do I. I should also say that unlike Euerges I do not spend time with my clients trying to determine what you least would call their true interests. Of course, I do go over and over their problems with them, trying to help them figure out what they want to do, and I will suggest considerations, questions and facts they seem to have left out. But their decision, if it is legal, is final with me. The most I do is to help them organise their affairs in ways that will suit them in the long as well as the short run.

I also have to say that I have no faith that our system of justice has been proven by experience to be the best possible one. I'm not sure what Euerges means when he speaks of our 'system' or that justice is its 'end', and I don't know whose experience he is talking about, whom it teaches, how it teaches, or what it teaches. As for the rules and principles of law that we apply and argue about, I certainly do not think they are the perfection of justice: some of them seem to be right, others pointless or wasteful, and some of them seriously evil.

Nor do I think that their origins in our version of a democratic system of government entitle them to automatic veneration.

Euerges justifies the activities of his life not in their own terms but by claiming that they are part of a larger system, which has been shown by experience to be the best possible one. But I do not share his faith in the perfection of our legal system, whether it is measured by results achieved or standards applied, and I dare say no one else does either who is not forced to such a position by his choice of profession.

Moreover, I know I do not represent only the noble and the good. Most of my clients are good enough in an ordinary way, but basically unthinking and rather selfish; some are in my view pretty despicable people engaged in pretty despicable enterprises. I help them not only when I think they are in the right, but when I think they are in the wrong, so long as it is not legally wrong or so morally wrong as to be intolerable. In many of the cases, I have litigated I am inclined to believe that justice was on the other side, though I have not really asked myself that question in a disciplined way.

In our arguments, whether made to judge and jury at trial or to other lawyers in negotiation, we do not say what we believe justice requires but whatever we think will persuade our audience, subject only to the ethical constraints already mentioned by Euerges. I have to say that while these constraints to some degree civilise the process, they do not change its fundamental nature. Indeed, they permit, and may even be thought to require, a lawyer to discredit witnesses whom he knows to be telling the truth and to suggest false inferences that may plausibly be drawn from true facts, and they give at least some play to motives of bigotry and prejudice of various kinds.

I said before that I do not spend time with my clients trying to determine their true interests, and I acknowledge that sometimes they, and others, are injured by the increase in power they get through my successes. Moreover, I agree that this is important, for it is a question of who they are and who they become. I also think it is important to what kind of person I am and what sort of community I help to constitute, and I know that to make myself a lawyer is to give myself a mind of a certain character or cast and that this is in large measure determined by what happens in the argument. But I would describe these things somewhat differently from you and Euerges.

Notwithstanding what you may take to be the implications of what I have just said, I do not think that to practise law is to deform the self. In fact, the character of the trustworthy lawyer seems to me thoroughly admirable, difficult to attain, and, what may surprise you most, to be acquired not in spite of his daily work in the law, but in large measure because of it, by virtue of its discipline and experience. Of course, there are really bad people in the law, as in every profession, and perhaps very few people, or even none, fully attain the possibilities I mean to point to with the phrase 'trustworthy lawyer'.

But my point, like yours, has to do with the tendency of the practice of the profession, and I think that its tendency is not to injure but to improve the character and that it offers possibilities in this respect that most other ways of living lack. I should add that I do not think that this tendency is much affected by the nature of one's clientele, nor even by the substantive rules with which one must deal, but that it is greatly affected by the nature of the ethical community that one establishes with other lawyers and judges.

I think you and Euerges have simply misunderstood the enterprise in which lawyers are engaged. I would put it this way: in our professional lives we lawyers preserve and improve a language of description, value, and reason—a culture of argument—without which it would be impossible even to ask the questions that you think are most important, questions about the nature of justice in general or about what is required in a particular case. This is because 'doing justice', 'arguing about justice', and 'deciding what justice requires' are never wholly abstract activities but are always culturally conditioned. They are ways of doing things with pre-existing materials and expectations, just as 'doing music' and 'doing architecture' are; what we lawyers do is to maintain the materials essential to these cultural activities and the conventions and understandings that make them possible.

The first essential resource for the activity of talking about what justice requires is a language in which the social world can be constituted and described so that a story can be told and an issue stated. At the simplest level, we need words to describe the various parties, their situations, and their motives before we can even state a question about what justice requires in a particular case. Similarly, we need procedures and understandings to regulate our talk, such as conventions about representation, the order of speech in the court or assembly, and the like. We need as well a pre-existing language of right and wrong, of expectation and prohibition—rules and maxims and proverbs and stories, and, perhaps, cases—before we can go to work. Let me try to make this point by using an example familiar to you, Socrates.

If I remember my undergraduate reading correctly, the Iliad begins with a dispute that arises when Agamemnon is forced to give up his prize girl to her father, the priest of Apollo, after Agamemnon originally refused the ransom request for her. Achilles and Agamemnon divide over whether Agamemnon should bear the loss alone, or whether the community of warriors should in some way make it up to him. Now one could not accurately state the question presented by this situation, let alone think about what right and justice require here, without words to describe the prize girl, her father the priest, the ransom, and the warriors and their chief. Not just any words will do—think how weakly the English words given above permit one to understand these actors and events; we need the Homeric words themselves, the language that defines the social world and the values that give particular meaning to the dispute. Only in the language of this culture can argument proceed about the issue of justice that has arisen within it.

You yourself, Socrates, show that you know that we need a language of social fact and value, for you invite your auditors not to a language less looking at the eternal essence of justice, but to a taking-apart and putting-together of the materials of existing culture, a reconstitution of language in a community of two to which all your loyalties extend. What we lawyers do is both similar and different: in working on our cases we constantly test our language against new facts and circumstances, against its own hidden or overt tensions, against common experience and new formulations, and in this sense can be said repeatedly to take it apart and put it together again. But our loyalties extend beyond the community of individuals with whom we talk to our legal world, indeed to our culture as a whole.

The object of our work is not to make a new language good only for two interlocutors, as yours is, but to leave the language we have remade in a condition fit for use by others. It is in fact our method of argument, which you deplore, that enables us to do this, for as we articulate our points of disagreement in a particular case, at the same time we necessarily perform an agreement with the rest of the language in which are disagreement is stated and our arguments framed. In order to assert our differences on some points, that is, we must acquiesce in the language we use to make these differences intelligible and meaningful. The effect of this is to convert the raw human materials of greed, fear and the desire for power, and the like, into questions presented in the language that we maintain. Our work is what makes possible the connections between one case and another, between past and present, that constitute this branch of our civilisation.

I say that we not only maintain but improve our language, and in one sense I am sure I am right. This process ensures, as nothing else could, that congruence between the terms and assumptions of our language and the conditions of social and natural reality that is essential to the survival of a language of justice and the culture it enacts. But we also improve it in another way, I think, for the law as I describe it becomes a repository of shared experiences, a set of experiments and trials and failures, which are by the law made intelligible and shareable. This is a culture of experience and experiment; it is a way of giving experience to ourselves, individually and collectively, the experience of making and remaking language under pressure.

In the law, our language of facts and law is constantly being tested against the real world, against common sentiment, against cases and arguments, and remade in light of what is discovered. This means that the law is a way in which the community defines itself, not once and for all, but over and over, and in the process, it educates itself about its own character and the nature of the world. The limits of our minds and imaginations are reached and tested, and a new step is taken. That is what the law is about. The lawyer is not a dialectician, but neither is a poet or an architect, and as is true of them, the meaning and pleasure of the lawyer's life arise from his participation in making and remaking the world of shared significance.

What this view of the law means about the ethics of legal argument is this. First, while I am in a sense 'insincere' when I say to a judge, for example, that 'justice requires' or the 'law requires' such and such result, this insincerity is a highly artificial one, for no one is deceived by it. No one in the courtroom would be surprised to learn that this is a form of argument and not a statement of personal beliefs. But at the same time, I am implicitly saying something else, with respect to which I am by any standard being sincere: that the argument I make is the best case that my capacities and resources permit me to make on this side of the case. This is a statement made by performance rather than in explicit conceptual terms, and it is a statement not about the nature of 'justice', but about the nature of the resources our legal culture affords for defending or attacking a particular result. But it is a statement honestly made.

In making this statement, the lawyer's audience is the judge, and we serve him directly not by telling him what we actually think he ought to do, but by *showing him something about the nature of his own situation in our culture. Together, the arguments of the two lawyers define the boundaries within which the judge operates by showing what even these parties, opposed as they are, must agree to, and they tell him what topics the culture requires him to face and deal with. Our arguments also provide him with a testing ground for his own thoughts.*

As the judge thinks through the case, at first inclined one way, then the other, he will take up the opposing arguments, oral or written, to learn what he has not yet dealt with in his own thinking and what he has. The briefs and arguments help him think his way into a problem and provide a kind of checklist to tell him when he has thought all the way through it. There is room for art and invention, too. We tell the judge truthfully not that we think a judgment for our client is the best result—that conclusion is determined by our role—but that the formulations we offer are the best version of our discourse in support of this result that we can find or make.

This kind of rhetoric, despite what you claim, leads to a kind of knowledge and not to mere belief—knowledge about the ways in which the materials of persuasion in our culture can be mobilised. The 'trustworthy' lawyer of whom I speak is one who can be trusted to perform this task honestly and intelligently, making the best case he can in light of what can most persuasively and fairly be said on the other side. It is the incompetent or sleazy lawyer who misrepresents or fudges the nature of the material, and his work is of little assistance to anyone.

Though on one occasion or another, he may prevail through the confusion he creates, over the long run he will fail, in part because those to whom he speaks will see what he is doing. The competent lawyer is by nature trustworthy in the sense I describe, for trustworthiness is essential to his professional standing and success, not only in the long run but in the short run too. It is not too much to say that in his presentation of the best case that can be made in the circumstances the good lawyer loves to tell the truth.

I have said that the judge is our ultimate audience, and this is true even in negotiating transactions and planning a client's affairs, for the judge is the final authority to whom recourse may ultimately be taken. Although it is true, as you say, that the persuader becomes like the object of his persuasion, it is our practice to address the judge not as the bundle of biases and feelings and predispositions and ideas that he in some sense is, but as if he were an ideal judge. It is what the best judge we can imagine would want to hear and know that we try to provide. (The practice of speaking to the best in the judge we address is in fact enforced by considerations of prudence, for to be caught addressing him any other way is obviously very dangerous indeed.)

Thus, while at first there may seem to be a huge difference between the justice-loving judge and the advocate who merely wants his client to win, in fact, the mind of the advocate is deeply formed by his own conception of what the best judge would be and what he would want to know: it is to his own ideal that he gives what you call the attentions of a lover. To do this is not to injure but to improve the self; it is very close to what you mean, **Socrates***, when you speak of your devotion to philosophy.*

This is a way of justifying the lawyer's life by understanding the process of which his activities form a part, as Euerges' was too. But unlike his justification, mine does not depend upon faith that the substantive rules we work with are the best of all possible rules, or even that they are substantially just. Nor does it claim that our particular procedures for inquiring about and deciding questions of justice are most likely to lead to results that are just. In fact, the justification I advance would support the activity of being a lawyer in almost any legal system, however unjust its rules might be on the merits, for the lawyer's task will always be to make the best case he can out of the materials of his culture in addressing an ideal judge. By its very nature, this is to improve his materials, both by ensuring their congruence with the world of facts outside the law and by moving them toward greater coherence, fairness, and the like.

Socrates*: So it may be Euphemes but have you not simply substituted one faith for another? Euerges has faith that the present legal system, as measured by its rules and results, is the best one possible; you have faith in your capacity to make arguments the tendencies of which will always be to improve rather than to damage the culture you have inherited. But upon what does your faith rest? May it not happen, for example, that your particular audience, say your judge, will be persuadable by distinctions and appeals that are in your view, not better but worse? And in such a case you will make those arguments, for they are what will work, and in doing so you will contribute not to the improvement but to the degeneration of the discourse. Is this not so?*

As I understand your claim, it is like that of an artist. You are like the musical composer who makes the best kind of music that can be made, or that he can make, out of the cultural and physical materials available to him. By 'materials', I mean the musical instruments on the one hand and the expectations that people bring to musical performance on the other, for it is with both of these that the composer must work. Indeed, every artist makes his artefact partly out of the materials of nature—stones, bricks, sounds—and partly out of the materials of culture—those expectations that define his audience and enable him to surprise, to please, and to instruct them. These expectations form a kind of language through which, and only through which, his work can be intelligible. We do not praise or blame the artist for the nature of his materials, of either kind, but only for what he does with them, and the same can be said of the lawyer, and perhaps of the judge as well.

Thus, the musical artist—and the same is true of the architect as well, and perhaps of the painter or dramatist—does not collapse into his culture, as Euerges did, when he appealed to the supposed perfection of the system and the respect due to the products of a democratic society, and so forth, but in some measure breaks himself out of his culture, distancing himself from it by claiming to maintain and improve it. The artist, and according to you the lawyer, thus assimilates himself not to the culture as it is, but to his own ideal version of it, and to the processes by which he attempts to make and remake it in that image.

But how can this be so? Where the conventions of art are not beautiful but ugly, will the work of the artist not be ugly too? And where do the standards by which he establishes his ideal come from? Are they not also formed by the musical or legal culture itself, with all of its defects? Either as a lawyer or musician, then, how can you have any confidence that the changes you make are true improvements, that the ideal to which you assimilate yourself is a proper one? The questions of beauty and justice are in the end the most important ones, and for them, rhetoric is plainly useless: only dialectic will suffice.

Euphemes: You state my claim well enough, Socrates, but you evaluate it wrongly, in part because you evaluate dialectic itself wrongly. Of course, I do not 'know' that my arguments are improvements or that my conception of the ideal judge is best, and of course, these are important questions. But you do not know these things either, and what we are really talking about is how such questions ought to be addressed, which is itself another version of the question we have been asking from the beginning: how ought we to lead our lives? The first claim I have been making is not that I do the best possible work with my materials—that is the kind of claim Euerges makes for the 'system'—but that this is what I strive for. It is a question of aim and motive, as if proper when the issue is how we lead our lives.

I also make a second claim about our method, especially as compared with dialectic. For the questions you have asked me—whether the particular argument improves the culture, or the particular conception of the ideal judge is a proper one—dialectic is valueless because in dialectic you confine your responsibilities to yourself and one another; you remake your language and community on the scale of two. For these questions, dialectic can produce no answer at all, because the questions themselves presuppose a larger world, in which alone they can have meaning. The answers must be good not only for the two of us but for our whole community, for the others who act in our universe and speak our language.

To say, as you do, that it is never good to have any relationship with any person that has any object other than discovering what is ultimately good for each of those two would in fact mean the end of culture; the lawyer is one whose aim it is to maintain and improve the culture that makes possible a larger life, in a larger world.

Socrates: *Let us put aside for the moment what you say about dialectic, for you still have not answered my question about what you yourself do. How can you claim to be constantly improving your discourse and culture? Suppose for example that in a particular legal system the ideals to which appeals can be made, the materials for the 'best case', are vicious ones? You will then move the discourse in the direction of vicious ideals rather than just ones, will you not? And once you concede that this is so, you will have to tell me how you can possibly know that your own culture is not one of the vicious ones. When you do, you will engage in dialectic, not rhetoric.*

Euphemes: *To start with, I do have to say that I am not sure that it is a good thing to be a lawyer in any imaginable culture. There is always the possibility that a culture is so horrible that it should be destroyed rather than improved, that one must become an enemy of the political system in order to be a friend to the nation. But I do mean to suggest how that question ought to be thought about, and I think my answer may lead as well to a response to your question about standards and ideals.*

In deciding whether we ought to be lawyers in a particular legal culture, we ought to ask not whether there is injustice there, or even serious injustice, for these will be part of any culture. Instead, we should ask about the materials for argument the culture makes available. Does this culture afford the materials with which one can appeal to its better side, establishing and reinforcing standards and values that are incompatible with its evils, and thus counteract them? Think for example of the lawyer in apartheid South Africa and the importance of his continually affirming the aspects of that tradition that honour individual autonomy and liberty, that respect each person as an individual, and that are thus wholly incompatible with the country's racist laws.

Or think of a lawyer in a Soviet satellite or Hong Kong state affirming the principles of legality with which the Party sometimes, but not always, interferes. Or of a lawyer in the historic southern states of America appealing to our traditional ideal of equality to correct the hideous inequalities, especially racial inequalities, with which we live. The question for the lawyer is not, does my system achieve justice, but rather, does it afford materials for the idealisation which, when mobilised by lawyers on both sides of a case, will tend to improve the culture itself? This view corresponds with the common feeling that it is of great importance to have conscientious and high-minded lawyers in regimes that are illegal or corrupt.

Will the answer ever be that the culture must be abandoned? I am not sure it will, for the very act of speaking about justice in a particular case on behalf of one of the parties always affirms the possibility of justice under law, and it necessarily entails, even if it also frustrates, the process of idealisation of which I speak. Such speech also makes real an essential equality between the speakers, if only for a moment, and it affirms the practice of reasoned judgment, and that entails certain ethical consequences as well. It may indeed be that it is good to be a lawyer whenever one can speak for another and sincerely make the best case that one's materials afford.

This is also, as you can see, a partial answer to your question about my faith in the improvements to be worked by law. Some elements of what we mean by justice are not complex but simple, and the practice of law as I have defined it continually affirms these. The values of equality, of reason, and of the very idea of appealing to right and justice against brute power. I have described the process of idealisation that is involved in legal argument, and I think it is a part of all legal argument: if an argument lacked that quality, it would no longer be legal, but purely instrumental or expedient. While it is true that some of the particular ideals appealed to may be undesirable or ugly, it is better that the practice itself should exist than that it should not. Indeed, as I said before, only if it does exist can one seriously ask the question that ultimately concerns you, namely, what ideals we ought to pursue.

All this assumes, as you point out, that the lawyer has standards and ideals by which to judge the possibilities for expression and action that a particular culture makes available to him. This returns us to the questions, of where these standards and ideals come from, how they are to be tested and explained and defended, and so on.

It is implicit in what I have said that at a certain level, these things are easy enough, for some injustices are plain and brutal enough to be self-evident to anyone. At this level, what we mean by justice is a community that maintains the minimal standards of the rule of law. It is better to have a hearing than no hearing, better to have a tribunal that claims obedience to authorities external to its will than no such tribunal, and so on. As for more complicated issues of justice—the right result in a particular case, for example, or in a particular class of cases, or the proper standards of distributive justice—the question for both of us is not whose answers are right, for neither of us has answers, but how to go about living and thinking in the conditions of uncertainty in which we find ourselves. With respect to these questions, what we mean by justice is a community of a certain sort, a community that proceeds to examine, talk about and decide these questions in a promising way. What really divides us is how to judge the lawyer's way of doing these things.

Here, I must return to my earlier claims that the activity of talking about justice requires the existence of a language in which factual and moral problems can be coherently and meaningfully stated and that what we lawyers do is to maintain that language in a condition in which it can be used for those purposes by ourselves and others.

What do I mean by a 'condition in which it can be used'? To start with, a language of justice must have within it room for claims both of expediency or self-interest on the one hand, and of justice or virtue on the other, if it is to have a life in the world. You show that you know this when you show that Callicles' attempts to strip his value words of all but their selfish meanings are doomed to failure, leading to intolerable intellectual and moral confusion. The attempt to use a purely pragmatic language, and to reject the limits imposed by a language of justice, destroys one's capacity to reason sensibly and to function coherently. Indeed it destroys the very idea of a self upon which the language of selfishness itself depends.[190]

But the converse of this is also true: to strip a language of justice of its congruence with actual facts and sentiments, with the felt needs of those who use it, is to strip it of any force in the world. This is what you do. You find an intolerable conflict within the central value terms of your own Greek language (agathos, kalos, and the like) and seek to strip them of those elements of meaning that reflect the competitive or success-oriented culture in which they had their origins. But when you do that you make a language that is 'paradoxical', impossible for others to speak.

The function of the law is to maintain a language that keeps alive this very tension between fact and ideal, expediency and justice, self and other; this tension is in fact essential to the practice of talking about what justice requires. You can see this tension in my own defence of law: when I say that the lawyer makes the 'best case' that can be made in the circumstances, does that mean the case that is most persuasive or most just?

You would draw a sharp line between them; I would not say that they are the same, but I would say that the answer to that question is always, or almost always, unclear. To be the 'most just' argument, it must be a workable one; to be workable, it must be just, at least in the sense that it must maintain the possibility, essential to the existence of self and community, of appealing to ideals that limit the will.

In other words, it is the object of our work to ensure that the language of the law has both the congruence with reality and the element of aspiration that are together essential to any meaningful talk about what justice requires in an actual community. As for the improving character of a particular argument, that is a matter that must be examined in the context of a particular discourse and a particular case; what we do is establish the conditions and means for that examination. We cannot guarantee the results, but no one can do that. What we can do is justify the practices that make possible thought about justice of a kind that is at once realistic and idealistic.

In the process that I describe, the law converts the raw materials of human nature and conflict into another form of life and language, into an argument about justice. This conversion is in fact what marks us as human beings, for it is this above all upon which the life of the polis, of the human community itself, depends. Indeed, what is true of the city is true of the self as well; both for the lawyer and for his client, the passions of ambition and conquest and competition are put to work in the service of a larger enterprise, the practice of arguing about what justice requires, without which we would have no city at all, no community, and no philosophy.

The mind the lawyer gives himself is one that loves this process of conversion and translation: the making of a certain kind of conversation and the maintenance of the conditions upon which it can proceed. You should understand the pleasure and meaning of such a life, Socrates, if anyone can.

Socrates: *But even if all that you say is true, Euphemes, none of it justifies what you do when you present evidence and argue about the facts, as opposed to engaging in the sort of argument about the law that you have been discussing. Surely making the 'best case' on the facts has a different ethical meaning from making the best case that the resources of the law permit you to make on a question of standards or norms. How can you possibly call yourself a friend to the jury when you cross-examine with great skill a witness you know to be telling the truth, or ask them to draw plausible but erroneous inferences from true facts? Whatever may be the case with respect to the judge, then, with respect to the jury you are a pure rhetorician with all that that means: the flattering pleaser and deceiver. Is that not so?*

Euphemes: Certainly not in the way you claim, Socrates. It is true that there are important and problematic differences between arguments about the law and arguments about facts, and I will say something in a moment both about the nature of these difficulties and about what it means to address them correctly. But first I need to correct your assumption that the lawyer will—that he professionally should—do whatever the law permits him to do on behalf of his client. Although some lawyers of course take that attitude, not all do so, and you and I have agreed that our subject is not the ethical quality of the majority of those who actually engage in the practice of law (though that is an interesting question) but the ethical possibilities of the profession.

Let us take the cross-examination of the truthful witness. To some degree what I said about judicial argument also obtains here, for the jury knows that each lawyer is trying to present his case in its strongest light, and the combined efforts of the lawyers do in fact aid the jury in its decision of the case as a whole, for they now know the most that can legitimately be claimed on each side. In both cases, there is a similar duty not to mischaracterise the law or the facts.

But you are quite right that there is a critical difference between the two kinds of argument as well, for the judge or other lawyer can effectively check and challenge your characterisations of law since all have access to the same material, but with respect to the facts some of what you know is simply not available to the other side. This means that the lawyer must indeed take special care in making factual claims, and many lawyers do so. Although it is true that the law would permit the savage cross-examination of a truth-telling witness, that does not mean that every lawyer would do it, or should do it.

Socrates: *How can that be? Do not your conventions of argument require you to do for your client whatever the law permits you to do?*

Euphemes: No of course not, that is what I am trying to tell you. Although most lawyers would be reluctant to admit it even to themselves, different lawyers would respond quite differently to the cross-examination question: some would cross-examine as rigorously as they could, others more softly, and some might in fact not cross-examine at all but concede the factual point being made.

Socrates: *But how could a lawyer justify to his client any course of action other than the first?*

Euphemes: The process of justification would begin with the beginning of their relationship, when the lawyer let the client know that although the client had employed his professional skill he had not obtained the right to dictate how that skill should be exercised. This can be made clear by an explicit statement, something like this: "If you want my services you must understand that I observe what I regard as the decencies of life in my relations to other lawyers and parties and witnesses. I will not treat you shabbily; do not expect me to treat others so. I will not be your mouthpiece, but your lawyer."

That is, of course, rather pompous, and in many contexts, a lawyer would feel that he could establish the essential point implicitly rather than explicitly— by the way he dealt with the client and spoke about the other lawyer, the other party, and the process itself. This kind of statement is not only possible, but it is far more common than most people, including most lawyers, are actually aware: think how often a lawyer refuses to take advantage of a procedural default, for example, or how often, at least in certain branches of the practice—divorce comes particularly to mind—the lawyers on both sides refuse, despite great pressure from their clients, to engage in childish and vindictive litigation.

If challenged, the lawyer could explain his position on two grounds. The first, suggested above, is contractual: this is what I offer you, and you have the right to reject it and go elsewhere. The second is more difficult to talk about, but if anything, even more important; it is ethical in the fullest sense of the term, and also from another point of view strategic. The lawyer might say something like this:

In the next several months, I will repeatedly be speaking on your behalf to a wide range of audiences: the other lawyer, the judge, the jury, witnesses, other officials, and so on. I want these audiences to take seriously what I have to say. I am not a chameleon or an actor but a single person, and my capacity to ask them to listen to me in the way I want them to, on the merits of the questions I discuss, is in large part a function of my sense of myself. If I were habitually sleazy and manipulative, signs of that would appear and make me less effective as a speaker for you; if I were habitually ethical but occasionally sleazy, I am sure that my discomfort would be less than completely hidden.

I can hardly exaggerate the importance of what I am saying: what the Greeks called the 'ethos' or character of the speaker is among the most powerful sources of persuasion. In any case, in which I act, my own sense that I am speaking properly, asking for what I am entitled to ask for, and functioning out of a sense of fairness, is essential to my ethos and therefore to my success. For success in two ways: not only in the material sense of gaining so much money by settlement or trial but in the much larger sense of helping you to give this difficulty a meaning that is most valuable and appropriate to you.

Let me give you a couple of examples of what such a lawyer would mean. Often a particular dispute is one of a series of matters with respect to which the parties must deal with one another; in such cases, proper management of one dispute will lead to quicker and easier resolution of others, and to the establishment of relations outside the adversarial context that are of real value, economic and otherwise. This is in fact the case whenever there are continuing relations, by reason of commercial connection, common children, or even because the parties simply live in the same community.

And even when one puts such considerations aside there is the question of the meaning of the result in the particular case for this client. What kind of victory does he really want? Here it is a great mistake to assume, as many people do, that clients naturally want victory at any cost, including that of unscrupulous behaviour from their lawyers. Some do, of course, have no doubt about it, but others realise that such an attitude is childish, impractical, and inconsistent with their basic sense of themselves.

Many clients in fact want what they are entitled to and no more, and welcome the opportunity to deal with a lawyer who respects the decencies of life, as they themselves do. They know in addition that the lawyer who is a shyster to others will often be a shyster to his client. They know that they can have little confidence in the judgment, knowledge, or skills of such a person.

All this, of course, does not answer the next question, which is how one decides what the decencies of professional life are and what practices are beneath them. On such questions, categorical rules are of little help, and they must be thought through on the merits each time, or rather, since they arise continually, in surprising ways, and without notice, they must be instinctively responded to by the character that the lawyer has gradually given himself over time by his habits of ethical reflection and action.

My point is not to make the ethical dilemmas of the lawyer's life seem to disappear but to establish that the lawyer is free to address them as true ethical issues for which he is responsible. Indeed, so far am I from denying the intractable difficulties of the lawyer's ethical life, that I would say that they are an important merit of it. Every day the lawyer faces questions of right and wrong that have no ready answer and no authoritative resolution, and this means that his professional life offers the opportunity for the building of a character that less problematic lives would lack.

It is true that in our relations with our clients, we do fall short of the standard you would have us meet, in that we do not engage our clients in a dialectical investigation of what their best interests really require; in a sense, we use them as the material of our art. But it is a corollary to what I have just said about the lawyer's ethical responsibilities that there are important senses in which this relationship, at least in its ideal form, is one of friendship, for it constantly presents questions, for both of us, of how we should behave and who we should be; it involves mutual education and respect and is based upon honesty. As Euerges said, in leaving certain questions of choice to the client, the lawyer respects his autonomy; likewise, in reserving some to himself the lawyer insists upon his own autonomy, and this reservation is a valuable form of teaching.

The lawyer is constantly forcing upon the client new understandings of the nature of the world in which he lives and of his situation within it, either showing him the limits that reality places upon his desires or expanding his sense of what is possible, and he is himself always learning about these things too. On these matters, everyone needs continual teaching. The fact that the lawyer finds himself taking one side, now another, without much regard for his personal predisposition is in fact an important source of education for him. It teaches him how much can be said for positions with which he is originally inclined to disagree.

For this reason, it is a great mistake to think, as some do, that the law professor is somehow freer or better than the lawyer. The danger for the professor is that he will spend his life writing articles or books that are really little more than a series of briefs all on the side of his own unexamined biases and attitudes, something a lawyer can almost never do. Any lawyer will tell you that compared with at least some of his clients, his role is to insist upon the truth, upon the facts that cannot be wished away. The lawyer is not only a fiction-maker, but a truth-respecter.

And one other thing: the good lawyer is faithful to the obligations he has assumed, to the client and to the law, and there is at once a kind of virtue and a kind of education in that. When he gives advice to his client, makes an argument to the jury, or drafts an instrument, he is engaged in making the world in which others live, and at every moment he is subject to obligations to others and to the law. His advice must be based upon a fair and accurate assessment of a situation; his argument must be punctiliously truthful in every statement of fact; his drafting must meet the needs of those whose lives it will affect.

A lawyer's life is a constant assumption of responsibility to others, and no one can have contempt for that. I might sum up what I have said by saying in his relations with both his culture and his client, the lawyer leads a life that at once requires and makes possible that he has an education of the fullest sort, and, if he takes his responsibilities seriously, he can offer such an education to others. Unlike the life of Callicles, Socrates, is not a life 'worthy of no one', but a life worthy of anyone.

Chapter 21

We all know here that the law is the most powerful of schools for the imagination. No poet ever interpreted nature as freely as a lawyer interprets the truth.
Jean Giraudoux, La Guerre de Troie n'aura pas lieu (1935)

When a proposition is made true for things, if two things suffice for its truth, it is superfluous to assume a third.
Occam's Razor—Quod Libet 1323–1325

That is the beauty of the common law; it is a maze not a motorway.
Lord Diplock, Morris v. Martin (1966)

In actual practice, two cases are rarely, if ever alike that a judge may have a wide discretion in deciding in a given case to follow either precedent A, or precedent B, both of which seem to have considerable bearing on this case but which, unfortunately, are completely contradictory to one another.
Robert Carr, The Supreme Court and Judicial Review (1942)

There is no useful rule without exception.
Thomas Fuller

I will now consider some aspects of legal reasoning. It is convenient for the purposes of this discussion to consider three processes of legal reasoning, at least one of which is involved in any but the simplest cases:

1. Deciding the facts, i.e., what actually happened;
2. Deciding the applicable law; and

3. Applying the law to the facts i.e., deciding what is the appropriate description or categorisation of the facts for the purposes of the relevant rules of law.

Deciding the Facts

Facts have to be decided on the basis of evidence given by witnesses, and documentary and other 'real' evidence in the case. Even if there is no substantial conflict in the evidence, it might be necessary to make a decision about the accuracy of certain evidence, which (even in the absence of direct conflict) may raise questions about the accuracy of observation and recollection of witnesses, and about their veracity. Assessment of these matters may depend on such things as the demeanour of a witness; the answers he gives to various questions, for example about events not centrally involved in the case but of which (if he is telling the truth) he should have similarly detailed recollection; his motives for either telling the truth or misrepresenting the position in one way or another; the plausibility (as a matter of common sense and experience) with other evidence in the case, which all must be similarly assessed.

The evidence in the case may include documents prepared at the time of the events in question: these may be extremely reliable evidence of what happened, but even here the possibility of accidental or deliberate inaccuracy has to be considered, in the light, for example, of the means of knowledge of the person preparing the document, the apparent time and care taken to ensure accuracy, the motives of such person to record matters truthfully or untruthfully, etc.

It is clear that many of the factors I have outlined could point in different directions, even in the absence of outright conflict in the evidence. When there is outright conflict in the evidence, the same factors arise in assessing all the evidence on both sides, and it is necessary to weigh them all, and ultimately come to a decision about what in fact happened. The decision can rarely be absolutely certain: in common-law jurisdictions, it has to be 'beyond reasonable doubt' in criminal cases, and 'on the balance of probabilities' in civil cases. In some cases, this decision has to be made by a judge or magistrate, in others by a jury with the assistance of legal directions from a judge.

It is clear that, in reaching a decision on such matters, factors of entirely different types have to be taken into consideration: demeanour, apparent ability to observe and remember, motives, plausibility of the story, coherence with other evidence, etc. There is no way in which these factors can be systematically reduced to a common scale so that points awarded for each can be weighted and added up, and totals for different versions compared. In assessing such matters as demeanour, acuity, motives, plausibility and coherence, one does not and cannot put such factors completely into words. An assessment is made on the basis of one's experience and common sense, the result of which can be partially expressed in words.

But such words do not exhibit the whole basis of the assessment: the actual 'weight' to be given to each factor cannot be explicitly stated. In all these matters, the reasoning process ultimately has to be expressed in terms of weighing various factors and coming to a conclusion on the basis of one's judgment, which one may support by exhibiting as best one can one's reasons. These reasons generally do not support the conclusion as a matter of logic, and if one looks for premises egumey which together with those reasons would do so, generally one cannot find premises egumey which one accepts as readily as one accepts the conclusion.

Deciding the Law

In common-law jurisdictions, the sources of law are essentially statutes and previous court decisions. Even the application of statutes may involve uncertain plausible reasoning about the meaning of words: this may be considered as a problem of deciding the law, or of applying it.

In relation to previous court decisions, there is greater room for plausible reasoning. Generally, a court is bound to apply a rule stated in a previous court decision only if it both was stated by a superior court in the same hierarchy of courts and was part of the *ratio decidendi* of the case in which it was stated, i.e., a rule on the basis of which that superior court actually decided the case. (Other rules stated by courts, called *obiter dicta*, generally carry less 'weight').

Otherwise, the rule has merely persuasive force, which may vary from very slight (e.g. if stated by an inferior court, and not in any event part of the *ratio decidendi* of the case but merely *obiter dicta*) through moderate (e.g. *ratio decidendi* of courts of equivalent status in related hierarchies) and strong (e.g. *ratio decidendi* of courts of superior status in related hierarchies or the same status in the same hierarchy) to overwhelming (e.g. if included in carefully considered *obiter dicta* given unanimously by a superior court, being the highest court in the particular hierarchy).

It sometimes happens that conflicting previous decisions can be found on particular points, and it sometimes happens that previous decisions on related points, while not actually conflicting, do not cohere or make good sense when considered together. It sometimes happens that no previous decision states a rule which applies precisely to the case presently to be decided, but that there are two or more rules which could be extended to cover the case, giving different results; or that two or more rules have been stated in contexts different from each other and from that of the present case, each of which literally applies to the present case, giving different results.

Even from this brief and inadequate outline of what is involved in deciding questions of law, there is obviously considerable indeterminacy as to what is *ratio decidendi* and what is *obiter dicta*, particularly in a decision of a superior court in which more than one judgment is given, and the reasons for the decision are expressed differently. There is also indeterminacy in considering whether rules, which do not actually conflict, cohere or make good sense when considered together.

Thus, one may have a rule that is arguably but not certainly part of the *ratio decidendi* of a decision of the superior court of a related hierarchy giving one result in the instant case, and something that is only an *obiter dictum* of one judge given in a decision of a superior court in the same hierarchy giving another result. The former may cohere well with some established rules, and not with others; the latter may cohere reasonably well with all established rules. There is no way in which such consideration (and there may be many others) could be reduced to a common scale.

One is certainly reasoning with words here since all the legal sources are expressed in words. However, when assessing the weight to be given to particular rules according to who stated them and in what circumstances, and assessing how well two rules or groups of rules cohere, one is dealing with ideas which are generally not fully and accurately put into words in one's reasoning, and one's conclusions and reasons for them generally express such ideas only partially and imperfectly.

In any event, when one comes to deciding what rule or rules to apply to the present case, where countervailing considerations of the type being discussed apply, the most important parts of the reasoning are not logically valid inferences, but matters of weighing the conflicting considerations and coming to a decision on the basis of one's judgment. Further premises which could make the inference a logical one are not stated. Indeed, courts generally avoid basing their decision on rules which are any wider than necessary for deciding the particular case and often advise counsel against doing so.

Some discussions tend to treat decisions as based on strict legal reasoning in so far as the reasoning is logically valid and to treat the residue as something else, such as the expression of non-rational values or preference. In some cases, there is no unique correct solution, and some examples show better legal reasoning than others, but virtually all exhibit informal rationality.

Applying the Law

In many cases, applying the legal rules to the facts involves deciding whether the facts as proved fall within categories such as the following: reasonable case, reasonable times, reasonable notice, consideration (for a contract), merchantable quality and substantial interference with competition. In order to decide whether facts do or do not fall into such categories, it is often necessary to consider countervailing considerations of different types; to envisage, in ways not fully expressible in words, the reality of what has been proved, and actual human beings acting in the circumstances proved; to weigh the various considerations and come to a judgment on them.

Even when the categories involved are apparently more precise, similar problems arise and similar reasoning occurs. The question may be whether a person has been caused loss by fraud. It may be proved that the defendant made a representation to this person which was true in some respects and not in others, which may complicate the question of whether the misrepresentation was material. It may not be proved that the defendant knew that the representation was false, and so there may be a question of whether the defendant was reckless, that is, knew that the representation might have been false but proceeded to make it not caring whether it was true or false.

There may be a question of whether the plaintiff relied on the representation, perhaps where he had some suspicions about the matter and/or had some other reasons to act as he did irrespective of his belief in the representation. Then there might be questions concerning the causation of the plaintiff's loss and foreseeability of it. At each stage, there may be difficulties in finding primary facts (process (1) at the beginning of Section 5.4) and further difficulties in deciding if they fit into the relevant legal categories (process (3)).

The conscious brain-mind uses rational procedures which have not yet been fully expressed as formal procedures by philosophers, scientists or lawyers and which probably cannot be expressed. The point is that a non-conscious computer (or a mechanistic brain) could not reason, or process information, except in accordance with algorithms and formal procedures expressed by definite rules. If the brain-mind does use rational procedures which cannot be fully expressed as formal procedures, then it is not mechanistic. In short: human reason cannot be formalised: therefore, it cannot be mechanised: therefore, the brain-mind is not mechanistic.

Some human reasoning proceeds in accordance with algorithms; that is, if follows precise and unambiguous rules. In particular, some human reasoning explicitly follows the extensive and valuable rules of logic and mathematics. These rules have greatly assisted rational human thinking, both extending its range and assisting in the detection of errors. However, formal reasoning in accordance with such rules is only a small part of human reasoning: another part is informal plausible reasoning, which is both ubiquitous and important.

Mathematician George Polya, in his book on *Mathematics and Plausible Reasoning*,[191] tells us that "the inductive evidence of the physicist, the circumstantial evidence of the lawyer, the documentary evidence of the historian, and the statistical evidence of the economist belong to plausible reasoning."[192] In fact, most of human reasoning is non-logical plausible reasoning. For example:

1. Scientific and philosophical works. If one examines almost any scientific or philosophical book or article, one will find that (mathematics aside) most arguments which are presented are not valid logical arguments but are informal plausible arguments. It may be possible to put such arguments, or at least some of them, into a valid logical form; but this will generally only be by supplying major premises which may well be less acceptable than the informal arguments themselves. Generally, at some stage in any such argument, one will find some appeal made to terms requiring judgment, weighing, preference, reasonableness etc.
2. Law. The decisions which are continually made and set out at length by judges presiding over court cases generally involve the weighing of countervailing considerations, which are of different types, and which

apparently cannot be expressed as commensurable quantities. Such decisions are reasoned, but cannot be expressed as the application of algorithms to accepted premises.
3. Practical reasoning. More generally, in many situations, a person has to decide what to do on the basis of non-commensurable considerations. Judges and lawyers are constantly faced with this dilemma. For example, duty may point one way, and expediency may point another way. In each case, assuming that both opposing contentions are accepted as having weight, and in the absence of a single scale on which the opposing considerations could both be measured, a choice between them could not be made, otherwise than randomly, by any algorithm or by any mechanistic process. We make sure choices by some process of 'weighing' these incommensurable considerations, and this process is generally considered rational.

Polya also asserts that 'Strictly speaking, all our knowledge outside mathematics and demonstrative logic …consists of conjectures' and that 'we support our conjectures by *plausible reasoning*' (p.v.).

Certainly, all such knowledge which goes beyond particular observations or perceptions can be supported only by plausible reasoning; formal or logical or deductive reasoning, as Polya reminds us, is 'incapable of yielding…new knowledge about the world around us'. Even particular observations depend in part upon theories accepted by the observer, and those theories themselves must go beyond particular observations or perceptions, so much also depends on plausible reasoning.

There are respected views put forward that such plausible procedures as induction cannot show even a probability of approximate truth of general statements, notably by Sir Karl Popper in *The Logic of Scientific Discovery* (Popper 1959).[193] However, the mainstream of scientific and philosophical thought is to the contrary: it is generally accepted that, although scientific theories must go beyond what can be established by observation and logic, such theories can be supported by plausible reasoning and thereby shown to have a probability of approximate truth. Otherwise, having regard to the theory-dependent character of observation, there would be no sound basis for believing anything. Indeed, the main arguments used by Popper to support his own position are plausible arguments; so, if he asserts his position as true (as he does), how can he deny that plausible arguments can support the truth of scientific theories?

The whole edifice of human knowledge is based in part on plausible reasoning, and our confidence in human knowledge generally can be no greater than our confidence in plausible reasoning.

There are no hard-and-fast rules for plausible reasoning. As Poly says:

Plausible reasoning is hazardious, controversial, and provisional... The standareds of plausible reasoning are fluid, and there is no theory of such reasoning that could be compared to demonstrative logic in clarity or which would command comparable consensus (p.v.).

Efforts have been made to formulate rules for, and thereby formalise, aspects of plausible reasoning: Bayes's probability calculus and Carnap's work on induction are examples. However, such efforts do not and cannot capture informal rationality.

So an important part of rational human thought including legal reasoning is plausible reasoning: plausible reasoning does not explicitly follow precise and unambiguous rules; it has not as yet been possible to formulate rules such that to follow them would be equivalent to engaging in plausible reasoning, and it is probable that such rules cannot be formulated.

The area of plausible reasoning which has received the most attention from philosophers is induction, the process of supporting general statements, such as hypotheses or theories stating laws of nature, on the basis of particular or singular statements, such as reports of observations or experiments. Sometimes, induction is regarded as including the formulation of general statements on the basis of particular statements, but I am not so concerned with this: the plausible reasoning with which I am concerned relates to justification rather than to discovery.

The question of whether inductive references are or may be justified, and if so under what conditions, is called the problem of induction. An early exposition was by eighteenth-century British philosopher David Hume. Hume, in fact, concentrated on one particular aspect of the problem, the respect in which inductive references involve begging the question or (to look at it another way) infinite regress. In *An Enquiry Concerning Human Understanding*,[194] Hume writes:

all inferences from experience suppose, as their foundation, that the future will resemble the past and that similar powers will be conjoined with similar sensible qualities. If there be any suspicion that the course of nature may change, and that the past may be no rule for the future, all experience becomes useless and can give rise to no inference or conclusion. It is impossible, therefore, that any arguments from experience can prove this resemblance of the past to the future; since all these arguments are founded on the supposition of that resemblance.

In *The Logic of Scientific Discovery*, Popper restates this argument in terms of an infinite regress: if there is a principle of induction which can, in combination with particular statements, justify universal statements, then this principle must itself be a universal statement, requiring a principle of induction to justify it, and so on *ad infinitum*.

Hume (and Popper) extend this argument so as to apply it to inferences from particular statements to the *probability* of universal statements. In his *Abstract of a Treatise of Human Nature*,[195] Hume writes:

Nay I will go further and assert that he could not so much as prove by any probable arguments that the future must be conformable to the past. All probable arguments are built on the supposition that there is this conformity betwixt the future and the past, and therefore can never prove it (Hume 1962: 294).

Plausible reasoning is related in various ways to language, and to questions concerning language.

The application of words. The very application of language often involves plausible reasoning, for example in that it is not possible to specify unambiguous rules for the application of even commonly used words, such as 'tree' or 'chair' or 'table': in borderline cases, the application of such words is a matter of judgment, which cannot be formalised, but *can* be supported or challenged by inconclusive but persuasive plausible reasoning.

This sort of problem occurs in everyday life; but is particularly well illustrated by a common task of lawyers: the interpretation of legal documents and of statutes. In many court cases, there is a legal document (a contract, a will, etc.) or a statute, whose application to the facts of the case is unclear: no algorithms can determine the result, but extensively plausible arguments can be advanced for rival interpretations. The result is a matter of judgment, very often one on which minds can reasonably differ; although very often also there can be a considerable degree of consensus on the 'correct' or 'best' interpretation. Furthermore, the fact that cases like this continually arise, notwithstanding the best efforts of the lawyers who draw contracts and wills, and of statutory draftsmen, points up the difficulty, I would say impossibility, of providing, by means of rules, an unambiguous result for all fact situations which can arise.

Wittgenstein in his *Philosophical Investigations*,[196] Wittgenstein examined the question of how it is possible to determine the correct application of a word. There is an illuminating discussion of the question in Nozick from which it can be seen how this problem is very similar to the problem of induction, and how Wittgenstein's solution can be likened to Hume's appeal to habit in relation to induction:

We do have a record of (some) past applications of the word, correct applications and incorrect ones. Does that fix how the word is to be applied in the future? Just as through any finite set of points, an infinite number of curves can be drawn, so different hypotheses or rules about applying the term are compatible with all past data points of application... Adding verbal instructions to past applications does not eliminate all but one way to apply the term, for these instructions themselves need to be applied in one of the many different possible ways...

In Wittgenstein's view, correctness in the application of a term is constituted by the way we actually go on to apply it. Nothing past fixes, logically determine, an application as correct, but it is just a fact about us that confronted with past teachings and applications we will go on a certain way, and we will all go on the same way.

In the note to this, Nozick suggests that 'The most plausible view is that certain underlying processes cause us to apply the term in a certain way in a new instance, given the past applications, these underlying processes being similar in all human beings because of our physical (i.e., neuro-physiological) similarities (presumably having been selected as useful by evolution)' He goes on to hint at, but not really get to grips with, the problems raised by such an attempted 'naturalisation' of plausible reasoning.

Consistently with my view of induction, I contend that such an appeal to habit, or to non-rational processes or structures in human beings, *cannot* explain our application of words to new situations. It is in fact just not true that in all cases we 'all go on the same way': for example, as mentioned earlier, real questions about the meaning of words constantly arise in courts of law, in relation to which minds can and do reasonably differ, and which are resolved by the application of inconclusive, but plausible, informal reasoning.

I am not here saying that a computer could not be given rules which would enable it to use a concept such as 'table': of course, it could, and by using such rules, it could probably apply the word correctly in most clear cases, and could perform reasonably in many borderline cases (e.g. whether the word 'table' applies in a particular context to a counter top at which people sit to eat meals). I do suggest, however, that we in fact use *informal* reasoning in this area, which a computer could not use, and I do suggest that we thereby do *better* than a computer could do, especially in difficult cases.

Indeterminacy of translation. Similar questions are raised by W.V.O. Quine's views on translation. In *Word and Object*,[197] he argues for the indeterminacy of translation: that we can know everything about the circumstances in which sentences of an unfamiliar language are assented to by users of that language, yet still not know but that 'it is a measure of the rationality of *accepting*, tentatively, a problematic guess' (pp. 414–15).

I do not propose to go deeply into these problems here. I will be proceeding on the assumption that there is a sense in which the probability of a general statement is a measure of the rationality of a belief in the truth, or approximate truth, of that general statement. This is roughly the sense used in courts of law, where decisions are often expressed as being made 'on the balance of probabilities', or on the basis of facts which are found to be true 'more probably than not'. In relation to probability in this sense, I take it that confirmation or corroboration or degrees of confirmation or corroboration is relevant and that in general terms the greater the confirmation or corroboration of a statement, the greater the probability of its approximation to the truth. To adopt the words of Putnam:

The very factors that make it rational to accept a theory 'for scientific purposes' also make it rational to believe it, at least in the sense in which one ever 'believes' a scientific theory—as an approximation to the truth which can probably be bettered, and not as a final truth.[198]

What I do not assume, but will now consider, is whether there are (as suggested by the work of Bayes and Carnap) satisfactory formal ways of assigning numerical values to probability in this sense, or to degrees of confirmation, in connection with inductive inference.

However, the computer's representations or models would be in its own code, as would any words it might use, and its reasoning would be limited to the manipulation of this coded material. The computer's code is relevantly similar to a language, and I suggest that 'reasoning' limited to the manipulation of coded material can be in no better case than reasoning limited to the manipulation of words: there is still no non-verbal or non-coded access to reality.

The Use of Analogy

Another characteristic of plausible reasoning especially in legal reasoning is the use of analogy. An analogy is a partial likeness between things, which forms a basis for comparison. Arguing or reasoning by analogy is using known similarities between things and/or events and/or states of affairs to suggest or justify conjectures or conclusions about further similarities between them. (This is, I think, the usual meaning of the term now, although it is somewhat different from the argument from analogy described by Greek philosophers, which had to do with equality of ratios and/or proportions).

An analogy may (like induction) be useful in a process of discovery. Observed similarities between item A and B, when one knows item A has property x, may suggest as something to be investigated that item B also has property x. Subsequently, one may seek to justify a hypothesis that item B has property x, and in this case, the original analogy which suggested the hypothesis may be part of that justification (although it need not be). I am concerned with justification by plausible reasoning, rather than discovery.

Justification through analogy is closely related to other types of plausible reasoning:

1. An inductive argument, for example, from the observation of many (and only) black ravens to the conclusion that all ravens are black, may be compared to an argument by analogy from the same observation to the conclusion that all other objects which are similar to those observed in being ravens will also be similar to them in being black.

2. The application of a term like 'table' to an uncertain case (say, the countertop mentioned earlier) will be guided to a considerable extent by similarities and differences between this case and things which are clearly tables. In cases of legal interpretation of words in legal documents and statutes, this process is used; indeed, in many areas of legal reasoning analogy is used extensively.
3. The analogy is also relevant in the case of a person seeking to understand an unfamiliar language, as exemplified by Quine's linguist. He will presumably proceed from observed similarities in circumstances of use of words, phrases, and sentences (as between his own language and that of the native tribe) to conclusions about similarities in meaning.

In some cases of reasoning by analogy to a conclusion, one step is to consider what is the closest or best analogue or analogy to a given item. For example, a judge may be faced with a situation which is not covered exactly by any established legal rule, and there may be two different established legal rules each governing slightly different circumstances: then, one question which the judge may well consider is 'which class of these situations governed by the established rules is the best analogy to the subject situation?'

In some types of informal reasoning, the very object is to find the best analogy. An important case (discussed in Hofstadter 1986):[199] is that of translation from one language to another by a person familiar with both languages. There will generally be a range of possible translations, some more literal, some more idiomatic, some which perhaps more than others capture the 'flavour' that the original has by reason of such things as puns, rhymes, consonances, associations, etc. A translation will seek the 'best' translation (or analogue, in the new language, of the original) having regard to the nature of what is translated and the purpose of the translation.

The use in reasoning of the concept of similarity (and thus the use of analogy) has been criticised by philosophers.

For example, Nelson Goodman in 'Seven Strictures on Similarity' contends in effect that the concept is either hopelessly vague or else superfluous. His fifth and seventh strictures are respectively: 'Similarity does not account for our predictive, or more generally, our inductive practice', and 'Similarity cannot be equated with, or measured in terms of, possession of common characteristics'.

The role of emotion. Indeed, I believe that emotional feelings are an essential part of our general rationality in all fields. For example, scientists talk of the beauty of theories such as the theory of relativity, relying on aesthetic judgements (and thereby on emotional feelings) as indicia of truth. Emotions can be highly irrational; but such irrationality in oneself may be identified, controlled, and perhaps eliminated, by application of one's general rationality (which, as I say, itself includes emotion). In making rational decisions, one attends to 'feelings' of similarity and difference, rightness and wrongness, beauty and ugliness, clarity and confusion, coherence and repugnance, simplicity and complexity, and so on. The totality of rational appraisal comprehends such things as dialectic and rhetoric (to mention some traditional categories) as well as logic.

One correct answer? Of course, when what is required for a decision is a choice between factors which cannot precisely and reliably be reduced to a common scale, there may in some cases be no unique 'correct' decision. In some cases, all or most reasonable human beings would agree on the 'correct' decision; in others, there would not be such agreement.

It might be contended that accordingly, all that is necessary (and probably all that occurs) is that the brain should instantiate a formal system which decides the obvious cases correctly—that is, in accordance with what most reasonable human beings would decide—and the balance at random. This formal system need only be capable of roughly scaling the competing factors, perhaps assigning a range to each: then if all calculations using the extremities of each range give the same result, it could be treated as correct. Otherwise, the result could either be given by calculations based on averages, or else at random: it would not really matter. At its formal substratum, the brain might work that way, and a computer could simulate it.

That is a possibility, but I think it is unlikely. It overlooks *inter alia* what has been called 'the infinity of argument'. That is, any propositions and any step of reasoning may be questioned and made the subject of plausible reasoning, quite possibly involving competing non-commensurable considerations. Any basis of scaling, any value judgment, can be reconsidered. Conscious decision-making enables one to adopt and change any method of dealing with such competing considerations: such flexibility may depend on people being effective, being able to make value judgments which are in a sense ultimate and unsupported, but which may nevertheless be challenged and changed on the basis of plausible reasoning.

Reliance on Weighing and Judgment

It has already been noted that in so far as our ordinary reasoning is not logically valid, it will on examination be seen to involve steps which come down to what is usually referred to as judgment, weighing alternatives or the like. I have already suggested that most of our reasoning, in science, philosophy, practical reasoning, and law (*inter alia*), involves such steps, and indeed, in many cases, those steps are the most significant ones. If such steps are tested on the basis of formal logical validity, they are seen to be invalid: from that point of view the likelihood that the conclusion is false (given the truth of thepremises) is no different from the likelihood that it is true: neither the conclusion nor its negation is entailed, and on the basis of formal logic no more can be said. However, the argument involving these steps is put as being persuasive and is generally accepted as such. Such persuasiveness cannot depend on logic: it must depend on some informal judgment or weighing.

To avoid the last conclusion, one or both of two propositions could be put:

1. Such steps in argument really involve unstatedpremises, and when these are supplied, such steps become a valid logical inference.
2. Formal systems with rules of inference wider than the rules of logic could be used, so as to make conclusions, which are not logically entailed bypremises, plausible or probable; for example, rules of induction as formalised by Carnap.

As regards (1), this does seem to be a satisfactory explanation either of how plausible reasoning actually works or of why it has persuasive force. In relation to induction, it is vulnerable to the Hume-Popper infinite regress. In many, perhaps most, cases, the conclusion of plausible reasoning seems more readily acceptable than any premiseswhich might be suggested in order to convert the argument into a logically valid one. Particularly is this so where there are two countervailing considerations, and one is judged to have greater weight in the particular case: for example, the convincing demeanour of one witness in a court of law who tells one story, and the plausibility of the different story told by another witness.

One may be able to give any number of reasons why a judgment is made in a particular case and be confident that it is correct: but find it impossible to formulate a statement or rule of more general application which can be mechanically applied in such cases, and which one accepts to be correct as readily as one accepts the result in the particular case.

As regards (2), I have already discussed the problem of induction. Furthermore, this does not reflect how plausible reasoning actually works. Such a system *may* underlie such reasoning and explain its persuasive force. However, I suggest that we could not reasonably be persuaded of this. Any argument seeking so to persuade us will itself be a plausible argument appealing to rational judgment and weighing of reasons: that is, it will depend upon the very sort of argument it seeks to explain away.

The crucial step of judgment or weighing is of its nature inconclusive, as is all plausible reasoning. This is my most fundamental disagreement with Penrose. He adopts a Platonic view of mathematical truths and suggests that 'consciousness is closely associated with sensing of necessary truths'.

Analytical Thought

Lawyers are often acclaimed for their powers of analytical thought. Leonard Mlodinow has said:

We tend to praise analytical thought as being objective, untinged by the distortions of human feelings, and therefore tending toward accuracy. But though many praise analytical thought for its detachment from emotion, one could also criticise it as not being inspired by emotion, as elastic thinking is.[200]

His view is the relative lack of an emotional component is one reason analytical thought is simpler than elastic thought and easier to analyse. He identifies our first modern insight into its nature as coming more than a century and a half ago, when, in 1851, the dean of faculty at Queen's College Cork, in southwestern Ireland, gave the annual address for the start of the college session. In that address, he asked, "Whether there exists, with reference to our mental faculties, such general laws as are necessary to constitute a science... I reply that this is possible and that [the laws of reason] constitute the true basis of mathematics. I speak here not of the mathematics of number and quantity alone, but mathematics in its larger, and I believe, truer sense, as universal reasoning expressed in symbolic forms."

At that time, he suggests no one made too much of the difference between playing a chess game from start to finish and composing an original symphony, starting from the blank page. But from today's point of view, a huge distinction is drawn. The former can be accomplished through the linear application of rules and logic, Boole's laws of thought. The latter requires more—namely, the ability to generate new and original ideas. The former can be reduced to algorithms, while the latter when we attempt to reduce it to algorithms, falls flat.

Traditional computers can do the former better than any person but cannot do the latter very well at all. In that gap lies a key to the difference between analytical thought and the greater power of elastic thinking. Mlodinow's opinion: the analytical approach we've worshipped in Western society ever since the Age of Reason is a low-level god, while the Zeus of human thought is elastic thinking. After all, logical thought can determine how to drive from your home to the grocer most efficiently, but it's elastic thought that gave us the automobile.

A chair is difficult to define via a rational, rule-based description because the definition must embrace not just typical chairs, but a great variety of novel versions. So how does a third grader make the identification? The elastic thinking of the brain is non-algorithmic, by which I mean that we achieve our ideas and solutions without a clear definition of the steps needed to get there. (I say this regardless of whether or not the brain can be simulated by a Turing Machine, as some believe.) Instead, rather than rely on a well-thought-out and easily stated definition of a chair, the neural networks in our unconscious minds, through years of seeing examples, somehow learn to weigh complex object traits in a manner of which we are not even aware.

He identifies key differences in the architecture of brains and digital computers, which in turn tells us something important our ourselves. In contrast to our brains, computers are made of interlinked switches that can be understood through circuit and logic diagrams, and they execute their analysis by following a well-defined series of steps (a program or algorithm) in a linear fashion that is specified for the task at hand by a programmer. The Google scientists who linked a thousand such computers in a neural net performed an impressive feat, and it's a promising approach. But our brains do something vastly more impressive, forming neural nets from *billions* of cells, each connected to thousands of others. These networks are organised into larger structures, which are in turn organised into larger structures, and so on, in a complex hierarchical scheme that scientists are only beginning to understand.

Such biological brains can process information in a top-down manner, as a traditional computer does, or from the bottom up, which is important in elastic thinking, or in some combination of the two modes. Bottom-up processing arises from the complex and relatively 'unsupervised' interaction of millions of neurons and can produce wildly original insights. Top-down processing, in contrast, is directed by the brain's executive regions and produces step-by-step analytical thought.

He cites an example of legal elastic thinking. Our executive brain is good at quashing ideas that are non sequiturs. But if we are problem-solving and happen to be plodding along in the wrong direction, non-sequiturs—steps that don't follow—are exactly what we need. Sanford Perliss, a well-known American defence attorney, tells of a case he heard in law school. A defendant was on trial for murdering his wife. The circumstantial evidence was strong, but the police had never found the body. When writing his closing argument, the defence attorney first tried the usual approach, summing up the evidence in an effort to persuade the jury to find reasonable doubt. But the logic wasn't working. The attorney feared he would convince no one. Then he got an idea 'out of left field'.

When he finally stood before the jury to make his argument, the attorney made a dramatic announcement: The supposed victim had been located. She was there, in the courthouse. He asked the jurors to turn toward the back of the room. In just a moment, he told them, she would walk through the doors, proving his client's innocence. The jurors turned in anticipation. A few seconds passed, but no one walked in.

The attorney then pronounced with great bravado that unfortunately they had *not* located the woman—but if the jurors turned to look, then in their hearts there was reasonable doubt, and they should vote to acquit. It was a brilliant example of a lawyer's mind abandoning the usual step-by-step approach and taking a new direction. Unfortunately for the defendant, his attorney had not clued him in on the ruse. As a result, he himself, having *no* doubt that his wife was dead, did not turn toward the back of the room. The prosecutor pointed this out in his rebuttal, and the defendant was convicted.

As Mlodinow has again stressed:

You don't solve riddles through a step-by-step linear approach, nor is that how J.K. Rowling invented the Harry Potter world, or how Chester Carlson thought of the idea for the Xerox machine. It's our unsupervised bottom-up thinking that provides us with the unexpected insights and new ways of looking at situations that produce that kind of accomplishment.[201]

Kurt Vonnegut wrote that we humans "have to constantly be jumping off cliffs and developing our wings on the way down."

Frozen thinking occurs when you have a fixed orientation that determines the way you frame or approach a problem. Our challenge is to turn off that mode of mental operation, to defrost and re-examine our 'frozen thoughts' when it is appropriate. Arendt called the kind of thinking we engage in when we rise above frozen thought 'critical thinking'. To Arendt, who was interested in the origins of evil, thinking critically was a moral imperative. In its absence, a society can go the way of Nazi Germany, a risk that is still present in many countries today. Yet Arendt noted a surprising number of people don't think critically. "[The] inability to think [critically] is not stupidity," she wrote, "It can be found in highly intelligent people."

Our conscious brains can process about forty to sixty bits per second, roughly the information content of a short sentence. Our unconscious has a much greater capacity. Your visual system, for example, can handle about ten million bits per second. As a result, your primary visual cortex can pass only a small fraction of that to your conscious mind. So, between your vast unconscious sensory perception and your limited conscious awareness stands a system of 'cognitive filters'. Those filters make their best guess regarding what is relevant or important. They pass that along to our awareness and censor the rest.

In my experience, the best lawyers and especially advocates are original thinkers. They think the arguments that lesser advocates never dream of.

To have original thoughts, you have to let the ideas flow first and worry about their quality (or appropriateness) later. Even then, the value of an idea can be difficult to ascertain, for it is one of the ironies of science, the arts, and the law, that the brilliant and the nutty are not always easily distinguished.

As Mlodinow recalls: Two-time Nobel laureate Linus Pauling encapsulated the process of innovation when he said, "The way to get good ideas is to get lots of ideas and throw out the bad ones. It's a process full of blind alleys and dead ends."

Law is a creative pursuit. Different creative pursuits require varying degrees of unconscious elastic thinking, in combination with various degrees of the conscious ability to modulate it and shape it through analytical thinking. In music, for example, at one end of the creative spectrum are improvisational artists, such as jazz musicians. They have to be peculiarly talented at lowering their inhibitions and letting in their unconsciously generated ideas. Although the process of learning the fundamentals of jazz would require a high degree of analytical thought, that thinking style is not as big a factor during the performance.

On the other end of the spectrum are those who compose complex forms, and as a symphony or concerto, that require not just imagination but also careful planning and exacting editing. We know, for example, through his letters and the reports of others, that even Mozart's creations did not appear spontaneously, wholly formed in his consciousness, as the myths about him portray. Instead, he spent long, arduous hours analysing and reworking the ideas that arose in his unconscious, much as a scientist does when producing a theory from a germ of insight. In Mozart's own words: "I immerse myself in music… I think about it all day long—I like experimenting—studying—reflecting…"

That's true, too, of another chemical that many eminent artists, musicians, and writers have claimed played a role in their success, alcohol. As musician Frank Varano said, "On some days, my head is filled with such wild and original thoughts that I can barely utter a word. On other days, the liquor store is closed." Such testimonials go back at least as far as 424 BC, when Aristophanes wrote, in his play *The Knights*, "When men drink, then they are rich and successful… Quickly, bring me a beaker of wine so that I may wet my mind and say something clever."

This may explain why there is a close relationship between drinking and the law!

Recent science seems to confirm that alcohol can have beneficial effects on elastic thinking. For example, in a 2012 study that paralleled the marijuana study done that same year, forty social drinkers in their twenties were recruited through Craigslist. Half were served enough vodka and cranberry juice to bring them to the border of being legally drunk. The others drank just cranberry juice. They were all then given problems whose solutions required elastic thinking. The drunk subjects solved about 60% of the problems; the sober ones, 40%. What's more, the tipsy students completed the test faster.

The problem with alcohol as a thinking aid is that while the defocusing it provides can loosen the thought processes, they can easily become so loose that they fall off their tracks. The same is true of marijuana. In both cases, the trade-off is much like that in schizotypy versus schizophrenia. Having a drink or two, or a hit of pot, while formulating your business strategy could increase the breadth of ideas that come to you—but if you are too far gone, those ideas might prove useless or incoherent.

The Silver Lining of Fatigue

Fatigue which lawyers often suffer from is enhancing. In 2015, a group of researchers in France showed, for example, that the simple act of exhausting your executive brain before you start pondering a challenging intellectual issue can unleash your elastic brain to mount a more effective attack.

The key to the experiment is that, in order to focus on the central arrow, the subjects must suppress the influence of the other arrows. That suppression is accomplished by the subjects' prefrontal cortex, and to perform that task over and over without a break for forty minutes, as the subjects were asked to do, is mentally exhausting.

Though success in science requires original ideas, once you have an idea, it takes quite a long time to work out its consequences, and it is in that analytical mode that you spend most of your time. By contrast, the need for elastic thinking is almost constant.

Many advocates will speak to that feeling of euphoria that results from the exhaustion of preparing a case. George Carman told me that often he would go out drinking on the night before a case and then work into the early hours of the morning and then go into court, mentally refreshed and 'in the zone'.

Chapter 22

Injustice anywhere is a threat to justice everywhere.

Martin Luther King, Jr

Justice is truth in action.

Joseph Joubert

Injustice is relatively easy to bear; what stings is justice.

H L Mencken

Justice is like a train that is nearly always late.

Yevtushonko

Justice will not condemn even the Devil himself wrongfully.

Thomas Fuller

Justice is impartiality; only strangers are impartial.

George Bernard Shaw

Natural justice languished a little in the UK during the first half of the twentieth century with the assistance of such decisions as *Local Government Board v. Arlidge* in which Lord Shaw uttered the following damning words of faint praise:

"In so far as the term 'natural' justice means that a result or process should be just, it is harmless though it may be a high-sounding expression in so far as it attempts to reflect the old jus natural[202] it is a confused an unwarranted transfer into the ethical sphere of a term employed for other distinctions; and, in so far as it is resorted to for other purposes, it is vacuous."[203]

It was in the 1960s in the UK that natural justice, as procedural fairness, was brought out into the full sunlight initially by the Privy Council in *University of Ceylon v. Fernando* and thereafter by the House of Lords in *Ridge v. Baldwin*.[204]

The House of Lords in the latter case repudiated the continuing requirement that decision-makers had to be characterised as acting judicially before attracting the application of the rules of natural justice. It reinstated the approach to the requirement of natural justice taken in *Cooper v. Wandsworth Board of Works*. From that time onwards, the language of 'fairness' in decision-making gained prominence.

It has been argued that individuals who are legally trained tend to be preoccupied with the adversarial adjudicative model of decision-making.[205] The lawyer not only claims that third-party review is a necessary component of a legal system, but he asserts that only control by judicial institutions is a guarantee of the reviewing agency's independence. The argument against this is that the adversarial model of adjudication is not a decisional structure well suited to the development of procedure norms.

It is said that the psychology of confrontation, delay and 'winner-take' all inherent in this system should have no place in the procedural review process. I have thought long and hard about this and have come to the conclusion that the adversarial system may not be perfect but the Socratic and dialectical approach of laws of the legal system which I discussed earlier in Chapters 18 and 19 is the most likely to be the most effective means of preventing the abuse of administrative action and the most likely to achieve 'fairness' in decision-making in our society.

In *Ryanair v. Aer Rianta* (2003) IR 264, Fennelly J. said, "The public interest in the proper administration of justice is not confined to the relentless search for perfect truth. The just and proper conduct of litigation also encompasses the objective of expedition and economy."

What Does It Mean to Be Fair?

According to Shakespeare, 'All's fair in love and war' but not in law!

This raises one of the fundamental issues of legal philosophy: to what extent is human conduct governable by rules, and to what extent can rules provide a structure within which responsible decision-making can take place? The positivist view of legal decision-making has been under attack for a number of years. I was brought up on Hart and his *Concept of Law* and I remember him shambling around Oxford always it seemed carrying a large carrier bag. He was a great eccentric genius. But his view of law simply being a system of rules is now a bit suspect.

Many lawyers now believe that rules can only operate as guidance to decisions. It is now acknowledged that legal rules operate in a broader context. Not only do other normative systems condition the meaning of legal rules but the concept of a legal rule is that it is descriptive of a past decision or a series of past decisions (a posteriori) and only secondarily prescriptive. What is truly distinctive of a legal system is not the structure and context of its rules, but the expectations and assumptions shared by participants committed to the legal process.

The implications of this attitude for procedural review are significant in that they show that the principles of fairness must consist of more than the establishment of rules. Due process for decision-makers will not alone promote fairness. It must perform an educative function, encouraging the development of certain paradigms of decision-making and engendering commitment to them.

The remedy of judicial review is often confused with the appellate function of courts. Even judges and lawyers who can list the differences between the two regimes often permit the assumptions of one judicial function to permeate others. In principle, a motion for judicial review involves the allegation of a lack of jurisdiction (error of law on the face of the record excepted) which is to say that it involves an indirect attack on the substance of the decision, through a direct challenge to the policy of the decision-maker to act as he did. Unlike appeals, review implies that for some formal reason, the decision-maker had no authority to decide, not that his decision was wrong on its merits.

While the blurring of this distinction between appellate and review functions may not be totally inappropriate in cases involving formal ultra vires review, it is generally misconceived in cases of procedural impropriety. In the latter instances, the original decision-maker will invariably be faced again with the same issue, and the reviewing court must therefore be prepared to provide guidelines as to the manner of decision-making that can be applied consistently and impartially. Hence the remedial assumptions underlying the judicial appellate process do not necessarily apply to procedural review.

There are three principal groups of judicial review for 'illegality', 'procedural impropriety' and 'irrationality'.

The concept of 'fairness' is generally characterised as being concerned with 'procedural impropriety' and will for the most part focus on that aspect of judicial review. But 'fairness' is not all about procedure. It is a broader concept than that. The courts have yet to grapple with developing a paradigm and principled approach to fairness.

Arguably, it is well time they did. As the historian E.P. Thompson said in response to the claim made by some 'structuralist' Marxists that law is simply a device for mystifying the masses and masking the reality of class dominance:

People are not as stupid as some structural philosophers suppose them to be. They will not be mystified by the first man who puts on a wig. It is inherent in the especial character of law, as a body of rules and procedures that it state and apply logical criteria with reference to standards of universality and equity... The essential precondition for the effectiveness of law, in its function as ideology, is that it shall display an independence from gross manipulation, and shall seem to be just. It cannot seem to be so without upholding its own logic and criteria; indeed, on occasion, by actually being just.[206]

Key Principles of Fairness

What does it mean to be fair?

It has been said that the "highest morality almost always is the morality of process."[207]

The legalistic view of fairness was that stated by Jackson J of the United States Supreme Court:

Procedural fairness and regularity are of the indispensable essence of liberty. Severe substantive laws can be endured if they are fairly and impartially applied.[208]

Looked at in that way the law does not see any special relationship existing between procedural and substantive justice.

As I have said, this perspective is characteristic of the ethical attitude of 'legalism'.

Essentially, it is that the courts are preoccupied with the instrumentalities, rather than the content of obligations.[209]

Much constitutional theory is dominated by this conception. To quote another American jurist, Frankfurter J.

The history of liberty has largely been the history of the observance of procedural safeguards.[210]

John Rawls saw substantive justice formulated in terms of the voluntary assumption of general principles in order to achieve a just society. He stated:

Justice begins…with one of the most general of all choices which persons might make together, namely, with the choice of the first principles of a conception of justice which is to regulate all subsequent criticism and reform of institutions.[211]

Even Hart was content to articulate a 'formalist' theory of procedural justice. He concluded that the maxims audi alteram partem and nemo index in causa sua are justified simply "because they are guarantees of impartiality or objectivity, designed, to secure that the law is applied to all those and only to those who are alike in the relevant respect marked and by the law itself."[212]

It was Lon Fuller who developed frameworks which linked the concepts of procedural review with those of substantive justice. He was concerned with uncovering what he labelled the 'inner morality' of the law and various legal institutions. He attempted to derive procedural principles from the instrumental rationality of the decision-making institution (adjudication, negotiation, mediation, legislation) itself. He believed that these institutions imposed upon decision-makers duties which could be characterised as role morality. He concluded:

When I speak of legal morality, I mean just that. I mean that special morality that attaches to the occupant of that office, not from murdering people, but from undermining the integrity of the law itself.[213]

While Fuller's writing was primarily directed to the elucidation of the special duties of rule-makers, it also deals with the analysis of other decisional processes.[214]

Implicit in Fuller's evaluation of legal institutions is the belief that the distinguishing feature of each institution is the mode of participation it affords to the affected party.

Hart saw in the two rules of natural justice a guarantee of the minimum conditions of impartial adjudication. Fuller extended this process across the entire range of legal decision-making.

Fuller's view was that institutions have an 'inner morality' which is coherent with and productive of substantive justice.

So what are the key principles of fairness? That question may be unpacked into a contemporary taxonomy which poses a number of propositions:

1. It is a theory of judicial review.
2. It is a theory which is essential in orientation.
3. It is a theory of review or implied grounds.
4. It is a theory the applicability of which is not limited to judicial or quasi-judicial decision-making processes.
5. It is a theory which is informalist, in that standards of review are neither fixed nor capable of specific *a priori* articulation.

The last two features represent a significant departure from earlier theories of review; previously supervision had been limited to 'judicial' functions, and as the epithet suggests the 'rules' of natural justice were relatively formalised.

But still, some advocates of fairness see no fundamental differences between the concept of fairness and that of natural justice.

The concept of fairness is part of our cultural heritage. It is deeply rooted in our law. It now lies at the heart of the judicial function and conditions the exercise of a large array of administrative powers affecting the rights, duties, privileges and immunities of individuals and organisations.

At the conceptual level, it is a first principle of justice and, arguably, it is democracy's guarantee of the opportunity for all to play their part in the political process. But compare Jeremy Waldron's views that it is undemocratic.

Ever since Aristotle's political philosophers have tried to mitigate or qualify that image, politics, they have argued, need not be the arbitrary rule of man over man. Perhaps we can imagine a form of political life in which everyone is a subject and everyone is ruled not by a person or by any particular group of people, but by a shared set of abstract rules. If I am subject to another person then I am at the mercy of his whims and passions, his angers and prejudices. But if we are both subject to the same law, then the personal factor is taken out of politics. By subjecting everyone to the law, we make ourselves less equal again.[215]

At a practical level, it is instrumental, that is to say, an aid, and good decision-making supports the rule of law by promoting public confidence in official decision-making and giving due respect to the dignity of individuals.

However, there is a tendency in some quarters to regard procedural fairness as a species of ethical ornamentalisation, a moral luxury, which is a drag on official decision-making.[216]

It has been observed that "it is natural that administration should be tempted to regard procedural restrictions, invented by lawyers, as an obstacle to efficiency."[217]

The rules of fairness, as rules of natural justice were derived from natural law as demonstrated by English cases of the seventeenth and eighteenth centuries. The natural justice hearing rule appeared in many cases in the Year Books.

Chief Justice Coke ('a seventeenth century Denning') inferred it from the provision of the Magna Carta that:

No free man shall be taken or imprisoned ruined or disseised or outlawed or exiled or in any way ruined, nor will we go or send against him, except by the lawful judgement of his peers or by the law of the land.[218]

By this provision, he said, "no man ought to be condemned without answer."[219]

It was stretching it a bit, but Coke, like Denning was nothing, if not creative.

It was Chief Justice Coke who in 1615 forcefully asserted the rule and at the same time dramatically extended the power of the Court of King's Bench.

The case concerned municipal behaviour. The Mayor and Chief Burgesses of the Borough of Plymouth had removed one of their number, James Bagg, from the office of Chief Burgess on the grounds of his misconduct. They made a number of allegations against him. They said that he had called the previous Mayor, Mr Trelawney, a 'cozening knave' and 'an insolent fellow'. They said that he had threatened to crack the neck of the current Mayor, Thomas Fowens. Worst of all they said that:

In the presence and hearing of... Thomas Fowens...and very many others of the burgesses and inhabitants of the borough...and in contempt and distain of the said Thomas Fowens, then Mayor, turning the hinder part of his body in an inhuman and uncivil manner towards the aforesaid Thomas Fowens, scoffingly, contemptuously and uncivilly, with a loud voice, said to the aforesaid Thomas Fowens, these words following, that is to say ('come and kiss').[220]

Mr Bagg (appropriately named) commenced proceedings in the Court of King's Bench challenging his removal from office by the mayor and other burgesses to either restore Mr Bagg to office or to show cause why he was removed. An answer was given referring to Mr Bagg's very bad behaviour. However, the court was not satisfied that the reasons given in the return to the writ justified his removal. On the question of how and by whom and in what manner a citizen or burgess should be disenfranchised, Coke C.J. said:

...although they have lawful authority either by charter or prescription to remove anyone from the freedom, and that they have just cause to remove him, yet it appears by the return, that they have proceeded against him without...hearing him answer to what was objected, or that he was not reasonably warned, such removal is void and shall not bind the party.[221]

For what may properly be called moral support, he quoted from Seneca's tragedy, the Medea, a passage which as translated in 1648, read:

Who ought decrees, nor heares both sides discust,
Does but unjustly, though Doome be just.[222]

The principle propounded in those lives was that even though a decision is right, it is not just if made without the decision-maker first hearing from the person to be affected by it.

Bagg's case was probably most notable as one of the first occasions on which mandamus was used as a tool for judicial review of administrative action. In justifying the issue of the writ, Coke asserted the jurisdiction of the Court of King's Bench in broad terms:

> *not only to correct errors in judicial proceedings, but other errors and misdemeanours [sic] extra-judicial, tending to the breach of peace, or oppression of the subjects, or to the raising of faction, controversy, debate, or to any manner of misgovernment; so that no wrong or injury, either public or private, can be done but that it shall be (here) reformed or punished by due course of law.*[223]

It is noteworthy that the requirement for a hearing outweighed any consideration of the merits of the decision under review.

To effect in 1723, the Court of King's Bench issued a mandamus to the University of Cambridge requiring the restoration to one Dr Bentley of the degrees of Bachelor of Arts and Bachelor and Doctor of Divinity of which he had been deprived by the University without a hearing. Dr Bentley had been served with a summons to appear before a university court in an action for debt. He said the process was illegal, that he would not obey it and that the Vice-Chancellor was not his judge. He was then accused of contempt and without further notice deprived of his degrees by the 'congregation' of the University.

The judgment of Fortescue J. in the case is often cited as an example of the way in which the idea of natural law informed the concept of natural justice.

Fortescue J. said:

> *The law of God and man both give the party an opportunity to make his defence, if he has any. I remember to have heard it observed by a very learned man upon such an occasion, that even God himself did not pass sentence upon Adam, before he was called upon to make his defence.*[224]

The notion that God thought up procedural fairness may be worth reflecting upon!

It was a notion which was extant a long time before Dr Bentley's case.

Writing in defence of St Athanasius in the fourth century, Bishop Lucifer of Cagliari invoked the example of a divinely converted hearing in the Garden of Eden:

How do you believe it divinely permitted to punish a person unheard when you see that Adam and Eve, the origin of our race, were heard before they were struck by the sentence of God? Then God called Adam and said to him, Adam, where are you? And Adam said, I heard your voice, Lord, in paradise and I was afraid, because I am naked, and I had myself. And God said to him, who showed you that you are naked, except that you have eaten from the tree from which alone I commanded not to eat? And Adam said. The woman that you gave me, she gave me from the tree and I ate. And God said to the woman why did you do this? And the woman said. The serpent persuaded me, and I ate ...[225]

It does not appear that the serpent was asked to testify. Being omniscient, God had no need to hear from anybody. If His exchange with Adam and Eve reflected respect for the hearing rule, that respect did not depend upon its practical utility.

After *Dr Bentley's case*, the hearing rule was reinforced in 1799 by Lord Kenyon in *R. v. Gaskin*.[226] It was Lord Kenyon who apparently coined the Latin term 'audi alteram partem' to encapsulate the rule, of which he said:

It is to be found at the head of our criminal law, that every man ought to have an opportunity of being heard before he is condemned...[227]

The Rule Against Bias

The second aspect of procedural fairness, the rule against bias surfaced in 1610 in *Dr Bonham's case*.[228] The case is best known for another vaulting claim by Coke in his assertion of the superiority of judge-made law over the parliamentary variety thus "when an Act of Parliament is against common right and reason, or repugnant, or impossible to be performed, the common law will control it, and adjudge such Act to be void."[229]

The Royal College of Physicians had tried Dr Bonham and secured his imprisonment when he had continued to practice in London after being refused permission to do so by the College. He brought a suit for false imprisonment in the Court of Common Pleas.

In the course of the judgment, Coke said of the college, which was entitled to keep some of the fine which it imposed, that:

the censors cannot be judges, ministers, and parties; judges to give sentence or judgment; ministers to make summons; and parties to have the moiety of the forfeiture.[230]

The character of the rule against bias as a kind of natural or constitutional limit upon parliamentary power was also asserted by Lord Chief Justice Hobart in 1614 in *Day v. Savadge* when he said that a statute "made against natural equity, as to make a man judge in his own cause, is void in itself, for jura naturae sunt immutabilia [the laws of nature are unchangeable] and they are leges legum [laws that apply to laws]."[231]

The passage demonstrates that the rule against bias, like the hearing rule, was treated as an expression of the natural law regarded by Roman legal scholars as "that ideal body of right and reasonable principles which was common to all human beings."[232]

Those principles are said to have emerged from Cicero's Latin renderings of Greek stoic philosophy, written in the first century BC.[233]

They became the underpinnings of Thomas Aquinas's philosophy and were regarded as divine law informing creation and binding human beings.

Despite his exalted status the constitutional force is given to natural justice and natural law by Chief Justice Coke in Dr Bonham's Case and by Chief Justice Hobart in *Day v. Savadge*, did not survive the rise of the doctrine of parliamentary supremacy.

In *City of London v. Wood*,[234] Chief Justice Holt reaffirmed the rule against bias as an expression of natural law. By that time, the idea that a person could not be a judge in his own cause was well established.

Natural law as an emanation of the divine had taken its place alongside the theories of Thomas Hobbes in which it was treated "not as traditional right-reason, but rather as a mode of reasoning about the liberty of individuals in the state of nature."[235]

Chief Justice Holt expressed support for *Dr Bonham's case* saying:

…it is a very reasonable and true saying; that if an Act of Parliament should ordain that the same person should be party and judge, or, which is the same, judge in his own cause, it would be a void Act of parliament; for it is impossible that one should be judge and party, for the judge is to determine between party and party, or between the government and the party; and an Act of parliament

can do no wrong, although it may do several things that look pretty odd; for it may discharge one from his allegiance to the government he lives under, and restore him to the state of nature; but it cannot make one that lives under a government judge and party.[236]

One might ask in contemporary terms how far distant from that proposition is the proposition that the rules of procedural fairness qualify the exercise of statutory powers as an implied limitation which requires clear words for its displacement.

There would seem to be a small 'c' constitutional dimension to the common law rule of interpretation, which supports procedural fairness in the exercise of statutory powers.

The suggestion that the natural law could invalidate or avoid statutes which were contrary to its norms fell before the rising tide of parliamentary supremacy following the Glorious Revolution of 1688.

The rule against bias was no exception to it.[237]

Nevertheless, the rule against bias was well established.

It was rather dramatically deployed against the Lord Chancellor himself in *Dimes v. Grand Junction Canal* in 1852.[238]

The House of Lords in that case set aside a decision involving a canal company in which the Lord Chancellor, Lord Cottenham, who had presided, was a shareholder. There was no suggestion that he was influenced by his pecuniary interest in the case.[239]

The appearance of bias sufficed. Lord Campbell after stating that Lord Cottenham would not be in the remotest degree influenced by his interest took the opportunity to deliver a stern warning to all lesser dispenses of justice.

This will be a lesson to all inferior tribunals to take care not only that in their decrees they are not influenced by their personal interest, but to avoid the appearance of labouring under such an influence.[240]

Embarrassingly, the House of Lords revisited the question again with one of its own in 1999.[241]

Their Lordships held that Augusto Pinochet, the former dictator of Chile, was amenable to arrest and extradition for crimes committed when in office. One of the intervenors in the case was Amnesty International. Lord Hoffman, who sat on the case, was a director of a related organisation, Amnesty International Charity Ltd. That fact was not disclosed to the parties.

The decision was set aside by a differently constituted panel of the Law Lords. The relevant principles were enunciated by Lord Browne-Wilkinson.

A judge who was a party to an action or had a financial proprietary interest in its outcome was automatically disqualified from hearing it. If a judge's conduct or behaviour could give rise to a suspicion of partiality, for example, because of friendship with a party, then the judge would be disqualified. Significantly, the automatic disqualification rule was extended to a judge involved whether personally or as a director of a company, in promoting the same causes in the same organisation as is a party to a suit.[242]

The principle so enunciated has been the subject of some debate referred to by Justice Grant Hammond of New Zealand in Judicial Recusal (2009).[243]

The criticism of the decision, as Justice Hammond explained it, was that the House of Lords had applied a formalistic per se rule to avoid any inquiry into whether Lord Hoffman could be said to have been likely to be biased. This approach was contrasted with that of the High Court of Australia in *Ebner v. Official Trustee in Bankruptcy*.[244] There the focus of the court was on reasonable apprehension of bias.

In *Cooper v. Wandsworth Board of Works*[245] decided in 1863, Byles J, in a frequently quoted passage, said:

...a long course of decisions, beginning with Dr Bentley's case, and ending with some very recent cases, establish that although there are no positive words in a statute requiring that the party be heard, yet the justice of the common law will supply the omission of the legislature.[246]

That passage and other judgments in *Cooper v. Wandsworth Board of Works* anticipated the question—Just how does the justice of the common law supply the omission of the legislature?

The English court's approach was to treat the problem as one of statutory interpretation. In *Wiseman v. Borneman*, Lord Guest said:

> *...the courts will imply into the statutory provision a rule that the principles of natural justice should be applied. This implication will be made upon the basis that parliament is not to be presumed to take away parties' rights without giving them an opportunity of being heard in their interest.*[247]

In Australia, the emphasis on the common law is to be found in the case of *Kioa v. West* decided (sometime later) in 1985.

Sir Anthony Mason said:

> *The law has developed to a point where it may be accepted that there is a common law duty to act fairly, in the sense of according procedural fairness, in the making of administrative decisions which affect rights, interests and legitimate expectations,*[248] *subject only to the clear manifestation of a contrary statutory intention.*

It may be that the distinction between the common law and a common law rule of statutory implication approaches a distinction without a real difference. The ultimate question is whether the obligation asserted is compatible with the terms of the relevant legislation. In either view, the obligation to accord procedural fairness is an obligation affecting how the decision-maker is to go about the task of decision-making. It is a limitation on the power to decide.

Perhaps Mason J. in *Kioa v. West* (ibid)[249] distilled the essence of the modern approach:

> *It has been said on many occasions that natural justice and fairness are to be equated... And it has been recognised that in the context of administrative decision-making it is more appropriate to speak of a duty to act fairly or to accord procedural fairness. This is because the expression 'natural justice' has been associated, perhaps too closely associated with procedures followed by courts of law. The developing application of the doctrine of natural justice in the field of administrative decision-making has been very largely achieved by reference to the presence of characteristics which have been thought to reflect important characteristics of judicial decision-making.*[250]

The requirements of fairness are not fixed and the concept has to be flexibly applied according to the context. These requirements "are not engraved on tablets of stone."[251]

Fairness is a 'constantly evolving concept'.[252] The categories of unfairness are not closed.

But the issue is a matter of law for which the court is the sole arbiter. Though the decision depends upon its context it is not a question of mixed law and fact which might allow a number of different possible conclusions. The conclusion is one of principle and for the court to decide itself.[253] The courts have not adopted a 'free for all' and 'go everywhere approach'. The vocabulary of the courts may have changed but the concerns which produced the quasi-judicial/administrative dichotomy remain.

In my view as a practitioner, the courts while saying that they are adopting a flexible approach still rely on a modified classification of function framework to structure the process by which procedural formalities are implied. In large part, this can be explained by reference to the traditional 'rule of law' thesis which underlines the common law system. Applying a principle of fairness requires a court to engage in a purposive balancing of interests which runs contrary to the assumptions of common law adjudication. Judges appreciate that activism in applying a theory of fairness would vest them with the power to determine how administrative decisions should be taken.

Since these determinations cannot be characterised as judicial decisions, in so far as they do not involve the invocation of a pre-existing normative structure, judges tread carefully in these areas. They have therefore resisted an over-informalist approach and have still maintained the distinctiveness and moral force of decision-making such as adjudication, and avoid administrative chaos by over-judicialisation of decision processes.[254].

The courts adopt an ad hoc approach to fairness which closely resembles classical adjudication and avoid the projection of adjudicative assumptions into non-adjudicative processes. Some writers have been at pains to list facts likely to affect the extent of the procedural safeguards that must be in place before a decision-making process[255] will be fair. This reflects the empirical approach adopted by many judges but helps little in the elucidation of principle.

As a result, the concept of fairness is directed to what may broadly be identified as participation in decision-making. The conditions under which any form of participation should be permitted, the precise nature of such participation in individuals' cases, and the constraints placed on decision-makers in order to guarantee the effectiveness of this participation are the fundamental elements of a theory of fairness. But fairness is also a theory of implied due process review; consequently, it is invoked subsidiarily in the interstices of a statutory procedural framework. But the courts have still not developed a paradigm-based general theory of fairness.

It seems to me that in order to determine the precise requirements of fairness, it is necessary to work out what could be an appropriate paradigm for each possible decisional process. Rather than ask what aspects of adjudicative procedure can be grafted onto this decisional process, the court should ask: what is the nature of the process here undertaken, what mode of participation is envisioned by such a decisional process, and what specific procedural guidelines are necessary to ensure the efficacy of that participation and the integrity of the process under review.[256]

The failure to develop such a theory has resulted in conceptual difficulties being caused in cases involving the arguments that while a decision may have been made unfairly it could have made no difference to the result and therefore the court should grant no relief.[257] The courts have varied in their approach often depending upon the nature of the decision being challenged.[258]

In cases involving terrorism, the courts have shown a greater willingness to conclude that the result would have been no different if a fair procedure had been adopted. But no clear principles have emerged from either the House of Lords or Supreme Court in this regard.[259] Further conceptual problems are caused by cases involving legitimate expectation, proportionality, waiver of a breach of procedural fairness and cases under the Convention and Human Rights Act 1998.

Finally, it has been said, "law is symbol as well as system… Law need no longer symbolise what it has been in the past. However potent a symbol is, it can change."[260]

Of course, it can change for better or worse. But the evolution of the principles of fairness have evolved with a few ups and downs in an upward direction which demonstrates that law is not merely a collection of signs, words and concepts having only a discursive meaning but is a symbol, a metaphor of human society. It will continue to evolve, and as lawyers, we all have a role to play in the participation of that process. The legal profession is particularly concerned with tradition and precedent, with formalism and settled ways of acting. Undoubtedly, the further development of the criteria of procedural fairness puts a premium on inventiveness, flexibility and experimentation.

There is also the other prospect that the courts might soon have to develop some sort of substantive rule of law based on fairness. As Jeffrey Jowell has commented[261]: "When the Rule of Law allows judicial interference on grounds of 'unreasonableness', 'irrationality', or 'oppressiveness', it does become a substantive doctrine, one that is less easily accepted than the procedural, particularly in a society without a written constitution. Courts therefore tread carefully on a substantive Rule of Law and seek to exclude (or disguise) policy considerations from the decision." As he says, "the 'unreasonableness' doctrine itself carefully avoids judicial second-guessing of the administration on the grounds of mere disagreement and only permits interference if the official decision verges on the outlandish."[262]

However, the Human Rights Act 1998 made a significant change to our unwritten constitution. Section 6(1) states, "it is unlawful for a public authority to act in a way which is incompatible with a convention right" (that is a right protected by the European Convention on Human Rights, as defined in the HRA itself). This represented a new, substantive, head of illegality, subject to the exceptions in the HRA. Under both the developing common law of judicial review and the HRA, the courts might justifiably in the interests of justice, extend their protection beyond acts without lawful authorisation, or undertaken without a fair procedure or which are plainly irrational.

The law now affords protection, through judicial review, for a set of substantive rights—personal liberty, freedom of speech, privacy and the like—in this new guise judicial review (arguably) protects not just the Rule of Law (it will do so through the Convention requirement that interference with Convention rights must be 'prescribed by law' but also a substantive set of civil and political rights).

Why should the courts on an application for judicial review not interfere with an executive decision which although intra vires, is not in breach of any procedural requirements and not irrational is simply unjust? Chief Justice Coke in *Bagg's Case* 1615 saw the Court of King's Bench's jurisdiction as being there to ensure "that no wrong or injury, either public or private, can be done but that it shall be (here) reformed or punished by due course of law."

Nearly 400 years later in the twenty-first century, the courts might well reflect on what he believed justice and therefore fairness meant.

Ultra vires review protects individuals from unauthorised exercise of governmental power and allows review of decisions for errors of law. It controls the substantive legal framework of decisions in particular instances; both usually have no longer-term effect on the internal management of decision-making bodies. By contrast, procedural impropriety review speaks neither to the statutory limits of a decision-making power nor to the pre-existing law it must apply but theoretically only to the institutional procedures by which decisions are made.

Review on grounds of jurisdiction functions principally in the same manner as an appeal; it protects individuals from unjustified interference and reproaches abuses of power. Jurisdictional review also provides a second, but more limited opportunity for dissatisfied persons to advance substantive claims. By contrast, procedural review does not check power but structures its exercise: it aids in redefining administrative decision-making in conformity with traditional concepts of judicial decision-making.

Administration may be characterised as the management of specified tasks and problems in order to achieve a determined policy; legal rules of jurisdiction and procedure only limit the framework within which activity is undertaken and are peripheral concerns of the administration. To the judge or lawyer, however, questions of policy are peripheral; ambivalent to the needs and constraints of administrative bodies. Courts tend to be preoccupied with the outer limits of administrative power and decision-making.[263]

Procedural review serves the political function of enfranchisement. While the judicial review on jurisdictional grounds is concerned with the protection of the substantive rights of those who are party to a decisional process, the procedural review is by its very nature directed to guarantee the effective participation of persons likely to be affected by administrative decisions. In one sense, an essential element of freedom is "the opportunity to participate in decision-making processes."[264]

When judicial review is sought on procedural grounds, the applicant is in fact claiming to be enfranchised; the argument advanced is not that a decision was itself unlawful, but that one has a right to participate in a certain manner in a decision.

Procedural review consequently serves an important purpose in constitutional theory, that is, to stimulate and guarantee creative and meaningful democratic participation in administrative government. While ultra vires review protects fundamental concepts of legality in any system of law, procedural review enshrines a theory of participation in political institutions which is peculiar to liberal democratic systems.[265][266]

Is Judicial Review Undemocratic?

J.R. Waldron summarises his argument that it is by saying:

Judicial review is vulnerable to attack on two fronts. It does not, as in often claimed, provide a way for society to focus clearly on the real issues at stake when citizens disagree about rights… And it is politically illegitimate, so far as democratic values are concerned by privileging majority voting among a small number of unelected and unaccountable judges, it disenfranchises ordinary citizens and brushes aside cherished principles of representation and political equality.[267]

Is there an argument that judicial review might provide a legitimate avenue of political activity for those seeking to rectify historic injustice, and might promote political equality and participation even in democracies with an adequate, conscientious legislature? Waldron claims "courts are expected to behave in the ways I have criticised focussing on precedent, text, doctrine and other legalisms…" (pp. 1376–1338).

NB. *Exegesis* reasoning—from text to gloss on text—new text—legal reasoning.

There are two types of judicial review strong/weak according to Waldron.

Judicial review of legislation by courts, according to Waldron, is unjustified in a reasonably functioning democracy. He characterises strong and weak judicial review as follows:

Strong

1. Declining to apply a statute in a particular case even though the statute on its own terms plainly applies in that case
2. Modifying the effect of a statute to make its application conform with individual rights in ways that the statute itself does not envisage.

Weak

Weak involves ex ante scrutiny of legislation by courts to determine whether it is unconstitutional or violates individual rights, "but courts may not decide to apply it or moderate its application simply because rights would otherwise be violated."

Examples of strong judicial review are found in the USA and Canada, while weak judicial review exists in the UK and New Zealand.

The concept of the 'Rule of Law' has also been criticised by Horowitz. He argues:

By promoting procedural justice, it enables the shrewd, the calculating and the wealthy to manipulate its forms to their own advantage. And it ratifies and legitimates an adversarial competitive, and altruistic conception of human relations.

Horowitz is wrong and confused in conflating the Rule of Law[268] with the substance of particular laws. Claiming that unjust laws and their rigorous enforcement demonstrate that the Rule of Law is an instrument of oppression is profoundly misleading.

Weak vs. Strong Judicial Review and Human Rights

Britain incorporated most of the rights of the European Convention of Human Rights (ECHR) into national law through the Human Rights Act 1988. The Act authorised the courts to make a "declaration of incompatibility whenever a legislative provision is incompatible with convention rights. A declaration of incompatibility, however, does not affect the validity, continuing operation or enforcement of the provision in respect of which it is given and is not binding on the parties to the proceedings in which it is made."[269]

A minister may use such a declaration as authorisation to initiate a fast-track legislative procedure to remedy the incompatibility. This is a power the minister would not have but for the process of judicial review that led to the declaration in the first place. A declaration of incompatibility creates a legislative opportunity to rectify an abuse of rights where otherwise there would be none. However, there is no guarantee that a minister will take advantage of the opportunity or will do anything to stop rights from being violated. In that sense, the British system of judicial review arguably is inadequate. Short of taking a case to the European Court of Human Rights, it is not clear what wronged individuals can do to vindicate their rights.

Epilogue

The supreme accomplishment of life is to blur the distinction between work and play.

Arnold J. Toynbee

Identify your passion make it your profession and you will never do another day's work in your life.

Originally attributed to Confucius, subsequently adopted by Mark Twain.

A man is not idle because he is absorbed in thought, there is visible labour and there is invisible labour.

Victor Hugo

Originality and a feeling of one's own dignity are achieved only through work and struggle.

Dostoevsky, A Diary of a Writer (1873)

Most good lawyers live well, work hard and die poor.

Daniel Webster

There is only one thing for a man to do who is married to a woman who enjoys spending money and that is to enjoy earning it.

Edgar Watson Howe, Country Sayings (1911)

Oratory is nothing but judicious imitation.

Voltaire

Fairness is what justice really is.
Potter Stewart, Justice of the Supreme Court of the United States of America

The principle of fairness considered in the preceding chapter pervades our legal thinking. As I look back at my career as a barrister, I reflect on that principle in practice. This book is a result of that reflection. It was the guiding light that shone brightly and never faded; it was and remains an abiding passion. Aristotle wrote in his *Politics*, "Whereas the law is passionless passion must ever sway the heart of man." I understand what Benjamin Franklin meant when he commented, "God works wonders behold a lawyer an honest man."

Richard Dawkins lacked insight when he failed to see the poetic beauty in legal thinking and the wonder of the law. If he reads this book, I do hope he will change his mind about the nature of a legal mind with a true love of legal thinking and the practice of law. My final gentle riposte to his criticism of the legal mind is that in my opinion, the greatest danger to which modern thought is exposed is domination by scientific thinking and the consequent distortion of the mind's view.

An Ode to Law*

In chambers where wisdoms glow,
Lies written in the books,
I found a love I didn't know
Among the legal nooks.

In courtrooms filled with measured tones,
Where justice sways and bends,
I saw beyond the legal tomes,
A profession that comprehends.

With every case and argument,
Passion brightly shone,
Minds so sharp, souls well-meant,
In you, I found my home.

Voices, a beacon in the night,
With reasons clear and strong,

But in chambers a softer light,
Where legal dreams belong.

You weave the ways with gentle care,
In battles just and true,
Yet, in your jurisprudence, love laid bare,
A world that I fell into.

In motions and in filed briefs,
A heart beats fierce and warm,
A love that finds its sweet relief,
In every legal storm.

For though the work may rule my days,
In you, I've found much more,
A passion that lights my darkest ways,
And opens every door.

Here in the court of life I stand,
With law, my heart's defender,
A barrister's love of court, so true,
A bond that will not render.

***R.S. Ramsey Owens (2025)**

---

[1] Unweaving the Rainbow by Richard Dawkins, p. 85, published by Allen Lane, The Penguin Press 1998.

[2] Observations in this direction may often be met with. As an example, I may mention *H.O. Christophersen*: Some Remarks on the Contents and Method of the History of Ideas (in Norwegian), in Congratulatory Publication to Francis Bull (1937), especially p. 45— Cp. On the contrary *Windelband*: Präludien, II (5th edition, 1915), pp. 9-10.

[3] *Stammler* has developed his doctrine of legal philosophy in several writings. Those which chiefly need to be considered here are: Theorie der Rechtswissenschaft (191) and Begriff and Bedeutung der Rechtsphilosophie, in Zeitschrift für Rechtsphilosophie, 1914, pp. 1 foll., particularly pp. 4, 36, 37-38. Cp. Also *Morris Ginsberg:* Stammler's Philosophy of Law, in Modern Theories of Law (1933), pp. 38 foll.

[4] *Del Vecchio*: Lehrbuch der Rechtsphilosophie (1937), pp. 228-229 and 231.

[5] *Stammler*, especially, sometimes expresses himself divergently; cp. Particularly the above-quoted treatise in Zeitschrift f:r Rechtsphilosophie, 1914, p. 9.

[6] *Ross*, the above quoted work, p. 196.

[7] <<Recht ist nicht ein wissenschaftlicher Begriff innerhalb eines Systems, sondern giebt dieses System selber an.>> (p. 198).

[8] *Tegen*: New Tendencies in Legal Philosophy and Criminal Law (in Swedish) (Formu, 1921), p. 545.

[9] Logische Untersuchungen, I (2nd ed., 1913), p. 48.

[10] Cp. the correct remarks on the irrelevance of the form of expression in *Bierling*: Juristiche Prinzipienlehre, I (1984), p. 29.

[11] For notions of value and notions of duty, cp. the just remarks in *Ross* Kritik der sogenannten praktischen Erkenntnis, pp. 88-89.

[12] *Hägerström*: Concerning the Question of the Notion of Existing Law (in Swedish). Tidsskrift for Rettsvidenskap, 1931, p. 74.

[13] The same treatise, p. 89.

[14] *Hägerström*: Der römische Obligationsbegriff im Lichte der allgemeinen römischen Rechtsanschauung, p. 605 and elsewhere.

[15] Cp. *Hägerström*'s review of Kelsen: Allgemeine Staatslehre, in Litteris," 1928, p. 39.

[16] *Lundstedt*: Lectures on Selected Parts of the Law of Obligations. III. The Notion of Obligation (Swedish), 2. p. 91.

[17] *Lundstedt*: Criticism of Scandinavian Doctrines of Injury (in Swedish), Tidsskrift for Rettsvidenskap, 1923, p. 74.

[18] *Lundstedt*: Lectures, III, 2. P. 92.

[19] *Lundstedt*: Criticism, p. 118.

[20] Quoted from Morris R. *Cohen*: Law and the Social Order. Essays in Legal Philosophy (1933), p. 209.

[21] *Olivecrona*: Law as Fact.

[22] Pp. 43, 44 and elsewhere.

[23] Pp. 56, 106 and 134.

[24] P. 104.

[25] P. 76.

[26] *Astrup Hoel*: The Modern Method of Law (in Norwegian) (1925).

[27] *Ross*: Theorie de Rechtsquellen, pp. 270-71.

[28] *Alf Ross*: Kritik der sogenannten praktischen Erkenntnis (1933); Reality and Validity in the Theory of Law (in Danish) (1934): cp. also the treatise: The Twenty-Fifth Anniversary of the Pure Theory of Law (in Danish), in Tidskrift for Rettsvidenskap, 1936, pp. 304 foll.

[29] *Ross*: Kritik, p. 20—A clear exposition of the main thoughts in this work of Ross', has been given by *Tegen* in a review in Tidsskrift for Rettsvidenskap, 1934, pp. 296 foll.

[30] *Ross*: Reality etc., p. 69.

[31] *Ross*: Reality etc., pp. 74 foll. It is first and foremost this problem that presents itself in Ross's thinking in connection with the traditional opposition between 'Sein' and 'Sollen'. As far as I can see, it is due to a misunderstanding that *Vinding Kruse*, in Tidsskrift for Rettsvidenskap, 1934, pp. 276-77, characterises the opposition between 'Sein' and 'Sollen' as the opposition "between the existing positive law and the law as it shall or ought to be".

[32] *Ross*: Reality etc., p. 146.

[33] Cp. above p. 5, note 2.

[34] It is therefore not quite accurate when one often speaks about the law living in the minds of the legal subjects. Cp., for instance, *Bierling:* Juristische Prinzipienlehre, I, pp. 47 and 145.—The expression may be allowed if one merely wishes to denote that law has in foundation in a psycho-physical reality, which to a great extent consists in the legal conviction of the legal subjects. But it is not correct if one means by it that law is nothing else than a sum of factual contents of consciousness.

[35] The different theories of the law as an expression of will are subjected to a thorough examination and a penetrating criticism by *Hägerström*. Cp. Chiefly: Is Existing Law an Expression of Will? (in Commemorative Publication Dedicated to Vitalis Nordström, 1916); Concerning the Question of the Notion of Objective Law (1917), and the treatise: Natural Law is the Science of Criminal Law, Svensk Juristtidning 1920, especially p. 340 (All in Swedish). Hägerström's criticism is based on his anti-normativistic conception of law. On the other hand, we meet the recognition of the traditional notion of the norm as different from the notion of command, among other places in *Bierling*: Juristsche Prinzipienlehre, I, p. 27 and *Hasserl*: Logische Untersuchungen, I, p. 41.

[36] Cp. *Husserl*: Logische Untersuchungen, I, p. 69, and von *Kries*: Logikk, p. 5.

[37] Cp. *Husserl*: Logische Untersuchungen, I, p. 238.

[38] Concerning the productive work of the mind as a "real object" in juridical thinking cp. *Knoph*: The Law of the Mind (in Norwegian), pp. 600-601. "The law of the mind" in Knoph's terminology covers the law of the literary, artistic and industrial property.

[39] Among those who have tried to refute this 'idealistic' view, I will mention: *H. Hartmann*: Über die sogenannten Sinn- und Normgehalte, zumal als Gegenstände der Rechtswissenschaft, in Zeitschrift für Rechtphilosophie, VI (9132-34), pp. 157 foll.

[40] In the same way as law 'exists' in this sense of the word, one may speak or moral of aesthetic values as subsisting or existing, in the sense that they have validity even if they are not comprehended. Cp. *Rikert*: Allgemeine Grundlegung der Philosophie, p. 134 and elsewhere.—Truth and beauty 'exist' as values regardless of whether they rouse adhesion and pleasure, says *Hugo Münsterberg*: Philosophie der Werte (1908), pp. 34, 37, 75 and elsewhere.—*Morris R. Cohen*: Law and the Social Order, p. 210, says, "Far from its being absurd, as Bingham asserts, to suppose that principles and rules can exist independently of the comprehension of the individual observer, that is exactly what we

all assume whenever we undertake to teach any science or systematic truth. And the law is no exception."

[41] I here chiefly sum up the concentrated exposition on p. 249.

[42] A brief exposition of the legal philosophy of Kelsen's school has been given by Kelsen himself in Statsvetenskaplig Tidskrift, 1933, pp. 193 foll., in the treatise: "The Pure Theory of Law. Its Method and Fundamental Notions" (in Swedish). Cp. Also the lucid exposition of *Lauterpacht*, in Modern Theories of Law (1933), pp. 105 foll.

[43] *Kelsen* and his adherents, the so-called Vienna school in legal philosophy, like to speak of the Stufenbau" of law, because the validity of every legal act depends, as it does, on the validity of a norm of a higher order, until we must stop at the fundamental norm itself, the validity of which is a postulate of legal logic.

[44] Theorie der Rechtsquellen, especially pp. 331-32.

[45] Cp. *Hägerström*: Concerning the Question of the Notion of Objective Law (1917, in Swedish), pp. 50-51. Cp. also by the same author: Concerning the Question of the Notion of Existing Law (in Swedish) in Tidsskrift for Rettsvidenskap, 1931, pp. 48 foll., particularly p. 50.

[46] Cp. above, p. 23.

[47] Cp., however, a remark by Ross in Reality and Validity in the Theory of Law (in Danish), p. 161.

[48] "The jural postulate asserts, not that the rule of every case is known and understood before the case arises (which leads to what is called the phonograph theory of the judicial function), but simply that the decision of every case is logically subsumed under general legal rules, which may not be thought of until after the decision, and which may, in fact, never the thought of at all. A postulate that asserts no more than this cannot be refuted. As a methodologic principle, it may serve the same function that the postulate of causality serves in the natural sciences." *Morris R. Cohen*: Law and the Social Order, p. 233.

[49] *Max Weber*: Wirtschaft und Gesellschaft (1922), pp. 393-94.

[50] Particularly *Simmel*: Das individuelle Getsetz, Logos, 1913, pp. 117 foll. Cp. also his writing: Lebensanschauung, 1918.

[51] *Simmel*, in Logos, 1913, p. 137. Cp. Lebensanschauung, p. 167.

[52] Logos, 1913, p. 150.

[53] Cp. an interesting treatise by *G. Radbruch*: Klassenbegriffe und Ordnungsbegriffe im Rechtsdenken; Revue Internationale de la Théorie du Droit, 1938, pp. 46 foll.

[54] Above, p. 48-49.

[55] I cannot see it otherwise than as implying a logical contradiction, when *Ross*, who, in his Theorie de Rechtsquellen, bases himself on the Kelsenian doctrine of the '*Stufenbau*' of law, yet at the same time disputes the logical possibility of concluding from the general to the special (p. 336). The conception of law as a system, in which norms of a lower order derive their validity from norms of a higher order (or vice versa), naturally assumes

the logical justification of conclusions from the validity of one norm to the validity of another.

⁵⁶ Cp. *Gustav Rümelin*: Werturteile and Willensentscheidungen im Civilrecht (1901), pp. 40-41.

⁵⁷ Concerning the open questions of subsumption, cp. *Von Kries*: Logik, pp. 574-75. Cp. also *Astrup Hoel*: The Modern Method of Law (1925), in Norwegian), p. 34.

⁵⁸ Modern jurists often express themselves as if the testing of the results of legal thinking might be carried out by a quite factual verification, of the same kind as that which is used in dealing with a statement of a real connection. Cp., for instance, *Finding Kruse's* remarks in the treatise: Concerning the Theory of the Sources of Law (in Danish), in Tidsskrift for Rettsvidenskap, 1930, p. 138.

⁵⁹ *Arnholm*: Excursions in Obligatory Law (1939, in Norwegian), p. 167.—Concerning such different possibilities of subsumption, cp. *Cardozo*: The Nature of the Judicial Process (1925, pp. 40-41).

⁶⁰ G. *Astrup Hoel*: The Modern Method of Law (1925, in Norwegian).

⁶¹ *Ross*: Theorie der Rechtsqueeelen, p. 202.

⁶² Cp. *Cardozo*: The Nature of the Judicial Process, p. 129. Even in the cases that come before the courts, Cardozo takes such a bright view of the matter that he thinks himself justified in establishing: "of the cases that come before the court in which I sit, a majority, I think, could not, with semblance of reason, be decided in any way but one" (p. 164).

⁶³ Cp., to the same effect, concerning formal and material justice *Ibering*: Der Zweck in Recht, I (3rd edition), pp. 366-67.

⁶⁴ Cp. below, ch. 4, paras.1, II.

⁶⁵ *Ross*: Theorie der Rechtsquellen, pp. 62-63 and elsewhere.

⁶⁶ *Olivecroma* differs: Law as Fact, p. 164.

⁶⁷ *Knoph*: The Law of Mind (in Norwegian), p. 558.

⁶⁸ "The view occasionally held that probability is concerned with degrees of truth, arises out of a confusion between certainty and truth." *J.M. Keynes*: A Treatise on Probability (1921), p. 15, note 1.

⁶⁹ Cp. *Astrup Hoel*: The Modern Method of Law (in Norwegian), pp. 33-34.

⁷⁰ Cp. *Knoph*: Legal Standards (in Norwegian), pp. 97-99.

⁷¹ *von Kries*: Logik, p. 12, speaks of "eine *stetige Abstufung*" from the cases in which the subsumption of a sensation under a general conception is indubitable, to the cases in which it is doubtful, and further to the cases in which it may be denied with certainty.

⁷² This seems to be regarded as fully established in modern physics. Cp. *Hylleraas*: The Position of the Principle of Causality in Modern Physics (in Norwegian) (The Christian Michelsen Institute for Science and Intellectual Freedom. Reports. V. 7. 1935), p. 20. It was also acknowledged to a great extent during the reign of classical physics. Cp. *Jevons*: The principles of science, I (1874), pp. 168 foll. Cp. also above, pp. 38-39.

[73] Cp. the invocation of the "principle of truth" in *Knoph's* The Law of the Mind (in Norwegian), p. 531.

[74] Above, p. 23.

[75] Cp. for instance, *Kristine Bonnevie*: A View of Life—a Natural Attitude to Life (in Norwegian), in Samtiden, 1938, especially p. 445.

[76] The Norwegian radical socialist leader, the late Professor *Edv. Bull* has, in his writing "Communism and Religion" (in Norwegian), acknowledged this himself. He says: "But the very fact that we find, in the causally determined, necessary course of development, a wandering towards 'higher' forms of society, implies that we, too, operate with a purpose or a 'meaning' of existence. And any such belief in 'progress' or 'development' or whatever one chooses to call it, is in its deepest nature related to religion" (p. 15).

[77] Cp. *Paton*: Fashion and Philosophy (1937), p. 11, where it is said: "A moral philosophy which professes to ignore metaphysics too often rests on a bad metaphysics which is little more than a hurried generalisation from a limited side of human experience."

[78] Above, p. 83.

[79] Concerning this, cp. *Kàre Foss*: Ludvig Holberg's Natural Law on the Background of the History of Ideas (in Norw.), p. 336.

[80] Cp. the dogmatic-historical survey in *Ross*: Theorie der Rechtsquellen, p. 23.

[81] The MacMillan Company, New York, 1968.

[82] Arendt, *On Revolution* (New York, The Viking Press, Inc., 1965 ed.), p. 22.

[83] Pierre Teilhard de Chardin, *The Future of Man* (New York, Harper & Row, Publishers, 1964), p. 119.

[84] R.D. Laing, *The Politics of Experience* (Harmondsworth, Eng., Penguin Books, 1967), p. 64.

[85] C.A.W. Manning, *The Nature of International Society* (New York, John Wiley & Sons, Inc., 1962).

[86] *cf.* remarks of Professor Myres McDougal, *Proceedings of the American Society of International Law*, April 1963, p. 163-65.

[87] *Corfu Channel Case*, 1949 L.C. J. 4 at 35.

[88] *Proceedings*, supra, p. 14.

[89] *Littledale v. Scaith,* I Taunt. 243n.

[90] *Fennings v. Grenville* (1808) 1 Taunt. 241.

[91] For a similar process also concerning whole salvage see *Ghen v. Rich*, 8 Fed. 159 (1881).

[92] Deut. 16:19 and 1:17.

[93] Deut. 19:15.

[94] 3.1.16.

[95] See Scott, *The Civil Law: A Translation of Enactments of Justinian*, Vol. XII.

[96] See J.H. Ralston, *International Arbitration from Athens to Locarno* (Stanford University, Calif., Stanford University Press, 1929), pp. 153-298. For a review of the

history of arbitration see Julius Stone, *Legal Controls of International Conflict* (New York, Rinehart & Co., 1954), Chap. 4, and authorities cited therein. For a full discussion of the arbitration under the Jay Treaty, see J.B. Moore, *Digest of International Arbitrations* (Washington, D.C., Govt. Printing Office, Modern Se4ries, 1898), Vol. 1, pp. 299-349. For treaty text see W.M. Malloy, *Treaties, Conventions, International Arts, Protocols and Agreements* (Washington, D.C., Govt. Printing Office, 1910), Vol.1, p. 590.

[97] Johnson, Coleman, Norton, and Bourne, *Ancient Roman Statutes* (1961), pp. 46, 47.

[98] Revised in 1907.

[99] Agreement between Great Britain and France providing for the settlement by arbitration of certain classes of questions which may arise between the two governments, Oct. 14, 1903, *Hertslet's Commercial Treaties*, Vol. XXIII, p. 492. First Hague Peace Conference, Convention for the Pacific Settlement of International Disputes, Malloy, *supra*, Vol. II, p. 2016; and Second Hague Peace Conference, Convention of Pacific Settlement of Disputes, *ibid*, p. 2220.

[100] The Statute of the Court, which entered into force on August 10, 1921, may be found in M.O. Hudson, *International Legislation* (1931), Vol. I, No. 37a, p. 530, as amended (1942-45), Vol. IX, No. 654, p. 510.

[101] Jenks, *The Prospects of International Adjudication*, 1964. Stevens & Sons Ltd., London, p. 765.

[102] Pound, *The Spirit of the Common Law* (The Beacon Press Inc., Boston, 1963, Edition, p. 99).

[103] Mr Justice Benjamin Cardozo, "Jurisprudence," Address to the New York State Bar Association, January 22, 1931.

[104] G. Hughes, "Rules, Policy and Decision Making" (Ms.)

[105] De Jouvenel, *On Power* (Boston, The Beacon Press, Inc., 1962 Edition), p. 313.

[106] Pound, *The Spirit of the Common Law* (Boston, The Beacon Press Inc., 1963 Edition), p. 78.

[107] 15 Cox C. C. 624, 14 Q.B. 273 (1884).

[108] *Ibid*, p. 287.

[109] *Ibid*, p. 287-88.

[110] *Ibid*, p. 279.

[111] 14 Q.B. 273 (1884), p. 288.

[112] *Summa Theologica*, "The Various Kinds of Law," Q. 91, Art.4.

[113] *cf.* Greece, Act 1492 of 17 Aug. 1950, art.32; art 24 of the Criminal Code of (Nationalist) China; arts. 36-37, Criminal Code of Japan; Para. 54, German Penal Code of 1871, revalidated 1953.

[114] 14 Q.B. 273 (1884), p. 283.

[115] *Ibid*, p. 288.

[116] 1 Wall Jr. 1, 26 Fed. Cas. 360 (1842).

[117] 347 U.S. 483 (1954).
[118] 163 U.S. 537 (1896).
[119] *Ibid.*, p. 544.
[120] *Ibid*, p. 551.
[121] 147 U.S. 483 (1954) at p. 490.
[122] *Ibid*, p. 492.
[123] *Ibid.*, p. 494.
[124] Sir Edward Coke, Institutes: Commentary Upon Littleton, First Institute, para. 80.
[125] 349 U.S. 294.
[126] *Ibid.*, p. 298.
[127] *Ibid.*, p. 300.
[128] *Summa Theologica*, "The Eternal Law," Q. 93, Art.3.
[129] J. Bronowski, *The Identity of Man* (Garden City, N.Y., Natural History Press, 1965) p. 15.
[130] Ruskin, *The Stones of Venice*, vol. 1 (London, George Allen, 1906), p. 35.
[131] John Dewey, *The Quest for Certainty* (New York, G.P. Putnam's Sons, 1960 ed.), p. 19.
[132] Bronowski, *The Identity of Man* (Garden City, N.Y., Natural History Press, 1965), pp. 100, 104, 85, 36.
[133] *Ibid.*, at 101.
[134] Holmes, "The Path of the Law" 10 Harvard L. Rev. 457 at 460.
[135] Cardozo, New York State Bar Address, *supra* note 1b, citing Dr Lyna Thorndike, *Science and Thought in the Thirteenth Century*.
[136] Thayer, *Preliminary Treatise on Evidence* (Boston, Little Brown & Co., 1898), p. 43.
[137] B & Ald. 405.
[138] 59 Geo. III, c. 46.
[139] King Charles's Statement to the Trial Court, 1649, Hughes and Fries, *Crown and Parliament in Tudor-Stuart England* (New York, Putnam, 1959), p. 238.
[140] Roscoe Pound, *The Spirit of the Common Law*, 1963 ed. (Boston, The Beacon Press, Inc., 1921), p. 82.
[141] Bentham, *The Principles of Morals and Legislation* (Oxford, The Clarendon Press, 1879), p. 17.
[142] *Summa Theologica*, Part II, First Part, transl. by the Fathers of the English Dominican Province, vol. 1 (1947) p. 998.
[143] *Ibid.*, p. 1011.
[144] Times Law Reports, 6 December 1962, Times, p. 7.
[145] *Summa Theologica*, Dominican transl., p. 1014.
[146] Blackstone, *Commentaries*, Andrews-Cooley, 4th Edition, vol. I, p. 69, 1899.
[147] Hegel, "Natural Law and Political Science on Outline."
[148] *Nicomachean Ethics*, Book V, Ch. 3.

[149] *Ibid.*, Ch.4.

[150] M. Merleau-Ponty, *The Phenomenology of Perception* (New York, Humanities Press, 1962), p. xii.

[151] Coomaraswamy, *Buddha, and the Gospel of Buddhism* (Bombay, India, Asia Publishing House, 1956), at 156.

[152] *Ibid.*

[153] *Ibid*, at 157.

[154] *Ibid*, at 159, quoted Suzuki, *Outlines of Modern Buddhism.*

[155] B.L. Suzuki, *Mahayana Buddhism* (New York, Collier Books, 1963), p. 40.

[156] *Ibid*, at 41.

[157] *Ibid*, at 69.

[158] *Ibid*, at 71.

[159] Merleau-Ponty, *supra*, pp. xvi, xvii, xviii.

[160] *Ibid*, at xx.

[161] Feng Yu-Lan, *A History of Chinese Philosophy*, vol. 1 (Princeton, N.J., University of Princeton, 1952), p. 373.

[162] E. Pound, *Confucian Analects* (London, Peter Owen, Ltd., 1956), p. 103.

[163] *Ibid*, at 84.

[164] Benjamin N. Cardozo, *The Nature of the Judicial Process* (New Haven, Conn., Yale University Press, 1921) paperback edition pp. 33-34; quote within extract from W.G. Miller, *The Data of Jurisprudence*, p. 335.

[165] Wechsler, "Toward Neutral Principles of Constitutional Law," 73 Harv. L. Rev. 1 at 11.

[166] Certain Expenses of the United Nations (1962) ICJ 151.

[167] Certain Expenses of the United Nations Advisory Opinion, ICJ Reports 1962, p. 151 at 254.

[168] U.N. Charter, Article 94.

[169] Wechsler, "Toward Neutral Principles of Constitutional Law," 73 Harv. Law Rev. 1 at 19.

[170] Fuller, *The Morality of Law* (New Haven, Conn., Yale University Press, 1964), p. 20.

[171] *Ibid*, p. 21.

[172] Lecture given by Robert Griffiths QC on Democracy and Judicial Review at the Law Society, Summer 2015.

[173] *Oneworld Publications 2018 p. 15*—James Miller.

[174] The *Gorgias* is one of Plato's early dialogues, written probably in the 380s (B.C.). The standard Greek text is PLATO, GORGIAS (e. Dodds ed. 1959). In addition, PLATO, GORGIAS (T. Irwin trans. 1979), provides a recent English translation with careful analysis of particular passages.

[175] This chapter and the following chapter are a version of a chapter by James Boyd White in his book, *When Words Lose Their Meaning: Constitutions and Reconstitutions of*

Language, Character, and Community (published in 1983 by the University of Chicago Press).

[176] *See* Plato, Gorgias 6-15 (E. Dodds 1959); *see also* 3 W. Guthrie, *A History of Greek Philosophy* 262-74 (1962). On Gorgias himself, see G. Kennedy, The Art of Persuasion In Greece 61-68 (1963).

[177] *See* PLATO, GORGIAS 17-19 (E. Dodds ed. 1959).

[178] On the nature of dialectic, see R. Robinson, Plato's earlier dialectic (1953); H. Sinaiko, love, knowledge, and discourse in Plato (1965).

[179] Socrates supports the distinction between "what one wants to do" and "whatever one thinks best" by distinguishing between an activity and its object (466e-68e). People take medicine to get well, make a voyage to get wealthy, and so on. And when a person does something on account of something else, he wants not what he does, but what he does it for. Who would want to take medicine or cross the mountains in winter for themselves alone? In the world, there are only good (*agathon*) (in the sense of 'advantageous') things, bad (*kakon*) things, and neutral (*metaxu*) things. And when people do neutral (*metaxu*) things on account of the good (*agathon*) things it is the good *(agathon)* things that they really want. Tbhis is how it is possible for a dictator to do "whatever he thinks best" and at the same time "what he does not want," that is, by being wrong about what he really wants, namely, the good (*agathon*). He cannot have much power if he cannot do what he wants (467c-68c).

[180] With respect to the desirability of being punished, Socrates leads Polus to agree that if someone punishes another justly (*dikaios kolazein*), the other suffers what is just *(dikaion)*, and what is just (*dikaion*) is also kalon (admirable, noble, beautiful) and what is *kalon* is *agathon* (good), i.e., either pleasant or useful. Since punishment is no pleasure it must be beneficial. And the benefit is enormous because it is a relief from the greatest of evils *(kakon)*, a miserableness not merely of body or condition, but of the very self (477a). All these things being true, to use rhetoric to avoid just punishment is pointless; if it has a proper use, it is only to bring just punishment upon oneself and to deflect it from one's enemies (480c-80d).

There is of course a possibility not considered here: that rhetoric might be used to deflect *unjust* punishment from oneself and one's friends. It is characteristic of Polus that he misses the point; it is later raised by Callicles and addressed by Socrates. See *infra* pp. 859-60.

[181] It is a tendency of the dialogues to call whatever kind of bad reasoning is at issue 'sophistic' or 'eristic' and to label any good reasoning 'dialectic'. *See* R. Robinson, *supra* note 1, at 70. For our purposes, it is the way dialectic is defined in the performance that matters. In any event, it would be inconsistent with the way dialectic is exemplified here to expect a systematic definition.

[182] *See supra* pp. 860-61.

[183] *See supra* pp. 860-61.

[184] See, for example, his 'proof' to Polus that whatever is *aischron* must be *kakon* (475a-75e).

[185] See, for example, how gently Socrates lets Gorgias off the hook after refuting his arguments (462e-62c).

[186] *See supra* note 8 and accompanying text.

[187] *See supra* pp. 855-56.

[188] What might Polus do with his experience: remember some of Socrates' propositions, or some of his moves, and try to repeat them? Or will he merely remain disturbed in his relationship with his teacher, Gorgias, and with his language? Or perhaps not even that?

[189] *See supra* pp. 859-61.

[190] For an elaboration of this point, see chapter 3 of the book When Words Lose Their Meaning by James Boyd White, 1984.

[191] Mathematics and Plausible Reasoning, i and ii (Princeton University Press, Princeton NJ), 954.

[192] Polya, 1951, vol.1, p.v.

[193] K.R. Popper (1959), The Logic of Scientific Discovery (Hutchinson, London).

[194] On Human Nature and Understanding (Collier, New York).

[195] A Treatise of Human Nature (Oxford University Press, Oxford).

[196] (1974) Philosophical Investigations, 3rd edn. (Blackwell, Oxford).

[197] Word and Object, Quine 1960 (MIT Press, Cambridge, Mass.).

[198] Putnam 1979: 356.

[199] 1986—Metamagical Themas (Penguine Harmondsworth) p. 586-9.

[200] Flexible Thinking by Leonard Mlodinow Elastic Allen Lane 2018.

[201] Ibid.

[202] (1915) AC 120.

[203] Ibid ibid at 138.

[204] (1964) AC 40.

[205] See two excellent Articles by Associate Professor R.A. Macdonald in Vols. McGill Law Journal.

[206] E.P. Thompson "Whigs and Hunters" (1977) pp. 262-63.

[207] Bickel, The Morality of Consent (1975).

[208] Shaughnessy v. U.S. 206, 224 (1953) per Jackson J. (dissenting).

[209] Shklar, Legalism (1964).

[210] McNabb v. U.S. 318, U.S. 332, 347 (1943).

[211] Rawls, A Theory of Justice (1971) p. 13.

[212] Hart, The Concept of Law, 1961, 156.

[213] Fuller, A Reply to Professors Cohen and Dworkin (1965), 10 Villanova L. Rev 655, 660.

[214] Fuller, The Forms and Limits of Adjudication (1978) 92 Harvard Law Review.

[215] J. Waldron, The Law (1990), p. 31.

[216] Noted in Lecture of Chief Justice Robert S. French, 7 October 2010, The University of Melbourne Law School.
[217] Wade and Forsyth. Administrative Law (8th edn. OVP 2000) at 435-436.
[218] J.C. Holt, Magna Carter (2nd ed., Cambridge University Press, 1992), at 461.
[219] Co. Inst. IV, 37 cited in Marshall, fn.5, at 18.
[220] Bagg's Case (1916) 11 Co. Rep. 95b 177 ER 127 (at 1275).
[221] Bagg's Case, at 99a [77 ER 1271 at 1279-1280].
[222] Medea: A Tragedie Englished by ES Esq (1648).
[223] Bagg's Case at 98a [77 ER 1271 at 1277-1278].
[224] R. v. Chancellor of the University of Cambridge (Dr Bentley's case (1723).
[225] J.M. Kelly "Audi alteram partem (1964) a Natural Law Forum 103 at 109.
[226] (1799) 8 TR 209 [101 ER 1349].
[227] Ibid p. 210.
[228] (1610) 8 Co Rep. 113b [77 ER 646].
[229] Ibid at 118a [77 ER 646 at 652].
[230] Ibid at 118a [77 ER 646 at 652].
[231] (1614 Hob 85 at 8) [80 ER 235 at 237].
[232] I. Holdsworth, A History of English Law (4th ed. 1936) Vol.2, at 6.
[233] Lloyd L. Weinreb, Natural Law and Justice (Harvard University Press, 1987.
[234] (1702) 12 Mod 669 [88 ER 592].
[235] P.A. Hamburger, "Revolution and Judicial Review: Chief Justice Holt's Opinion in City of London v. Wood (1994) 94 Columbia Law Review.
[236] 12 Mod 669 at 687-688 [88 ER 1592 and 1602].
[237] Lee v. Bude and Torrington Junction Railway Co (1871) 1LR 6 CP 576 at 582—Wilkes T.
[238] (1852) 3 HLC 759.
[239] Ibid at p. 793.
[240] Ibid at 793-794.
[241] R v. Bow Street Magistrates, Ex Parte Pinochet Ugarten (No.2) (2000) 1 AC 119.
[242] Ibid at 135.
[243] Hammond, Judicial Recusal; Principles, Process and Problems (Hart Publications).
[244] (2000) 205 CLR 337.
[245] (1863) 14 CB (NS) 180 [143 ER 414].
[246] Ibid at 193 [143 ER at 420].
[247] (1971) AC 297 at 310.
[248] 1985 159 CLR 520 at 584.
[249] Ibid p. 583.
[250] Ibid p. 583.
[251] Lloyd v. McMahon (1987) C 625 HL 702 per Lord Bridge.
[252] R v. H (2004) 2 AC 134, para.11 Ibid.

[253] Laws LJ (2008) EWCA Civ 353 paras 26-27, see also AK (Iran) v. Secretary of State for Home Department (2008) EWCA Civ 941 CA Ibid.

[254] R.A. Macdonald Vol.26 McGill Law Ibid.

[255] Ibid

[256] Ibid R.A. Macdonald.

[257] Secretary of State for the Home Department v. MB (2008), 1 AC para. 90.

[258] Ibid

[259] R (Smith) v. Secretary of State for the Home Department (2004), 3 WLR 341 CA para. 93.

[260] Vining: Legal Identity: The Coming of Age of Public Law (1978), p. 181.

[261] Jeffrey Jowell "The Rule of Law today" p. 13-19.

[262] Ibid Jowell.

[263] Wilson "Direction in the Analyses of Administrative Process (1972), 10 Osgoode Hall, 117 137-9 gives an excellent summary of this distinction.

[264] Fuller, Freedom as a Problem of Allocating Choice (1968), 112 Proc. Am. Phil. Society 101, 103.

[265] Rostow, The Democratic Character of Judicial Review (1952), 66 Harv L. Review 193 cf. Male The Anti-Democratic Character of Judicial Review (1972).

[266] Col. L. Rev. 1140. Jeremy Waldron (2006) 115 Yale Law Journal 1346. Also Annabelle Lever in Judicial Review Undemocratic 2007.

[267] J. Waldron, "The Core of the Cause Against Judicial Review" (2006), 115 Yale Law Journal 1346 at 1353.

[268] M.J. Horowitz, "The Rule of Law on unjustified human good" (1977), 86 Yale LJ 591.

[269] Human Rights Act 1998 Section 4(2)(b).

The Manufacturing o

Different types of markets exist throughout the world but how are they created? In this book, an interdisciplinary team of authors provide an evolutionary vision of how markets are designed and shaped. Drawing on a series of case studies, they show that markets are far from perfect and natural mechanisms, and propose a new view of markets as social construct, explaining how combinations of economic, political, and legal constraints influence the formation and performance of markets. Historical trajectories and interdependencies among institutional dimensions make it difficult to build costless, non-biased coordination mechanisms, and there are limitations to public and private attempts to improve the design of markets. The authors show that incomplete and imperfect modes of governance must be improved upon and combined in order for markets to work more efficiently. This timely book will interest practitioners and academics with backgrounds in economics, law, political science, and public policy.

ERIC BROUSSEAU is Professor of Economics and Management at Paris-Dauphine University. He is a member of Dauphine Research in Management (DRM), a Joint Research Center between the CNRS and Paris-Dauphine. He is also the founder and director of the European School for New Institutional Economics (ESNIE), and President of the International Society for New Institutional Economics (ISNIE). His research focuses on the economics of governance, with applications to innovation, digital economics, the environment, development, and global governance.

JEAN-MICHEL GLACHANT is Director of the Florence School of Regulation, and Holder of the Loyola de Palacio Chair at the European University Institute in Florence. He has been coordinator or scientific adviser for several European research projects such as THINK, Optimate, SESSA, CESSA, Reliance, EU-DEEP, RefGov, TradeWind, and Secure. He is Chief Editor of *EEEP: Economics of Energy and Environmental Policy*, the new academic journal of the International Association for Energy Economics, and is a member of the board of IAEE.

Eric Brousseau and Jean-Michel Glachant have assembled a fascinating set of contributions that discuss the institutional arrangements that contribute to the "manufacturing" of markets for goods and services. Traditional microeconomics textbooks implicitly assume that "free markets" somehow have emerged as if by "immaculate conception." These markets may in turn have "market imperfections" that might be mitigated by a variety of government regulatory interventions. In fact, markets never exist in an institutional vacuum. At the very least, laws defining and institutions for enforcing property rights, for defining liability for damages, determining and enforcing responsibilities for allocating the associated costs, and institutions governing the enforcement of contractual commitments are necessary for markets to function at all. Laws and institutions responding to market power, externalities, imperfect information, uncertainty, transactions costs and other attributes of bilateral exchange are necessary for markets to perform well. Choices must be made among alternative governance arrangements that apply to markets in the real world and to help to define the boundaries between firms and markets. The chapters in this book provide important insights about how these institutional choices have been made in many different contexts, drawing on lessons from economics, political science, organizational behavior, psychology, and law. There is much to learn from these chapters for both scholars and policymakers.

Paul L. Joskow, Massachusetts Institute of Technology, and President, Alfred P. Sloan Foundation

Market design, regulation and competition policy have never been more important for policy-makers confronting footloose business and finance. They must continually renegotiate public–private relations while endeavoring to maintain the trust needed for future-oriented decisions, whether for investment or environmental policy. This wide-ranging book challenges, enlightens and provides timely guidance on these and many other problems confronting market economies.

David Newberry, University of Cambridge

This impressive collection of chapters, focused on the creation and operation of markets, takes seriously the critical connection between economics and politics. All markets depend on political institutions, all markets adjust and develop in ways that reflect economic interests, and any approach that privileges one side at the expense of the other is unlikely to understand how markets are actually manufactured.

Douglass C. North, Washington University in Saint Louis, Nobel Laureate

The chapters in this collection greatly advance our understanding of how markets are embedded in a complex system of social technologies. Together they provide a surprisingly accessible introduction to the cutting edge of the social scientific analysis of institutions.

*Henry E. Smith, Harvard Law School, and
Director, Project on the Foundations of Private Law*

There is no one interested in markets and the role they play in our economies, societies and polities who will not learn, be challenged (and at times enervated!) by this wide ranging collection of often fresh, even scintillating chapters.

*Joseph H.H. Weiler, President,
European University Institute, Florence*

The Manufacturing of Markets

Legal, Political and Economic Dynamics

Edited by
ERIC BROUSSEAU AND
JEAN-MICHEL GLACHANT

CAMBRIDGE
UNIVERSITY PRESS

University Printing House, Cambridge CB2 8BS, United Kingdom

One Liberty Plaza, 20th Floor, New York, NY 10006, USA

477 Williamstown Road, Port Melbourne, VIC 3207, Australia

314-321, 3rd Floor, Plot 3, Splendor Forum, Jasola District Centre, New Delhi - 110025, India

79 Anson Road, #06-04/06, Singapore 079906

Cambridge University Press is part of the University of Cambridge.

It furthers the University's mission by disseminating knowledge in the pursuit of education, learning and research at the highest international levels of excellence.

www.cambridge.org
Information on this title: www.cambridge.org/9781107677326

© Cambridge University Press 2014

This publication is in copyright. Subject to statutory exception and to the provisions of relevant collective licensing agreements, no reproduction of any part may take place without the written permission of Cambridge University Press.

First published 2014
First paperback edition 2019

A catalogue record for this publication is available from the British Library

Library of Congress Cataloging in Publication data
The manufacturing of markets : legal, political and economic dynamics / edited by Eric Brousseau, Jean-Michel Glachant.
    pages cm
Includes bibliographical references and index.
ISBN 978-1-107-05371-7 (hardback)
1. Industrial management. 2. Marketing. I. Brousseau, Eric, editor of compilation. II. Glachant, Jean-Michel, editor of compilation.
HD30.4.M3696 2014
381–dc23
2014004085

ISBN 978-1-107-05371-7 Hardback
ISBN 978-1-107-67732-6 Paperback

Cambridge University Press has no responsibility for the persistence or accuracy of URLs for external or third-party internet websites referred to in this publication, and does not guarantee that any content on such websites is, or will remain, accurate or appropriate.

Contents

List of figures	*page* x
List of tables	xii
Notes on contributors	xiii
Acknowledgments	xxiii

1 Introduction: manufacturing markets – what it means and why it matters 1
ERIC BROUSSEAU AND JEAN-MICHEL GLACHANT

Part I Public and private complementarities in securing exchange **11**

Introduction to Part I 13
ERIC BROUSSEAU AND JEAN-MICHEL GLACHANT

2 Measurement systems as market foundations: perspectives from historical markets 17
AASHISH VELKAR

3 How to manufacture quality: the diversity of institutional solutions and how they interact in agrifood markets 37
MARTA FERNÁNDEZ-BARCALA, MANUEL GONZÁLEZ-DÍAZ, AND EMMANUEL RAYNAUD

4 The law of impersonal transactions 58
BENITO ARRUÑADA

Part II Path dependency and political constraints in establishing property rights systems **79**

Introduction to Part II 81
ERIC BROUSSEAU AND JEAN-MICHEL GLACHANT

5	"Manufacturing markets": the efficiency advantages of grandfathering allocations over auctions TERRY L. ANDERSON, RAGNAR ÁRNASON, AND GARY D. LIBECAP	85
6	Allocation in air emissions markets A. DENNY ELLERMAN	102
7	Auction versus negotiation in public procurement: looking for empirical evidence ESHIEN CHONG, CARINE STAROPOLI, AND ANNE YVRANDE-BILLON	120

Part III The political origin of competition — 143

	Introduction to Part III ERIC BROUSSEAU AND JEAN-MICHEL GLACHANT	145
8	Why competitive markets aren't self-actuating: the political economy of limited access JOHN JOSEPH WALLIS	149
9	The creation of a market for retail electricity supply STEPHEN LITTLECHILD	166
10	The institutional design of European competition policy ANTONIO MANGANELLI, ANTONIO NICITA, AND MARIA ALESSANDRA ROSSI	199

Part IV The myopia of the public hand — 223

	Introduction to Part IV ERIC BROUSSEAU AND JEAN-MICHEL GLACHANT	225
11	Third-party opportunism and the theory of public contracts: operationalization and applications MARIAN W. MOSZORO AND PABLO T. SPILLER	229
12	The cycling of power between private and public sectors: electricity generation in Argentina, Brazil, and Chile WITOLD J. HENISZ AND BENNET A. ZELNER	253

13 Politics and the manufacturing of a transatlantic market
    for civil aviation (1944–2010) 271
    YANNIS KARAGIANNIS AND ADRIENNE HÉRITIER

    Part V The challenge of balancing public and private
    ordering 289

    Introduction to Part V 291
    ERIC BROUSSEAU AND JEAN-MICHEL GLACHANT

14 The microstructure of the first emerging markets in
    Europe in the eighteenth century 295
    LARRY NEAL

15 Money reconstructed: Argentina and Brazil after
    hyperinflation 315
    JÉRÔME SGARD

16 For a renewal of financial regulation 333
    MICHEL AGLIETTA AND LAURENCE SCIALOM

    Part VI The daily adjustment of market technology 353

    Introduction to Part VI 355
    ERIC BROUSSEAU AND JEAN-MICHEL GLACHANT

17 Antitrust liability in the US for unilateral refusals to
    deal in intellectual and other property 359
    HOWARD A. SHELANSKI

18 How do firms exercise unilateral market power?
    Empirical evidence from a bid-based wholesale
    electricity market 390
    SHAUN D. MCRAE AND FRANK A. WOLAK

19 Exchanges: the quintessential manufactured markets 421
    CRAIG PIRRONG

20 Conclusion: tâtonnement in the manufacturing of
    markets 441
    ERIC BROUSSEAU AND JEAN-MICHEL GLACHANT

References 470
Index 512

Figures

2.1	Proportion of domestic sales to imported wheat, UK (1828–1885)	page 27
5.1	Economic rents	93
5.2	The creation of rents via innovation and investment	94
5.3	The effects of increased cost of capital (at a point of time)	96
6.1	Waxman–Markey allocation by broad use	116
7.1	Evolution of award procedures according to the administrative level of public buyers	130
7.2	Distribution of the number of proposals received per contract (2007)	132
7.3	Distribution of contract duration and contract value	134
7.4	Distribution of award procedures for different categories of contract value	136
7.5	Distribution of award procedures for different categories of contract duration	136
7.6	Distribution of amendments to contract values according to award procedures	140
8.1	A simple schematic of a natural state	152
8.2	A slightly more complicated natural state	156
11.1	Third-party opportunism costs, and contracting and enforcement costs	239
11.2	Governmental opportunism	250
14.1	Exchange Alley	301
14.2	Castaing's *Course of the Exchange*, January 8, 1720	303
16.1	The vicious circle of the euphoric drive	338
18.1	Derivation of offer curve (steep residual demands)	397
18.2	Derivation of offer curve (flatter residual demands)	397
18.3	Elasticity calculation for Firm B, peak half-hour period in February 2006	400

18.4 Half-hourly inverse semi-elasticities by firm, 30-day
rolling average 401
18.5 Mean inverse semi-elasticities and system price, 30-day
rolling average 402
18.6 Derivation of offer curves with and without fixed-price
contracts 403
18.7 Half-hourly net inverse semi-elasticities by firm, 30-day
rolling average 406
18.8 Mean net inverse semi-elasticities and system price,
30-day rolling average 407

Tables

3.1	Manufacturing quality	page 44
7.1	Award procedure and contractual experience	131
7.2	Number of propositions received by awarding procedures (2007)	133
7.3	Contracts value and duration by award procedures	135
7.4	Award procedures and contractual amendments	139
10.1	The institutional design of European competition policy: a summary chart	219
18.1	Dependent variable = offer price at dispatch quantity for supplier j	412
18.2	Dependent variable = offer price at dispatch quantity for supplier j	412
18.3	Dependent variable = offer price at dispatch quantity for fossil fuel plant/unit k	418

Contributors

MICHEL AGLIETTA is Emeritus Professor at the University of Paris West Nanterre La Défense and Scientific Advisor for the Center of International Studies and Forecasting (CEPII). His research agenda focuses on modern finance and monetary theory.

TERRY L. ANDERSON is the president of the Property and Environment Research Center (PERC) in Bozeman, Montana, and a senior fellow at the Hoover Institution, Stanford University. He is the author or editor of 37 books including most recently *Tapping Water Markets* with Brandon Scarborough and Lawrence R. Watson (RFF. 2012). Anderson has published widely in professional journals and the popular press including the *Wall Street Journal*. He received his BS from the University of Montana in 1968 and his PhD in Economics from the University of Washington in 1972. Anderson is an avid outdoorsman who enjoys archery, hunting, fishing, horseback riding, skiing, and hiking.

RAGNAR ÁRNASON is a professor of fisheries economics and the chairman of the Institute of Economic Studies at the University of Iceland. Professor Árnason has also been a visiting professor in several schools in Europe and America. His research has primarily been in the field of natural resource economics especially fisheries economics and property rights. He has a publication record of over 150 scientific articles and several books.

BENITO ARRUÑADA is Professor of Business Organization at Pompeu Fabra University, Barcelona, and former president of the International Society for New Institutional Economics. His research lies in the conjunction of organization, law, and economics. Many of his works focus on the organizational conditions that facilitate impersonal exchange, covering from property titling or business regulation to moral systems.

ERIC BROUSSEAU is Professor of Economics and Management at Paris-Dauphine University and at the European University Institute (Florence, Italy). He is a member of Dauphine Research in Management (DRM), a Joint Research Center between the Centre National de la Recherche Scientifique (CNRS) and Paris-Dauphine. He is the founder and the director of the European School for New Institutional Economics (ESNIE), and Vice-President of the International Society for New Institutional Economics (ISNIE). His research agenda focuses on the economics of governance, with three main applied fields: innovation and intellectual property, Internet and digital economics, environmental governance. In matters of institutional economics, Eric Brousseau has been working extensively on the economics of contracts, multi-level governance, public vs. self-regulation, and on the dynamic of institutions. He has been involved in researches funded by the French Government, the European Commission, the US National Science Foundation, the UN, and the OECD.

ESHIEN CHONG is Assistant Professor of Economics at the Sorbonne Business School (Paris 1 University), and the Economics of Public–Private Partnership Chair at the Institut d'Administration des Entreprises. His research interests include public–private partnerships, economics of regulation, and economics of contracts, applied to the question of organization of the water industry and to public procurement.

A. DENNY ELLERMAN is an internationally recognized expert on energy and environmental economics with a particular focus on climate policy, emissions trading, and interactions with energy markets. He is a part-time professor at the Robert Schuman Centre for Advanced Studies at the European University Institute in Florence, Italy, and is retired from MIT, where he was for many years a senior lecturer and executive director of the Center for Energy and Environmental Policy Research and of the Joint Program on the Science and Policy of Global Change.

MARTA FERNÁNDEZ-BARCALA is Associate Professor of Management at the University of Oviedo, Spain. Her research agenda focuses on organizational design and total quality management. Her papers have been published in journals such as *International Journal of Research in*

Marketing, Tourism Economics, Economía Industrial, and Cuadernos de Economía y Dirección de la Empresa.

JEAN-MICHEL GLACHANT is Director of the Florence School of Regulation and Holder of the Loyola de Palacio Chair at the European University Institute, Florence. He is Professor in Economics and holds a PhD from La Sorbonne University, Paris. Jean-Michel Glachant is a Member of the EU–Russia Gas Advisory Council of Commissioner Oettinger (EC), he is or has been Advisor to DG TREN, DG COMP, DG RESEARCH, and DG ENERGY of the European Commission, and Coordinator/Scientific Advisor of several European research projects such as THINK, SESSA, CESSA, Reliance, EU-DEEP, RefGov, TradeWind, Secure, and Optimate. He is a Member of the Advisory Board of the E-Price project and Research Partner of CEEPR (MIT, USA), EPRG (Cambridge University, UK), and Chief Editor of *EEEP: Economics of Energy & Environmental Policy*, a new journal of the International Association for Energy Economics.

MANUEL GONZÁLEZ-DÍAZ is Associate Professor of Business Economics at the University of Oviedo, Spain. He is now the Dean of the School of Economics and Business at the University of Oviedo. His research focuses on the economics of organizations and particularly how incentives and contracts shape inter-organizational relationships. His papers have been published in journals such as *Journal of Business Venturing, Journal of Small Business Management, International Journal of Research in Marketing, Industrial and Corporate Change*, and *Journal of Economic Behavior and Organization*.

WITOLD J. HENISZ is the Deloitte & Touche Professor of Management in Honor of Russell E. Palmer, former Managing Director at the University of Pennsylvania. His research examines the impact of political hazards on international investment strategy including efforts by multinational corporations to engage in corporate diplomacy to win the hearts and minds of external stakeholders. This research has been published in journals in international business, management, international studies, and sociology. He served as a departmental editor at *The Journal of International Business Studies*, has won multiple teaching awards at the undergraduate and graduate levels, redesigned the global component of the required curriculum in the Wharton

MBA program, and is a principal in the risk management consultancy PRIMA LLC.

ADRIENNE HÉRITIER is Joint Chair Political Science, Department of Political and Social Sciences and Robert Schuman Centre for Advanced Studies, European University Institute, Florence. Her main publications extend knowledge in the field of European policy making, European institutions, comparative public policy, institutional theory, regulation of network industries in Europe, and new modes of governance.

YANNIS KARAGIANNIS is Assistant Professor of Political Science at the Institut Barcelona d'Estudis Internacionals (IBEI), having previously been Marie Curie Research Fellow at the University of Exeter (UK), and Visiting Scholar at the University Pompeu Fabra in Barcelona. His research agenda focuses on European Union politics, international political economy, political game theory, and the political economy of antitrust laws.

GARY D. LIBECAP is Distinguished Professor of Economics and Corporate Environmental Management at the Bren School of Environmental Science & Management and the Economics Department, University of California, Santa Barbara. He is also a research associate at the National Bureau of Economic Research, Cambridge, Massachusetts; Sherm and Marge Telleen Research Fellow, Hoover Institution, Stanford University; and Senior Research Fellow, Property and Environment Research Center, Bozeman, Montana. His PhD is from the University of Pennsylvania. His research focuses on how or under what circumstances property rights to natural and environmental resources can be defined and enforced to address the problems of open access and how or when markets might be developed as options for more effective resource management and allocation. He examines the bargaining and transaction costs involved in collective action to establish property institutions and markets. His work encompasses economics and law, economic history, natural resource economics, and economic geography. His latest books are *Owens Valley Revisited: A Reassessment of the West's First Great Water Transfer* (Stanford University Press, 2007), *The Economics of Climate Change: Adaptations Past and Present*, co-edited with Richard Steckel (University of Chicago Press and NBER, 2011), and *Environmental Markets: A Property Rights Approach* with Terry L. Anderson (Cambridge University Press, 2014).

Notes on contributors

STEPHEN LITTLECHILD was previously Professor of Commerce (1975–1989) at the University of Birmingham, UK, Member of the Monopolies and Mergers Commission (1983–1988), Director General of Electricity Supply and Head of the Office of Electricity Regulation (1989–1998), and nonexecutive Member of the Postal Services Commission (Postcomm) (2006–2011). Since 1999 he has been an international consultant on privatization, regulation, and competition, including in the electricity, telecommunications, water, and airport sectors. He is also Emeritus Professor at the University of Birmingham and fellow at the Judge Business School, University of Cambridge.

ANTONIO MANGANELLI is Programme Manager at the BEREC Office (Body of European Regulators of Electronic Communications). He was a research associate at the European University Institute, where he coordinated the Electronic Communications and Media area of the Florence School of Regulation. He also worked as a consultant in the regulation and antitrust of network industries, carrying out research and reports for the Independent Regulators Group (IRG), the Italian Electronic Communications Regulator (AGCOM), and private stakeholders. He holds a PhD in Law and Economics from the University of Siena and was Visiting Researcher at the University of Texas at Austin.

SHAUN D. MCRAE is an assistant professor in the Department of Economics at the University of Michigan. His research is at the intersection of industrial organization, energy economics, and development economics, with particular interests in the design of energy subsidy programs, the effects of unreliable electricity supply, and the behavior of firms in wholesale and retail electricity markets.

MARIAN W. MOSZORO is an Assistant Professor at Kozminski University and Policy Research Fellow of the Public–Private Sector Research Center at IESE Business School in Barcelona and Visiting Scholar at the Haas School of Business, University of California, Berkeley. He was Undersecretary of State and Deputy Minister of Finance of Poland, Chairman of Bank Gospodarstwa Krajowego and the Export Credit Insurance Policy Committee, and a member of several governmental committees. His areas of current research are business and public policy, corporate finance and public–private partnerships.

LARRY NEAL is Emeritus Professor of Economics at the University of Illinois at Urbana-Champaign, Research Associate of the National Bureau of Economic Research, and Visiting Professor at the London School of Economics. Specializing in financial history and European economies, he is author of *The Rise of Financial Capitalism: International Capital Markets in the Age of Reason* (Cambridge University Press, 1990), *The Economics of Europe and the European Union* (Cambridge University Press, 2008), *The Origin and Development of Financial Institutions and Markets* (co-edited with Jeremy Atack, Cambridge University Press, 2009), and *"I Am Not Master of Events": The Speculations of John Law and Lord Londonderry in the Mississippi and South Sea Bubbles* (Yale University Press, 2012).

ANTONIO NICITA is Professor of Economic Policy at the University of Roma "La Sapienza." In 2013 he was appointed by the Parliament as member of AGCON, the Italian regulator of telecommunications and media. He is a member of the Board of Directors of the Italian Society of Law and Economics and of the European Association of Law and Economics. He is also Secretary of the International Society for New Institutional Economics (ISNIE). In 2006–2007 he was an economic adviser to the Italian Minister of Communications and a member of the Governmental Unit for the Improvement of Regulation. He has been OECD Consultant and Economist at the Italian Antitrust Authority. His research interests cover industrial organization, law and economics, competition economics and regulation, as well as communications and media.

CRAIG PIRRONG is Professor of Finance and Director of the Global Energy Management Institute at the Bauer College of Business at the University of Houston. He has published extensively on the industrial organization of financial markets. This research examines the determinants of the number of financial exchanges; the scale and scope of these exchanges; exchange ownership form and governance; vertical integration between trade execution and clearing; and the economics of counterparty default risk allocation mechanisms. He also researches the economics of commodity pricing and market manipulation.

EMMANUEL RAYNAUD is a research fellow at the National Institute for Agronomical Research (INRA) in France and a member of the Centre d'Economie de la Sorbonne at the University of Paris I. His research focuses on contracting and governance practices in topics such as franchising, vertical coordination in agrifood chains related to quality strategies, hybrid organizations, and multilevel governance. His papers have been published in journals such as *International Journal of the Economics of Business*, *Industrial and Corporate Change*, *Journal of Economic Behavior and Organization*, and *Journal of Management and Governance*.

MARIA ALESSANDRA ROSSI is Assistant Professor of Economic Policy at the University of Siena. She was Visiting Researcher at the University of Oxford, the Council of Europe, the Department of Economics at UC Berkeley, the Santa Fe Institute of Technology, the University of Paris X, and the European University Institute in Florence. She carried out research and reports for OECD, the Independent Regulators Group (IRG), the Italian telecom national regulatory agency (AGCOM), and the Italian Ministry of Finance. She has written numerous essays in national and international journals such as: *Cambridge Journal of Economics*; *Telecommunications Policy*; *Economics of Innovation and New Technologies*; *Communications & Strategies*; *European Journal of Law and Economics*.

LAURENCE SCIALOM is Professor of Economics at the University Paris West Nanterre la Défense and a member of the executive board of EconomiX, a joint Research Center between the Centre National de la Recherche Scientifique (CNRS) and the University. Her research agenda focuses on financial crisis, micro- and macro-prudential policy, and the emergence of a new central banking.

JÉRÔME SGARD is Professor of Political Economy at Sciences Po, where he also teaches Economic History. After obtaining a PhD in Economics at the Université de Paris-Nanterre, he worked as a country-risk economist at a private bank, later for a government think tank. He then went to CEPII (1993), a public research center in applied international economics, also based in Paris. There, he worked on transition in Eastern Europe and on emerging-market crises, for instance in Asia and Latin America. Since he joined Sciences Po, in 2008, his main research topics have revolved around the architecture and regulation of markets, as seen from a micro-level perspective. Hence his interest in the history and the political economy of judges, arbiters, or bureaucrats. Currently his research interests are industrial policy during the

French Ancien Regime, bankruptcy, international trade arbitration, and sovereign debt restructuring.

HOWARD A. SHELANSKI is Professor of Law at Georgetown University Law Center. His research focuses on antitrust and regulation, with an emphasis on high technology industries. Before joining the Georgetown faculty, Shelanski was Professor of Law at the University of California at Berkeley from 1997 until 2011, where he was also Co-director of the Berkeley Center for Law and Technology. Since July 2012 he has been Director of the Bureau of Economics at the US Federal Trade Commission, on leave from his teaching position. Previously, he was Deputy Director of the FTC's Bureau of Economics from 2009 to 2011, Chief Economist of the Federal Communications Commission from 1999 to 2000, and Senior Economist at the President's Council of Economic Advisers from 1998 to 1999.

PABLO T. SPILLER is the Jeffrey A. Jacobs Distinguished Professor of Business & Technology at the Haas School of Business, University of California, Berkeley, Research Associate, National Bureau of Economic Research (NBER), and Visiting Professor of Law, Columbia University. He has held academic positions at the University of Pennsylvania and the University of Illinois, at Urbana-Champaign. He has been Senior Research Fellow at the Hoover Institution, Stanford University and Visiting Professor at NYU Law School, Universitè Paris I, Universidad de San Andrés, and Tel Aviv University. His research interests lie at the intersection of economics, politics, and the law. His current research is on the institutional foundations of public policy. He is Editor-in-Chief of the *Journal of Law, Economics, & Organization*, Associate Editor of the *Journal of Applied Economics* and *The Regulation Magazine*, Board Member of the *Journal of Comparative Studies*, and Member of the Advisory Board of the Institute for Transnational Arbitration, the University CEMA, and of the Center for Global Prosperity. He is the former president of the International Society for New Institutional Economics, and was a special advisor to the Bureau of Economics of the US Federal Trade Commission, and an elected member of the board of directors of the American Law & Economics Association.

CARINE STAROPOLI is Associate Professor of Economics at Paris School of Economics (Paris 1 University). She works on the economics of regulation applied to infrastructure industries (particularly the energy sector) using experimental economics to address market design issues.

She is also interested in the economics of public–private partnerships from a political economy perspective, notably concerning public procurement and energy efficiency contracting.

AASHISH VELKAR is Lecturer in Economic History at the University of Manchester, UK. In 2012, he published his first monograph with Cambridge University Press titled *Markets and Measurements in Nineteenth Century Britain*. He has also published in leading international journals such as *Business History* and *Enterprise and Society*. He won the 2010 Thirsk-Feinstien PhD Prize in Economic History and the 2010 Coleman Prize for Business History after completing doctoral research at the London School of Economics. He was the first recipient of the new researchers' award for "best paper" at the 2007 European School on New Institutional Economics.

JOHN JOSEPH WALLIS is Professor of Economics at the University of Maryland and a research associate at the National Bureau of Economic Research. He is an economic historian and institutional economist who focuses on the dynamic interaction of political and economic institutions over time. As an American economic historian, he has collected large data sets on government finances and on state constitutions, and has studied how political and economic forces changed American institutions in the 1830s and 1930s. In the last decade his research has expanded to cover a longer period, wider geography, and more general questions of how societies use institutions of economics and politics to solve the problem of controlling violence and, in some situations, sustaining economic growth.

FRANK A. WOLAK is the Holbrook Working Professor of Commodity Price Studies in the Economics Department and the Director of the Program on Energy and Sustainable Development at Stanford University. From 1998 to 2011 Wolak was the Chair of the Market Surveillance Committee (MSC) of the California Independent System Operator. In this capacity, he prepared numerous reports and opinions on the market design, performance, and oversight of the California electricity market for the management and Board of Governors of the California ISO and the Federal Energy Regulatory Commission (FERC). He has also testified numerous times at the FERC, and at various Committees of the US Senate and House of Representatives on issues relating to market monitoring and market power in energy markets. Wolak has worked on the design and regulatory oversight of the electricity markets internationally in Europe, Australia/Asia, and Latin America, as well as the US and Canada.

ANNE YVRANDE-BILLON has been Associate Professor in Economics at the University of Paris I (Sorbonne) since 2003 and Senior Economist at the French Competition Authority since 2011. Prior to joining the French Competition Authority, she worked at the French Council of Economic Analysis, an independent advisory body reporting to the Prime Minister. She holds a PhD in Economics from the University of Paris I. Her research and publications are mostly in the fields of economics of contracts and organizations, and regulation of utilities, with a particular interest in the public transport sector. Her research has been published in high-ranked, peer-reviewed journals such as the *Journal of Economic Behavior and Organization*, the *Review of Industrial Organization*, and the *Journal of Transport Economics and Policy*.

BENNET A. ZELNER is Associate Professor of Logistics, Business and Public Policy at the Robert H. Smith School of Business, University of Maryland. His research focuses largely on infrastructure industries recently subject to market-oriented reform – such as privatization, deregulation, and liberalization – and the challenges that these environments pose for private investors. Prof. Zelner teaches classes in emerging-market strategies and global economics. He also sits on the editorial review board of several journals, and is a principal in the risk management consultancy PRIMA LLC. Prof. Zelner previously taught at Duke University's Fuqua School of Business and Georgetown University's McDonough School of Business.

Acknowledgments

The editors would like, first and foremost, to thank warmly the contributors to this collective endeavor. The process of manufacturing this collective book was particular since we really requested from the contributors to adopt a common – while not single – perspective in thinking on how markets are generated, and how they evolve, to result in the complex machineries that policy makers, the economic agents, and the public attempt to understand and master. Not only did the various authors accept to share with us their immense expertise and knowledge, but also they played the game in designing their contributions so as to "interact" with the other chapters of this book, that is therefore truly collective. This humility deserves our gratitude.

This book is an outcome of the REFGOV (Reflexive Governance) Integrated Project, funded by the European Commission under the 6th Framework Program. The editors would like to thank the DG Research from the European Commission for its financial support. Also they are grateful to Jacques Lenoble, the scientific coordinator of this program, who allowed the participants in the IFM (Institutional Frames for Markets) project within this program to benefit from a unique opportunity to exchange and cooperate for five years.

The realization of the book itself relied upon a workshop organized at the Villa Finaly, a conference center from the universities of Paris in Florence, the team of which is warmly thanked. The setting allowed intensive and fruitful exchanges among the contributors to the book that were a condition of the success of this collective endeavor. The organization of the workshop benefitted from the kindness and efficiency of Maria Breidy.

The publication of the book was significantly supported by the Florence School of Regulation and Loyola de Palacio Chair from the European University Institute in Florence. We are indebted in particular to Emanuela Michetti and Marta Joanna Czeladzka who provided assistance in the editing of the book.

1 Introduction: manufacturing markets – what it means and why it matters

ERIC BROUSSEAU AND JEAN-MICHEL GLACHANT

1.1 Designing markets: an essential policy tool

Designing and implementing markets aimed at fostering the efficient provision of all kinds of private and public goods has become a major challenge for contemporary economic policies. First, the processes of transition to a market economy, or the movement towards economic integration – like that occurring at the EU level – or technical change and innovations, have been leading to the creation and organization of all kinds of new markets. Second, the design of efficient markets has become an essential policy tool. Until the 1980s, the usual remedy for so-called "market failures" was either the public provision of services, or the design of command-and-control regulations. The resulting bureaucratic and political failures led to the creation of more sophisticated markets. These innovations even led to the implementation of "pure" public policies, such as environmental protection or limitation of climate change, through the design of ad-hoc markets. Third, as pointed out by the far-reaching impact of the performance of some markets – above all finance, but also energy, information, technology, etc. – on the dynamic and on the stability of the economy, the issue of controlling the sophistication of products, the interactions among agents, the fluidity of adaptations, and of course systemic collapse have become central.

Contemporary economics made major progress in departing from the traditional vision of the discipline in which institutions were exogenous to the analysis. However, the dominant vision today is still a "mechanical" one. Market mechanisms are seen as turn-key tools available on the shelves. It is often assumed that a given instrument should produce a given economic outcome, with little understanding of implementation constraints and interplay between various institutional components. More "biological" visions also remain too crude. Evolutions are too often seen through the lenses of the efficient processes of the selection of the fittest, and cumulative learning.

At the same time, analyses at the frontier of other disciplines (in particular law and political science) have highlighted the various logics at play in the dynamic of institutions. In a nutshell, institutions result inherently from the interplay among the economic quest for efficiency, the political fights for strength and rewarding positions, and the legal constraints of security and stability. It seems therefore relevant to build a framework to analyze the interplay between the economy, politics, and the law. This is the aim of this book.

1.2 Markets as manufactured devices

1.2.1 Complex social technologies ...

Modern economic thinking draws largely from the "invention" of the concept of markets by the moral and political philosophy of the eighteenth century. The analysis of the performance and of the *modus operandi* of this specific social technology led to the emergence of economics as a specific body of knowledge (and academic discipline) in the nineteenth century. In addition, the strong development of the free market led many analysts to consider it as a "natural" coordination device. The market became the starting point for the analysis of many economic issues, including the question of nonmarket coordination. The economics of the firm and the analysis of organizations started by trying to understand how firms could emerge in a market economy (Coase, 1937). Also, many of the early developments in the economics of organization – i.e., the managerial and the behavioral approaches of the firm – were aimed at understanding firms' strategies in the context of imperfect/monopolistic competition and market failures rather than understanding the economics of organized collective action.

It was only in the late 1980s with the contributions of scholars like North, Williamson, Barzel, Greif, and Weingast that the institutional foundations of markets were brought into the limelight. These developments benefitted from the earlier contributions of law and economics (or how agents act in a given institutional setting and react to it) and political economy/public choice (which is about how individual interests and economic transactions shape/bias political and bureaucratic actions). They resulted in the idea that, far from being "natural," markets are organized and constructed in all their dimensions. Indeed, markets require the establishment of "measurement systems" aimed at establishing the various dimensions of the quality of the goods and services that are exchanged. Systems of property rights are also needed to establish what exactly is exchanged (rights of use, access, transformation, and consumption, etc.) and also to make it clear who is entitled to do what with the traded resources. Lastly, all kind of rules of interactions must determine how traded quantities, qualities, and prices are decided: Do agents meet directly or via an intermediary? What are they allowed to negotiate? Are prices customized or not? For all these "dimensions" in the organization of exchanges, rules must be established, processes to negotiate additional rules or amendments have to be agreed upon, and some mechanisms have to be designed to ensure enforcement and to resolve disputes.

Basically four "families" of organizational arrangement deal with these issues. Agents can negotiate bilateral contracts, they can follow self-regulation emerging in communities, they can delegate to a third party – a platform – the management of their interactions, they can be submitted to public rules. Usually, both because needs are contrasted, but also because most markets result from the addition of compromises on different issues established at different periods in time, the institutional framework that makes a market possible is a combination of alternative arrangements dealing with the various dimensions mentioned above.

Markets are complex social technologies, in the very sense of the notion of complexity. They are made of a significant number of interacting components influencing each other in a non-ergodic way. They are also *manufactured* in the sense that they draw from human action. This explains many of their "imperfections" because human beings' rationality is inherently bounded, and also because conflicting interests, and therefore compromises, lie behind the design of markets. The combination of complexity, of bounded rationality, and of compromise among conflicting interests results in systems, which are difficult to master, and rarely the result of optimization processes.

1.2.2 ... designed by trembling hands

The contributions to this book all start from this premise. Markets are built by the trembling hands of human action. The "s" here is important since markets are the result of collective, sometimes contradictory, actions. Most markets are built on a piecemeal basis and rational design is often of little help both for understanding and for action.

Since markets are compromises, potential efficiency gains are not sufficient conditions for guaranteeing implementation of reforms. Beyond the confrontation of individual interests, it is important to take into account the myopic dimensions of interacting actors. These actors attempt to influence the design of markets on the basis of their own interests, but at the same time are unable to anticipate the result of the interactions among the various stakeholders; namely the users and the suppliers, but also innovators and new entrants, and the public actors including the government, the judiciary, and the various ad-hoc agencies.

Contributions to collective action are therefore often shortsighted. This explains why so many balances are needed in the evolution of markets. In fact, two types of balances exist: *de facto* and *de jure*. *De facto* balances are linked to the fact that institutional frameworks of markets translate into decisions of investment and specialization by economic agents. These agents cannot change their capabilities and capacities overnight. Moreover, they cannot write off investments and switch to other activities so easily because it might result in disequilibria on other markets (through defaults of payment, but also misadjustments of supply or demand). Thus coalitions might easily form to defend the status quo, and in any event the inertia of economic agents plays a strong role. *De jure* balances are linked to the logic of the rule of law. Markets are based on rights and rules. The ability to modify them might be bounded by the principle of the hierarchy of norms that prevent social actors and decision makers from overwhelming the distribution of rights. Such principles protect against the tyranny of the majority, or of the dominant interests. It is an essential pillar of trust in most advanced societies, at the basis of the long-term planning capability of economic agents. This is at least a strong factor of civil peace in any society, which is valued by large fractions of the population; even by the disadvantaged minorities, because at least some of their interests are guaranteed. This is the reason why legal constraints of stability are so pregnant in market reforms.

However, "political" compromises about the genesis and sharing of all kind of rents, and the "legal" preferences for, and necessity of, stability are permanently challenged by the quest for economic efficiency.

If "wider in scope," "more competitive," "less costly to run" markets might allow for a deeper division of labor, a higher pace of innovation, and boosted incentives to perform efficiently, then the generated surplus might well be shared among the various stakeholders to allow the adoption of new principles of organization and/or to form coalitions able to implement change. All kind of scenarios might occur in the complex game between customers, providers, new entrants, and rulers. "Economic" efficiency is thus a third driver of market evolution.

1.3 A set of analytical case studies …

This book groups various essays, based on in-depth case studies, attempting to highlight the various dimensions of the dynamics driving the building of markets. Indeed, if we admit that we are facing path-dependent processes concerning complex systems, it is essential to be informed about the true nature of the dynamics and interdependencies at stake. Moreover, it is not enough to claim that human rationality is bounded, or that we are dealing with "games" involving a great many "players" with different logics. It is essential to dig deeper by examining carefully who those players are, what their actual behavior is, and how in practice they interplay by examining specific experience in the real world. This is quite in line with the methodological legacy of the founding scholars of the modern economics of institutions, and above all the four Nobel Laureates – Ronald Coase, Douglass North, Elinor Ostrom, and Oliver Williamson – who all relied upon meticulous observations of real world problems.

These case studies provide us with complementary visions of the dynamics explaining the forming of markets. They enable both us and the readers to understand better how the economic, political, and legal drivers combine in various circumstances. It also leads to the better identification of the relevant categories of players and through what lenses they should be analyzed to understand better their actual role. For instance, it is very clear that most of the time, it is irrelevant to analyze those issues with an actor that would be the "government" or the "state" or the "public bureaucracy." At least, relying on the horizontal division of power "à la Montesquieu" is necessary. Moreover, it is often relevant to isolate the agencies – the competition authority and the regulatory bodies, or ad-hoc entities like the central bank – that play such a strong role in the design and performance of contemporary markets. Lastly, in the context of globalization and regional integration, it is often pertinent to take into account the multilevel character of governance, with interactions between the national, the subnational, and the international public mechanisms.

The contributions also address different "dimensions" of the institutional foundations of markets (measurement, property rights, rules of interaction) and analyze them in different industrial contexts. Among the industries covered, there are agro-food, energy, telecommunications and media, real estate and land, water provision, transportation, banking and finance, etc. We mix contributions dealing with the organization of various markets for the provision of private goods; and also consider public and club goods, or common pool resources. In addition, contributions focus on different historical, geographic, or institutional contexts, highlighting both the specificity of each of them and the common features.

1.4 ... structured into six topics

We chose to group these different chapters under six analytical headings whose logic is presented below. In a sense, the first three relate to the institutional characteristics that influence the performance of markets; namely the securization of exchange, the attribution of property rights, and the organization of the exchange. They highlight the strong and multichanneled interdependencies among institutional dimensions, and therefore the difficulty to align each of them to benefit from costless and nonbiased coordination mechanisms. The three latter parts of the book consist of an investigation into the constraints characterizing public action, when attempting to design and control markets. While markets might rely on self-organization and self-regulation, these techniques are inherently flawed by weaknesses, inconstancies, and capture. At the same time, however, public action is also biased and imperfect. The contributions to the book, therefore, highlight how the combination of two incomplete and imperfect modes of governance should be understood and could be improved.

1.4.1 The "mechanics" of markets

We start with one of the most familiar problems to economists (and laymen), which is the uncertainty over the characteristics of what is exchanged, which might prevent exchange from happening. Above all, a market aims at enabling impersonal exchange, since it is the condition for fostering the division of labor and competition (through new entry). Hence the issue of building mechanisms to objectivize the characteristics of what is exchanged. This is the purpose of the part entitled "Public and Private Complementarities in Securing Exchange."

The second necessary condition for making markets possible is the attribution of property rights to players. Markets have the strong advantages, when not failing, of obliging participants to make decisions grounded on a cost/benefit analysis. Moreover the market aggregates individual choices and thus "internalizes" interdependencies among them. This is why they can be good arbiters among conflicting claims when decisions have to be taken about use of and access resources that are costly or exhaustible. Yet stakeholders must be granted with an initial endowment to allow the performance of the market. The process by which the initial distribution of property rights is decided – say auction vs. grand-fathering (or first claim–first served) – impacts on the distribution of the benefits among stakeholders of market creation/enhancement. Since market players are not all characterized by the same capabilities, this might impact on the efficiency of the process of market implementation. The related debates are developed in the second part of the book entitled "Path Dependency and Political Constraints in Establishing Property Rights Systems."

Competition is often considered as a "natural" characteristic of biological and economic systems. What can be drawn from many of the contributions to this book is that, while rivalry is "natural," there is nothing "natural" in competition in general, that is "organized" rivalry, and even less in "fair competition." Competition has to be organized and implemented. It is a condition for the efficiency of markets, but it is not necessarily a stable equilibrium; i.e., a situation to which a system will automatically converge. In the part entitled "The Political Origin of Competition" the contributors point out the difficulties with which an efficient process of competition can be implemented and guaranteed. Moreover they show that it is never achieved and that the process by which competition is developed is both piecemeal and myopic. The resulting market structure and its institutional framework are thus highly path-dependent.

1.4.2 Challenges for the "visible hand" of the state

The paradox with markets is that they are not built against the state or the government, but by the public rulers or in cooperation with them. Historically they emerged from societies structured by social casts, professional guilds, and communities in which there were exchanges, but few competitive markets (North et al., 2009). On-going negotiations between the society and the rulers led, in certain circumstances, to the development of modern anonymous and competitive markets (Brousseau et al., 2011; Wallis, this volume). The point is that the public ruler is strongly constrained in their actual actions. First, public decision-making is always subject to potential reversal, because the mandate of the ruler can evolve with the balance of powers that establishes their capability to rule. The lack of consistency of public decision-making over time inherently impacts upon the ruler's capability to implement reform and therefore the credibility of reforms, opening the door to all kinds of strategic maneuvers, which include of course the aforementioned inertia. Second, political competition favors a logic of winner takes all by which a dominant coalition tends to implement reforms without redistributing gains to losers. This generates cycles of reforms and counter-reforms that favor neither the quest for first best, nor the fine-tuning of the second-best "feasible" solution. Third, the "ruler" is not a simple entity, but a divided organization. This is an essential point: Modern states are empowered with huge bureaucratic capabilities and extended legitimacy to rule, because they are full of checks and balances that inherently result in inconsistencies in decision-making. Thus most markets are far short of the perfect competition target. These are the arguments developed in the part entitled "The Myopia of the Public Hand."

Another challenge of public action is that the capability of the ruler to substitute for private action is in actual fact very limited. Even when the ruler can suspend the market mechanism and redesign from scratch a new allocation mechanism – a solution that is often called for in the case of major systemic crisis, especially in the case of financial and monetary crisis – the ruler experiences difficulties in monitoring the economy because they cannot adjust efficiently all individual demand and supply. This is the famous risk of paralysis or inefficiency of any central planner as identified by Hayek from the 1920s. Thus, when the ruler attempts to control the functioning of a market, a public authority has to play with the incentives and anticipation of the various "players" in the markets. The point is that their aggregated capability is far beyond the capacity of any public ruler. At the same time, the public ruler is often the only entity able to mobilize consistently this energy. Hence, the difficult balance between public ordering and private initiative that is addressed by the contributions grouped under the heading "The Challenge of Balancing Public and Private Ordering." On the one hand, public regulation and intervention is difficult to implement, while on the other hand self-regulation or the absence of regulation inevitably lead to major crises.

The contributions to the last part of the book highlight how market players can rely on all types of strategies aimed at colluding, or abusing dominant positions, or hijacking the mechanisms supporting exchange in order to create bottlenecks and implement tolls. They point out, hence, that besides the role of public ordering to avoid and fix systemic crisis, the day-to-day operation of markets can lead to major captures that justify public intervention. This does not call, however, for overly strict and detailed regulations and checks, because they are too costly to design and implement ... and because public bureaus – beyond the problem of incentives and motivations – do not master the detailed and evolving knowledge that is needed. What the contributors to this last part show is that there are two pillars to deal with "the Daily Adjustments of Market Technology." First, competition among platforms of exchange/self-regulated markets is a major inhibitor of potential capture. Second, judicial settlement of conflicts among stakeholders is an essential tool to guarantee the implementation of generic principles of competition, beyond the technical and economic-commercial specificities of any markets. There is a strong call, therefore, for an ongoing supervision of the performance of markets, both by specialized entities and by judges; which is consistent with the idea that efficient competitive markets are a never reached objective.

PART I

Public and private complementarities in securing exchange

Introduction to Part I

ERIC BROUSSEAU AND JEAN-MICHEL GLACHANT

Yoram Barzel's framework (1989), which lies behind Douglass North's analysis of the relationship between institutions and economic performance (1990), insists on the idea that institutions may contribute to the "measurement" of the various dimensions of the mutual agreements among agents that are necessary to perform any exchange. "Measuring" applies both to the physical attributes of the goods (and services) and to the "rights" that are traded. Indeed, trade is not about physically circulating goods among individuals, but about transferring various rights of access, of use or of benefits among economic agents, which can either be individuals or organizations. It results in systems of "property rights" that may recognize alternative rights granted to different agents over the same resource.

Public and private institutions may save individual efforts to "measure" the characteristics of what is exchanged. Indeed when quality is defined and certified, it saves traders' cost in negotiating and inspecting the characteristic of goods and services. In the same vein, when property rights are clearly established, the negotiation, the writing, and the enforcement of contracts is simplified. This has a double impact. First, it reduces the level of uncertainty, hence of risks, inherent to an exchange. Agents save then on transaction costs, because not only they might save on the measurement efforts, but also because they save on the costs associated with lack/errors of measurement that translate into mechanisms to protect against risk (guarantees and insurance). Second, when institutions contribute to "objectivize" the exchange, it allows impersonal exchange; i.e., trade between parties which do not know each other. To put it another way, it allows extension of markets beyond the boundaries of social networks.

All in all, "measurement" institutions combine to determine the extension of markets, which impacts upon economic performance through two drivers: the division of labor on the one hand, and the fostering of competition on the other. Competition potentially brings benefits because it tends to erode rents, and favor the implementation of innovation. The three chapters in this first part of the book deal with various dimensions of this objectivization of exchange.

Aashish Velkar's chapter investigates how measurement systems – characterized by the nature of the actors who assess the property of traded goods, the technology they rely upon, and the rules framing the exchange – are designed and established. The case study analyzes the dynamic of changes in the British wheat markets in the nineteenth century, which led to a shift from a largely domestic market in the early 1800s to an internationally integrated one by 1880. What is highlighted here is twofold. First, the integration of markets is strongly dependent upon the development of impersonal and nonmanipulable systems of measure; hence the *scientific grounding* and *third-party certification* characterizing modern measurement systems. Formal and objective measurement systems allow for the increasing of the variety of both commodity and players. That said, it is clear that no complete systems of measurement can be developed to avoid any uncertainty in the exchange. Dispute resolution mechanisms are then a component of any system of measurement. Their aim is not only to deal with strategic manipulations, but also to solve honest disputes based on biases in the mutual interpretation of the other contribution(s) in the exchange.

Second, while measurement systems tend to become less and less manipulable and grounded on specific tacit knowledge, their emergence is the result of processes by which economic players and private interests promote their preferred systems of measure. Indeed, the way quality is assessed, including the moment at which goods are inspected, impacts greatly on the incentives and ability to shirk of the various players in the transaction chains, hence the strategic stakes in designing measurement systems. However, the successful measurement standards are integrated by market players which establish their strategies and invest in assets according to the established standards, which deliver positive feedback on the credibility of these norms. Compliance is linked to their acceptance by all the players, which makes them quite difficult to manipulate *ex post*, even if they result from manipulation *ex ante*… This emphasizes why norms are such essential stakes and why it is relevant for market players to invest heavily in strategies to establish them and ensure their diffusion; as was the case in the nineteenth century for the British flour milling industry. From that perspective, the dynamic of market integration mechanically increases the bargaining power of the demand side since buyers face a greater number and variety of suppliers, hence their ability to force the supply side to comply with measurement standards and technologies that decrease the manipulability of trade.

Since measuring the attributes of goods is so central in any exchange, because otherwise information asymmetries trigger all kinds of strategic behavior that ruins the benefits of trade, Marta Fernández-Barcala, Manuel González-Díaz, and Emmanuel Raynaud survey and analyze how various institutions solve or at least mitigate the challenge of assessing quality. The authors disentangle and classify alternative ways of manufacturing quality either through state intervention (regulation), or through private investments (e.g., brands) or thanks to organized collective actions by networks and communities (e.g., certification). The analysis of the interactions between these various solutions highlights more complementarities than substitutability, while the latter does exist. Hence the difficulty of building consistent systems of quality assessment.

Fernández-Barcala and her co-authors suggest that the governance of quality necessarily combines a great diversity of mechanisms because the attributes to be measured are so numerous and so different that the cost-minimizing solutions for each of these dimensions differ. They also insist on the respective relative performance of public vs. private governance solutions, in particular by pointing out that public standardization is the best solution in easy to measure issue, while private arrangements are more effective when measure is complex. One could add that public institutions are better when there are externalities beyond transacting parties; while private solutions outperform public ones when it is a question of matching the two parties' utility functions (e.g., consumer satisfactions vs. firm's profit).

The difficulty of building consistent systems of quality assessment is magnified, as in any institution-building problem, because all kinds of strategies may lead to the development of mechanisms that tend to be redundant, and sometimes destructors of preexisting ones. The point, however, is to balance the benefits of reshaping more consistent institutional frameworks (and destroying inefficient solutions) and the actual costs of malfunctioning and redundancies.

Benito Arruñada points out that exchange generally takes place between more than two agents because the (property/decision) rights of one of the parties in the exchange are impacted by previous contracts. There are therefore general interdependencies among agents due to their *ex ante* negotiated agreements. This generalized mutual dependence generates uncertainty in the exchange. This uncertainty is not solved by the intervention of the judge in the case of incidents – such as the default of payment, sale by unauthorized agents, and the like – because parties cannot know in advance what will be decided by the judge *ex post* given the evidence he will get, and his interpretation of the web of mutual commitments among agents. Thus the existence of public registries of these mutual commitments is essential for the securization of exchange and more generally for the foundation of a system of exchange.

With this contribution, Benito Arruñada highlights that the type of uncertainty to be managed in building market infrastructures is far from being due solely to the characteristics of goods, because agents do not trade goods, but rights which are fundamentally mutual commitments among members of a society; hence the centrality in a market economy of reliable and wide scale available systems of "objectivization" of actual rights. In this context, the development of modern systems of exchange can be pictured as a competition between two different technologies and the actors operating them: the artisan manufacturing of contracts by lawyers and notaries and the industrial production of "legal commodities" by default contract rules and organized registries. In this context, something close to a Luddite attitude is still observable when legal professionals oppose standardization of legal acts and services, or when they claim the higher quality of personalized service.

Generally speaking, protecting third parties produces a legal commodity, which is easy to trade impersonally, improving the allocation and specialization of resources. Historical delay in generalizing this legal commoditization paradigm is attributed to path dependency – the law first developed for personal trade – and an imbalance in vested interests, as Luddite legal professionals face weak public bureaucracies.

2 | *Measurement systems as market foundations: perspectives from historical markets*

AASHISH VELKAR

2.1 Introduction

This chapter explores the significance of measurement systems as foundational elements of trade and market exchange and reviews the dynamics through which such institutional systems emerge. It specifically investigates how measurement systems help in overcoming fundamental measurement problems, the degree to which they emerge or change endogenously, and how they help in coordinating trade and market activity.

2.2 The fundamental measurement problem

Economic systems face a fundamental measurement problem in that delineating complete information about a product is costly, since such information is usually based upon multiple product attributes (Barzel 1982; Cheung 1983). This creates potential for information asymmetry – a classic principal-agent problem. The asymmetry becomes amplified for a heterogeneous product or commodity. For instance, apples can be measured on the basis of their color, weight, size, juiciness, etc.; manufactured commodities like wire can be measured on the basis of its diameter, weight, metal composition, tensile strength, conductivity, etc.; CD players can be measured on the basis of number of functions, shape and size, power or output rating, sound quality, etc.; restaurants can be measured on the basis of ambience, reputation of the chef, service, cleanliness, authenticity, etc. Thus, the greater the number of measurable attributes, the costlier it is to measure the product *ceteris paribus*.

Measurement costs also depend upon the *ease* with which these attributes can be measured. Thus, *search* attributes (e.g., color, weight, etc.) are easier to measure at the time of transaction, whereas *experience* attributes (e.g., taste, functionality, etc.) can usually be measured on an *ex post* basis. *Credence* attributes (e.g., method of production) cannot be measured even on an *ex post* basis and are based upon trust, reputation, or third-party certification (Tirole 1988). Measurement costs also depend upon whether measurable attributes capture information about a product's *condition* (freshness or newness, color, size, etc.) or *composition* (strength, purity, etc.) or *functionality* and performance ("does it do what it says on the tin?"). It is easier, and therefore less costly, to measure the product's condition rather than its composition or functionality.

Measurement costs form a part of overall transaction costs, and determine the extent to which people are willing to engage in economic exchange (North 1990). The challenge, therefore, is how to manage or minimize the measurement problem. Organizational approaches including branding and product warranties, vertical integration, share contracting, futures exchange, help economic groups manage measurement costs (Barzel 1982). Standardization is also an effective tool to overcome information asymmetry by ensuring that measurements are made on the basis of common or summary criteria (Daviron 2002; Ponte and Gibbon 2005). Such common criteria could emerge due to negotiation and compromise, and are not solely dependent upon economic or technical factors. Third-party organizations, such as commodity exchanges, reduce potential costs by eliminating the need for repeated or duplicative measurements (Pirrong 1995a).

This chapter explores how measurement problems are solved through the study of measurement *systems*. The argument developed here is that measurement systems act as coordinating mechanisms and solve the fundamental measurement problem by ensuring effective circulation of information within markets. Such systems are not only technological systems, but rather embody the "rules of the game" within a given market. The embodiment of institutional rules (regulations, norms, conventions, etc.) implies that measurement systems establish links between people who measure and the measurement tools they use. Such systems are dynamic and change over time and this dynamic change is often the product of negotiation, cooperation, and consensus between different actors within a market, i.e., the change is endogenous.

These arguments are systematically explored in this chapter using an analytical framework, which is described in Section 2.3. The framework considers a particular definition of measurement systems and the important elements that comprise such systems. The historical case study that is used to develop the arguments is described in Section 2.4. Section 2.5 deconstructs the important analytical elements of this case study. Section 2.6 offers a summary and several concluding remarks.

2.3 Analyzing measurement systems

Measurement systems could be defined in very broad terms to include "all elements associated with measuring," including systems and instruments of counting, methods of using instruments, different methods of measuring in different social situations, as well as the interlinked, varied, and conflicting social interests (Kula 1986). A narrower definition by the National Measurement Office, UK suggests that a measurement system is "a network of laboratories and processes that provide measurement standards and calibration testing facilities."[1] Measurement systems considered in this chapter lie somewhere between these two extreme definitions – between systems that include everything associated with how people measure and a hierarchy of organizations conducting measurement activity for industrial or commercial use.

Measurement systems comprise several analytically relevant elements. For instance, measurement *units* are often considered public goods because they are non-rivalrous, i.e., they are available for use by all and use by one does not diminish the amount available to others (Kindleberger 1983). Yet, measurement *standards* could be nonpure private goods, i.e., they are nonrivalrous but can be made excludable by restricting access to them (Romer 1990). While the excludability of measurement standards implies tradability between interested economic agents, measurements as standards have transaction costs reducing properties, i.e., an institutional flavor (Antonelli 1994; Helgesson et al. 1995). This duality places severe demands on analyzing measurements exclusively as economic goods or as institutions. A useful definition of measurement systems must incorporate both the technological attributes of measurement *standards* as well as the institutional attributes of measurement *practices*.

For this chapter, measurement systems are considered to comprise three distinct elements. First, the system comprises people or groups of people (organizations) who make or use measurements in an economic

---

[1] www.bis.gov.uk/nmo/about (accessed February 20, 2014).

setting. Second, it comprises tools that enable people to make measurements, to make comparisons, and to contextualize the measurements in a useful manner for a given economic activity. These tools include metrological units (such as weights and measures), instruments (such as gauges, scales, etc.), and standards (to make comparisons). Third, the system comprises a set of rules –formal and informal, legal and customary, mandatory and voluntary – that connect the people to the tools, that direct the use of the tools in specific contexts, and that enable the transformation of measurements as observations into useful information (Velkar 2012).

This framework is used to analyze a historical case study of how a measurement system overcomes the fundamental measurement problem, and how the system itself changes dynamically and concurrently with shifting market equilibrium. The study is a historical reconstruction of various institutional elements of a measurement system based upon detailed textual analysis. The study follows the historical institutional analysis approach described by Greif (1998) and Greif and Laitin (2004).

Specifically, the measurement system within the British wheat markets of the nineteenth century is studied and the changes in this system from the early 1800s to the latter part of that century are analyzed and explained. The trajectories of the three important elements within the system, viz. economic structure of groups, technological changes surrounding measurement tools, and the evolution of measurement practices and rules, are analyzed. The economic groups included are fairly heterogeneous: producers of grain, merchants and middlemen, industrial buyers (e.g., millers), industry and trade associations, commodity exchanges, business media, etc. Measurement artifacts considered are similarly broad ranging from the system of weights and measures, to measuring instruments (including gauges and scales), to measurement standards (including quality grades), etc. The rules and practices that are analyzed can be described as those that regulate the *mensuration* activities, in contrast to the *metrological* activities. The difference is that while mensuration deals with the practice of measurement, metrology refers to the science of measurement.[2] Both the formal regulations as well as informal norms or conventions are considered for analysis.

---

[2] The analytical distinction is often difficult to discern practically. Briefly, metrology deals with the accuracy of artifacts (e.g., units such as the *kilogram* or the *bushel*), whereas mensuration deals with the selection of artifacts for

Rules could be *de jure* (legal) in nature, those which emerge *de facto* in the process of exchange, or which are agreed upon voluntarily. The entire investigation is based on micro-level and detailed examination of evidence collected from several archival sources.

2.4 Quality measurements in British wheat markets

The case of the British wheat markets of the nineteenth century shows how the markets addressed the fundamental problem of measuring quality of a highly heterogeneous commodity and how the system was able to transform quality measurements from *de facto*, decentralized practices to a set of more centralized practices. In doing so, the case study demonstrates how institutions and institutional changes facilitated trade and market exchange. This case also helps to show how measurement systems, as institutions, were the foundational elements of the markets, and how they ensured effective circulation of product information. On the whole, the study shows how the measurement system within this market was crucial in enabling the shift from a given equilibrium position in the early nineteenth century (mainly domestic trade) to a radically different equilibrium position (internationally integrated markets) by the end of the nineteenth century.[3]

2.4.1 Measurement issues and de facto *solutions*

In the nineteenth century, the British wheat markets faced two major measurement issues. There were no uniform standards for measuring quality *ex ante* and buyers depended upon their tacit knowledge to assess quality of wheat: "The eye, nose and hand were necessary [in] judging the value of grain and [the buyers determined] its quality by 'merely taking up and poising a small quantity of it in their hands.'" (Dumbell 1925). Thus, individual buyers made quality measurements through sampling and visual inspection. The other issue was that a *bushel* of wheat, the most commonly used measurement unit, uniformly did not mean the same measure of quantity across domestic

---

a particular economic activity (e.g., measuring the weight as opposed to volumetric capacity of wheat).

[3] See Velkar (2012) for more details regarding the measurements used in wheat markets of the nineteenth century.

markets in Britain.[4] This was a well-recognized fact by the nineteenth century. The *bushel* could be used either as a volumetric unit or as a weight unit and often varied across geographical locations (BPP 1820 Vol. VII, p. 483).

Nevertheless, there were well-established commercial (mensuration) practices for navigating through this metrological maze. Wheat was sold using a combination of volume and weight measurements in many British wheat markets, i.e., based on the density of a *bushel* of wheat. In such cases, the *bushel* was guaranteed to weigh a specified amount, say 60 *lbs*. If the actual weight was more or less than the guaranteed weight per volume, the contract price was adjusted proportionately. A contract for wheat from Boston c.1830 guaranteed delivery weight to be 18 *stone* per *quarter* and specified price and terms as 54s 6d "pay or be paid," i.e., the farmer was to make a "proportionate allowance" to the merchant in case the net weight on delivery was under 18 *stone* 4 *lbs*, and conversely the farmer was to receive an allowance from the merchant in case the net weight on delivery was found to exceed 18 *stone* 4 *lbs* (BPP 1834 Vol. XLIX).

Such practices reflected the reasoning that grain of higher density was of better quality than grain of lower density, and had better bread-making ability (BPP 1834 Vol. VII, p. 87). The use of density to assess the quality of wheat was not unique to Britain. French bakers regularly used this method in the eighteenth century to distinguish between good and average quality wheat (Kaplan 1984).

This brief survey shows how domestic British markets managed two key informational requirements – the amount of wheat traded and the quality of the grain – through the practice of making wheat contracts based on the grain's density. This was a *de facto* grading practice that emerged before commodity exchanges began establishing formal quality grades in the latter half of the nineteenth century. The *de facto* practice was an effective way for the trade to make a rapid and straightforward assessment of quality (BPP 1834 Vol. VII). The density of any given variety of wheat was notoriously difficult to maintain, as it was sensitive to climatic and other conditions. Even under controlled conditions the density of a specific wheat variety could vary over time. The density measurement system was designed basically to

---

[4] 1 *Imperial bushel* = 1.03 *US bushels* (approx.) = 36.36 *liters* (approx.) and 1 *quarter* = 8 *bushels*. Also, 1 *stone* = 14 *lbs* and 1 *lb* = 0.45 *kg* (approx.).

capture such variations in quality from one season to another for the same variety or between two stocks of the same variety.

Managing the issue of quality measurements became critical by the second half of the nineteenth century when new wheat varieties were added to the existing low yielding British varieties. There were 16 different domestic wheat types available for sale in English grain markets in the 1850s. Wheat imports had added about 40 or so foreign varieties to the growing number of domestic varieties by c.1880 (Jago and Jago 1911).

2.4.2 Quality measurements by commodity exchanges

Until the mid-nineteenth century, quality of wheat was ascertained by inspecting samples submitted for inspection, in markets such as Mark Lane in London, where quality was measured on the basis of other important physical attributes, such as the presence of impurities, dryness or moisture content, texture, etc., in addition to the density of grain. However, inspecting samples was problematic as samples would often hide the extent of variation in the quality. There were frequent complaints against corn factors who exposed only a selection of their samples so that the buyers did not get a complete picture of the actual quality of the stock (Fay 1925; Merrill 1911).

From the mid-nineteenth century onwards, commodity exchanges began to develop detailed mechanisms to measure and grade this complex commodity. The British exchanges, such as the London Corn Trade Association (LCTA) and the Liverpool Corn Trade Association, were primarily concerned with grading imported wheats, not domestic ones: there is no evidence that either of these exchanges developed formal grades for the domestic trade.

The Fair Average Quality or FAQ method was one of the mechanisms that was most commonly adopted by LCTA for grading wheat quality. Under this method, samples of all wheat imported into the UK, including from several ports in Europe, were periodically collected before fixing the grades for any given year. The grades were developed on a responsive basis, i.e., based on annual samples collected, and effectively functioned as ranked categories – into which the different samples could be sorted – rather than as fixed standards.

FAQ quality descriptions varied according to the source of the produce and different sets of criteria were used. For instance, when Indian grain was graded on FAQ terms, allowance was made for dirt and other impurities (such as non-farinaceous seeds). Similarly, grades for New Zealand wheat were described separately for round berried and long berried wheat. LCTA would also take into account the differences in the densities of wheat from Argentina, Australia, California, or other locations. For example, while fixing the standard for Australian wheat in 1894, the LCTA fixed an average weight of 63 *lbs* per *bushel* for that season's wheat. On the other hand, the average weight of Californian White was assumed to be 60.5 *lbs* per *bushel* while fixing the standards for 1895 (LCTA committee minutes).

These developments in Britain mirrored those in the US where commodity exchanges, such as the Board of Trade of the City of Chicago (CBT), had begun classifying grades of grain according to descriptions of color, quality, and general condition around c.1860 (Merrill 1911). Before the turn of the century, a national system of grading the various varieties of red, white, winter, and spring wheat had begun to emerge in the US. Nevertheless, quantification of quality attributes as well as standardization across the various commodity exchanges and trading centers continued to remain problematic and elusive. Even by 1914, US grades used descriptions such as sound, dry, reasonably clean, sweet, mature, plump, etc. The issue of fixing numerical grades would continue to dodge the trade and the US state well into the third quarter of the twentieth century (Hill 1990). North American grain was gradually accepted in the UK on the basis of "official certificate of inspection to be final as to quality," i.e., according to the quality guaranteed by the inspection certificates issued on the basis of grades developed by American exchanges.

Commodity exchanges in the UK and US thus independently developed distinct practices to measure the quality of wheat. As the number of hands through which the commodity passed increased with the internationalization of grain markets, quality measurements increasingly came within the purview of these meso-level institutions. In other words, lengthening of international value chains was accompanied by centralization of measurement practices.

2.4.3 Quality from the buyers' perspective

In the latter half of the nineteenth century, there were corresponding and equally significant changes in the milling industry – the largest buyers of wheat in the UK. Throughout most of the nineteenth century millers had relied upon the visual inspection of samples to purchase grain. Wheat of lower density was known to yield a lower quality of flour and the millers, and bakers, preferred the hard, denser wheat varieties to the soft, less dense wheat varieties (BPP 1834 Vol. VII). In addition, the strength of the grain or flour was crucial to the miller. Strength was initially defined as the ability to absorb and retain moisture, which later was modified to indicate the quantity and quality of gluten the grain contained (Jago and Jago 1911). Stronger flour was preferred because a greater number of loaves was obtained from a given weight of such flour than from weaker flour. Hard wheat varieties of the high densities were considered to be stronger wheats, whereas softer wheats were considered to be of the weaker kind; British wheats, on the whole, were considered to be of the weaker kind (Percival 1934). The miller basically had to balance both the density as well as moisture characteristics of the grain, as those varieties with the highest bushel weight with low moisture content usually gave the greatest amount of flour.

The miller's craft continued to demand a great deal of experimentation and risk even towards the end of the nineteenth century. Millers had to consider, for each variety of wheat, whether it would contribute to one or more aspect of flour quality: strength, color, taste, or general appearance. Assessing the quality of grain depended upon the "empiricism of the practical miller" (Jones 2001). Consequently, wheat buying was governed by experience, general principles, and a considerable degree of detailed knowledge, and no two millers agreed on what constituted good quality. When the volume of imported grain increased and the number of varieties available multiplied, the millers, like the merchants, began to rely upon the grades and measurement standards set by the various commodity associations, such as the LCTA or the Liverpool Corn Trade Association.

There continued to be dissonance amongst the millers as to the quality differences between the various varieties, and quality was a relative rather than an absolute measure in this industry. This dissonance is particularly evident in the practice of mixing grain to produce flour acceptable to the miller (Velkar 2012, p. 197). Mixing was one of the most basic skills the miller had to possess as it eked out the supply of expensive best quality wheat, and enabled the miller to enhance his margin by mixing expensive and inexpensive wheats. In this way, the miller could still sell the mixed flour at a price higher than that of inferior quality flour (BPP 1814–15 Vol. V, p. 1353). When the availability of foreign wheat increased, good quality imported wheat was mixed with lower quality domestic varieties.

As the milling process became more specialized and sophisticated after c.1880, the *differences* in quality between varieties as well as the *consistency* of quality in a given variety became crucially important. Revolutionary changes in milling technology after 1880 were accompanied by development and improvements in testing and measuring the different quality attributes of wheat. At the same time, scientific study of the wheat grain and the nutritive value of its different parts focused on understanding the chemical and physical properties of its proteins, especially gluten (Chick 1957; Jago and Jago 1911). The increased understanding of the chemical composition and properties of gluten aided the developments of various testing methods and instruments for assessing the quality of flour: Pekar's method of assessing whiteness of flour, Boland's aleurometer to test the strength of gluten, and Robine's method for estimating quantity and likely bread output are some examples (Jones 2001).

Even so, each miller had to independently discover the strength of any given flour, as there was "no satisfactory method of numerically registering strength except through a baking test" (Jago and Jago 1911, p. 291; Jones 2001). Notwithstanding the increasing use of LCTA or CBT grades, wheat buying continued to be governed by experience and general principles and millers continued to assess the quality of grain using *ex post* measurements.

2.5 Measurement systems as foundational elements

The foregoing reveals important shifts that occurred during the nineteenth century in the wheat markets. Measurement of quality transformed from a decentralized activity situated in local markets into a centralized activity coordinated by the commodity exchanges. Further, the standards used to measure the quality of wheat were transformed from the *de facto* standards used within local and regional markets to voluntary consensus standards that were acceptable on an international basis. Finally, the role of quality standards gradually transformed from measurement of quality to that of guaranteeing or

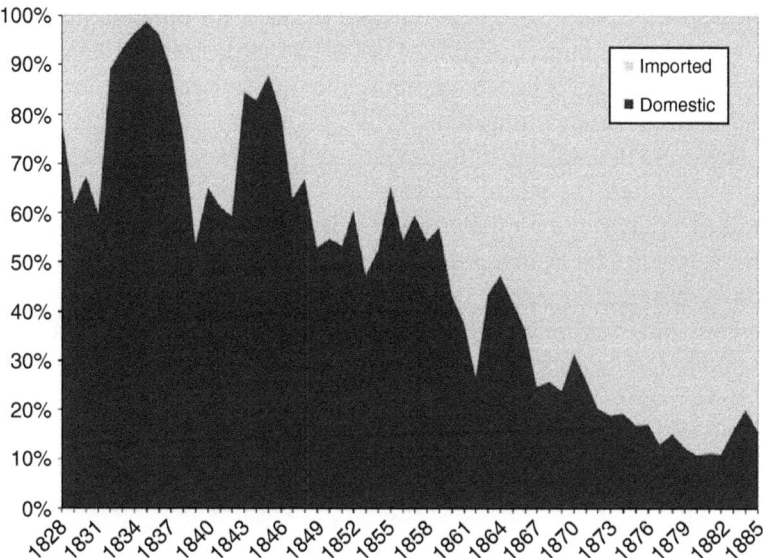

Figure 2.1 Proportion of domestic sales to imported wheat, UK (1828–1885)

assuring quality. These shifts armed the British wheat markets to transition to a new equilibrium: international specialization and dependence upon imported wheat after c.1860 (Figure 2.1).

2.5.1 From inspection to grading: an institutional change

Wheat buyers (traders as well as millers) had traditionally preferred to sort the commodity as finely as possible, into a greater number of categories, and on attributes that indicated the grain's bread-making ability. In contrast there was little incentive for the seller (i.e., both farmers and traders) to sort the commodity, into any more categories than was necessary, such as by variety, port of origin or the season (winter, spring, etc.). Practically, grain with certain undesirable attributes, e.g., high moisture content, high impurities, etc., could be corrected and re-sorted into higher grades. But, grain with undesirable compositional attributes (density, color, texture) could not be corrected for (Barzel 1982). Sampling and inspection of grains at multiple points along the commodity chain were therefore common practices. Grading by commodity exchanges effectively *increased* the categories in which the product was sorted, and eliminated the need for potentially duplicative sampling and inspection. The direct involvement of commodity exchanges also signaled an important shift in terms of third-party measurements and certification.

This fundamental institutional change – from inspection to grading – impacted the wheat markets in at least four significant ways. Product standards or quality grades helped to reduce overall measurement costs by avoiding costly, repeated, and duplicative examination by buyers and sellers, an argument proposed by Pirrong (1995a). Further, quality grades helped to standardize commercial contracts enabling the commodity exchanges to become "clearing houses" (Forrester 1931).[5] Standard contracts potentially eliminated the need to negotiate commercial terms regarding product specifications, quality measurements, etc. They also helped to institutionalize arbitration mechanisms within the commodity exchanges, and reduce monitoring and enforcement costs (Chattaway 1907; Ferguson 1980). The third impact was that third-party or "official" grades helped in the creation of trust as they were better able to *guarantee* quality than individual inspection. In other words, official grades economized on the measurement of credence attributes, such as region of origin or the season in which it was produced, e.g., Canadian Club, or American No. 1 Winter grades of wheat grains. Finally futures trading could develop on the basis of quality grades aiding the internationalization of this primary commodity by managing risk. A futures market helped to transfer the price risk to a specialized group of speculators (the broker-merchants), and helped to link local farms in producer regions to the international buyers along the highly specialized commodity chain (Daviron 2002).

More directly, *differences* in the way grain from the various foreign sources was graded helped to reduce overall measurement costs as the structure of the trade changed. US wheat was graded at source (prior to shipment) whereas wheat from other overseas regions was graded in the UK. The elevator-based storage system that developed in America required grading at source as wheat had to be graded at the point when the farmer brought it for storage at the elevators at the shipping point. This was because grain was stored in the elevator

---

[5] The "clearing house system" refers to the activities of passing shipping and other commercial documents between traders, settlement of contracts, clearing of differences, etc.

along with grain of similar quality, thus segregating the identity of the grain parcels from that of the individual sellers. The seller (farmer) received value according to the lowest quality that the grain could be graded into. This strengthened the incentives of those shipping the grain to elevators to maintain quality before storage (Pirrong 1995a; Stewart 1923). Once the graded grain was loaded onto ships or railway cars for transport it was nearly impossible to mix grain of varying qualities. Such opportunism problems and malpractices were possible prior to storage. The only dissipation of quality could occur due to damage caused by moisture and poor storage conditions. The incentives to maintain quality prior to shipment was high, but not during the transportation of the already graded grain. This problem was alleviated when the US government begun supplying moisture content certificates, which could then be used to compare with the actual condition of the grain when it arrived at its destination (Merrill 1911).

In contrast, handling facilities for grain imported from other countries such as Argentina and Australia were extremely crude. Crude handling methods exposed the grain to varying weather and insect condition and the absence of elevators meant that it was most efficient to ship grain in bags.[6] This made it virtually impossible to create parcels of grain of standardized grades by combining grain from individual growers prior to shipment, as was possible in the elevator based storages of North America. Further, with individual shipments retaining their identity, inspecting quality at the importing country economized on the number of measurements necessary along such a trade route. There were few incentives to prevent dissipation of quality prior to bagging and storage. But all things being equal, this system would have given the shipper an incentive to take care of the cargo at sea.[7] In such practices quality could not be guaranteed prior to shipment. The FAQ system, an *ex post* method of grading, was particularly suited in these instances. It adjusted standards to reflect systematic factors affecting the quality of grain from a particular location (level of quality due to grain composition as well as condition due

---

[6] Bagging made it easier and less costly to unload at the importing ports prior to the introduction of mechanical unloading devices such as pneumatic elevators; see Cunningham (1923).

[7] This would also have depended upon the contract and shipping terms, i.e., who had the residual property rights on the cargo and who paid for insurance, freight, etc.

to storage, transport, handling, etc.). The method also minimized the number of potential disputes regarding product quality (Chattaway 1907; Ferguson 1980).

2.5.2 Endogenous institutional changes

The international wheat trade, in the second half of the nineteenth century, expanded enormously due to declining transaction costs: removal of tariffs and other trade barriers, a stable exchange rate regime pegged to the gold standard, reduction in freight, transportation and communication costs, etc. – many of which were exogenously determined factors. However, several of the factors that fueled the transition of grain markets into a mature and information rich market were endogenously determined (Ejrnæs et al. 2008; Jacks 2006; Jacks et al. 2010). The argument offered here, that changes to the measurement systems were largely endogenously determined, resonates with such existing views on commodity market integration. The endogeneity argument is further illustrated using two examples: changes to business processes within the trade, and the emergence of industry associations and trade journals.

Technological improvements at the ports, changes in milling techniques, introduction of newer testing methods for wheat quality, etc., enabled fundamental changes to business and trade practices. For example, improvements in the loading/unloading technologies at the ports changed the incentives for measuring quality during the unloading process. As a bulk commodity, determining the density of grain (to indicate its quality) required measuring the same stock of grain twice, once in terms of its volume and again in terms of its weight. For a bulky commodity like wheat this implied a considerable increase of effort and time at the importing ports where grain from coastwise routes as well as foreign grain was unloaded. Towards the beginning of the nineteenth century, grain transported on ships would usually be put into sacks in order to ease its removal from the ship's hold, and also during delivery on the wharves. This process involved using the *bushel* measure, as each sack was expected to hold a specific capacity (Broomhall and Hubback 1930; Dumbell 1925). If grain had to be weighed, it was done once it was sacked and hoisted on to the deck. Each sack, or a sample of sacks, would then be weighed using scales to arrive at the density estimates (BPP 1834 Vol. VII, pp. xix–xx). Changes in the transport and discharging technology in the latter half of the nineteenth century altered this unloading process. The sacking process in UK ports could be eliminated when foreign grain began arriving in sacks that did not require re-bagging. The introduction of pneumatic elevators in the 1890s further made the sacking process redundant. Grain could be vacuumed from the ship's hold and poured onto scales for weighing, from where it would eventually be discharged out of the ship (Driel and Schot 2005).

The elimination of sacking meant that quality measurements did not have to occur during the unloading of grain at ports. In fact, it increased the incentives for conducting quality measurements more centrally by institutions such as the LCTA. De-linking the distribution (i.e., unloading) and quality assessment processes thus made third-party quality measurements economical. This further made it practical to expand the summary criteria for measuring quality and increase product segmentation by sorting the grain into finer categories. Additionally, third-party grading meant that associations could function as quality assurance and dispute resolution centers. The increasing number of disputes involving the quality and condition of the grain in international trade could now be resolved relatively transparently through arbitration mechanisms that depended upon these grades. For a long time, London (UK) buyers resisted and challenged the practice of US exporters to dispatch American wheat on the basis that inspection certificates were "final as to quality." LCTA continually helped British merchants to address quality problems concerning US graded grain by raising these issues directly with the US exchanges. The eventual acceptance of US grades in the UK was the result of continuing negotiations between the LCTA and the US exchanges, as well as changes to the measurement practices at the importing ports in the UK. There can be no doubt that such changes to business practices contributed greatly in the overall reduction of transaction costs in the international trade between the UK and wheat producing nations, particularly the US.

While measurement practices in the international wheat *trade* undoubtedly underwent radical shifts, practices in other parts of the wheat *markets* changed in different ways. Millers began to use quality grades specified by commodity exchanges. However, such quality measurements provided the millers with only *partial* information about quality. Even the increased categorization and finer product segmentation was insufficient as far as the miller's profession was concerned.

This is illustrated by an example from more recent times that stresses the economics of flour extraction. In 1973, the Chicago (CBT) grade number 2 soft red winter wheat (SRW) specified 58 *pound* per *bushel* density as a grading criterion. A miller usually bases grain price to flour ratios on the assumption of a 73 percent flour extraction rate, implying that 2.36 *bushels* would be required to produce 100 *pounds* of flour. A reduction of density from 58 *pounds* to 57 *pounds* per *bushel* has two implications. First, at the same extraction rate, the miller now needs 2.40 *bushels* of wheat to produce 100 *pounds* of flour. Second, a reduction of test weight, and hence quality of the grain, is likely accompanied by a reduction of extraction rate to say 70 percent which further increases the quantity of grain required, 2.50 *bushels*, to produce the same quantity of flour. The resulting cost differential of wheat to flour is not always reflected in the price discounts for the different wheat qualities (Jones 1999). Similarly, millers in the nineteenth century could not base grain price to flour ratios solely on the basis of stated product grades. To complicate things further, British millers in the nineteenth century had to also account for the *relative* cost differences between the individual varieties (and qualities) of wheat due to the practice of mixing wheat varieties (Kirkland 1896). Millers thus had to depend upon other methods of measuring wheat quality in addition to the wheat grades specified by the exchanges.

As commodity grades captured only partial information about wheat quality, as far as the millers were concerned, other institutions emerged to overcome this information deficit. After 1870, several industry associations were set up, which became a forum to establish procedures and governance mechanisms, as well as to serve as nodes to disseminate knowledge and information (Macrosty 1903). The association that undoubtedly had the greatest impact on the milling industry was the National Association of British and Irish Millers (NABIM) formed in 1878. The association functioned as a "clearing house" for knowledge and information. For instance, a series of annual conventions were organized by NABIM between 1884 and 1890 on topics such as "Bookkeeping for millers," "Gradual reduction milling," "The Carter and Zimmer sorting system," "The world's wheat crop and wheat values," etc. (Jones 2001). It also acted as the "educator" and a promoter of milling as a "science" beyond its obvious industrial origins. The association complemented the various efforts that were under way to establish some sort of organizational structure for technical education.

NABIM also acted as a "pressure or lobby group" on behalf of its members, and the milling industry more generally. For instance, NABIM wrote to the Board of Trade in 1878 expressing the opinion of the milling trade regarding the metrological units to be used in the sale of wheat and other grain. It had canvassed the regional and local millers associations, corn merchants, and agriculturists through a series of more than 20 meetings held across the country throughout 1878 (Board of Trade Papers, BT 101/43, letter dated Nov 7, 1878). NABIM was also involved in the quality standardization and grading process for wheat. For example, it proposed various amendments to the LCTA standard contract forms in 1896. Its suggestion regarding the proportion of dirt and foreign matter allowed in grain imports from India was nevertheless rejected by the LCTA as "impracticable" (LCTA Arbitration Subcommittee Papers, 1896).

Other institutions of importance were the various technical and trade journals such as *Miller*, started in 1875 by William Dunham, and *Milling* started in 1891 by G. J. S. Broomhall. The publications served as forums to exchange information, knowledge, opinions, developments, etc. that directly affected the millers and how they conducted their trade. In it one would find information about new developments in the milling process pioneered by milling engineers such as Herbert Simon, or about the state of the wheat crop in Britain or its foreign sources, letters seeking opinions about the best method of mixing grain to get the ideal flour, news articles on developments affecting the wheat, milling, and baking trades, etc. The editorial, technical, commercial, and correspondence content was supplemented by the growing amount of advertising. Such journals provided much of the basis of news, ideas, and discussion for both formal and informal networks of communication throughout the industry (Jones 2001).

Thus, the changes to the measurement system were largely endogenous. The different elements of the system (the economic groups, the measurement tools, and the institutional rules) underwent important changes. The roles of the different groups changed, with respect to who made the measurements and who guaranteed them. The tools that were used and the manner in which the measurements were made were considerably altered during this period. Changes involving the measurer as well as the measurement practices were largely endogenous to the system. An interesting aspect of this case is that not all parts of the system changed uniformly. Centralized quality measurements through grading were largely restricted to imported wheat in the UK; domestic markets continued to measure quality using the traditional *de facto* practices in contrast to the North American markets where centralized grading increasingly became the norm. Similarly, millers continued to depend upon other industry-specific methods to assess grain quality on an *ex post* basis. The endogenous change was nonergodic indicating a strong element of path dependency. Nevertheless, such dynamic changes had the effect of ensuring that crucial, more complete, information circulated within the markets in a cost-effective manner.

2.5.3 Measurements and institutional change: impact on trade and markets

The significance of such a dynamic measurement system can be considered in light of two important perspectives. The commodity changed hands a number of times along the chain as it traveled from the producer to the consumer. Also, value addition to the commodity occurred in various forms and along the various stages in this chain: sorting and grading, mixing and storage, transport and distribution, milling and baking, etc. These activities gradually dispersed internationally as the chains lengthened along international routes. Thus, grain milled into flour in Britain was most likely to have been grown, sorted, graded, and mixed in transcontinental locations, such as the Americas, by the end of the nineteenth century.

These facts highlight two important and related developments within the commodity chain. For the commodity to efficiently change hands a number of times and to go through the various stages of value addition along the chain, the commodity had to become fungible. Simultaneously, the exchanges between the buyer and the seller had to be efficiently coordinated. Fungibility depended both upon the degree to which the product was standardized throughout the chain as well as the extent to which the producer's identity was alienated from the produce (Daviron 2002). Efficient coordination implied, among other things, the reduction in search costs as well as the emergence of effective dispute resolution mechanisms. Both these became possible in the British wheat markets with the changes in the measurement system.

As declining transaction and information costs are an important driver of international specialization and product market integration, the dynamic measurement system helped British wheat markets to shift equilibrium from a largely domestic market to an internationally integrated one. The equilibrium shift not only ensured price efficiency and a considerable expansion in trade volumes, but it enabled the markets to deal with an unprecedented *scope* of product variety. The markets had to, and did, deal with an explosion in the variety of wheats that were available in British markets due to the internationalization: from 16 domestic varieties in c.1850 to over 65 domestic and imported wheat varieties in c.1880. This explosion would have potentially amplified the fundamental measurement problem and only a dynamic institutional change in the measurement system ensured that information circulated cost-effectively.

These two aspects, coordinating equilibrium shifts and endogenous change, underlie the claim that measurement systems were an important foundational element of British wheat markets in the nineteenth century.

2.6 Conclusions

Measurement issues are pervasive across economic systems and have historically constituted a fundamental problem of exchange (Velkar 2012). Measurement costs are part of monitoring and enforcement costs that characterize any exchange (Barzel 1982; North 1990). The chapter has shown that markets are able to solve measurement problems dynamically and endogenously. This was possible as a result of several institutions and institutional changes, including the centralization of quality measurements through grading, emergence of voluntary consensus standards, the shift from measuring quality to guaranteeing it, greater role of commodity exchanges and industry associations in coordinating international trade, etc.

Institutional changes ensured that the different elements of the measurement system – the economic groups, the measurement tools, and the measurement practices – underwent important changes. As a result, the markets were able to shift equilibrium from a largely domestic market to an internationally integrated one. Pushing this point further, the institutions and institutional changes analyzed in this chapter suggest that markets coordinate equilibrium shifts in several different ways simultaneously, i.e., there is no single set of rules to coordinate behavior (Wilkinson 1997).

Dynamic measurement systems and equilibrium shifts also provide an insight into understanding market integration and the extent to which integration can be enduring. Measurement systems (or other similar systems) make it possible for networks of diverse (heterogeneous) groups to be better integrated, increase both the scale and scope of market activity, and manage information costs more effectively.

3 How to manufacture quality: the diversity of institutional solutions and how they interact in agrifood markets

MARTA FERNÁNDEZ-BARCALA, MANUEL
GONZÁLEZ-DÍAZ, AND EMMANUEL RAYNAUD

3.1 Introduction

One of the great achievements of New Institutional Economics (NIE hereafter) has been to investigate and describe the myriad of coordination hazards that might plague a market economy while explaining how the different devices that form the institutional framework can mitigate them (see among others, Dixit, 2004; Greif, 2005; Williamson, 1985). The definition and security of property rights and the enforcement of contractual arrangements are examples of what Coase called the "institutional structure of production." As the title of the book suggests, from this perspective, markets are "produced," or "manufactured." In other words, even if some markets have a spontaneous origin, a market economy is based on human design and this design is anything but costless.

In this chapter, we develop this perspective on a more narrow issue, namely, the hazards and solutions involved in "manufacturing" product quality. As we see it, *manufacturing* quality is about the operations that are necessary for defining and differentiating products related to particular characteristics or attributes and for enforcing the exchange of the promised set of attributes. This is not a simple task because quality is a multidimensional concept and definitions require a common understanding (sometimes called a "quality convention") so that various products can be graded and ranked within the same category

---

A first version of this chapter was presented at the workshop "Manufacturing Markets: legal, political and economic dynamics," Florence, June 2009. We thank Céline Bignebat, Jean-François Sattin, and especially Eric Brousseau and Jean-Michel Glachant for useful comments. The research has received support from the European Commission through the "Reflexive Governance" Integrated Project (CIT3–513420). Usual disclaimers apply.

under a common heading and, sometimes, a common label. Even the quality of the sort of "simple" products that standard textbooks use as examples approximating perfect competition may quite often be described in a variety of ways. Take wheat, for example: many buyers and sellers, worldwide competition, simple and (apparently) homogeneous product. Previous studies suggest, however, that defining wheat quality is not easy (see Pirrong, 1995b).

Industrial organization (IO) and Walrasian economy implicitly assume that the task of defining and enforcing quality has already been set. Unfortunately, this is not always the case and, thanks to the NIE contribution, we now have better knowledge of the consequences of a poor assessment of quality for the efficiency of market exchanges. Our aim is therefore to review the main mechanisms used in order to manufacture product quality. We start by suggesting that manufacturing quality can be fruitfully analyzed through the lens of Transaction Cost Economics, in particular the "measurement" branch as explored by Barzel in various contributions (Barzel, 1982, 2002, 2004). We disentangle alternative "families" of manufacturing quality devices and rank them on a "public/private" continuum. More importantly, we analyze the interactions among these devices by describing some of their complementarities.

In order to provide empirical contents for our analysis, we analyze the specific sector of agrifood in which, we believe, product quality issues are highly relevant. Agrifood sectors, in particular fresh food products, are characterized by natural variability and heterogeneity of raw products that lead to uncertainty on product quality for consumers. Furthermore, consumers are becoming increasingly sensitive to a "broader" conception of quality. By this we mean that they value not only the attributes of products (like meat tenderness) but also some dimensions of the production process itself (like organic production or fair trade), thus raising new issues. Finally, a series of high profile food safety issues (like the Bovine Spongiform Encephalopathy [BSE] scare) have heightened public awareness in various countries and triggered new reflections on the regulation of product quality.

This chapter is organized as follows. First, we describe the typical problem regarding the definition and enforcement of quality for agrifood products (Section 3.2). Then we describe (Section 3.3) the range of institutional solutions that have been designed to make quality exchanges possible. Section 3.4 explores the way these solutions interact to show that they both complement and substitute each other,

How to manufacture quality   39

creating complex patterns of interactions. Section 3.5 is an attempt to operationalize the analysis by matching quality aspects and institutional solutions. The conclusion follows.

3.2 The nature of the problem: measuring quality

In this section, we analyze the main contractual hazard involved in exchanging products of varying and sometimes unknown quality (at least for one side of the transaction), and we relate this problem with the dimension of the transactions that seems the most relevant: the measurement problem. We start by briefly reviewing the "measurement approach" in general (3.2.1) before applying it to quality issues (3.2.2).

3.2.1 Measurement issues as the core of economic transactions

It is quite usual among NIE scholars to disentangle two branches of Transaction Cost Economics (hereafter TCE). First, the "governance" branch mostly associated with the works of Coase (1937) and Williamson (1985). The focus here is on the description of the properties of alternative governance structures and the alignment between transactional attributes and alternative (mostly bilateral) governance structures. The classical "make or buy" problem is the canonical example of this approach. The second, "measurement" branch, is mainly associated with the work of Barzel (1982, 2002) and the prominent contribution of Alchian and Demsetz (1972). At the root of this second approach is the combination of three factors:

(i) Products and assets have a bundle of attributes embodied in them. These attributes are the characteristics of the products themselves, like size and color, but also attributes of the production process (eco-friendly products, animal welfare) or even the organization of the supply chain (for instance, fair trade). Consumers derive utility from these attributes.[1] For instance, environmentally friendly production processes are gaining increasing popularity among European consumers.

---

[1] The emphasis of the multidimensional nature of any economic good is also the core of Lancaster's approach to consumer theory (Lancaster, 1966). However, Lancaster did not discuss the possibility that each specimen of a given

(ii) The level of each of these characteristics may vary from one specimen of a product to another. Both external factors and factors directly under the control of economic agents are behind this variability. For instance, the protein content of wheat may vary from one year to another because of climate variations or because of the care taken during harvesting and storage. Without any supporting devices, the level of attributes in a product bought on date t is not a perfect predictor of these attributes for the same product bought on t+1.

(iii) It is difficult and costly to ascertain the value of goods before the transaction is performed. For instance, the amount of juice in an orange or the taste of a tomato are difficult to predict by simply looking at the product. According to Barzel, "virtually no commodity offered for sale is free from the cost of measuring its attributes" (Barzel, 1982, p. 28). Economic agents need to spend resources to make a more or less accurate initial assessment.

Thus buyers decide how much to purchase on the basis not only of the posted price but also the measurement costs they have to bear. It should be noted that both sides of the deal need to incur measurement costs. "In every exchange, both the seller and the buyer will require some verification of the measurements of the exchanged goods: the seller to assure himself he is not giving up too much, the buyer to assure himself he is not receiving too little" (Barzel, 1982, p. 32). More generally, the measurement branch emphasizes the true value that factors of production bring to an exchange (like in Alchian and Demsetz, 1972), or uncertainties as to the value of the outcome of an exchange, which inevitably give rise to contracting and monitoring problems.

The presence of this type of costs creates contractual problems. Given that information is not symmetrically allocated among transactors for a number of reasons (knowledge, expertise, opportunity cost of time, natural skills, etc.), less informed parties should bear search and information costs to solve this disadvantage. Furthermore, opportunistic sellers may take advantage of their informational advantage by, for instance, promising "good" quality but providing "bad" quality. Akerlof's (1970) paper takes the market for used cars as an example of consumers' adverse selection.

commodity might vary. Neither did he integrate in his analysis the possibility of asymmetric information between buyers and sellers on these attributes.

3.2.2 Measuring quality and related quality uncertainty

The notion of product quality is not easy to define even if we all have (but do not necessarily share) a kind of common sense idea as to what quality means. For the rest of this chapter, quality will be defined as the measurement of the various attributes that make up a product. This measurement activity requires three complementary steps:

(i) The creation of a metering or grading device. Reference to the economics of standards (David, 1987; Kindleberger, 1983), which describes various types of standards, is relevant here. First, there are definitional or measurement standards like currency, weights, sizes. Second, there are standards for minimal admissible attributes or minimum quality standards, like safety level or minimal educational requirements in some professions. Finally, there are standards assuring technical compatibility like the physical design of interfaces.

(ii) Comparison of individual product quality with standards or with a grading system. This measuring activity is not always an easy task. The intensity of this problem depends on the characteristics of the product. Three types of product attributes that determine their potential controversial and uncertain nature have been identified in the industrial organization literature: search, experience, and credence.[2] Search attributes are those that the consumer, before purchasing, can check on (for example, color or shape). Experience attributes are difficult to observe in advance but can be ascertained upon consumption (for example, the taste of a fruit). Finally, credence attributes are difficult or impossible to ascertain even after consumption (for example, the effect that consumption of a product has on one's health). Most agrifood products combine experience and/or credence attributes which make asymmetric information a great concern, especially when food safety issues are at stake. This is especially relevant as consumers nowadays have become more sensitive not only to the attributes of products but also to the production process involved. Consumption of the product does not provide any information on the production process itself.

(iii) Facilitating enforcement of the defined quality. The idea is to ensure that once the transaction is performed, parties have

---

[2] See Darby and Karni (1973) and Nelson (1970).

the devices to force the other party to fulfill its commitment at the lowest cost (transaction costs). We explain this in the next section.

3.3 Mitigating measurement issues

One of the major consequences of the "lemon problem" described by Akerlof (1970) is that asymmetric information prevents mutually advantageous transactions from taking place and thus reduces total value. From a Coasean perspective, rational agents therefore have strong incentives to develop safeguard mechanisms to mitigate contractual hazards and exploit all gains from trade. Definition and implementation of these safeguards generate transaction costs which reduce the total exchange surplus. Parties have a mutual interest in mitigating such transaction costs. In this section, we describe and contrast different "families" of institutional solutions for guaranteeing quality in any transaction.

3.3.1 Describing the institutional landscape

In this section, we cover the diversity of institutional solutions used to mitigate the quality measurement problem. We do so by describing various institutional alternatives observed in various agrifood chains along a "public/private" axis. Sorting institutional solutions like this is a simple way to emphasize some of their structural differences. One of these differences is the involvement of the state as a mitigator of the different dimensions of the measurement problem. In our description, "public manufacturing" of quality means the involvement of the "public machinery" in the definition/enforcement of quality. The state is involved in the production of quality mostly through *ex ante* actions like defining the relevant attributes and measurement scales and fixing minimum requirements for using some particular labels or names which have valued reputational capital. The state is also involved in defining and setting a minimum of liability issues to facilitate *ex post* transaction enforcement. This enforcement is also based on state *ex post* actions through the judicial system. "Private manufacturing" mostly relies on a more refined quality definition and on enforcement that loosely relies on the mandatory nature of norms. It requires the use of extralegal mechanisms to induce compliance, including such things as reliance on reputation, third-party verification, and even vertical integration.[3] These two options are just polar forms as there is a variety of mixed or "hybrid" solutions combining properties of polar forms. It is even frequent to find transactions in which different solutions coexist because they are not mutually exclusive categories. For instance, the definition of product quality may rely on voluntary initiatives while enforcement of the specifications may be done through the judicial system. Table 3.1 summarizes the main families of institutional solutions, components of quality, and examples.

3.3.2 "Public ordering" institutional solutions

In most developed countries, national regulations establish the main principles concerning food quality, food safety, and consumer protection. Generally speaking, the state provides both definition of relevant attributes and minimum requirements for them, i.e., devices to assess and meter quality. Such public regulation may also define the product itself or product eligibility to carry a particular "label" or denomination. For instance, the French "baguette" has a regulated definition. Only shops with particular characteristics can call themselves a "bakery" (bread has to be made "in house"), while stores that only heat frozen loaves cannot called themselves bakeries. These regulatory definitions indirectly define a quality ranking, or at least differentiate generic categories. Another issue that is important for our purpose is how information is provided by firms (Rubin, 2000). For instance, the state heavily monitors marketing programs in specific markets in order to avoid confusion on the consumer side.

Regulation also fixes minimum requirements and producer responsibility for not cheating on their promised quality. Although this is a solution defined *ex ante*, it is mostly relevant *ex post* because its aim is to punish firms that have sold defective products. In this sense, it acts as a direct incentive for quality assurance, and seems especially relevant for food safety. In all cases, dedicated public bodies or product liability are the main devices used to enforce minimum requirements.

---

[3] Another form of private ordering is, of course, violence as used for transactions governed by illegal organizations like mafias. While we do not analyze this possibility, it should be stressed that violence, boycott, or embargo are sometimes used in European agrifood sectors, mostly in transactions between farmers and large retailers.

Table 3.1 Manufacturing quality

Components		Institutional solutions		
		Public ordering	"Mixed" ordering	Private ordering
Quality definition (measurement costs)	Disclosure of attributes/ Setting of metering and grading devices	Regulation (e.g., compulsory conservation information, definition of yogurt/baguette)	GI regulation (e.g., months of maturity and % of milk types in a PDO cheese) GI private brand names and GI certification bodies	Brand name-specific attributes (also by private certification brand names), voluntary nutritional information, health-giving properties of functional yogurt drinks
	The action of comparing with standards or grading systems	Regulation (e.g., cost per kg/liter, which is relevant when products are sold in different sizes), the obligation of signing the original price, and the sale price during sales	Classification of GI products according to different standards (the strength of taste in a cheese, the type of feeding of chickens or pigs, etc.)	Brand names, private rankings from brand names or private certifications (e.g., Parker's wine guide)
Enforcing quality (enforcement costs)	Enforcement	Regulation (e.g., the judicial system based on producers' legal responsibility)	GI regulation on monitoring quality (who, how, when) and self-enforcement (e.g., termination at will by the GI regulatory council)	Brand names (e.g., additional responsibility based on self-enforcement)

Note: GI means "Geographical Indicators" which is a catchword to describe situations such as Protected Designation of Origin (PDO) and Protected Geographical Indicator (PGI) (see below for further details).

Most of these regulatory requirements have costs and benefits. Some costs are already well known, as testified by the extensive literature on pressure groups initiated after the work of Stigler (1971). In addition, regulatory error in establishing mandatory standards is also an issue. There is substantial asymmetry amongst the consequences of regulatory errors (laxity or excessive strictness). The risk of laxity can be corrected, at least in part, by the market (by switching decisions to other providers). Moreover, it does not pose obstacles for the use of other types of device, like a private standard, additional warranties, or particular monitoring. For example, infant milk may be sold in any supermarket but several private brands differentiate their product by selling only in pharmacies. The risk of excessive strictness is more difficult to correct: all firms, whatever their quality, are forced to fulfill the mandatory standards, regardless of real demand by consumers (Arruñada, 2000). Finally, any breach of the standard must be verifiable by third parties in order for litigation to be possible, leading to a (potential) legal sanction.

Regulation also has benefits. Barzel (2004) points out that both definitional and minimum quality standards reduce buyers' measurement costs. On the one hand, the definitional standard and the definition of scale make it easier to measure and compare products and, on the other hand, fixing minimum attributes reduces variance in product quality because such attributes truncate the distribution of quality and therefore mitigate the search and measurement costs borne by individual consumers.

3.3.3 *"Private ordering" institutional solutions*

Mandatory regulation on product quality is not the only device used in modern economies to mitigate measurement hazards. Firms spontaneously adopt various standards and organizational patterns with a view to reducing quality hazards. Sellers may offer nonmandatory warranties to consumers. They give the purchaser direct insurance against defaults and help minimize the probability of defects because an extensive warranty may be expensive for the seller if the goods are likely to go wrong (Barzel, 1982).[4]

---

[4] Other devices that enhance the value of reputation in the same way are money-back assurances, free trials, and long-term warranties.

Private systems also include various forms of certifications by a third party. In "markets for certification," individual or collective profit-oriented organizations facilitate and frame the competitive landscape by providing information on quality to consumers, based on private standards.[5] Outsourcing of this monitoring activity to an *independent monitor* aims to give credibility by limiting collusion between the "auditor" and the "auditee."[6] Such voluntary certifications are important in agrifood sectors. Some firms specialize in providing consumers with information about the quality of particular products and/or the reliability of particular firms.[7]

Other firms may also decide to adopt a quality assurance scheme such as International Organization for Standardization (ISO) norms or collective codes of good practices. These schemes are voluntary and are certified by a third party. Another interesting voluntary quality assurance device in the agribusiness sector is the EurepGAP (now GlobalGAP) system founded as an initiative of some of the larger European retailers. EurepGAP members include retailers, producers/farmers, and associate members from the input and service sides of agriculture. The system aims to develop widely accepted standards and procedures for the global certification of "Good Agricultural Practices" (GAP).

Another solution mainly relies on "relational" incentives. Brand name and its related reputation is a canonical example of such a relational agreement (Barzel, 1982; Klein and Leffler, 1981; Shapiro, 1983). Brands act first as cognitive support devices summarizing the definition of quality. Brands' goodwill is also a powerful "self-enforcing" device as emphasized in the seminal contribution by Klein and Leffler (1981). The fear of losing the consumer's patronage and the corresponding

---

[5] Some practices that were originally voluntary may become compulsory if moral hazard is an increasing concern or if they become the norm in the industry. One example is auditing, which today is mandatory for firms of a certain size.

[6] There is extensive industrial organization literature on issues such as the revelation of information by certifiers (sometimes called middlemen), the welfare implications of provision of information on quality by a third-party certifier, and so on (see, for instance, Biglaiser and Friedman, 1994 and Fernández-Barcala et al., 2010). Recent controversies about the role of rating agencies in the financial crisis remind us that this issue is still under debate.

[7] For instance, in the wine sector, Robert Parker's guide is an important source of information for consumers with little knowledge of wine quality. The Michelin guide is another example.

loss of reputation make the promise on quality transmitted by the brand name credible without any third-party intervention. However, the ability of reputation-based mechanisms to safeguard quality is limited. The price premium necessary to provide sellers with the correct incentives increases with the lag between two transactions and the time needed to discover the "true" attributes (Klein and Leffler, 1981; Shapiro, 1983). Similarly, if most of the relevant quality attributes of a product are credence attributes, the necessary price premium may be too large. In other words, the greater the quality measurement problem, the higher the reputational capital must be. Furthermore, if competition among firms increases, the necessary price premium may become difficult to sustain.

The last "private" solution to measurement issues is integration (Barzel, 1982). The idea is that if only one party is involved, there is no interest conflict and therefore no opportunism. In business-to-consumer transactions, this takes the form of "home or self-production" by consumers. In business-to-business transactions, it takes the form of vertical integration. There is a trade-off here between the mitigation of the measurement problem and gains from specialization. As all stages of the production process are carried out by the same entity, it is not necessary to measure the product. This saves on transaction costs but comes at the cost of losing specialization and economies of scale. Stigler (1951) argues that specialization is determined by the size of the market and internal transaction sizes are usually smaller than in market transactions (Williamson, 1985).

3.3.4 *"Hybrid" solutions mixing public and private components*

This last family of institutional solutions is probably the most complex to describe and study because it is not always easy to draw a sharp line between this family and the two polar cases. There are two common factors among the examples we will describe. First, the definition of quality largely has a private nature above some minimum mandatory requirement. Second, enforcement relies heavily on the introduction of a third (or external) party as the main enforcer of quality. We briefly describe the example of "Geographical Indicators" (GI). "Geographical Indicators" is a catchword to describe situations where a group of firms in the supply chain both rely on a common quality label related with a geographical area and are involved in a collective organization managing the brand (called a "regulatory council"). It is nowadays one of the prominent quality brands used in various EU agricultural sectors and for various products (wine, cheese, meat, etc.).[8] From a legal point of view, GIs were established at the European Union level in 1992, when it created the systems known as Protected Designation of Origin (PDO) and Protected Geographical Indicator (PGI) to promote and protect food products (regulation EEC 2081/92 of July 1992).[9] The European regulation on PDO products is similar to a trademark registration that protects property rights on brand names (here geographical names).[10]

The EU's GI system is structured around three types of participant: firms involved in the production process, local or national regulators, and inspection agencies. Firms that take part directly in the production process and want to create and promote a GI need approval by the local or national regulator. As real owners of the GI, local or national governments delegate to the "regulatory council" the task of running the GI, namely drafting the quality specification, promoting the GI, enforcing the rules which are agreed on collectively. This council is made of up representatives of each step of the supply chain (farmers, processors). Authorization is conditional on fulfillment of certain requirements, which focus mainly on the definition of the geographical limits of the designation, technical and health aspects of production, evidence on the connections between the characteristics of the final product and some characteristics of the local area (like specific soil condition, traditional know-how, etc.), and finally on strict control of the products to be labeled with the GI. Members of the GI have to nominate a public or private inspection body that will certify the quality requirements for the production process. These inspection bodies must be registered and authorized by national and EU regulators. After acceptance by regulators, the group of firms can use the

[8] Today, around 1,000 products rely on GI and many more are pending registration.
[9] Some European countries like France and Italy already have a long tradition of geographical designation. Moschini et al. (2008) provided a more detailed presentation of the GI institutional framework.
[10] A PDO covers the term used to describe foodstuffs that are produced, prepared, and processed in a given geographical area using recognized know-how. In the case of the PGI, the geographical link must occur in at least one of the stages of production, processing, or preparation.

label and benefits of the legal framework. It is quite common to have the final products carrying several labels, for instance the name of the GI as well as the name or brand of the processor.

3.4 Interactions among solutions: complements or substitutes?

Up to now, we have focused on describing the "institutional landscape" related to the manufacturing of quality. We now look at the interactions among the various institutional solutions. Do we need private solutions when public ones are available and run smoothly? Is there any benefit from the coexistence of different solutions? The point is that we actually do observe all the described solutions at any given time and for the same types of products. What we suggest is that these institutional solutions both substitute and complement each other. This is very similar in spirit to the analysis of the interactions between formal and informal (or relational) contracts provided by Klein (1996).[11] The mere presence of public solutions provides support for private-based solutions. But, at the same time, what is done at the public level probably does not need to be replicated by private solutions. The rest of this section illustrates these interactions among institutional solutions.

The substitution effect is based on the idea that all institutional solutions aim to solve the same measurement problem. Given that all these devices yield transaction costs, it is enough for a single one of them to work properly. For example, given that regulations do not allow sales of meat products that have not been slaughtered in an authorized slaughterhouse, no meat retailers inform consumers that all mandatory hygiene requirements have been complied with during slaughter. Such a notification would be costly and would not add any

---

[11] This analysis illustrates a fundamental complementarity between court-enforcement and self-enforcement. The two enforcement mechanisms are substitutes in demand in the sense of a positive cross elasticity of demand, so that an increase in the price of one of the mechanisms leads to an increased use of the other mechanisms ... But the two enforcement mechanisms are complements in supply, in the sense of a positive cross elasticity of supply, so that an increase, for example in the quantity of reputational capital, leads to an increase in the marginal productivity of court-enforcement. That is, the two mechanisms work better together than either of them do separately. (Klein, 2000, p. 75)

value because consumers can be expected to be informed about the regulations.

The "complement" perspective, on the other hand, emphasizes the benefits of simultaneously relying on formal/public and informal/private arrangements. From this perspective, the mere presence of, for instance, public solutions enhances the benefits of relying on private ones. These have been described by Aoki (2001) as situations of institutional complementarities. While it is outside the scope of this chapter to provide an extensive analysis of such complementarity, we provide several examples.

On the one hand, the efficiency of private brands as quality safeguards extensively relies on public institutional support. For instance, intellectual property rights and trademark laws are critical "support" factors for brand names. They provide incentives to invest in such intangible assets because they reduce the likelihood of falsification and insure brand owners against exploitation. Similarly, the mere existence of public quality standards may make reputation-based solutions more effective. For some attributes, such as food safety, it is difficult to know, even *ex post*, whether the product is safe or not. Relying on public control/standardization for safety attributes mitigates the weaknesses of the reputation system.[12] The brand name will not inform consumers that the firm's reputation backs its product attributes, but firms will communicate their performance in public controls.

We described some examples of public solutions supporting private ones. The interaction, however, probably runs both ways in that private solutions may also help to improve public solutions.[13] This is particularly important when product attributes are costly to measure and consequently the transaction creates a quality query. Given that not all attributes are equally relevant for all consumers because of their personal taste, preferences, and/or information, regulation hardly affects the more exclusive, or select, attributes. Following the traditional argument from regulation economics, norms will only be approved if

---

[12] The emergence of global safety standards initiated, among others, by large retailers is an example of safety hazards dealt with by intermediate or mixed governance. These standards have a collective and voluntary basis, stating the minimum safety requirements that suppliers (worldwide) must respect in order to sell to (mostly) European large retailers.
[13] In some cases, private initiatives may even try to bypass public rules if private actors feel that public solutions are inappropriate and/or corrupt.

a large number of persons lobby politicians. So mandatory norms will only apply to attributes that are "minimum requisites" for a majority of consumers, not to sophisticated attributes which are only valued by a small minority. Private ordering mechanisms quickly fill the gap, emphasizing more fine-grained attributes. Advertising does not need to explain all (generic) attributes but only the *incremental*, most brand-specific attributes. Furthermore, like most public institutions, public standards are slow to evolve and there is quite often a gap between compulsory criteria and the evolving needs of private actors. One way to reduce this gap is to empower private actors to participate in the drafting of quality regulations. This is quite often described as "regulatory capture" in the economic literature. While this literature (rightly) emphasizes the danger of having a regulatory design partly driven by private interests, involvement by the private sector might also offer some benefits. Bringing the private sector into the "regulatory game" may reduce possible maladjustment of public rules.[14] The point is that the enhancement of initial public regulation may heavily rely on feedback from the private sector.

3.5 Matching quality dimensions with institutional solutions

One of the great strengths of the TCE "governance branch" has been its capacity to provide empirically testable propositions. The most famous is the "alignment principle" linking transactional attributes to alternative governance structures (Williamson, 1985). Although progress has been made in generating and testing the empirical predictions of the measurement branch, in particular to explain payment schemes (see, for instance, Leffler and Rucker, 1991; Leffler et al., 2000), it is fair to say that many things remain to be done in order to reach a significant amount of empirical confirmations. Quality concerns or problems are an example because the literature about this topic is rather scarce. We attempt to match quality measurement hazards with the institutional solutions described in Section 3.3. However, this should

---

[14] This point is emphasized in the literature on self-regulation. One of the advantages of self-regulation vis-à-vis public regulation lies in firms' superior knowledge of the regulatory issue at stake and the related lower transaction costs of the self-regulatory process (see Grajzl and Murrell, 2007, for more on this).

be considered just as a preliminary theoretical reflection requiring empirical validation.

Two preliminary considerations are relevant here. First, standard industrial organization describes the differing intensity of the quality measurement problem by disentangling search, experience, and credence *products*: The harder it is to *ex ante* easily assess product quality, the larger the measurement problem. However, Barzel's work suggests focusing on the *attribute* level instead of the product level. Consumers consider a variety of attributes in each product and the severity of the measurement problem depends on these attributes. For instance, the appearance of a tomato (a simple attribute valued by consumers) does not give us too much information on its organoleptic attributes nor on its production process (for instance, organic or not, which has become a relevant attribute for many consumers). The direct consequence is that we cannot state that the quality of a particular product is better managed by a particular institutional solution. Rather, *certain attributes* are probably better guaranteed in a transaction using certain institutional solutions. Second, this shift in the unit of analysis (from the products to the attributes) has a consequence for any attempt to match or align quality measurement problems with institutional solutions. Given that all products are made of various attributes, multiple institutional solutions coexist most of the time for a given good because, as Table 3.1 shows, manufacturing quality requires solving both measurement and enforcement problems and there exist particular devices which are more appropriate for solving each type of problem. Taking the product globally, all these institutional solutions complement each other and are probably partially specialized. For instance, while the definition of quality might be governed easily by private agreements, its enforcement might rely more frequently on public institutions. This is this "division of tasks" that we now briefly explore by first analyzing the definition of quality and then looking at its enforcement.

On the quality definition side, we argue that private ordering is more effective for *detecting* relevant attributes (i.e., attributes that some consumers are ready to pay for) but public ordering is more effective for *setting* standards and definitions (i.e., fixing the requirements for each category, concept, or definition). To put it differently, thanks to the incentives provided by the price system, private initiatives are good at discovering new combinations of relevant attributes for some segments of consumers. We have to note that consumers' preferences evolve quickly and not all attributes are equally relevant for all of them. This means that a continuous effort is needed to disclose to the market these "new" attributes. For instance, some consumers now base their purchasing decisions on firms' operating practices like fair trade or organic production. Firms are more able to discover them in order to gain (temporary) competitive advantages. Private brands may even be interested in comparing themselves with rivals to differentiate their products, thus *initiating* comparison (second level in Table 3.1).

However, public institutions are needed to "institutionalize" some of these definition and comparisons, i.e., to provide them on a larger scale. As time goes by and the economic volume of transactions increases, these definitions, scales, standards, and concepts become relevant for a substantial part of the consumers and arouse interest in the regulators in standardizing them.[15] The unquestionable advantage of such regulation is the individual measurement cost saving because the diversity of concepts and measurements may raise opportunism and the individual need to protect transactions by investing in measuring. Regulation reduces this type of transaction costs and facilitates exchanges. There are however two risks related with public involvement: one, when choosing among alternatives (i.e., the coexistence of several definitions for the same product as for example the definition of yogurt)[16] and, two, when fixing arbitrary reference levels (e.g., percentage of cacao for a product to be considered "chocolate"). Regarding the former risk, one consequence of this multiplicity of definitions is that consumers remain uncertain about some critical attributes. Given that there is no

---

[15] The example of organic food regulation in France is interesting in that respect. Organic production initially emerged as a "private initiative" promoted by both consumer and producer "activists" without any public involvement. When the market share of organic products reaches a certain size, several definitions of what an organic product should be coexist, some being more stringent than others. Many agents involved in the production of organic food thus called for a public definition of organic product.

[16] Yogurt definition is controversial. The World Health Organization's recommendation that fermented, pasteurized dairy products should not be accepted under the heading of "yogurt" is accepted by many countries worldwide but is rejected by the Spanish government: see for instance www.elpais.com/articulo/sociedad/ONU/rechaza/nombre/yogur/postre/lacteo/pasteurizado/elpepisoc/20030704elpepisoc_3/Tes/, accessed July 19, 2010.

guarantee that the solution chosen by the regulator is correct, it seems clearly preferable to have lax regulation, focusing on how to compare and offering tools to reduce measurement costs. In the example of the yogurt definition, the relevant point is to inform the consumers about the pros and cons of pasteurizing the fermented milk instead of just forbidding the use of the name "yogurt" in these products. Regarding the latter risk, we have already argued that regulation laxity is better than strictness because its errors can be partially corrected by private ordering (e.g., private brands using rich compositions of cacao in their chocolates may clearly advertise this aspect). Conversely, excessively strict regulation might crowd out transactions which might be profitable for the parties.

The other problem regarding manufacturing quality is the enforcement of the quality definition. Barzel (2004) suggests that the enforcement of quality aspects or attributes that are relatively easy to monitor directly can be more cheaply reached through explicit specifications like public standardization (e.g., measuring the volume of the container, the weight of the packaging, or the minimum percentage of cacao in the chocolate). Other attributes that are more difficult to contractually define (such as the health-giving properties of functional yogurt drinks) are more cheaply enforced through implicit arrangements among parties that rely heavily on self-enforcement (our private-ordering solutions). Three arguments can, at least, support this assertion. First, the law and judicial systems facilitate legal enforcement of transaction commitments, particularly when quality is easily measured and verifiable. In other circumstances, such systems are not particularly efficient. One reason is that the court will lack the specialized knowledge and industry expertise that is needed to accurately assess products' quality. This is one of the key aspects emphasized by Bernstein (2001) when she tries to explain why most transactions in the US cotton industry are governed by a body of "private law" despite the existence of a well-defined legal system.[17] It is therefore more efficient to rely on private ordering in which compliance is ensured by self-enforcement, either by a party's brand name (Danone) or by a public (GI) or private third party (Max Havelaar logo or GlobalGAP)

---

[17] According to her interviews with business people in this industry, cotton grading is a very subjective process in which many factors are involved. Expert knowledge seems very important.

How to manufacture quality   55

which certify that one party has complied.[18] Second, public solutions are probably too expensive and ineffective to enforce transactions that involve only small dollar amounts and are very time-sensitive (Richman, 2004). Fresh fish and most fruits and vegetables are good examples of those types of products which are highly perishable. If public courts are slow in handling and resolving disputes about quality, private contractors will not find it economical to rely on public courts to enforce their deals. Finally, we can argue that what is easily measurable is easy to standardize. Standardization of quality operates mostly on a large scale, when the volume of transactions is high. Dixit (2004) argued that public ordering systems are characterized by high fixed costs but low marginal costs of enforcement while private orders have opposite characteristics. Once the volume of transactions reaches a certain level, it is cheaper to rely on public systems because of lower marginal costs of enforcement. As easy to measure quality attributes are prevalent in many transactions, they should be enforced through public ordering.

3.6 Conclusions

We have surveyed and analyzed how various institutions solve, or at least mitigate, the information asymmetry about quality and related measurement costs. First, we highlight that both quality definition (defining attributes and scales and comparing with standards) and quality enforcement are key factors in this process of "manufacturing quality." Second, we show that the economic literature has traditionally considered two ways to solve the informational asymmetry problem. First, the noninformed party should invest resources in obtaining any hidden information (measurement costs). Apart from direct consumer observation and supervision, the most important mechanisms are certification and standardization, such as ISO certifications or rating companies. The second solution relies on an alignment of parties' interests in such a way that a well-informed party has no incentive to take advantage of its better knowledge. Credible signaling through, for example, brand names is probably the main safeguard.

---

[18] The Max Havelaar logo is a private certification which offers consumers fair trade guarantees, so is a credence attribute and avoids high measurement costs. The GlobalGAP system described above is another illustration of a (worldwide) private certification system.

Real problems regarding quality require a complex combination of both types of solution because products comprise various attributes and the severity of measurement problems varies among attributes. We disentangle and classify alternative families of institutional solutions: public ordering, private ordering, and hybrid solutions. We then describe the interactions between these various solutions claiming that they substitute and complement each other in guaranteeing product attributes in exchanges. If one of these devices is absent or not effective (e.g., a low requirement of cacao for using the denomination of "chocolate"), actors may initiate other individual (advertising richer compositions) or collective solutions to handle the problem at stake. On the other hand, private solutions such as branding depend heavily on public institutions such as trademark law.

We end this chapter with some predictions as to which institutional solutions are most effective for dealing with the particular problems involved in manufacturing quality. We suggest that private ordering is more effective for *detecting* attributes, measures, and scales (because of the high-powered incentives of the price system) but that public ordering is more effective for *setting* standards and definitions (because of the economies of scale), particularly when quality is relatively easy to define *ex ante* and to verify. Conversely, if quality is difficult to verify, it is more efficient to rely on private ordering in which compliance is ensured by self-enforcement. Finally, when several alternatives coexist in the market, it is preferable to have lax regulation, focusing on informing parties about how to compare and offering tools to reduce measurement costs.

The complementarity/substitutability among alternative solutions has important implications for regulatory design and policy makers. Let us describe two of them. First, designing effective quality regulation is a complex issue because of important interactions among various regulatory instruments. When deciding to rely on a particular regulatory instrument, the regulator must take into account not only the direct effects of this instrument but also the range of indirect consequences the decision will have. Any other devices that have a complementary relationship with the targeted one will be affected. For instance, let us assume that there is a complementary relation between the credibility of GIs and certain vertical restraints (e.g., price fixing, control of supply, exclusive territories) within a supply chain. Such vertical restraints might be a tool to create and share the rents of a good reputation among firms and thus act as an incentive to produce high quality (Kranton, 2003). The regulator may decide to ban such contractual restraints because it fears that this might be used as a strategic tool to reduce competition. By preventing firms from using such a provision, the regulation might increase the costs of monitoring quality along the chain, threatening the sustainability of GIs as quality assurance for consumers.

Second, it is possible, for the same reasons, that in order to reach a given target, the regulator will strategically use the substitution among various instruments. For instance, the regulator might want to improve the health of the population by decreasing the consumption of "junk food." Banning this activity is an option, although an unpopular one. Taxing junk food is the most evident option the regulator has. This may well be strongly opposed both by food sector firms and some consumers concerned about the increase in price. Other regulatory options might be to increase the informational content of labeling by explicitly stressing the negative health effects of such products or to run public campaigns to promote healthy food. The important point is that the regulator can try to bypass direct opposition by relying on an instrument that substitutes the one it cannot use in order to reach a particular target.

4 | The law of impersonal transactions

BENITO ARRUÑADA

4.1 Introduction

This chapter develops a theory of the institutions supporting impersonal transactions by publicly registering private contracts. It sees contract registration as a public intervention on private contracts that allows judges to apply market-friendly rules when adjudicating disputes over subsequent contracts ex post. This solution protects innocent third parties and thus obviates the information asymmetry that they suffer when entering into such subsequent contracts. In so doing, it facilitates impersonal market transactions.

The starting points for the analysis are sequential exchanges in which, first, one or several "principals" – owners, employers, shareholders, creditors, etc. – voluntarily contract with one or several "agents" – possessors, employees, company directors, and managers – in an "originative" transaction; and, second, the agent then contracts "subsequent" transactions with third parties.[1] Sequential exchanges

This chapter draws on arguments presented in greater depth in Arruñada (2012). I thank Eshien Chong, Ricard Gil, Henry Hansmann, P. J. Hill, Fernando Gómez-Pomar, Fernando Méndez, Henry Smith, John Wallis, Giorgio Zanarone, and participants at several workshops and conferences for their comments. The usual disclaimers apply. This study received financial support from the European Commission and the Spanish Ministry of the Economy, through projects CIT3-513420 and ECO2011-29445.

[1] Using an agency conceptual framework allows me to pose the theory in general terms, encompassing both business and property transactions. This agency structure is clearer in company registries than in property registries because, for property, which party plays the role of agent or of principal depends on the type of fraud. But the agency structure is also present in all property transactions. This becomes clear when we observe, for instance, that in a second sale the seller is acting as an "agent" for the first buyer, even if this use of the agency concept is unconventional in legal terms, as the first buyer does not intend the seller to act in this capacity and the seller does not portray herself as an agent of the buyer.

The law of impersonal transactions 59

are needed to obtain the benefits of specialization in the tasks of principals and agents: between landowners and farmers, employers and employees, shareholders and managers, etc. However, they give rise to substantial transaction costs, because third parties suffer information asymmetry with respect to the previous originative contract. In particular, third parties are often unaware if they are dealing with a principal or an agent, or if the agent has sufficient title or legal power to commit the principal. This constitutes a grave impediment, especially for impersonal transactions.

Moreover, principals also face a serious commitment problem when trying to contain this asymmetry because their incentives change after the third party has entered the subsequent contract. Before contracting, principals have an interest in third parties being convinced that agents have proper authority but, if the business turns out badly, principals will be inclined to deny such authority. This is why the typical dispute triggered by sequential transactions is one in which the principal tries to elude obligations committed by the agent in the principal's name, whether the agent had legal authority or not.

The law can adjudicate in such disputes in favor of the principal or the third party. Favoring the third party will be referred to here as enforcing "contract rules," as opposed to the seemingly more natural "property rules" which favor the principal. The terms "property rule" and "contract rule" echo the property and contract rights that the original owner retains in each case.[2] Their effects are clear. Take the simple case in which an agent exceeds his legal powers when selling a good to an innocent third party (that is, a good-faith party who is uninformed

---

[2] These rules are similar but distinct from the "property" and "liability" rules defined in a classic work by Calabresi and Melamed (1972) because here the rules are defined in the context of a three-party sequence of two transactions instead of a taking affecting only two parties. Moreover, my analysis focuses on the role played by the parties in each transaction, disregarding that current third parties will often act as principals in a future sequence of transactions. Consequently, when good-faith third parties win a dispute over their acquisitive transaction (i.e., when they are given a property right), they do not win as a consequence of applying a property rule, which – by definition – would have given the good to the original owner. In such a case, the third party does not pay any monetary damages to the original owner, as in Calabresi and Melamed's liability rule. Moreover, Calabresi and Melamed's property rule is weaker, referring only to the ability to force a would-be taker to bargain for a consensual transfer similar to specific performance, and thus arguably has little to do with a right *in rem* (Merrill and Smith 2001a).

about the matter in question). Applying the "property rule" that no one can transfer what he does not have, the sold good returns to the principal (the "original owner") and the third party (supposed here to be a "good faith purchaser for value") wins a mere claim against the agent. This will maximize property enforcement – the owner held a right *in rem* so his right is not damaged without his consent[3] – but will worsen the information asymmetry suffered by all potential third parties with respect to legal title. Conversely, the law can apply an indemnity or "contract rule" so that the sold good stays with the third party and the principal only wins a claim against the agent. This will then minimize information asymmetry for potential third parties but will also weaken property enforcement.

In principle, the choice of rule involves a tricky trade-off between property enforcement and transaction costs. On the one hand, enforcing contract rules obviates the information asymmetry usually suffered by third parties and encourages them to trade. It thus transforms the object of complex transactions into legal commodities that can be traded easily, thus extending the type of impersonal transaction that characterizes modern markets. On the other hand, enforcing contract rules dilutes the principals' property rights, endangering investment and specialization in the tasks of principals and agents.

To overcome this trade-off between property *in rem* enforcement and transaction costs, expanding the set of viable contractual opportunities without damaging property rights, the law tends to apply contract rules, but allowing principals to opt for property rules when they make their choice public. Principals can produce this publicity by various means, such as keeping possession of movable assets or filing their claims to immovables in a public registry. This way, when principals opt for a property rule, their rights become safer while, thanks to publicity, third parties will suffer little information asymmetry. Similarly, when principals choose a contract rule, third parties' rights are safe while principals' rights are weaker. But this weakening of property is limited since principals choose the agent who, for instance, they entrust with possession or appoint as their representative, this being the moment when they implicitly "choose" a contract rule.

---

[3] See Merrill and Smith (2001b: 780–789). Note that the economic literature often uses a broader concept of "property rights" that includes both property and contract rights.

The smooth operation of this switching of rules poses varying degrees of difficulty for different transactions. The difficulty is minor when the originative contract inevitably produces verifiable facts, such as the physical possession of movable goods or the ordinary activity of an employee. For these cases, judges can base their decisions on this public information, which is produced informally. Conversely, greater difficulty arises when the originative contract produces less verifiable facts, making this "informal" solution harder to apply. Such an informal solution may even be impossible if the contract remains hidden and its consequences are not observable. Consider, for example, the difficulties for clearly establishing by purely private contract the existence of a corporation, distinguishing the corporation's assets from the personal assets of its shareholders.

In such contexts of harder verifiability, it helps to enter and preserve at least some information on the originative contract in a public registry. Registration is costly so is not universally efficient, especially in situations of low demand for impersonal exchange, and it requires independence and public access. First, to prevent interested manipulation and thus provide verifiability, the registration process necessarily has to be independent of all the parties involved, including parties to the originative contract. (This requirement of independence makes registration wholly different from documentary formalization, which is designed to safeguard the relation between parties to the same contract.) Second, at least the key features of the originative contract need to be made available to the public or at least to potential third parties, so that they can know beforehand which rules are applicable to any subsequent contracts. In essence, registration becomes the means to make the voluntary choice of market-enabling contract rules verifiable by courts and therefore commits principals to their choices.

The analysis is close to several theories of property – meaning, *in rem* – rights, such as, mainly, Hansmann and Kraakman (2000, 2002), Merrill and Smith (2000), and Arruñada (2003). It departs from part of the previous literature (e.g., Medina 2003; Armour and Whincop 2007) by focusing on the cases and solutions that are prevalent in the population of transactions instead of those most represented in the litigated sample. Its main goal is to explain the role of institutions in modifying the problem's information structure, with the intention of reaching global optimality. It pays relatively little attention to how parties' incentives and costs drive the local optimality of alternative rules, which is the main line in most analyses of exceptions in this area.

The rest of this chapter proceeds as follows. Section 4.2 clarifies the nature of impersonal exchange. Section 4.3 introduces the main concepts used in the analysis: single and sequential exchange, and originative and subsequent transactions. Section 4.4 points out the importance of sequential exchange for specialization and examines a representative sample of sequential exchanges in business and real property. Section 4.5 identifies the nature of the title problem present at the core of all these exchanges and the solutions that are applied to solve it. Lastly, Section 4.6 explores the difficulties involved in developing these institutional solutions, which are attributed to historical path dependency – the law first developed to support personal exchanges; sunk costs by jurists, who often keep thinking in terms of personal transactions; and the vested interests of law professionals, who in this area are often able to prevail over relatively weak public bureaucracies.

4.2 The nature of impersonal exchange

Modern economies prosper on the basis of specialization and trade. More specialized resources and firms are more productive, but this greater specialization only makes sense when producers can sell their production in a larger market. Specialization and, therefore, economic growth becomes more feasible when trade goes beyond the personal circle of known people. By expanding the market, impersonal exchange opens all sorts of new specialization opportunities which are essential to economic growth.[4]

However, in most economic exchanges, contractual performance is based on personal characteristics of the parties, such as their wealth, solvency, and reputation. First, most trade between parties who know each other is clearly personal as it relies on their mutual knowledge and expectations of their future trade. Similarly, much of the trade with strangers also requires gathering information to know which performance assurances – for instance, reputation – they offer; so it is also personal.

---

[4] See mainly North and Thomas (1973), Hayek (1982), Granovetter (1985), North (1990), and Seabright (2004).

Second, trade also retains key personal elements when performance assurances are not produced by the parties themselves but by specialized assurance intermediaries, such as financial institutions or rating agencies. In such cases, trade remains personal to the extent that it is based on the reputation of the intermediaries and their knowledge of their clients. Similarly, trade is also personal under community responsibility systems, when all members of a group (for instance, all merchants of a particular city in late medieval times) are liable for the behavior and contractual obligations of each of its members (Greif 2002, 2006a). Such a system allows strangers to trade with group members on the basis of limited personal information, just enough for them to unambiguously know which individuals are members of which groups and which groups are dependable. Moreover, it also requires personal monitoring within each group. Both assurance intermediaries and community responsibility therefore make transactions more impersonal but still retain important personal attributes.

Lastly, trade is often considered to be impersonal when parties can solve their conflicts before an independent judge (e.g., North 1990: 34–35; 1991). However, this reliance only reduces the amount of personal information required for transacting, as parties still need to ascertain at least how solvent their obliged counterparties are. Even with perfect judges, creditors must worry about how likely it is that their debtors might become judgment proof. Insolvency carries little stigma today but even in old times, when insolvent debtors ended up in prison, jailing them must have provided little joy to their creditors. Therefore, as in the previous cases, judicial enforcement still depends on personal attributes, and judicially supported trade still remains substantially personal in nature.

To the extent that personal attributes are present in all these cases, parties must spend resources on developing personal guarantees and producing knowledge about them. Also, to the extent that such guarantees remain weak, contractual enforcement is unreliable, prone to conflict, and thus costly. Lastly, where there is a risk of contractual default, parties withdraw and waste trade opportunities. Therefore, relying on personal exchange precludes profitable exchanges between unknown parties and limits specialization opportunities and efficient reallocation of resources, hindering economic growth.

To expand the scope of transactions and exploit the benefits of comparative advantage more fully, parties must be able to trade without any knowledge of their respective characteristics, which requires making contractual performance independent of such characteristics. This greatly simplifies the parties' information problem but it can be achieved only by defining rights in respect of assets instead of persons. Furthermore, several caveats are in order. First, defining rights directly on assets makes trade harder because they survive any trade unless the rightholder consents to the trade. Second, this characterization in terms of assets is superficially inexact for some business transactions in which no real assets are involved, as we will see below. Yet the substance of the case is the same to the extent that the nature of rights hinges on the actions available to the rightholder to enforce them. Third, impartial judicial enforcement is a necessary but insufficient condition for this fully asset-based impersonal exchange. Given that, to be secured, rights on assets have to be respected by everyone, they require some sort of public or judicial enforcement, which is therefore a necessary condition. But this is not sufficient in itself because, without some form of registration, judges would have a hard time applying efficient rules, as we will see shortly.

4.3 The information structure of single and sequential exchange

Judges solve two main types of conflict, which correspond to two different exchange structures – single and sequential exchanges. Single exchange involves two or more parties in only one transaction – for instance, a principal and an agent who will provide services to the principal. Sequential exchange additionally involves in a subsequent transaction at least a third party to the originative transaction – some other person who now contracts with the agent. Both exchanges pose different problems of information asymmetry.

Information asymmetry in single exchange is well represented by Akerlof's (1970) market for "lemons," in which the owner of a used car is trying to sell it. Prospective buyers are reluctant to buy because, given that owners know the quality of their own car better, used cars on sale tend to be those of poorer quality. This information asymmetry with respect to material quality poses a serious threat to trade, and parties must dedicate plenty of resources to produce information and provide all sorts of quality assurances. Many of these solutions may be implemented by parties alone by, for instance, verifying quality

The law of impersonal transactions 65

and investing in reputation. They can also rely on a judge to complete and enforce the contract. In particular, to overcome the information asymmetry about quality, parties may specify in the contract the car's expected level of performance. Also, the seller can guarantee a minimum level of quality, promise to pay future repairs, or give back part of the selling price in case of a major breakdown. Specifying and verifying these relevant dimensions of performance would be costly. For instance, parties would have to write them down and keep a copy of the contract for future use. If contract obligations are not fulfilled, the aggrieved party could call on the judge to enforce the contract, using it as a source of primary evidence for the judge's decision.

An aspect of this single-exchange "lemons" example illustrates the information asymmetry problem posed by sequential exchange. How does the buyer know that the seller is really the owner or, in general, has legal power to sell the car? If he does not have such power, the buyer faces the loss of the full purchase price. Therefore, this information asymmetry about what I am referring to as legal "title" (about the prior originative transaction between the previous owner and the current seller) may be even more serious than that about material quality, which most often only causes a partial loss. It is also harder to solve by parties alone because, however much title examiners strive to clarify title, title evidence may remain hidden in the absence of registries. And developing registries faces a collective action problem whose solution exceeds the power of individual parties.

The task of the judge is also harder and more critical. Harder because the judge must decide based on the originative contract between the principal-owner and the agent-seller, which they can easily manipulate, especially when it is not available to the third-party-acquirer. More critical because, instead of simply solving a conflict between the parties to the contract, by comparing actual and promised performance, the judge now has to adjudicate the car to one of the two claimants – the previous owner and the buyer – granting the losing party a mere claim for indemnity against the seller. In fact, cases of title conflict start because such a claim is much less valuable than its alternative or is unenforceable.

The gap in value explains that the effect of this type of judicial decision is substantial. Expectations about how similar cases will be decided define the incentives of all parties potentially involved with this type of asset and transaction to invest, trade, and specialize. Potential buyers will be more reluctant to purchase if they think judges will rule for the owner (that is, if judges apply a property rule and assign the asset to the owner); and owners will be less willing to invest if they think judges will rule for the buyer (if, applying a contract rule, judges assign the asset to the buyer). Both will also take more precautions in case judges rule against them: buyers will investigate title more and will prefer to contract with people they know. Consequently, there will be less impersonal exchange. Similarly, owners will be more careful about choosing agents and, when possible, will prefer those they know personally or who, more generally, offer good personal guarantees. Owners' attempts to avoid putting themselves in a position where they may risk being dispossessed will hinder specialization: owners will contract more directly instead of using intermediaries, given that it is separation of ownership and control that creates such a risk. Furthermore, many of these effects impose invisible costs in terms of lost trade opportunities, especially but by no means only in less developed economies.

All these effects mean that judicial decisions on sequential exchange cases exert a major effect on economic activity. It is therefore crucial to optimize them, so they must be applied selectively, on the basis of reliable contractual evidence. The rest of the chapter presents a general theory of the institutions used to produce such evidence: contractual registries. Their function is, in essence, to provide reliable evidence for judicial decisions when such evidence is not readily available as a by-product of the contracting and productive processes. Using this evidence, judges can decide litigated cases by applying rules that favor innocent uninformed parties, which should encourage them to trade impersonally, and, in turn, encourage all participants to specialize. Furthermore, such evidence allows judges to apply such rules efficiently, without damaging property rights.

The next step in our analysis clarifies the differences between single and sequential exchange and explains why sequential exchange is essential for economic specialization.

4.4 The prevalence of sequential exchange

The scope of single exchange is severely limited because most specialization necessarily involves sequential exchange – both originative and subsequent transactions. This is mainly so when one of the parties to the contract is the agent of someone else. Furthermore, even simple transfers of durable assets implicitly involve originative transactions in the form of previous transfers and principals in the form of alternative claimants – e.g., potential legal owners and, in general, any potential claimants of other rights on the asset. Most exchange thus involves several parties in a sequence of transactions, because of the desire of economic participants to reach specialization advantages and the chain of asset transfers. As a minimum, exchanges therefore involve at least three parties in a sequence of at least two transactions.

Sequential exchange encompasses specialization in the tasks performed by principal and agent, including all types of delegation and separation of ownership and control – e.g., between shareholders and managers, owners and possessors, mortgagors and mortgagees, etc. This specialization creates new transaction costs, driven mainly by the risks that the agent may lack or exceed the powers to commit the principal or that either the owners or the third-party acquirers may be dispossessed or deceived. These acquiring third parties now suffer much greater information asymmetry than if there was only uncertainty about the good's material quality. This information asymmetry about the agent's legal title or power to contract needs to be overcome for impersonal markets to function properly.

Let us now examine a representative sample of business and property transactions in different markets, to observe how they differ from single exchange, how they are present in most markets, what they have in common, and how they differ from each other.

Perhaps the simplest sequential exchange is one in which a producer relies on a distributor to sell its products to the distributor's customers. First, an originative transaction takes place between the producer and the distributor and then a subsequent transaction happens between the distributor and the customer. This arrangement achieves specialization advantages because using distributors allows producers to focus on production and to reach a larger market. In turn, distributors can focus better on distribution, sell a wider set of products, and be closer to their customers.

But it also causes transaction costs. Customers are generally unaware of the quality of the seller's legal title. Ideally, in case of a dispute (arising, for instance, from default of payment by the distributor to the producer), they would like the judge to decide that the good remains with the customer and the producer gets only a claim for indemnity against the distributor. This is probably a sensible solution if the producer has chosen the distributor voluntarily, especially if both the producer and the distributor are professionals repeatedly playing this game. Producers will then have good incentives to choose reliable distributors, and distributors will have good incentives to develop proper safeguards.

Our second case is equally simple: in an employment relation we have an originative transaction by which an employer hires an employee, leading to subsequent transactions in which the employee interacts with a third party. This third party should worry about the power of the employee to commit the employer, and how the judge will decide when the employee exceeds such power. For similar reasons to the previous case, it will be reasonable for the judge to protect the third party. The rationale, as before, is that employers are the ones freely choosing and controlling employees.

In these two cases, the judge has little difficulty verifying that both the producer and the employer had consented to be committed by, respectively, the legal acts of the distributor and the employee. Such consents are made verifiable by the visible fact that the good had been entrusted to the distributor and the employer had been publicly acting as such.

In contrast, things are different with company contracts, as they often lack such public, verifiable consequences. Imagine for instance a third case in which two persons create a limited liability partnership, LLP, with a general partner under unlimited liability and a limited partner under limited liability. Consider the possibility that, in a subsequent transaction the general partner borrows from company creditors falsely claiming that the limited partner is subject to *unlimited* liability. In cases like this third example, the judge will face serious difficulties if the originative contract remains private and, as a consequence, does not produce unequivocal consequences. In previous examples, possessing a good and acting as an employee were publicly observable facts. In contrast, a partner's liability regime is an abstract feature of the originative contract, which could remain private and, therefore, be manipulated in an opportunistic manner. At the least, it would need to be explicitly included in all subsequent contracts for these to be implemented with a modicum of guarantees.

Many other corporate transactions pose similar difficulties, as it is often unclear who has legal power to commit a company. Typically, partners or shareholders delegate to a corporate board or manager, who then enter into all sorts of contracts with third parties: they may, for instance, sell unauthorized shares to new shareholders, or exceed the limits of the company's legal purpose – what lawyers call the "objects clause." For some of these transactions, the authority of the company agents may be easy to verify for some companies. For many others, however, it will remain hidden and nonverifiable. Other attributes of companies may also be hard to verify. In particular, both company and partners' creditors will be most interested in knowing which assets are owned by the company and which by its partners. Furthermore, participants often have incentives for opportunistic behavior. Besides incentives to exaggerate the assets at the time of contracting credit, shareholders also have incentives to move assets in or out of the company depending on company and personal financial circumstances.

In principle, as with partners' and shareholders' limited liability, clauses on all these aspects could be explicitly included in subsequent company and personal contracts. But this inclusion would be costly and unreliable. A much more efficient solution is provided by entering originative corporate contracts in a public register. Registering these contracts implicitly includes them in all subsequent contracts in an easy-to-verify (i.e., hard-to-manipulate) manner.[5]

The structure of exchanges in real property is identical to that of the previous business cases: (1) a principal and an agent subscribe an originative contract – sale, mortgage, lease, etc., (2) the agent contracts with a third party in a subsequent contract – e.g., the owner sells or mortgages the land again; and (3) a judge may be called to decide. In real property cases, the agent often cheats by hiding a previous transaction and pretending to transfer a given right that is apparently unaffected by the hidden transaction; for example, pretending to convey full title or to grant a first mortgage, or to sell the land free of encumbrances. The judicial decision will, in essence, allocate priority access to the asset, between the principal and the third party, awarding the losing party a mere claim against the agent.

However, compared to the business cases, in real estate exchanges the roles of principal and agent are more implicit and alternating. For

---

[5] It thus offers a modular design for economic activity. See, mainly, the pioneer work by Simon (1962), and, closer to our topic, Smith (2006, 2007, 2008, and 2009).

example, in a double sale of land the owner who sells the same land twice can fruitfully be seen as cheating on his duties as an agent of the first buyer, to whom he has a duty to not sell again. The judge will give the land either to the principal (the first buyer) or to the third party (the second buyer), while leaving the losing party with the right to claim an indemnity from the former owner (the agent). Something similar happens with second mortgages: the first mortgagee acts as principal, the owner as agent, and the second mortgagee as the third party.

4.5 Common problem and common solution

All these transactions share a common structure: an originative contract between principal and agent, and a subsequent contract between the agent and a third party who suffers information asymmetry about the legal title of the agent. Given that the agent's title is a product of the originative contract, the third party suffers information asymmetry about the originative contract. Fraudulent subsequent transactions are made possible because, as a consequence of the originative transaction, agents become in possession of assets or are placed in a position in which they seem to have power to contract on behalf of the principal. For example, a lease of land gives the lessee the possession of the land and puts him in a good position to pretend to be the owner when selling to an innocent third party. Similarly, an employee will tend to be seen as authorized to commit the firm.

Merely optimizing this trade-off of transaction costs and property rights statically is a losing proposition. In the static trade-off, applying property rules would favor earlier owners to the detriment of later owners and, vice versa, applying contract rules would favor later owners to the detriment of earlier owners. Economic growth benefits from and may often require both secure property rights to encourage investment, and low transaction costs to improve the allocation and specialization of resources. Therefore, it is often efficient to develop institutions that, at a cost, are capable of *overcoming* the trade-off, maximizing value for acquirers without damaging owners.

They do so by applying contract or property rules in a given context but with the appropriate conditions, which greatly reduce damaging side effects for, respectively, security of property or transaction costs. When the law applies a contract rule, it does so after the owner has consented, and granting or denying their consent allows owners to protect their property. This is the solution invented in the Middle Ages under the Law Merchant: when merchants entrust possession of their goods to other merchants, the judge will grant the goods to third-party innocent acquirers in subsequent transactions. Similarly, when shareholders incorporate a company and appoint its representatives they are consenting to their property rights being weakened in favor of the third parties who will start contracting with the company. But, since this potential weakening of property rights is decided on by the owners, it should not cause much damage. Conversely, when the law applies a property rule, it does so only after the owner has complied with verifiable publicity requirements that greatly reduce transaction costs for all potential third parties in the market. For example, in a double sale of land the judge will give the land not to the first buyer but to the first buyer to make the purchase public. In other words, by not making the purchase public, the first buyer is implicitly consenting to his property right being weakened, so that a contract rule will be applied to adjudicate a possible second sale that is made public first. Similar solutions are applicable to all previous examples.

The key issue is that the judge does not apply these rules automatically: they are subject to conditions, which are needed to overcome the trade-off between property enforcement and transaction costs. In particular, given the sequential nature of the exchange, all systems must make sure that principals remain committed to their choices. To illustrate this point, imagine a merchant who, after placing his merchandise in the hands of a distributor who does not pay him, claims that the distributor was not authorized to sell it; or think of a shareholder who grants full powers to a manager but, when he makes a huge mistake, reneges from him and claims that he lacked legal powers. If their point is upheld by the judge, the third party would get only a claim for indemnity against the distributor or the manager. Commitment is the key in these examples. It is also key in land transactions. For example, in a double sale, the owner and the first buyer could easily collude and announce the first sale only when land value moves above the expected indemnity cost. Moreover, when a property rule is to be applied, commitment must also reach all potential third parties.

The common condition is that the judge has to be able to verify the consent given or the publicity produced in the originative transaction. This can be done informally, when the originative transaction itself or the activities it gives rise to inevitably publicize the relevant information as a by-product. An informative transaction in this regard is, for example, that leading to a commercial seller gaining possession of merchandise. Similarly, the scope of employees' powers can often be easily ascertained by observing them perform the usual tasks of their jobs. Otherwise, explicit procedures need to be implemented to, in essence, make public the consensual elements that may affect third parties. Such elements include, at least, the date and the information necessary to apply the corresponding rule. For example, the incorporation of a company also requires the name, founders, capital, decision rules, etc; and purchases and mortgages of land also require, at least, to identify the parcel and the transactors.

The solution is therefore one of relying on public knowledge of originative contracts and, when such knowledge is not available, registering the contracts to make their content verifiable. Broadly speaking, when the law applies a contract rule, which reduces transaction costs in subsequent transactions, it protects owners by having them choose the agent and triggering an agent-mediated contract rule only as a consequence of the agent's appointment. Conversely, when the law enforces a property rule, which guarantees *in rem* enforcement of owners' rights, it does so with the condition that the originative transaction has been made public and verifiable, which also reduces transaction costs for subsequent transactions. Of course, many situations are not all-or-nothing and, instead, there is a continuum. For instance, some degree of automatic publicity may be sufficient for low-value transactions and, in other cases, a mixture of publicity mechanisms is applied for different dimensions. For example, possession of real property may play a publicity-and-verifiability role for some real rights which produce notice (e.g., some leases) but not for others which are abstract in nature (e.g., ownership, mortgage). In any case, having some elements of the originative contract public and verifiable ensures, either that parties to that originative contract are committed to the contract rule – that is, rightholders cannot deny they have given consent to weakening of their rights, or that enforcing the property rule will not harm innocent third parties. In essence, it makes sure that judges and third parties base their decisions on the same information.[6]

---

[6] A key characteristic of these judicial decisions is that they are based on information about the consent given by rightholders, not about the possible

4.6 Difficulties faced by the law of impersonal transactions

Our overview of transactions suggests that the solution for impersonal market exchange is to make it possible for rightholders to voluntarily dilute their property rights. More precisely, the solution is to either condition the enforcement of property rules to publicity, as in real property, or to directly enforce contract rules. Both solutions aim to protect innocent third parties in subsequent contracts, reducing transaction costs, without damaging property rights. Damage to property rights is limited because rightholders still have to grant their consent. Even in business transactions, they exercise their consent when activating the contract rule through explicit legal acts faced by the law of impersonal transactions such as entrusting possession of movable goods, employing a worker, or filing documents in a company registry.

Property rules can thus be seen as playing a declining role in both corporate and property law, and unconditional enforcement of them as an exception. In corporate law, most jurisdictions now protect innocent third parties against legal defects in the corporate decision-making process; and, even if shareholders are free to introduce limitations in articles of incorporation and representation powers, these limitations are increasingly ineffective against innocent third parties.[7] In real property, privacy plays a decreasing role, and recording of deeds is being replaced in many countries by land registration, which tends to guarantee indefeasible title to innocent acquirers.

Significantly, contract rules covering many commercial and financial areas were applied for business trade early on within the medieval Law Merchant (Berman 1983: 348–350). However, Western law has taken more than ten centuries to apply market-enabling rules when applying them efficiently requires supporting organizations. Governments have

---

values of the disputed resources in the hands of the competing claimants. The latter problem is analyzed in the literature on property versus liability rules (see, for instance, Ayres and Talley 1995; Kaplow and Shavell 1996; as well as Krauss 1998, for an overview), which focuses on a situation in which a disputed right must be allocated between its owner and a taker (instead of an innocent third party), and the liability (instead of contract) rule has this second party compensating the owner.

[7] For instance, when a board of directors goes beyond its powers (Grossfeld 1973: 39–45; Lutter 1973: 131–135), and in cases of defective incorporation (Buxbaum 1973: 23–29). Armour and Whincop also assert a shift in English law towards granting more protection to third parties (2007: 459).

struggled for most of these ten centuries to organize land registries that could make their application to real property possible (Arruñada 2003). Similarly, company registries, also invented within the Law Merchant, were adopted by most governments only in the nineteenth century (Arruñada 2010). This difference is explained by the fact that applying efficient default rules (such as applying a contract rule to commercial exchange) does not require organizational support: they work on the basis of verifiable publicity produced in the market, without any organization. This explains why they were widely applied after their inception in the Middle Ages.

The delay has arisen in developing the public organizations needed for efficient enforcement of market-enabling rules: mainly public registries for recording and/or registering companies, land conveyances, mortgages, and other security interests. They, too, started to be proposed by cities and merchants back in the Middle Ages but were only created much later, often unsuccessfully. Most countries in the world have in fact run company and land registries for more than a century; however, only a few have achieved functional registries, and some of these only recently. In addition to the common difficulties of public administration, functional legal registries face two additional hurdles. First, the value of their services disappears altogether when they are unreliable, because of corruption or poor organization. Second, they compete head-on with lawyers and notaries who, both as individual professionals and as a group, prefer a weak or dysfunctional registry, which increases the demand for most of their services.

The struggle for market institutions can thus be pictured as a battle between two different technologies and the specialized resources using them: the artisan manufacturing of contracts by lawyers and notaries and the industrial production of "legal commodities" by default contract rules and organized registries. In this context, something close to a Luddite attitude is still observable when legal professionals oppose standardization of legal acts and services, or when they claim the higher quality of personalized service. It is revealing that the Law Merchant, by which contract rules were created, developed without relying on and, in fact, in disdain of the established legal professions: "In all types of commercial courts ... not only were professional lawyers generally excluded but also technical legal argumentation was frowned upon" (Berman 1983: 347).

The law of impersonal transactions 75

Obviously, the desire to preserve rents and quasi-rents constitutes a major stumbling block for most efforts to create or reform public registries. The added twist in this "Institutional Revolution" is that Luddites are not opposing business entrepreneurs, as they did in the Industrial Revolution, but mostly civil servants. In this conflict, the side of modern formalization technology is especially weak, even after a registry is created, when registrars are paid a fixed salary and, consequently, have little interest in providing a valuable service to users. Understandably, in many countries registries end up being captured by and subordinated to lawyers and notaries.

Therefore, the delay in the institutional support of impersonal exchange is probably related to the simple fact that mainstream law first developed for facilitating personal exchange. Consequently, most legal resources are still adapted to personal exchange, including not only the human capital of judges, scholars, and all sorts of law practitioners, but also other intangible assets, such as conceptual frameworks and academic curricula. Owners of these intellectual resources resist change, but sunk costs and the conflicts of interest they generate are not the only difficulty. Conceptual and theoretical models are also important obstacles to the introduction of market-enabling legal changes.

Furthermore, contractual registries have been paid uneven attention: substantial by development experts, little by scientists who are better placed to advance knowledge in this field. This lack of scientific attention is partly explained by the focus of both economics and law on the type of transaction that hardly needs registration. Both have focused their attention on solving the problems between parties to the contract. Both disregard the fact that a key problem for impersonal transactions is the information asymmetry faced by third parties who are entering into a transaction affected by a previous, originative, transaction. This applies to economic analyses which do not distinguish between contract and property rights (Merrill and Smith 2001a), dealing instead with contract rights that are enforceable only between the parties to the originative contract; or, perhaps most often, with the conditions for private rights on property, whether they are enforced as property or as contract rights.

More importantly, it also affects most legal treatments, which take as their references cases in which legal effects are triggered by private contract alone. They thus disregard the fact that for most transactions in today's economy private contracts alone do not have effects against third parties. Alternatively, in the best of cases, they treat such third-party effects as mere exceptions, despite being by far the general case. For example, it is considered that transactional documents that provide evidence of the bargain between company founders or property transactors actually incorporate a company or transfer property rights, when in fact in modern legal systems – whatever type of registration law is used – such documents either have no effects against third parties or have them only exceptionally. In order for this traditional paradigm to keep a framing role, first it is stated that, for example, a memorandum of association or a transfer deed have effects creating a company or transferring property. Second, the protection provided to third parties by the fact that the parties to the originative contract omitted a "requirement" to record such documents is treated as a mere exception regarding such effects.[8] In a nutshell, the exception becomes the general rule, and the rule an exception, as if the treatment of third parties were not really the key issue.

Consequently, both economic and legal analyses often fail to provide a sound basis for understanding the function and organizational requirements of formalization institutions. Framing the analysis with this traditional paradigm leads to underestimation of the role played by public registries and, correlatively, to overestimation of the function of informal solutions (possession, apparent authority) and documentary formalization. The latter, in most cases, can at most play a complementary role. The unsuitability of the paradigm makes it difficult to adapt formalization systems to meet the demands of the modern economy. It also helps explain the survival of unfounded legal exceptions, which generate gray areas in which impersonal contracting becomes impossible.

Mainly, the traditional paradigm sustains all sorts of private palliatives, both prior to and subsequent to the contract – mainly, lawyering to draw up personal safeguards and validate private contracts or to litigate in any additional conflicts arising. These solutions are idiosyncratic and therefore costly, and are of doubtful effectiveness and variable quality. They can be judged as "artisan," in contrast to

---

[8] The good faith third parties who are unaffected by the private contract are, for example, company creditors of unregistered companies, personal creditors of their founders, or the purchasers of land from the owners on record who have previously sold to persons who did not record their deeds.

the "industrial" solutions required for impersonal transactions, which require low unit costs and standard legal attributes for subsequent transactions. This institutional development is thus similar to the standardization achieved by mass production in the nineteenth century and the secured quality provided by "zero-defect" manufacturing in the late twentieth century. This is precisely the type of solution that nineteenth-century legal experts started to build but which their successors do not always grant all the value it deserves.

PART II

Path dependency and political constraints in establishing property rights systems

Introduction to Part II

ERIC BROUSSEAU AND JEAN-MICHEL GLACHANT

As illustrated by the contribution of Benito Arruñada in Part I, new institutional economics pays extended attention to the efficiency of alternative systems of rights establishment; essentially by contrasting centralization vs. decentralization of property rights settlements (Barzel, 1989). According to this approach, centralization impacts upon efficiency by impacting upon the level of transaction costs borne by agents when attempting to use or trade resources, because their efforts to settle and secure property rights are not invested in production, and also because transaction costs determine the extension of markets, and hence division of labor. In this second part of the book, we do not consider the alternative social technologies relied upon to build a system of property rights. Rather, we consider how, when a market is created, property rights should be attributed to the various participants. Indeed, if transaction costs are not zero, Coasean bargaining will be limited, leading to an absence of redistribution of assets to the most productive stakeholders and a loss of potential benefits for society. Given this, we will contrast auctions and grandfathering.

In Chapter 5, Terry Anderson, Ragnar Árnason, and Gary Libecap point out that, worldwide, markets, and more precisely rights-based management systems, tend to replace command-and-control centralized regulation, which generally has not been successful in managing many natural resources and the environment. Denny Ellerman's analysis of markets of air emission permits (Chapter 6) highlights that the creation of markets does not impact only the traders involved in these markets, i.e., their costs, benefits, and risks. It impacts more largely on many potential stakeholders outside the markets, through various transmission mechanisms.

Denny Ellerman's contribution also points out one consequence of the complexity of the mechanisms of transmission between market players and the citizens/consumers when radically new markets are created. It makes it difficult for the social players to anticipate properly and manage the distribution of these benefits. The resulting political negotiations and battles are then played out by stakeholders who neither share the same vision of the situation, nor have complete knowledge. "Efficiency" in trade and "justice" in distribution have therefore little chance of being the main driver of market manufacturing.

Ellerman's chapter hence illustrates once more the biases introduced by political intervention in the manufacturing of markets. That said, this is not only due to the logic inherent to political decision making (see Part IV). This is also due to the very structure of economic issues in our second best world as it is: there is always a balance between economic and equity issues. The most efficient arrangements result in rents captured by some categories of players. These rents could be allocated differently, but political intervention does not guarantee at all a fairer distribution, nor that the resulting dynamic will lead to greater efficiency. It might even hinder the efficiency of the arrangement.

That said, markets could yield wealth because they favor the revelation of shadow prices that exist in nonmarket mechanisms and favor all kinds of inefficiencies and capture or rents. Whether it is a question of airborne emissions control, fisheries management, fresh water allocation, or habitat preservation, rights-based management generally involves setting a cap on total output, the assignment of shares of the cap as property rights, and their subsequent trade. These arrangements demonstrate effectiveness in mitigating the losses of open access; providing incentives for efficient resource use and investment; generating information regarding alternative options; and creating a mechanism to direct resources to their highest valued uses.

Of course, creating markets is not a first best solution because property rights are inherently incomplete and because transaction costs are always positive. It is however often an excellent second best due to the incentives and information deficiencies of (pure) public provision. Nevertheless the way property rights are allocated when markets are created to provide public goods, or mitigate the production of public bads, impacts strongly on the distribution of the benefits of the social innovation. Creating markets to favor a better use of resources raises two issues: What mechanisms will guarantee a better alignment of incentives and the revelation of information? And how should the benefits be distributed? Both Ellerman and Libecap point out that the citizens-consumers are most of the time those who ultimately pay for the harm and benefit from the wealth associated with the creation of a market. Alternative options in distributing property rights when building markets from scratch impact however on the ability of the various stakeholders to capture, temporarily or definitively, rents that delay or reduce the benefits to be expected from the more efficient mechanism.

First possession or grandfathering is by far the most common mechanism, but it is controversial. There are equity concerns as rights holders gain new wealth and status, and potentially, political influence. Auctions, which have been rarely used for open access resources thus far, are argued to be a more equitable allocation method or one that can transfer rents to the state to reduce distortive taxes.

Anderson, Árnason, and Libecap, however, advocate that the advantages of grandfathering over auctions have been underestimated in the scientific literature and in policy recommendations. First, as resource rents are not fixed, but depend upon investment, innovation, and production decisions, grandfathering presents the advantage to allocate property rights to those who have the more extended knowledge and capability to manage the resources in consideration, because they have been historically in charge of them. Simply, the "new" property rights provide them with better incentives to manage them efficiently according to the collective goals. On the contrary, when the rents of the rights-based management (RBM) mechanism are extracted via auctions, the likelihood is high that these "windfall profits" in the hands of the politicians will be distributed according to a pure political bargaining logic. This is far from guaranteeing an efficient distribution and use of resources in society.

In their chapter Eshien Chong, Carine Staropoli, and Anne Yvrande-Billon review the theoretical literature on the relative efficiency of auctions and negotiations in public procurement – which is a different issue from the one dealt with by the two other chapters, while it highlights the difficulties of implementing actual auctions – and provides some empirical evidence confirming that auctions are generally not very efficient when projects are complex, when the competencies of the public authorities are limited as compared to those of the suppliers, and when it is difficult to prevent collusion among bidders, especially because the supply side is made up of a limited number of competitors that repeatedly interact. However, because of a general atmosphere of mistrust against public authorities and public bureaus, most public policies worldwide favor the awarding of public projects to private entities through these types of competitive mechanisms.

The contributions by Ellerman and Árnason and his co-authors highlight that the best principle of distribution of the allowance when a market is created may be dependent on the nature of the resources; namely whether it is a "good" or a "bad." In the case of goods, producers benefitting from grandfathering will transmit efficiency gains to the customer if markets are competitive. Since they have the accumulated capital and experience to manage the concerned resources efficiently, providing them with property rights over the now scarce and valuable resources is the most efficient way to guarantee the realization of social benefits. In the case of bads, however, producers will always pass on to taxpayers the cost of the reduction of bad production ... without any incentive to use the best technique and more generally to balance the costs of bads and the costs of their reductions. In that case, auctioning is the best way to reveal shadow prices and to guarantee a quick return or the social benefits to the citizens ... if indeed the majority of the allowance value is assigned directly to consumers.

This illustrates two essential facts when markets have to be built by public authorities. First, despite undeniable progress in social science about alternate "social technologies," knowledge about the matter is still quite imperfect. Indeed only little is known about the relative costs of public decision-making biases (i.e., the cost of a limited level of corruption in a well-organized bureaucracy, given the costs of incentives and deterrence mechanisms to prevent corruption and encourage right decisions) vs. the cost of inefficient auction procedures (wrong awarding, re-negotiation, potential collusion must be taken into account). Second, while knowledge remains incomplete, ideological and political fashions play a strong role in policy-making even in those types of area where, at first glance, public opinion has few established preferences. This reinforces the need for a better understanding of the political processes by which "social technologies" are selected to frame economic activities in general, and the design of market processes in this particular book.

5 "Manufacturing markets": the efficiency advantages of grandfathering allocations over auctions

TERRY L. ANDERSON, RAGNAR ÁRNASON, AND GARY D. LIBECAP

5.1 Introduction

There is a general move toward rights-based management regimes (RBM) worldwide for natural resources and the environment. These regimes typically involve a form of cap and trade in airborne emissions control (carbon markets), fishery management (individual transferable quotas [ITQs], individual vessel quotas [IVQs]), fresh water allocation (water rights and markets), and the provision of other forms of environmental services, such as development credits obtained through land set-asides for habitat preservation.[1] Rights-based management generally includes setting a cap on total output, the assignment of shares of the cap as property rights, and their subsequent trade. These arrangements replace command-and-control centralized regulation, which generally has not been successful (Libecap, 2008). The creation or "manufacturing" of these markets requires the allocation of property rights. We argue that grandfathering the allotments of local users can be the most efficient distribution mechanism. We differ from the standard support among economists for auctions. Although we focus on emerging resource and environmental markets, our arguments likely apply to other settings.

The authors thank Eric Brousseau, Jean-Michel Glachant, Raphael Soubeyran, Tom Dederwaerdere, Denny Ellerman, Sandy Klassa, Corbett Granger, and Zach Donohew for helpful comments on earlier drafts of the chapter. This chapter builds on Anderson and Libecap (2009) and Anderson, Árnason, and Libecap (2011).

[1] See Stavins (2007) for discussion of the movement toward market-based instruments. Other discussions are found in Anderson and Hill (2004) and Libecap (2007, 2008). Consider the success under the Clean Air Act Amendments of 1990 in designing air pollution emission permits that lowered the cost of meeting air quality targets (Tietenberg, 2005, 395–402; Stavins, 2007, 23).

We argue that grandfathering promotes investment and rent creation principally by lowering the cost of capital. By contrast, auctions, by extracting rents for the auctioneer – typically the state – can raise the cost of capital for less diversified firms and thereby retard investment. There are other reasons to question the efficiency of auctions that we point to below. If we are correct, the allocation mechanism is not neutral, and this factor should be considered in determining how property rights will be distributed as markets are "manufactured."

For resource and environmental problems, the move to property rights and markets is designed to reduce the dissipation of rents through a "tragedy of the commons."[2] Maximizing the rental stream requires a system of property rights that avoids a competitive race for rents and instills incentives for conservation of the resource, investment, and efficient production from it. The alternative of open access leads to excessive short-term output, underinvestment, and limited trade. The adoption of property rights assumes an allocation mechanism, and this process has not received sufficient attention by researchers.

Especially with environmental and natural resources where there often is localized information, the direct involvement of incumbent users is critical not only for management success, but for increasing rents. Locals often have the most complete information about the asset and the most effective and low-cost ways of producing from it and investing in it. Indeed, the capturing of additional resource rents created by entrepreneurial activities provides incentives for innovation.

Accordingly, rents are not a *fixed* stock given by nature as is commonly assumed, but rather depend upon the actions of those who use the resource in the provision of valuable goods and services. First-possession allocation assigns ownership and rents to existing users, reinforcing their incentives for effective management and potentially lowering the cost of capital, encouraging greater investment and the *growth* of rents.[3]

In this chapter, we describe the allocation mechanisms that are available; discuss the nature of rents; outline the investment advantages of grandfathering, relative to auctioning; and, finally, illustrate some of

---

[2] Resources solely with amenity values may not require investment and production for value. For the losses of open access, see Hardin (1968).
[3] See discussion of first possession in Epstein (1979), Rose (1985), and Lueck (1995, 1998).

the problems associated with auctions by presenting a political model that outlines opportunity for rent seeking with proposed CO_2 emission permits. The efficiency arguments for auctions, whereby revenues are used to reduce distortive income taxes, are weakened by overriding political incentives to divert revenues to influential constituencies and the underlying wasteful competition this encourages.

5.2 Alternative allocation systems

As noted above, the "manufacturing" of markets requires an allocation mechanism for the assignment of property rights, and as we argue, the method chosen can have significant implications for rent maximization. Below are the major allocation options:

5.2.1 Political allocation

All formal property rights are political institutions (Libecap, 1989) because they require recognition and enforcement by the state. But here the political allocation of property rights refers to the assignment of ownership based purely on political influence. These assignments may not be to local users, but to political cronies or supporters of the government. Political allocation may also be molded by particular equity or distributional concerns whereby targeted groups are given preference in the granting of property rights, such as has been the case of administrative allocation of spectrum rights in the US.[4] We are not aware of a general survey of the use of political allocation, but it seems especially likely for valuable, fixed natural resources in developing countries where the rule of law and other political institutions are weak, allowing for rent-seeking corruption.[5]

5.2.2 First possession

First possession or grandfathering is by far the most common allocation mechanism (Árnason, 2002; Libecap, 2007). It assigns ownership to incumbents who generally obtained their claim on a first-come,

---

[4] See Libecap (2007) for a brief overview and reference to the broader literature.
[5] This observation underlies the "resource curse" argument. See Humphreys, Sachs, and Stigliz (2007).

first-served or first-in-time, first-in-right basis. Having a direct stake in access to the resource, first possessors are important constituents in the property rights distribution because they want consideration of past investments – physical or human capital – in specific, non-deployable assets. But recognition of incumbents is more than political expediency. Generally, first-possession rules recognize current parties, who have experience in exploiting the resource and, hence, are likely to be low-cost, high-valued users, having outcompeted less-efficient parties.[6] Previous investments in human and physical capital and the development of exceptional skills among heterogeneous parties generate inframarginal rents, even under open access conditions (Johnson and Libecap, 1982).[7]

To the extent that restrictions on entry under RBM are granted to first possessors in accordance with these past investments and historical production shares and that the allocation is not anticipated so as to have caused a race for rights, the efficiencies gained in the first-possession process will remain.[8] Further, by recognizing historical production patterns and capital outlays, first-possession rules in RBM can signal security in property rights and encourage future investments.

First possession also may encourage efficiency because as it draws upon existing local knowledge and defines a clear set of ownership, it encourages production of additional information and cooperation once rights are established. These actions can increase resource rents. First possessors have an historical understanding of the resource and efficient production from it. This knowledge can be valuable for coordinating production practices to enhance private returns and it can be a basis for collaborating with regulators (or replacing them) in setting the cap or total allowable production, reducing industry resistance to the output controls.[9]

---

[6] See Lueck (1995). To the extent that existing companies reflect a distorted exploitation structure due to open access, this argument might be weakened. Internal adjustment within the industry will take place under the RBM regime. For an example in fisheries, see Grafton, Squires, and Fox (2000).

[7] Johnson and Libecap (1982) show that heterogeneity among fishers limits rent dissipation even under open access and the rule of capture.

[8] For discussion of the potential for rent dissipation in the establishment of property rights, see Haddock (1986) and Anderson and Hill (1990).

[9] In a similar setting, Johnson (1995) has shown that the imposition of taxes on quota rents in ITQ (individual transferable quota) fisheries could lead to reduced incentives for fishers to conserve (invest in) the fish stock.

Establishing rights based on first possession necessarily requires reducing the access of some parties. It is this restriction and the associated reduction in output that is an initial source of rent creation by RBM, as we show below. Further, transferring rents from the first possessors to the polity, as through competitive auctions, will not reduce the efficiency gains from restricting access. The rental losses that we emphasize below come from subsequent changes in dynamic investment patterns.

First possession has been criticized on fairness grounds because it discriminates against new entrants and may encourage large holdings. If first-possession ownership is viewed as rewarding those who by luck and connections got early access, such criticism may be warranted and may lead to political opposition to sanctioning of claims based on first possession (Alesina and Angeletos, 2005, 960–980).

5.2.3 Uniform allocation

Equal sharing rules avoid the distributional concerns associated with first possession and better reflect egalitarian goals, but they have not been used to any extent in RBM. If there are no restrictions on subsequent exchange of property rights and transaction costs are low, there are few efficiency implications. The resource still migrates to high-valued users and rents remain within the industry. Uniform allocations also avoid the measurement costs of verifying claims of past production or use or of documenting precedence claims that are part of first-possession assignments. They can circumvent the costly pursuit of or rush for property rights when first possession is known to be the allocation rule.

Lotteries are examples of uniform allocations because each claimant is given an equal, random draw in the assignment of rights to the resource, and the allocation granted generally is partitioned equally among lottery winners. Uniform allocations via lotteries are most effective when applied to new resources where there are no incumbent claims and all parties are relatively homogeneous. They can also be used when the access and use rights granted are short-term and no long-term ownership is implied, such as with lotteries for annual hunting licenses.

5.2.4 Auction

Auctions are another allocation method in RBM, although as noted above they have been used only on limited occasions. There are efficiency and equity arguments for auctions. For example, see Bromley (2009) for fisheries.[10] First, auctions may place the resource directly into the hands of those who have the highest value for it and thereby avoid the transaction costs of reallocation. Second, auctions generate information about the value of the resource. And, finally, auctions transfer rents to the state (as the seller), and the funds could be used to address equity concerns if there were strong political arguments for doing so.

The amounts and distribution of rents created by an auction depend upon auction design, which can be complex. The net amount of the rents created depends on the auction costs, on measurement and enforcement costs following the auction, and on the lobbying costs invested in influencing the terms that may provide specific advantages to certain groups during or after the auction.[11]

In practice, auctions have been adopted more rarely than economists who espouse their virtues might like. For example, ITQs in fisheries have generally been grandfathered rather than auctioned, and SO_2 permits under the Clean Air Act Amendments of 1990 were granted to existing emitters (Joskow and Schmalensee, 1998). Nonetheless, auctions have been called for to allocate CO_2 emission permits to limit greenhouse gas emissions under cap-and-trade regimes. Parry, Williams, and Goulder (1999), Burtraw and Evans (2009), and other economists (see the petition signed by prominent economists to be delivered to the House Energy and Commerce Committee, March 3, 2009) argue for auctioning CO_2 permits in the US, rather than grandfathering the permits to past polluters.[12] Auctions are favored both for their simplicity and transparency, as well as the raising of funds that can be used to lower preexisting distortive taxes.[13] Auction revenues also could be used to support R&D or to compensate parties particularly harmed by the policy. If this happens, society could achieve both the public good of fewer carbon emissions and a more efficient tax structure. Whether this happens, however, depends on the political framework

---

[10] For summary of auction issues, complications, and applications, see McAfee and McMillan (1987), Milgrom (1989), and Klemperer (2002).
[11] See discussion by McMillan (1994) regarding the experimentation and costs of designing auctions for the spectrum.
[12] Led by the Southern Alliance for Clean Energy, www.cleanenergy.org.
[13] Parry, Williams, and Goulder (1999) refer to this effect as the revenue-recycling effect.

that actually determines the allocation of auction revenues. Later we will analyze the probable allocation results in the context of a realistic model of political rent allocation.

5.3 "Manufacturing" markets and resource rents: the efficiency advantages of grandfathering

Although there is consensus among economists and resource managers that RBM is the most practical way of reducing losses from open access and of generating wealth associated with environmental and natural resources, questions remain about whether the rents created by RBM will be subsequently captured, enhanced, or dissipated. Here we focus on how allocation of the rents to users or to government will affect the rents spawned by RBM.

There are many notions of "rent" in economics.[14] Classical resource rent is payment for a fixed resource in excess of opportunity costs or what is necessary to induce production. The resource is viewed as having inelastic supply. A related concept is economic rent or returns beyond a normal rate of return due to restrictions on entry and production. These include monopoly returns or short-term gains from first-mover, competitive advantage acquired through innovation.

It is often argued that resource allocation is invariant to lump-sum rent taxation and that an auction (which can be thought of as a form of lump-sum or fixed-cost tax) is the preferred method for assigning rights because it ensures that they will go to those users who value them the most.[15] Agents will continue to produce efficiently even if the rents are eliminated. In fisheries, for example, Clark, Major, and Mollett (1989, 138) argue that the economic rent generated by the creation of transferable fishing quotas "can either be taxed away by the government or left in the fishery to be capitalized into the value of the ITQ." If the right is auctioned, the winning bid will be determined by the highest expected future value of the rental stream. In this context, rents are returns over and above opportunity costs, and therefore their distribution will not affect resource allocation.

---

[14] Classical or economic rent, Schumpeterian rent, Hotelling rent, and so forth.
[15] An important exception is Johnson (1995) who challenges the view that resource rents can be taxed without distortionary effects.

We argue, however, that the amount of rents created and saved through RBM is not invariant to allocation for at least three reasons. The first is that the rents created by RBM and transferred to government, whether by auction or taxation, will be competed for in a potentially rent dissipating political process. As we discuss below there are theoretical and empirical reasons to believe that such rent dissipation is likely.

The second reason lies in the process whereby rents are created. The notion of *in situ* resource rents suggests that they arise simply from the natural existence of the resource to which homogeneous units of other inputs are applied. Computing the rents is a matter of subtracting the cost of other inputs from the value of the output created. As long as the resource remains open to access by all, rents at the margin will be fully dissipated by competing entrants. Hence, rents are dissipated or created by increasing or reducing the amount of additional factors employed in resource use.

Ignored in this reasoning is the role that heterogeneous resources play in the production process. As argued in Johnson and Libecap (1982) and Johnson (1995), it is important to recognize that even under a completely open access regime, some rents will be captured by inframarginal users. These users might be first entrants who recognized the value of the resource before others, users who apply superior management skills to the resource production process, or those who have invested in human capital most likely through learning-by-doing. In any case and especially for a resource that has been exploited for a long time by users who have acquired time- and place-specific information about the resource, there will be a sorting process that leaves some rents for the inframarginal, more efficient producers.

The amount of these rents depends upon the contribution that heterogeneous inputs make to the value of the production process. Not all resource rents arise solely from the mere existence of the asset. Some additional rents are generated by the productive investment activity of inputs that turn the resource into valuable products and services. Figure 5.1 illustrates the contribution of resource and Ricardian or inframarginal rents to the resource at any point in time.[16]

---

[16] These arguments are developed in more detail in Anderson, Árnason, and Libecap (2011).

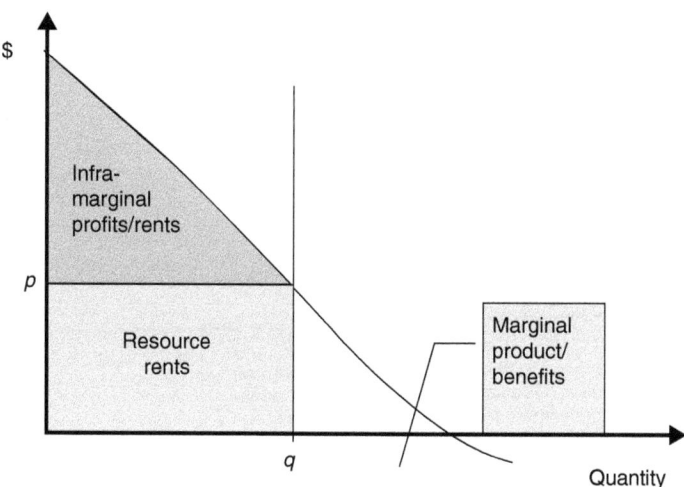

Figure 5.1 Economic rents

In a dynamic sense there is the possibility of creating *additional* rents through innovation and investment by inframarginal users. The process is illustrated in Figure 5.2.

In light of this, consider the incentive effects of redistributing these rents to government whether by auction or taxation. What are the implications for the inframarginal, low-cost producer who has managerial or entrepreneurial talent that generates additional value? Such talents may have alternative uses. If rents are eliminated in the resource sector, the entrepreneur/manager may shift effort elsewhere where the inputs are somewhat lower valued, but earn rents, thus creating an allocation effect. Of course, exit by one resource user will open the door for another, but the new user may be less efficient and therefore will create fewer rents from the resource and less social value.

The third and related reason that rent distribution matters for rent creation relates to the cost of capital and the dynamic investment patterns described above. Grandfathering promotes investment by sustaining rents in the industry and signaling long-term investment opportunities and security, and by lowering borrowing costs. In contrast, by reducing rents in the industry, auctions can fail on both accounts.

As noted above, the anticipation of rewards (rents) encourages research and development of new products and production methods;

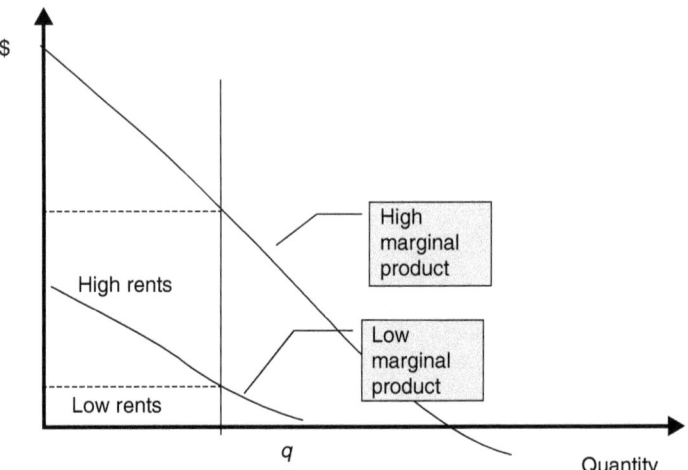

Figure 5.2 The creation of rents via innovation and investment

long-term investment in human and physical capital; and in low-cost production practices. The retention of rents in the industry not only confirms the value of past production and investment decisions, but signals opportunities for future wealth-increasing actions. High rates of return attract productive resources to the industry, making it innovative and dynamically efficient.

Further, retained rents can fund risky investments in industry-specific capital or the resource and/or lower the cost of capital in accessing external funding. Early investments are likely to involve asymmetric information and high transaction costs of assessing economic performance and risk. In the case of new, "manufactured" markets, the optimal capital and labor configuration will not be known because it is unlikely to correspond with that which was used under regulation or open access. Moreover, new production methods, products, and marketing options, previously not feasible under regulation or open access, will require experimentation. None of these is likely to be easily conveyed to external lenders until more information is generated in a later period. Accordingly, self-financing via retained rents may be the low-cost method of funding investment. In this way, retained rents play a role similar to retained earnings in industrial enterprises for in-house financing of speculative new products and markets and operating capital requirements.

The finance literature and the associated literature on contracts and transaction costs provide supportive insights. All firms rely on internal financing, but risky new activities particularly depend upon internal financing (Myers and Majluf, 1984).[17] Additional theoretical and empirical work (Calomiris and Hubbard, 1995) on the importance of internal financing (retained earnings, retained profits) when there is asymmetric information reveals significant declines in investment following increases in the undistributed profits tax in the US.

The absence of retained earnings also increases firm-specific risk because of the greater likelihood of bad earnings' outcomes, and hence raises the cost of capital for external financing. Stated differently, for undiversified firms, as is likely to be the case in many new "manufactured" markets, the loss of rents via auction can increase the total volatility of expected firm earnings. This outcome raises the cost of capital, and reduces investment in the environmental or natural resource.

These factors appear to be recognized by franchisers in allocating franchises. For example, Kaufmann and Lafontaine (1994) report that McDonald's and other franchisers do not extract all *ex ante* rents via their royalties and franchise fees. The firm leaves initial rents with the first franchisees to provide an incentive mechanism for good operations and R&D in the site and the overall franchise reputation that is captured by the parent firm. Additionally, McDonald's seeks undiversified, small operators to be their franchisees, who have focused incentives on the new franchise. These operators, however, would face downstream liquidity constraints with high borrowing costs. Accordingly, they must rely on cash flow and the rents that are part of it.

Figure 5.3 shows the impact of the higher cost of capital on investment and the associated reduction in overall rents associated with the resource. To the extent that these factors are important, the allocation system can have significant efficiency effects. We cannot directly test this argument because auctions have been used so rarely in environmental and natural resource markets. Our arguments, however, provide reasons for pause in arguing for auctions, as many economists do, for emerging markets.

---

[17] There is a "pecking order" theory of corporate finance that says that corporations first use retained earnings, then debt (senior claims on the firm have lower asymmetric information costs), and then equity when debt capacity is exhausted.

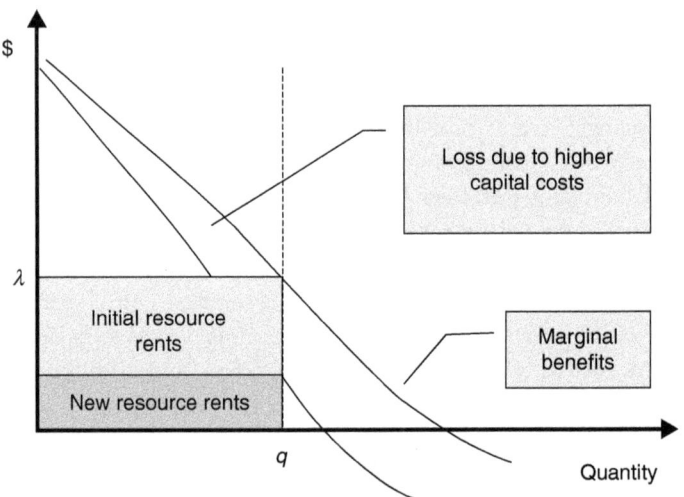

Figure 5.3 The effects of increased cost of capital (at a point of time)

5.4 "Manufacturing markets": the political economy of allocating resource rents and another reason to question the efficiency advantages of auctions

5.4.1 The political economy of allocation

The literature in economics and political science indicates that government delivery of collective goods for the broad public and particularistic goods for private constituencies results from a complex political process.[18] The mix depends upon political bargaining among legislators who prefer public goods or private goods or some combination of both. Politicians have to weigh the political benefits and costs of the trade-offs associated with these choices, issues that have not been carefully addressed by auction advocates. Accordingly, it is not possible to assert that auction revenues will be targeted to income tax reduction or other public goods activities, rather than to interest group transfers. They may, or may not, depending on political preferences and negotiations.

In the United States vote-maximizing politicians represent narrow jurisdictions and must be responsive to them, at least to some extent,

---

[18] This material is drawn from Anderson and Libecap (2011).

in considering broader policy objectives. Volden and Wiseman (2007) describe how politicians trade off the political returns from providing various combinations of collective and particularistic goods, subject to the constraint of a fixed budget. A winning congressional coalition must be assembled before any proposed mix can be selected.[19] Proponents of a particular policy must offer budget distributions to constituencies and projects favored by their colleagues in order to win their support. These necessary political exchanges reduce the funding available for the initial public objective.

Volden and Wiseman (2007, 84) argue that the greater the value placed on the public good, the more it will be under-provided by Congress. Those who support the public good will be willing to pay even more to entice the backing of their reluctant colleagues. In the case of auction revenues, this argument suggests that even if tax reduction is highly valued by many members of Congress, at least some and perhaps a large share of the funds will be directed to particularistic constituent services valued by those who otherwise would oppose providing the public good. Moreover, in this case, politicians prefer an open rule allowing for amendments in debate, making it more difficult *ex ante* to lock in income tax reduction as part of legislation authorizing a permit auction.[20]

Because auction revenues are likely to be diverted to private constituent services, we must ask how revenues are allocated among competing demands and to what extent this competition for transfers will dissipate rents. Following Peltzman (1976) and Becker (1983), vote-maximizing politicians must trade off the marginal votes gained from providing transfers to interest groups with votes lost from taxpayers. Under their models none of the parties get all that they want; taxpayers pay more taxes than they would otherwise prefer; and constituent groups get fewer transfers. In this process, politicians balance the incremental gains or losses in votes as tax-funded transfers are provided to interest groups.

---

[19] Volden and Wiseman (2007) begin with a homogeneous legislature where politicians have similar preferences and then relax that assumption. In either case, the predictions hold.

[20] Volden and Wiseman's argument is in contrast to Baron and Ferejohn (1989) who argue that politicians generally prefer closed rules (no amendments) to reduce bargaining costs, when a single good is valued.

Consider a scenario where politicians distribute revenues from a lump-sum tax on a well-defined group – for example, revenue from auction of resource use rights – rather than revenue from an income tax. In this case, because the revenues are generated as part of a regulatory process to control access to a resource, the marginal votes lost from using the revenues to fund constituent transfers may be less than if taxes are explicitly levied for these transfers. Hence, tax revenues so generated will be considered a windfall by politicians. Political theory suggests that revenue windfalls result in expenditure increases that exceed those that would be funded through taxes on similar increases in income (Gramlich, Galper, Goldfeld, and McGuire, 1973; Fisher, 1982; Hines and Thaler, 1995).[21] Accordingly, Congress may use an auction windfall to provide more transfers than would otherwise be the case.

Rent seeking becomes an issue in this context. To determine the distribution of the revenue windfall, following Peltzman (1976) and Becker (1983), as well as the insights of Krueger (1974), Buchanan, Tollison, and Tullock (1980), and Murphy, Shleifer, and Vishney (1993), interest groups will compete for transfers by lobbying. The more homogeneous, wealthy, and small the group, the more likely it will be successful because the group's interests are aligned, because the group has resources, and because there is less opportunity for free-riding (Olson 1965). Under these conditions, a large, heterogeneous group of taxpayers, who might prefer the income tax reductions suggested by auction proponents, are at a relative disadvantage in political bargaining, making less money available for tax reduction than auction proponents have suggested. Making matters worse, competition among interest groups preferring particularistic goods from auction revenues will further dissipate rents.

5.4.2 Tobacco trust fund allocations

To understand how politicians actually have distributed funds between public and particularistic goods and the rent dissipation involved in determining who receives those transfers, we consider the case of the tobacco trust fund allocations. In November 1998 a settlement was

---

[21] This is the so-called "flypaper effect," a description of how government block grant money "sticks where it hits" (Hines and Thaler, 1995, 218).

reached between the major US tobacco producers and 46 states.[22] The lawsuit was brought by the states' attorneys general on behalf of their state's Medicaid programs seeking compensation for healthcare expenditures attributed to smoking. The Master Settlement Agreement (MSA) between the states and four major tobacco companies, representing over 99 percent of the domestic cigarette market, required that the tobacco companies make annual payments to the states in perpetuity.

It also restricted the marketing and advertisement of cigarettes and required a five-year, $1.5 billion contribution toward the establishment of the American Legacy Foundation for antismoking education. In exchange, state lawsuits against the participating tobacco manufacturers were dropped.[23] Total payments were projected to be $206 billion over the first 25 years (Schroeder, 2004). Funding first became available in 2000. To date, $79.2 billion from tobacco settlement money has been received by the states.

The MSA stated that the awards were to provide "significant funding for the advancement of public health, the implementation of important tobacco-related public health measures" (National Association of Attorneys General, 1998), and most states indicated their intent to use the funds to pay for the costs of Medicaid from smoking-induced illnesses and pay for tobacco control programs (Schroeder, 2004). Indeed, part of the formula determining the allocation of payments across states was based on smoking-related medical costs and expenditures.[24] These latter costs are paid in annual installments from 2008 through 2017 (Singhal, 2008).

---

[22] Four other states, Florida, Minnesota, Mississippi, and Texas, had previously reached individual settlements with tobacco companies that totaled $40 billion. Also the District of Columbia, Puerto Rico, and four territories joined the 46 states in the Master Settlement Agreement.
[23] The four major tobacco companies to initially settle were Brown & Williamson, Lorillard, Philip Morris, and R.J. Reynolds. Since 1998, other tobacco companies have joined the MSA.
[24] There are three types of payments under the settlement: an initial allocation distributed across the first five years of payments, 1999–2003; annual payments, which are paid in perpetuity; and contributions to a Strategic Contribution Fund that compensates states' previous lawsuit costs. $86.1 billion will go into the Strategic Contribution Fund, according to the National Conference of State Legislatures 2003 report "State Management and Allocation of Tobacco Settlement Revenue."

The annual payments states receive are adjusted in two ways – inflation and volume. The volume adjustment is based on the total volume of cigarettes shipped nationally and is not state specific. State allocations of the initial and annual funds are based on two equally weighted factors: a state's share of smoking-related medical costs and a state's share of smoking-attributable Medicaid expenditures (Singhal, 2008). The Centers for Disease Control and Prevention (CDC) provided states with a minimum funding recommendation for tobacco control programs based on the demographics of each state (CDC, 1999).

Given the focus on tobacco-related health expenses, tobacco control programs to reduce smoking, and compensation for communities adversely affected by the settlement, it is instructive to follow how the states have actually used the settlement funds. As described by Anderson and Libecap (2009, Table 1), states used their allocations to cover budget shortfalls, debt service, and other expenditures for areas unrelated to tobacco health or control issues.

A report titled "A Decade of Broken Promises" written by four antismoking lobbies found that from 1998 to 2008 states spent only 3.2 percent of total tobacco-generated revenue (MSA funds and tobacco taxes) on tobacco prevention and cessation programs.[25] No state tobacco prevention programs were funded at the CDC-recommended level, and only nine states fund them at over 50 percent of the recommended levels (Campaign for Tobacco-Free Kids, 2012).[26]

It is apparent that much of the tobacco trust fund allocations support activities unrelated to tobacco health or control despite the spirit of the MSA. The associated political allocation likely involves rent-seeking activities as lobby groups mobilize to channel funds in their direction or to protect existing allocations. Windfall allocations attract lobbying from interested parties who seek to direct funds their way.

---

[25] The report "A Decade of Broken Promises: The 1998 State Tobacco Settlement Ten Years Later" was written by the Cancer Action Network, Campaign for Tobacco-Free Kids, the American Lung Association, and the America Heart Association.

[26] The nine states funding tobacco prevention programs at greater than 50 percent of the CDC recommended levels are Alaska, Delaware, Wyoming, Hawaii, Montana, Maine, Vermont, South Dakota, and Colorado.

5.5 Conclusion

The movement toward RBM and the "manufacturing" of markets for environmental and natural resources is based on its demonstrated effectiveness in mitigating the losses of open access; providing incentives for efficient resource use and investment; generating information regarding alternative options; and creating a mechanism to direct resources to their highest valued uses. The development of markets, however, raises the question of the allocation of property rights. First possession or grandfathering is by far the most common mechanism, but it is controversial. There are equity concerns as rights holders gain new wealth and status and, potentially, political influence. Auctions, which have been rarely used for open access resources heretofore, are argued to be a more equitable allocation method or one that can transfer rents to the state to reduce distortive taxes. This notion is strengthened by arguments that resource rents are fixed and that the allocation rule does not have efficiency consequences. Auction bids are fixed costs.

In this chapter, however, we argue that the allocation rule can have efficiency implications that have been overlooked both in the scientific literature and in policy recommendations. Resource rents are not fixed, but depend upon investment, innovation, and production decisions. These decisions are motivated by the expectation of higher rates of return. To the extent that rents are extracted via auctions, these returns are reduced. Moreover, the costs of capital rise, potentially reducing rent-creating innovation, and investment. Grandfathering, by retaining rents in the industry and by maintaining incumbents with specialized knowledge and skills, on the other hand, avoids these problems. Accordingly, it is likely to be the most effective allocation mechanism for "manufacturing" markets.

6 | Allocation in air emissions markets

A. DENNY ELLERMAN

6.1 Introduction

The past two decades have witnessed the increasing use of a new form of environmental regulation, cap-and-trade, that consists of creating limited property rights in emissions, known as allowances, and organizing a market for their exchange. Public policy attention has been directed principally to the two features emphasized by the catchy label, that is, the cap – the limit on aggregate emissions – and trading – the flexibility and least-cost properties associated with this instrument. Until recently, relatively little interest has been directed to the creation and distribution of the property rights, more commonly known as allocation, which is the essential mechanism by which cap-and-trade systems operate.

This chapter focuses specifically on allocation and it takes Libecap's *Contracting for Property Rights* (1989) as the point of departure. A central theme in Libecap (1989) is that the creation of property rights in common pool resources is a response by those benefiting from open access to the losses incurred, either actually or prospectively, as a result of overuse. This chapter argues that air emissions markets are different in important aspects from the common pool resource problems that inspired Libecap's insight. Furthermore, this difference explains the unsettled nature and continuing evolution in the assignment of property rights in air emissions markets.

The following section of the chapter explains how air emissions markets are different. The next section seeks to clarify the nature and possible uses of the allowance value that is created by these systems. The following section describes and analyzes the evolution in the

I am indebted to Jean-Michel Glachant, Eric Brousseau, Gary Libecap, Freddy Huet, and participants in the Workshop on Manufacturing Markets held in June 2009 in Florence, Italy, for comments on an earlier version of this chapter. The usual disclaimer applies.

Allocation in air emissions markets 103

assignment of these property rights in the early US programs, the EU ETS, and in actual and proposed US GHG programs. The final section summarizes and concludes.

6.2 How air emissions markets are different

Air emissions markets are different in that their motivation is the avoidance of ancillary harm (externalities) instead of the preservation of profit. In the usual common pool resource problem, developing property rights and facilitating exchange is a means of tapping, maintaining, or increasing the profits that can be obtained from exploitation of the resource. Examples are fisheries, grazing and timber lands, and mineral deposits. Typically, the main actors are those who have been drawing profit from exploitation of the resource. In the case of air emissions, the motivation is avoiding the harm to others that results when the common pool resource, the use of the atmosphere as a repository for emissions streams, is overexploited. In this instance, the main actors are those being harmed or agents working on their behalf for the public good.

Two important characteristics distinguish the problem of assigning property rights in air emissions markets. The first is that the firms whose production processes contribute to the overuse of the common pool resource draw little if any profit from its exploitation. Their profits arise from the successful organization of the requisite factors of production to provide something of value. Use of the atmosphere as a sink for emissions is accidental and rarely if ever the motivation of the economic activity that causes the harm. The second characteristic is that the beneficiaries of the unrestricted access to the common pool resource are not the firms themselves, but the firms' customers, or more broadly speaking, the public. At least as a first approximation in a competitive economy, the cost savings from free access are passed on to consumers in lower product prices.

These two characteristics of air emissions markets set up a very different institutional dynamic from other common resource problems. First, those who benefit from free access to the common pool resource are not those whose access is to be rationed, at least directly. Second, these latter – producing firms – have little interest in constructing a market since they draw no profit from the use of the resource. Their concern focuses on the consequences for existing profits of pricing their current and expected continuing access to the common pool resource. Understandably, these firms tend to adopt a defensive posture with respect to proposals that would price or otherwise limit their access. Third, those demanding action will as often as not fail to perceive that the public, as the ultimate consumers of the goods being produced, receive a compensating benefit in the form of lower prices for the harm being caused by overuse. The common slogan that the "polluter should pay" misses this point to the extent that it is aimed at the firm, which is only the agent of consumers' desires for goods at the lowest possible price. The agency problems created by these circumstances are quite unlike those in other common resource problems where existing use and benefit are more directly aligned.

Two other aspects complicate the creation of air emissions markets. The first is that the value to be distributed in the creation of an air emissions market is an accidental but unavoidable consequence of removing the harm. Creation of this value is not the purpose of the cap and the absence of obvious claimants for that value can greatly complicate the assignment of property rights and the creation of air emissions markets.[1]

The second complicating factor is that a market-based approach is not the only or necessarily the preferred means of removing the harm. The harm from air emissions has been an observable problem calling for collective action from as early as the thirteenth century with the formation of cities and limitations on coal-burning, but the first impulse for dealing with the problem has always been prohibition or some other form of legal prescription that seeks to limit emissions to a tolerable level by mandates instead of by the establishment of explicit property rights.

6.3 The potential recipients of allowance value

Allowance value is the scarcity rent created by a cap-and-trade program and it is equal to the total number of allowances (= the cap) times the market price of allowances. Since a binding cap creates a price, allowances are valuable and their assignment endows the recipient

---

[1] Raymond (2003) provides an excellent discussion of the potential claimants, grounded in political philosophy, as well as an accompanying, insightful analysis of how these competing claims have been settled in actual cases where property rights in public resources have been established.

Allocation in air emissions markets 105

with some expected value. One common way of thinking about the distribution of this value is that it can be either auctioned by the government or allocated for free, typically to the owners of the covered facilities who will henceforth be required to surrender allowances equal to their emissions. This dichotomy is oversimplified in focusing more on the means of distribution than on the ultimate recipients, but it captures what has until recently been the main line of debate. To identify the recipients, we must look beyond the legal entities of corporations and government to the households who receive payments from these legal shells.

When allowances are assigned for free to a corporate owner of a covered facility, profits are increased by approximately the value of the endowment, and a third or so of that increment is returned to government as corporate profit tax (and thence to households as government expenditure) and the rest to shareholders either as dividends or increased equity value. If the corporate entity is price-regulated on a cost-of-service basis (such as is the case for many electric utilities), the value of the free allocation is presumed to be passed through to rate-payers since no cash cost is incurred for these allowances. Rate-payers are also the presumed ultimate recipient when allowances are assigned to non-profit owners, such as rural coops, municipalities, and government-owned corporations. If cost-of-service regulated and non-profit entities operate as usually assumed, households capture the allowance value as rate-payers instead of as shareholders and the government receives nothing since there is no allowance value to be taxed.

The auctioning alternative potentially involves four sets of recipients. One frequent proposal is to use the auction revenue to reduce existing taxes on the returns from labor and savings in order to encourage a greater supply of these factors of production to help to pay for the costs of the constraint on emissions. This approach is said to produce a "double dividend" since a "bad" is taxed and taxes on a "good" are reduced. Most economists are thinking of this approach when they argue that auctioning would be more efficient than free allocation (Goulder, Parry, and Burtraw 1997; Parry, Williams, and Goulder 1999). It is the only use of allowance value that has these efficiency attributes,[2] but it is not the only use for auction revenues. All the other

---

[2] An exception is offered in this volume by Anderson, Árnason, and Libecap (Chapter 5), who argue for free allocation to incumbent emitters based on investment and innovation effects.

public uses of auction revenues share the lump-sum inefficiency that is attributed to free allocation.

A second possible use of auction revenue is a per capita distribution of the auction revenues to citizens, now called "cap-and-dividend."[3] To many, this approach is desirable for offsetting the regressive effect of a carbon price on lower income quintiles, unlike either free allocation or the double dividend, which distribute allowance value disproportionately to the upper income quintiles where most stockholders and taxpayers are found (Dinan and Rogers 2002). Serious proposals have been made to reduce taxes on income for only the lower income quintiles (Metcalf 2007); however, these proposals implicitly introduce the further issue of the progressivity of the tax code and at best they would increase only the supply of labor.

A third use of the allowance value created by a cap is increased government expenditure often for some use related to the environmental problem being addressed. In proposed US climate change legislation, examples are R & D incentives, promotion of new lower carbon technologies, and adaptation including transitional payments to workers who are adversely affected by the introduction of a carbon price. The ultimate recipients of this use of auction revenues would be households receiving some direct payment or employed or investing in the designated activities. Payments could also be made to the corporate entities who are the usual recipients of free allowance allocations, thereby replicating the effect of free allocation, but this alternative never figures in arguments concerning the use of auction revenues.

The final potential recipient of auction revenues is the Treasury, thereby reducing deficits, borrowing needs, and interest rates currently, as well as reducing the tax burden on future generations.

6.4 The evolution of allowance allocation

Three distinct phases can be identified in the evolution of the assignment of emission rights in cap-and-trade programs. The first phase includes all of the early US cap-and-trade programs targeting conventional emissions. Their distinguishing characteristic is the

---

[3] This idea was first advanced in Barnes (1999) with the label of "SkyTrust." It has re-emerged in the current US debate (see www.capanddividend.org) and received serious consideration as a viable alternative for allocation in, for instance, Congressional Budget Office (2007) and Orszag (2007).

non-controversial assignment, usually in perpetuity, of all the allowance value to the owners of the emission sources that were required to surrender allowances against emissions. The second phase is best represented by the European Union's CO_2 Emissions Trading Scheme in which a similar initial assignment to incumbent emitters led in very little time to the adoption of measures that will phase out free allocation. The current debate in the US for a GHG cap-and-trade program constitutes the third phase in which auctioning vs. free allocation has become an after-thought and the focus of the allocation debate is squarely on the intended recipients of the allowance value created by the cap.

6.4.1 The early US programs: non-controversial allocations[4]

All of the early US programs assigned 100 percent of the allowances to the owners of the emissions sources required to surrender allowances. Moreover, these assignments were of indefinite duration with no scheduled phase-out, although the right of the regulator to change the allocation subsequently was always implicit and sometimes explicitly asserted.[5]

These early allocations were remarkably non-controversial in comparison to what was to come. One reason is that allocation was poorly understood by the general policy community, even if participants, including the legislators or regulators who enacted the programs,

---

[4] The Acid Rain or SO_2 trading program is by far the most studied of the US programs. The standard reference is Ellerman et al. (2000) and useful shorter summaries are provided by Schmalensee et al. (1998), Stavins (1998), Burtraw and Palmer (2004), and Ellerman (2004). Harrison (2004) provides a good summary of the RECLAIM programs. The NOx programs, which are usefully summarized by Aulisi et al. (2005), are the orphans from the standpoint of academic research. The interested reader is well served by consulting the Annual Progress Reports published by the US Environmental Protection Agency for both the SO_2 and NOx programs (US EPA various). General reviews of early US experience with emissions trading are provided by Ellerman, Joskow, and Harrison (2003) and Tietenberg (2006).

[5] For instance, sec. 403(f) of the 1990 Clean Air Act Amendments authorizing the SO_2 Trading Program states that "an allowance ... is a limited authorization to emit sulfur dioxide ... [which] does not constitute a property right." This wording protects the government from charges of an unconstitutional taking when modifying the program while not obstructing the treatment of allowances as de facto property rights.

were aware of the distributive aspects.[6] As a result, the debate focused almost exclusively on the motivating environmental concerns and on the effectiveness and least-cost aspect of a cap-and-trade approach.

A second reason for the lack of controversy is the command-and-control precedent in air emissions regulation. The value created by prescriptive, source-specific limits on emissions was rarely an explicit issue in these regulatory proceedings and that value was invariably assigned to the incumbent, usually by the imposition of more stringent standards on new entrants. This feature was pointed out by economists, as well as the potential for regulatory capture and manipulation; however, the economic critique emphasized the perverse effects of these provisions and their inefficiency. The distributive effects were rarely if ever noted. An important exception was Buchanan and Tullock (1975) who hypothesized that the capture of this value was the reason that emission sources preferred command-and-control to the usual economic prescription of a Pigouvian tax. Thus, when the first air emissions markets were being constructed, the command-and-control precedent, which had always obscured the magnitude and value of the scarcity rents created by the constraint on emissions, predisposed most to ignore the distributive aspects of allowance allocation.

This regulatory precedent was also an important factor in explaining the generally favorable attitude of emitters towards cap-and-trade as an alternative. Not only did free allocation preserve the rent for those who would have received it under the command-and-control approach, but the value of that rent could be more easily monetized. The value could now be either used to avoid the purchase cost of allowances or turned into cash for other financial purposes. For instance, in the SO_2 program, scrubbers were financed in part by the sale of the allowance streams that would no longer be needed once the scrubber was installed and operating (Ellerman 2004).

A third and final reason for the non-controversial nature of the allowance assignment is the price-regulated status of the allowance recipients. Nearly all of the recipients in the three major US programs were electric utilities subject to cost-of-service regulation. In theory, a free allocation of allowances to these cost-of-service regulated entities

---

[6] Joskow and Schmalensee (1998), largely reprinted as chapter 3 in Ellerman et al. (2000), remains the best discussion and analysis of how allowance value was allocated in the legislative process.

meant that electricity prices would be lower and the allowance value conveyed to rate-payers. Whether this was the reality of electric utility regulation is another thing, but this idealized picture was firmly fixed in most people's minds and it put to rest any questions concerning the ultimate recipients of the allowance value being created by the cap.

The non-controversial nature of allocation in these early cap-and-trade programs allowed them to be debated almost exclusively on their environmental and economic merits. In all of these instances, cap-and-trade provided a welcome alternative to the conventional regulatory approach that was becoming increasingly unable to effect further emission reductions. The clearest example is the RECLAIM program. The regulatory authority, the South Coast Air Quality District, had developed a detailed source-specific, command-and-control program to reduce NOx and SO_2 emissions sufficiently to bring Los Angeles into compliance with the National Ambient Air Quality Standards, but the plan was viewed as very costly and infeasible politically. Cap-and-trade provided the answer with a cap equal to the emissions level that would have been achieved by this prescriptive plan and the flexibility that would avoid the outlandish instances of impracticality that could be used politically to weaken the program, if not to block its implementation entirely.

The issue here was not legal authority. The Clean Air Act endowed regulators with plenty of authority in theory; the issue was always the practicality of exercising that authority. Cap-and-trade provided a preferred approach both to the regulators, who were more interested in achieving the emission reductions than in the distribution of allowance value, and to the regulated, who realized that cap-and-trade provided better protection against the potentially adverse effects of further regulation on existing profits than the always possible command-and-control alternative.

A similar situation obtained with the nearly contemporaneous Acid Rain SO_2 Trading Program. The 1970 Clean Air Act was not well designed for dealing with inter-state pollution and a decade of failed legislative proposals in the 1980s for controlling acid rain precursor emissions, all of the command-and-control variety, prepared the way for the acceptance of this radically different approach when advanced in 1989 by the newly elected Bush Administration. As was the case with RECLAIM, legislators and the owners of affected facilities welcomed the ability to solve the environmental problem while being able to deal with distributional and equitable concerns in a low-key way through allowance allocation.

No better evidence exists of the preference for cap-and-trade when further emission reductions had to be made than the NOx Budget Program where the conventional regulatory alternative remained an explicit option. States were assigned a "budget" or limit on NOx emissions from within-state sources that would have to be met either by the conventional source-specific regulations or by adopting the common Model Rule and thereby participating in the regional NOx emissions trading program. All but one state chose to join the regional trading program and the exception proved the rule. The few sources in New Hampshire were already in compliance with the assigned budget so that there was no need to take additional measures.

The striking common feature of all these early US programs is that the allowances and the value embodied by them were granted for free to those required to surrender allowances equal to emissions, regardless of the process by which the program was created. This assignment met the concerns of all involved. For the regulated, their essentially defensive concern about the effect of an emissions constraint on their profits was met in a manner that was as good as, if not better than, the usual command-and-control alternative, and certainly better than a tax. For the legislators and regulators, allowances provided a quickly appreciated means of solving problems of equitable treatment without detracting from achievement of the environmental goal. Moreover, distributing allowances for free to those who would be required to surrender allowances, and who could be expected as a whole to undertake the desired abatement, was a lot easier than issuing a prescriptive rule and then having to amend it to fit the heterogeneous circumstances of the real world in which the rule had to be applied.

In these early programs, assigning both the obligation to surrender allowances and a certain number of free allowances to the regulated firms seemed an obvious way to proceed given the dominant regulatory mode of imposing obligations directly on emitting sources and not thinking about the distribution of a scarcely perceived scarcity rent. The newly affected sources had been freely exercising the right to emit before and they would be the entities requiring allowances afterwards. These firms were not clamoring for the cap, but given its adoption, the receipt of free allowances calmed their fears about the effects of the new policy on their profits. Moreover, since nearly all the

Allocation in air emissions markets 111

affected sources were in the cost-regulated electric utility sector, such an allocation was the more acceptable from a political point of view for lightening the cost burden on rate-payers.

6.4.2 The EU ETS: controversy appears[7]

The uncontroversial nature of allowance allocation in the early US programs was stripped away as using cap-and-trade came to be viewed as the means of limiting GHG emissions. The European Union's CO_2 Emissions Trading Scheme (EU ETS) marks the transition. It was the first cap-and-trade program to address GHG emissions and also the first to include sources outside of the electricity generation sector in a significant manner (about 40 percent of covered emissions). The EU ETS started out in 2005 with virtually 100 percent free allocation to regulated entities, as had been done in the early US programs, but this policy choice was an issue from the beginning, and auctioning soon became the basic rule.

In response to initial stakeholder consultations, the European Commission did not include auctioning in its initial proposal to establish a CO_2 cap-and-trade system. However, in the next step in the EU legislative process, the European Parliament initially insisted upon some degree of mandatory auctioning with amendments that went so far as to make auctioning the only means of distributing allowances in the second (2008–12) period. In the subsequent back-and-forth between the Council of Ministers and the Parliament, the percentage of auctioning was whittled down and, in the end, the mandatory inclusion of auctioning fell victim to mandatory participation in the first (2005–07) period. At the urging of strong industry lobbies, both the UK and Germany had held out for member-state opt-outs for the first period

---

[7] A symposium in the initial issue of the *Review of Environmental Economics and Policy* provides a good introduction to the EU ETS (Convery and Redmond 2007; Ellerman and Buchner 2007, and Kruger, Oates, and Pizer 2007). Other summary introductions are Ellerman (2008) and Ellerman and Joskow (2008). A comprehensive evaluation of the early years of the program is provided by Ellerman, Convery, and de Perthuis (2010). The experience of allocating allowances is the subject of ten member-state case studies in Ellerman, Buchner, and Carraro (2007). Delbeke (2006) provides a clear and thorough explanation of the development and resolution of issues that arose in implementation. The political context and history is superbly presented in Skjærseth and Wettestad (2008).

based upon their own climate-change programs that relied largely on voluntary agreements with industry. In the final agreement, these two largest countries agreed to mandatory participation in the first period, but the price was the ability to issue all allowances free of charge to incumbent emitters (Skjærseth and Wettestad 2008, pp. 126–132).

As a consequence, auctioning was no more than an option in the final Directive (European Union 2003). Member states could auction up to 5% of the member-state total for the first period (2005–07) and up to 10% in the second period (2008–12). In other words, free allocation was mandatory for 95% and 90% of the member state's allowances and 100% free allocation was not precluded. The member-state uptake of the auctioning option was slight. Only four member states (Denmark, Ireland, Hungary, and Lithuania) chose to auction in the first period for a total of 0.13% of the total cap. In the second period, four more member states (Germany, the UK, the Netherlands, and Austria) auctioned some allowances and the percentage rose to 3.0%.

The combination of free allocation and high prices in the early years of the first trading period created a huge outcry over what came to be called "windfall profits," which was seen as a direct consequence of free allocation.[8] The initial Directive provided an opportunity to address such concerns in its requirement that the Commission consult with stakeholders and propose revisions to the Directive in light of experience during the first period. The resulting proposal to amend the Directive included provisions (European Commission 2008b) that

- established auctioning as the basic principle of allocation for the EU ETS;
- prohibited free allocation to electric utilities beginning in 2013;
- phased out free allocation to industrial facilities from 80 percent of baseline in 2013 to 0 percent in 2020; and
- allowed up to 100 percent free allocation for facilities in industrial sectors found to be trade-impacted.

---

[8] Curiously, this critique was directed at electric utilities, often by non-utility industrial concerns, who logically were themselves also recipients of "windfall profits." A notable difference in Europe, when compared to the circumstances of the early US programs, is that electricity markets had become deregulated in some large member states and that industrial concerns were often exposed to wholesale electricity prices even in those countries where retail electricity rates continued to be regulated.

The subsequent legislative process softened these provisions by allowing some East European countries to phase out free allocation to electric utilities between 2013 and 2020 and extending the industrial phase out from 2020 to 2027. Still, about half of the allowances issued in 2013 will be auctioned and the remaining free allocation progressively phased out in favor of auctioning.

What had not been possible politically when the initial Directive (European Union 2003) was adopted became so five years later in December 2008 when agreement on the amended Directive (European Union 2009a) was reached. The main issue in 2003 was whether to adopt a system and especially whether it would be mandatory for all member states in the first period. In 2008, when the system was established and had even become the source of some pride, the issue was not whether to continue it, but how to amend it in light of the experience in the first few years. Not having to battle over whether the system should be continued made it possible to focus on these details of system design.

The controversy over windfall profits, which greatly facilitated the adoption of changes in the allocation rules, revealed a countervailing concern to that of industry about the effects of pricing access to the commons on their profits, namely, that allocation should not *increase* their profits. At the same time, the continuing free allocation to "trade-impacted" sectors indicated a continuing concern that the profits of regulated firms should not be diminished as a result of pricing their access to the commons. In effect, a more nuanced view of allocation, based squarely on the *status quo ante*, has evolved. Allocation should not disadvantage the owners of affected facilities, but it should also not make them better off.

This distinction was foreshadowed in the initial free allocation to affected facilities, where a clear distinction was drawn between industrial firms, which were subject to extra-EU competition, and electric utilities that were not. When EU member states first confronted the task of allocating allowances, which implicitly involved assigning the expected shortage to affected facilities, they assigned the shortage of electric utilities and provided industrial facilities as many allowances as they were expected to need (Ellerman, Buchner, and Carraro 2007, pp. 357ff). This differential treatment is evident not only in the public explanations offered in nearly every National Allocation Plan, but also in any ex post examination of the differences between allocations and emissions at affected facilities (Ellerman and Buchner 2007; Kettner et al. 2007; Ellerman and Trotignon 2009).

The EU ETS marks an important stage in the evolution of allocation in air emissions markets. The practical exigencies of getting a program started resulted in an initial free allocation to regulated entities that mirrored the American example, but circumstances quickly changed. Not only was auctioning formally adopted as the basic principle of distribution in response to the perceived windfalls to regulated entities, but a more refined criterion for free allocation was developed. A vague concern for effects on profits would no longer suffice; a more specific, plausible concern would have to be established, such as competition with firms not facing similar charges. The implied criterion is that free allocation is justified to compensate for these competitive effects, but not otherwise.

6.4.3 The US GHG proposals: focusing on the ultimate recipients

The debate in the EU ETS between free allocation and auctioning has focused on the means of distributing allowances without paying much attention to the ultimate recipients of the allowance value created by the cap. There is a good institutional reason for this limitation on the debate in the European Union. The European Commission, which had become the central agent in implementing the EU ETS, cannot raise its own revenue and does not tell member governments how to spend the revenue they receive.[9] Allowances might be auctioned from a central platform, but the revenues would go back to the member states to decide how they should be spent, in the same way that free allocation had been left to member states in the first two periods. Since no such institutional barrier exists in the United States, the debate has moved directly to the identity of the final recipients of the newly created allowance value.

---

[9] A reaffirmation of this point can be observed in the evolution of a provision in the Commission's initial proposal for amending the ETS Directive (European Commission 2008b) that would require member states to reserve 20 percent of auction revenues for climate-related purposes. In the final compromise (European Union 2009a) this requirement was made into an aspirational goal (at an even higher percentage) but with a firm reassertion of a member state's right to decide how to dispose of its auction revenues.

The change in allocation first appeared in the Regional Greenhouse Gas Initiative (RGGI) in the north-eastern states from whence it progressed to the legislative proposals developed in the Senate in the last years of the Bush Administration and became fully exposed in the more serious discussion engaged in Congress after President Obama's election. Also, in this Congressional phase of the debate, a new claimant has appeared: direct compensation to households.

RGGI entered into effect at the beginning of 2009 and it is the only state or regional cap-and-trade program implemented so far in the US. The Model Rule, which was developed to guide participating states in implementing the program, called for reserving 25 percent of allowances for public auction to be used for "consumer benefit or strategic energy purpose" (RGGI 2006, p. 43). Reserving a quarter of the allowances for public auction was a radical departure from prior US experience, but the final choices of all the participating states was even more surprising: auctioning 100 percent (or slightly less in some cases) of the allowances and using the revenue exclusively for funding energy efficiency and renewable energy programs. The foremost advocates of this allocation were the environmental non-governmental organizations who successfully coupled auctioning with increased government expenditure for specified environmental purposes.

As the debate over GHG cap-and-trade measures moved to the federal level and to Congress in 2007–08, a compromise was developed that split the anticipated allowance value approximately equally between the RGGI example of auctioning with revenue assigned to public uses and the free allocation to covered sources. This compromise failed to satisfy anyone. Advocates of auctioning were dismayed at the continuing free allocation, while conservatives were appalled by the unprecedented expansion of government expenditure outside of the usual budgetary and appropriations process.

The only proposal so far to gain a majority for passage in either chamber of Congress, the Waxman–Markey Bill, which was approved by the House of Representatives in June 2009, differs significantly in its allocation of allowance value.

- Free allocation to firms required to surrender allowances is conditional and limited to trade-impacted industry as in the EU ETS.
- Funding of climate-related programs is scaled back considerably from the RGGI example and what had been previously proposed in Congress.

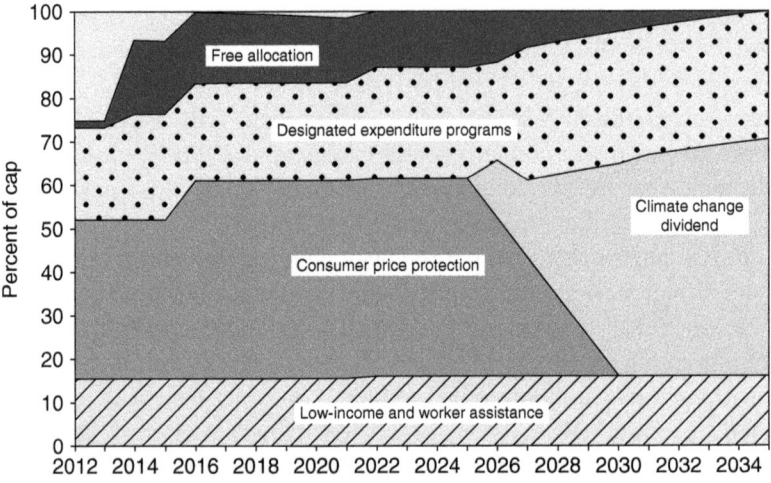

Figure 6.1 Waxman–Markey allocation by broad use
Source: Developed by the author

- The majority of allowance value is dedicated to compensating consumers directly for the effects of a carbon price.

Figure 6.1 illustrates these broad categories.

The most striking feature of this proposal is the extent to which direct compensation to consumers has replaced free allocation to incumbents and the funding of climate-related programs. Consumer compensation starts out at 52 percent of allowance value and rises to 71 percent by 2035. It consists of three components:

- a continuing 15 percent tranche to be auctioned with the revenues used to compensate low-income households for the presumed regressive effects of carbon prices;
- a large initial allocation to local electricity and natural gas distribution companies to use for shielding consumers from electricity rate increases; and
- a later auction with the proceeds returned to households on a per capita basis as a climate change dividend.[10]

In contrast, expenditures on climate-related programs and free allocation to affected facilities, which had split the pie in earlier

---

[10] Since all local distribution companies are price regulated, the initial distribution of allowances to these entities effectively delegates the allocation

Congressional proposals, have less than half the pie to share among themselves. Special expenditure programs start out at 21% and rise eventually to 29%, while free allocation to firms starts out with 1.5% of the cap, rises to a maximum of 17% when the industrial sector enters the program in 2014, declines to 12% in 2026, and is then phased out in 10% increments by 2035.

Whether these allowances are to be auctioned or freely allocated is hardly mentioned and the link between having an obligation to surrender allowances against emissions and receiving a free allocation of allowances is completely severed. The bulk of the allowance value for the initial fifteen years will be directly allocated to entities that have no obligation to surrender allowances against emissions. The presumption is that these recipients will sell them to realize the allowance value, but the legislation is silent on this matter other than indicating that entities receiving these allowances may consign them to the federal auction that will be required for the 15 percent tranche designated for low-income households and for the later climate change dividend. Only 15 percent of total allowance value is reserved for entities that have an obligation to surrender allowances against emissions and only for those considered to be trade-impacted. Even so, the free allocation cannot be taken for granted. Eligible industrial sectors will be defined by a rule based on the trade and carbon intensity of each sector's output and qualifying installations will not receive allowances up front but be rebated annually on a product-output basis.[11]

The Senate must now act and the evolution of the debate there highlights even more the emergence of the consumer as a new claimant for allowance value. At the end of 2009, Senators Cantwell and Collins introduced a bill that has received much attention and has been dubbed a "cap-and-dividend" bill for requiring all of the allowances to be auctioned and 75 percent of the resulting value to be returned to households in a quarterly dividend check. The details of

---

decision to the state public utility commissions which regulate the prices of electricity and natural gas distributed to retail household customers.

[11] The only exception would be the refining sector whose allocation of 2 percent from 2014 to 2026 is not dependent on a determination of trade impact. The allocation represents process emissions and it is a small proportion of the total number of allowances that refineries would be required to surrender since they must also cover the carbon content of all refined products sold for domestic consumption.

what is expected to be the main legislative vehicle in the Senate, to be introduced by Senators Kerry, Graham, and Lieberman, have yet to be revealed, but the sponsors have indicated that a cap-and-dividend feature may account for as much as 60 percent of allowance value.

The current proposals for a US GHG program move beyond the familiar auctioning vs. free allocation debate with its unspoken presumption that auctioned allowances would be used for public uses and that freely allocated allowances would be awarded to corporate entities. Whether to auction or to allocate freely has become a technical detail as the debate focuses squarely on the intended recipient of allowance value. Perhaps not surprisingly, free allocation to public entities, which would sell the allowances and use the revenues for designated public purposes, has given conservatives reason to oppose free allocation with the same intensity that liberals have inveighed against free allocation to private entities. The beneficiaries of this emerging stand-off will be consumers, who are broadly speaking the origin of the demand for the goods and services that cause the harm and those who will bear the final cost of measures taken to reduce these harmful effects. This consumer interest in compensation has been slow to assert itself, but it appears finally to have done so.

6.5 Conclusion

If the final US GHG cap-and-trade program resembles the current lead proposals in the Congress, the assignment of property rights in air emissions markets will have undergone a complete transformation in form. From being assigned entirely to the emitting sources included within the program through free allocation, allowances are now to be mostly auctioned and the proceeds returned directly to households. This evolution reflects the special characteristics of air emissions markets. When a market is to be created from scratch and the motivation is the avoidance of social harm, there are no obvious claimants for the value created. The early claims of producing firms for free allocation were motivated not so much by attempts to preserve benefit from the exploitation of the common pool resource as by an essentially defensive concern for the effects of the proposed constraint on their preexisting profits. While this concern is justifiable and one that must be addressed, the EU ETS has shown that finding the right balance is not easy. Finally, it has taken a long time for the public, broadly speaking,

Allocation in air emissions markets

to realize that they are those benefiting from free access to the common pool resource as well as those harmed by its overuse. The slow but inevitable recognition of this circumstance is forming the basis for assigning most of the allowance value directly to consumers.

At a deeper level, the evolution in the assignment of property rights in air emissions markets represents a return, after some stumbling through agency problems, to the principle recognized by Libecap. The proximate motivation for creating air emissions markets has not been preserving profits from the exploitation of a common pool resource, but their further development appears likely to require an assignment of the property rights created by the cap to those who are both the causes of overuse through their demand for goods and services at lowest cost and the beneficiaries of the non-pricing of access to the common pool resource. Or, as expressed more colloquially and pithily by Pogo: "We have met the enemy and he is us."

7 Auction versus negotiation in public procurement: looking for empirical evidence

ESHIEN CHONG, CARINE STAROPOLI, AND ANNE YVRANDE-BILLON

7.1 Introduction

Public procurement refers to the public authorities' activities of purchasing goods, works, and services. These purchases range from simple items such as pens and paper clips through to complex goods or construction works. Hence public procurement markets represent a major part of economic activities. For instance, in the European Union, total public procurement is estimated at about 17 percent of EU GDP (€2,000 billion) in 2007,[1] while in France it represents 16.6 percent of GDP.[2]

Procurement policy also plays an important role in addressing social and environmental problems (EU 2005) and in developing the private sector in general and specific segments of the industry (SME notably). Additionally, in the European context, an effective public procurement policy is fundamental to improve the functioning of the Internal Market and enable the EU to reap the full benefits from an enlarged Internal Market. For that purpose, community rules on public procurement have been set up (Directives 2004/18/EC and 2004/17/EC).

As in the US, the rules organizing public procurement in Europe strongly advocate the use of auctions to award contracts and select

---

This chapter benefited from comments received at various seminars and conferences, including the ISNIE 2010 conference, the conference on Applied Infrastructure Research in Berlin, and the workshop "Manufacturing Markets" in Firenze. In particular, we would like to thank Ricard Gil, Leonardo Meeus, Jean-Michel Oudot, Pablo Spiller, and Frank Wolak for very helpful comments on earlier versions of the chapter.

[1] Internal Market Scoreboard, n°19, July 2009.
[2] Source: http://ec.europa.eu/internal_market/publicprocurement/docs/public-proc-market-final-report_en.pdf (accessed June 1, 2012).

final providers of goods and services to public entities while the circumstances when negotiation can be used are strictly restricted. Such preference for competitive tendering over negotiated procedures in public procurement is justified by the assumption that auctions allow finding supply sources at the cheapest price and at acceptable quality. Auctions are also favored because they are seen as a way to prevent favoritism and ensure equal opportunity to potential suppliers. As a matter of fact, auctions remain the dominant award mechanism for public procurement contracts. Thus, in France, from 2005 to 2007, auctions were used to award 70 percent of the procurement contracts in the public works sector while in Europe they corresponded to 82 percent in 2008 (European Union 2009b).

Yet, recent empirical and theoretical contributions show that auctions are not a *panacea*, as already pointed out by Williamson (1976). Interestingly, while public and private procurement share the same essential purpose of obtaining the lowest price without loss of quality, the practices of each sector are different. Thus, as documented by Bajari et al. (2009), "from 1995 to 2000, almost half of private sector non-residential building construction projects in Northern California were procured using negotiations, while the rest were procured with some form of competitive bidding. Only eighteen percent were procured using unrestricted open competitive bidding, which is what FAR dictates for the public sector" (p. 1). In other words, while auctions are the prescribed procedures and the most used ones for public procurement, in the private sector – where buyers are free to choose their purchasing method – competitive tendering is far from being their preferred option.

In addition, as shown by several recent empirical works (Guasch 2004; Guasch et al. 2008; Estache et al. 2009), public procurement contracts awarded via competitive tendering are frequently renegotiated, which generates significant additional costs and questions the efficiency of the procedure itself. Thus for instance, Guccio et al. (2008), in a study of public works procurement contracts in Italy in 2005, estimate that, for about a quarter of all works, adaptation costs consequent to renegotiations increase the original costs by 10 percent. Additionally, the main argument justifying the use of auctions for public procurement (to prevent collusive practices and corruption) is severely called into question. Numerous theoretical developments indeed show that competitive tendering procedures are not immune to corruption, collusion, and/or favoritism (Compte et al. 2005; Lambert-Mogiliansky and Sonin 2006; Auriol et al. 2009).

These paradoxical observations regarding the use of auctions and negotiation in public procurement are the starting point of our chapter which aims at empirically investigating the determinants of award procedures. For this purpose, we use an exhaustive dataset of 76,188 French public works contracts attributed at various levels of decisions (central government, including agencies, universities, hospitals, etc., and local governments) between 2005 and 2007. Based on these data, our chapter highlights empirical regularities on what motivates public buyers when choosing a given procedure. In line with recent developments in the transaction cost literature, our work contributes to the discussion on the relative merits of alternative awarding mechanisms in a context where the will to implement competition to avoid corruption and favoritism should favor auctions, while the effective governance for complex and sometimes unique work should be "relational contracting" or negotiations. From a theoretical perspective, this debate has received a lot of attention since the seminal papers by Demsetz (1968) and Williamson (1976) who expressed opposite views on the efficiency of franchise bidding for natural monopolies. However, very few empirical works have been done to confront their propositions with facts, which is precisely what motivates the present work.

The chapter is organized as follows. Section 7.2 summarizes the theoretical arguments developed in the procurement literature regarding the respective merits of auction and negotiation. This survey allows us to identify the conditions under which auctions are more efficient than negotiation procedures. Section 7.3 presents public procurement practices in the construction sector in France thereby emphasizing the nature of the transactions and the governance problems that characterize the construction process. Section 7.4 is devoted to empirically investigate the main determinants of the choice of procedure in the French construction sector. We first deal with the impact of buyers' experience and expertise on the choice of award procedure. Then, we assess the role of projects' size and contracts' duration. Section 7.5 is dedicated to the analysis of the renegotiations that have occurred which is a first step towards an efficiency analysis of the trade-off between auction and negotiation. Section 7.6 concludes on the economic rationale behind the choice of awarding procedures.

7.2 Auction versus negotiation: the theoretical debate

Besides the traditional literature on auctions which emphasizes the efficiency properties of such attribution mechanisms as means to introduce competition and prevent corruption (Bulow and Klemperer 1996), a growing body of the procurement literature supports the promotion of alternative award procedures (more particularly negotiation) or at least questions the conditions under which auctions can efficiently be used. The arguments put to the front to qualify the efficiency of auctions echo the ones used by the proponents of the Transaction Cost Economics view in the now classical "franchise bidding of natural monopolies" debate which opposed, in the 1970s, Demsetz (1968), on the one hand, to Williamson (1976) and Goldberg (1976, 1977), on the other hand. While Demsetz (1968) considered that competitive tendering was the ideal mechanism to regulate natural monopolies, Williamson (1976) and Goldberg (1976, 1977) highlighted the failures of auction procedures, arguing that in the presence of relationship-specific investments and high uncertainty the contractual disabilities of the parties mitigate the efficiency of the franchise bidding mechanism and militate in favor of the use of alternative coordination devices, like utilities regulation.[3]

In the broader context of public procurement, the trade-off between regulation and franchise bidding translates into a trade-off between negotiation and auction. While regulation and franchise bidding are two ways to select and/or control a natural monopoly, the literature on procurement, in its recent developments, views auction and negotiation as alternative ways to select a provider of goods and services, each one presenting its own advantages and limitations (Manelli and Vincent 1995; Bajari et al. 2009).

In a nutshell, while auctions are supposed to ensure transparency, selection of the lowest cost bidders by benefiting from competition and prevent biased awarding of contracts, it may have some undesirable self-selection consequences and fail to respond optimally to *ex post* adaptation. On the contrary, negotiations may easily be suspected of corruption and favoritism but at the same time these "relational" contracting modes allow public buyers and suppliers to spend more

---

[3] See Priest (1993) or Crocker and Masten (1996) for a detailed review of the debate.

time discussing *ex ante* the characteristics of the project to be delivered, and the appropriate design of the contract thereby reducing the risk of *ex post* opportunistic haggling. Hence, according to this literature, the trade-off between auctions and negotiations in public procurement is assumed to depend on (1) the buyers' level of expertise and competencies regarding the organization of competitive tendering, (2) the potential for competition, and (3) the level of complexity of the project to be procured. In what follows, we present the theoretical arguments regarding these three aspects. In the next section, we investigate whether we can find empirical regularities suggesting that these aspects influence French public buyers' decision regarding the choice of an award procedure for works contracts.

7.2.1 Buyers' competencies

A first challenge buyers have to face is to define the characteristics of the work to be procured. This task may be particularly difficult when buyers have no clear preferences or lack the technical expertise (e.g., knowledge of construction techniques, materials, process) required to describe the project. In such circumstances of limited capabilities of the buyers, negotiation should be the preferred awarding procedure because it allows the buyers to discuss the project with the potential suppliers and hence improve its design and specification before work begins. Conversely, experienced buyers, because they build more frequently and/or have competent technicians and engineers in-house, are expected to use auctions more frequently, all else held constant (Goldberg 1977; Bajari et al. 2009).

The second challenge linked to buyers' competencies concerns the organization of the awarding procedure itself. Many public procurement processes are carried out by municipalities or small agencies which may have neither the experience nor the knowledge of how to organize an efficient award procedure that is respectful of the rather complex and changing legislation and may then be afraid of being suspected of favoritism or corruption. Furthermore, the increasing number of recourses notably by eliminated candidates increases the fear of being suspected of favoritism or any kind of discretionary power.[4] In

---

[4] For instance, the European Court of Justice published 200 judgments and orders containing the keywords "public procurement" and "award" between 1997 and 2009. Of these judgments, 27.5 percent were made between 1997 and 2003 and 72.5 percent between 2004 and 2009. Moreover the recent EU

order to avoid such suspicions, public buyers are inclined to choose auction. This last argument echoes the one developed by Spiller (2008) on the incidence of public scrutiny on the choices made by public contractors. In particular, he argues that the pressure exerted by interested third parties (e.g., political competitors) might lead public bodies to avoid negotiation and relational contracting and prefer rigid procedural processes such as auctions.

7.2.2 Potential for competition

There are critical pitfalls in auction design since, depending on the circumstances, auctions are very vulnerable to collusion and may deter entry into the auction (Porter and Zona 1993; Klemperer 2002). The benefits for auctioning may thus be reduced if not totally cancelled in case of collusive market since there might not be enough bidders to assure that the winning price will differ significantly from the monopoly price. Among the various circumstances that participate to increasing the risks that participants may explicitly or tacitly collude, the number of potential respondents to the competitive tender is a crucial determinant for the success of auctioning. In a nutshell, if the market is highly concentrated – few potential respondents – auction may be less attractive than negotiation.

7.2.3 Complexity

The variable that has undoubtedly deserved the most attention in the literature on public procurement is the complexity of the goods/works to be procured. Defined as the difficulty to provide a rather complete set of plans and contingencies of a project, complexity is considered in the literature as a key determinant of the choice of an awarding procedure. More precisely, negotiation is advocated when the project is complex, that is when *ex ante* design is hard to complete and *ex post* adaptations are expected. By contrast, competitive tendering is the recommended awarding mechanism for projects and services that are simple to describe and for which there are no objective reasons for *ex post* adaptations (Mougeot and Naegelen 1988; Bajari et al. 2009).

Directive 2007/66/EC seeks to allow potential candidates to legally contest award decisions made by public buyers. Therefore, the legal risks supported by public buyers can be expected to become higher.

Auctions are thus an effective way of determining the lowest cost supplier where the price of the project being procured is the buyer's only concern.

But auctions work less well for complex projects or services for which a vector of prices is to be determined and/or for which the buyer highly cares about other attributes of procurement like quality or reliability (Manelli and Vincent 1995). In such cases, the selection principles of the winning bidder are indeed difficult to determine. Although multidimensional auctions theoretically appear as a natural practical solution to deal with such circumstances, they are very often too complex to implement in practice because of their lack of transparency and their greater vulnerability to corruption and favoritism (Burguet and Che 2004; Estache et al. 2009).

Another risk incurred when auctions are used for complex projects is the increase of the bidding costs. Indeed, if the buyer fails to specify the subject matter of the bid with precision then uncertainties will result, costs of bidding will be increased, and applicants will be discouraged. The number of bidders being limited, the expected benefits of competitive tendering would consequently be affected. Or, as shown by Bajari et al. (2007), the number of bidders may not be limited but, since they anticipate future renegotiation due to contractual incompleteness, their bid may incorporate high risk premia for them to be able to recover potential adaptation costs.[5]

Finally, if the description of the project is not sufficiently clear, competitive tendering may also lead to situations of adverse selection and end up with the selection of the most opportunistic bidder (Bajari et al. 2009). If contractual design is incomplete and service is complex, auction may indeed lead to choosing the bidder who is the most aware of the contractual blanks he could exploit, that is to say the one who is able to determine where contracts will fail. Anticipating that he will be able to take advantage of situations that are unforeseen in the contract by renegotiating the initial arrangement, this strategic candidate will not hesitate to propose an unrealistically low price. This type of bidding behavior (low-balling strategy) jeopardizes allocative efficiency, which is the most important objective of tendering.

---

[5] In their study of highway construction and maintenance contracts in California, Bajari et al. (2007) estimate these risk premia to represent, on average, 10 percent of the value of the contract.

To sum up the propositions derived from the literature, the trade-off between auction and negotiation in public procurement is assumed to depend on (1) the competencies of public buyers regarding the design of the project and the organization of competitive tendering, (2) the potential for competition, (3) the level of complexity of the project to be procured. Moreover, it has been argued theoretically that auction-based procedures are more likely to lead to *ex post* adjustments, and these adjustments are potentially more costly. In the next section, we intend to identify and document such regularities in the French public procurement practices using data on public procurement work contracts. To this end, we first investigate the determinants of award procedures using variables that may serve as proxies for the three classes of determinants identified above. In a second subsection, we look into the occurrence of contract amendments to understand whether *ex post* adjustments occur as the theory predicts.

7.3 Public procurement in the construction sector in France

7.3.1 Work contracts

Our study focuses on works contracts, which represent 35 percent of the procurement contracts in 2007 in France. Given the definition provided by the EU Directive works cover the whole range of construction works from site preparation, complete or part construction and civil engineering utility sectors, building installation (electrical, plumbing and sanitary, mechanical, etc.), and building completion. This diversity translates into various situations regarding the level of complexity, coordination problems, uncertainty, or potential opportunistic behaviors from contracting parties.

Thanks to the rich and exhaustive data provided by the Economic Observatory of Public Procurement of the French Ministry of Finance (OEAP), we have been able to build a comprehensive database covering the public work procurement activities undertaken by public buyers during three consecutive years, from 2005 to 2007. More precisely, the database contains information on some characteristics of the projects (e.g., type of work) and their afferent contract (e.g., value, duration, identity of contractors, awarding procedure, price, number of subcontractors, renegotiation). During this period, a total of 76,188 procurement contracts have been passed by 8,216 public buyers in

France. However, for motives of coherence and robustness, we had to reduce our sample to 72,283 procurement contracts on public works.

7.3.2 Buyers

Buyers can be distinguished between central administrations (i.e., ministries, museums, universities, hospitals and other bodies governed by public law, or associations formed by one or more of such authorities or bodies governed by public law) and local administrations (e.g., regions, *départements*, municipalities, etc.). For simplicity, we will refer to the former as "central buyers" and the latter as "local buyers."

There are 7,645 local buyers and 517 central buyers who have awarded at least one procurement contract on public work during the three years of our sample. Over this period, the bulk of procurement activities stems from local buyers (90.1 percent of total procurement contracts). However, the average number of procurement contracts per central buyer is 13.83 and only 8.5 per local buyer. Procurement activities as measured by the value of contracts are more important on the whole for local buyers, even if the average value of a public work contract is more important for central buyers (the average contract for a central buyer amounts to about €508,898 while for a local buyer it is about €407,949). In terms of contract duration, the average duration for a public work contract is about 12.21 months long.

7.3.3 Procedures

The French Public Procurement Code holds that public buyers may choose among eight formalized awarding procedures for work contracts between €4,000 net of VAT and €5,150,000 net of VAT.[6] These procedures differ in various dimensions including publication rules, openness to effective competition, selection criteria and process.

In order to stick to the literature, we focus on five procedures that can be grouped into two main categories: "auction," which gathers the open and restricted auction procedures, and "negotiation," which gathers the three procedures for which selection is made after consultation of the candidates and negotiation of contracts' conditions.

---

[6] These thresholds are those used in 2007; they have been slightly modified in 2010, the upper threshold being €4,845,000.

Open competitive tender is by far the favorite choice of French public buyers and, altogether, open and restricted auctions are used for about 72 percent of public work contracts over the three years 2005–2007. Even if the use of negotiated procedures is somehow restricted to specific situations, it still represents about 17 percent of award procedures, negotiation with prior publication and call for competition being by far the most popular negotiated procedure.

Over the years, there has been a slight evolution in the type of procedure used by public buyers. Indeed, over the period 2005–2007, there is a decrease in the use of competitive tender procedures overall: while this procedure accounts for 73 percent of total procurement contracts in 2005, this ratio falls to 63 percent in 2007. Thus, despite the growing emphasis in the EU directives on the merits of competitive tendering, there seems to be a trend in France towards less competitive procedures, namely negotiated procedures. The remainder of this chapter helps in assessing this evolution.

7.4 Auctions versus negotiations: an empirical analysis

7.4.1 The determinants of award procedures for French public work procurement contracts

In the following, we investigate how various determinants may impact the public buyers' choice of award procedure by examining correlations between the observed award procedures and proxies for each of the identified determinants using simple statistics and/or distribution graphs.

7.4.1.1 Public buyers' expertise

To explore the incidence of buyers' capabilities on the choice of award procedures, we rely on two different proxies. Firstly, we compare award procedures used by central and local buyers, and secondly, we rely on the number of public work contracts previously awarded as a measure of the buyer's experience. The former variable may reflect buyers' expertise as central buyers are usually better staffed than local ones (OECD 1999). Therefore, one may expect central buyers to be more competent in defining their projects. The latter variable captures potential learning effects that a buyer could acquire by frequently

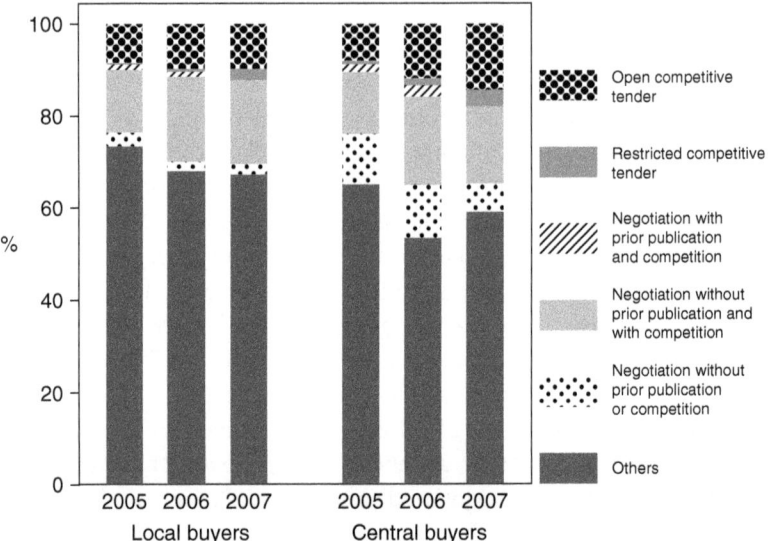

Figure 7.1 Evolution of award procedures according to the administrative level of public buyers

dealing with public work procurement contracts. Based on our theoretical discussion, we expect central buyers to rely more on auction based procedures.

Figure 7.1 shows the use of various award procedures by central and local buyers. It reveals no great differences in the choices made by these two categories of buyers: both use competitive tendering and negotiation in the same proportions. The only noticeable difference concerns the use of restricted competitive tendering which is much more frequent for central buyers. This may be explained by the size of the projects launched by central buyers which requires them to restrict the number of bidders. This is consistent with the results obtained by Bajari et al. (2007) and Ye (2007) who find that, for projects involving large bidding costs, buyers should restrict competition in order to give qualified bidders an incentive to participate by maximizing their chance to win the project.

As a measure of buyers' experience, we use the cumulative sum of public works contracts awarded by a buyer (up to a given year) and check whether more experienced buyers tend to rely more on auctions.

Auction versus negotiation in public procurement

Table 7.1 *Award procedure and contractual experience*

Awarding procedures chosen at year t	Public buyer's contractual experience (cumulative sum of public works contracts signed up to year t)	
	Mean	Standard deviation
Open auction	78.05	126.33
Restricted auction	71.51	108.74
Negotiation with prior publicity and competition	68.50	114.36
Negotiation without prior publicity and with competition	66.67	87.30
Negotiation without prior publicity nor competition	112.65	156.50
Others	62.34	131.79
Total	75.09	124.77

Table 7.1 shows that more experienced buyers tend to use competitive tendering more frequently.[7] On average, the contractual experience of buyers who choose open auctions is significantly higher than the experience of those who choose restricted auctions (resp. 78.05 contracts and 71.51 contracts). This result corroborates that auction is chosen by public buyers that have the highest experience in terms of cumulative number of contracts.

7.4.1.2 The potential for competition

A second determinant of buyers' choices relates directly to competitive pressure. If available, we would use the number of potential respondents per tender, as well as various measures of industrial concentration and barriers to entry to explore the link between the potential for

---

[7] We conducted a Student's t-test to check whether the mean public buyers' experience when competitive tendering is used is significantly different from the mean public buyers' experience for the three types of negotiation-based procedures. The test statistic is −5.6002, indicating that the difference in means is significant at less than 1 percent.

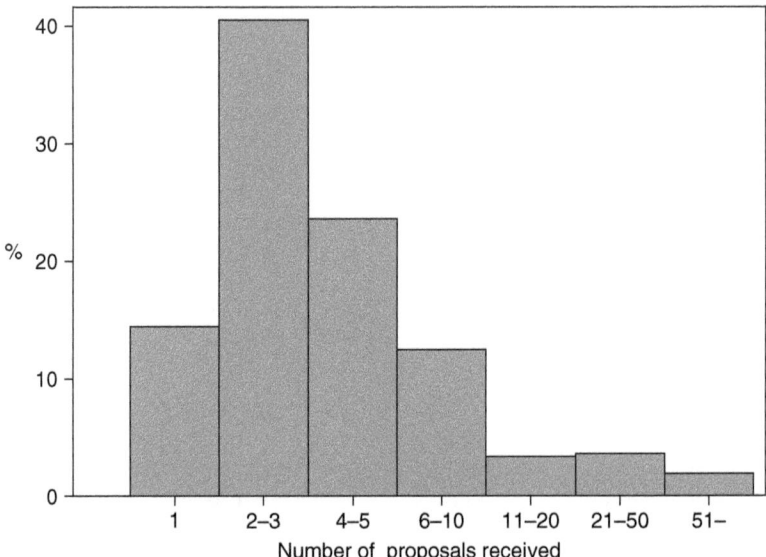

Figure 7.2 Distribution of the number of proposals received per contract (2007)

competition and the chosen award procedure. Unfortunately, we do not have information on the pertinent market and consequently on these various measures. Still, for each contract attributed in 2007 we have data on the number of proposals received by buyers. Even if it cannot be considered as a concentration index, this variable still gives some indications on the intensity of competition and thereby might affect the relative efficiency of award procedures. Indeed, fewer propositions submitted in a tender may reflect either a lack of potential candidates (and thus a concentrated market), or the fact that potential candidates refuse to submit or consider the tender as unsuited to them. Such refusals may be due to real or supposed entry barriers linked to the bidding costs imposed on bidders or to suspicions of favoritism by the buyer towards a particular competitor (reducing the expectation to be selected). It may also reflect collusive or entry-deterring behaviors from competitors.

Our data reveal that the intensity of competition is moderate (Figure 7.2): in about 40% of the cases, public buyers have received two to three propositions, which may reflect limited competition, and in about 25% of the cases they have received four or five propositions.

Table 7.2 *Number of propositions received by awarding procedures (2007)*

Procedures	N	Mean
Open auction	10,091	6.60
Restricted auction	395	4.55
Negotiation with prior publication and competition	2,670	6.30
Negotiation without prior publication nor competition	298	2.85
Others	1,542	3.66
Total	14,996	6.12

Cases with more than eleven propositions represent 12% of the cases, while cases where buyers received only one proposition – which by definition reflects a lack of competition – represent 15%. A more detailed analysis also reveals that the picture is relatively similar for both local and central buyers even if the market seems to be more competitive at the local level.

It is also worth noting that on average the number of propositions received under negotiation with prior publication and call for competition and under open competitive tenders are almost the same (6.3 and 6.6 respectively) (Table 7.2). This suggests that even with negotiated procedures, competition may not be altogether absent.

7.4.1.3 The complexity of a procurement project

As explained below, we would expect that more complex projects are associated with negotiation-based procedures.

Complexity is difficult to measure, especially given the vast amount and the wide diversity of contracts we have in the database. As such, we use contracts' value and duration as proxies for complexity in our empirical analysis: arguably, both dimensions are closely related to the complexity of a project and this is consistent with previous works on the subject (e.g., Bajari et al. 2007). Indeed, considering that complex projects often involve a higher number of tasks and more collaborators, one may assume that more complex projects are more expensive. Moreover, as uncertainty is a key determinant of complexity and as the

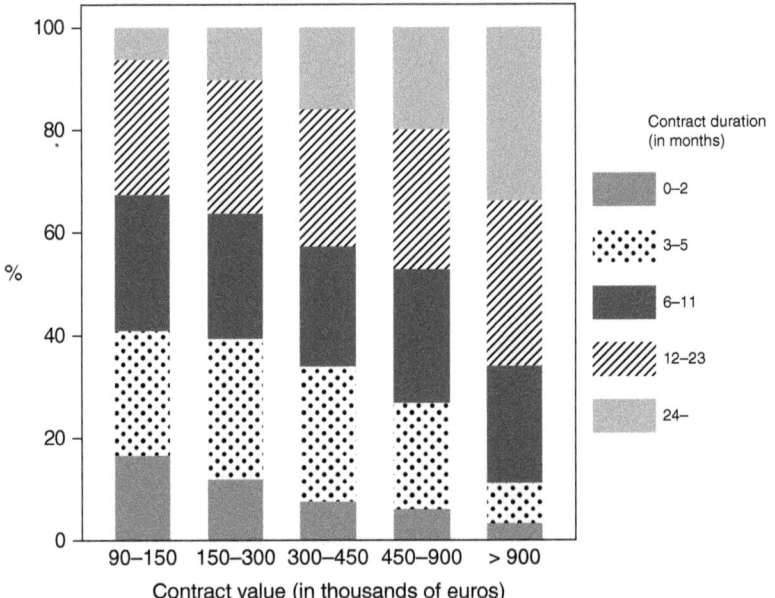

Figure 7.3 Distribution of contract duration and contract value

former increases with time, one may consider that long-term projects are likely to be complex. Figure 7.3 plots the distribution of contract duration by categories of contract value. It illustrates that longer contracts are often associated with a higher initial contract value. This positive correlation between contract value and duration may be driven by the same underlying process – the degree of complexity.

Table 7.3 shows simple statistics on contracts' value and contracts' duration according to the various award procedures. These statistics do not corroborate the proposition according to which complex projects are more likely to be awarded via negotiated procedures. Indeed, contracts awarded via auctions are longer and more expensive on average than contracts awarded via negotiation with prior publication and competition. Furthermore, contracts' value and duration are highest on average when restricted competitive tendering is used. Lastly, auctioned contracts are on average longer than contracts awarded through negotiated procedures.

Figures 7.4 and 7.5 respectively show the share of award procedures used for different categories of contract value and contract duration. Unsurprisingly, for all categories of contract values and

Table 7.3 *Contracts value and duration by award procedures*

Procedures	Contract value (€) Mean	Contract duration (months) Mean
Open auction	447,963	12.86
Restricted auction	670,536	15.40
Negotiation with prior publicity and competition	361,323	11.62
Negotiation without prior publicity and with competition	461,808	11.95
Negotiation without prior publicity nor competition	451,731	11.93
Others	206,784	7.52
Total	**417,934**	**12.21**

durations, open auctions seem to be the favored procedure. However, what is interesting is that the share of auctioned contracts increases with contract value. In terms of duration, one may observe a surge in the use of auction-based procedures for contracts longer than 24 months. Overall, even when we break down award procedures according to contracts' value and duration, higher contract values and longer contracts are more often associated with auction-based procedures.

If contract value and duration can be taken as an indication of project complexity, then our statistics indicate that more complex projects are associated with auction procedures. Such an observation, however, is the opposite of what the theoretical literature predicts and departs from the procurement practices observed in the private sector (Bajari et al. 2007). A plausible explanation may be driven by a specific characteristic of public procurement: the need to avoid suspicions of corruption or favoritism. Expensive and long-term projects may be particularly prone to such suspicions, and the need for a public buyer to show that the contract is awarded fairly may therefore be stronger. For such projects, auctions may be favored by public buyers as these

136   *Establishing property rights*

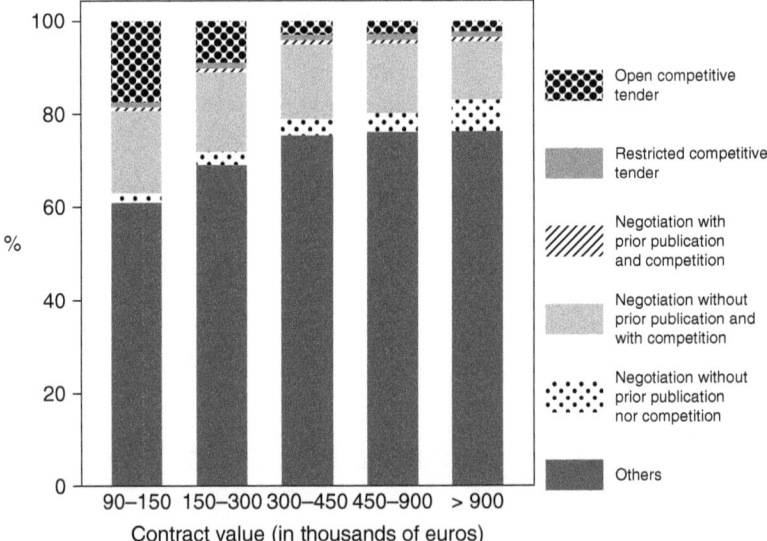

Figure 7.4 Distribution of award procedures for different categories of contract value

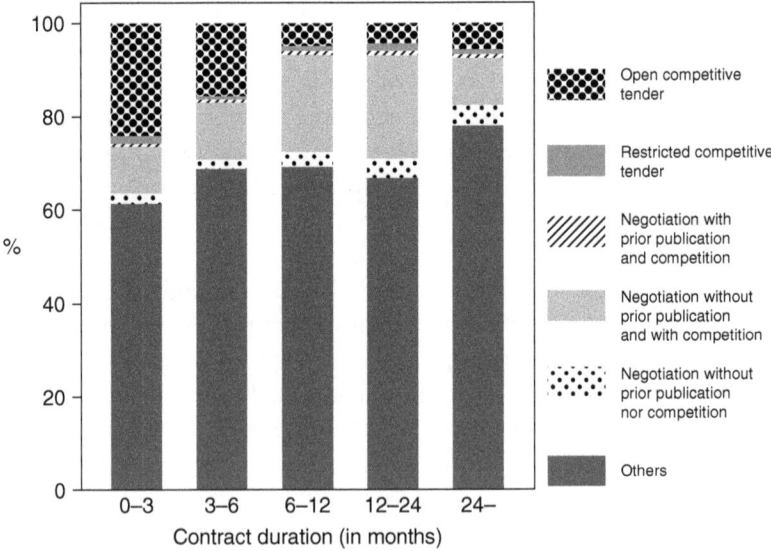

Figure 7.5 Distribution of award procedures for different categories of contract duration

procedures are commonly seen as instigating greater transparency and fair competition.

7.5 Award procedures and contract amendments

A second set of predictions put to the forefront in the recent economic literature is the relation between *ex post* coordination and award procedures. In particular, it has been argued that contracts awarded through auction-based procedures are more prone to *ex post* adaptations (Guasch 2004; Bajari et al. 2007, etc.). This leads us to empirically investigate *ex post* modifications to the initial contracts in the public works procurement.

Using our data, we assess whether auction-based procedures actually lead to more *ex post* modifications, and whether these modifications are more costly. These aspects may be captured in our database by the number of amendments to the initial contracts and by the outcome of these amendments. Economic theory leads us to expect a higher occurrence of contract amendments and more important changes in amended value and/or duration to the initial contract associated with auction-based procedures.

A total of 9,264 amendments to the initial contracts have been made between 2005 and 2007, representing about 13 percent of total procurement contracts within these three years.[8] Such contractual amendments may lead to a change in contract value. The total amount of amendments to the contracts' value represents about 15 percent of the total value of public works contracts. This is significant and suggests that public works procurement contracts are not renegotiation-proof.

Table 7.4 provides some statistics on contract amendments according to award procedures. One can observe that about 73 percent of amended contracts were awarded using open competitive tenders, while about 11 percent of amended contracts were awarded via a negotiation-based procedure with prior publication and competition. This may be due to the fact that auction procedures are more widely used than negotiation-based procedures. However, if we compare these figures to the share of each procedure used to award public work

---

[8] Relative frequencies are computed with respect to *all* procurement contracts in our database between 2005 and 2007, i.e., inclusive of all contracts whose initial value is above the legal threshold of €5,150,000,000.

procurement contracts, the frequency of amendments when contract is awarded through an open competitive tender tends to be higher than the share of initial contracts awarded through this procedure (69 percent of total initial contracts), and the share of amendments to contracts awarded through negotiation with prior publication and competition tends to be lower than the share of initial contracts awarded through this procedure (16 percent of total initial contracts). The frequency of amendments for contracts awarded through various other available procedures seems to reflect the share of their use accordingly. Thus, our statistics on the occurrence of amendments seem to be consistent with findings from the economic literature. They suggest that negotiation-based procedures allow a public buyer to better specify a project *ex ante*. In turn, this leads to a lower need for *ex post* adjustments for these projects.

The impact of amendments on contracts' value also seems to be consistent with the general economic literature. From Table 7.4, one may indeed conclude that such amendments generally result in an increase in the contract's value, even if some amendments also lead to a reduction of the initial amount of projects. Yet, this latter case tends to be quite marginal. When we break down the modification to contract value according to the award procedure used, one finds that open competitive tenders induce more costly renegotiations. Indeed, Table 7.4 shows that 81 percent of the total amount induced by amendments concern contracts that were awarded using open competitive tenders, whereas only 6 percent of the renegotiated amounts stem from contracts that were awarded using negotiations with prior publication and competition. Interestingly, contracts awarded through restricted competitive tenders account for about 8 percent of total amended value, whereas such a procedure is used to award only 3.2 percent of initial procurement contracts.

Figure 7.6 looks at the distribution of amended contract values for each type of procedure. The figure shows that most amendments lead to increases in the contract's value. More importantly, the figure also shows that the share of auction-based procedures in our sample is associated with more contracts whose amendments increase substantially the value of the initial contracts. About 25 percent of amended contracts awarded using open auction result in an increase of over €500,000. This applies to about 35 percent of amended contracts

Table 7.4 *Award procedures and contractual amendments*

Award procedure of the initial contract	Amendments (number)	%	Total value (millions €)	%	Mean value (millions €)
Open auction	6,746	72.82	5,228	81.17	0.775
Restricted auction	503	5.43	531	8.25	1.056
Negotiation with publication and competition	992	10.71	380	5.91	0.383
Negotiation without publication and with competition	46	0.50	56	0.88	1.237
Negotiation without publication nor competition	152	1.64	98,067	1.52	0.645
Others	825	8.91	146	2.27	0.177
Total	9,264	100	6,442	100	0.695

awarded through restricted competitive tenders. In contrast, the share of amended contracts which result in an increase of over €500,000 of the contracts' initial value represents less than 20 percent of the contracts awarded through negotiation with prior publication and competition.[9]

---

[9] We have conducted the same exercise distinguishing between central buyers and local buyers and found the same result, i.e., the share of contractual amendments leading to a change of more than €500,000 of the contracts' initial value is larger when the amended contracts were initially auctioned.

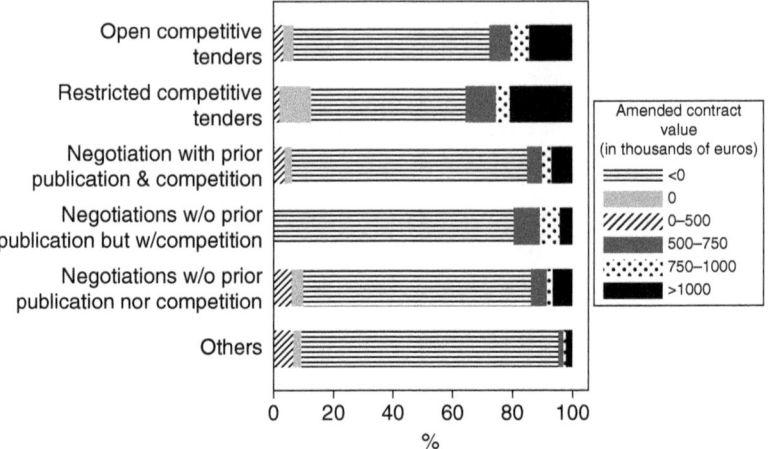

Figure 7.6 Distribution of amendments to contract values according to award procedures

This observed difference between the amended values of contracts awarded under different procedures corroborates the main insights from the economic literature: firstly, amendments to contracts awarded under auction procedures may result in a greater change in contracts' value because renegotiations may be more costly overall.[10] One plausible explanation for the higher amended value associated with auction procedures may therefore reflect more costly renegotiations when contracts were initially awarded using such procedures. Such an observation is also consistent with the hypothesis of opportunistic *ex post* renegotiations. Secondly, amended values of contracts awarded using auction-based procedures may be higher simply because such contracts involve more complicated projects from the outset. As mentioned before, higher contract value may mean more complex projects, and since such contracts are more likely to be awarded using an auction procedure, it is not surprising that there are more amendments to these contracts.

In a nutshell, statistical observations suggest that there is a link between contract amendments and award procedures. Furthermore, these statistical observations do not provide strong evidence against

---

[10] This is because rents are dissipated during the initial auction procedure. Hence, *ex post* adaptations to the initial contracts are met with more resistance (Bajari et al. 2007; Bajari et al. 2009).

Auction versus negotiation in public procurement 141

the major insights from economic literature: a majority of amended contracts were awarded using auction-based procedures, and contracts awarded through auction-based procedures seem to be associated with higher amended values.

7.6 Concluding remarks

Although public procurement markets represent a major stake for economic activity and a large part of public spending, few empirical works have been made so far to investigate the procurement practices of public buyers. Yet, theoretical academic papers and regulations are full of recommendations regarding the way to organize such markets. Their advice can be summed up shortly as they largely emphasize the use of auctions to manufacture these markets.

However, a recent literature, mostly relying on transaction cost theory, highlights the potential difficulties (public) buyers may encounter if they systematically choose competitive tendering to award their procurement markets. More precisely, this literature points out the inefficiency of auction procedures to select providers of complex goods or services for which contracting is often subject to renegotiations.

What we intended to do in this chapter is to describe the practices of French public buyers and try to find empirical regularities in the way they attribute procurement contracts. Our study is based on an original database gathering the entire set of public works procurement contracts in France over the period 2005–2007. The results of our preliminary statistical investigations question the efficiency of the French public buyers' choices. Indeed we show that their choices of awarding procedures are independent of their level of expertise, which, in line with Spiller (2008), can be interpreted as a consequence of third-party opportunism. We also point out that public buyers' decisions are not rational as they appear to depend neither on the value of the projects nor on their length although these variables are crucial determinants of projects' complexity. More precisely, auction-based procedures happen to be largely favored, whatever the characteristics of the project to be procured, and our data reveal that this translates into costly renegotiations. However, whether these renegotiations could have been avoided through the use of negotiation instead of auction is still an open question.

Further investigations are to be done to distinguish between "needed" and opportunistic contractual renegotiations and to deepen the analysis of the determinants of renegotiations. However, given the values at stake and the quasi-absence of rationale behind the buyers' choices, one can reasonably bet that changes in the way procurement markets are manufactured may lead to significant savings.

PART III

The political origin of competition

Introduction to Part III

ERIC BROUSSEAU AND JEAN-MICHEL GLACHANT

This part of the book develops the idea that competition – i.e., organized and domesticated rivalry – is nothing but natural. It gathers chapters highlighting how it is difficult to implement it. On the basis of the very long-run history of civilization, John Wallis clearly highlights that markets result from political compromises and that therefore it is "natural" that their (inefficient/specific) organization generates rents for the political coalitions that support the existence of the market and, eventually, for the organizations that enable the market to perform. This thesis is in addition illustrated and complemented in several other chapters of this book.

One of the essential outcomes of his chapter is to change the perspective through which the concept of market efficiency should be considered, at least by economists. To a certain extent, it is meaningless to consider rents generated by the limited competitiveness of markets as inefficient, since they remunerate the political coalition that make the market possible. At the same time, these rents correspond to resources that could be allocated to expand the stock of productive assets if they were not used to remunerate the political coalition, which explains the superior efficiency of more open, transparent, and integrated markets.

While competitive markets enhance the efficiency of social exchange, they are not the condition for market exchange, then the division of labor. This is why many social actors are satisfied with non-competitive markets. Limited openness allows the social division of labor and provides security. What competition brings is incentives and innovation, but also potential social disorder since established positions are challenged and since various stakeholders can be expelled from markets, not to mention crises that are inherent to markets, especially in phases of transition when stabilizers are not yet built and operators are learning new rules of the games and adapting their capabilities and strategies. This echoes many political debates in post-crisis economies where many politicians and large fractions of society support the development of all kind of barriers to head-on competition; from regulations to trade barriers. Competitive markets are far from being stable social equilibriums. The fear of a more unstable, then risky economy, is a strong element that might bring wide political support, even from those over which rents are captured, for the limited implementation of competition on markets. This explains why implementing competition policies is so difficult from a political point of view.

In a sense, the chapter by Stephen Littlechild, a central actor in the reform of the electricity industry in Great Britain, provides us with an illuminating modern illustration of the political origin of competition. More precisely, his narrative of the process that led to the implementation of a fully competitive market at the retail level in an industry in which it had long been considered that it was useless and impossible to implement, illustrates well the interplay between economic considerations (the implications of competition for prices, profits, and flotation values), political ones (the trade-offs between competition and electricity flotation proceeds and the subsequent flotation of the coal industry), and the legal logic (the specification of the franchise and the removal of monopoly). This multi-field multi-player game was clearly too complex to allow any reformer both to envisage and implement any plan. Thus, the UK electricity reforms should better be considered as a specific process of incremental reforms leading to discoveries and collective learning, modifying the framework of the bargaining process among interest groups and various public bodies, and leading to implement a set of reforms that was not at all envisioned at the early beginning, than as the result of a concerted and smart plan.

One of the key drivers of the reform was however a belief by politicians that the benefits of privatization were conditioned by the implementation of extended competition. The point is that nobody knew at the beginning what it meant, and almost no interest group was calling for competition at the retail level. The UK reform, however, deeply transformed the beliefs of many actors in the electricity industry worldwide and has become the blueprint of many reforms in network industries today.

A side conclusion of the analysis proposed by John Wallis is that since a political order is necessary to allow a market to exist, it is not a big surprise that it is so difficult to create an integrated market at the international – for instance at the European – level. This point is in a sense deepened by the chapter proposed by Antonio Manganelli, Antonio Nicita, and Maria Alessandra Rossi. The authors deal with the web of formal institutions involved in the implementation of competition policy in Europe. There are not only vertical coordination stakes between the European (federal) competition authorities and the national ones, but also potential horizontal problems. The co-authors highlight the contrasted logic of the various bodies involved in the enforcement of competition policies. In a nutshell, competition authorities tend to consider collective (at least public policy) goals and focus in particular on the interest of the consumers as a whole. Regulatory authorities focus on the efficiency of the supply side and might consider also the long-term interest of providers. Courts are aimed at enabling the various stakeholders to claim for their rights. Moreover, their logic of action is different. Competition authorities rely on the logic of deterrence when they deal with individual cases, while courts tend to focus on the infringements of the rights of the stakeholders involved in the case. On their side, regulatory authorities tend to focus more on long-term considerations in order to "build the future," while competition authorities and courts act *ex post* and are more short-termist. The authors show that conflicts of logic and overlapping authorities are likely to prevent any "efficiency" in the actual performance of competition policies. In particular, the actual power is so divided among so many different entities, that most of them cannot figure out how their behavior will impact on the authority of others. Lack of coordination is not only a question of incentives. It is also a question of complexity.

To put it another way, there is neither a clear hierarchy of norms, nor a rational design of the bureaucratic and political bodies in charge of their enforcement. This is clearly due to path dependent processes of institutional building, without clear and integrated vision of what is done. The result is that most agencies and courts in charge of the implementation are very unlikely to have the appropriate incentives, and the adequate scope of competences to deal with actual issues, as well as the ability to coordinate with others so as to provide the players with a consistent and neutral set of "rules of the game" with blind enforcement.

In the case of the European Union, however, there is a strong imbalance between the Commission's antitrust power and regulatory authorities and courts. One of the reasons is obviously the logic of the building of the union around a unified market, which provided the EC with strong legitimacy to develop its authority in the domain; in contrast with others. The Commission had the opportunity to develop a strong antitrust capability and legitimacy, relatively well coordinated in a multilevel perspective with the national competition authorities. On the contrary, regulations are relevant at the industry level, with a much stronger heterogeneity of logics across industries and across countries (especially because the structure of the regulated industries and the "national interest" might differ greatly from one country to another). Thus a well-organized system of competition authorities faces a much less organized system of regulation agencies, which might explain why "industrial policies" are so weak in balancing the logic of antitrust in Europe (as compared to the US for instance).

8 | Why competitive markets aren't self-actuating: the political economy of limited access

JOHN JOSEPH WALLIS

8.1 Introduction

Markets are ubiquitous in recorded human history. Until recently, however, markets tended to be subordinate to other social institutions and thriving, open, competitive markets were the exception rather than the rule. Why don't open competitive markets automatically create the conditions for their continued existence? In their brief for this conference, Eric Brousseau and Jean-Michel Glachant point out that at least six categories of actors interact simultaneously on three levels to produce the social frameworks that manufacture markets. This chapter follows Brousseau and Glachant by taking as given that markets are complicated social institutions comprised of elements that are intentionally and unintentionally designed; that market institutions persist over time only if the dynamic relationships between political, economic, and legal interests and institutions provide incentives for social actors to maintain specific markets; and that the power of markets to coordinate behavior and allocate resources may be used for purposes other than maximizing social welfare through gains from trade, and so how we evaluate the "efficiency" of any set of market arrangements should not necessarily be limited to the internal operation of markets. Why aren't competitive markets self-actuating?

The chapter builds on several unoriginal insights. First, markets are always embedded in organizations. At one extreme markets may be embodied in a single formal organization that creates and sustains the market and a marketplace, like modern stock or commodity exchanges. Medieval European cities, for example, often organized and operated

My thanks go to Larry Neal, Yannick Perez, Mushtaq Khan, Steve Webb, Doug North, and Barry Weingast for comments and conversations, and to Eric Brousseau and Jean-Michel Glachant for their encouragement.

markets. In these limiting cases, the organization that makes the market exists independently of the market participants. In most markets, however, market structure results from the interaction of several or many organizations. Second, all markets are connected to other markets. In neoclassical economics it is the ability of the price mechanism to signal costs and benefits that enables all of these markets to simultaneously coordinate market participants in widely dispersed and apparently independent lines of endeavor. Finally, and least original, is that most markets require a modicum of rules and organizations that enforce the rules. Open competitive markets require open entry and impersonal rules that are credibly enforced by an unbiased third party. Most markets are not open and competitive because entry is limited, rules are not impersonal, and enforcement is uneven.

These insights are slightly off the main lines of thinking about markets in institutional economics.[1] Nonetheless, their combination generates new insights into the dynamic relationships between the social institutions that manufacture markets. The sections that follow first lay out a way of thinking about how societies use organizations to structure social order by creating incentives for powerful and dangerous individuals to cooperate, drawing on the framework of North, Wallis, and Weingast (2009, hereafter NWW). The coalition of powerful individuals is the organization capable of providing third-party enforcement of rules and is, therefore, critical to our understanding of markets. Next, the connectedness of markets is exploited to show how organizations that promote markets can serve as conduits for structuring incentives within and between powerful organizations and their leadership, even in societies where access to both organizations and markets is limited. This section provides an answer to the question posed in the chapter title, why competitive markets are not self-actuating. The social forces that support the emergence of markets on a larger scale, generating economic growth through higher productivity

[1] Institutional economics sees markets as the interaction of individual actors (even if those actors are legal persons that represent an organization). Institutions make possible contractual forms which are available to the actors at some cost. Political organizations frame the possible contracts and finance enforcement resources, including courts, which are charged with interpreting the contractual rules, guiding enforcement, and applying penalties in cases of contractual breach. Contracts are not costless and neither is transacting, but contracts provide tools that individual actors can use to shape their relationships. Markets are usually treated in isolation, *ceteris paribus*.

and gains from specialization and division of labor, inherently generate counter forces that limit access to organizations and, therefore, limit some aspects of markets. The counter forces are part of the dynamic relationship between politics and economics in most societies, what NWW call natural states.

The final two sections of the chapter consider these social dynamics in greater detail, with a particular eye to the question of why competitive markets do not automatically generate patterns of economic interest that inherently lead political actors to maintain open access markets. One element of social dynamics is the formation of interests and the process of rent formation. The other element is the nature of impersonal relationships, or more accurately for most societies, the inability to sustain impersonal relationships.

8.2 Order, organizations, and coalitions

Human societies rarely exceeded sizes of 100 people for any sustained period of time until about 10,000 years ago. It seems safe to say that while exchange between groups certainly occurred, markets are a development of larger societies and are an integral part of the way in which larger societies capture gains from specialization, division of labor, and trade. The first question to ask, therefore, is how societies managed to organize or reorganize themselves to sustain larger scales, since larger scale is a prerequisite for markets. This section lays out a simple version of the conceptual framework of NWW, which situates the problem of social scale in the context of violence.[2]

NWW begin their analysis in a world of small societies of 50–100 people in which individuals base trust on personal interaction, and ask how, in a world where violence is a viable option, some individuals can deal with dangerous and potentially violent individuals with some degree of confidence. NWW begin with specialists in violence, who mistrust one another, and will not lay down their arms and coexist because they believe such behavior will lead the other specialist to destroy or enslave them. Armed conflict is the equilibrium outcome. The solution to ongoing violence, in simple terms, is for the violence specialists to agree to divide the land, labor, and capital in their world between themselves and agree to enforce each other's privileged access

---

[2] See NWW (2009, chapter 2). This exposition follows Wallis (2011).

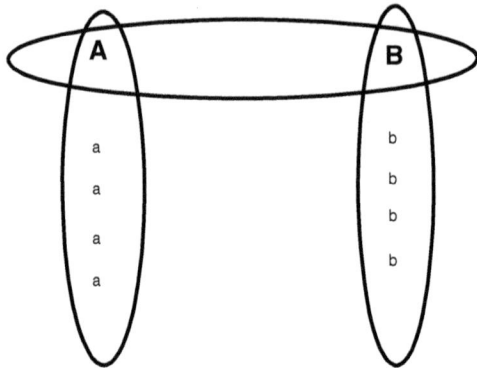

Figure 8.1 A simple schematic of a natural state

to their resources. If the difference in the value of the rents they earn from their privileges under conditions of peace rather than violence are large enough, then each specialist can credibly believe that the other will not fight. The specialists remain armed and dangerous and can credibly threaten the people around them to ensure each other's rights.

The arrangement is represented graphically in Figure 8.1, where A and B are the two violence specialists, and the horizontal ellipse represents the arrangement between the specialists that create their organization/institution. The vertical ellipses represent the arrangements the specialists have with the labor, land, capital, and resources they control: their "clients," the a's and b's. The horizontal arrangement between the specialists is made credible by the vertical arrangements. The rents the specialists receive from controlling their client organizations enable them to credibly commit to one another, since those rents are reduced if cooperation fails and the specialists fight.[3] It is the rents from peace that are lost if any of the specialists fight, that shape incentives that limit violence.

There is also a reciprocal effect. The existence of the agreement between the specialists enables each of them to better structure their client organizations, because they can call on each other for external

---

[3] Note that the rents received from client organizations are classically rents, the return to an asset or activity above its opportunity costs. These are explicitly not Directly Unproductive, Profit-Seeking (DUP) rents à la Bhagwati or Krueger. The question of rents is taken up in more detail in Section 8.3.

support. The specialist's organization is what NWW call the "dominant coalition."

There is a fundamental difference between the nature of the horizontal and vertical organizations. An *adherent organization* is one where all of the members have an interest in cooperating with each other (on the relevant dimensions of the organized activity) at all points in time. In an adherent organization interests are structured in such a way that all individuals have an interest in belonging to the organization, without the external intervention of a third party. In contrast, a *contractual organization* is one where relationships between the group members are not inherently self-sustaining, and the group maintains itself only through the presence (or potential presence) of an external third party. The third party may enforce relationships within the organization or between the organization and other external parties.[4]

In Figure 8.1, the horizontal relationships between the violence specialists create an adherent organization, the dominant coalition, an organization held together only by the interlocking interests of its members. The vertical relationships between the violence specialists and their clients are contractual organizations, shaped and organized by the external presence of the other violence specialists. The dominant coalition acts as a third party for each of the member organizations. The vertical organizations might be organized as kin groups, ethnic groups, patron-client networks, or crime families. The combination of multiple organizations, the "organization of organizations," mitigates the problem of violence between the really dangerous people, the violence specialists, creates credible commitments between the specialists by structuring their interests, and creates a modicum of belief that the specialists and their clients share a common interest because the specialists have a claim on the output of their clients. The figure is a very simple representation. In a functioning society, members of the dominant coalition include economic, political, religious, and educational specialists (elites) whose privileged positions create rents that ensure their cooperation with the dominant coalition and create the organizations through which the goods and services produced by the population can be mobilized and redistributed.[5]

---

[4] In Greif's terms a contractual organization is only an institutional element, since it depends on other institutional elements to sustain its integrity.

[5] NWW (2009, chapter 2). Earle (1997 and 2003) and Johnson and Earle (2000) provide a series of anthropological examples of how chiefs come to power

The key to the whole arrangement is that the rents A and B derive from their organizations enable them to credibly commit to one another. The interests created by these organizations must interlock, that is, the ability of A and B to form organizations depends on their coordination and cooperation, since the vertical/contractual organizations are structured by the third-party enforcement of the dominant coalition. The most valuable privilege members of the dominant coalition enjoy is the exclusive ability to form organizations, and among the organizations that elites form and the coalition supports are markets. The primary source of rents within the coalition is the ability to use the third-party services of the dominant coalition to enforce arrangements within the organizations of the coalition members. The rules that help sustain markets, therefore, are inherently tied to the dynamic relationships within the dominant coalition. The rents created by those exclusive privileges are part of the glue holding the agreements between the specialists together. Limiting access to rules enforced by the coalition creates rents and shapes the interests of the players in the coalition.

At the same time, the institutional structure gives leaders of organizations tools to shape the interests of their clients. The nature of the (vertical) client organizations is critical to the whole structure. Because the specialists can call on the dominant coalition to enforce agreements within their client organizations, those organizations are contractual. The markets provided by client organizations depend on rules enforced by the organization, which in turn depends on the rules supported by the larger coalition.

Markets are one part of the entire complex of organizations that create incentives and interests for powerful individuals leading to cooperative outcomes. Organizations occupy the central place in this process and limiting access to organizations shapes interests. Organizations are a primary driver of both the shape of institutions and their change over time. Cooperation cannot be sustained unless powerful individuals believe that cooperation is in the interest of other powerful individuals. Organizations structure interests and so facilitate cooperation.

and the scale of society increases by the systematic manipulation of economic interests.

8.3 Market connections, rent creation, and the political economy of dominant coalitions

Figure 8.1 is too simple. The dominant coalition is never made up of just violence specialists. The whole point of the coalition is to create an interlocking set of rents and mobilizing rents requires other specialists: economic, political, and religious at the very least. It cannot be overemphasized that the creation of organizations that enable larger societies to form immediately creates the possibility of increasing productivity through specialization and division of labor. Once powerful individuals establish a social organization capable of sustaining a larger society, they have strong interests to promote trade and markets.

Figure 8.2 portrays a slightly more realistic dominant coalition with four members. There are two violence specialists, A and B, two economic specialists (traders) A_t and B_t, and their associated client networks. A_t and B_t are part of the dominant coalition, they enjoy rents from the control of a function, trade, to which access is limited, and the existence of those rents ties them into the dominant coalition and creates incentives for them to support the coalition. A_t and B_t are also specialists who are able to exploit a comparative advantage in trade that stems from their position in the coalition. A_t and B_t are also market makers. They are able to draw on their position within the coalition to socially and physically create and administer markets and marketplaces.[6] Perhaps even more important, A_t and B_t are able to draw on A and B to provide third-party enforcement of agreements. Not only are A_t and B_t able to access enforcement of agreements between themselves, A_t and B_t can enforce agreements between a's and b's as well.

There is little doubt in the historical record that when larger societies form trade is an integral part of the social structure, that trade is always controlled by the dominant coalition, and that some individuals within the social hierarchy enjoy privileged positions with respect to trade and markets.[7] As the anthropologist Timothy Earle

---

[6] By "socially" create markets I mean that the market makers are able to structure repeated interactions of individuals, including rules, laws, norms, and courts; by "physically" creating markets I mean that they literally invest in the physical infrastructure, including market places, transportation, and storage facilities, that enable exchange to take place over larger stretches of time and space.

[7] For studies of "pristine" civilizations, that is the first large civilizations that arose without a geographic predecessor in Mesopotamia, Egypt, India, China,

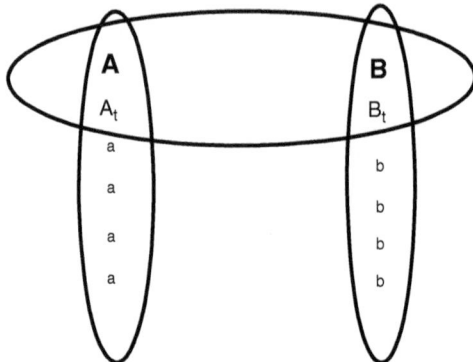

Figure 8.2 A slightly more complicated natural state

puts it when discussing the emergence of chiefdoms (groups of over 200 or so):

> In chiefdoms, control over production and exchange of subsistence and wealth creates the basis for political power ... Economic power is based on the ability to restrict access to key productive resources or consumptive goods ... Control over exchange permits the extension of economic control over broader regions ... The real significance of economic power may be that the material flows through the political economy can be used by the chief to nurture and sustain the alternative power sources ...
>
> Earle (1997: 7)

The point is not to quibble about which came first, larger societies, social hierarchies, or trade and markets, but to acknowledge that all three elements of societies appear to have been intrinsically linked historically. Their simultaneous relationship, their endogeneity, is not in question, but instead forms the basis for thinking about the dynamics of the relationships that support markets.

The first dynamic element is that the use of trade, markets, and economic privileges to create economic rents that are then used to secure more stable political coalitions and social order turns the way we often think about limits on access and markets on its head. Limits on entry, both in terms of entry of organizations that make markets

---

Meso America, and South America, see Service (1975) and Trigger (2003). For the anthropological record on the emergence of larger societies see Earle (1997 and 2003) and Johnson and Earle (2000).

and in terms of market participants, typically create rents for specific actors but also reduce the efficiency of markets. Since, however, the first requirement for markets is a large enough society with some measure of order, without a social order that manipulates economic rents to coordinate powerful individuals and groups, the formation of a stable coalition that can provide the political underpinnings of market exchange is impossible (or hindered), and so markets do not come into being at all or exist at a much simpler level. The relevant comparison is not between efficient and inefficient markets, but between inefficient markets and no markets at all. We must be careful not to think of the dominant coalition as just a political organization independent from economic organizations, since the close integration of economics and politics glues the coalition together. The ability of the dominant coalition to provide a modicum of peace and physical security, as well as third-party enforcement of arrangements and agreements within the coalition, depends on manipulating economic rents. At the same time, the ability of markets and organizations to generate rents depends on the provision of those services by the coalition.

NWW call this dynamic relationship between economic and political arrangements the "double balance." Political arrangements must be consistent with economic arrangements, and vice versa. The structure of rents in the economic system is an inherent part of the interconnected balance of interests in the political system, and the balance of interests in the political system is an inherent part of the economic system.[8] In this sense, the efficiency of a market cannot be evaluated solely with respect to factors internal to the market. If markets depend on third-party support from the dominant coalition, then market inefficiencies that create rents used to stabilize the coalition are not, in the larger sense, social inefficiencies. If the dominant coalition destabilizes without the rents, and the market cannot function without the coalition, then evaluating the efficiency of a market solely in terms of the way it allocates resources is problematic.

The second dynamic aspect of markets that plays a critical role in the politics of the dominant coalition is their interconnectedness. The

---

[8] In an open access order both the political and economic systems are open to entry. The concept of the double balance suggests that an open political system cannot be stable with a limited access economy, nor can an open economy be stable with a limited access political system.

market for wheat is connected to the market for land, the market for transportation services, and the market for bread. The stability of the relationship between the players within the dominant coalition depends on the fact that the actions of one player affect the other: if one is violent both lose rents. The expansion of markets is both a way to increase rents and to coordinate the interests of elites. If the dominant coalition includes individuals with privileged access to or control of land, border crossings, ships, bakeries, and markets then a well-functioning market for wheat means changes in circumstances that affect the price of wheat affect all of those elites and their interests, simultaneously. By promoting the formation of markets, elites directly raise the productivity of the assets they control at the same time that they are able to better coordinate incentives within the dominant coalition. The benefit does not come without a cost, however. At times, markets may transmit signals to elites that move their interests in directions that reduce cooperation rather than increase it.

8.4 Rents and social dynamics[9]

The foregoing provides a basic answer to the question posed by this chapter: why aren't competitive markets self-actuating? The answer has to do with the dynamic relationship between political, economic, and other social forces. Markets require larger social institutions and structures in order to function. In particular, the scale and efficiency of any market depends on the provision of third-party enforced rules. The extent to which rules are sophisticated, dependable, transparent, and enforced in an unbiased manner determines how well a market works. The dynamic relationships between powerful groups and individuals that makes a larger social structure possible, creates strong incentives for the coalition to support the formation of some organizations within the coalition that promote trade and establish markets, so there are many more markets in natural states than in hunting and gathering societies. If the dominant coalition has strong incentives to promote markets, however, why don't all societies promote markets with open entry, well-defined property rights, and the social

---

[9] My understanding of rents and social dynamics has developed in conversation and cooperation with Mushtaq Khan and Steve Webb, for a paper currently titled "Rents and Development in Limited Access Orders."

Why competitive markets aren't self-actuating 159

infrastructure necessary to support free exchange of goods and services? One part of the answer concerns the way in which rents affect the dynamic relationship between politics and economics. The other concerns the nature of impersonal rules and relationships necessary to sustain open markets, the subject of the next section.

A key implication of rents is that rents make people's behavior more predictable. Classic economic rents exist whenever the benefits to an action exceed the opportunity costs of the action. The predictability of behavior depends on the size of the rent. The behavior of a person for whom a particular action produces very small rents is not predictable. Any small change in any of a number of variables could lead to a change in behavior. Competitive markets are flexible because, as neoclassical economics emphasizes, in a competitive market there are not rents for consumers or producers at the margin, so their behavior flexibly responds to changing conditions. As rents increase, behavior becomes more predictable. The choices individuals make are more robust to changes. Societies have no interest in making people just indifferent to using violence, societies have a strong interest in creating large rents from not using violence. The NWW logic of the natural state uses the creation of rents to incentivize powerful individuals and groups, and make their behavior more predictable and thus their commitments to each other credible.

While greater rents make behavior more predictable, the effect of rents has nothing to do with whether the rent makes the larger society better off or worse off. Within the dynamic relationships of the dominant coalition, whether the rents are good or bad for the rest of society is of secondary importance. It is not the size of the rents in aggregate terms that matters, it is the size of the individual rents relative to the choice sets of members of the coalition.

Markets always involve organizations, either as formal market makers or as the significant participants that make the market work. In natural states, the ability to control and participate in markets is a major source of rents. Indeed, the fact that rents come from markets and markets work better under conditions of relative stability and in the absence of violence, is a strong inducement for the members of the dominant coalition to maintain cooperation and make markets work more efficiently. At the same time, the world is a constantly changing place. Dominant coalitions must continuously adjust their organizations and their privileges to maintain stability within the coalition.

There is no *a priori* reason to expect that these adjustments will always be in the direction of making markets work better or making organizations more productive. Rents can be generated by making markets work less efficiently, e.g., creating market power, limiting entry, or regulating prices or quality.

In general, rents can be created both by extending the third-party services to elite organizations, or by withdrawing or reallocating third-party service from some elite organizations. There is a continuous play of political forces and of economic forces that reflect the underlying notion of a double balance. Societies that are able to increase the productivity of their political, economic, and social organizations at the same time that they maintain or increase the stability of their social arrangements are societies that manage to grow. Societies that find it necessary to maintain (or restore) stability by reducing the productivity of their political, economic, and social organizations are societies that manage to shrink. These processes are not mutually exclusive, they go on in every society all the time. Given the dynamics of these processes, we should not be surprised that open and competitive markets are not inherently self-sustaining.

8.5 Anonymous and impersonal relationships and social dynamics[10]

The dynamics of rent creation enable us to understand why there is no inherent tendency for natural state societies to become more productive, or for more open and competitive markets to emerge, just as there is no inherent tendency in the opposite direction. But what if a society moves over a period of time toward more productive organizations and markets and experiences economic growth as the result of incremental changes in institutions? Will the organizations and markets in those societies necessarily move closer to the kinds of institutions that support open access, namely free entry, rule of law, and support for impersonal relationships between individuals? The point at issue is the nature of the third-party rules that a society can support.

A central tenet of the new institutional economics is that the ability to support impersonal relationships is a critical, if not the central, element of open access economies and polities. The new institutional

---

[10] The argument of this section is based on Wallis (2011).

economics has not, however, been precise about the definition of impersonality or how it develops. Impersonal relationships occur when two individuals interact in a way that does not depend on their personal identity. Another way of saying this is that societies are capable of creating and sustaining an impersonal identity of citizen or resident that applies equally to a large class of people.[11] The essence of impersonality is *treating everyone the same*.

While there is nothing controversial in this definition of impersonal relationships, it is not always the one used in the new institutional economics. In practice, institutional economists have defined impersonality as *dealing with people you do not know*. The two definitions are not the same and to keep them separate I will denote relationships between people who do not know each other personally as *anonymous* relationships.

The working definition of impersonal as "not personal" is usually motivated by considering how two individuals who do not know each other personally and have no expectation of a continuing relationship in the future can come to agree on a social relation. Greif and North both place impersonality at the heart of modern institutional development, but the point holds for a much wider literature.[12] North has long stressed the importance of impersonal exchange for economic development and he clearly had impersonality, not anonymity, in mind when he defined institutions as the rules of the game and the methods of enforcement: rules in an athletic event should apply equally to all participants.[13] North started with the genetic human endowment that enabled people to use face to face interaction and repeated dealings to develop credible relationships.[14] The rise of impersonal exchange, therefore, involved dealing with people who one "didn't know" personally and, therefore, impersonal was implicitly defined as "not personal" or "not known."

---

[11] Impersonal rules do not have to apply to everyone universally. Whether a rule is impersonal or not always depends, in part, on the identity of the people it applies to.
[12] See Cook, Hardin, and Levi (1995), Fukuyama (1995), and Lupia and McCubbins (1998) for a discussion of trust between individuals.
[13] Specific discussions of North's approach to personal and impersonal exchange can be found in North (1981, pp. 182 and 204); North (1990, pp. 22, 34–35, and 55–60); North (2005, pp. 70–71, 84, and 119).
[14] The genetic endowment argument is clearly laid out in his 2005 book. The ability of people to deal with one another in small groups forms the basis

Greif motivates impersonality as a relationship between two individuals who did not know each other personally, but could nonetheless reach agreements that spread across space and time. Greif shows how communal courts in medieval Italian city-states, which were biased against outsiders and non-citizens, were nonetheless capable of providing unbiased judicial decisions on a narrow range of matters.[15] In order for the community responsibility system to work, however, all the traders had to be able to identify each other as citizens of a specific city, e.g., Genoa, Pisa, or Hamburg. If one trader from a city cheated, all traders from that city were punished. It was the rents created within the merchant organizations of their own cities, which were inherently personal, that enabled city merchants and their courts to deliver unbiased justice for a limited number of contracts. What Greif described was a type of anonymous exchange. A trader from Genoa could trade with confidence in Hamburg, even if he had never been to Hamburg and would never go again. But he could only do so because the merchants in Hamburg *knew that he was a merchant from Genoa*.

Greif shows how it is possible to enable anonymous relationships between people who do not know each other personally, by embedding individuals in a social context that is personal, not impersonal. Awareness of the larger social situation in which their interactions take place is part of the shared beliefs that make anonymous exchange possible.[16] This is the same logic that NWW use to show how creation of personal privileges can create rents that enable powerful individuals to credibly commit to non-violent relationships and thus can order a larger society. The privileges cannot be impersonal: if they were they would not be privileges and they would not create rents.

Impersonality underpins all modern developed societies. It is a necessary condition for open and competitive markets. In order for people to believe that they will be treated impersonally, and therefore have an incentive to treat other people impersonally, enforceable impersonal

---

for the "foraging" order in NWW. The evolutionary heritage plays a central role in evolutionary psychology and the general notion that modern humans are evolved to deal with small groups and are, therefore, maladapted for the complex societies that have developed over the last 10,000 years; Cosmides and Tooby (1992) and Pinker (1997).

[15] "Partial communal courts were thereby motivated to provide impartial justice" (Greif 2006b, p. 310).
[16] Granovetter's (1985) concept of social "embeddedness" is relevant here.

rules with two characteristics must be present. First, the same rules must apply in the same manner to all people (or all citizens). Second, the rules must be enforced impersonally, impartially, and without bias. Even societies that have unbiased third-party enforcement of rules will not be able to sustain impersonal exchange if different rules apply to different people.[17]

The dynamics of institutional change involve competing organizations and their attempts to shape institutions, both formal and informal, to their own ends. In most societies these dynamics are constrained by the threat of violence. In natural states, even in very sophisticated and successful natural states, political, economic, and social relationships are embedded in a network of organizations that sustain those relationships through identifying individuals with the group or organization they belong to. As in Greif's community responsibility system, the incentives facing individuals within their own organizations enable them to credibly deal with individuals in other organizations. This mirrors the dynamics represented in Figure 8.1, where the rents elites derive from their client organizations enable them to credibly commit to each other the adherent organization of the dominant coalition. These relationships, however, are not impersonal, they are anonymous relationships.

The fundamental process of creating and supporting organizations, including the organizations that manufacture markets, embed individual relationships in a social framework of anonymous, rather than impersonal, interaction. This social dynamic helps us understand why competitive open markets are not self-sustaining. Even as societies become capable of supporting larger organizations with more complex structures operating over wider reaches of space and time, those organizations are not driven to create and sustain impersonal relationships, instead they create and sustain more complex and sophisticated anonymous relationships. Increasing productivity and economic growth does not inevitably lead to institutions capable of supporting impersonal exchange, because creating and enforcing rules that treat everyone the same strikes at the very heart of the rent creation process. We must be careful not to confuse the ability of natural states to dramatically increase the degree of specialization and division through

---

[17] NWW consider the difference between biased enforcement and unique identity on pp. 154–158.

anonymous exchange, with the assumption that greater specialization necessarily requires greater impersonality.

8.6 Conclusions

The chapters in this volume illustrate a wide range of markets and the institutions that make them possible. I have tried to cast some light on the dynamic interaction of political, economic, and social forces that underlie markets with a focus on why thriving, open, and competitive markets do not seem to emerge spontaneously in societies and when they do appear are rarely sustainable. I have not addressed why only a handful of open access societies in our contemporary world appear to be able to sustain competitive markets.

The tension between the use of markets to stabilize political and social arrangements and the uses of markets to increase productivity and the efficiency of resource allocation is the heart of the argument. Markets require larger social institutions and structures to operate. At the same time, the ability to construct larger societies depends upon the development of incentives for powerful individuals and groups to cooperate and refrain from the use of violence. As societies increase in size, there are strong incentives for powerful groups to promote the development of markets (and productivity and efficiency). But there are also strong incentives to preserve rents that markets create that serve to balance interests within the dominant coalition of the powerful. These two forces constantly affect social arrangements. This is the logic of the natural state laid out by North, Wallis, and Weingast that explains, in basic terms, why competitive markets are not self-actuating in natural states.

Why don't the obvious benefits of more efficient markets for social productivity lead societies to reach arrangements that redistribute the gains from better markets in a way that mollifies the interests of the powerful? This is a matter of social dynamics. Arrangements within the dominant coalition depend on the existence of rents to provide credible incentives. Whether those rents make the larger society better or worse off, however, is of second order importance to maintaining stable relationships within the coalition. Since the world is constantly changing, the use of markets to create rents by limiting entry and other regulations is always a possibility. Hampering markets and enhancing markets can both produce rents, or shift rents within the dominant coalition, and as a result both are likely to occur through time. The efficient market force that inexorably pushes for the enhancement of markets is counterbalanced by the need for stable political arrangements, an example of the double balance between economics and politics.

Even when societies move to enhance markets, they are likely to do so in a way that increases specialization and division of labor by embedding exchange relationships in organizations. More sophisticated organizations provide more predictable rules and norms for exchange, as in Greif's example of the community responsibility system. But the kind of anonymous relationships developed by the interlocking interests of organizations and their members are not the kind of impersonal relationships we associate with competitive markets. There is no inherent social dynamic that leads societies to "treat everyone the same." That appears to be a relatively rare outcome associated with the transition to open access societies that first appear in the nineteenth century.

9 The creation of a market for retail electricity supply

STEPHEN LITTLECHILD

9.1 Introduction

Until 1990 UK electricity supply was provided by state-owned entities with regional monopolies. A retail electricity market (sometimes called supply competition or retail choice in the US) did not exist; even the concept was alien. Yet in September 1989, as part of its privatization program, the Government laid down a timetable for opening up to retail competition the entire electricity market of England and Wales. There were three stages: large users on March 31, 1990 (Vesting Day), medium-sized users in April 1994 and all other users including domestic (residential) in April 1998.

The response was dramatic. In April 1990 about one third of the largest business users in the country chose a different electricity supplier. By 1997/8 the proportion had roughly doubled. In April 1998 the smallest (residential) users were allowed to choose supplier. By April 2009 over half had changed supplier. Other countries have followed suit. Full retail electricity competition (that is, choice of supplier for all customers regardless of size) is now official policy in the European Union.

It might be assumed that the way in which the market was created in England and Wales was part of a considered policy to facilitate the introduction and regulation of competition; that the Government as owner of the nationalized electricity industry would be in a position to specify the precise arrangements for opening the market; that the phasing over time was designed to facilitate implementation; and that

An earlier version of this chapter was presented to the Workshop on "Manufacturing Markets: legal, political and economic dynamics," Villa Finaly, Florence, June 11–13, 2009. I am grateful to conference discussants Carine Staropoli and Yannick Perez; to Michael Brocklehurst, Paul Kitcher, David Walker and George Yarrow for clarifying pre-privatization arrangements; to John Baker, Willy Rickett and Lords Lawson, Parkinson and Wakeham for further insights; to several referees; and to Jean-Michel Glachant for editorial suggestions.

The creation of a market for retail electricity supply

the contractual arrangements that accompanied the timetable would provide a basis for the future development of the industry. It might even be thought that this would be a model case study of how governments can successfully create a competitive market. Certainly, other countries have generally phased in the opening of their own retail electricity markets.

Two accounts of electricity privatization paint a rather different picture. Henney (1994) says that the Regional Electricity Companies (RECs, formerly known as Area Boards) agreed a deal with the generators whereby competition would be limited to very large customers. "Leaving the obligation to supply to market forces would not ensure that sufficient capacity would be built ... This arrangement would ensure that the proposed nuclear plants could be built, and that everyone would be spared the inconvenience of having to compete" (p. 116). The Department of Energy rejected this deal, but agreement was reached later on the timetable mentioned above, with an associated set of long-, medium- and short-term contracts between the RECs and the generators.

Helm (2004) suggests that "the concept and design of the transition to full retail competition was an article of faith rather than a well-worked out plan." In the event it provoked a series of crises for all the parties:

Why, then, did its architects pick such a rigid timetable in ignorance of its practicality? Although there was a strong dose of cynicism in fixing dates which were carefully designed to be beyond the successive general elections, there was a clear rationale behind the plan ... The role of the deadlines is to give companies (and regulators) targets. ... The industry then had to be bound to the mast of an ever more liberalized market, with companies, regulators and government forced to come up with solutions, or face the criticism which inevitably follows delay. (pp. 152–4)

The extensive *History of Electricity Privatisation* (United Kingdom Department of Energy 1992), only now available, enables us to evaluate the above propositions.[1] The *History* contains a frank and detailed

---

[1] Unless otherwise indicated, the numbers in parentheses refer to paragraphs in this *History*. The relatively few redactions in the public version of the *History* do not impinge on the narrative and analysis of the present chapter. David

account of advice given by the Department of Energy (henceforth the Department) to its ministers, and of exchanges of view between senior ministers, the Prime Minister and other parties involved.

As we shall see, the *History* suggests that actual events were almost the opposite of the first picture painted above, and broadly consistent with the accounts given by Henney and Helm. It also reveals a richer picture. It documents (from sources not available to the other authors) not only the evolving views within the Department but also the differing views and influence of other ministers and advisers.

This chapter focuses on the creation of a retail electricity market, one of the least understood yet most controversial aspects of electricity privatization. I have sought to put the concept into a slightly broader historical and academic context than other authors, and to bring some personal perspective to bear.[2] Nonetheless, it will be apparent that retail competition cannot be considered as an isolated part of the novel competitive electricity market that was created around 1990, nor of the Government's economic and political strategy as a whole. For convenience, a timeline of relevant events is given as an appendix to the chapter.

9.2 Background

The Electricity Act 1947 nationalized the electricity industry in Great Britain. It created a British Electricity Authority and 12 Area Electricity Boards in England and Wales (plus 3 in Scotland). The Electricity Act 1957 replaced the British Electricity Authority by the Central Electricity Generating Board (CEGB).

The CEGB was required to develop and maintain an efficient, co-coordinated and economical system of supply of electricity in bulk to all parts of England and Wales. To that end it generated almost all the electricity it needed (supplemented by a small proportion imported from Scotland and France) and transmitted it, through its high voltage power lines and cables, to the Area Boards.

The 12 Area Boards bought bulk supplies of electricity from the CEGB. Each Area Board distributed electricity to consumers in its own

---

Parker's *Official History of Privatisation*, Volume II, 1987–1997, which covers electricity privatization, has since been published (Parker 2012).

[2] The author played a small part in this story, initially as adviser to the Secretary of State from November 1987, and then (from 1989 to 1998) as the first electricity regulator. He was also an early proponent of the concept of retail competition in electricity supply (Littlechild 2009).

The creation of a market for retail electricity supply 169

geographical area, where it had a statutory monopoly. The CEGB was allowed to supply electricity to any other body if authorized by the Minister, though such direct supply was not used on a significant scale. It was open to a large industrial user to generate its own electricity, but there was no wholesale or retail market for electricity, and no concept of competition in retail supply.

9.3 Early views: 1979 to 1987

A new Government brought a new approach.

The Conservative administration of 1979 set out to reverse the policy of centralized public sector planning. In 1982, the Secretary of State for Energy (Nigel Lawson) set out the new objective: to create a market for energy. The Oil and Gas (Enterprise) Act 1982 sought, inter alia, to liberalize the gas market and, in particular, to provide for competition through common carriage. The Energy Act 1983 extended the same principles to the electricity supply industry. (1.02)[3]

Although important forerunners of privatization, the 1982 and 1983 Acts were nonetheless limited in effect (Hammond et al. 1986; Helm 2004 p. 64).

In initial thinking on privatizing and liberalizing the electricity industry, two major and influential views emerged. As the *History* remarks, they were to recur throughout the debate on the future structure of the industry.

- A study by consultants Coopers & Lybrand Associates (1983) in May 1983 concluded that the only scope for introducing competition lay in generation, and saw a breakup of the CEGB as the only means of achieving this. It identified the nuclear program as the main obstacle to this. It assumed that long-term contracts with Area Boards that continued to have a monopoly of supply would ensure sufficient investment in new generation. (1.04–1.08)[4]

---

[3] This principle of common carriage was being developed elsewhere too, including in Chile. But neither Chile nor the Energy Act 1983 envisaged retail competition for all customers as an alternative (or complement) to regulation of electricity or gas supply.
[4] The study was commissioned by Nigel Lawson, who refers approvingly to it in his memoirs (Lawson 1992, p. 179).

- Sir Walter (later Lord) Marshall, chairman of the CEGB, took a quite different view, also in May 1983. He resisted breakup of the CEGB and favored amalgamating the Area Boards into a single distribution company (the so-called "two-company solution"). He "saw no advantages in licensing the Area Boards' territorial monopoly," and envisaged the CEGB effectively competing with this Board in supply to large users. (1.09)

By 1983, the Treasury, now under the leadership of Nigel Lawson who had moved there from the Department of Energy, was actively taking forward the development of policy on privatization and competition generally (Parker 2009, pp. 172–7). It commissioned a paper that contains what seems to be the first suggestion of retail competition for *all* electricity customers (Beesley and Littlechild 1983).[5]

In contrast, Peter Walker, the new Secretary of State at the Department of Energy, was of a different disposition to Nigel Lawson. He privatized British Gas as a single entity in 1986, which did not take forward thinking or practice on competition (Helm 2004 pp. 108, 116, citing Hammond et al. 1985a; see also Hammond et al. 1985b). The Department's report to the Secretary of State in April 1987 "cast doubt on the competitive benefits of fragmenting the industry" and noted "considerable support within the industry for the 'two company' solution." (2.10) Inter alia, "independent generators should continue to have the right to supply customers direct, but the option of restricting this right to large customers should be seriously considered, as should be the possibility of preventing the CEGB from supplying direct." (2.12)

In March 1987, Henney (1987) argued for breaking up the CEGB into nine or ten successor generating companies and a separate grid company. He proposed that there should be competition in supply for

---

[5] I discussed the electricity part of this paper with some industry contacts in December 1983, and then expanded it into a separate paper on electricity privatization (Littlechild 1984). Amongst other things, these papers proposed to separate the electricity Area Boards into distribution networks and competing private retailers that would buy and sell power over the distribution networks. This would make new use of common carrier obligations on the distribution networks. The aim was to use competition rather than regulation to pass through to retail customers as a whole the increased efficiencies in generation (that we expected would flow from privatization, competition and new entry into the wholesale market). See also Littlechild 2009; Parker 2009, p. 175 fn 64.

large (but not small) electricity users, using the distribution network as a common carrier.[6]

A Department paper identified many difficulties that Henney's restructuring proposal would raise and the time it would take (nearly ten years, covering two Parliaments). It "expressed worry about the disruption caused by such a long drawn out process, especially for the large investment programme in generating capacity that was foreseen." (2.14)

A meeting with the Prime Minister on 28 April 1987 concluded that electricity privatization was feasible, but reached no conclusions on the appropriate option. The election was called for June 11, 1987. The Conservative manifesto contained a commitment "to bring forward proposals for privatizing the electricity supply industry subject to proper regulation." It also said that a Conservative Government intended to go on playing a leading role in the task of developing abundant, low-cost supplies of nuclear electricity. (2.18)

9.4 Exploration of options: June 1987 to February 1988

Following the election, Cecil Parkinson was appointed as the new Secretary of State for Energy on June 13, 1987. The day after taking up his post he discussed a Department paper on the options for electricity privatization. It was agreed that further work should concentrate on the "two company" option (which was subsequently dropped) and the breakup of the CEGB. Financial, technical, legal, regulatory and accounting advisers were to be appointed. Further discussions among the Department, its advisers and the industry, and a seminar presentation to the Prime Minister and other leading ministers at Chequers (the Prime Minister's official country residence) on September 14, 1987, explored the implications of four main options:

- Option A privatize the CEGB as it stood;
- Option B as for option A, except that a block of power stations would be sold off as a competing company;

---

[6] Henney (1987, p. 40) suggested that customers taking more than 0.25m kWh per annum should be able to choose their supplier. He did not quantify the implications, but at a typical load factor of 57 percent this might correspond to a maximum demand of about 500 kW (= 0.5 MW). This might represent the largest 20,000 or so out of some 22 million customers, perhaps accounting for about 40 percent of total demand.

- Option C as for option B, except that ownership and control of the grid would be transferred to the distribution companies;
- Option D as for option C, except that the CEGB would be broken up into four or five generating companies.

All these options assumed the privatization of the Area Boards as existing separate entities. (3.15)

The Chequers seminar agreed that option A should be ruled out, and that options C and D should in particular be studied, though option B could not be ruled out. Major issues for study included the feasibility of separating the grid from the other CEGB generating stations, the implications for the nuclear investment program, for coal, for prices and for Scotland, and the possibility of privatizing the industry in one Parliament rather than two.[7]

After further analysis and discussions, the Secretary of State held a weekend seminar at Nuneham Park on November 21/22, 1987. The seminar explored in turn the options earlier presented to the Prime Minister. There was still considerable pressure from the CEGB for option A.[8] Nevertheless, the Secretary of State decided that his tentative preference was option C, given the political imperative to introduce competition into the industry. Option D was envisaged to involve too much disruption and to take two Parliaments to complete.[9]

There was subsequent analysis of how to produce the desired level of new nuclear investment, which was in doubt under any of the options. Possibilities included retaining nuclear in the public sector, subsidizing

---

[7] Cecil Parkinson adds that it was also decided to include nuclear in the package, and that the ongoing nuclear program must proceed. "Finally, it was agreed that if there was a conflict between introducing competition into the industry and getting the best price for it then competition should take precedence over price. Nigel Lawson [Chancellor] ... was particularly insistent on this" (Parkinson 1992 ch. 13, cited in Henney 1987, p. 59).

[8] "Lord Marshall had told the Permanent Secretary that most, if not all, of the Board of the CEGB would resign if any decision was reached that did not leave the CEGB intact. ... The Permanent Secretary informed the Secretary of State of Lord Marshall's message in the margins of the seminar." (3.30) I have been told that Lord Marshall's Board colleagues were not aware of his message.

[9] The Nuneham Park seminar was my own introduction to the scene. (3.26) I regret that it did not present the Secretary of State with a feasible and defensible option for a competitive industry structure. The *History* does not indicate that the four or five successor generator companies in option D would jointly own the nuclear generating stations and would be precluded from subsequently divesting (or specializing in) this nuclear ownership.

The creation of a market for retail electricity supply 173

the building of nuclear plant, and imposing some form of obligation on generators or distributors to generate or take X percent of electricity from non-fossil sources. This was not a trivial issue, particularly for the Prime Minister, who "expressed great concern about the future of the nuclear program and skepticism that a statutory obligation on the Area Boards would work." (3.41)

There were still differences of view among ministers, with the Chancellor and the Trade and Industry Secretary favoring something closer to option D. The Prime Minister too had concerns about structure, and "was at first not prepared to accept that privatization should proceed on a basis opposed by Lord Marshall." (4.01)[10] These issues were not resolved until a Cabinet Meeting on February 25, 1988. And indeed important new issues began to surface, such as the potential impact of coal imports on British Coal. (4.06)

9.5 The *White Paper* February 1988 and competition in supply

The *White Paper* entitled "Privatising Electricity" (United Kingdom Secretary of State for Energy 1988) was published on February 25, 1988, after the Cabinet Meeting just mentioned. Effectively, it announced the decision in favor of option C. Two privatized generators would be formed from the CEGB, with the larger one owning some 70 percent of existing capacity including the nuclear stations, and the smaller one owning the remaining 30 percent of existing capacity. The transmission grid would be separated off, and owned jointly by the distribution companies. The two successor generating companies were known as Big G (later National Power) and Little G (later PowerGen).

The *White Paper* discusses the strengths and limitations of the existing industry structure, the proposals for restructuring and competition in generation, the need for nuclear power, and the implications for regulation, customers and employees. It says that customers should be given new rights. But at no point in this period of policymaking – that is, from the election in June 1987 to the *White Paper* in February

---

[10] She had appointed him Chairman of the Atomic Energy Authority in 1981, Chairman of the CEGB in 1982, knighted him later that year, and made him a life peer in 1985 "on successful completion of his crusade to 'keep the lights on' no matter what moves Arthur Scargill's striking miners made against the power stations" (Baker 1996). See also Thatcher (1993, pp. 683–4).

1988 – does the *History* mention the concept of competition in supply (or retail competition or choice of supplier). There is no discussion of the implications of generators being able to sell direct to customers, whether large users or others. An influential view in the Department was that this would not be of interest to suppliers or any but the very largest users (Littlechild 2009, p. 760). There was also concern that it could prejudice the delivery of some of the policy objectives, such as securing value from the sale of the industry (proceeds) and timely completion of the privatization within the lifetime of the 1987 Parliament.

Although I pressed for some explicit recognition of the potential importance of competition in supply, the emphasis in the *White Paper* was on restructuring to create competition in generation, with a focus on the privatized Area Boards driving the competitive action by seeking out competitive tenders. There was reference to "other existing and potential private generators, who will generally contract with the distribution companies, the grid company, or large customers." But with respect to competition in supply, there were only a few sentences about distribution companies competing for large users, possibly using common carriage.

The *White Paper* included a commitment to strengthening the common carriage arrangements, which it recognized as an important area for regulation. It also acknowledged the need to ring-fence the various activities of the privatized companies, together with separate accounts. So there was an emphasis at this stage on putting in place the conditions necessary to make competition in supply effective. And the regulator would have a duty to promote competition. But such competition was still regarded as a matter for large users, and was not regarded as unduly significant, let alone as a threat to privatization.[11]

The *White Paper* asserted that, "in the new structure, the commercial relationship between the distribution companies and generators will be governed by contracts" (p. 8). Thus, "the grid company will operate on the basis of contractual relationships with generating and distribution companies," which "will be for them to negotiate." It was left open whether the distribution companies would contract for supply from the grid company (analogous to the single buyer model),

---

[11] "Even after privatization, the supply activities of the distribution companies … will remain, in large part, natural monopolies" (*White Paper* para 50).

or from the generating companies, or from both. But the statutory obligation to supply would be placed on the distribution companies rather than on a generator. (The Area Boards and the Department consistently maintained that the latter would prevent competition from developing.)

9.6 Regulation and competition in supply

The Department put a paper to the industry in March 1988 setting out proposals for the broad structure of regulation. It noted that "The monopoly areas of retail supply and transmission would need to be regulated." (7.01) Thus, at this stage no distinction is drawn between distribution and retail supply, and retail supply is assumed to be a monopoly rather than a competitive activity.[12]

Four months later, some of the implications of retail competition began to dawn. For example, the *History* now refers to an "Alternative Approach to Price Formula," namely the argument that I had been making for separate and different types of price controls on distribution and supply businesses rather than a single price control. (7.20)

And for the first time the *History* has a subheading with the phrase "Competition in Supply."

The new structure of the industry seemed likely to create more competition in electricity supply than was envisaged in the *White Paper*: there would be no permanent monopolies of supply; and the distribution companies' ownership of their wires would give them a natural monopoly of distribution, but not of supply.

Competition in supply faced the distribution companies with the risk of "stranded investment." The proposed regime dealt with this problem in two ways:

- Large customers would be obliged to take supply on contract, rather than by tariff. The contracts could contain suitable exit clauses to deal with stranded investment.

---

[12] Nevertheless, in some respects the Department seemed to be thinking boldly. Henney (1994, p. 94) says that although the Area Board chairmen "were aware that the White Paper talked of competition to supply large customers, they were very surprised at the first meeting of the Joint Department/REC Regulation Working Group in March 1988 when the Department said that the entire market would be open to competition."

- In deciding whether to grant a second-tier license to an alternative supplier, the regulator would need to take account of the impact on the distribution company of stranded investment. (7.11, 7.12)

It would soon become apparent that this was an optimistic assessment as a result of the limited interpretation of the stranded investment issue, and of the concept of retail competition.[13]

9.7 Decisions: February to December 1988

The *History* refers to the period leading up to the *White Paper* decisions as the "political" phase. Next, from February to November 1988 came the "creative" phase: "the ground-breaking work on regulation, licenses and contracts, the initial attempt to square nuclear liabilities with privatization," culminating in the introduction of the Electricity Bill. From then until Vesting was the "executive" phase.

An early decision (in March 1988) was the timetable for privatization, beginning with Vesting Day (when the restructuring of the industry and the new regulatory arrangements would take effect) on January 1, 1990.[14] On June 9, 1988 the designate chairmen and chief executives of the CEGB successor companies were announced. On June 17 the CEGB proposed an allocation of power stations between Big G and Little G successor companies. Some new appointments were made to the boards of the Area Boards, especially finance directors. Plans for a new Office of Electricity Regulation (Offer) were developed by September 1988. My appointment as Director General of Electricity Supply (DGES), and head of Offer, was announced in May 1989 (to take effect as from September 1989).

Among the regulatory issues to be resolved were the scope (coverage) of price control, and whether there should be a single price

---

[13] It was expected that each "alternative supplier" would have a license to supply "defined premises." (7.08) The initial licenses did indeed list the specific customers that the Secretary of State allowed each company to supply beyond its own area, and the companies had to apply for approval to serve other customers. One of my earliest actions as regulator was to remove the need for this, by granting licenses enabling the recipients to supply any customer with maximum demand over 1 MW (Littlechild 2000, pp 24–5).

[14] After that would be flotation of the distribution companies in Spring 1990, the larger generator (Big G) in Autumn 1990 and the smaller one (Little G) in Spring 1991. (6.39)

control or separate controls on distribution and supply. There also surfaced the possible regulation of initial contracts between successor generators and distribution businesses.[15] The main issues here were the duration of contracts and the level of prices, on which industry views differed markedly.[16]

A seminar on Regulation on July 6, 1988, attended by the Department's Ministers, seemed to settle some of these issues. Price control would be applied to all customers. Initial contracts would be for five to ten years. Aggregate revenue from these contracts should be constrained so that there was no discontinuity with the Bulk Supply Tariff. (7.33) (The Bulk Supply Tariff was the basis on which the CEGB sold electricity to the Area Boards.) But much remained to be resolved. Moreover, views differed within the Department and between its advisors. (7.35–7.36)

On September 29, 1988 the Secretary of State proposed the way ahead to his ministerial colleagues. Reversing the July decision, regulation of electricity supply would be limited to prices in the tariff market. (7.38) The concept of separate price formulae applying to the distribution tariff and to the price of electricity supplied "won favour." Initial contracts would be limited to 10 years except for nuclear stations. Distribution companies would also be limited to owning no more than 15 percent of their contracted capacity.

The Chancellor was broadly content, but (with a view to flotation proceeds) had concerns about profits in view of the surplus capacity, and suggested the possibility of longer contracts than 10 years. The Trade and Industry Secretary was more concerned about competition and prices, and preferred contracts shorter than 10 years. (7.46)

---

[15] In principle the contracts were for negotiation between the CEGB and the Area Boards. But the Department was concerned to avoid unjustified price increases arising simply from privatization.

[16] The Area Boards were concerned that the CEGB prices were excessive, and that the two CEGB successor generating companies might discriminate by loading the Area Boards with high cost capacity charges while offering contracts at marginal cost to large customers. The CEGB was arguing for contracts to provide capacity payments for the remaining life of its stations, and for freedom to allocate capacity between distribution companies and large customers. It said that, with shorter contracts, flotation proceeds would be reduced unless capacity charges were appropriately increased, and when the time came to renegotiate the contracts, distribution companies would prefer to bring in new entrants or establish their own capacity. (7.21–7.24)

The Secretary of State responded on November 14, 1988. He noted that the industry was now proposing two types of contract (see below) to deal with the problem of surplus capacity. He accepted the possibility of "some initial contracts of up to 15 years to provide stability for some time after flotation." (7. 49) After some further discussion, the Secretary of State circulated draft licenses in December 1988, implementing the policy decisions in his letters of September and November.

9.8 Contract negotiations in 1988

This apparent progress does not reveal the extent of the differences of view that were emerging during this period. Thinking on contracts evolved as the parties began to come to terms with the implications of competition in supply.

Progress on contracts during 1988 was hampered by the Area Boards' worries about the opportunity for generators to pick off large industrial customers, particularly given a surplus of generating capacity. To mix the metaphors in vogue, "cherry picking" by the generators would result in demand "walking away" from the distributors, leaving them with "stranded" contracts and investment. A number of ways of dealing with or preventing "cherry picking" were canvassed, resulting in much argument between the two sides and in justifications to the Department of their positions. (9.03)

The CEGB put forward two contractual solutions. In the contract market, distribution companies' contracts, with those large customers whom they feared might be poached, could be back-to-back with contracts with generators. In the tariff market, contracts with generators would include some provision for "winding-down" the distribution companies' obligation to buy capacity and energy if generators began poaching customers. The Area Boards were not attracted to these solutions. Wind-down failed to address their concern about the proper level of electricity prices. Back-to-back contracts would hardly be practicable as they would need to be in place for all customers above 1 MW (compared with the CEGB's suggestion of nearer 10 MW). (9.04)

The Area Boards responded to the CEGB by proposing a "two-tier" approach to contracting, involving the concept of "net-back" or "spot-price" contracts.

The creation of a market for retail electricity supply 179

A substantial amount of capacity would be contracted for at prices approximating to present Bulk Supply Tariff levels. For the remainder of the capacity required, the capacity element of the contract would be determined retrospectively by reference to system marginal price. These "net-back" contracts would enable distribution companies to offer prices to large customers sufficiently low to remove the threat of poaching by the generators. (9.05)

The Area Boards also suggested the possibility of "a temporary limitation on grant of second-tier licenses to supply customers below a certain size." (9.06)

The CEGB initially argued strongly against the net-back contracts. But by December 1988 the CEGB and the Boards had agreed on the broad principles of the contracts. There was still some disagreement over the size of the net-back tranche and the duration of such contracts, but the way ahead seemed clear.[17]

9.9 The first contract package: July 1989

Despite the apparent agreement, a number of important issues needed to be resolved. The implications for coal privatization also needed to be considered, and Coal Division was becoming very concerned about the possible magnitude of the net-back tranche. (21.04) By May 1989 it had become apparent that decisions on contracts were urgently needed if the timetable was to be met. Following a seminar with the Department and advisers, on June 14 the Secretary of State sent the Prime Minister a paper on Electricity Contracts, Prices and Proceeds. (21.18)

The paper reflected a greater emphasis on competition. Competition in supply would be implemented at Vesting, despite the preferences of the Area Boards. (21.20) There would be life-of-station contracts for nuclear, with the additional costs over and above those of fossil plants being financed by a levy on all customers. There was a new approach to deal with the concerns about stranded contracts. Instead of long-term contracts (up to 15 years) with provisions for winding down (as advocated by the CEGB), or two-tier contracts with a tranche of

---

[17] "The generators were offering 10% of capacity and a [net-back] contract length of three years. The Area Boards were seeking 20% and five to eight years. (9.07) It was agreed that the generators would offer 'indicative' contract prices by the end of January 1989 on the assumption of a 15% tranche of net-back contracts." (9.08) A timetable for negotiating contracts was also agreed.

net-back/spot contracts (as advocated by the Area Boards), the initial contracts for fossil generation would all be for five years and the Area Boards would have options to terminate 10 percent of these contracts every six months (in effect, their minimum duration would range from six months to five years). This would also benefit independent generators by preventing the two main generators from tying up the market on long-term contracts.

Each fossil-fired generating set would receive a market-related price equivalent to the price expected to be offered by a new entrant generator. This amounted to a 10 percent reduction on the Bulk Supply Tariff. "The Department's financial advisers believed that a contractual package based on broadly competitive prices provided the only sound basis for flotation if competition was to be introduced." (21.21)

The price estimates assumed British Coal price moving to world coal prices in five years, with a phased reduction in the annual volume purchased. This would help to secure the future of British Coal. Additional measures were suggested for limiting the increase in prices to industrial customers. With these, and the introduction of the nuclear levy, average prices to domestic and commercial customers would rise by only about the rate of inflation.

Ministers including the Prime Minister broadly supported the package, albeit with some reservations about prices (some considered them too high, others too low). The Prime Minister was concerned about the impact on pits worked by members of the Union of Democratic Mineworkers (UDM), who had stayed at work during the coal strike. (21.25) The package was agreed on July 18, 1989. The *History* makes no reference to discussions with the industry, let alone agreement. This would turn out to be important. Nonetheless, the industry reportedly accepted the package with some reservations, though British Coal was aggrieved.[18]

The package meant that retail competition would start at Vesting, then scheduled for January 1, 1990, only five months hence. There was no restriction on the extent and nature of such competition. Although the package referred explicitly only to large customers, this seemed to include customers with a maximum demand over 1 MW. There was no statutory or license barrier to competition to supply smaller customers

---

[18] British Coal was concerned at having been kept in the dark about the package, and about the proposed tapering to world prices. The company continued to hold out for a 10-year contract for the greater part of its supplies.

as and when the companies or competitors thought it worthwhile to do so.

9.10 Rethinking: August to September 1989

In retrospect, this seems to have been a high point for the prospects of retail competition. Events were soon to undermine these expectations. For example, as a result of further work on nuclear, the costs and risks of the older Magnox stations became increasingly apparent. On July 24, 1989, his last day as Secretary of State, Cecil Parkinson explained that he was withdrawing the Magnox stations from the privatization. (20.39) Eventually, on November 9, the remaining nuclear stations were pulled from the privatization. (20.40–20.90)[19]

On taking up his appointment, the new Secretary of State John Wakeham was concerned to discover that all was not what it seemed. Progress was behind schedule. Vesting by January 1, 1990 had become unrealistic, as had flotation in Spring 1990. In September he announced a revised timetable: Vesting on March 31, 1990 and flotation of the distribution companies in Autumn 1990 followed by the two generating companies in the first half of 1991.

This in itself would have meant only a three-month delay in the opening of full retail competition. However, two other aspects of the July 1989 arrangements – the two-Pool system and the first contract package – soon began to unravel.

During the first half of 1989, the CEGB and Area Boards had been working on the basis of a two-Pool system, involving a generators' G Pool and distributors' D Pool.[20] As discussions developed, the Area Boards became concerned that this approach would lead to the loss of their largest customers, since the generators could bypass the D Pool and sell direct. (21.12) The generators, for their part, were concerned that the D Pool with its attempt to mirror the actual dispatch of plant

---

[19] A week later Lord Marshall resigned the Chairmanship of the CEGB and his position as Chairman-designate of National Power (formerly Big G). (20.92) It has been suggested to me that he was intransigent and unreceptive to negotiation, and that his disappearance opened the door to all the industry players getting to a workable solution with all the various compromises that were needed.

[20] The generators' G Pool would allow generators to trade so as to meet their contractual obligations at lowest cost. The distributors' D Pool would allow the distribution companies to trade their contract entitlements so as to meet demand at the lowest contract price.

via detailed contracts amounted effectively to the leasing of plant to the distributors. This would also be complex, inefficient and unduly restrictive on the generators and on large users wanting load management terms. There was a question whether the proposed rules on contracts were pro-competitive or anti-competitive. Area Boards found difficulty in producing a less restrictive solution.[21] At the beginning of August 1989 they came up with a completely revised single-Pool approach: a Unified Settlements System.

This in itself was not a problem for the Department's policy – indeed, the Department saw advantages in the Unified Pool proposal. However, there was more. "Truly open competition" in retail supply presented a problem for the industry.

At about the same time [early August 1989], Mr. Duncan Ross, Chairman of Southern Electric, wrote to Mr. Guinness [Department of Energy] about the basic issues between generators and distributors. He believed that the generators were concerned that in a world of truly open competition there would be a severe risk of generating capacity failing to be adequately remunerated on a long-term basis. The Area Boards' new proposal for a unified pool did not itself address this concern. Mr. Ross suggested that there were only two ways of addressing it:

Either

1) long-term contracts between distributors and generators, with both capacity remuneration and fixed prices for energy, allied to a distributors' monopoly over supply to regulated customers within their licensed areas;

or

2) open competition in supply, with a flotation value for the generators reflecting the resultant volatility of profits.

The Area Boards believed that it could well be possible to reach agreement with the generators on pooling, settlement, contracts, etc., on the basis of

---

[21] In May 1989 the Area Boards had tabled proposals involving "nine rules" governing pooled and unpooled contracts. In July the Secretary of State rejected these proposals as too restrictive on the nature of contracts. He asked the industry "to develop the two-Pool approach in accordance with three principles which any pooling, contractual and regulatory arrangements should satisfy," and also indicated that "he was willing to consider some restrictions on the generators' freedom to supply customers direct." (21.17) The Area Boards concluded that the two-Pool approach could not be satisfactorily adapted to comply with the Secretary of State's objectives.

option 1), but option 2) would require the Department to intervene strongly. (22.01)

The generators confirmed their concerns.[22] They envisaged "alternative ways in which their concerns could be allayed: either a) persuading the Area Boards to sign a proportion of longer-term contracts at the outset, so that the range of duration of contracts was up to fifteen, rather than five years; or b) accepting substantially lower prices in the initial contracts, so that they faced less risk of declining profits when those contracts expired." (22.03)

To put the issue another way, the "broadly competitive contract prices" proposed by the Department and its financial advisers in July 1989 seem to have been based on calculations of a long-run new entry price. In contrast, the generators and Area Boards argued that the perceived excess capacity at the time meant that, in the short run, competitive prices could well be below that level.

For the Department, both options presented problems.

The difficulty with a) was that the Area Boards would refuse to sign long-term contracts without a monopoly of some part of the market. (It was thought this [monopoly] would be very unattractive to Professor Littlechild, the No. 10 Policy Unit and possibly to the DTI and the European Commission.) The difficulty with b) was that it could make the generators unflotable, would greatly reduce proceeds, could require cash injections into the generators' balance sheets and would not enable them to sign long-term high-priced contracts with British Coal. (22.03)

At the beginning of September, the Department recommended that the industry should proceed on the basis of the single Pool. There should be further analysis of the viability of the generators depending on the extent of long-term contracts, and an assessment of the Area Boards' argument that they could only accept long-term contracts if

---

[22] [T]hey were worried that it would encourage distributors and other customers to buy from them on a spot basis only. Given the surplus of capacity, the spot price would be low. In addition, low spot prices for sale of electricity would be inconsistent with high prices on a long-term basis for British Coal, which the Government might want to insist on. Also, low spot prices would not fund FGD investment. (22.03) Flue Gas Desulphurization (FGD) was required in order to clean up the emissions of coal-fired power stations.

they had a monopoly of part of their market. The Secretary of State agreed. But the Department was overtaken by events.

9.11 The industry proposal: September 1989

The generators and distributors scented a solution to their problems, and were working faster than the Department's processes envisaged. They accepted competition in supply above 1 MW but not below. On September 6 they proposed a set of contracts agreeable to both sets of parties. The key features were a monopoly franchise for each Area Board for customers in its area with maximum demand up to 1 MW, covering about 70 percent of the total market;[23] long-term contracts with fossil stations for supply to the franchise market (average 10 years, maximum 15 years), with a tapering surcharge to British Coal; short-term contracts (6 months to 5 years) for at least half the non-franchise market and spot price purchases for the balance; and restrictions on the generating companies selling direct into the non-franchise supply market (in aggregate, not more than 15 percent of their total capacity and not more than 15 percent of any one Area Board market). (22.05)

Generators and distributors were united in the belief that this package would remove sources of uncertainty, facilitate rapid progress on contracts and allied matters, preserve substantial competition and permit successful flotations. (22.05)

9.12 The Department's dilemma

Given the strong disagreements between Area Boards and generators, the prospect of agreement within the industry must have been attractive. However, the Department was soon faced with concerns about this proposal. The Prime Minister's office noted "the crucial importance of achieving genuine competition in contractual and operating arrangements, so that the consumer secured proper benefits from privatization." (22.06)[24]

---

[23] Henney (1994, p. 116) says that the package envisaged that "competition would be limited to customers above 10 MW for five years then extended to customers above 5 MW." That would have been even more restrictive than the package described in the *History*.

[24] In addition, the Trade and Industry Secretary "was concerned about reports that the industry wanted to have long-term supply contracts and a distributors'

The creation of a market for retail electricity supply 185

However, the Department was reluctant to reject the proposal. The Secretary of State replied to the Prime Minister's office on September 12, suggesting that "achievement of the prime objective of privatization might mean some modification of other objectives in the short term." (22.07) While the industry's recent proposals "represented a major initial limitation of the competitive structure which Mr. Parkinson had agreed with officials in July, the industry maintained that they were indispensable to privatization proceeding on the current timetable." And they had other advantages.[25]

The Secretary of State met with the Prime Minister on September 13. She reaffirmed that achieving privatization had to be the first priority. "At the same time it was important to avoid the extent of competition being over-diluted, resulting in a rerun of the British Gas privatization. But she recognized that some degree of compromise on competition was likely to be necessary in striking the overall balance." (22.08)

9.13 The Department's response

The Department noted that these proposals "were unique in that it was the first time that the Area Boards and the generators had agreed on the principles on which the new contractual, operating and settlement regime should be based." Although the industry was nationalized, it was statutorily run at "arm's length" from government. All the parties therefore had to be satisfied before signing the contracts (and personally signing the prospectus statements) on which the new regime depended. Hence it was not feasible to contemplate imposing a solution on the industry. The Department therefore advised that "some deal with the industry was essential if privatization was to be achieved during the present Parliament; but that an attempt ought to be made to limit the restriction on competition that the proposals represented." This might be with a smaller franchise market, a shorter

---

monopoly of small customers. This would run counter to the pro-competitive approach agreed in the summer. A move to long-term initial contracts would jeopardize the chances of proper competition developing and would be especially hard on emerging private generators." (22.07)

[25] "The proposals retained competition in generation; were likely to be welcomed by independent generators; and could well make it easier to accommodate the costs of reducing sulphur emissions. Longer-term contracts with distributors would enable the generators to enter into longer-term commitments to British Coal." (22.07)

franchise period or shorter initial contracts. (22.09) This approach perhaps reflected the inclinations of the new Secretary of State, who had a reputation as a "fixer" of difficult political problems.

Meanwhile other departments reaffirmed their concerns about competition. (22.10) The Department had "extensive discussions with all sides of the industry and two discussions with Professor Littlechild." On September 22 it identified two options. (22.11, 22.12)

- The first option involved a five-year restriction on competition in supply to premises consuming less than 1 MW. This would be reviewed at the end of five years. If the Government decided to remove the restriction, the transition to a fully competitive market would be phased over three years.
- The second option involved a three-year restriction on competition in supply to premises consuming less than 1 MW; after the three years were up, a phased reduction of the 1 MW limitation to 0.1 MW (100 kW) over the next two years; the 0.1 MW limitation being phased out altogether over a further three years.

Whereas the first option provided the *possibility* of competition for all customers within eight years, the second provided a *commitment* to allow the phased introduction of such competition over the same period. In other respects, especially contracts, the two options were essentially the same.[26] The main difference from the industry proposal was that long-term contracts would cover 50 percent rather than 70 percent of the total market.

The Department envisaged that the industry would accept the first option but that Professor Littlechild would not.[27] PowerGen was

[26] They both envisaged a) life-of-station contracts for nuclear (which had already been agreed) and 10–15-year contracts for 12 GW of fossil-fuel capacity. In total, these longer-term contracts would cover about 50% of the total market; b) the remainder of the initial franchise market (about 20% of the total market) would be met by shorter-term (3–5-year) contracts; c) the initial non-franchise market (about 30% of the total market) being met by a mixture of spot and six-month to five-year contracts, as proposed by the industry; and d) a limit of 15% on the generators' aggregate direct sales in any one distributor's licensed area. (22.11) The reduction in the franchise to 0.1 MW would extend competition to about 50,000 customers accounting for about 50% of the total market.

[27] He thought that a five-year monopoly in the market below 1 MW would provoke much criticism, particularly on the part of larger retailers and other commercial operators who would be excluded for some time from the benefits

relaxed about the second option but the Area Board chairmen and National Power reacted adversely. Professor Littlechild responded favorably. The Department recommended that the Secretary of State should seek to persuade the industry to accept the second option, on the same basis as they put forward their own proposals, "i.e. that they would cooperate constructively and effectively to deliver privatization during the present Parliament," otherwise the only proposal remaining on the table would be that agreed by Ministers in July.

At his crucial meeting with the industry Chairmen on September 25, the Secretary of State explained why the industry's proposal of September 6 presented him with difficulties: he did not believe he could persuade colleagues to accept it, there would be considerable difficulties with the European Commission and difficulties, too, with the DGES. He was prepared to put to colleagues the alternative proposal tabled by the Department (the second option) if he could tell them the industry was united behind it. (22.14)

The industry Chairmen raised various objections, which were generally countered.[28] Nevertheless, as the industry appeared to be dissatisfied with the Department's proposal, the Secretary of State asked the Chairmen to come forward with a modified proposal by the end of the day, otherwise he would take the Department's proposal unmodified to the Prime Minister.

9.14 The industry's modified proposal

The Chairmen worked on this issue during the afternoon and presented a package which the Secretary of State believed there was a reasonable chance of colleagues accepting. (22.14)

---

of competition in supply. The Department's advisers considered that opposition from Professor Littlechild, or even reluctant acquiescence, would unsettle investors and lead to lower proceeds. (22.11) On September 25 Professor Littlechild confirmed his strong reservations about the industry's proposals. (22.13)

[28] E.g., "The Area Boards said that ... under the Department's proposal, they would not be able to offer independent generators sufficiently long-term contracts to make investment worthwhile, though this might be different if the distributors were given a permanent monopoly below 0.1 MW. The Secretary of State said that he would not be able to secure colleagues' agreement to a permanent franchise." (22.14)

The modified proposal had the following features:
1) a <u>four</u>-year limitation on the issue of second-tier supply licenses for supply to premises taking 1 MW or less;
2) a further <u>four</u>-year limitation on issue of second-tier licenses for supply to premises taking 0.1 MW or less;
3) thereafter no limit on the issue of second-tier licenses;
4) life of station contracts for supply from nuclear stations;
5) <u>four- to eight</u>-year contracts for 12 GW of supply from fossil-fueled stations, equivalent to the extent of the distributors' monopoly franchise;
6) the distributors to secure the balance of their requirements under contracts with the generators of <u>up to five years;</u>
7) during the first four years, National Power and PowerGen would, in aggregate, be limited to supplying no more than 15 percent of the demand in any one distributor's territory. This limit would be <u>raised to 25 percent for the next four years and then be completely lifted</u>. (22.15, underlining in original)

Professor Littlechild argued for a faster reduction in the distributors' monopoly.[29] Nonetheless, on September 26, 1989 the Secretary of State recommended the industry's modified proposals to his colleagues. They gave a qualified acceptance, inviting him to seek a shorter transitional period (six rather than eight years). (22.24) The Department advised that this would make the coal contract negotiations very difficult. The Secretary of State wrote to the industry chairmen on September 29, 1989, accepting the package they had put forward. He described the discussions as "the most productive since the Electricity Act was passed." (22.26)

9.15 Subsequent contracts and prices

As the *History* remarks, "there remained the enormous task of translating the principles and framework now agreed into contracts, codes and agreements." (22.28) This had to be complete by Vesting on March 31, 1990, just six months hence.

---

[29] Via one or more of the following: "removal of the 1 MW to 0.1 MW franchise within two rather than four years; the DGES to have discretion to allow aggregation of premises; and the timetable for removal of monopoly to be reviewed by the DGES after two years." (22.16)

The creation of a market for retail electricity supply 189

In particular, the coal and electricity contracts that had driven the supply competition timetable had to be negotiated. The Secretary of State indicated that "he had accepted the eight year limitation on competition within the electricity industry because that would make it easier for long-term coal contracts to be signed." (26.03) In the event, British Coal and the generators were unable to reach agreement on the envisaged four- to eight-year contracts. The final contract package brokered by the Secretary of State was limited to three years. British Coal declined to sign longer contracts on the terms on offer. This in turn led to three-year contracts between generators and distributors, despite the franchise having been agreed at eight years. (26.24) In December 1989 the contract package was modified accordingly. (26.12, 26.13, 26.25)

The Government considered it important to assess the implications for prices.[30] Steps were taken to reduce the projected price increases to large users to a politically acceptable level, notably by rebalancing between franchise and non-franchise customers. (26.22–26.38) The Area Boards eventually announced average price increases of 9.0% nominal for franchise customers (presented as below the rate of inflation, then 9.4%) and average price reductions of 8.47% nominal for non-franchise customers.

9.16 The broader context, the evolution of thinking and the learning process

The Government "created" the market for retail electricity supply in the sense that it removed the statutory monopoly of the Area Boards. This step has to be seen in its broader context. The Government's aim was to turn a state monopoly as far as possible into a privately owned and competitive market. This necessitated restructuring the industry, creating competition in generation and in supply, creating a wholesale spot market (the Pool), writing initial contracts, setting up a regulatory framework, and so on. There were also many goals

---

[30] Calculations just before the December contract package suggested a 6–8% nominal price increase for domestic (residential) consumers, reductions in real terms for the majority of commercial and industrial customers, but price increases of 15% nominal for large users and up to 30% nominal for the dozen or so very large users. "Such increases were clearly unacceptable." (26.21)

to achieve: a better deal for customers, ensuring security of supply, taking forward the nuclear program, obtaining value from the sale of the industry and completing the privatization within the lifetime of the 1987 Parliament – and enabling the subsequent transition to a privatized and competitive UK coal industry as well. Creating a retail electricity market was important, but it was only a part of the total picture, and could not be allowed to jeopardize the other objectives.

The Department's thinking on what creating this retail market would mean, and therefore how to do it, evidently went through several significantly different stages.

- The *White Paper* in February 1988 saw supply competition as hardly worth mentioning, irrelevant other than for a few large users.
- Even by December 1988 it was still a minor issue: the Government envisaged long-term (5–15-year) contracts in the industry, with any concerns about stranded contracts being met by a small tranche of spot-price contracts.
- By July 1989 the Government attached greater importance to both wholesale and retail competition. It proposed to remove the retail monopoly immediately and entirely. Instead of long-term contracts, short-term (six-month to five-year) contracts and options to terminate contracts would offset the risks to investors and facilitate new entry into generation.
- The industry argued that the resulting contract prices (and flotation proceeds) would be unduly low, and would not facilitate coal privatization. Generators and distribution companies proposed a package that they had agreed between themselves, limiting retail competition to customers over 1 MW, with a franchise monopoly below 1 MW enabling long-term contracts up to 15 years.
- The Government was now torn. It was concerned to ensure proceeds, investment and coal privatization. And it felt unable to dictate terms to the industry parties because it needed their acceptance of the contracts that would underpin privatization. Nevertheless, the continuation of a franchise monopoly was no longer acceptable.
- The Government therefore accepted the principle of a temporary franchise monopoly but insisted on a transition to full retail competition. In September 1989 agreement was reached on a phased

The creation of a market for retail electricity supply 191

three-stage opening, with provision for contracts of four and eight years to match this.

There was certainly a learning process.[31] Henney (1994) brings out well the particular structure to the process. "The parties to the negotiation were grappling with how to break the traditional 'utility deal' and reconstruct relationships in a competitive manner." (p. 104) Some preferred the "utility deal," others preferred the competitive model.[32] The Government in principle preferred the competitive model – but also wanted the concomitants of a utility deal (subsidies for coal and nuclear power and an obligation to supply) that were ultimately inconsistent with competition. A learning process was inevitable, on the part of all concerned.[33] This was particularly true with respect to the significance of retail competition.

Above all few understood the extent to which introducing competition in supply – in addition to competition in generation – changed the fundamental risk allocation and hence economics of the industry, and was opening Pandora's box. Initially competition in supply was treated like an add-on, and it took a long time for people to appreciate that it was central to the system, and that many of the proposals to restrict competition would unwind like a ball of string. It took some time for the profound significance of

---

[31] "[E]conomic policy making is a dynamic game, whose conditions are uncertain and changing, and whose rules are at least partially made up by the participants as they go along" (Dixit 1996, p. 30).

[32] Throughout this phase of the work and indeed up to the agreement on the contractual package in September 1989, there was continual conflict between the proponents (to exaggerate) of the "competitive model" (who included the government), who advocated open access for all customers, a rapid move to market prices, shorter term contracts between the generators and the RECs, ready access for new entrants, and a low flotation value for National Power and PowerGen, and the proponents of the "franchise model." They advocated limiting competition to customers with a load over 10 MW and the retention of a permanent franchise for smaller customers, relatively higher electricity prices, longer contracts between the generators and RECs (which could if necessary incorporate subsidies for nuclear power and coal and perforce restricted access for new entrant generators), and a higher valuation for National Power and PowerGen. (Henney 1994, p. 93)

[33] "People had to go down the traditional path to see that it got them nowhere; it took time to change from conventional electricity supply industry thinking the world over to more 'normal' commercial thinking. The people involved were creating a whole new way of doing business – it was not surprising that the learning process was somewhat confused and tortuous" (Henney 1994, p. 105).

competition in supply to be fully understood, and that among other things it had fundamental financial implications and made traditional capacity planning (indeed any form of decentralized capacity planning) impossible, and for people to appreciate that competition in supply was the most radical part of the proposed new system. (Henney 1994, pp. 93–4)

9.17 A negotiated settlement?

The Department of Energy was leading the electricity privatization, but eventually found itself not in a position to dictate terms. It needed to gain the agreement not only of other Departments, but importantly of the relevant economic and political actors. This included especially the generators and Area Boards, who were incumbents in their own markets but potential entrants into the markets of the other parties. As nationalized industries whose agreement was needed to sign contracts and the privatization prospectus, they were not pawns of the Government, but ultimately became "veto players" in the "game." However, they were reluctant to exercise veto power insofar as they too wished to bring about a timely privatization.

It became apparent that the solution proposed by the Department in July 1989, and agreed by ministers, was not viable. The parties were unable to reach agreement within that framework, at least not without jeopardizing proceeds, timely completion and coal contracts. The breakthrough was in effect a negotiated settlement, a package comprising only a partial opening to competition but also a mix of long-term and short-term contracts negotiated between the industry parties themselves. The latter were no doubt interested to protect their markets from competition, but they were also offering deliverability of the Government's policy as a whole.

Remarkably, in view of the stance just a year earlier, the Government insisted on the parties modifying the agreed package to meet the concerns of ministers and the DGES about retail competition. As Helm (2004) observes, the point of an agreed timetable for opening the whole of the market was to commit not only the industry and the regulator but also subsequent governments. The choice made in September 1989 turned out to be critical. Suppose the industry's initial proposal had been accepted, or the Department's first option (review of the retail monopoly after five years) had been chosen. The political pressures posed by the coal industry in the mid-1990s would undoubtedly have led to deferral or abandonment of the prospect of full competition and of the ending of the coal subsidies. It would have saddled more customers with the costs of high-priced contracts for a longer period of time. Again, when some distribution companies argued against full market opening after the new (Labour) Government was elected in 1997, the committed timetable provided a defense against such opportunism.

Was the decision to insist on a timetable inevitable? Was it independent of the personalities involved? It seems likely that there would have been pressure to allow retail competition for the largest users, maybe even as far as industrial users over 1 MW. But would the extent of retail competition have gone much further without key ministers (and advisers) as committed to the principle of competition as Cecil Parkinson, Margaret Thatcher (and Sir Alan Walters), Nigel Lawson and Lord Young? Or without a prospective DGES who had actually proposed the novel policy of full retail competition some five years earlier?

In the event, the longer contracts specified in the package were not delivered. A critical interested party, British Coal, was not a party to the package. Should it have been involved in this negotiation? If so, it is not clear that agreement would have been reached consistent with the Government's emphasis on competition. The eight-year package was not irrelevant: when the three-year coal contracts came up for renewal the Government took full advantage of the remaining franchise to broker new contracts to cope with a difficult political situation and to enable coal privatization. By the same token the Government was constrained by the timetable with respect to both quantity and duration of subsidy.

In the end, some phasing of competition was not necessarily a bad idea, even from the perspective of those who argued for the "competitive model." It enabled electricity privatization to take place on time, with manageable risks to the companies, and later coal privatization. It allowed time for all parties to learn from experience, and for later regulatory provisions (e.g., metering, profiling and data transfer) to make retail competition effective for residential users. Against this, the phasing did force medium-to-large users (for four years) and smaller and residential customers (for eight years) to bear a very considerable burden of subsidizing the British coal industry.

In contrast to all the agonizing over the design, duration and pricing of initial contracts, the subsequent competitive market process in the UK has so far selected vertical integration between generation and supply, rather than long-term contracts, as the main means of survival. Ironically, the early contributors to the discussion all dismissed the possibility of vertically integrated regional power boards. Yet that concept is perhaps closest to the eventual outcome today (albeit without the regional element, except in Scotland). If the concept of retail competition had been better elaborated and understood in the 1980s, power boards might have received more sympathetic consideration, though any regional nature would not have been so conducive to effective competition.

9.18 Was it worth it?

The question is inevitably asked: was it worth it? Did the benefits of full retail competition outweigh the costs? There is not space to address this question fully here, but a few remarks may be in order.

Non-franchise customers fared very well when the market opened.[34] Generators proved keen to offer attractive terms and large users proved keen to respond. Within the first month or so, 28% of non-franchise (over 1 MW) customers, accounting for 43% of non-franchise load, had signed up for an alternative (second-tier) supplier. Within eight years these proportions had increased to 63% and 75%, respectively (Offer 1997, p. 28). In 1994, medium-sized industrial users (with maximum demand over 0.1 MW or 100 kW) showed that they too were willing to switch supplier.[35] It does not seem to be disputed that retail competition has been of benefit to industrial and commercial users.

Would residential customers and other small users be interested in competition in supply? Some in the Department and the industry had doubted it.[36] But in 1998, when they were at last allowed a choice,

---

[34] "A survey of industrial users on behalf of the Major Energy Users Council reported that for the year ending March 1991, 76% of consumers with sites consuming 1 MW or more had experienced price reductions of at least 10%, and 31% had had reductions of over 20%. (*Power in Europe* 18 July 1991)." (26.38)

[35] In 1994/5 some 25% of 100 kW customers, accounting for 30% of the total 100 kW load, switched supplier. By 1997/8 those proportions had increased to 41% and 53% respectively (Offer 1997).

[36] One of the most senior Area Board chairmen had responsibility for coordinating the arrangements for retail competition. I told him that I could

residential customers moved to new competing suppliers at the rate of more than 1 percent per month. A decade later, more than half the residential customers in the UK are supplied by non-incumbent suppliers.

But numbers of customers changing supplier is only one aspect. Are the benefits to residential customers worth the costs involved? In the UK today there is particular concern whether retail profit margins are excessive and whether prices follow wholesale prices down as quickly as they should do. Some call for reintroducing regulation of retail prices.

Various attempts have been made to analyze these costs and benefits, and to construct counterfactual prices (e.g., Green and McDaniel 1998; Littlechild 2002; Newbery 2006; Defeuilley 2009; Littlechild 2009). Just two brief observations here. First, retail competition means that customers do not have to "take what they are given," or rely on regulation being able and willing to discover what different customers want and to identify and enforce a "fair" or "competitive" price. It gives all customers (and suppliers) the ability to act for themselves. Each individual customer is able to choose the combination of price, risk, duration of contract and other terms that best suits that customer's needs. The variety can be remarkable (e.g., Littlechild 2006).

Second, in assessing the level of retail prices, the level of wholesale price that is observed in the market should not be taken as given. The question is what that wholesale price would have been in the absence of retail competition for residential customers. The relevant comparison is with a monopoly franchise covering between one third and one half the total market, with associated investments, contracts, wholesale and retail prices determined by government and/or regulator rather than by the competitive market. The evidence from the process of opening the UK retail market, and from experience elsewhere, does not suggest that the interests of customers would be the only or most important consideration. This is not to say that other considerations – related to fuel mix, climate change or affordability, for example – cannot be justified as a matter of public policy. But with full retail competition any restrictions on the competitive market now have to be justified explicitly and are thereby subject to more informed

envisage domestic (residential) customers choosing their own electricity supplier, perhaps selecting from entries in the Yellow Pages telephone book. "It will never happen," he said firmly, "It will never happen."

analysis, costing and debate. That is surely a significant benefit of retail competition.

Is the British approach to creating a retail market a model for others? Maybe not, even though the concept of a timetable has set a precedent followed by many governments worldwide. Each country will have its own specific issues to address. However, the multi-faceted nature of the market, the multiple goals of policy, the somewhat unpredictable process of balancing conflicting objectives and emerging practical constraints, the substantial learning over time, the role of negotiated agreement within the industry, and the delivery of some but not all the initial aims of policy – all this may not be unrepresentative of how governments actually operate, including in creating markets. What was perhaps distinctive at a critical time was the commitment to competition exhibited by the leading actors in this particular drama. And, I would argue, with justification.

Appendix

Timeline of events related to the creation of the market in retail electricity supply

1947, 1957 Electricity Acts creating CEGB and Area Boards with regional monopolies
1979 May General Election, Conservative victory
1982 June Oil and Gas (Enterprise) Act liberalizing gas market and enabling competition through common carriage

1983

May Energy Act extending the same principles to electricity
May Coopers & Lybrand report to Department of Energy proposing breakup of CEGB to enable competition in generation but continued monopoly in supply
May Sir Walter Marshall letter opposing breakup of CEGB and proposing "two company solution" with competition to supply large users
June General Election, Conservative victory

The creation of a market for retail electricity supply 197

November Littlechild and Beesley paper to Treasury proposing full retail competition

1987

March Henney monograph for CPS advocating restructuring of CEGB and competition to supply large users
April Department report to Mr. Walker noting support for "two company solution"
June Conservative Party Manifesto commitment to electricity privatization
October General Election, Conservative victory, Mr. Parkinson appointed as Secretary of State for Energy
September Chequers seminar
November Nuneham Park seminar

1988

February *White Paper* "Privatising Electricity"
March Department paper (to industry) on structure of regulation
July Department seminar on regulation
September Mr. Parkinson's proposals on regulation
November introduction of the Electricity Bill
December draft licenses

1989

January divisionalization of CEGB
March embryo Office of Electricity Regulation (Offer)
May appointment of Director General of Electricity Supply announced
June Mr. Parkinson's proposals (to PM) on contracts, prices and proceeds
July Magnox nuclear stations withdrawn from privatization
July John Wakeham replaces Cecil Parkinson as Secretary of State for Energy
July Royal Assent to Electricity Act
August Area Boards propose Unified Pool instead of two-Pool system

September appointment of Director General of Electricity Supply effective

September franchise and contract package negotiated and agreed, including eight-year timetable to full retail competition

September Mr. Wakeham's proposals on revised contract package

September decision on revised privatization timetable

November remaining nuclear stations withdrawn from privatization

November agreement between British Coal and generators on initial contracts

December Mr. Wakeham's proposals on revised (three-year) contract package, contract prices and nuclear revenue

1990

March revised Vesting Day

November Offer for sale of distribution company shares

1991

March Offer for sale of 60 percent of generation company shares

10 The institutional design of European competition policy

ANTONIO MANGANELLI[1], ANTONIO NICITA, AND MARIA ALESSANDRA ROSSI

10.1 Introduction

Competition policy constitutes an important facet of "market manufacturing." Indeed, it consists of a system of actors and rules explicitly meant to protect and enhance the competitive dynamics of markets and their efficient functioning. In Europe, competition policy has played an even deeper role in "manufacturing" the market than elsewhere, since its development has historically been influenced by the aim to contribute to the creation of a single market space – the common internal European market.

Notwithstanding its relevant role in the design of markets and antitrust rules, European competition policy has not been characterized by a rationally designed enforcement system and its evolution seems rhapsodic in many ways. It may be more properly described as the result of more or less unintended evolutionary patterns linked to political forces. In this chapter we investigate whether, in spite of this tortuous evolution, the current EU competition policy framework is nonetheless evolving towards an efficient institutional design.

In order to evaluate the characteristics of the EU competition policy system, we adopt (and adapt, where appropriate) a framework of analysis based on the notion of "multilevel governance," originally derived from the political science literature and more recently cast in economic terms (Brousseau and Raynaud 2006). The notion of "multilevel governance" has gained wide currency both in Europe and elsewhere. It refers to a system of allocation of powers and responsibilities among

---

[1] BEREC Office. DISCLAIMER: The drafting of the present work was completed by Antonio Manganelli before his employment in the BEREC Office and the opinions expressed are based solely on his personal views and understandings of the subject matter.

vertically related policy layers (EU institutions, nation-states, regions, etc.), each of which is autonomous from the others, yet it cannot be considered completely free to exercise such powers and responsibilities (Grande 1996; Marks et al. 1996; Scharpf 1994).

The EU competition policy system, similarly to most aspects of the EU institutional framework,[2] does fit this description, although only a few contributions have adopted this approach in the analysis of EU competition policy (Budzinsky 2009; Budzinsky and Christiansen 2005; McGowan 2000; Walzenbach 2006), and generally not from an economic perspective (with the exception of some works by Kerber, and particularly Kerber 2003 and 2009).

The EU competition policy system has traditionally been characterized by a rather strong centralization of competences and powers held by the EU Commission. Indeed, as many National Competition Authorities (hereinafter NCAs) were born after the Commission started playing its role in competition policy, the bulk of the Commission's decisions shaped the evolution of national antitrust approaches. However, recent policy developments have strengthened the "multi-level" nature of the system. In particular, the so-called "modernization" of competition policy, whose main step has been the enactment of Regulation 1/2003 (hereinafter REG),[3] has increased the extent of decentralization of competition policy enforcement, thus fostering the role played by NCAs. As a result, powers and responsibilities in relation to either the definition of substantive competition rules or competition enforcement are currently shared among actors, placed at different governance levels, none of which can operate independently from the others.

This vertical dimension is crucial to understanding the institutional design of European competition policy, yet an exclusive focus on it would entail the risk of missing important features of the overall picture. Indeed, the vertical dimension of the multilevel governance interfaces horizontally with at least two other very important "parallel

---

[2] The principal focus of the multilevel governance literature has for some time been on policy areas that primarily involve budgetary issues, as this literature developed to provide an account of the evolution of the relationships among EU decision-making layers, with specific regard to the allocation of structural funds and to regional policies (Marks 1993).

[3] Council Regulation of December 16, 2002 on the implementation of the rules on competition laid down in articles 101 and 102 of the Treaty.

The institutional design of competition policy 201

domains" of competition policy. First, besides administrative bodies (the EU Commission and NCAs), national courts too can apply competition law, giving rise to the so-called private enforcement. Second, within regulated sectors, such as for instance the Electronic Communications or the Energy sectors, National Regulatory Authorities (hereinafter, NRAs) play an important role in the design of competition rules. This is because EU policy has been recently pushing towards a convergence of competition law and sector-specific regulation, formally defining competition enhancement as a main goal of NRAs.[4]

Therefore, the EU competition policy system amounts to a dense web of vertical and horizontal relationships among a large set of relevant actors, all concurring to define the institutional environment in which competition takes place. These relationships, governed by both formal and informal coordination rules, imply significant competence overlaps and strong interdependencies. This institutional design raises two fundamental questions: How do these overlaps and interdependencies affect the overall effectiveness and efficiency of the system? What problems, if any, do they solve or, on the contrary, do they cause?

In order to assess the implications and trade-offs associated to these overlaps and interactions, our analysis highlights whether the actions of the different subjects involved in competition policy enforcement are complements or substitutes from the perspective of the achievement of a competitive EU market. The analytical focus is placed on "core" competition policy enforcement (i.e., to activities relating to art. 101 and 102 TFEU), and particularly on the three aspects of the system that we deem most significant, namely: (i) the design and the vertical allocation of competences and powers among the European Commission and NCAs (Section 10.2 below); (ii) the horizontal allocation of competences and powers among parallel competition policy domains, that is the interactions between administrative and judicial enforcement (Section 10.3) and between competition law enforcement and sector-specific regulation (Section 10.4) (see also Table 10.1).

---

[4] A complete analysis of the multilevel system would also take into account the fact that all the competition policy decisions adopted by administrative bodies (Commission and NCAs) are subject to judicial revision by the General Court (previously the Court of First Instance), the European Court of Justice or national (administrative) courts. In this chapter we have chosen to disregard this aspect.

10.2 The vertical design and allocation of competences and powers within the EU multilevel competition policy system

The vertical design of the EU competition policy system can be described by reference to two main aspects: (i) the allocation of competences in the design of substantive competition law and (ii) the allocation of competences in the enforcement of competition policy. The current EU system is characterized by: (a) a high degree of harmonization of substantive law; (b) a relatively high degree of enforcement decentralization, mitigated by a strong unifying role played by the European Commission.

As for (a), the provision of substantive competition law was envisaged by the founders of the European Community as a key instrument to ensure the integrity of the internal common market and has therefore been a longstanding feature of the EU competition policy system. Consequently, European competition law is uniformly applied to all behaviors and practices affecting "trade between member states."[5] At the same time, this design does not exclude the existence of national laws and the possibility that these may to some extent diverge from European law, although the importance of these divergences has been substantially reduced through the modernization process.[6]

As for (b), the current design of the system is the result of more recent developments, as it follows the enactment of Regulation 1/2003 (REG), pursuant to which Member States must designate competition authority(ies) responsible for the application of articles 101 and 102 TFEU (art. 35 REG), which can apply articles 101 and 102 of the Treaty in their entirety in individual cases[7] (art. 5) with powers very similar to those held by the Commission.[8]

---

[5] As a matter of fact, the European Court of Justice has always adopted a wide interpretation of this general concept, e.g., ECJ, 13/07/66, *Consten and Grundig/Commission EC*, C-56 and 58/64. More recently, the Commission has adopted a Communication aimed to clarify and delineate the concept. Communication 2004/C 101/07.

[6] Indeed, art. 3(1) REG states that where NCAs and national courts apply national competition law to illicit behaviors within the meaning of European competition law, they shall also apply the latter to such behaviors. This naturally tends to reduce conflicts among substantive normative systems. Moreover, art. 3(2) REG also reduced abstract divergences of EU and national competition rules.

[7] Before REG the exemption of art. 101(3) could be enforced only by the Commission.

[8] From art. 7 to 10 REG for the Commission's powers and art. 5 REG for NCAs'.

Both aspects of the vertical design of the EU competition policy system could in principle be analyzed from an economic perspective. However, we believe that focusing on the allocation of enforcement competences allows us to grasp more relevant insights in terms of efficiency of the overall system. This is for at least two reasons. First, substantive law has been rather static in the past few decades within developed economies' jurisdictions, thus placing at the center stage of the analysis the way in which the law is enforced rather than its substance. Second, competition law is principle-based, which implies that relevant norms are filled of concrete significance only when the principle is applied, i.e., at the enforcement stage.

Therefore, in what follows, we will focus on competition policy enforcement and analyze the current EU system in terms of optimal degree of enforcement decentralization, following insights offered by the fiscal federalism literature (Oates 1972; Tiebout 1956) and the relatively less developed legal federalism literature (see, for instance, Faure 2004; Kerber 2003 and 2009; Van den Bergh 1998).

The choice of the optimal degree of enforcement decentralization involves relevant trade-offs. On the benefits side, a first advantage of decentralization may reside in the reduction of the Commission's workload that may allow it to selectively focus on the most relevant cases. Second, decentralization provides further benefits in terms of the effective use of dispersed information. Enforcement requires identifying rule-breakers by observing their behavior and measuring the anticompetitive effects locally generated, sometimes evaluating the lawful/unlawful nature of observed practices on the basis of sector- and context-specific information. As NCAs may have easier access to such information than a centralized enforcer (the Commission), they are in a better position to apply competition rules. In this respect, a decentralized system appears comparatively more efficient than alternative arrangements. Finally, a decentralized enforcement system may favor dynamic efficiency because it entails a learning process that, through the comparison of the costs and benefits of competing legal rules and precedents, leads to the emergence of the most efficient rules. This has been highlighted, in particular, by the literature on regulatory competition (see, for instance, Ogus 1999; Sinn 1997; Sun and Pelkmans 1995; Van den Bergh 2000) and, with specific regard to the competition policy domain, by Kerber (2003 and 2009) and Van den Bergh and Camesasca (2006, ch. 10).

A further advantage of decentralization focused upon in the fiscal federalism literature – the greater ability of a decentralized system to meet local preferences – is more questionable when applied to the competition policy domain, since satisfaction of consumers' short-term preferences is not necessarily consistent with long-term welfare maximization (assuming this is the objective of competition policy)[9] and the risk of "regulatory capture" is possible also for competition authorities.

On the opportunity costs side, enforcement decentralization has some negative implications created by the uncoordinated interplay among the actions of several decentralized enforcers that would, of course, not represent an issue in a centralized system. In particular, we refer to (a) possible duplication of enforcement costs, as multiple NCAs may intervene in the same case; (b) legal uncertainty associated to the possibility of treating differently – in different EU countries – similar cases; and (c) the externalities created by the positive or negative external effects of the control of anticompetitive behavior not taken into account by a single NCA.

The latter is a particularly important issue. Externalities among the actions of different NCAs arise in presence of two joint conditions: (i) anticompetitive behavior concerns a relevant geographic market that crosses national boundaries; and (ii) either joint action by multiple national authorities is needed to effectively control anticompetitive behavior (so that NCAs' actions are complementary) or a single case is investigated by multiple NCAs but action by one NCA is sufficient to ensure adequate enforcement (so that NCAs' actions are substitutes).

The conventional approach to externalities in this context (Depoorter and Parisi 2005; Van den Bergh and Camesasca 2006) assumes a symmetric setting where NCAs have identical objective functions and are self-interested and where optimality is exclusively defined in terms of enforcers' joint interests rather than in terms of some broader notion of social welfare. In this "private interest" framework, (a) when NCAs' actions are complements, enforcement activity is assumed to involve a positive externality: enforcement by one NCA raises the benefits obtainable by enforcement by the other concerned NCA(s); and (b) when NCAs' actions are substitutes, enforcement activity is assumed

---

[9] This could be the case of some exclusionary price practice, like predatory pricing or selective "win-back" offers; Nicita (2009).

to involve a negative externality: action by one NCA eliminates the utility associated to further actions. As a consequence, within this framework, positive externalities entail a sub-optimal level of enforcement action (leading to under-restriction and free-riding), while negative externalities involve an excessive level of enforcement (leading to over-restriction and rent-dissipation).

Alternatively, it is possible to make different assumptions on NCAs' objective functions, by assuming that each NCA's objective function includes social welfare (i.e., consumer welfare plus firm profits), but only of their own country. Under this alternative "public interest" framework, externalities arise because of the divergence of the specific interests of different NCAs whose actions are complementary or substitutes. In this case, actions that would improve overall efficiency of the internal market may not be adopted because their costs are borne by a given NCA, while their benefits are enjoyed in a different country. Alternatively, NCAs may adopt actions that are sub-optimal for overall efficiency at the European level because they entail benefits for a given NCA's own country, while the costs fall predominantly on different countries.

However, irrespective of the specific objective function assumed, the important point to stress is that decentralization involves opportunity costs, due to externalities that would be absent if enforcement were performed by a single entity. These costs result from the attainment of a second best level of enforcement, which can be either higher or lower than it is socially optimal.

What is crucial to us is to highlight how the current EU multilevel competition policy system scores in terms of the highlighted trade-offs. The analysis of the rules disciplining the vertical allocation of competition policy competences allows us to reach two broad conclusions. The first is that the vertical design of the allocation of competences within the EU multilevel system appears to reflect awareness of the above-mentioned trade-offs, as it incorporates some features typical of a centralized system and some coordination rules susceptible to mitigate the costs of decentralization. The second is that a hybrid system that involves some competence overlaps such as the current EU institutional framework may be considered a relatively more efficient system than a fully centralized or a fully decentralized one.

This hybrid multilevel system incorporates rules that may overcome the risk of duplication of enforcement costs and of legal uncertainty associated to the adoption of a fully decentralized system. This is the case, for instance, for art. 11(6) REG, providing that the initiation by the Commission of proceedings for the adoption of a decision shall relieve NCAs of their competence to apply those articles, and of art. 16(2) REG, providing that NCAs' rulings on agreements, decisions or practices under article 101 or article 102 of the Treaty which are already the subject of a Commission decision, should not run against the decision adopted by the Commission.

Most importantly, the EU multilevel system incorporates rules that may address the negative implications of the existence of externalities in a decentralized system. First of all, the European Commission exerts exclusive jurisdiction when anticompetitive practices within the meaning of art. 101 or 102 affect more than three Member States, whereas the EU Commission Notice on cooperation within the Network of Competition Authorities provides for parallel enforcement by multiple NCAs if two or three domestic markets are affected. Thus, the multilevel system seems to foresee centralization when externalities are particularly relevant.

Moreover, rules minimizing the negative effects of externalities by promoting cooperation and coordination among NCAs and between NCAs and the Commission have been set in place. The Commission and the NCAs compose a network of public authorities (European Competition Network – ECN) that is supposed to "apply the Community competition rules in close cooperation." To this purpose, art. 11 and 12 REG establish information exchanges and coordination procedures. Further arrangements for information and consultation have been set up. In this regard, if an NCA is already scrutinizing a case, the Commission has the obligation to consult with that NCA before initiating its own proceedings. Art. 13 REG provides incentives for cooperation affirming that where NCAs of two or more member states have received a complaint or are acting on their own initiative under article 101 or article 102 of the Treaty against the same practice, the fact that one authority is dealing with the case shall be sufficient ground for the others to suspend the proceedings before them or to reject the complaint. The same applies for the Commission. These rules have the additional effect of reducing duplication of enforcement costs.

Thus, the vertical competence overlaps characterizing the EU multilevel competition policy system are governed by coordination rules

The institutional design of competition policy 207

aimed at minimizing to some extent the negative implications of decentralization. The overall structure of the multilevel system may therefore turn out to be more efficient than a fully centralized or fully decentralized system.

Moreover, the competence overlaps among different NCAs and between NCAs and the Commission in a context characterized by a given level of substitutability may help to mitigate the risks of regulatory capture with respect to either a completely centralized or a completely decentralized system. A decentralized system with vertical competence overlaps may, at the same time, increase accountability, since it allows closer monitoring by citizens and firms and it may raise the "minimum efficient scale" of investment in rent-seeking activities to subvert effective antitrust decisions and indeed makes renegotiation harder (Laffont and Martimort 1999; Martimort 1999).

10.3 The interaction between administrative and judicial competition law enforcement

Another relevant feature of the European competition policy system is the interface between public and private enforcement, i.e., between application of competition law by the Commission and NCAs, which initiate proceedings *ex officio* (public enforcement), and by national courts, which act following complaints by private parties (this is the reason why it is generally called private enforcement).

The interplay between public and private enforcement concerns both the relationship between the Commission and national courts, and the relationship between NCAs and national courts. From a more general standpoint, the whole interaction is based on a horizontal relationship between administrative and judicial enforcement, where the nature and the instruments of enforcement are different and generally considered complementary. Indeed, while courts protect the "interests of private parties" (or, more accurately, the rights that Community laws confer upon them), NCAs and the Commission safeguard the Community's public interest. Thus, private and public enforcement are complementary in the sense that the former ensures direct compensation to the victims of EC antitrust infringements through the payment of damages and is therefore not necessarily concerned with the issue of general deterrence, while the latter is concerned with general deterrence at the market level, and the fines it imposes are punitive in nature and not compensatory.

While conventionally interpreted as complementary, public and private enforcement should also be considered substitutes from at least two perspectives. First, they are alternative tools that may be used to ensure legal certainty, as either one would be sufficient to clarify what is the licit behavior in a given circumstance. Second, more important for our purposes, they are to some extent substitute tools from the point of view of deterrence and fair compensation. In fact, public enforcement of competition law (both at the supranational and at the national level) is often "regulatory" in nature, as it may impose compensatory remedies in the form of positive obligations to infringing companies, which may be implicitly assessed as a component of victims' lost profits (as it is the case, for exclusionary abuses, for remedies providing access to an essential facility at a non-discriminatory price to the benefits of the plaintiffs). Conversely, damages compensation through private enforcement can indirectly pursue public interests, because of the indirect deterrence effect that compensatory damages can cause.

The increasing extent of horizontal competence overlaps among NCAs, the Commission and national courts derives from the mentioned Regulation 1/2003 (art. 6) and from the 2008 Commission White Paper – that has called attention to the need to strengthen the complementarity between public and private enforcement of antitrust law, foreseeing a further strengthened role of national courts.[10] In particular, the White Paper's aim is to set out measures to address the current ineffectiveness of antitrust damages actions due to "various legal and procedural hurdles in Member States' rules governing actions for antitrust damages before national courts."[11]

By increasing the role of private enforcement, the Commission seeks to: (a) provide for compensation of the victims of antitrust infringements; (b) increase the level of deterrence of anticompetitive behaviors; and (c) decrease the probability of false negatives

---

[10] White Paper on Damages Actions for Breach of the EC Antitrust Rules – COM(2008) 165 final.
[11] The Commission points, in particular, to "the very complex factual and economic analysis required, the frequent inaccessibility and concealment of crucial evidence in the hands of defendants and the often unfavorable risk/reward balance for claimants" (White Paper, p. 2).

by increasing the number of parties that may initiate antitrust proceedings and by giving incentives to victims to reveal relevant information.

The benefits from the increased role played by private enforcement follow from the fact that the latter may address some of the concerns expressed by the Commission. At the same time, though, its overlap with public enforcement may give rise to a number of costly coordination failures, such as: (a) the possibility of inconsistent decisions and therefore the lack of uniformity in the application of EU competition law; (b) the poorly coordinated overlapping between sanctions in the form of antitrust fines and the compensatory damages awarded to victims; and (c) the scarcely coordinated overlapping between remedies in the form of commitments before antitrust authorities and the liquidation of damages.

As for (a), the possibility that national courts take decisions that are to some extent different for similar cases and eventually in contrast with Community law is a general feature of a system that envisages a high degree of decentralization of enforcement, to an even greater extent than it is the case in relation to decentralized enforcement by NCAs. However, the possibility of inconsistencies or even of outright mistakes appears particularly likely in regard to the enforcement of art. 101(3), which involves articulated economic reasoning and the delicate balancing of efficiencies and anticompetitive effects that courts may not be best positioned to perform.

As for (b), the very fact that the objectives of public and private enforcement are intrinsically different – the first being aimed at deterrence, the second at compensation – are bound to give rise to inevitable negative effects in terms of the ability of the system to determine and enforce optimal deterrence, that is the ability to minimize social costs, including the costs of both antitrust violations and of antitrust enforcement action. Indeed, even assuming that the fines imposed through public enforcement are optimally determined, i.e., leading therefore to optimal deterrence, the very overlap with private enforcement before courts could undermine such optimality since, from the point of view of deterrence, public and private enforcement should be considered substitutes. This holds if the actors involved – the Commission or the NCAs and the courts – do not take into account each other's decisions, as the amount of damages added to the amount of the (optimal) fine clearly would generate over-deterrence.

Finally, as for (c), the (opportunity) cost of commitments accepted by an NCA or the Commission should be clearly quantified and taken into consideration for the definition of the optimal amount of damages awarded by national courts, which rarely happens.

The three issues raised above call for a substantial extent of coordination between private and public enforcement. To some extent, there are rules currently in place that appear to reflect awareness of these concerns. However, coordination is currently only partly achieved through formal means (i.e., through legislative provisions) and the debate on how to improve such coordination is still in its infancy.

In particular, some formal rules of coordination contained in Regulation 1/2003 are meant to reduce the possibility of inconsistencies and conflicts between decisions of national courts and Community law. This is the case for the leading role held by the Commission in the general enforcement of competition policy also with respect to the judicial application of antitrust law. In fact, the mentioned art. 16(1) REG states that when national courts rule on agreements, decisions or practices under article 101 or article 102 of the Treaty which are already the subject of a Commission decision, they cannot take decisions running against the decision adopted by the Commission. They must also avoid giving decisions that would conflict with a decision contemplated by the Commission in proceedings it has initiated. To this purpose, the national court may assess whether it is necessary to stay its proceedings.

Moreover, similarly to the rules disciplining the relationship between the Commission and NCAs, the Commission and national courts have a reciprocal duty of cooperation, mainly in terms of information exchange, communication and consultation procedures stated by art. 15 REG. Due to the principle of "independence" of national courts, however, and to the fact that national courts protect individual rights conferred by art. 101 and 102, the Commission does not have the power to relieve national courts of their power to apply art. 101 and 102, as it is the case for NCAs.

The interactions between the Commission and national courts are governed by two types of coordination mechanisms, succinctly described in art. 15(1) REG. The first is activated by national courts and relates to the Commission's *amicus curiae* role, played by (a) transmitting relevant information to national courts; and (b) giving its opinion on the application of the competition rules, albeit without considering

The institutional design of competition policy 211

the merits of the case pending before the national courts (the opinion given to national courts thus differs from that which may be requested by NCAs, perhaps in order to limit the Commission's intervention).[12] In order to give its opinion, the Commission may "request the relevant court of the Member State to transmit or ensure the transmission to them of any documents necessary for the assessment of the case" (art. 15(3) REG).

The second type of coordination mechanism can be activated by the Commission *ex officio* (and by NCAs as well) and consists of two monitoring mechanisms. Art. 15(3) entitles the Commission to submit written observations to courts of the Member States "where the coherent application of art. 101 or 102 of the Treaty so requires," both if judgment is pending and if it is appealed. It is important to note, however, that national courts are not legally bound to follow the "opinions" and the "observations" of the Commission, as they are not part of a binding act and are not subject to review by the Court of Justice.

However, these formal rules of coordination are not sufficient for at least two reasons. First, the issue of coordination is largely left to Member States' law relative to the relationship between national courts and NCAs, which is much less well developed than those existing between the Commission and national courts. More specifically, European competition law, while attributing to Member States the power to submit observations to national courts on issues relating to European competition policy (but not to national competition policy), does not at present specify how a national authority should be informed on judgments applying Community antitrust law given by national courts.

As a matter of fact, only in some Member States can victims of the infringement of art. 101 or 102 rely on the NCA's decision as a binding proof in civil proceedings for damages. Indeed, this has led the Commission to suggest in its "White Paper" that such a rule should be included in each national antitrust law.

---

[12] In this regard a specific but relevant information exchange issue is related to the interaction between leniency programs and actions for damages. The Commission in the aforementioned White Paper suggests that an adequate protection against disclosure in private actions for damages must be ensured for corporate statements submitted by a leniency applicant in order to avoid placing the applicant in a less favorable situation than the co-infringers.

Second, while the issues of the internal coherence of the system and of the creation of the internal market through homogeneous application of competition policy are explicitly addressed through the formal rules described above, the issue of economic efficiency, in terms of fulfillment of optimal enforcement, is left to the (potential) presence of informal means of coordination that are, at present, mostly lacking and highly debated.

An increased recourse to informal means of coordination should thus be called for, especially having regard to the horizontal dimension of the interface between public and private enforcement. A number of measures in this direction could be envisaged such as, for instance, the possibility for NCAs to play an *amicus curiae* role along the lines of the role that may be played by the Commission, the possibility for the NCAs to distinguish between punitive and "efficiency" components of the fine or to provide a (non-binding) estimate of the damages caused by infringements and, finally, means to ensure that national courts take explicitly into account the adoption of commitments before the NCA in calculating damages. These measures, while not decisive, may improve the current situation.

10.4 The interaction between competition law enforcement and regulation: the case of the Electronic Communications sector

Competence overlaps also exist across parallel domains of competition policy, in the interplay between NCAs and National Regulatory Authorities (NRAs). The EU policy framework envisages the coexistence of competition policy and sector-specific regulation, interpreting them as complementary tools.[13] In the US, by contrast, competition policy and sector-specific regulation are perceived as substitutes, so that competition policy intervention is ruled out in regulated sectors.[14]

---

[13] Commission decision of 4 July 2007, case COMP/38.784 – *Wanadoo Espana v. Telefónica*; General Court decision of April 10, 2008, *Deutsche Telekom v. Commission*, confirming the appealed Commission decision 2003/707/CE of May 21, 2003. As a matter of fact, the legal basis of this decision is represented by the primacy of competition law (primary law) over sector-specific regulation (secondary law).

[14] In this regard the US Supreme Court Decision, on January 13, 2004, *Verizon Communications Inc. v. Law Offices of Curtis Trinko*.

Within this framework of coexistence, thus of competence overlapping between competition law enforcement and sector-specific regulation, a recent trend, in Europe, is increasing the degree of substitutability of the two activities. This trend, falling under the label of "convergence" of antitrust and sector-specific regulation, implies that NRAs should be included within the competition policy system since they are explicitly attributed by recent EU directives a competition-enhancing role.

For the sake of concreteness, the implications of this convergence and the ensuing overlaps and interdependencies will be illustrated by reference to a specific regulated sector, the Electronic Communications[15] sector, where attribution to NRAs of competition-enhancing aims and competition law-inspired powers is more advanced and clear.

In the Electronic Communications sector, the extent of substitutability characterizing the action of enforcers belonging to the parallel domains of antitrust and regulation has increased from two angles. On the one side, European competition law allows public enforcement bodies (both at the supranational and at the national level) to adopt decisions which can be classified as regulatory, in that they prescribe behavioral obligations. On the other side, NRAs' decisional practice, whose main aims are, by statute, the promotion of competition and the enhancement of consumer welfare, tends to be based to a significant extent on concepts and categories drawn from competition policy.

As for the first aspect of the convergence – competition policy enforcers' regulatory powers – (a) the vagueness of art. 7 REG leaves the Commission, in applying art. 101 and 102, the possibility to impose on dominant undertakings, in particular in recently liberalized industries, behavioral or structural remedies that not only bring infringement to an end but also design a more competitive market where that infringement will not be possible; (b) art. 9 REG gives the Commission the power to render binding commitments "formally" proposed by undertakings; (c) art. 101(3) states the possibility for the Commission to exempt illicit agreements from the application of art. 101(1) when these could imply productive or dynamic efficiency gains.

---

[15] In Electronic Communications sectors a very complex regulatory system has emerged in Europe, after 2002. The main act is represented by the Directive 2002/21/EC on a common regulatory framework (FD), recently amended by the "Better Regulation Directive" 2009/140/EC.

Similar regulatory powers are assigned to NCAs by art. 5 REG when they apply EU competition law. Moreover, NCAs – when acting as European administrative bodies – can "disapply" national rules, substantially de-regulating.[16] As for the second aspect – regulators' use of competition policy tools – *ex ante* obligations can be imposed by NRAs only on operators having significant market power (SMP), a concept stated to be equivalent to a dominant position in antitrust analysis. Furthermore, besides basic interconnection and interoperability obligations, NRAs can impose obligations on firms with SMP that correspond to typical antitrust remedies against abuse of dominant position.[17]

Thus, the actions by the Commission and NCAs, on one side, and by NRAs, on the other, generally overlap. Moreover, since they pursue the same public interest – "a competitive market" – and adopt similar policy tools, they are increasingly designed as substitute tools for the pursuit of a competitive EU market. Yet, they still coexist.

This policy framework entails both benefits and costs. The benefits follow from the elements of complementarity that competition law enforcement and regulation still maintain and that justify their coexistence. In fact, *ex ante* regulation and *ex post* antitrust intervention would be perfect substitutes if either (a) *ex ante* regulation was perfectly effective (i.e., no regulatory failures are possible) or (b) *ex post* competition law enforcement had the same probability to fail as *ex ante* regulation. These circumstances, however, do not seem to hold, since the effectiveness of regulation is necessarily limited by imperfect and incomplete information, higher *ex ante* – before abusive conducts actually materialize – than *ex post*.

Thus, regulation, restricting and specifying the set of dominant firms' licit behaviors, increases the likelihood of their compliance with competition law in markets where otherwise the probability of their abusive behavior is very high. However, competition law still plays a role (being complementary to regulation) when regulation is not effective,

---

[16] In several circumstances, the European Court of Justice confirmed the duty of each national body enforcing European law to "disapply" national law contrasting with art. 101(1) and art. 102 of the Treaty in combination with art.10 and 86. For example, ECJ C-198/01.

[17] In particular, art. 8(1) Access Directive (Directive 2002/19/EC) give NRAs powers to impose: transparency obligations (art. 9), non-discrimination obligations (art. 10), obligation of accounting separation (art. 11), obligations of access to, and use of, specific network facilities (art. 12), price control and cost accounting obligations (art. 13).

i.e., when *ex post* it turns out that regulation has not restricted or specified enough the set of dominant firms' licit behaviors.

The costs of the current institutional solution derive from coordination problems analogous to those relative to the optimal degree of decentralization of enforcement, namely: (a) the possible duplication of enforcement costs; (b) externalities; and (c) legal uncertainty.

The issue of cost duplication appears, in this specific context, a second-order problem. This is because, strictly speaking, cost duplication would ensue if Commission/NCAs' and NRAs' actions were perfect substitutes, i.e., they were alternative means to achieve exactly the same outcome while, for the reasons mentioned above, they should rather be considered complementary to some extent.

As for externalities, the analysis developed with reference to the competence overlaps among different NCAs in Section 10.2 offers useful insights also in the present context. In particular, the nature of the externalities and strategic interactions varies according to whether we assume that authorities' actions are characterized more by complementary or substitute features. Moreover, the final outcome of the interaction among different authorities may be influenced by the fact that the two authorities may include in their objective functions different notions of social welfare (for example, NCAs' objective function may have a pro-consumer bias while that of NRAs may have a pro-companies one). In both cases, we should expect to observe a level of enforcement different from the optimal level, with the most likely outcome being an empirical question (Barros and Hoernig 2004).

The issue of the legal uncertainty associated to the possibility of the adoption of inconsistent decisions is likely to constitute a more serious problem, as the multilevel system does not incorporate explicit rules or mechanisms aimed at ensuring full coordination. Moreover, the occurrence of inconsistencies resides in the substitutability characterizing the action of NRAs and competition law enforcers (Commission and NCAs) and in particular in the possibility that the latter choose to intervene *ex post*, modifying the market outcome determined by regulation, not just because regulation failed but rather because they intend to pursue a different regulatory outcome for idiosyncratic, eventually country-specific, reasons.[18]

---

[18] A limit to substitutability and thus legal uncertainty in this context is represented by the ECJ statement affirming that it is possible to enforce competition law when the illicit behavior depends on autonomous

The risk of such strategic interactions is particularly high with regard to the interactions between the Commission and NRAs, although it exists also for interactions between NCAs and NRAs. Indeed, this sort of issue has emerged within recent margin squeeze cases under regulated wholesale and retail prices.[19] This is because of the regulatory design of Electronic Communications, where enforcement is decentralized (through NRAs) and the Commission manages mechanisms of harmonization, similarly to the competition policy domain.[20] Differently from the competition policy domain, however, the Commission cannot directly intervene to change regulatory choices made at the national level.[21] The rationale of this different institutional design can be found in the greater discretion necessary to positively prescribe behaviors and the greater importance in this procedure of dispersed information and dynamic adaptation of regulation to market changes. Given this institutional design, competition policy intervention may be improperly used to modify regulatory choices adopted at the national level. However, in these cases it is particularly hard to detect strategic behavior, as it may be difficult to assess whether *ex post* intervention is motivated by the perception of a failure of regulation or by the pursuit of idiosyncratic objectives.

---

    decentralized private choice, yet it is somehow constrained by specific regulation. See, for instance, the General Court decision of 10 April 2008, *Deutsche Telekom* v. *Commission*, confirming the appealed Commission decision 2003/707/CE of May 21, 2003.

[19] Case T-271/03, *Deutsche Telekom AG* v. *Commission*. Case COMP/38.784, *Wanadoo España* v. *Telefónica*.

[20] As a matter of fact, also horizontal mechanisms of coordination between NRAs are defined by the framework directive. That is (a) the exchange of relevant information (art. 3.5); (b) the possibility for an NRA to raise comments about a market analysis held by another NRA (art. 7.3). However, those mechanisms have been extremely scarcely used. On the contrary, institutional coordination mechanisms, such as the establishment of ERG (European Regulators Group, Decision 2002/627/EC) and recently substituted by BEREC (Body of European Regulators of Electronic Communications, Regulation 1211/2009/EC), have been more effective. Actually, these mechanisms have envisaged both vertical and horizontal coordination dimensions.

[21] The EU Commission covers a fundamental role in the regulatory procedures, *ex ante* generally defining relevant market subject to national regulation and *ex post* controlling the national regulatory procedure, whose outcome cannot though be substituted but only partially inhibited.

The previous analysis suggests that some modifications are needed to the current system to increase institutional efficiency. First, in order to avoid the highlighted risks of legal uncertainty, the Commission should adopt a different legal tool to modify an undesired national regulatory outcome. Rather than applying competition law (enforcing art. 102 TFEU), the Commission could for example initiate an infringement proceeding against a Member State under art. 226. Second, formal and more effective mechanisms of coordination between NCAs and NRAs are necessary, while at present, from the perspective of both competition and regulatory substantive law, NCAs' and NRAs' activities are basically independent and characterized by mere obligations of reciprocal consultation (often not binding). This very much contrasts with the substantial interdependences previously described.

10.5 Concluding remarks

In this chapter we have made a first attempt at evaluating the overall efficiency of the institutional design of European competition policy. This has been interpreted as a multilevel and multidimensional system, i.e., as a hybrid institutional system characterized by relevant interdependencies among the involved actors. In particular, emphasis has been placed on the relevant competence overlaps existing at both the vertical and horizontal level.

The existence of overlapping competences at both the vertical and the horizontal level entails both benefits and costs. The cost-benefit balance seems to be more clearly favorable to the current institutional arrangement when analyzing the vertical dimension of the system. Indeed, our main conclusion in this regard is that the evolution of this institutional design appears today more consistent with the objectives of the creation of the internal market and of the promotion of efficient market outcomes than full centralization or full decentralization, given the substantial harmonization of substantive competition rules. By contrast, the overall cost-benefit balance appears more uncertain when considering the horizontal competence overlaps across parallel domains of competition policy – private vs. public enforcement and competition law enforcement vs. regulation.

Our analysis thus suggests the need to pay greater attention to these (mainly) horizontal aspects of the institutional design, that have so far been relatively neglected. Indeed, the relatively scarce attention paid to the issue of the efficient overall design of European competition policy has been devoted predominantly to the vertical dimension, and particularly to the issue of the optimal degree of decentralization in the design and enforcement of competition law.

With regard to the issue of the interface between public and private enforcement, the brief overview we have provided points to the need for more refined coordination mechanisms. Formal rules of coordination do exist, but they address mainly the issues of the internal coherence of the system and of the creation of the internal market through homogeneous application of competition policy. Informal mechanisms of coordination are, by contrast, scarcely developed at present. Since it is to these mechanisms that the issue of economic efficiency, in terms of fulfillment of optimal enforcement, is mostly left, care should be taken to ensure that they develop through time.

As for the overlaps among competition law enforcement and regulation, our analysis has highlighted the tension existing between institutional actors who tend to attribute greater weight to industries' long-term constraints (i.e., regulators) and actors who tend to be more short-term and consumer oriented (i.e., antitrust authorities). This tension can be easily explained by two complementary observations. On one side, because of the necessity to build the internal market, deeply ingrained into the founding documents of the Community, the Commission had, over the years, the opportunity to develop a strong antitrust capability and legitimacy, relatively well coordinated in a multilevel perspective with the NCAs. On the other side, the historical heterogeneity across industries and across countries of market conditions, resources, constraints and national interests that affects regulatory choices has prevented the full development of a truly harmonized regulatory environment. Addressing the shortcomings emerging from the coexistence of a relatively well-harmonized multilevel system of NCAs and a much less harmonized system of NRAs constitutes an important challenge for European decision-makers.

Given the importance of the design of rules for the process of market manufacturing, it is essential that the rules disciplining the enforcement of competition policy are well designed and lead to efficient outcomes. This suggests that the shortcomings identified in this chapter should be taken seriously in the future evolution of the European multilevel competition policy system.

Table 10.1 The institutional design of European competition policy: a summary chart

	Actions and actors	Dimension of analysis	Current EU Policy	Evaluation of EU Policy
Level of Competition Law Public Enforcement (Section 10.2)	**Centralized public enforcement (A)** EU Commission / **Decentralized public enforcement (B)** NCAs	Vertical dimension: decentralization vs. centralization → different level of enforcement (governance)	Decentralized public enforcement, jointly with coordination mechanisms between NCAs and Commission playing a role of functional superiority	The hybrid public enforcement system reaps most decentralization benefits: i) Commission can focus on selected actions; ii) Effective use of dispersed information; iii) Dynamic efficiency benefits → **while mitigating its potential problems, through some degree of centralization and coordination mechanisms**, which: i) internalize some externalities; ii) avoid enforcement costs duplications; iii) favor legal harmonization and certainty; iv) decrease risk of regulatory capture

Table 10.1 (*Cont.*)

	Actions and actors	Dimension of analysis	Current EU Policy	Evaluation of EU Policy
Nature of Competition Law Enforcement (Section 10.3)	**Public enforcement (C=A+B)** EU Commission and NCAs **Private enforcement (D)** National courts	Mainly Horizontal: administrative vs. Judicial enforcement → different nature of the enforcer and different interest protected	Public enforcement jointly with an enhanced private enforcement and coordination mechanisms between Commission and judges	The increasing overlap between public and private enforcement implies positive effects: i) protects "privates" interests" through infringements compensation; ii) increase incentives to victims to reveal information → **but formal rules of coordination are insufficient**, implying: i) sub-optimal deterrence; ii) unfair compensation of damages; iii) costs of legal uncertainty

Set of Norms Applied (Section 10.4)	Competition law enforcement (E=C+D) EU Commission, NCAs and national courts Sector-specific regulation (F) EU Commission and NRAs	**Mainly Horizontal:** Competition law enforcement vs. Regulation → application of a different set of norms (by a different administrative body)	Coexistence of regulation and competition law enforcement and convergence of the two domains	The COEXISTENCE of regulatory and antitrust actions (justified by complementarity features) jointly with CONVERGENCE (which leads to substitutability): → makes regulation pro-competitive in nature → but gives rise to coordination problems, particularly in terms of: i) legal uncertainty; ii) externalities. → since formal rules of coordination are insufficient: i) need for more effective coordination between NRAs and NCAs; ii) necessary restraint of competition policy intervention aimed at modifying regulatory outcomes for idiosyncratic reasons.

PART IV

The myopia of the public hand

Introduction to Part IV

ERIC BROUSSEAU AND JEAN-MICHEL GLACHANT

In this part, three main reasons are highlighted as being essential causes of public myopia when implementing markets. More precisely, the authors of the chapters grouped here develop why the "public hand" fails in designing and implementing first best solutions. First, public rulers are challenged by political competitors and stakeholders in the society. Their commitments are always subject to future amendment and even reversals due to the potential evolution of political coalitions. In turn, they are not fully reliable, which leads rulers to pay risk premiums under the form of rents, and henceforth loss of efficiency (as compared to a first best). Second, the political game tends to favor "winner takes all" type of behavior, especially because in the future the reverse is expected to happen. This self-reinforcing cycle leads to the implementation of inconsistent institutional infrastructure over time. Third, the division of power among all kind of authorities in actual government systems may lead to inconsistent and ineffective policies.

Marian Moszoro and Pablo Spiller introduce the notion of third-party opportunism as the quintessential hazard of public transactions. Their fundamental idea is that public decision making is subject to all kind of checks and balances, making any decision uncertain because it can be challenged by third parties who judge that their interests are harmed and who have some bargaining capabilities. Their chapter focuses on public contracting because the credibility of commitment is essential in featuring in the characteristic of contracts. They show that the whiff of corruption and the concern for misuse of other people's money makes challenging public contracts feasible. High *ex ante* payment volatility or *ex post* flexibility in implementation may trigger implementation challenges, leading to contract failure or to costly adaptation by the public officials. Thus, even though the enactment and performance of a contract may be honest and legal, public agents may fear politically motivated challenges, and hence will *ex ante* adjust the nature of the contracts so as to limit those features whose probity may be questioned. These adjustments will imply more contract specificity in design and rigidity in implementation. Such contractual adaptation, however, is not costless. Contractors' perception of specificity and rigidity will translate into *ex ante* higher prices as well as the enactment of stronger compensating clauses. The contractual complexity and adaptation required to limit the potential for third-party challenges, whether opportunistic or not, make public contracting look "inefficient."

Moszoro and Spiller's analysis is however much broader in scope than public contracting. Indeed, the authors highlight and discuss the implication of third-party opportunism for public decision making in general, which includes regulation of markets, institutional design, and so on. They henceforth provide us with a general theory of the consequences of the limits in commitment capabilities of public rulers.

Witold Henisz and Bennet Zelner, on their side, highlight the iron rule of political cycles. Studying the back and forth movement between public and private ownership and monitoring of an industry and its related markets – namely the electricity industry – these scholars highlight how fine-tuning in the manufacturing of the market is difficult to perform. This is because market and industrial reforms tend to result in winners and losers. According to them, most "regulatory reforms" are not managed according to a Pareto improving logic, implementing Hicks-Kaldor compensations so that there are no losers. The logic of political decision making, indeed, leads the temporarily dominant coalition to capture much of the benefits of the reform, generating a significant group of losers whose interests can be ignored by the policy makers or other interest groups in the short run. As illustrated by Latin American case studies, these losers attempt to undermine the reform by calling for patches aimed at softening the harm they experience. These patches are implemented in an inconsistent way, under a purely political logic of avoiding the formation of a too large and too strong coalition of opponents, leading inevitably to inconsistencies in the institutional framework, then in significant sources of inefficiencies. These inefficiencies trigger the formation of a reverse coalition that precisely implements another "radical" reform generating the same type of cycle.

The myopia of the public hand 227

Such an understanding of the processes of reform calls for the development of governance systems more immune to political pressures by interest groups. This is, of course, one of the major justifications for the establishment of powerful independent regulators in all domains. The truth is however that regulators are inherently "subsidiaries" of governments and parliaments whose actual power and status can be reconsidered when power shifts. It is therefore very unlikely that the process of manufacturing markets could escape the pendulum movement described by Henisz and Zelner.

The paradox of the case analyzed by Yannis Karagiannis and Adrienne Héritier is that the air transportation industry has long been considered a model of liberalization driven by market forces – with new entrants calling for more deregulation to oust incumbents – while it is in fact a story of deregulation mainly based on political competition among sovereign states. These states have been promoting national carriers for years, due to the benefit of such national champions in terms of political independence and prestige, industrial policy, employment, etc. The actual and most aggressive competitors were probably not the new entrants, but the incumbents, whose weapons were not only their ability to master costs and commercial innovation, but also to lobby efficiently their government and its various agencies. Not only do their historical narratives of the case highlight the importance of the geo-strategic drivers of this battle among sovereign nations, but they also show how the dynamics of international relations have been influenced by the infra-national equilibriums among components of the government.

Incidentally, their chapter highlights also how these multi-player games are difficult to anticipate, and then to control. While most players invest a lot of capabilities to play such games with huge stakes, tiny changes in the balance of power between components of divided governments – by departments in the US, by nations in the case of the "EU government" (i.e., the Commission) – can lead to unanticipated effects. Indeed, the case points out how the hegemonic US government ended up losing control of the international air transportation market, because the competition among government departments led the US to play too aggressively. This favored the unification of Europe which was able to obtain conditions much more favorable to European carriers than in the past.

11 | Third-party opportunism and the theory of public contracts: operationalization and applications

MARIAN W. MOSZORO AND PABLO T. SPILLER

11.1 Introduction

In contrast to private contracts, public contracts are open to challenge by third parties. The whiff of corruption and the concern for misuse of other people's monies[1] make challenging public contracts feasible. High *ex ante* payment volatility or *ex post* flexibility in implementation may trigger implementation challenges, leading to contract failure or to costly adaptation by the public official, whether in terms of time or political career. Thus, even though the enactment and performance of a contract may be honest and legal, public agents may fear politically motivated challenges, and hence will *ex ante* adjust the nature of the contracts so as to limit those features whose probity may be questioned. These adjustments will imply more contract specificity in design and rigidity in implementation. Such contractual adaptation, however, is not costless. Contractors' perception of specificity and rigidity will translate into *ex ante* higher prices as well as the enactment of stronger compensating clauses. The contractual complexity and adaptation required to limit the potential for third-party challenges, whether opportunistic or not, make public contracting look "inefficient" (Spiller 2008:16).

The higher level of contract specificity and rigidity in public contracting can be understood, then, as a political risk adaptation by public agents.[2] It is not that civic-oriented legislation limits public agents'

---

[1] What Williamson (1999:311) calls the hazard of probity posed by transactions organized in the public sector.
[2] As Eggers and Goldsmith (2004:122) underscore, "when something goes wrong in a public sector network, it tends to end up on the front page of the newspaper, instantly transforming a management issue into a political problem."

discretionary actions with "red tape," but rather that public agents limit the risk of third parties' challenges through contracting formalities and rigidities, externalizing the associated costs to the public at large.

This chapter provides an operationalization of Spiller's (2008) third-party opportunism (TPO), towards an understanding of the organizational foundations of pricing, specificity, and rigidity – the outer features – of public contracts. Spiller's theory of public organization is rooted in a transaction cost-*cum*-positive political theory, where the nature of organizational adaptation of public contracts results from their inherent hazards. Spiller's framework follows Williamson's (2005) four cornerstones of the economics of governance – namely, governance,[3] transaction costs,[4] adaptation,[5] and interdisciplinary social science[6] – and introduces third-party opportunism as the quintessential hazard of public transactions.

11.2 Prior literature

Third-party opportunism relates to a threefold literature on public contracting: industrial organization, public administration, and political economy.

In the industrial organization literature, public contract pricing is determined by informational costs, arising from informational asymmetries, the extent of verifiability of information, and the presence of repeated interactions (Bajari and Tadelis 2001; Laffont and Tirole 1993; Loeb and Surysekar 1994; Macaulay 1963; Marshall, Meurer, and Richard 1994a). Hart and Moore (2008) present a model with a trade-off between flexibility and rigidity in relational contracts, where the combination of *ex ante* competition and *ex post* lock-in makes the initial contract a useful reference point. In a flexible contract, a party may feel entitled to different outcomes within the contract and thus "shades by providing perfunctory rather than consummate performance" if she

---

[3] Williamson (2005:3) defines governance as "the means by which to infuse order, thereby to mitigate conflict and realize mutual gains."
[4] Acknowledging that hierarchies and procurement are "alternative methods of coordinating production" (Coase 1937:388).
[5] Not only though the price system, but also as a managerial decision.
[6] The need to incorporate insights from law, political science, and sociology to understand what the rough price theory cannot fully capture.

does not get what she expected (Fehr, Hart, and Zehnder 2011:494). It is, however, the nature of the hazards involved in public–private relations that determines the fundamental features of public procurement and contracting (Williamson 1979). Not only is "the nature of the agreement ... carefully delimited, and the more formal features govern when ... terms are contested" (Williamson 1979:236), but the potential for a contest from an excluded seller impacts the nature of the agreement (Marshall et al. 1994a). Whereas private parties in private-private relations adapt to new information as it becomes available in order to save litigation cost (Williamson 1975), and courts are rather used to termination disputes (Macaulay 1963:65–66), public contracts appear bureaucratic and over-monitoring in situations in which contractual rigidity is not needed (Prendergast 2003:932–933).

According to the public administration view, contracting inefficiencies are associated with the large number of formal processes that appear to be essential to ensure the public sector's functions as well as with "red tape," i.e., costly and compulsory rules, regulations, and procedures with no efficacy for their functional object (Bozeman 1993:274).[7] Bureaucrats are used only for "hard" agency problems, where consumers cannot be trusted (Prendergast 2003:933). Extensive rules and regulations arise from dividing authority among the separate branches of government (executive, legislative, and judicial), designed to prevent abuses of power, protect people's rights (Baldwin 1990:10–11), and reflect equity values not necessarily present in private firms, including educational, health-related, legal, and environmental (Forrer, Lee, Newcomer, and Boyer 2010:480). Red tape regulations are intended to decrease public employees' uncertainty about how they

---

[7] A report to Congressional Committees on a Congress-authorized test program to simplify the procedures for the acquisition of commercial supplies and services that allowed government buyers to eliminate certain procedural requirements when purchasing commercial items not exceeding $5 million, i.e., allowing contract flexibility, indicated that although

> data was not collected to provide a basis for measuring whether the test program produced the desired results of maximizing efficiency and economy and minimizing burden and administrative costs for both the government and industry, ... the Office of Federal Procurement Policy survey of procurement executives in 1999 showed that these executives believed that the program has had a positive impact on the federal procurement process. ... However, the survey did not collect empirical data that would have supported these views. (United States Government Accountability Office [GAO] 2001)

should behave (Kurland and Egan 1999:440). Both formalities and red tape are the instruments by which bureaucracies restrict public agents' discretion (Boyne 2002; Lan and Rainey 1992) and "overcome the temptation to capitulate to consumers simply to avoid complaints" (Prendergast 2003:932).

The political economy profession has long been divided into advocates of public interest theory (in line with the public sector motivation literature), and "capture" or interest group theory of government intervention in industries, seeded by Buchanan (1965) and Olson (1965), and elaborated by Stigler (1971). This positive approach, both in its Chicago school (Becker 1983; Peltzman 1976; Stigler 1971) and Virginia school (Buchanan 1975; Buchanan, Tollison, and Tullock 1980) modalities, concentrates on the demand-side, "black-boxing" the supply-side of political decision-making (Laffont and Tirole 1993:475–476). On the other hand, positive political theory scholars, led by Riker (1963), focused on the supply-side of political decision-making, studying how politics – legislative procedures, administrative procedures, and bureaucratic oversight – affects legislative, judicial, and regulatory behavior.[8] Positive political scholars have also studied the use of interested parties (de Figueiredo, Spiller, and Urbiztondo 1999; McCubbins and Schwartz 1984) and consumers (Prendergast 2003) as instruments of oversight.

In addition to the mainstream political economy view of public contracting, there is an increasing literature on the crucial role of political motives in shaping public–private long-term relations. According to Hammami, Ruhashyankiko, and Yehoue (2006), private participation (from procurement to privatization) is positively correlated with less corruption and with an effective rule of law. Engel, Fisher, and Galetovic (2006) suggest that public agents, to increase their chances for re-election, prefer direct spending instead of more complex contracts subject to scrutiny. In developing countries, new administrations tend to renegotiate or unilaterally change concession agreements (Brench et al. 2005; Guasch, Laffont, and Straub 2007; Lobina and Hall 2003), i.e., reshape contract terms and appropriate rents. Iossa and Martimort (2008) conclude that long-term contracting can help to prevent cost overruns, but it requires institutions with

---

[8] See, for example, Ferejohn (1990), Gely and Spiller (1990), McCubbins, Noll, and Weingast (1987, 1989), Weingast and Moran (1983).

strong commitment power and, as the risk of regulatory opportunism increases, the case for long-term contracting is weaker.

Laffont and Tirole (1993:9) emphasize that the link "between procurement and regulation and the associated administrative and political constraints is still unknown to us or is still in a state of conjecture. … Institutions are endogenous and should as much as possible be explained by primitive considerations." This chapter is an attempt to operationalize the basic features of public contracting from its primitive considerations: its fundamental hazards.

11.3 A heuristic model of third-party opportunism

11.3.1 Signaling process: hazards into rigidity

We focus our analysis on the public agent's perspective. We ignore sunk costs to abstract from governmental opportunism,[9] and to make the argument on TPO straightforward.

There are four agents explicitly and implicitly involved in public contracting:

1) Incumbent public agent
2) Private contractor
3) Third-party challengers, i.e., political opponents to the incumbent public agent, competitors to the contractor, and interest groups[10]
4) Public at large, i.e., voters and courts.

The signaling process starts before the signing of a contract. The public agent is commissioned to use public monies and contract for goods and services. The public agent perceives the threat of potential third-party challenges and tries to minimize political risks and maintain political support. Contract outcomes affect voters' opinions, thereby affecting electoral outcomes. If a public contract does not meet the expectations of the public, political consequences may include

---

[9] See Spiller (2008) and references therein.
[10] In our understanding, the closest to a third-party challenger – reversing Buchanan's (1975:229) and Williamson's (1985:29) nomenclature – is an "anti-arbitrator," i.e., an outsider who tries to create conflict between parties who have reached an agreement. As an arbitrator lessens frictions and transaction costs, so a challenger to a public contract increases political costs to the public agent.

weakened chances of re-election for incumbent public agents. The private contractor may not be directly aware of the hazards faced by the public agent, but observes contract specificity and rigidity. Specificity and rigidity equal less adaptability, higher contracting and implementation costs, and hence higher final prices charged to the public agent.

11.3.2 Conceptualizing contract specificity and rigidity

Contract specificity refers to *ex ante* complexity of subject, completeness of clauses, technical provisions, and processing costs (Laffont and Tirole 1993:307). Contract rigidity refers to *ex post* enforcement, penalties, hardness, and intolerance to adaptation of contracts,[11] and normally correlates with contract specificity: the more specific the contract is, the more rigid its implementation and enforcement is expected to be. Otherwise, if the contract is specific and then the parties agree to deviate, third parties can accuse the contracting parties of collusion.

Complex public contracts have more contractual rigidities than simpler contracts. The cost of *ex post* enforcement increases in complexity (Bajari and Tadelis 2001:393). Because the public sector has more ambiguous objectives than private organizations (Boyne 2002), and it is difficult to assess to what extent these objectives are achieved (Lan and Rainey 1992), public high specificity and rigidity mitigate ambiguity and problematic evaluation. For example, Department of Defense directives specify in great detail source selection policies, including the development of objective technical, cost, schedule, manufacturing, performance, and risk criteria, the auction techniques, the organization of the selection committee, and the pertinence of contacts with contractors.[12] Public agents must also follow imposed standards of evidence, and may be constrained to formulate standards and follow their own rules to avoid discriminating between distinct situations on the basis of non-verifiable information (Laffont and Tirole 1993:5).

---

[11] In this regard, contract rigidity is the opposite of a "best efforts" clause.
[12] See the Department of Defense's memorandum on "Source Selection Procedures," issued on March 4, 2011, and effective July 1, 2011. Available at: www.acq.osd.mil/dpap/policy/policyvault/USA 007183–10-DPAP.pdf (accessed May 19, 2011).

11.3.3 Modeling hazards, rigidity, and pricing

Third-party challenges may arise from honest attempts to control costs and from opportunistic attempts to replace the public agent. Third-party costs, then, have two components: third-party costs T related to political costs of loss of office, reputation, and support that surge from contract discretionary terms (flexible contracting), and third-party costs K that rise with expenses related to the contract. Part of these contracting costs is borne directly by the contractor (K_{pr}) and reflected in the contract price, and part borne only by the public agent. If a third-party challenge is successful, there are also costs associated with the financial and social costs of a new tender, i.e., time and documentation,[13] or settlement awards made by the winning bidders to protesters in exchange for a promise to drop their protest (Marshall, Meurer, and Richard 1994b). We underline political[14] costs as the main cost for public agents concerning third-party challenges, and these costs are difficult to appraise, let alone to measure financially. The more discretionary the contract terms are, the more room there is for third parties to challenge the contract. Therefore, third-party costs T – both honest and opportunistic – can be mitigated by contract specificity and rigidity R.

Contract design (*ex ante* specificity), and implementation and enforcement (*ex post* rigidity) costs are subject to time needed for contract preparation, lawyers, documentation, and control, and can be measured financially. Contracting and enforcement costs K rise with contract specificity and rigidity R. The public agent wants to keep K low, because the more expensive a contract is, the more subject the public agent is to third-party challenges for misuse of funds.

---

[13] Marshall et al. (1994a) sustain that allowing excluded bidders to challenge the outcome of a procurement process inefficiently reduces sole-sourcing.

[14] Maser, Subbotin, and Thompson (2010) study the efficiency of the bid-protest mechanism in the US. In underlining "fairness" in contracting, i.e., that giving equal treatment to "*all* potential suppliers matters, not only to winners, but to losers as well" (Maser et al. 2010:2; their emphasis), they characterize the challenger as a loser bidder and focus on the transaction-cost side of TPO, ignoring the political context of public agents. They make this point more explicitly next, recalling the rule-of-law doctrine: "official duties are supposed to be defined primarily by neither instrumental aims nor political pressure, but by law" (Maser et al. 2010:3).

In order to illustrate and operationalize the third-party opportunism theory of public contracts, we introduce some simple notation. Hazards faced by the public agent are subject to the likelihood of TPO challenge σ and the likelihood of success of TPO challenge τ,[15] which are driven by contract complexity (sector-specific) and political contestability.

The price P bid by the contractor is the sum of operating costs (company-specific), contracting costs for the private contractor (contract-specific subject to rigidity R), and a mark-up (economic profit). To simplify our argument, we assume a uniform technology across firms and a competitive bidding market, such that P is the lowest possible cost and follows private contracting and enforcement costs K_{pr}. We also assume away governmental opportunism, i.e., government direct or incremental expropriation (Spiller and Savedoff 2000:9).

The likelihood of TPO challenge σ is assumed to increase in complexity of transactions, as inherent public–private information asymmetries increase with complexity (Spiller 2008); "open accessibility" (North, Wallis, and Weingast 2006), as in open democracies there is more public participation, scrutiny, and accountability; proximity to elections, since political challengers arise as potential political gains increase; and decrease in cost of challenge (costs of court litigation, new elections campaign) relative to the gains and value of a contract, and rigidity R, as there is less room for challenge.

Given that it is harder to prove wrongdoing when there is less room for discretionary actions, the likelihood of success of TPO challenge τ is also assumed to decrease in rigidity R, as the courts are more likely to dismiss and the public to ignore challenges to more specific and rigid – "narrower" – contracts. As both σ and τ decrease in R, expected third-party costs $E(T)$ fall as well in R. The simple intuition that $E(T)$ costs fall in R is that the likelihood of a successful TPO challenge can

---

[15] We use the term "likelihood" instead of "probability" to underline that we refer here to singular public contracts, which have no statistical distribution of possible opportunistic behavior or third-party challenges. The likelihood of third-party challenge and the success of the challenge can be compounded, since what makes a challenge actual is its likelihood of success (likelihood of third-party challenge σ increases in the likelihood of success of the challenge τ). Every challenge has some probability of success; otherwise the challenger would lose resources and reputation.

be reduced to negligible by extreme contract rigidity – all deviations are observed and hence directly prosecuted.

$E(T)$ costs are decreasing in R, while K costs – both public and private – are increasing in R. The optimal level of rigidity R^* is, therefore, driven by TPO costs, actual contracting and enforcement costs, and beliefs of the public agent about σ and τ.

The position of the $E(T)$ curve depends primarily on the political costs of a successful challenge to the incumbent public agent, and also on the costs of a new tender (documentation, new analyses), cost of externalities (including the value of lost time for users),[16] and the public agent's reputation. The slope of $E(T)$ is a function of the likelihood of a successful TPO challenge. As both σ and τ are decreasing in R, $E(T)$ is decreasing and strictly convex in R.

The position of the K curve is a function of materials and labor costs to be incurred, and also cost of time to close a contract, professionals needed (lawyers, engineers, consultants), required documentation, and control. The slope of the K curve is a function of the marginal cost of contracting and enforcement – what Laffont and Tirole (1993:307) call "processing costs." By assuming them to be non-decreasing in contract specificity and rigidity, K is rising and convex in R.

We assume that the public agent fully internalizes expenses related to the contract, i.e., at the end, she is politically accountable, directly or indirectly, for all costs borne.[17] She has to pay contractors' costs and her own costs, and she has also to minimize political costs. The sum curve of the expected third-party opportunism costs $E(T)$ plus contracting and enforcement costs K is U-shaped. It implies that the optimal contract is non-flexible and of finite rigidity. A too-flexible contract would be politically too risky while an over-rigid contract would be too expensive. The corollary is that, in the presence of

---

[16] E.g., highway repair generates significant negative externalities for commuters through increased gridlock and commuting times. Lewis and Bajari (2011:1174) take the example of Interstate 35W, a main commuting route in Minneapolis carrying over 175,000 commuters per day. If a highway construction project results in a 30-minute delay each way for commuters on this route, the daily social cost imposed by the construction would be 175,000 hours. If we value time at $10 an hour, this is a social cost of $1.75 million per day. Most public contracts affecting the public at large, from sewage disposal to worse service because of a delay in buying IT equipment, carry externalities.

[17] Our main argument also holds for partial internalization by the public agent of expenses related to the contract.

third-party opportunism, the optimal public contract that minimizes political and contracting costs is specific and rigid, ergo more expensive in its design, implementation, and control than the theoretical first-best price in a non-opportunistic world.[18] A direct outcome is that the higher the expected political costs of challenge, *ceteris paribus*,[19] the higher the optimum contract rigidity and price will be.

11.4 Contract price under TPO

In every tender under budgetary constraints, the public agent sets – explicitly in tender information, announcements or the budget, or implicitly in internal regulations – a maximum price P^{bud} that she can pay the contractor. To lessen TPO, she also adjusts contract specificity and rigidity at R^*. The acceptable contracting price-rigidity sets for the public agent are below the maximum contract price P^{bud}, i.e., contracts "in the budget," subject to low TPO costs. The contractor sees specificity and rigidity R^* in the tender documentation and bids accordingly. On the contractor's side, the acceptable price-rigidity sets are those on and above her private contracting costs K_{pr}. Therefore, the contracting area – i.e., the sets acceptable to both the public agent and the contractor – is given by price-rigidity combinations above K_{pr} and below P^{bud}. At a given R^*, the minimum price required by the contractor is P^{min}. Figure 11.1 plots $E(T)$ and K curves, bid and budgeted and minimum prices, optimal rigidity, and the price-rigidity contracting area.

Before the tender, especially in complex contracts and given the contracting rigidities, the public agent only has an estimation of the contractor's costs K_{pr}, but does not know them with certainty. If P^{bud} budgeted by the public agent is below the minimum acceptable price $P^{min} = K_{pr}$ for the contractor at a given R^*, then there will be no

---

[18] Thus, TPO does not lead to a "vicious cycle" as suggested by Maser et al. (2010:4). In a game theory set, this state can be described as a Bayesian Nash equilibrium.
[19] A certain degree of specificity and rigidity is inherent to every contract, even in the absence of TPO, to avoid the standard contractual opportunism by the contractor (e.g., shading on quality) and the public agent (e.g., delay in payments, haggling). For simplicity, and to underscore TPO, we abstract from relational opportunism. The degree of specificity and rigidity R presented in Figures 11.1 and 11.2 are beyond the levels of specificity and rigidity inherent to relational contracts.

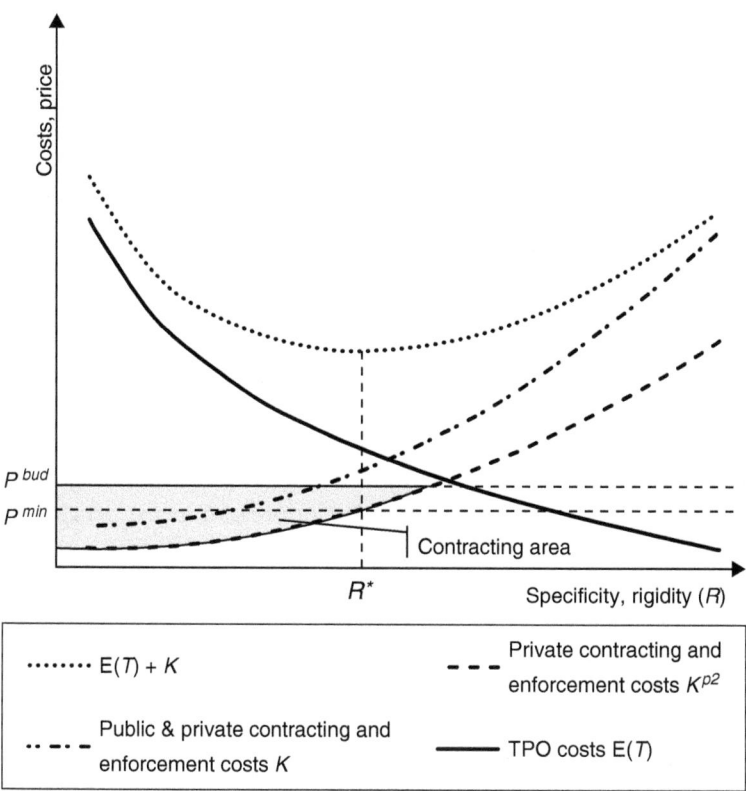

Figure 11.1 Third-party opportunism costs, and contracting and enforcement costs

bidders at that level of R, or – in the case that P^{bud} is not known by bidders prior to the tender – bidders will bid $P > P^{bud}$ and the tender will be annulled. Therefore, "no contract" is a possible outcome if political risks are significant and budgeted expenses are too low at a given rigidity.[20] In this case, the tender will have to be redesigned at a lower rigidity level at the risk of higher TPO for the public agent; the budget reconsidered, creating room for third-party challenges attempting to control budget expenses; or terms negotiated after bidding, increasing TPO on suspicion of collusion.

[20] Scarce budgeted expenses for transport infrastructure along with excessive contract specificity and rigidity due to continuous TPO can explain the paralysis in highway development in Poland during the last decade. See "Poles repositioned," *Project Finance Magazine*, October 23, 2010.

11.5 Applications and empirical implications

The base case that our model tackles is a simple public procurement contract. There are other situations, however, where TPO can explain the mechanisms related to public procurement and efficiency. We now apply and extend the framework to practical settings to derive empirical implications.

11.5.1 Bureaucracies

Civil servants are subject to more specific and rigid contracts (e.g., regulated hiring, list of duties and responsibilities) than their peers in the private sector.[21] A private company can hire whoever it wants and a typical employment contract may simply say "follow the instructions of your principal," while in a public institution the process of employment of civil servants is highly formalized and procedural, and responsibilities are detailed in civil service laws and internal regulations of the agency, department, office, and section in question (Horn 1995:20, 88, 112), and subject to independent ordinary and extraordinary controls (Horn 1995:98).[22] Both specific employment procedures and rigid contracts in the civil service are aimed at avoiding challenges of favoritism (GAO 2003; Horn 1995:101), but nonetheless result in civil servants being allowed less discretion, less initiative in offering solutions, and lower productivity[23] (analogous to higher price in public tenders). TPO thus provides a consistent explanation of civil service inefficiencies broader than the public administration view on red tape.[24]

---

[21] In this instance, bureaucrats as individuals are the private party contracting with the public agency.

[22] For example, controls may be overseen by the Government Accountability Office in the US, the Australian National Audit Office in Australia, the Tribunal de Contas da União in Brazil, or the Bundesrechnungshof in Germany, to name a few.

[23] According to the British Office for National Statistics (ONS), public sector productivity fell by 3.4 percent in 1997–2006, compared with a rise of 28 percent in the private sector over the same 10-year period (see Robert Watts, "Public sector pay races ahead in recession," *The Sunday Times*, January 3, 2010).

[24] See Bozeman (1993). See also Laffont and Tirole (1991), Pfiffner (1987), and Spiller and Urbiztondo (1994).

Bambaci, Spiller, and Tommasi (2007) describe the Argentine bureaucracy as a combination of constitutional protections of civil servants, relative low wages,[25] and low accountability to "short lived" political public agents,[26] which produces unresponsive bureaucrats with few incentives to invest in their own capabilities. Precisely because political public agents do not last long, TPO is not a prevalent hazard for them. The institutional adaptation that emerged is the large use of a "parallel bureaucracy,"[27] i.e., temporary contracted professionals, better paid, more responsive to their principals, under a more flexible regime than permanent bureaucrats, and whose appointments are left to the discretion of the principal public agent in office (Bambaci et al. 2007:172–174; Iacoviello et al. 2002). Thus, political public agents in Argentina blend permanent bureaucracy with temporary bureaucrats who respond more flexibly and efficiently.

11.5.2 Fixed-price vs. cost-plus contracts

In theory, fixed-price contracts are preferable when the adverse selection problem decreases relative to the moral hazard problem (e.g., in the procurement of standardized goods and services, or in projects involving a low level of informational asymmetry between the contracting parties), while cost-plus procurement is preferable when the adverse selection problem increases relative to the moral hazard problem (i.e., when uncertainties related to technological requirements are unknown and bigger than the inefficiencies arising from incomplete monitoring and insulation of the contractor from cost overruns) (Loeb and Surysekar 1994).

---

[25] In 1999, Federal Government wages divided by GDP per capita equaled 1.65 in Argentina, compared with 3.70 in Brazil, 3.25 in Colombia, 3.05 in Chile, and 1.99 in Mexico. See Carlson and Payne (2003).
[26] The low accountability of the Argentinian administration is to a large extent due to the high turnover of political public principals: ministers, secretaries, and undersecretaries of state. For instance, the average tenure of Ministers of Finance in 1950–1989 was 1 year, compared with 2.4 years in developed countries and 2.0 in developing countries (Bambaci et al. 2007:165).
[27] In 1998–1999, parallel bureaucrats accounted for 17 percent in the Presidency office, but 63–88 percent in ministries (see "Estudio exploratorio sobre la transparencia en la Administración Pública Argentina: 1998–1999," Oficina Anticorrupción, Ministerio de Justicia, 2000, cited in Bambaci et al. 2007:172).

In practice, cost-plus contracts have been criticized by the administration, lawmakers, and taxpayers for frequent and substantial cost overruns in government contracting. A GAO (2008) study of 95 major defense acquisition projects found cost overruns of 26 percent, totaling $295 billion over the life of the projects. Cost-plus contracts are more flexible to adaptation, but also subject to potential abuse[28] and shading (Fehr, Hart, and Zehnder 2011). The Presidential Memorandum of March 4, 2009, for the Heads of Executive Departments and Agencies on Government Contracting, explicitly stated that "there shall be a preference for fixed-price type contracts. Cost-reimbursement contracts shall be used only when circumstances do not allow the agency to define its requirements sufficiently to allow for a fixed-price type contract."[29] In the presence of closer third-party oversight and fear of TPO,[30] public agents will prefer fixed-price contracts in settings where cost-plus contracts could prove to be more efficient.[31]

11.5.3 Public–private partnerships and key performance indicators

A public–private partnership (PPP) is a public service business operated under a long-term contract or license associated with a degree

---

[28] Cost-plus contracts are seen as a "blank check" for contractors and the root cause of procurement inefficiencies. A notable exception is the case of London's Heathrow Airport Terminal 5, which was delivered on schedule and under budget, under a cost-plus regime (see www.airport-technology.com/projects/heathrow5/; accessed July 10, 2011).

[29] See Presidential Memorandum of March 4, 2009, for the Heads of Executive Departments and Agencies on Government Contracting, retrieved from www.whitehouse.gov/the_press_office/Memorandum-for-the-Heads-of-Executive-Departments-and-Agencies-Subject-Government/ (accessed July 11, 2011).

[30] As stated in the Presidential Memorandum (op. cit.), "reports by agency Inspectors General, the Government Accountability Office (GAO), and other independent reviewing bodies have shown that noncompetitive and cost-reimbursement contracts have been *misused*, resulting in wasted taxpayer resources, poor contractor performance, and inadequate accountability for results" and "improved *contract oversight* could reduce such sums significantly" (emphasis added).

[31] Analyzing major defense acquisition programs, Wang and San Miguel (2011) argued that fixed-price contracts do not provide adaptable risk-sharing mechanisms and may lead to an unintended increase in government payments. See also Tony Purton, "The case for a return to 'cost plus'," *Defense Viewpoints*, March 24, 2007, www.defenceviewpoints.co.uk/articles-and-analysis/the-case-for-a-return-to-cost-plus (accessed July 10, 2011).

of exclusivity within a certain geographical area. It may involve the transfer to the private contractor of the right to use some existing infrastructure required to carry out a business (such as a water supply system in a city) and commonly the private contractor assumes substantial financial, technical, and operational risk in the project.

PPPs allow for *ex ante* flexibility in contracting to gain efficiency. To control quality *ex post*, key performance indicators (KPIs) are used, i.e., measures specifically tailored for each sector, under which the private partner is evaluated. At the same time, KPIs constitute a signal for the public at large (consumers and voters) that the service, although privately provided, remains publicly accountable. KPIs are thus crucial to third-parties' perception of PPPs.

Ex ante flexibility, however, makes PPPs vulnerable to third-party challenges (higher σ), a hazard that private investors translate into higher prices. A number of Australian studies of private investment in infrastructure (Economic Planning Advisory Commission 1995; Harris 1996; House of Representatives' Standing Committee on Communications Transport and Microeconomic Reform 1997; Industry Commission 1996; Quiggin 1996) reached the conclusion that, in most cases, the PPPs were inferior – overall more expensive for the public or delivered lower quality of services – than the standard model of public procurement based on competitively tendered construction of publicly owned assets. One response by public agents to these negative findings was the development of formal procedures for *ex ante* assessment of PPPs using the Public Sector Comparator (PSC) and Value-for-Money (VfM) methodologies, i.e., introducing more contractual *ex ante* specificity and contractual costs.[32]

In 2009, the Treasury of New Zealand, in response to inquiries by the new National Party government, released a report on PPPs that came to the conclusion that "there is little reliable empirical evidence about the costs and benefits of PPPs" and that "the advantages of PPPs must be weighed against the *contractual complexities and rigidities* they entail."[33]

---

[32] See, for example, Department of Treasury and Finance of Victoria, "Partnerships Victoria Guidance Material: Public Sector Comparator – Technical Note," Melbourne 2001.

[33] Brian Rudman, "Promised electric trains derailed by misguided enthusiasm," *The New Zealand Herald*, June 1, 2009. Emphasis added.

In the presence of TPO, public agents would pursue private provision of public goods mostly in projects where – assuming internalization of contract expenses by the public agent – expected political benefits gains from better private management offset increased *ex ante* contracting costs related to compliancy with cost-benefit assessment and higher *ex post* rigidity related to KPIs.

11.5.4 Public-to-public contracts

When a public agent engages in a contract with another public agent (e.g., a state contracting a service from a government-owned enterprise) or a quasi-public agent (e.g., a state negotiating salaries with a public-employee union),[34] both sides have to respond to their constituencies (i.e., the public agent to voters; the union leader to union members). TPO costs rise because of double scrutiny and higher likelihood of political challenge on both sides. Higher expected TPO costs result in higher contract rigidity. If the public agent subsidizes the government-owned company, higher contract rigidity might not be directly reflected in higher prices, but indirectly, e.g., through taxes or lower delivered quality of services. Public agents and government-owned companies or public-employee unions can agree to low contract specificity and rigidity only if there is strong political leadership and low political contestability (low TPO costs), as in authoritarian regimes.[35]

11.5.5 External consultants and certification of contractors

The engagement of independent consultants (e.g., multilateral agencies, international advisers, especially in countries with weak law

---

[34] See *The Becker-Posner Blog* entry for March 27, 2011: "Public-Employee Unions" by Richard Posner and "Government Sector Unions" by Gary Becker (www.becker-posner-blog.com/, accessed March 28, 2011). As Becker notes,

> even without the strike threat – indeed, possibly even without unions – public employees can often extract considerable benefits from local, state, and the federal government in the form of higher earnings and generous pensions and health benefits. Public employees form a sizable voting bloc with formidable resources of money and the time of members to spend on supporting political candidates who they expect will be generous when it comes time to bargain over compensation.

[35] See discussion in Section 11.5.6 below.

Third-party opportunism and public contracts 245

systems) strengthens the objectivity of procurement processes and prevents third-party challenges that cooperation between public agents and private contractors has crossed the line and become collusion.

Moszoro and Krzyzanowska (2008) report the use of external consultants in the city of Warsaw in the pre-procurement planning phase when it wanted to introduce novel PPP contracts: first, to overcome the lack of expertise in complex contracting (to reduce K) and, second and most importantly, to "safeguard the city authorities against complaints and criticism by subsequent administrations." While the city authorities could have designed the tender process in-house, they seem to have outsourced it to reduce TPO. The use of external consultants, however, came at a cost: PLN 10 million ($3.2 million), i.e., 1.2 percent of the estimated budget for those projects.

Similarly, certain public tenders require certification of contractors and subcontractors (Lewis and Bajari 2011), increasing contract specificity and the price of the tender. In May 2010, a public procurement for the "Canal Safety and Drainage Improvements Project" in Antioch, Pittsburg, Bay Point, Clyde, and Walnut Creek (California), tendered by the Contra Costa Water District Construction Department, was objected to by JMB Construction.[36] JMB Construction argued that the apparent low bidder Con-Quest Contractors included a non-certified subcontractor. According to Contra Costa Water District Construction Department, the relevance of the works the alleged subcontract would provide was minimal for the project overall; however, the challenger argued that the inclusion of a non-certified subcontractor allowed Con-Quest Contractors to bid a lower price ($756,000 compared with JMB Construction's $852,000, i.e., 11 percent cheaper) than if it had included only certified subcontractors.[37]

In both cases – the use of external consultants and certification of contractors – the implicit aim is to lessen the likelihood of TPO challenge (σ). There is a trade-off for the public agent between lower TPO hazards and additional contracting costs K of external consultants and certification. The public agent will employ external consultants and certification when additional contracting costs K incurred

---

[36] See: www.ccwater.com/buscenter/109067_results.pdf (accessed May 28, 2010).
[37] Based on an interview held in May 2010 with a Contra Costa Water District engineer.

are lower than price gains in contract flexibility due to lower $E(T)$ and R^*.

11.5.6 Efficient small communities and authoritarian regimes

Small local governments (towns, counties) can be more efficient in public contracting than larger governments (metropolises, states). Due to lower value of contracts in comparison to larger governments, the benefits from political challenge are relatively low. Thus the likelihood of challenge is lower and subsequently potential TPO costs are lower. The public agent can therefore engage in more discretionary contracts and incur lower transaction costs.

Coviello and Gagliarducci (2010) present a study covering 3,825 Italian municipalities and 27,537 auctions, where an increase in the mayor's tenure of one term is associated with fewer bidders per auction (−23.28%), higher probability that the winner is local (+3.20%), and that the same firm is awarded repeated auctions (+25.52%), i.e., more discretionary contracting (lower R^*) correlated with longer tenure. They also find evidence that a high level of heterogeneity within the government coalition reduces the possibility of favoritism in shaping the procurement process, that less "colluded"[38] mayors are more likely to gain reelection and survive longer, and that citizens and competitors are more likely to closely monitor large public projects.

Two reasons can be given why mayors with longer tenure show low concern about TPO and contract discretionarily. First, the Italian electoral system in municipalities is a simple majority regime. Consequently, in very small municipalities, more political contestability results in more dispersed voting and relative advantage of incumbent mayors.[39] Second, procurement protests in Italy go through courts, where penalties for breaking procurement laws are hardly enforced.[40] When K

---

[38] Coviello and Gagliarducci (2010) argue that mayors' time in office progressively leads to a long-term relation ("collusion") with a few favored bidders, and propose two interpretations: one based on favoritism and bribes in procurement, and another based on a learning process of mayors about the quality of contractors and a preference for highest-quality contractors with work (2010:26–27).

[39] If m is the population and n the number of candidates, a candidate needs $m/n + 1$ votes to win the election.

[40] During the period 2005–2008, the Italian central purchasing authority CONSIP made 4,095 random inspections on the *ex post* renegotiations of

increases more rapidly than E(*T*) decreases in *R*, or E(*T*) are insignificant due to lack of political contestability (as seems to be the case in Italian municipalities), the outcome is discretionary procurement.[41]

Authoritarian regimes, where the likelihood of challenging the incumbent public agent is low, can contract public works more discretionarily and, thus, cheaper and quicker. The lack of opportunities for TPO can help to explain the rapid contracting and development of infrastructure in Paraguay during the Stroessner regime. Molinas et al. (2006:12–13) report the significant ability of the regime

> to reap the benefits offered by long-term economic opportunities. ... [Development programs were] possible because of the intertemporal "cooperation" of the key actors (the government, the Party and the Armed Forces). The adaptation of the development model to allow for increasing integration with Brazil would have been unlikely under short-lived governments like the ones characterizing the post-Chaco war period (1936–1954). During that 18-year period, there were 12 different presidents, and political volatility prevented an adaptation to changing economic environments. ... During the 1960s and the 1970s, Paraguay built roads, silos and, most importantly, the biggest dam in the world, the Itaipú Hydro-electric Dam, built jointly with Brazil. The long-term growth strategy turned out to be effective. During the 1960s, real GDP growth was 4.2 percent. During the 1970s, Paraguay had one of the highest growth rates in the region, with real GDP increasing at 8 percent over the decade.

That ability to move policy decisively and effectively by an authoritarian regime, however, also funneled most of the benefits from this fast development period to a few contractors and subcontractors – companies owned by the dictator's followers (Fogel 1993:16).

---

procurement contracts for goods and services, and found a total of 1,455 contractual infringements. Only 4 percent of the associated penalties were paid (Coviello and Gagliarducci 2010:27). Anecdotally, it takes on average more than 10 years for juries to come to a verdict on contract protests. How public contracting can actually take place in an environment in which penalties are seldom paid remains a subject of future research.

[41] Coviello and Gagliarducci (2010) also report – contrary to our predictions – an increase in contract prices (reduction of winning rebate by –12.68 percent) along with an increase in contract discretion. According to these authors, higher prices are not due to higher cost of procurement and contract terms (the study analyzed the procurement of standardized items), but are driven by mayors' favoritism and colluded renegotiations (corruption) or preference for higher-quality contractors.

11.5.7 Privatizations of government-owned companies

Privatizations of government-owned companies[42] are usually subject to clauses of commitment of the private acquirer over labor retention, modernization processes, future investments, and other socially sensitive issues. On the one hand, rigid privatization contracts (high $R*$) take place in the fear of TPO challenges to the incumbent public agent by labor unions, the local community, and the political opposition. In order to minimize TPO challenges to privatizations, public agents embed in privatization contracts clauses and golden shares that allow them to limit "cream skimming" (Kolderie 1986) and the discretion of the private investor. On the other hand, such privatization clauses limit the governance of the company and, consequently, lower its value (analogous to a high price in a public procurement). If the revenue to the public budget from privatization is low, the public agent can be accused of collusion with the private agent or of "selling off the family silver" (Kolderie 1986). The corollary is that privatizations' aftermath regarding price and efficiency appears to be a sell-off from a government's valuation standpoint and rigid from a private managerial perspective.

11.5.8 Immunity for public agents

Many countries guarantee public agents a degree of immunity from legal prosecution as a way to insulate them from threats of media smear campaigns, courts, and legal harassment (Dal Bó, Dal Bó, and Di Tella 2006). Dal Bó et al. develop a model in which the public agent cares about money, punishment, and the political cost of getting involved in a corrupt deal, e.g., the result of a detection probability (2006:45). They show (2006:49) that, by limiting the potential for pressure from interested groups, immunity may indirectly lead to an increase in the quality of public officials, and hence better public policies. Congruently, from a TPO theory perspective, immunity lowers the likelihood of successful TPO challenges σt because the public

---

[42] PPP and privatization differ in that the former is a transfer to the private sector of a right (which may or may not come with a physical asset) to perform the public function, while the latter usually refers to the sale of an asset which is not necessarily idiosyncratic to the public sector (e.g., liquor stores in Pennsylvania).

agent will not have to prove probity and, consequently, provides flexibility that leads to an increase in efficiency of public agents.

11.6 An extension: governmental opportunism

In this chapter, our goal was to highlight third-party opportunism implications for public contracting. However, the model can also serve to analyze the impact of governmental opportunism (G) as a hazard to public contracts (Moszoro 2010).

Let I be sunk investments and A be the rents of the public agent from expropriation (whereas $A = I$ represents total expropriation and $A < I$ represents partial expropriation) and ψ the likelihood of governmental opportunism of appropriating A. Expected costs of governmental opportunism equals $E(G) = A\psi(R)$, where ψ is assumed to decrease in contract specificity and rigidity ($\delta\psi/\delta R < 0$).

In the presence of governmental opportunism, the private contractor will respond by seeking further specificity and rigidity R and charging an additional $A\psi(R)$ to her private contracting costs K_{pr}. For any $\psi > 0$, the higher sunk investments I, the higher possible expropriation rents A and expected costs of governmental opportunism $E(G)$ (Troesken 1996), specificity and rigidity of the contract $R' > R^*$, and final price $P' > P^{min}$ charged to the public sector (see Figure 11.2). A corollary of the interrelation of third-party and governmental opportunism is that higher price P' due to governmental opportunism makes the contract more vulnerable to third-party challenges, or not feasible, if the P' is above the maximum price P^{bud} that the public agent is willing or is able to pay.

The contractor's taking out insurance against adverse political events (e.g., governmental expropriation, confiscation of assets, or repudiation of contracts) mitigates the expected costs of governmental opportunism, but shifts up the cost of contracting K by the insurance premium. In a competitive insurance market, the political risk insurance premium equals the insurer's expected expropriation rents $E_S(G)$, while the contractor's willingness to pay for political risk insurance equals her expected expropriation rents $E(G)$. Political risk insurance will be beneficial for the public agent only if the political risk insurance premium, compounded now in the contract price, amounts to no more than the differential between contract prices with and without political risk insurance, i.e., $E_S(G) \leq P' - P^{min}$, this differential being

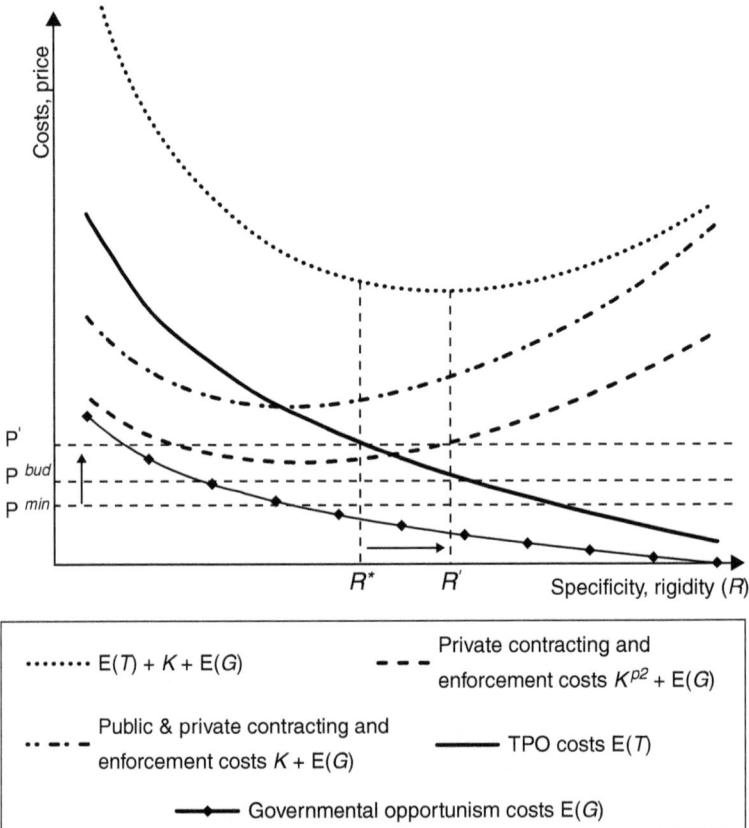

Figure 11.2 Governmental opportunism

due to further rigidity and the contractor's expected cost of governmental opportunism at R'. Political risk insurance will be cost-efficient for the contractor if the political risk insurance premium is lower or equal to her expected cost due to governmental opportunism, i.e., $E_S(G) \leq E(G)$.

If political risk insurance premiums are too low, contractors that face opportunistic-type governments will take out insurance, increasing the average claims. Contractors may also lower rigidity below the optimal level without political risk insurance due to moral hazard, sparking more governmental opportunism and further increasing the average claims. Advancing this result, the insurer will increase political risk premiums. If political risk insurance premiums are too high, it will not be cost-efficient for contractors of non-opportunistic-type governments to take out political risk insurance. In equilibrium without informational asymmetry on the government type, contractors will be indifferent about taking out political risk insurance. In the presence of informational asymmetry about the likelihood of governmental opportunism ψ, an adverse selection screening game – largely described in the literature on insurance markets – will take place, which explains high political risk insurance premiums, the existence of tiny private markets for political risk insurance, and the indispensable involvement of multilateral agencies (MLAs).[43]

11.7 Concluding remarks

TPO theory combines political hazards and transaction costs to explain apparent inefficiencies in public contracts. A paramount conclusion of our analysis is that public contracts cannot be directly compared to private contracts. Instead, they can only be compared to analogous public contracts, and should pass Williamson's (1999) "remediableness criterion"[44] to attest to their efficiency.

That public contracting is more expensive and rigid than private contracting, however, does not mean that transferring those activities to the public sector would reduce political risks and hence make them more efficient. Not only, as Williamson (1999:320) discussed, do certain transactions have special needs for probity and require the security of the state,[45] but the privatization of public functions itself involves TPO hazards, making them less preferable for public agents than public contracting itself.

---

[43] See, for example, the Multilateral Investment Guarantee Agency (MIGA), a member of the World Bank Group (www.miga.org/; accessed July 15, 2011), or the Overseas Private Investment Corporation (OPIC), a US Government's development finance institution (www.opic.gov/insurance; accessed July 15, 2011).

[44] "The "remediableness criterion" holds that "an extant mode of organization for which no superior *feasible* alternative can be described and *implemented* with expected net gains is *presumed* to be efficient" (Williamson 1999:316; emphasis is original).

[45] See, also, Prendergast (2003:930–933) who claims that public procurement is used for "hard" agency problems where consumers cannot be trusted and "when bureaucracies work poorly, consumer choice works worse."

In this chapter we have analyzed public procurement in a variety of environments to show that much of its outer features can be understood as political adaptations to the fundamental hazard of third-party opportunism prevalent in public contracting.

12 The cycling of power between private and public sectors: electricity generation in Argentina, Brazil, and Chile

WITOLD J. HENISZ AND BENNET A. ZELNER

12.1 Introduction

As public discourse and public policy have shifted away from unfettered confidence in free markets in the wake of the global economic and financial crisis that began in 2008, academics, policymakers, and practitioners have struggled to define the shifting boundary between the public and private sectors. State ownership and operation have extended to industries previously perceived to be inviolably market-oriented. The extent and longevity of this seemingly abrupt change in the economic role of government are still unclear, however. While some have advanced the radical notion that bulwarks of capitalism such as the United States are veering toward "socialism," others view the financial crisis as having instigated a cathartic last gasp of state intervention.

Neither extreme view is likely correct. In this chapter, we propose an alternative view that we illustrate with a century-long historical analysis of the electricity generation industry of three Latin American nations – Chile, Argentina, and Brazil – that have each cycled back and forth between the poles of private ownership and operation at one extreme, and public ownership and operation at the other. Building on recent research in the field of Political Science (Baumgartner et al. 2009) and our own prior research on the diffusion and sustainability of market-oriented infrastructure reform (Henisz, Zelner, and Guillén 2005; Zelner, Henisz, and Holburn 2009) we attribute this policy cycling to the manner in which interest group pressures and institutional constraints interact to produce long policy cycles characterized by "punctuated equilibrium" (Baumgartner et al. 2009). Although electricity's substantial political salience and economic importance may amplify such political dynamics (Levy and Spiller 1994; Henisz and Zelner 2005), we expect that this pattern holds in many policy areas (see Baumgartner et al. 2009). For this reason we are skeptical of declarations that the boundary between the public and private sectors has permanently shifted toward one extreme or the other.

The adoption of a new policy necessarily produces winners and losers. The organized interest groups suffering the most adverse economic consequences of the new policy – as well as those most ideologically opposed – likely fought adoption in the first place and now seek to repeal the new policy. Other groups – both organized groups that are only marginally affected by the policy as well as diffuse, unorganized groups – remain relatively unengaged at this point (Henisz and Zelner 2005).

Policymakers' ability to consider only a limited range of issues at one time, together with the procedural costs of changing policy and the recency of the new policy's adoption, provide sufficient "institutional friction" (Baumgartner et al. 2009) to sustain the new policy despite opposed groups' entreaties to repeal it. Over time, however, pressures to repeal the policy mount as adverse effects on specific groups become more visible. The groups that initially opposed the policy enlist the support of unengaged groups by demonstrating the policy's negative consequences for these groups or its inconsistency with their engrained values and beliefs (Henisz and Zelner 2005). Policymakers subject to institutional friction – but also cognizant of the growing chorus of dissatisfied voices – manage the pressures for repeal by applying targeted "patches" to alter specific policy elements, effectively deferring the costs of wholesale policy change by compensating the policy's most vocal or powerful opponents. Over time, these adjustments cumulate to produce an incoherent patchwork rife with new inefficiencies and inequities, which in turn draw additional interest groups into the opposition coalition. Moreover, exogenous forces – broader ideational influences or specific "focusing events" – may further influence the legislative agenda, effectively reducing the institutional friction holding the skeleton of the original policy in place by sensitizing policymakers to the entreaties of the growing coalition seeking repeal.

When the pressures exerted by the policy's opponents grow strong enough to overcome institutional friction – a process that may take years or decades – policymakers repeal the policy and adopt a replacement (Oliver 1992). The replacement policy reflects built-up interest group pressures that have cumulated over time, including some provisionally held in check by patches, and thus typically represents a drastic departure from its predecessor. This "stick-slip" dynamic is similar to that associated with earthquakes and other natural events where pressure builds against friction. Because policymakers previously "under-responded" to mounting pressures for repeal, they "now rush to make up for past inattention by dramatically increasing policy outputs directed to [the issue]" (Baumgartner et al. 2009: 608). The cycle then begins anew.

The three country cases we discuss below illustrate how the interest group dynamics surrounding the electricity generation industry combined with institutional friction to produce a pattern of cycling between the poles of private ownership and operation at one extreme, and public ownership and operation at the other. Policy cycling in the electricity industry is especially germane in the context of the broader policy debates instigated by the financial crisis because the core dimension around which much political conflict revolved was that running from operational and economic efficiency to targeted income redistribution. Private ownership and operation promoted the former objectives, whereas public ownership and operation facilitated the latter through practices such as price subsidization, over-employment, and the construction of "white elephants" (Henisz and Zelner 2006). The costs of these redistributive practices, which cumulated over time, were operational and financial inefficiency. Relative to the public sector model, private ownership and operation promoted efficiency and reliability, but without serving the same redistributive ends (and possibly even furthering the concentration of wealth by facilitating monopolization).

In each case, electricity generation began in the private sector and grew so rapidly that the three countries' penetration rates were among the highest in the world by the mid 1920s. Subsequently, each country's national government responded to perceived monopoly abuses by implementing a series of policy initiatives to control price, limit returns, and target investment. These interventions so stymied private investors that investment eventually came to a standstill and the government in each case nationalized the electricity generation industry. While investment and employment levels subsequently surged and price levels remained low – especially for politically salient constituencies – the economic cost of politicized investment and operating decisions grew ever larger in the form of massive government debt, supply shortages and disruptions, and even full-blown crises. Struggling governments responded by (re)introducing market-oriented policies, but when crisis conditions receded, they soon began applying politically motivated "patches" as well (Victor and Heller 2007).

12.2 Unfairness of private provision and creeping government involvement

Prior to the 1930s, private owners and operators were the first to generate, transmit, and distribute electricity throughout Latin America, leading to rapid but uneven growth in its availability. In Chile electricity was provided exclusively by private producers through 1925, and the country enjoyed the second highest rate of per capita consumption in the world, behind only France. Private owners and operators were similarly dominant in Argentina and Brazil. However, growing concerns about the pricing and supply decision of natural monopolies, which might be both inefficient and violate norms of distributive justice, subsequently led to government intervention, albeit with limited operational or economic success. Such intervention was particularly aggressive in the presence of foreign private ownership, which provided a ready basis around which those calling for greater fairness and local control could coalesce in support of greater state intervention. Eventually, all three countries turned to state-owned and operated systems following one or more "focusing events" (Kingdon 1984) that served as additional rallying points for opponents of the private sector model.

In Chile in 1925, the government created the "fondo de servicios publicos" to channel additional capital to companies whose output benefited the nation and which would be subsequently regulated as a result. By 1931, the Chilean government became concerned that they were subsidizing investment without accountability and began to regulate prices to ensure access for new customers. Unfortunately, they chose a price level that made investment in new capacity by the 190 active subsidized private firms in the industry unprofitable. When Chilean private investors responded to these controls by refusing to invest what the government perceived as sufficient sums in new capacity, the government channeled public funds to the newly created state-owned enterprise Emresa Nacional de Electricidad S.A. (Endesa). The Chilean government also instituted a rate-of-return-based compensation scheme for remaining private producers.

In the 1930s, the new Vargas administration in Brazil began to contest the largely foreign control of electricity generation which it perceived was similarly failing to meet the needs of the non-urban population particularly the rural and suburban poor. In 1931, Vargas abrogated all private contracts governing the use of water to generate electricity and in 1934 established a new Code that required government authorization and concession for the use of water to generate electricity even if the waterway was privately owned (Marques 1997). Rate of return regulation was introduced allowing for 10 percent return on investment calculated at historical (not replacement) cost (Baer and McDonald 1998) though actual returns were often far lower due to the political control of pricing to end consumers (Hamaguchi 2002). The military government expanded the scope of government authority in the sector by decree in 1937, 1938, and 1939 to deal with growing supply shortages (Marques 1997). Such shortages were aggravated by a price freeze during World War II and a prohibition on the granting of new licenses to foreign-owned firms (Baer and McDonald 1998).

The Brazilian government responded with a National Electrification Plan and created state-owned enterprises to implement this plan in the Northeast and Southeastern regions. Provincial governments not covered by these new entities created their own power companies which received preferential cost of capital via the National Economic Development Bank (BNDE). From 1952 to 1965, the share of private generating capacity plummeted from 82.4% to 33.6% while the public sector soared from 6.8% to 65.6%. Control over this growing public capacity was consolidated in the state-owned enterprise Electrobras in 1962 (Hamaguchi 2002). After a series of disputes regarding the investment in new capacity by private generators, the Brazilian government nationalized the two largest remaining private firms in 1964 and 1979.

From 1910 to 1930, foreign-owned electric holding companies consolidated municipal power contracts in three large utilities that together controlled 74 percent of the Argentinean national generating capacity (Lanciotti 2008). Unlike their Chilean and Brazilian counterparts, the Argentinean utilities largely escaped the 1930s unscathed despite costly local adjustments to international shifts in currency values. In 1943, however, a nationalist military government approved of local efforts to expropriate foreign utilities and introduced a national regulatory agency for the first time. These initial steps towards nationalization were accelerated under the Peronist government beginning in 1946 as was an acceleration of public investment in new generating capacity targeting the non-urban poor.

12.3 Inefficiency of public provision

The growth in indirect public intervention through the regulation of prices or returns and direct public intervention through state-owned generation and distribution politicized investment, hiring, and pricing policies as affordable supply and full employment came to dominate the economic objectives of reliability and cost recovery (World Bank 1995; Savedoff and Spiller 1999). Pricing cross-subsidies, power plant construction decisions made on the basis of providing jobs rather than fulfilling unmet demand or lowering costs, and the freezing of nominal electricity prices during inflationary periods caused chronic operating deficits that necessitated cutbacks in maintenance and economically necessary new construction, resulting in increasingly obsolete plants, high network line losses, and recurring blackouts (International Energy Agency 1999).

Under state ownership, investment levels soared far beyond what was needed to satisfy demand. One interviewee described to us the quintessential white elephant, a power facility that he had just purchased from the government in a neighboring country that was full of useless marble and soaring atriums that were good for the filming of the movie *Highlander* but little else. In Argentina, with the assistance of World Bank financing and repeated optimistic projections for demand growth, the state-owned enterprises continued to expand their capacity until, in 1989, the nominal reserve margin peaked at over 45 percent, versus industry standard levels of 15–20 percent. Moreover, new capital investment typically consisted of dated technology favoring domestic fuel supplies, which resulted in low productivity growth and inflexibility.

Governments systematically manipulated prices for political gain. Brazilian pricing was explicitly tied to broader income redistribution and industrial policies (Baer and McDonald 1998). One prominent example was the decision to equalize electricity prices nationally despite substantial cost differences, which varied according to consumer class and region by as much as 133 percent (Pires Rodrigues and Braga Monteiro 1991). Politicians also used the electricity industry to balance pressures within the governing coalition and across regions. According to De Souza Costa of Banco Pactual, "Each piece of Escelsa used to represent a different political party, which meant that political considerations, rather than need, drove managers' decisions and the president was not in command of the whole company" (Independent Power Report 1996).

The Argentine system of pricing was also explicitly employed to accomplish a multitude of political objectives, including income redistribution and the reduction of costs for favored industries and geographic constituencies. Trade-offs among these and other conflicting political objectives yielded high price volatility, which deterred private investment. Political battles between the Ministry of Economics, which sought to limit spending, and the Ministry of Public Works, which sought to promote new investment, compounded these problems. Differences between the tariff policies of the Department of Energy (responsible for national companies) and provincial regulatory authorities (responsible for local companies) combined with incessant political intervention in the determination of firms' allowed capital costs to further increase investor uncertainty (Bastos and Abdala 1993).

Perhaps even more damaging to state-owned enterprises' (SOEs) financial health than tariff imbalances was the practice of freezing prices to control inflation, which typically led to a drastic decrease in the real price of electricity often at a time of sharply increasing real input prices. As fuel costs soared in the 1970s and early 1980s, real prices of electricity in Argentina fell by almost one-quarter. The Allende government in Chile pursued a similar policy during the hyperinflation of 1971–1973 (Soto 1999). Beginning with the first oil shock in 1973, control over electricity prices became one of the Brazilian government's primary inflation-fighting tools (Baer and McDonald 1998).

Politicized pricing also yielded perverse economic and even political outcomes. An example can be found in the actions of the Chilean utility Chilectra during the winter of 1978. Concerned that its new thermoelectric unit would not operate at capacity and thus engender criticism for investing in a white elephant, the company offered a subsidy to those users who exceeded their electricity consumption of the previous year. Unsurprisingly, a large number of consumers shifted to electric heating, leading demand to spike beyond even the new level of capacity and causing blackouts that led to high-level political intervention in the pricing reform (Philippi 1991: 30–31).

This combination of politicized investment and pricing led to low operational and financial performance. While network losses averaged 6.7% in the European Union and 7.2% in the US, line losses ranged between 10 and 14% in Argentina, Brazil, and Chile. Despite the huge capacity overhang in Argentina described above, actual reserves were far lower than these headline figures as over one-third of capacity was typically under repair (Vecchia 1993).

In terms of financial performance, Spiller and Martorell (1996) report calculations undertaken by Pires Rodrigues and Braga Monteiro (1991) that in 1989 the average price of billed power in Brazil was more than one-third below the average long-run marginal cost, causing the financial costs of operation for the industry to rise as much as 50% above average revenues. Estache and Rodriguez-Pardina (1998) report that the 65 vertically integrated monopolies in the Brazilian state sector had operating costs 20–30% above efficient levels. Similarly, in Argentina, financial operating losses for the three largest state-owned enterprises over the period 1980–1987 averaged $800 million per annum with return on assets consistently negative and ranging as low as –21% with national rolling blackouts required in 1989 to prevent systemic failure. Chilean utilities Endesa and Chilectra also reported negative returns on assets in 1973 (–4.3 and –3.2% respectively) (Soto 1999).

12.4 Neoliberal reform

By the 1990s, the accumulated negative economic and operational consequences of decades of politically motivated management had in many places reached a level that threatened the financial and physical stability of the electricity supply system. Deteriorating system performance threatened broader macroeconomic growth, both because electricity is a critical input to economic growth, and also as the result of rising public sector debt burdens (Little et al. 1993) driven partly by the borrowing of state-owned electricity companies (Petrazzini 1995). Indeed, the burden was so large in some countries that it precipitated major blackouts or even a full-blown macroeconomic crisis. It was in the face of such focusing events that industrial consumers and other organized interest groups long opposed to state ownership and operation began to collaborate with entrepreneurial politicians, who assembled new broad-based coalitions in favor of reform to successfully attack the state-centered model. The increased dependence of fiscally distressed countries on the international financial community, which strongly advocated neoliberal policies, further accelerated the market-oriented policy reform (Henisz, Zelner, and Guillén 2005).

In response to the growing evidence of government failure, Chile (1978), Argentina (1992), and Brazil (1993) began concerted efforts to increase the emphasis on economic efficiency within the electricity industry by creating a more independent regulatory authority, opening the door to new private investment and privatization of state-owned assets, and compensating new private investors based on long-term private contracts or market-determined spot prices subject to some minimal government regulation. Dr. Bruno Phillipi, later Chief Executive Officer of GENER, described the impetus for the design of the initial Chilean reform of the electricity sector and the creation of the independent National Energy Commission (NEC) in 1978 as an attempt to preempt the political intervention that had occurred in the 1930s. The government knew it would face short-term political pressure from.

private or public industrial groups, whose productivity or sale of services lies on artificial comparative advantages, ... unions of the companies of the [electricity] sector, which [perceive] a threat to the security and privileges of their employment, ... commercial banks and international creditors, who wish to ensure repayment of their credits [and] equipment suppliers who see opportunities to sell their products. (Philippi 1991: 7)

Several years after its inception, the NEC introduced a new, ostensibly apolitical system of price determination for regulated consumers that used a relatively simple dynamic programming model (Spiller and Martorell 1996: 113–114). In addition, the 1982 law also sought to stimulate private investment by reducing unnecessary regulation and promoting a competitive generation sector in which both long-term contracts and a spot market could function. "The law also includes detailed regulations with explicit mechanisms for settling disputes between the regulators and the utilities, with the judiciary as the final arbiter" (Estache and Rodriguez-Pardina 1998: 3). In the words of Fischer and Serra (2000: 189),

> the legislature was interested in assuring potential investors that their investment would not be expropriated by the regulator. Decision power was therefore taken away from the regulators and embedded into the law ... At the time, this revolutionary approach seemed a good bargain: in the early 1980s, Chile needed to convince investors that the rules of the game would not change according to regulatory whim.

Once the regulatory system was established, the government restructured its state-owned assets, separating the functions of regulation, generation, transmission, and distribution in multiple independent entities. Privatization of the resulting firms began in 1981 and continued through 1996, by which point the system had been transformed from one in which the state owned 90% of generation and 80% of distribution (Philippi 1991) to one in which the private sector owned 90% of all generation assets, accounted for 70% of new investment, and owned the transmission grid and virtually all distribution facilities.

The Argentine reforms sought to borrow from the successes of the Chilean model and also to extend them. Argentina's 1992 law established an independent regulatory body with a complex apolitical appointment process for its board of directors and a fee-based budgetary mechanism (Estache and Rodriguez-Pardina 1998). The industry was broken up into multiple generation and distribution companies prior to privatization and restrictions were placed on reintegration (Davis 1997). Complex bands and rules as well as myriad charges and subsidies sought to provide equity to end users and incentives to investors. According to Matty Vengerik, CS-Boston Vice President, the benefits of this "marketization" of the industry included putting "an end to the building of white elephants, since market forces will determine what construction is necessary." Also, "it discourages the return to a policy of nationalization of politically set prices" (Lagniappe Letter Latin American Information Services 1993).

The Brazilian government also declared its privatization objectives in 1992, but plans to privatize Electrobras were quickly shelved due to a corruption investigation that ultimately led to the President's resignation (Independent Power Report 1993). The Brazilian reform effort began in earnest the next year with the passage of laws permitting the state to assume state-owned enterprises' liabilities, abolishing uniform pricing rules, and allowing open access to the national transmission grid (Baer and McDonald 1998). The government also announced its intention to privatize as much as 40 percent of the nation's generating capacity, which officials saw as the "the only way ...[to] raise enough funds to make much needed investments in new generation facilities to meet growing demand" (Independent Power Report 1993). In 1995, another new law was passed to permit the establishment of independent power producers (Maia 1999).

Notably, privatization in Brazil occurred in the absence of a clearly defined regulatory framework and in a system in which considerable uncertainty remained about future pricing and even asset ownership. Early investors therefore relied upon the government's need to attract future investment to mitigate the threat of opportunistic behavior on the part of the state (Baer and McDonald 1998). In 1996, the regulator ANEEL was finally established, with a board of directors serving noncoincident four-year terms and funding from an independent user fee that ensured the regulator's independence (Estache and Rodriguez-Pardina 1998).

12.5 Economic efficiency gains

Reforms in all three countries produced dramatic efficiency gains. In the case of Chile, Galal et al. (1994) document a striking decrease in the average variable cost of one privatized generating company (CHILGENER, later GENER) due largely to increased efficiency in the amount of electricity generated per unit of coal input. Further, total costs declined even more sharply due to an increase in the capacity utilization of CHILGENER's plants from approximately 50% in 1985 to 83.4% in 1989. Data from Estache and Rodriguez-Pardina 1998: 5 and Rudnick 1998: 3 indicate that energy line losses fell from 20.9% in 1986 to 8.6% in 1996 or almost 60%. Fischer and Serra (2000: 184) report that labor productivity increased from 376 clients per worker in 1987 to 703 in 1997. Rudnick (1998) reports that the ratio of GWh to employees at Endesa increased from 2.23 in 1989 to 7.62 in 1996.

As in the case of Chile, substantial efficiency gains were reported in Argentina, especially for the period 1992–2002, during which time the private sector invested $7.5 billion in the sector (Pollitt 2008) and the number of private generators increased from 7 to 33. Investment costs plummeted by over 80%, from $6,000/kW to $1,000/kW (Badaraco 1998), and reliability improved as the number and duration of failures decreased by 30–60% and the average repair time for an outage fell 80% (Badaraco 1999). Electricity theft fell from 28% to 10% of generation. Thermal plant availability, the cause of the 1988–1989 power crisis, quickly rose from 45% to 75% while the number of employees per megawatt was cut in half (Solanet 1994). Given the rise in capital, labor productivity nearly tripled (Pollitt 2008).

In Brazil, efficiency gains from the more modest privatization program were also evident. In the case of the Escelsa, energy losses have fallen from 12% to 9% while staffing has fallen 30%. Profits have tripled from $15.6 million to $47.9 million and the company has no debt (Independent Power Report 1996). In the case of Light, the workforce was slashed by 40% while the average duration of shortages fell by 26.3%, rates were slated to fall by 15%, investment increased 13%, and profits doubled (Moffett 1998). CEMIG laid off 2,200 of 14,594 workers while providing service to 53,000 new consumers and increasing net income by 168%.

12.6 Re-emergent concerns over fairness

Despite the efficiency gains, the reformed systems in the three countries still attracted criticism. In Chile, critics argued from the outset that wealth had effectively been transferred from the state and the people to shareholders and managers of the newly privatized enterprises (Murillo 2009). As evidence, they pointed to the thousandfold appreciation of electric utilities' shares between 1984 and 1994 (Jadresic 1997: 60); rates of return of 30% and rerun on assets as high as 20% in the mid-1990s (Britan and Serra 1998: 951); and the large gap between the 11.4% reduction in tariffs and the 37.4% decline in the cost of generation (Fischer and Serra 2000).

High returns and prices were often alleged to be the result of market power stemming from the lack of restrictions on cross-ownership of assets. Over the course of several years, Endesa had amassed 60 percent of the installed capacity in Chile, control over the largest distributor, ownership of the national transmission grid, and 60 percent of allocated non-consuming water rights (Britan and Serra 1998: 949). The remaining two generators accounted for another 33 percent of installed capacity.

Market power concerns also arose in the negotiations between new entrants into the generation segment and the transmission and distribution companies on which they had to rely to deliver power. So great were the problems that one generator, Colbun, built two parallel high-voltage transmission lines of its own between its plant and Santiago rather than pay the rates charged by Endesa (Diaz and Soto 2002).

The perception that private investors were benefiting at the expense of the broader population eroded popular support for private participation in the electricity industry. In Argentina, a blackout in Buenos Aires caused by a power station fire served as a focusing event to crystallize opposition. Customers who had been without power for more than a week threatened to file a $700 million lawsuit, and the case was dismissed only after Edesur was fined more than $60 million. This outcome satisfied no one: customers felt that they were unfairly compensated for their losses and began to explicitly question the model of private power provision, while politically motivated breach of the $10 million cap on fines in Edesur's contract spooked investors in an uncertain market climate (Wing 1999).

Political support for reform waned especially quickly when narrow segments of the population were forced to bear higher costs. Argentina again provides an example. The national market rules there included price adjustments to reflect capacity constraints on the transmission system, but provincial actors undermined these rules. Demand from Brazil and Uruguay had led to a growing electricity export market that placed strains on the existing transmission infrastructure in the provinces of Cordoba and Mesopotamia. One provincial governor affected by the Brazilian exports responded by rejecting the price increase designed to signal transmission congestion and unilaterally reducing the price to his constituents by 14 percent.

In Brazil, the higher costs that undermined support for the privatization program took the form of layoffs from the recently privatized San Paolo electric utility. A blackout during the 1997 Christmas holiday served as a focusing event that spread this group's unhappiness with the new system. Although record heat and a poor pre-privatization maintenance history certainly contributed to the blackout, the press and public focused on the 40 percent staff cuts, record profits, and weak regulatory supervision. The penalty assessed on the utility (0.1 percent of sales) was seen as only a token punishment (Moffett 1998). Popular support subsequently decreased to the point where Electrobras' remaining generating assets could not be sold and the privatization program was put on hold (Electric Utility Week International 2000).

Another prominent dispute pitted Itamar Franco, the newly elected provincial governor of Minas Gerais and ex-President of Brazil, against Southern Corporation and AES, which had purchased the local utility CEMIG in 1997. Although AES and Southern together owned enough board seats to block board decisions, Franco made the popular case that the national government had failed to pursue the national interest when it structured the agreement to permit the blocking rights. AES and Southern subsequently lost their blocking rights after a legal battle, and Duke and AES both suspended their participation in an auction for the utility Cesp Tiete as a result. According to Luiz Fernando Rolla, the investment relations manager for Cemig, however, Franco sought only "to undermine the President's authority and to be selected as the Presidential candidate for the PMDB for the next election. Politicians' strategies are above any logical thought. He doesn't care if the state is damaged by his strategy" (Euromoney 1999: 46).

12.7 Patchwork policy

Evidence from Brazil and Argentina illustrates both the nature of the "patches" applied by political officials to mollify a contested policy's most vocal and disaffected opponents, as well as the potential for the resulting "patchwork" to reduce other sources of support for the policy. Speaking of Argentina, one interviewee declared: "The theory of how the market would work here has been tinkered, modified, and altered so much in the two years since its introduction that it is difficult to consider the system transparent. We started with a model that looked interesting and well-designed and ended up having one that worked in a completely different manner." Another interviewee opined that "we had laws and the regulatory authority was supposed to act independently, but increasingly they are acting as a consumer watchdog and squeezing the investors like crazy." Related concerns arose in Brazil, where one interviewee contended that, "The implicit message to private investors is that you need to check [industry regulator]

ANEEL's website every Thursday because if you have 290 resolutions already totaling 900 pages, you can be confident that there will be Resolution 291." An industry analyst in Brazil elaborated: "Who is going to ensure that the state will not manipulate prices if the country is faced with a complicated situation – a rise in inflation, for example?" (Pereira 2001).

The cumulative effect of investors' mounting concerns in response to the evolving policy patchwork was ultimately to thwart the attainment of one of the primary objectives – attracting capital – that privatization had originally been intended to achieve. One Enron manager summarized the situation as one in which "chronic uncertainty about the future rules of the market" had halted new development (Global Power Report 2001a). Another Enron official interviewed in a local business daily elaborated: "Investors are comfortable running market risks. But regulatory risks like indefinition [sic] or the possibility of changes in the rules are not risks they are disposed to run" (Global Power Report 2001b). Enron employees were not alone in making such pronouncements. An AES official, for example, put the matter succinctly: "We will not invest in the future [in Brazil] if the rules continue the way they are" (Wisnefski 2001).

A local consultant provided a more nuanced viewpoint: "We Brazilians believe that these regulations will come out sooner or later. If you want to invest in Brazil, you have, to some extent, to make a leap of faith. You can't wait for all the rules to be made – you'll be dead by that time! Most of the time things in Brazil are in a gray zone" (Kaplan 1997). Another explained that "the regulatory environment in Brazil is an ever-changing scenario. That's the way we do things." "Deregulation has a speed limit in Brazil. We have to consolidate investment capacity at a reasonable pace otherwise the economy will be completely dominated by foreign investors. Competition is good so long as it is controlled by the government."

The problems in Argentina were even more pronounced, especially after the 2002 financial crisis, when the government fixed electricity prices in pesos in direct violation of contractual guarantees made to foreign investors whose debts were denominated mainly in dollars. When many of these investors declared bankruptcy and new investment ground to a halt, customers again confronted shortages, rationing, and blackouts as pricing subsidies caused demand to surge. One interviewee explained that, "The only thing that the government cares about is the tariff faced by consumers so that they can say that they are helping their constituents." Other interviewees emphasized the incompatibility of "market" and "political" objectives: "They don't understand the system. They just don't like it. Even worse, instead of letting the rules and regulatory framework work and then change the rules when they don't like the outcome, the government gives the regulator the outcome that they want for political reasons and then forces the regulatory rules and framework to produce that outcome." Public-sector interviewees were equally cynical: "The government lacks commitment to the market and to the private sector. It is always trying to solve problems in a regulatory or administrative manner. The government is still trying to drive the economy as a central planning team. The new government hasn't accepted the change in the role of the market in Argentina."

12.8 The future of electricity generation in Argentina, Brazil, and Chile

Politicians' interest in investment, employment, and electricity pricing does not end with the adoption of privatization and other market-oriented reforms, and no regulatory design can permanently eliminate political influences from the electricity generation industry, especially in the aftermath of focusing events around which various groups rally to promote their interests. Writing in 1993, former Argentine electricity minister Carlos Bastos aptly summarized:

All government administrations are always interested in public utilities, whether privately- or state-owned. The chief executive officers of the sector enterprises know that they are exposed to potential government interference such as expropriation, price controls, significant changes in the terms of the concession, or simply intervention in the form of central planning ... The temptation for the government and the regulators to make business decisions that affect the behavior of the power sector is always present. (Bastos and Abdala 1993)

In Argentina, Brazil, and Chile, political officials in recent years acted at the behest of a growing coalition of consumers, workers, and other stakeholders who perceived the distribution of the returns from privatization to be unfair or illegitimate. Also writing in 1993, Nobel Laureate Vargas Llosa declared that:

With the type of privatization that is pursued at the moment, the principal benefits of [economic] growth favor exclusively small elite. This is a big mistake because in ten years we will have a contrary reaction against the free market and privatization. Populism will again find a propitious round in Latin America ... The only way to avoid this effect is to assure that the market takes its roots in the practical life of the majority of the population. Otherwise, everything is reversible, because the economically underprivileged population will not believe in the market as an instrument of progress. (quoted in Manzetti 1999: 330)

Governments in all three countries have chipped away at the private sector model, implementing patches to market-oriented policy frameworks to restore objectives associated with the public sector model. It is likely that, as has occurred in the past, the resulting patchwork will eventually collapse under the weight of its rising costs. When such a collapse occurs, a new cycle will begin.

12.9 Conclusion

The cases of the Argentinean, Brazilian, and Chilean electricity generation industries illustrate the model of policy cycling outlined at the beginning of this chapter. What lessons do this model and the three countries' experiences provide for the future? The most obvious is the difficulty of sustaining the "pure" public or private sector model given the realities of the policymaking process. Although a hybrid system that balances conflicting preferences for efficiency and redistribution holds theoretical appeal, the dysfunction that such systems have exhibited when implemented on a *de facto* basis, together with the formal policymaking process's "stick-slip" dynamics and consequent overshooting, suggest that cycling may itself may be the most stable outcome possible over the long term.

If correct, this prognosis may not be as dire as it at first blush sounds. By implementing appropriate strategies, private investors who explicitly recognize the cyclicality of public policies governing the generation of electricity may reap economic rewards for themselves, and in the process provide gains for consumers as well. As one investor explained to us:

> I try to treat the problem [with the government officials] as one that needs to be managed. I am still objecting to the new price and trying to put it up [*sic*], but I know that the contracts are likely to be changed. If there is a regulated price, the price will be used for political purposes. If anyone assumes that there will be no changes, it is naïve. It is more than naïve, it is stupid. Any kind of regulation should contain fundamental elements and changing elements. In any pattern of change, you have waves. Now, we are in a transient period. There will be times with disputes and discussions, and times to focus on the market. It is possible, in such a system, to have investment.

13 | Politics and the manufacturing of a transatlantic market for civil aviation (1944–2010)

YANNIS KARAGIANNIS AND ADRIENNE HÉRITIER

13.1 Introduction

This chapter focuses on the manufacturing of markets in transatlantic aviation. For half a century between the mid-1940s and the mid-1990s, transatlantic trade in air transport services was one of the tightest-regulated markets in the industrial world. Much of this changed in April 2007: in one of the most economically and politically important instances of manufacturing international markets in recent years, the European Union (EU) and the US signed an Open Skies Agreement (OSA). That OSA plans the liberalization of transatlantic air transport, and the European Commission (Commission) has described it as "historic," marking a "new era" where "the benefits for consumers could reach €12 billion over the first five years [and] the Agreement could lead to the creation of 80,000 jobs" (European Commission 2007). But, if the OSA is so beneficial, why did it not occur earlier? Why wasn't the Commission, whose instrumental involvement brought such benefits, called upon in the 1990s or even before that?

To answer these questions we examine the literature on the history of transatlantic aviation from 1944 to 2010. We present a narrative that covers more than sixty years of international aviation politics, but our focus is on specific interactions between identifiable actors. We wish to understand how the preferences of various actors combined with the strategic environment in which they act played out to produce the institutional and policy outcomes we observe. By doing so, we hope to contribute to an improved understanding of the political economy of manufacturing markets in aviation – and beyond.

We explain the events that led to the liberalization outcome using the techniques of analytic narratives:

1) An extensive review of the literature to (a) gain a deep understanding of the policy stakes involved in various events; (b) build a preliminary narrative; and (c) find points of divergence and/or weak points in existing explanatory accounts; and
2) Use of game-theoretical concepts, especially subgame perfection, to adjudicate between competing social-scientific explanations and/or fill in incomplete claims (Levi 2004).

From the extant literature we retain three lessons: (1) the US and various European countries have often been antagonistic in aviation matters; (2) some authors interpret this history in rationalistic terms, whereby policy outcomes are determined jointly by the strategies of various actors; others adopt a constructivist perspective, whereby policy outcomes are determined by the joint effect of radical uncertainty and social processes; and (3) the OSA of 2007 was made possible by the successful involvement of the Commission in aviation, which corresponded to a pooling of sovereignty at the EU level to counteract the US's divide and rule strategy to conquer European markets. On these bases, we ask two questions: (1) is the evidence advanced by constructivist accounts compelling enough to abandon the assumption of rationality? And (2) if the OSA of 2007 was the result of Europe's unity against the US aggression, why was the latter an equilibrium strategy for the US? Why, that is, didn't the US correctly anticipate the backlash that their aggressive strategy would create?

Our discussion is organized as follows. Section 13.2 offers a presentation of all the analytical tools we use in assessing the narrative. Section 13.3 reviews the recent literature to start building a preliminary narrative; to identify and discuss the most relevant arguments. Section 13.4 answers the two main questions identified from the narrative. Section 13.5 concludes.

13.2 Our analytical toolbox

This section presents the tools we employ in our reading of the extant literature, and in our selection of particular events for further analysis. We present our concepts of (1) "events"; (2) equilibrium; (3) actors' (unobserved) preferences; and (4) nested games.

13.2.1 Carefully defined events

In the analysis of public policies it is often tempting to focus on long-term, complex processes. William H. Riker (1957: 61) defined events as "the existence ... of some sort of perceived motion or action, sometime, somewhere" in a larger context of an infinitely moving reality imagining "starts and stops. What lies between the starts and stops we call events" consisting of a situation as (1) "an arrangement and condition of movers and actors in a specified, instantaneous, and spatially extended location" and (2) an event as "the motion and action occurring between an initial situation and a terminal situation such that all and only the movers and actors of the initial situation ... are included in the terminal situation." Riker demonstrated that arguments about ambiguously defined events carry the danger of wrong inferences, and argues that "[o]ne sensible way the scientist can minimize unnoticed entrance and exit is to work with small events."

13.2.2 Equilibrium and subgame perfect equilibrium

We use the concept of Nash equilibrium (NE) as a situation where two or more players adjust their strategies so as to make them mutually optimal so that no one has an incentive to unilaterally deviate from their strategy given what the others are doing (see Osborne 2004: 11–52). The conversion of simultaneous games (where NEs are found) into sequential games, which may represent more accurate descriptions of reality, creates subgames and makes some strategies non-credible; subgame perfection and the definition of subgame perfect equilibrium (SPE) serve to eliminate such strategies and therefore reduce the number of NEs. The identification of preferences and incentives are central in finding SPE (see Osborne 2004: 164–168).

13.2.3 Actors' preferences

Preferences are a tricky subject in political science because (1) they are unobservable; and (2) the 1980s invasion of sociological and historical "new institutionalism" has driven scholars' attention to institutions. Yet, although institutions are obviously central for explaining political-economic outcomes they are only part of the story and the two building blocks and the equation central to politics is said to be:

Preferences × *Institutions* = *Outcomes*

We take the difficulties associated with researching the preferences as a warning: (1) we operate an analytical distinction between the actors' preferences and their actions; (2) we resist the double temptation of imputing preferences by assertion or by *ex post hoc* observation of distributive outcomes; and (3) we check for the observational equivalence of different social-scientific theories.

13.2.4 Nested games

Often, political games are too complex to be reduced to the analysis of a single event. Interactions may involve too many actors and be too complex to be described as tractable games and/or simple subgames. For example, politicians who bargain over the terms of a trade agreement play a bargaining game at the international arena; but they also play a delegation game with those on behalf of whom they negotiate in the national arena. Therefore, the payoffs of the game in the principal arena are influenced by the prevailing conditions in the secondary (secondary for the analyst) arena. The "inputs" of one game into another are often encouraged by a country's constitution, and often themselves the object of strategizing. A player's actions may appear sub-optimal or irrational in one arena if one fails to take into account his motivations in a sub-arena (Tsebelis 1990: 5).

13.3 The narrative: method, history, and remaining questions

Some detailed scholarship has been devoted to the analysis of the politics of transatlantic air transport liberalization that we use to build a preliminary narrative, and to evaluate extant arguments. We then analyze the narrative with the help of game-theoretical concepts (especially subgame perfection) to arrive at a more accurate explanation (e.g., Milgrom and Roberts 1982; Weingast 1998). In building the narrative we prioritize works which (1) are recent and incorporate

The transatlantic market for civil aviation (1944–2010)   275

previous findings; (2) are political-scientific or political-economic; and (3) present the basic concepts of aviation economics. Using these criteria, the most relevant works for us here are those of Kassim and Stevens (2010), Meunier (2005), Rhoades (2008), Staniland (2003), and Woll (2008).

Because commercial aviation across the Atlantic did not develop before World War II, our starting point is the Convention on International Civil Aviation, decided in Chicago in December 1944. Participants from more than 40 countries aimed at establishing world air routes, and the regulatory framework for international commercial aviation for the post-war period. On economic matters, the US advocated full liberalization with some restrictions on the freedom to pick and discharge traffic at intermediate points. Liberalization was opposed by the UK, Australia, New Zealand, and to a lesser extent the Continental Europeans, all of whom advocated an international order based on absolute national sovereignty. The UK, in particular, was strongly opposed to liberalization because its control of numerous airports across the globe, at which most aircraft operating international routes still had to land, gave it a formidable bargaining tool in bilateral negotiations with the US and France. The US then proposed separate agreements embodying the extent to which nations would grant each other reciprocal air rights, referred to as the "Freedoms of the Air."

The "Chicago Convention" was not as biased in favor of the US as the country's political and economic clout would imply. On the one hand, Chicago did set out various possibilities for trade in air rights. Since the Europeans would not support a multilateral system based on the liberal "Freedoms," countries were allowed to exchange traffic rights using bilateral Air Service Agreements (ASAs). ASAs typically contained provisions on traffic rights, capacity, number of carriers to serve routes, and prices. This meant that the US could affect the strategies, and therefore the competitiveness, of those foreign carriers wishing to fly there.

On the other hand, the US made many concessions: The Convention defined strict national sovereignty rights over airspace; created the United Nations' International Civil Aviation Organization (ICAO) to supervise agreements; and obliged the US to effectively accept a cartel – which was formed with the creation of the International Air Transport Association (IATA). The latter would stabilize prices and fix quantities, thereby limiting the scope of efficient US carriers to compete with smaller European ones. On these legal bases, bilateral inter-governmental agreements known as ASAs rapidly proliferated and fixed all "market" conditions. The most influential of them was the Bermuda agreement, signed in 1946 between the US and the UK. And the most important feature of these agreements is the "nationality clause," which restricts access to carriers that are owned by nationals of the contracting states. Considering the narrative on Chicago, the questions remain: *Why did the US give in to European (especially British) demands in Chicago? What credible threat did the Europeans make?*

These anti-competitive ASAs mirrored the conditions within most countries. In the UK, the two largest carriers, the British Overseas Airways Corporation and British European Airlines, were not only nationalized in 1946, but also allowed to engage in market-sharing. In France, the 1945 wave of nationalizations saw the creation of Air France, which received a monopoly over the management of the entire French air transport network, as well as advantageous (monopolistic) regulation, especially from 1963 to 1986. Even in ordo-liberal Germany, Lufthansa was under state ownership, and air transport was exempt from the normal application of antitrust rules. In the US, where carriers were private, the Civil Aeronautics Board (CAB) regulated both entry and prices. Crucially, it was also responsible for the antitrust scrutiny of international agreements and mergers. Hence, restrictive as the ASAs may have been, they were not more so than national rules and regulations.

In the meanwhile, the equilibrium reached in Chicago and the ensuing ASAs became increasingly unstable. In the US, in 1950 Pan Am, one of the two main US carriers engaged in international operations, invented the "economy class," thereby signaling its intention to cut prices. In Europe, the German carrier Lufthansa was re-created in 1955, thus putting pressure on the Dutch carrier KLM, which could not rely on its small domestic market, and had therefore heavily invested in Germany. KLM pressed for improved access to US airports, and lesser competition by US airlines in its home market. After the US government granted these conditions to KLM, US carriers became more conscious of international politics. When France asked for the recognition of the principle of reciprocity, as well as the right to fly to the West Coast and then on to the Pacific, the US refused. France accused the US of developing a hypocritically liberal rhetoric, which failed to mask protectionist policies favoring Pan Am and TWA. The protracted negotiations that followed ended up with the denunciation by the French government of the 1946 ASA.

Another crucial development of the 1950s concerned the invention of a new airline business model by Delta Air Lines in 1955, namely the hub-and-spoke model (HSM). HSM is a system of connections arranged like a chariot wheel, in which all traffic moves along spokes connected to a central hub. The spread of the HSM affects the cost structure of carriers, hence their incentives to consolidate, and hence the fear of national governments to see their flag carriers be absorbed by foreign competitors. To grasp the political-economic consequences of HSM, it is useful to understand how the HSM – given the cost structure of carriers[1] – contributes to economies of scope. Modern international carriers seek to achieve economies of scope by growing horizontally. Economies of scope occur when a multi-product firm can produce a given range of differentiated goods at a lower total cost than the total cost of producing that variety in separate firms. In international aviation, the average cost of a multi-product carrier decreases with the number of origin-destination pairs it serves. This is precisely the function of the HSM, which spread in the US in the late 1970s, and then throughout the world in the 1980s and 1990s. In HSM a carrier flies passengers from a set of "spoke" airports through a central "hub," where passengers change planes and then fly to their outbound destinations. This system increases traffic volume between the spoke airports and the hub, increasing the load factor (passenger/seat ratio) of aircraft, which in turn makes the use of comparatively cheaper large aircraft profitable, and thus spreads flight-specific fixed costs.

The next important step concerns two exogenous shocks in the first half of the 1970s: the commercialization of wide-body jets and the OPEC crisis of 1973. Wide-body jets were introduced in 1970 and

---

[1] The bulk of costs of carriers falls under three categories: (1) fixed overhead costs (e.g., general and administrative expenses, advertising); (2) flight-sensitive costs, a function of the number of flights (e.g., fuel); and (3) traffic-sensitive costs, a function of the number of passengers (e.g., food). Once a schedule is set, only traffic-sensitive costs are variable. This shows that aviation is a capital intensive industry and that a carrier operating short of capacity must cover at least its variable costs by disposing of unsold seats at a low price. This creates a strong incentive to reduce prices and even risk price wars, which in turn means that carriers are particularly vulnerable to cyclical lows in demand. Hence the incentive to form cartels (private or public).

represented big increases in efficiency. For similar load factors, they made flights considerably cheaper for those carriers who could invest in the new technology. Those, like the UK's BOAC (British Airways' long-haul state-owned predecessor), which could not switch fast were at big risk. Combined with the effect of the oil crisis and the enduring crisis regarding rights to fly over the Pacific, this put insurmountable pressure on the original 1946 Bermuda ASA between the US and the UK. In a prolonged bargaining process, the UK asked for (1) tighter controls on capacity; (2) the end of double designation (i.e., the authorization of services by more than one airline per country on a particular route); (3) the curb on Fifth Freedom rights exercised by Pan Am and TWA through Heathrow;[2] and (4) rights to more US cities for British carriers. The new ("Bermuda II") agreement reached in 1977 abolished American Fifth Freedom rights from Heathrow to four major European cities, allowed for annual approval of capacity, granted the UK the right to fly to six additional US cities, and limited the liberal arrangements for the new competitors of incumbent European flag carriers, the charter airlines. These particularly favorable conditions, coupled with the extraordinary importance of Heathrow in the transatlantic aviation market, enabled the UK to resist the pressure that led other countries to open skies agreements with the US from the late 1970s to the present.

The 1980s were also marked by two highly significant developments. On the one hand stands the completion of the full liberalization of the US domestic market, and on the other hand the progressive development of a European air transport policy. Regarding US policy developments, the CAB and its anti-competitive regulatory policies was progressively phased out, until the organization was finally absorbed by the Department of Transportation in 1985. The end of entry and price regulation in the domestic US market signified the beginning of a competitive era of industry growth, coupled with frequent price wars and numerous reorganization bankruptcy filings. It also meant that, whereas the US had been able to cope for four decades with the nationality clause in international ASAs, and in particular with the convention of designating one or at most two airlines to operate from

---

[2] "Fifth Freedom" rights allow an airline to carry traffic between foreign countries as part of services connecting the airline's own country. In this case, Pan Am and TWA could carry passengers and cargo from London to various other European airports, including Frankfurt.

each state, it now had to re-negotiate its ASAs to allow for more US firms on each route. But, would a country like the UK or France allow three or four US carriers with deep pockets to operate commercial flights in exchange for the same rights as before, for the same single state-owned airline as before? As we shall see, the answer is no. The US had to find a way to make these countries accept the fact that there were now more and more competitive US carriers.

At the same time in Europe, the Commission took certain important liberalizing initiatives. Although neither the 1985 Commission White Paper on the Completion of the Internal Market nor the 1986 Single European Act were long on aviation, the tacit alliance between the Commission and the ECJ allowed the former to force the hand of national governments into accepting its three legislative packages. This raises the question: *Why did the Europeans accept American ideas about the benefits of liberalized aviation markets in the mid-1980s?* Kassim and Stevens (2010) and Woll (2008) also talk of important ideational changes, whereby protectionist governments and survival-minded carriers gradually came to accept more liberal views because they considered the US deregulation policy a success. Taken together, these packages (1987, 1990, and 1992) formed the basis of a pro-competitive European aviation policy. Coupled with a series of important liberalizing rulings by the ECJ, the commercialization of public carriers, and the development of an important low-cost industry, they helped create a competitive European market.

There was, however, much less progress regarding the role of the EU in transatlantic aviation. In a 1994 ruling the ECJ held that international agreements on air transportation did not fall under the Community's trade policy competence, because they were covered by separate articles in the EU Treaty. This drawback for the Commission meant that the US could still attempt to divide and rule the Europeans. But the way this strategy was implemented was crucial to its success. Despite their liberal rhetoric within Europe, the British would not negotiate more rights to Heathrow. The strategy had to initiate from elsewhere. The new "Open Skies" initiative of the 1990s therefore started from the conveniently located Netherlands. The US idea consisted in gaining foothold in Amsterdam Schiphol, from where they would threaten to divert international traffic outbound from the UK, France, and of course Germany – unless, that is, these countries signed their own OSA with the US. In order to lure the Dutch into the plan, the US reminded them that their international cost-saving and market-enlarging alliance with Northwest Airlines benefited from an antitrust immunity which was not set in stone. The same combination of incentives could be used elsewhere. *But why was the American "carrot" of conditional antitrust immunity for alliances between a US and a European carrier credible?* Despite loud protests from the Commission, which feared that a series of small bilateral OSAs would endanger the unity of the European market and prevent the possibility of mergers in Europe due to the nationality clause in OSAs, the plan worked. A "domino effect" swept Europe, reaching first small countries (bilateral OSAs were signed with the Netherlands in 1992; Belgium, Luxembourg, Denmark, Finland, and Austria in 1995) and then, as predicted, larger ones (Germany in 1996, and France and Italy in 1998). "KLM-nomics" had apparently worked. Thus, *KLM's business strategy seems to have been crucial in undermining European unity. Yet, if it is explained by the country's colonial past, why didn't France, the UK, Portugal, or Belgium have similar preferences? If the small size of its domestic market explains liberal preferences, why didn't Portugal or Belgium have the same preferences as the Netherlands?*

But the US strategy backfired. Starting at the end of the 1990s, the Commission, the ECJ, and eventually even the national governments adopted a different strategy. Particularly important in that process was the ECJ's 2002 "Open Skies" ruling, according to which (1) several provisions in the bilateral OSAs infringed EU law, and (2) certain provisions in OSAs with third countries could only be negotiated by the Commission. This gave the Commission a lever to force member governments to give it a mandate to negotiate an OSA with the US.

As Kassim and Stevens note:

The second open skies initiative launched by the US in the 1990s … played a major role in the battle between the Commission and the member states over the development of an external dimension to EU action. Washington's aggressive policy of divide-and-rule vis-à-vis the European governments allowed the Commission to mobilize support for, and ultimately to persuade member governments of the advantages of, granting the Community a mandate to negotiate traffic rights with third countries. Its previous failed attempts suggest that, without the manoeuverings by the US, the Commission may not have been able to strategize as effectively. (Kassim and Stevens 2010: 7–8)

This begs the question: If three factors explain why the Commission could previously not acquire a role in aviation (the presence of efficient incumbent actors, the national governments' preferences, and the ambiguous provisions of the Treaty), what explains its success in defining such a role in 1997? And, if the US strategy consisted in "dividing and ruling" the Europeans, why did the US press so hard with it as to provoke the involvement of the EU?

In February 2003, the Commission's new-found role allowed it to announce a plan to negotiate a new, EU-wide agreement with the US. In March 2003, the Council of Ministers endorsed it unanimously. And, four years later, a new OSA was agreed with the US, to the Europeans' (partial) satisfaction.

13.4 Theoretical analysis

In this section we present a theoretical explanation offering an answer to the open questions, while seeking to avoid (1) ambiguous events, and (2) unsubstantiated assumptions about actors and their preferences. We first adjudicate between the competing claims of constructivists and rationalists, then develop an explanatory model based on what we learned from the narrative.

13.4.1 Rational profit-maximizers or sociological identity-seekers?

The literature is divided between rationalistic and constructivist arguments. On the one hand, international aviation is depicted as a "strategic, politically sensitive, and highly visible sector" (Kassim and Stevens 2010: 4), where even non-majoritarian bureaus, where incentives are presumably low-powered, are utility-maximizers. On the other hand, some authors argue that actors learn ideational lessons that change their materially defined preferences, or that big carriers are often caught in a situation of radical ("Knightian") uncertainty (Woll 2008). This renders the behavioral status of the main actors unclear. Moreover, actors' preferences are mostly asserted or "observed" rather than derived. It is assumed that governments are (1) unitary actors with no conflicts between departments, and (2) faithful representatives of their domestic carriers. One exception is the derivation of carriers' preferences from the economics of scale and scope in aviation economics.

Kassim and Stevens (2010) and Meunier (2005), for example, both analyze the politics of transatlantic aviation from an institutionalist viewpoint, but refer to both rationalistic and sociological institutionalist assumptions. More explicitly Woll claims that "the preference formation of economic actors is socially embedded. ... I dispute policy models that assume that the activities of economic actors are materially determined" (Woll 2008: 3–4). She adds, "I do not claim that firms behave in ways that conflict with their economic self-interest. Rather, how firms make sense of their economic interests in a complex setting depends on the historical and structural embeddedness of the relations they maintain with governments and competitors" (Woll 2008: 8). When it comes to specific interactions, however, airlines, officials, and even consumers were all able to depart from existing structures and advocate innovative policies. The evidence offered in favor of constructed identities is (1) low-cost JetBlue's public support of Virgin America's entry in the US market; and (2) European airlines' conversion to free trade following the first OSAs (for the narrative on JetBlue and European airlines' preferences, see Woll 2008: 97–125).

Methodologically, the constructivist claims rest on three unjustified assumptions. First, they assume that preferences are observable and genuinely revealed. This confuses preferences and actions.[3] Second, they attribute a causal role to evolving preferences without controlling for institutions. For example, Kassim and Stevens argue that US deregulation changed the opportunity structure for EU involvement because of its favorable ideational impact, but do not control for institutional developments inside the EU (Kassim and Stevens 2010: 7). Third, the inferences rely on the analysis of complex and lengthy "events." In a long period the observation of evolving preferences is neither surprising nor particularly useful, because such lengthy episodes include too many strategic situations.

Empirically, it may be argued that cognitive shifts may be accounted for by another than the constructing of identities. The hypothesis of cognitive shifts is observationally equivalent to well-known results in industrial organization economics. Using the instances of JetBlue's public support for Virgin America's entry into the US market, and European carriers' supposed conversion to liberalism, one can argue

---

[3] For example, Woll infers from the fact that government officials say so that the US government's foremost concern is consumer welfare (Woll 2008: 111).

that firms often play signaling games of deterrence, where an incumbent is challenged by a potential competitor who seeks a license to operate. Both the potential competitor and investors want to know the incumbent's ability to compete, but this is private information. The incumbent has two options: (1) lobby to protect its rent; or (2) publicly welcome competitors. Lobbying may seem less costly, but it does not send the right signal of competitiveness. Because welcoming competition seems irrational if undertaken by a weak firm, signaling is like playing "chicken": if you refuse to play, you have already played and lost. The upshot is that JetBlue's actions (or European carriers in general) did not reveal its (their) true preference(s) for sharing its (their) profits; it is at least as likely that exactly the opposite occurred.

13.4.2 Our explanatory model: rationality and political limit pricing

We start from the observation in Kassim and Stevens: "Its emergence as a decision-making arena and regulatory actor has established the Union as an international actor in key areas of air transport and the partner (and rival?) of the US, which has been the hegemonic power in aviation since 1945" (Kassim and Stevens 2010: 8). We expect our model to explain: (1) why did the US pursue their divide-and-rule strategy so aggressively as to provoke the emergence of the EU as an antagonistic force? And (2) why didn't that outcome occur earlier?

We define a "political limit pricing" nested game with two stylized actors and develop it based on core insights of the presented narrative. One actor is a US bureaucrat ("bureaucrat"). The US department with responsibility for international aviation (the CAB from 1944 to 1979, then the DoJ 1979–1984, and from then onwards the DoT), together with the State Department, defined the form of ASAs and OSAs which were subsequently adopted by all countries. The other actor is a European government, British, French, and to lesser extent German governments ("government"). From the fact that this is international politics, the game is non-cooperative, not a coordination game, but an area of traditionally antagonistic interests between the US and European governments.

The bureaucrat seeks to maximize a utility function with two arguments, one representing her career concern, and the other the US public interest. Ever since the 1970s there has been antagonism between

DoJ and DoT, each advocating a policy closer to its own mandate (antitrust and competitiveness respectively). At the same time all US departments have defended an international aviation policy based on a vague "public interest," which includes foreign policy objectives. In general international aviation is a policy area where most governments, including those with liberal policies like the US after 1978, protect and represent their own carriers. The US pursue a liberal rhetoric on some issues (e.g., access, price-fixing), but not on others (ownership).

Given that most governments protect and represent their own carriers, and given that international transatlantic aviation has traditionally been an area of antagonistic interests, ever since the 1980s there have been calls by the European Commission for greater involvement in international aviation policy issues. However, national governments have been reluctant to oblige, each preferring to negotiate directly with the DoT and State Department since delegating powers to the European Commission comes at a cost in terms of sovereignty and ideal policy point.

Henceforth, we refer to the US bureaucrat as "bureaucrat," to the European government as "government," and to the European Commission as "Commission." The bureaucrat moves first and makes an offer for the exchange of traffic rights. She can either follow an aggressive bargaining strategy, offering an uneven division of the gains from trade, or she can make a "limit" offer. *A limit offer is a more generous proposal that makes it just preferable for the government to accept it than to reject it.* Having received the bureaucrat's offer, the government moves second. It can either accept or reject the offer. If it rejects it, it delegates international negotiating powers to the Commission. Finally, if the government delegates powers to the Commission, the bureaucrat gets a chance to play again, and she can either follow an aggressive bargaining position against the Commission, or be accommodating and collaborative.

Having specified the players and their strategies, our description of this "event" will be complete if we specify payoffs. Regarding the bureaucrat, her career concern and public interest mandate are served better when she negotiates agreements with individual governments than when she negotiates with the Commission, because of the divide-and-rule effect. She thus prefers keeping the Commission out of the aviation arena. Regarding the government, delegating powers to the

Commission comes both at a sovereignty cost and at the cost of a movement away from its ideal policy point. It too thus prefers keeping the Commission out, provided the bureaucrat makes a credible fair offer.[4]

The question is under what circumstances the bureaucrat's limit pricing offer is credible: When can it discourage the government from involving the Commission by making a marginally good-enough offer? Will the government observe the good-enough offer and infer that it would not be as well off if the Commission got involved? This question is worth asking particularly given that Chicago, IATA, ASAs, and OSAs are relatively stable institutions which tend to last decades. Nevertheless, an ASA or an OSA can be denounced at a relatively low cost. A first line of argument is to propose that the government delegate negotiating powers to the Commission just once, to see what happens. Because of the sunk sovereignty and policy costs, however, this is not an attractive solution: there is no experimentation option.

A second line of argument is to examine the *subgame perfection* of the bureaucrat's offer. A limit offer is effectively one where the bureaucrat makes a promise and a threat, and still maximizes its utility function. The promise is to not denounce the agreement immediately after the spectre of the Commission has gone; the threat is to negotiate harder against the Commission than with individual governments; and the optimality condition is that these strategies still allow her to further her career concern and her public interest mandate. Under these conditions, the limit offer will work if the bureaucrat does not need to make too many concessions to the government in order to avoid the involvement of the Commission. This occurs where the Commission is a relatively unattractive option for the government, i.e., where the government's threat to delegate powers to the Commission is not subgame perfect, either because the government is nationalistic or because the Commission holds policy preferences too far removed from the ideal policy point of the government.

The limit offer will only be a subgame perfect equilibrium if the government expects that the bureaucrat will carry out her threat to

---

[4] In this setting, any calls by the US bureaucrat in favor of the involvement of the Commission, sometimes interpreted as sincere in the literature, are intended to make the government more suspicious of that strategy.

negotiate harder with the Commission than with the individual government, *even once the latter has delegated powers to the Commission.* For this it has to know that the bureaucrat benefits from systematically opposing the Commission rather than collaborating with the latter. Specifically, if the concessions the bureaucrat can make to the government are not very important, and the latter's cost of delegating powers to the Commission are not very high, the latter option of aggressive bargaining, delegation to the Commission, and accommodation is more likely. For, if the bureaucrat cannot benefit from systematically opposing the Commission, then the government cannot rationally believe the opposite. On the contrary, the government should anticipate that if it delegates to the Commission, the bureaucrat will collaborate. Thus, the government should do so, even where the bureaucrat has made a limit offer at the first stage of the game. And the bureaucrat should anticipate that it cannot prevent the involvement of the Commission, even with a limit offer.

Against the background of this theoretical argument our reading of the historical narrative is that, for most of the post-World War II era, the US developed a non-renegotiation commitment technology, which consisted in setting the standard for ASAs and OSAs. Because these documents were drafted by the US, the US favored their becoming the international standard. And their becoming the international standard assured individual national governments that the US would not renege. At the same time, a commitment technology for ASAs did not mean that the US could not go further. The French case in 1958 and, above all, Bermuda II and the Dutch OSA of 1992 prove that further concessions were possible – and indeed useful to the US, who could thereby signal good intentions, and thereby further remove the threat of a unified European answer.

Finally, if the US could profitably engage in limit offers, why do we observe the increasing involvement of the Commission from the mid-1990s onwards? We argue that the US ceased its limit offer strategy, asked for terms which the Europeans perceived as excessively aggressive and divisive, and thus provoked the delegation of powers to the Commission. But why didn't the US correctly anticipate this? Our answer rests on the concept of nested games: the US were involved simultaneously in games of international bargaining and in games of domestic politics. We know that the DoJ has been very antagonistic to the DoT. Since the DoT's payoffs in the international bargaining game depended on the prevailing conditions in the game played against the DoJ, the DoT faced a variable payoff structure.

Just as the 1982 presidential election led to a redistribution of roles in favor of DoT, the approach of the 1996 presidential election and the prospect of renewed antitrust enforcement efforts highlighted the DoJ's claim on the antitrust immunization powers of DoT. For that reason, DoT had to act fast to (1) get the immunities out, and (2) present a record of service to the public interest. Hence, domestic political struggles led to too aggressive a policy towards the Europeans. At the same time, a similar nested game – not discussed here – was at work in Europe: despite its ambiguity, the ECJ ruling of 2002 led to a situation where the Commission by systematically threatening infringement procedures could force member states to grant it the long requested sole negotiation mandate with the US.

Finally, our model captures important elements of more distant events, throwing light on why many concessions were made by the US to the Europeans with a weak fallback position in Chicago in 1944; why the 1958 concessions were made to France regarding rights to the West Coast and beyond, just as the entry into force of the EEC Treaty signaled the renewed prospects of European integration; and the signing of Bermuda II with the UK in 1978, just as the UK started its tumultuous life as a member state of the EU.

13.5 Conclusion

We have presented a method to systematically summarize and assess the literature on the politics of manufacturing markets in transatlantic aviation. We have outlined what we know or can infer about this history, and of questions which are still beyond our knowledge. We then theorized many apparently distinct events in a sixty-year-old history by presenting a nested game of political limit-pricing where the US offers policy concessions (Bermuda I, Bermuda II, OSAs) in return for negotiating market conditions with individual European states. Finally, we have discussed the rationality behind this materially important instance of institutional change, and how the nestedness of political games has brought about a liberalization of transatlantic markets which did not seem very probable a few years ago. A nested game of political limit-pricing, *mutatis mutandis*, holds for other sectors of trade liberalization such as the energy markets. Here, too, the outcome over a contest of who negotiates a bilateral agreement of liberalization of markets with whom may be accounted for by looking at political limit-pricing in a context of nested arenas.

PART V

The challenge of balancing public and private ordering

Introduction to Part V

ERIC BROUSSEAU AND JEAN-MICHEL GLACHANT

The three chapters in this section deal with the regulation of financial markets. On the one hand, the specific characteristics of these markets – which are central in an economy because they mediate the various markets of goods and services and they also interconnect markets across time – might justify grouping these contributions together to point out the specificities of financial regulation. In particular, the far-reaching effect of financial crises and the importance of trust in financial systems justify for many a specific thinking on the issue. On the other hand, the commonalities between financial markets and other markets can be well highlighted. Systemic collapses threaten many other markets. Behind the idea of trust lies the question of the balance between the private capabilities and the public ones. In most markets, the government means are much weaker than those of the private actors if they coordinate or massively bypass regulations, for instance by off-shoring key components of their activities. What unifies these three contributions and makes them complementary to the other contributions in this book, then, is the fact that they discuss this complex relationship between the public regulatory capabilities and the market forces. They highlight the narrow path for public ordering between ineffective command and control and inefficient "laissez faire." The art of market regulation consists in leveraging the animal spirit of agents, to avoid having them coordinating on fallacies. This is true in finance, but also in the electricity industry, in digital networks, as well as in several other domains.

The historical narrative by Larry Neal provides an illuminative analysis of the obstacles facing those who attempt to build markets by rational design. While there were no formal stock exchanges in London, Paris, or Amsterdam to handle the increase in transactions that accompanied the Mississippi and South Sea bubbles of 1720, the Beurs in Amsterdam and Exchange Alley in London were already the sites where trading in financial securities took place. These places developed on the basis of innovations in contractual arrangements. When John Law attempted to combine the best features of the Dutch and British financial systems in France from 1715 to 1720, he placed extraordinary pressures on pre-existing informal market structures. The differences among the British and French approaches to the collapse of their stock market bubbles lies in the will of the British to ensure the continuity of contracts. The government was involved in the restructuring of the corporations of that time, and many debts were renegotiated, but everything happened under the shadow of the legal order within which conflicts were settled. It took years to do so, with enormous transactions costs. However, this salvaged the emerging capital market and resulted in a homogenization and sophistication of financial assets, which ensured both the existence of a mass financial market in London and the development of an active and profitable financial industry. By contrast, the involvement of the French government in the design of Law's System led it to manage its divestiture, which resulted in an authoritarian writing-off of debts and tight regulation of financial and banking activities. This eliminated the possibility to develop both financial markets and the industry. Typically a more decentralized, progressive, and "biological" management of the crisis favored the resilience and the adaptation of the proto-stock exchange in London, while rational and central design prevented France from building a solid micro-foundation for its financial sector.

In a very parallel spirit, Jérôme Sgard compares the 1994 Brazilian Real Plan, which rebuilt a working, national monetary order, and the bi-monetary Argentine Currency Board regime, which collapsed in 2001 and caused a major dislocation of both the real economy and the financial sector. Both experiences of monetary destruction and reconstruction shed light on how policy or regulatory intervention interacts with private choices in the building of market infrastructures. Policy efficiency is conditional upon the willingness of the agent to keep using the national currency; but using it as a policy variable also contradicts the agent's perception that its stability is a condition for their own continuing private capacity to calculate and optimize. Hence the path for policy-makers in managing monetary policy is very narrow.

The point is that individual agents – both citizens and firms – play a strong interactive role in the process of money building or destroying. The shaping of their contracts reflects their strategy, depending on the

The challenge of balancing public and private ordering 293

context, in trying to manipulate the currency either to protect their wealth or to benefit from transfers of value. Their aggregated (while uncoordinated) forces are well beyond that of any government, which produce the permanent risk of catastrophic evolution. At the same time, the only tool to channel these forces to avoid the collapse of the monetary system and to make monetary stability a focal point and mutually shared belief, is to have the government mixing threats and incentives to push the convergence of beliefs on the un-profitability of diverging strategies, hence their ineffectiveness. The role of the ruler as the builder of converging expectations and beliefs appears essential; hence the centrality of the credibility of authorities in building markets.

In their discussion of the needed reforms for financial regulation, both in Europe and in the US, Michel Aglietta and Laurence Scialom highlight the relationship between innovation and systemic risk in a world of bounded rationality. In the specific case of financial instruments, incomplete information and difficulty in understanding the actual characteristics of innovative financial instruments trigger uncertainty because it is impossible for most market participants, and regulators, to measure objective probabilities in using past accumulated knowledge. In such an environment, economic agents are driven by animal spirit. Their rationality being bounded, market participants rely on heuristic patterns that select and integrate the knowledge relevant to their type of activity (Akerlof and Shiller, 2009). However, they are aware of the limits of their knowledge. They are thus induced to enlarge it in taking account of the opinions of others that they presume might have better information. Since these others are on the same footing, strategic complementarities arise, leading to herd behavior and resulting in the potential collapse of the market, since mutual trust disappears. Exactly the same can occur in other systems characterized by strong complementarities and generalized mutual dependencies among members of the industry; as is the case in most network industries. It is not the complexity and the interdependencies per se but the pace of innovation that makes the system vulnerable to the fact that nobody really has a clear vision of the real state of interdependencies, and then is able to take the appropriate action in the case of (endogenous or exogenous) perturbation.

Yet, the problem is the implementability of remedies. Indeed, Michel Aglietta and Laurence Scialom rightly insist on two essential characteristics of regulatory remedies. First a central public regulator with strong capabilities to impose top-down constraints and to centralize information is needed to assess systemic risks and impose on players the burden of the systemic risk they individually generate. Second, this regulator (or set of regulators) should be submitted to strong bidding rules to be credible. Hence their propositions for a contingent regulation to refer to contingent contracting; imposing *ex ante* designed constraints on players in the function of their risk as assessed by the central and independent authority.

This contribution highlights again the strong "political" constraint on the capability to "manufacture" totally perfect – in this case resilient – markets. Regulation inevitably comes after crisis, in the sense that it aims to deal with the roots of the last crises, while market participants are likely to invent new forms of technologies or contracts that create new coordination and systemic problems. The problem facing any "benevolent dictator," beyond the standard question of its actual benevolence, is that it is very unlikely that it will be able to learn fast enough to anticipate adequately the next crises, and their cure.

Also its ability to benefit from enough political authority to be an actual dictator is questionable. In a post-crisis context, a majority can emerge to support the devolution of more power to independent regulators. However, as time goes by, innovations can sustain an evolution of beliefs, which may trigger the development of new coalitions of interests, pushing for binding the authority of the regulator(s) so as to allow this coalition to benefit from the spread and development of innovation. This is exactly what happened with the real estate bubble in the US, Spain, and many other countries in recent years.

14 | The microstructure of the first emerging markets in Europe in the eighteenth century

LARRY NEAL

14.1 Introduction

By the end of the seventeenth century, secondary markets for shares in joint stock corporations were well established in Amsterdam, London, and Paris. Starting in 1719, however, the participants in these early emerging markets were caught up in the rise and demise of John Law's System in Paris, then the South Sea Company's scheme to imitate the French success in refinancing government debt by issuing new equity stock, and finally some belated attempts by various Dutch cities and provinces to imitate the apparent successes of the French and British experiments. By this time, the wealth derived from the burgeoning commercial activities in the Atlantic port cities of Europe was sufficiently dispersed to allow capital market access to those well down the social hierarchy, not just to those in the nobility or peerage but to merchants and tradesmen, widows and spinsters (Carlos and Neal 2006; Earle 1989; Grassby 2001; Hart 2006; Hoffman et al. 2000; Zahediah 1994). Although most individuals active in the markets in 1720 lived in the immediate metropolitan regions of Amsterdam, London, and Paris, participation was not limited to these regions. Indeed, all three markets were dedicated to encouraging investors from other parts of the Netherlands, Britain, France, and the rest of Europe. Many of them responded by using trusted agents in Amsterdam, London, and Paris (Gelderblom and Jonker [2004, 2009] for Amsterdam; Carlos and Neal [2006)] for London; and Velde [2009] for Paris).

14.2 The "Big Bang" of financial capitalism

The Mississippi and South Sea bubbles during the years 1719 and 1720 were the original "Big Bang" of financial capitalism. Across Europe, governments whose finances had been exhausted by the demands of large-scale warfare fought nearly continuously over the previous century sought to refinance their accumulated debts by resorting to a variety of financial innovations. The most thoroughgoing innovations, foreshadowing in many ways the financial techniques that created a global financial market at the end of the twentieth century, were the product of John Law's implementation in France of his theories of finance-led growth. The speculative fervor exhibited in response to the issues of new stock in his *Compagnie des Indes* and then to the new issues of stock in the South Sea Company in London amazed contemporaries. The collapse of the speculative bubbles that arose in 1719–20 generated an alternative literature at the time that argued that stock markets were essentially useless diversions from productive labor, merely pretending to add value through securitization of projected schemes. By luring in innocent and ignorant investors, the prices of the new securities were subject to "the madness of crowds," which inevitably led to collapse of prices, disillusion of the masses, and general economic distress. Nevertheless, scholars in recent years have examined the quantitative evidence left in the price currents and in occasional business accounts of early times and found that even these early, informal, unregulated, and ill-organized securities markets performed their job of "price discovery" in a reasonable fashion (Murphy 2009; Shea 2007a, 2007b).

Somehow, financial markets did recover in Europe then as they have eventually after each major financial crisis since. Further, economic progress in the form of greatly expanded international trade and industrialization accompanied by technological advances across the entire spectrum of human endeavors has accompanied each recovery in financial markets since 1720. Perhaps some confidence in our collective future may be restored by examining more closely how these early markets all collapsed, but then recovered in different ways thanks to the different policies pursued by each government. With hindsight, it is clear that the British were the most successful in responding to the collapse, the French least, with the Dutch in between. Analysis of the microstructure of the respective markets that remained after the respective regulatory and fiscal reforms helps explain why.

Essentially, Britain built on the existing architecture of the stock market that had been increasingly active over the previous thirty years, maintaining open access for foreign investors. In reorganizing the

South Sea company after its collapse, the British government actually enlarged the customer base for its debt, kept a large and diverse network of experienced stock traders in business, and created the largest stock of a homogeneous, transparently priced financial asset available anywhere in the world – the South Sea Annuities (Carlos, Neal, and Wandschneider 2007). France, by contrast, recoiled from its brief experiment with Dutch and British financial market techniques and constrained the market for its government debt for the next century to a privileged group of financiers who maintained monopoly rights over both the taxes and the debt service of the monarchy, to the long-run disadvantage of both the state and the economy (Bonney 2010). The Dutch, already heavily taxed and politically constrained by the fiscal independence of the individual provinces, left Holland, their most advanced province, to its own fiscal devices in the future. Holland's debt stagnated, became increasingly short-term and locally held, and the government was unable to respond effectively to challenges by either the British (Fourth Anglo-Dutch War 1780–84) or the French, who absorbed the Netherlands after 1795 and finally imposed general taxes and a truly national debt.

14.3 The emerging stock markets of Europe in 1715

There was no doubt in the minds of contemporaries when the bubbles collapsed in 1720 that the trouble had begun with the financial innovations of John Law in his efforts to reshape the public finances of France. The South Sea bubble in England that followed was seen as a response to the apparent success of Law's System by the end of 1719. Minor ripples of proposed projects throughout the provinces of the Netherlands followed in response to the early successes of the Mississippi and South Sea Companies. John Law was unique among contemporaries in his first-hand observation of the operation of financial markets in Europe. The oldest son of an established goldsmith-banker in Edinburgh, he traveled with his paternal inheritance to London shortly after the "glorious revolution" that brought William III and Mary to the throne of England, Scotland, and Ireland in 1688. War finance and overseas mercantile adventures were the main concerns of his contemporaries in both Edinburgh and London, as the military enterprises of William III quickly exhausted the treasuries of both capitals. William was forced to rely increasingly upon his Dutch financiers that he had brought with him from Holland, finding ways to ship silver from London to Amsterdam where it could be used to finance his armies waging war against Louis XIV. Law was aware of the many proposals for reorganizing British finances, both in England when the Bank of England was chartered in 1694 and in Scotland where the Bank of Scotland was formed in 1695. His ideas for stimulating the economy of Scotland by issuing banknotes backed not by a hoard of silver or gold, but by real assets earning a stream of income were being formed at the time. His classic work, *Money and Trade Considered* (1705), made his reputation as a theorist of first rank; his personal ventures in subscribing to the South Sea Company shares in London, organizing lotteries in Amsterdam, and dealing in foreign exchange in Genoa, made him respected by the leading moneymen of those financial centers. When he arrived in Paris in the summer of 1715, offering his services to the French authorities for curing their financial difficulties created by the War of the Spanish Succession, his authority on financial issues, both in theory and practice, was unquestioned (Murphy 1997).

In terms of "manufacturing a market" in securities, Law had observed the importance of a large and varied base of customers, most of whom hold one or two of the chief securities available for trade; then providing access to the market directly through financial intermediaries; and maintaining monitor information about their investments indirectly through print media and personal networks. The three stock markets of Amsterdam, Paris, and London varied considerably in terms of these three ingredients, but each had a reasonable customer base, a sizeable stock of tradable securities, and knowledgeable intermediaries. This was due mostly to the large-scale issuance of various forms of debt by each government to finance their nearly constant warfare during the previous century.

14.3.1 Amsterdam

Amsterdam had the oldest tradition of active stock trading, primarily in the shares of the largest joint-stock company in the world at the time, the Vereenigde Oost-Indische Compagnie (VOC hereafter), created in 1602. Unlike its precursors in the Dutch trade with Asia, the VOC did not pay off its shares from the returns of each voyage. Instead, shareholders had to be content with either the dividends that the company might, or might not, declare and the willingness of someone else to purchase the shares in turn. As the company became increasingly profitable over the course of the seventeenth century, dividends became regular and generous, stimulating competing companies in the rest of Europe, especially England and France (Gelderblom and Jonker 2004). In addition, each city and province in the Netherlands found it necessary to issue new bonds with each war, leading to an active secondary market in these various securities at a local level (Gelderblom and Jonker 2009).

As the most important port for transshipments of products between northern and southern Europe by the beginning of the seventeenth century, Amsterdam was also the main source of mercantile information (Flandreau et al. 2009; McCusker and Gravesteijn 1991; Morineau 1985). The Dutch regularly published price currents that focused on wholesale prices of the major commodities that flowed through the Amsterdam markets. The price currents included current exchange rates on the major cities in Europe and occasionally the prices of shares in the major Dutch corporations, the Dutch East Indies Company, and later the West Indies Company (McCusker and Gravesteijn 1991). One suspects that there were daily or at least twice-weekly ephemera published in Amsterdam that gave exchange rates and forward prices of the major Holland securities. While only occasional copies have been found in personal archives, the gazettes in other Dutch cities such as Utrecht, Leuven, and Delft did publish securities prices from the Amsterdam Beurs by the end of the seventeenth century (Frehen, Goetzmann and Rouwenhorst 2009). As ephemera, the various price currents were regularly included in correspondence among European merchants and bankers to verify the legitimacy of the prices at which transactions had been completed for their principals. The gazettes were included in the regular mails carried on packet boats between Amsterdam (Hook of Holland) and London (Harwich) and by express coach between Amsterdam and Paris.

To provide a central place where customers could find willing intermediaries to advise them and then execute their trades, Amsterdam's Beurs contained a section where dealers in securities could ply their trade. During periods of financial speculation when the crowds grew so large and boisterous that they interfered with the commodity traders who occupied most of the Beurs, the stockjobbers (*actionistes*) moved sometimes to a bridge connecting the Beurs to Kalverstraat and from there in the coffee houses along Kalverstraat. Josef de la Vega's classic work, *Confusion de Confusiones*, first published in Spanish in Amsterdam in 1689, presumably for the edification of wealthy Sephardic Jewish patrons, describes in vivid detail the operations of the various investors, speculators, and their intermediaries. These included options and occasional bear and bull operations, much as in modern markets.

While de la Vega's work described various categories of *actionistes*, according to whether they were men of substance acting as market makers or brokers relying on commissions to make their income, recent work on the early trading of shares in the VOC indicates that a competent core of active professionals trading in the Dutch securities was difficult to detect, at least in the early seventeenth century. Part of the reason was the uncertainty over enforcement of forward contracts, when the original seller did not maintain ownership of the security during the period of the contract (Petram 2009). By 1715, it is doubtful the situation was much better for outsiders wishing to initiate trading in the Amsterdam Beurs. An eyewitness report to Lord Londonderry, whose experiences with John Law and each of the major stock exchanges emerging in Europe in 1720 are described below, indicated that Amsterdam lay well behind both London and Paris in terms of public accessibility.

14.3.2 London

By all accounts, London's secondary market for government bonds and corporate securities was the most advanced in Europe, possibly the world, by 1715. While the Royal Exchange was a deliberate imitation of the Amsterdam Beurs, it appears that little of the actual trading of government debt took place there. Rather, when the Bank of England was established in 1694 to handle the government's finances, an important part of its duties was to pay out the annual or semi-annual dividends owed to the government's creditors. As a result, its facilities became an important meeting place where actual transfers of ownership of securities recorded in the stock ledgers maintained by the bank could take place. The various coffee shops and company offices nearby in Exchange Alley provided meeting places between potential customers and the active stockjobbers and brokers.

Emerging financial markets in the eighteenth century 301

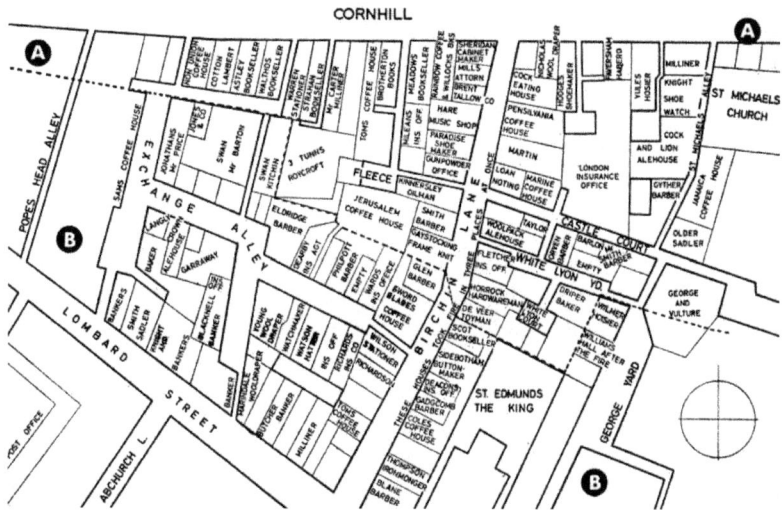

Figure 14.1 Exchange Alley

In his *Collection for Improvement of Husbandry and Trade (1692–1703)*, John Houghton described the mechanics of the emerging stock market in London for the new investor as well as how s/he could access the market and learn the prices of the various securities on offer. He explained that securities could be purchased either by going directly to someone who wanted to sell or by using a broker who would help guide the new investors through the process. Houghton noted that an investor could find out "what Prices the Actions bear for most of the Companies trading Joynt-stocks" at Garraways and two years later he noted "brokers as being 'chiefly upon the Exchange, and at Jonathan's Coffee-house, sometimes at Garaways's and at some other Coffee-Houses" clustered around Exchange Alley behind the Royal Exchange (Figure 14.1). These "brokers" provided both expertise and information about the market, but generally were not regarded as useful professionals in Houghton's time. Some of the antipathy might have come from the threat to the social order and status quo possible from the very anonymity of the impersonal market (Dickson 1967, p. 490).

In London, printers were allowed general freedom with the accession of William of Orange to the throne of England in 1688/89 so a number of print sources emerged to keep potential investors informed of developments in its emerging securities market. Newspapers regularly inserted paragraphs to report on the latest prices for the major forms of government debt available. Perhaps even more useful, a specialized publication, John Castaing's *Course of the Exchange*, began regular appearance at least by 1698 (Figure 14.2). Castaing was followed by competition from John Freke's *The Price of Several Stocks*, the last issue of which appeared June 22, 1722, while Castaing's *Course of the Exchange* continued through to 1810. It appeared twice-weekly, on Tuesdays and Fridays, which also happened to be the days that mail packet boats left from Harwich to the Dutch port at Hook of Holland. Each issue contained the prices of the major securities over the prior three days, as well as the latest exchange rates for bills of exchange in major European cities. It concluded with notes on the days of dividend payment for the major government stocks and the numbers on tallies that currently paid off at the Exchequer.

Finally, the creation of the United East India Company in 1708 and the South Sea Company in 1710 had created two huge joint-stock companies in addition to the Bank of England, the shares of which provided potential investors in government bonds a variety of choices among easily transferred and transparently priced assets. All three companies had issued their initial capital stock in exchange for short-term government bills whose promises to pay had fallen well behind the flow of tax revenues committed to pay them off with interest. Their separate monopolies promised investors the possibilities of higher dividends than the government was paying on the debt it owed to the companies, plus the possibility of capital gains when the government's remaining debt rose in value. The mass of government "funds" provided everyone concerned a convenient intervention asset that could be pledged as collateral, left as a secure source of regular earnings, or liquidated as a source of ready cash when needed.

14.3.3 France

By contrast to the regularly printed price lists for securities traded in Amsterdam and London, in Paris the prices for bills of exchange and stocks in the government sponsored trading companies were only included in the official publication, the *Mercure de Paris*, after 1724 when the official Paris Bourse was opened. Its opening followed completion of the Visa, the process that determined under French law how much credit each shareholder of John Law's company could claim in

Emerging financial markets in the eighteenth century 303

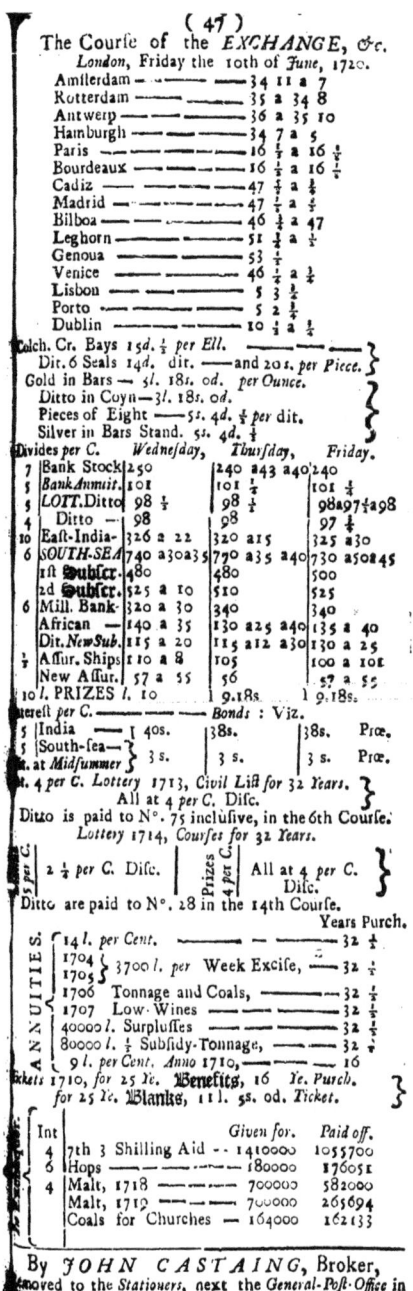

Figure 14.2 Castaing's *Course of the Exchange*, January 8, 1720

the bankruptcy proceedings begun in 1721. Before 1724, there may have been ephemeral price sheets issued by licensed *agents de change* to their favored customers, but economic historians now are forced to rely on occasional archival sources.[1] The relative paucity of price evidence for securities traded in Paris is evidence of the stultification of a secondary market for financial assets throughout the eighteenth century in France.

While a royal decree in 1638 had established a corporation of official *agents de change* in Paris, they focused on the business of drawing and accepting foreign bills of exchange more than trading in securities. In common with the monarchy's technique of selling remunerative offices to well-to-do bourgeoisie and nobles, the agents were required to make a forced loan to the Crown. When the Crown needed more revenue, it either increased the size of the bond required or the number of agents. By 1720, trade in securities had gravitated to rue de Quincampoix, where trading among individuals could take place without the intermediation of the official *agents de change*. At the height of speculative frenzy in John Law's *Compagnie des Indes* in autumn 1719, all available space along the street had been leased to speculators. In contrast to the Amsterdam and London markets, there was no well-established core of traders with the expertise and capital needed to keep a liquid market functioning in what government bonds existed.

These were available in huge quantities and were widely held among the French population, but they circulated hand to hand as bearer obligations and at erratic discounts to their face value when issued. The London *Course of the Exchange* published twice-weekly the numbers on the new short-term bills being issued by the British government to compare with numbers of the bills that were being paid off, so that the general public could determine what delay there might be before their bill was redeemed and so have a fair idea of what its market value might be. There was nothing comparable to these details that was available to the French holders of the *billets d'état* and even the most knowledgeable financiers of the French state were caught periodically in the devaluations of the unit of account in which the *billets* were denominated. Such was the situation when John Law appeared

---

[1] For example, Giraudeau's "Variations Exactes de tous les effets en papier qui on eu cours sur la place de Paris a commencer au mois d'Août 1719 jusques au dernier Mars 1721," found in the Bibliothèque Mazarine, MS. 2820.

in France in 1715 to offer his expertise in bringing France's financial sector up to and beyond the levels already reached in Amsterdam and London.

14.4 The financial innovations of John Law in France

Law's System, as he termed it, essentially combined the best features of British and Dutch finance and then took the next step as he saw it to improve on them. The Bank of England, established in 1694, had improved on the Bank of Amsterdam, established in 1609. In addition to providing giro services for account holders while maintaining a fixed monetary unit of account for them, just like the Bank of Amsterdam, the Bank of England issued bank notes in excess of its actual specie reserve. This gave it the possibility of expanding the money supply beyond its reserves in metallic coin and bullion, an advantage it put to use in discounting domestic and foreign bills of exchange for London merchant-bankers as well as for the British government. Instead of requiring all wholesale payments to be made through the bank as in Amsterdam, and forcing merchants to establish accounts by deposits of specie or bullion, the Bank of England took on a large amount of the government's outstanding war debts, agreeing to take a lower rate of interest than the government was currently paying.

Law's improvement on the English and Dutch examples was to create a bank of issue with fractional reserves, but with the authority to issue more in case of need. As in the English case, its capital was based on accepting outstanding government debt and receiving a lower rate of interest from the government. As in the Dutch case, it created a monopoly for itself of an important part of the payments system, but with the remittances of tax payments and government outlays going through Law's Banque Générale, rather than the wholesale payments made by merchants in Amsterdam. Eventually, when he created the Banque Royale, he went beyond both the Dutch and British cases by making its bank notes subject to royal edicts that would determine their value in exchange. In other words, he created true fiat money for the French government.

The New English East India Company, chartered under William III in 1698, took on a similar amount of government debt in exchange for being granted the privilege of competing with the Old East India Company in the trade with Asia by establishing new bases on the sub-continent. In the War of the Spanish Succession, the success of those two corporations in clearing up the British finances of the previous war led to the creation of an even larger joint-stock corporation, the South Sea Company in 1710 and the uniting of the two East India Companies in 1708, again on the basis of absorbing short-term government debt trading at substantial discounts and charging a lower rate of interest in return for the monopoly privileges being granted to the new corporation.

Meanwhile, the Dutch East India Company and the Bank of Amsterdam had been unable to expand their capital stock or offer the same kind of support to the war efforts of the United Netherlands. Neither organization was able to expand its capital stock by absorbing new government debt because each was set up to be governed by local political authorities – the seventeen representatives of the six cities making up the United East India Company in the case of the VOC and the city council of Amsterdam in the case of the Bank of Amsterdam.

The joint-stock company that John Law created in France ended up absorbing all of the government's outstanding debt in return for absorbing all of its previous state monopolies by issuing new stock repeatedly. The resulting Compagnie des Indes included the monopoly of trade with the Mississippi drainage in North America, the tobacco monopoly, the slave trade, the trade with the East Indies, the royal mints, and in the final stage, the united tax farms of France charged with collecting all the royal taxes. As a final initiative, Law combined his Banque Royale with the Compagnie des Indes in February 1720, setting the price of shares in the Compagnie at 9,000 livres as issued by the Banque Royale.

The previous inflation created by Law's excessive note issues from the Banque Royale led to a continued drop in the foreign exchange rate of the *livre tournois* against all other European currencies. To redress the situation, an edict in May 22, 1720 declared that the Compagnie's shares would be reduced in monthly stages of 500 livres to a level of only 5,000 livres by December 1, 1720. The alarm caused by the announcement of this edict led to a quick reversal of the edict on May 31, 1720. The two combined to discredit both the system and Law's ability to control it, leading to an irretrievable collapse of nominal prices for the Compagnie's shares along with a rapid fall in the exchange rate as investors scrambled to find safe havens for what

Emerging financial markets in the eighteenth century 307

remained of their capital (Murphy 1997, ch. 17). So ended the initial experiments with fiat money and rapid credit expansion in France.

Prior to the edicts, however, Law had wreaked more serious damage on the personal networks of contracts among individuals that had arisen during the bubble period. Everyone participating in buying shares in his new company could use the new security as collateral against their default on personal loans made in varying amounts for a wide range of purposes. When Law combined the two companies in February, he also eliminated the business of scores of stock dealers who had descended on Paris to act as intermediaries for the throngs of new customers eager to participate in the new market. Law closed down the rue Quincampoix by a decree of March 22, 1720 and brought all stock trading inside his company's offices at the Hotel Soissons. He declared by a decree of July 20, 1720 that his headquarters was now the official bourse for all trading in government securities. He even suppressed the offices of the *agents de change* in August and replaced them with sixty "commissions" of his own choosing. The terms for withdrawing sums from the bank account then varied with the edicts being issued to counter the continued fall of the livre tournois on the foreign exchanges. By substituting the bank's fiat currency for clearing transactions in the stock of the Compagnie, Law effectively put all the stockbrokers in Paris out of business. By October, Law again changed course, closing the bourse on October 29 and creating sixty new offices for *agents de change*. Thereafter, all business simply ceased while the Visa was carried out to determine what losses would be imposed on each investor, a process not completed until 1725 (White 2003).

14.5 Lord Londonderry (the Money Pitt) invests in all three markets

Evidence from a series of lawsuits revolving around the actions of Lord Londonderry during the rise and collapse of the Mississippi bubble and then the South Sea bubble, followed by his desperate efforts in Amsterdam to restore his lost fortunes in Paris and London help to highlight the differences among the internal architecture of the three stock markets as well as the contrasts among their legal regimes. At the time, all three countries were military and political allies, as each was vitally interested in restraining the power of Philip V of Spain, while retaining the support of the Habsburg Emperor in Vienna.

Londonderry's brother-in-law, James Stanhope, was the English minister responsible for establishing and then sustaining the Quadruple Alliance. Londonderry's experiences as an eminent speculator on all three exchanges during the critical years of the financial booms and busts highlight nicely the issues that arise when "Manufacturing Markets."

Londonderry, born Thomas Pitt, Junior, was the second son of Governor Thomas Pitt of diamond fame. Thanks to his skill in initiating and completing the sale of the Regent diamond to France in 1717, he became his father's business attorney and handled all the Pitt family's stock dealings. Many of these turned sour, the result of failed counterparties in each case, but the result was a series of lawsuits, some initiated by Londonderry against his defaulters and some initiated against him by disappointed partners, including eventually members of his own family, which included his nephew, William Pitt, the future Lord Chatham. We take up his misfortunes in France, then turn to his various successes and mishaps in London, and conclude with a minor recoup of his affairs in Amsterdam.

Pitt's initial dealings in Exchange Alley in London began in 1714 with the stock brokers George Cradock and Nathaniel Shepherd. Most of his affairs dealt with the personal accounts of the Pitt family, reflecting the increasing trust his father was placing in him, but occasional glimpses of his future adventures in Paris and Amsterdam appear. Londonderry's accounts show him variously extracting a usurious rate of interest on a loan made on the security of South Sea stock; making a small return on a forward contract speculating on a rise in the price of South Sea stock; and earning substantial sums from the resale of hundreds of lottery tickets, the favorite investment for small investors in England. In October 1715, his accounts begin to show credits from and payment to the order of John Law in Paris and his associates in both Paris and London. Londonderry's increasing dealings with France were a natural outgrowth of an enthusiastic endorsement of John Law's recently opened *Banque Générale* in Paris that he received from the secretary to the British ambassador in Paris:

In the last letter I had the honour of from you, you desire me to let you know what Mr. Law's bank is a doing. All I can tell you in that matter, is that every body here thinks it will do well. The Credit of it is established and they do a vast deal of business every day. It has ruined all the Banquiers here for it discounts bills and gives and takes bills upon every foreign place at one per cent cheaper than any of them and by the force of their money and the privileges it has, is already master of the Exchange with every country till trade force a change in that matter. Letter to Londonderry from Thomas Crawford, Paris, 16 September 1716, C108/418/10

There is little evidence that Londonderry took up Crawford's recommendation to invest in Law's schemes at that time, but it is clear that Crawford's enthusiasm for Law's financial innovations in Paris persuaded Londonderry and his father, Thomas Pitt, to rely on Law's good reputation to pay for the exorbitant price they agreed on for the Pitt/Regent diamond in 1717. Payment of 2 million livres tournois was arranged in several installments from June 1717 through June 1719. At the time, this amounted to over £130,000, and the later payments all bore 5 percent annual interest as well. Londonderry clearly invested part of his commission in the Compagnie des Indes, and made a substantial gain over the next two years, reputedly becoming one of the new "millionaires" created by the Mississippi bubble. Just before the final surge of the price of Mississippi stock in late August 1719, Law and Londonderry entered into a huge forward contract in which Law promised to deliver a year hence £100,000 of English East India Company stock to Londonderry at 10 percent under its current price, namely at 180 percent of par. The details of this incredible contract require separate treatment, but the point to be made here is that both Law and Londonderry deposited the equivalent of £30,000 as earnest money. Law appointed his agent in London, George Middleton, to make this sum available to Londonderry and Londonderry deposited his earnest money in Law's bank.

In January 1720, as the price of Mississippi stock was clearly going to fall, Londonderry made a hurried trip to Paris and entered into contracts with a number of speculators in Paris, mostly British expatriates, to sell his holdings at the end of May 1720. In buying both shares and options on new subscriptions in the Mississippi Company, Londonderry relied on the firm of E. Burgess and David Lyon. These were evidently experienced stockjobbers from London. Their commissions were regularly charged at 1/8 percent, the same as Londonderry paid to his stockbrokers in London.

Shortly after Londonderry's visit to Paris, however, Law carried his next maneuver to preserve his System. In February, he merged the *Compagnie des Indes* and the *Banque Royale* while requiring all stock dealings to be done through accounts in the bank. Londonderry made another trip to Paris in March and entered into a new round of private forward contracts to dispose of his holdings of Mississippi stock. No fewer than twenty-five separate contracts were copied out later for the benefit of his lawyers afterwards, because none of the private forward contracts made by Londonderry to cover his risks in Paris were completed.

The failures of Londonderry's contracts in Paris went beyond issues of idiosyncratic risk with his various counterparties. Although some of the counterparties were notorious for their brazen speculations such as Joseph Gage and Lady Mary Herbert, others were serious merchants and officials, including none other than Lord Stair, the British ambassador. Thanks to the bankruptcy of the *Banque Royale* in July, the subsequent recapitalization of the *Compagnie des Indes*, and the destruction of all documentation of the Visa when it was completed in 1723, there was no possibility left for Londonderry to salvage the remains of his French fortune. Ultimately, he cashed out in 1726, realizing only 5 percent of his original holdings. At the final liquidation in Paris, moreover, his French *agent de change* charged him a full 1 percent commission, adding insult to injury.

While assessing the situation in Paris in March 1720, Londonderry turned to one of his father's merchant correspondents in Amsterdam, Bernard VanderGrift. Eventually, Londonderry was able to sell part of his East India Company stock to various Dutch and English investors lined up by VanderGrift at a substantial profit over the 180 percent of par promised by Law. In addition, Londonderry made a substantial gain on stock in the Dutch West Indies Company, although the sums involved in both transactions were small compared to his dealings in Paris and London. More interesting is that Londonderry was able to use VanderGrift as an agent for disposing of shipments of various goods he had consigned to VanderGrift in Amsterdam. These were clearly actions taken to realize some of the gains from his dealings in Mississippi stock, but by transferring the terms of his stock contracts into settlement by taking up delivery of various goods, including cascarilla from the Bahamas and tobacco from Virginia. VanderGrift was a capable agent for all Londonderry's dealings in Amsterdam,

Emerging financial markets in the eighteenth century 311

although his commission was ¼ percent on the stock deals, rather than the 1/8 percent Londonderry was accustomed to paying in both London and Paris.

In his dealings on Exchange Alley in London, however, Londonderry made a substantial killing on the fresh issue of capital made by the Royal African Company at the beginning of 1720, won a huge bet with none other than John Law in August 1720 on the stock of the East India Company, and sold out of South Sea stock at the height of that bubble. But then he had to deal with the bankruptcy claim of his final counterparty on South Sea stock, the goldsmith bank, Mitford & Merttins. Londonderry filed suit as one of the creditors against the bankrupt firm but that firm lodged a countersuit against Londonderry, accusing him of a usurious loan. The details of the case and its resolution give us more insights into the how and why the London stock market was able to recover from the collapse of the South Sea bubble, while the Paris market was essentially moribund for the next century.

The specifics of each case were laid out by Londonderry's lawyers with a list of the witnesses to be brought in on each side. On August 24, 1720, Londonderry had sold the goldsmith bankers, Mitford & Merttins, £6,000 of South Sea stock at 540 pct. to be delivered and paid for on October 24, 1720. In the meantime, they declared bankruptcy, so Londonderry sold the £6,000 to the highest bidder he could find on October 24, taking a loss of £18,000. He filed a claim against the bankrupt firm as one of their creditors for this amount. Mitford & Merttins then filed a countersuit, claiming that there never was any South Sea stock in play, but the contract had been done to disguise a usurious loan to them by Londonderry. (If so, the rate really was usurious – 48 percent on an annual basis!) Years went by, but eventually Londonderry's lawyers were able to tell him that his case had won and he would receive his share of the payout by the bankruptcy commissioners to the line of creditors. Unfortunately, by that time, Londonderry had died, but the case was made for all such stock market contracts in the future in London (details in Neal 2011).

The case of Londonderry's claim against Mitford & Merttins is interesting in several dimensions. Mitford & Merttins was a prominent goldsmith bank in London that had been at the center of bubbles created during the year 1720. Throughout the bubble year of 1720, their name appeared regularly in the London newspapers as the agents designated to receive subscription moneys paid into various bubble companies – the Rose insurance company, a sail cloth company, a company to produce salt with a new invention, and a company to build ships for lease or freight. When subscribers demanded their moneys back, or the projectors wished to withdraw the money paid in, the bankers were clearly strapped for liquidity. If we accept the argument of the goldsmiths that they had borrowed £30,000 from Londonderry on such usurious terms, the first implication is that they were increasingly desperate for cash by the end of the summer of 1720. Borrowing large sums of cash from a valued customer and an active participant in transactions of all kinds in Exchange Alley and then declaring bankruptcy may have served as an object lesson for London's stockjobbers thereafter. The rules of the London Stock Exchange throughout the nineteenth and twentieth centuries, until the "Big Bang" in October 1986, expressly forbid any of its members (or wives or immediate family) from having any formal business relationship with a bank.

Second, it appears that the practice of selling out when a buyer who had contracted to purchase a security failed to appear at the time specified for transfer of the security was clearly established at this early date. It took nearly a century before the procedures for "selling out" and "buying in" were written into the rules and regulations of the formal London Stock Exchange. Those rules, which persisted throughout the nineteenth century, required the disappointed seller or buyer to confirm the price at which he had been forced to sell or buy to the clerks of the Settling Room. Assuming that the seller had to sell at a lower price than agreed or the buyer had to buy at a higher price than contracted, the absent buyer or seller who had contracted to be present was then required to make good the difference in price. Later, when Londonderry's case had wound its way through the English legal system, his lawyers informed him that his claim in the bankruptcy case had been upheld, conforming under common law to the practices of Exchange Alley. The letter with this good news reached the Leeward Islands, unfortunately, only after Londonderry had died.

Third, an experienced trader, promoter, and speculator (i.e., a stockjobber) such as Londonderry managed to accumulate such a complicated web of offsetting contracts and commitments during this first financial crisis of modern capitalism that it took a first-rate law firm decades to sort out. In contrast to the French case, where the authorities handling the bankruptcy of Law's Banque Royale and Compagnie des Indes destroyed all documents once they had made their decisions final, the British legal system maintained the important principle of "continuity of contract," a principle sustained in common law through the subsequent centuries.

Over the next several years, Law's System was gradually broken up and the investors in the company paid off at substantial write-downs, amounting to as much as 95 percent in the case of rich foreigners, such as Lord Londonderry. The *Banque Royale* was closed, and no public bank permitted thereafter in France until the *Banque de France* was created by Napoleon in 1801. The *Compagnie des Indes* was reduced to trading with the East Indies in competition with the more established companies of the Dutch and English, and eventually forced out altogether at the conclusion of the Seven Years War in 1763. More importantly, the idea of assigning real value to a claim on a financial asset, as explained by Isaac de Pinto in 1771, was eliminated by royal decree under Louis XV as a means of reassuring the remaining investors in French government debt.

The response of the British government to the collapse of the South Sea bubble is a study in contrasts. Despite the efforts of the South Sea Company to sustain the level of their overpriced stock with the Bubble Act of June 1720, the bubble collapsed and the South Sea Company was restructured under government supervision. Robert Walpole's government managed, with the self-interested help of the Bank of England, to restore the vitality of the London stock market by converting one-half of the South Sea stock into perpetual annuities offering 5 percent interest for five years, to be reduced then to 4 percent (and eventually to 3 percent). In this manner, Walpole salvaged the emerging capital market in London because at a stroke he created an enormous stock of homogenous, readily transferable, and fungible financial assets that were widely held by at least 35,000 individuals (Carlos et al. 2007).

While the remaining stock of the South Sea Company was gradually wound up due to the resistance of the Spanish Empire against allowing it to expand upon its monopoly of the slave trade, both the Bank of England and the East India Company periodically increased their capital stock. The business of the London stock market continued to be active and profitable for a growing number of specialist traders, despite the absence of volatility in the prices of the various securities. Meanwhile, the attention of *actionistes* in Amsterdam turned as well to the English securities, which now represented the largest mass of tradable securities available to European investors. The continued aversion to securities markets for government debt in France was to plague the monarchy's finances for the rest of the century.

In Amsterdam, the various projects that had been initiated in the various cities and provinces in belated imitation of the exciting innovations occurring in Paris and London, mostly withered away as investors sought safety in the form of hard cash in the form of silver and gold, whether in bullion or specie. Only the marine insurance company created in Rotterdam survived to compete with the London Assurance and Royal Assurance companies that had been chartered in Britain. Even the shares of the West India Company, which had enjoyed a brief boom, fell back to previous levels. Thereafter, the interests of Dutch investors focused on the huge supply of government bonds now available on the London market. Later in the century, the Dutch agent of the British East India Company in Amsterdam, Isaac de Pinto, argued that the expertise of the stockbrokers in Amsterdam had helped the British government finance their wars with France by investing heavily in each new issue of government debt (de Pinto 1771).

Ultimately, the secondary market for government debt was consolidated and re-established on the basis of a wholesale refinancing of existing older forms of government debt that were illiquid, i.e., not easily marketed, in the British case. The French first inflated away the existing stock of unserviceable debt under John Law's System, and then destroyed all three elements of a successful secondary market in government debt by eliminating the corps of professional stock traders, restricting future debt issues to various forms of life annuities not easily transferable, and discouraging broad-based holding of government debt (Bonney 2010; White 2003). The Dutch maintained active secondary markets in government debt, mainly Holland's, but concentrated on short-term debt that required frequent rolling over (Gelderblom and Jonker 2009). Dutch investors turned increasingly to British debt or high-yield debt issued by surrounding monarchies and the newly formed United States of America (Riley 1980; Wilson 1941).

15 | *Money reconstructed: Argentina and Brazil after hyperinflation*

JÉRÔME SGARD

15.1 Introduction

Money is usually seen in action but rarely in construction. For instance, one may observe the issuing policy of central banks or the trade-offs faced by agents when buying or selling on a foreign exchange. Here money is a given, and it is also closely attached to the most synchronic and self-referential outcomes of economic analysis: market equilibrium and the formation of relative prices. Clearly, it is difficult to reconcile this view with a more "genetic" approach that is centered on the constitution of money, its evolution, and its possible breakdown.

Two classical narratives of money's emergence reflect this constraint in that both are very much ad hoc. One version is followed by those who think within the neoclassical or orthodox paradigm and so envisage money exclusively as a medium of exchange. That is, money is just the $(n-1)$th good, which theoretically allows decentralized agents to shift from barter to integrated markets. In this view, money springs fully formed out of private exchange and its essential function is to reduce transaction costs.[1] This natural history of markets then encounters well-known logical difficulties. If markets predate money, then how can one account for aggregation and the operation of a price mechanism in the premonetary era? And if money is a commodity, what can be said of fiat money? What, then, is the point of having a central bank? In other words, this narrative may serve as a low-cost prologue to, say, the analysis of monetary policy, but it is not a promising start for a comparative or historical approach to explaining how money is established.

This contribution draws from Sgard (2008), with less empirical material and a revised analytical discussion. This version benefited from comments made by Céline Bignebat and Witold Henisz.

[1] Ostroy (1973), Jones (1976), Bell (2001).

The second narrative derives from Knapp's so-called Chartalist approach.[2] Here, money results from the act of a state, or a "charter": a declaration by the sovereign that this or that piece of metal or paper constitutes "money." The obligation to pay taxes in this currency typically gives the statement some muscle. Historical records confirm parts at least of this story and document, for instance, the long fight of premodern states to establish their monopoly on money issuing and minting. Still, one struggles to account on this basis for the long-standing capacity of agents to create private monies or institutions that are supplementary or complementary to public ones – or, perhaps, substitutive or dilutive of them.

Both of these narratives, the natural and the statist, raise the risk of "hypostasis of money."[3] That is, money tends to be considered not as an institution but rather as some essence, of an extraordinary social quality, that was obscurely created some time after humans emerged from the state of nature. Beyond the largely unanswerable question regarding the ultimate origin of a social institution, the open theoretical question is how public regulators and private agents jointly shape the evolution of money, and affect over time its overall stability and the quality of its services: how money supports private contracting and the proper operation of markets, and whether it offers the government an effective policy instrument. Money in its modern form is altogether a highly regulated institution that is closely tied to core government prerogatives, and an instrument of private contracting that cannot be imposed upon agents. In fact, the effectiveness of money-as-policy instrument depends entirely on their willingness to rely on it when buying goods, negotiating prices, or raising debt. Hence, its regulation is not only about policy making, whether one looks to central banking, foreign exchange regimes, banking regulation or accounting norms; it is also about contractual practices and private ordering. In other words, rather than being constructed as some ahistorical or essential invention, money should be envisaged as a downstream, historically conditioned institution. Exploring what early monies, say in the Pacific Islands, have in common with the recent experience of the Federal Reserve may not be a highly rewarding enterprise.

In this contribution I look however at an indeed exotic and comparatively rare experience, namely hyperinflation – an experience

---

[2] Knapp (1924), Lerner (1947).   [3] Cartelier (2007).

where money as an institution is debased, sometimes destroyed, and possibly later stabilized and reconstructed. Hyperinflations are indeed occasions when this institution becomes highly fluid and unstable: bifurcations and collapses may emerge in the very short run and then exert long-term constraints on its "re-institutionalization," therefore on the future conditions of private choices and policy options. For instance, "dollarization" typically progresses by leaps and bounds, under the pressure of brutal monetary crisis and more or less improvised policy reactions; but it is then extremely difficult to undo so that the decisions of both public and private agents will reflect over the long run this institutional constraint. They will have to adjust in order to act consistently with the new environment.

This chapter explores how a working monetary order was reestablished in Argentina and Brazil after the hyperinflations that marked the 1980s and early 1990s. What's of interest here is not just the technique that ended inflation but also the process whereby money recovered its capacity to support economic calculability and market operations while serving also as a useful policy instrument. Comparing two nearly simultaneous experiences also allows accounting for the qualitatively different outcomes obtained over the long run as a consequence of the interplay between policy initiatives and the decentralized (informal) institutional choices made by private agents.

The starting point in this comparison is that during the years of high inflation each country adopted a different response to the massive redistributive threats it experienced. Argentina largely transferred its monetary functions to the dollar. Brazil, in contrast, opted for a more inward strategy of protection, relying on price indices as an accounting hedge while the domestic, highly inflationary instrument of payment (i.e., cash) remained widely in use. Thus the two countries coordinated around two different monetary rules through a mix of decentralized or informal institutional choices and policy actions that triggered, confirmed, or curbed these choices. After stabilization (i.e., after 1991 and 1994 in Argentina and Brazil, respectively), the two contrasting regimes built on these legacies exercised entirely different micro- and macro-economic constraints. The regimes also proved to be unequally sustainable: whereas Brazil succeeded in gradually modernizing its market institutions and expanding its economy, in 2001–2002 Argentina experienced a second major crisis that once again raised the threat of a major destruction of the existing monetary order.

As a matter of convenience, I use the term *monetary order* to refer to the broad set of institutions and rules (both private and public) that provides stability and consistency to monetary relations and allows a national money to deliver its expected private and public benefits. I use *monetary regime* or *policy regime* to refer to the conventions and public organizations that are specifically related to monetary policy in the standard macroeconomic perspective: interest and foreign exchange policies, convertibility rules, policy commitments, issues of credibility, procedures, and so forth.

Section 15.2 explains how money consists of a unit of account and a unit of payment as well as how these units may be split under high inflation. Section 15.3 discusses the Brazilian *Plano Real* of 1994, which succeeded in reestablishing a working national money; and Section 15.4 addresses the Argentine 1991 Currency Board and its eventual collapse in 2001. Section 15.5 concludes.

15.2 Protection against high inflation: theoretical issues

15.2.1 Two monetary functions: accounting and payment

Generations of social scientists – starting with Max Weber, Georg Simmel, and Ludwig von Mises – have analyzed the key role that money plays in the development of individual agency, microeconomic calculations, and the capacity to leverage private resources across large social fields. Money empowers agents and therefore supports the dynamics of the division of labor: to the extent that it remains stable, money facilitates lending, investment decisions, and the sale and purchase of goods and services.

However, money in action differs from a broadband network, a technical norm, or even a stock exchange: if debased, the externalities caused by its decline or collapse are potentially much larger. This is because once it has been established, money is seized and invested by decentralized agents who rely on it as they exchange on markets for goods and debt; that is, money enables the coordination of a decentralized division of labor based on contracts and payments, so that if its capacity to coordinate market exchange fails then the whole social machinery is affected. In the worst cases, the breakdown of the payment system may make it impossible to settle any type of transaction beyond barter; this is the endpoint of uncontrolled hyperinflation *and* a systemic liquidity crisis (i.e., the two paradigmatic crises for money). Conversely, restoration of the monetary order is typically associated with a recovery in private contracting and hence in economic activity. The prospect of falling into barter and getting out of it does not however surreptitiously reintroduce the "natural history of money" that has been criticized in the introduction. Barter is the ultimate default option when money breaks down. But how the collapse of money may affect social exchange is conditional upon how money had been used by agents and, beforehand, how it had been socially constructed.

If we move one step further in the exploration of monetary crisis, we have to consider the two main functions of money. First is the *unit of payment*, which is the instrument for settling contractual liabilities, like cash or cheques typically: it is provided in exchange for goods or services and it circulates as a medium of multilateral exchange. Therefore this unit is at stake when agents opt for barter: in some way, they cannot or they do not want to use it anymore. The unit of payment is thus the instrument of monetary policy, which is primarily about how much instruments of payments will be put in circulation in the economy (given the multiplier effect). Money's unique capacity to settle debts explains why profligate governments have so much interest in issuing it: if the state controls the manufacture of money, then it can pay salaries and service its own debt without visibly raising revenue from the population. Hence money is about seignorage but is subject to inflation.

Money's second function is as a *unit of account*, in which real term economic values, or terms of trade are measured as a reflection of market forces (i.e., relative scarcities). Hence this function affects agents when they negotiate contracts, set prices, or substitute an input for another in their production function. For this reason, highly volatile relative prices, which are by-products of high inflations, reduce the capacity of agents to optimize decisions and trade off competing offers. Foreign exchange is another example: if its short-term evolution is highly volatile, hence unpredictable, owing to high domestic inflation, then setting the price of imported goods in terms of the domestic unit of account may become all but impossible. Traders may then decide to post only dollar prices or stop trading altogether.

However, the unit of account does not only support exchange on spot markets, where the transfer of goods and money are simultaneous. It also records financial commitments: stocks of assets and liabilities. It formalizes future obligations of payments, hence intertemporal wealth transfers. The unit of account then bears strongly on a firm's performance, hence on its sustainability, i.e., its solvency. It is one of the key institutions that build the time-horizon of agents, specifically via their capacity to calculate economic choices over a more or less extended time-frame. High inflation is then associated with a considerable weakening of financial obligations, typically via large and informal or extracontractual wealth transfers between debtors and savers. Under such conditions, agents are driven less by solvency constraints than by protecting themselves in the short run against inflationary erosion (or by benefiting from the losses incurred by others).

In summary terms, the unit of account supports two generic dimensions of economic calculation associated with two principles of market discipline.[4] First is the relative price structure, which is synchronic (i.e., observed at a given instant in time) and which primarily reflects the efficiency of competing producers – that is, their production function, or the supply side of the economy. Second is the intertemporal financial structure of firms, which determines their time-horizon, profitability, and solvency, and thus the distribution of wealth.

In principle, money's "payment" and "accounting" units should be closely anchored one on the other: this is how a standard, well-functioning, trusted money works, in which case inflationary erosion would affect both units. Firms would first negotiate terms for one work week (accounting function) and later pay for that work in the same money (payment function). Other things equal, intermediary inflation would cause a loss of revenue for the worker. In this normal, stable circumstance, agents are like price takers on a competitive market or beneficiaries of a pure, nonexclusionary public good: they may either use this currency (and support the inflation risk) or exit.[5] Under high

---

[4] These two dimensions of calculability are embodied by two classes of accounting books. On the one hand are *inflows and outflows of payments* as reported on the income statement, which reflects (a) the production function's efficiency at prevailing prices and (b) the firm's liquidity constraints and hence its capacity to avoid immediate default. On the other hand are *stocks of assets and debts*; these are recorded on the balance sheet, which shows how future income flows will be shared among capital providers and thus reflects their individual risk in the case of solvency *or* bankruptcy. See Cartelier (2006).

[5] After Cagan (1956), we say that *hyperinflation* exists whenever the monthly inflation rate exceeds 50% for two consecutive months. However, many of the dynamic patterns evident at rates of only 20–30% per month are much like those observed at 50%. On hyperinflations in general, see Sargent and Wallace (1981), Sargent (1982), Dornbusch and Fischer (1986), Dornbusch et al.

inflation, however, agents tend to act strategically and to hedge their transactions, the effect of which is to split the two monetary functions: they will typically include in their contracts ad hoc revaluation clauses that automatically adjust payments to reflect monetary devaluation as the contract matures. By definition this strategy concerns only intertemporal contracts. It may easily be applied not only to debt contracts, bank deposits, and wages but to virtually all financial transactions, including bonds, tax liabilities, insurance polices, rents, and so forth.

The overall conseqence of these strategic behaviours is that the payment and accounting functions of money may be transferred independently of one another to substitute support, so each may gain a life of its own. Agents would then act strategically with respect to the respective monetary units, though they could not ignore the choices of other agents – monetary substitution is also about coordination, hence it is by definition a collective choice. Within a given economy, if prices were set in five different substitute currencies then markets would segment unless one money emerged as the dominant one.

15.2.2 Relative prices and economic adjustment

Over the medium term, the key problem with a split money is that the economy loses a key micro- and macroeconomic adjustment mechanism. Normally, a one-off permanent adjustment of the exchange rate (or, more generally, any change in relative prices) leads to a corresponding permanent change in relative profit rates across sectors. For instance, a lower foreign exchange rate will cause domestic nontraded services to become less expensive and less profitable vis-à-vis internationally traded goods. Production factors will be progressively reallocated to the more profitable (exporting) sectors. Hence, the economy's supply side will adjust to market signals and recover some growth potential, while the demand side will support more directly the short-run adjustment of the current account.

However, this mechanism does not work if agents systematically protect their purchasing power against *any* price movement. Suppose all producers, including hairdressers and plumbers, set their prices in dollars; then any change in the exchange rate of the national peso will

(1990), and Vegh (1992). On currency substitution, Calvo and Vegh (1992), Rennhack and Nozaki (2006).

be immediately reflected in *all* peso prices. Producers will simply adjust their price list as soon as they learn of the market movement. Rather than allowing for a correction in relative prices, the whole episode will end up in pure inflation, that is an homothetic drift of the whole price structure covering both the traded and the nontraded sectors. There will be no gain in price competitiveness, the balance of payments will not move, and the supply side will not adjust. In other words, even if the economy is flexible and open, a split and dysfunctional money may severely impact the way agents respond to market signals, hence the adjustment pattern in the real economy. Money is not a natural, neutral institution: how it works and the services it offers depend upon how agents use it. This is the experience that Argentine and Brazilian agents made first-hand, although in a different manner.

From the early 1970s onward, Argentina chose the dollar as a dominant monetary substitute.[6] This is by far the most common strategy in developing or socialist economies, if only because it does not require much in the way of institutional investments or capacity for collective action: a basic exchange bureau can handle the job with little or no policy guidance. Then this collective choice typically comes with large foreign exchange and banking crisis that cause large jumps in the overall level of dollarization. Argentina had its share of it.

In contrast, Brazil already during the 1960s opted for domestic price indices as a hedge against inflation.[7] This made it easier to preserve the state's monopoly of the national money on payments: the bank could not readily open dollar deposits to domestic agents and, contrary to the experience of Argentina, cash transactions in dollars did not develop much, even informally. Capital controls also remained tight and imposed short-term constraints on private agents, although the point should not be overplayed. The sheer magnitude of revenue transfer under high inflation implies that domestic hedging instruments were actually available, for otherwise agents would also have taken the road of de facto dollarization.

Compared with dollarization, indexation clearly demands better foresight and stronger domestic institutions, both public and private.

---

[6] Llach (1985), Giorgio (1989), Baliño (1991), Sturzenegger (1991).
[7] See Fishlow (1974, 2005), Lara Resende (1990), and Simonsen (1995).
   Actually, in each country both indexation and dollarization were observed simultaneously; at issue in this chapter is the *dominant* form of monetary substitution around which institutions and regulations were built.

Price indices must be timely, resilient, and widely trusted. The Brazilian solution was a decentralized and competitive supply of price indices. For years, agents could freely contract on the basis of monthly or weekly indices as well as of consumer and production indices, or sectoral and regional ones; some indices were provided by state institutions and others by trade unions, professional organizations, or chambers of commerce. Though the *cruzeiro* remains the dominant unit of payment, it largely lost its accounting function, which was altogether privatized, fragmented, and opened to competition. Yet the system still functioned insofar as it coordinated agents and allowed markets to function.

Another example of institution-building under systematic indexation was the interbank payment system, which should be highly efficient under high inflation; if not, enterprises may rapidly lose large parts of their working capital as a consequence of inflationary transfers.[8] Or take the domestic bond market: Brazil's 1987 introduction of indexed Treasury bills was the basis for strong growth in the supply of a broader array of private, indexed financial assets. Despite accelerating rates of inflation, the following years witnessed rapid growth in private balance sheets, in technical know-how, and in the use of high-tech equipment in Brazilian banks. Public regulation accompanied the whole process, which featured economies of scale and other positive network externalities. During this period, Argentine banks were nearly destroyed by hyperinflation.

The catch, however, is this: given the exponential nature of anticipated inflation, high inflation cannot be sustained over time; in fact, efficient hedging can serve only to postpone eventual stabilization (whether hedging takes the Argentine or Brazilian route). Nonetheless, choices made under high inflation by agents and policy makers may shape their ulterior trade-offs. Under the pressure of economic crisis, financial intermediaries offered adapted financial services and firms and households built up their balance sheets accordingly (i.e., they accumulated savings and investments contracts designed to limit the risk of decapitalization). Regulators then responded to these strategies by supporting, accommodating or restricting them, or by trying

---

[8] See Listfield and Montes-Negret (1996). In Argentina until the end of the 1990s, settlements between commercial banks and the central bank were still made largely in cash (i.e., via armored trucks). See also Angelini (1998).

to influence them. All these factors later affected how stabilization was envisaged and how a monetary order was reconstructed. Path-dependency is primarily founded on the mutual consistency between public regulations, market institutions, and the structure of individual balance sheets which reflect past trade-offs and also shapes present private interests. We now look at how the post-inflationary effects played in Brazil and Argentina, respectively.

15.3 The Brazilian *Plano Real*

Beyond nominal stabilization, reconstructing national money is about reanchoring the accounting and payment units to each other. That is: inducing agents to rely on the same money as a coordinating institution for their payment and accounting operations. After a series of programs in the 1980s that aimed to destroy (or at least weaken) the "parasitic" link between the national money and its substitutes,[9] both Argentina and Brazil eventually opted for what was actually a much less ambitious strategy: *a complete anchoring of the economy to its alternate unit of account*, to which the unit-of-payment function would then be legally transferred. Neither country relied on a policy surprise or any shock on expectations: the measures were widely discussed and voted on by the Parliament weeks before their inception, so agents had nearly complete knowledge of the stabilization's logic before it was implemented. Therefore, coordination was not entirely the *ex post* result of individual market-based reactions to the plan when introduced. It relied very much on an *ex ante* coordination based on open, public deliberation.

The strategy in the *Plano Real* (1994) was to begin by reconstructing the unit of account, which carries the highest risk because of the underlying redistributive stakes.[10] Between February and June 1994, the plan sought to re-coordinate agents on a new daily accounting

---

[9] The policy debate of the 1980s on inflation stabilization opposed orthodox monetarists, who argued that money control should be the sole anchor, and the so-called heterodox, who argued for multi-anchor programs (e.g., the exchange rate coupled with a freeze on wages and prices). See Dornbusch and Simonsen (1987), Heymann (1987), Bruno et al. (1988), Kiguel and Liviatan (1988), Giorgio (1989), Modiano (1990), and Bruno et al. (1991).

[10] Arida and Lara Resende (1985) were the first to detail the logic of this program, more than a decade before it was actually tried. For a full description of its implementation, see Franco (1995); see also Garcia (1996).

index, the *Unidade Real de Valor* (URV). It was published by the central bank and was linked to the dollar but with no underlying commitment. At the same time, laws stipulated that all wages and all *new* contracts must be anchored solely to the new URV, and agents were given strong incentives to convert *old* contracts into the new unit – especially financial contracts, which carry the highest redistributive stakes.

The consequences of this strategy were twofold. First, the fragmented unit of account was reunified or "re-nationalized," so that it became again a coherent public institution. Second, the ongoing process of indexation (active since the mid-1960s) was almost fully completed, with the account and payment functions entirely separated. Everyone was now using the unified new unit of account, which supported the whole price structure, while continuing to use the *cruzeiro*, the old unit of payment. Practically all domestic private contracts and relative prices were accounted for in the URV, with no link whatsoever to the actual instrument of payment and to monetary policy, which was still run in the old, highly inflationary *cruzeiro*.[11] Hence, in June 1994, the *cruzeiro*'s 48 percent monthly inflation rate then amounted to a homothetic shift in the price structure. This was a most extraordinary and dangerous situation: the economy had no monetary anchor, and monetary policy could have no impact on relative prices and real term revenues.

Once the re-coordination on the URV was obtained, a standard monetary reform was implemented. On July 1, the unit-of-payment function (i.e., the legal tender) was transferred to the URV; this became the *real*, which replaced the old *cruzeiro*. The old fiduciary money was withdrawn, and the central bank began to conduct both monetary and foreign exchange policy in *reals*. Monthly inflation fell from 48% in June to 7.8% in July and to 1.9% in August; it remained below 2% during the two following years. In other words, a single, integrated monetary unit had been created that formally was as perfectly disindexed as the *cruzeiro* was indexed (on the URV) at the end of June 1994. The key intuition here is that – because individual hedging strategies had taken a decentralized, contractual form – overcoming the accounting unit's fragmentation required starting from contracts and

---

[11] Inflation in the UVR was estimated at 3.7 percent between February and June, according to Sachs and Zini (1996).

voluntary agreements. Thus, rebuilding money could not be a declarative, unilateral act of the sovereign; it had to accommodate the existing structure of financial contracts and the private trade-offs of agents.

The critical question the day after was whether the new *real* could itself lose the unit-of-account function: whether the two monetary functions were now strongly anchored one on the other, or whether they may easily split again. When confronted with a large foreign exchange shock, for instance, would the public hang on to the new national money? Or would agents once again shift their price list to an alternate accounting unit in order to protect themselves against revenue transfers? In this latter case, then the *real* would have failed to establish itself as a viable, integrated national money: its capacity to adjust relative price movements and transfer market signals would not be restored, and inflation could easily ratchet up.

This question was answered in January 1999, when a foreign exchange crisis was followed by a 35 percent depreciation in the exchange rate. Yet by the second quarter, annualized inflation had reached only 8 percent and remained at that level until the year's end – under a fairly restrictive policy mix.[12] In these conditions, a textbook "J-curve" scenario of stabilization and export-led recovery could progressively take hold; at the same time the central bank adopted a standard inflation-targeting policy framework that explicitly assumed that the country could now run its own monetary policy, with no commitment as regards the exchange rate.[13]

15.4 The Argentine monetary experiments

15.4.1 *Monetary reconstruction, I: the Currency Board*

The Argentine Currency Board, established in April 1991, shared many features of the Brazilian *Plano Real*. The main principle was to anchor the national peso at par on its parasitic substitute, here the dollar. By law, both monies became perfect substitutes: all the peso's functions (including that of legal tender) were assumed as well by the dollar. In other words, it was implicitly conceded that the dollar had achieved an almost complete monopoly on the unit-of-account function, plus a large

---

[12] IMF (1999), Baig and Goldfajn (2000).
[13] Bogdanski et al. (2001). Before 1999, Brazil followed a succession of monetary and foreign exchange rules with no a priori commitment; see Franco (2000).

part of payment services; hence, the peso's last chance for survival – as a (part-time) unit of payment – was to be anchored as solidly as possible to the dollar. At least some seignorage revenue would be kept, along with the unspoken option of returning to a single national currency. In order to maximize its commitment to the anchor, the Argentine central bank was required to follow strict rules of emission: the stock and flow of reserve money was to be fully backed by dollar assets.[14]

The main consequence of this monetary regime was that domestic interest rates were driven exclusively by the US Federal Reserve policy and the "country risk premium" as measured by international capital markets. Via the credit multiplier, capital inflows (resp. outflows) implied an automatic expansion (resp. contraction) of money supply and credit distribution. In principle, there could be no "sterilization" and no lender of last resort.[15]

At first, the Argentine Currency Board was quite effective and allowed for some catch-up growth, which was fueled by large capital inflows. Its success in weathering the 1994–1995 Mexican crisis seemed, at the time, to signal its long-term sustainability.[16] But the Asian crisis (1997–1998) and, more directly, the Brazilian 1999 devaluation proved too hard to absorb. The eventual collapse of this regime reflected the real term appreciation of foreign exchange (i.e., a loss of competitiveness) as well as increasing pressure on the budget and hence on the public debt. The result was a painful recession followed by a full-scale systemic crisis: the country lost access to the international capital market in March 2001, and starting in October growing capital outflows led to a drastic liquidity and credit crunch. This was followed by a full-blown run on the banks and, in a context of severe social and political instability, a default on the public debt (December 2001) and a panicked exit from the fixed exchange rate (January 7).[17] The peso then lost 72% of its value against the dollar;

---

[14] Actually, 20–30 percent of the central bank's foreign reserves could be in the form of dollar-denominated Treasury bills issued by the Argentine government.

[15] See Canavese (1992) and Cavallo and Cottani (1997) for a description of this monetary regime.

[16] See Caprio et al. (1996) regarding the extreme measures taken to avert a full collapse of the banking sector during the 1995 Tequila crisis; also Calomiris and Powell (2000).

[17] The year 2002 featured much debate (not recounted here) on the main cause of Argentina's abandoning its Currency Board. See, among others, della Paollera and Taylor (2003), Fanelli and Heymann (2002), Hausmann and Velasco (2002), and Mussa (2002).

over the first half of 2002, GDP contracted by 15%, investment by 44%, and imports by 56%.

15.4.2 Monetary reconstruction, II: pesification

Simultaneously, with these developments, a unique process of monetary disintegration was observed. First, starting in mid-2001, many provinces started to issue parallel monies, such as the *patacones* of the Province of Buenos Aires. Unable to enter capital markets or to tap the central bank's cash, the insolvent and illiquid provinces settled an increasing share of their payment obligations (in particular, their wage bill) with this new type of IOU. The liquidity of these securities increased once they could be used to pay local taxes, at which time a number of enterprises (especially in retail trade) also began accepting them.[18] This history is in line with Knapp's (1924) views. The second aspect of the monetary disintegration affected the payment system through which agents should settle decentralized transactions: bank deposits were frozen on December 3, and foreign payments remained de facto blocked for more than three months.

However, floating the peso also implied the sudden breakup of a ten-year-old institutional arrangement hence a mass of private arrangements, network externalities, and stocks of financial contracts that were premised on the assumption that the bimonetary constitution would hold. Critically, floating the peso was doomed to result in a highly unstable, two-equilibria situation in light of the open competition between peso and dollar, both of which were used extensively by the public. Agents could quickly and fully re-coordinate around one of the currencies, causing the other's value to plunge toward zero – and there was little mystery regarding which currency would fall. For this reason, the main risk was not hyperinflation, as was commonly supposed; rather, the risk was destruction of the peso on the foreign exchange market leading to a domestic price explosion – regardless of whether the money supply could be controlled.

This was the third component of the monetary crisis in Argentina: once the unit of payment had been fractured and the payment system frozen, the national unit of account could be destroyed almost

---

[18] This monetary phenomenon had been observed locally during the 1980s as well as recurrently in Argentina during the nineteenth century; see Irigoin (2000) and della Paollera and Taylor (2003).

instantly.[19] In Brazil, this risk had been fully controlled: until July 1, 1994, agents had no other choice than to pay in the old, inflationary *cruzeiro* until its entire stock was exchanged for *reals* in a one-off, nonmarket conversion. In practice, the Argentine government tried to take the same road in order to forestall a destructive open competition between the dollar and the peso: in February 2002 it decided to "pesify" the economy, i.e., to convert into pesos all domestic prices, wage contracts, financial assets, private debts, interbank payments, etc. In a chaotic context marked by unprecedented levels of improvisation, the objective was to give the peso the full monopoly again over the accounting and payment functions, after it had been lost since the 1970s.

By the end of 2002, the results of pesification were quite remarkable from the viewpoint of an institutionalist theory of money. On the one hand, inflation was down and the price for goods and services responded positively: the nontrade sector exhibited only limited nominal price increases; traded goods remained anchored to international prices and so producers made large terms of trade gains.[20] This is exactly what theory predicts and what Brazil experienced in 1999: the economy recovered, although at the cost of massive revenue transfers between sectors of the economy.

On the other hand, pesification had a destructive impact on the financial side of the economy. The main reason is that many agents in Argentina hold large debts and assets denominated in dollars; hence a precipitous fall in the exchange rate entailed a major redistribution of wealth. Dollar savers became nominally much richer, and those who had taken on dollar debt (because of its lower interest rate) faced insolvency. Hence pesification was implemented with two objectives: it aimed to rebuild a national money with a capacity to support intertemporal contracting *and* to reverse, mitigate, or reallocate individual wealth losses due to declines in the exchange rate (i.e., between early

---

[19] The Hungarian hyperinflation following World War II is a rare comparable experiment in which the economy had become de facto bimonetary so that the population could freely arbitrate between a strong unit and an inflationary currency. In July 1946, inflation of the unprotected money reached 4.2×10^{16}; at the end of the month, when that unit was withdrawn, the total corresponding monetary aggregate for the whole country could be converted on the black market to 2,300 US dollars (Bomberger and Makinen 1983).

[20] See Burstein et al. (2005) for a detailed analysis of price adjustments in Argentina after 2001.

January and late February). Reshuffling capital losses between agents and sectors became the key political economic issue. Violent proxy fights between interest groups and lobbies dominated the policy scene for over a year.

For a concrete example, take the "asymmetric pesification" of banks' balance sheets. In March and April 2002, dollar credits to enterprises were exchanged at a different rate than dollar deposits; enterprises were thereby subsidized at the expense of banks and their depositors. The government then decided to recapitalize the banks with the equivalent of 15 percent of GDP in Treasury bills – and this at a time when the state was already in default (and patently insolvent). The utterly bizarre result was that, by the end of 2002, the only agents in Argentina who could measure their net wealth were those who had nothing (the majority) and the happy few who had everything abroad. Again and again the same questions were raised: Who owns what? Who is solvent and who is not? Who should exit the market and who may still trade and enter into new contracts?

The sheer impossibility of answering these questions was finally reflected in the suspension of bankruptcy law, the ultimate regulatory institution in any capitalist economy. Whether applied to banks, enterprises, private consumers, or state entities, bankruptcy could not operate because of the confusion that reigned about how financial accounts should be established and settled. This was the endpoint of the collapse of firms' intertemporal contractual structure and hence of the socially constructed norm – namely, solvency – that confirms their viability or sanctions their failure.

15.5 Conclusion

From the late 1960s onward, Argentineans and Brazilians adopted contrasting strategies for hedging against high and unstable inflation. In Argentina, agents re-coordinated around the dollar as a dominant unit of account and unit of payment. However, the Brazilian economy re-coordinated on a variety of inflation indices; hence a more inward-looking regime took hold that better protected the private financial system and the real economy. The 1994 *Plano Real* may then contend as the most sophisticated (and the most baroque) monetary reform ever attempted. It first reassembled the unit of account by allowing a gradual, voluntary transfer of existing financial contract terms to

Money reconstructed after hyperinflation 331

a new, countrywide index. Then the unit-of-payment function was added; thus, virtually overnight a single, nonindexed national money was reborn that integrated both monetary units. An active issuing and foreign exchange policy was instituted at the same time.

In Argentina, the informal process of dollarization was confirmed by the establishment of a Currency Board in 1991: a tight, bimonetary regime of a permanently fixed exchange rate whose aim was to "import" low-inflation credentials via perfect substitutability between the dollar and the national peso. Over the medium term, this solution proved unviable as it led to a large-scale monetary and economic collapse by 2002. At that time, the authorities tried to duplicate Brazil's strategy of reintegrating the two monetary functions into a single, national currency – except that Argentina tried to "pesify" its economy by fiat and in most chaotic context, both economically and politically. Adoption of the new payment unit was not difficult, and few producers resisted setting prices in pesos. What proved to be much trickier was dealing with financial contracts, which by definition carry the greatest redistributive risks. In Brazil, agents had the time and a road map for renegotiating contracts privately: the microeconomic foundations of the monetary reform, as summarized in the balance sheets, were built *before* the new currency was introduced and monetary policy shifted to the new regime. In Argentina the authorities intervened in these contracts and reallocated private wealth on a large scale *after* pesification had been edicted and after the peso had been floated.[21]

One highly orthodox conclusion of these two experiences is that the capacity to adjust relative prices is indeed decisive in any market economy. But there is a caveat: the loss of this capacity may reflect a policy choice (e.g., a fixed exchange rate) but may also result from private strategies (e.g., monetary substitution). This fact confirms that money as a market institution is neither exogenous nor "natural." It is jointly affected by regulatory and microeconomic decisions. Both influence how markets work but also constrain, in the short run and at the margin, the agent's and the policy maker's trade-offs.

Agents respond, sometimes strongly, to regulatory changes such as a stabilization program or monetary reform. Yet the impact of money on market dynamics depends on agents' *continued* willingness to use it in ways that confirm the expectations of monetary reformers. A

[21] Cartelier (2006).

currency is institutionally binding only insofar as it (a) coordinates all private exchanges and contracts and (b) imposes itself at the margin as the self-evident monopoly provider of both the payment function and the accounting function. This is how money acquires its institutional character. It is formalized by statute but it is also the outcome of a decentralized process of coordination and strategic behavior.

An integrated and uncontested money works through the whole division of labor and affects all market exchanges, via relative price signals and financial contracting. This is why its collapse is so costly for society and why it may affect behaviors over the long run. But because it affects individual trade-offs in such a comprehensive, symmetric, and nondiscriminatory manner, money also offers to policy makers a unique capacity to bear on virtually all individual decisions. It is a most remarkable policy-making instrument just because it affects agents as they freely calculate their market decisions. Hence, monetary policy can shape aggregate outcomes without impairing competition and private rights.

Still, the very attempt to police or manipulate money (i.e., to use it as a variable in the policy makers' optimization) is contradictory to the agents' assumption that money is a given: that is, a parameter, both permanent and nonnegotiable, that conditions their own continuing private capacity to calculate and optimize. The experience of hyperinflation indicates that this ambiguity is constitutive of modern monetary orders and that it may also lead to their destruction.

16 For a renewal of financial regulation

MICHEL AGLIETTA AND LAURENCE SCIALOM

16.1 Introduction

Since the eighties, capital requirement has been the cornerstone of bank regulation. Basel 2 is based on the principle that the purpose of regulation is to ensure the soundness of individual institutions against the risk of losses on their assets. The rationale for this prudential choice is to preserve bank solvency and thus to protect the interests of creditors – especially small depositors who are lacking in the expertise, incentives and ability to discipline bank managers efficiently (Dewatripont and Tirole 1993). This micro-prudential perspective treats risks as "exogenous" and considers that for a financial system to be sound it is necessary and sufficient for each institution to be sound. This proposal is liable to the fallacy of composition. It is possible and often likely that attempts by individual institutions to remain solvent can push the system to collapse. Financial risk depends on the collective behavior of institutions; it is endogenous. This is because collectively institutions can affect the prices of financial assets, the quantities transacted and hence the global financial stability. This in turn has powerful effects on the soundness of the institutions (Danielsson, Shin and Zigrand 2009). Moreover, it has been widely admitted that the key determinant of capital buffer size should be the riskiness of the assets with a crude valuation of risk with Basel 1 and a more sophisticated one with Basel 2. This general principle governing bank solvency regulation is based on the dissemination of the "best practices" of optimal risk management. Indeed, self-regulation largely governs bank capital requirements. The first step in this direction was made in the 1996 amendment to the Basel 1 agreement which aimed at determining regulatory capital for market risk on the basis of quantitative risk models built by the banks themselves. This move towards self-regulation was extended to credit risk in pillar 1 of Basel 2. However, bank regulation based on individually optimal risk management behavior makes systemic financial crisis sharper, larger and more costly. It constitutes a strong factor for homogenization of financial behaviors and therefore a worsening channel for financial instability in a context of increased perceived risks (Danielsson et al. 2001). Thus, the current design of micro-prudential regulation is highly procyclical and as such serves to amplify aggregate financial fluctuations.

One of the key foundations of this kind of prudential design is that the roots of potential solvency problems are strictly located on the assets side, because deposit insurance schemes protect banks from depositors' runs. This reasoning leads to a sharp distinction between solvency and liquidity. Unfortunately for the framework of regulation based on this distinction, market finance has blurred the dividing line between banks and non-banks. A shadow banking system has arisen in the wake of financial innovations, which depends entirely on market liquidity for its funding. In this gray zone between financial intermediation and pure market finance, credit and illiquidity risk are closely intertwined. With mark-to-market accounting, changes in asset prices rapidly impair the net worth of all the participants in the financial system. Consequently, in times of stress, a tightening in market liquidity quickly translates into changes in the equity base of banks and market intermediaries. There is a dynamic interaction between the liquidity and solvency of financial institutions (Adrian and Shin 2008b).

During the 2007/08 financial turmoil, micro-prudential regulations revealed their weaknesses, ineffectiveness and pernicious effects, partly because of their pro-cyclicity. So the financial crisis seriously challenges this conception of financial regulation which seems to ignore systemic risk. The reflexivity between individual actions and the reactions of others makes the objective of overall financial stability paramount. From our point of view, this reorientation towards systemic concerns and the correlative addition of a higher level of regulation is essential but not enough. The philosophy of micro-prudential regulation also needs an overhaul. In other words, a new layer of financial regulation, let us call it macro-prudential, must be built and its relation to more traditional micro-prudential policy needs to be envisioned in a top-down approach.

In the first part of this chapter, the basic concepts that underline the framework of macro-prudential policy are presented: the bounded rationality and strategic complementarity governing behaviors in the financial markets, the destructive dynamics of systemic risk and the reason why the innovation of structured credit has exacerbated it. Then we explain why the containment of systemic risk requires countercyclical prudential policy to control credit expansion in the financial cycle and how a macro-prudential policy could be implemented in a top-down approach under the leadership of central banks. The perimeter of banks subject to the macro approach should be enlarged to encompass all systemically important institutions, be they in the regular or in the shadow banking system. Both macro capital requirements and liquidity management tools should be used to implement dynamic macro control at the micro level. In the second part of the chapter, we link macro- and micro-prudential policy so as to avoid regulatory capture. We also advocate the generalization of prompt corrective action on the enlarged banking system subject to macro-prudential policy. Finally, we discuss how the proposals for implementing macro-prudential policy might be adapted in Europe along the lines of the De Larosière Report.

16.2 Foundations of macro-prudential policy

The dynamics which exacerbated and spread the present crisis led to systemic risk. Systemic risk is a situation of widespread market failure, whereby the rational responses of individual economic agents to the financial stress they undergo are highly correlated and magnify the stress of everyone (Aglietta and Moutot 1993). As a consequence, in a systemic risk situation, the social cost of the failure of any large and complex financial institution, be it a commercial bank or not, is much higher than the private cost. It makes government responsibility for overall financial stability not only desirable, but compelling.

16.2.1 Behavioral underpinnings of systemic risk

Systemic risk can occur under uncertainty, i.e., an environment intractable to the measurement of objective probabilities by using accumulated knowledge from the past. In such an environment, economic agents are driven by animal spirits. Since their rationality is bounded, market participants rely on heuristic patterns that select and integrate the knowledge relevant to their type of activity (Akerlof and Shiller 2009). However, they are aware of the limits of their knowledge and are thus induced to enhance it by paying attention to the opinions of others that they presume might have better information. Because others are on the same footing, strategic complementarities arise.

Whenever reflexivity is prevalent, strategic complementarities are the interrelationships that coordinate the interactive game between economic agents. Coordination under strategic complementarities gives rise to multiple self-fulfilling equilibria of mutual validation of expectations on one another's decisions (Cooper and John 1988). A system embodying multiple equilibria is liable to shifts in regime.

16.2.2 Banks' behavior under uncertainty in credit markets

Credit markets are markets of promises, and the game that is played is the confidence game. Trust or mistrust is what matters. Strategic complementarities were once described metaphorically by a prominent investment banker:[1] "As long as the music is playing, we all must go on dancing." Strategic complementarities are inbuilt in the heuristic pattern of banking.

The pattern is composed of two thresholds that determine the supply of credit of an individual bank. Banks have different degrees of risk tolerance which are distributed stochastically. The trigger threshold determines the entry of a bank in an asset market. It is the volume of credit already granted by other banks, more tolerant to risk, that induces a bank of a given risk tolerance to grant credit. Obviously this process leads to a self-feeding momentum. To what limit? What determines the decision of exit in a particular asset market?

It is the solvency threshold. A bank leaves the market when its non-expected loss reaches its value-at-risk (VaR). The VaR depends on a common factor, the asset price taken as collateral for loans. In turn asset purchases by borrowers depend on aggregate credit, i.e., on collective bank behavior.

In modelling credit supply along these lines, it can be demonstrated that credit is a stable rising function of the borrowing interest rate as long as a critical rate is not reached. All the way up, leverage increases, but inflating asset prices conceal the risk. Beyond the critical rate, which is impossible for the banks to assess because it is the outcome of the strategic complementarities of all banks, the credit regime becomes

---

[1] Mr. Prince, the former Citygroup CEO.

chaotic (Aglietta and Scialom 2010). A systemic crisis can erupt at any time.

16.2.3 Financial fragility: disaster myopia and erosion in security margin

As long as asset prices are fast-rising, endogenous credit risk amongst all lending institutions, or a large subset of them, seems to be low, all the more so as it rarely erupts. It is a tail risk with catastrophic losses when it strikes. Confronted with such a profile, the players in finance hold the risk to be nil, because the perception of this immeasurable risk is below their heuristic threshold. Fragility creeps into the system because market participants perceive large opportunities for capital gains and so undervalue risks, resorting to ever higher leverage to maximize their profits.

Therefore strategic complementarities lead to a disaster myopia (Guttentag and Herring 1986), which feeds a vicious circle to the apex of the speculative bubble. This roundabout process has been hugely magnified by the crazy development of the market-based credit system.

Figure 16.1 exhibits the procyclical roundabout process of mark-to-market leverage that spurred the portfolio of securitized credit in the ascending stage of the real estate cycle. Financial market intermediaries finance the purchase of credits to be structured with market borrowing (repos and commercial paper issuance). They prod the surge of credit to households by a host of banks and unregulated credit brokers. The originators sell the credits to the arrangers of mortgage-backed securities (MBS) for a fee. The process can be replicated with any credit eligible to pooling and repackaging in asset-backed securities (ABS).

16.3 Macro-prudential policy: a breakthrough in prudential regulation

At the London Summit, the G20 communiqué hinted at the need for macro-prudential policy. If correctly understood and effectively implemented, macro-prudential policy will cause a sea change in central bank doctrine and financial regulation. On the one hand, central banks will no longer rely exclusively on inflation targeting. On the

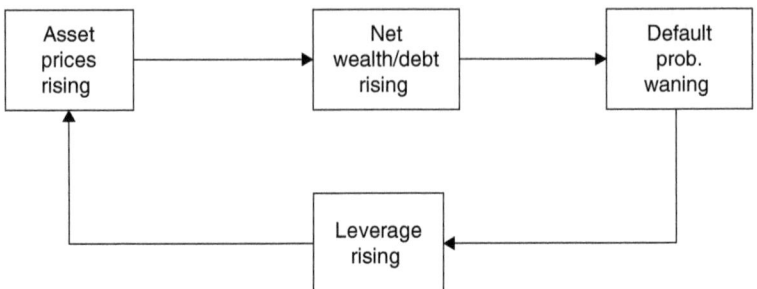

Figure 16.1 The vicious circle of the euphoric drive

other hand, systemic prevention will impinge upon capital regulation and liquidity management.

16.3.1 Central banks should control credit aggregates for the sake of financial stability

The focus solely on price stability has made central banks insensitive to the build-up of financial imbalances stemming from credit dynamics. The belief underpinning central bank policy in the last three decades has been the inherent stability of efficient financial markets. According to this view, exogenous shocks are taken care of by financial market adjustments. Only disruptions in the money supply can trigger inflation, and only inflation can have a long-lasting disorderly impact on financial markets.

Not only is this assertion contradicted historically by repeated episodes of financial crises in deflationary regimes, but it is logically inconsistent as well. Price stability is a necessary condition of financial stability, because high inflation is volatile and spreads uncertainty, as monetarists forcefully claim. It does not follow that it is a sufficient condition, as long as the hypothesis of perfect capital markets is rejected. It can even be argued that low and stable inflation is propitious to aggressive risk-taking that fosters financial instability. Indeed, price stability cum deep-rooted financial globalization entail low credit cost, high leverage and booming asset prices.

The inescapable conclusion is that central banks should pursue a dual objective of financial and price stability and should be empowered with enlarged responsibilities (Borio and Lowe 2002). It is well-known that it is impossible to achieve two objectives with a single

For a renewal of financial regulation 339

instrument; other tools must be forged to handle financial instability. Controlling global credit expansion throughout the financial cycle is the key to mitigating its perniciousness (Borio 2004).

Excessive credit growth must be measured against a benchmark, which is a long-run trend in inflation-adjusted credit growth co-integrated with long-run real GDP growth. This is the credit expansion that sustains a steady-state regime, consistent with a given rate of GDP growth. Excessive credit growth in the upward stage of the financial cycle is defined as the cumulative positive gap between actual credit expansion and the cumulative expansion that would have occurred if credit growth had followed the benchmark track.

To take the rise of the shadow banking system into account, the measurement of aggregate credit growth can be completed with new findings about liquidity and leverage (Adrian and Shin 2008c). They pertain to the behavior of financial intermediaries and impact the risk-taking channel of monetary policy.

16.3.2 Tools of macro-prudential policy: countercyclical capital against systemic risk and restraints on liquidity management

Moderating excess aggregate credit growth and regulating liquidity are the operating objectives of central banks when they implement macro-prudential policy to keep systemic risk at bay. The proper tools must affect the balance sheets of financial intermediaries. They are micro-economic instruments to achieve macroeconomic objectives, since a macro constraint on credit growth must be distributed to suppliers of credit that indulge in leverage. A top-down approach is in order. Two questions immediately arise: what is the perimeter of financial entities that should be subjected to this new layer of financial regulation? What are the specific instruments to be used and how are they related to the operating objectives?

The sub-system to be regulated should compound all systemically important financial entities (Acharya and Richardson 2009). They should be placed under the macroeconomic oversight of the central bank, though their microeconomic supervision might remain within the competence of supervisory bodies that are specific to each country. However, since firms belonging to the shadow banking system should be supervised as banks, the reach of supervisory authorities should be enhanced. Furthermore, a top-down approach can only be implemented if a permanent institutional arrangement is established between the central bank and the supervisory authorities, whenever they are separated from the central bank.

Every financial entity, which generates or transmits endogenous risk in credit and derivatives markets, whether due to its size, its interconnections or its leverage, should be labeled a systemically important financial institution (Brunnermeier et al. 2009). Such an institution should be subjected to countercyclical capital requirement to offset its contribution to systemic risk. This requirement is a proportion of the macro capital requirement deemed necessary by the central bank in the buoyant stage of the financial cycle to keep systemic risk in check. The overall capital requirement determined by the central bank is a function of the aggregate excess credit defined above. What has to be done to implement the top-down approach is to estimate the contribution of individual institutions to systemic risk resulting from the spill-over effect of their own excessive risk-taking.

Endogenous risk is due to contagion triggered by extreme losses hitting one firm via counterparty network and polarized distress sales, or is due to exposure to common macro risk factors. Because bank risk control models are inadequate to measure endogenous risk, it should be estimated by supervisors. Three methods can be applied: structural modeling of balance sheet interdependencies to simulate the chain reaction of a shock occurring in one institution (Goodhart, Sunirand and Tsomocos 2005); macro stress testing conducted by the central bank with all systemically important institutions to determine their likely losses and capital requirements under extreme scenarios defined by the central bank; statistical measures of co-risk, using market data, to estimate how much the deterioration of the financial situation in one institution impinges upon the risk of extreme losses in others (Adrian and Brunnermeier 2009; IMF, 2009).

To determine the countercyclical capital assigned to a systemic financial entity, the supervisor can compute the contribution of this entity to systemic risk, using any of the three methods.

Besides, banks are vulnerable to the interaction between credit and liquidity risk. This is particularly troublesome with shadow banks, which depend entirely on market liquidity for funding. Their potential fragility can be measured by two indicators, once off-balance-sheet items have been reintegrated into the balance sheets: the maturity mismatch and the ratio of leverage.

The most sensitive exposures to liquidity risk are illiquid asset pools in mark-to-market trading accounts. Asset pools are backed by liabilities financing them. An obvious drawback of mark-to-market accounting is the fact of valuing assets independently of the maturity of the debts that finance them. A pool of illiquid assets will have the same mark-to-market value whether the liabilities have a maturity of one week or T years.

A way to induce better liquidity management stems from the design of accounting norms closer to fair value, namely mark-to-funding accounting. Pools of illiquid assets should be paired with the liabilities financing them in the process of valuation. A pool of assets in a trading portfolio, financed by short-term debts (less than a year), should be marked-to-market. The same pool, financed by T-year bonds, should be priced according to the discounted expected future average price of the assets over T years. In a crisis, this method will be rewarded, because the mark-to-funding value in the balance sheets of the assets whose financing is carefully managed will be higher than the market price of the assets. Proper accounting will give an incentive to manage liquidity wisely, instead of relying blindly on market liquidity which can dry up abruptly.

16.4 Prompt corrective action: the cornerstone of micro-prudential policy

Reorienting financial prudential policy towards systemic concern involves a top-down approach. However, this type of inflexion should be backed by a drastic reshaping of micro-prudential policy. Indeed, laxity in supervision largely contributed to the regulatory capture by investment bankers that led to the financial meltdown in the US and in the EC. The principle of prompt corrective action (PCA), introduced in the US to discipline deposit banks (Benston and Kaufman 1998), should be extended to all systemically important institutions. The Financial Stability Board (FSB) should promote the application of PCA beyond the US. Indeed, PCA has a triple merit: being partly automatic, it escapes the pressure of bank lobbies; being progressive, it addresses the deterioration in bank balance sheets early enough to avoid involving the taxpayer most of the time; using simple tools, it is transparent and shielded from the bad faith of the supervisees.

Although PCA is a matter for micro-prudential policy, it is nevertheless consistent with the systemic reorientation in financial regulation if it has the potential to limit the build-up in leverage that leaves the financial system vulnerable to a sudden reversal. The rationale for a ceiling on the leverage ratio, which is a constituent of PCA, is that it is binding during the euphoric period of the cycle. It forces the banks either to raise new equity (costly but easy during the expansion stage of the cycle) or to restrain balance sheet growth. Of course, these two options are onerous in terms of profitability but it is exactly what should be done. Besides, they can be justified and interpreted as a Pigovian tax.

Moreover, the implementation of PCA involves the adoption of a special resolution regime for financial institutions in order to give credibility to the closure rule which is the cornerstone of PCA policy. Giving the regulator the legal set of tools to resolve all the issues related to systemic financial institutions (acquisition by a private sector purchaser, creation of a bridge bank, partial transfer of deposits and assets to a good bank, temporary public control, etc.), this new resolution regime could become a powerful instrument to alleviate the too-big-to-fail problem and so to contribute to the objective of global financial stability.

16.4.1 A benchmark: the American PCA framework

US banking supervision, introduced in 1991 under the Federal Deposit Insurance Corporation Improvement Act (FDICIA), is a landmark to be developed in a general framework to back up the macro-prudential reshaping of financial regulation. The general idea is the following: the banks are classified according to simple capital/asset ratios (from well-capitalized to critically under-capitalized) and each category is associated with both mandatory and discretionary provisions. When a bank is downgraded to a lower level of capital zone, the regulatory constraint is consequently reinforced. Supervisors are empowered to close down a bank within 90 days after it has crossed the threshold of critical undercapitalization. At this point, the Federal Deposit Insurance Corporation (FDIC) is vested with the powers of the receiver which is the liquidator, or with the capacity of a conservator that acts as an

For a renewal of financial regulation 343

administrator in order to resolve the institution's crisis. The advantages of this procedure are twofold: on the one hand, it reduces moral hazard in bank behavior; on the other hand, it discourages the regulator's forbearance. Requiring and enforcing resolution at a pre-specified low but positive capital level constitute a closure rule.

16.4.2 What should the trigger thresholds for early intervention be?

What could the closure rule be? Obviously, a risk-based capital measure cannot be elected as a trigger point for early regulatory intervention. Most of the banks which were bailed out during the 2007–08 financial crisis were found to be well capitalized according to Basel 2. For instance, the two largest Swiss banks (UBS and Credit Suisse) were among the best-capitalized large international banks in the world (Hildebrand 2008); according to a simple leverage ratio, they were among the worst capitalized. When leverage is interpreted strictly as the ratio of total assets to common equity, UBS reached a leverage ratio of 53 at the end of 2007. This is a very high figure, even compared to US investment banks, which were heavily leveraged (Lehman at the same date had a leverage ratio of 30.7). Therefore, had UBS been an American bank and were investment banks enrolled under the same principles of supervision as deposit commercial banks, UBS would have been classified as critically under-capitalized.

On the basis of these observations, the Basel 2 measurement of capital adequacy cannot claim to provide the trigger thresholds for early coercive intervention.

From our point of view, the macro-prudential measurement of capital adequacy is not a direct substitute either. Indeed, the *ex ante* influence of the regulator on the future behavior of banks is strengthened by the *ex ante* knowledge of prompt corrective action associated with each threshold of intervention. The credibility of supervision is grounded on the predictability of the coercive action, which requires immutability of the trigger points in the course of time. In particular, the closure rule should be pre-determined and non-adjustable. This is not the case for the macro-prudential capital ratio which varies during the cycle. So we can imagine a double criterion. Banks and other systemic financial institutions have to respect both their macro-prudential capital adequacy ratio (responsibility of the systemic regulator) and a simple leverage ratio defining in particular the closure rule (responsibility of micro-prudential regulator). A crude leverage ratio, i.e., a leverage ratio on common equity,[2] provides a safeguard against the shortcomings of risk-weighted requirements. It protects individual banks against their underestimation of risk and the incapacity of their models to capture endogenous risk.

The proposal presents at least three main advantages:

- A simple leverage ratio is a trigger threshold for early regulator interventions, coupled with a special bank bankruptcy regime. Conceptually and operationally, there is a continuum between regular prudential policy – the gradual process of supervisory coercive actions with pre-specified sanctions associated with prudential triggers – and bank insolvency proceedings. The credibility and severity of the pre-insolvency measures (early interventions) protect the taxpayer against the moral hazard generated by the financial safety net and arm the supervisors against regulatory capture (Scialom 2007).
- The leverage ratio is easy to measure, publicly verifiable and hard to manipulate. It operates fully independently of any complex modeling assumption and calibration procedures. Hence it alleviates the risk of regulatory capture and of regulatory arbitrage.
- Although it is a tool of micro-prudential policy, it is nevertheless consistent with the systemic reorientation in financial regulation. It contributes to limiting the build-up in leverage and subsequently reinforces the resilience of the financial system to unexpected large losses. The rationale for a simple leverage ratio is that it is binding during the euphoric period of the cycle and forces the banks either to raise new equity (costly but easy during the expansion stage of the cycle) or to restrain balance sheet growth.

Nevertheless, episodes of crisis in Citigroup, Bank of America and several other US banks, Northern Rock, the largest Swiss banks and many German banks, underline a thorny problem. Although the adoption of a simple leverage ratio as a trigger point of intervention might

---

[2] For a discussion on the need to adopt this kind of crude leverage ratio based on the most basic form of equity (held by the owners of the bank with voting power and hence who have the right to exercise control over the bank) excluding hybrid claims such as subordinated debts or preferred shares see: Geneva Report, chapter 4 "counter cyclical regulation" (Brunnermeier et al. 2009).

be a good solution for "traditional banks" with essentially a banking book, it does not constitute an efficient solution for the systemically important shadow banks. The proposal of extending PCA policy to the new market intermediaries involves a renewal of the gradual coercive device in a way that takes the lessons of the current crisis into account. For systemically important financial institutions, a set of simple, publicly verifiable and hard to manipulate indicators should provide early warnings for the various dimensions of risk in investment banking (including maturity mismatches, funding liquidity risk, risk of large losses in trading books). A battery of indicators can act as trigger points for regulatory intervention. They include quantity indicators: gross leverage ratio extending to off-balance-sheet items, maturity mismatch of different asset classes measured by the discrepancy between mark-to-funding and mark-to-market value, liquid assets/short-term debt (Aglietta and Scialom 2010). They also encompass market price indicators such as funding spreads and CDS spreads.

The extension of the PCA framework to systemically important shadow banks also involves alterations in the mandatory and discretionary coercive provisions associated with each downgraded category. Concerning the trading book, a rule imposing that issuers of securitized products retain a certain proportion of the underlying risk (non-hedged) on their books for the life of the instrument, with the amount depending on the regulator's assessment of the bank's – or shadow bank's – situation, could be introduced in the set-up. Gradual capital charges against illiquidity could also be included in the PCA mechanism.

16.4.3 The required legal and institutional changes in bank resolution framework

The implementation of prompt corrective action requires the adoption of specific insolvency laws for all banks and more generally for systemic financial institutions at the domestic level. One of the main challenges for financial stability is to create a regulatory framework to overcome the too-big-to-fail problem (Dewatripont and Rochet 2009; Eisenbeis and Kaufman 2005), which has paradoxically been exacerbated by the methods of resolution used during the 2007–08 financial crisis. Currently, when a large interconnected financial firm is in severe distress, there are only two options: either it obtains outside capital or funding from the government, or it files for bankruptcy under the general corporate bankruptcy law. This is not appropriate and can dramatically affect financial markets, as the Lehman Brothers case illustrates. Therefore, the adoption of a specific resolution regime for all systemic financial institutions is the keystone for comprehensive regulatory reform in order to mitigate systemic risk (Squam Lake Working Group on Financial Regulation 2009b).

The resolution authority (regulator or separate institution) would be vested with the legal powers to put the firm into conservatorship or receivership and then to administer its effective orderly reorganization or wind-down. This task would be facilitated by forcing the biggest financial institutions to pre-plan for their own demise (living wills) and so to clarify and simplify their legal structures, whose complexity has been conducive to regulatory and tax arbitrage (Avgouleas, Goodhart and Schoenmaker 2010). As underlined by Cihak and Nier (2009), the main goals of the resolution process should be, on the one hand, the minimization of the impact of the potential failure on the financial system, and on the other hand, the reduction of the need for taxpayer funds. The trustee of the conservatorship or receivership should be endowed with broad powers. It should be able to create a bridge financial institution, to sell or transfer the assets or liabilities of the distressed institution, to renegotiate or repudiate the institution's contracts (including with its employees), to deal with the derivative book and more generally to drastically restructure the institution and replace its Board of Directors and senior officers. None of these actions should be subject to the approval of the stakeholders or creditors of the failed institutions.

This kind of new legal resolution mechanism could be reinforced by the introduction of automatic recapitalization, involving private creditors in the resolution process, thus reducing moral hazard in the financial system shares (Squam Lake Working Group on Financial Regulation 2009a). This could be done via a new debt contract with a covenant stipulating a compulsory conversion clause into common equity when the crude leverage ratio is low enough. For this forced recapitalization mechanism to be effective, it needs to impose an issue rule on banks for this new type of debt (called "recap-bonds"). For each euro of core tier 1 capital, banks could be required to issue a minimum of n euros of recap-bonds outstanding. These new bonds would be classified as hybrid claims. The yield spread between "recap-bonds" and senior bonds would constitute a market-generated indicator of the counterparty risk and so could become an early warning indicator of the risk of regulator mandated debt-for-equity swap. Under this proposal, the threat of expropriation of the shareholders is replaced by the threat of an extreme dilution of their ownership. This type of device would be conducive to a great improvement in the complementarity between market and regulatory discipline to alleviate the too-big-to-fail problem.

16.5 Proposals for a renewed prudential architecture in Europe

While the proposed regulatory framework – combining a top-down approach in capital requirement and a PCA procedure in supervision – is relevant for all major jurisdictions in the world, it cannot be implemented straightaway in the fragmented European organization that weakens supervision in Europe. Major institutional changes are badly needed.

16.5.1 The current EU prudential framework

The present EU supervisory arrangements focus mainly on the supervision of individual firms and place too little emphasis on macro-prudential issues. The present system is grounded on minimal harmonization of prudential rules,[3] as required by the Commission Directive on financial regulation and mutual recognition of national regulatory standards and practices. As such, the single passport system is based on two related pillars:

- the principle of control by the home country for domestic operation and overseas branches;
- the host regulator's responsibility for subsidiaries of foreign banks.

It follows that crisis management primarily depends on national authorities, as well as the fiscal burden for bailing out the banks they

---

[3] As the De Larosière Report points out, the present regulatory framework in Europe lacks cohesiveness. The main reason for this situation stems from the option provided to EU members in the enforcement of the Directive, which led to a wide diversity of national transpositions.

regulate. The flaws in the loose coordination of domestic institutions are aggravated in the Euro zone. A monetary union with a plurality of national supervisors requires tighter cooperation among them.

The so-called De Larosière Report published in February 2009, which presents a detailed and relevant diagnosis of the shortcomings of the European prudential and regulatory framework and proposes substantial reforms, could constitute an adequate framework for implementing our regulatory and supervisory proposals.

16.5.2 A three-tiered approach for European prudential architecture

The De Larosière Report comes up with a three-tiered approach:

- a systemic regulator at the "top": the European Systemic Risk Council (ESRC) located at the European Central Bank (ECB);
- functional regulators in the "middle tier": a European Banking Authority, a European Securities Authority and a European Insurance Authority;
- three functional regulators at the domestic level at the bottom.

At the top, in the proposed model of central bank-based systemic risk regulator, the current Banking Supervision Committee of the ECB would be replaced by the ESRC, which would benefit from the logistical support of the ECB. The ESRC/ECB, with access in real time to information generated in financial centers and transmitted to national central banks and domestic supervisors, will be in a position to trace fast changes in exposure of the main market makers with operations in several integrated markets. Moreover, the ESRC would work as a warning agency and in times of crisis would be in the best position to assist the ECB Board and Council of Governors to arrive at a diagnosis and work out a mode of intervention to deal with a liquidity crisis at the most appropriate time. It could also help the Council to coordinate rescue operations for major cross-border bank failures, involving more than one country and national central bank.

What about the middle level? Currently, the main means by which the EU Council deals with EU cross-border financial groups are the supervisory colleges. They are established when a financial group operates in another member state through one or more branches, or subsidiaries. The college is chaired by the home country supervisor of the group's parents and functions on the basis of ad hoc mandatory written arrangements, agreed upon by the competent authorities to allow the home country to implement consolidated supervision of the group. Theses colleges raise two major issues: the legal power of the lead regulator can be insufficient to enact coercive measures in the host country and the quality and quantity of information shared in the college can be deteriorated in the event of financial distress and so the trust between the members of the college can be highly jeopardized precisely when it needs to be strong (Centre for European Policy Studies 2008). The disastrous rescue of Fortis substantiates this fear.

To overcome those shortcomings, the De Larosière Report proposes the establishment of an integrated European System of Financial Supervision (ESFS) through the creation of three European Authorities: a European Banking Authority, a European Insurance Authority and a European Securities Authority. While, at the bottom, it can be argued that national supervisors are best-equipped to carry out day-to-day supervision and to be responsible for reporting to the European level, the ESFS is indispensable at the upper level. The ESFS is designed as an integrated but decentralized network, which fully respects the subsidiarity principle. Indeed the powers of the new "Authorities" would be significantly reinforced, compared with the present arrangements. The main key competences of the Authorities would be the following:

- adoption of binding supervisory standards;
- oversight and coordination of colleges of supervisors and legally binding mediation between national supervisors;
- licensing and supervision of EU-wide institutions considered as systemic;
- binding cooperation with the ESRC to ensure adequate macro-prudential supervision; and
- a coordinating role in crisis situations.

In June 2010, the European Commission proposed a new framework for a coordinated – rather than unified at EU level – macro- and micro-prudential device along the lines proposed by the De Larosière Report. The proposal has to be put to a vote in parliament to be set up in 2011. Even if this new prudential architecture constitutes a substantial improvement compared to the current supervisory and regulatory arrangements, it reveals weaknesses. The European Systemic Risk Board (ESRB), which would be headed by the President of the ECB, will be in charge of EU-level macro-prudential regulation and supervision. Although it would identify risks with a systemic dimension, issue risk warnings and if necessary recommend specific actions to avoid the build-up of deeper problems, the ESRB would not have any binding power to impose measures on member states. Moreover, in contrast with the Obama administration's regulatory reform proposal, the ECB will not be the supervisor of the systemic cross-border financial groups directly. These limitations could significantly weaken the role and performance of the ESRB as Europe's regional systemic regulator. The EU agreement also establishes a new micro-prudential authority at the EU level: the European system of financial supervisors in accordance with the De Larosière Report. Importantly, this new EU level supervisory authority will be endowed with binding decision-making power in the case of disagreement between the home and host state supervisors, including within the college of supervisors.

16.6 Conclusion: a comprehensive framework

The global financial crisis has pinpointed the relevance and the virulence of systemic risk in modern innovative finance. It is based on the propensity of credit markets to drift to extremes in close correlation with asset price spikes and slumps. In turn, this propensity is nurtured by the heuristic behavior of market participants under severe uncertainty. When plagued by disaster myopia, market participants spread systemic risk. Such adverse conditions have been magnified by financial innovations that have made finance able to annihilate micro-prudential policies.

Malfunctioning in finance is so deep and disorders are so widespread that sweeping reforms are the order of the day. Macro-prudential policy should be the linchpin of relevant reforms but micro-prudential regulations also need to be reshaped to become consistent with this financial stability priority. Consequently, bank supervisors should broaden their oversight to a much larger perimeter, encompassing all systemically important institutions. Countercyclical capital provisions should be required and linked to the control of the aggregate credit supply. Leveraged institutions without any deposit base should be offered incentives for much stricter liquidity management. A prompt corrective action policy enlarged in its scope and adapted to mark-to-market financial intermediaries coupled with a systemic financial institution resolution framework could be an effective institutional design. It could alleviate the too-big-to-fail problem which feeds systemic risk and avoid the currently prevailing regulatory capture.

Implementing macro-prudential policy entails institutional changes. Central banks, bank supervisors and other financial regulators need to work much more closely than before, because the spread of systemic risk is not deterred by institutional and geographical frontiers. The changes that need to be made are particularly drastic in Europe, where national parochialism makes the resolution of orderly cross-border bank crises all but impossible.

PART VI

The daily adjustment of market technology

Introduction to Part VI

ERIC BROUSSEAU AND JEAN-MICHEL GLACHANT

The three chapters in this part develop the idea that, in practice, markets are highly complex (social) technologies, in which fine-tuning is difficult to manage, because it requires an in-depth understanding of the logic of each component and of its interplay with the other components. Many actors can play on this complexity to manage strategies aimed at generating rents and capturing value. The various chapters discuss how it can be institutionally managed.

Howard Shelanski's chapter focuses on an in-depth analysis of the doctrine to be implemented regarding a (dominant) firm's unilateral refusal to deal with a competitor. More precisely he analyzes whether intellectual property could be the basis of a de facto recognition of a right not to refuse to deal. Indeed, some advocate that the long-term general interest is to encourage investments in R&D and creation, which might result in strong protection of the rights of the IP owners. Shelanski convincingly argues that there are no reasons to overprotect IP owners. Indeed, antitrust authorities and courts should apply a rule of reason principle and analyze case by case the social cost and benefits of having the owner of an "essential facility" denying access to its competitors. While such a situation may occur, there are no reasons to consider that works of creation and inventions should be presumed to be more strategic and risky investments than other assets.

This case illustrates well a central argument developed during the course of this book. (Performing and efficient) markets are most of the time the result of institutional bricolage, because of the sophistication of the underlying social technology. Markets are not the simple implementation of general and simple principles like "competition" and "optimal trade-off between the protection and diffusion of new knowledge." Rather, they are produced by specific adjustments made to a set of technological, historical, and local constraints that may lead to contrasted solutions here and there. Thus the judicialization of the building of markets is much more preferable to the implementation of too rigid and detailed rules, because it allows adaptation to specific circumstances such as the actual competing and investment capabilities of actors, the existence of bottlenecks and alternatives, the relevant horizon to be considered (short vs. long termism), etc. Basically, Howard Shelanski argues that the number of variables and situations to be considered is so huge that it is more relevant, from a governance point of view, to allow market players to sue and negotiate the structure of the market, than to let any social planner design optimal institutional frameworks, that would always rely on incomplete or not sufficiently up-dated information about users' needs, and suppliers' techno-economic constraints.

On the other hand, an independent and powerful third party is needed. Indeed, direct negotiation among market players and self-regulation could indeed lead to the capture of the process of market building by dominant players that could well promote technologies and infrastructures extending their domination (Brousseau and Glachant, 2011). This is why conflicts and competition about the establishment of market rules and structures should occur under the shadow of a public ruler oriented toward the promotion if not of the general interest, then at least of a reasonable balance of interests among the various stakeholders.

The chapter by Shaun McRae and Frank Wolak contributes to the explanation of why in certain circumstances the judicial system might have a limited capacity to oversee market activities. In their chapter entitled "How Do Firms Exercise Unilateral Market Power? Empirical Evidence from a Bid-Based Wholesale Electricity Market" they illustrate well how difficult it is to build competitive markets. Their analysis of the concrete exercise of market power by firms shows how subtle and invisible strategies can be developed, making it quite a complex task to assess, and therefore oversee the behavior of market players. Indeed they show that the implementation of what is the most competitive type of mechanism – auctions – did not prevent firms exercising market power. Without breaking the law, and simply to maximize their profits, New Zealand electricity suppliers were able to capture significant rents over consumers. This raises the issue of development of methods to detect and measure the exercise of market power. This also raises the issue of developing capabilities to guarantee effectively fair competition. All in all their analyses call not only for sophisticated models to assess the behavior of market players, and then the involvement of experts like engineers and economists in the process of market framing, but also the need for specialized entities, like regulators, to specialize in the assessment of marketing strategies due to the specificity of each market.

In his chapter on the economics of exchanges Craig Pirrong highlights the central role of intermediaries, organizers, and platforms. He points out that any exchange results from a trade-off between the collective will to reduce transaction costs and the "natural monopoly" characteristics of the three main and complementary activities that allow such a reduction. Indeed trade execution, clearing, and settlements are all characterized by strong economies of scale and of scope, and those involved in these activities rely on network effects to provide efficiency gains to the market players. All this gives agents involved in these platforms a strong ability to capture all kind of rents. They do so both by vertically and horizontally integrating activities and by setting pricing schemes for trading services as well as rules. That said, Craig Pirrong also highlights the various elements that combine to prevent perfect collusion among those who control the trade of securities and derivatives. First, their heterogeneity – they play different roles, but also some traders are directly operating in exchanges – results in competition and a lack of consensus in manipulating instruments to capture and distribute rents. Second, technology, and in particular digital technologies, tends to reduce the traditional informational and reputational advantages of those operating on the floor. Third, competition among exchanges prevents full capture. Lastly, the government can also be the arbitrator of conflicts among interest groups. All in all, none of these factors guarantees full efficiency, but they all combine to mitigate rent seeking by market operators.

17 | Antitrust liability in the US for unilateral refusals to deal in intellectual and other property

HOWARD A. SHELANSKI

17.1 Introduction

In recent years there has been an increasing shift away from command-and-control regulation and toward legal regimes that foster the development of competitive marketplaces over which regulation is no longer, or at least much less, necessary. To an increasing degree, then, regulation can be said to have changed its orientation from restraining market failures to manufacturing markets that will overcome those failures (Kearney and Merrill 1998). One way in which regulation has made this transformation is to focus more on mandating that incumbent, dominant firms provide access to their facilities to new entrants than on restraining the market behavior of the incumbents. The local competition provisions of the Telecommunications Act of 1996 in the United States provide one example of such an access-oriented approach. More generally, antitrust law can also be used to govern the relationships among dominant firms and their rivals in such a way to avoid monopoly and to "manufacture" more competitive market structures, although the conditions under which this can and should be done are both limited and controversial. This chapter will address such use of antitrust law in innovative industries in which intellectual property may be the critical asset for competitive entry and success.

A firm's unilateral refusal to deal with a competitor has always been a shaky foundation upon which to build a case for liability under Section 2 of the Sherman Act, the relevant statute in the United States. American antitrust law nonetheless has long recognized a duty to deal with rivals in some limited circumstances. The recent trend in the federal courts has been to further diminish potential exposure for dominant firms that individually refuse to supply their competitors with goods or services that the latter need to compete. That shift has been strongest in cases in which the refusal to deal involves intellectual property (IP), creating differences among courts in the extent to which they allow antitrust to reach refusals to supply property protected by IP rights. Put most plainly, the question that has prompted divergent answers from the courts is whether a firm's unilateral refusal to supply a rival with IP should be judged under the Section 2 approach that applies to other (non-IP) property or instead should be exempted from normal antitrust scrutiny.

If one thinks as a matter of precedent or policy that antitrust law should impose a duty to deal in some cases, then eliminating refusal-to-deal liability for IP needs justification. If one takes the position that there should never be liability for refusals to deal in any property, this emerging shift is troubling because it represents only piecemeal progress toward a general antitrust rule of per se legality for unilateral refusals to supply competitors. In this chapter, I take as given that under current doctrine unilateral refusals to deal can sometimes be illegal under Section 2 of the Sherman Act. Instead, I focus upon the federal courts' varying approaches to refusals to deal in IP and how those approaches differ from the courts' treatment of refusals to supply rivals with other kinds of property.

As discussed below, some circuit courts treat refusals to supply IP as susceptible to rule-of-reason inquiry under Section 2 of the Sherman Act whereas at least one court, the US Court of Appeals for the Federal Circuit, essentially exempts refusals to deal in IP from that antitrust inquiry. This chapter argues in favor of the former and against the latter; it argues that neither economics nor IP policy considerations provides a sound basis for exempting refusals to supply IP from antitrust law's general liability standard for unilateral refusals to deal. This is not to say that IP should not sometimes be treated deferentially in antitrust enforcement. That deference, however, should flow from the same factors that in most cases weigh against antitrust mandates to deal in any property: deterrence of innovation or of investment in procompetitive strategies. Sometimes those factors will be magnified where IP is at stake; but they are not so systematically different for intellectual property that refusals to supply IP should be exempted from the antitrust standard applicable to other property.

17.2 Why might unilateral refusals to deal matter?

There are both policy and doctrinal reasons why unilateral refusals to deal might matter for antitrust enforcement. On the normative side, there is a reasonable consensus that, at least in theory, a firm's refusal to supply its rivals can under some conditions harm both short-term and long-run consumer welfare (Carlton 2001;[1] Frischmann and Waller 2008;[2] MacKie-Mason 2002[3]). There is also consensus that the short-term and long-run effects of refusals to deal often, if not usually, move in opposite directions. While there may be short-run harms to price and output levels, there are likely to be longer run increases in investment and innovation (MacKie-Mason 2002: 2–3). Where the consensus breaks down is over views of how successfully courts and antitrust agencies can identify and balance the effects of a monopolist's refusal to deal.

The static concern with refusals to deal is that they can create allocative inefficiencies with higher prices and lower output than would result in a competitive market. Thus, a refusal to supply a necessary input to a downstream rival could reduce price competition in the downstream market and deprive consumers of any comparative efficiencies the denied firm might have. For example, foreclosure of access to distribution channels owned by the upstream firm could prevent the downstream firm from achieving viable economies of scale (Carlton 2001). Strategic denials of complements to a rival's product could exclude the rival from the product market in which the two firms compete (Whinston 1990).

The dynamic concerns with refusals to deal are primarily that requiring a firm to trade with its rivals might reduce the firm's incentive to invest and innovate. It is commonly argued that if a firm must share with competitors the gains derived from costly innovation, it will innovate less than if it can decide for itself when, with whom, and on what terms it will trade. To the extent a refusal to deal reduces innovation in the downstream market there also could be harmful dynamic effects from withholding supply from rivals. But most commentary and court

---

[1] Identifying limited circumstances where refusals to deal cause net harm to consumers.
[2] Taking a broader view of refusal-to-deal harms.
[3] Finding consensus.

decisions have focused upon the deterrent effect of antitrust liability on upstream investment and innovation, and the accompanying dynamic harms to consumer welfare.[4]

The doctrinal reason to be concerned with refusals to deal is that, as a matter of current law, they can sometimes lead to antitrust liability. There has been vigorous and ongoing debate over whether courts and antitrust agencies are capable of separating harmful from non-harmful refusals to deal with sufficient accuracy to improve consumer welfare. In the shadow of that debate, the federal courts in the United States have long recognized a limited duty to deal with competitors under Section 2 of the Sherman Act (Frischmann and Waller 2008). Since the Supreme Court's 1912 decision in *Terminal Railroad*,[5] which required a group of rail carriers to provide competing companies with equal access to its bridge and terminal facilities, the federal courts have attempted to prevent unacceptably anticompetitive refusals to deal while recognizing a firm's general prerogative not to cooperate with its rivals. To this end, the federal circuit courts have offered several iterations of a multi-factored "essential facilities" doctrine through which cases warranting liability for refusal to supply a competitor could be identified[6] (Pitofsky et al. 2002; Robinson 2002). While some commentators have attacked that doctrine as lacking standards and providing a vehicle for baseless or unmanageable antitrust claims (Phillip Areeda famously labeled the doctrine "an epithet in search of a limiting principle"; Areeda 1989), others have argued that the essential facilities doctrine is no less manageable than the general rule-of-reason inquiry in monopolization cases and that courts are capable of applying it effectively (Popofsky 2006; Robinson 2002; Waller 2008).

The Supreme Court never expressly adopted the essential facilities doctrine or used the term affirmatively in its Section 2 jurisprudence. Until its decision in *Verizon Communications Inc. v. Law Offices of Curtis V. Trinko*,[7] however, the Court had never rejected the doctrine

---

[4] See, e.g., *Verizon Commc'ns Inc. v. Law Offices of Curtis V. Trinko, LLP*, 540 US 398, 414 (2004).

[5] *United States v. Terminal R.R. Ass'n*, 224 US 383 (1912).

[6] The essential facilities doctrine typically has four main elements: "(1) control of the essential facility by a monopolist; (2) a competitor's inability practically or reasonably to duplicate the essential facility; (3) the denial of the use of the facility to a competitor; and (4) the feasibility of providing the facility." *MCI Commc'ns Corp. v. AT&T Co.*, 708 F.2d 1081, 1132–33 (7th Cir. 1983).

[7] 540 US 398 (2004).

either. On several occasions the Supreme Court had upheld lower courts' reliance on essential-facilities tests and denied *certiorari* in cases where plaintiffs had prevailed on such claims.[8] In deciding refusal-to-deal cases, the Court has focused more on whether the particular facts of a case warrant liability under a rule-of-reason test than on crafting a systematic doctrine or test for such conduct.[9] In 1985, for example, the Court held in *Aspen Skiing Co. v. Aspen Highlands Skiing Corp.* that under a narrow set of conditions – notably, a profitable prior course of dealing with the plaintiff coupled with absence of a procompetitive explanation for changing course – unilateral refusals to deal could be illegal under Section 2.[10]

Prior to *Aspen*, the Court had imposed duties to deal in some cases where a monopolist held bottleneck control over inputs necessary for competition to exist.[11] While one might read *Aspen* or the Court's earlier decisions in *Otter Tail, Terminal Railroad*, or *Lorain Journal* implicitly to recognize some form of essential facilities doctrine, in no case did the Court try to establish a set of factors for consideration as the lower courts have done in proposing forms of an essential facilities test. In *Trinko*, the Court bluntly rejected any reading of its precedent to approve the essential facilities doctrine and asserted more forcefully than in the past that US antitrust law strongly disfavors the imposition of unilateral duties to deal.[12] The *Trinko* Court did not, however, reverse any of its prior duty-to-deal decisions or find refusals to deal to be legal per se. The federal courts' general approach to refusal-to-deal claims under Section 2 can therefore be fairly described as highly restrictive but not entirely preclusive.

---

[8] *Lorain Journal Co. v. United States*, 342 US 143 (1951); *Otter Tail Power Co. v. United States*, 410 US 366 (1973); *MCI Commc'ns Corp. v. AT&T Co.*, 708 F.2d 1081 (7th Cir. 1983), *cert. denied*, 464 US 891 (1983).

[9] As the Department of Justice explains the rule-of-reason approach to antitrust liability, the courts must undertake an extensive evidentiary study of (1) whether the practice in question in fact is likely to have a significant anticompetitive effect in a relevant market and (2) whether there are any procompetitive justifications relating to the restraint. Under the Rule of Reason, if any anticompetitive harm would be outweighed by the practice's procompetitive effects, the practice is not unlawful.

[10] 472 US 585 (1985).

[11] See *Terminal R.R. Ass'n*, 224 US 383; *Otter Tail*, 410 US 366.

[12] *Trinko*, 540 US.

17.3 Divergence in IP and non-IP refusal-to-deal cases

Over the past decade – starting even before the Supreme Court in *Trinko* narrowed the scope of liability for unilateral refusals to deal generally – US courts of appeals began to craft a different approach for refusal-to-deal cases involving intellectual property (Weiser 2002).[13] Those decisions have mostly made it harder for plaintiffs to win antitrust suits for refusal to supply IP, although they have done so to different degrees and in very different ways. The important difference that has developed is between courts that still find refusals to deal in IP susceptible to antitrust scrutiny under Section 2 (the First, Ninth, and Tenth Circuits) and courts (the Federal Circuit) that withhold such scrutiny and essentially exempt unilateral refusals to supply IP from antitrust liability. The split among the circuits is therefore not just a difference in the stringency of conditions plaintiffs must meet to prove anticompetitive refusals to deal under Section 2, but in whether plaintiffs can bring the antitrust claim at all when intellectual property is at issue. The key cases that illustrate this distinction are the First Circuit's decision in *Data General v. Grumman*[14] and the Federal Circuit's decision in *CSU v. Xerox*.[15]

At issue in *Data General* was whether copyright should fully shield a firm from antitrust liability for refusal to deal in the copyrighted product or whether such a refusal should still be examined under Section 2 of the Sherman Act. Put in terms of the rule of reason's balancing of pro- and anticompetitive effects, the questions before the First Circuit were whether an antitrust plaintiff should even "be allowed to demonstrate the anticompetitive effects of a monopolist's unilateral refusal to grant a copyright license" and, if so, whether the defendant would then have to justify its conduct as advancing consumer welfare.[16]

Two years before the First Circuit addressed *Data General*, the Tenth Circuit in *Rural Telephone Service Co. v. Feist Publications* at least implicitly answered both of the above questions affirmatively.[17] *Feist*

---

[13] "As some courts and commentators would have it, intellectual property development deserves different treatment under antitrust than real property."
[14] *Data Gen. Corp. v. Grumman Sys. Support Corp.*, 36 F.3d 1147 (1st Cir. 1994).
[15] *CSU, LLC v. Xerox Corp.*, 203 F.3d 1322 (Fed. Cir. 2000) (*CSU*) (*In re Independent Service Organizations Antitrust Litigation*).
[16] *Data General*, 36 F. 3d at 1186.   [17] 957 F.2d 765 (10th Cir. 1992).

involved a firm's refusal to sell its copyrighted directory listings to a competitor. In assessing the plaintiff's refusal-to-deal claim, the court never questioned the applicability of antitrust law to the IP at issue and proceeded to examine the defendant's refusal to deal under Section 2's rule of reason.[18] The Tenth Circuit did not specifically examine the relevance of IP to the defendant's burden of justification because the court ended the inquiry upon finding that the plaintiff could not meet its initial burden of showing harm to competition. But it would have been pointless for the court to have made even that initial inquiry if it thought that the mere existence of IP rights in the goods at issue would have freed the defendant of any burden and blocked antitrust liability.

The First Circuit's *Data General* decision is consistent with *Feist* but specifically addresses the defendant's burden to provide a procompetitive business justification in a case involving IP. As the Tenth Circuit did in *Feist*, the First Circuit found that unilateral refusals to deal with a rival in copyrighted works do not fall outside antitrust scrutiny and can violate Section 2.[19] But the Court found that in providing its countervailing justification for any exclusionary harm from the conduct, the defendant should receive a heightened presumption that its refusal to license IP was procompetitive within the meaning of the antitrust laws.[20]

How the First Circuit's procompetitive presumption would work is unclear from the decision. The court rejected Data General's attempt to make the procompetitive presumption for its refusal to deal irrebuttable.[21] The court instead characterized the balance of pro- and anticompetitive effects of a refusal to deal in IP as an empirical question whose answer should be informed but not predetermined by intellectual property law's underlying premise that the ability to exclude competitors is an important inducement to innovation.[22] For the First Circuit, that underlying premise supported a presumption that long-term innovation gains from a refusal to supply IP could compensate for short-term harms to competition "in a particular market for a particular period of time," but did not suffice to make the presumption conclusive for all markets at all times.[23] As the court put it,

---

[18] *Feist*, 957 F.2d at 767–69.   [19] *Data General*, 36 F.3d at 1184–85.
[20] *Id.* at 1188.   [21] *Id.* at 1184.   [22] *Id.*
[23] *Id.* at 1184.

"by no means is a monopolist's refusal to license a copyright entirely 'pro-competitive' within the ordinary framework of the Sherman Act. Accordingly, it may be inappropriate to adopt an empirical assumption that simply ignores harm to the competitive process caused by a monopolist's unilateral refusal to license a copyright."[24] The First Circuit thus adopted a rebuttable presumption that a desire to exclude others from using copyrighted work was a valid business justification that would outweigh the anticompetitive effects of a unilateral refusal to license a copyright.[25]

Under *Data General* the status of the goods at issue as IP therefore matters in refusal-to-deal cases, but in a very particular way: the more innovation and investment that goes into a product, the greater the risk that liability for refusal to deal in that product will deter procompetitive economic activity. The government grants intellectual rights only after a showing of certain levels of innovation, a showing that has not been made *ex ante* for other kinds of property. Therefore, the procompetitive elements of a firm's refusal to supply a rival with IP should receive greater presumptive, but still rebuttable, weight in the "ordinary" antitrust analysis than should non-IP-protected property. Section 2's rule-of-reason balancing test applies to refusals to supply IP, but the presumed weights of costs and benefits differ from cases involving property not subject to IP protections.

In *CSU v. Xerox*, the Federal Circuit took the step the First Circuit expressly declined to take and adopted a virtually preclusive presumption against liability for refusals to license IP or to sell IP-protected products (Melamed and Stoeppelwerth 2002).[26] At issue in *CSU* was Xerox Corporation's refusal to provide certain copyrighted material to independent, aftermarket repair organizations. The case was virtually identical on its facts to *Image Technical Services, Inc. v. Eastman Kodak Co.* ("*Kodak*"), in which the Ninth Circuit had found that the protection of IP rights could be a valid business justification for refusing to supply a competitor but that the justification could fail if found to be a pretext for anticompetitive conduct.[27] The *CSU* court rejected the Ninth Circuit's reasoning and ruled that for a refusal-to-deal claim

---

[24] *Id.* at 1185.   [25] *Data General*, 36 F.3d at 1147, 1187.
[26] *CSU, LLC v. Xerox Corp.*, 203 F.3d 1322 (Fed. Cir. 2000) (*CSU*) (*In re* Independent Service Organizations Antitrust Litigation).
[27] 125 F.3d 1195 (9th Cir. 1997).

involving IP to be heard in the Federal Circuit, a plaintiff must show either that the IP was obtained by fraud (i.e., is not legally IP) or that the claim involves tying of IP to non-IP (i.e., is not a pure refusal-to-deal claim). The Federal Circuit therefore closed the door in its jurisdiction to antitrust inquiry into refusal-to-deal claims involving IP-protected products; claims that might be heard were the products other than IP or the case brought in another circuit.

Taken together, the cases discussed above reveal several fault lines in the law governing unilateral refusals to deal in IP. One set of differences among courts is in the degree of special deference they afford to intellectual property rights as counterweights to exclusionary harm in refusal-to-deal cases, with the First Circuit falling between the apparent absence of special status for IP in the Tenth Circuit to the complete deference to IP as a justification in the Federal Circuit. Beneath those varying approaches is a more fundamental difference among the circuits on the question of whether a refusal to deal in IP should be an allowable basis for an antitrust claim at all. On this question the Federal Circuit departs from other courts in withholding antitrust scrutiny from a firm's refusal to supply a rival with IP.

The divergence highlighted by *Data General* and *CSU* might not matter if the circuit courts were either to converge on one approach toward refusals to supply IP or to eliminate refusal-to-deal liability generally as an antitrust claim. Neither prospect appears likely. Other circuits do not appear to have followed the Federal Circuit's lead in making refusals to deal in IP legal per se, but neither the First Circuit's *Data General*'s presumption nor any other approach appears to have become common currency in the federal courts either.

Moreover, the federal courts have not moved toward wholesale elimination of refusal-to-deal liability from antitrust law. While the Supreme Court in *Trinko* took a narrow view of refusal-to-deal precedent it did not eliminate such claims from the scope of Section 2.[28] The *Trinko* decision restricted *Aspen* to its unusual facts and placed the case "at or near the outer boundary" of Section 2 liability,[29] but it stopped short of overruling the case and in a back-handed manner left open the possibility of "adding ... to the few exceptions from the proposition that there is no duty to aid competitors."[30] The extent to

---

[28] 540 US 398 (2004). [29] *Trinko*, 540 US at 409.
[30] *Trinko*, 540 US at 411.

which the Court will eventually let stand any such exceptions by lower courts remains to be seen. As Section 2 doctrine currently stands, however, under appropriate conditions a unilateral refusal to deal is a valid antitrust claim. Just the year after *Trinko* the D.C. Circuit overturned the district court's dismissal of a refusal-to-deal claim by Covad Communications against Bell Atlantic.[31] The D.C. Circuit made clear that it found only that Covad's pleading stated its claim sufficiently to survive Rule 12(b)(6) dismissal, not that Covad would be successful in proving the factual conditions for refusal-to-deal liability under Section 2.[32] While the burden on the plaintiff to prove those conditions is high given the "sometimes considerable disadvantages"[33] of imposing antitrust liability in refusal-to-deal cases, the burden is not so high as to be the practical equivalent of the per se legality *CSU* confers where IP is involved.

The law governing refusals to deal in IP is therefore in an uncertain state. Courts that follow *CSU* for single-firm refusals to deal in IP while applying *Trinko*'s guidance for refusals to supply other kinds of property might in some circumstances treat the two kinds of cases differently, eliminating the possibility of liability in the IP cases but leaving open the possibility otherwise. Other courts might reject *CSU*'s permissive standard in IP cases and use what discretion *Trinko* leaves them to consider liability in all refusal-to-deal cases, while yet others could use that same discretion to move all unilateral refusals to supply in the direction of *CSU* and impose no liability except, perhaps, for the very rare case that exactly replicates the circumstances of *Aspen*.[34] Taken together, *CSU* and *Data General* raise the broad question of how the status of property as IP should matter in refusal-to-deal cases and the more specific question of whether courts should exempt unilateral refusals to deal in IP from liability under Section 2 of the Sherman Act.

Were the Supreme Court to take up the above questions, it would have four choices. First and least probably, it could adopt

---

[31] *Covad Commc'ns Co. v. Bell Atl. Corp.*, 398 F.3d 666 (D.C. Cir. 2005).
[32] *Id.* at 676.   [33] *Id.* at 412.
[34] In not overruling *Lorain Journal* or *Otter Tail*, the Court in *Trinko* leaves ambiguous whether a refusal-to-deal claim that replicates the facts of either of those cases would survive dismissal. The *Trinko* Court's emphasis on *Aspen* and its facts would appear to make the prospects for such claims doubtful, however.

a refusal-to-deal approach to IP that is friendlier to plaintiffs than the approach *Trinko* establishes, i.e., the Ninth Circuit's intent-based test from *Kodak* or something similar. It seems unlikely, however, that the Court would adopt a rule for IP that would let a case go to a jury when that same case would have had no basis for liability had it involved property other than IP. Second, the Court could adopt the *CSU* rule or one that similarly creates per se legality for a firm's refusal to supply IP to a rival, without making any effort to harmonize that rule with *Trinko*. Third, the Court could further reduce the potential for liability in all refusal-to-deal cases, taking *Trinko* a step further and possibly overruling *Aspen*. Finally, the Court could reverse *CSU* and rule that Section 2 applies to all refusals to deal, with no exemptions for cases involving intellectual property.

This chapter will argue for the last alternative above. The next section will examine several legal and economic justifications for a special rule for refusals to deal in IP and argue that they are unconvincing. The chapter will then turn to a discussion of general standards for refusal-to-deal liability. That section will explain why both policy considerations and available evidence weigh against further movement toward per se legality for unilateral refusals to deal under Section 2 of the Sherman Act.

17.4 One standard or two?

Both economic and legal reasons could exist for exempting refusals to deal in IP from the antitrust inquiry that applies to refusals to deal in other kinds of property. An economic justification would require reason to think that the harmful consequences of mandatory dealing in IP are systematically greater than the harms from mandatory supply of other products; moreover, those harms must be so much greater that it is not worth balancing them against the harms from refusal to deal in a rule-of-reason inquiry. Such a difference in economic effects could follow from a difference in how mandatory dealing affects the economic and competitive incentives regarding the different categories of property. Alternatively, the basis for differential treatment of IP could lie in a legal conflict between general antitrust law and the statutory regimes that specifically govern intellectual property. In the sections that follow, I will briefly address the potential statutory basis for withholding antitrust scrutiny from a firm's refusal to supply rivals with IP, and will then turn to the relevant economic arguments for treating IP and other property differently under Section 2.

17.4.1 Statutory basis for differing liability

I assume in this chapter that the legal fact of a patent or copyright is not in itself a sufficient basis for differentiating the antitrust treatment of IP from that of other property. That assumption is consistent with the case law, which generally holds that intellectual property protection is not a barrier to enforcement of the antitrust laws.[35] The D.C. Circuit in *Microsoft* wrote colorfully that the claim that IP rights insulate a firm from antitrust liability is "no more correct than the proposition that the use of one's personal property, such as a baseball bat, cannot give rise to tort liability."[36] That decision is only the most emphatic in a line of cases establishing that intellectual property law does not confer immunity from antitrust liability for conduct involving IP. The Supreme Court, for example, made clear in *Square D Co. v. Niagara Frontier Tariff Bureau, Inc.*, that it "strongly disfavor[s]" repeal of the antitrust laws by implication.[37]

The intellectual property statutes provide little support for the implied repeal the Supreme Court warned against in *Square D*. Section 271(d)(4) of the Patent Act prohibits a court from using a refusal to deal as grounds for denying an IP owner damages for infringement.[38] But that statutory provision does not expressly bar antitrust counterclaims by the infringer and does not appear to apply at all to Section 2 claims by a non-infringing plaintiff.

The case law to date does not fully specify the relationship between Section 271(d) and the antitrust laws. However, section 271(d)(4) might be read to preclude refusal-to-deal counterclaims in infringement litigation altogether where the defendant (who would be the antitrust plaintiff) has infringed the IP rights at issue, although that would be a very strong reading. Alternatively, the provision might be interpreted to bar the defendant from recovering damages on a refusal-to-deal counterclaim, because the damages would amount to

---

[35] See, e.g., *Data General*, 36 F.3d at 1147, 1184; *United States v. Microsoft Corp.*, 253 F.3d 34, 62–63 (D.C. Cir. 2001).
[36] *Microsoft*, 253 F.3d 34, 62–63.   [37] 476 US 409, 421 (1986).
[38] 35 USC § 271(d) (2003).

an offset and, hence, an effective reduction in the original plaintiff's infringement damages. That reduction in infringement damages would be in tension with the statute. Yet, the latter interpretation would not bar the defendant in the infringement case from obtaining an injunction against the IP owner's continued refusal to deal. Finally, infringement damages and antitrust damages could be viewed independently and non-exclusively under Section 271. While the choice of interpretation is unresolved, only the most expansive reading of the statute would preclude refusal-to-deal counterclaims altogether and, as noted, the statute has no application where the refusal-to-deal claim is being made in the absence of alleged infringement.

Similarly, the Patent Act's authorization in Section 154 for patentees "to exclude others from making, using, offering for sale or selling the invention throughout the United States" says nothing about exempting such exclusions from the antitrust laws.[39] Moreover, Section 154 provides patentees with no greater property rights than those that attach to tangible property under common law (Melamed and Stoeppelwerth 2002; Weiser 2002).[40] The government appears to share this latter view; in opposing *certiorari* in *CSU*, the Solicitor General stated that the government would "have serious concerns ... and not be prepared to endorse" a holding "that a refusal to sell or license property protected by a valid patent may never be the basis of an antitrust violation" except under the Federal Circuit's narrow exceptions.[41] Any argument for treating IP differently for purposes of refusal-to-deal liability therefore needs some basis other than the legal fact that the property involved in such conduct was protected by patent or copyright.

17.4.2 *The economic rationale for limited antitrust liability*

The underlying economic rationale for antitrust law's general presumption against mandatory dealing provides insight into whether antitrust law should apply at all to a firm's refusal to deal in IP. That rationale centers largely on economic incentives for initial investment and innovation. In discussions of why refusals to deal should be legal,

---

[39] 35 USC § 154(a)(1) (2003).
[40] Discussing similar objectives of intellectual and real property rights.
[41] Brief for the United States as Amicus Curiae: *Data General*, 36 F.3d at 10.

courts and commentators usually emphasize the potential deterrent effect of mandatory dealing on the investment incentives of the would-be defendant and of all others who would see imposition of liability as a signal of what might await them should their business succeed too well. This emphasis makes sense: If a firm is deciding whether to invest in an asset or in the research and development to produce an innovative product, it will be less favorably inclined to do so if it faces limits on its future economic exploitation of that property.

Limits on economic exploitation may come in many forms: taxes, land-use restrictions, and regulatory standards are some prominent examples. Society generally imposes such burdens because under the right circumstances their net benefits are worth the costs of whatever investment or beneficial economic activity they deter. Moreover, to the extent regulation does not handicap market competition, its deterrent effect on investment and innovation is likely to be muted, because firms can still gain on their rivals through such activities. Most taxes and regulations do not handicap market competition. There are exceptions, but in most cases regulatory and fiscal burdens are of general applicability and all rivals in the market must live with them equally. All pharmaceutical companies doing business in the United States must go through the Food and Drug Administration's drug approval process; all US telecommunications carriers must contribute to the universal service fund; and all American industrial workplaces must comply with Occupational Health and Safety Administration (OSHA) regulations.

Other regulations may target specific firms in ways that reduce their competitive advantages and diminish their incentives to invest in the innovations that give rise to such advantages. Such regulations nonetheless may be socially beneficial. Moreover, whether selective regulation will in fact deter desirable activity will depend on the facts and circumstances of particular cases. Nevertheless, policy makers should implement regulation that falls asymmetrically among firms within a market more cautiously than they approach rules of general applicability. The imposition of liability for refusing to deal falls within this cautionary category. Mandatory dealing requires the defendant, by virtue of its dominant position in the market for a particular product, to bear asymmetric regulatory burdens and to provide assistance to a competitor. Whereas some limits on exercise of market power may be neutral with respect to a firm's market position, mandatory dealing risks reducing a firm's profitable exploitation of its dominant position. Whatever intended benefits might motivate such rules, limits on a particular firm's market exploitation can create stronger investment disincentives than rules of general applicability. As Dennis Carlton and Kenneth Heyer explain, enforcement based on the static competitive effects of a firm's refusal to supply its rivals carries the risk of harm to dynamic efficiency that would reduce economic growth and welfare over time (Carlton and Heyer 2008). That rationale is reflected in the *Trinko* Court's concern with counterproductive enforcement that reduces firms' incentives to engage in the very competition and innovation the antitrust laws are designed to encourage and preserve.[42] It is also reflected in the First Circuit's grounding of *Data General*'s heightened presumption against mandatory dealing in IP in an assumed empirical link between IP and the pro-consumer innovation that antitrust law promotes.

One can imagine cases in which mandatory dealing would not interfere with investment incentives and where imposing liability for a firm's refusal to deal would not be economically harmful. For example, there may be cases in which dealing would be more profitable over the long run than not dealing with a rival and in which the only plausible motive for refusing to deal is anticompetitive. That was the lower court's finding in *Aspen*. In other cases, the firm already may be earning returns on its investment well in excess of the expected earnings upon which the firm based its decision to make the investment in the first place. In such cases the right to exclude is stronger than would have been necessary to prompt the innovation at issue *ex ante*, although mandatory dealing in that good may still raise a red flag for future investments. In yet other circumstances the benefits of competitive access to the product in question could have long-run benefits for competition and innovation that outweigh the costs of deterred initial investment and innovation.

The policy challenge lies not in theoretically identifying the above possibilities but, first, in identifying them with sufficient generality that mandatory dealing won't deter innovation by non-parties and, second, in implementing the details of any mandatory dealing arrangement. Both are fraught with difficulty. It can be hard for courts to distinguish the above categories of cases from those where harmful deterrence will

[42] *Trinko*, 540 US at 414.

occur. Even if they do, the remedy may turn the court into a regulator. These concerns about the role and capabilities of the courts are well known and were important motivators of the Supreme Court's decision in *Trinko* to restrict the established scope of Section 2 refusal-to-deal liability.

There is a further reason to be concerned about mandatory dealing, this one involving incentives of the would-be buyer rather than the owner of the property at issue in a case. When a firm obtains something through a mandate to deal, it neither produces the product for itself nor induces a third party to do so. While there may be cases in which it is economically inefficient for any firm other than the defendant to produce the good at issue, in most cases consumers gain in two ways from having the buying firm create a source of supply separate from the refusing monopolist. First, consumers obviously get the benefit of a second producer in the market and the possibility of competition that either directly or indirectly (in the case of upstream inputs) lowers retail prices and/or improves quality. Second, with two suppliers the long-run level of innovation in the product at issue is likely to be higher than under monopoly. While the relationship between market structure and innovation is complex, there are good reasons to expect a monopolist to have less incentive to innovate than a firm facing competition does (Arrow 1962). Any liability standard for refusals to deal should therefore avoid providing firms with an artificial or unnecessary way around self-supplying or finding an alternative to the refusing seller. The law should preserve the innovation incentives of potential buyers and third-party suppliers just as it does those of the original producer who is refusing to deal; denying antitrust claims aimed at refusals to deal might avoid the error of deterring anyone's innovation incentives, although with possible trade-offs in the form of under-enforcement errors.

Consequently, a minimum (but not sufficient) condition for Section 2 to mandate dealing with a competitor is that any potential competitor face either a legal or economic barrier to any alternative source of supply. The essential-facilities test generally contained a similar requirement that the plaintiff prove its inability to practically or reasonably duplicate the essential facility. The minimum condition I am suggesting requires that the barrier be one that any firm would face, not just the particular firm making the refusal-to-deal claim. For example, a plaintiff firm might have a financial structure that makes it unable to attract the capital to invest in producing the good at issue for itself, but such a firm-specific capital constraint should not count as a general economic barrier if another firm could plausibly enter the relevant market. Moreover, the kind of economic barrier that would satisfy the minimum condition is one that would make entry by any firm "uneconomic," which essentially means that the incumbent producer – i.e., the refusing seller – enjoys something akin to a natural-monopoly cost structure in production of the good or a physical monopoly over a necessary resource.

Similarly, any legal barriers must be of general impact and block any potential alternative to the refusing supplier. Such barriers may take a variety of forms, with primary examples being zoning rules that preclude alternative production and intellectual property protections that cannot be circumvented. An individual firm's inability to meet permitting requirements or invent around an IP barrier should not count unless it can be shown that no firm could reasonably overcome those legal hurdles.

One can imagine barriers to production other than economic and legal ones. Competitors might lack the technological know-how or other human capital necessary to produce the refusing seller's good. Although capability barriers might render it impossible as a practical matter for competitors to enter the market, such barriers should not be grounds for mandatory dealing by the firm that happened to take the initiative and develop the skills to innovate. Even where the requisite know-how is subject to trade secret protection, nothing legally prevents a firm from independently developing and deploying the same technology and the minimum condition for mandatory dealing would not be met. As an economic matter, a contrary approach would diminish the incentives for buyers and sellers alike to invest in improving their technology and workforce.[43] As a doctrinal matter, even in the past era of competitor-focused Section 2 jurisprudence, the case law was clear that a monopolist may exploit advantages that

---

[43] An interesting question might arise if a capability barrier to entry existed simultaneously with an economic or legal barrier. If competitors could not produce the good at issue even if any economic or legal hurdles were removed, then there is a good argument that the latter barriers should not count and the minimum condition for refusal-to-deal liability is not satisfied. So the real minimum condition is that there must be a *determinative* legal or economic barrier to alternative production by any firm.

are purely the result of "superior skill, foresight and industry."[44] For this reason, existing antitrust standards for refusal-to-deal liability incorporate the minimum requirement of a genuine barrier to competitive supply. The general rule-of-reason inquiry for claims under Section 2 requires the plaintiff to prove monopoly power (or its substantial probability) and the essential facilities doctrine requires proof of the practical impossibility of competitive provision of the good or input at issue.

In sum, the rationale for the presumption against mandatory dealing is grounded in economic incentive effects. While that rationale generally emphasizes the economic incentives of possible sellers, the anti-liability presumption for refusals to deal also finds justification in preserving beneficial incentives for competition and innovation by the would-be buyers.

Do the above considerations about the incentives of both buyers and sellers to invest in competition and innovation provide the basis for a withholding antitrust law's liability standard for refusals to deal from cases involving IP? At first look it might appear that the producer-incentive criterion is more important for IP than for other property. The prospects of successful development of IP and of its commercial utility may be more uncertain *ex ante* and make research and development riskier than other productive investments a firm might make. Moreover, the economic lifecycle of IP is uncertain, and firms can anticipate that rival innovators will seek to improve the technology at issue, potentially not just taking market share from the firm refusing to deal but knocking that firm from the market altogether. The investment hurdle for IP may also be higher than for other economic opportunities, because IP investments may be (although need not be) less reversible or recoverable than other investments. More generally, there could be many reasons why certain innovations might require inventors to expect to appropriate a larger benefit from their discoveries than other innovations require. Intellectual property rights are one means of strengthening expected appropriations.

Taking a more critical look, however, it is unclear that most or even the most valuable investments in IP need stronger economic incentives

---

[44] See *United States v. Aluminum Co. of Am.*, 148 F. 2d 416, 430 (2d Cir. 1945).

than other property investments. Development of IP does not always require higher capital or risk than, for example, construction of specialized manufacturing facilities, natural resource exploration, or real estate. Moreover, not all IP investment improves social welfare. Many patents lack economic value and are never practiced or enforced (Allison et al. 2004). Other IP may be developed for purely defensive purposes of protecting markets and blocking competition (Dogan and Lemley 2009)[45] although such cases may be hard to distinguish from bona fide innovation efforts (Gilbert 2007). On the other side, much valuable innovation is never patented, and scholars have cast doubt on the link between innovation incentives and IP protections (Arundel and Kabla 1998;[46] Hall 2002[47]). As a result, any refusal-to-deal liability standard that differentiated IP from other property on grounds of innovation incentives would miss much, if not most, industrial innovation. Moreover, a rule like *CSU*'s that exempts refusals to deal in IP from antitrust liability might induce innovators to seek IP protections where they otherwise would not. A more permissive approach to IP refusals under Section 2 is therefore hard to rationalize on grounds that IP investment requires systematically stronger economic incentives than other investments do.

The criterion of buyer incentives may even weigh in the other direction, toward a less lenient, more pro-plaintiff, antitrust approach to refusals to deal in IP, because refusals to supply IP will more likely satisfy the minimum conditions for mandatory dealing than will other refusals to deal. As discussed above, only when would-be buyers face an insurmountable economic or legal barrier to alternative provision of the good at issue should courts even consider a unilateral refusal-to-deal case. Otherwise they could weaken incentives for buyer-side investments in innovation and competition that, while entailing higher private costs to the would-be buyers, improve consumer welfare. Intellectual property protection is, by virtue of the legal exclusivity it confers on the inventor, more likely to impose such legal barriers on alternative supply sources. One cannot assume that IP imposes such

---

[45] A good example is "product hopping" in the pharmaceutical industry.
[46] Finding patenting rates at less than 50 percent across important industrial sectors.
[47] Concluding that IP protection in the United States cannot be justified by empirical data on innovation.

barriers because IP rights do not necessarily create market power for the rights holder.[48] Moreover, other kinds of protections, for example state trade-secret laws, might provide similar legal barriers for property not protected by patent or copyright. But in those cases where the refusing firm's market power does stem from its IP rights in the product at issue, potential buyers face a legal barrier to self-provision even in the absence of any economic barrier.

Even if one presumes that IP protections raise the likelihood of preclusive legal barriers to competitive entry, mandatory dealing should be an exceptional remedy. Concerns about seller-side investment incentives and the difficulty of enforcing and administering mandatory-dealing remedies remain. The point of the above discussion is not to argue for especially stringent (i.e., pro-plaintiff) antitrust review of refusals to deal in IP, but simply to show that when buyer-side incentives are taken into account, there is no reason for courts to place refusals to deal in IP beyond the reach of the antitrust analysis that would apply to other refusals to deal.

17.4.3 IP validity concerns and refusal-to-deal liability

The Federal Circuit's *CSU* decision implicitly raises the issue of patent validity in refusal-to-deal cases involving IP. Under *CSU* it appears that a defendant's assertion of an invalid but non-fraudulent patent would still supply a conclusively acceptable business justification for the refusal to supply a rival. From a competition policy perspective this presumption is troubling. Evidence suggests that a significant proportion of patents should never have been granted in the first place. While some such patents are obtained or maintained through fraud and might be screened out under *CSU* or otherwise violate the Sherman Act,[49] most invalid patents probably result not from fraud but from procedural flaws that make it impossible for the current patent-granting system accurately to separate strong from weak patent applications. The problems with the patent review process are well

---

[48] US Dep't. of Justice and FTC, Antitrust Guidelines for the Licensing of Intellectual Property § 2.2 (Apr. 6, 1995); *Illinois Tool Works Inc. v. Indep. Ink, Inc.*, 547 US 28 (2006).

[49] See, e.g., *Walker Process Equip., Inc. v. Food Mach. & Chem. Corp.*, 382 US 172 (1965).

documented⁵⁰ (Thomas 2001⁵¹). What is significant for current purposes is that invalid patents may comprise a substantial proportion of all patents held in the economy. One comprehensive study found that 46 percent of litigated patents between 1989 and 1996 were held to be invalid (Allison and Lemley 1998). Estimates from older studies show even higher proportions of patents being invalidated through litigation (Leslie 2006).⁵² To the extent barriers to entry result from IP protections that never should have been granted, refusals to deal in such "IP" are particularly harmful with no redeeming virtues for the economic incentives of sellers or buyers. The more invalid patents there are, the greater the likelihood that the balance between costs and benefits of mandatory dealing in IP weighs in favor of a legal standard more likely to result in liability. Imprecision in the patenting process is another reason not to have a conclusive presumption that an assertion of IP rights constitutes a valid business justification for otherwise anticompetitive conduct.

One possible response to the high rate of invalid patents is to allow plaintiffs to challenge the validity of patents upon which defendants rely to justify anticompetitive refusals to deal. A court's finding that a patent should not have been granted and the defendant's assertion of the invalid patent was a prohibitive barrier to competitive supply would weigh in favor of liability for having refused to deal in the invalid IP. Injunctive relief would not be necessary with the IP barrier removed, but retroactive damages could be awarded.

There are several problems with such an approach, however. Validity determinations in refusal-to-deal cases would be costly for litigants and the courts. Courts have generally relied on a presumption of validity where patents have been central to questions of antitrust liability.⁵³ Any special rule requiring validity determinations in refusal-to-deal cases that hinge on intellectual property rights would likely create bad incentives for both courts and parties. Courts would

---

⁵⁰ Numerous studies have found that patent examiners are constrained to spend very little time – estimates range from eight to twenty-five hours – on each application.
⁵¹ Noting that "the average time allocated for an examiner to address one application is understood to be between sixteen and seventeen hours."
⁵² Citing older empirical estimates.
⁵³ See, e.g., In re Tamoxifen Citrate Antitrust Litigation, 466 F.3d 187, 208–09 (2nd Cir. 2006).

have greater incentive to dispose of IP-related refusal-to-deal claims pre-trial regardless of the underlying antitrust merits in order to avoid time-consuming IP issues. Plaintiffs might file more, and weaker, refusal-to-deal claims against IP owners in the hope that putting IP validity into play will induce the defendant to settle even if antitrust liability is unlikely.

More fundamentally, the inquiry into IP validity presupposes that the legal status of property as protected IP should matter for the antitrust liability standard, a difference this chapter argues is unwarranted. Once one moves away from the *CSU* rule of essentially per se legality for refusals to deal in IP, the validity of IP should matter to the antitrust inquiry only insofar as it creates a legal barrier to alternative sources of supply (and hence creates the necessary, but not sufficient, minimum condition for refusal-to-deal liability). For that purpose, a presumption of IP validity does not help the defendant and may help the plaintiff meet its minimum, threshold burden. Because the error costs from invalid patents here fall on the defendant (who could choose not to assert its false IP protections) rather than the plaintiff, there would be no need for the court to undertake an invalidity determination.

Invalid patents might still create competitive problems, because they can improperly confer market power and otherwise have anticompetitive consequences when unchallenged (Leslie 2006, note 61). The more invalid patents there are in the economy, the more likely are such harms. Invalid patents might therefore be taken as reason to make it easier for antitrust plaintiffs to remedy refusals to deal that depend on market power acquired through illegitimate IP rights. Yet such an adjustment of the overall liability standard for refusals to deal to address invalid IP is a bad idea, for some of the same reasons applied above to invalidity determinations.

More generally, antitrust is a poor vehicle for addressing broader problems caused by invalid IP, which should ideally be left to IP policy to address. In this regard there have been some hopeful, if still preliminary, developments. For example, with respect to intellectual property quality reforms, the Supreme Court's 2007 decision in *KSR* v. *Teleflex* clarified the non-obviousness standard and made it harder to obtain a patent for an invention or combination of prior art that could have been achieved by a person having "ordinary skill" or "ordinary creativity" in the art.[54] With respect to intellectual property enforcement reforms, the Supreme Court in *E-Bay, Inc. v. MercExchange, LLC* held that a finding of infringement should not presumptively lead to an injunction against the infringer's use of the patented technology.[55]

To the extent intellectual property doctrine – as reflected in cases such as *KSR* and *E-Bay* – is starting to reduce validity concerns and the anticompetitive aspects of IP enforcement, antitrust law should not try to compensate for IP-related concerns through its approach to unilateral refusals to deal. Even if one were to assume narrower patent protections and broader antitrust liability to be individually beneficial, their combined welfare effects may not be additive if they too easily afford refusal-to-deal plaintiffs an alternative to competitive self-supply. Given both practical considerations and the fact that intellectual property reform could mitigate the special anticompetitive concerns that arise from invalid patents, antitrust law needs neither to have an exemption for refusals to supply IP nor to make IP-validity determinations part of refusal-to-deal cases.[56]

17.4.4 Toward a single liability standard for unilateral refusals to deal

For the reasons discussed above, refusals to deal in IP should be treated neither more leniently nor more stringently under antitrust

---

[54] *KSR Int'l Co. v. Teleflex, Inc.*, 550 US 398 (2007). In *KSR*, the Court reversed the Federal Circuit's upholding of a patent for the connection between an adjustable vehicle control pedal and an electronic throttle control. Application of the heightened non-obviousness requirement established in *KSR* led the Federal Circuit to invalidate the petitioner's patent on a toy switching mechanism in *Leapfrog Enter., Inc. v. Fisher-Price, Inc.*, 485 F.3d 1157 (Fed. Cir. 2007).

[55] 547 US 388 (2006).

[56] An interesting question outside the scope of this chapter is the effect that IP reforms might have on firms' incentives to deal with rivals. One possibility is that reducing IP protections might increase incentives to deal because firms would rather sell to rivals than have competitors invent around them. But the effect could also work in the opposite direction, with firms keeping a closer hold on technology when they lose the ability to protect their investment through infringement suits. The answer will likely vary case by case, with perhaps the greater incentive to keep a close hold on technology that is most easily copied or invented around and for which, in turn, the inventor's refusal to deal is ultimately less consequential for competition. These, however, are questions for further research.

law than refusals to deal in other property. The criterion of preserving producers' innovation incentives provides little economic justification for placing refusals to deal in IP outside the reach of antitrust enforcement. This recognition does not mean either that such incentives are unimportant or that liability should be imposed in any but exceptional circumstances; the point is simply that the circumstances are not so much more exceptional for IP that antitrust standards should not apply.

17.5 Which approach to refusals to deal should prevail?

The broader question of what standard should govern the treatment of unilateral refusals to deal under US antitrust law is a matter of substantial debate. Proposals range from resurrection of an essential-facilities approach to effectively per se legality. Along the spectrum are several rule-of-reason approaches that vary in stringency. One proposed approach would impose liability only where a firm's refusal to deal would not be profitable or make economic sense absent the exclusionary effect the refusal has on competition (Melamed 2005;[57] Werden 2006). A competing approach finds the "profit sacrifice" test to be both over- and under-inclusive in its categorization of anticompetitive conduct and focuses instead upon the consumer-welfare consequences of refusals to deal and other exclusionary conduct (Salop 2006; Popofsky 2006[58]). The European Union has recently embraced a consumer-welfare framework for refusal-to-deal cases.[59] The EU's rule-of-reason approach focuses upon how a dominant firm's individual conduct affects consumer welfare, while allowing the defendant the possibility of rebutting the evidence of consumer harm with evidence

---

[57] [T]he sacrifice test asks whether the allegedly anticompetitive conduct would be profitable for the defendant and would make good business sense even if it did not exclude rivals and thereby create or preserve market power for the defendant. If so, the conduct is lawful. If not – if the conduct would be unprofitable but for the exclusion of rivals and the resulting market power – it is anticompetitive.

[58] Critiquing both the profit-sacrifice and rule-of-reason approaches as general standards.

[59] European Comm'n, DG Competition, *Guidance on the Commission's Official Enforcement Priorities in Applying Article 82 EC Treaty to Abusive Exclusionary Conduct by Dominant Undertakings* (Dec. 3, 2008), available at http://ec.europa.eu/competition/antitrust/art82/guidance.pdf.

of compensating efficiencies. The D.C. Circuit applied such a test in its 2005 *Covad* decision.[60] An alternative approach would examine the relationship between the exclusionary conduct and the defendant's economic efficiency (Elhauge 2003).[61] A common thread in many proposed approaches is to balance producer and consumer concerns by requiring defendants to advance a pro-competitive business justification for refusals that harm competition (Kolasky 2006).

The Supreme Court's much less plaintiff-friendly approach in *Trinko* can be thought of as a stringent rule-of-reason approach that would permit liability only if, at a minimum, a plaintiff could prove facts analogous to those of *Aspen* or some other compelling circumstances warranting liability and its accompanying overdeterrence and enforcement costs. The Court's emphasis in *Trinko*, like that of the Department of Justice in its 2008 report on enforcement of Section 2,[62] is on preventing the administrative burdens and error costs from false positives in antitrust enforcement.

While there are good institutional and economic arguments against imposing liability for unilateral refusals to deal, courts should reject standards that, like that of *CSU*, effectively make refusals to deal per se legal. They should instead examine refusals to deal in IP and other property under a standard that is demanding of plaintiffs but not preclusive of antitrust liability. A detailed analysis of alternative rule-of-reason approaches to unilateral refusals to deal is beyond the scope of this discussion. At a minimum, however, I argue in this chapter that should the Supreme Court again address the question of refusal-to-deal liability, it should adopt a unified approach for IP and other property that is no more lenient to defendants than that of *Trinko*. That standard should allow lower courts enough discretion to add to the circumstances that, like those of *Aspen*, constitute exceptions to anti-

---

[60] *Covad Commc'ns Co. v. Bell Atl. Corp.*, 398 F.3d 666, 675–76 (D.C. Cir. 2005).

[61] The proper monopolization standard should focus on whether the alleged exclusionary conduct's ability to increase monopoly power depends on the defendant improving its own efficiency, or whether it would do so by impairing the efficiency of rivals whether or not defendant efficiency were enhanced, permitting the former and prohibiting the latter.

[62] US Dep't of Justice, Competition and Monopoly: Single Firm Conduct Under Section 2 of the Sherman Act 16–18 (Sept. 2008), available at www.usdoj.gov/atr/public/reports/236681.pdf.

trust law's strong presumption against liability for single-firm refusals to deal.

Moreover, the Court should reject per se legality (or its practical equivalent) for unilateral refusals to deal. First, there can be refusals to deal that are unacceptably anticompetitive, as discussed above and as the Supreme Court and numerous circuit courts have found. While *Trinko* emphasizes the costs of false positives in enforcement, precluding liability would ensure at least some number of false negatives in which conduct antitrust would deem harmful would go unpunished. The risk of false negatives in enforcement should not be ignored. To the extent the cases involving conduct that causes net harm to competition can be separated from others in which false positives are more likely, it would reduce consumer welfare were the courts to adopt an over-inclusive rule against liability. The Supreme Court takes the view that the risk and cost of such false negatives is minor compared to the risk of false positives, especially with the treble damages that follow from liability in private suits. Even if it were true that any individual false positive result is on average more costly than any individual false negative, it is not necessarily true that the overall costs of false positives from antitrust enforcement are higher than the costs of false negatives. That balance depends on the likely frequency of false positives. Both substantive and procedural developments in antitrust law over the past thirty years have reduced the likelihood that cases will reach trial and the probability that plaintiffs will win once they get there. In its 2007 Report and Recommendations, the Antitrust Modernization Commission discussed the importance of avoiding both overdeterrence and underdeterrence of anticompetitive conduct but noted in its discussion of treble damages that "[n]o actual cases or evidence of systematic overdeterrence were presented to the Commission."[63]

On the procedural side, the Supreme Court has over the years placed limits on who can sue under the antitrust laws[64] and has raised the pleading requirements for those who can.[65] More fundamentally, the

---

[63] Antitrust Modernization Comm'n, Report and Recommendations 247 (2007) (Recommendation 42), available at http://govinfo.library.unt.edu/amc/report_recommendation/amc_final_report.pdf.

[64] See, e.g., *Atlantic Richfield Co. v. USA Petroleum Co.*, 495 US 328 (1990); *Illinois Brick Co. v. Illinois*, 431 US 720 (1977); *Brunswick Corp. v. Pueblo Bowl-O-Mat, Inc.*, 429 US 477 (1977).

[65] *Bell Atl. Corp. v. Twombly*, 550 US 544 (2007).

Court has increased the substantive burdens on plaintiffs for a number of antitrust claims, in particular those alleging monopolization under Section 2 of the Sherman Act. The Court has ruled against plaintiffs in sixteen consecutive antitrust cases since 1992.[66] In so doing the Court has made it harder for plaintiffs to get to the merits, never mind win, on claims ranging from predatory pricing,[67] vertical price restraints,[68] and, of course, refusals to deal.[69] Those are only examples, and the Court has raised barriers to plaintiffs for numerous other kinds of antitrust claims as well (Dogan and Lemley 2009). The point here is not to debate the merits of any of those particular decisions, but to show that antitrust jurisprudence has evolved to reduce the likelihood of false positives. The assumption that even more preclusive rules against liability are necessary to protect against investment deterrence and other costs of over-enforcement requires more justification than the Court has offered in light of these developments.[70]

The case law provides additional empirical evidence that the prospect of false positives is not so great as to warrant a rule of per se legality. There have been relatively few successful claims for refusal-to-deal liability and the overall number of cases has not been so great as to suggest the administrative and deterrence costs of a rule-of-reason test will be higher than the benefits of such a rule. Glen Robinson has shown that from 1980 to 2000, there were a total of seventy-one district and circuit court opinions addressing essential-facilities claims. Although essential-facilities claims are a subset of refusal-to-deal claims, they are a large subset and serve as a reasonable proxy for the volume of the latter (Robinson 2002). In only five of twenty-eight circuit court opinions and six of forty-three district court opinions did the courts find there to be even a triable issue of fact as to the existence of an essential facility (Robinson 2002). I updated the data for this chapter and found twenty-two circuit court opinions from 2001 to 2008 addressing essential facilities claims, of which only three found

---

[66] The last antitrust plaintiff's victory in the Supreme Court was in *Eastman Kodak v. Image Technical Serv.*, 504 US 451 (1992).
[67] *Brooke Group, Ltd. v. Brown & Williamson Tobacco Corp.*, 509 US 209 (1993).
[68] *Leegin Creative Leather Products, Inc. v. PSKS, Inc.*, 551 US 877 (2007).
[69] *Trinko*, 540 US at 398.
[70] As Dogan and Lemley point out, the landscape of antitrust law has changed significantly since Judge Frank Easterbrook's 1984 critique of antitrust law's propensity toward false positives.

a triable issue on the merits. Those three include the Second Circuit's *Trinko* decision that the Supreme Court later reversed. During that same recent period there were forty district court cases (distinct from the circuit-court cases just mentioned) that dealt to differing degrees with the essential facilities doctrine, only eight of which declined to dispose of the claim on dismissal or summary judgment.

The case precedent therefore shows that even under the essential-facilities approach the Court disdained in *Trinko*, the courts have been able to weed out the majority of cases, and potential liability will not necessarily be a broad deterrent to innovation. To be sure, even the majority of cases that ended with dismissal or summary judgment entailed costs for defendants and the courts, although those costs are presumably much less than those that would have resulted from mistaken findings of liability. But the overall number of essential-facilities cases, which I take as a proxy for the broader universe of refusal-to-deal cases, has been modest. As precedent develops, courts and plaintiffs gain increased guidance for the disposition of future cases. To the extent specific factual circumstances (like those of *Aspen*) can be identified in which refusal-to-deal liability may be warranted, those facts can become elements that inform the rule-of-reason inquiry and limit the incidence of false positives in enforcement. In sum, the evidence from past experience does not on its face suggest such indiscriminate disposition by the courts or such a large number of cases that the deterrent and other costs of enforcement justify a prophylactic rule against antitrust liability for unilateral refusals to deal.

Another reason for courts to reject per se legality for refusals to deal is that not all refusal-to-deal cases implicate the investment incentives with which the Supreme Court was so concerned in *Trinko*. In a number of key cases like *Otter Tail*,[71] *MCI v. AT&T*,[72] and the *AT&T* divestiture case[73] (and not to mention *Trinko* itself), the source of monopoly power lay in facilities the defendant had long had in place and in which an obligation to deal would not likely interfere with recoupment of its investment. Of course, even long-established telecommunications and power distribution networks require ongoing investment and innovation and it can be risky to assume duties to

---

[71] *Otter Tail*, 410 US 366 (1973).
[72] *MCI Commc'ns Corp. v. AT&T Co.*, 708 F.2d 1081 (7th Cir. 1983).
[73] *United States v. AT&T Co.*, 552 F. Supp. 131 (DDC 1982).

deal to be free of deterrent effects. But to the extent the defendant has had the facility in place long enough to gain the actual or probable market power necessary for a Section 2 monopolization claim, the relationship between original investment and the duty to deal may be remote and marginal. The question of the relationship between duties to deal and investment incentives is complex, and policy makers need to consider not just the specific case but the signaling effect liability may have on investment and innovation in the broader economy. But the evidence to date does not warrant absolute preclusion of liability to protect those dynamic incentives and suggests that the lower courts can develop a discriminating enough screen to balance the various welfare considerations at stake.

Finally, the emphasis on seller-side investment incentives in *Trinko*, *CSU*, and other decisions may miss important factors for long-term consumer welfare. As the First Circuit found in *Data General*, the question of the relationship between long-term innovation effects and short-term competition effects is an empirical one. Because the path of innovation is likely much harder to predict than short-term changes in price and output levels, it will be impossible in most cases definitively to calculate the comparative static and dynamic welfare effects of economic conduct. Because the economic benefits of innovation may be comparably large and knowable only in hindsight, a bias toward dynamic benefits in substantive liability standards makes sense to counteract the evidentiary bias toward static effects. For that reason, liability for unilateral refusals to deal should be an uncommon exception. But uncommon in this case should not mean nonexistent. Neither theory nor empirical evidence provides reason to eliminate Section 2 liability to preserve technological innovation (Katz and Shelanski 2007).[74] This is particularly true when one considers that there is also an empirical question not just about comparative static and dynamic benefits but about the relationship between initial and follow-on innovation benefits as well.

Over-protection of a potential seller's innovation incentives affects not just short-run competition but long-run innovation as well. The welfare trade-offs in unilateral refusal-to-deal cases may therefore be more complex than meet the eye. Firms that obtain access to a

---

[74] Surveying theory and evidence on the relationship between competition and innovation.

monopoly-produced product will not only compete in selling that product today, but may compete by innovating to improve that product tomorrow. There are good reasons to think that competition is beneficial for follow-on innovation, as a monopolist may hesitate to innovate if the improved product only cannibalizes customers from the monopolist's own earlier-generation product (Arrow 1962). A monopolist may find innovation unnecessary to maintain customers and irrelevant to its market share, while a competitor more likely finds innovation necessary to increase its market share. Of course, without initial innovation there can be no follow-on innovation, so it is essential to preserve incentives for the former even while trying to create possibilities for the latter. But from a consumer welfare standpoint there is no evidence that the choice between initial and follow-on innovation needs to be as absolute as that embodied in a rule of per se legality for unilateral refusals to deal and as argued by strong proponents of the "Schumpeterian" school of competition policy (Katz and Shelanski 2005); and there is nothing in the relevant theory or evidence that would lead to different liability standards for refusals to deal in IP and other property on innovation grounds.

17.6 Conclusion

Refusals to deal raise important challenges under Section 2 of the Sherman Act. In most cases there should be little controversy over a firm's decision not to supply a rival. A dynamic competition policy that looks beyond short-term competitive effects should avoid imposing liability that would impede longer-run incentives for innovation and investment. In some cases, however, the competitive effects of refusals to deal can be both severe and long-lasting, while the effects of mandatory dealing on the refusing firm's incentives may be minor. The likelihood of such harmful cases may increase with industrial consolidation, concentration of IP ownership, and deregulation of dominant firms in network industries. Antitrust law's approach to refusals to deal will therefore invariably involve trade-offs between the costs of false negatives and the costs of false positives in enforcement. In this chapter I argue that while antitrust law correctly imposes a high bar to success for plaintiffs complaining of refusals to deal, the standard should not become preclusive of liability and the availability of antitrust enforcement should not depend on what kind of property – IP or other – is at issue in the case. Neither economics nor practical experience with antitrust enforcement counsels exemption from antitrust liability for refusals to supply IP or a general rule per se legality for refusals to deal. Antitrust law has steadily evolved in a direction that reduces the likelihood of improvident enforcement and costly false positives. Courts should not take antitrust precedent or antitrust policy's objective of promoting innovation to block them from continuing this winnowing process in addressing unilateral refusals to deal.

18 | How do firms exercise unilateral market power? Empirical evidence from a bid-based wholesale electricity market

SHAUN D. MCRAE AND FRANK A. WOLAK

18.1 Introduction

Empirical examination of the implications of profit-maximizing firm behavior in imperfectly competitive markets is complicated by the fact that the primitives of the economic environment, such as market demand functions and firm-level cost functions, are not directly observable. Moreover, the researcher rarely knows the strategic variables that firms use to influence market prices or often even the details of how market prices are set. As a result, researchers rely on parametric models of market demand, firm-level cost functions, and equilibrium models of strategic interaction such as non-cooperative quantity-setting or price-setting behavior to understand how firms behave in imperfectly competitive markets. Consequently, any conclusions about firm behavior or the extent of market power exercised are conditional on these functional form assumptions and the assumed model of strategic interaction between firms.

We pursue an alternative approach that relies on a data-rich environment where many of these economic primitives are observable and both the strategic variables that firms choose and the exact mechanism that translates these strategic variables into market-clearing prices are known. This economic environment allows us to examine many implications of expected profit-maximizing behavior in imperfectly competitive markets without relying on functional form assumptions for market demand or a specific model of strategic interaction among firms.

To understand the advantages of the approach we pursue, it is useful to review the traditional approach from the perspective of the rapidly expanding literature in what Bresnahan (1989) calls the new empirical industrial organization. This approach uses market-clearing prices and quantities and variables assumed to shift demand and production costs along with three economic and behavioral assumptions to recover estimates of the extent of market power exercised in an imperfectly competitive market.

The three main econometric and behavioral assumptions necessary for validity of the traditional approach are: (1) parametric functional forms for the market demand and firm-level or market-level variable cost functions; (2) a model of firm-level strategic interaction, such as monopoly, quantity-setting competition, or price-setting competition; and (3) profit-maximizing or expected profit-maximizing behavior. Using a cross-section of monopoly newspaper markets, Rosse (1970) was the first to demonstrate that the combination of these three assumptions can allow a researcher to recover the firm's marginal cost function from market-clearing prices and quantities and demand and cost shifters. The results of this modeling effort can then be used to estimate the marginal cost of the highest cost unit of output produced by the firm. This marginal cost equals the market-clearing price if the firm were unable to exercise any market power. Consequently, the difference between the market price and this estimated marginal cost measures the extent of market power exercised.

Porter (1983) applied this basic approach to an oligopolistic industry – nineteenth century railroads. He assumed that actual market outcomes are the result of non-cooperative quantity-setting behavior between market participants. Bresnahan (1981 and 1987) measures the extent of market power exercised in the United States' automobile industry using the assumption of price-setting competition.

All of these studies and many more recent ones employing these techniques rely on an assumed parametric model of demand and a model of competition among firms to derive an estimate of the extent of market power exercised from market-clearing price and quantity data. As has been emphasized by a number of authors, most forcefully by Bulow and Pfleiderer (1983), the estimate of the extent of market power exercised depends on the functional form assumed for the market demand. The assumed model of competition can also exert a substantial influence on the estimate of the extent of market power exercised.

All of these studies quantifying the extent of market power exercised do not explicitly address the question of how firms exercise market power, specifically what factors determine the extent of market power that firms are able to exercise and the amount of market power they choose to exercise. Because the amount of market power exercised is identified from market-clearing prices and quantities (and demand and cost shifters) using the functional form assumed for demand and the assumed model of competition among firms, any conclusions about how firms exercise market power or what factors enhance their ability and incentive to exercise market power are conditional on these two assumptions.

The recent world-wide trend toward introducing bid-based wholesale electricity markets has created an increasing number of data-rich economic environments where it is possible to study how firms behave in imperfectly competitive markets using only the assumption of expected profit-maximizing behavior. Participants in these multi-unit auction markets submit their willingness-to-sell or willingness-to-purchase curves to the market operator and these curves are used to compute market-clearing prices and the quantities bought and sold by each market participant. A willingness-to-sell or willingness-to-buy curve gives the amount of the good a market participant is willing to sell or buy for each possible market-clearing price. If the researcher is willing to assume that a supplier constructs its willingness-to-supply curve to maximize the expected profits that it earns given the offers of its competitors and the bids of demanders, then it is possible to infer a supplier's variable cost function from the bid and offer curves that it and its market participants submit without having to resort to functional form assumptions for aggregate demand or an assumed model of competition among firms.

For the case of a multi-unit auction market, the offers submitted by other suppliers besides the supplier under consideration and the bids of all demanders determine the realized residual demand curve faced by that supplier. For the case that the researcher only has data on market-clearing prices and quantities, the residual demand curve a supplier faces is determined by the functional form assumption for aggregate demand and an assumed model of competition among firms.

For a multi-unit auction market, because a supplier does not know the offers of other suppliers or all demand bids at the time it submits its willingness-to-supply curve, this supplier must construct its offer curve to maximize the profits that it expects to earn given the distribution of residual demand curves that it faces. Wolak (2003a) demonstrates that the assumption that the supplier chooses the form of its offer curve to maximize its expected profits given the distribution of residual demand curves that it faces identifies that supplier's marginal cost function.

Wolak (2003a) applies this logic to a multi-unit auction market for wholesale electricity to estimate generation unit-level variable cost functions without the first two assumptions described above. The information contained in the offer curves submitted by all market participants and the assumption of expected profit-maximizing offer behavior by the supplier under consideration are sufficient to estimate generation unit-level marginal cost functions for a supplier. Wolak (2007) extends this cost function estimation framework to the case of multivariate cost functions in order to quantify the extent to which marginal costs for a specific generation unit in a given half-hour of the day vary with the level of output during that half-hour and during other half-hours of the day. Wolak (2003b) shows that the information contained in the offer curves and demand bids can also be used to compute a measure of the ability of a supplier to exercise unilateral market power.

This chapter uses the framework in Wolak (2003a, 2003b, and 2007) and data on half-hourly offer curves and market-clearing prices and quantities from the New Zealand wholesale electricity market over the period January 1, 2001 to June 30, 2007 to characterize how the four large suppliers in this imperfectly competitive industry exercise unilateral market power. To accomplish this we introduce half-hourly measures of the firm-level ability and incentive of an individual supplier to exercise unilateral market power that are derived from a model of expected profit-maximizing offer behavior in a multi-unit auction market. We then show that half-hourly market-clearing prices are highly correlated with the half-hourly values of the firm-level and across firm-average measures of both the ability and incentive of the four large suppliers in New Zealand to exercise unilateral market power.

We then present evidence consistent with the view that this increasing relationship between the ability or incentive of individual suppliers to exercise market power and higher market-clearing prices is caused by the four large suppliers submitting higher offer prices when they have a greater ability or incentive to exercise unilateral market power. We show that after controlling for changes in input fossil fuel prices and other factors that impact the opportunity cost of producing electricity during that half-hour, each of the four suppliers submits a higher offer price into the wholesale market when it has a greater ability or incentive to exercise unilateral market power.

18.2 The New Zealand wholesale electricity market

In October 1996, a wholesale electricity market was formed by the New Zealand electricity supply industry. This market was a contract between market participants – generation unit owners, retailers, and energy traders – that specified how generation units were dispatched and wholesale prices were determined.

Prior to the start of the wholesale market, the transmission and generation sectors were dominated by the state-owned Electricity Corporation of New Zealand ("ECNZ"), which owned and operated more than 95 percent of the total New Zealand electricity generating capacity. ECNZ was broken up in three stages. First, in July 1994, the national transmission grid was separated into a stand-alone State-Owned Enterprise ("SOE") Transpower. In February 1996, before the start of the wholesale electricity market, Contact Energy was formed out of ECNZ generation assets that represented roughly 22 percent of total electricity production. Contact Energy was a stand-alone SOE in competition with ECNZ until it was privatized in 1999. Finally, about the same time as the privatization of Contact Energy, the remainder of ECNZ was split into three competing SOEs: Genesis, Meridian, and Mighty River Power. All three firms, as well as Transpower, remain state-owned during our sample period.

In response to a perceived lack of competition in both the wholesale and retail markets, the Government announced a series of reforms of the electricity supply industry in April 1998. In addition to the final split of ECNZ, these reforms included the forced separation of distribution and retailing businesses. At the time there were more than 40 distribution firms, each with a very high market share in retailing for customers on their networks. The separation of distribution and retail led to rapid vertical integration between the generation and retail sectors, as Contact Energy and the newly formed SOE generators bought the retail businesses from the network owners. Two new privately owned generation and retail firms were created out of the industry reorganization – TransAlta New Zealand and TrustPower – although the former firm disintegrated in 2001.

Since 2001 the industry market structure has been relatively stable. There are five major generation owners: Contact Energy, TrustPower, and the three SOEs, Genesis, Meridian, and Mighty River Power. Each of these generation owners is vertically integrated with a retail business serving a mix of residential, commercial, and industrial users. With the exception of TrustPower, all of these firms have more generation capacity than their average retail load obligation, although there are half-hours during our sample period when each of these retailers has retail load obligations that exceed their sales in the short-term wholesale market.

More than 99% of the energy produced in the South Island comes from hydroelectric sources. There is sufficient generation capacity in the South Island to serve its annual electricity requirements, as well as export a substantial amount of energy to the North Island using a submarine transmission line. Approximately 24.4% of the North Island supply came from hydroelectric sources in 2007, with the remaining 75.6% split between natural gas-fired (44.6%), coal-fired (11.6%), geothermal (13.0%), wind (3.4%), wood (2.1%), and less than 1% from biogas facilities.

Annual electricity consumption for the entire country in the year ending December 2007 was approximately 38.5 Terawatt hours (TWh), with the commercial sector consuming 23.3% of this total, the industrial sector 43.7%, and the residential sector 33.0%. An important aspect of the New Zealand electricity industry is that much of the population resides in the northern part of the North Island in the Auckland metropolitan area, whereas many of the major hydroelectric resources are in the southern part of the South Island. As a result, transmission and distribution accounts for a relatively large fraction of the cost of delivered electricity compared to the rest of the world.

18.3 Empirical evidence on how suppliers exercise unilateral market power

This section uses supplier offers, water reservoir levels, and market outcomes to demonstrate a number of empirical regularities in the behavior of the four large suppliers and market outcomes in the New Zealand market. First, summary statistics are presented on the behavior of half-hourly measures of both the unilateral ability and incentive to exercise unilateral market power for each of the four large suppliers. These half-hourly measures of the ability and incentive to exercise unilateral market power are shown to be highly positively correlated with the value of the quantity-weighted average half-hourly market-clearing price.

To demonstrate that this observed positive correlation between the average half-hourly firm-level unilateral ability and incentive to exercise market power and half-hourly market prices is the direct result of market participant behavior, a second line of empirical evidence is introduced. Expected profit-maximizing offer behavior implies that a supplier's half-hourly offer price – the price at which it is willing to sell a pre-specified amount of energy to the short-term wholesale market – should be positively correlated with both its ability and incentive to exercise unilateral market power during that half-hour. Econometric analysis is then used to quantify the empirical relationship between the half-hourly offer price of each supplier and the half-hourly value of an index of that supplier's unilateral ability to exercise unilateral market power (after controlling for other exogenous factors impacting half-hourly market outcomes such as water levels and input fossil fuel prices). Further econometric analysis examines the empirical relationship between the half-hourly offer price of each supplier and the half-hourly value of an index of that supplier's unilateral incentive to exercise unilateral market power. We find that when each of the four suppliers has a greater ability or greater incentive to exercise unilateral market power, they submit substantially higher half-hourly offer prices for a pre-specified quantity of energy.

18.3.1 Market outcomes and the unilateral ability and incentive to exercise market power

Measures of the ability and incentive of a supplier to exercise unilateral market power can be computed on a country or system-wide basis or separately for the North and South Islands using the half-hourly level of demand and the willingness-to-supply curves of all market participants. The form of the residual demand curve that a supplier faces determines its ability to exercise unilateral market power. The inverse of the elasticity of the residual demand curve evaluated at the market-clearing price is one measure of the ability of a supplier to exercise unilateral market power. This inverse elasticity measures the percent change in the market-clearing price that would result from

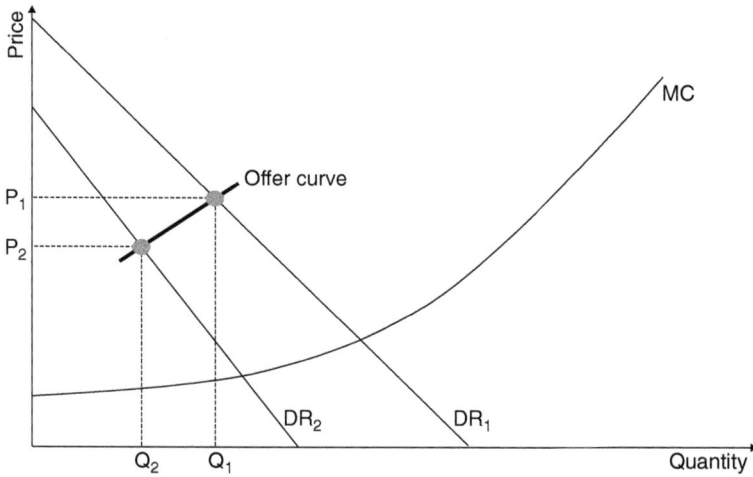

Figure 18.1 Derivation of offer curve (steep residual demands)

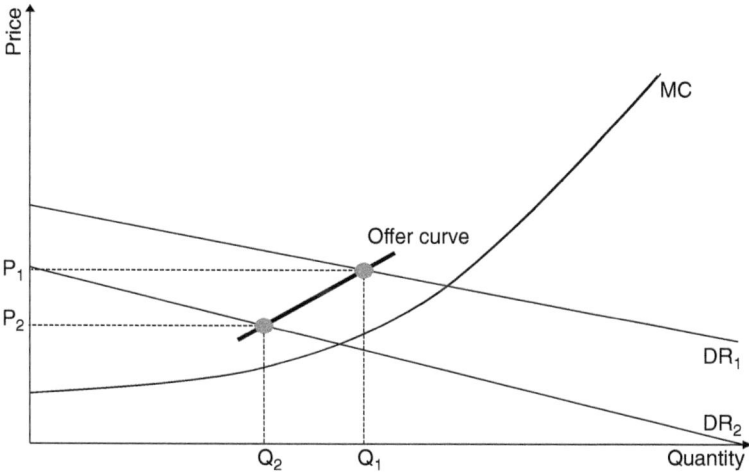

Figure 18.2 Derivation of offer curve (flatter residual demands)

the supplier producing 1 percent less output than it actually produced during that half-hour period.

Under a simplified model of expected profit-maximizing offer behavior described in Figures 18.1 and 18.2 and discussed in detail in Wolak (2000), this inverse elasticity measure can be directly related to the market-clearing price and the marginal cost of the highest cost unit owned by that supplier operating during that half-hour period.

The logic underlying the construction of the expected profit-maximizing offer curve in Figure 18.1 implies that the point (P_1, Q_1) is the ex post profit-maximizing price/quantity pair for the firm for the residual demand realization $DR_1(p)$ and the point (P_2, Q_2) is the ex post profit-maximizing price/quantity pair for the firm for the residual demand realization $DR_2(p)$. The first-order conditions for ex post profit-maximization for these two residual demand realizations are:

$$(P_1 - C_1)/P_1 = -1/\varepsilon_1 \text{ and } (P_2 - C_2)/P_2 = -1/\varepsilon_2 \tag{3.1}$$

where C_i (i=1,2) is the marginal cost for supplier i at output level Q_i (i=1,2) and $-1/\varepsilon_i$ (i=1,2) is the inverse of the elasticity of the residual demand curve for that residual demand realization.

Recall that the inverse elasticity is defined in terms of the residual demand curve as:

$$-1/\varepsilon_i = [DR_i(P_i)/P_i] \times [1/DR_i'(P_i)] \tag{3.2}$$

where $DR_i'(P_i)$ is the slope of residual demand curve i evaluated at price P_i, and $DR_i(P_i)$ is the value of residual demand curve evaluated at price P_i. Using this definition of the inverse elasticity, the two equations in (1) can be rearranged to equal:

$$P_i = C_i - [DR_i(P_i)/DR_i'(P_i)], i=1,2. \tag{3.3}$$

Equation (3.3) implies that the market-clearing price is equal to the marginal cost of the highest cost unit owned by that supplier operating during that half-hour plus the level of the residual demand curve divided by the absolute value of the slope of the residual demand curve.

Define η_i (i=1,2), the inverse semi-elasticity of the residual demand curve i, as:

$$\eta_i = -(1/100)[DR_i(P_i)/DR_i'(P_i)]. \tag{3.4}$$

This magnitude gives the $/MWh increase in the market-clearing price associated with a 1 percent reduction in the amount of output sold by the supplier. In terms of this notation, equation (3.3) becomes

$$P_i = C_i + 100\eta_i, i=1, 2. \tag{3.5}$$

Thus, the simplified model of expected profit-maximizing offer behavior implies that higher market-clearing prices should be associated with higher values of the inverse semi-elasticity.

How do firms exercise unilateral market power? 399

Because offer curves in the New Zealand wholesale market are step functions, residual demand curve realizations do not strictly satisfy the assumptions implied by the simplified model of expected profit-maximizing offer behavior presented there, so that equation (3.5) will not hold with equality. However, the general model of expected profit-maximizing offer behavior implies that when a supplier has a greater ability to exercise unilateral market power as measured by the size of η_i, the \$/MWh price increase that results from reducing the amount it sells in the wholesale market by one percent, that supplier's offer price is likely to be higher.

Computing the slope of the residual demand curve at the market-clearing price for a step-function residual demand curve requires choosing the output change used to compute the finite-difference approximation to the slope. These output changes should be large enough to ensure that enough price steps on the residual demand curve are crossed so that a non-zero slope is obtained, but not too large that the implied output change is judged as implausible for the supplier to implement. We also want to choose a procedure for selecting the output changes to ensure that the value of the slope obtained is not sensitive to the size of the output changes used to compute it.

Figure 18.3 describes the details of the process we use to compute the slope of the residual demand curve for Firm B for a peak half-hour period in February 2006. Suppose that $Q^* = 901$ MW is the output sold by Firm B at the market-clearing price for this half-hour period of $P^* = \$145/\text{MWh}$.[1] We want to approximate the slope of the residual demand curve in the vicinity of (P^*, Q^*). Consider a 10 percent price change window on either side of P^*, and look for the closest steps on the residual demand curve to (P^*, Q^*) that lie outside this 10 percent price window. The closest point below P^* that has price less than 0.9 times P^* is ($129, 969$). Call this point (P_1, Q_1). Above P^* the closest point with price greater than 1.1 times P^* is ($164, 871$). Call this point (P_2, Q_2). The slope of the residual demand curve DR(P^*) at (P^*, Q^*) according to this procedure is given by the formula:

$$DR'(P^*) = (Q_1 - Q_2)/(P_1 - P_2) = (969 - 871)/(129 - 164) = -2.8 \quad (3.6)$$

---

[1] All dollar (\$) magnitudes reported in this chapter are in units of New Zealand dollars.

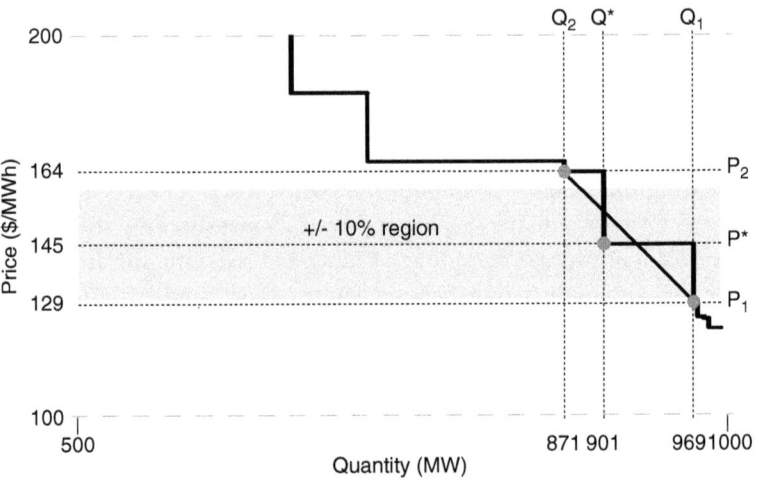

Figure 18.3 Elasticity calculation for Firm B, peak half-hour period in February 2006

The resulting inverse semi-elasticity at (P^*, Q^*) for this residual demand curve gives the \$/MWh price increase from a 1 percent reduction in output and is equal to:

$$\eta = -(1/100)DR(P^*)/DR'(P^*) = -(1/100)Q^*/DR'(P^*) = -(1/100)\ 901/(-2.81) = 3.21 \qquad (3.7)$$

This semi-elasticity quantifies the ability of Firm B to raise prices during this half-hour period by reducing its output by 1 percent. This magnitude implies that if Firm B reduces its output by 1 percent relative to $Q^* = 901$ MW, keeping the offers of all other firms and the level of demand constant, the increase in the market price would be \$3.21/MWh.

To compare time series behavior of the inverse semi-elasticities[2] across firms, Figure 18.4 plots the 30-day moving average of the half-hourly values of the inverse semi-elasticities for the four largest firms from January 1, 2001 to June 30, 2007. The half-hourly inverse semi-elasticities follow a very similar pattern across the four firms and certain suppliers have persistently larger values than other suppliers. The maximum value of the smoothed inverse semi-elasticities shown in the

---

[2] A comparison of the results from calculating the inverse semi-elasticity for the four large suppliers in each half-hour from January 1, 2001 to June 30, 2007, using four different values for the price change window: 1%, 5%, 10%, and 15% can be found in Wolak and McRae (2009).

How do firms exercise unilateral market power? 401

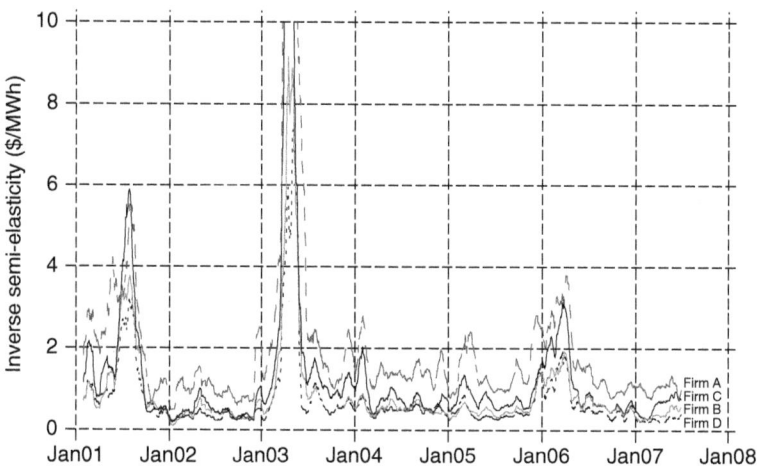

Figure 18.4 Half-hourly inverse semi-elasticities by firm, 30-day rolling average

figure is 10, with the values for Firm A peaking at close to 20 during early 2003 and the peak values for Firm C for this time period also exceeding 10. Over the entire sample period, Firm A's smoothed inverse semi-elasticities tend to be the highest, followed by Firm C, then by Firm B, and finally by Firm D.

To demonstrate the very close relationship between half-hourly market-clearing prices and the half-hourly ability of the four large suppliers to exercise unilateral market power (as measured by the inverse semi-elasticity of their residual demand curves), Figure 18.5 plots the 30-day moving average of the half-hourly values of the quantity-weighted average of the nodal prices and a 30-day moving average of the half-hourly values of the unweighted average of the four values η_{ihd} for Firms A to D, which is equal to $\eta_{hd}(\text{firm}) = \frac{1}{4}\sum_{i=1}^{4} \eta_{ihd}$.

Define p_{hdm} as the price at transmission grid node m during half-hour h of day d and q_{hdm} as the total amount of energy injected at transmission node m during half-hour h and day d. Figure 18.5 shows that the time series pattern of $p_{hd}(avg) = \dfrac{\sum_{m=1}^{M} p_{hdm} q_{hdm}}{\sum_{m=1}^{M} q_{hdm}}$, the quantity-weighted average of the nodal prices for half-hour h of day d, closely tracks $\eta_{hd}(\text{firm})$. During periods when the average index of the ability of these suppliers to exercise unilateral market power is high, the quantity-weighted average of the nodal prices they are paid is also

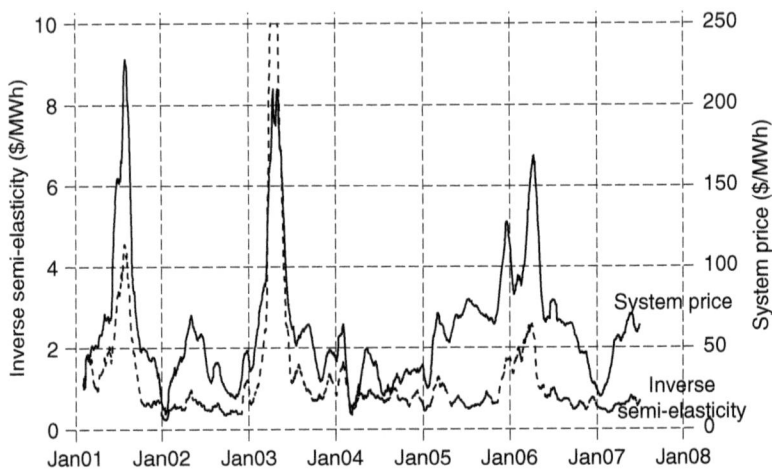

Figure 18.5 Mean inverse semi-elasticities and system price, 30-day rolling average

very high. Specifically, during mid-2001, early 2003, and early 2006 the average index of the ability of suppliers to exercise unilateral market power is high and the quantity-weighted average nodal price is high. Conversely, during periods when the average index of the ability of these suppliers to exercise unilateral market power is low, the quantity-weighted average of the nodal prices is significantly lower. This occurs during 2002, 2004, and 2005.

Even if a supplier possesses a substantial ability to exercise unilateral market power, it may not submit willingness-to-supply curves that reflect this ability if it has no incentive to exercise unilateral market power. A supplier with fixed-price forward market obligations approximately equal to its sales in the short-term wholesale market has little incentive to exercise unilateral market power, even if it has a substantial ability to do so. This logic suggests that half-hourly measures of the unilateral incentive of each supplier to exercise unilateral market power should be correlated with both market-clearing prices and the level of offer prices that each supplier submits. Wolak and McRae (2009) discuss how fixed-price forward market obligations, either in the form of fixed-price retail load obligations or fixed-price forward contracts, impact the incentive of a supplier to exercise unilateral market power, even if that supplier has a substantial ability to exercise unilateral market power. They show that the inverse semi-elasticity of the net-of-forward market obligation residual demand curve summarizes the incentive a supplier has to exercise unilateral market power.

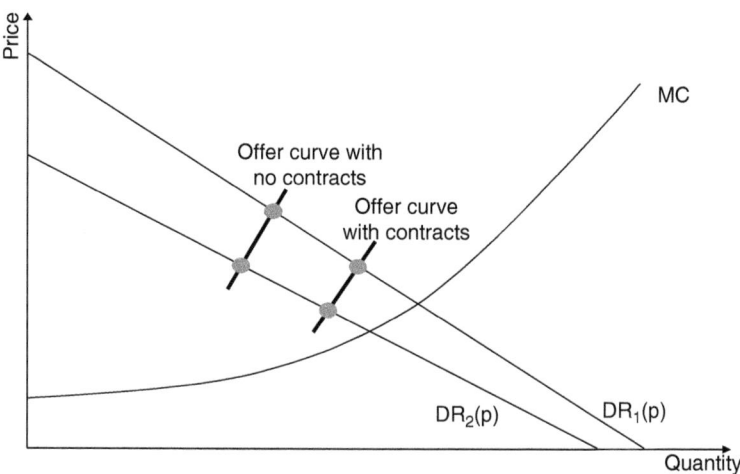

Figure 18.6 Derivation of offer curves with and without fixed-price contracts

Inverse semi-elasticities for the net-of-forward market obligations residual demand curves can be computed from these inverse semi-elasticities to obtain measures of the incentive (as opposed to ability) of individual suppliers to exercise unilateral market power. Wolak and McRae (2009) demonstrate that under a simplified model of expected profit-maximizing offer behavior, the inverse semi-elasticities of the net-of-forward obligations residual demand curve can be directly related to the market-clearing price and the marginal cost of the highest cost unit owned by that supplier operating during that half-hour period.

The logic underlying the construction of the expected profit-maximizing offer curve with forward market obligations drawn in Figure 18.6 implies that the point of intersection between the offer curve and each residual demand realization is an ex post profit-maximizing price/quantity pair for the firm for each residual demand realization given the forward market obligations of the supplier, Q_C. For the two residual demand curve realizations in Figure 18.6, the first-order conditions for ex post profit-maximization for these two residual demand realizations are:

$$(P_1 - C_1)/P_1 = -1/\varepsilon_1^C \text{ and } (P_2 - C_2)/P_2 = -1/\varepsilon_2^C \qquad (3.8)$$

where C_i (i=1,2) is the marginal cost for supplier i at the output level Q_i (i=1,2) and $-1/\varepsilon_i^c$ (i=1,2) is the inverse elasticity of the net-of-forward market obligations residual demand curve for that residual demand realization. The inverse elasticity of the net-of-forward market obligations residual demand curve at price P_i and forward market obligation Q_C is equal to:

$$-1/\varepsilon_i^C = [(DR_i(P_i) - Q_C)/P_i] \times [1/DR_i(P_i)]$$
$$= -1/\varepsilon_i \, [(DR_i(P_i) - Q_C)/DR_i(P_i)]$$

By replacing in equations (3.2) to (3.4) $DR_i(P_i)$ by $DR_i^C(P_i) \equiv DR_i(P_i) - Q_C$ and define η_i^C (i=1,2), the net inverse semi-elasticity of the net-of-forward market obligations residual demand curve i, we can find that:

$$P_i = C_i + 100\eta_i^C, \, i=1,2. \tag{3.9}$$

The net inverse semi-elasticity of the net-of-forward market obligations residual demand curve i, is:

$$\eta_i^C = -(1/100)[(DR_i^C(P_i)/DR_i^{C'}(P_i)]$$
$$= \eta_i[(DR_i(P_i) - Q_C)/DR_i(P_i)] \tag{3.10}$$

The first equality defines η_i^C in terms of the net of fixed-price forward market obligations residual demand curve. The second equality demonstrates that it is equal to the inverse semi-elasticity of the residual demand multiplied by the supplier's exposure to short-term prices. This value of η_i^C gives the $/MWh increase in the market-clearing price associated with a 1 percent reduction in the net position of the supplier, the difference between its short-term market sales and its fixed-price forward market obligations.

Equation (3.9) demonstrates that the simplified model of expected profit-maximizing offer behavior with fixed-price forward market obligations implies that higher offer prices and higher market-clearing prices are associated with higher values of the inverse semi-elasticity of the net-of-fixed price forward market obligations residual demand curve after controlling for the variable cost of the highest cost generation unit in that supplier's portfolio of generation units operating during that half-hour period, C_i in equation (3.9).

To compute the half-hourly value of the inverse semi-elasticity of the net-of-forward market obligations residual demand curve for each of the four largest suppliers, we use the second equality in equation (3.10), with η_i^C instead η_i, which computes this index of the incentive of a supplier to exercise unilateral market power by multiplying the inverse semi-elasticity of the residual demand curve by that supplier's exposure to short-term wholesale prices at the market-clearing price P*, (DR(P*) − Q_C), divided by the supplier's short-term market sales, DR(P*). This approach to computing η_i^C ensures that the same estimate of the slope of the step-function residual demand curve is used to compute both η_i and η_i^C.

The assumptions required for the validity of the simplified model of expected profit-maximizing offer behavior with fixed-price forward market obligations do not hold because suppliers submit non-decreasing step functions rather than increasing continuous functions as their willingness-to-supply curves. It is important to emphasize that even if the assumptions necessary for the strict validity of the simplified model of expected profit-maximizing offer behavior do not hold, η_i^C is still a valid measure of the half-hourly incentive of a supplier to exercise unilateral market power. It equals the $/MWh increase in the market-clearing price that results from a 1 per cent increase in the supplier's net position relative to what it actually had during that half-hour period. As shown in the first equality of equation (3.10), this measure depends on the half-hourly offers of all other suppliers and the supplier's short-term market sales minus its fixed-price forward market obligation.

Figure 18.7 graphs the 30-day moving average of the net inverse semi-elasticities over the sample period of January 1, 2001 to June 30, 2007 computed as described above. For the value of Q_C, we use the half-hourly value of the retail load obligation of that supplier. Because there is a small, but sometimes important, fixed-price forward contract market in New Zealand and a small amount of retail load pays a retail price that varies with the half-hourly wholesale price, there is the potential for a small amount of measurement error between the true value of Q_C and the supplier's retail load obligation.

Figure 18.7 demonstrates the mitigating influence of fixed-price forward market obligations on the ability of suppliers to exercise unilateral market power. All of the inverse semi-elasticities of the residual demand curve are reduced significantly in absolute value as a result of multiplying them by the half-hourly value of the net exposure of the supplier to short-term prices, $[(DR_i(P_i) − Q_C)/DR_i(P_i)]$. This net exposure can be negative if the supplier sells less in the short-term market than its fixed-price forward market obligations, Q_C. This explains why some of the smoothed values of η_i^C are negative for certain suppliers during portions of the sample period.

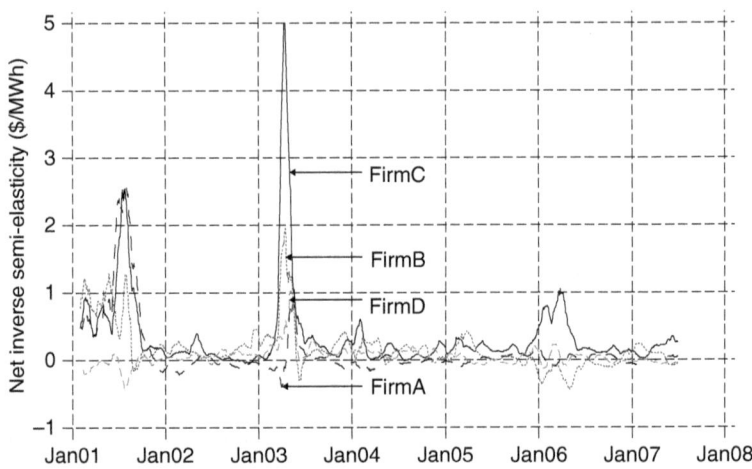

Figure 18.7 Half-hourly net inverse semi-elasticities by firm, 30-day rolling average

As shown in Figure 18.4, all four suppliers had more than double the ability to exercise unilateral market power in early 2003 relative to mid-2001, as measured by smoothed half-hourly semi-elasticities during the two time periods. Only Firm C translated this larger ability into a large incentive to raise short-term prices as measured by the value of η_i^C. Consequently, one explanation for the slightly longer period of higher prices that prevailed during mid-2001 is that a larger number of suppliers had a significant incentive to exercise unilateral market power during mid-2001 versus early 2003.

Figure 18.8 plots the 30-day moving average of the half-hourly values of the quantity-weighted average of the nodal prices and a 30-day moving average of the half-hourly values of $\eta_{hd}^C(firm)$. Figure 18.8 shows that the time series pattern of $p_{hd}(avg)$, the quantity-weighted average of the nodal prices for half-hour h of day d, closely tracks the time series pattern $\eta_{hd}^C(firm)$, which is defined analogously to $\eta_{hd}(firm)$. During the half-hour periods when this average index of the incentive of these suppliers to exercise unilateral market power is larger, the quantity-weighted average of the nodal prices is high. Specifically, during mid-2001, early 2003, and early 2006 the average index of the incentive of suppliers to exercise unilateral market power is high and the quantity-weighted average nodal price is high. Conversely, during periods when the average index of the incentives of these suppliers to

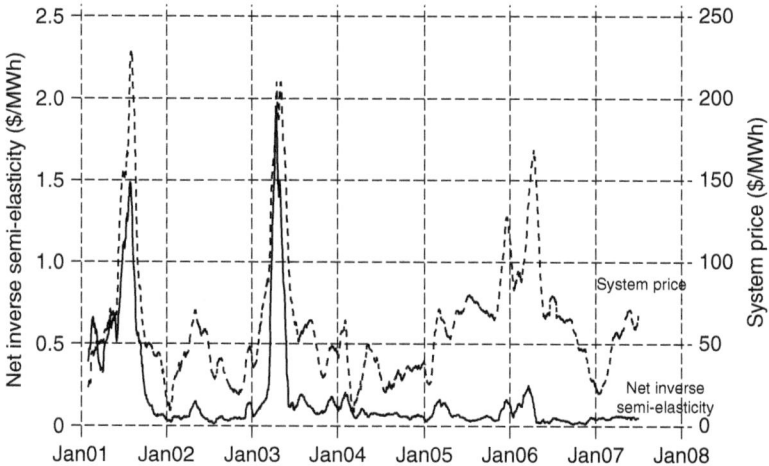

Figure 18.8 Mean net inverse semi-elasticities and system price, 30-day rolling average

exercise unilateral market power is close to zero, the smoothed quantity-weighted average of the nodal prices is significantly lower. This occurs during 2002, 2004, and 2005.

This section has shown that both the ability and incentive of all four suppliers to exercise unilateral market power are positively correlated with market-clearing prices. The ability to exercise unilateral market power is clearly a necessary condition for a supplier to exercise unilateral market power because a supplier must face an upward-sloping residual demand curve to be able to raise market prices by withholding its output. However, even a supplier with a substantial ability to exercise unilateral market power may not exploit this ability unless it has an incentive to do so. As noted above, the difference between a supplier's short-term market sales and its fixed-price forward market obligations determines the supplier's incentive to exercise unilateral market power.

18.4 Offer behavior and ability and incentive to exercise market power

The previous section has demonstrated that the ability and incentive to exercise unilateral market power is very highly correlated with the level of market prices. This section explores the extent to which this relationship is due to suppliers exercising unilateral market power by raising their offer prices (during periods when they have an increased ability and incentive to exercise market power). The theory of expected profit-maximizing offer behavior implies that suppliers exercising all available unilateral market power will submit higher offer prices when they have a greater ability and incentive to exercise unilateral market power. This section provides empirical confirmation for this implication of expected profit-maximizing behavior.

We find that after controlling for differences over days of the sample and half-hours of the day or half-hours of the day during each month of our sample period in an individual supplier's opportunity cost of producing electricity from their generation units, higher values of η, a supplier's unilateral ability to exercise unilateral market power, are associated with a higher offer price for the quantity of energy dispatched during that half-hour period by that supplier. A similar statement holds for η^C, a supplier's incentive to exercise unilateral market power. After controlling for opportunity cost differences over time, higher values of this index of the incentive to exercise unilateral market power are associated with a higher offer price for the quantity of energy dispatched during that half-hour period by that supplier. The absolute values of the regression coefficient estimates – associated with the incentive of a supplier to exercise unilateral market power – are uniformly higher for all market participants than the corresponding coefficient estimates for the regressions using the unilateral ability measure. This outcome is consistent with the assertion that the incentive to exercise unilateral market power is a key determinant of a supplier's offer price if it has significant fixed-price forward market obligations, as is the case for all of the four large suppliers under consideration.

As equations (3.5) and (3.9) in Section 18.3 demonstrate, the simplified model of expected profit-maximizing offer behavior by a supplier facing a distribution of downward sloping residual demand curves implies that, after controlling for the opportunity cost of the highest cost generation unit operating during that half-hour period (the term C_i in these two equations), a supplier's offer price at the quantity of energy that it sells in the short-term market should be an increasing function of the value of the inverse semi-elasticity, and increasing in the net inverse semi-elasticity. Although the conditions necessary for the strict validity of the simplified model of expected profit-maximizing offer behavior do not hold for the New Zealand market, we still expect these two implications of the simplified model to hold. Specifically, when a supplier has a greater unilateral ability or incentive to exercise unilateral market power, after controlling for its opportunity cost of selling energy from its highest cost generation unit operating during that hour, the offer price it sets for the amount of energy that it sells in the short-term market should be higher.

Let P_{jhdm}(actual) equal the offer price at the actual level of output sold by supplier j during half-hour h of day d during month of sample m, η_{jhdm} the inverse semi-elasticity of supplier j's residual demand curve during half-hour h of day d during month of sample m, and η^C_{jhdm} the inverse net semi-elasticity of supplier j's net-of-forward-market-obligation residual demand curve during half-hour h of day d during month of sample m. We take two approaches to controlling for differences across half-hours during our sample period in the variable cost of the highest cost generation unit owned by that supplier operating during that half-hour period. The first approach assumes that this variable cost can be different for each supplier for every day during our sample period and each half-hour during the day. The following regressions are estimated for each supplier j:

$$P_{jhdm}(\text{offer}) = \alpha_{dmj} + \tau_{hj} + \beta_j \eta_{jhdm} + \varepsilon_{jhdm}$$
$$\text{and } P_{jhdm}(\text{offer}) = \gamma_{dmj} + \mu_{hj} + \delta_j \eta^C_{jhdm} + \nu_{jhdm}, \tag{4.1}$$

where the α_{dmj} and γ_{dmj} are day-of-month d for month-of-sample m fixed effects and the τ_{hj} and μ_{hj} are half-hour-of-the-day fixed effects. The ε_{jhdm} and ν_{jhdm} are mean zero and constant variance regression errors. Input fossil fuel prices and water levels change at most on a daily basis. Because there is a different fixed effect for each day and month combination during our sample period, these fixed effects completely account for the impact of daily changes in fossil fuel prices and water levels during our sample period on the variable cost of the highest cost generation unit owned by supplier j that is operating during each half-hour period in the day. Consequently, these day-of-sample fixed effects completely control for any differences across days of the sample in input fossil fuel prices and water levels. The half-hourly fixed effects account for differences across half-hours of the day in this variable cost. This strategy for controlling for variable cost changes across half-hours of the sample implies more than 2,400 possible variable cost values over the sample period for each supplier. Multiplying this figure by four implies more than 9,600 possible variable costs of the highest cost generation unit operating during a half-hour that could set the market-clearing price during our sample.

Our second strategy for controlling for the opportunity cost of producing electricity from the highest variable cost unit (operating during half-hour period-of-the-day h during month of the sample m for supplier j) uses different half-hour-of-the-day fixed effects for each month of the sample period. The two equations estimated are:

$$P_{jhdm}(\text{offer}) = \alpha_{hmj} + \beta_j \eta_{jhdm} + \varepsilon_{jhdm}$$
$$\text{and } P_{jhdm}(\text{offer}) = \gamma_{hmj} + \delta_j \eta^C_{jhdm} + v_{jhdm}, \quad (4.2)$$

where α_{hmj} and γ_{hmj} are half-hour-of-the-day for each month-of-the-sample fixed effects to control for the differences in the opportunity cost of producing electricity from the highest variable cost unit operating during half-hour period-of-the-day h during month-of-the-sample m for supplier j. The ε_{jhdm} and v_{jhdm} are once again mean zero and constant variance regression errors. Because there are 48 half-hour periods in the day and 78 months during our sample period from January 1, 2001 to June 30, 2007, there are 48 × 78 = 3,744 values of the α_{hmj} and the same number of values of the γ_{hmj} for each supplier j. These fixed effects imply that the variable cost of producing electricity from the highest cost generation unit operating during half-hour 12 in month 3 of the sample period can be different from this same variable cost during all other months of the sample period. Moreover, the variable cost of producing electricity from the highest cost generation unit operating during half-hour 12 in month 3 can differ from the variable cost of producing electricity in any other half-hour of any other month of the sample period, including month 3.

These fixed effects allow for a substantial amount of variability in the time path of the variable cost of the highest cost unit operating in the North and South Island of New Zealand during each half-hour of our sample period. There are 3,744 fixed effects for each supplier to account for differences in the variable cost of the highest cost unit in their portfolio operating during each half-hour of the sample period. Multiplying this figure by 4 implies 14,976 different possible variable costs of the highest cost unit operating owned by the four large suppliers that could set prices during our sample period.

The fixed effects in model (4.1) and model (4.2) should be more than sufficient to account for differences in the variable cost of the highest cost generation unit operating during each half-hour of the sample period in the portfolio of generation units owned by each of the four large suppliers. The opportunity cost of producing electricity from hydroelectric generation units should not differ significantly across half-hours of the day or days of the month in a hydroelectric dominated system. The opportunity cost of water depends on current water storage levels and the distribution of future water inflows and outflows. New information about these variables arrives daily, but the best estimates of future inflows and outflows changes slowly as do water storage levels. Our day-of-sample fixed effects are more than sufficient to account for changes in the opportunity cost of water over our sample period.

The variable cost of producing electricity from individual fossil fuel generation units is unlikely to change significantly during individual months of our sample period. It implies that fixed effects that allow these half-hourly variable costs to change each month of the sample period should provide for far more fluctuations in the variable cost of the highest cost unit producing electricity during each half-hour of our sample period than is likely to be necessary to capture the amount of variability that actually exists in these variable costs. Regressions of model (4.1) including the value of the relevant daily fossil fuel price and daily water levels (to account for daily changes in the variable cost of operating fossil fuel generation units and daily changes in the opportunity cost of water) did not quantitatively change any of our results. This outcome is not surprising given the high level of agreement between our estimates of β_j and δ_j using day-of-sample and half-hour-of-the-day fixed effects and different half-hour-of-the-day fixed effects for each month of the sample period.

Table 18.1 presents the estimated values of β_j and δ_j and the estimated standard errors for each of the four suppliers using the day-of-sample and half-hour-of-the-day fixed effects. Table 18.2 presents estimates of the same parameter values for the different half-hour-of-the-day fixed effects for each month of the sample period. The values of β_j and δ_j are positive, precisely estimated and economically meaningful for all regressions. Focusing on the day-of-sample and half-hour-of-the-day fixed-effects model, holding all other factors constant, if the residual demand curve faced by Firm C has an inverse semi-elasticity that is one unit higher, the offer price associated with the amount of output that it sells in the short-term market is predicted to be $1.41/MWh higher. This is because of the greater ability Firm C

Table 18.1 *Dependent variable = offer price at dispatch quantity for supplier j*

	Firm A	Firm B	Firm C	Firm D
β_j	0.46	0.56	1.41	3.81
(s.e.)	(.017)	(.040)	(.031)	(.062)
δ_j	5.08	4.02	4.31	21.63
(s.e.)	(.108)	(.146)	(.101)	(.335)

Note: Day-of-sample and half-hour fixed effects are included in all regressions.

Table 18.2 *Dependent variable = offer price at dispatch quantity for supplier j*

	Firm A	Firm B	Firm C	Firm D
β_j	0.67	0.73	1.16	4.54
(s.e.)	(.020)	(.040)	(.029)	(.064)
δ_j	7.27	3.39	3.38	22.86
(s.e.)	(.129)	(.154)	(.092)	(.354)

Note: Month-of-sample interacted with half-hour fixed effects are included in all regressions.

has to exercise market power as implied by the inverse semi-elasticity of its residual demand curve.

We compute the half-hourly sample mean and standard deviation of η_{jhdm} for each h to demonstrate the economic significance of our estimates of β_j. Table 5.3 of Wolak and McRae (2009) presents these half-hour-of-the-day means and standard deviations. For example, for Firm C, the standard deviation of η_{jhdm} for h=37 is equal to 6.811. This implies that holding the opportunity cost of water and the price of the input fossil fuel constant, a one standard deviation change in the value of η_{jhdm} for half-hour number 37 implies a $9.60/MWh higher offer price and a two standard deviation change a $19.20/MWh higher offer price according to the parameter estimates in Table 18.1. For Firm A, the mean and variance of the inverse semi-elasticities over the sample period are even higher. The value of β_j for Firm A implies that a one standard deviation change in the value of the inverse semi-elasticity of its residual demand curve during half-hour number 23, holding all other factors constant, implies an offer price increase of $4.50/MWh.

Changes of this magnitude in the value of its inverse semi-elasticity for half-hour number 23 for Firm A during our sample period are not unusual.

For Firm D the value of β is significantly higher than it is for all of the other suppliers, on the order of \$3.81/MWh. However, the mean value of the inverse semi-elasticity is the lowest of all of the suppliers and the variance is also the smallest. Nevertheless, the magnitude of β for Firm D implies that even for a one standard deviation change in the value of its inverse semi-elasticity, economically significant changes in Firm D's offer price are predicted to occur because of its increased ability to exercise unilateral market power.

The values of δ, the coefficient associated with η^C_{jhdm}, the inverse semi-elasticity of the net of forward market obligations residual demand curve, are substantially larger in absolute value than the corresponding value of β, the coefficient associated with η_{jhdm}, for all suppliers. The value of δ for Firm C implies that if the value of the inverse semi-elasticity of the net forward market obligations residual demand curve for Firm C increases by one unit, then Firm C's offer price for the amount it sells in the short-term market is predicted to increase by \$4.31 because of the substantially greater incentive Firm C has to exercise unilateral market power. Table 5.4 of Wolak and McRae (2009) presents the half-hour-of-day means and standard deviations for η^C_{jhdm}. This table shows that a one unit change in the value of η^C_{jhdm} is a fairly frequent occurrence. For a number of half-hours of the day, a 3 unit change in η^C_{jhdm} is less than a two standard deviation change. For example, during half-hour number 37, a two standard deviation change in the value of η^C_{jhdm} implies a more than \$20/MWh increase in Firm C's offer price.

It is important to emphasize that, different from the case of the inverse semi-elasticity of the residual demand curve, which can only be positive, the inverse semi-elasticity of the net-of-forward-market-obligations residual demand curve can be negative if the supplier's fixed-price forward market obligations exceed the amount of energy that it sells in the short-term market. As shown in Figure 18.7, this was frequently the case for Firm A as well as for Firm B and Firm D during the sample period. The results in Table 18.1 for Firm A imply that, keeping all other factors constant, if a negative value of η^C_{jhdm} for Firm A becomes larger in absolute value by one unit, Firm A's offer price is predicted to be \$5.08/MWh lower because of its greater incentive to exercise unilateral market power by driving the price down. A one unit change in η^C_{jhdm} is less than a one standard deviation change for many half-hours of the day. The results in Table 18.1 also imply that – keeping the opportunity cost of water and the price of the input fossil fuel constant – if the value of the inverse semi-elasticity of the net-of-forward-market-obligations residual demand curve facing Firm A increases by one unit, the offer price for the amount of energy it sold in the short-term market is $5.08/MWh higher because of the greater incentive Firm A has to exercise unilateral market power.

Thus, once fixed-price forward contract obligations are introduced into a wholesale market, suppliers with the ability to exercise unilateral market power can do so either by increasing or decreasing prices. A supplier with a substantial ability to exercise unilateral market power that is net short relative to its forward market obligations (meaning that it has more fixed-price forward market obligations than the amount of energy it sold in the short-term market) has an incentive to exercise market power by driving down the wholesale price, which reduces the cost of closing out its net short position through purchases from the short-term market. The results shown in Tables 18.1 and 18.2 confirm this for logic for all suppliers. Alternatively, when a supplier is long relative to its forward market position, meaning that its sales in the short-term market exceed its fixed-price forward market obligations, a higher value of the η^C_{jhdm} implies that it will raise its offer price because it has an incentive to use its ability to exercise market power to raise the market-clearing price.

The estimate for δ_j for Firm D is by far the largest of the five values reported in Tables 18.1 and 18.2. However, as shown in Wolak and McRae (2009), the standard deviations of the inverse elasticity of the net of fixed-price forward market obligations for Firm D are very small in absolute value relative to the values for the other three suppliers. Nevertheless, even multiplying the estimate of δ_j for Firm D by a one standard deviation change in the value of its inverse elasticity yields predicted offer price changes of more than $10/MWh for many half-hours of the day. Because the η^C_{jhdm} for Firm D takes on both positive and negative values during the sample period, there are times when Firm D submits a substantially lower offer price, all other factors held constant, because it has an incentive to use its ability to influence market prices to lower the market-clearing price because its short-term market sales are less than its forward market obligations. Alternatively, when it is long relative to its forward market position, a higher value of the η^C_{jhdm} for Firm D implies that it will raise its offer price because it has an incentive to use its ability to exercise market power to raise the market-clearing price.

It is important to emphasize that the goal of our modeling effort is to determine whether higher offer prices are systematically associated with higher values of η_{jhdm} and η^C_{jhdm} and whether the magnitude of this relationship is economically significant. The results of our analysis presented in Tables 18.1 and 18.2 provide strong confirmation of a positive and economically significant relationship between a supplier's half-hourly offer price and the half-hourly values of η_{jhdm} and η^C_{jhdm}. The magnitude of this relationship is substantially larger for the measure of the incentive to exercise unilateral market power relative to the measure of the ability to exercise unilateral market power. This result is consistent with the logic that a supplier with the ability to exercise unilateral market power must also have the incentive to do so in order to find it expected profit-maximizing to submit offer prices that exploit it.

It is important to emphasize that the regressions (4.1) and (4.2) are predictive regressions in the sense discussed in Reiss and Wolak (2007). As noted above, the economic theory of expected profit-maximizing offer behavior described in Wolak (2003a and 2007) does not imply these regressions yield the precise causal relationship between half-hourly offer prices and the half-hourly indexes of the ability and incentive of market participants to exercise unilateral market power. This fact does not invalidate the interpretation of these regressions as providing predictive statistical evidence consistent with the view that after controlling for the level of input fossil fuel prices and the opportunity cost of water, when any of the four suppliers has a greater ability or incentive to exercise unilateral market power as measured by these indexes, each supplier submits a significantly higher half-hourly offer price and this higher offer price results in a substantially higher market-clearing price.

18.5 Do thermal suppliers behave as if they have no ability to exercise market power?

The final piece of evidence in favor of the view that the four large suppliers exercise all available unilateral market power is a test of the null hypothesis that thermal suppliers behave as if they had no ability or incentive to exercise unilateral market power. A supplier that has no ability or incentive to exercise unilateral market power can be expected to submit an offer curve equal to its aggregate marginal cost curve of supplying electricity. The complication with implementing this test for hydroelectric suppliers is that estimating their no-market-power opportunity cost of supplying energy is a massively complex computational problem related to the actual opportunity cost of stored water. However, for fossil fuel suppliers we know that the opportunity cost of producing electricity from their generation units depends on the price of the input fossil fuel, the heat rate of the generation unit, and the variable operating and maintenance cost of the generation unit. Consequently, a fossil fuel supplier with no ability to exercise unilateral market power will submit an offer price for each fossil generation unit equal to the unit's variable cost.

Our test of the null hypothesis that no supplier has the ability or incentive to exercise unilateral market power is based on the simple insight that offer prices of fossil fuel generation unit owners with no ability to exercise unilateral market power should not be predicted by any other factors besides those that impact the variable cost of the generation unit. In particular, if fossil fuel suppliers do not have any ability to exercise unilateral market power, the offer price for the amount of energy they sell into the short-term market should not be impacted by the system hydro storage level. In contrast, if higher offer prices are associated with lower water levels, then this is consistent with a supplier that has the ability to exercise unilateral market power taking advantage of this fact to raise their offer prices and market-clearing prices in response to the incentives that it faces.

To investigate this null hypothesis we regress the offer price for the quantity of energy sold from each fossil fuel generation unit during the half-hour periods of the sample when the unit was available to supply energy on a number of factors that control for the variable cost of producing electricity from this generation unit at different levels of output and daily hydro storage levels in Terawatt-hours (TWh). Let P_{khdm}(offer) equal the offer price of the energy sold in the short-term market from fossil fuel generation unit k during half-hour h of day d and month m. Let $Hydro_{dm}$ equal the amount of hydroelectric energy in storage on day d of month m. Let $QINC_{ikdhm}$ equal a set of I(k) dummy variables each of which equals 1 if the dispatch quantity from fossil fuel generation unit k during half-hour h of day d in month m lies in the 10 MW quantity increment i. For each generation unit we take the maximum and minimum output observed during the sample period and divide this range into 10 MW increments. For example, if 250 MW is the lowest output level and 360 MW is the highest output level, then I(k) equals 11, meaning that there are 11 possible 10 MW bins that the supplier could produce in during the sample period. These quantity bins are chosen to account for the fact that the heat rate of fossil fuel units can be different for different output levels. Define YR_{zdhm} as an indicator variable that equals one if half-hour h of day d and month of sample m is in year z, where z=2001, 2002,...2007. Define MTH_{wdhm} as an indicator variable that equals 1 if half-hour h of day d and month-of-sample m is in month-of-the-year w=1, 2, 3..., 12. We estimate the following regression for each fossil fuel unit:

$$P_{khdm}(offer) = \sum_{i=1}^{I(k)} \alpha_{ik} QINC_{ikdhm} + \sum_{z=2001}^{2007} \gamma_{zk} YR_{zkdhm}$$
$$+ \sum_{i=1}^{I(k)} \sum_{z=2002}^{2007} \theta_{izk} YR_{zkdhm} QINC_{ikdhm} + \sum_{i=1}^{12} \delta_{ik} MTH_{ikdhm}$$
$$+ \beta_k Hydro_{dm} + \varepsilon_{khdem}.$$

(5.1)

This linear regression controls for differences in the variable cost of fossil fuel units across the 10 MW quantity increments of output levels for the unit (the first summation), across each year of the sample (the second and third summations), and within the months of the year (the fourth summation) in order to assess whether the level of hydroelectric storage provides incremental explanatory power, beyond these variables that control for differences in the generation unit's variable cost of production, in predicting the offer price.

Table 18.3 presents the results of estimating (5.1) for the major fossil fuel units (or, in one case, group of units) operating in the New Zealand market during our sample period. In all cases, the estimated value of β_k, the coefficient associated with the value of system hydro storage for unit k, is found to be negative and precisely estimated. The null hypothesis that β_k is equal to zero is overwhelmingly rejected for all eight units, which provides strong evidence against the null hypothesis that the owners of these fossil fuel units behave as if they had no ability to exercise unilateral market power. The implied change in

Table 18.3 *Dependent variable = offer price at dispatch quantity for fossil fuel plant/unit k*

	Plant 1	Plant 2	Plant 3	Plant 4
β_k	−17.40	−2.34	−19.61	−21.13
(s.e.)	(.457)	(.135)	(.340)	(.448)
	Plant 5	Plant 6	Plant 7	Plant 8
β_k	−8.05	−24.31	−11.01	−24.12
(s.e.)	(.674)	(.377)	(.459)	(.335)

Note: Regressions include year-of-sample fixed effects interacted with generation quantity in 10 MW bins, as well as month-of-year fixed effects. The dependent variable in each regression is the offer price from either a single generation unit, or a group of units.

offer behavior from these generation units as a result of changes in the water level are also economically meaningful. For example, if the value of system hydro storage decreases by 1 TWh, then the offer price for the Plant 6 is predicted to increase by $24.31 and by $24.12 for the Plant 8. The predicted increases in the offer prices for a 1 TWh reduction in the value of system hydro storage for Plant 5 and Plant 7 are roughly half these values. Plant 1 and Plant 3 have predicted offer price increases for a 1 TWh reduction in system hydro storage of $17.40 and $19.61, respectively. Note that the difference between the minimum and maximum system hydro storage levels during our sample period is 3.1 TWh, so these estimates predict very large changes in the offer prices of fossil fuel units for the observed changes in hydrological conditions.

Although these parameter estimates are inconsistent with the hypothesis that these fossil fuel generation unit owners have no ability to exercise unilateral market power, the signs and magnitudes of the estimated values of the β_k are consistent with the hypothesis that the owners of these generation units have a significant ability to exercise unilateral market power and that this ability to exercise unilateral market power decreases with the level of system hydro storage. These results are also consistent with the results presented in the previous section which showed that the offer price for the quantity of energy sold in the short-term market by each of the four suppliers is increasing in that supplier's ability and incentive to exercise unilateral market power.

18.6 Conclusions about how firms exercise market power

The several lines of empirical inquiry presented in this chapter are broadly consistent with the implications of expected profit-maximizing offer behavior by the four large suppliers in response to the extent of competition they face from other suppliers on a half-hourly basis. This conclusion does not depend on any assumptions about the functional form of aggregate demand in the market or any model of strategic interaction among firms. Because of the data-rich multi-unit auction environment that we study, ex post half-hourly measures of the ability of a supplier to exercise market power using the offers submitted by all suppliers and the level of system demand can be computed without either of these assumptions. We find that each of the four large suppliers submits a higher half-hourly offer price when it has a higher half-hourly unilateral ability to exercise market power. The half-hourly offer price increases predicted by the parameter estimates from our econometric model (for typical changes in the half-hourly ability of each supplier to exercise market power) are economically significant in the sense that the implied offer price increases can be in the range of $10/MWh to $20/MWh during peak periods of the day.

We find even larger (in absolute value) predicted changes in a supplier's half-hourly offer prices in response to changes in its half-hourly incentive to exercise market power for typical changes in the values of these indexes. Our index of the half-hourly incentive of a supplier to exercise market power can be positive or negative, depending on the supplier's exposure to short-term market-clearing prices during that half-hour period. If a supplier is net long – its short-term market sales exceed its fixed-price forward market obligations for that half-hour – then its index of the incentive to exercise market power is positive. If a supplier is short – its sales are less than its fixed-price forward market obligations for that half-hour – then its index of the incentive to exercise market power is negative. Our regression results predict that sizeable increases in the supplier's offer price occur during half-hour periods when this index of the supplier's incentive to exercise market power is large and positive. They also predict that sizeable decreases in the supplier's offer prices occur during the half-hour periods when this half-hourly index of the supplier's incentive to exercise market power is large in absolute value and negative. These results emphasize that the extent a supplier actually exploits a lower degree of competition from other firms depends on the incentive it has to do so, as measured by the degree to which the revenues the supplier receives depend on the short-term market-clearing prices. In addition, how the supplier exploits its ability to influence the short-term market price depends on the sign of its exposure to short-market prices. This result implies that a portion of the high degree of volatility in half-hourly short-term wholesale electricity prices is the result of changes in the sign of the half-hourly incentive of suppliers to exercise unilateral market power. Finally, we provide strong evidence against the null hypothesis that the half-hourly offer curves submitted by owners of fossil fuel generation units are the result of those suppliers behaving as if they have no ability to exercise market power.

Taken together, the empirical results in this chapter demonstrate that although prices in a multi-unit auction wholesale electricity market depend on supply and demand conditions, actual supply conditions depend on the offer curves submitted by market participants to the wholesale market. These offer curves are a direct result of the unilateral expected profit-maximizing actions of suppliers given factors that they are unable to control such as the level of demand at all locations in New Zealand, amount of water inflows to hydroelectric generation units, and the price of fossil fuels and other inputs consumed to produce electricity. Therefore, the ability and incentive of large suppliers to exercise unilateral market power are important determinants of the supply conditions that determine short-term wholesale prices, even after the impact of exogenous factors such as water availability and fossil fuel prices have been taken into account.

19 | Exchanges: the quintessential manufactured markets

CRAIG PIRRONG

19.1 Introduction

Financial exchanges such as the Chicago Mercantile Exchange or the New York Stock Exchange are often identified as the epitome of a free market. The price competition on an exchange superficially resembles a Walrasian market. But this competition takes place within a dense web of deliberately chosen rules, and organizational and governance structures. These formal rules and structures are supplemented by intricate informal norms that also constrain and guide the actions of the agents who trade on exchanges.

Thus, although the process of buying and selling that takes place on exchanges appears to approximate the ideal competitive market, a focus on the transaction process itself is misleading. Upon examination, it is apparent that exchanges are, in fact, the epitome of a manufactured market. The agents who own and control exchanges manufacture a complex institutional infrastructure that shapes the more visible trading process.

This immediately suggests the question: What economic forces determine the organizational and governance structures; the formal rules; and the informal norms?

Answering these questions requires a detailed analysis of the micro-foundations of the transacting process. This analysis demonstrates that both efficiency and distributive considerations affect the organization, governance, and rules of exchanges.

In an Arrow-Debreu-Walras world, all relevant attributes of commodities and securities are completely and costlessly specified; information is costless and uniformly distributed; and contracts are costlessly self-enforced. In reality, however, there are measurement costs; information is costly and distributed asymmetrically; and parties have incentives to renege on contractual commitments. Economizing on measurement, information, and enforcement costs permits more beneficial trades to occur. Exchanges have historically been at the forefront of devising ways to economize on such costs. By creating and enforcing rules, exchanges make anonymous trade over time and space possible. They provide an infrastructure that supports trade.

Although such transactions-cost reducing considerations explain some exchange rules, they cannot explain all of them. Nor can they explain exchange organization or governance. Understanding these features requires a detailed understanding of the trading process and the agents who participate.

This analysis demonstrates that: (a) the consummation of even a simple financial transaction requires the performance of several complementary tasks; (b) there are advantages to specialization in the performance of these tasks, these specialists have specific capital, and even agents within a particular specialization are heterogeneous due to different endowments of capital; (c) there are economies of scale and scope; and (d) due to these strong scale and scope economies, there are strong natural monopoly tendencies in exchange trading, and that exchanges possess market power.

These ubiquitous features have important implications that largely determine the salient features of exchange organization, governance, rules, and norms. Exchange market power generates economic rents. Moreover, specialization and task-specific skills and capital give rise to rents and quasi-rents. These rents and quasi-rents create incentives to engage in rent-seeking behavior – which in turn, provides an incentive to devise organizational and governance structures, and rules and norms, that economize on it. Moreover, the existence of rents provides a motive to craft rules and structures to share them among market participants, and to protect the agreed upon division.

Thus, exchanges are the product of a complex variety of efficiency and rent-seeking considerations. In this chapter, I illustrate this conclusion by examining exchange organizational form, vertical integration, the committee dominated governance of traditional exchanges, the content of exchange rules, and the difficulties that exchanges have faced in addressing inefficient conduct that has profound distributive consequences.

The analysis of exchange organizational form is particularly illuminating, because it illustrates how a technological shock that affected the distribution of rents among the suppliers of complementary transactional services, the move to electronic trading, led to a complete and rapid change from not-for-profit to for-profit form at exchanges throughout the world.

The remainder of this chapter is organized as follows. Section 19.2 discusses measurement, information, and enforcement cost issues, and how exchanges have, or have not, addressed them. This motivates a discussion of how such failures have shaped government regulation of exchanges, and how governments have become an important part of the market manufacturing process.

Section 19.3 presents an overview of the process of executing the purchase or sale of a financial instrument. This analysis identifies the complementary components that are required to consummate a financial transaction, and identifies the scale and scope economies inherent in supplying them.

Section 19.4 analyzes the technology for performing these complementary functions in a traditional "open outcry" trading environment; shows how this technology gave rise to rents and quasi-rents, which in turn created a need to devise institutional protections to mitigate rent seeking; and then demonstrates that not-for-profit organizational form and committee dominated, political governance structures were well-adapted to provide these protections. The section concludes by examining how technological change affected the distribution of rents, and how organizational form changed in response.

Section 19.5 examines how transactions cost, and technological and competitive considerations determine the extent of vertical integration on exchanges.

Section 19.6 provides a brief summary.

19.2 Exchanges as transactions cost-reducing institutions

Economic agents incur costs to make trades. Consider an apparently simple commodity, such as wheat. Wheat varies in crucial qualities, such as protein content or foreign matter. Given such heterogeneity, it is insufficient for a buyer to say to a seller "I want to buy some wheat." The buyer and the seller need to come to an understanding about the qualities of the wheat actually being bought and sold. They need a language to describe wheat, and a means of assessing the attributes of the actual wheat that is sold. Moreover, to the extent that there are myriad buyers and sellers, there are often benefits to creating a standard language, and a standard measurement technology.

The buyer and the seller also need to arrive at a price. The value of the wheat depends, in part, on information about supply and demand. To the extent that information is not necessarily uniformly distributed among all buyers and sellers gives rise to adverse selection costs that impede trade.

The buyer and the seller need to ensure that the agreements that they make are adhered to. For reasons related to risk or logistics, it is often desirable to negotiate today transactions that will be completed at some future date, or which involve some future contingency. The separation in time of agreement and performance creates the possibility of non-performance. For instance, a wheat futures buyer may want to renege if the price of wheat falls. Moreover, even if agents do not want to renege opportunistically, they may be unable to perform due to some event, such as bankruptcy.

It is possible for parties to negotiate terms related to commodity definition and measurement, information disclosure, and contract enforcement. However, since (a) transactions are often repeated over time, (b) many agents engage in these transactions, and (c) certain activities have public goods attributes, there are reasons to engage in collective action to reduce transactions costs. Indeed, the genesis of most commodity and securities markets is traceable directly to the efforts of market participants to reduce measurement, information, and enforcement costs through collective action.

For instance, many famous commodity exchanges, such as the Chicago Board of Trade, were created in large part to economize on the costs of commodity measurement. Prior to their establishment, there were no standards, even for things as prosaic as the definition of the term "bushel." Since the same grain was often bought and sold repeatedly, agents repeatedly incurred measurement costs. To economize on these costs, market participants formed exchanges that defined the attributes of commodities; created a standard language for describing them; and operated inspection systems to economize on measurement costs.

Pirrong (1995a) demonstrates that these systems were often elaborate, and exhibited variations that reflected differences in the quality-control technologies. For instance, technological and infrastructure differences affected the cost of quality control across producing and exporting regions, and grading standards reflected this, specifying measurement in export countries with developed storage technologies, and in the importing countries for shipments originating in more primitive regions where quality control was more costly.

Exchanges also mediated quality disputes between traders. For instance, in the late-nineteenth and early-twentieth centuries virtually all cotton traded internationally was bought and sold under contracts specifying the resolution of disputes through Liverpool Cotton Exchange arbitration (Simpson 1991; Bernstein 2001).

Historically, exchanges also implemented measures to mitigate information costs and asymmetries. Exchanges often collected and distributed information about production, prices, imports, exports, and supplies. The central collection and dissemination of this information economized on information production costs, and reduced information asymmetries, thereby reducing adverse selection costs.

Arguably the most important exchange initiatives to reduce transactions costs related to contract enforcement. In volatile commodity futures markets, both trader insolvency, and opportunistic efforts by traders to escape losing trades, were serious problems. The earliest rules of the Chicago Board of Trade included provisions regarding the posting of performance bonds. Over time, rules regarding contract performance became more elaborate. Futures exchanges also pioneered the collective sharing of performance risk via the innovation of the clearinghouse, first developed in 1891.

In brief, exchanges have historically implemented a variety of rules, policies, and practices to reduce transactions costs. But not all exchange efforts met with success. An examination of the failures sheds light on the types of issues that make it difficult for exchanges and their members to consummate mutually beneficial Coasean bargains. In particular, these episodes illustrate how distributive conflicts over rents can interfere with the negotiation of such deals.

The best example is the conflict over the regulation of grain "warehousemen" by the Chicago Board of Trade in the 1860s. Warehousemen were essential to the efficient handling of grain in bulk. Merchandisers of grain would purchase it in the country and ship it to Chicago to be stored until it was efficient to market it to consumers in markets in the eastern US. In performing their functions, warehousemen could affect the quality of grain through the care they took in handling and storing it. Moreover, they could influence the process of measurement, and engage in processes like the "mixing" of grain that allowed them to exploit the discreteness of grain grades (Pirrong 1995a). Finally, warehousemen had an information advantage arising from their ability to monitor the quantity and quality of grain in store. The resulting "lemons problem" created additional deadweight losses.

The merchandisers and futures traders on the Chicago Board of Trade attempted to use the rules of the exchange to compel the warehousemen to implement improved grading systems, and to disclose information about grain in store. The Board also attempted to negotiate with the warehousemen to craft mutually acceptable rules and enforcement mechanisms. The attempts to compel and the negotiations both failed. Compulsion failed because the rents warehousemen captured from their exploitation of the grading system and information advantages exceeded the benefits of exchange membership. Negotiations failed in large part because side payments were impractical.

In the end, the Board turned from negotiations with the warehousemen to appeals to the Illinois legislature which passed rules regulating the warehousemen. The warehousemen's lawsuit resulted in a landmark legal decision in the case *Munn v. Illinois*, which granted states broad powers in regulating private economic activity.

This episode illustrates that large distributive effects can interfere with the ability of exchanges to implement transaction cost reducing rules. Many exchange rules improved welfare without imposing large distributive effects. For instance, traders do not know whether they will be a bankrupt, or the counterparty of a bankrupt. They anticipate that they will capture a proportionate share of the reduction in transactions costs associated with more efficient rules regarding contract performance, and hence all benefit from the adoption of such rules. In contrast, in the elevator battle, the efficient rules redistributed wealth from warehousemen to merchandisers and futures traders, and hence achieving a Coasean bargain required the payment of compensation. The available technology for manufacturing rules did not permit the production of enforceable deals to provide such compensation.

This problem is not a relic of the distant past. While working with exchanges to re-design futures contracts, I have learned that seemingly small changes – like adding a particular city as a delivery point on a futures contract – can have major distributive effects. As a result of these distributive effects, negotiations over adjustments to delivery design are typically rancorous, and lead to the persistence of clearly inefficient incumbent delivery systems.

Exchange difficulties in controlling the exercise of market power by large traders – market manipulation – provide another example of the challenges posed by distributive conflicts. Market power is inefficient not only because of the welfare losses associated with the exercise of market power, but because the unpredictability of its occurrence and its large effects on prices undermines the roles of futures contracts as hedging instruments, and beacons for price discovery (Pirrong 1995b). Nonetheless, exchanges were almost uniformly unsuccessful in creating and enforcing rules to reduce the frequency of corners and squeezes. Pirrong (1995c) shows that this was in large part due to the distributive effects of manipulation. Any exchange action would have led to large transfers of wealth among traders. Furthermore, exchange members were fearful that the power to intervene selectively to alter contractual obligations during a corner could be misused. Exchange members concluded that it was better to live with the inefficiencies associated with periodic corners, than to undermine contract enforcement.

Efficiency and distributive effects influence virtually every aspect of exchange rules, organization, and governance. I next turn to a detailed examination of the technology of trading. This examination helps highlight a series of other possible efficiency and distributive effects which I will demonstrate help explain other salient aspects of the manufacture of financial markets.

19.3 The technology of trading of financial instruments

The completion of a financial transaction typically involves a variety of complementary activities.

The first function is the execution; that is, the consummation of an agreement between a buyer and a seller. In exchange markets, orders to buy and sell are directed to a central marketplace. In a traditional floor-based, open outcry exchange, orders to buy or sell are represented by agents (floor brokers) on the exchange floor, or by exchange members physically present on the exchange dealing on their own account. Buyers and sellers (or their agents) on the exchange floor agree to the terms of a transaction through a negotiation or auction process. In newer, computerized exchanges, orders are routed to a central computer that matches buy and sell orders.

Once the buyer and seller agree to terms, a transaction must be cleared. The clearer first establishes that the buyer and seller indeed transacted by verifying that all terms submitted by the buyer and seller match. In most centralized markets, the clearing entity is then substituted as a principal to the transaction, becoming the buyer to the seller, and the seller to the buyer. That is, the clearer becomes the central counterparty ("CCP") that bears the risk of default by those with whom it transacts.

In their role as CCP, "clearinghouses" engage in a variety of activities, including: calculation and collection of collateral (margin); determination of settlement obligations; determination of default; collection from defaulting parties; and remuneration of participants in the event of a default. The CCP usually determines the net amount each party owes or is owed which typically reduces the flows of cash (and securities) between transacting parties.

Settlement is the process whereby transactors complete their obligations to pay cash or deliver securities. Presently, delivery is performed by debiting or crediting the securities and cash accounts of the counterparties to transactions. This typically involves the maintenance of a central register that records ultimate ownership of securities.

A securities or derivatives transaction involves all three functions. Thus, these functions are complementary, and the demand for each service is a derived demand. This has important implications for the organization of financial markets.

It should also be noted that there is an exquisite division of labor within the various complementary activities just described. An exhaustive discussion of this division in each of these functions is impractical, but the point can be illustrated by considering specialization in the function of executing transactions in a traditional floor-based exchange.

A customer's order to buy and sell is typically directed to a brokerage firm. This firm: evaluates the creditworthiness and performance risk of the customer; manages the customer's position by keeping records of trades and positions and receiving cash due and paying cash owed; and provides the customer with advice and information. The brokerage firm, in turn, directs the order to a floor broker for execution. The floor broker is typically an independent contractor whom the brokerage firm pays a commission. The broker represents the order to the trading crowd. Members of the trading crowd may include other floor brokers representing customers, but independent traders buying or selling on the own accounts ("locals") also participate. These locals provide liquidity by absorbing temporary order imbalances, buying (selling) when more customer sell orders than buy orders (buy orders than sell orders) flow to the floor.

All of these activities within the execution function are highly complementary. A customer consumes a bundle of brokerage firm, floor brokerage, and local trader services; each is essential to the completion of a trade.

What's more, even within a particular specialization practitioners are heterogeneous. They differ in their human and financial capital. Due to these differences, inframarginal members earn rents.

Furthermore, human capital in these functions tends to be highly specialized, and non-redeployable. As a result, floor traders tend to earn far more in this activity than they could in their next best alternatives. Moreover, a floor-based exchange is a dense social network in which reputation and social capital are quite important. These assets are specialized to trading on the floor of a particular exchange.

The physical capital of a floor-based exchange is also highly specialized. The trading building is specially designed to facilitate floor trading.

There is another aspect of financial trading that exerts an influence on the organization of exchanges: market power arising from extensive scale and scope economies in each of the three major functions. First consider the execution of transactions. Liquidity effects make trading of a particular financial instrument a natural monopoly. Due to informational considerations, the cost of liquidity is lower when all trading in a particular instrument is concentrated on a single exchange.[1] That is, liquidity costs (of which losses to the informed are a major component) in a particular market are lower, the larger the number of uninformed traders in that market.

Put differently, informational and liquidity considerations create a network effect. The prospect of achieving lower trading costs by trading on the biggest market for a particular instrument creates a centripetal force that tends to "tip" all trading activity in that instrument to a single exchange. Moreover, the difficulty of coordinating the simultaneous defection of traders from an incumbent exchange creates

---

[1] Admati and Pfleiderer (1991); Pirrong (1999, 2002).

a switching cost that provides the incumbent exchange with market power.

The other functions also exhibit scale and scope economies. Consider clearing. Basic diversification considerations imply that the risks a clearinghouse bears per trader in a particular instrument are decreasing with the number of traders (Pirrong 2008). Similarly, diversification across different instruments reduces risk, and generates a scope economy. Due to these considerations, clearing exhibits strong natural monopoly characteristics.

The specialization and heterogeneity of those involved in floor trading creates economic rents. Moreover, the extensive economies of scale in various aspects of the trading of financial instruments can create market power that also generates rents. The specialization and limited redeployability of physical and human capital creates quasi rents. The extensive complementarity of the various activities involved in floor trading, and the heterogeneity of the participants, creates opportunities to redistribute these rents through exchange rules, policies, and norms. Moreover, these rules, policies, and norms can have efficiency effects.

Thus, exchange members face a complex challenge in choosing forms of organization, modes of governance, rules, policies, and norms that diminish wasteful rent seeking and encourage wealth-enhancing bargains. The next sections examine in some detail the institutional implications of market power and the extensive complementarity and division of labor inherent in the technology of trading financial instruments.

19.4 Trading technology and exchange organization and governance

The consequences of trading technology discussed above decisively affect the organization and governance of exchanges.

First consider the effects of scale economies, entry barriers, and the resultant market power. Exchanges have an incentive to exploit this market power and can do so by limiting membership. Pirrong (2002) demonstrates that due to the liquidity cost advantage that a larger exchange possesses, a group of traders that supplies just more than half of the total available capacity to execute transactions is immune from competition from other exchanges. By restricting membership, an exchange can enhance its members' profits without fear of competitive entry.

Thus, network effects imply that exchanges will limit entry to extract a monopoly rent. The historical record is consistent with this implication. With the primary exception of the London Stock Exchange, which was prohibited from limiting entry by an Act of Parliament, exchanges have limited entry. Pirrong (1999, 2000) presents evidence that these entry restrictions generate rents for members.

Exchanges have employed other means to exploit the market power arising from network effects. For instance, prior to the 1970s and 1980s, when regulatory pressure stopped the practice, exchanges around the world operated and enforced brokerage cartels (Pirrong 2000).

Network effects, entry restrictions, cartels, and other measures create rents. As noted previously, rents also arise from heterogeneity among exchange members. The existence of such rents, of course, creates the incentive to engage in rent seeking. Exchange members have incentives to mitigate these wasteful activities. They can do so through the choice of ownership and organizational forms, and the nature of exchange governance.

Consider who should own the exchange, examining first a traditional open outcry exchange. Since human capital and physical capital involved in the trading process is highly specialized, and that its value in alternative uses is low compared to its value in trading, there are considerable quasi rents in trading. Separation of ownership of the physical and human capital creates the potential for opportunistic holdups. Therefore, transactions costs considerations imply that exchanges should be organized as mutuals, where the members who trade on the exchange own its physical and financial assets. And indeed this has historically been the case. Exchanges are typically member-owned mutual firms.

Next consider whether the mutuals should be organized as for-profits or not-for-profits. The crucial difference between these forms is that for-profit mutuals can distribute surplus to members, but non-profits cannot. At first blush, one would think that highly profit-motivated individuals would choose the for-profit form. But distributive considerations in the presence of large rents and quasi rents strongly suggest otherwise.

In a traditional firm, shareholders are relatively homogeneous and agree that the firm should choose price to profit and be free to distribute it to the shareholders. In contrast, the heterogeneous members of an exchange do not necessarily agree on pricing and distribution policies because these policies can be used to redistribute rents among the members. In particular, pricing and distribution policies can be used to transfer rents from one group of members to another group providing a complementary service.

For instance, suppose that the supply of brokerage services is less elastic than the supply of locals' services. A tax incidence-type analysis implies that given these conditions, charging a per trade fee that generates revenues in excess of the costs of operating the exchange, and distributing the surplus equally among the members would tend to redistribute rents from the brokers to the locals. The fee would reduce the prices both locals and brokers can charge for their services, but the impact on brokers would be greater due to the smaller elasticity of supply of broker services. Brokers and locals would participate equally in the proceeds of the fee, however, and this would effectively transfer rents from the brokers to the locals.

The non-profit form precludes this sort of rent extraction and redistribution. The distribution constraint inherent in the non-profit form implies that profits generated by exchange fees cannot be used to shift rents among groups. Thus, the non-profit form reduces incentives to use the exchange fee structure in ways that distort exchange output to redistribute wealth to a powerful constituency in the exchange.

In fact, open outcry exchanges almost uniformly were organized as non-profits (Pirrong 2000).

Now consider exchange governance. Elimination of the use of exchange pricing and distribution policies to redistribute rents does not foreclose all avenues for rent seeking. Exchange rules also have distributive consequences. For instance, a seemingly innocuous rule, such as the size of the minimum price increment (the "tick"), can redistribute rents. Locals make a profit by buying at the bid, and selling at the offer. The difference between these, the tick size, determines the profitability of supplying liquidity. Raising the tick size tends to increase the profitability of making markets as a local, but given the complementarity of the services of exchange members, this tends to reduce the derived demand for brokerage services, and reduce the wealth of brokers.

Rent seeking through the rule-making and enforcement process involves costs, and provides a reason for creating governance structures that mitigate waste and support the consummation of wealth enhancing Coasean bargains. The literature on the industrial organization of legislatures (Weingast and Marshall 1988) demonstrates that the use of committees that have exclusive jurisdiction over specified rules, and the requirement that all proposed changes to rules gain approval of the committees whose constituents are affected, can support these goals. Requiring the acquiescence of affected committees to rule changes prevents ex post reneging on Coasean bargains, and therefore helps enforce such deals. Furthermore, the effective veto power of committees over rules that adversely affect its constituents mitigates the possibility of using rule changes to extract rents from them. Thus, organizations that have the ability to redistribute large rents by changes in rules should utilize political, committee-dominated governance structures.

Exchanges do just this. Indeed, exchanges are notorious for the reliance on committees, and the byzantine nature of their governance. These mechanisms create checks and balances that mitigate rent-seeking battles among exchange members.

The efficient organizational form and governance structure may be technology-dependent because technology affects the magnitude of rents and quasi rents, and their distribution. A major shock to trading technology provides a test of the foregoing implications. Starting in the 1990s advances in computing capability and communications technologies made computerized trading of securities and derivatives feasible. Indeed, electronic trading has many advantages over traditional floor-based trading. For one thing it is much more rapid. Moreover, errors and mistakes are less likely in computerized markets. Furthermore, and perhaps most importantly, computerized markets allow anyone in the world with a computer and cash to supply liquidity to the markets on effectively equal terms, whereas in a floor-based system, those on the floor have preferential access to information and can act on it more rapidly, giving them a substantial advantage over those located off-exchange in supplying liquidity.

Electronic trading also reduces some information disparities. Those on the exchange floor observe prices, bids, and offers directly and in real time, whereas those off-the floor must rely on the process of relaying information from the floor to them. Floor traders also can observe who is trading, and other forms of "soft" information that is not available to those away from the floor. In contrast, in an electronic market everyone with a trading screen sees the same price and quantity information at the same time. Whereas floor traders have the advantage of seeing more information sooner, no such disparity exists in an electronic market.

Thus, technological change reduced the cost of providing transactional services. At the same time, however, it (a) reduced the heterogeneity of the suppliers of transactional services, and (b) reduced the rents that some of these suppliers could earn. With respect to heterogeneity, note that electronic trading eliminates the need for some kinds of agents altogether, notably floor brokers. Moreover, electronic trading that permitted the entry of large numbers of liquidity suppliers trading "upstairs" reduced the time, space, and information advantages, and hence the rents, of traditional locals on floor exchanges.

This technological shock had two major effects, both related to its effect on exchange member rents and their distribution.

First, the fact that electronic trading devalued the specialized human capital and the rents attributable to advantages of time and place made traditional exchanges resist fiercely the move to electronic trading. The advantages of incumbency arising from network effects and switching costs allowed them to do so successfully for some time. However, the evident and growing efficiencies of electronic trading credibly threatened the open outcry exchanges with extinction. As a result, open outcry exchanges in the United States and elsewhere were compelled to transition to electronic trading.

Second, electronic trading's effect on rents and their distribution undermined the need for the elaborate organizational and governance structures devised to protect rents. Specifically, since in an electronic environment it was possible to trade in large volumes without relying on a group of very specialized intermediaries located in a highly specialized physical facility, intermediary ownership of an exchange was no longer an efficient adaption to production technology. Similarly, absent a set of specialized, heterogeneous intermediaries, non-profit ownership and politicized exchange governance were no longer required to protect rents.

Thus, this major technological change to electronic trading eliminated the need for member ownership, non-profit form, and political governance. As a result, in parallel with the adoption of electronic trading, exchanges converted from non-profit mutuals to for-profit investor owned firms.

This does not mean that rents disappeared altogether. Nor did the technological change eliminate all sources of complementarity in the trading process. Network effects and switching costs are important in electronic markets, just as in open outcry ones. These give rise to economies of scale, market power, and the associated rents. Moreover, the economies of scale and scope in clearing and settlement also remain, and these functions remain complementary to trade execution. I next discuss how this affects exchange vertical organization.

19.5 Vertical relations and exchange organization

The earlier analysis of execution, clearing, and settlement noted that each of these functions is characterized by strong scale economies. If these services are supplied by firms that specialize in a single function, the strong scale economies in each tend to result in the survival of a single firm in each function, each of which has some market power. Due to the complementarity of clearing, settlement, and execution, separate ownership, control, and pricing of these functions therefore creates a trilateral monopoly problem which creates the potential for inefficiencies.

First, due to complementarity, multiple-marginalization problems arise. Independent price setting by the three firms results in a price that exceeds the monopoly price that an integrated monopoly firm would charge.

Second, even if the exchange, clearer, and settlement agent enter into a set of contracts that avoid multiple-marginalization and ensures that the ultimate customer of financial transaction services pays the price which maximizes the rent to be divided between the three entities, wasteful opportunism can arise. Each entity employs specific capital, and this capital is likely to be quite durable. These considerations lock the suppliers of execution, clearing, and settlement services into long-term, trilateral relationships. Due to the long-term nature of the relationships, the parties are likely to rely on long-term contracts to govern their interactions. However, the specific assets of the clearer, exchange, and settlement firm give rise to quasi rents, and each firm has the incentive to engage in ex post opportunism to expropriate them. Unpredictability in the economic environment makes complete contracts impossible, and parties can exploit this incompleteness to profit at the expense of their contracting partners.

Integration of the complementary trading functions abolishes the deadweight losses arising from multi-marginalization and opportunism. Although integration does not result in a first best outcome (because the integrated entity is a monopoly) it offers some advantages over a disintegrated structure because it avoids the costs associated with inefficient pricing and rent seeking. It can also adapt to unpredictable changes in conditions, such as technology or regulatory shocks, which challenge contractual governance of the relationships between distinct execution, clearing, and settlement firms.

This is not to say that vertical integration is free. Due to their inability to precommit to a high powered incentive system, integrated divisions are typically operated subject to low powered compensation schemes that attenuate incentives to reduce costs and innovate. Moreover, information asymmetries between managers give rise to costly information rents and the use of low powered incentives.

Thus, standard transactions cost considerations imply that integration of trade execution, clearing, and settlement offers several advantages. Assuming the existence of separate execution, clearing, and settlement firms, vertical merger increases the rents to be split among their owners. Thus, integration is plausibly a second-best response to the natural monopoly characteristics of trading, clearing, and settlement.

Although vertical integration is a well-recognized way to mitigate transactional hazards, there are other ways to organize firms and to govern relationships between them in order to control transactions costs in the presence of small-numbers and specific asset problems such as those inherent in trade execution, clearing, and settlement.

For instance, a user cooperative can eliminate multiple marginalization problems.[2] Brokerages can form a cooperative firm that supplies clearing. It is possible for this cooperative to choose prices that eliminate double marginalization.

---

[2] Hansmann (1996). Hausman, Leonard, and Tirole (2003) present a model showing how a non-profit cooperative can induce an efficient outcome in a network industry.

This does not mean that this alternative is as efficient as, or more efficient than, integration. Several potential problems arise, including:

- The clearing cooperative cannot internalize all benefits from investments to improve productivity or service quality because some of these benefits accrue to the monopoly exchange if this investment is non-contractable. This reduces at the margin the cooperative's incentives to invest, and leads to underinvestment.
- The foregoing analysis assumes that (a) the cooperative implements an open access policy, and (b) the per unit fee it charges members is set competitively, that is, the cooperative does not enforce a broker cartel. Both assumptions are subject to challenge. For instance, financial exchanges were non-profit mutuals that enforced broker cartels that set minimum commissions and restricted membership.[3] Elsewhere (Pirrong 1999) I show that a cooperative natural monopoly firm can exercise market power, and allow its members to earn economic rents, by restricting membership. To avoid this, it is necessary to constrain the cooperative's ability to limit membership. This is not a straightforward task, as in the case of clearing and settlement it is economically sound to impose financial requirements on members to mitigate moral hazard; it is no mean feat to determine whether a given financial requirement is justified as a prudent way to maintain the solvency of the clearing and settlement firm, or is instead set inefficiently high in order to restrict membership.
- Separation of trade execution and post-trade services can impede coordination. For instance, a change in a trading or clearing system often requires changes in the other. The incentives to adopt efficient changes may not be well aligned when trade execution and post-trade services are carried out by different firms. Similarly, sometimes there is a need to coordinate responses to market shocks or regulatory changes. Implementation of such changes requires negotiation across firm boundaries, which can provide an opportunity for hold-ups to extract the quasi rents that arise from specific investments.

---

[3] Hansmann (1996) and Philipson and Posner (2001) argue that even non-profits may exercise market power even though they cannot distribute profits to their owners. For instance, they can charge supracompetitive prices for goods over which they have market power, and use the resulting profits to subsidize the production of other goods for their owner-members.

This impairs incentives to introduce efficiency-enhancing innovations or to respond efficiently to shocks.
- Effectively operating as a non-profit, the clearing firm's management is subject to low powered incentives.

A vertically integrated exchange is not vulnerable to expropriation of the returns to investment, or to hold-ups that impede coordination. The integrated exchange has no incentive to limit brokerage participation in the clearinghouse for strategic purposes, as this reduces the derived demand for its services. On a priori grounds it is not possible to determine whether incentive power is weaker in an integrated exchange than with an effectively non-profit clearer. However, on balance, unless the costs of low powered incentives for an integrated firm are substantially higher than for the post-trade processor, integration dominates supply of post-trade services by a cooperative.

These problems with the cooperative solution can be mitigated by extending control and ownership rights in the cooperative to the exchange. That is, shared governance – partial integration – is one means of attenuating the transactions costs associated with the separation of trade execution and post-execution service providers.

In sum, although a vertically integrated exchange does not result in a first best outcome, alternative arrangements in which clearing and settlement are separated from execution incur deadweight costs as well. These alternatives might have some merit, as compared to vertical integration, to the extent that regulation or cooperative ownership of one segment of the industry (such as clearing and settlement) facilitates competition in another (such as trade execution), and even then only to the extent that the associated efficiency gains outweigh any efficiency losses that arise in a disintegrated industry. However, in the case of financial transactions, each of the three segments of the industry has strong natural monopoly elements. The creation of a clearing cooperative, for instance, does not eliminate the centripetal force of liquidity that gives execution venues considerable market power, but incurs costs from low powered incentives, weak incentives to reduce costs, entry restrictions, or some combination thereof; again, this arrangement is preferable to integration only if these costs are lower than the transactions costs incurred by the integrated firm.

In fact, vertical integration of trade execution, settlement, and clearing in a single firm is the modal form of organization in centralized securities and derivatives markets (Pirrong 2008). In most cases, the clearing and settlement operation is a division or wholly owned subsidiary of the exchange where transactions are executed. In most of the remaining instances, the execution venue has an ownership stake or governance role, or both, in the clearing and settlement entities.

Pervasive economies of scope in clearing and settlement are leading to diminished exchange roles in some clearing and settlement entities, such as LCH.Clearnet in Europe. The scope economies in clearing and settlement extend across multiple exchanges, and also across centralized exchange and decentralized OTC markets. In particular, the consolidation in banking and intermediation, whereby large intermediaries participate in myriad exchange and OTC markets, has increased these scope economies in clearing and settlement. This provides a strong incentive to consolidate clearing and settlement across exchanges and OTC markets. This has raised the opportunity cost of vertical integration and exchange control over clearing and settlement, relative to the alternative form of organization, clearing and settlement cooperatives owned and operated by users of clearing and settlement services. The decline in exchange ownership and control over clearing and settlement entities that span exchange and OTC markets is consistent with this change in relative costs.

Thus, consistent with the theory just outlined, integration is the primary means of organizing these functions except where scope economies in clearing and settlement encompass markets where scope economies in execution are absent (such as across exchange and OTC markets).

19.6 Summary and conclusions

Exchanges for financial instruments are often held out as the archetypal competitive market. In fact, they are the quintessential manufactured market. They are institutions deliberately designed to support financial transactions. Historically, and into the present, they have adopted measures to reduce transactions costs, such as measurement and contract enforcement costs.

The technological characteristics of trading have exerted a decisive influence on the way these markets are manufactured. Trading of financial instruments involves complementary functions requiring specialized human and physical capital, and which are subject to very strong scale economies. These features create rents, and create coordination challenges. Exchange operators have responded by crafting organizational and governance structures that reflect complex trade-offs between efficiency and rent seeking considerations. Many exchange rules, organizations, and governance structures are clearly intended to enhance efficiency by reducing transactions costs and mitigating rent seeking. Other rules, however, are less laudable, being best understood as means to create and secure rents by exploiting the competitive impediments that arise from extensive scale and scope economies. Moreover, the voluntary nature of exchanges and the difficulty of crafting and enforcing some Coasean bargains has precluded them from creating and enforcing rules that would mitigate certain forms of inefficient conduct.

The facts that exchanges (a) are organizations designed to advance the interests of the intermediaries who trade on them, (b) sometimes implement inefficient rules that benefit their member-owners, and (c) sometimes are incapable of implementing efficient rules, have led governments to impose extensive regulations on exchanges. Regulation has increased substantially the complexity of the manufacturing process. In particular, it has altered the bargaining process that ultimately determines exchange rules, and shifted the nexus of many of the negotiations from exchange board rooms to legislative chambers and regulators' offices. As a result, exchange rules now reflect the influence of a broader collection of interests, including those who do not participate directly on exchanges. Indeed, the foregoing discussions of the elevator controversy in Chicago (ultimately resolved by legislative intervention) and manipulation (the prevention of which being the motivation for much US regulation of derivatives and securities markets) provide excellent illustrations of how regulatory interventions have altered the content and character of exchanges.

But although regulatory intervention has substantially altered exchange rules and the processes of exchange governance, the fact remains that these rules and processes reflect a balance between efficiency and distributive considerations. These are the materials from which the archetypal markets are manufactured.

20 | Conclusion: tâtonnement in the manufacturing of markets

ERIC BROUSSEAU AND JEAN-MICHEL GLACHANT

20.1 Why the manufacturing of markets matters

Markets are key social technologies since they are the vector of impersonal exchange and competition. Implementing markets or developing more efficient markets are essential factors of growth since they lead to a deeper social division of labor, favor a better use of resources due to the combination of incentives and the ability to do so, and foster innovation. Obviously, the division of labor as well as innovation might exist without markets, but anonymous exchange and competition boost them. Also, markets might fail to deliver welfare, because they are manipulated by specific interests, or because they may enter a perverse loop of crisis, even leading to their own collapse. However, the most dynamic economies are all characterized by the development of market exchange, and to a large extent economic development is due to the development of a market economy. Understanding how markets are built is therefore essential to understand many policy and societal issues.

20.1.1 Economics as the science of market performance ...

In a sense, economics is THE science of markets. It became an autonomous domain of knowledge with the development of the concepts of the market and market economy. This led to the development of a considerable domain of knowledge on the mechanisms leading to the setting of economic quantities, of the dynamic and effects of competition, on the source of maladjustments in decentralized systems, etc. At the same time, all of these developments of both traditional and modern economics were based on a fiction of what markets are. Traditionally they are a mechanism allowing the meeting of demand and supply, then the establishment of prices; hence the volume of production and exchange and the distribution of the wealth among economic agents. However, nothing is said about the origin and nature of this social technology. It is simply there under the different assumed myths as the Smith's "Invisible Hand" or the Walras' "Auctioneer."

Dissatisfactions about the capability to understand the performance of actual economies thanks to this model led economists to develop considerably their understanding of market microstructures from the 1970s, when they started to take into account seriously the insight of the young Ronald Coase (1937) about the cost of market exchange. If markets are costly, then they can be considered as a social technology (of exchange), with competition from alternative technologies. From the 1970s, a generation of economists worked on the understanding of the essence of transaction technologies in a decentralized economy. In particular they developed contract theories and later market microstructure analysis to understand how agents seeking to benefit from the opportunities of trade, solve the various challenges linked to the intrinsic risks and difficulties of exchanges: the costs of identifying the best match between needs and capabilities, constraints in adjusting plans in time and space, opportunistic behavior resulting from information asymmetries, low incentives to comply with commitments if new opportunities come up, etc.

20.1.2 ... and of market design

From the late 1980s economists developed a vast body of knowledge that could be grouped under the heading of "market design." They accumulated a wide set of theories and evidence on the properties of alternative ways to govern bilateral exchange or to organize markets. This resulted in an in-depth understanding of the technology of markets, as well as of the techniques to implement and develop competition. Indeed, one of the factors that boosted the development of this body of knowledge was the liberalization of many industries and trade from the 1980s in most OECD countries, then worldwide after the collapse of the planned economies. Economists were consulted on implementing markets and competition in components of the economy that were previously either not commoditized (e.g., the environment), or operated by governments (e.g., services of general interest), or at least strictly regulated (e.g., network services). Contemporary economics is therefore, among other things, a science of the social technology of market exchange.

While the profession and society as a whole benefit from fairly extended knowledge on the performance of alternative market designs, the way this social technology is actually designed and implemented remains under-explored. Yet, this is an essential link in the implementation of policies based on the knowledge accumulated by economists on market technologies. Moreover, it might also be an essential factor of understanding of the very nature of this technology. Contributing to the exploration of how markets are built is the "raison d'être" of this book.

20.1.3 The need to analyze processes of market building and market reforms

What this book highlights is that markets are complex systems articulating several interacting components contributing to a facilitation of economic exchange. Altogether these elements determine the level of transaction costs, hence the extension of impersonal exchange and the intensity of competition. Both have a huge impact on the level and distribution of wealth since they impact on social actors' ability to specialize and to benefit from position and opportunities. The design of markets is therefore not a neutral game, and all kinds of stakeholders form coalitions and play strategies to influence the genesis and the capture of rents and positions to control potential evolutions of market structures and market designs. The case studies articulated in this book attempt to highlight how these strategies interplay, and question the ability to monitor market building dynamics, both for social planners and organized interests. They demonstrate that we are definitively in a second best and evolutionary world where efficiency gains are just one of the drivers of the process of market building.

This last chapter attempts to draw conclusions. First, in sections 20.2 to 20.4, we look through analytical lenses to present some positive outcomes about our understanding of the manufacturing of markets. We show that markets are articulating mechanisms that are built on a piecemeal basis by contrasted interests interacting according to a complex combination of logics. This results in processes, whose evolutionary nature has to be highlighted. Markets are indeed in a permanent process of reform and rebuilding. Second, in sections 20.5 to 20.7, we attempt to derive normative conclusions for political actions and actors' strategies. Our goal is not to propose any "optimal" policy since we are in a second best world where alternative policies have not only efficiency effects but also distribution impacts: they are truly political choices. Rather, we draw guidelines for political action, either by a benevolent ruler or by social actors. We therefore insist on the idea that markets are not neutral social technologies, which explains why they always correspond to imperfect compromises. On the one hand, social actors logically attempt to distort them to their benefits. On the other hand this results in a permanent need to monitor, adapt and reform – in brief to govern – markets. That said, there is no way to design a perfect (public) body that would be able to monitor market evolutions. The regulation of markets must be thought of in terms of multi-stakeholder mechanisms facilitating coordination while maintaining the possibility to challenge any positions in the long run. In other words, markets request pluralistic and reflexive governance.

20.2 Markets as architecture

20.2.1 Three governance dimensions: objectivization, impersonalization and interindividual adjustments

The market is not "a" mechanism but an architecture of mechanisms. Those mechanisms aim, first, at objectivizing the exchange, thus making it less manipulable by parties thanks to systems of measure and certification clarifying the characteristics of the traded goods and services. Second, these mechanisms allow the impersonalization of exchange, which means that trade can occur between parties which have no personal and social ties, simply because their mutual commitments are governed under the shadow of a system of enforced rights (see Chapter 4 by Benito Arruñada). Mutual agreements about the use/transfers of resources do not request that the parties are involved in repeated exchange or belong to the same community because the complex web of mutual commitments about the use, access and benefit of resources, which are essential in providing credibility to agreements, are neutrally registered. Third, these mechanisms favor the adjustment of individual plans to produce or use resources because they implement principles, according to which agents can compare them,

Tâtonnement in the manufacturing of markets

negotiate adjustments and guarantee compliance with the resulting agreements (and resolve disputes if any). The question here is whether individual traders can rely on socialized mechanisms – either a third party acting as platform, facilitator or guarantor, or a set of collective rules about the way to meet, to share information and to negotiate – to settle deals and perform transactions.

When generic mechanisms contribute to the objectivization and impersonalization of the exchange, transaction costs tend to be reduced since agents can save on their individual efforts to negotiate and check the characteristics of trade and to guarantee the enforcement of promises. When collective mechanisms contribute to the impersonalization of exchange and the adjustments of plans, the quality of matching in the economy is enhanced, which allows a deeper division of labor. When social means combine to allow the objectivization and impersonalization of exchange and adjustment of plans, then transparency of the social exchange is boosted. The resulting competition provides actors with incentives to be more efficient, and with opportunities to introduce innovations.

Objectivization, impersonalization and adjustments of plans largely draw from the building of three families of mechanisms – based on the acceptance of common rules and related enforcement capabilities – aimed at measuring the commodity's characteristics, registering and transferring rights (i.e., recognized legitimacy to access, use or benefit of resources), setting and settling prices and quantities. To perform these tasks, four types of "governance regimes" are available. They can be ranked according to a logic where the performance of the related tasks is increasingly managed at a collective level and by specialized entities.

20.2.2 Four regimes of governance: contractualization, intermediation, self- and public regulation

The first regime corresponds to a world of Coasean bargaining, where the parties contract on the basis of established rights (Coase 1960). This is a world of maximum flexibility for the actors who can arrange customized deals. At the same time, such a regime requires a great deal of adjustments once rights have been established – either through the negotiation and signature of sophisticated contingent contracts, or thanks to renegotiation or conflict – which result in high transaction costs borne by the parties, either ex ante or ex post. Of course fine graining in the definition of property rights, as well as detailed liability laws, result in greater ease in contracting and in a higher level of security. However, as compared to the other regimes below, this is clearly the regime with the least collective and specialized governance, letting the burden of transaction performance fall on the shoulders of transacting parties and judges or arbitrators.

The second regime can be qualified as "Williamsonian" in the sense that it relies essentially on third party/intermediaries providing "interested" exchange services. This is the realm of brokers, private conflict settlers, platforms, exchange service providers, wholesalers and retailers. It is a world of bilateral arrangements, in which design and management are delegated to a third party. These third parties can contribute to the reduction of transaction costs because they benefit from economies of scale and specialization (see Spulber 1996; Brousseau 2002). At the same time they capture rents because of their central positions (see Chapter 19 by Craig Pirrong). As pointed out by the literature on two-sided markets (Rochet and Tirole 2007) and on assemblers (Brousseau and Pénard 2007), there is even a correlation between their ability to capture rents and to provide efficiently transactional services. There is therefore a trade-off.

The third type of governance, "self-regulation" has been extensively analyzed, in particular by Elinor Ostrom (1990, 2005), on the provision of public goods and by Avner Greif (2006b) on the organization and securization of exchange. This regime relies on the accumulated knowledge, repetition of transaction and convergence of interests within a group (characterized by proximities in terms of geography, social network, economic interests, etc.) to implement efficient collective coordination solutions. The limit of these solutions is that they are based on the adhesion of participants (and on the ostracization of infringers). If exit/exclusion costs are low, then the self-implemented order is weak. From a social planning point of view, the limit of self-regulation is that they generally do not take into account externalities transferred to other stakeholders in the society. To put it another way, self-regulation aims at maximizing the efficiency of exchange for the members of the community, while it is not implemented to increase collective welfare.

The fourth type of arrangement corresponds to public ordering and state regulation. Douglass North and Barry Weingast in particular have highlighted the central trade-off here (North and Weingast 1989; Weingast 2004). On the one hand, public rulers might be powerful and impose rules on social actors targeting specific objectives. Moreover, in some political configurations these objectives can be collective wealth, innovation and growth. At the same time, public rulers are not always benevolent and might favor specific interests. Moreover, as pointed out by the literature on public bureaucracy and public decision makers, the government and its various components might lack adequate capabilities (from information and knowledge to human capital) to govern efficiently economic exchanges and production. That said, the historical experience of the development of the Western world highlights that in some conditions, an efficient articulation between a Weberian bureaucracy and the rise of the rule of law might trigger the development of capabilities that allow traders to benefit from a dramatic decrease in transaction costs.

20.2.3 A continuum toward more rule-based impersonal exchange

In one sense, and in this order, the four governance regimes highlighted here correspond to a continuum along which the exchange becomes increasingly impersonal and increasingly collectively managed. From the traders' point of view, they are decreasingly free to choose the conditions of exchange, because they increasingly rely on collective rules that state most of them ex ante. This results in more "standardized" products and transactions, which increase transparency, and hence competition and security. This "standardization" of transaction and commoditization of all types of service provision favor the division of labor, the extension of markets and also the multiplication of markets. In a sense, the complete public regulation of the quality of merchandise, of the contractual arrangements and of the meeting between demand and supply would result in the fiction of the Walras-Arrow-Debreu markets, where the traders have only to decide the quantities they buy and sell on the various markets since everything else is managed by the shadow institutional framework which defines the various markets (hence the conditions of exchange) and manages the "tâtonnement" process.

Beyond the reduction of transaction costs, it is important to point out that the socialization and specialization of the governance of exchanges result in an ability to perform a more sophisticated exchange, which is a key driver of a deeper division of labor and the securization of transaction. Securization, which is also dependent upon the quality of the property right systems, is a key enabler of the lengthening of the time horizon of the players and therefore an essential driver of long-term investments, both in physical infrastructures and in efforts to innovate, two strong drivers of growth. As pointed out above, however, the more the governance of exchange is socialized and specialized, the easier it is for those in charge of this governance to establish positions and capture rents; hence the sensitivity of the organization of checks and balances in the governance of a market economy.

20.2.4 Modular governance architectures, and their specific dynamic

Beyond this general discussion on the trade-offs concerning the centralization of the organization of markets, it is important to point out that the three domains mentioned above – the certification of the commodity characteristics, the guarantee of the rights to access, use, benefit from and contract resources, and the mechanisms aimed at determining the terms of trade – can be governed by the four different arrangements. There are thus at least 12 (3×4) configurations of market organization, but in fact there are more if one considers that these broad categories of components can themselves be split into more fine-grained ones (as it is done, for instance, in Chapter 3 by Marta Fernández-Barcala, Manuel González-Díaz and Emmanuel Raynaud, in the case of the measures of quality).

This is one of the outcomes of the contributions to this book to highlight the truly complex nature of the resulting architecture. Markets are made of various components that could be governed following contrasting logics. At the same time, these components influence each other, both in synchrony and in diachrony. Indeed, the way one component is organized might impact on the performance of another. For instance, the efficient performance of an auctioneer market requires clear property rights. Also, change in the organization of one component may induce evolutions in another. This is, for instance, illustrated by the contribution by Aashish Velkar (Chapter 2), who showed how the objectivization of the measure of quality transformed the bargaining power between supply and demand on the wheat market, allowing the latter to progressively transform the market from a face-to-face contracting system into anonymous commodity exchanges.

This vision of markets allows for a sophistication of the analysis initiated by scholars such as Yoram Barzel (1989) or Harold Demsetz (1967). The question is not simply to decide the optimal combination of levels of governance to establish property rights, nor the best procedure to distribute them. The idea of complexity brings other dimensions into the analysis. From an analytical point of view, it raises the issue of the consistency among the components of a given market. What is the likelihood that the complex system is consistent? Do mechanisms exist which push for more consistency across components? Also, is efficiency – whatever efficiency means: transaction cost minimization or more intense competition – a driver of evolution? What are the selection mechanisms between alternative market organizations? From a policy-making perspective, the question is the ability to monitor the process of market building. Is rational design helpful both to understand what the objectives should be and how to reach them? To put it another way, do optimal forms of market really exist, and if so, are they implementable? Is it relevant to target one simple and single objective when attempting to build markets? As pointed out in the next two sections, the vision of the market that is drawn from the studies proposed in this book leads to a modest vision of what is possible or should be expected when attempting to influence the organization of markets.

20.3 Markets as a result of complex games

20.3.1 A game between traders, intermediaries and rulers

The case studies proposed in this book highlight that the rules and organization that end up governing market exchanges are the results of multiplayer games among which at least three categories of agents are identifiable.

First, one can identify the trading parties. Suppliers, which include new entrants, play a strong role in designing and implementing systems facilitating trade. The demand side is often less active in designing solutions, except in markets between professionals. It should be noted, however, that the bargaining power of the demand side tends to increase with the degree of competition. Thus, the ability of the users to influence the process of market design is strongly dependent upon the degree of socialization and specialization of market exchange. One can suspect irreversibilities, there. Traditional systems of exchanges are generally opaque. New entrants can however contribute to implementing more transparency and objectivity, as they need to inform the demand side of their competitive supply. Above a certain threshold, the united users have enough bargaining power to push for the design of more transparent, efficient and competitive market mechanisms.

Second, there are the specific agents providing exchange services either because they are market organizers (platforms), facilitators of trade (brokers, intermediaries), or third parties providing transaction services (lawyers, certifiers, payment services providers, conflict settlers, etc.). History books are full of cases in which private service providers became the central organizers of markets. This is the case for most stock exchanges. Yet even when they do not fully organize the market, the role of exchange service providers is essential. As pointed out by the contribution of Craig Pirrong to this book (Chapter 19), they contribute to reducing transaction costs, to the "cost" of capturing rents. They therefore are active, both in implementing innovation and in lobbying the other actors involved in the manufacturing of markets in the design of market components. Their goal is obviously to establish their position, both against their competitors and vis-à-vis the trading parties, to consolidate their sources of rents. Of course, the competition among them is a major factor of the erosion of these rents. Also, trading parties and the government may have interests in reducing these rents. At the same time, these service providers contribute to the efficiency and security of trade. They are not easily substituted, in particular because beyond their technical capabilities, one of their essential assets lies in the fact that the various stakeholders trust them (due to a mix of confidence built up from past interactions, and of the anticipation that they want to maintain their reputation). Moreover, this trust is established on a very "micro" basis, at the level of the interactions among traders and these third parties. While, generally speaking, "intermediaries" have a bad name, agents retain trust in their local shopkeeper, lawyer, banker, etc. This contributes to maintaining the centrality of those actors in the day-to-day operations of many markets, which is the source of their capability of action and negotiation when it comes to the question of discussing evolutions.

Third, there are the public rulers. Public authorities are central in the organization of trade because it is a major source of power and rents. As pointed out by the contribution of John Wallis to this book (Chapter 8), in all societies the ruling elite controls the organization of economic activities because it is both a way to establish its power, especially by distributing rents to organize a coalition, and a central means of transforming political influence into concrete benefits. There is however a trade-off in the manipulation of markets to the exclusive benefits of political rulers, since it leads to discouraging entrepreneurs and more generally to hindering trade, hence the division of labor and innovation. Thus rulers may not only enfranchise economic agents, but also provide them with infrastructure facilitating or supporting trade. They may even end up developing sophisticated organizational architecture including "independent" agencies aimed at organizing markets, providing exchange services and guaranteeing security and stability (Brousseau et al. 2010).

The (vertical and horizontal) division of the public authority is a "mechanical" consequence of the development of the strengths of modern governments. It is explained by the necessity of checks and balances within the powerful state, but also by the complexity of the question dealt with that leads to the development of different skills and to making sure that the various logics are taken into account in decision-making. At the same time the division of modern states into many (partly independent) entities results in autonomization of the components of the fragmented government (in a standard self-justifying organizational logic). In addition, to legitimize and strengthen their autonomy, these entities can build alliance with a coalition of stakeholders outside the government, in a way which reinforces their legitimacy (well illustrated by the contribution of Yannis Karagiannis and Adrienne Héritier in Chapter 13). In the end, the various components of the government can defend specific interests, which may not be the general interest, or the simple interest of the political coalition in power. One of the illustrations of this in our contemporary world is the "consumerist" orientation of antitrust authorities as compared to the "industrialist" biases of regulatory agencies pointed out, for instance, by Antonio Manganelli, Antonio Nicita and Maria Alessandra Rossi in Chapter 10.

20.3.2 Political strategies, economic competition and the rule of law

These three categories of stakeholders – i.e., traders, intermediaries, the government – interact according to a combination of three logics of actions: the political logic of settling coalitions aimed at securing equilibriums establishing a hierarchy among individuals' agendas; the economic logic of organizing the circulation and use of resources so as to get a surplus, while of course each player is mainly motivated by increasing his individual wealth and reinforcing his competitive advantage; and the legal logic of maintaining stability in a social system in guaranteeing participants rights and a foreseeable and challengeable process of modifying or clarifying them. It is important to note that all the categories of stakeholders listed above act simultaneously in the framework of these logics, because they are not referring to individual motivations, preferences or patterns, but to coexisting logics in the social game.

While rivalry is inherent to human behavior, and while exchange exists in any human society, markets – that is, policed competition and anonymized exchange – are inherent to institutionalized societies. This is why markets are intrinsically political in the sense that rulers oversee their organization, when they do not simply establish them. As pointed out by North et al. (2009) markets are initially organized to generate and distribute rents, so as to maintain a minimal social consensus, and to bring revenue into the hands of the rulers and their allies. Thus, for most members of a society, negotiating with the rulers and also with the other stakeholders about the organization of markets is a way to challenge the pre-existing distribution of rents and to secure access to future rents. It is very likely, therefore, that any market organization results in rents; and that any market reorganization translates into the redistribution of rents (even if they might also erode). The first consequence of this is that the design of market is intrinsically political since it requires the building of coalitions to impose the change on the losers. The second consequence is that, because the stability of the institutional framework of a market results in the consolidation of rents, reforms trigger a dynamic of competition. Lastly, it is very unlikely that market organization remains stable over a long period of time since the stakeholders whose interests are neglected – and in particular new entrants and users – have incentives to form a coalition to reverse the dominating one.

That said, everything is not "pure politics." Indeed, motivated by their individual wealth, all kinds of stakeholders push for evolutions in the architectures of markets by promoting changes that increase economic efficiency. Either the costs of transaction decrease, or degree of competition increases, resulting in net gains at the collective level. The resulting reforms are Pareto improving, while this does not mean that Hicks-Kaldor compensation (of the losers) is implemented. The same logic applies when markets are created to substitute for alternative regimes of access and benefits. In practice, a large set of institutional entrepreneurs – either trading parties, or intermediaries, or political/bureaucratic decision makers – invent new social technologies to reduce transaction costs or enhance the performance of social exchange. They are driven either by local efficiency gains in their daily practice, or by the will to enhance collective efficiency through meso/macro-economic reforms, even if in the latter case they also consider the individual benefits that they might get. In any case, as in any issue in economics, individual motivations should not be confused with social outcomes. Since alternative organization of markets does not result in the same level and distribution of benefits, there is always room for proposals by entrepreneurs. Competition among them and between them and incumbents (that is those currently mastering the organization of a given market) may result in erosion of rents and reduction of inefficiencies.

Torn between political games and economic progress, the architectures of markets could be subjected to permanent, violent and unpredictable evolutions. This would be a major issue, since the current organization of markets shapes the inter-temporal arbitrages of agents. Indeed, they chose to specialize and invest, to act on a given set of markets, the timing of their economic decision under the shadow of the established systems of measure, of guarantee of commitments, of the meeting between demand and supply. When their choices can be questioned overnight, they limit involvement in markets and prefer autarky. This is what happens, for instance, in the case of hyperinflation or civil war.

This is why it is essential to establish strongly the credibility of the institutional frameworks guaranteeing the commodities' characteristics, the rights and contracts, and the establishment of values. The rule of law imposes therefore its own logic – against the winning coalition or the profitable innovation – because guaranteeing both the persistence and the smooth evolution of the pre-existing order is the condition of trust, which is necessary to guarantee adhesion. Without adhesion, there is no market, and no social exchange, depriving the society of the benefits of the division of labor and competition. While often considered as a constraint by reformers or entrepreneurs, the rule of law is simply a condition of the existence of markets. As a consequence market evolutions are always difficult to manage because stakeholders lean on their "rights" to protect their past investments and positions. Also, when public action tends to neglect trust in (market) institutions – as is the case in revolutions – it may have far-reaching effects, since agents dramatically revise their decision in matters of investments and specialization. Larry Neal shows this clearly in the case of financial markets (Chapter 14). The development of markets requires a large volume of reference security widely held by a diverse customer base, a corps of professional traders that form personal networks that support exchange, and a microstructure for contract enforcement. These elements are sustainable only if all actors share mutual and reciprocal beliefs of the convergence of their interest in maintaining this infrastructure by complying with their commitments.

Glachant et al. (2011) provide a detailed analysis of the interplay between the political will to implement more integrated and competitive energy markets in Europe, the game played by operators to deal with risk and long-term investments, and the specific logic of the competition and antitrust legal frameworks.

20.4 The logic of evolutionary institutional equilibria

Markets result therefore from the meeting of strategies carried out by three categories of players acting according to the mixed-logic of the establishment of coalitions, generation and capture of efficiency gains, and protection of past investments. All this results in non-ergodic processes of evolution, whose future is unpredictable, while the logics are identifiable.

20.4.1 (Social) innovations and their adoption

Markets are diverse because they are empirical constructions without plans (at least, plans that would be consistent over several periods of time). As biological patterns, their emergences and evolutions come both from chance and necessity, to echo Jacques Monod (1971). However, coincidence does not mean that market components draw from random innovations; and necessity does not translate into the idea that a process selects the more efficient forms.

In the specific case of mechanisms of exchange, the notion of coincidence corresponds to the idea that there are "spontaneous" developments of transaction technologies fitting to the specific needs of sub-sets of economic agents which need workable solutions to face, for instance, a technological shock or the aftermath of a crisis, or simply to increase their wealth. All these phenomena are usually very local and not aimed at reshaping the whole system of exchange. However, they can have far-reaching effects, because local innovations in the technology of exchange may spread to wider communities and reshape the logic of exchange due to network externalities.

Indeed, necessity lies in the requirement for consistency along transaction chains and across dyads of traders when exchange systems lead agents to perform transactions with a wide set of counterparts. The norms that "organize" the daily performance of some specific and local markets can then be adopted by other traders, simply because they exist and are requested in the exchange with some categories of players.

Also, norms (of exchange) tend to become self-sustainable because of the division of labor. To specialize, invest and operate, players need to rely on norms. Even if they might disagree on their preferred norms, they tend to agree on the superior necessity of norms. Then, even if not the best, pre-existing norms tend to be complied with by incumbents; even if they were initially imposed by a dominant player or a non-benevolent ruler. Sunk costs make adopters reluctant to switch to alternative norms when the latter leads to past investments being written off (including specialization). This makes established norms strong and difficult to reverse. Anticipating future irreversibilities explains why strong conflicts might exist in the establishment of norms of all kinds.

20.4.2 Competition among institutional entrepreneurs and trading communities

This does not mean that markets are inherently inefficient because self-reinforcing loops of adhesion would lead to the domination of ANY norm. As analyzed in Brousseau and Raynaud (2011), the competition among institutional entrepreneurs triggers a permanent challenging of existing norms/governance regimes. These entrepreneurs can be trading parties, intermediaries or political rulers and they can have all sort of motivations. However, they are all interested in improving their strategic position against other entrepreneurs. From that perspective they articulate the logic of local initiatives, and the forming of coalitions to leverage network effects.

In a given state of market organization, individual behavior balances between compliance with the existing social technology, and the tentative implementation of local "patches"; i.e., innovative coordination practices. These innovations can give birth to new collective practices and institutions by adhesion/imitation. Collective action also can arise. Markets being social technology, collectives can also form to implement a technology of exchange that enhances the performance of trade, or gives a competitive position to the coalition. While these initiatives are not systematically driven by a movement of rationalization, and while there is no "natural" selection process that would allow the survival of only the cost-minimizing solutions in the long run, these initiatives might trigger situations which are irreversible.

20.4.3 Institutional irreversibilities

By the end, the main source of irreversibility is the division of labor, which makes it difficult to get back to a more autarkic form of social organization (Brousseau et al. 2011). Not only would it induce the loss of collective benefits, but also it would request the reinvention of forgotten techniques and the renouncement of many technologies. Yet, other (intermediary) mechanisms are at play. In particular the development of markets induces the building of institutions and norms that benefit enough players to create coalitions supporting their perpetuation. This concerns both the objectivization of exchange and the development of competition.

20.4.3.1 The balancing of power among market players

The objectivization of exchange induces non-manipulability of its essential dimensions. Whether it is a question of the physical characteristics of goods, or of the legal delineation of the rights that are transacted, non-manipulability is supplied either by third parties – which are themselves led to be neutral and competent because they rely on some (ethical/scientific) principles enforced by communities and networks; see Greif (2006b) – or by mutual bodies – where the plurality of interests is considered; see McCubbins et al. (1987) – or by organizations – structured by checks and balances and procedures "à la Weber"; see de Figueiredo et al. (1999) – that end up by being essential coordination service providers. Once they are present in the economy, they modify the ability to manipulate the terms of exchange, they make conditions of exchange more transparent and they enhance the verifiability of trade. They therefore change the balance of power between the various market players and, in particular, contribute to increasing the capability of influence of the demand side.

20.4.3.2 Innovation and new entrants

The impact of the development of competition is less straightforward. On the one hand, the same logic applies. More competitive markets tend to give more bargaining power to the demand side. It can result in strong legitimacy for the bodies in charge of guaranteeing access to new entrants, and fighting collusion and the exercise of monopoly power. On the other hand, market crises and failures to control the collusive strategies of some dominant players lead all kind of interests to voice against competition and free markets, resulting in the erection of regulations and legal barriers to trade. Alternation of these two patterns might give the impression that there is a pendulum moving between phases of liberalization and phases of regulation; which correspond to the dominant wisdom. This ignores, however, that the creation of "new" markets as well as the "liberalization" of existing markets result in the advent of new products, new players, new technologies of production, new ways to access resources that are not destroyed ex post, even when it becomes necessary to "regulate" competition or the functioning of the exchange. Indeed, new assets, opportunities and expectations give strong incentives to continue to trade, even if trading mechanisms might need to be amended. This is why it is preferable to think in terms of market evolutions and development.

20.4.4 The double face of redundancies and overlaps

That said, the process of market construction is not centrally and rationally monitored. The institutional framework of markets is influenced both by the necessity to maintain some stability in the system – then the existence of de facto consensus about common norms and procedures – and the will of agents and reformers to modify (locally) the shape of the existing framework. This results in the coexistence of systems performing closely related tasks, systems that are not always well adjusted to each other (also illustrated in the coexistence of many alternative social technologies to assess the quality of traded goods; see Fernández-Barcala et al., Chapter 3). Markets are full of overlapping and redundant imperfect components that all in all control each other to avoid major drifts, catastrophic evolutions and systemic collapse. At the same time, redundancies and overlapping avoid optimization and prevent costs minimization. This could be considered in such a perspective as the irreducible costs of reliability and sustainability in the long run.

Also, redundancies and overlaps among (public and private) authorities within the institutional framework of a market (i.e., between the components of the regulatory framework), can be seen as a mechanism favoring liberalization. Indeed, it is a factor of competition among authorities and also of possibilities of evolution of the framework. Imperfect institutional design generates uncertainties that give room for maneuver to the players, which can surf on ambiguities, missing links and fuzziness to erode the rents of their competitors (suppliers or users).

20.4.5 Decentralized evolution as source of inconsistencies

The logic of politico-economic cycles in the building of markets should not be forgotten. Indeed, since the shape of markets can be deeply affected by political coalitions, and since the implementation of market reforms results in irreversible situations through the development of assets and institutions, the various economic and political players might rationally attempt to implement reforms aimed at capturing rents and distorting "definitely" the shape of the evolutionary path in their favor. The dominant reaction of losers is not only to resist these evolutions radically *ex ante*, but also to erode them *ex post*. This might result in inconsistencies that undermine the performance of the framework, and also result in crises (as pointed out in Chapter 12 by Witold Henisz and Bennet Zelner).

The second source of endogenous inconsistencies is the local innovations mentioned above. Technical, organizational and marketing innovations always challenge the consistency/effectiveness/efficiency of the existing institutional framework, triggering a permanent flow of tensions that may result in crises.

20.4.6 Crises as opportunities to reshape institutional frameworks

Crises are important in the process of market building because they are occasions on which the gravitational forces that lead to stability – including the influence of the legal frameworks – can be overwhelmed by factors of transformation. In Aoki's and Greif's terms, crises are periods during which the mutual expectations about each other's consistent behaviors are no longer effective in enabling (satisfactory) coordination (see Greif and Laitin 2004; Aoki 2011).

Leadership is essential in those periods to discover and implement new focal points on which to coordinate. Intermediaries, on the one hand, and governments, on the other, are typically those which can reorganize markets on these occasions. The problem of intermediaries is that they might be powerless. They can neither order nor force adhesion to new rules and norms by traders. Moreover, there might exist competition among intermediaries.

On the contrary, the government may have the capability to "convince" market players to adopt new rules. They can indeed play on several levers, including political force. At the same time, their main weakness is that they do not have the relevant knowledge to build the adequate market microstructure. They must therefore cooperate with the players to explore new solutions and to foster adoption, with (again) the obvious risk of capture ... especially when the necessity to act in emergency prevents the consultation of all stakeholders and the building of consensus. The narrow path of government in their effort to rebuild institution and trust is well analyzed in Chapter 15 by Jérôme Sgard on monetary regimes.

All in all, while the analyst can point out the various intrinsic characteristics of markets – that are thus complex, evolutionary and unstable systems – action is made difficult by the fact that these features translate into barely predictable systems. Not only are malfunctioning and crises difficult to foresee, but when reforms/changes are needed the right action is difficult to decide, both because the requested transformations are not easy to identify and also because the complexity of the chains of strategic reactions is difficult to anticipate. In the next sections we nevertheless discuss the essential policy questions raised by the contributions to our collective analysis of market manufacturing.

20.5 Pro-competition reforms

20.5.1 *The political difficulty and uncertainty of rebalancing interests*

One of the central points made in this book is that competition is not "natural" and has to be built. It results from a political process, and rents have to be secured to create coalitions supporting (more) open competition. Indeed, implementing market mechanisms challenges established interests and requires huge costs of adoption from many of the players, that include writing off investments, reshaping capabilities and adapting to rising uncertainty (see the example of the EU integration of the electricity market discussed by Glachant and Lévêque 2009). Thus, there is always strong resistance to the implementation of pro-market and pro-competitive reforms.

Reforms are also complicated by the process of reform itself, as perfectly illustrated by Stephen Littlechild's narrative of the reform of the electricity industry in Great Britain (Chapter 9). First, since markets are complex mechanisms, they are hardly designable from scratch and hardly implemented overnight, because a lot of fine-tuning is necessary in each component of the machinery. Thus implementation is necessarily piecemeal, with resistance and compromises at each step. Second, the logic of politics shapes the process of reform. Rulers are subject to political cycles. Political reformers need to stabilize their coalition to keep power (and among other things ensure the non-reversibility of their reforms). They therefore rarely manage reforms according to a Hicks-Kaldor logic by which the losers would be compensated thanks to the collective efficiency gains. To stabilize the pro-reform coalition, the winners often share the generated efficiency gains, and

Tâtonnement in the manufacturing of markets 461

benefit from the windfall profits linked to the redistribution of assets and rights. A corollary is that since losers tend not to be compensated, they play hostile strategies. Initially, they frontally oppose reforms and are in favor of the status quo. Then, they resist reforms at the implementation stage. Ex post, they try to establish a coalition to reverse reforms. This might give the rulers incentives to adapt their reforms as time goes by, and to accept amendments aimed at reducing opposition (often in a divide and conquer logic). As a result, reforms can be seriously undermined by inconsistencies.

20.5.2 *The intrinsic limits of governmental action*

This trend may be emphasized by two institutional characteristics of public decision-making in liberal states. First, the division of power leads governments to be composite organizations influenced by a wide set of interests. Governmental action is rarely fully consistent, resulting in overlaps, missing links and inconsistencies in the resulting institutional framework. Second, to prevent corruption and to allow democratic control, public action is severely bounded by procedures and behavioral norms, as well as characterized by risk of future reversal. The notion of "third party opportunism" developed by Marian Moszoro and Pablo Spiller (Chapter 11) reflects this idea. Basically, politicians and bureaucrats cannot always implement the first best solution simply because they lack the credibility and the legitimacy to commit to implementing certain solutions. In particular, when flexibility or progressivity is needed, public decision makers can be deprived of the discretion that would be required. Constitutions and citizens prefer rigidity because judicial and democratic ex post monitoring is not trusted. Hence, clearly political constraints prevent "rational" public decision makers governing in function of the public interest, even if they would like to be "benevolent dictators."

20.5.3 *Insulation of the authority as an imperfect solution*

These elements explain why a united power with a clear vision of the benefits linked to impersonal exchange and competition is key in the implementation of pro-markets reforms. Divided policy making tends to dilute and delay reforms, and to implement in any case inconsistent market infrastructures. On the contrary, a united power, with a clear vision, is able both to manage acceptability at each step and to coordinate gradual reforms so as to adapt the institutional framework to the path of evolution. The united power thus needs to be backed by a strong political coalition, which might undermine the reforms if the later attempts to capture too much benefit. So the reformers clearly have a complex mandate to keep the support of the pros and to redistribute part of the reform's benefits to the cons at the implementation stage. This is the condition of non-reversibility of the reform, since as time goes by economic agents adapt to the new norms and market organizations. At the same time, it might be reversed by the evolution of coalitions with swinging interests between the pros and cons.

Making (economic) reforms (relatively) independent of the electoral process has been a key issue in most countries for the last thirty/forty years. This explains why pro-market forces have been heavily investing in building consensus – especially the so-called "neo-liberal consensus" – within the elites. In a sense it has been very effective in the OECD countries. Both the conservative and the social-democrat elites adhere to the idea that competitive markets are greatly preferable to an administrated economy. It resulted in the continuity of reforms beyond electoral cycles, thanks in particular to the creation of (semi-) independent regulatory agencies aimed at managing the transition to more competitive markets in many industries that were operated previously either by regulated monopolies or by state-owned firms.

That said, it should never be forgotten that the design and implementation of markets remain severely restricted by constraints that prevent the implementation of the most efficient solutions. Also, a given market organization inevitably generates rents, whose distribution is not neutral, both for collective efficiency and political equilibriums. Markets are therefore never first best technologies. The actual relative performances of alternative market mechanisms should therefore be systematically assessed, both among themselves and with alternatives to markets that include administrative or collective management.

20.6 Creating/implementing new markets: the issues in establishing private property rights systems

Among the most emblematic markets reforms since the 1980s, the creation of markets aimed at managing all kind of (formerly) "commons"

Tâtonnement in the manufacturing of markets 463

(especially natural resources) or the provision of public goods is certainly central. Right-based management systems trigger incentives to lower costs and to innovate. Yet, again, efficiency has a price: the allocation of rents to some players. This raises fairness and equity issues.

20.6.1 The inherent biases of privatization processes

Markets require the attribution of property rights. This is the condition for providing incentives for efficient resource use and investment ... and to create a mechanism favoring the directing of resources towards their highest valued uses. In a Coasean world, however – that is a world different from the one of the "Coase theorem" – the mechanism relied upon to distribute property rights – i.e., to privatize – is not neutral. Indeed, when transaction costs are not zero, market redistribution is imperfect. Alternative mechanisms result thus in different distributions of the rents generated by the implementation of markets. Also, since the different potential users of the resources may have different abilities in managing them, the initial distribution of property rights influences the generated surplus. Thus, the process of "privatization" impacts upon its efficiency, while by the end the customers/citizens are always those who pay for inefficiencies, as pointed out by Denny Ellerman (Chapter 6).

Implementing the most efficient privatization mechanisms is difficult for one essential reason: the scope of the conflict among private interests. The rents generated by processes of privatization might be so huge that it makes it difficult for any process not to be manipulated. Even a "benevolent dictator" would have difficulties in resisting the pressures, which include corruption, falsification of information, lobbying, etc. In addition, since conflicts and reversal of coalitions might occur, the evolution of these processes tends to be random, making it difficult to drive them efficiently because of a lack of foreseeability.

20.6.2 Auction vs. grandfathering: the implementability issue ...

In the context of market creation, an auction is the solution that is often recommended by economists, as well as by policy consultancy bodies (such as inter-governmental organizations). Indeed, auctions are supposed to be subject to a lower degree of political and economic manipulation. Moreover, auctions allow the "owner" of the assets/commons that are privatized to benefit from revenue that can be redistributed to provide public goods. Due to implementation constraints, however, auctions are not always the best solution, not in the "first best" sense but in the "alignment" sense. Given the actual constraints – the capabilities of the auctioneer, those of the bidding parties, the understanding of the public at large and, in consequence, the political acceptability of sophisticated mechanisms, the potential inefficiency of the distribution of the rent generated by the auction, etc. – grandfathering (in the case of property rights distribution; see Chapter 5 by Terry Anderson, Ragnar Árnason and Gary Libecap) or negotiated contracts (in the case of public procurement analyzed by Eshien Chong, Carine Staropoli and Anne Yvrande-Billon in Chapter 7) might appear as preferable solutions. They obviously require, however, neutral and competent public bureaus to avoid capture of those processes by corrupt political and bureaucratic elites in collusion with business ... and we know that it is a "strong" assumption (on the debates around the status of "bureaus," see Beuve et al. 2013).

20.6.3 ... and the nature of the collective action dilemma

The best principle of distribution of the allowance when a market is created may be dependent on whether the concerned resource is a "good" or a "bad." In the case of goods, since the current exploiters of the resource have the accumulated capital and experience to manage the resources efficiently, they should be the most able to value it efficiently, and will transmit efficiency gains to the customer if markets are competitive. Grandfathering seems therefore the most efficient way to guarantee the realization of the social benefits of a system aimed at distributing more efficiently a scarce and valuable resource.

In the case of bads, however, producers will always transfer the cost of the reduction of their production to taxpayers ... without any incentive to use the best technique and more generally to balance the costs of bads and the costs of their reductions. In that case auctioning is the best way to reveal shadow prices and to guarantee a return of social benefits to citizens ... if indeed the majority of the allowance value is assigned directly to consumers.

20.7 The paradoxes of regulating/mastering markets

Once markets are created, the remaining question is whether policy makers and bureaucrats should be involved in their monitoring. Against this vision, a vast literature on public choice highlights the limited ability and the non-benevolence of public decision makers, and claims that all in all market failures are preferable to political ones. On the contrary, of course, the other vast literature on market failures calls for the regulation of markets.

20.7.1 The permanent risk of capture and inefficiency

This book results in a balanced vision. Indeed, it highlights three justifications for public oversight of the performance of markets. First, the political origin of markets translates into rents attached to any market organization. It may justify the permanent monitoring of markets so as to implement reforms aimed at eroding the sources of these rents to guarantee redistribution to all stakeholders, to maintain pressure on players and to favor innovation. Second, since institutional frameworks are inherently imperfect, they are characterized by inefficiencies and the risk of systemic collapse. It is justified to try to fix the former, and to prevent the latter as advocated in particular in Chapter 16 by Michel Aglietta and Laurence Scialom. Lastly, market participants, including intermediaries, are all involved in a daily activity of micro-innovation aimed at capturing some wealth (well illustrated by the analysis of the New Zealand electricity market proposed by Shaun McRae and Frank Wolak in Chapter 18). Not only can eroding these permanently re-created source of rents result in efficiency gains, but also those local innovations may also seize up the performance of the market, and even be the source of crises (think of the innovative products in financial markets).

20.7.2 Two challenges for regulation: innovation and authority

All these elements call for some supervision of markets to avoid major drifts due to capture by specific interests of the levers of their design, and to prevent systemic crises. This does not lead, however, to the conclusion that a public agency should implement detailed regulation and exercise strict supervision. Various stakeholders, and in particular citizens, new entrants and third parties, have both competencies and incentives to be involved in the process of market organization and supervision.

Moreover, the efforts of regulations are constrained by a double challenge. First, the entities in charge of the regulation are confronted with the permanent innovations by market players that bind their capacity to design appropriate rules, and to identify the specific behaviors to be scrutinized. Second, these entities need to be able to resist pressure, while at the same time independence may limit their actual authority.

20.7.2.1 The challenge of learning without being captured

Innovation generates a challenge both for regulation and for competition policy. On the one hand, the idea of an ex ante designed set of constraints to control risks and prevent crises is irrelevant in a context of permanent innovation. Players invent new instruments and contracts that bypass the constraints aimed at preventing the repetition of the past crises. So the entities in charge of preventing market collapse and systemic crises should be aware of the evolution of actual practices to try to identify potential drift, warn the actors and help them to coordinate to fix the issues. These require strong capabilities of investigation, analysis and conviction.

On the other hand, in the daily operations of markets, competitors tend to develop subtle and difficult to observe behaviors that can harm consumers or discourage entry. This calls for specialized capabilities of supervision, since competition (and the threat of entry) does not automatically eliminate this kind of behavior ... and since not combating it would encourage even more open capture.

The need for specialized supervision does not mean, however, that regulatory agencies should be created to provide it. Supervision can also rely upon analytical expertise, such as a dedicated institute or a consultant firm. The point however is that the organization in charge of enforcement should combine three characteristics. First, it has to accumulate an in-depth knowledge of the industry, its players, its technologies, its markets. Second, it has to be able to access data, including the private data of operators. Third, it has to be independent in the sense that it has to be able to investigate any subject. Indeed, if the list of issues it could deal with were limited, it would be very likely that operators on the market would be able to collude on un-verified variables. Public and specialized agencies are thus well gifted to play the role of supervisor.

20.7.2.2 Independence vs. authority

This leads to the second issue: the relationship between independence and authority. To address the issues pointed out above, the usual reply is to empower market regulators and to grant them independent status to protect against pressure. An extended authority is requested to allow the regulator to investigate the situation generated by the aforementioned innovations, and to impose evolving rules on the industry. The question becomes then the probability of such a "delegation of authority" in the world as it is. What government would accept to deprive itself of such degree of sovereignty, both internally and a fortiori in the context of international federalism? Moreover, would citizens in democratic countries waive their right to influence economic policy making to grant it to "independent" administrative authorities; especially in the case where these authorities are populated by individuals with ties with the industry? And the industry itself? Would the powerful market players let the development of powerful and skilled regulators bind their ability to play at the margin, where risks are as spectacular as profits? It is obviously very unlikely that fully powerful and independent regulators will emerge, especially in an internationally fragmented context.

The challenges of innovation and authority call for the implementation of multi-stakeholder based mechanisms aimed at reducing information asymmetries, favoring the convergence of beliefs and expectations, and stimulating trust to allow cooperation (among competitors and among the stakeholders) to prevent maladjustment, systemic crises and, when they do occur, to favor their fixing. Regulatory authorities can play a role in favoring cost sharing, coordinating agendas and stimulating cooperation. Regulators tend then to become organizers of forums, rather than market organizers per se (see Brousseau and Glachant 2011).

20.7.3 *The rule of law as an ultimate guarantee*

Judicialization is also key in the regulation of markets. Indeed, the specificity of each market, the potential collusion among market players (because reciprocity is at play), the biases of regulators in favor of a stable industry (to prevent crises), can combine to develop specific (informal) norms that would be contrary to superior norms. In particular, preference for the status quo might hinder competition, depriving entry and consolidating rents. The ability of the judiciary to review and challenge decisions made by all sorts of authorities as well as agreements among parties is therefore essential. The discussion of the interplay between antitrust and intellectual property by Howard Shelanski (Chapter 17) highlights how potential conflicts of norms play in the daily operations of markets regulations. The second argument in favor of a judicialization of the oversight of markets is linked to the permanent innovation by industry players. Regulations are always late in detailing what should be authorized or forbidden. Ex post assessment by judges applying principles like the rule of reason is essential to guarantee compliance with some fundamental principles, and in particular the ability to challenge any position.

20.8 Concluding comments: the key role of expectations and beliefs

Once markets are established, market forces are much more powerful than any government. Governments have in practice a limited capability to act concerning markets, both in terms of knowledge and in terms of administrative capabilities. Governments and public decision makers in general can simply influence players by generating focal points and favoring convergence of behaviors. Hence the strong role of beliefs in the building and governance of markets, since players have to trust the public agents in their ability to convince the other players to adhere to norms and to rely on common focal points.

While beliefs have non-rational aspects, hence their potential volatility, they are also grounded in past experience and their revealing capabilities about how future issues will be dealt with. This is a question of regularity of behavior as well as accumulated capability. While we pointed out earlier the lack of consistency of the accumulated capabilities shaping the performance of markets, we also insisted on the extreme sophistication of their components. The accumulated institutions in the most developed economies might be considered as an ensemble of strong stabilizers of market mechanisms. All in all, the resilience of the market and of the economy today is much stronger than in the nineteenth century "free market economy" of the industrial revolution. Moreover, crises are scarcer and less violent. This partly results from an evolution of beliefs in the long run. As pointed out by the strong "confidence" of citizens in Western countries in many components of their social environment – from money, to street corner security – this might well be due to the relative efficiency of the imperfect institutions that frame their life, which all in all protect them from the essential risks borne by their ancestors, or by their contemporary peers in developing countries. Thus, while attempting to implement perfect regulatory frameworks is hopeless, the permanent quest to improve the quality of our current framework is an essential factor of social and market performance since it influences the confidence of citizens which favor the stability of their (economic) behavior.

On the contrary the erosion of belief in the government's ability to ensure a satisfactory performance of the economy is a potential endogenous driver of the destabilization of a market economy. When policy makers, bureaucrats and players succeed in controlling the inherent instability of markets, most of them and the general public may progressively forget that systemic crises can occur: they tend to be considered as historical relics. This results in a progressive erosion of the consensus in favor of constraints on the performance of markets, and in particular in favor of an extension of these constraints, resulting in the inevitable surfacing of a new crisis fundamentally driven by innovations that overwhelm the logic of the pre-existing market mechanisms.

Thus the belief that the government and, beyond it, the united stakeholders can succeed in regulating markets efficiently tends to be precisely the main limit on the actual capability of the governance of our economies.

References

Acharya, Viral, and Matthew Richardson, eds. 2009. *Restoring Financial Stability: How to Repair a Failed System*. Hoboken, NJ: Wiley & Sons Publishing.

Admati, Anat, and Paul Pfleiderer. 1991. "Sunshine Trading and Financial Market Equilibrium." *Review of Financial Studies* 4(3): 443–481.

Adrian, Tobias, and Markus Brunnermeier. 2009. "CoVaR." *Federal Reserve Bank of New York Staff Reports* 348.

Adrian, Tobias, and Hyun Song Shin. 2008a. "Liquidity, Monetary Policy and Financial Cycles." *Current Issues in Economics and Finance. Federal Reserve Bank of New York Issues in Economics and Finance* 14(1).

———. 2008b. "Liquidity and Financial Contagion." *Banque de France Financial Stability Review Special Issue on Liquidity* 81(11): 1–7.

———. 2008c. "Financial Intermediaries, Financial Stability and Monetary Policy." *Federal Reserve Bank of New York Staff Reports* 346.

Aglietta, Michel, and Philippe Moutot. 1993. "Le Risque de Système et Sa Prévention." *Cahiers Economiques et Monétaires de la Banque de France* 41: 21–53.

Aglietta, Michel, and Laurence Scialom. 2003. "The Challenge of European Integration for Prudential Policy." LSE Financial Market Group Special Paper 152.

———. 2010. "A Systemic Approach to Financial Regulation – A European Perspective." *Economie Internationale (International Economics)* 3(123): 31–65.

Akerlof, George A. 1970. "The Market for 'Lemons': Quality Uncertainty and the Market Mechanism." *Quarterly Journal of Economics* 84(3): 488–500.

Akerlof, George A., and Robert J. Shiller. 2009. *Animal Spirits: How Human Psychology Drives the Economy, and Why It Matters for Global Capitalism*. Princeton University Press.

Alchian, Armen, and Harold Demsetz. 1972. "Production, Information Costs and Economic Organization." *American Economic Review* 62(5): 777–795.

Alesina, Alberto, and George-Marios Angeletos. 2005. "Fairness and Redistribution." *American Economic Review* 95(4): 960–980.

Allison, John R., and Mark A. Lemley. 1998. "Empirical Evidence on the Validity of Litigated Patents." *AIPLA Quarterly Journal* 26: 185–276.

Allison, John R., Mark A. Lemley, Kimberly A. Moore, and R. Derek Trunkey. 2004. "Valuable Patents." *Georgetown Law Journal* 92: 435–480.

Anderson, Terry, and Peter Hill. 1990. "The Race for Property Rights." *Journal of Law and Economics* 33(1): 177–197.

2004. *The Not So Wild, Wild West: Property Rights on the Frontier.* Stanford University Press.

Anderson, Terry, and Gary Libecap. 2009. "The Allocation and Dissipation of Resource Rents: Implications for Fishery Reform." ICER Working Paper 13/2009.

Anderson, Terry, Ragnar Árnason, and Gary Libecap. 2011. "Efficiency Advantages of Grandfathering Allocations in Rights Based Fishery Management." *Annual Review of Natural Resource Economics* 3: 159–179.

Angelini, Paolo. 1998. "An Analysis of Competitive Externalities in Gross Settlement Systems." *Journal of Banking and Finance* 22(1): 1–18.

Antonelli, Christiano. 1994. "Localized Technological Change and the Evolution of Standards as Economic Institutions." *Information Economics and Policy* 6(3–4): 195–216.

Aoki, Masahiko. 2001. *Toward a Comparative Institutional Analysis.* Cambridge, MA: MIT Press.

2011. "Institutions as Cognitive Media Between Strategic Interactions and Individual Beliefs." *Journal of Economic Behavior & Organization* 79(1–2): 20–34.

Areeda, Phillip. 1989. "Essential Facilities: An Epithet in Need of Limiting Principles." *Antitrust Law Journal* 58: 841–854.

Arida, Persio, and Andre Lara-Resende. 1985. "Inertial Inflation and Monetary Reform: Brazil." In John Williamson, ed. *Inflation and Indexation: Argentina, Brazil, and Israel*, 27–45. Washington, DC: Institute for International Economics.

Armour, John, and Michael J. Whincop. 2007. "The Proprietary Foundations of Corporate Law." *Oxford Journal of Legal Studies* 27(3): 429–465.

Árnason, Ragnar. 2002. "A Review of International Experiences with ITQ." Annex to: *Future Options for UK Fishing Management*, Report prepared by CEMARE, University of Portsmouth for the Department for the Environment, Food and Rural Affairs of the United Kingdom.

Arrow, Kenneth. 1962. "Economic Welfare and the Allocation of Resources for Innovation." In Nelson, Richard R., ed. *The Rate and Direction of*

Inventive Activity: Economic and Social Factors, 609–626. New York: Arno Press.

Arruñada, Benito. 2000. "Audit Quality: Attributes, Private Safeguards and the Role of Regulation." *European Accounting Review* 9(2): 205–224.

— 2003. "Property Enforcement as Organized Consent." *Journal of Law, Economics, & Organization* 19(2): 401–444.

— 2010. "Institutional Support of the Firm: A Theory of Business Registries." *Journal of Legal Analysis* 2(2): 525–576.

— 2012. *Institutional Foundations of Impersonal Exchange: The Theory and Policy of Contractual Registries*. University of Chicago Press.

Arundel, Anthony, and Isabelle Kabla. 1998. "What Percentage of Innovations are Patented? Empirical Estimates for European Firms." *Research Policy* 27(2): 127–141.

Aulisi, Andrew, Jonathan Pershing, Alexander E. Farrell, and Stacy Van Deveer. 2005. *Greenhouse Gas Trading in US States: Observations and Lessons from the OTC NOx Budget Trading Program*. Washington, DC: World Resources Institute.

Auriol, Emmanuelle, Thomas Flochel, and Stéphane Straub. 2009. "'La Patria Contratista': Public Procurement and Rent Seeking in Paraguay." IDEI mimeo.

Avgouleas, Emilios, Charles Goodhart, and Dirk Schoenmaker. 2010. "Living Wills as a Catalyst for Action." Duisenberg School of Finance Working Paper 4.

Ayres, Ian, and Eric Talley. 1995. "Solomonic Bargaining: Dividing a Legal Entitlement to Facilitate Coasean Trade." *Yale Law Journal* 104 (5): 1027–1117.

Badaraco, E. P. 1998. "Transformation of the Argentine Electricity Industry." Mimeo.

— 1999. "Presentation of the Electric Power Sector." Mimeo.

Baer, Werner, and Curt McDonald. 1998. "A Return to the Past? Brazil's Privatization of Public Utilities: The Case of the Electric Power Sector." *Quarterly Review of Economics and Finance* 38(3): 503–523.

Baig, Taimur, and Ilan Goldfajn. 2000. "The Russian Default and the Contagion to Brazil." IMF Working Paper 00/160.

Bajari, Patrick, and Steven Tadelis. 2001. "Incentives versus Transaction Costs: A Theory of Procurement Contracts." *RAND Journal of Economics* 32(3): 387–407.

Bajari, Patrick, Stephanie Houghton, and Steve Tadelis. 2007. "Bidding for Incomplete Contracts: An Empirical Analysis." NBER Working Paper 12051.

Bajari, Patrick, Robert McMillan, and Steve Tadelis. 2009. "Auctions versus Negotiations in Procurement: An Empirical Analysis." *Journal of Law, Economics, & Organization* 25(2): 372–399.

Baker, John. 1996. "Obituary: Lord Marshall of Goring." *The Independent*, February 26.

Baldwin, J. Norman. 1990. "Perceptions of Public versus Private Sector Personnel and Informal Red Tape: Their Impact on Motivation." *The American Review of Public Administration* 20(1): 7–28.

Baliño, Tomás. 1991. "The Argentine Banking Crisis of 1980." In Vasudevan Sundararajan and Tomás Baliño, eds. *Banking Crises: Cases and Issues*, 58–112. Washington, DC: IMF Publications.

Bambaci, Juliana, Pablo T. Spiller, and Mariano Tommasi. 2007. "The Bureaucracy." In Pablo T. Spiller and Mariano Tommasi, eds. *The Institutional Foundations of Public Policy in Argentina*. New York: Cambridge University Press.

Barnes, Peter. 1999. "The Pollution Dividend." *The American Prospect* 44: 61–67.

Baron, David P., and John A. Ferejohn. 1989. "Bargaining in Legislatures." *American Political Science Review* 83(4): 1181–1206.

Barros, Pedro Pita, and Steffen H. Hoernig. 2004. "Sectoral Regulators and the Competition Authority: Which Relationship Is Best?" CEPR Discussion Paper 4541.

Barzel, Yoram. 1982. "Measurement Cost and the Organization of Markets." *Journal of Law and Economics* 25(1): 27–48.

  1989. *Economic Analysis of Property Rights*. Cambridge University Press.

  2002. *A Theory of the State: Economic Rights, Legal Rights and the Scope of the State*. Cambridge University Press.

  2004. "Quality Standards and the Form of Agreement." *Economic Inquiry* 42(1): 1–13.

Bastos, Carlos Manuel, and Manuel Angel Abdala. 1993. *Reform of the Electric Power Sector in Argentina*. Buenos Aires: World Bank and the Secretary of Energy of Argentina.

Bates, Robert A., Avner Greif, Margaret Levi, Jean-Laurent Rosenthal, and Barry Weingast. 1998. *Analytic Narratives*. Princeton University Press.

Baumgartner, Frank R., Christian Breunig, Christoffer Green-Pedersen et al. 2009. "Punctuated Equilibrium in Comparative Perspective." *American Journal of Political Science* 53(3): 603–620.

Becker, Gary S. 1983. "A Theory of Competition Among Pressure Groups for Political Influence." *Quarterly Journal of Economics* 98(3): 371–400.

Beckers, Torsten, Andreas Brenck, Maria Heinrich, and Christian von Hirschhausen. 2005. "Public–Private Partnerships in New EU Member Countries of Central and Eastern Europe." *European Investment Bank* 10(2): 82–111.

Beesley, Michael, and Stephen Littlechild. 1983. "Privatization and Monopoly Power." Paper submitted to HM Treasury, November.

Bell, Stephanie. 2001. "The Role of the State and the Hierarchy of Money." *Cambridge Journal of Economics* 25(2): 149–163.
Benston, George, and George Kaufman. 1998. "Deposit Insurance Reform in the FDIC Improvement Act: The Experience to Date." *Economic Perspectives* 22(2): 2–20.
Berman, Harold J. 1983. *Law and Revolution: The Formation of the Western Legal Tradition.* Cambridge, MA: Harvard University Press.
Bernstein, Lisa. 2001. "Private Commercial Law in the Cotton Industry: Creating Cooperation through Rules, Norms, and Institutions." *Michigan Law Review* 99(135): 1724–1755.
Beuve, Jean, Eric Brousseau, and Jérôme Sgard. 2013. "Bureaucracy, Collegiality and Public Decision-Making: The Case of Eighteenth-Century France." Mimeo, University Paris Panthéon-Sorbonne/ University Paris-Dauphine/Sciences-Po.
Bhagwati, Jagdish. 1982. "Directly Unproductive, Profit-Seeking (DUP) Activities." *Journal of Political Economy* 90(5): 988–1002.
Biglaiser, Gary, and James Friedman. 1994. "Middlemen as Guarantors of Quality." *International Journal of Industrial Organization* 12(4): 509–531.
Board of Trade Papers (BT 101/43), The National Archives, London.
Bogdanski, Joel, Paulo Springer de Freitas, Ilan Goldfajn, and Alexandre Antonio Tombini. 2001. "Inflation Targeting in Brazil: Shocks, Backward-looking Prices, and IMF Conditionality." Central Bank of Brazil Working Paper 24.
Bomberger, William A., and Gail E. Makinen. 1983. "The Hungarian Hyperinflation and Stabilization of 1945–1946." *Journal of Political Economy* 91(5): 801–824.
Bonney, Richard. 2010. "The Apogee and Fall of the French Rentier Regime, 1801–1914." In Luis Cardoso and Pedro Lains, eds. *Paying for the Liberal State: The Rise of Public Finance in Nineteenth Century Europe.* Cambridge University Press.
Borio, Claudio. 2004. "Market Distress and Vanishing Liquidity: Anatomy and Policy Options." BIS Working Paper 158.
Borio, Claudio, and Philip Lowe. 2002. "Asset Prices, Financial and Monetary Stability: Exploring the Nexus." BIS Working Paper 114.
Borio, Claudio, and Haibin Zhu. 2008. "Capital Regulation, Risk-taking and Monetary Policy: A Missing Link in the Transmission Mechanism?" BIS Working Paper 268.
Borio, Claudio, Craig Furfine, and Philip Lowe. 2001. "Procyclicality of the Financial System and Financial Stability: Issues and Policy Options." BIS Working Paper 1.
Boyne, George A. 2002. "Public and Private Management: What's the Difference?" *Journal of Management Studies* 39(1): 97–122.

Bozeman, Barry. 1993. "A Theory of Government 'Red Tape'." *Journal of Public Administration Research and Theory* 3(3): 273–303.
Brench, Andreas, Thorsten Beckers, Maria Heinrich, and Christian von Hirschhausen. 2005. "Public – Private Partnerships in New EU Member Countries of Central and Eastern Europe." *European Investment Bank* 10(2).
Bresnahan, Timothy. 1981. "Departures from Marginal-Cost Pricing in the American Automobile Industry." *Journal of Econometrics* 17: 201–227.
   1987. "Competition and Collusion in the American Automobile Market: The 1955 Price War." *Journal of Industrial Economics* 45(4): 457–482.
   1989. "Empirical Methods for Industries with Market Power." In Richard Schmalensee and Robert D. Willig, eds. *Handbook of Industrial Organization*, Vol. II. Amsterdam: North-Holland.
Britan, Eduardo, and Pablo Serra. 1998. "Regulation of Privatized Utilities: The Chilean Experience." *World Development* 26(6): 945–962.
British Parliamentary Papers 1814–15. Vol. V. *Report of Select Committee on Manufacture and Sale of Bread*.
   1820. Vol. VII. *Second Report of the Commissioners on Weights and Measures*.
   1834. Vol. VII. *Report from the Select Committee on the Sale of Corn*.
   1834. Vol. XLIX. *Returns from Corn Inspectors*.
Bromley, Daniel W. 2009. "Abdicating Responsibility: The Deceits of Fisheries Policy." *Fisheries* 34(6): 280–302.
Broomhall, George J. S., and John H. Hubback. 1930. *Corn Trade Memories: Recent and Remote*. Liverpool: Northern Publishing.
Brousseau, Eric. 2002. "The Governance of Transaction by Commercial Intermediaries: An Analysis of the Re-engineering of Intermediation by Electronic Commerce." *International Journal of the Economics of Business* 9: 353–374.
Brousseau, Eric, and Jean-Michel Glachant. 2011. "Regulators as Reflexive Governance Platforms." *Competition and Regulation in Network Industries* 12(3): 194–209.
Brousseau, Eric, and Thierry Pénard. 2007. "The Economics of Digital Business Models: A Framework for Analyzing the Economics of Platforms." *Review of Network Economics* 6: 81–114.
Brousseau, Eric, and Emmanuel Raynaud. 2006. "The Economics of Multilevel Governance." Paper presented at the 2006 ISNIE Conference, Boulder, University of Colorado.
   2011. "Climbing the Hierarchical Ladders of Rules: A Life-cycle Theory of Institutional Evolution." *Journal of Economic Behavior and Organization* 79: 65–79.

Brousseau, Eric, Pierre Garrouste, and Emmanuel Raynaud. 2011. "Institutional Changes: Alternative Theories and Consequences for Institutional Design." *Journal of Economic Behavior and Organization* 79(1–2): 3–19.

Brousseau, Eric, Yves Schemeil, and Jerome Sgard. 2010. "Constitutions, States and Development." *Journal of Comparative Economics* 38: 253–266.

Brunnermeier, Markus, and Lasse H. Pedersen. 2007. "Market Liquidity and Funding Liquidity." LSE Financial Market Group Discussion Paper 580.

Brunnermeier, Markus, Andrew Crocket, Charles Goodhart, Avinash Persaud, and Hyun Shin. 2009. "The Fundamental Principles of Financial Regulation." ICMB-CEPR Geneva Reports on the World Economy 11. London: CEPR.

Bruno, Michael, Guido di Tella, Rudiger Dornbusch, and Stanley Fischer, eds. 1988. *Inflation Stabilization: The Experience of Israel, Argentina, Bolivia and Mexico*. Cambridge, MA: MIT Press.

Bruno, Michael, Stanley Fischer, Elhanan Helpman et al. 1991. *Lessons of Economic Stabilization and Its Aftermath*. Cambridge, MA: MIT Press.

Buchanan, James. 1965. "An Economic Theory of Clubs." *Econometrica* 33: 1–14.

1975. "A Contracting Paradigm of Applying Economic Theory." *American Economic Review* 65(May): 225–230.

Buchanan, James M., and Gordon Tullock. 1975. "Polluters' Profits and Political Response: Direct Controls versus Taxes." *American Economic Review* 65(1): 139–147.

Buchanan, James M., Robert D. Tollison, and Gordon Tullock. 1980. *Toward a Theory of the Rent-seeking Society*. College Station, TX: Texas A&M University Press.

Budzinski, Oliver. 2009. "An International Multilevel Competition Policy System." *International Economics and Economic Policy* 6(4): 367–389.

Budzinski, Oliver, and Arndt Christiansen. 2005. "Competence Allocation in the EU Competition Policy System as an Interest-Driven Process." *Journal of Public Policy* 25(3): 313–337.

Bulow, Jeremy, and Paul Klemperer. 1996. "Auctions versus Negotiations." *American Economic Review* 86(1): 180–194.

2009. "Why Do Sellers (Usually) Prefer Auctions?" *American Economic Review* 99(4): 1544–1575.

Bulow, Jeremy, and Paul Pfleiderer. 1983. "A Note on the Effect of Cost Changes on Prices." *Journal of Political Economy* 91(1): 182–185.

Burguet, Roberto, and Yeon-Choo Che. 2004. "Competitive Procurement with Corruption." *RAND Journal of Economics* 35(1): 50–68.

Burstein, Ariel, Martin Eichenbaum, and Sergio Rebelo. 2005. "Large Devaluations and the Real Exchange Rate." *Journal of Political Economy* 113(4): 742–784.

Burtraw, Dallas, and David A. Evans. 2009. "Tradable Rights to Emit Air Pollution." *Australian Journal of Agricultural and Resource Economics* 53(2): 59–84.

Burtraw, Dallas, and Karen Palmer. 2004. "SO_2 Cap-and-Trade Program in the United States: A 'Living Legend' of Market Effectiveness." In Winston Harrington, Richard D. Morgenstern, and Thomas Sterner, eds. *Choosing Environmental Policy: Comparing Instruments and Outcomes in the United States and Europe*, 41–66. Washington, DC: Resources for the Future.

Buxbaum, Richard M. 1973. "The Formation of Marketable Share Companies." In Alfred Conard, ed. *Business and Private Organizations*, Vol. XIII in the *International Encyclopedia of Comparative Law*. Tubingen: Mohr Siebeck.

Cagan, Phillip. 1956. "The Monetary Dynamics of Hyperinflation." In Milton Friedman, ed. *Studies in the Quantity Theory of Money*, 25–120. Chicago University Press.

Calabresi, Guido, and A. Douglas Melamed. 1972. "Property Rules, Liability Rules, and Inalienability: One View of the Cathedral." *Harvard Law Review* 85(6): 1089–1128.

Calomiris, Charles, and R. Glen Hubbard. 1995. "Internal Finance and Investment: Evidence from the Undistributed Profits Tax of 1936–37." *Journal of Business* 68(4): 443–482.

Calomiris, Charles, and Andrew Powell. 2000. "Can Emerging Market Bank Regulators Establish Credible Discipline? The Case of Argentina, 1992–1999." NBER mimeo.

Calvo, Guillermo, and Carlos Vegh. 1992. "Currency Substitution in Developing Countries: An Introduction." IMF Working Paper 92/40.

Campaign for Tobacco-Free Kids. 2012. *A Broken Promise to our Children: The 1998 State Tobacco Settlement 13 Years Later*. Available at: www.tobaccofreekids.org/what_we_do/state_local/tobacco_settlement/?utm_source=home&utm_medium=carousel&utm_campaign=home (accessed May 30, 2012).

Canavese, Alfredo. 1992. "Hyperinflation and Convertibility-based Stabilization in Argentina." In Alvaro Antonio Zini, ed. *The Market and the State in Economic Development in the 1990s*, 181–199. Amsterdam: North Holland.

Caprio, Gerard, Michael P. Dooley, Danny Leipziger, and Carl E. Walsh. 1996. "The Lender of Last Resort Function Under a Currency Board: The Case of Argentina." World Bank Policy Research Working Paper 1648.

Carlos, Ann, and Larry Neal. 2006. "The Micro-Foundations of the Early London Capital Market: Bank of England Shareholders During and After the South Sea Bubble, 1720–1725." *Economic History Review* 59(3): 498–538.

Carlos, Ann, Larry Neal, and Kirsten Wandschneider. 2007. "Networks and Market Makers in Bank of England Shares, 1720." Unpublished.

Carlson, Ingrid, and J. Mark Payne. 2003. "Estudio comparativo de estadísticas de empleo público en 26 países de América Latina y el Caribe." In K. Echebarría, ed. *Red de gestión y transparencia de la política pública. Servicio civil: temas para el diálogo*. Washington, DC: Inter-American Development Bank.

Carlton, Dennis W. 2001. "A General Analysis of Exclusionary Conduct and Refusal to Deal – Why Aspen and Kodak Are Misguided." National Bureau of Economic Research, Working Paper 8105/2001. Available at: www.nber.org/papers/w8105.pdf (accessed May 30, 2012).

Carlton, Dennis W., and Ken Heyer. 2008. "Appropriate Antitrust Policy Towards Single Firm Conduct." National Bureau of Economic Research. Economic Analysis Group Discussion Paper EAG 08-2. Available at http://papers.ssrn.com/sol3/papers.cfm?abstract_id=1111665 (accessed May 30, 2012).

Cartelier, Jean. 2006. "Comptabilité et Pensée Economique: Introduction à une Réflexion Théorique." *Revue Economique* 57(5): 1009–1032.

2007. "The Hypostasis of Money: An Economic Point of View." *Cambridge Journal of Economics* 31(2): 217–233.

Cavallo, Domingo F., and Joaquin Cottani. 1997. "Argentina's Convertibility Plan and the IMF." *American Economic Review* 87(2): 17–22.

Centers for Disease Control and Prevention. 1999. *Tobacco Control Activities in the United States: 1994–1999*. Washington, DC: US Department of Health and Human Services.

Centre for European Policy Studies. 2008. *CEPS Task Force Report: Concrete Steps Towards More Integrated Financial Oversight*. Brussels: CEPS Publications.

Chattaway, Chris. 1907. "Arbitration in the Foreign Corn Trade in London." *Economic Journal* 17(67): 428–431.

Cheung, Steven S. 1983. "The Contractual Nature of the Firm." *Journal of Law and Economics* 26(1): 1–22.

Chick, Harriette. 1957. "Wheat and Bread: A Historical Introduction." *Proceedings of the Nutrition Society* 17: 1–7.

Cihak, Martin, and Erlend Nier. 2009. "The Need for Special Resolution Regimes for Financial Institutions – The Case of the European Union." IMF Working Paper WP/09/200.

Clark, Ian N., Philip J. Major, and Nina Mollett. 1989. "The Development and Implementation of New Zealand's ITQ Management System." In Ragnar Árnason, Philip A. Neher, and Nina Mollett, eds. *Rights Based Fishing*, 117–145. London: Kluwer Academic Publishers.

Coase, Ronald. 1937. "The Nature of the Firm." *Economica* 4(16): 386–405.

———. 1960. "The Problem of Social Cost." *Journal of Law and Economics* 3: 1–44.

———. 1978. "Economics and Contiguous Disciplines." *Journal of Legal Studies* 7(2): 201–211.

———. 1994. *Essays on Economics and Economists*. University of Chicago Press.

Compte, Olivier, Ariane Lambert-Mogiliansky, and Thierry A. Verdier. 2005. "Corruption and Competition in Procurement Auctions." *RAND Journal of Economics* 36(1): 1–15.

Congressional Budget Office. 2007. "Trade-offs in Allocating Allowances for CO_2 Emissions." *Economic and Budget Issue Briefs* April 25. Washington, DC: Congressional Budget Office.

Convery, Frank J., and Luke Redmond. 2007. "Market and Price Developments in the European Union Emissions Trading Scheme." *Review of Environmental Economics and Policy* 1(1): 88–111.

Cook, Karen S., Russell Hardin, and Margaret Levi. 1995. *Cooperation without Trust?* New York: Russell Sage Foundation.

Cooper, Russell, and Andrew John. 1988. "Coordinating Coordination Failures in Keynesian Models." *Quarterly Journal of Economics* 103(3): 441–464.

Coopers & Lybrand Associates. 1983. *Structural Options for the EFI*. Report to the Department of Energy. Unpublished.

Cosmides, Leda, and John Tooby. 1992. "The Psychological Foundation of Culture." In Jerome H. Barkow, J. Leda Cosmides, and John Tooby, eds. *The Adapted Mind: Evolutionary Psychology and the Generation of Culture*, 19–136. New York: Oxford University Press.

Coviello, Decio, and Stefano Gagliarducci. 2010. "Tenure in Office and Public Procurement." CEIS Research Paper 179, Tor Vergata University.

Crocker, Keith J., and Scott Masten. 1996. "Regulation and Administered Contracts Revisited: Lessons from Transaction-Cost Economics for Public Utility Regulation." *Journal of Regulatory Economics* 9(1): 5–39.

Cunningham, Bryson. 1923. *Cargo Handling at Ports: A Survey of the Various Systems in Vogue, with a Consideration of their Respective Merits*. London: Chapman & Hall.

Dal Bó, Ernesto, Pedro Dal Bó, and Rafael Di Tella. 2006. "Plata o Pomo? Bribe and Punishment in a Theory of Political Influence." *American Political Science Review* 100(1): 41–53.

Danielsson, Jon. 2009. "The Myth of Riskometer." Available from VoxEU. org: www.voxeu.org/index.php?q=node/2753 (accessed May 30, 2012).

Danielsson, Jon, Paul Embrechts, Charles Goodhart, Con Keating, Felix Muennich, Olivier Renault, and Hyun Shin. 2001. "An Academic Response to Basel 2." LSE Financial Market Group Special Paper 130.

Danielsson Jon, Hyun Shin, and Jean-Pierre Zigrand. 2009. "Risk Appetite and Endogeneous Risk." Available at: http://papers.ssrn.com/sol3/papers.cfm?abstract_id=1360866 (accessed May 30, 2012).

Darby, Michael, and Edi Karni. 1973. "Free Competition and the Optimal Amount of Fraud." *Journal of Law and Economics* 16(1): 67–88.

David, Paul A. 1987. "Some New Standards for the Economics of Standardization in the Information Age." In Partha Dasgupta and Paul Stoneman, eds. *Economic Policy and Technical Performance*. Cambridge University Press.

Daviron, Benoit. 2002. "Small Farm Production and the Standardization of Tropical Products." *Journal of Agrarian Change* 2(2): 162–184.

Davis, Neal. 1997. "The Transformation of Argentina's Electricity Industry." In US Department of Energy, ed. *Electricity Reform Abroad and US Investment*. Washington, DC: US Department of Energy.

Defeuilley, Christophe. 2009. "Retail Competition in Electricity Markets." *Energy Policy* 37(2): 377–386.

de Figueiredo, Rui J. P. Jr., Pablo T. Spiller, and Santiago Urbiztondo. 1999. "An Informational Perspective on Administrative Procedures." *Journal of Law, Economics, & Organization* 15(1): 283–305.

De Larosière Group. 2009. *Report of the High-level Group on Financial Supervision in the EU*. Brussels: EU Commission.

De La Vega, José. 1957. *Confusion de Confusiones*. Reprinted in Boston: Baker Library, Harvard Graduate School of Business.

Delbeke, Jos, ed. 2006. *EU Environmental Law: The EU Greenhouse Gas Emissions Trading Scheme*, Vol. IV in *EU Energy Law*. Leuven: Claeys & Casteels.

Della Paollera, Gerardo, and Alan M. Taylor 2003. "Gaucho Banking Redux." NBER Working Paper 9457.

Demsetz, Harold. 1967. "Toward a Theory of Property Rights." *American Economic Review* 57(2): 347–359.

1968. "Why Regulate Utilities." *Journal of Law and Economics* 11(1): 55–66.

De Pinto, Isaac. 1771. *Traité de la Circulation et du Crédit*. Amsterdam: Marc Michel Rey.
Depoorter, Ben, and Francesco Parisi. 2005. "The Modernization of European Antitrust Enforcement: The Economics of Regulatory Competition." *George Mason Law Review* 13(2): 309–323.
Dewatripont, Mathias, and Jean Charles Rochet. 2009. "The Treatment of Distressed Banks." In Mathias Dewatripont, Xavier Freixas, and Richard Portes, eds. *Macroeconomic Stability and Financial Regulation: Key Issues For the G20*, 149–164. London: CEPR Ebook.
Dewatripont, Mathias, and Jean Tirole. 1993. *The Prudential Regulation of Banks*. Cambridge, MA: MIT Press.
Diaz, Carlos, and Raimundo Soto. 2002. "Open-Access Issues in the Chilean Telecommunications and Electricity Sectors." In Federico Basañes and Robert Willig, eds. *Second-generation Reforms in Infrastructure Services*, 193–222. Washington, DC: IDB Publications.
Dickson, Peter G. M. 1967. *The Financial Revolution in England: A Study in the Development of Public Credit, 1688–1756*. New York: St. Martin's Press.
Dinan, Terry, and Diane Lim Rogers. 2002. "Distributional Effects of Carbon Allowance Trading: How Government Decisions Determine Winners and Losers." *National Tax Journal* 55(2): 199–221.
Dixit, Avinash K. 1996. *The Making of Economic Policy: A Transaction-Cost Politics Approach*. Cambridge, MA: MIT Press.
  2004. *Lawlessness and Economics: Alternative Modes of Governance*. Princeton University Press.
Dogan, Stacey L., and Mark A. Lemley. 2009. "Antitrust Law and Regulatory Gaming." *Texas Law Review* 87: 685–730.
Dornbusch, Rudiger, and Stanley Fischer. 1986. "Stopping Hyperinflations, Past and Present." *Weltwirtschaftliches Archiv* 122.
Dornbusch, Rudiger, and Mario Henrique Simonsen. 1987. *Inflation Stabilization with Incomes Policy Support*. New York: Group of Thirty.
Dornbusch, Rudiger, Ferico Sturzenegger, and Holger Wolf. 1990. "Extreme Inflation: Dynamics and Stabilization." *Brookings Papers on Economic Activity* 21(2): 1–84.
Driel, Hugo Van, and Johan Schot. 2005. "Radical Innovation as a Multilevel Process: Introducing Floating Grain Elevators in the Port of Rotterdam." *Technology and Culture* 46(1): 51–76.
Dumbell, Stanley. 1925. "The Sale of Corn in the Nineteenth Century." *Economic Journal* 35(137): 141–145.
Earle, Peter. 1989. *The Making of the English Middle Class: Business, Society and Family Life in London, 1660–1730*. London: Methuen.
Earle, Timothy. 1997. *How Chiefs Come to Power*. Stanford University Press.

2003. *Bronze Age Economics: The Beginnings of Political Economies.* Boulder, CO: Westview Press.
Easterbrook, Frank H. 1984. "The Limits of Antitrust." *Texas Law Review* 63: 1–40.
Economic Planning Advisory Commission. 1995. *Final Report of the Private Infrastructure Task Force.* Canberra: Australian Government Publishing Service.
Eggers, William D., and Stephen Goldsmith. 2004. *Governing by Network: The New Shape of the Public Sector.* Washington, DC: Brookings Institution Press.
Eisenbeis, Robert, and George Kaufman. 2005. "Bank Crisis Resolution and Foreign Owned Banks." *Federal Bank of Atlanta Economic Review* 2005(4).
      2006. "Cross-border Banking: Challenges for Deposit Insurance and Financial Stability in the European Union." Federal Reserve Bank of Atlanta Working Paper 2006(15).
Ejrnæs, Mette, Karl Gunnar Persson, and Søren Rich. 2008. "Feeding the British: Convergence and Market Efficiency in the Nineteenth-century Grain Trade." *Economic History Review* 61(s1): 140–171.
Electric Utility Week International. 2000. *Brazil, Rejecting True Privatization, Opts to Sell Furnas in Small Blocks.*
Elhauge, Einer. 2003. "Defining Better Monopolization Standards." *Stanford Law Review* 56: 253–344.
Ellerman, A. Denny. 2004. "The US SO_2 Cap-and-Trade Programme." In OECD, *Tradeable Permits: Policy Evaluation, Design and Reform*, 71–97. Paris: OECD Publishing.
      2006. "Are Cap-and-trade Programs More Environmentally Effective Than Conventional Regulation?" In Charles Kolstad and Jody Freeman, eds. *Moving to Markets in Environmental Regulation: Lessons from Twenty Years of Experience*, 48–62. Oxford and New York: Oxford University Press.
      2008. "Lessons for the United States from the European Union's CO_2 Emissions Trading Scheme." In Denny A. Ellerman et al., eds. *Cap-and-Trade: Contributions to the Design of a US Greenhouse Gas Program*, 2–35. Cambridge, MA: MIT Center for Energy and Environmental Policy Research.
Ellerman, A. Denny, and Barbara K. Buchner. 2007. "The European Union Emissions Trading Scheme: Origins, Allocation and Early Results." *Review of Environmental Economics and Policy* 1(1): 66–87.
      2008. "Over-allocation or Abatement? A Preliminary Analysis of the EU ETS Based on the 2005–06 Emissions Data." *Environmental & Resource Economics* 41(2): 267–287.

Ellerman, A. Denny, and Paul L. Joskow. 2008. *The European Union's Emissions Trading System in Perspective.* Washington, DC: Pew Center on Global Climate Change.

Ellerman, A. Denny, and Raphael Trotignon. 2009. "Cross-border Trading and Borrowing in the EU ETS." *Energy Journal* 30(2): 53–78.

Ellerman, A. Denny, Barbara K. Buchner, and Carlo Carraro, eds. 2007. *Allocation in the European Emissions Trading Scheme: Rights, Rents and Fairness.* Cambridge and New York: Cambridge University Press.

Ellerman, A. Denny, Frank J. Convery, and Christian de Perthuis. 2010. *Pricing Carbon: The European Union Emissions Trading Scheme.* Cambridge and New York: Cambridge University Press.

Ellerman, A. Denny, Paul L. Joskow, and David Harrison, Jr. 2003. *Emissions Trading: Experience, Lessons, and Considerations for Greenhouse Gases.* Washington, DC: Pew Center on Global Climate Change.

Ellerman, A. Denny, Paul L. Joskow, Richard Schmalensee, Juan-Pablo Montero, and Elizabeth M. Bailey. 2000. *Markets for Clean Air: The US Acid Rain Program.* Cambridge and New York: Cambridge University Press.

Emmons, William III. 1997. "Credence Goods and Fraudulent Experts." *RAND Journal of Economics* 28(1): 107–119.

2000. *The Evolving Bargain: Strategic Implications of Deregulation and Privatization.* Boston, MA: Harvard Business School Press.

Engel, Eduardo, Ronald Fischer, and Alexander Galetovic. 2006. "Renegotiation Without Holdup: Anticipating Spending and Infrastructure Concessions." Cowles Foundation Discussion Papers 1567, Cowles Foundation for Research in Economics, Yale University.

Epstein, Richard. 1979. "Possession as the Root of Title." *Georgia Law Review* 13: 1221–1242.

Estache, Antonio, and Martin Rodríguez-Pardina. 1998. "Light and Lightning at the End of the Public Tunnel: Reform of the Electricity Sector in the Southern Cone." World Bank Policy Research Paper 2074.

Estache, Antonio, Jose Luis Guasch, Atsushi Iimi, and Lourdes Trujillo. 2009. "Multidimensionality and Renegotiation: Evidence From Transport-Sector PPP Transactions in Latin America." *Review of Industrial Organization* 35(1): 41–71.

Euromoney. 1999. "Minais Gerais, Franco the Noisy Populist." *Euromoney*, October, p. 46.

European Commission. 2007. "EU-US Open Skies. A New Era in Transatlantic Aviations Starts on March 30." Available at: http://europa.eu/rapid/pressReleasesAction.do?reference=IP/08/474&guiLanguage=en (accessed May 30, 2012).

2008a. *White Paper on Damages Actions for Breach of the EC Antitrust Rules.* COM(2008) 165 final.

2008b. *Proposal for a Directive of the European Parliament and of the Council Amending Directive 2003/87/EC so as to Improve and Extend the Greenhouse Gas Emission Allowance Trading System of the Community.* COM(2008) 16 final.

European Commission. DG Competition. 2008. Guidance on the Commission's Official Enforcement Priorities in Applying Article 82 EC Treaty to Abusive Exclusionary Conduct by Dominant Undertakings (December 3, 2008). Available at: http://ec.europa.eu/competition/antitrust/art82/guidance.pdf (accessed May 30, 2012).

European Union. 2003. "Directive 2003/87/EC of the European Parliament and of the Council of 13 October 2003 Establishing a Scheme for Greenhouse Gas Emission Allowance Trading within the Community and Amending Council Directive 96/61/EC." *Official Journal of the European Union* L275: 32–46, October 25, 2003.

2005. *Buying Green Handbook.* Available at: http://ec.europa.eu/environment/gpp/pdf/buying_green_handbook_fr.pdf (accessed May 30, 2012).

2009a. "Directive 2009/29/EC of the European Parliament and of the Council of 23 April 2009 Amending Directive 2003/87/EC so as to Improve and Extend the Greenhouse Gas Emission Allowance Trading Scheme of the Community." *Official Journal of the European Union* L140: 63–87, June 5, 2009.

2009b. *Internal Market Scoreboard,* July 2009 No. 19. Available at http://ec.europa.eu/internal_market/score/docs/score19_En.pdf (accessed May 30, 2012).

Fanelli, Jose, and Daniel Heymann. 2002. "Dilemas Monetarios en la Argentina." *Desarrollo Económico* 42(165): 3–24.

Faure, Michael. 2004. "Economic Analysis of Tort Law and the European Civil Code." In Arthur Hartkamp and Carla Joustra, eds. *Towards a European Civil Code – Third Fully Revised and Expanded Edition,* 659–676. London: Wolters Kluwer.

Fay, Charles R. 1925. "The London Corn Market at the Beginning of the Nineteenth Century." *American Economic Review* 15(1): 70–76.

Fehr, Ernst, Oliver Hart, and Christian Zehnder. 2011. "Contracts as Reference Points – Experimental Evidence." *American Economic Review* 101(2): 493–525.

Ferejohn, John. 1990. "Congressional Influence on Bureaucracy." *Journal of Law, Economics, & Organization* 6: 1–20.

Ferguson, Robert B. 1980. "The Adjudication of Commercial Disputes and the Legal System in Modern England." *British Journal of Law and Society* 7(2): 141–157.

Fernández-Barcala, Marta, Manuel González-Díaz, and Juan Prieto-Rodriguez. 2010. "Hotel Quality Appraisal on the Internet: A Market for Lemons?" *Tourism Economics* 16(2): 345–360.

Fisher, Ronald. 1982. "Income and Grant Effects on Local Expenditure: The Flypaper Effect and Other Difficulties." *Journal of Urban Economics* 12(3): 324–345.

Fischer, Ronald, and Pablo Serra. 2000. "Regulating the Electricity Sector in Latin America." *Economia* 1(1): 155–198.

Fishlow, Albert. 1974. "Indexing Brazilian Style: Inflation without Tears?" *Brookings Papers on Economic Activity* 1: 261–280.

2005. "Thirty Years of Combatting Inflation in Brazil, from the PAEG (1964) to the Plano Real (1994)." Oxford University – Center for Brazilian Studies (CBS) Working Paper 68–05.

Flandreau, Marc, Christophe Galimard, Clemens Jobst, and Pilar Nogués-Marco. 2009. "Monetary Geography before the Industrial Revolution." *Cambridge Journal of Regions, Economy and Society* 2(2): 149–171.

Fogel, Ramón. 1993. "La estructura social paraguaya y su incidencia en la transición a la democracia." In D. Abente Brun, ed. *Paraguay en Transición*. Caracas: Editorial Nueva Sociedad.

Forrer, John, James E. Kee, Kathryn E. Newcomer, and Eric Boyer. 2010. "Public–Private Partnerships and the Public Accountability Question." *Public Administration Review* May/June: 475–484.

Forrester, R. B. 1931. "Commodity Exchanges in England." *Annals of the American Academy of Political and Social Science* 155(1): 196–207.

Franco, Gustavo. 1995. *O Plano Real e Outros Ensayos*. Rio de Janeiro: Francisco Alves.

2000. "The Real Plan and the Exchange Rate." Princeton University Essays in International Finance 217.

Frehen, Rik G. P., William N. Goetzmann, and K. Geert Rouwenhorst. 2009. "New Evidence on the First Financial Bubble." Yale ICF Working Paper 09–04.

Friedman, Milton. 1953[1970]. *Essays in Positive Economics*. University of Chicago Press.

Frischmann, Brett M., and Spencer Weber Waller. 2008. "Revitalizing Essential Facilities." *Antitrust Law Journal* 75: 1–66.

Fukuyama, Francis. 1995. *Trust: The Social Virtues and the Creation of Prosperity*. New York: Free Press.

Galal, Ahmed, Leroy Jones, Pankay Tandon, and Ongo Vogelsang. 1994. *Welfare Consequences of Selling Public Enterprises*. New York: Oxford University Press (for the World Bank).

Ganuza, Juan-José. 2007. "Competition and Cost Overruns in Procurement." *Journal of Industrial Economics* 55(4): 633–660.

Garcia, Marcio. 1996. "Avoiding the Costs of Inflation and Crawling Towards Hyperinflation: The Case of the Brazilian Domestic Currency Substitute." *Journal of Development Economics* 51(1): 139–159.

Gelderblom, Oscar, and Joost Jonker. 2004. "Completing a Financial Revolution: The Finance of the Dutch East India Trade and the Rise of the Amsterdam Capital Market, 1595–1612." *Journal of Economic History* 64(3): 641–672.

— 2009. "With a View to Hold: The Emergence of Institutional Investors on the Amsterdam Securities Market during the Seventeenth and Eighteenth Centuries." In Jeremy Atack and Larry Neal, eds. *The Origins and Development of Financial Markets and Institutions: From the Seventeenth Century to the Present*, 71–98. Cambridge and New York: Cambridge University Press.

Gely, Rafael, and Pablo T. Spiller. 1990. "A Rational Choice Theory of Supreme Court Statutory Decisions with Applications to the State Farm and Grove City Cases." *Journal of Law, Economics, & Organization* 6(2): 263–300.

Gilbert, Richard J. 2007. "Holding Innovation to an Antitrust Standard." *Competition Policy International* 3. Available at: www.competitionpolicyinternational.com/file/view/4602 (accessed May 30, 2012).

Giorgio, Luis Alberto. 1989. "Crisis Financiera, Reestructuracion Bancaria y Hiperinflacion en Argentina." Banco Central de la Republica de Argentina, mimeo.

Glachant, Jean-Michel and François Lévêque, eds. 2009. *Electricity Reform in EU. Towards a Single Energy Market*. Cheltenham: Edward Elgar.

Glachant, Jean-Michel, Dominique Finon, and Adrien de Hauteclocque, eds. 2011. *Competition, Contracts and Electricity Markets. A New Perspective*. Cheltenham: Edward Elgar.

Global Power Report. 2001a. *Brazil's Power Crisis Due to Bad Regulations, Market Participants Say*.

— 2001b. *Enron Says 2 Brazil Projects, 980MW, On Hold Until Market Rules Clarified*.

Goldberg, Victor P. 1976. "Regulation and Administered Contracts." *Bell Journal of Economics* 7(2): 426–448.

— 1977. "Competitive Bidding and the Production of Precontract Information." *Bell Journal of Economics* 8(1): 250–261.

Goodhart, Charles. 2008. "The Regulatory Response to the Financial Crisis." *Journal of Financial Stability* 4(4): 351–358.

Goodhart, Charles, Pojanart Sunirand, and Dimitrios Tsomocos. 2005. "A Risk Assessment Model for Banks." *Annals of Finance* 1(2): 197–224.

Gordy, Michael, and Bradley Howells. 2004. "Procyclicality in Basel II: Can We Treat the Disease Without Killing the Patient?" *Journal of Financial Intermediation* 15(3): 395–417.

Goulder, Lawrence H., Ian W. H. Parry, and Dallas Burtraw. 1997. "Revenue-raising vs. Other Approaches to Environmental Protection: The Critical Significance of Pre-existing Tax Distortions." *RAND Journal of Economics* 28(4): 708–731.

Grafton, R. Quentin, Dale Squires, and Kevin J. Fox. 2000. "Private Property and Economic Efficiency: A Study of a Common-pool Resource." *Journal of Law and Economics* 43(2): 679–713.

Grajzl, Peter, and Peter Murrell. 2007. "Allocating Lawmaking Power: Self-regulation vs. Government Regulation." *Journal of Comparative Economics* 35(3): 520–545.

Gramlich, Edward M., Harvey Galper, Stephen Goldfeld, and Martin McGuire. 1973. "State and Local Fiscal Behavior and Federal Grant Policy." *Brookings Papers on Economic Activity* 4(1): 15–66.

Grande, Edgar. 1996. "The State and Interest Groups in a Framework of Multi-level Decision-making: The Case of the European Union." *Journal of European Public Policy* 3(3): 318–338.

Granovetter, Mark. 1985. "Economic Action and Social Structure: The Problem of Embeddedness." *American Journal of Sociology* 91(3): 481–510.

Granovetter, Mark, and Soong Roland. 1986. "Threshold Models of Interpersonal Affects in Consumer Demand." *Journal of Economic Behaviour and Organization* 7(1): 83–99.

Grassby, Richard. 2001. *Kinship and Capitalism: Marriage, Family, and Business in the English Speaking World, 1580–1720*. New York: Cambridge University Press.

Green, Richard, and Tanga McDaniel. 1998. "Competition in Electricity Supply: Will '1998' Be Worth It?" *Fiscal Studies* 19(3): 273–293.

Greif, Avner. 1998. "Historical and Comparative Institutional Analysis." *American Economic Review* 88(2): 80–84.

2002. "Institutional Foundations of Impersonal Exchange: From Communal to Individual Responsibility." *Journal of Institutional and Theoretical Economics* 158(1): 168–204.

2005. "Commitment, Coercion and Markets: The Nature and Dynamics of Institutions Supporting Exchange." In Claude Ménard and Mary M. Shirley, eds. *Handbook of New Institutional Economics*, 727–786. New York: Springler-Verlag.

2006a. "The Birth of Impersonal Exchange: The Community Responsibility System and Impartial Justice." *Journal of Economic Perspectives* 20(2): 221–236.

2006b. *Institutions and the Path to the Modern Economy*. New York: Cambridge University Press.

Greif, Avner, and David D. Laitin. 2004. "A Theory of Endogenous Institutional Change." *American Political Science Review* 98(4): 633–652.

Greif, Avner, Paul Milgrom, and Barry R. Weingast. 1994. "Commitment, Coordination, and Enforcement: The Case of the Merchant Guilds." *Journal of Political Economy* 102(4): 745–776.

Grossfeld, Bernhard. 1973. "Management Control of Marketable Share Companies." In Alfred Conard, ed. *Business and Private Organizations*, Vol. IV in the *International Encyclopedia of Comparative Law*. Tubingen: Mohr Siebeck.

Guasch, J. Luis. 2004. *Granting and Renegotiating Infrastructure Concessions: Doing it Right*. Washington, DC: The International Bank for Reconstruction and Development of the World Bank Institute.

Guasch, J. Luis, Jean-Jacques Laffont, and Stéphane Straub. 2007. "Concessions of Infrastructure in Latin America: Government-led Renegotiations." *Journal of Applied Econometrics* 22(7): 1267–1294.

2008. "Renegotiation of Concession Contracts in Latin America, Evidence from the Water and Transport Sectors." *International Journal of Industrial Organization* 26(2): 421–442.

Guccio, Calogero, Giacomo Pignataro, and Ilde Rizzo. 2008. "Adaptation Costs in Public Works Procurement in Italy." Proccedings of the 3rd International Public Procurement Conference, Amsterdam.

Guttentag, Jack, and Richard Herring. 1986. "Disaster Myopia in International Banking." Princeton University Essays in International Finance 164.

Haddock, David D. 1986. "First Possession versus Optimal Timing: Limiting the Dissipation of Economic Value." *Washington University Law Review* 64: 775–791.

Hall, Bronwyn H. 2002. "Patents and Innovation." Testimony for the Federal Trade Commission & Department of Justice Antitrust Division Hearings on Competition & Intellectual Property Law in the Knowledge-Based Economy on Feb. 26, 2002. Available at: www.ftc.gov/opp/intellect/020226bronwynhhall.pdf (accessed May 30, 2012).

Hamaguchi, Nobuaki. 2002. "Will the Market Keep Brazil Lit Up? Ownership and Market Structural Changes in the Electric Power Sector." *The Developing Economies* 40(4): 522–552.

Hammami, Mona, Jean-François Ruhashyankiko, and Etienne B. Yehoue. 2006. "Determinants of Public–Private Partnerships in Infrastructure." IMF Working Paper 06/1999.

Hammond, Elizabeth, Dieter Helm, and David Thompson. 1985a. *Regulation of the Gas Industry: Memorandum 27*. Submitted by the Institute of Fiscal Studies to The Energy Committee.

———. 1985b. "British Gas: Options for Privatisation." *Fiscal Studies* 6(4): 1–20.

———. 1986. "Competition in Electricity Supply: Has the Energy Act Failed?" *Fiscal Studies* 7(1): 11–33.

Hansmann, Henry. 1996. *Ownership of Enterprise*. Cambridge: Harvard University Press.

Hansmann, Henry, and Reinier Kraakman. 2000. "The Essential Role of Organizational Law." *Yale Law Journal* 110(3): 387–440.

———. 2002. "Property, Contract, and Verification: The Numerus Clausus Problem and the Divisibility of Rights." *Journal of Legal Studies* 31(2): S373–S420.

Hardin, Garrett. 1968. "Tragedy of the Commons." *Science* 162(3859): 1243–1248.

Harris, A. C. 1996. "Financing Infrastructure: Private Profits from Public Losses." In *Public/Private Infrastructure Financing: Still Feasible?* Sydney: Audit Office of NSW, Public Accounts Committee, Parliament of NSW.

Harrison, David, Jr. 2004. "Ex-post Evaluation of the RECLAIM Emissions Trading Programmes for the Los Angeles Basin." In OECD, *Tradeable Permits: Policy Evaluation, Design and Reform*, 45–69. Paris: OECD Publishing.

Hart, Marjolein t'. 2006. "Money and Trust. Amsterdam Moneylenders and the Rise of the Modern State, 1478–1794." Paper presented at the International Economic History Congress, Helsinki, University of Helsinki.

Hart, Oliver, and John Moore. 2008. "Contracts as Reference Points." *Quarterly Journal of Economics* 123(1): 1–48.

Hart, Oliver, and Luigi Zingales. 2009. "To Regulate Finance, Try the Market." Posted in Foreign Policy on September 30, 2010. Available at: http://experts.foreignpolicy.com/posts/2009/03/30/to_regulate_finance_try_the_market (accessed May 30, 2012).

Hausman, Jerry, Gregory K. Leonard, and Jean Tirole. 2003. "On Nonexclusive Membership in Competing Joint Ventures." *RAND Journal of Economics* 34(1): 43–62.

Hausmann, Ricardo, and Andrés Velasco. 2002. "Hard Money's Soft Underbelly: Understanding the Argentine Crisis." *Brookings Trade Forum* 2002: 59–104.

Hayek, Friedrich A. von. 1982. *Law, Legislation, and Liberty: A New Statement of the Liberal Principles of Justice and Political Economy.*

University of Chicago Press. Reprint, London: Routledge & Kegan Paul.
Helgesson, Claes-Fredrik, Steffan Hultén, and Douglas J. Puffert. 1995. "Standards as Institutions: Problems with Creating All-European Standards for Terminal Equipment." In John Groenewegen, Christos Pitelis, and Sven-Erik Sjöstrand, eds. *On Economic Institutions: Theory and Applications*, 164–182. Cheltenham: Edward Elgar.
Hellwig, Martin. 2009. "Systemic Risk in the Financial Sector: An Analysis of the Subprime Mortgage Financial Crisis." *De Economist* 157(2): 129–207.
Helm, Dieter. 2004. *Energy, the State and the Market: British Energy Policy Since 1979*. Oxford University Press.
Henisz, Witold J., and Bennet A. Zelner. 2005. "Legitimacy, Interest Group Pressures, and Change in Emergent Institutions: The Case of Foreign Investors and Host Country Governments." *Academy of Management Review* 30(2): 361–382.
  2006. "Interest Groups, Veto Points, and Electricity Infrastructure Deployment." *International Organization* 60(1): 263–286.
Henisz, Witold J., Bennet A. Zelner, and Mauro. F. Guillén. 2005. "The Worldwide Diffusion of Market-oriented Infrastructure Reform, 1977–1999." *American Sociological Review* 70(6): 871–897.
Henney, Alex. 1987. *Privatise Power: How to Restructure the Electricity Supply Industry*. London: Centre for Policy Studies.
  1994. *A Study of the Privatisation of the Electricity Supply Industry in England and Wales*. London: EEE.
Heymann, Daniel. 1987. "The Austral Plan." *American Economic Review* 77(2): 284–287.
Hildebrand, Philipp. 2008. "Is Basel 2 Enough? The Benefits of a Leverage Ratio." Lecture at the LSE Financial Market Group.
Hill, Lowell D. 1990. *Grain, Grades and Standards: Historical Issues Shaping the Future*. Urbana and Chicago: University of Illinois Press.
Hines, Jr. James R., and Richard H. Thaler. 1995. "Anomalies: The Flypaper Effect." *Journal of Economic Perspectives* 9(4): 217–226.
Hoffman, Philip, Jean-Laurent Rosenthal, and Gilles Postel-Vinay. 2000. *Priceless Markets: The Political Economy of Credit in Paris, 1660–1870*. University of Chicago Press.
Hooghe, Liesbet, and Gary Marks. 2001. *Multilevel Governance and European Integration*. Lanham, MD: Rowman and Littlefield.
Horn, Murray. 1995. *The Political Economy of Public Administration: Institutional Choice in the Public Sector, Political Economy of Institutions and Decisions*. Cambridge University Press.
Houghton, John. 1692. *A Collection for Improvement of Husbandry and Trade*. London: Randall Taylor.

House of Representatives Standing Committee on Communications Transport and Microeconomic Reform. 1997. *Planning not Patching: An Inquiry Into Federal Road Funding*. Canberra: Australian Government Publishing Service.

Humphreys, Macartan, Jeffrey D. Sachs, and Joseph E. Stiglitz, eds. 2007. *Escaping the Resource Curse*. New York: Columbia University Press.

Iacoviello, Mercedes, Mariano Tommasi, and Laura Zuvanic. 2002. "Diagnóstico institucional de sistemas de servicio civil: caso Argentina." Working Paper 8962, Inter-American Development Bank.

Independent Power Report. 1993. *International Power Brazil to Privatize Part of 1,457MW Sao Paulo Utility*.

1996. *One Year After Privatization, Brazil Escelsa Has Cut Losses and Raised Profit*.

Industry Commission. 1996. *Competitive Tendering and Contracting by Public Sector Agencies*. Canberra: Australian Government Publishing Service.

Ingham, Geoffrey. 1996. "Money is a Social Relation." *Review of Social Economy* 54(4): 507–529.

International Energy Agency. 1999. *Energy Statistics*. Paris: OECD Publishing.

International Monetary Fund. 1999. *Brazil: Selected Issues and Statistical Appendix*. Staff Country Report 99/97, September.

2009. "Assessing the Systemic Implications of Financial Linkages." Chapter 2 in: *Global Financial Stability Report: Responding to the Financial Crisis and Measuring Systemic Risks*. Washington, DC: IMF Publications.

Iossa, Elisabetta, and David Martimort. 2008. "The Simple Micro-Economics of Public–Private Partnerships." *CEIS Tor Vergata Research Paper Series* 6(12).

Irigoin, Maria Alejandra. 2000. "Inconvertible Paper Money, Inflation and Economic Performance in Early Nineteenth Century Argentina." *Journal of Latin American Studies* 32(2): 333–359.

Jacks, David S. 2006. "What Drove 19th Century Commodity Market Integration?" *Explorations in Economic History* 43(3): 383–412.

Jacks, David S., Christopher M. Meissner, and Dennis Novy. 2010. "Trade Costs in the First Wave of Globalization." *Explorations in Economic History* 47(2): 127–141.

Jadresic, Alejandro. 1997. "Regulating Private Involvement in Infrastructure: The Chilean Experience." In Harinder S. Kohli, Ahoka Mody, and Michael Mody, eds. *Choices for Efficient Private Provision of Infrastructure in East Asia*, 54–68. Washington, DC: The World Bank.

Jago, William, and William C. Jago. 1911. *The Technology of Bread-making*. London: Kent & Co.

Johnson, Allen W., and Timothy Earle. 2000. *The Evolution of Human Societies*. Stanford University Press.
Johnson, Ronald N. 1995. "Implications of Taxing Quota Value in an Individual Transferable Quota Fishery." *Marine Resource Economics* 10(4): 327–340.
Johnson, Ronald N., and Gary Libecap. 1982. "Contracting Problems and Regulation: The Case of the Fishery." *American Economic Review* 72(5): 1005–1022.
Jones, Eluned. 1999. "The Role of Information in US Grain and Oilseed Markets." *Review of Agricultural Economics* 21(1): 237–255.
Jones, Glyn. 2001. *The Millers: A Story of Technological Endeavour and Industrial Success, 1870–2001*. Lancaster: Carnegie Publishing Limited.
Jones, Robert A. 1976. "The Origin and Development of Media of Exchange." *Journal of Political Economy* 84(4): 757–775.
Joskow, Paul, and Richard Schmalensee. 1998. "The Political Economy of Market-based Environmental Policy: The US Acid Rain Program." *Journal of Law and Economics* 41(1): 37–83.
Kaplan, Michael. 1997. "Energy Restructuring in Brazil." *Journal of Project Finance* 3(2): 43–63.
Kaplan, Steven Laurence. 1984. *Provisioning Paris: Merchants and Millers in the Grain and Flour Trade During the Eighteenth Century*. Ithaca, NY and London: Cornell University Press.
Kaplow, Louis, and Steven Shavell. 1996. "Property Rules Versus Liability Rules: An Economic Analysis." *Harvard Law Review* 109(4): 713–790.
Kassim, Hussein, and Handley Stevens. 2010. *Air Transport and the European Union: Europeanisation and its Limits*. London: Palgrave-Macmillan.
Katz, Michael L., and Howard A. Shelanski. 2005. "Schumpeterian Competition and Antitrust Policy in High-Tech Markets." *Competition* 14: 47–67.
  2007. "Mergers and Innovation." *Antitrust Law Journal* 74: 1–86.
Kaufmann, Patrick J., and Francine Lafontaine. 1994. "Costs of Control: The Source of Economic Rents for McDonald's Franchises." *Journal of Law and Economics* 37(2): 417–453.
Kearney, Joseph D., and Thomas W. Merrill. 1998. "The Great Transformation of Regulated Industries Law." *Columbia Law Review* 98: 1323–1409.
Kerber, Wolfgang. 2003. "An International Multi-Level System of Competition Laws: Federalism in Antitrust." In Josef Drexl, ed. *The Future of Transnational Antitrust – From Comparative to Common Competition Law*, 269–300. Berne: Staempfli – Kluwer Law International.

2009. "The Theory of Regulatory Competition and Competition Law." In Karl Meessen, ed. *Economic Law as an Economic Good, Its Rule Function in the Competition of Systems*, 27–44. Munich: Sellier.

Kettner, Claudia, Angela Koeppl, Stefan Schleicher, and Gregor Thenius. 2007. "Stringency and Distribution In the EU Emissions Trading Scheme: The 2005 Evidence." FEEM Working Paper 22/2007.

Kiguel, Miguel, and Nissan Liviatan. 1988. "Inflationary Rigidities and Orthodox Stabilization Policies: Lessons from Latin America." *World Bank Economic Review* 2(3).

Kindleberger, Charles. 1983. "Standards as Public, Collective and Private Goods." *Kyklos* 36(3): 377–396.

Kingdon, John W. 1984. *Agendas, Alternatives, and Public Policies*. New York: Addison-Wesley Longman.

Kirkland, J. 1896. "The Relative Prices of Wheat and Bread." *Economic Journal* 6(23): 475–484.

Kiyotaki, Nobuhiro, and John Moore. 2005. "Liquidity and Asset Prices." *International Economic Review* 46(2): 317–349.

Klein, Benjamin. 1996. "Why Hold-ups Occur. The Self-Enforcing Range of Contractual Relationships." *Economic Inquiry* 34(3): 444–463.

2000. "The Role of Incomplete Contracts in Self-Enforcing Relationships." *Revue d'Economie Industrielle* 92(1): 67–80.

Klein, Benjamin, and Keith B. Leffler. 1981. "The Role of Market Forces in Assuring Contractual Performance." *Journal of Political Economy* 89(4): 615–641.

Klemperer, Paul. 2002. "What Really Matters in Auction Design." *Journal of Economic Perspectives* 16(1): 169–189.

Knapp, Georg F. 1924. *The State Theory of Money*. London: Macmillan and Company.

Kolasky, William. 2006. "Refusals to Deal with Rivals: A Proposed Synthesis." Presentation at the Federal Trade Commission & Department of Justice Joint Workshop on Monopolization (July 18, 2006). Available at: www.wilmerhale.com/files/upload/kolasky_07_2006.pdf (accessed May 30, 2012).

Kolderie, Ted. 1986. "The Two Different Concepts of Privatization." *Public Administration Review* 46(4): 285–291.

Kranton, Rachel. 2003. "Competition and the Incentive to Produce Quality." *Economica* 70(3): 385–404.

Krauss, Michael I. 1998. "Property Rules vs. Liability Rules." In B. Bouckaert and G. de Geest, eds., *Encyclopedia of Law & Economics*, Vol. II: 782–794. Cheltenham and Northampton: Edward Elgar.

Kregel, Jan. 2008. "Minsky's Cushions of Safety." Levy Economics Institute of Bard College Public Policy Brief 93.

Krueger, Anne O. 1974. "The Political Economy of the Rent-seeking Society." *American Economic Review* 64(3): 291–303.

Kruger, Joseph, Wallace E. Oates, and William A. Pizer. 2007. "Decentralization in the EU Emissions Trading Scheme and Lessons for Global Policy." *Review of Environmental Economics and Policy* 1(1): 112–133.

Kula, Witold. 1986. *Measures and Men*. Princeton, NJ: Princeton University Press.

Kurland, Nancy B., and Terri D. Egan. 1999. "Public v. Private Perceptions of Formalization, Outcomes, and Justice." *Journal of Public Administration Research and Theory* 9 (3): 437–458.

Laffont, Jean-Jacques, and David Martimort. 1999. "Separation of Regulators against Collusive Behavior." *RAND Journal of Economics* 30(2): 232–262.

Laffont, Jean-Jacques, and Jean Tirole. 1991. "The Politics of Government Decision-Making: A Theory of Regulatory Capture." *Quarterly Journal of Economics* 106(4): 1089–1127.

1993. *A Theory of Incentives in Procurement and Regulation*. Cambridge, MA: MIT Press.

Lagniappe Letter Latin American Information Services. 1993. *Power Privatization Established Argentina on Innovative Path*.

Lambert-Mogiliansky, Ariane, and Konstantin Sonin. 2006. "Collusive Market Sharing and Corruption in Procurement." *Journal of Economics and Management Strategy* 15(4): 883–908.

Lan, Zhiyong, and Hal G. Rainey. 1992. "Goals, Rules, and Effectiveness in Public, Private, and Hybrid Organizations: More Evidence on Frequent Assertions About Differences." *Journal of Public Administration Research and Theory* 2(1): 5–28.

Lancaster, Kelvin. 1966. "A New Approach to Consumer Theory." *Journal of Political Economy* 74(2): 132–157.

Lanciotti, Norma. 2008. "Foreign Investments in Electric Utilities: A Comparative Analysis of Belgian and American Companies in Argentina, 1890–1960." *Business History Review* 82(3): 503–528.

Lara Resende, A. 1990. "Estabilizacão e Reforma: 1964–1967." In Marcelo Paiva Abreu, ed. *A Ordem do Progresso, Cem Anos de Politica Economica Republicana, 1889–1989*. Rio de Janeiro: Elsevier.

Law, John. 1705. *Money and Trade Considered: with a Proposal for Supplying the Nation with Money*. Edinburgh: Andrew Anderson.

Lawson, Nigel. 1992. *The View from No. 11: Memoirs of a Tory Radical*. London: Bantam Press.

Leffler, Keith B., and Randal R. Rucker 1991. "Transaction Costs and the Efficient Organization of Production: A Study of Timber-Harvesting Contracts." *Journal of Political Economy* 99(5): 1060–1087.

Leffler, Keith B., Randal R. Rucker, and Ian A. Munn. 2000. "Transaction Costs and the Collection of Information: Presale Measurement on Timber Private Sales." *Journal of Law, Economics, & Organization* 16(1): 166–188.

Leijonhufvud, Axel. 2008. "Keynes and the Crisis." CEPR Policy Insight 23.

Lerner, Abba P. 1947. "Money as a Creature of the State." *American Economic Review* 37(2): 312–317.

Leslie, Christopher R. 2006. "The Anticompetitive Effects of Unenforced Invalid Patents." *Minnesota Law Review* 91: 101–183.

Levi, Margaret. 2004. "An Analytic Narrative Approach to Puzzles and Problems." In Ian Shapiro, Rogers Smith, and Tarek Masoud, eds. *Problems and Methods in the Study of Politics*, 201–226. New York: Cambridge University Press.

Levy, Brian, and Pablo Spiller. 1994. "The Institutional Foundations of Regulatory Commitment: A Comparative Analysis of Telecommunications Regulations." *Journal of Law Economics and Organization* 10(2): 201–246.

Lewis, Gregory, and Patrick Bajari. 2011. "Procurement Contracting with Time Incentives: Theory and Evidence." *Quarterly Journal of Economics* 126(3): 1173–1211.

Libecap, Gary D. 1989. *Contracting for Property Rights*. New York: Cambridge University Press.

2007. "The Assignment of Property Rights on the Western Frontier: Lessons for Contemporary Environmental and Resource Policy." *Journal of Economic History* 67(2): 257–291.

2008. "Open-access Losses and Delay in the Assignment of Property Rights." *Arizona Law Review* 50(2): 379–408.

Listfield, Robert, and Fernando Montes-Negret. 1996. "Brazil's Efficient Payment System: A Legacy of High Inflation." World Bank Policy Research Working Paper 1680.

Little, Ian, Richard Cooper, W. Max Corden, and Sarath Rajapatirana. 1993. *Boom, Crisis and Adjustment: The Macroeconomic Experience of Developing Countries*. New York: Oxford University Press.

Littlechild, Stephen C. 1984. "Restructuring and Privatisation of the UK Electricity Supply Industry." Unpublished.

2000. "Privatisation, Competition and Regulation." Institute of Economic Affairs Occasional Paper 110 (Wincott Lecture).

2002. "Competition in Retail Electricity Supply." *Journal des Economistes et des Etudes Humaines* 12(2/3): 379–402.

2006. "Competition and Contracts in the Nordic Residential Electricity Markets." *Utilities Policy* 14(3): 135–147.

2009. "Retail Competition in Electricity Markets – Expectations, Outcomes and Economics." *Energy Policy* 37(2): 759–763.

Llach, Juan J. 1985. "La Naturalezza Institucional e Internacional de las Hiperinflaciones." Instituto Torcuato di Tella, mimeo.

Lobina, Emanuele, and David Hall. 2003. "Problems with Private Water Concessions: A Review of the Experiences in Latin America and Other Regions." In Inter-American Development Bank, *Water Pricing and Public–Private Partnership in the Americas*. Washington, DC: IADB.

Loeb, Martin P., and Krishnamurthy Surysekar. 1994. "On the Optimality of Cost-Based Contracts in Sole Source Procurement." *Management Accounting Research* 5(1): 31–44.

London Corn Trade Association, Committee Minutes, Papers and Reports (MS23186/1, MS23177 and MS23175), Corporation of London Records Office, London.

Lueck, Dean. 1995. "The Rule of First Possession and the Design of the Law." *Journal of Law and Economics* 38(2): 393–436.

1998. "First Possession." In Peter Newman, ed. *The New Palgrave Dictionary of Economics and the Law*, 132–44. London: Macmillan Press.

Lupia, Arthur, and Mathew D. McCubbins. 1998. *The Democratic Dilemma: How Can Citizens Learn What They Need to Know?* New York: Cambridge University Press.

Lutter, Marcus. 1973. "Limited Liability Companies and Private Companies." In Detlev Vagts, ed. *Business and Private Organizations*, Vol. XIII of the *International Encyclopedia of Comparative Law*. Tubingen: Mohr Siebeck.

Macaulay, Stewart. 1963. "Non-Contractual Relations in Business: A Preliminary Study." *American Sociological Review* 28(1): 55–67.

MacKie-Mason, Jeffrey K. 2002. "What to Do About Unilateral Refusals to License?" At 2 Testimony for the Federal Trade Commission & Department of Justice Hearings on Competition & Intellectual Property Law and Policy in the Knowledge-Based Economy on May 1, 2002. Available at: www.ftc.gov/opp/intellect/020501mackie2.pdf (accessed May 30, 2012).

Macrosty, Henry. 1903. "The Grainmilling Industry: A Study in Organization." *Economic Journal* 13(51): 324–334.

Maia, Fernando. 1999. "Some Regulatory Tools to Deal With Competition in the Brazilian Electricity Sector." Working Paper of the Institute of Brazilian Business and Public Management Issues at the George Washington University.

Majone, Gaindomenico. 2001. "Non Majoritarian Institutions and the Limits of Democratic Governance: A Political Transaction-Cost

Approach." *Journal of Institutional and Theoretical Economics* 157(1): 57–78.
Manelli, M. Alejandro, and Daniel R. Vincent. 1995. "Optimal Procurement Mechanism." *Econometrica* 63(3): 591–620.
Manzetti, Luigi. 1999. *Privatization: South American Style.* New York: Oxford University Press.
Marks, Gary. 1993. "Structural Policy and Multi-level Governance in the EC." In Alan Cafruny and Glenda Rosenthal, eds. *The Maastricht Debate and Beyond,* Vol. II in *The State of the European Community,* 391–410. Boulder, CO: Harlow Longman.
Marks, Gary, Liesbet Hooghe, and K. Blank. 1996. "European Integration from the 1980s: State-Centric v. Multi-Level Governance." *Journal of Common Market Studies* 34(3): 341–378.
Marshall, Robert C., Michael J. Meurer, and Jean-François Richard. 1994a. "Curbing Agency Problems in the Procurement Process by Protest Oversight." *RAND Journal of Economics* 25: 297–318.
  1994b. "Litigation Settlement and Collusion." *Quarterly Journal of Economics* 109(1): 211–239.
Marques, Geider L. 1997. "Restructuring the Brazilian Electrical Sector." Working Paper of Institute of Brazilian Issues at the George Washington University.
Martimort, David. 1999. "Renegotiation Design with Multiple Regulators." *Journal of Economic Theory* 88(2): 261–293.
Maser, Steven M., Vladimir Subbotin, and Fred Thompson. 2010. "The Bid-Protest Mechanism: Effectiveness and Fairness in Defense Acquisitions?" Available at: http://papers.ssrn.com/sol3/papers.cfm?abstract_id=1616424 (accessed May 30, 2012).
McAfee, R. Preston, and John McMillan. 1987. "Auctions and Bidding." *Journal of Economic Literature* 25(2): 699–738.
McCubbins, Matthew D., and Thomas Schwartz. 1984. "Congressional Oversight Overlooked: Police Patrols versus Fire Alarms." *American Journal of Political Science* 28 (1): 165–179.
McCubbins, Matthew D., Roger D. Noll, and Barry R. Weingast. 1987. "Administrative Procedures as Instruments of Political Control." *Journal of Law, Economics, & Organization* 3(2): 243–277.
  1989. "Structure and Process, Politics and Policy: Administrative Arrangements and the Political Control of Agencies." *Virginia Law Review* 75: 431–482.
McCusker, John, and Cora Gravesteijn. 1991. *The Beginnings of Commercial and Financial Journalism: The Commodity Price Currents, Exchange Rate Currents, and Money Currents of Early Modern Europe.* Amsterdam: NEHA.

McGowan, Francis. 2000. "Competition Policy." In Helen Wallace and William Wallace, eds. *Policy-Making in the European Union*, 115–148. Oxford University Press.

McMillan, John. 1994. "Selling Spectrum Rights." *Journal of Economic Perspectives* 8(3): 145–162.

Medina, Barak. 2003. "Augmenting the Value of Ownership by Protecting It Only Partially: The 'Market-Overt' Rule Revisited." *Journal of Law, Economics, & Organization* 19(2): 343–372.

Melamed, A. Douglas. 2005. "Exclusionary Conduct under the Antitrust Laws: Balancing, Sacrifice, and Refusals to Deal." *Berkeley Technology Law Journal* 20: 1247–1268.

Melamed, A. Douglas, and Ali M. Stoeppelwerth. 2002. "The CSU Case: Facts, Formalism, and the Intersection of Antitrust and Intellectual Property Law." *George Mason Law Review* 10: 407–428.

Merrill, J. C. F. 1911. "Classification of Grain into Grades." *Annals of the American Academy of Political and Social Science* 38(2): 58–77.

Merrill, Thomas W., and Henry E. Smith. 2000. "Optimal Standardization in the Law of Property: The Numerus Clausus Principle." *Yale Law Journal* 110(1): 1–70.

   2001a. "What Happened to Property in Law and Economics?" *Yale Law Journal* 111(2): 357–398.

   2001b. "The Property/Contract Interface." *Columbia Law Review* 101(4): 773–852.

Metcalf, Gilbert E. 2007. "A Proposal for a US Carbon Tax Swap: An Equitable Tax Reform to Address Global Climate Change." Brookings Institution Discussion Paper 2007-12.

Meunier, Sophie. 2005. *Trading Voices: The European Union in International Commercial Negotiation*. Princeton University Press.

Milgrom, Paul. 1989. "Auctions and Bidding: A Primer." *Journal of Economic Perspectives* 3(3): 3–22.

Milgrom, Paul, and John Roberts. 1982. "Limit Pricing and Entry under Incomplete Information." *Econometrica* 50(2): 443–459.

Minsky, Hyman. 1986. *Stabilizing an Unstable Economy*. New Haven, CT: Yale University Press.

Modiano, Eduardo. 1990. "A Opera Dos Três Cruzados: 1985–1989." In Marcelo Paiva Abreu, ed. *A Ordem do Progresso, Cem Anos de Politica Economica Republicana, 1889–1989*. Rio de Janeiro: Elsevier.

Moffett, Matt. 1998. "Sour Juice: In Brazil, A Utility Dims Public Enthusiasm for Privatizations." *Wall Street Journal*, April 27.

Molinas, José, Anibal Pérez-Liñán, Sebastian M. Saiegh, and Marcela Montero. 2006. "Political Institutions, Policymaking Processes and Policy Outcomes in Paraguay, 1954–2003." IDB Working Paper 201.

Monod, Jacques. 1971. *Chance and Necessity*. New York: Alfred A. Knopf, Inc. (translated from Jacques Monod, *Le hasard et la nécessité. Essai sur la philosophie naturelle de la biologie moderne*, Paris: Le Seuil, 1970).
Moran, Mark J., and Barry R. Weingast. 1983. "Bureaucratic Discretion or Congressional Control? Regulatory Policymaking by the Federal Trade Commission." *Journal of Political Economy* 91(5): 765–800.
Morineau, Michel. 1985. *Incroyables Gazettes et Fabuleux Métaux: Les Retours des Trésors Américains d'après Les Gazettes Hollandaises (XVIe-XVIIIe Siècles)*. London and New York: Cambridge University Press.
Moschini, GianCarlo, Luisa Menapace, and Daniel Pick. 2008. "Geographical Indications and the Competitive Provision of Quality in Agricultural Markets." *American Journal of Agricultural Economics* 90(3): 794–812.
Moszoro, Marian. 2010. "Opportunism in Public–Private Project Financing." IESE Business School Working Paper 887. *SSRN eLibrary*.
Moszoro, Marian, and Magdalena Krzyzanowska. 2008. "Striving for the Quality of Public Services Through Public–Private Partnerships. The Case of 7 Projects in the City of Warsaw." Paper read at *4th International Conference: An Enterprise Odyssey: Tourism – Governance and Entrepreneurship*, at Cavtat (Croatia).
Motta, Massimo. 2004. *Competition Policy*. Cambridge University Press.
Mougeot, Michel, and Florence Naegelen. 1988. "Analyse Micro-Economique du Code des Marchés Publics." *Revue Economique* 39(4): 725–752.
Murillo, Maria Victoria. 2009. *Political Competition, Partisanship and Policy Making in Latin American Public Utilities*. New York: Cambridge University Press.
Murphy, Anne S. 2009. "Trading Options before Black-Scholes: A Study of the Market in Late Seventeenth Century London." *Economic History Review* 62(s1): 8–30.
Murphy, Antoin E. 1997. *John Law: Economic Theorist and Policymaker*. New York: Oxford University Press.
Murphy, Kevin M., Andrei Shleifer, and Robert W. Vishny. 1993. "Why is Rent-seeking So Costly to Growth?" *American Economic Review* 83(2): 409–414.
Mussa, Michael. 2002. *Argentina and the Fund: From Triumph to Tragedy*. Washington, DC: Institute for International Economics Publishing.
Myers, Stewart, and Nicholal S. Majluf. 1984. "Financing and Investment Decisions When Firms Have Information that Investors Do Not Have." *Journal of Financial Economics* 13(2): 187–221.
National Association of Attorneys General. 1998. Master Settlement Agreement. Available at: http://ag.ca.gov/tobacco/pdf/1msa.pdf (accessed May 30, 2012).

National Conference of State Legislatures. 2003. State Management and Allocation of Tobacco Settlement Revenue 2003. Available at: www.stpnd.com/UserFiles/File/NCSL_2003_report_on_the_MSA.pdf (accessed May 30, 2012).

Neal, Larry. 1990. *The Rise of Financial Capitalism: International Capital Markets in the Age of Reason*. Cambridge and New York: Cambridge University Press.

2011. *"I Am Not Master of Events": The Adventures of John Law and Lord Londonderry in the Mississippi and South Sea Bubbles*. New Haven, CT: Yale University Press.

Nelson, Philip. 1970. "Information and Consumer Behavior." *Journal of Political Economy* 78(2): 311–329.

Newbery, David. 2006. "Electricity Liberalization in Britain and the Evolution of Market Design." In Fereidoon P. Sioshansi and Wolfgang Pfaffenberger, eds. *Electricity Market Reform, An International Perspective*, 109–144. Oxford: Elsevier.

Nicita, Antonio. 2009. "Consumers Win-back as Exclusionary Conduct. Some Insights for Antitrust Law." Quaderni del Dipartimento di Economia Politica – University of Siena – 565.

North, Douglass C. 1981. *Structure and Change in Economic History*. New York: Norton.

1990. *Institutions, Institutional Change and Economic Performance*. Cambridge University Press.

1991. "Institutions." *Journal of Economic Perspectives* 5(1): 97–112.

2005. *Understanding the Process of Economic Change*. Princeton University Press.

North, Douglass C., and Robert Paul Thomas. 1973. *The Rise of the Western World: A New Economic History*. Cambridge University Press.

North, Douglass C. and Barry R. Weingast. 1989. "Constitutions and Commitment: Evolution of Institutions Governing Public Choice." *Journal of Economic History*, 44: 803–832.

North, Douglass C., John Joseph Wallis, and Barry R. Weingast. 2006. "A Conceptual Framework for Understanding Recorded Human History." NBER Working Paper 12795.

2009. *Violence and Social Orders: A Conceptual Framework for Interpreting Recorded Human History*. New York: Cambridge University Press.

Nugent, Neil, and William Paterson. 2003. "The Political System of the European Union." In Jack Hayward and Anand Menon, eds. *Governing Europe*, 92–113. Oxford University Press.

Oates, Wallace E. 1972. *Fiscal Federalism*. New York: Harcourt Brace Jovanovich.

OECD. 1999. "Procurement Markets." *OECD Journal of Competition Law and Policy* 1(4): 83–123.
Office of Electricity Regulation (Offer). 1997. *Annual Report*. London: Offer Publications.
Ogus, Anthony. 1999. "Competition between National Legal Systems: A Contribution of Economic Analysis to Comparative Law." *International and Comparative Law Quarterly* 48: 405–418.
Oliver, Christine. 1992. "The Antecedents of Deinstitutionalization." *Organization Studies* 13(4): 563–588.
Olson, Mancur. 1965. *The Logic of Collective Action: Public Goods and the Theory of Groups*. Cambridge, MA: Harvard University Press.
  1982. *The Rise and Decline of Nations*. New Haven, CT: Yale University Press.
Ondo Ndong, Sonia, and Laurence Scialom. 2009. "Northern Rock: The Anatomy of a Crisis – The Prudential Lessons." In Robert Bliss and George Kaufman, eds. *Financial Institutions and Markets: 2007–8 The Year of Crisis*. Houndmills: Palgrave Macmillan.
Orszag, Peter R. 2007. "Approaches to Reducing Carbon Dioxide Emissions." Written testimony before the Committee on the Budget, US House of Representatives, November 1, 2007.
Osborne, Martin. 2004. *An Introduction to Game Theory*. New York: Oxford University Press.
Ostrom, Elinor. 1990. *Governing the Commons: The Evolution of Institutions for Collective Action*. Cambridge University Press.
  2005. *Understanding Institutional Diversity*. Princeton University Press.
Ostroy, Joseph M. 1973. "The Informational Efficiency of Monetary Exchange." *American Economic Review* 63(4): 697–710.
Parisi, Francesco, Norbert Schulz, and Jonathan Klick. 2006. "Two Dimensions of Regulatory Competition." *International Review of Law and Economics* 26(1): 56–66.
Parker, David. 2009. *The Official History of Privatisation*, Vol. I: *The Formative Years 1970–1987*. Government Official History Series. London and New York: Routledge.
  2012. *The Official History of Privatisation*, Vol. II: *Popular Capitalism 1987–1997*. Government Official History Series. London: Routledge.
Parkinson, Cecil. 1992. *Right at the Centre*. London: Weidenfeld and Nicolson.
Parry, Ian W. H., Robertson C. Williams III, and Lawrence H. Goulder. 1999. "When Can Carbon Abatement Policies Increase Welfare? The Fundamental Role of Distorted Factor Markets." *Journal of Environmental Economics and Management* 37(1): 52–84.

Peltzman, Sam. 1976. "Toward a More General Theory of Regulation." *Journal of Law and Economics* 19(2): 211–240.
Percival, John. 1934. *Wheat in Great Britain*. London: Duckworth.
Pereira, R. 2001. "Brazil: Analysts Divided over Furnas Privatization Model." *World News Connection*, April 13.
Petram, Lodewijk. 2009. "How the World's First Stock Exchange Developed into a Well-Functioning Market: The Amsterdam Market for VOC Shares, 1602–1700." Paper presented at the World Economic History Conference, University of Utrecht.
Petrazzini, Ben. 1995. *The Political Economy of Telecommunications Reform in Developing Countries: Privatization and Liberalization in Comparative Perspective*. Westport, CT: Praeger.
Pfiffner, James P. 1987. "Political Appointees and Career Executives: The Democracy-Bureaucracy Nexus in the Third Century." *Public Administration Review* 47(1): 57–65.
Philippi, D. B. 1991. "The Chilean Electric Power Sector in the Last Decade: The Design and Implementation of a New Policy." Unpublished.
Philipson, Tomas J., and Richard Posner. 2001. "Anti-Trust and the Not-For-Profit Sector." NBER Working Paper 8126.
Pinker, Steven. 1997. *How the Mind Works*. New York: Norton.
Pires Rodrigues, A., and F. Braga Monteiro. 1991. "Electricity System in Brazil." Paper presented at CERES Workshop on Electricity Regulation in the Southern Cone, Montevideo.
Pirrong, Craig. 1995a. "The Efficient Scope of Private-Transactions-Cost-Reducing Institutions: The Case of Commodity Exchanges." *Journal of Legal Studies* 24(1): 229–255.
  1995b. "Mixed Manipulation Strategies in Commodity Futures Markets." *Journal of Futures Markets* 15(1): 13–38.
  1995c. "The Self-Regulation of Commodity Exchanges: The Case of Market Manipulation." *Journal of Law and Economics* 38(1): 141–206.
  1999. "The Organization of Financial Exchange Markets: Theory and Evidence." *Journal of Financial Markets* 2(4): 329–357.
  2000. "A Theory of Financial Exchange Organization." *Journal of Law and Economics* 43(2): 437–471.
  2002. "Securities Markets Macrostructure: Property Rights and the Efficiency of Securities Trading." *Journal of Law, Economics, & Organization* 18(2): 385–410.
  2008. "The Economics of Clearing in Derivatives Markets: Netting, Asymmetric Information, and the Sharing of Default Risks Through a Central Counterparty." University of Houston Working Paper.

Pitofsky, Robert, Donna Patterson, and Jonathan Hooks. 2002. "The Essential Facilities Doctrine under US Antitrust Law." *Antitrust Law Journal* 70: 443–462.
Pollitt, Michael. 2008. "Electricity Reform in Argentina: Lessons for Developing Countries." *Energy Economics* 30(4): 1536–1567.
Ponte, Stefano, and Peter Gibbon. 2005. "Quality Standards, Conventions and the Governance of Global Value Chains." *Economy and Society* 34(1): 1–31.
Popofsky, Mark S. 2006. "Defining Exclusionary Conduct: Section 2, the Rule of Reason, and the Unifying Principle Underlying Antitrust Rules." *Antitrust Law Journal* 73: 435–482.
Porter, Robert H. 1983. "A Study of Cartel Stability: The Joint Executive Committee, 1880–1886." *Bell Journal of Economics* 14(2): 301–314.
Porter, Robert, and Douglas Zona. 1993. "Detection of Bid Rigging in Procurement Auctions." *Journal of Political Economy* 101(3): 518–538.
Prager, Robin. 1990. "Firm Behaviors in Franchise Monopoly Market." *RAND Journal of Economics* 21(2): 211–225.
Prendergast, Canice. 2003. "The Limits of Bureaucratic Efficiency." *Journal of Political Economy* 111(5): 929–958.
Priest, George. 1993. "The Origins of Utility Regulation and the 'Theories of Regulation' Debate." *Journal of Law and Economics* 36(1): 289–323.
Quiggin, John. 1996. "Private Sector Involvement in Infrastructure Projects." *Australian Economic Review* (1st quarter): 51–64.
Raymond, Leigh. 2003. *Private Rights in Public Resources: Equity and Property Allocation in Market-based Environmental Policy*. Washington, DC: Resources for the Future.
Regional Greenhouse Gas Initiative (RGGI). 2006. *Model Rule* (8/15/2006). Available at: www.rggi.org/docs/Model%20Rule%20Corrected%20 8.15.06.pdf (accessed April 20, 2010).
Reiss, Peter, C., and Frank A. Wolak. 2007. "Structural Econometric Modeling: Rationales and Examples from Industrial Organization." In James J. Heckman, and Edward E. Leamer, eds. *Handbook of Econometrics*, Vol. 6A: 4277–4415. London: Elsevier.
Rennhack, Robert, and Masahiro Nozaki. 2006. "Financial Dollarization in Latin America." IMF Working Paper 06/7.
Rhoades, Dawna L. 2008. *The Evolution of International Aviation: Phoenix Rising*. Aldershot: Ashgate Publishing.
Richman, Barak. 2004. "Firms, Courts, and Reputation Mechanisms: Toward a Positive Theory of Private Ordering." *Columbia Law Review* 104(8): 2328–2367.

Riker, William. 1957. "Events and Situations." *Journal of Philosophy* 54(1): 57–70.
Riker, William H. 1963. *The Theory of Political Coalitions*. New Haven, CT: Yale University Press.
Riley, James C. 1980. *International Government Finance and the Amsterdam Capital Market, 1740–1815*. Cambridge University Press.
Robinson, Glen O. 2002. "On Refusing to Deal with Rivals." *Cornell Law Review* 87(2001–2002): 1177–1232.
Rochet, Jean-Charles, and Jean Tirole. 2007. "Two-sided Markets: A Progress Report." *RAND Journal of Economics* 37: 645–667.
Romer, Paul M. 1990. "Endogenous Technological Change." *Journal of Political Economy* 98(5): S71–S102.
Rosamond, Ben. 2003. "New Theories of European Integration." In Michelle Cini, ed. *European Union Politics*, 109–127. Oxford University Press.
Rose, Carol M. 1985. *Possession as the Origin of Property*. University of Chicago.
Rosse, James N. 1970. "Estimating Cost Function Parameters Without Using Cost Data: Illustrated Methodology." *Econometrica* 38(2): 256–275.
Rubin, Paul. 2000. "Information Regulation (Including Regulation of Advertising)." In Badewijn Bouckaert and Gerrit De Geest, eds. *The Regulation of Contracts*, Vol. III in the *Encyclopedia of Law and Economics*. Cheltenham: Edward Elgar.
Rudnick, Hugh. 1998. "The Electric Market Restructuring in South America: Successes and Failures on Market Design." Paper presented at the Harvard Electricity Policy Group, San Diego.
Sachs, Jeffrey, and Alvaro Zini. 1996. "Brazilian Inflation and the Plano Real." *World Economy* 19(1): 13–37.
Salop, Steven C. 2006. "Exclusionary Conduct, Effect on Consumers, and the Flawed Profit-Sacrifice Standard." *Antitrust Law Journal* 73: 311–374.
Sargent, Thomas J. 1982. "The Ends of Four Big Inflations." In Robert Hall, ed. *Inflation: Causes and Effects*, 41–98. Chicago University Press.
Sargent, Thomas J., and Neil Wallace. 1981. "Some Unpleasant Monetarist Arithmetic." *Federal Reserve Bank of Minneapolis Quarterly Review* Fall.
Savedoff, William, and Pablo Spiller. 1999. "Government Opportunism and the Provision of Water." In William Savedoff and Pablo Spiller, eds. *Government Opportunism and the Provision of Water*. Washington, DC: InterAmerican Development Bank.
Scharpf, Fritz. 1994. "Community and Autonomy: Multilevel Policy Making in the European Union." *Journal of European Public Policy* 1(2): 219–242.

Schmalensee, Richard, Paul L. Joskow, A. Denny Ellerman, Juan-Pablo Montero, and Elizabeth M. Bailey. 1998. "An Interim Evaluation of Sulfur Dioxide Emissions Trading." *Journal of Economic Perspectives* 12(3): 53–68.

Schroeder, Stephen A. 2002. "Conflicting Dispatches from the Tobacco Wars." *New England Journal of Medicine* 347(14): 1106–1109.

2004. "Tobacco Control in the Wake of the 1998 Master Settlement Agreement." *New England Journal of Medicine* 350(3): 293–301.

Scialom, Laurence. 2007. "Les Propositions du European Shadow Financial Regulatory Committee Sur l'Action Corrective Précoce en Europe – Une Analyse Critique 'Amicale'." *Revue Economique* 58(5): 1127–1138.

Seabright, Paul. 2004. *The Company of Strangers: A Natural History of Economic Life*. Princeton and Oxford: Princeton University Press.

Service, Elman R. 1975. *Origins of the State and Civilization: The Process of Cultural Evolution*. New York: Norton.

Sgard, Jérôme. 2008. "L'Hyperinflation et la Reconstruction de la Monnaie Nationale: Une Comparaison de l'Argentine et du Brésil, 1990–2002." In Bruno Thérêt, ed. *La Monnaie Dévoilée Par Ses Crises*. Paris: Presses de l'EHESS.

Shapiro, Carl. 1983. "Premiums for High Quality Products as Returns to Reputations." *Quarterly Journal of Economics* 98(4): 659–679.

Shea, Gary. 2007a. "Understanding Financial Derivatives during the South Sea Bubble: The Case of the South Sea Subscription Shares." *Oxford Economic Papers* 59(1): 73–104.

2007b. "Financial Market Analysis Can Go Mad (In the Search for Irrational Behaviour during the South Sea Bubble)." *Economic History Review* 60(4): 742–765.

Simon, Herbert A. 1962. "The Architecture of Complexity." *Proceedings of the American Philosophical Society* 106(6): 467–482.

Simonsen, Mario H. 1995. *30 Anos de Indexaçao*. Rio de Janeiro: Fundaçao Vargas Editora.

Simpson, Alfred W. B. 1991. "The Origins of Futures Trading on the Liverpool Cotton Market." In Peter Cane and Jane Stapleton, eds. *Essays for Patrick Atiyah*. Oxford: Clarendon Press.

Singhal, Monica. 2008. "Special Interest Groups and the Allocation of Public Funds." *Journal of Public Economics* 92(3–4): 548–564.

Sinn, Hans-Werner. 1997. "The Selection Principle and Market Failure in Systems Competition." *Journal of Public Economics* 66(2): 247–274.

Skjærseth, Jon Birger, and Jørgen Wettestad. 2008. *EU Emissions Trading: Initiation, Decision-making and Implementation*. Farnham: Ashgate Publishing.

Smith, Henry E. 2006. "Modularity in Contracts: Boilerplate and Information Flow." *University of Michigan Law Review* 104: 1175–1222.
———. 2007. "Intellectual Property as Property: Delineating Entitlements in Information." *Yale Law Journal* 116(8): 1742–1822.
———. 2008. "Governing Water: The Semicommons of Fluid Property Rights." *Arizona Law Review* 50(2): 445–478.
———. 2009. "Modularity in Property, Intellectual Property, and Organizations." Harvard Law School mimeo.
Solanet, Manuel. A. 1994. "Privatization: The Long Road to Success in Argentina." *Business Forum* Winter/Spring: 28–31.
Soto, R. 1999. "Institutional Reforms in the Electricity Sector." Manuscript.
Spiller, Pablo T. 2008. "An Institutional Theory of Public Contracts: Regulatory Implications." NBER Working Paper 14152.
Spiller, Pablo T., and Luis V. Martorell. 1996. "How Should it Be Done? Electricity Regulation in Argentina, Brazil, Uruguay and Chile." In Richard Gilbert and Edward P. Kahn, eds. *International Comparison of Electricity Regulation*, 82–125. New York: Cambridge University Press.
Spiller, Pablo T., and William D. Savedoff. 2000. "Oportunismo gubernamental y suministro de agua.". In P. T. Spiller and W. D. Savedoff, eds. *Agua perdida: compromisos institucionales para el suministro de servicios públicos sanitarios*. Washington, DC: Inter-American Development Bank.
Spiller, Pablo T., and Santiago Urbiztondo. 1994. "Political Appointees vs. Career Civil Servants: A Multiple Principals Theory of Political Bureaucracies." *European Journal of Political Economy* 10(3): 465–497.
Spulber, D. 1996. "Market Microstructure and Intermediation." *Journal of Economic Perspectives* 10: 135–152.
Squam Lake Working Group on Financial Regulation. 2009a. *An Expedited Resolution Mechanism for Distressed Financial Firms: Regulatory Hybrid Securities*. Washington, DC: Council on Foreign Relations.
———. 2009b. *Improving Resolution Options for Systemically Relevant Financial Institutions*. Washington, DC: Council on Foreign Relations.
Staniland, Martin. 2003. *Government Birds: Air Transport and the State in Western Europe*. Lanham, MD: Rowman and Littlefield.
Stavins, Robert N. 1998. "What Can We Learn from the Grand Policy Experiment? Lessons from SO2 Allowance Trading." *Journal of Economic Perspectives* 12(3): 69–88.
———. 2007. "Market-based Environmental Policies: What Can We Learn From US Experience (and Related Research)?" In Jody Freeman and Charles D. Kolstad, eds. *Moving to Markets in Environmental Regulation:*

Lessons from Twenty Years of Experience, 63–94. New York: Oxford University Press.
Stewart, James. 1923. "Marketing Wheat." *Annals of the American Academy of Political and Social Science* 107: 187–192.
Stigler, George. 1951. "The Division of Labor Is Limited by the Extent of the Market." *Journal of Political Economy* 59(3): 185–193.
   1971. "The Theory of Economic Regulation." *Bell Journal of Economics and Management Science* 2(1): 3–21.
Sturzenegger, Federico. 1991. "Description of a Populist Experience: Argentina, 1973–1976." In Rudiger Dornbusch and Sebastian Edwards, eds. *The Macroeconomics of Populism in Latin America*, 77–121. Chicago University Press.
Sun, Jeanne-Mey, and Jacques Pelkmans. 1995. "Regulatory Competition in the Single Market." *Journal of Common Market Studies* 33(1): 67–89.
Thatcher, Margaret. 1993. *The Downing Street Years*. London: Harper Collins.
Thomas, John R. 2001. "Collusion and Collective Action in the Patent System: A Proposal for Patent Bounties." *University of Illinois Law Review*: 305–354.
Tiebout, Charles. 1956. "A Pure Theory of Local Government Expenditure." *Journal of Political Economy* 64(5): 416–424.
Tietenberg, Thomas. 2005. *Environmental and Natural Resource Economics*. Boston, MA: Pearson, Addison-Wesley.
   2006. *Emissions Trading: Principles and Practice*. Washington, DC: Resources for the Future.
Tirole, Jean. 1988. *The Theory of Industrial Organization*. Cambridge, MA: MIT Press.
Trigger, Bruce G. 2003. *Understanding Early Civilizations*. Cambridge University Press.
Troesken, Werner. 1996. *Why Regulate Utilities? The New Institutional Economics and the Chicago Gas Industry, 1849–1924*. Ann Arbor: University of Michigan Press.
Tsebelis, George. 1990. *Nested Games: Rational Choice in Comparative Politics*. Berkeley, CA: University of California Press.
United Kingdom Department of Energy. 1992. *History of Electricity Privatisation (England and Wales)*. London: Department of Energy.
United Kingdom Financial Services Authority. 2009. *The Turner Review: A Regulatory Response to the Global Banking Crisis*. London: Financial Services Authority.
United Kingdom Secretary of State for Energy. 1988. *Privatising Electricity: The Government's Proposals for the Privatisation of the Electricity Supply Industry in England and Wales*. London: HMSO, Cm 322, February.

United States Antitrust Modernization Commission. 2007. Report and Recommendations. Available at: http://govinfo.library.unt.edu/amc/report_recommendation/amc_final_report.pdf. (accessed June 1, 2012).

United States Department of Defense. 2011. *Source Selection Procedures*. Available at: www.acq.osd.mil/dpap/policy/policyvault/USA007183-10-DPAP.pdf (accessed May 19, 2011).

United States Department of Justice. 1997. *Antitrust Resource Manual*. Available at: www.justice.gov/usao/eousa/foia_reading_room/usam/title7/ant00000.htm (accessed June 1, 2012).

——— 2008. Competition and Monopoly: Single Firm Conduct under Section 2 of the Sherman Act (Sept. 2008). Available at www.usdoj.gov/atr/public/reports/236681.pdf (accessed June 1, 2012).

United States Department of Justice and Federal Trade Commission. 1995. *Antitrust Guidelines for the Licensing of Intellectual Property*. Available at: www.ftc.gov/bc/0558.pdf (accessed June 1, 2012).

United States Environmental Protection Agency (US EPA) (various). *Progress Report*. Various years by program, available at www.epa.gov/airmarkets/progress/progress-reports.html (accessed April 20, 2010).

United States Federal Trade Commission. 2003. "To Promote Innovation: The Proper Balance of Competition and Patent Law and Policy. Executive Summary." Available at: www.ftc.gov/os/2003/10/innovationrptsummary.pdf (accessed June 1, 2012).

United States Government Accountability Office. 2001. *Contract Management. Benefits of Simplified Acquisition Test Procedures Not Clearly Demonstrated*. Washington, DC: United States General Accounting Office (GAO). Available at: www.gao.gov/new.items/d01517.pdf (accessed July 11, 2011).

——— 2003. *Equal Employment Opportunity. SSA Region X's Changes to Its EEO Process Illustrate Need for Agencywide Procedures*. Washington, DC: United States Government Accountability Office (GAO). Available at: www.gao.gov/new.items/d03604.pdf (accessed July 18, 2011).

——— 2008. *Defense Acquisition. Assessments of Selected Weapon Programs*. Washington, DC: United States General Accounting Office (GAO). Available at: www.gao.gov/new.items/d08467sp.pdf (accessed July 11, 2011).

Van den Bergh, Roger. 1998. "Subsidiarity as an Economic Demarcation Principle and the Emergence of European Private Law." *Maastricht Journal of European and Comparative Law* 5(2): 129–152.

——— 2000. "Towards an Institutional Legal Framework for Regulatory Competition in Europe." *Kyklos* 53(4): 435–466.

Van den Bergh, Roger, and Peter Camesasca. 2006. *European Competition Law and Economics: A Comparative Perspective*. London: Sweet and Maxwell.

Vecchia, G. 1993. "Power Connections: Privatization of Electricity Surges Ahead in Argentina." *LatinFinance*.

Vegh, Carlos. 1992. "Stopping High Inflation: An Analytical Overview." IMF Staff Paper 39(3).

Velde, François. 2009. "Was John Law's System a Bubble? The Mississippi Bubble Revisited." In Jeremy Atack and Larry Neal, eds. *The Origins and Development of Financial Institutions and Markets*, 99–120. Cambridge University Press.

Velkar, Aashish. 2012. *Markets and Measurements in Nineteenth Century Britain*. Cambridge University Press.

Victor, David, and Thomas C. Heller, eds. 2007. *The Political Economy of Power Sector Reform: The Experiences of Five Major Developing Countries*. New York: Cambridge University Press.

Volden, Craig, and Alan E. Wiseman. 2007. "Bargaining in Legislatures over Particularistic and Collective Goods." *American Political Science Review* 101(1): 79–92.

Waller, Spencer Weber. 2008. "Areeda, Epithets, and Essential Facilities." *Wisconsin Law Review*: 359–386.

Wallis, John Joseph. 2011. "Institutions, Organizations, Impersonality, and Interests: The Dynamics of Institutions." *Journal of Economic Behavior and Organization* 79(1–2): 48–64.

Walzenbach, Gunter P. E. 2006. "European Competition Policy: Governance as Graduated Coordination." In Gunter Walzenbach, ed. *European Governance. Policy Making between Politicization and Control*, 17–34. Aldershot: Ashgate Publishing.

Wang, Chong, and Joseph San Miguel. 2011. "Unintended Consequences of Advocating Use of Fixed-Price Contracts in Defense Acquisition Practice." Paper read at the *Eighth Annual Acquisition Research Symposium: Creating Synergy for Informed Change*, May 11–12, 2011, at Monterey, CA.

Weingast, Barry. 1998. "Political Stability and Civil War: Institutions, Commitments and American Democracy." In A. Bates, A. Greif, M. Levi, J.L. Rosenthal, and B. Weingast, eds. *Analytic Narratives*, 148–193. Princeton University Press.

Weingast, Barry R. 2004. "The Constitutional Dilemma of Economic Liberty." *The Journal of Economic Perspectives* 19(3): 89–108.

Weingast, Barry, and William Marshall. 1988. "The Industrial Organization of Congress; Or, Why Legislatures, Like Firms, Are Not Organized As Markets." *Journal of Political Economy* 96(1): 132–168.

Weingast, Barry R., and Mark J. Moran. 1983. "Bureaucratic Discretion or Congressional Control? Regulatory Policymaking by the Federal Trade Commission." *Journal of Political Economy* 91(5): 765–800.

Weiser, Philip J. 2002. "Law and Information Platforms." *Journal on Telecommunications & High Technology Law* 1: 1–36.

Werden, Gregory J. 2006. "Identifying Exclusionary Conduct Under Section 2: The 'No Economic Sense' Test." *Antitrust Law Journal* 73: 413–434.

Whinston, Michael D. 1990. "Tying, Foreclosure, and Exclusion." *American Economic Review* 80: 837–859.

White, Eugene. 1989. "Was There a Solution to the Financial Crisis of the Ancien Régime?" *Journal of Economic History* 49(3): 545–568.

———. 2003. "The Paris Bourse, 1724–1814." In Stanley L. Engerman, Philip T. Hoffman, Jean-Laurent Rosenthal, and Kenneth L. Sokoloff, eds. *Finance, Intermediaries and Economic Development*, 34–74. Cambridge and New York: Cambridge University Press.

Wilkinson, John. 1997. "A New Paradigm for Economic Analysis?" *Economy and Society* 26(3): 305–339.

Williamson, Oliver E. 1975. *Markets and Hierarchies: Analysis of Antitrust and Implications*. New York: Free Press.

———. 1976. "Franchise Bidding for Natural Monopolies: In General and with Respect to CATV." *Bell Journal of Economics* 7(1): 73–104.

———. 1979. "Transaction-Cost Economics: The Governance of Contractual Relations." *Journal of Law and Economics* 22(2): 233–261.

———. 1985. *The Economic Institutions of Capitalism: Firms, Markets, Relational Contracting*. New York: The Free Press, Macmillan, Inc.

———. 1999. "Public and Private Bureaucracies: A Transaction Cost Economics Perspective." *Journal of Law Economics and Organization* 15(1): 306–342.

———. 2002. "The Theory of the Firm as Governance Structure: From Choice to Contract." *Journal of Economic Perspectives* 16(3): 171–195.

———. 2005. "The Economics of Governance." *American Economic Review* 95(2): 1–18.

Wilson, Charles. 1941 (Repr. 1966). *Anglo-Dutch Commerce & Finance in the Eighteenth Century*. Cambridge University Press.

Wing, L. K. 1999. "Painful Lessons." *Latin Finance*.

Wisnefski, S. 2001. "Brazilian Power Rationing Highlights Regulatory Challenge." Dow Jones Wire Service, May 23.

Wolak, Frank A. 2000. "An Empirical Analysis of the Impact of Hedge Contracts on Bidding Behavior in a Competitive Electricity Market." *International Economic Journal* 14(2): 1–39.

2003a. "Identification and Estimation of Cost Functions Using Observed Bid Data: An Application to Electricity Markets." In M. Dewatripont, L. P. Hansen, and S. J. Turnovsky, eds. *Advances in Economics and Econometrics: Theory and Applications (Eighth World Congress)*, Vol. II: 133–169. New York: Cambridge University Press.

2003b. "Measuring Unilateral Market Power in Wholesale Electricity Markets: The California Market 1998 to 2000." *American Economic Review* May 2003: 425–430.

2007. "Quantifying the Supply-Side Benefits from Forward Contracting in Wholesale Electricity Markets." *Journal of Applied Econometrics* 22: 1179–1209.

Wolak, Frank A., and Shaun D. McRae. 2009. "How Do Firms Exercise Unilateral Market Power? Evidence from a Bid-Based Wholesale Electricity Market." EUI Working Paper RSCAS 2009/36, 2009.

Woll, Cornelia. 2008. *Firm Interests: How Governments Shape Business Lobbying in Global Trade*. Ithaca, NY: Cornell University Press.

World Bank. 1995. *Bureaucrats in Business: The Economics and Politics of Government Ownership*. New York: Oxford University Press.

Ye, Lixin. 2007. "Indicative Bidding and a Theory of Two-Stage Auctions." *Games and Economic Behavior* 58(1): 181–207.

Zahedieh, Nuala. 1994. "London and the Colonial Consumer in the Late Seventeenth Century." *Economic History Review* 47(2): 239–261.

Zelner, Bennet A., Witold J. Henisz, and Guy L. F. Holburn. 2009. "Contentious Implementation and Retrenchment in Neoliberal Policy Reform: The Global Electric Power Industry, 1989–2001." *Administrative Science Quarterly* 54(3): 379–412.

Index

accounting, 318–321, 323
mark-to-market, 334, 341
  norms, 316, 341
adjudication, 59
  approach, 71
  contracts ex post, 58
  title conflict, 65
advertising, 33, 51
agency relationship, 17
  principals, and, *see* principal
agents
  authority, 59, 69
  categories, 449
  competition policy, 13, 58, 60, 81
  different, 284
  economic, 4, 19, 293, 335, 455, 462
  exchanges, 421
  immunity, 248
  interdependencies, 16
  interests, own selfish, 4
  legal authority, 67
  money building, 292
  organization, 3
  principal, and, *see* principal
  public, 59, 229–251, 468
  rulers, and, 451
  sequential exchange, 66–70
  specialist, 4, 60
  strategies, 336
  trading parties, 449
agrifood, 37, 41, 46
  chains, 42
  quality assurance, 46
allocation/distribution, 7
  allowance, principle of, 84, 464
  assumed mechanism, 86
  efficiency, 82, 95, 164, 444
  first-possession, 87–89
  franchises, 95
  innovation, 82

managing, 82
political, 87
political economy, 96–98
preferred method, 86
quality, 45
rule, 101
tobacco trust fund, 98–100
uniform, 89
antitrust/competition, 147, 199, 218, 378, 388, 466
anticompetitive behaviors, 209, 382
applicability, 365
authorities, 147, 206, 209, 218, 355
aviation, 276
benefits, 14
compensation, 207–210
consumerism, 373, 451
consumers, effect on, 195, 454
costs, 209
damages, 207
economic, 452–454
economic rationale, 371
efficiency, 7, 454
emphasis, 179
enforcement, 208, 213, 361, 381, 389
European policy, *see* European competition policy
exchanges, 357
false positives, 383, 384, 385
fines, 209
generation, in, 173, 174, 189, 191, 196
immunity, 280
immunization powers, 287
innovation, 457
institutional entrepeneurs, 456
intellectual property, *see* intellectual property
judicial application, 210

Index

judicial controls, 386
law, 211, 359–360, 381, 382, 384
liability, 367, 376
local, 359
mandatory dealing, *see* mandatory dealing
national law, 200, 211
natural, as, 7
new entrants, 457
procedural law, 384
public law enforcement, 208
purchasing power, 321
regulation, 166
regulatory convergence, 213
remedies, 214
retail, concept of, 194
rules, 199
substantive law, 202
supply, in, 170, 173–176, 178, 182, 184, 186, 191, 194
trading communities, 456
unilateral refusals, 355, 359, *see* unilateral refusals
victims, 208
violations, 209
attributes
brand-specific, 51
checks and balances, *see* checks and balances
commodities, 421, 424
credence, 18, 28, 41, 47
personal, 63
procurement, 126
products, 52
quality, 24, 26, 47, 55
safety, 50
search, 17
true, 47
auctions, 89–91, 356
basic rule, as, 111–118
competitive, 89
efficiency, 84, 87, 90, 96–100, 121
equity, 90
implementability, 463–464
mandatory, 112
multi-unit market, 392, 393
negotiation, and, 123–127
procedures, 84, 123, 128, 135, 137, 140, 141
public procurement, and, 83, 141

rents, 92, 93
revenues, 97, 105
aviation, transatlantic, 271
constructivist, 281–283
divide and rule strategy, 279
EU's role, 279
Heathrow, 278, 279
history, 271, 275–281
liberalization, 278–280
nationality interests, 276, 284
open skies, 278, 279–281
political limit pricing, 283–287
rationalism, 281–283

balances
buyer/seller, 429
checks and, *see* checks and balances
efficiency, 269, 440
individual behavior, 456
mandatory dealing, and, 379
need for, 4
political power, 457, 460
public/private, 291
bankruptcy, 304, 346
bank, 344
emerging markets, 310
investment, and, 267
law, 330
reorganization, 278
stock markets, and, 312
banks, 305–307
American framework, 342
behavior, 336
central policy, 338
credit aggregation, 338–339
credit regime, 336
crude leverage ratio, 344
dispute resolution, 346
early intervention, 343–345
gross leverage ratio, 345
Prompt Corrective Action, 341–347
resolution mechanisms, 346–347
risk control models, 340
supervision, 351
trigger thresholds, 343–345
vulnerability, 340
brand, 18
names, 46, 47, 48, 50, 54
private, 45, 50, 53, 54
public institutions, 56

brand (cont.)
  signaling, credible, 55
bureaucracies, 240–241
  bureaucrat, 283
  design, 147
  politics, and, 283–286
  public agents, 232

capitalism, 295–297
centralization/decentralization
  advantages/disadvantages, 203–205
  commodity exchanges, 26
  competences, 200
  competition policy
    enforcement, 200
  division of labor, 318
  efficiency, and, 81
  enforcement, 202
  European competition policy, 200
  externalities, 204, 206
  grading, 34
  inconsistencies, source of, 458
  legal uncertainty, 206
  measurement practices, 24
  opportunity costs, 204
  property rights, 81
  quality measurements, 34, 35
  regulation, 81
  trade-offs, and, 448
checks and balances, 8, 225, 433, 448, 451, 457
collective action, 104, 322
  balances, 4
  costs, reducing, 424
  innovations, 456
  nature, 464
  power, 65
commodity
  asymmetry, and, 17
  chain, 27, 28, 34
  characteristics, 445, 448
  definition, 424
  grading, 27–30, 32
  language, 424
  legal, 16, 60, 74
  markets, 30, 425
  sorting, 27
  value addition, 34
competition policy, *see* antitrust/ competition
consumer compensation, 116–119

consumers
  lobbying, 261
  product attributes, 38
  short-term preferences, 204
  unilateral refusals, and, 361
contractors, 244–246
contracts
  characteristics of parties, 62
  comparative advantage, 63, 155
  conflicts, 65
  cost-plus, 241–242
  enforcement, 37, 63
  fixed-price, 241–242
  flexible, 230, 237
  informative, 72
  inter-temporal, 321
  judicial decisions, 65
  long-term, 232, 233
  originative, 59–70, 72, 76
  price, 238
  public, *see* public contracting
  public-to-public, 244
  registration, 58, 61, 64
  registries, 74–75
  relational, 230
  rights, 75
  rigidity, 234
  share, 18
  simplification, impact of, 13
  specificity, 234
copyright, 364, 370, 371, 378
  refusal to licence, 366
corruption
  auctions, 121, 122
  legal registries, 74
  negotiations, 123
  preventing, 123, 461, 463
  public contracts, 225, 229, 232
  rent-seeking, 87
  suspicions, 124, 135
  vulnerability, 126
costs, 18
  allocation, 89
  duplication, 215
  enforcement, 35, 205
  information, 35
  measurement, 17, 19
  opportunity differences, 408
  policy, 285
  procedural, 254
  sunk, 62, 75

Index

third-party, 235
trade-offs, 60, 70
transaction, 18, 35, 67, 81, 82
criteria
  common, 18
  compulsory, 51
  grading, 32
  remediableness, 251
  risk, 234
  selection, 128
  summary, 18, 31

delegation, 3, 48
  authority, 467
  European Commission, 285–286
  political power, 69, 274
deregulation, 267, 279, 282
  liberalization, and, 388
  pro-competition reforms, 227
dispute resolution, 31
  mechanisms, 14, 35
distribution, *see* allocation/distribution
division of labor
  benefits, 5, 165, 318, 454
  drivers, 13, 448
  irreversibility, 456
  market exchange, 145, 332, 428, 441, 445
  norms, 455
  politics, 451
  productivity, 151, 155
  social, 145
  standardization, 447
  trading instruments, 430
dominant position, 9, 214

economic adjustment, 321–324
economies
  scale and scope, of, 422, 430, 435
efficiency
  driver of evolution, as, 5
  dynamic, 373
  economic, 212, 218, 255, 263–264, 453
  markets, 145, 157, 158
  need for, 2
electricity industry
  Argentina, 257, 259, 262, 264, 265, 266, 268
  blackouts, 258, 260–261, 267

Brazil, 257, 258, 262, 264, 265, 266, 267
Chile, 256, 259, 261, 263, 264
competition, 174, 175, 191
contract negotiations, 178–179
creation, market, 189
departmental concerns, 184, 186
development, 169–175, 191
first contract package, 179–184
fossil fuel suppliers, 416–418
franchising, 186
goals of reform, 189
implementation, market, 176–178
market power, 416, 419–420
modified proposal, 187–188
neoliberal reform, 260–263
New Zealand wholesale market, 394–395
options, 171, 182, 186
privatization, 167–168, 171, 192, 193, 197
problems, contract, 183
profit-maximizing behavior, 407–415
public provision, 258
retail market background, 166, 169
structure, new, 175
studies, 392
timeline of market creation, 196–199
timetable, 192–193
Unified Pool proposal, 182
utility deal, 191
vertical integration, 194
White Paper, 173–175, 190
wholesale market, 393
entrepreneurial activities, 86
equilibrium, 273
  aviation, 276
  market, 20, 315
  models, 390
  punctuated, 254
  shift, 21, 27, 35, 36
  social innovation, 455
  stable, 7
  subgame perfect, 273, 285
European competition policy
  competences, 207
  convergence, 201, 213, 218
  coordination rules, 209–211, 218
  costs, 214, 217
  decentralization, 203–207
  design, 200, 202, 203, 216, 217

European competition policy (*cont.*)
  Electronic Communications
    sector, 213
  enforcement, 200, 201, 203
  framework, 213
  horizontal competences, 208, 217
  informal coordination, 212
  law enforcement and regulation,
    interplay, 212–217, 218
  multilevel system, as, 205–207
  objective functions, 205
  private enforcment, 208
  public and private, 207–212, 218
  vertical competences, 200, 202,
    206, 217
exchange rates, 299, 302, 321
  fixed, 327, 331
exchanges, 21
  agents, 435
  anonymous, 162, 164, 441
  characteristics, 440
  committees, 433
  commodity, 18–30, 31, 35, 149,
    424, 449
  control over clearing and
    settlement, 439
  difficulties, 427
  economics, 357, 421
  efficiency, 145, 422, 423–427, 431
  electronic trading, 433–435
  enforcement, 425
  floor-based, 428, 429
  foreign market, 328
  futures, 18
  governance, 430, 448
  grain regulation, 425
  impersonal, *see* impersonal
    exchanges
  information, 425
  mechanisms, 455
  mediation, 425
  network effects, 431
  open outcry, 432, 434
  organization, 3, 422, 429, 430,
    435–439
  ownership, 431
  proportionality, 426
  roles, 439
  sequential, *see* sequential exchanges
  services, 432
  single, 64, 66
  stock, 291, 450
  structures, 69
  trading, 427–430
  vertically integrated, 438
execution function activities, 429
experts, 75, 77, 357
external consultants, 244–246

favoritism, *see* corruption
financial crisis, 253, 255, 267,
    334, 343
  first, 312
  market building, 459
  market recovery, 296
  regulation, 345
  risk, and, 350
  systemic risk, and, *see* systemic risk
first possession, 87–89
  efficiency, 88, 89
  implementability, 463–464
franchises, 95
  bidding, 122, 123
  customer, 189
  monopoly, 184, 191, 195

Geographical Indicators, 47–49
governance
  alignment principle, 51
  architectures, 448–449
  Coasean bargaining, 445
  contractual, 436
  dimensions, 444–445
  exchanges, 422, 430–431
  limits, 461
  make or buy problem, 39
  multilevel, 199
  public authority, 451
  reflexive, 444
  regimes, 445–447, 456
  regulators, and, 227
  structures, 39, 51, 56, 421, 422, 423,
    432, 433, 434, 440
  systems, 227
grandfathering, *see* first possession
guarantees, 63
  personal, 63, 66

hierarchy of norms, 4, 147
hyperinflation, 259, 316, 332
  rates, accelerating, 323
  uncontrolled, 318, 328

Index

impersonal exchanges, 441, 444
 benefits, 461
 delay, 75
 demand, 61
 extension, 443
 importance, 161
 nature of, 62–64
 rule-based impersonal, 447–448
 sustaining, 13, 163
impersonalization, 444–445
incentives, 31
 buyer, 377
 electricity industry, 416–418
 exchanges, 430
 information advantages, 42
 innovation, 374, 377, 382, 387
 investment, 372, 373, 378, 386, 387
 mandatory dealing, 374, 376
 market power, 396–407
 opportunistic behavior, 69
 relational, 46
 rent-seeking behavior, 422
 structures, 422
 vertical integration, 436
industrial organization, 38, 41, 52, 230
 cognitive shifts, and, 282
 empirical approach, 391
 legislatures, 433
information
 adapting, 231
 asymmetry, 17, 18, 40, 55, 58–60, 64–70, 75, 203, 241, 251
 incomplete, 214, 293
 labeling, 57
 partial, 31, 32
 structure, 61
 trading differences, 433
institutional change, 35
 dynamics, 163
 endogenous, 30–34
 inspection to grading, 27–30
 markets, impact on, 34–35
 measurement system, 35
 public/private, 42–43
 rationality, 287
 theory, 20
instruments, 19, 20, 232, 322, 466
 bureaucratic, 232
 derivatives, 346, 428
 diversification, 430
 exchanges, and, 439

 financial, 293
 hedging, 427
 manipulating, 357
 payments, of, 319
 quality, assessing, 26
 securities, 428
 substitution, 57
 trading, 427–430, 439
insurance, 13, 45, 249, 250, 312
 deposit schemes, 334
 political risk, 249, 250, 251
 premiums, 249
intellectual property, 50, 355, 359, 360, 365, 468
 antitrust, 370
 case law, 370
 economic rationale, 371–378
 exclusivity, 377
 innovation, 377
 investments, 376
 judicial approach, 367, 368
 protections, 375
 quality reforms, 380
 refusal to deal, 360, 364, 366, 369, 378–381
 statutory basis, 370–371
 validity concerns, 378–381
interest groups, 96, 146, 232, 255
 conflict, 357
 dynamics, 255
 economic consequences, 254
 pressures, 253
 theory, 232
interindividual adjustments, 444–445
international activities, 34
International Organization for Standardization (ISO), 46
international trade, 35, 296
 disputes, 31
investment, 4
 allocation, and, 86
 anti-trust liability, 371–374
 banking, 343, 345
 electricity, 255–264
 first-possession, 85–88
 future, 248
 innovation, and, 361
 institutional, 322
 intellectual property, 376–378
 politicizing, 258, 259, 260
 stranded, 175, 176, 178

investment (*cont.*)
  sunk, 249
  upstream, 362

judicial decisions
  conditions, and, 70, 71
  consent, 68
  effect, 65
  evidence, 66
  real property, 69
  sequential exchanges, 65–66

key performance indicators, 242–244

leadership, 150, 170, 244, 335, 459
legal uncertainty, 204, 205, 215–217
liberalization, 457, 458
liquidity management, 429
  asset pools, 341
  restraints, 339
  risk, 340, 345
  tools, 335
lotteries, 89, 298

mandatory dealing
  barriers, 375
  concerns, 374
  consequences, 369
  deterrence, 373
  effects, 372, 388
  exception, as, 378
  investment, 373
  minimum conditions, 377
  presumption against, 371, 376
markets
  aviation, *see* aviation, transatlantic
  certification, for, 46
  commonalities, 291
  complexity, 3
  components, 448
  constructs, as, 3
  contractualization, 445–447
  credit, 336, 340
  demand, 390–391
  derivatives, 340, 439, 440
  designing, 1–2, 442–443
  economy, 2, 16, 331, 469
    coordination hazards, 37
  efficiency, *see* efficiency
  electricity, *see* electricity industry
  electronic communications, 213
  failures, 1, 2, 359, 465
  free, 253, 421, 457
  homogenization, 292
  human action, 3–5
  innovation, and, 374
  intermediation, 445–447
  liberalization, 226, 443–444
  manufactured devices, as, 2–9
  mechanics of, 6–7
  natural history, 315
  performing, 1, 355, 441–442
  policy tool, as, 1
  prices, 396–407
  reorganization, 452
  retail, 169, 190, 195, 196
  securities, 296, 298, 314, 424, 439, 440
  structure, 374
  variety, and, 35
measurement
  application, 13
  branch, 39
  costs, *see* transaction costs
  institutions, 13
  practices, 19, 24
  private, 45–47
  problem, fundamental, 17–19
  standards, 14, 15, 19, 20, 25, 41
  substitution effect, 49
  units, 19
measurement systems
  analyzing, 19–21
  dynamic, 36
  elements, 19–20
  problem solving, 18
  significance, 17
mensuration activities, 20
metrological activities, 20
models, economic, 391
modern economics, 2
money
  account, unit of, 318, 319–321, 324–326, 330
  action, in, 318
  anchoring, 324–326
  bimonetary constitution, 328
  capital losses, 330
  charter, as, 316
  commodity, as, 315

Index

crisis, 319
currency, 331
disintegration, 328
dollarization, 317, 322, 331
effectiveness, 316
effects, 332
emergence, 315
exchange, medium of, 315
functions, 319–321
hypostasis of, 316
indexation, 322, 325
national, 318, 322, 324, 326, 329, 331
order, 292, 317, 318, 319, 324
order, monetary, 318
path-dependency, 324
payment, 318–321, 323
payment, unit of, 318, 319–321, 324–326, 330
pesification, 328–330
reconstruction, 326–330
reform, 325, 330–332, 350
renationalization, 325
stabilization, 317, 318, 323–326, 331
substitutes, 322
monopolies
exchange trading, 422
innovation, 388
natural, 123, 175, 357, 429, 430, 436, 437, 438
power, 374–376, 386, 457
price, 435
regulated, 462
rent, 431
rights, 297
rule of reason, 362
statutory, 169, 189
trade, 306
unilateral refusal, 366
multi-marginalization, 436

negotiation
third parties, 356
New Institutional Economics (NIE), 37, 39

objectivization, 444–445
characteristics, 7
exchange, of, 13, 14, 457

rights, of, 16
oligopolistic industries, 391
open access
auctions, 83, 101
conditions, 88
consequences, 86
foreign investors, 296
losses, 82, 91, 102
markets, 151, 164
rents, 92
resources, 83
support, 160

patents, 377
costs, 380
granting system, 378
invalid, 378, 379, 380, 381
obtaining, 378
protections, 381
validity, 379
policy, and
cycles, 254–255, 269
economic safeguards, 372
efficiency, 292
electricity industry, 195, 255
macro-prudential, 334, 335–341, 351
micro-prudential, 334, 335, 341–347
patches, 254, 266
pressures, 254
private investors, and, 270
rationality, and, 449
political economy, 2, 96, 149, 155, 156, 230
literature, 232
politics
actors' preferences, 273
authority, 294
cycles, 226, 460
failures, 1
games, 2, 274, 287, 453
limit pricing, 283
nested games, 274
positive theory, 230, 232
pricing, 258–260
strategies, 452–454
prices
competitiveness, 322
independent setting, 435

prices (*cont.*)
  margin squeeze cases, 216
  market-clearing, 390–394,
    398–407, 416
  relative, 321–324
  retail, 195, 374
  wholesale, 195, 405, 414
principal, 58
  agent, delegation to, 67
  owner, 65
  rules, choice of, 60
  specialization, 59
  substitute, 428
  third parties, 59, 60
private goods, 6
  measurement standards, 19
  preferences, 96
privatization
  allocation/distribution of property rights, *see* allocation/distribution
  benefits, 146
  bias, 463
  contracts, 248
  electricity, *see* electricity industry
  government-owned companies, 248
  reform, 260–264
pro-competition reform
  liberalization, 203, 226, 288, 460–462
procurement
  activities, 127, 128
  buyers, 124–125, 128
  competition, 125, 131–133
  competitive tendering, 121
  complexity, 125–126, 133–137
  contracts, 121, 137–141
  efficiency, 243
  negotiations, 122
  procedures, 128
  public buyer's expertise, 129–131
  regulation, and, 233
  rules, 120
  work contracts, 127–128
production factors, 40, 103, 105
products
  attributes, 41–42, 50, 52
  composition, 17, 18, 26, 29, 333
  condition, 18
  credence, 52
  experience, 52
  functionality, 18
  information, 17
  labeling, 43
  measurement of attributes, 41
  regulation, 48
  responsibility, 43
  search, 52
  segmentation, 31, 32
profit-maximizing behavior
  expected, 392–394, 395–407
  implications, 390, 419
  incentives, and, 407–415
property rights, 7, 83, 85, 88, 101
  allocation/distribution,
    see allocation/distribution
  cap, 82, 85
  contract, and, 75
  damaging, 73
  definition, 37, 158, 446
  distribution, 464
  established, 13
  incomplete, 82
  transferring, 76
property theory, 61
public
  administration, 74, 230, 231, 240
  bureaucracy, 5
  debt, 256, 297, 302, 305–307, 314
  hand failings, 225
  institutionalization, 53
  interest, 205, 284
  interest theory, 232
  intervention, 9, 15, 58, 253, 256, 258
  ordering, 43–45
  private axis, 38, 42
  private partnerships, 242–244
  procurement, *see* procurement
  product definition, 43
  transactions, 225
public contracting
  adjustments, 226
  agents, 233
  authoritarian regimes, 247
  corruption, 225
  efficiency, 251
  governmental opportunism, 249–251
  hazards, 233

Index   521

implications, 249
inefficiency, 229
literature, 230, 232
pricing, 230
private, and, 251
rigidity, 229, 234
small communities, 246
public goods, 1
  activities, 96, 120
  allocation, 464
  attributes, 424
  distribution, 82
  exchange, 446
  measurement units, 19
  preferences, 96
public rulers, 8, 225, 447, 451
publicity, 60, 71
  automatic, 72
  mechanisms, 72
  property rules, 73
  verifiable, 74

quality
  assessing, 21
  assurance, 31, 43, 46, 57
  buyers' perspective, 24–26
  consumers, and, 38
  definition, 13, 37, 41, 52
  enforcement, 47, 54
  FAQ method, 23
  hazards, 45
  manufacturing, 15, 38, 52, 54, 55, 56
  measurements, 21–24, 28, 31
  milling process, 24–26
  private nature, 47
  solutions, 56
  standards, 21, 26

rationality, 3, 5
  agents, 293
  assumption, 272
  bounded, 293, 334, 335
redistribution
  market, 463
  rents, 432, 452, 465
  targeted, 255
  wealth, 329
  windfall profits, 461
reforming markets, 226

regulation, 123
  bank, 333–351
  benevolence, and, 294
  challenges, 465–467
  command and control, 1, 81, 85, 107–111, 291, 359
  competences, 349
  current EU prudential framework, 347
  designing, 56
  electricity, 166–198, 253–271
  European competition, *see* European competition policy
  exploitation, restricting, 372
  lax, 56
  mandatory, 45
  micro-prudential, 334
  money, 316, *see* money
  public, 445–447
  reflexivity, 334
  requirements, 45
  self, 3, 9, 333, 356, 445–447
  systemic risk, 334
  targets, 372
  three-tiered approach for EU, 348
remedies, 213, 293
  antitrust, 214
  compensatory, 208
  mandatory dealing, 378
  overlapping, 209
rent seeking
  activities, 100, 207
rents
  additional, 93
  anticipation, 93
  distribution, 93, 357
  ex ante, 95
  in situ resource, 92
  loss, 95
  maximizing, 86
  resource, 83, 86, 88, 92, 96, 101
  retained, 94
  seeking, 87, 98, 357, 430, 432, 436, 440
  technology, 435
  users, 92
reputation
  capital, investing, 42, 47, 65, 429
  maintaining, 450
  solution, based, 18, 47, 50, 63

rights-based management regimes, 85–101
rule of law, 160, 232, 452–454, 467
rules
　contract, 59, 73
　equal sharing, 89
　exchange, 426, 430, 440
　expectations, 293
　first-possession, 88
　market-enabling, 74
　property, 59, 73
　switching, 61
　transaction cost reducing, 426

self-enforcement, 54, 56
sequential exchanges, 58
　definition, 64
　distributors, and, 67
　employment, in, 68
　information asymmetry, 65
　prevalence of, 66–70
　specialization, 67
　third parties, 64
settlement of transactions, 428, 435–439
signaling process, 233
social hierarchy, 295
social technology
　alternatives, 81, 84, 442, 458
　complex, 2–3, 355
　market exchange, 441, 443
specialization
　advantages, 47, 62, 67, 422, 446
　agents, 4, 60
　exchanges, 62, 448, 450
　floor-based, 428, 430
　heterogeneity, 429
　human capital, 434
　increasing, 165
　international, 27, 35
　productivity, 151, 155
　rents, and, 422
　resources, 16, 70
　sequential exchange, 66
standardization
　commercial contracts, 28
　commodity exchanges, 24
　grading, and, 28–30, 33
　information asymmetry, 18
　law, 16

public, 15, 54
quality, 55
reputation, and, 50
transactions, 447
state, *see* public
　autonomy, 451
　challenges for, 8–9
　market building, 84
　ownership, 258, 261, 276
stock markets, 292, 301
　Amsterdam, 298–300, 314
　Britain, 296
　differences between, 307–314
　emerging, European, 297–298
　France, 302–305
　inflation, and, 306
　London, 300–302, 313
　money, and, 318
　recovery, 311
subgame perfection, 275, 285
systemic risk, 293, 294
　agents, 335
　behavioral underpinnings, 335
　capital, and, 339, 340
　centralization, 348
　dynamics, 335
　methods, 340
　regulation, 334, 346, 351
　spread, 351

taxation, 91, 92, 93
　independence, 297
　politics, and, 98
technology
　analysis of performance, 2
　dependence, 433
　digital, 357
　electronic trading, 433–435
　externalities, 455
　improvements, 30
　industrialization, 296
　innovation, 1
　non-renegotiation commitment, 286
　quality-control, 424
　social, *see* social technology
　trading, 430, 433, 439
third-party opportunism, 141, 230, 233–238, 249, 252, 461
trade
　associations, 32–33

Index 523

costs, and, 423
derivatives, 357
execution, 357, 435, 436, 438
impersonal exchanges, 63
journals, 30, 33
meaning, 13
securities, 357
trademark
  laws, 50, 56
  registration, 48
trade-offs
  costs, 70
  efficiency, 440
  European policy, 201
  flexibility, 230
  welfare, 387
trading
  electronic, 423, 433, 434, 435
transaction costs
  measurement branch, 18, 39, 51, 251, 443, 463
  New Institutional Economics, *see* New Institutional Economics
  theory, 141, 230

uniformity
  allocation, 89
  European competition law, 202, 209
  information, 421, 424
  market power, 408
  pricing rules, 263
  quality, 21, 34
  technology, 236

unilateral refusals, 360, 361, 363
  antitrust, 368
  balancing, 383
  concerns, 361
  damage, 377
  discretion, 368
  doctrine, 362
  effects, 366, 382
  exception, as, 387
  importance, 361–363
  intellectual property, 367
  judicial approach, 362, 381, 383
  legality, 369, 384, 386, 388
  liability, 364, 381
  profit sacrifice, 382
  rule-of-reason approach, 382, 383
  standard, 382
  US cases, 364–367

vertical integration, 18, 43, 47, 394, 422, 435–439
  opportunity cost, 439
  problems, 437
voluntary
  agreement, 21
  contracts, 58
  quality assurance, 46
  standards, 26

Walrasian economy, 38
warranties, 18
  additional, 45
  non-mandatory, 45

Lightning Source UK Ltd.
Milton Keynes UK
UKHW021254291219
356021UK00023B/774/P

FRIEDRICH NIETZSCHE AND THE POLITICS OF HISTORY

Friedrich Nietzsche is now widely recognised as being among the most important and influential European thinkers of the past two centuries. In this major new addition to Ideas in Context, Christian Emden explores Nietzsche's understanding of modern political culture and his position in the history of modern political thought. Professor Emden surveys Nietzsche's entire intellectual career from his years as a student in Bonn and Leipzig during the 1860s to his genealogical project of the 1880s, and challenges current, exclusively philosophical interpretations of Nietzsche's political thought that tend to pay little attention to the complex historical settings within which his ideas gain momentum. Nietzsche's repeated demand for a "historical philosophizing" that connects our understanding of modern political culture to a critical examination of modernity's historical emergence stands at the center of this study, which combines a detailed contextual reading of Nietzsche's writings and notebooks with a philosophical assessment of his political thought. By focusing on the influence that fundamental themes of nineteenth-century intellectual and political culture exerted on the development of his political thinking – from classical scholarship and German historicism to the rise of cultural anthropology, the growing importance of the life sciences, and the politics of nationalism – Christian Emden argues that Nietzsche's actual position is best understood as an exercise in political realism, which seeks to transcend the traditional idealogical faultlines of modern political culture. By contributing to a more historically informed discussion of Nietzsche's critical response to the political predicaments of modernity, this study also sheds new light on the state of historical and political culture in Germany at a time when the ideals of the Enlightenment gave way to the demands of the modern nation state.

CHRISTIAN J. EMDEN is Associate Professor of German Studies at Rice University.

IDEAS IN CONTEXT 88

Friedrich Nietzsche and the Politics of History

IDEAS IN CONTEXT

Edited by
Quentin Skinner and James Tully

The books in this series will discuss the emergence of intellectual traditions and of related new disciplines. The procedures, aims and vocabularies that were generated will be set in the context of the alternatives available within the contemporary frameworks of ideas and institutions. Through detailed studies of the evolution of such traditions, and their modification by different audiences, it is hoped that a new picture will form of the development of ideas in their concrete contexts. By this means, artificial distinctions between the history of philosophy, of the various sciences, of society and politics, and of literature may be seen to dissolve.

The series is published with the support of the Exxon Foundation.

A list of books in the series will be found at the end of the volume.

FRIEDRICH NIETZSCHE AND THE POLITICS OF HISTORY

CHRISTIAN J. EMDEN
Rice University

CAMBRIDGE UNIVERSITY PRESS
Cambridge, New York, Melbourne, Madrid, Cape Town, Singapore,
São Paulo, Delhi, Dubai, Tokyo, Mexico City

Cambridge University Press
The Edinburgh Building, Cambridge CB2 8RU, UK

Published in the United States of America by Cambridge University Press, New York

www.cambridge.org
Information on this title: www.cambridge.org/9780521155076

© Christian J. Emden 2008

This publication is in copyright. Subject to statutory exception
and to the provisions of relevant collective licensing agreements,
no reproduction of any part may take place without the written
permission of Cambridge University Press.

First published 2008
First paperback edition 2010

A catalogue record for this publication is available from the British Library

Library of Congress Cataloguing in Publication Data

Emden, Christian.
Friedrich Nietzsche and the politics of history / Christian J. Emden.
p. cm. – (Ideas in context ; no. 88)
Includes bibliographical references and index.
ISBN 978-0-521-88056-5 (hardback : alk. paper)
1. Nietzsche, Friedrich Wilhelm, 1844–1900. 2. Political science–Germany–
History–19th century. 3. Political science–Philosophy.
4. Political culture. I. Title. II. Series.
JC233.N52E53 2008
320.01–dc22
2008003908

ISBN 978-0-521-88056-5 Hardback
ISBN 978-0-521-15507-6 Paperback

Cambridge University Press has no responsibility for the persistence or
accuracy of URLs for external or third-party internet websites referred to in
this publication, and does not guarantee that any content on such websites is,
or will remain, accurate or appropriate.

It is impossible to understand the present without knowing the past, and, to compare them with each other, one would need more time and fewer distractions.
Johann Wolfgang von Goethe
Italienische Reise (January 25, 1787)

I go along the new streets of our cities and think how, of all these gruesome houses which the generation of public opinion has built for itself, not one will be standing in a hundred years' time, and how the opinions of these house-builders will no doubt by then likewise have collapsed.
Friedrich Nietzsche, *Schopenhauer als Erzieher* (1875)

Contents

Acknowledgments	*page* xi
Abbreviations and translations	xiv

	Introduction	1
1	The failure of neo-humanism	17
	Philologists, liberals, and the nation	20
	The Austro-Prussian War in Leipzig	36
	The demands of history	42
	Toward a cautious materialism	53
	Teleology and the laws of history	64
2	The formation of Imperial Germany, seen from Basel	79
	Intellectual culture in Basel	80
	The practice of cultural history	82
	The need for philosophical education	102
	The "German spirit" and the Franco-Prussian War	112
3	The crisis of historical culture	129
	The crisis of historicism	130
	What is orientation in history?	140
	The political mobilization of myth	150
	"The soul of the antiquarian"	156
	The impossible critical historian	163
4	Political lessons from cultural anthropology	174
	The view from outside	175
	Lessons from anthropology	181
	Metaphor, myth, and cultural reality	190
	"Survivals" – religion and the nation state	199
	Political realism and the "Free spirit"	216
5	Genealogy, naturalism, and the political	229
	The path to genealogy	230

	A natural history of moral communities	237
	Sovereign individuals and the ethic of responsibility	248
	The task of genealogy	260
	"To translate humanity back into nature"	269
6	The idea of Europe and the limits of genealogy	286
	"The creation of the European individual"	287
	Beyond the modern nation state	299
	Political realities in Imperial Germany	308
	Modernity and the limits of genealogy	316

Bibliography 324
Index 366

Acknowledgments

This book is much longer than I originally thought it should be. While it started out as an article, a short addendum to my *Nietzsche on Language, Consciousness, and the Body* (2005), since I felt that I had not paid enough attention to the historical strategies Nietzsche employed throughout his writings, it quickly grew into a much larger project. One of the reasons for this was the prominent role Nietzsche's intellectual and political environment played for both his historical thought and his understanding of the political. In short, the topic of this book is Nietzsche's response to the historical and political culture of Europe in the age of the modern nation state. As such, it seeks to fill a notable gap in recent, and not so recent, scholarship and seeks to situate Nietzsche firmly in the history of modern political thought.

From the initial stages of this project I was privileged to receive support from many sources. As a Fellow at Sidney Sussex College, Cambridge, I was able to rely on the College's generous support for research in Germany, and I also have to thank the Trustees of the Tiarks Fund at Cambridge University's Department of German. At Rice University three President's Faculty Research Awards made the completion of this book much easier than anticipated and facilitated, among other things, a crucial trip to the Niedersächsische Staats- und Universitätsbibliothek Göttingen, Germany.

Work in an area such as intellectual history is possible only because of the hard work of librarians, locating and making available even the most obscure sources. I wish to express my gratitude, once again, to the enormously helpful staff at the university libraries in Cambridge, Konstanz, Göttingen, and Basel, at Harvard, Rice, and at the Goethe-und-Schiller Archiv in Weimar, Germany. In the final stages of this project, Anna

Shparberg at Rice's Fondren Library jumped over every administrative hurdle to make available publications in German intellectual history more quickly than any university library could normally do.

The final version of this book owes much to discussions with friends, teachers and colleagues, whose personal encouragement, intellectual example, and wit contributed a great deal to the completion of this book. For many critical interventions, surprising hints and uncomfortable questions, I am grateful to Aleida Assmann, Nicholas Boyle, Thomas Brobjer, Peter Burke, Peter C. Caldwell, Steven Crowell, John Flower, Ulrich Gaier, Duncan Large, Anthony LaVopa, David Midgley, David Mikics, Gregory Moore, Hugh Barr Nisbet, David Owen, Gabriele Rippl, Richard Schacht, Quentin Skinner, Uwe Steiner, James Tully, Sarah Westphal, Joachim Whaley, Harvey Yunis, John H. Zammito, and Rachel Zuckert. The argument has also benefited from passing conversations with Maudemarie Clark, Jean Grondin, Paul Michael Lützeler, John Richardson, and Dermot Moran, which took place at conferences or during guest lectures.

Most importantly, though, Steven Crowell, David Mikics, David Owen, and James Tully have been extraordinarily generous in reading, dissecting and commenting upon several drafts; their keen attention to detail has forced me to readdress central issues and prevented several mistakes that would have otherwise gone unnoticed. Also, I would like to express my gratitude to the two anonymous reviewers for Cambridge University Press, whose criticisms and suggestions were of considerable help, and to my enormously patient editor, Richard Fisher, who had to wait for several months until all revisions were completed. Finally, I have to thank Jodie Barnes, Rosanna Christian and Sue Dickinson, my copyeditor, for guiding me through the entire production process.

The Master and Fellows of Sidney Sussex College, Cambridge provided the ideal environment for finishing an early draft of this book, as did the Department of German at the University of Cambridge. The congenial atmosphere at Rice University, especially the debates in the History of Philosophy Workshop at the Center for the Study of Cultures, now the Humanities Research Center, allowed me to learn much from neighboring disciplines and sharpened my understanding of issues I might have simply overlooked. Likewise, I have profited greatly from discussions with colleagues in the research group Cultural History & Literary Imagination at Cambridge, some of which took place within the context of a two-year collaboration between Rice and Cambridge on "Changing Perceptions of the Public Sphere." In an increasingly specialized academic environment it is all too rare to be able to exchange ideas with colleagues from other fields, and many of these exchanges – often over lunch or dinner – have made academic life more bearable and the argument of this book, I hope, more lucid.

Portions of this book have been presented on different occasions at the University of Cambridge, England, at the University of Glasgow in Scotland, at the University of Sussex in Brighton, England, and at the Annual Conference of the German Studies Association in Pittsburgh, USA. I am grateful to the audiences, whose critical questions forced me to rethink central arguments. Some of the themes I could only touch upon in Chapter 1 are discussed in more detail in "Learning How to Read: Nietzsche in Leipzig," *Oxford German Studies* 35 (2006), 97–110. An abridged version of Chapter 3 has been published as "Toward a Critical Historicism: History and Politics in Nietzsche's Second *Untimely Meditation*," *Modern Intellectual History* 3 (2006), 1–31, and parts of Chapter 6 have been published as "The Uneasy European: Nietzsche, Nationalism and the Idea of Europe," *Journal of European Studies* 38/1 (2008), 27–51. I am grate-ful to the editors for their permission to reuse and reshape this material.

Over the last years my students at Cambridge and Rice had to listen to what must have seemed to them a variety of obscurities about German and European intellectual history, which they often forced me to clarify. A seminar on German nationalism and another seminar on Nietzsche, the latter of which I had the pleasure of co-teaching with Steven Crowell, left them sufficiently bewildered. I hope they continue to have patience with my digressions.

As always, this book is for Carla, a proper *Wissenschaftlerin*, who has tolerated, often with her eyes rolling, the many late nights it took to turn a wild draft into a readable book. Without her smile, patience and intelligence it would not have seen the light of day. But it is also for my parents, who have made these intellectual travels possible.

Houston, USA
Winter 2007/8

Abbreviations and translations

Friedrich Nietzsche's writings and notes are quoted according to the following abbreviations:

AC *The Anti-Christ*, in *"Twilight of the Idols" and "The Anti-Christ,"* trans. R. J. Hollingdale (Harmondsworth: Penguin, 1968), pp. 113–87. Quoted according to section.

BAW *Werke und Briefe: Historisch-Kritische Gesamtausgabe*, ed. Hans Joachim Mette (Munich: C. H. Beck, 1933–40). Quoted according to volume and page number.

BGE *Beyond Good and Evil*, trans. Judith Norman, ed. Rolf-Peter Horstmann and Judith Norman (Cambridge: Cambridge University Press, 2002). Quoted according to section.

BT *The Birth of Tragedy*, in *The Birth of Tragedy and Other Writings*, trans. Ronald Speirs, ed. Raymond Geuss and Ronald Speirs (Cambridge: Cambridge University Press, 1999), pp. 1–116. Quoted according to page number.

D *Daybreak: Thoughts on the Prejudices of Morality*, trans. R. J. Hollingdale, ed. Maudemarie Clark and Brian Leiter (Cambridge: Cambridge University Press, 1997). Quoted according to section.

EH *Ecce Homo*, trans. Walter Kaufmann (New York: Vintage Books, 1989). Quoted according to part and section.

GM *On the Genealogy of Morality*, trans. Carol Diethe, ed. Keith Ansell-Pearson (Cambridge: Cambridge University Press, 1994). Quoted according to essay and section.

GS *The Gay Science*, trans. Josefine Nauckhoff, ed. Bernard Williams (Cambridge: Cambridge University Press, 2001). Quoted according to section.

GSA	Unpublished Notes in the Goethe- und Schiller-Archiv, Weimar, Germany. Followed by signature and page reference.
HA	*Human, All Too Human*, trans. R. J. Hollingdale, intro. Richard Schacht (Cambridge: Cambridge University Press, 1996). Quoted according to volume, part and section, except for vol. 1 which has no parts.
KGB	*Briefwechsel: Kritische Gesamtausgabe*, ed. Giorgio Colli and Mazzino Montinari (Berlin: Walter de Gruyter, 1975–). Quoted according to volume and page reference.
KGW	*Werke: Kritische Gesamtausgabe*, founded by Giorgio Colli and Mazzino Montinari, ed. Volker Gerhardt, Norbert Miller, Wolfgang Müller-Lauter, and Karl Pestalozzi (Berlin: Walter de Gruyter, 1967–). The *Philologica* are quoted according to volume and page number. The *Nachlaß* is quoted according to volume and fragment number.
TGS	*The Greek State* in *On the Genealogy of Morality*, trans. Carol Diethe, ed. Keith Ansell-Pearson (Cambridge: Cambridge University Press, 1994), pp. 176–86. Quoted according to page number.
TI	*Twilight of the Idols*, in *"Twilight of the Idols" and "The Anti-Christ,"* trans. R. J. Hollingdale (Harmondsworth: Penguin, 1968), pp. 19–122. Quoted according to part and section.
TL	*On Truth and Lying in a Non-Moral Sense*, in *The Birth of Tragedy and Other Writings*, trans. Ronald Speirs, ed. Raymond Geuss and Ronald Speirs (Cambridge: Cambridge University Press, 1999), pp. 139–153. Quoted according to page number.
UM	*Untimely Meditations*, trans. R. J. Hollingdale, ed. Daniel Breazeale (Cambridge: Cambridge University Press, 1997). Quoted according to part and section.
Z	*Thus Spoke Zarathustra: A Book for Everyone and Nobody*, trans. and ed. Graham Parkes (Oxford: Oxford University Press, 2005). Quoted according to part and section.

All translations from Nietzsche's *Philologica*, correspondence, and *Nachlaß* are my own, although other translations have been consulted whenever possible.

As a general rule, I have simply referred to, or quoted from, standard English translations of any given source when they were available. In some cases, I have also referred to sources in their original language, for instance, when it was necessary to clarify a particular passage. On a very few occasions I have quoted from the original source even though an English translation is available. I have done so for three reasons: either the text was translated only partially, the translation was seriously out of date, or I found the translation to be somewhat misleading. When no English translations are available, I have quoted from standard editions in the original language. All translations, unless otherwise noted, are my own.

For reasons of consistency, all titles in a language other than English have been left in the original. This includes all references to Nietzsche's writings.

Introduction

This is a study in intellectual history and, more precisely, the history of modern political thought. It examines the link between history and politics in the writings of the German philosopher Friedrich Nietzsche. Its goal is to assess the role that historical thought, and his notion of "historical philosophizing," play in his understanding of modern political culture. As much as this is reasonably possible, it seeks to cover his entire intellectual career from his years as a student in Bonn and Leipzig during the 1860s to his genealogical project of the 1880s. Part of my effort in this book is to shed light on the state of historical and political culture in Germany at a time when the neo-humanist and cosmopolitan ideals of the Enlightenment gave way to the demands of the modern nation state. In following this line of inquiry, which sets this study somewhat apart from recent more philosophical scholarship on Nietzsche, I hope to contribute to a more historically informed discussion of his critical response to the historical and political predicaments of the nineteenth century and, more generally, modern political culture.

Given that the political is a central aspect of Nietzsche's work, it is not surprising that much recent philosophical scholarship sought to address the value of his critique of morality and to draw lessons from this critique with regard to both the possibilities and the limits of liberalism. At the same time, there is little agreement about the actual orientation of Nietzsche's political thought. Daniel Conway, for instance, has suggested that Nietzsche "wishes to return to the very ground of politics itself, to excavate the site of politics, and to retrieve the founding question of politics." While Conway's interpretation does not necessarily follow the principles of philosophical liberalism in the narrow sense of the term, his conclusion that Nietzsche ultimately delivers a "philosophy of resistance," which is continued in the work of Michel Foucault, is based on accepting the pluralist orientation of Nietzsche's political thought.[1] Mark Warren has likewise argued for taking the latter seriously as a "preface to critical, postmodern political theory," which would include "the values of individuation, communal intersubjectivity, egalitarianism, and pluralism."[2] Most recently, Bernard Reginster suggested that Nietzsche's interest in the will to power does not exclude a developed understanding of benevolence.[3]

Other commentators, however, have sought to highlight the ways in which Nietzsche's political ideas center on the limits of liberalism. For Bruce Detwiler, Ofelia Schutte and Richard Wolin, Nietzsche remains a reactionary political thinker with authoritarian desires and direct spiritual affinities to fascism.[4] In a more balanced account, Fredrick Appel contends that at the heart of Nietzsche's thought lies "an uncompromising repudiation of both the ethic of benevolence and the notion of the equality of persons in the name of a radically aristocratic commitment to human excellence." Although critical of Nietzsche's conclusions, Appel portrays his political thought as "genuinely torn between two competing ideals: a stoic notion of autarchy and an Aristotelian sense of our dependence on the right sort of company for the fullest cultivation of our virtue."[5] This assessment is in many ways echoed by Don Dombowsky's recent study on Nietzsche's proximity to Machiavelli, which argues that an "aristocratic liberal critique of democratic society lies at the heart of his political philosophy."[6]

---

[1] Daniel W. Conway, *Nietzsche and the Political* (London: Routledge, 1997), pp. 2 and 141–2.
[2] Mark Warren, *Nietzsche and Political Thought* (Cambridge, Mass.: MIT Press, 1988), pp. 12 and 247.
[3] See Bernard Reginster, *The Affirmation of Life: Nietzsche on Overcoming Nihilism* (Cambridge, Mass.: Harvard University Press, 2006), pp. 148–200 and 228–68.
[4] See Bruce Detwiler, *Nietzsche and the Politics of Aristocratic Radicalism* (Chicago: University of Chicago Press, 1990), pp. 4–5; Ofelia Schutte, *Beyond Nihilism: Nietzsche without Masks* (Chicago: Chicago University Press, 1985), p. 161; Richard Wolin, *The Seduction of Unreason: The Intellectual Romance with Fascism from Nietzsche to Postmodernism* (Princeton, N.J.: Princeton University Press, 2004), pp. 28–30 and 54–8. While Schutte and Wolin present a literal reading with little contextualization and attention to the complexity of Nietzsche's political thought, only Detwiler's argument is philosophically convincing.
[5] Fredrick Appel, *Nietzsche contra Democracy* (Ithaca, N.Y.: Cornell University Press, 1999), pp. 2 and 13.
[6] Don Dombowsky, *Nietzsche's Machiavellian Politics* (New York: Palgrave Macmillan, 2004), pp. 3–4.

Much of the disagreement about the actual orientation of Nietzsche's political ideas is a result of the way in which recent political faultlines tend to overshadow the context within which Nietzsche's own ideas developed. It is, indeed, remarkable that his ideas have rarely been situated in their own intellectual and political setting. While there are some exceptions to this trend – such as the studies by Henning Ottmann and Urs Marti, which have largely been ignored in English-speaking scholarship[7] – many recent investigations into Nietzsche's political ideas lack a willingness to take the political culture of nineteenth-century Germany into account. The latter is, however, crucial for Nietzsche's understanding of the political.

Political culture in Germany between the 1850s and 1880s is to a considerable extent marked by the historical identity and self-conception of the emerging nation state. It is precisely in this respect that the importance of historical thought for Nietzsche's philosophical and political criticism should not be underestimated. Surprisingly, Nietzsche's historical thought has rarely been examined in sufficient detail and is primarily treated as a philosophical, or epistemological issue, that comes to the fore in his second "Untimely Meditation," *Vom Nutzen und Nachtheil der Historie für das Leben* (1874) and his genealogical project of the 1880s.[8] What I attempt to show in the following chapters is that Nietzsche's political ideas cannot be really understood properly without linking them to the crucial importance he attached to historical knowledge and to the historical strategies that constitute a central part of his philosophical criticism. As such, it is necessary to address in more detail the intellectual configurations within which his political thought gained momentum. Nietzsche's political orientation

---

[7] See Henning Ottmann, *Philosophie und Politik bei Nietzsche* (Berlin: Walter de Gruyter, 1987), and Urs Marti, *"Der grosse Pöbel- und Sklavenaufstand": Nietzsches Auseinandersetzung mit Revolution und Demokratie* (Stuttgart: J. B. Metzler, 1993).

[8] See, for instance, Ofelia Schutte, "The Place of History in Nietzsche's Thought," in Bernard P. Dauenhauer (ed.), *At the Nexus of Philosophy and History* (Athens, Ga.: University of Georgia Press, 1987), pp. 97–115, and the contributions in Dieter Borchmeyer (ed.), *"Vom Nutzen und Nachteil der Historie für das Leben": Nietzsche und die Erinnerung in der Moderne* (Frankfurt/M.: Suhrkamp, 1996). For notable exceptions, see Aldo Lanfranconi, *Nietzsches historische Philosophie* (Stuttgart: Frommann-Holzboog, 2000), and Thomas H. Brobjer's articles, "Nietzsche's View of the Value of Historical Studies and Methods," *Journal of the History of Ideas* 65 (2004), 301–22, "Nietzsche's Relation to Historical Methods and Nineteenth-Century German Historiography," *History and Theory* 46 (2007), 155–79.

undergoes crucial and at times even radical changes from the early 1860s to the late 1880s. Needless to say, these changes respond to developments in the environment within which his ideas gained momentum.

While the philosophical discussion of Nietzsche has made substantial achievements over the last few decades, on which I will draw throughout this study, the image of Nietzsche among intellectual historians is still surprisingly marked by his presumed aestheticism and his longing for myth as an alternative to modernity and liberalism. Even though Allan Megill, for instance, has emphasized the complexity and ambivalence of Nietzsche's arguments, he concludes that myth and art remain the main foci of the latter's thought.[9] More recently, George S. Williamson has followed this example in a detailed study, which seeks to outline the development of mythical thought in nineteenth-century Germany, examining "the influence of a persistent discourse on myth from the era of early Romanticism (*Frühromantik*) up through the later thought of Friedrich Nietzsche."[10] Nevertheless, his assessment of Nietzsche's position remains highly problematic: Williamson reduces the entire corpus of Nietzsche's writings to an elaborate aestheticist mythology that seeks to counter the negative effects of modernity. Nietzsche, he argues, was mainly interested in "articulating a new sacred narrative" within which myth served "as the necessary condition for cultural life in any future Germany."[11] Along somewhat different lines, Henning Ottmann has suggested that, during the early 1870s, Nietzsche sought to correct the political consciousness of his time with a homogeneous notion of culture that was based on a peculiar mixture of neo-humanist ideals and aestheticist beliefs and that was rooted in an imaginary ancient Greece as opposed to the modern technocratic nation state of the new Imperial Germany.[12] But in contrast to Williamson, Ottman rightly points out that, by the mid-1870s, Nietzsche had adopted a position that came increasingly close to cosmopolitan Enlightenment ideals, thus leaving his earlier aestheticism behind.[13]

---

[9] See Allan Megill, *Prophets of Extremity: Nietzsche, Heidegger, Foucault, Derrida* (Berkeley, Calif.: University of California Press, 1985), p. 30.
[10] George S. Williamson, *The Longing for Myth in Germany: Religion and Aesthetic Culture from Romanticism to Nietzsche* (Chicago: University of Chicago Press, 2004), p. 4.
[11] Ibid., pp. 235 and 275.
[12] See Ottmann, *Philosophie und Politik bei Nietzsche*, pp. 22–42 and 75–99.
[13] See ibid., pp. 99–108.

The popular image of Nietzsche as a myth-maker that still influences much work on nineteenth-century German intellectual history in the English-speaking world remains indebted to a particular reading of German history as a somewhat precarious case within an otherwise liberal and democratic Western world. While there are clearly specific circumstances that influence the formation of the nation state and the rise of nationalism in nineteenth-century Germany, the vision of an essentially illiberal Germany is oddly one-sided.[14] The idea of Germany's *Sonderweg*, or "special path," is suggestive of an autonomy of German history that never existed in the first place and that, like any other national history, was only able to gain currency as a politically motivated fiction.[15] As such, it is more than questionable to assume that Nietzsche's reflections on history and political culture are part of an overall "longing for myth" in German intellectual history which culminates in the political catastrophes of the twentieth century. Taking the link between Nietzsche's historical critique and his response to the political situation of his time seriously will show that he in fact sought to dismantle the imaginary mythical conjectures that characterize nineteenth-century political culture, from the Austro-Prussian War of 1866 via the formation of a German nation state after the Franco-Prussian War of 1870–71 to Imperial Germany as an authoritarian nation state in the 1880s. I will argue that Nietzsche's conception of the political, and his critique of contemporary political culture, are closely related to his demand for "*historical philosophizing*," as he notes in 1878 in the first volume of *Menschliches, Allzumenschliches* (*HA* I: 2). His political thought, in other words, is inextricably linked to historical strategies

---

[14] Nevertheless, as far as the second half of the nineteenth century is concerned, even German historians have insisted on a *Sonderweg* of German history. See Hans-Ulrich Wehler, *Deutsche Gesellschaftsgeschichte, III: Von der "Deutschen Doppelrevolution" bis zum Beginn des Ersten Weltkrieges, 1849–1914* (Munich: C. H. Beck, 1995), and Heinrich August Winkler, *Der lange Weg nach Westen* (Munich: C. H. Beck, 2000). Such interpretations seem mainly interested, however, in delivering a "national history" for a "Berlin Republic" after 1990 as a hard-won teleological process on the road to "normality." See Anselm Doering-Manteuffel, "Eine politische Nationalgeschichte für die Berliner Republik: Überlegungen zu Heinrich August Winklers *Der lange Weg nach Westen*," *Geschichte und Gesellschaft* 27 (2001), 446–62.

[15] See Michael Geyer, "Historical Fictions of Autonomy and the Europeanisation of National History," *Central European History* 22 (1989), 316–42: 341. See also Michael Geyer and Konrad H. Jarausch, *Shattered Past: Reconstructing German Histories* (Princeton, N.J.: Princeton University Press, 2002), pp. 37–59 and 221–43.

that enable him to take stock of the political conditions and foundations of European modernity.

In a thick contextual reading I will argue that one of the most central concerns of Nietzsche's work is a direct response to the crisis of modern German and, ultimately, European historical and political culture. This crisis unfolds in the period between the 1840s and 1900 and thus runs parallel to Nietzsche's intellectual career. Three overlapping developments have contributed to this crisis. It is these developments that furnish the background to this study. First, the neo-humanist ideals that originated in the cosmopolitanism of the Enlightenment, and that were rooted in a specific understanding of the classical tradition around 1800, had to face new political realities in the aftermath of the Napoleonic Wars, which ultimately led to their demise. Second, the formation of Imperial Germany as a modern nation state after the Franco-Prussian War of 1870–71 was deeply connected to the emergence of cultural foundation myths that stabilized the uncertain political identity of the new German nation state, which was still marked by older federal structures as well as regional differences and confessional tensions. The status of nationalism in the political culture of Imperial Germany needs to be viewed against this background. Third, while history was widely seen as being able to provide cultural and political orientation, on a theoretical level the historical disciplines at large had to face the so-called crisis of historicism. Marked by the tension between, on the one hand, the need for causal explanation and teleological models, and on the other, the growing realization that historical knowledge and social experience were irreducibly contingent, the crisis of historicism posed the question of how to think about history and politics under conditions of flux.

While there are many other political and social trends that shape the intellectual and political landscape of nineteenth-century Germany, especially after 1870, it is these three developments that constitute a substantial part of the environment within which Nietzsche's political thought gains momentum. I will develop this argument in six steps that roughly follow Nietzsche's intellectual biography. The first chapter focuses on Nietzsche's educational experience at the universities of Bonn and Leipzig between 1864 and 1869. Nietzsche turns to classical scholarship, one of the most prestigious historical disciplines with a professional ethos like few

Introduction 7

others, at precisely that moment when its neo-humanist ideals were increasingly pushed aside by the new political demands of the modern nation state. It is within this context, I contend, that Nietzsche, in his correspondence and his early notebooks, begins to pay attention to the political constellations of his time, such as the problem of national identity, the Austro-Prussian War, and Bismarck's vision for Prussia's German vocation.

The wider developments at stake in this context are, of course, closely related to the question of Germany's historical identity and political culture.[16] Of course, historical identity is formed within the public realm of political culture.[17] Classical scholarship and neo-humanism were part of this public realm and sought to redefine themselves vis-à-vis the political demands of the emerging nation state.[18] At the same time, a religious version of historical consciousness, which was rooted in German Romanticism and which fell on fertile ground after the Napoleonic Wars, aestheticized political realities into mythical conjectures. Nietzsche responds to precisely this context, which will continue to shape his own interest in the value of historical knowledge for a critical assessment of the foundations of modern political culture.

A crucial concern in Nietzsche's notebooks between 1866 and 1869 is the philosophical status of historical knowledge and the historical method. I wish to suggest that these notebooks in fact constitute a decisive turning point within Nietzsche's intellectual development. On the one hand, they highlight the importance of his practical experience as a student of classical scholarship and lead him to question the foundations of the historical method as it is applied by his teachers and peers. The problem of what it means to think historically, which has a profound influence on his genealogical project of the 1880s, emerges first in the pages of these notebooks. On the other hand, it is in these notebooks that we can

[16] See Georg G. Iggers, *The German Conception of History: The National Tradition of Historical Thought from Herder to the Present*, 2nd, rev. edn. (Middletown, Conn.: Wesleyan University Press, 1983); Bernd Faulenbach, *Ideologie des deutschen Weges: Die deutsche Geschichte in der Historiographie zwischen Kaiserreich und Nationalsozialismus* (Munich: C. H. Beck, 1980); Stefan Berger, *The Search for Normality: National Identity and Historical Consciousness in Germany since 1800* (Oxford: Berghahn, 1997), pp. 1–18.
[17] See John E. Toews, *Becoming Historical: Cultural Reformation and Public Memory in Early Nineteenth-Century Germany* (Cambridge: Cambridge University Press, 2004), pp. 117–206.
[18] See Suzanne L. Marchand, *Down from Olympus: Archaeology and Philhellenism in Germany, 1750–1970* (Princeton, N.J.: Princeton University Press, 1996), pp. 3–74.

observe the formation of Nietzsche's philosophical interests, especially his encounter with the work of Arthur Schopenhauer and Friedrich Albert Lange. It is necessary to point out, however, that these philosophical interests are more ambiguous than commonly assumed and they furthermore influence his understanding of the value of historical knowledge. But it is his reading of Kant, and his interpretation of "teleology," that finally forces Nietzsche to take the problem of historical knowledge seriously.[19] In Kant he finds the philosophical instruments to formulate a critique of the contemporary status of historical knowledge: rejecting the explanatory value of teleological models in history, and German idealism's obsession with the philosophy of history, he needs to address the intellectual value of historical knowledge within modern culture from a different angle. It is within this context that Nietzsche also encounters the political implications of a teleological notion of historical development, including the emancipatory ideals of Enlightenment cosmopolitanism.

Standard accounts of Nietzsche's first years as a professor of classical scholarship at the University of Basel in Switzerland are by and large dominated by the scandal surrounding his first book, *Die Geburt der Tragödie aus dem Geiste der Musik*, published in 1872. The latter is seen as representing Nietzsche's emphasis on art and aesthetics as guiding philosophical paradigms. While these are undoubtedly important issues, in the second chapter I will provide an alternative account of Nietzsche's orientation during the early 1870s, which will focus on the intellectual environment of Basel. In the period between 1869 and 1873, one of Nietzsche's main concerns is the political formation of Imperial Germany as a unified modern nation state and the consequences of this development for the outlook of German political culture. Nietzsche's observation of these developments is predominantly shaped by the lasting presence of neo-humanist ideals in the slightly anti-modern intellectual setting of Basel, represented by Johann Jakob Bachofen and Jacob Burckhardt.[20] Indeed, after his short experience of the

---

[19] On Nietzsche's early reading of Kant, see R. Kevin Hill, *Nietzsche's Critiques: The Kantian Foundations of his Thought* (Oxford: Clarendon Press, 2003), pp. 1–37.

[20] My discussion of this area has profited enormously from Lionel Gossman, *Basel in the Age of Burckhardt: A Study in Unseasonable Ideas* (Chicago: University of Chicago Press, 2000).

Franco-Prussian War, Nietzsche begins to adopt a more critical stance toward the political imagination and the historical foundation myths of Imperial Germany, which even in the early 1870s were still marked by references to the Wars of Liberation against Napoleon as a historical turning point that dominated the cultural politics of a Prussian-led Germany.[21] While his scholarly work, such as the lectures on *Encyclopaedie der klassischen Philologie* (1871), deepened his understanding of the historical method and of history's cultural value, his public lecture series *Ueber die Zukunft unserer Bildungsanstalten* (1872) and his four "Untimely Meditations" (1873–76) increasingly seek to advance a cultural critique of modernity's political conditions. It is in this respect that he conceives of philosophical education as a basis for the critique of modernity, which differs sharply from the aestheticist outlook often attributed to Nietzsche's writings of this period.

The third chapter investigates how this new emphasis on cultural critique through historical awareness shapes Nietzsche's views about the political dimension of historical knowledge, which stand at the center of his second "Untimely Meditation," *Vom Nutzen und Nachtheil der Historie für das Leben*. In this essay he reacts to rather specific developments within the contemporary intellectual context, such as the establishment of historical foundation myths for a new German nation state, exemplified by the public monuments and commemorations of the 1870s, and the effect of such foundation myths on the political imagination of historical scholarship.

My interest in this issue is related to the crisis of historicism that begins to take shape in Germany from the 1840s onward. It is often argued that this crisis only emerges around 1900, that is, once Georg Simmel's *Die Probleme der Geschichtsphilosophie* (1892) and Ernst Troeltsch's *Der Historismus und seine Probleme* (1922) begin to give this crisis a name and once the neo-Kantians Wilhelm Windelband and Heinrich Rickert have separated the historical sciences from other fields of knowledge, most notably the natural sciences.[22]

---

[21] On the Wars of Liberation as a cultural point of reference, see Frank Becker, *Bilder von Krieg und Nation: Die Einigungskriege in der bürgerlichen Öffentlichkeit Deutschlands, 1864–1913* (Munich: Oldenbourg, 2001), pp. 306–21.

[22] See Iggers, *The German Conception of History*, pp. 124 and 128, and Charles R. Bambach, *Heidegger, Dilthey, and the Crisis of Historicism* (Ithaca, N.Y.: Cornell University Press, 1995), p. 22.

It is possible to argue, however, that the much-debated crisis of historicism surfaces already during the 1830s as an intellectual constellation within German Protestant thought.[23] In any event, it is reasonable to assume that the crisis of historicism begins as soon as we can observe a historical turn among disciplines that were traditionally outside the historical profession in the narrow sense of the term.[24] Most importantly, though, the cultural politics of the Prussian state between 1814 and the late 1840s always linked the historicization of knowledge to its political self-definition.[25] As soon as the direct influence of German idealism, especially Hegel and Schelling, began to wane, and as soon as historical consciousness and Protestantism began to define political identity in an attempt to turn a vague notion of "the people" into a modern state, the question about the cultural value and the integrity of historicism came to the fore. It is this complex intellectual constellation that Nietzsche responds to in his second "Untimely Meditation." His own position during the mid-1870s can best be described as a cautious or critical historicism. But the second "Untimely Meditation" is also a transitional piece in that it formulates a set of problems with regard to the cultural relevance of historical knowledge and the political dimension of historical consciousness without really being able to deliver a convincing solution. Nevertheless, this essay is an important step on the way to the genealogical project that gains shape in *Die fröhliche Wissenschaft* (1882/87), *Jenseits von Gut und Böse* (1886), and *Zur Genealogie der Moral* (1887).

Although this has rarely been discussed in sufficient detail, from around 1875 Nietzsche begins to become interested in contemporary cultural anthropology.[26] Given the rise of anthropological thought in Europe and its institutionalization from the middle of the nineteenth century onward, this is not really surprising. Classical scholarship itself often entertained a close

---

[23] See Allan Megill, "Why Was There a Crisis of Historicism?" *History and Theory* 36 (1997), 416–29: 419–29.
[24] See Theodore Ziolkowski, *Clio, the Romantic Muse: Historicizing the Faculties in Germany* (Ithaca, N.Y.: Cornell University Press, 2004), and Peter Fritzsche, *Stranded in the Present: Modern Time and the Melancholy of History* (Cambridge, Mass.: Harvard University Press, 2004).
[25] See Toews, *Becoming Historical*, pp. 19–65.
[26] One of the few exceptions is Andrea Orsucci, *Orient – Okzident: Nietzsches Versuch einer Loslösung vom europäischen Weltbild* (Berlin: Walter de Gruyter, 1996).

relationship to the anthropological debates of the time.[27] In the fourth chapter, I will link Nietzsche's reception of cultural anthropology to his emerging historical strategies of political critique. Examining Nietzsche's anthropological interests in *Menschliches, Allzumenschliches* and his notebooks of the time, I propose that it is in fact these interests, especially the work of Edward Burnett Tylor, that allows him to gain a more independent perspective. Anthropology, in other words, enables him to adopt an artificial outside perspective on European modernity, its cultural mentalities, and political absolutes: Nietzsche, I will show, concludes that, instead of being marked by an increasing disenchantment with reality and the retreat of religion into the private sphere, the cultural conditions of modernity, and of the modern nation state, remain shaped by complex mythical conjectures.

Nietzsche's understanding of the political importance of myth can be seen especially with regard to his account of the relationship between religion and the nation state in *Menschliches, Allzumenschliches* as well as with regard to his clear insight into the dynamics of nineteenth-century German nationalism: in both cases Nietzsche examines the way in which the political identity of the nation state is based on what amounts to a hidden political theology. However, while it is often claimed that Nietzsche rejects the modern state as a whole and that he is particularly critical of democratic political participation, I contend that his position is more complex: the state he rejects is Imperial Germany as an authoritarian nation state. As a consequence, he begins to adopt a position that can be described as a political realism that seeks to understand the limits both of the authoritarian state and of a mass democratic civil society.

Against this background, the fifth chapter seeks to present a new interpretation of Nietzsche's genealogical project. The latter is understood not only as a strategy of philosophical critique as it is presented in *Die fröhliche Wissenschaft* and the first few paragraphs of *Jenseits von Gut und Böse*. Rather, I wish to emphasize from the point of view of the essays in *Zur Genealogie der Moral* that genealogy entails a realist critique of the political that is grounded in a historically oriented philosophical naturalism: genealogy deals with

---

[27] See Renate Schlesier, *Kulte, Mythen und Gelehrte: Anthropologie der Antike seit 1800* (Frankfurt/M.: Fischer Taschenbuch Verlag, 1994).

the natural history of moral norms as well as with that of moral communities, such as the modern state. Nietzsche's naturalism, however, does not rest on substantive claims about morality; he merely seeks to emphasize that the formation of moral values implies a psychology that is closely connected to the body and that therefore cannot be seriously detached from the rest of the natural world.[28] Ethical judgments can become normative not because they are detached from nature, but precisely because they are shaped by an interaction between that which we regard as "natural" and that which we regard as "social."[29] As such, the formation of moral norms is not fundamentally different from the formation of other aspects of human knowledge.[30] Nietzsche, thus, undercuts the traditional dualism of nature and normativity. This also implies, however, that the distinction between historical critique and natural science, as it was formulated in the nineteenth century, begins to break down: because of its naturalist background, Nietzsche clearly envisions genealogy as a scientific enterprise. This does not mean, however, that his naturalism is an exercise in reductionism. It simply implies that, in relation to the rest of nature, human beings, including their moral norms, are not a special case.[31] The political conclusions of genealogy are rooted in this naturalist perspective: the seemingly universal value commitments of moral communities, including the modern nation state, need to be regarded as the outcome of a natural history that genealogy seeks to uncover and trace back to its sites of emergence.

Of course, the claims of the genealogical enterprise also have practical consequences. While genealogy clearly relies on philosophical arguments Nietzsche advances during the 1880s, it is equally concerned with the historical formation of the political.

---

[28] See Bernard Williams, *Truth and Truthfulness: An Essay in Genealogy* (Princeton, N.J.: Princeton University Press, 2002), pp. 22–7.

[29] See Joseph Rouse, *How Scientific Practices Matter: Reclaiming Philosophical Naturalism* (Chicago: University of Chicago Press, 2002), pp. 19 and 180–3.

[30] See Christian J. Emden, *Nietzsche on Language, Consciousness, and the Body* (Urbana, Ill.: University of Illinois Press, 2005), pp. 124–62, and Christoph Cox, *Nietzsche: Naturalism and Interpretation* (Berkeley, Calif.: University of California Press, 1999), pp. 69–106.

[31] See John Richardson, *Nietzsche's New Darwinism* (Oxford: Oxford University Press, 2004), pp. 70–94. Needless to point out, Nietzsche's naturalism is a result of his reception of contemporary biological thought. See Gregory Moore, *Nietzsche, Biology, and Metaphor* (Cambridge: Cambridge University Press, 2002), pp. 21–111.

Indeed, the absolutism of theological and metaphysical notions of morality becomes particularly manifest in the realm of the political – and, for Nietzsche, this means that they become manifest in the political culture of the modern nation state. As I show in the final chapter, genealogy, then, not only deals with the problem of moral values and their evolution but also with the political culture of the nineteenth century, which is often cached in religious terms and moral absolutes. This becomes especially obvious in Nietzsche's observation of political events in Imperial Germany, especially as far as the consolidation of nationalism and the rise of anti-Semitism are concerned. But he also begins to outline an alternative political culture, an imagined European tradition, which stands in sharp contrast to what he perceives to be the political illusions of his time, such as nationalism, socialism, and liberalism. Nevertheless, by allowing Nietzsche to examine the foundations of the political, genealogy also prevents him from formulating a valuable and coherent alternative to what he perceives to be the crisis of modern political culture: as an intellectual experiment, Nietzsche's political realism clearly highlights the fragile and illusory foundations of modern political culture, but in a tragic turn it also shows that it is impossible to break with these illusions, since the latter are the result of long-term historical developments which we are unable to escape.

The argument I have outlined above does not always sit easily with current philosophical interpretations of Nietzsche's thought. While I draw on these interpretations throughout the following chapters, this study seeks to enrich the philosophical debate about Nietzsche with a historical framework that attempts to understand why and how he has opted for genealogy as one of the centerpieces of his philosophical criticism. In a letter to his friend Heinrich Köselitz from July 1887, Nietzsche might have described *Zur Genealogie der Moral* as merely "a small polemical pamphlet," thus downplaying, as is so often the case in his correspondence, his true intentions. But in the same letter he also leaves little doubt about the actual importance of this rather slim volume: it "clearly *shows*" the fundamental "problem" that he sought to approach in his previous publication, *Jenseits von Gut und Böse*, which initially had not sold very well (*KGB* III/5, p. 112). The problem he speaks about, however, is not only his lack of public success, but also his reflections on what he believes to be the philosophers of the future, that is, the "*good Europeans* and free, *very* free spirits," who would be able to overcome the metaphysical dogmatism that had originated with Plato and, subsequently, the Judeo-Christian tradition (*BGE*, preface). Indeed, the essays of *Zur Genealogie der Moral* are characterized by precisely that "critical discipline" which Nietzsche presents in *Jenseits von Gut und Böse* as the most important step toward the second centerpiece of his later philosophical criticism, namely the task of the philosopher "to *create values*" (*BGE* 210 and 211). But the development of genealogy does not take place in a historical and political vacuum. This is particularly significant because, after Nietzsche's untimely mental decline in early 1889, other observers of modernity – most notably Georg Simmel, Max Weber, Karl Mannheim, and Walter Benjamin – followed similar lines of inquiry well into the twentieth century. It is in this sense that Nietzsche's reflections on historical knowledge and political culture are of crucial importance within the development of modern social and political thought.

There are, of course, difficulties any approach to Nietzsche's historical thought has to face. While philosophers have showed limited interest in Nietzsche's historical thought, professional historians – after the "theory wars" of the 1970s and 1980s, which in both the German and Anglo-American context have led to a rediscovery of nineteenth-century historicism – have occasionally sought to come to terms with Nietzsche's uncomfortable views about the uses and disadvantages of history.[32] As such, it is not surprising that Nietzsche should be presented as a quasi-postmodern critic of traditional historicism, who was in search of a "posthistoricist innocence" that is "ahistorical or antihistorical in implication."[33] In contrast, I shall argue that Nietzsche's intellectual world is more complicated than it may seem at first sight, but this will only become clear in a thick contextual reading. This study, then, follows an approach that the historian of science Peter

---

[32] See, for instance, Otto Gerhard Oexle, "Von Nietzsche zu Max Weber: Wertproblem und Objektivitätsforderung der Wissenschaft im Zeichen des Historismus," in *Geschichtswissenschaft im Zeichen des Historismus: Studien zu Problemgeschichten der Moderne* (Göttingen: Vandenhoeck & Ruprecht, 1996), pp. 73–94, and Annette Wittkau, *Historismus: Zur Geschichte des Begriffs und des Problems*, 2nd edn., corr. (Göttingen: Vandenhoeck & Ruprecht, 1994), pp. 45–60.

[33] David D. Roberts, *Nothing But History: Reconstruction and Extremity after Metaphysics* (Berkeley, Calif.: University of California Press, 1995), pp. 58–80, especially 78–9.

Galison described as "at once conceptual *and* contextual."[34] This approach is based on the assumption that, as Joseph Rouse has argued, knowledge "is always shaped by the goods, practices, and projects whose allocation and pursuit are at issue, and by the institutions and social networks that are organized around those pursuits."[35] While Rouse here mainly refers to the methodological problems posed by the cultural study of science, the writing of intellectual history has to face the very same issues. This becomes particularly obvious in the work of Michel Foucault and Quentin Skinner, who have approached this problem from different angles, but who have both emphasized the need for what we might term reflective contextualization – despite the obvious differences in the subject matter that their writings are concerned with.[36] Contextualization, however, always means that it is necessary to accept that contexts themselves are never really stable, which poses serious problems on a practical level. Although intellectual historians might wish for a more complete treatment of their subject, giving a voice to the enormous complexity of the issues at hand, they will necessarily need to economize in order to achieve a description of their subject that is able to link the conceptual and the contextual in a coherent manner. To put it more bluntly, books need to remain readable.

Finally, although this is a study in intellectual history, I hope to show that there is indeed much to be learnt from Nietzsche with regard to the uncertain foundations of the political in our own time. Many of the problems he seeks to come to terms with are as relevant at the beginning of the twenty-first century as they were in the nineteenth century. It is in this respect that the practice of intellectual history has inherently political implications that

---

[34] Peter Galison, "Multiple Constraints, Simultaneous Solutions," *PSA: Proceedings of the Biennial Meeting of the Philosophy of Science Association* (Chicago: University of Chicago Press, 1988), vol. II, pp. 157–63: 162.

[35] Joseph Rouse, "Beyond Epistemic Sovereignty," in Peter Galison and David J. Strump (eds.), *The Disunity of Science: Boundaries, Contexts, and Power* (Stanford, Calif.: Stanford University Press, 1996), pp. 398–416: 413.

[36] See the articles collected in Quentin Skinner, *Visions of Politics, Volume 1: Regarding Method* (Cambridge: Cambridge University Press, 2002), and Michel Foucault, *The Archaeology of Knowledge*, trans. A. M. Sheridan Smith (New York: Pantheon, 1982). The parallels between Skinner and Foucault have already been pointed out by James Tully, "The Pen is a Mighty Sword: Quentin Skinner's Analysis of Politics," in Tully (ed.), *Meaning and Context: Quentin Skinner and His Critics* (Princeton, N.J.: Princeton University Press, 1989), pp. 7–25: 16–17 and 24.

should not be underestimated – regardless of whether we wish to follow the "Cambridge School," the German traditions of *Geistes-* and *Begriffsgeschichte*, Michel Foucault's project of an *archéologie du savoir*, or any other such paradigm. Although I do not wish to go into the necessary details to make such an argument, at least not on this occasion, Quentin Skinner is entirely correct in noting that intellectual history, at the very least, is able to show how our present values and, in Foucault's term, episteme "reflect a series of choices made at different times between different possible worlds." It is precisely this awareness of the *longue durée* of intellectual configurations and their political consequences that can "liberate us from the grip of any one hegemonial account" and that invites us to "ask ourselves what we should think of them."[37] It is not entirely surprising that Skinner himself should refer to a famous passage in the preface of Nietzsche's *Zur Genealogie der Moral* in order to highlight this task of intellectual history: "interpretation," especially the interpretation of history, requires something that is akin to "*rumination*" (*GM*, preface, 8).

[37] Quentin Skinner, *Liberty before Liberalism* (Cambridge: Cambridge University Press, 1997), pp. 116–17.

CHAPTER 1

The failure of neo-humanism

In 1841, the political economist Friedrich List, one of the main architects of the German Customs Union that harmonized trade and tariffs between the German states, cast a critical eye on the export products of several European nations. List – himself a harsh critic of what he believed to be the economic hegemony of the British Empire – quickly realized that the German states were not doing particularly well. Suffering from the effects of British free-trade doctrines the German states were able to offer only a limited range of products to an emerging European market: "children's toys," "wooden clocks" and that most eccentric item on his list – "philological writings." Apart from traditional craftsmanship, there was too much "thinking" going on in Germany.[1]

Whether the young philologist Friedrich Nietzsche, who occasionally attended the lectures of another prominent political economist, Wilhelm Roscher, at the University of Leipzig during the 1860s, was aware of List's acerbic assessment can be doubted. In any case, neither for Nietzsche, born two years before List's untimely death in 1846, nor for most of his educated contemporaries did classical scholarship represent some form of deficiency, economic or otherwise. As a historical discipline philology was regarded as one of the most prestigious fields of research at German universities throughout the nineteenth century. Before Nietzsche was born, philologists such as Friedrich August Wolf, Gottfried Hermann and August Boeckh were able to

---

[1] See Friedrich List, *Das nationale System der politischen Ökonomie: Der internationale Handel, die Handelspolitik und der deutsche Zollverein*, in *Schriften, Reden, Briefe*, ed. Erwin von Beckrath, Karl Goeser, Friedrich Lenz, William Notz, Edgar Salin, and Artur Sommer (Berlin: Hobbing, 1927–35), vol. VI, pp. 171 and 196. On List's economic protectionism, see Keith Tribe, *Strategies of Economic Order: German Economic Discourse, 1750–1950* (Cambridge: Cambridge University Press, 1995), pp. 32–56.

17

re-invent a discipline which had existed since antiquity itself, but which from the Renaissance onward often lacked a coherent theoretical framework, a clear historical perspective and, above all, a systematic practice. All this, it seems, was achieved in roughly ninety years between the 1780s when Wolf began to lecture on *Alterthumswissenschaft* at the University of Halle and the 1870s when philological scholarship itself became an increasingly specialized subject that bore little resemblance to its origins.

The changing political and scientific culture of the nineteenth century left many traces in the self-conception of classical scholarship as a historical discipline. With the waning influence of the grand philosophical systems of German idealism, the historical disciplines as a whole entered a time of intellectual ferment. Vis-à-vis the tremendous success of research in the natural sciences in Germany, especially physics and the life sciences, from the 1840s onward, and against the background of a rapidly changing political landscape, the study of history was clearly in need of new orientation. Considering the self-conception of historical scholars throughout the nineteenth century, this might be surprising. Indeed, much like classical scholarship, German *Geschichtswissenschaft* seems to have reached its height during the 1800s, when historians such as Leopold von Ranke, Theodor Mommsen, Heinrich von Treitschke, Heinrich von Sybel and Johann Gustav Droysen set standards of scholarly method and presentation that were to shape historiography deep into the twentieth century. But the rise of the historical disciplines in nineteenth-century Germany culminated in what is now called the "crisis of historicism." Between the 1840s and 1860s, the first symptoms of this crisis already appeared on the horizon. By the 1870s and 1880s, even Nietzsche could ignore neither the signs of the times, nor their irony: at the very moment the study of history, because of its political and ideological implications as well as its achievements, was considered to be one of the most prestigious fields of study, the foundations of historical knowledge became increasingly problematic.

Despite these developments, the ideological framework of classical scholarship remained rooted in the ideals of Johann Joachim Winckelmann's classicism and Wihelm von Humboldt's neo-humanism. While the work of classical scholars was often marked by increasing specialization, their professional presentation continued to appeal to ideals of totality, seeking to bridge the widening gap that appeared around 1840 between *Bildung* and *Wissenschaft*, between self-cultivation and scientific rationalization.[2] Wolf's *Vorlesungen über die Alterthumswissenschaft*, published posthumously between 1831 and 1839, and Boeckh's highly influential lectures on *Encyklopädie und Methodologie der philologischen Wissenschaften*, delivered at the new University in Berlin from 1810 onward, provided a framework for the rise of a culture of professional authority and generated the formation of highly specialized approaches and sub-disciplines within a relatively short time.[3]

Nietzsche's relationship to his chosen profession was never easy. At the end of April 1866, several months after he had arrived at the University of Leipzig leaving behind him the rather conservative and provincial atmosphere at the University of Bonn in the Rhineland, he did not seem to have been particularly content with his situation. On April 27, he sent a long letter to his friend Hermann Mushacke in Berlin, in which he complained bitterly about academic life in Leipzig and toyed with the idea of transferring to the Prussian capital (*KGB* I/2, p. 129). To a young classical scholar in the 1860s, Berlin would not have been the center of political power it was to become during the 1870s. Rather, the image of Berlin was still steeped in the neo-humanist ideals of Wilhelm von Humboldt, who several decades earlier had assembled a formidable cast of scholars in a new university that – according to Humboldt's own words – was to have a decisive influence on the "intellectual and moral development" in Germany.[4]

Nietzsche certainly never made it to Berlin. His fragmented intellectual and artistic pursuits contributed to the general

---

[2] See Marchand, *Down from Olympus*, pp. 7–35, and Anthony J. LaVopa, "Specialists against Specialization: Hellenism as Professional Ideology in German Classical Studies," in Geoffrey Cocks and Konrad H. Jarausch (eds.), *German Professions, 1800–1950* (New York: Oxford University Press, 1990), pp. 27–45.
[3] See Axel Horstmann, "Die 'Klassische Philologie' zwischen Humanismus und Historismus: Friedrich August Wolf und die Begründung der modernen Altertumswissenschaft," *Berichte zur Wissenschaftsgeschichte* 1 (1978), 51–78, and *Antike Theoria und moderne Wissenschaft: August Boeckhs Konzeption der Philologie* (Frankfurt/M.: Campus, 1992).
[4] See Wilhelm von Humboldt, "Antrag auf Einrichtung der Universität Berlin, Mai 1809," in *Werke*, ed. Andreas Flitner and Klaus Giel (Darmstadt: Wissenschaftliche Buchgesellschaft, 1960–81), vol. IV, pp. 29–37: 30.

impression that he did not exactly resemble the usual student of philology and that his philological studies were relatively inconsequential with regard to the future development of his philosophical thought. As a result, it is easy to underestimate his fervent interest in historical scholarship. In fact, Nietzsche's understanding of the value of history, and his continued emphasis on the importance of historical knowledge for a more critical assessment of modernity's political culture, were very much indebted to the intellectual environment he encountered in Bonn and Leipzig.

PHILOLOGISTS, LIBERALS, AND THE NATION

Nietzsche's philological career began early. Already at the neo-humanist boarding school at Pforta, which he attended from 1858 to 1864, he was exposed to a wide range of topics from Greek and Roman antiquity, which mirrored the educational canon of the time and shaped the highly regimented atmosphere at the school.[5] Founded in 1543, Schulpforta, as it is commonly known, saw itself as serving the interests of the state of Saxony, and since 1815 also those of Prussia, by preparing its pupils for entry into the ranks of the civil service, the Protestant clergy, and higher education. Financially supported by the state, pupils were accepted largely irrespective of their social background, Nietzsche himself coming from rather modest means. As an elite institution with a growing reputation Schulpforta was also the place where some of the main representatives of the German cultural canon received their initial schooling, among them the poets Friedrich Gottlieb Klopstock and Friedrich Schlegel, but also the philosopher Johann Gottlieb Fichte and the historian Leopold von Ranke. Likewise, an impressive cast of prominent classical scholars attended the school at some time in their life, such as Otto Jahn and Ulrich von Wilamowitz-Moellendorff. Classical languages formed the most important part of the curriculum, and despite his rather poor command of English, French and Hebrew, Nietzsche excelled in Greek and particularly in Latin. The library at Schulpforta, filled with seemingly endless rows of books stretching from floor to ceiling, was the ideal starting point for any historian,

---

[5] See Curt Paul Janz, *Friedrich Nietzsche: Eine Biographie* (Munich: Hanser, 1978–79), vol. I, pp. 65–132.

philosopher or philologist. Nietzsche's last essay as a school-boy, "De Theognide Megarensi" (1864), was already a philological piece in its own right and was used in his later paper "Zur Geschichte der Theognideischen Spruchsammlung," which was to be published in the prestigious journal *Rheinisches Museum für Philologie* in 1867.

In 1864, Nietzsche entered the University of Bonn and read theology, some German literature, philosophy, and classical philology. During the fairly short period he spent in the academic center of the Rhineland – itself a decisive period of his intellectual biography – he frequented a variety of different courses from Anton Heinrich Springer's lectures on the history of art and on eighteenth-century literature and Wilhelm Ludwig Krafft's lectures on ecclesiastical history to the extremely influential lectures on politics by the serene but passionate historian Heinrich von Sybel, attended regularly by almost three hundred students. Although the direct influence of these lectures on Nietzsche's further development was relatively limited, and although he did not seem to have taken extensive notes, he nevertheless was attracted by the magisterial authority of his teachers. Krafft, for instance, was not only a well-known expert on the early history of the Christian Church among the Germanic tribes in late antiquity, but he also directed the Protestant theological seminary in Bonn and was a prominent figure in the cultural politics of the Rhineland.[6] Springer, on the other hand, might have been less influential in terms of political authority, but as the author of the highly successful *Handbuch der Kunstgeschichte* (1855) he belonged to the founders of academic art history in Germany.[7]

In contrast to Krafft and Springer, Sybel was probably Nietzsche's most famous teacher in Bonn, although their personal contact remained limited. Nevertheless, in one of his early letters home, Nietzsche singled out Sybel's lectures on politics as particularly impressive (*KGB* 1/2, p. 18). A pupil of Leopold von Ranke and, in 1859, one of the founders of the highly influential *Historische*

---

[6] See Wilhelm Ludwig Krafft, *Die Topographie Jerusalem's, mit Inschriften, Ansichten, Plänen und Karten* (Bonn: König, 1846), and *Die Anfänge der christlichen Kirche bei den germanischen Völkern* (Berlin: Hertz, 1854).

[7] See Anton Heinrich Springer, *Handbuch der Kunstgeschichte: Zum Gebrauche für Künstler und Studierende und als Führer auf der Reise* (Stuttgart: Rieger, 1855).

Zeitschrift, which had a strong commitment to German idealism, Sybel had just published the first volumes of his history of revolutionary Europe, *Geschichte der Revolutionszeit* (1853–68).[8] When Nietzsche attended his lectures, Sybel was already one of the leading members of the so-called *kleindeutsch* or Prussian school of political historiography, which sought to integrate historical scholarship into the political agenda of national liberalism. After all, Sybel was a member of the Prussian chamber of deputies where his national liberalism, also reflected in his lectures on politics in Bonn, was initially opposed to Bismarck's idea of a unified German nation. Argumentative and popular, and clearly catering to a specific political environment, his lectures attracted a large number of students, Nietzsche among them.[9]

Although Nietzsche's intellectual interests in 1864/65 were fairly wide, after a short while he began to concentrate on the history of philosophical thought and on classical scholarship – a combination that was to have a profound impact on his later critique of European modernity and German political culture. On the philosophical side much of his initial knowledge was provided by Karl Schaarschmidt's comprehensive introductory course on the history of philosophical thought, "Allgemeine Geschichte der Philosophie." In these early-morning lectures, Nietzsche was able to gain much-needed guidance through the meandering history of European thought from the pre-Socratics up to Kant and Schopenhauer with occasional references, for instance, to philosophical thought in India.[10] Like Nietzsche, Schaarschmidt had graduated from Schulpforta, and Nietzsche himself had received a favorable reference from his former philology teacher Karl Steinhart intended to facilitate contact with Schaarschmidt, whom he also met socially on several occasions before he actually began

---

[8] See Heinrich von Sybel, *Geschichte der Revolutionszeit* (Düsseldorf: Buddeus, 1853–68). On the *Historische Zeitschrift*, see especially Helen P. Liebel, "Philosophical Idealism in the *Historische Zeitschrift*, 1859–1914," *History and Theory* 3 (1964), 316–30, and Theodor Schieder, "Die deutsche Geschichtswissenschaft im Spiegel der *Historischen Zeitschrift*," *Historische Zeitschrift* 189 (1959), 1–104.

[9] See Hellmut Seier, "Sybels Vorlesung über Politik und die Kontinuität des 'staatsbildenden' Liberalismus," *Historische Zeitschrift* 187 (1959), 90–112.

[10] See Johann Figl, "Nietzsches frühe Begegnung mit dem Denken Indiens: Auf der Grundlage seiner unveröffentlichten Kollegnachschrift aus Philosophiegeschichte," *Nietzsche-Studien* 18 (1989), 455–71.

to attend the latter's lectures in the summer semester of 1865 (*KGB* II/1, pp. 18, 21–2 and 35–6).

Schaarschmidt was undoubtedly more of a second-rate academic philosopher. But through critical editions of Spinoza and Leibniz, he exerted considerable influence on the philosophical curriculum and proceeded to become the main editor of the influential periodical *Philosophische Monatshefte*, criticizing the emerging neo-Kantianism in the German philosophy departments from the mid-1870s onward.[11] His lectures gave Nietzsche a solid grasp of the historical outlines of European philosophy. It was, after all, in Schaarschmidt's lectures that he became more familiar with the European metaphysical tradition, and Schaarschmidt also recommended much secondary material – above all Hegel's *Vorlesungen über die Geschichte der Philosophie* (1816–30) and Albert Schwegler's *Geschichte der Philosophie im Umriß* (1848). Thus, before Nietzsche studied the writings of Schopenhauer and Kant himself, he had already acquired a taste for the analytical sophistication of philosophical argument. This analytical sophistication, as we shall see, was also to inform his increasing skepticism with regard to the status of historical knowledge.

With regard to classical scholarship we are safe in assuming that the main influences on Nietzsche's early philological education were Friedrich Ritschl and Otto Jahn. In November 1864, somewhat overexcited and overwhelmed, Nietzsche remarked:

That men like Ritschl, who gave me a speech on philology and theology, and like Jahn, who, like myself, does philology and music without denigrating either to a mere side issue, exert an enormous influence on me, anybody can imagine who has experienced these heroes of scholarship [*Heroen der Wissenschaft*]. (*KGB* I/2, p. 18)

Nietzsche's "heroes of scholarship" saw themselves as continuing a tradition of neo-humanist ideals, but Humboldt would not have always been pleased about their academic *Realpolitik*.

Ritschl had studied in Leipzig and Halle and held professorial positions in Breslau and Halle before he arrived in Bonn in 1839, where he also became head librarian and, together with his colleague Otto Jahn, director of the archaeological collections.

---

[11] See Karl Schaarschmidt, *Der Entwicklungsgang der neueren Speculation als Einleitung in die Geschichte der Philosophie* (Bonn: Marcus, 1857), and "Vom rechten und vom falschen Kriticismus," *Philosophische Monatshefte* 14 (1878), 1–12.

His conception of classical scholarship was marked by a combination of textual and historical criticism, embedded in precisely the neo-humanist framework of *Bildung* that Wilhelm von Humboldt envisaged for the reform of the Prussian university system in the early 1800s.[12] Beginning with studies on the Greek grammarians, he later turned to the Latin tradition where his scholarly efforts resulted in a seminal edition of Plautus' works and several related monographs.[13] His most lasting and, for Nietzsche, most interesting contribution was, however, his epigraphic research. Ritschl's voluminous *Priscae Latinitatis monumenta epigraphica* (1862–64) was a ground-breaking work with lithographic reproductions of Roman public inscriptions, which opened up a new perspective on the history of the Latin language and in particular on the development of archaic Latin.[14]

For Nietzsche, Ritschl's emphasis on the close relationship between, on the one hand, a study of textual material that focuses on details, and on the other, the cultural history of antiquity as a whole, will prove to be as instrumental as his stress on classical scholarship as a humanist discipline within the increasingly specialized scientific culture of the nineteenth century. After attending his lectures on Plautus (1864–65) and Latin grammar (1865), it is of little surprise that Nietzsche held Ritschl – whose students also included some of the most influential classical scholars of the nineteenth century, such as Georg Curtius, Jacob Bernays, Erwin Rohde, and Hermann Usener – in very high regard. Even in *Ecce Homo*, written in 1888 and published only in 1908, Nietzsche stressed the influence of his former teacher, although it is certainly true that his appreciation of Ritschl was of a slightly hyperbolic nature: Ritschl, he noted, was the "only ingenious scholar" he ever met (*EH* III: 9).

In contrast to his unstinting admiration of Ritschl, Nietzsche's relations with Jahn were of a more ambivalent nature. There is no doubt that, during his time in Bonn, Nietzsche regarded Jahn as an

---

[12] See Rudolf Vierhaus, "Bildung," in Otto Brunner, Werner Conze, and Reinhart Koselleck (eds.), *Geschichtliche Grundbegriffe: Historisches Lexikon zur politischen Sprache in Deutschland* (Stuttgart: Klett-Cotta, 1972–97), vol. I, pp. 508–51.

[13] See, for example, Friedrich Ritschl, *De Oro et Orione commentatio: Specimen historiae criticae grammaticorum Graecorum* (Breslau: Schulze, 1834), and *Neue Plautinische Exkurse: Sprachgeschichtliche Untersuchungen* (Leipzig: Teubner, 1869).

[14] See Friedrich Ritschl, *Priscae Latinitatis monumenta epigraphica, ad archetyporum fidem exemplis lithographis repraesentata* (Berlin: Reimer, 1862–64).

important archaeological scholar and he attended his lecture-course on the history and the methods of classical archaeology, while complaining in a letter to his mother and sister in Naumburg, written in March 1865, about the "colossal" workload of Jahn's seminars (*KGB* 1/2, p. 48).[15] Nevertheless, in *Die Geburt der Tragödie* (1872), he denounced Jahn as a "liar" and "hypocrite" (*BT* 94). But this harsh criticism was based more on Jahn's outspoken rejection of Richard Wagner, which Nietzsche was unable to tolerate in the early 1870s, than on the quality of his scholarly work.[16] Nevertheless, Jahn was also a slightly controversial figure, because of his involvement in liberal politics during the 1840s and 1850s. After an initial professorship in classical archaeology at the small but renowned University of Greifswald on the shores of the Baltic Sea, Jahn moved on to the more metropolitan Leipzig in 1847. Four years later he ran into difficulties with the state authorities of Saxony because of his liberal political convictions, which questioned the state control of higher education and cultural life in nineteenth-century Germany. That these difficulties led Jahn to lose his *venia legendi*, his permission to teach, was exactly the way in which German authorities unsuccessfully sought to regulate the political climate in higher education.

Ritschl supported Jahn's subsequent application for a professorship in Greek at the University of Bonn, which was on Prussian territory, and Jahn arrived in 1855 as the designated successor to the eminent philologist Friedrich Gottlieb Welcker. Together with August Wilhelm Schlegel, Welcker had built up the archaeological collections of the Akademisches Kunstmuseum, and, together with Ritschl, Jahn became its director from 1855 onward.[17] Three

---

[15] See Hubert Cancik, "Otto Jahns Vorlesung *Grundzüge der Archäologie* (Bonn, Sommer 1865) in den Mitschriften von Eduard Hiller und Friedrich Nietzsche," in Hubert Cancik and Hildegard Cancik-Lindemaier, *Philolog und Kultfigur: Friedrich Nietzsche und seine Antike in Deutschland* (Stuttgart: J. B. Metzler, 1999), pp. 3–33. For Jahn's archaeological work, see his *Archäologische Aufsätze* (Greifswald: Koch, 1845), *Archäologische Beiträge* (Berlin: Reimer, 1847), and *Griechische Bilderchroniken, bearbeitet von Otto Jahn*, ed. Adolf Michaelis (Bonn: Marcus, 1873).
[16] See Barbara von Reibnitz, "Otto Jahn bei Friedrich Nietzsche: Der 'Grenzbotenheld' als Wagner-Kritiker," in William Calder III, Hubert Cancik, and Bernhard Kystler (eds.), *Otto Jahn (1813–1869): Ein Geisteswissenschaftler zwischen Klassizismus und Historismus* (Stuttgart: Steiner, 1991), pp. 204–33.
[17] See Wolfgang Ehrhardt, *Das Akademische Kunstmuseum der Universität Bonn unter der Direktion von Friedrich Gottlieb Welcker und Otto Jahn* (Opladen: Westdeutscher Verlag, 1982), pp. 87–123.

years later, Jahn was rector of the university and his more general lectures, such as "Die Bedeutung und Stellung der Alterthumsstudien in Deutschland" (1859), became hugely popular, since they appealed to the "Germanness" of classical scholarship and provided students with much ideological support at a time when the outlook of their discipline seemed uncertain: the "classical cultures" (i.e. Greek and Roman antiquity), Jahn suggested, were to be seen as unique, and although classical scholarship gained much from the work of Italian humanists and English scholars, the main foundation was clearly German and to be traced back to Christian Gottlob Heyne, Friedrich August Wolf, and August Boeckh.[18]

Jahn largely saw himself as following in the footsteps of Winckelmann's "philhellenism" by interpreting predominantly visual material – e.g. vases, reliefs, murals – through its relationship to literary texts and mythological motifs, thereby linking the study of art history and religious culture. For Jahn, this historicization of Greek religious culture culminated in an anthropologically oriented study of mythology as, for instance, in his famous essay "Über den Aberglauben des bösen Blicks bei den Alten" (1854).[19] This does not mean, however, that he intended to change the historical perspective of archaeology away from Winckelmann's stylistic paradigms of aesthetic and cultural wholeness. Rather, he continued to regard Greek antiquity as an ideal and specific cultural environment that was largely independent of "oriental" influences, in much the same way as Winckelmann regarded the "Hellenic" style as superior, for instance, to Egyptian art.[20] Jahn's debt to Winckelmann, or rather his debt to the classicist image of Winckelmann, renders it obvious that much of his archaeological criticism was inspired by the neo-humanist milieu of the early nineteenth century: he ordered the statues in the Akademisches Kunstmuseum not according to historical principles but merely

---

[18] Otto Jahn, "Die Bedeutung und Stellung der Alterthumsstudien in Deutschland," in *Aus der Alterthumswissenschaft: Populäre Aufsätze* (Bonn: Marcus, 1868), pp. 3–50: 27–8, 30–2 and 50.

[19] See Otto Jahn, "Über den Aberglauben des bösen Blicks bei den Alten," *Königlich-Sächsische Gesellschaft der Wissenschaften, philologisch-historische Klasse: Berichte über die Verhandlungen* 7 (1855), 28–110. On Jahn's anthropological perspective, see Schlesier, *Kulte, Mythen und Gelehrte*, pp. 33–64.

[20] See, for instance, Jahn, "Die hellenische Kunst," in *Aus der Alterthumswissenschaft*, pp. 115–82.

according to their presumed stylistic quality and also inaugurated the annual celebrations of Winckelmann at the universities of Greifswald and Kiel. Jahn's work thus leaves an ambiguous impression: from a political point of view he might be regarded as representing a liberal modernity, but as an archaeological scholar he opted for a more traditional stance, albeit with decisive anthropological innovations. Taking into account that Nietzsche's own decision, in early 1865, to transfer from theology to classical scholarship was mainly influenced by Jahn and Ritschl, we are safe in assuming that the historical perspective of their work left traces in Nietzsche's own intellectual development.

Throughout the nineteenth century, the professional authority of German *Alterthumswissenschaft* was deeply connected to the German political imagination. In the minds of a generation of students like Nietzsche this heightened the prestige of classical scholarship as a discipline that, without being overtly political along the lines of "nation" and "religion" like the Prussian historians, was able to provide a utopian intertwining of Germany and Greece.[21] Classical scholarship was thus a truly modern enterprise that had many hidden links to the political imagination of the time. There are indeed many convergences between the political aspirations of historians such as Sybel and the neo-humanist interests of classical scholars such as Jahn and Ritschl, for their respective ideological orientations in fact share much common ground dating back to the early 1800s.

Regardless of their political differences, the way liberal scholars like Jahn and more conservative scholars like Ritschl conceived of their work in terms of *Wissenschaft* is embedded in a notion of neo-humanist *Bildung* that implies a political orientation grounded in the ideal of a "classical tradition." It is easy to see how the establishment of such a "classical tradition," emphasizing the presumed "freedom," "harmony" and "unity" of Winckelmann's imaginary Hellenic Greece, provided a powerful counter-image to the political and cultural particularism of the German states in the earlier nineteenth century and beyond. Already in the final decades of the previous century, the aesthetic idealization of antiquity

---

[21] A prominent example for a historiography along the lines of "nation" and "religion" that ultimately seeks to legitimize the German vocation of Prussia is Heinrich von Sybel's programmatic "Über den Stand der neueren deutschen Geschichtsschreibung," *Preußische Jahrbücher* 1 (1858), 349–64.

provided an opportunity to oppose the social norms of the day, but it also established an almost religious vision of things Greek, blending scholarship and literary aesthetics into one. By the early 1800s, and against the backdrop of the Napoleonic Wars, Greek antiquity was thus able to become a prominent factor within the political consciousness of German intellectuals, academics, and writers.[22] The discussion concerning the origin of a classical Greek culture was in many ways a discussion about the possibilities of cultural and, by implication, political autonomy, which stretched deep into the nineteenth century.[23] Especially the belief that classical studies would ultimately serve the advancement of an ideal "humanity," which was introduced by Friedrich Schlegel and Wilhelm von Humboldt, was reactivated toward the middle of the nineteenth century, for instance, in Ritschl's lecture "Ueber die neueste Entwickelung der Philologie," first delivered in Breslau in 1833. Not surprisingly, Ritschl continued this neo-humanist stance throughout the 1850s and 1860s, and Jahn adopted this perspective in his rectorial address "Die Bedeutung und Stellung der Alterthumsstudien in Deutschland" in Bonn.[24] Thus, despite their many differences, Jahn and Ritschl can be seen as representing, in person as well in their work, the ideological convergence of Greece and Germany. Nevertheless, Nietzsche was aware of the political and historical ambiguities of this imaginary classical

---

[22] See Christian J. Emden, "History, Memory, and the Invention of Antiquity: Notes on the 'Classical Tradition'," in Christian J. Emden and David Midgley (eds.), *Cultural Memory and Historical Consciousness in the German-Speaking World since 1500* (Oxford: Peter Lang, 2004), pp. 39–67; Wilhelm Voßkamp, "Klassik als Epoche," in Reinhardt Herzog and Reinhardt Koselleck (eds.), *Epochenschwelle und Epochenbewußtsein* (Munich: Wilhelm Fink, 1987), pp. 493–514; Manfred Fuhrmann, "Die Querelle des Anciens et des Modernes, der Nationalismus und die deutsche Klassik," in *Brechungen: Wirkungsgeschichtliche Studien zur antik-europäischen Bildungstradition* (Stuttgart: Klett-Cotta, 1982), pp. 129–49.

[23] See Brian Vick, "Greek Origins and Organic Metaphors: Ideals of Cultural Autonomy in Neo-Humanist Germany from Winckelmann to Curtius," *Journal of the History of Ideas*, 63 (2002), 483–500.

[24] See Friedrich Schlegel, "Vom Wert des Studiums der Griechen und Römer," in *Kritische Friedrich-Schlegel-Ausgabe*, ed. Ernst Behler, Jean-Jacques Anstett, and Hans Eichner (Paderborn: Schöningh, 1958–), vol. I, p. 639; Wilhelm von Humboldt, "Ueber den Character der Griechen, die idealische und historische Ansicht desselben," in *Werke*, vol. II, pp. 65–72; Friedrich Ritschl, "Ueber die neueste Entwickelung der Philologie," in *Opuscula philologica* (Leipzig: Teubner, 1866–79), vol. V, pp. 1–18; Jahn, "Die Bedeutung und Stellung der Alterthumsstudien in Deutschland," in *Aus der Alterthumswissenshaft* pp. 3–50. See, in a similar vein, another teacher of Nietzsche, Georg Curtius, "Ueber die Bedeutung des Studiums der classischen Literatur," in *Kleine Schriften*, ed. Ernst Windisch (Leipzig: Hirzel, 1886), pp. 89–109.

tradition. Already in a notebook entry from spring 1869, he was to lament that the concept of "antiquity" was rather vague (*KGW* I/5, 75 [3]) and in the fragments under the title "Wir Philologen" of March 1875 he was going to describe this imaginary classical tradition as a superficial and historically unsound idealization (*KGW* IV/1, 3 [4]).[25]

Considering the ambiguity of Nietzsche's remarks about the "classical tradition" and its imaginary intermingling of Germany and Greece, it is not entirely correct to assume, as some commentators have done, that Nietzsche "outs" the "racism" and "nationalism" that supposedly pervades German classical scholarship as a whole.[26] On the one hand, notions of "race" and "nation" were less prominent in German classical scholarship than in the parallel development of German linguistics and ethnography, and it would be historically unsound to reduce the debate about "nationhood" in nineteenth-century Germany to a purely racist discourse. On the other hand, Nietzsche's growing suspicions about the "classical ideal" promoted by the glorification of Winckelmann and Schiller in the nineteenth century were directed less against its presumed "nationalist" tendencies than against the homogeneous idealization of ancient Greece. To be sure, it is debatable whether there ever really was a "tyranny of Greece over Germany" as has often been suggested, since such catchphrases tend to obfuscate the complexity of the historical and political processes involved.[27] But the ideological convergence of Greece and Germany throughout the 1800s is difficult to ignore. Furthermore, classical scholarship was right from the beginning embedded in a political program, largely due to Wilhelm von Humboldt's role in the Prussian state: neo-humanist ideals of *Bildung* can only have an effect once they are part of an institutional setting.

---

[25] See also *KGW* III/3, 3 [76] and *KGW* III/4, 32 [67]. On the ambiguity of Nietzsche's position, see Christian J. Emden, "The Invention of Antiquity: Nietzsche on Classicism, Classicality, and the Classical Tradition," in Paul Bishop (ed.), *Nietzsche and Antiquity: His Reaction and Response to the Classical Tradition* (Rochester, N.Y.: Camden House, 2004), pp. 372–90. On Nietzsche's discussion of the classical as an aesthetic category, see Helmut Pfotenhauer, *Die Kunst als Physiologie: Nietzsches ästhetische Theorie und literarische Produktion* (Stuttgart: J. B. Metzler, 1985), pp. 123–35.
[26] See James I. Porter, *Nietzsche and the Philology of the Future* (Stanford, Calif.: Stanford University Press, 2000), p. 274.
[27] See Eliza M. Butler, *The Tyranny of Greece over Germany* (Cambridge: Cambridge University Press, 1935).

The close institutional relationship between scholarship and state is only one part of the story, however, for the legitimacy and long-term success of Humboldt's concept of *Bildung* were also connected to the political tropes of national "freedom" and "unity" that shaped the world-view of most German intellectuals and academics deep into the 1870s and beyond. By the time Nietzsche arrived in Bonn, questions concerning national identity and national unity were not only part of daily political debate, but they were still symbolically linked to the so-called "Wars of Liberation." Considering that 1865 is half a century after Napoleon's abdication and the Vienna Congress, this might be somewhat surprising. But influenced by the quasi-religious sentiment of "freedom" that ran through German Romanticism, and inspired by the ideological "rediscovery" of a specifically "German antiquity," the call for a united "German" resistance against Napoleon's imperialism triggered a far-reaching change in the cultural consciousness of German intellectuals that neither the politics of restoration nor the Carlsbad Decrees of 1819 were able to reverse. The nostalgic vision of Greek antiquity that can be detected in the writings of Winckelmann, Schlegel and Humboldt contains a utopian dimension that, almost automatically, politicized any appreciation of antiquity.[28] As a consequence, the metaphors of "freedom," "harmony" and "unity" that pervaded the political consciousness of German classicism could easily move into the discourse of national liberalism. In this respect, German national liberalism also stood in some contrast to the British and French varieties of liberalism, which were based either on economic ideals or on the universal validity of political ideals, such as liberty and equality. In the aftermath of the French Revolution and the Napoleonic Wars, however, liberty and equality as specific political demands were not seen as representing a German identity, which was supposedly rooted in an organic concept of community and which had a more nationalist tendency.[29] It is also

---

[28] On this utopian dimension, see Annemarie Gethmann-Siefert, "Das Klassische ist das Utopische: Überlegungen zu einer Kulturphilosophie der Kunst," in Rudolf Bockholdt (ed.), *Über das Klassische* (Frankfurt/M.: Suhrkamp, 1987), pp. 47–76: 62–7.

[29] See Frederick C. Beiser, *Enlightenment, Revolution, and Romanticism: The Genesis of Modern German Political Thought, 1790–1800* (Cambridge, Mass.: Harvard University Press, 1992), p. 334.

in this respect that German national liberalism did not really continue the cosmopolitan ideas of the Enlightenment.

The rise of national liberalism in the period between the 1840s and 1860s, which ultimately questioned the legitimacy of the existing social order but was quickly absorbed into German nationalism after 1871, was an integral part of the cultural consciousness among the intellectual elite and among academics at German universities. This was perhaps nowhere more obvious than in the historical disciplines, where Heinrich von Treitschke, Johann Gustav Droysen, and Heinrich von Sybel began to establish a political historiography that emphasized state, nation and political authority as its main reference points. Especially Sybel's liberal-conservative constitutionalism, evident in the lectures on politics Nietzsche attended in Bonn in 1864/65, contributed to the national sentiments among students and intellectuals, which in the long run were to transform initially liberal ideas into a reactionary ideology, supporting not only the German vocation of Prussia but also the establishment of a German Empire.

Although much later Nietzsche was to condemn this foggy glorification of the Prussian state in a colorful aside on Sybel and Treitschke in *Jenseits von Gut und Böse* (*BGE* 251), he was far more appreciative of such national sentiments in 1865. On July 30, 1865, Nietzsche attended a public speech Sybel delivered in front of an exalted audience that celebrated the unveiling of a monument honoring Ernst Moritz Arndt on the so-called Alter Zoll in Bonn. Arndt was the author of highly polemical essays, collected under the title *Geist der Zeit* (1805–18), which argued for the organic unity of the German *Volk* in order to compensate for the lack of national consciousness and to shore up resistance against Napoleon.[30] His highly symbolic political activism shared in the wider rhetorical demonization of Napoleon and France, which was at the core of Germany's historical mythology throughout the nineteenth century and which is also the reason why Arndt's monument in Bonn, erected in 1865, is a direct expression of the contemporary political culture in the Rhineland.[31] In fact, as soon

---

[30] See the remarks in Ernst Moritz Arndt, *Geist der Zeit*, in *Werke: Auswahl in zwölf Teilen*, eds. August Leffson and Wilhelm Steffens (Berlin: Bong & Co., 1912), vol. VII, pp. 81–2 and 91.

[31] On Arndt's position within the political culture of nineteenth-century Germany, see Hans-Ulrich Wehler, *Deutsche Gesellschaftsgeschichte, I: Vom Feudalismus des "alten Reiches"*

as Nietzsche had arrived in Bonn in autumn 1864, he embarked on an expedition to the local cemetery in order to visit Arndt's grave (*KGB* I/2, p. 15).

In contrast, for instance, to Johann Gottlieb Fichte's lectures, *Reden an die deutsche Nation* (1808), which despite their nationalist tone were still rooted in the philosophical ideals of the eighteenth century, Arndt's rhetoric was far more reactionary: the German "hatred" of the French was to become manifest in a "bloody" war that would rid Germany of its "shame."[32] In many ways, Arndt's political propaganda did not accurately reflect the situation on the ground, since the presence of Napoleonic troops in the Rhineland, despite obvious economic exploitation, also brought clear advantages, such as a centralized administrative infrastructure and the French *code civil*. While such administrative integration was certainly a means of conquest, stabilizing political claims over occupied territory, it also supported the modernization of previously absolutist states.[33] Although not entirely opposed to such reforms, Arndt contributed considerably to the formation of an anti-French, and occasionally also anti-Semitic, sentiment that stayed at the core of German nationalism throughout much of the nineteenth century – even among the liberals, which Bismarck was able to exploit in the period before the Franco-Prussian War. Ironically, Arndt was also a victim of the restoration politics in the aftermath of the Vienna Congress of 1814/15, which made him even more attractive to the national liberal camp in the Rhineland: appointed to a professorship in history at the University of Bonn in 1818, he began to criticize the restoration politics and argued for a united Germany as a constitutional monarchy safeguarding the freedom of the press and the political participation of its citizens.[34] Since the Vienna Congress sought to

---

bis zur "defensiven Modernisierung" der Reformära, 1700–1815 (Munich: C. H. Beck, 1987), pp. 523–5, and Wulf Wülfing, Karin Bruns, and Rolf Parr, *Historische Mythologie der Deutschen, 1798–1918* (Munich: Wilhelm Fink, 1991), pp. 22–3.

[32] Arndt, *Geist der Zeit*, in *Werke*, vol. VIII, p. 169.

[33] See Michael Rowe, *From Reich to State: The Rhineland in the Revolutionary Age, 1780–1830* (Cambridge: Cambridge University Press, 2003), pp. 243–81, and Stuart Woolf, *Napoleon's Integration of Europe* (London: Routledge, 1991), pp. 83–132.

[34] See Arndt, *Geist der Zeit*, in *Werke*, vol. IX, pp. 29 and 40–91. Arndt's emphasis on political participation and rights, however, mainly developed within a strong national program that excluded, for instance, German Jews from such participation. See Paul Lawrence Rose, *Revolutionary Antisemitism in Germany from Kant to Wagner* (Princeton, N. J.: Princeton University Press, 1990), pp. 127–8.

re-establish a pre-revolutionary political order in Central Europe, and since the Carlsbad Decrees of 1819 substantially restricted public political debate, Arndt suddenly found himself in opposition to the very forces he had so vehemently supported in previous years. He immediately lost his position in Bonn and was allowed to resume teaching only when Friedrich Wilhelm IV ascended to the Prussian throne in 1840.

Considering the irony of Arndt's relationship to Prussia, it is indeed fitting that Sybel – about to switch from opposing Bismarck to supporting his grand vision for a German state – should have delivered a speech in front of Arndt's monument. Although Nietzsche experienced the "Arndt-Fest," with its processions through the city of Bonn, as a rather tedious example of nationalist Kitsch, he nevertheless regarded Sybel's speech as the highlight of the whole affair (*KGB* 1/2, p. 76).[35] Nietzsche's bewilderment about the festivities honoring Arndt, which lasted for several days, mirrors another experience, two months earlier, of the enthusiasm among the population of Cologne, gathered to celebrate the visit of the Prussian King Wilhelm I on the occasion of the fiftieth anniversary of a "Prussian Rhineland" liberated from Napoleonic occupation (*KGB* 1/2, p. 66). Again, this was an occasion where Sybel, at the neighboring University of Bonn, delivered a lecture, this time emphasizing that the political freedom of the Rhineland was only possible under Prussian guidance.[36]

Although it is difficult to judge how seriously Nietzsche took Sybel's ideas, the latter's view of Arndt linked the national liberalism of the Rhineland, represented in particular by the intellectual culture at the University of Bonn, to neo-humanist ideals.[37] Like Jahn, who himself was a member of the committee planning the monument for Arndt, Sybel thus saw national liberalism as a continuation of Humboldtian neo-humanism, perhaps even as its political manifestation. For a generation of classical scholars,

---

[35] See also the excerpts from Max Eyfferth's diary reprinted in *BAW* III, p. 413. Eyfferth was a friend of Nietzsche's in Bonn and Leipzig.
[36] See Heinrich von Sybel, "Preussen und Rheinland," in *Kleine Schriften*, vol. II (Munich: Cotta, 1869), pp. 383–406. Nietzsche and Eyfferth seem to have attended this lecture. See Eyfferth's diary in *BAW* III, p. 405.
[37] Sybel makes this particularly clear in a later speech: "Die Gründung der Universität Bonn: Festrede zum Fünfzigjährigen Jubiläum der Rheinischen Friedrich-Wilhelms-Universität," in *Kleine Schriften*, vol. II, pp. 407–73: 423 and 426.

coming of age in the period between the 1840s and 1860s, this was an attractive model able to keep the neo-humanist framework alive in a time of political uncertainties.[38]

By the time Nietzsche decided to move from Bonn to Leipzig – together with Bonn, Göttingen and Berlin one of the main centers of philological and historical research in nineteenth-century Germany – the intellectual climate in the Prussian Rhineland had undergone a considerable change. Sybel's repeated idealization of the University of Bonn as a safe haven for intellectual debate did not really reflect the realities of academic intrigue that came to a head in the course of 1865 and forced Ritschl to leave for Leipzig. From a distance, it even seems that Nietzsche followed his teacher Ritschl, who had left the Rhineland for Leipzig after a heated controversy with Jahn, which soured their initially cordial relationship and administrative collaboration. But upon closer inspection the situation is more complicated, and in order to understand this particular aspect of Nietzsche's intellectual biography, it might be helpful to reconsider the developments which led to Ritschl's departure from Bonn.

Although, at the beginning, Ritschl supported Jahn's position at the University of Bonn, their relations cooled quickly, and in 1861 – four years before Nietzsche arrived on the scene – Ritschl left the direction of the archaeological collections to Jahn. Over the following years, the tensions between them turned into a full-blown personal battle, an intrigue only possible in the realm of academe. By 1865, the so-called "Bonner Philologenkrieg," with many ironic turns and bizarre misunderstandings, was in full swing and polarized not only the university but almost the entire intellectual community of Prussia.[39] Even Sybel, who was not directly involved in this quarrel, took an active interest in the developments, since he sought to emphasize the educational ideals of the nation state. Although he regarded the whole controversy as trivial, he ultimately sided with Jahn, with whom he shared many of

---

[38] See, for instance, Wilhelm Herbst, *Das classische Alterthum in der Gegenwart: Eine geschichtliche Betrachtung* (Leipzig: Teubner, 1852), pp. 4–33.

[39] See Christian Benne, *Nietzsche und die historisch-kritische Philologie* (Berlin: Walter de Gruyter, 2005), pp. 274–8; Hans Herter, "Aus der Geschichte der klassischen Philologie in Bonn," in *Kleine Schriften*, ed. Ernst Vogt (Munich: Wilhelm Fink, 1975), pp. 648–64: 652–4; Friedrich von Bezold, *Geschichte der Rheinischen Friedrich-Wilhelms-Universität von der Gründung bis zum Jahre 1870* (Bonn: Marcus & Weber, 1920), pp. 504–12.

his liberal political views, and openly opposed Ritschl – only to turn against Jahn once Ritschl had left Bonn for Leipzig.[40] In May 1865, Nietzsche pointedly remarked in a long letter to his friend Carl von Gersdorff in Göttingen that the atmosphere at the University of Bonn had been transformed into one of scandal and personal hatred (*KGB* 1/2, p. 56).

The initial reason for the quarrel was of a rather profane administrative nature: the appointment of another professorial chair in Latin, with Jahn also contemplating a move to Vienna for largely financial reasons. The actual quarrel began with neither Jahn nor Ritschl but was triggered by students of the latter who attacked Jahn's position within the university. Nevertheless, both Jahn and Ritschl were quickly regarded as representing incompatible political camps that reflected the gridlock of 1860s Germany: Jahn, the liberal, was seen as standing for the political autonomy of the university and for the democratization of political representation in Prussia, whereas Ritschl, who was well known as a master of administrative intrigue with good connections to the ministerial world, was regarded as the conservative opponent. Surprisingly, it was not Jahn who had to leave Bonn but Ritschl, who decided to accept an appointment at Leipzig.

Whether Nietzsche really left Bonn for Leipzig because of Ritschl's departure can be doubted. In a letter to his mother and sister from May 3, 1865, he merely remarked that the quarrel between Ritschl and Jahn had reached an unfortunate state of mutual personal attacks, while in the letter to Gersdorff mentioned above he sided with Jahn but already indicated that he would be leaving Bonn once the summer semester of 1865 was over (*KGB* 1/2, pp. 49 and 56). In another letter to his sister in June 1865 Nietzsche left the impression that he changed sides once again, intending to follow Ritschl to Leipzig (*KGB* 1/2, p. 64). This impression becomes even stronger in a letter written toward the end of June, when he finally reported to an old school friend that, in the following semester, he would be in Leipzig, since it had become clear that his teacher Ritschl intended to go there as well (*KGB* 1/2, p. 68). Although it might seem that

---

[40] See Paul Egon Hübinger, "Heinrich von Sybel und der Bonner Philologenkrieg," *Historisches Jahrbuch* 83 (1964), 162–216.

Nietzsche's decision to leave Bonn for Leipzig was taken before Ritschl made his own intentions public, he was increasingly willing to suggest that he in fact followed in Ritschl's footsteps.

Whatever the effect of the "Philologenkrieg" on Nietzsche's future career decisions, it was in many ways his first direct personal encounter with the political predicaments of academic culture in nineteenth-century Germany. The quarrel between Jahn and Ritschl mirrored more general trends within the precarious intellectual and academic landscape of nineteenth-century Germany: what Wilhelm von Humboldt, during the early 1800s, envisaged as a reform of German higher education along the lines of liberal *Bildung* was ultimately unable to materialize within the rapidly changing political conditions after the failed revolutions of 1848/49. By the time Nietzsche entered the University of Bonn, the educational ideals of the early nineteenth century had been increasingly emptied. New demands for the specialization of scientific and scholarly endeavors began to emerge within the German university, running parallel to the much-discussed "rise of academic illiberalism" which was to become increasingly manifest during the 1880s and 1890s.[41] As we shall see, several years later when Nietzsche had already left Germany behind, he was still grappling with these issues in a series of public lectures with the title "Über die Zukunft unserer Bildungsanstalten" (1872) and in the essay *Vom Nutzen und Nachtheil der Historie für das Leben* (1874).

THE AUSTRO-PRUSSIAN WAR IN LEIPZIG

Moving from Bonn to Leipzig, from the industrial and intellectual center of the Rhineland to the more metropolitan environment of a city that already in the eighteenth century took a central part in the intellectual life of the German Enlightenment, also meant that Nietzsche was beginning to situate himself in a completely different tradition. Symbolically speaking, Ernst Moritz Arndt was replaced by Goethe. And indeed, when Nietzsche enrolled at the University of Leipzig on October 19, 1865, he was quite pleased

---

[41] On the effects of these developments, see Konrad H. Jarausch, *Students, Society, and Politics in Imperial Germany: The Rise of Academic Illiberalism* (Princeton, N.J.: Princeton University Press, 1982), pp. 78–159 and 399–416.

about the fact that Goethe, that epitome of German *Bildung* and *deutsche Klassik*, had become a student at the very same institution exactly one hundred years earlier (*BAW* III, p. 295).[42] It was, however, several months later that Nietzsche had a more direct historical experience and realized how Prussian *Realpolitik* saw itself as shaping German history and identity.

By the mid-1860s, Otto von Bismarck had turned the internal problems of the shaky German Confederation, established in the aftermath of the Vienna Congress to provide political stability among the thirty-six German states, into a more fateful struggle for political dominance between Prussia as a rising European military and industrial power and an Austrian Empire that was largely regarded as backward-looking. While the latter had little interest in a unified German nation under Prussian leadership, Bismarck was keen on turning into a historical fact what he perceived to be the German vocation of Prussia.[43] Prussia's proclamation, on June 10, 1866, to form a new German federation under Prussian leadership was intended not only to polarize the German states, with some of them siding with Austria, while others welcomed the initiative from Berlin, but also to provoke Austria into a military response. Nietzsche himself was aware of this precarious situation. In a letter to his mother and sister, he complained about Bismarck's political strategies that were bound to force Austria into a war with Prussia merely in order to achieve the unification of the German states (*KGB* I/2, pp. 134–5). What Bismarck had in mind was what Heinrich von Sybel, despite his initial opposition to the Prussian chancellor, postulated several years earlier as the so-called *kleindeutsch* solution: the unification of the German states and the long-term survival of Austria could only be achieved by a German federation that excluded the Habsburg Empire.[44]

In the ensuing conflict, however, Saxony, separating Prussia from Austria and sharing a common border with the then Austrian province of Bohemia, allied itself with the Habsburg Empire,

---

[42] See Nicholas Boyle, *Goethe – The Poet and the Age, I: The Poetry of Desire (1749–1790)* (Oxford: Oxford University Press, 1991), pp. 62–6.
[43] See the documents in Otto von Bismarck, *Ausgewählte Werke*, ed. Gustav Adolf Rein, Wilhelm Schüßler, Eberhard Scheler, Alfred Milatz, and Rudolf Buchner (Darmstadt: Wissenschaftliche Buchgesellschaft, 1962–83), vol. III, pp. 746–66.
[44] See Heinrich von Sybel, *Die Deutsche Nation und das Kaiserreich: Eine historisch-politische Abhandlung*, 2nd edn. (Düsseldorf: J. Buddeus, 1862), p. 124.

and Bohemia was precisely where the looming war against Austria was going to be decided. Shortly before the Prussian army entered Bohemia, a large contingent of troops from Prussia and Mecklenburg was already stationed in Leipzig and gave the city a more militaristic atmosphere. Although there was no resistance in Leipzig against this deployment and life went on as usual, the military presence triggered nationalist sentiments among Leipzig's students, since many of them came from outside Saxony. By then, even Nietzsche's attitude had changed, and in contrast to many of his friends he favored not Saxony or Austria, but Prussia. Perhaps he did so because Thuringia, where he had grown up and which also included Weimar as the home of Goethe, was on the Prussian side; perhaps he did so because one of his closest friends, Carl von Gersdorff, had just left Leipzig to begin a career as an officer in the Prussian army.

Two days before military operations began in earnest and Prussian troops crossed the border into Bohemia, Nietzsche declared himself to be a "fervent Prussian" and asked his mother to notify him as soon as the Prussian authorities decided to mobilize volunteers (*KGB* 1/2, p. 135). After the battle at Sadová, just outside Königgrätz, on July 3, 1866, which completely destroyed the armies of Austria and Saxony, there clearly was no need for volunteers. But although Nietzsche and the other Prussian students were thus unable to join in the war effort and, in Nietzsche's words, unable to carry the "blood-splattered insignia of honor," he saw himself as serving his "fatherland" through his philological "studies" (*KGB* 1/2, pp. 137–8). The professional ethos and authority of German classical scholarship were a continuation of politics by different means. And if classical scholarship was indeed a historical discipline, then it took part in the establishment of historical continuities that, as Sybel noted in one of his most programmatic articles, connected "past and present" in the idea of "nationhood."[45] As a result, Nietzsche began to regard the unification of the German states as the "German hope" and watched the war "in breathless excitement," arguing that one needed to "take pride" in the victories of the Prussian army and in a government that sought to realize a "national program" that

---

[45] Heinrich von Sybel, "Ueber den Stand der neueren deutschen Geschichtsschreibung," in *Kleine Schriften*, vol. I, 2nd edn. (Munich: Cotta, 1869), pp. 343–59: 346.

was bound to culminate in an even more important war against France (*KGB* 1/2, pp. 140 and 142–3).

Aware of the human cost of war, but also somewhat exalted by the political options opened up by the defeat of Habsburg Austria, Nietzsche echoed these ideas in a long letter to his friend Carl von Gersdorff, which is worth quoting at length, since it has never been discussed in detail:

> But proud we must be, to have such an army, even – horribile dictu – to have such a government, that follow the national program not only on paper, but that maintain this program, with the highest energy and with an enormous effort of money and blood, even against the great French tempter Louis le diable. ... Now at least ... comes the great time of trial, the acid test for the seriousness of the national program. ... A war against France has to call for a unity of conviction in Germany; ... Never within the last 50 years have we been so close to fulfilling our German hopes. Slowly I begin to realize that there was no other, milder way than the terrible one of an annihilating war. ... Our national efforts will not be able to avoid turning the European condition upside-down, or at least trying to. If this should fail, we hopefully will have the honor of falling on the battlefield, hit by a French bullet. (*KGB* 1/2, pp. 142–4)

Glorifying Prussia's German vocation, and anticipating the Franco-Prussian War of 1870/71, Nietzsche seems to have embraced Prussian expansionism. After reading Heinrich von Treitschke's political pamphlet *Die Zukunft der norddeutschen Mittelstaaten* (1866), which was prohibited in Saxony for good reason, Nietzsche even suggested that being annexed by Prussia would be in the best interest of Saxony (*KGB* 1/2, pp. 158–9).

The political remarks in Nietzsche's correspondence of the mid-1860s suggest that, in the period between 1858 and 1868, Nietzsche held essentially conventional political views that corresponded entirely to the conservative program of national liberalism in Germany.[46] While it is undoubtedly the case that Nietzsche did not yet have any independent point of view from which to judge the contemporary political circumstances more critically, it is crucial to understand that the political environment he encountered in the mid-1860s was to provide the background of his later views. This does not mean, however, that he continued along the

---

[46] See Ottmann, *Philosophie und Politik bei Nietzsche*, pp. 11–16, and Marti, *"Der grosse Pöbel- und Sklavenaufstand"*, pp. 93–4.

lines of a conservative, or even reactionary, political program. Rather, he became increasingly aware that Prussia's *Machtpolitik* stood in some contrast to the neo-humanist tradition he was exposed to in his work as a student of classical scholarship. His political interests during the 1860s allowed him to gain a first insight into the tension between the late-Enlightenment ideals of neo-humanism and the authoritarian streak of the emerging German nation state. Much later, once he had seen the battlefields of the Franco-Prussian War, and once he had moved from Leipzig to Basel, he was to grow more suspicious of Prussia's ambitions and revised his enthusiasm for the national cause. It is precisely Nietzsche's emerging historical vision that will incline him to question the foundation myths of "imagined communities," such as "nation," "culture," and "religion."[47]

During his time in Leipzig, Nietzsche's interests also turned to the theoretical foundations and the historical perspective of classical scholarship, which will have been triggered by Ritschl's convictions about the cultural benefit of classical studies within a wider neo-humanist framework. That Ritschl's conception of classical scholarship was indebted to Humboldt's notion of *Bildung* is difficult to ignore. On many occasions Humboldt emphasized that the inherently human drive to knowledge through a form of self-cultivation transformed this drive into an ethically informed moral education, which was based on the unity of human experience.[48] As such, *Bildung* was not merely individual self-cultivation, but its close relationship to moral judgment highlights an intrinsically social dimension. Along these lines Ritschl sought to justify the philological enterprise as a program of moral education. Ritschl's move is hardly surprising, especially once we take into account the enormous influence of Humboldt's educational program on the self-conception and administrative structure of German universities until the 1860s.[49] Humboldt's emphasis on *Bildung* is, however, in

---

[47] On the notion of "imagined communities," see Benedict Anderson, *Imagined Communities: Reflections on the Origin and Spread of Nationalism* (London: Verso, 1983), pp. 11–40.
[48] See Humboldt, "Theorie der Bildung des Menschen," in *Werke*, vol. 1, pp. 235 and 237–8.
[49] For Humboldt's position within the history of classical philology and his influence on the German university system, see Ada Hentschke and Ulrich Muhlack, *Einführung in die Geschichte der Klassischen Philologie* (Darmstadt: Wissenschaftliche Buchgesellschaft, 1972), pp. 65–74, and Charles E. McClelland, *State, Society, and University in Germany, 1700–1914* (Cambridge: Cambridge University Press, 1980), pp. 99–149.

many ways connected to the idea of the "state," in this case Prussia, as a unified moral entity, so that *Bildung* itself is a form of *Aufklärung*, enlightenment, realized in the public realm of education, scholarship, and science. This connection between neo-humanism and the state was plagued by a variety of political problems that Humboldt could not foresee, but that later contributed to the collapse of intellectual liberalism in Imperial Germany. The national orientation of German liberalism represented by historians such as Heinrich von Treitschke, Theodor Mommsen, and Johann Gustav Droysen, which was removed from the more cosmopolitan outlook of the Enlightenment, was in many ways all too ready to accept the dominant state policies under Bismarck, while Bismarck himself was able to use the liberals for the advancement of his own more conservative goals.

In letters written in the immediate aftermath of the fateful clash between Prussia and Austria on the Bohemian battlefield, Nietzsche shows himself to be a keen observer of these political developments. Only a few days after the Prussian victory at Sadová he wrote to his friend Carl von Gersdorff, himself training to become an officer in the Prussian army, that the emergence of a national political program during the Austro-Prussian War, which ultimately excluded Habsburg Austria once and for all from any future German nation state, blurred the traditional boundaries between the liberals and the conservatives:

Generally speaking, every party which accepts these policy goals [i.e. national unification] is a liberal party, and even among the important conservative block in the chamber of deputies I cannot but recognize a new shade of liberalism. For I am unable to believe that all these men are simply men of the government, people that blindly snuggle up to the governing power, detect in Austria 6 months ago the sanctuary of conservative interests, only to declare a national war against the latter 6 months later. (*KGB* 1/2, p. 143)

A month later he remarked in another letter to Carl von Gersdorff that the "old party lines, i.e., the extreme positions, have been completely destroyed," and Nietzsche began to identify with what he regarded as a historical shift in the political landscape:

To speak openly, it is also for me a rare and completely new delight to be in agreement with the government of the time. Of course, one needs to let certain dead sleep, and furthermore one needs to realize that Bismarck's game was of a particularly daring nature; a political strategy that shouts "va banque" can be cursed as much as revered, depending on its success. But this time, there is success: great things have been achieved. Sometimes I try to detach myself for several minutes from the spirit of the age, from the subjective and natural sympathies for Prussia, and then I have in front of my eyes a colossal political spectacle, the kind that can only be provided by history, perhaps not morally acceptable, but quite beautiful and edifying for the observer. (*KGB* 1/2, pp. 158–9)

Although the last sentence of this quotation seems to suggest Nietzsche's increasing willingness to understand the political in aesthetic terms, this passage merely expresses his fascination with the effects of Bismarck's policies and their underlying conception of power. It is within this conext that Nietzsche begins to learn a crucial lesson that will become increasingly important during the 1870s and 1880s and that influences what I shall be discussing later as his political realism: political life is predominantly concerned with the acquisition, stabilization, and growth of power in terms of both *Macht* and *Herrschaft*.

THE DEMANDS OF HISTORY

Within Nietzsche's chosen discipline, classical scholarship, the political tensions that came to the fore around 1866 were not without effect. Although Ritschl largely refrained from making direct political statements in his lectures, his own political leanings inclined him to regard an idealized version of neo-humanist self-cultivation as the best foundation for classical scholarship. Even though there were fundamental differences, the ideological justification of classical scholarship ran parallel to that of the modern German nation state. Already in his 1833 lecture "Ueber die neueste Entwickelung der Philologie," which was also published in the same year as the entry on "philology" in Brockhaus's widely distributed *Conversations-Lexikon der neuesten Zeit und Litteratur*, Ritschl pointedly remarked that, despite its lack of conceptual unity, classical scholarship could not be regarded anymore as a purely scholarly undertaking that might happen to possess some vague educational value. Rather, the study of philology demanded a new awareness for the cultural importance of scholarship. Philology itself, he continued, was not only a specialist field of research in its own right, but at its very center stood an anthropological claim, symbolizing the totality and unity of human knowledge as a whole: the "ideas" of the "good," the "sacred," "beauty," and "truth" as they relate to the four "spheres" of "morality," "religion," "art," and "science" and also to the human ability to "act," "feel," "see," and "think."[50]

Whether classical philology, as Ritschl believed, really was able to deliver a link between morality, religion, art and science is somewhat doubtful, at least with regard to its institutional politics. The personal attacks and general fractiousness that marked German classical scholarship throughout the 1800s were hardly a harbinger of such educational ideals.[51] Nevertheless, like many of his colleagues Ritschl held on to the general educational value of the philological enterprise. In a series of fragments, "Zur Methode des philologischen Studiums," composed in the late 1850s, he wholeheartedly maintained that the "study of classical antiquity" is a "revitalizing force [*Neubelebung*]", without which "all higher culture of modern times would become narrow, muddy and wither away."[52] To be sure, Ritschl was not the first and not the only philologist to argue along these lines, especially in the nineteenth century.[53] But his emphasis on the connection between past and present, itself a historicist position, had a profound impact on Nietzsche's historical thought and educational ideals; it will lead him to reformulate the very relationship between past and present against the background of far-reaching philosophical problems of historical knowledge – problems that Ritschl himself clearly underestimated.

More than twenty-five years ago, R. J. Hollingdale noted in a highly influential study that "Nietzsche was primarily a philosopher" and that his philological writings are "something of interest to classical scholars rather than students of Nietzsche."[54] But if we

---

[50] See Ritschl, "Ueber die neueste Entwickelung der Philologie," pp. 3 and 8.
[51] On this aspect, see Glenn W. Most, "One Hundred Years of Fractiousness: Disciplining Polemics in Nineteenth-Century German Classical Scholarship," *Transactions of the American Philological Association* 127 (1997), 349–61.
[52] See Ritschl, "Zur Methode des philologischen Studiums," in *Opuscula philologica*, vol. v, pp. 19–32: 15.
[53] See, for instance, Friedrich August Wolf, *Vorlesungen über die Alterthumswissenschaft*, ed. Johann Daniel Gürtler (Leipzig: Lehnhold, 1831–39), vol. I, pp. 31–45; August Boeckh, *Encyklopädie und Methodologie der philologischen Wissenschaften*, ed. Ernst Bratuschek, 2nd edn. (Leipzig: Teubner, 1886), pp. 10 and 257; Curtius, "Ueber die Bedeutung des Studiums der classischen Literatur," in *Kleine Schriften*, pp. 89–109.
[54] R.J. Hollingdale, *Nietzsche* (London: Routledge & Kegan Paul, 1973), pp. 1 and 211.

wish to attain a better insight into the way his historical thought and his critique of contemporary political culture develops over a period of about twenty-five years, there is little justification for ignoring the link between his philological education and his philosophical interests during the 1860s. It is within this context that Nietzsche increasingly begins to realize the critical potential of historical knowledge. Surprisingly, at a time when Nietzsche was still a pupil of Ritschl at the University of Leipzig, he already began to question the practice of classical scholarship as a historical discipline. His main criticism was directed against the professional authority and ethos of contemporary classicists, which, as he believed, rested on the unquestioned assumption that the history of philology itself represents a steady accumulation of knowledge that culminates in a homogeneous image of antiquity. Among his colleagues, he noted, there is a tendency to "overestimate" the idea of philology as a "science," while "most philologists are merely factory laborers in the service of scholarship," unable to achieve a more comprehensive understanding of their own enterprise (*KGW* 1/4, 52 [30]). By the late 1860s, then, Nietzsche had become quite uneasy about the professional authority and ethos that had attracted him to classical scholarship in the first place. While this unease had immediate implications with regard to the way he conceived of the role of historical understanding in classical scholarship, it also opened the way for more philosophical questions regarding the status of historical knowledge. Nietzsche's practical experience as a student of classical philology was thus directly related to his philosophical interests, especially as far as the writings of Arthur Schopenhauer, Friedrich Albert Lange, and Immanuel Kant were concerned.

Throughout the 1860s and early 1870s Nietzsche began to consult works on the history of classical scholarship, from Arnold Hermann Ludwig Heeren's seminal *Geschichte des Studiums der classischen Litteraturen seit dem Wiederaufleben der Wissenschaften* (1797–1801) to Carl Hirzel's *Grundzüge zu einer Geschichte der classischen Philologie* (1872). By the late 1860s, the development of literary history as a scholarly discipline had become a particularly pressing concern. In spring 1868, Nietzsche began to consider a collection of his own philological papers under the title *Beiträge zur griechischen Litteraturgeschichte*, preceded by an introduction focusing on the study of literary history in ancient Greece (*KGW* 1/4, 57

[72]). While this project never came to fruition, it is remarkable that the introductory chapter seems to have slowly moved into the center of Nietzsche's attention (*KGW* 1/4, 58 [58]). What had originally been planned as an introduction had turned into a book-length project in its own right with a total of twenty-four chapters (*KGW* 1/4, 61 [2]). Needless to say, Nietzsche never completed this project, but in a letter to Erwin Rohde in Kiel, written at the beginning of February 1868, he remarked that his work on Democritus and his increasing interest in a "history of literary studies in antiquity and modern times" was meant "to tell the philologists some uncomfortable truths" (*KGB* 1/2, p. 248). At the very center of Nietzsche's interest in literary history stood a reflection on the status of historical knowledge, that is, a reflection on the "chains of theorems that have been constructed about history itself" (*KGW* 1/4, 52 [30]).

In order for the philological enterprise to achieve a more coherent vision, Nietzsche remarked in his notebooks, it must pay attention to factors such as the social status and aesthetic ideas of contemporary writers, which indirectly influence our image of antiquity. It must also take into account the philosophical, religious and moral framework of different historical epochs, the ways in which historiography is practiced as well as its underlying conception of history, and finally also the capacity of any culture to accommodate and accept that which is perceived as "foreign" and "ancient" (*KGW* 1/4, 52 [31]).[55] Only if we grant that our image of antiquity, and of any other historical period for that matter, is immersed in the complex intellectual fabric of our own cultural mentalities, would we be in a position to accomplish a more critical understanding of the past – at least this is what Nietzsche believed in the summer of 1867. As a consequence, he begins to align himself with what we might term a philosophically oriented historicism: "The medium through which the historian sees consists of his own ideas (also those of his time) and those of his sources." The implications of this are obvious enough: "We have enough to do, perhaps even more than we ever could, if we wish to strip off the 'subjectivity' of our own appearances and that

---

[55] See Benne, *Nietzsche und die historisch-kritische Philologie*, pp. 66–7, and Brobjer, "Nietzsche's Relation to Historical Methods and Nineteenth-Century German Historiography," 161–5.

of sources: the kind of 'objectivity' we are able to achieve is far from being any. It is nothing but 'subjectivity' on an elevated level" (*KGW* 1/4, 56 [6]).

By the late 1860s, then, Nietzsche began to adopt a form of historicism that stressed the heterogeneity of historical knowledge and that was opposed to the fastidious collection of "factual data." On the one hand, there are always more "facts," "events" and "processes" than historians would be able to integrate in their narratives. On the other, historical narratives themselves need to be situated in a broader context, and this very context is by definition always too complex and also marked by a constant lack of accurate information. Historical narratives have to introduce hypothetical statements with regard to more or less probable interconnections. Of course, Hegel had already described these problems with regard to what he called "reflective historiography:"

> This kind of thing inevitably happens with any historical work which tries to cover long periods or indeed the whole of world history; it is compelled *to dispense more or less with individual accounts of reality* and to make do with abstractions, summaries, and *abridgements*. This [means] not only that *many* events and actions must be *omitted*, but also that thought or understanding, the most effective means of abridgement, must intervene. [56]

Hegel clearly believed that this is an unproblematic issue as long as we follow the unfolding of human consciousness and freedom in history. Nietzsche, we shall see, was a little more skeptical with regard to this.

In any case, while Hegel does not believe that historiography is in any way a deficient enterprise, Nietzsche is not so sure about this. Indeed, the problem that will continue to plague Nietzsche's historical vision until the late 1870s is the central question as to whether history is an "art" or whether it belongs to the realm of "science." One of the sources for the way in which he encounters this problem is Arthur Schopenhauer's idea that the poetic dimension of historical writing remains the main reason why historiography cannot be regarded, strictly speaking, as a "science." Of course, Schopenhauer points out, "the historian should accurately

---

[56] Georg Wilhelm Friedrich Hegel, *Lectures on the Philosophy of World History: Introduction, Reason in History*, trans. H. B. Nisbet, introd. Duncan Forbes (Cambridge: Cambridge University Press, 1975), p. 18.

follow the individual event according to life as this event is developed in time in the manifold tortuous and complicated chains of reasons or grounds and consequents." But what the historian should do differs markedly from what he actually can hope to achieve, for "he cannot possibly possess all the data" and "he cannot have seen all and ascertained everything." At first sight, Schopenhauer thus argues along the lines of Hegel. But he also reaches a startling conclusion that Hegel would certainly have been unwilling to even contemplate: "I think I can assume that in all history the false outweighs the true."[57] For Schopenhauer, this implies above all that, while historical discourse might generate knowledge (*Wissen*), it is unable to reach the same objective certitude as the exact sciences (*Wissenschaft*).[58] The consequences of this deficiency are obvious: literary accounts are far more successful in reconstructing the past than historiography, for as an inherently aesthetic discourse literary representation has, in one way or another, a relatively direct access to the "idea" of the past:

> Therefore, he who seeks to know mankind according to its inner nature which is identical in all its phenomena and developments, and thus according to its Idea, will find that the works of the great, immortal poets present him with a much truer and clearer picture than the historians can ever give. [59]

Schopenhauer's hopes in literature might be misplaced, but his remarks indeed seem to suggest that historical discourse needs to be replaced by literature.

Nietzsche's attraction to Schopenhauer is obvious and well documented, but it is also evident that Schopenhauer's position is of a more metaphysical nature than Nietzsche bargained for: aestheticizing history limits the critical potential of the study of history. Furthermore, with his demand to replace historiography with literature, Schopenhauer has maneuvered himself into a rather difficult position. This might not be quite as obvious in the first volume of *Die Welt als Wille und Vorstellung*, published in 1819, but twenty-five years later, in the second volume of 1844, his argument becomes increasingly inconclusive. While initially pointing out that historical discourse belongs to the empirical

---

[57] Arthur Schopenhauer, *The World as Will and Representation*, trans. E. F. J. Payne (New York: Dover, 1966), vol. 1, p. 245.
[58] See ibid., vol. 1, pp. 28–9 and 62–3. [59] Ibid., vol. 1, p. 246.

sciences, he suddenly reintroduces, on the basis of Aristotle's *Poetics*, the idea that, from a philosophical perspective, poetry is superior to historiography.[60] Again, this implies that historiography cannot be regarded as an empirical science, since empirical sciences establish objective and universal laws, while historical discourse can only account for individual events that lie in the past.[61] Schopenhauer's claim that historical discourse does not lead to any universal knowledge with regard, for instance, to the unfolding of reason and consciousness, is certainly directed against Hegel and, considering the publication date of the second volume, against the Hegelianism of the 1830s and 1840s.[62] The curious position Schopenhauer adopted had more to do with his aversion to Hegel than with the status of historical knowledge at large. Not surprisingly, several pages after a scathing attack on Hegel he suddenly softens his tone and argues that historical knowledge is not such a terribly deficient thing after all.[63]

As an attentive and critical reader of *Die Welt als Wille und Vorstellung*, Nietzsche was certainly familiar with the difficulties of Schopenhauer's position. Nevertheless, he shared with Schopenhauer a distaste for the Hegelian tradition. Several years later, in his essay *Vom Nutzen und Nachtheil der Historie für das Leben* (1874), he was going to deliver a straightforward attack on Hegel's philosophy of history as it was continued in Eduard von Hartmann's *Philosophie des Unbewussten* (1869), which sought to discover a metaphysical unity in the teleological "process of world-history [*Weltprozess*]."[64] As can be expected, Hartmann's philosophical ideas about the course of history have not gone unnoticed in his own time. Julius Bahnsen, for instance, whose *Zur*

---

[60] See ibid., vol. II, pp. 127–8 and 439. The passage that Schopenhauer has in mind is Aristotle, *Poetics*, 1451b5.
[61] See Schopenhauer, *The World as Will and Representation*, vol. II, pp. 440–1.
[62] See ibid., vol. II, p. 442.
[63] See ibid., vol. II, p. 445. Paul Gottfried, "Arthur Schopenhauer as a Critic of History," *Journal of the History of Ideas* 36 (1975), 331–8: 334–5, has suggested that Schopenhauer's changing ideas about historical knowledge are largely a result of his early quarrel with Hegel and his jealousy about the public success of Hegelianism. In contrast, Harry J. Ausmus, "Schopenhauer's View of History: A Note," *History and Theory* 15 (1976), 141–5, has argued that Schopenhauer's assessment of history is actually quite positive and should not be reduced to his negative experience of the Hegelians.
[64] Eduard von Hartmann, *Die Philosophie des Unbewussten* (Berlin: Duncker, 1869), pp. 454 and 637–8. See Federico Gerratana, "Der Wahn jenseits des Menschen: Zur frühen E. v. Hartmann-Rezeption Friedrich Nietzsches (1869–1874)," *Nietzsche-Studien* 17 (1988), 391–433.

Philosophie der Geschichte (1872) Nietzsche read shortly after it reached the booksellers, criticized Hartmann as presenting a Hegelianism in disguise that ran counter to Schopenhauer's position.⁶⁵ In his second "Untimely Meditation" on the "uses" and "disadvantages" of history for life, Nietzsche himself was to regard Hartmann as a Hegelian and duly rejected his teleological notion of historical progress (*UM* II: 9). But although Schopenhauer does not feature prominently in *Vom Nutzen und Nachtheil der Historie für das Leben*, Nietzsche's critical remarks about Hartmann were also a hidden rejection of Schopenhauer's views on history, since both Hartmann's and Schopenhauer's philosophical framework relied on the notion of an "unconscious will" underlying all appearances. After reading Rudolf Haym's critical essay "Arthur Schopenhauer" – first published in 1864 in the *Preußische Jahrbücher*, the series itself founded by the historian Heinrich von Treitschke with Heinrich von Sybel as one of the main early contributors – he grew increasingly disillusioned with the metaphysical speculations of *Die Welt als Wille und Vorstellung*.⁶⁶

It should be obvious that Nietzsche, in the 1860s as in the 1870s, was very much aware of the problems of historical knowledge. At times, his remarks from the late 1860s even seem to foreshadow some of the central ideas of *Vom Nutzen und Nachtheil der Historie für das Leben*, especially when he points out that "one currently tends to overestimate history" and that "humanity has more to do than making history" (*KGW*1/4, 56 [3] and 57 [30]). But his occasional impatience with history should not lead us to believe that he wished to abandon history altogether. On the contrary, while he was busy dismantling what he regarded as a wrong understanding of history, he read Herodotus and Thucydides, outlined future courses on "the beginnings of Greek historiography" and on "the development of historical scholarship among the Greeks" (*KGW* 1/4, 52 [66] and 56 [8]).⁶⁷

---

⁶⁵ See Julius Bahnsen, *Zur Philosophie der Geschichte: Eine kritische Besprechung des Hegel-Hartmann'schen Evolutionismus aus Schopenhauer'schen Principien* (Berlin: Duncker, 1872). Nietzsche borrowed this book twice from the University Library in Basel in February 1871 and in April 1872.
⁶⁶ See Sandro Barbera, "Eine Quelle der frühen Schopenhauer-Kritik Nietzsches: Rudolf Hayms Aufsatz *Arthur Schopenhauer*," *Nietzsche-Studien* 24 (1995), 124–36.
⁶⁷ Around the same time, a colorful collection of historical titles began to appear on Nietzsche's reading lists, including Christoph Meiners's *Geschichte des Ursprungs, Fortgangs und Verfalls der Wissenschaften in Griechenland und Rom* (1781–82) and

But from whichever way Nietzsche attempted to approach the nature of history and historical knowledge, he encountered the question as to whether historical studies should be seen in terms of *Kunst* or in terms of *Wissenschaft*. That Nietzsche had to confront this question has much to do with the theoretical tensions within contemporary historical thought itself. The emergence of historicist models within German historical scholarship during the final decades of the eighteenth century represented a fundamental change that could still be felt in the second half of the nineteenth century: the humanist principle of history as the "narration of actions" (*narratio rei gestae*), itself based on a strictly rhetorical model, had been transformed into a conception of history that was at once empirical in orientation and theoretically reflective.[68] Although "historical knowledge" (*cognitio historica*) was regarded deep into the nineteenth century as inferior to philosophical thought, the historicization of reason and culture in the course of the nineteenth century – together with obvious political factors, such as the French Revolution and the Napoleonic Wars – rendered it possible for history to become the dominant explanatory paradigm within the humanities in Germany. But this also meant that the study of history itself continued to be subject to the fundamental tension between "art" and "science."[69]

Considering the context of Nietzsche's notebooks of 1867/68, he clearly derived some inspiration for his ideas about the historical method from an unlikely source, Ferdinand Christian Baur, the founder of the so-called Tübingen School of Protestant theology, which sought to found theological principles upon historical and critical analysis.[70] In an inconspicuous note in which Nietzsche

---

Friedrich Creuzer's *Die historische Kunst der Griechen* (1803). See *KGW* 1/4, 38 [13] and [15], 52 [31], 58 [64], and 62 [48].

[68] See Horst Walter Blanke, Dirk Fleischer, and Jörn Rüsen, "Theory of History in Historical Lectures: The German Tradition of *Historik*, 1750–1900," *History and Theory* 23 (1984), 331–56.

[69] See Horst Dreitzel, "Die Entwicklung der Historie zur Wissenschaft," *Zeitschrift für historische Forschung* 8 (1981), 257–84.

[70] A summary of Baur's position can be found in his *Die Tübinger Schule und ihre Stellung zur Gegenwart*, 2nd edn., enlarged (Tübingen: Fues, 1860), pp. 3–85, and "Die Einleitung in das Neue Testament als theologische Wissenschaft: Ihr Begriff und ihre Aufgabe, ihr Entwicklungsgang und ihr innerer Organismus," *Theologische Jahrbücher* 9 (1850), 463–566, and 10 (1851), 70–94 and 291–329. Among Baur's pupils were the philosophers Eduard Zeller and Albert Schwegler as well as the theologian Albrecht Ritschl. See Horton Harris, *The Tübingen School: A Historical and Theological Investigation*

presents the view that the historical understanding of any source material is inevitably influenced by the historian's complex cultural and intellectual background, he discusses Baur's repeated demand for a critical reassessment of what it means to think historically (*KGW* 1/4, 56 [6]).

That Nietzsche, the son of a Protestant minister, should discover Baur is not surprising. Once biblical hermeneutics, influenced by the close institutional relationship between theology and philology at German universities – in particular at Göttingen and Halle – began to adopt the methods of textual criticism for the exegesis of the Scriptures in the later eighteenth century, the road was open for the rise of historicism within Protestant thought. Although the historicist turn of Protestant theology properly speaking is often dated to the 1890s, the first decades of the nineteenth century witnessed an intense debate about the status of historical knowledge, and about the uses of the historical method, among Protestant theologians. Within these debates, Baur and the Tübingen School – including Baur's pupil Albrecht Ritschl, a nephew of Nietzsche's teacher Friedrich Ritschl – embraced the historical nature of Christianity.[71] Although the members of the Tübingen School were often unable to reconcile Protestant dogma with the historicity of Christianity, the introduction of historical methods into Protestant theology promised a more critical account of theological orthodoxy. But as soon as Baur adopted the methods that already shaped the work of contemporary philologists and professional historians, he also needed to consider from a more philosophical point of view what it meant to think about cultural processes predominantly in terms of their historical development. This issue surfaced already in his *Lehrbuch der christlichen Dogmengeschichte* (1847), where he emphasized a "critical" approach to history that, in contrast to a mere "empirical" one, should ideally be able to deliver objective knowledge about the past.[72]

---

 into the School of F. C. Baur (Oxford: Clarendon Press, 1975), especially pp. 11–88, 101–12 and 137–80.
[71] See Baur, *Die Tübinger Schule*, pp. 13–14, and Albrecht Ritschl, "Ueber geschichtliche Methode in der Erforschung des Urchristenthums," *Jahrbücher für Deutsche Theologie* 6 (1861), 429–59.
[72] See Ferdinand Christian Baur, "Lehrbuch der christlichen Dogmengeschichte: Vorrede der ersten Ausgabe (1847)," in *Ausgewählte Werke in Einzelausgaben*, ed. Klaus Scholder (Stuttgart-Bad Cannstatt: Frommann, 1963–70), vol. II, pp. 303–8: 307.

Clearly, Baur did not wish to give up the teleological conception of historical development he encountered in the works of the idealists Hegel, Schelling and Schleiermacher. But in what was to become perhaps his most influential work, *Die Epochen der kirchlichen Geschichtsschreibung* (1852), which Nietzsche's own theology professor in Bonn, Wilhelm Ludwig Krafft, will have referred to in his lectures on church history, Baur began to realize the difficulties of his own historical approach: much like Hegel and Schopenhauer, albeit for different reasons, Baur concluded that it would be inevitable to avoid a fundamental tension between the "objective" reality of the past and our "subjective" knowledge about historical events. As a result, the historian will never really be able to present an account of history that corresponds to the events of the past, for history tends to dissolve into an "infinite web" of causes and effects that elude the historian's understanding. Only historical distance might allow us to overcome this limitation and grasp the "idea" of historical developments, that is, the successive unfolding of the "spirit" in the history of the Protestant Church.[73]

On the one hand, Nietzsche agreed with Baur's skepticism about the subjective nature of historical knowledge. On the other, he was unable to accept the Hegelian outlook of Baur's deliberations, since the latter still believed that it was indeed possible to detect a necessary and law-like process behind historical events, such as the course of ecclesiastical history and the history of Christian dogma. Nietzsche, however, who had just discovered Kant, clearly regarded such teleological speculations as plain nonsense: historical "events," he notes, do not follow any "necessary course," and the "historian" is in any case unable to show that historical processes are themselves "reasonable." Any attempt at describing teleological developments in history is an "illusion" (*KGW* 1/4, 56 [5]). For Nietzsche, this also implied that the idea of "progress" was not a necessary "law of history" – "neither in intellectual, nor in moral and economic terms" (*KGW* 1/4, 56 [4]).

To be sure, Nietzsche's skepticism with regard to the nature of history and the status of historical knowledge is not without its own problems. The main question he has to face is: Why should the

---

[73] See Ferdinand Christian Baur, *Die Epochen der kirchlichen Geschichtsschreibung* (Tübingen: Fues, 1852), pp. 13–14 and 18.

study of history still be of interest, if it is unable to lead to any certain knowledge? What is, in other words, the value of history? Only much later, in *Menschliches, Allzumenschliches* (1878–80), would he be able to provide a proper answer to this question when he noted that "historical understanding [*historischer Sinn*]" consists in isolating and comparing different epochs in such a way that they highlight not some kind of pre-established cultural continuity, but the tendency toward change (*HA* I: 274).[74] Nietzsche is thus far from rejecting history altogether: "Direct self-observation is not nearly sufficient for us to know ourselves: we require history, for the past continues to flow within us in a hundred waves; we ourselves are, indeed, nothing but that which at every moment we experience in this continued flowing" (*HA* II: i.223).

TOWARD A CAUTIOUS MATERIALISM

Nietzsche's interest in the problem of historical knowledge is clearly inspired by his practical experience of classical scholarship as, strictly speaking, a historical discipline. At the same time, we should not underestimate the relevance of Nietzsche's philosophical interests during the 1860s. Already in Carl Schaarschmidt's introductory lectures on the history of philosophy at the University of Bonn in the summer of 1865, he encountered the main historical and contemporary trends of philosophical thought. Schaarschmidt clearly devoted much time to familiarizing his students with the works of Kant, Hegel, and Schopenhauer. Underlying these lectures is in many respects the Hegelian assumption that the history of thought should be understood as a logical succession of different philosophical systems. "The history of philosophy," Nietzsche wrote in one of his notes on Schaarschmidt's lectures, "is an intellectual process, a specific struggle for the unfolding of reason [*Entwicklungskampf der Vernunft*]" (GSA 41/76, p. 3). The problem of teleology that Schaarschmidt highlighted with this remark was to play a central role within Nietzsche's own philosophical education and it also was to have a lasting influence on his historical thought.

---

[74] Hollingdale translates Nietzsche's expression *historischer Sinn* literally as "historical sense."

Nietzsche's early philosophical education was in many ways accidental. Once he had left Bonn for Leipzig, where he did not really attend any courses in philosophy, he began to project, in 1867/68, larger dissertations on Democritus and Kant, which sought to deal with contemporary philosophical topics, such as materialism, teleology, and organicist views of life. But shortly before he began to consider the possibility of a philosophical dissertation, he received what is often regarded as his main initiation into philosophical thought when he had famously stumbled in a bookshop upon the first volume of Arthur Schopenhauer's *Die Welt als Wille und Vorstellung*, which is rightly regarded as the most important document of post-Kantian idealism.[75] Subsequently he acquired the latter's *Parerga und Paralipomena* (1851), and in 1866, he also read Friedrich Albert Lange's *Geschichte des Materialismus*, which was to become one of the most influential documents for the rise of neo-Kantian thought in nineteenth-century Germany. Indeed, the encounter with Schopenhauer and Lange led Nietzsche toward a cautious materialism that was to resurface on several occasions throughout many of his later writings.

Schopenhauer's status as an early educator of Nietzsche is well documented and the details need not concern us here. It is nonetheless necessary to stress that Nietzsche's relationship to Schopenhauer is not without ambivalence.[76] Representing the world "as it is," in opposition to the world of "appearances" that largely shape human experience, Schopenhauer's notion of "will" as an unconscious striving force provided Nietzsche with a conceptual framework that was to have a considerable influence on both the philosophical perspective and the vocabulary of *Die Geburt der Tragödie*, (*BT* pp. 31–3 and 76–80). Praising Schopenhauer's victory over the presumed optimism of rational and logical thought, and interpreting ancient Greek culture through the lens of "pessimism," Nietzsche emphasized the importance of unconscious and dream-like appearances as indicative of the will, in very much the same way as the experience of music was supposed to be an expression of the will (*BT* pp. 14–19, 76–80 and 85–8).[77] We

---

[75] See Terry Pinkard, *German Philosophy, 1760–1860: The Legacy of Idealism* (Cambridge: Cambridge University Press, 2002), pp. 333–45.
[76] See the contributions in Christopher Janaway (ed.), *Willing and Nothingness: Schopenhauer as Nietzsche's Educator* (Oxford: Clarendon Press, 1998).
[77] See Schopenhauer, *The World as Will and Representation*, vol. I, pp. 255–67.

cannot help noticing, however, that, in comparison to his later philosophical criticism, the philosophical arguments Nietzsche puts forth in his book on tragedy are not particularly sophisticated. They have more to do, in short, with Nietzsche's enthusiasm for Schopenhauer as a philosophical outsider than with a sound reflection on the implications of the latter's position. Indeed, many years later, in *Ecce Homo*, written in 1888–89, Nietzsche pointed out that Schopenhauer's pessimism was rather questionable, like many other aspects of Schopenhauer's philosophy (*EH* v: 1). As a result, it has often been suggested that Nietzsche's thought falls into two distinctive periods: "with" Schopenhauer and "after" Schopenhauer. But again, such a distinction is awkward once we realize that, despite his glowing admiration for Schopenhauer's philosophical prose, already Nietzsche's early accounts of Schopenhauer's metaphysical speculations in 1867/68 betray a more critical perspective. He argued, for instance, that Schopenhauer's theory of the will is merely an "experiment," a speculative philosophical claim that ultimately "failed" (*KGW* 1/4, 57 [51]), and he continued to speak of the "contradictions" that ran through "Schopenhauer's system" (*KGW* 1/4, 57 [55]).

Against this background, we need to be cautious with regard to the assumption that Nietzsche's philosophy as a whole was largely inspired by Schopenhauer's metaphysics.[78] This clearly continues to be a widely held belief and also plays into an aestheticist reading of Nietzsche.[79] On the other hand, it also requires serious revision, since it is not difficult to show that Nietzsche's reception of Schopenhauer remains highly ambivalent.[80] Nietzsche's enthusiasm for Schopenhauer's metaphysics began to decline almost immediately after he had read *Die Welt als Wille und Vorstellung* in 1865. Nietzsche's notebooks from late 1867 and 1868 are

---

[78] This assumption can be found, for instance, in Martin Heidegger, *Nietzsche* (Pfullingen: Neske, 1961), vol. II, p. 239, and Hollingdale, *Nietzsche*, p. 51.
[79] See, for instance, Alexander Nehamas, *Nietzsche: Life as Literature* (Cambridge, Mass.: Harvard University Press, 1985), p. 42.
[80] See Manfred Riedel, "Ein Seitenstück zur *Geburt der Tragödie*: Nietzsches Abkehr von Schopenhauer und Wagner und seine Wende zur Philosophie," *Nietzsche-Studien* 24 (1995), 45–61, and Sandro Barbera, "Ein Sinn und unzählige Hieroglyphen: Einige Motive von Nietzsches Auseinandersetzung mit Schopenhauer in der Basler Zeit," in Tilman Borsche, Federico Gerratana, and Aldo Venturelli (eds.), *"Centauren-Geburten": Wissenschaft, Kunst und Philosophie beim jungen Nietzsche* (Berlin: Walter de Gruyter, 1994), pp. 217–33.

particularly interesting in this respect, since they show that he was not entirely comfortable with the metaphysical claims of Schopenhauer's work.[81]

It is nevertheless necessary to understand that one of the most crucial aspects of Schopenhauer's philosophy, his emphasis on the link between perception and knowledge, plays a fundamental role for Nietzsche's developing philosophical beliefs (*KGW* 1/4, 57 [62]): once we are able to realize, largely on Kantian grounds, that there are no "things-in-themselves" properly speaking, we also have to accept that intellectual operations are based on "nothing but images and names" (*KGW* 1/4, 57 [55]).[82] Nietzsche's early reception of Schopenhauer thus contributes to his growing epistemological skepticism, which gained momentum through his reading of Lange's *Geschichte des Materialismus* (1866).

Lange is undoubtedly a central figure in the philosophical discourse of nineteenth-century Germany. Like Nietzsche the son of a Protestant minister, Lange moved to Switzerland while still in his youth, where his father had been appointed Professor of Protestant Theology at the University of Zurich. The liberal climate of Zurich left many traces in Lange's political convictions, and he openly opposed Bismarck's politics by becoming involved in the labor movement, while at the same time favoring a vision of German unification along the lines of a democratic nation state. After studying philosophy, classical philology and theology in Zurich and Bonn, and after several short interludes as a high-school teacher, he was later to become the founder of the so-called Marburg School, which continued to influence the reception of Kant until the early twentieth century. As such, he is rightly regarded as one of the most central figures in the rise of neo-Kantianism from the mid-1860s onward.[83] At the beginning of the twentieth century, Wilhelm Windelband, another representative of the neo-Kantian tradition,

---

[81] See Hill, *Nietzsche's Critiques*, pp. 75 and 94–6.
[82] On Schopenhauer's theory of perception, see Christopher Janaway, *Self and World in Schopenhauer's Philosophy* (Oxford: Clarendon Press, 1989), pp. 157–65.
[83] See Klaus Christian Köhnke, *Entstehung und Aufstieg des Neukantianismus: Die deutsche Universitätsphilosophie zwischen Idealismus und Positivismus* (Frankfurt/M.: Suhrkamp, 1986), pp. 233–57, and Thomas E. Willey, *Back to Kant: The Revival of Kantianism in German Social and Historical Thought, 1860–1914* (Detroit, Mich.: Wayne State University Press, 1978), pp. 83–101.

The failure of neo-humanism 57

pointedly remarked that Lange's *Geschichte des Materialismus* exemplifies like no other work the general intellectual atmosphere among German philosophers in the second half of the nineteenth century.[84]

Active in social democratic political movements, and interested in questions of constitutional reform, Lange was a prolific writer able to link the intellectual developments of his environment to social issues, as in his *Die Arbeiterfrage* (1865), which separated his own liberalism from the national liberalism of Heinrich von Sybel. His most lasting contribution is, however, his profound influence on the formation of neo-Kantian thought from the late 1860s onward. Since 1870, he held a professorship in philosophy at the University of Zurich, after he failed to obtain a suitable position in Germany. Despite his status as an outsider, Lange was quickly able to establish himself, also through family connections, within the patrician environment of the Swiss city and only left in 1873, shortly before his death, to accept a chair in philosophy at the University of Marburg.

Lange's widely read account of materialism in European thought provided Nietzsche with a comprehensive historical narrative that traced the development of materialism from ancient Greek philosophy up to Kant, who, for Nietzsche, emerged as a viable and more sophisticated alternative to Schopenhauer.[85] More importantly, however, Lange also investigated the implications of materialism for the theory of knowledge in the context of nineteenth-century science, especially with regard to physiology and allied experimental disciplines. In contrast to a more positivist scientific materialism, intent on reducing human knowledge to the methodological framework of the natural sciences, Lange argued that the foundations of human knowledge cannot be reduced to rule-governed natural phenomena, for our very understanding of such rule-governed natural phenomena changes over time and is dependent on fairly complex conceptual arrangements:

> Those who ... wish to content themselves with building a temple of concepts, which might not really contradict the contemporary state of

---

[84] See Wilhelm Windelband, *Die Philosophie im deutschen Geistesleben des 19. Jahrhunderts*, 2nd edn. (Tübingen: J. C. B. Mohr, 1909), p. 82.
[85] See George J. Stack, *Lange and Nietzsche* (Berlin: Walter de Gruyter, 1983), pp. 195–223, and Stack, "Kant, Lange, and Nietzsche: Critique of Knowledge," in Keith Ansell-Pearson (ed.), *Nietzsche and Modern German Thought* (London: Routledge, 1991), pp. 30–58.

the positive sciences, but which might be destroyed by every methodically gained progress, and which might be torn down and rebuilt anew by any later architect, might certainly pride themselves with the construction of a charming and perfect work of art, but they also necessarily renounce the advancement of true and lasting knowledge in any field.[86]

Both a positivist notion of science and the metaphysical conjectures of idealism, thus, merely represent a numinous conceptual poetry unable to analyze the intricacies of human knowledge.[87] As a consequence, Lange repeatedly pointed out that neither things-in-themselves, nor the assumption of a direct access to reality, are feasible philosophical options, since the interplay between sensory perception and mental abstraction shapes our understanding of our environment.[88]

Much of Lange's argument undoubtedly rests on a detailed reading of Kant as the great watershed of philosophical thought which finally questions our preconceived ideas about the relationship between "subject" and "object."[89] This also means that Lange's argument goes one step further than Kant's "transcendental aesthetic" and "transcendental analytic" in suggesting that our notions of "space," "time," "causality," "force," "substance," and so on, are necessary fictions according to which we order our perceptions and mental images. Central to Lange's epistemological critique is, however, also the idea that our perception of reality is mostly a product of our biological organization and its interaction with the "intelligible world":

For the time being it is entirely irrelevant as to whether the phenomenal world can be reduced to mental representations or to the mechanism of our organs, as long as we regard it as a product of our organization in the widest possible sense of this term. As soon as this has become obvious not only with regard to individual perceptions, but is acknowledged as sufficiently universal, the following series of conclusions is the result:

(1) The world of sensory perception is a product of our organization.
(2) Our visible (bodily) organs are, like all other parts of the world of appearances, merely images of an unknown object.

---

[86] See Friedrich Albert Lange, *Geschichte des Materialismus und Kritik seiner Bedeutung in der Gegenwart* (Iserlohn: Baedeker, 1866), p. 471 (emphasized in the original).
[87] See ibid., p. 346.   [88] See, for instance, ibid., pp. 484, 490 and 492.
[89] See ibid., pp. 233–78.

(3) Our true organization is therefore as unknown to us as is external reality [*die wirklichen Außendinge*]. In all cases, we are merely faced with the product of their interaction.[90]

In Nietzsche's reading this leads to a heightened form of skepticism about the foundations of human knowledge that becomes particularly manifest in an early letter to Carl von Gersdorff from August 1866, in which he quotes the above passage from Lange almost verbatim and concludes:

> We are faced with a highly enlightened Kantian and natural scientist [*Naturforscher*]. ... The true being of reality, the thing-in-itself, is thus not only unknown to us, but even its concept is nothing more and nothing less than born from a contradiction within our organization of which we cannot say whether it makes any sense beyond our experience. (*KGB* I/2, pp. 159–60)

Lange undoubtedly provided Nietzsche with a thorough conceptual framework from which he was able to assail the claims of what he perceived to be metaphysical dogmatism. But it should also be obvious that this epistemological skepticism had a profound effect on the way in which Nietzsche sought to come to terms with the status of historical knowledge. If, in other words, our knowledge about ourselves cannot be based on any objective point of reference, then it might very well also be the case that our knowledge about historical epochs remains a complex imaginary construction equally dependent on the imaginary nature of "facts," "causes," and so on. Although Nietzsche is not yet ready to do this, Lange's account of materialism will ultimately force him to consider the cultural value of such illusions.

Lange's argument clearly develops against the background of the growing gap between the claims of the natural sciences, which were able to present universally valid laws, and the humanistic disciplines, which increasingly came to accept the contingency of human experience. This gap began to emerge already during the 1840s, gained prominence during the 1870s and 1880s, and continued to be of central importance at the beginning of the twentieth century in the work of neo-Kantians such as Wilhelm Windelband, Heinrich Rickert, and Max Weber. Lange's own position is ambiguous and can perhaps best be described as a cautious materialism.

---

[90] See ibid., p. 493.

Highlighting the epistemological difficulties of the contemporary natural sciences, especially physics and physiology, he is, on the one hand, clearly unwilling to reduce human knowledge to law-like processes and also unable to accept that science delivers any kind of objective knowledge properly speaking. On the other, he argues that we can only reach this conclusion, once we have gained a more detailed understanding of the way in which the natural world, including our own physiology, is connected to what we call knowledge. Many dimensions of human experience are bound to resist an explanation according to natural laws, or so he believes. Lange's position in many ways encapsulates central aspects of the intellectual environment within which Nietzsche himself began to discuss the nature of historical knowledge. More importantly, though, some of the questions that Lange raised with regard to the limits of materialism were to reappear many years later in the cautious philosophical naturalism that characterizes Nietzsche's genealogical project during the 1880s.

It is ironic to realize that, when Nietzsche was a student at the University of Leipzig, the university itself was slowly beginning to emerge as one of the main centers for the attempt to bridge the gap between the natural sciences and the human sciences on empirical grounds. Leipzig was home to Gustav Theodor Fechner, the founder of "psycho-physics," whose writings often focused on the functional interdependence of the physical and the intellectual world, but also to Ernst Heinrich Weber, whose work on nerve stimulation and human physiology can be regarded as the foundation of experimental psychology, which was continued by the work of Wilhelm Wundt, himself a pupil of Hermann von Helmholtz.[91] The philosophical implications of this research furnished much of the background to Lange's *Geschichte des Materialismus*.[92] We can thus reasonably assume that Nietzsche himself became aware of Fechner's and Weber's ideas, which were very much at the forefront of contemporary physiology, through Lange. Furthermore, Fechner was a close friend of the Leipzig astrophysicist Carl

---

[91] See Gustav Theodor Fechner, *Elemente der Psychophysik* (Leipzig: Breitkopf & Härtel, 1860), vol. I, p. 8. See also Michael Heidelberger, *Die innere Seite der Natur: Gustav Theodor Fechners wissenschaftlich-philosophische Weltauffassung* (Frankfurt/M.: Klostermann, 1993), pp. 217–37.

[92] See Lange, *Geschichte des Materialismus*, pp. 410–500.

The failure of neo-humanism 61

Friedrich Zöllner, who had made his own name in the area of optical research. Zöllner was, however, also the author of a series of essays on the theory of science, collected under the curious title *Über die Natur der Cometen* (1872), in which he devoted much time and energy to assessing contemporary debates in physiology, often referring back to the work of his Leipzig colleagues Fechner and Weber.[93] Nietzsche himself read Zöllner's treatise only several years after he had left Leipzig for the University of Basel. But it is important to realize that the epistemological issues discussed by both Zöllner and Lange develop against the background of precisely that kind of scientific materialism that was practiced at the University of Leipzig. These intellectual configurations were to introduce Nietzsche, perhaps more directly than Schopenhauer, to the complex relationship between consciousness and reality, which was to mark his epistemological skepticism during the early 1870s, especially in his notebooks of the time and the essay "Ueber Wahrheit und Lüge im aussermoralischen Sinne" of 1873: "The stimulation of a nerve is first translated into an image! first metaphor. The image is then imitated by a sound! Second metaphor. And each time there is a complete leap from one sphere straight into a completely different and new one" (*TL*, p. 144).[94] For Nietzsche this meant that, precisely because human physiology and the biological organization of the human body shaped human knowledge and experience, our understanding of the empirical was of a rather problematic nature. For his developing views on the status and value of historical knowledge this was bound to have serious implications.

At the University of Leipzig, however, scientific materialism was not limited to physiology and psychology.[95] One of the most prominent members among the faculty was the political economist

---

[93] See Johann Carl Friedrich Zöllner, *Über die Natur der Cometen: Beiträge zur Geschichte und Theorie der Erkenntniss*, 2nd edn. (Leipzig: Engelmann, 1872), pp. 329–34 and 378–425.
[94] See Christian J. Emden, "Metaphor, Perception, and Consciousness: Nietzsche on Rhetoric and Neurophysiology," in Gregory Moore and Thomas H. Brobjer (eds.), *Nietzsche and Science* (Aldershot: Ashgate, 2004), pp. 91–110.
[95] On the personal and institutional configurations in Leipzig, see Roger Chickering, "Das Leipziger 'Positivisten-Kränzchen' um die Jahrhundertwende," in Gangolf Hübinger, Rüdiger vom Bruch, and Friedrich Wilhelm Graf (eds.), *Kultur und Kulturwissenschaften um 1900, II: Idealismus und Positivismus* (Stuttgart: Steiner, 1997), pp. 227–45.

Wilhelm Roscher, who had studied under Georg Gottfried Gervinius and Arnold Ludwig Heeren at the University of Göttingen, two of the most prominent German historians of the time. Although Roscher's first academic work was on the Greek historian Thucydides, he soon turned to contemporary political economy (*Nationalökonomie*). As a discourse about the dynamics of value within society, political economy allowed Roscher to establish direct links between scientific and humanistic disciplines, even though he clearly regarded his approach as a "science," not as "scholarship."[96] Already as a lecturer in Göttingen in the early 1840s he outlined a program of political economy as a scientific enterprise properly speaking, which was to focus on the statistically measurable laws of economic development, on the one hand, and which sought to connect its results to insights derived from legal and cultural history, on the other.[97] As a consequence, Roscher proposed a view which was at once scientific and able to stress that the different stages in the history of economic development, from ancient societies to modern industrialism, were contingent upon their different institutional contexts and predominant political structures – factors which the laissez-faire view regarded as being outside the realm of economic interpretation.

Despite the historicist slant of his approach, Roscher was far from accepting any form of historical contingency: economic stages might be marked by differences in their historical setting, but there were clear developmental laws and factors that could be classified in objective terms.[98] Although the outlook of Roscher's approach often seems to be Hegelian in that he stipulates a teleological development of economic differentiation, the positivist environment in Leipzig during the 1850s and 1860s played a prominent role. Once Roscher had arrived at the city's university in 1848, he found himself in the company of Fechner and Weber, who highlighted much like Roscher that social and psychological reality could be dissolved into a set of abstract functional relationships that

---

[96] See David F. Lindenfeld, *The Practical Imagination: The German Sciences of the State in the Nineteenth Century* (Chicago: University of Chicago Press, 1997), p. 155.

[97] See Wilhelm Roscher, *Grundriss zu Vorlesungen über die Staatswirthschaft nach geschichtlicher Methode* (Göttingen: Dieterich, 1843), p. iv. This approach was more fully developed a decade later in the first volume of Roscher's *System der Volkswirthschaft* with the title *Grundlagen der Nationalökonomie* (Stuttgart: Cotta, 1854).

[98] See Lindenfeld, *The Practical Imagination*, p. 156.

required little, if any, foundation in the neo-humanist models still favored by the historical disciplines; cultural values were not a question of human experience and historical consciousness, but – once all factors were known – they could ideally be calculated according to specific, albeit very complex, laws.

Nietzsche himself seems to have been more aware of this background than generally assumed. While it is obvious that his reading of Schopenhauer, Lange and Kant occupied his philosophical interests during the late 1860s, he did in fact have some personal contact with Roscher (*KGB* I/2, p. 373). He realized the importance of the latter's work already in Bonn, when he recommended Roscher, of whom he had probably heard in the lectures of Heinrich von Sybel, to his close friend Carl von Gersdorff (*KGB* I/2, p. 55). Once he had arrived in Leipzig himself, Nietzsche also became a friend of Roscher's son Wilhelm Heinrich, who happened to study classical philology and who became, like Nietzsche, an ardent follower of Friedrich Ritschl. Despite some tension in their personal relations, Nietzsche stayed in contact with him until 1870. Furthermore, Ernst Windisch, another close friend of Nietzsche's in Leipzig, who started out as a philologist and who was to become one of the foremost comparative linguists in late nineteenth-century Germany, was soon to be engaged to Roscher's daughter (*KGB* II/1, pp. 306 and 320). Indeed, within the close-knit academic community of Leipzig it was difficult to avoid Roscher both personally and intellectually. As such, it should not be surprising that a student of classical scholarship like Nietzsche, who had already frequented Sybel's lectures on politics at the University of Bonn, would also attend Roscher's lectures on political economy, "Grundlagen der praktischen Politik als Einleitung in die gesamte Staats- und Rechtswissenschaft," in the winter semester of 1865–66 (*KGB* I/2, p. 129). Indeed, he found Roscher's lectures inspiring enough to make a partial transcript (GSA 49/84, pp. 88–92, 94–7, 100, and 102–5).[99] It seems that the political perspectives of Sybel's and Roscher's lectures provided an enriching alternative to the neo-humanist approach he found in the courses of Ritschl.

[99] In fact, Nietzsche's notes of Roscher's lectures are far more detailed than his notes of Ritschl's courses on Roman epigraphics and Aeschylus, which ran parallel to Roscher's lectures (*GSA* 49/84, pp. 3–8 and 27–33).

The atmosphere at the University of Leipzig, which was indicative of the wider intellectual configurations in nineteenth-century Germany, clearly exerted a lasting influence on Nietzsche. Within this context, the legacy of German philosophy, which was often quoted as the foundation for the neo-humanist outlook of much contemporary historical scholarship, emerged as increasingly troubled. As long as neo-humanism, suggesting a unity of human knowledge and experience, could be seen as providing orientation for the humanities, the cultural value of historical knowledge itself was not in question. But as soon as the program of neo-humanism was on the defensive, the status of historical knowledge became an increasingly serious problem. This becomes more evident once we take into account Nietzsche's growing interest in Kant during the years 1866–68.

TELEOLOGY AND THE LAWS OF HISTORY

Although Nietzsche's reception of Kant's critical philosophy is still under discussion, many of his philosophical ideas are, of course, strongly influenced by Kantian themes.[100] In the winter of 1867/68, when he was still a student in Leipzig, and once he had read Schopenhauer and Lange, Nietzsche turned to Kant's *Kritik der Urteilskraft* (1790). At first sight, it is certainly true that Nietzsche's early interests in Kant, in particular his notebook from April and May 1868, are largely linked to the problem of teleology in natural philosophy (*KGW* I/4, 62 [3]–[57]). His eclectic reading lists betray an attempt to link a reassessment of Kant's thought under the ambitious title "Die Teleologie seit Kant" to a more materialist emphasis on physiology and the life sciences (*KGW* I/4, 62 [6]).[101] Nietzsche's often cryptic remarks

---

[100] See Hill, *Nietzsche's Critiques*, pp. 1-37, 73–116 and 169–95. Nietzsche's knowledge of Kant's philosophical enterprise is to a considerable extent mediated by Schaarschmidt, Schopenhauer and Lange. But in an inconspicuous note from 1867/68, Nietzsche also mentions Karl Rosenkranz, *Geschichte der Kant'schen Philosophie* (Leipzig: Voss, 1840), and Kuno Fischer, *Immanuel Kant: Entwicklungsgeschichte und System der kritischen Philosophie* (Mannheim: Bassermann, 1860), which is the third and fourth part of the latter's *Geschichte der neuern Philosophie*, published in ten volumes since 1854 (*KGW* I/4, 58 [46]).

[101] Nietzsche's reading lists can be found in *KGW* I/4, 62 [48] and [53]. Apart from numerous references to Kant and Schelling, as well as to contemporary interpretations of their philosophical ideas, he obviously wished to include much new scientific material, including Hermann von Helmholtz, *Ueber die Wechselwirkung der Naturkräfte und die darauf bezüglichen neuesten Fortschritte der Physik: Populär-wissenschaftlicher Vortrag*

about the implications of Kant's concept of teleology are clearly inspired by his reading of Lange, and it is interesting to note that they are largely built around the central Kantian assumption of teleology as a mental construct projected onto nature (*KGW* 1/4, 62 [7]).[102]

In terms of a goal-oriented formative drive teleology served as an important explanatory model within the life sciences of the nineteenth century, and in the context of Jean Baptiste Lamarck's *Philosophie zoologique* (1809) and Charles Darwin's *The Origin of Species* (1859), teleological models were a central part of the dominant evolutionary arguments of the time. Theories of generation, epigenetic and otherwise, introduced teleological theories of growth and inheritance into the discourse of morphology, embryology, and *Entwicklungsmechanik*.[103] Although many of these positions can be traced back to the biological debates of the eighteenth century, we can witness an increasing popularization of such theories from around 1800 onward, which culminates in the second half of the nineteenth century; the very concept of "life" underwent drastic changes at the beginning of the nineteenth century and these changes had an effect on the way in which the notion of "vital forces" became a central paradigm in the biological sciences and beyond.[104]

Nietzsche's notebooks of 1867–68 show that he was aware of these trends. In fact, his tentative reading lists, which included Lorenz Oken's *Lehrbuch der Naturphilosophie* (1809–11) and Johannes Müller's famous *Handbuch der Physiologie des Menschen* (1833–40), show that his many reflections on Kantian teleology cannot really be separated from the contemporary popularization

---

(Königsberg: Gräfe & Unzer, 1854), and Rudolph Hermann Lotze, *Medicinische Psychologie oder Physiologie der Seele* (Leipzig: Weidmann, 1852).

[102] Nietzsche's notes on Kant's concept of teleology, together with his projected work on post-Kantian notions of teleology in the contemporary biological sciences, have received limited attention. See, however, Hill, *Nietzsche's Critiques*, pp. 83–94.

[103] See Lynn K. Nyhart, *Biology Takes Form: Animal Morphology and the German Universities, 1800–1900* (Chicago: University of Chicago Press, 1995), pp. 105–42, and Timothy Lenoir, *The Strategy of Life: Teleology and Mechanics in Nineteenth-Century German Biology* (Dordrecht: Reidel, 1982), pp. 156–94.

[104] See Michel Foucault, *The Order of Things: An Archaeology of the Human Sciences* (New York: Vintage, 1971), pp. 226–32 and 281, and Robert J. Richards, *The Romantic Conception of Life: Science and Philosophy in the Age of Goethe* (Chicago: University of Chicago Press, 2002), pp. 313–21.

of the life sciences. At the same time, he was aware of the enormous difficulties in reducing theories of organic growth to the vitalistic principle of a striving force that cannot really be known, and in an outline of his planned dissertation he had to leave open what this force was supposed to be: "living force =" (*KGW* 1/4, 62 [49]).[105]

Although Nietzsche had serious difficulties in coming to terms with the vitalistic and monistic outlook of the contemporary life sciences, evolutionary models continued to have a lasting impact on his philosophical enterprise as a whole, and he was unable to escape the logic of his own intellectual environment.[106] What is important, however, for his discussion of teleology in the late 1860s is the Kantian framework which leads him to conclude that the assumption of a purposive teleological constitution of nature is, above all, a mental construct projected onto natural phenomena (*KGW* 1/4, 62 [52]). As an explanatory and organizing paradigm within the natural sciences, and especially within the new life sciences, Kant argues, teleology is certainly a necessary part of our reasoning about the world: "For if we want to investigate the organized products of nature by continued observation, we find it completely unavoidable to apply to nature the concept of an intention, so that even for our empirical use of reason this concept is an absolutely necessary maxim."[107] For Kant, then, teleology is mainly a regulative principle, which safeguards the unity of knowledge according to what he terms "analogy of experience," that is, we cannot but help project the principles of human action and intentions onto our concept of nature.[108]

In 1868, Nietzsche wholeheartedly accepted Kant's position, at least as far as he found it discussed in Lange's *Geschichte des Materialismus*: since we cannot but construct an analogy between human experience and the natural world outside us, our interpretation of nature automatically follows teleological models.

---

[105] In contrast, Hill, *Nietzsche's Critiques*, pp. 93–4 and 112–16, suggests that Nietzsche did in fact believe in the actual existence of a determinate "life force."

[106] See Moore, *Nietzsche, Biology, and Metaphor*, pp. 21–84, and Wolfgang Müller-Lauter, *Nietzsche: His Philosophy of Contradictions and the Contradictions of his Philosophy*, trans. David J. Parent (Urbana, Ill.: University of Illinois Press, 1999), pp. 161–82.

[107] Immanuel Kant, *Critique of Judgment*, trans. Werner S. Pluhar (Indianapolis, Ind.: Hackett, 1987), p. 280.

[108] See Immanuel Kant, *Critique of Pure Reason*, ed. and trans. Paul Guyer and Allen W. Wood (Cambridge: Cambridge University Press, 1998), pp. 297–8 (B 222–3).

The rule-governed, law-like processes that seem to permeate both the organic and inorganic world are merely mental projections (*KGW* I/4, 62 [3] and [7]): "We are astonished about ... that which is complicated and assume (according to human analogy) that it contains a special kind of wisdom" (*KGW* I/4, 62 [15]). This position is clearly influenced by his reading of Lange, who notes, for instance, that the "notion of causality," which underlies a functional and heuristic understanding of teleology as it is present in Kant, "*is rooted in our* [physiological] *organization*," but that it cannot provide any access to natural laws and reality as such.[109] For Lange, this does not mean, however, that teleology and causality are irrelevant. On the one hand, it is obvious that the order of reality "is merely a product of the interaction between our organization and the real world, whose true essence remains hidden to us," so that any specific ideas we might have about this essence merely constitute a "phantasm [*Hirngespinst*]." On the other hand, the very fact that we can conceive of this interaction forces us to assume the existence of an " 'intelligible' world" beyond the "categories" that we project into the order of things.[110] In sharp contrast to both Kant and Lange, however, Nietzsche increasingly wonders whether teleological models are of any explanatory value in the first place, for they seem to suggest the existence of a higher being or some imaginary force beyond human experience. Realizing the artificial nature of teleological models, and thus discarding them, might have practical value: it forces us to accept, first, that there is no higher being (*KGW* I/4, 62 [16]) and, second, that our environment is wholly contingent, that is, marked by chance and flux (*KGW* I/4, 62 [45]). As we shall see later, Nietzsche increasingly changed his position under the influence of contemporary evolutionary thought, especially during the 1880s: but from this evolutionary point of view, teleology was not external to human beings, but rather part of what it meant to be human.

In his notes of April and May 1868, Nietzsche still refrained from drawing any general conclusions from his discussion of teleology. He knew all too well that his philosophical ideas still moved on thin ice. But his discussion of teleology did have a considerable impact on the way in which he began to question the

---

[109] Lange, *Geschichte des Materialismus*, p. 264.   [110] Ibid., pp. 274–5.

status of historical knowledge. His seemingly fleeting reference, for instance, to Johann Gottfried Herder's *Ideen zur Philosophie der Geschichte der Menschheit* (1784–91) not only indicates that he thought about widening his discussion of teleology to include cultural history; it also shows that he was indeed aware of the connection between, on the one hand, the rise of teleological models in German philosophy since the eighteenth century, and on the other, the parallel development of a specific philosophy of history within German idealism emphasizing the law-like structure of grand-scale historical processes (*KGW* 1/4, 62 [48]). After all, Kant himself established a direct link between teleology as a regulative principle for the understanding of natural phenomena and the general developmental laws projected onto historical events. His notion of a "universal history of the world in accordance with a plan of nature," presented most fully in the essay "Idee zu einer allgemeinen Geschichte in weltbürgerlicher Absicht" (1784), integrates teleology into the discourse of historical thought: the history of humanity needed to be regarded in terms of an ideal plan of natural causation, even though such a plan might not exist in history as such.[111] It is important to realize, however, that for Kant such a teleological argument is embedded in a wider political argument about the possibility of enlightenment and civil society. The latter, he claims, only makes sense from a historical point of view if we are able to attribute a "cosmopolitan goal" to historical developments:

> [I]f we assume a plan of nature, we have grounds for greater hopes. For such a plan opens up the comforting prospect of a future in which we are shown from afar how the human race eventually works its way upward to a situation in which all the germs implanted by nature can be developed fully, and in which man's destiny can be fulfilled here on earth. ... It would be a misinterpretation of my intention to contend that I meant this idea of a universal history, which to some extent [*gewissermaßen*] follows an *a priori* rule, to supersede the task of history proper, that of *empirical* composition. My idea is only a notion of what a philosophical

---

[111] Immanuel Kant, "Idea for a Universal History with a Cosmopolitan Purpose," in *Political Writings*, ed. Hans Reiss, trans. H. B. Nisbet, 2nd edn., enlarged (Cambridge: Cambridge University Press, 1991), pp. 41–53: 51. On Kant's link between the teleological interpretation of nature and history, see Rudolf A. Makkreel, *Interpretation and Imagination in Kant: The Hermeneutical Import of the "Critique of Judgment"* (Chicago: Chicago University Press, 1990), pp. 130–41.

mind, well acquainted with history, might be able to attempt from a different angle.¹¹²

Despite Kant's modest claim that his argument is merely a philosophical one, and that he does not at all wish to encroach upon the work of proper historians, there can be little doubt that his intentions are more ambitious. What he is interested in is the discovery of "a plan of nature aimed at a perfect civil union of mankind," which could serve as a "guide" for actual political progress.¹¹³ Much hinges on Kant's use of the word *gewissermaßen*, which is somewhat ambiguous. On the one hand, it suggests that such a plan of nature, at least to some extent, actually exists; on the other hand, it means that it is more reassuring for the observer of history to assume that there might be such a plan, whereas in actual fact there is none to be found.

Despite this ambiguity I would suggest that, six years before his more sophisticated discussion of teleology in the *Kritik der Urteilskraft*, Kant actually assumes the existence of such a plan, which has far-reaching political consequences: it is possible to "discover a regular process of improvement in the political constitutions of our continent (which will probably legislate eventually for all other continents)."¹¹⁴ Only a teleological understanding of historical developments, in other words, allows for the universal claims of both reason and the moral law to be realized in the realm of the political – even in the realm of international relations. Although Kant does not fully renounce such a strict reading of historical teleology in later years, his philosophical discussion in the *Kritik der Urteilskraft* is more cautious and clearly argues that teleology could only serve as a regulative explanatory model.

Kant's wording in the passage quoted above also has a second implication, especially when he speaks of "man's destiny [*Bestimmung*]" being "fulfilled here on earth." The term "destiny" is clearly suggestive of a more theological dimension of Kant's

---

[112] Kant, "Idea for a Universal History," in *Political Writings*, pp. 52–3. Compare the German text "Idee zu einer allgemeinen Geschichte in weltbürgerlicher Absicht," in *Werkausgabe*, ed. Wilhelm Weischedel, 11th edn. (Frankfurt/M.: Suhrkamp, 1990), vol. XI, pp. 49–50. See also Yirmiahu Yovel, *Kant and the Philosophy of History* (Princeton, N.J.: Princeton University Press, 1980), pp. 135–57.
[113] Kant, "Idea for a Universal History," in *Political Writings*, pp. 51–2.
[114] Ibid., p. 52.

argument, since the assumed plan of nature can be read as a form of predestination. He returned to this theme in *Die Religion innerhalb der Grenzen der bloßen Vernunft* (1793), which stipulated that the Christian Church – more so than the modern state – served as a model for the ideal of a civil union of humanity.[115] Of course, one should hesitate to see Kant's critical project exclusively through the lens of his religious and theological occupations, especially since his respective opinions are far removed from theological dogmatism.[116] His writings on religion during the 1790s in many ways react to a specific political setting and, like Gotthold Ephraim Lessing's *Die Erziehung des Menschengeschlechts* (1777/80) and Moses Mendelssohn's *Jerusalem oder über religiöse Macht und Judenthum* (1783), they also aim at convincing an educated public of the necessary link between religious and political freedom.[117] It is also obvious, however, that the convergence of church and society could have unintended consequences, which Nietzsche encountered in nineteenth-century Germany, such as the close link between the Protestant Church and the Prussian state or the idea that the German nation state after the Franco-Prussian War had been the result of historical predestination. Given that Kant's ideas almost invited such misunderstanding, it is not surprising that less pragmatic representatives of German idealism, such as Johann Gottlieb Fichte in his lectures "Die Grundzüge des gegenwärtigen Zeitalters" (1804–5), argued for a more literal understanding of a teleological "world plan [*Weltplan*]" that preceded the historical events themselves.[118] Nietzsche himself will encounter such arguments and their political consequences throughout the 1870s and 1880s, but for now it is sufficient to realize that, by the late 1860s, he was well aware of the problematic nature of teleological arguments.

---

[115] See Immanuel Kant, *Religion within the Bounds of Mere Reason*, in *Religion and Rational Theology*, trans. and ed. Allen W. Wood and George di Giovanni (Cambridge: Cambridge University Press, 1996), pp. 129–71, especially 133–6. For a somewhat contentious discussion of Kant's respective ideas and their effect on his political thought, see Ian Hunter, *Rival Enlightenments: Civil and Metaphysical Philosophy in Early Modern Germany* (Cambridge: Cambridge University Press, 2001), pp. 337–63.

[116] See Kant, *Religion within the Bounds of Mere Reason*, in *Religion and Rational Theology*, pp. 188–215.

[117] See ibid., pp. 136–41 and Manfred Kuehn, *Kant: A Biography* (Cambridge: Cambridge University Press, 2001), pp. 361–72.

[118] See Johann Gottlieb Fichte, *Die Grundzüge des gegenwärtigen Zeitalters*, in *Werke*, ed. Peter Lothar Oesterreich and Wilhelm G. Jacobs (Frankfurt/M.: Deutscher Klassiker Verlag, 1997), vol. II, pp. 76–7.

Leaving aside the political implications of such a philosophy of history, it seems that Nietzsche's reflections on Kant and teleology are often inconclusive and incoherent, but they clearly seek to come to terms with what has been called the "legacy of German idealism" in post-Kantian thought.[119] The tension between teleology and contingency within nineteenth-century German historicism in the aftermath of Kant and Hegel is a direct result of the insurmountable problems historians and philosophers encountered once they sought to reconcile nature and history. Nietzsche will not have missed the significance of these problems: teleological thought throughout the 1800s was marked by a convergence between nature and history, between organicist vitalism and historical causality, which followed either the model of a disguised eschatological theology or the new paradigms of the life sciences, such as physiology and morphology. Since they trace the development of living organisms either backward or forward in time, evolutionary models are certainly historical in orientation; they are connected to a much wider trend that we might describe as a "temporalization" of nature taking place in the course of the eighteenth century.[120] Although, for instance, Wilhelm von Humboldt felt somewhat uneasy about teleological models, his reflections on world history clearly show how the gap between the organizing principles of nature and those of history began to narrow around 1800. In his short "Betrachtungen über die Weltgeschichte," written in the early years of the nineteenth century, Humboldt speculated about a fundamental force, which becomes manifest in both nature and history, and which organizes both the physical conditions of our environment and the historical fate of human beings.[121] Several years later, in his address to the Prussian Academy of Sciences of 1821, "Über die Aufgabe des Geschichtsschreibers," he repeated this idea and stressed that the difference between nature and history was negligible:

All living forces – man as well as plants, nations, individuals and humanity, as well as the different peoples, even the products of the mind,

---

[119] See Pinkard, *German Philosophy*, pp. 356–67.
[120] See H. B. Nisbet, "Naturgeschichte und Humangeschichte bei Goethe, Herder und Kant," in Peter Matussek (ed.), *Goethe und die Verzeitlichung der Natur* (Munich: C. H. Beck, 1998), pp. 15–43.
[121] See Humboldt, *Betrachtungen über die Weltgeschichte*, in *Werke*, vol. I, pp. 572–3.

in the way in which they are based on a series of continued effects, such as literature, art, customs, the external form of civic society – have common characteristics, developments, laws.[122]

Humboldt's sweeping statement, combining virtually all forms of human activity and all natural phenomena into one quasi-organic whole, is undoubtedly representative of German idealism's fling with biological metaphors.

Through Schaarschmidt's philosophy lectures in Bonn, and through Albert Schwegler's introductory textbook *Geschichte der Philosophie im Umriß* (1848), both of which paid much attention to the general implications of Kant's critical project, Nietzsche was aware of the way in which especially Hegel, in his *Vorlesungen über die Philosophie der Geschichte* (1822–31), finally transformed Kant's more cautious teleological model into a fundamental "impulse of *perfectibility*," a "principle of development," governing the successive dialectical unfolding of "reason," "freedom" and "consciousness" in human history:

> The sole aim of philosophical enquiry is *to eliminate the contingent*. . . . We must bring to history the belief and conviction that the realm of the will is not at the mercy of contingency. That world history is governed by an ultimate design, that it is a rational process – whose rationality is not that of a particular subject, but a divine and absolute reason – this is a proposition whose truth we must assume; its proof lies in the study of world history itself, which is the image and enactment of reason.[123]

For Hegel, the "elimination of the contingent" was the true task of a philosophical understanding of history, and this remained a guiding principle for many German academic philosophers deep into the nineteenth century.

At the same time, it needs to be noted that such a teleological understanding of historical development, much like the eighteenth century's vision of humanity and civil society, was rooted in an essentially European perspective. Even though, for instance, Kant and Hegel undeniably sought to widen the scope of the philosophy of history, it was Europe, especially Protestant Europe, that had outpaced other cultures in its intellectual development.

---

[122] Humboldt, *Über die Aufgabe des Geschichtsschreibers*, in *Werke*, vol. 1, p. 598.
[123] Hegel, *Lectures on the Philosophy of World History*, pp. 124–7 and 28. See also Charles Taylor, *Hegel* (Cambridge: Cambridge University Press, 1975), pp. 389–427.

Johann Gottfried Herder, in contrast, was one of the few who suspected that the "European collective spirit" that was supposed to come to the fore in such a teleological understanding of world history posed a serious political problem: the superiority of Europe was at least in part based on "the *crime of abusing humanity* before almost all people of the earth."[124] In stark opposition to the optimism of the European Enlightenment, he proclaimed in his *Briefe zur Beförderung der Humanität* (1793–97): "Our part of the world ... has not cultivated but has destroyed the shoots of peoples' own cultures wherever and however it could. ... What is a measuring of all peoples *by the measure of us Europeans* supposed to be at all?"[125] Herder's answer to this question was a direct attack on the presumed "*innate superiority*" of European civil society as the imaginary goal of world history:

> The nature-investigator presupposes no *order of rank* among the creatures that he observes; all are equally dear and valuable to him. Likewise the nature-investigator of humanity. The negro has as much right to consider the white man a degenerate, a born albino freak, as when the white man considers him a beast, a black animal. Likewise the [native] American, likewise the Mongol.[126]

Indeed, from Herder's perspective, the task of a truly cosmopolitan history would thus entail the continuous attempt to think beyond Europe, or at least to see Europe itself as a historical and political problem.

Already toward the end of the eighteenth century, then, a teleological understanding of historical development that was inevitably based on the norms of what was seen as European civil society was more fragile than generally assumed. It was these political implications of historical thought that Nietzsche was to encounter from the early 1870s onward. Even before he began to study Kant in earnest, he remarked laconically: "Events, neither those of the individual nor those of history, take a necessary course, that is, a reasonable course" (*KGW* 1/4, 56 [5]).

The concept of "force" (*Kraft*) that Humboldt and others often employed when they sought to conceptualize cultural processes

---

[124] Johann Gottfried Herder, *Letters for the Advancement of Humanity*, in *Philosophical Writings*, ed. and trans. Michael N. Forster (Cambridge: Cambridge University Press, 2002), p. 381.
[125] Ibid., pp. 383 and 386.   [126] Ibid., p. 394.

was itself certainly a teleological principle par excellence: it was a "living force" or *vis viva*. Originally introduced by Gottfried Wilhelm Leibniz in an attack on Descartes's theory of motion, the *vis viva* was seen as that dynamic quantity, which described the force of a body in motion and, by implication, also the conservation of energy in the universe.[127] In the course of the eighteenth century, and triggered by the rise of the biological sciences from the 1750s onward, the assumption of a "living force" was transferred to the realm of the organic, where it constituted what Johann Christian Reil saw as a *Lebenskraft* and Johann Friedrich Blumenbach as a *Bildungstrieb*.[128] Outside the physical sciences strictly speaking, the notion of *Kraft* was notoriously difficult to define. The very problem that plagued the organicist teleology of biological vitalism, and which led Nietzsche to drop the idea of a "living force" in the late 1860s, was also present in teleological accounts of history: it was just impossible to find such a primordial *Kraft*. Nietzsche, of course, would reintroduce the concept of a shaping or plastic force in later writings, but the living force he referred to in his early notebooks was a more metaphysical construct.[129]

Already by the eighteenth century, when the debate about the *vis viva* was at its height, it was unclear whether such a dynamic quantity made scientific sense, since it was largely rooted in the abstract and essentially theological idea of the economy and simplicity of nature. As a consequence, Herder, for instance, remarked that we are simply unable to know anything about

---

[127] See Gottfried Wilhelm Leibniz, "Brevis demonstratio erroris mirabilis Cartesii et aliorum," in *Mathematische Schriften*, ed. C. I. Gerhardt (Berlin: Asher, 1848–63), vol. VI, pp. 117–23, and "Système nouveau de la nature et de la communication des substances," in *Philosophische Schriften*, ed. C. I. Gerhardt (Berlin: Weidmann, 1875–90), vol. IV, pp. 477–87. For a precise account of Leibniz's notions of force and motion, see Daniel Garber, "Leibniz: Physics and Philosophy," in Nicholas Jolley (ed.), *The Cambridge Companion to Leibniz* (Cambridge: Cambridge University Press, 1995), pp. 270–352: 309–21.

[128] See Johann Friedrich Blumenbach, *Über den Bildungstrieb und das Zeugungsgeschäfte* (Göttingen: Dieterich, 1781), and Johann Christian Reil, "Von der Lebenskraft," *Archiv für die Physiologie* 1/1 (1796), 66–7. On this debate, see Richards, *The Romantic Conception of Life*, pp. 218–29 and 255–61.

[129] On Nietzsche's notion of Kraft, see Günter Abel, *Nietzsche: Die Dynamik der Willen zur Macht und die ewige Wiederkehr* (Berlin: Walter de Gruyter, 1984), pp. 82–95 and 247–59; Peter Poellner, *Nietzsche and Metaphysics* (Oxford: Oxford University Press, 1995), pp. 266–88; Martin Bauer, "Zur Genealogie von Nietzsches Kraftbegriff: Nietzsches Auseinandersetzung mit J. G. Vogt," *Nietzsche Studien* 13 (1984), 211–27.

such a force.[130] Even though the notion of *Kraft* gained much importance in the discourse of nineteenth-century German physics, for instance, in Hermann von Helmholtz's *Über die Erhaltung der Kraft* (1847) and Wilhelm Weber's *Elektrodynamische Maassbestimmungen* (1846), Lange noted that *Kraft* was nothing but a metaphor.[131] If Lange should be right, and if teleological models were generally based on some form of personified striving force, then Nietzsche must have realized the obvious fallacy of such models, irrespective of whether they were applied to nature or to history: the conceptual unity of any form of reality, which underlies notions such as "force," is a construct *après coup* (*KGW* I/4, 62 [28]). Although Nietzsche remained somewhat uncertain about the role of teleological striving in nature, he seems to have been convinced that, with regard to historical reality, teleology did not hold much water.

Nietzsche was not alone in distinguishing between historical processes and the organization of nature. His evolving thoughts on the relationship between teleology and history mirror those of Jacob Burckhardt, his later colleague at the University of Basel. Burckhardt accepted the idea that "nature" worked according to "few primordial types [*Urtypen*]" that could be discovered in all evolutionary processes, but the life of "a people" should be regarded as the "slow development" of a "specific cultural mentality [*der spezifische Volksgeist*]." Natural archetypes and the contingency of cultural mentalities were simply incompatible. This led Burckhardt to reject what he regarded as the "bold anticipation of a world-plan," that is, the idea of a teleology of historical processes, which marked the writings of Fichte, Humboldt, and Hegel.[132] But by separating history from nature, Burckhardt introduced what was to become one of the central themes of German historicism in the later nineteenth century, namely the problem of cultural values. If the universal laws of nature could not be applied to historical events, cultural values might not

---

[130] See Johann Gottfried Herder, *Ideen zu einer Philosophie der Geschichte der Menschheit*, in *Werke in zehn Bänden*, ed. Martin Bollacher, Jürgen Brummack, Ulrich Gaier, Gunter E. Grimm, Hans Dietrich Irmscher, Rudolf Smend, and Johannes Wallmann (Frankfurt/M.: Deutscher Klassiker Verlag, 1985–2000), vol. VI, p. 349.
[131] See Lange, *Geschichte des Materialismus*, pp. 373–5.
[132] Jacob Burckhardt, *Weltgeschichtliche Betrachtungen*, ed. Rudolf Marx (Stuttgart: Kröner, 1978), pp. 24–5 and 5.

be universal either. Historicizing cultural processes culminates in questioning the legitimacy of morality and religion. An exclusively empirical study of history that wishes to restrict itself to the presumed objectivity of factual sources is unable to provide the kind of cultural orientation Kant and Hegel had in mind when they emphasized the role of "freedom."[133] Natural laws, and our recognition of such natural laws, are free from value statements, while the problem of values stands very much in the focal point of our attempts to interpret historical events and cultural processes. To interpret history in terms of nature, Nietzsche was going to point out, is thus to underestimate the importance of such cultural values.

Around 1868, Nietzsche's ideas about the precise relationship between nature and history were still inconclusive, but several years later, in his essay *David Strauss der Bekenner und Schriftsteller*, published in 1873, he revisited this issue:

an honest natural scientist believes that the world conforms unconditionally to laws, without however asserting anything as to the ethical or intellectual value of these laws: he would regard any such assertions as the extreme anthropomorphism of a reason that has overstepped the bounds of the permitted. (*UM* I: 7)

The idea of law-like and rule-governed processes that might be discovered in the realm of nature just could not be applied to culture and history. First of all, natural laws are independent from human interests, which govern historical and cultural developments. Second, accepting the explanatory power of natural laws does not entail that they have any value outside the realm of natural science strictly speaking. The epistemic value of natural laws does not at all mean that they have a moral value. For Nietzsche, it was the simplistic popularization of scientific discourse among philosophers and historians that essentially "moralized" the natural sciences and continued to support the myth of a teleology of history throughout the nineteenth century. His attack on the moralization of science on the basis of teleological arguments was indeed more than timely, since the idea that processes within organic nature

---

[133] See Wittkau, *Historismus*, pp. 42–4.

essentially embodied aesthetic and moral values, is a central, albeit much-neglected trait of nineteenth-century evolutionary biology.[134] In order to avoid this physicalist trap with regard to cultural processes, Nietzsche slowly began to adopt a historicist position that allowed him in subsequent years to move the problem of cultural values into the center of a genealogy of modern European mentalities.

Indeed, long after Nietzsche had left Bonn and Leipzig behind, and long after he had broken with German neo-humanism, he began to consider the direct political and social consequences of a law-governed grand narrative of human progress. In the fifth book of *Die fröhliche Wissenschaft*, which was added to the second edition in 1887, he provides a particularly pertinent example: by assuming that their profession and class, that is their "way of making a living," are historically and socially predestined, nineteenth-century Europeans have forgotten how much the choices they have made "were determined by accidents, moods, and arbitrariness." As such, their political and social life is entirely rooted in "that fundamental faith on the basis of which someone could calculate, promise, anticipate the future in a plan," that is, "the basic faith that man has worth and sense only in so far as he is *a stone in a great edifice*," such as history, humanity, or the modern nation state. Seen from this perspective, the egalitarian promise of a "future 'free society'," held by both nineteenth-century liberalism and socialism, neither corresponds to the political and social realities of the time, nor does its vision of freedom imply the existence of an autonomous individual (*GS* 356).

The assumption of a historical and political predestination – as it underlies, for instance, the retrospective justification of the modern German nation state as the goal of human history – is clothed in a false optimism. As a consequence, Nietzsche demanded of the "good European" to be, above all, "a pessimist" (*GS* 357). Such pessimism, however, is rooted in a form of historical critique that seeks to examine the way in which the present is fundamentally shaped by the past. Nietzsche, thus, slowly begins to rehabilitate a crucial insight that can be found in Herder's attack on Voltaire in 1774: any philosophy of history

---

[134] See Richards, *The Romantic Conception of Life*, pp. 533–40.

that conceives of historical developments as a goal-directed and law-governed process toward an ideal political and cultural constitution has to show disdain for the primitiveness of previous intellectual attitudes, thus underestimating the way in which the present remains haunted by whatever we believe to have overcome.[135] Indeed, if a historical grounded notion of humanity should be possible in the first place, it has to leave behind a merely emancipatory understanding of history. After Bonn and Leipzig, Basel proved to be the ideal intellectual setting within which this approach was able to gain momentum.

---

[135] See Herder, *This Too a Philosophy of History for the Formation of Humanity*, in *Philosophical Writings*, p. 279.

CHAPTER 2

The formation of Imperial Germany, seen from Basel

Nietzsche's appointment at the University of Basel as a relatively young professor of Greek language and literature – supported by Friedrich Ritschl in Leipzig and by Hermann Usener, Ritschl's successor in Bonn – was not a particularly unusual development.[1] Nevertheless, Nietzsche, who had not submitted any doctoral dissertation, was rather surprised about the offer. In a letter from December 1868 to his friend Erwin Rohde in Hamburg he lamented that he was unable to complete any serious work, and a month later he still bemoaned his solitary existence in Leipzig (*KGB* 1/2, pp. 349 and 356). But on January 16, 1869, boredom had given way to new excitement, since he had just heard from Ritschl about his likely appointment. The prospect of this position clearly changed his mind about philology: "only last week," he remarked to Rohde, "I wanted to write to you and suggest that together we may study chemistry and that we throw philology where it belongs: onto the rubbish heap of tradition [*Urväter-hausrath*]. Now the devil of 'fate' tempts me with a philological professorship" (*KGB* 1/2, pp. 359–60).[2] At the beginning of February, he finally took up contact with Wilhelm Vischer-Bilfinger,

---

[1] Gottfried Hermann, for instance, was twenty-three when he began to lecture on philology at the University of Leipzig in 1795, August Boeckh was twenty-five when he accepted a chair in classical scholarship at the University of Berlin in 1810, Heinrich von Sybel was promoted to a professorship in history at the University of Bonn at the age of twenty-seven, and Jacob Wackernagel was twenty-six when he succeeded Nietzsche in Basel.

[2] Nietzsche's use of the term "Urväter-hausrath" is a reference to the beginning of Goethe's *Faust I*, when Faust laments that his study is filled with useless "instruments" unable to bring him any true knowledge. See Johann Wolfgang von Goethe, *Faust: Eine Tragödie*, in *Werke: Hamburger Ausgabe*, ed. Erich Trunz, vol. III, 16th, rev. edn. (Munich: C. H. Beck, 1996), p. 21.

the chair of the search committee in Basel, and forwarded a short curriculum vitae which ended on quite a high note, notifying Vischer-Bilfinger that he was busy completing at the same time both his doctoral work and his professorial thesis, the German *Habilitation*. Only the "current academic regulations" prevented him from doing so "before Easter 1869" (*KGB* 1/2, p. 368). One can only wonder what the more serene and patrician scholars in the Swiss city of Basel thought of their ambitious new colleague from Leipzig.

INTELLECTUAL CULTURE IN BASEL

In comparison with the German states, especially Prussia, Nietzsche believed Basel to provide an exceptionally free-thinking environment of intellectual nobility, although things were more complicated than he realized (*KGB* 1/2, p. 360). It is rather difficult to imagine nineteenth-century Basel, dominated by a close-knit economic elite, as a particularly exciting place for any young scholar or scientist. Though surpassing most German cities in wealth, it lacked the fashionable metropolitan sophistication of Berlin or Leipzig. The overall atmosphere in Basel was of a rather tranquil, if not to say provincial nature marked by a small-town version of neo-humanism, which placed much emphasis on good relations between the educational institutions and the political authorities. Ironically, this also meant that the city was able to provide an intellectual exile from Europe's struggle with modernity and nationalism, while at the same time accommodating new intellectual trends, even fundamental social changes, without losing its civic identity.[3]

Founded in 1454, Basel's university ranks among the oldest in Europe, and it was shaped in almost every aspect by the political and economic interests of Basel's patrician families.[4] Academic culture was clearly linked to public interests and scholarly work was regarded as a direct contribution to civic life. But enrollment at the university remained low: until the mid-1840s it rarely

---

[3] See Gossman, *Basel in the Age of Burckhardt*, pp. 13–103, and Carl E. Schorske, "History as Vocation in Burckhardt's Basel," in *Thinking with History: Explorations in the Passage to Modernity* (Princeton, N.J.: Princeton University Press, 1998), pp. 56–70.

[4] On the social structure of Basel's patrician families during Nietzsche's time, see Philipp Sarasin, *Stadt der Bürger: Struktureller Wandel und bürgerliche Lebenswelt, Basel 1870–1900* (Basel: Helbing & Lichtenhahn, 1996), pp. 266–80.

exceeded sixty students, and even in the 1870s student numbers remained small in comparison with the emerging grand-scale research culture at German institutions in Berlin and elsewhere.[5] Perhaps such an environment was ultimately necessary to provide a breeding-ground for the extravagant intellectualism that is reflected not only in the work of Nietzsche but also in that of Jacob Burckhardt and Johann Jakob Bachofen, who were sidelined by the German philologists and historians in Berlin, Bonn, and Leipzig but who proved to be far more influential and long-lasting than many of their academic colleagues and adversaries in Prussia or Saxony.

To be sure, within the academic world of the nineteenth century, the University of Basel was largely insignificant. Nietzsche himself was appointed simply because his predecessor, Adolf Kiessling, had moved to Hamburg, and because the relatively low salaries, together with the fact that the University of Basel lacked any international prestige, made it difficult to attract prominent scholars from Germany, who were used to a different pay scale and career opportunities.[6] While Nietzsche must have been aware of this, he also profited from a unique intellectual atmosphere that was largely marked by three factors that set Basel apart from its German neighbors. First, the accumulation of wealth, based on a merchant economy, proved to be a decisive contributing factor to the city's cultural life. Second, an understanding of Protestant piety with a strict moral code that pervaded both public and private life not only stabilized the close relationship between clergy and political authorities, but it also informed the role of academics as representing a civic institution. Finally, Basel was also home to a neo-humanist ideal of education that sought to deliver a form of *Bildung* compatible with the interests of the city's patrician families; Basel's intellectual elite continued a cultural program that had been lost in Berlin soon after Humboldt's death. As a result, the curriculum of both the university and the so-called Pädagogium, the public preparatory school, reflected a lasting tension between a reluctant modernization and an anti-modern intellectualism

---

[5] For a comprehensive history of the university, see Edgar Bonjour, *Die Universität Basel von den Anfängen bis zur Gegenwart, 1460–1960* (Basel: Helbing & Lichtenhahn, 1971).
[6] See Andrea Bollinger and Franziska Trenkle, *Nietzsche in Basel* (Basel: Schwabe & Co., 2000), p. 23.

questioning the values of a technocratic modernity.[7] Nietzsche's own perspective on modernity's historical foundations and political dilemmas was in many ways a direct result of this tension.

THE PRACTICE OF CULTURAL HISTORY

In Basel, Nietzsche taught at both the university and at the Pädagogium, which stressed the value of the humanist canon as a form of cultural orientation in the midst of the political and social turmoil of the nineteenth century.[8] But most importantly, he was able to meet Bachofen and Burckhardt, who were already prominent figures in the field of cultural history. Both made a profound impact on Nietzsche. Although neither Bachofen nor Burckhardt were always impressed by Nietzsche's speculations and style, he referred to their work throughout his life and their influence on his historical vision should not be underestimated.

Bachofen in many respects shared Nietzsche's fate of being obscurely famous. Bachofen had initially studied law and classical philology at the universities of Basel, Berlin and Göttingen from 1834 to 1838. In the Prussian capital, his teachers included August Boeckh but especially Friedrich Carl von Savigny, one of the main representatives of the historical school of legal thought, who was an outspoken opponent of Hegel's philosophy of right. In Göttingen, one of the most important centers of classical scholarship in Germany since the days of Heyne, he studied under Karl Otfried Müller, whose *Prolegomena zu einer wissenschaftlichen Mythologie* (1825) rejected the philosophical interpretation of myth in favor of treating myths as historical sources.[9]

After travels through Europe, working for a law firm, and a short stint at Oxford's Magdalen College in 1839, Bachofen took up a professorship in Roman law at the University of Basel. Echoing Savigny and the legacy of Roman law in German Romanticism, his

---

[7] See Gossman, *Basel in the Age of Burckhardt*, pp. 77.
[8] See Janz, *Friedrich Nietzsche*, vol. I, pp. 277–849; Hans Gutzwiller, "Friedrich Nietzsches Lehrtätigkeit am Basler Pädagogium," *Basler Zeitschrift für Geschichte und Altertumskunde* 50 (1951), 148–224; Richard Meister, "Nietzsches Lehrtätigkeit in Basel 1869–1879," in: *Anzeiger der Österreichischen Akademie der Wissenschaften: Phil.-Hist. Klasse* 85 (1948), 103–21. For a fascinatingly detailed description of Nietzsche's daily life, see Bollinger and Trenkle, *Nietzsche in Basel*, pp. 61–70.
[9] See Karl Otfried Müller, *Prolegomena zu einer wissenschaftlichen Mythologie* (Göttingen: Vandenhoeck & Ruprecht, 1825), pp. 66–81, especially 79.

inaugural lecture, on May 7, 1841, emphasized the historical study of law over the idea of natural law. But three years later he was forced to resign from his position, since it was widely rumored that he was appointed only because of his family's political clout.[10] Although still active politically, his main interest continued to be the relation between law and religion in archaic societies, thus emphasizing an approach to cultural history which was not really compatible with the historical vision of the leading German scholars, such as Barthold Georg Niebuhr, Johann Gustav Droysen, and Theodor Mommsen. Influenced by the connection between mythology and symbolic forms, Bachofen underlined the importance of religious thought and ritual as a basis for the development of law, state, and culture. In an almost nostalgic view on antiquity, he also stressed the interconnection between "Orient" and "Occident," that is, of early Greek and Roman cultures and the societies of the Near East. Like Müller's work on Greek mythology, and much like Savigny's historical school of law, his approach was directed against the philosophical systems developed by German idealism, thus seeking to replace philosophical speculation about the cultural life of ancient societies with a framework that was inspired by archaeology and contemporary anthropological thought.

When Bachofen and his Basel colleague Franz Dorotheus Gerlach, a teacher at the Pädagogium, published the first volumes of their *Geschichte der Römer* in 1851, they experienced a hostile reaction from the establishment of German historiography in Berlin.[11] Mommsen, whose own *Römische Geschichte* (1854–56) was to become the standard reference text of the nineteenth century, wrote a devastating review of Bachofen's and Gerlach's account, which especially rejected their idea that the Roman political constitution rested on theocratic foundations.[12] For Mommsen,

---

[10] As a result, Bachofen also resigned from his position as a judge at the Criminal Court in 1842 and left the city's Senate in 1845. See Gossman, *Basel in the Age of Burckhardt*, pp. 122–3.
[11] See Franz Dorotheus Gerlach and Johann Jakob Bachofen, *Geschichte der Römer* (Basel: Bahnmaier, 1851).
[12] See Theodor Mommsen, *Römische Geschichte* (Berlin: Weidmann, 1854–56). Mommsen's anonymous review was published in *Literarisches Centralblatt für Deutschland*, 7 (November 16, 1850), cols. 138–9. On the quarrel between Bachofen and Mommsen, see Lionel Gossman, *"Orpheus Philologus:" Bachofen versus Mommsen on the Study of Antiquity* (Philadelphia: Transactions of the American Philosophical Society, 1983), pp. 21–6.

such an idea was anathema not only because it seemed to him unsound scholarship, but even more so because it contradicted his political interests. Like his later colleague Johann Gustav Droysen, whose work on Hellenism and Alexander the Great established an imaginary correspondence between ancient Macedonia and modern Prussia, Mommsen viewed the history of Rome through the lens of Prussia as a constitutional monarchy: the Roman state was part of a process of modernization that culminated in the European nation state. There was, in short, no room for theocratic foundations in Mommsen's image of a civic Rome. In turn, Bachofen began to regard his adversary's scholarship as indicative of Prussia's political aspirations to become the leading central European power, caricaturing Mommsen as the Bismarck of German scholarship, although as a member of the Prussian Deputy Chamber (1862–66, 1873–79) and the German Reichstag (1881–84) Mommsen was often in open conflict with Bismarck.[13]

Bachofen's main intellectual project rests on the affinity of historiography and mythology, on the assumption that both religious myths and law are a result of a symbolic interpretation of culture and nature; it also rests on an anthropological perspective, which becomes particularly obvious in his *Versuch über die Gräbersymbolik der Alten* of 1859 and in his chief work *Das Mutterrecht* published in 1861.[14] From Bachofen's point of view, the antipodean relationship between Basel and Berlin, at least as far as historical scholarship was concerned, mirrored the difference between an anthropological conception of history and a notion of historiography as serving the interests of the modern state.

That Nietzsche should have found Bachofen's attitude attractive goes without saying. Bachofen's work on myth and archaic culture provided Nietzsche, who was an occasional guest at Bachofen's rather magnificent house in Basel, with a scholarly ideal from which he derived much inspiration. But we also need to be cautious not to overestimate the personal relationship between

---

[13] On Bachofen's image of Mommsen, see Gossman, *Basel in the Age of Burckhardt*, pp. 160–8. For Bismarck's dismay about Mommsen, see Bismarck, *Ausgewählte Werke*, vol. VIII, p. 640.

[14] See Johann Jakob Bachofen, *Versuch über die Gräbersymbolik der Alten* (Basel: Bachmaier, 1859), and *Das Mutterrecht: Eine Untersuchung über die Gynaikokratie der alten Welt nach ihrer religiösen und rechtlichen Natur* (Stuttgart: Krais & Hoffmann, 1861).

Nietzsche and Bachofen; direct evidence of Bachofen's influence is often hard to come by.[15] At times, Bachofen was not too impressed by the direction the work of his young admirer took. His wife Luise, herself a member of the extended Burckhardt family, related how her husband's attitude to Nietzsche underwent crucial changes: while delighted about the image of archaic Greece that Nietzsche delivered in his *Die Geburt der Tragödie*, he grew increasingly frustrated with regard to Nietzsche's subsequent writings, so that even their personal contact became infrequent.[16]

Like Bachofen, Burckhardt came from one of Basel's more prominent families, even though they could not compete with the Bachofens' wealth. Initially destined, much like Nietzsche, to become a Protestant minister or theologian, he quickly turned to the study of history. In Berlin his teachers included not only the philologists Boeckh and Welcker, but also the historians Ranke and Droysen as well as one of the founders of art history in Germany, Franz Kugler, the author of the seminal *Handbuch der Kunstgeschichte* (1842), which competed with the handbooks of Nietzsche's former teacher Anton Heinrich Springer in Bonn.[17]

For Burckhardt's early historical thought Ranke played a pivotal role.[18] Initially Burckhardt accepted the latter's idea that the European nation state needs to be seen as the complex product of a long-term historical process, but his Swiss background prevented him from adopting the nationalist turn that was to shape the Prussian historians in subsequent years. Much like Bachofen, he thus grew increasingly disillusioned both with the political perspective of contemporary historical thought and with its thinly disguised Hegelian backbone, based on the idea of a teleological plan in the course of history to be uncovered by the work of the

---

[15] In fact, Bachofen does not feature prominently in Nietzsche's work, although Nietzsche refers to Bachofen's writings on matriarchy and to the later study *Das lykische Volk* (1862), for instance, in his introductory lectures on the history and methods of classical scholarship (*KGW* II/3, p. 429). For Bachofen's presence in Nietzsche's correspondence during the early 1870s, see *KGB* II/3, pp. 84, 123, 191 and 279.

[16] See Luise Bachofen-Burckhardt's account in Hermann Randa, *Nietzsche, Overbeck und Basel* (Berne: Haupt, 1937), pp. 17–18.

[17] See Franz Kugler, *Handbuch der Kunstgeschichte* (Stuttgart: Ebner & Seubert, 1842). On Burckhardt in Berlin, see Gossman, *Basel in the Age of Burckhardt*, pp. 215–18.

[18] On the relationship between Burckhardt and Ranke, see Horst Günther, "*Der Geist ist ein Wühler:*" *Über Jacob Burckhardt* (Frankfurt/M.: Fischer Taschenbuch Verlag, 1997), pp. 16–17.

historian. Indeed, Ranke's repeated emphasis on the objectivity of the historian and the empirical veracity of source material could barely camouflage the teleological orientation of his narrative. In his lectures "Über die Epochen der neueren Geschichte," tellingly delivered in front of the Bavarian King Maximilian II in October 1854, Ranke might have claimed that the value of each historical epoch rested merely in itself and should not be regarded primarily as part of an overarching plan. But the historical development he outlined from Imperial Rome to the political situation of the nineteenth century is all too obvious: at the end of this process, we can find the European nation state, especially Prussia, as an ideal social and political entity.[19]

From the perspective of Burckhardt, Ranke's approach – which shaped the outlook of the latter's historical vision from the *Deutsche Geschichte im Zeitalter der Reformation* (1839–43) and *Preußische Geschichte* (1847–48) to his unfinished *Weltgeschichte* (1881–88) – was clearly limited. It traced cultural processes back to the relationship between state and church within an epic narrative that was bound to reduce the complexity of what was at stake. When Burckhardt returned from Berlin to Basel, he soon began to argue for a more complicated model of historical processes, which sought to examine the actual and symbolic interrelations between "state," "religion," and "culture" as the three "forces," or "potencies," determining historical processes over longer periods in time.[20] Burckhardt's new approach became particularly obvious in his *Die Cultur der Renaissance in Italien* (1860) – a book Nietzsche admired, and referred to, for many years. Here, he presented a comprehensive account of the different cultural developments in the Italian Renaissance, which was opposed to the more unilinear models employed by Ranke and others.[21] Instead of following a grand narrative of human emancipation and political order, he constructed a typological model according to the three paradigms

---

[19] See Leopold von Ranke, *Über die Epochen der neueren Geschichte*, in *Aus Werk und Nachlaß*, ed. Walther Peter Fuchs and Theodor Schieder (Munich: Oldenbourg, 1964–75), vol. II, p. 60. For a detailed assessment of Ranke's wider claims, see Toews, *Becoming Historical*, pp. 372–416.

[20] See Burckhardt, *Weltgeschichtliche Betrachtungen*, pp. 27–69.

[21] On Burckhardt's turn to cultural history, see Gossman, *Basel in the Age of Burckhardt*, pp. 251–95, and Friedrich Jaeger, *Bürgerliche Modernisierungskrise und historische Sinnbildung: Kulturgeschichte bei Droysen, Burckhardt und Max Weber* (Göttingen: Vandenhoeck & Ruprecht, 1994), pp. 86–181.

of state, religion and culture, which was able to establish manifold hidden relations between a dazzling array of themes: the appropriation of antiquity in Renaissance scholarship; sepulchral cults; the meaning of ancient ruins in Rome; the combination of pagan and Christian beliefs; the political influence of the papacy; the writings of Petrarch, Dante, and Boccaccio; and the emergence of the Ciceronian canon at humanist universities. Burckhardt's historiographical enterprise put much emphasis on the *longue durée* of historical processes: these are not the product of revolutions, reformations, coronations and wars, but the result of slow transformations, of indirect links between different spheres of life, of a complicated network of historical and geographical influences, and also of lasting cultural "crises" in the face of such transformations.[22]

Nietzsche voiced his admiration for his older and already fairly prominent colleague as early as 1869/70 (*KGB* II/1, pp. 13, 22, 30 and 155), and he regularly attended Burckhardt's public lectures "Über das Studium der Geschichte" in the winter semester of 1870/71. In an enthusiastic letter to his friend Carl von Gersdorff, himself an officer somewhere on the frontline during the Franco-Prussian War, he even remarked:

> Yesterday evening I had the kind of pleasure that I would have granted especially to you. Jacob Burckhardt was freely delivering a lecture on "historical greatness," in fact from the perspective of our own intellectual and emotional horizon. This older, highly unusual man might not be inclined to misrepresentations of the truth, but nevertheless to discretion. But on walks I take with him, he calls Schopenhauer "our philosopher." Every week I attend his one-hour seminar on the study of history, and I believe to be the only one among the 60 listeners, who is able to understand the deep intellectual paths with their peculiar twists and turns when his presentation touches on the profound [*das Bedenkliche*]. For the first time I take pleasure in a lecture, but it really is of such a kind that I could give it myself if I were older. In today's lecture he focused on Hegel's philosophy of history in a manner that was suitable to the anniversary. (*KGB* II/1, p. 155)

That Nietzsche should situate Burckhardt's theoretical position between the names of Schopenhauer and Hegel is rather peculiar. Burckhardt was always keen on distancing himself from philosophical speculation; that he would have called Schopenhauer "our philosopher" is perhaps a projection of Nietzsche. Burckhardt

---

[22] On the notion of crisis, see Burckhardt, *Weltgeschichtliche Betrachtungen*, pp. 159–205.

might have been secretive about the truth, but this "truth" seems to have been mostly Nietzsche's "truth."

Although their relations were always cordial, we should not forget that Burckhardt never regarded Nietzsche as a particularly intimate friend, nor as a prospective collaborator. As Franz Overbeck pointed out more than once, the relationship between Burckhardt and Nietzsche was clearly one-sided. While Nietzsche continued to idealize Burckhardt, the latter seems to have found the writings and sweeping philosophical gestures of his younger colleague increasingly dreadful. After the publication of the Nietzsche's first "Untimely Meditation," *David Strauss der Bekenner und Schriftsteller,* in 1873, Burckhardt was openly annoyed about Nietzsche's visions of grandeur and began to shield himself from his intellectual advances. In a letter to Overbeck, Nietzsche's friend Heinrich Köselitz, better known under the pseudonym "Peter Gast," remembered many years later one of those episodes that betray the mundane humanity of academic life, when Burckhardt seems to have noted laconically: "This Nietzsche! He can't even fart healthily."[23]

There is little direct indication that Nietzsche immersed himself in Burckhardt's more theoretical speculations. But in May 1875, six years into his professorship in Basel, he was presented by two of his former students – the lawyer Louis Kelterborn and the historian Adolf Baumgartner – with a 488-page transcript of Burckhardt's popular lectures on Greek cultural history, which the latter delivered almost continuously over a period of fifteen years from 1872 to 1886 (*KGB* II/5, pp. 58 and 87). Burckhardt's lectures were enormously successful in their time. More than fifty students attended these lectures regularly – almost half of the students enrolled at the university in 1872.[24] But Nietzsche's remarks about this series of lectures are perhaps somewhat hyperbolic:

All history has thus far been written from the point of view of success and assuming the existence of reason in this success. Also Greek history: we do not really have one. But this is the way it generally is: where are the

---

[23] Franz Overbeck and Heinrich Köselitz, *Briefwechsel,* ed. David Marc Hoffmann, Niklas Peter, and Theo Salfinger (Berlin: Walter de Gruyter, 1998), p. 475. See also Franz Overbeck, "Erinnerungen an Friedrich Nietzsche," *Neue Rundschau* 17 (1906), 209–31 and 320–30: 228, and Jacob Mähly, "Erinnerungen an Friedrich Nietzsche," *Die Gegenwart* 58 (1900), 246–50: 249.

[24] See Gossman, *Basel in the Age of Burckhardt,* pp. 297–346.

historians whose perspective is not characterized by excuses? I see only one – Burckhardt. (*KGW* IV/1, 5 [58])

Clearly rejecting the Hegelian idea that history necessarily needs to be understood in terms of a teleological form of historical progress and a successful unfolding of reason, Nietzsche presents Burckhardt as the most formidable opponent of such "excuses." Undoubtedly, he appreciated, for instance, the way in which Burckhardt criticized as completely fraudulent the optimistic classicist image of an ideal and homogeneous Greek antiquity, which was still very much in vogue among German philologists.[25] But he must have also realized the importance of Burckhardt's view that the true task of cultural history was to describe the internal life and the mentalities of past epochs, rather than their material achievements.[26] This also separated Burckhardt's vision of cultural history from the emerging "cultural sciences" of the time. Inspired alike by evolutionary theories and the growing interest in ethnology, the latter presented a nomothetic discourse seeking to discover the laws of human society in its cultural manifestations, which supposedly could be studied empirically with regard to ethnic physiognomies, weapons, folkloric dress-codes, etc. Prominent examples of this trend, which began to gain momentum in the early 1840s and culminated during the 1870s, are Gustav Klemm's voluminous *Allgemeine Cultur-Geschichte der Menschheit* (1843–51) and Friedrich von Hellwald's *Culturgeschichte in ihrer natürlichen Entwicklung* (1875), which Nietzsche assailed on several occasions as the "wisdom of a frog's nose [*Froschnasen-Weisheit*]" (*KGW* V/2, 11 [299]).[27] The focus on seemingly empirical data certainly distinguished the early cultural sciences from a more abstract philosophy of history, but their emphasis on the idea of a unilinear historical progress aligned them with increasingly illiberal political positions that valued European "civilization" over non-European "primitive cultures" within the context of the

---

[25] See Jacob Burckhardt, *Griechische Culturgeschichte*, in *Gesamtausgabe*, ed. Emil Dürr et al. (Stuttgart: Deutsche Verlagsanstalt, 1930–34), vol. IX, pp. 343–4.
[26] See ibid., vol. VIII, pp. 2–4.
[27] See Gustav Klemm, *Allgemeine Cultur-Geschichte der Menschheit, nach den besten Quellen bearbeitet mit xylographischen Abbildungen der verschiedenen Nationalphysiognomien, Geräthe, Waffen, Trachten, Kunstproducte u.s.w. versehen* (Leipzig: Teubner, 1843–51), and Friedrich von Hellwald, *Culturgeschichte in ihrer natürlichen Entwicklung bis zur Gegenwart* (Augsburg: Lampart, 1875).

colonial ambitions of the main European powers.²⁸ Needless to say, Burckhardt's historical enterprise, together with his political beliefs, was hardly compatible with such a project.

That Nietzsche found Burckhardt's lectures and writings inspiring is difficult to overlook. After he had read the transcript of Burckhardt's lectures, he even felt the need to change the perspective of his own scholarship toward a more anthropological perspective by shifting his attention from literary history, for instance, to the role of religious cults and rituals in the formation of archaic cultures. In a letter of September 1875, he remarked: "I have just begun a cycle of lectures for the next seven years; this winter I am reading on 'Religious Culture of the Ancient Greeks' [*Religiöse Alterthümer der Griechen*]. They are *all new* courses, which is why they require my full attention" (*KGB* II/5, p. 116). That Nietzsche felt compelled to compose a complete series of new lectures which were supposed to run over several years, indicates that, despite his many harsh remarks about the state of contemporary scholarship, he still regarded historical studies as a worthwhile enterprise. The question is: what kind of historical studies did Nietzsche have in mind? In fact, this anthropological turn of Nietzsche's philological work in many ways continued a much earlier project that comes to the fore in his inaugural lecture at the University of Basel in 1869, "Homer und die klassischen Philologie." Already before he encountered Burckhardt's work in detail, he argues that "the most consequential discovery" of classical studies was the "discovery and appreciation of the *mentality of the people* [*Volksseele*]." As such, "the true carriers and levers of so-called world-history" were not single individuals, but the latter's cultural practices merely expressed "the great instincts of the masses, the unconscious drives of peoples" (*KGW* II/1, p. 260). These drives, or rather the cultural value of these drives, will also be one of the central themes of his later genealogy. In fact, the anthropological orientation that Nietzsche's own scholarly endeavors began to take during the 1870s prepared much of the ground for his genealogical project of the 1880s.

---

²⁸ It should be noted that not all trends of the cultural sciences in Germany were marked by political illiberalism. See Woodruff D. Smith, *Politics and the Sciences of Culture in Germany, 1840–1920* (New York: Oxford University Press, 1991), pp. 13–55.

Nietzsche's admiration for Bachofen and Burckhardt was, however, not the only reason why he continued to be interested in the value of historical thought for the interpretation of cultural processes. Another, more personal influence during the 1870s was the theologian Franz Overbeck, whose appointment at the University of Basel contributed to the city's extravagant intellectualism. By commenting on Nietzsche's writings on many occasions, Overbeck also sharpened the increasingly historical perspective of Nietzsche's thought. This is in many respects due to Overbeck's own position within an intellectual field in the aftermath of Schleiermacher's anonymously published speeches *Über die Religion* (1799), namely the encounter of theology and historicism.

Throughout the nineteenth century, the rise of historicist thought reshaped Protestant theology. Schleiermacher's successful combination of religion and hermeneutics was in many ways responsible for a secularized history of theological doctrine. Partaking in the wider historicist trends of the time, this approach marked much of the work of Protestant theologians, such as Ferdinand Christian Baur, Albrecht Ritschl and, somewhat later, Adolf von Harnack.[29] This development was not limited, however, to the German states, in particular Württemberg and Prussia. Even the relatively pious Protestant community in Basel was not immune from these trends, since the city often offered a safe haven to German professors whose liberal convictions had brought them into conflict with the authorities of the German states. One such scholar, who arrived in Basel long before Overbeck, was the theologian Wilhelm M. L. de Wette, who had the opportunity to meet Herder when he was a pupil at the Weimar *Gymnasium* and whose good relations with Schleiermacher helped him to become one of the rising stars of Protestant scholarship in Prussia. By 1810, Schleiermacher had arranged for de Wette to join the theological faculty at the new University of Berlin. Nine years later, however, the King of Prussia, Friedrich Wilhelm III, dismissed him from his post. With a compassionate letter to the mother of Carl Ludwig Sand – a theology student from Jena, who assassinated the writer and politician August von Kotzebue – the politically unassuming de Wette

[29] See Gunter Scholtz, *Ethik und Hermeneutik: Schleiermacher's Grundlegung der Geisteswissenschaften* (Frankfurt/M.: Suhrkamp, 1995), pp. 29–34.

had inadvertently left the impression that he sympathized with the revolutionary cause of precisely those liberals whom Kotzebue had targeted in his articles for the *Literarisches Wochenblatt*.³⁰ Invited to join the University of Basel in 1822, de Wette entered the same seemingly anti-modern intellectual world that was to become the breeding-ground for the ideas of Bachofen, Burckhardt, Nietzsche, and Overbeck.

Like the Tübingen School around Baur, de Wette increasingly rejected orthodox Protestant dogma in favor of a strictly historical interpretation that emphasized the role of mythology in Christian religion and that also had an effect on the young Burckhardt. It is in this respect that de Wette, who had published a highly influential *Lehrbuch der christlichen Dogmatik* (1813–16) and a *Lehrbuch der christlichen Sittenlehre* (1833), prepared much of the ground for the arrival of Franz Overbeck. Like de Wette, Overbeck was able to bridge the gap between the German and Swiss contexts. Representing the enormous prestige of the German research university system in the nineteenth century, he arrived in Basel in April 1870, after having studied theology at four of Germany's most prominent institutions: the universities of Leipzig, Göttingen, Berlin and Jena, where he had also completed his *Habilitation*, his professorial thesis, in 1864 and where he had taught until his move to Basel.³¹

Before Overbeck's arrival, Nietzsche seems already to have been quite interested in this new colleague (*KGB* II/1, p. 94), who was a close friend of the historian Heinrich von Treitschke, the author of the famous *Deutsche Geschichte im neunzehnten Jahrhundert* (1879–94) and Ranke's successor at the University of Berlin. That Overbeck, despite his later political disagreements with the Prussian historian, remained throughout his life as close a friend to Treitschke as to Nietzsche, is at first sight quite surprising. After all, Treitschke's political agenda and later anti-Semitic remarks were to bring him into conflict with many liberal scholars. As the editor of the conservative *Preußische Jahrbücher* he quickly established himself as one of the driving forces behind the nationalism of the

---

³⁰ See Thomas Albert Howard, *W. M. L. de Wette, Jacob Burckhardt, and the Theological Origins of Nineteenth-Century Historical Consciousness* (New York: Cambridge University Press, 2000), pp. 71–5.

³¹ See Curt Paul Janz, "Die Berufung Franz Overbecks an die Universität Basel 1870," *Basler Zeitschrift für Geschichte und Altertumskunde* 92 (1982), 139–65.

Prussian school of historiography. After the Franco-Prussian War of 1870/71, and throughout Bismarck's *Kulturkampf* during the early 1870s, which directly linked Prussian Protestantism to German nationalism, Treitschke's *Deutsche Geschichte* can indeed be read as the program for a specifically German national identity that retrospectively justified Prussia's dominance.[32] Even Overbeck felt uncomfortable with these tendencies. But his lasting friendship with Treitschke is also indicative of the way in which Basel's intellectual culture was able to accommodate contradicting ideological orientations.[33]

Perhaps inspired by Overbeck's close friendship with Treitschke, and certainly attracted by the status of Treitschke's *Preußische Jahrbücher* as one of the leading periodicals that shaped public discourse in nineteenth-century Germany, Nietzsche speculated in a letter to his friend Erwin Rohde that one of his shorter essays on tragedy might find an ideal home in this publication (*KGB* II/1, p. 197). In June 1871, Overbeck himself forwarded the manuscript of "Sokrates und die griechische Tragödie" to Treitschke, whose reaction was – to put it diplomatically – rather cautious: admitting that he might merely be a layman as far as Greek tragedy was concerned, Treitschke wrote back to Overbeck that he simply did not understand what the manuscript was about.[34] Nevertheless, Nietzsche continued to court Treitschke, for one year later he sent a copy of his first book, *Die Geburt der Tragödie*, to Treitschke, who was then a professor of history at the University of Heidelberg (*KGB* II/1, p. 280). Finally, when Overbeck married Ida Rothpletz in 1876, Nietzsche's close friend Carl von Gersdorff presented Overbeck with "a little monument to friendship," a *monumentulum amicitiae*, which was a colored, wooden plate

---

[32] On the link between Prussian Protestantism and German nationalism, see Helmut Walser Smith, *German Nationalism and Religious Conflict: Culture, Ideology, Politics, 1870–1914* (Princeton, N.J.: Princeton University Press, 1995), pp. 17–49. On the German vocation of Prussia, see Stefan Berger, "Prussia in History and Historiography from the Eighteenth to the Nineteenth Century," in Philip G. Dwyer (ed.), *The Rise of Prussia, 1700–1830* (Harlow: Longman, 2000), pp. 27–44: 34–40.

[33] See the discussion of Overbeck's reaction to Treitschke's *Deutsche Geschichte* in Niklaus Peter, *Im Schatten der Modernität: Franz Overbecks Weg zur "Christlichkeit unserer heutigen Theologie"* (Stuttgart: J. B. Metzler, 1992), pp. 105–18.

[34] On this peculiar episode, see Barbara Reibnitz, *Ein Kommentar zu Friedrich Nietzsche, "Die Geburt der Tragödie aus dem Geiste der Musik"* (Kap. 1–12) (Stuttgart: J. B. Metzler, 1992), pp. 47–8, and Brobjer, "Nietzsche's Relation to Historical Methods and Nineteenth-Century German Historiography," 176–7.

painted with symbols and initials, depicting the diverse circle of friends around the newly wed couple: Richard Wagner appeared as a genius with wings, Erwin Rohde as several dancing Satyrs, Nietzsche himself as a grimacing scholar, and Treitschke as the German Imperial Eagle (*KGB* II/5, p. 178 and *KGB* II/6, p. 358).[35]

The details of Nietzsche's friendship with Overbeck need not concern us here, but it is important to realize that Nietzsche's and Overbeck's intellectual developments from 1870 onward are marked by striking parallels.[36] In a later autobiographical note, Overbeck pointed out that, despite their age difference, they immediately found a mutual trust that was to protect them from later disagreements: "We are two scholarly characters, who want to transcend themselves."[37] Against this background, it is not surprising that their respective inaugural lectures – Nietzsche's "Homer und die klassische Philologie" (1869) and Overbeck's "Über Entstehung und Recht einer reinhistorischen Betrachtung der Neutestamentlichen Schriften der Theologie" (1870) – complement each other in that they both projected a critical attitude toward their respective disciplines. Likewise, Nietzsche's second "Untimely Meditation," *Vom Nutzen und Nachtheil der Historie für das Leben* (1874), mirrors Overbeck's polemical gesture in his pamphlet *Ueber die Christlichkeit unserer heutigen Theologie* (1873), which questioned the idea of Christianity in a similar way as Nietzsche questioned the value of history.[38]

In his inaugural lecture in Basel, Overbeck argued that the New Testament does not convey any theological or historical "facts," for the latter have been constructed by the different authors of the gospels, by their point of view, their historical distance, their

---

[35] This wooden disc is part of Franz Overbeck's estate at the University Library in Basel, item A 294. For the hint about its existence I am grateful to Martin A. Ruehl, "Basel and Nietzsche," *Nietzsche-Studien* 30 (2001), 499–503: 500. A fine representation can now be found on the back cover of Bollinger and Trenkle, *Nietzsche in Basel*.

[36] See Martin Arndt, "Die Basler Syntroglodyten Overbeck und Nietzsche: Eine Freundschaft im Dissens," *Zeitschrift für Religions- und Geistesgeschichte* 53/3 (2001), 193–226.

[37] Overbeck, "Erinnerungen an Friedrich Nietzsche," 320 and 322.

[38] See Andreas Urs Sommer, *Der Geist der Historie und das Ende des Christentums: Zur "Waffengenossenschaft" von Friedrich Nietzsche und Franz Overbeck, mit einem Anhang unpublizierter Texte aus Overbecks "Kirchenlexicon"* (Berlin: Akademie Verlag, 1997), pp. 29–43 and 83–108, and Franz Overbeck, *Ueber die Christlichkeit unserer heutigen Theologie: Streit- und Friedensschrift*, in *Werke und Nachlaß*, ed. Ekkehard W. Stegemann, Niklaus Peter, and Marianne Stauffacher-Schaub (Stuttgart: J. B. Metzler, 1994–), vol. 1, pp. 167–256.

personal inclinations.[39] A truly historical and, thus, "scientific" theology would need to align itself with the new paradigms of the historical method in the nineteenth century. Only the latter would be able to sufficiently counterbalance the rise of dogmatism, and Overbeck situates his own work in an intellectual field that also includes Ferdinand Christian Baur, Schleiermacher and de Wette.[40] This does not mean, however, that Overbeck wished to completely discredit religion as a whole: Overbeck accepted early Christianity as an authentic way of life that had been erased by the rise of theological dogma.[41] Being an agnostic at heart, he nevertheless valued religion over theology. But Overbeck's arguments also suggest that Christian theology needs to be regarded as an archaic mythical doctrine, and this is exactly the lesson Nietzsche drew from his friend's writings:

> With Christianity a religion became dominant that corresponded to a pre-Greek state of humanity: belief in ubiquitous magical processes, bloody sacrifices, superstitious fear of demonic tribunals, despair about oneself, ecstatic brooding and hallucinating, man himself turned into a playground for good and evil spirits and their warriors. (*KGW* IV/1, 5 [94])

Nietzsche's conclusion, as should be clear from his emphasis on superstition and animism, moved him into an increasingly anthropological direction that will become even more important in the later 1870s.

Considering Nietzsche's orientation during the early 1870s, it is more than obvious that the intellectual culture of nineteenth-century Basel left many traces that continued to shape central aspects of his later work. Against this background, it also becomes questionable whether *Die Geburt der Tragödie* should really be regarded as the main starting point for Nietzsche's later cultural and philosophical criticism, as has been claimed by some intellectual historians.[42] While art and aesthetics continue to be an

---

[39] See Franz Overbeck, "Über Entstehung und Recht einer rein historischen Betrachtung der Neutestamentlichen Schriften in der Theologie," in *Werke und Nachlaß*, vol. 1, pp. 83–106: 100.
[40] See ibid., p. 97 and 106.
[41] See ibid., pp. 84–91, and Franz Overbeck, "Über die Anfänge der patristischen Litteratur," *Historische Zeitschrift* 48 (1882), 417–72.
[42] See Megill, *Prophets of Extremity*, pp. 35–42, and Williamson, *The Longing for Myth in Germany*, pp. 234–83.

important concern in most of Nietzsche's writings, the presumed centrality of the aesthetic that is invariably attributed to his writings is in need of much revision. The short-hand conclusion that Nietzsche "looks at the world in general as if it were a sort of artwork" fails to really clarify the critical import of Nietzsche's writings.[43] Indeed, once we take a closer look at his manifold scholarly interests during the 1870s, we cannot but realize that his reflections on Greek tragedy constitute only part of his actual work.

Generally speaking, it is possible to discern five thematic trends in Nietzsche's scholarly work that seem to represent a slow shift away from textual criticism toward a more historicist and anthropological conception of classical studies.[44] First of all, a fair amount of his lectures, seminars and notebooks between 1869 and 1875 are concerned with Latin grammar and ancient rhetoric, but they also contain detailed examinations of rhythm and meter in Greek lyric poetry as well as epigraphic research dealing with Roman public inscriptions.[45] Second, we are able to observe a wide-ranging interest in the formation of Greek literature within a cultural context shaped by ritual and myth.[46] Third, he delivered substantial

---

[43] Nehamas, *Nietzsche*, p. 3. Most recently, Tamsin Shaw, "Nietzsche and the Self-Destruction of Secular Religions," *History of European Ideas* 32 (2006), 80–98: 83–6 and 91, has sought to reformulate the centrality of the aesthetic by arguing that Nietzsche's early thought represents an attempt at establishing a "post-Christian faith," that is, a secular religion based on the convergence of philosophical insight and art. Brian Leiter, "Nietzsche and Aestheticism," *Journal of the History of Philosophy* 20 (1992), 275–90, has already outlined the problems of such interpretations. Günter Abel, "Logik und Ästhetik," *Nietzsche-Studien* 16 (1987), 112–48, has convincingly shown that Nietzsche's aesthetic interests are completely intertwined with his epistemological concerns. This aspect is underplayed in Julian Young, *Nietzsche's Philosophy of Art* (Cambridge: Cambridge University Press, 1992).

[44] For a complete list of Nietzsche's lectures, seminars, courses and classes both at the University (1869–79) and the Pädagogium (1869–76), see Bollinger and Trenkle, *Nietzsche in Basel*, pp. 71–8.

[45] This area of Nietzsche's work is represented in particular by his *Vorlesungen über lateinische Grammatik* (1869–70), *Griechische Rhythmik* (1870–71), *Einleitung in die lateinische Epigraphik* (1871–72) and *Einleitung in die Rhetorik des Aristoteles* (1874–75, 1875, possibly also in 1877–78). Apart from his lectures and seminars, there is also a substantial range of notebooks, such as *Aufzeichnungen zur Metrik und Rhythmik* (1870–71), *Zur Theorie der quantitirenden Rhythmik* (1870–71), *Rhythmische Untersuchungen* (1870–71), *Geschichte der griechischen Beredsamkeit* (1872–73), and *Darstellung der antiken Rhetorik* (1872–74).

[46] See, for instance, Nietzsche's inaugural lecture *Homer und die klassische Philologie* (1869) as well as the lecture series *Prolegomena zu den Choephoren des Aeschylus* (1869–70, 1874, 1877–78), *Die griechischen Lyriker* (1869, 1871, 1873, 1874, 1874–75, 1878–79), *Einleitung in die Tragödie des Sophocles* (1870), and, above all, *Geschichte der griechischen Litteratur* (1874–75).

lectures on ancient Greek philosophy and its reception.[47] Like his lectures and notebooks concerned with language and rhetoric, these more philosophically inclined courses often tend to transcend the generally accepted boundaries of classical scholarship by introducing epistemological questions that are also present in the essays "Über Wahrheit und Lüge im aussermoralischen Sinne" (1873) and "Die Philosophie im tragischen Zeitalter der Griechen" (1873). Closely related to his work on Greek literary history during the early 1870s, a fourth thematic trend is represented by an increasing concern with the anthropological foundations of myth and ritual in archaic societies. This trend, which reflected the wider "anthropological turn" within classical scholarship during the second half of the nineteenth century, becomes particularly manifest from the mid-1870s onward, when he worked on "Der Gottesdienst der Griechen" (1875–78).

At the same time, it is necessary to realize that Nietzsche's philological work is also informed by considerable reflections on classical scholarship as a historical discipline. This becomes evident in his early lectures on "Encyclopaedie der klassischen Philologie," delivered for the first time in the summer semester of 1871, and is continued even after the publication of the first three "Untimely Meditations." His notes under the title "Wir Philologen," composed around March 1875, bear witness to his enduring concern with the value and perspective of philology as a critical discourse.[48]

While this is not the place to attempt a more comprehensive assessment of Nietzsche's philological writings and notebooks, it is nevertheless difficult to overlook the general importance of this work during the early 1870s.[49] There is no real evidence, that, as has often been suggested, Nietzsche was intent on rejecting

---

[47] See *Einführung in das Studium der platonischen Dialoge* (1871–72, 1873–74, 1876, 1878–79), *Ciceros Academica* (1870, 1870–71), and *Die vorplatonischen Philosophen* (1872, 1875–76, 1876, possibly already in 1869–70).

[48] See Hubert Cancik, "'Philologie als Beruf': Zu Formengeschichte, Thema und Tradition der unvollendeten vierten Unzeitgemäßen Friedrich Nietzsches," in Borsche, Gerratana, and Venturelli (eds.), *"Centauren-Geburten"* (Berlin: Walter de Gruyter,1994), pp. 81–96.

[49] See Fritz Bornmann, "Anekdota Nietzscheana aus dem philologischen Nachlaß der Basler Jahre (1869–1878)," in Borsche, Gerratana, and Venturelli (eds.), *"Centauren-Geburten,"* pp. 67–80, and Christian J. Emden, "Sprache, Musik und Rhythmus: Nietzsche über die Ursprünge von Literatur, 1869–1879," *Zeitschrift für deutsche Philologie* 121 (2002), 208–30.

classical philology and historical scholarship in general. Standard accounts of Nietzsche's scholarly work are distorted inasmuch as they tend to present his philological interests in sharp contrast to the dry and pedantic style of academic discourse in nineteenth-century Germany.[50] Even detailed expositions of Nietzsche's philological background tend to assume that his philological writings are a prime example of classical scholarship somehow gone wrong, while a more thorough appreciation of Nietzsche's philology has emerged only in recent years.[51]

Nietzsche himself, it should be added, was not completely unaware of his somewhat questionable reputation, especially after his first book, *Die Geburt der Tragödie*, was so vigorously attacked by Ulrich von Wilamowitz-Moellendorff. It is not really necessary to re-examine the quarrel between Nietzsche and Wilamowitz in any detail. Much has been said about this elsewhere.[52] It is sufficient to note that there was more at stake than scholarly disagreement. The harsh criticism that the young and ambitious Prussian scholar, who was later to become the most influential philologist of his time, leveled against Nietzsche's theory of tragedy accurately reflects the precarious situation of classical scholarship itself. Wilamowitz's attack was directed not only against the lack of rational scholarly method in Nietzsche's book on tragedy – exemplified most visibly by the absence of footnotes and any scholarly apparatus – but it also lamented that Nietzsche seemed to undermine the Greek myths.[53] But in fact, the discussion surrounding Nietzsche's book on tragedy laid bare the precarious

---

[50] See James Whitman, "Nietzsche in the Magisterial Tradition of German Classical Philology," *Journal of the History of Ideas* 47 (1986), 453–68: 453 and 461. In contrast, see Christian J. Emden, "Learning How to Read: Nietzsche in Leipzig," *Oxford German Studies* 35 (2006), 97–110.

[51] The questionable state of Nietzsche's philology has been emphasized by M. S. Silk and J. P. Stern, *Nietzsche on Tragedy* (Cambridge: Cambridge University Press, 1981), pp. 133 and 271.

[52] See Carsten Zelle, "Der Abgang des Herakles: Beobachtungen zur mythologischen Figurenkonstellation in Hinsicht auf Friedrich Nietzsche und Ulrich von Wilamowitz-Moellendorff," *Nietzsche-Studien* 23 (1994), 200–25; Jaap Mansfeld, "The Wilamowitz-Nietzsche Struggle: Another New Document and Some Further Comments," *Nietzsche-Studien* 15 (1986), 43–58; William M. Calder III, "The Wilamowitz-Nietzsche Struggle: New Documents and a Reappraisal," *Nietzsche-Studien* 12 (1983), 214–54.

[53] See Ulrich von Wilamowitz-Moellendorff, *Zukunftsphilologie! Zweites stück: eine erwiderung auf die rettungsversuche für Fr. Nietzsches "geburt der tragödie"* (1873), in Karlfried Gründer, *Der Streit um Nietzsches "Geburt der Tragödie:" Die Schriften von E. Rohde, R. Wagner, U. v. Wilamowitz-Moellendorff* (Hildesheim: Olms, 1969), pp. 115–35: 134.

state of those neo-humanist visions of the classical tradition that among German classical philologists, from Jahn to Wilamowitz, were directly connected to visions of national identity.[54] In 1871, Nietzsche had complained in his notebooks that the philhellenism that had been cultivated among his peers was both theoretically superficial and historically ill informed (*KGW* III/3, 3 [76]). A few years later, in the notes for "Wir Philologen," he described the historical vision of philhellenism as based on "ignorance, false judgments and deceptive conclusions" as well as on "the self-interests of a particular caste" (*KGW* IV/1, 3 [4]). The self-interests in question were, of course, those of the German philologists, whose prestige within the university system was increasingly threatened by the technocratic demands of the modern nation state.

Against the background of his experiences in Bonn and Leipzig, and influenced by the intellectual enviroment in Basel, Nietzsche was clearly uneasy about the use of neo-humanism as an ideological trope. In contrast, Wilamowitz demanded philological specialization without abandoning the aestheticized dream of a "classical Greece" that served as a mirror image of Germany. While Nietzsche pointed out that "*the drive for classical* antiquity can only come from knowledge of the present" (*KGW* IV/1, 3 [62]), it seems that, for Wilamowitz, the present of the modern German nation state was to be justified through an ideological conception of classical antiquity, which effectively sought to "Germanize" the Greeks and to "nationalize" the classical tradition.[55] Certainly, this dimension of Wilamowitz's approach to classical scholarship became more obvious only in subsequent years, when he began to influence the curriculum at German schools, when he delivered public speeches on the German Emperor's birthday, and when he justified Germany's entry into the First World War.[56] But in 1872 his resistance to any doubts about the predominant image of

---

[54] See, for instance, Herbst, *Das classische Alterthum in der Gegenwart*, pp. 149–65.
[55] See Bernhard vom Brocke, "'Von des attischen Reiches Herrlichkeit' oder die 'Modernisierung' der Antike im Zeitalter des Nationalstaats," *Historische Zeitschrift* 243 (1986), 101–36.
[56] See Ulrich von Wilamowitz-Moellendorff, *Griechisches Lesebuch* (Berlin: Weidmann, 1902); "Der griechische Unterricht auf den Gymnasien," in *Verhandlungen über Fragen der höheren Unterrichts, Berlin 6. bis 8. Juni 1900, nebst einem Anhange von Gutachten herausgegeben im Auftrage des Ministers der geistlichen, Unterrichts- und Medicinal-Angelegenheiten* (Halle: Verlag der Buchhandlung des Waisenhauses, 1901), pp. 205–17; *Reden aus der Kriegszeit* (Berlin: Weidmann, 1915).

classical Greece was already linked to the fear that criticizing the classical tradition automatically meant undermining those cultural tropes that safeguarded the historical identity of the German nation state.

Clearly, *Die Geburt der Tragödie* was not the high point of Nietzsche's philology, neither of his philosophy.[57] But the effects of the scandal it triggered shaped Nietzsche's difficult relationship to his own profession for years to come. In November 1872, Nietzsche sent a letter to his friend Erwin Rohde, which outlined his troubles at the University of Basel:

> The next fact that somewhat depresses me is that the *philologists have stayed away* from our university for this winter semester: a rather unique phenomenon, which you will interpret in the same way as I do. In one specific case I even know that one student, who wished to study philology here, has been kept back at Bonn, happily writing to relatives that he is grateful to God not to be at a university where *I* am professor. (*KGB* II/3, p. 85)

Although Nietzsche was able to count on the support of some of his colleagues in Basel, his scholarly position turned out to be challenging. Consequently, he seems to have been intent on leaving the impression that he wished to distance himself completely from both philological and historical scholarship:

> Precisely in those circles whose dignity could consist in drawing inexhaustibly from the Greek stream to the benefit of German education [*Bildung*], precisely the teachers in our institutions of higher education [*Bildungsanstalten*] have learned better than most how to reach a quick and comfortable accommodation with the Greeks, even to the extent of abandoning sceptically the Hellenic ideal and completely perverting the true aim of all classical studies [*Alterthumsstudien*]. In those circles one either exhausts oneself in the attempt to become a reliable corrector of old texts or a natural historian studying language in microscopic detail, or one perhaps seeks to appropriate Greek antiquity, alongside other antiquities, "historically," but at any rate adopting the method and the haughty demeanour of today's cultured [*gebildeten*] historiographers. (*BT* p. 96)

---

[57] See, however, the accounts of James I. Porter, *The Invention of Dionysus: An Essay on the Birth of Tragedy* (Stanford, Calif.: Stanford University Press, 2000), and John Sallis, *Crossings: Nietzsche and the Space of Tragedy* (Chicago: University of Chicago Press, 1991), which both emphasize the philosophical sophistication of Nietzsche's book as an early embodiment of his later philosophical criticism.

Judging from this passage, Nietzsche's criticism of traditional historical scholarship, as it was practiced in the specialized research environment at German universities, seems obvious. But, as is so often the case with regard to Nietzsche's polemical claims, we have to be cautious and resist taking them at face value. The passage in question can be found in the middle of the twentieth chapter toward the end of *Die Geburt der Tragödie*, when he has already left the territory of Greek antiquity and entered the numinous world of Richard Wagner's bourgeois aestheticism and his nationalist program of Germanic foundation myths. In contrast, the main argument of the first twelve chapters is philological and historical in orientation: despite the many references to Schopenhauer, Schiller and Shakespeare, Nietzsche in fact discusses the origin of Greek tragedy against the background of earlier philological studies, mainly the work of Jakob Bernays and Karl Otfried Müller.[58] In fact, the book was not supposed to end with Wagner at all but with Socrates – only in 1871, shortly after his return from the Franco-Prussian War, did he begin to link Wagner's aesthetics more directly to his theory of tragedy.[59]

Nevertheless, Nietzsche repeats his scathing criticism of classical scholarship in the early summer of 1875, when he attacked Otto Jahn, one of his former teachers in Bonn:

One does not learn anything from lectures on philology when these are given by philologists; they are complete twaddle, for instance, Jahn ("Bedeutung und Stellung der Alterthumsstudien in Deutschland"). No feeling for what is to be defended, what is to be protected: this is the way people speak who have not yet contemplated that they could be attacked. (*KGW* IV/1, 5 [125])

Nietzsche, it seems, was above all dissatisfied not with historical scholarship as such, but rather with its political orientation: Jahn's rectorial address at the University of Bonn in 1859, "Die Bedeutung und Stellung der Alterthumsstudien in Deutschland,"

---

[58] See Jakob Bernays, *Grundzüge der verlorenen Abhandlung des Aristoteles über Wirkung der Tragödie* (Breslau: Trewendt, 1857), and Karl Otfried Müller, *Aeschylos, "Eumeniden": Griechisch und deutsch, mit erläuternden Abhandlungen über die äussere Darstellung, und über den Inhalt und die Composition dieser Tragödie* (Göttingen: Dieterich, 1833). For a detailed assessment of Nietzsche's reading, see Thomas H. Brobjer, "Sources of and Influences on Nietzsche's *Birth of Tragedy*," *Nietzsche-Studien* 34 (2005), 278–99.

[59] See Reibnitz, *Ein Kommentar zu Friedrich Nietzsche*, pp. 45–6.

is a largely politically oriented piece intended for a wider audience to safeguard the already fairly fragile integrity of classical scholarship in the changing intellectual landscape of the nineteenth century. Historical scholarship and philology as the handmaiden of political interests – this was what Nietzsche sought to distance himself from. In sharp contrast, he demanded a reorientation of historical criticism as a philosophical critique of political culture.

THE NEED FOR PHILOSOPHICAL EDUCATION

Throughout the second half of the nineteenth century, most classical scholars, in Germany as elsewhere, viewed contemporary philosophical developments with much suspicion. From around 1860 onward, any serious reflection on the epistemological foundations of classical scholarship as a historical discipline was largely regarded as far-fetched speculation. There are, it seems, two main reasons for this development. First, the increasing disciplinary specialization within the German university system contributed to unforeseen tensions between philosophy and philology. Second, there was no need to reconsider the relationship between philology and philosophy, since eminent scholars like August Boeckh had already provided a relatively coherent theoretical framework for classical philology and other historical disciplines against the background of German idealism.[60] Upon closer inspection, however, the situation is more complex, for Boeckh sought to build "a comprehensive cultural history of antiquity" on the "knowledge of ideas."[61] With this emphasis on ideas over empirical evidence, Boeckh contributed to what has been called the "historicization of reason," the effects of which became particularly manifest in the second half of the nineteenth century.[62]

---

[60] See Boeckh, *Encyklopädie*, pp. 79–260, and also Friedrich Ast, *Grundlinien der Grammatik, Hermeneutik und Kritik* (Landshut: Thomann, 1808), pp. 1–16 and 165–226.
[61] Boeckh, *Encyklopädie*, pp. 175, 86, 20 and 57.
[62] See Ulrich Johannes Schneider, *Philosophie und Universität: Die Historisierung der Vernunft im 19. Jahrhundert* (Hamburg: Meiner, 1999), and Herbert Schnädelbach, *Philosophy in Germany, 1831–1933*, trans. Eric Matthews (Cambridge: Cambridge University Press, 1984), pp. 34–58. Köhnke, *Entstehung und Aufstieg des Neukantianismus*, pp. 402–3, provides an interesting statistical account of this "historicization of reason" with regard to the lectures and seminars given by neo-Kantian philosophers between 1870 and 1884: of 472 lectures in total, more than half are concerned with the history of philosophy.

One of the many effects of this historicizing trend was that the history of philosophy slowly replaced the philosophy of history as one of the main concerns within the humanities in nineteenth-century Germany. Hegel's and Schleiermacher's systematic work on the history of philosophy, which fell into the first two decades of the nineteenth century, introduced an unprecedented historical consciousness into German academic philosophy, which was continued in the publications of their pupils, most prominently August Heinrich Ritter.[63] But this development also brought along new questions with regard to the status of historical knowledge itself. First of all, the historicization of philosophical thought was directly connected to an increasing awareness of the hermeneutical problems any historian has to face. At the threshold between Enlightenment, German idealism, and the rise of historicism, this introduced into historical discourse at large what has been called a "polarization between contingency and teleology":[64] the contingency of individual events or developments often stood in contrast to the presumed progression of philosophical thought from ancient Greece to modern Europe. Second, the widespread historicization of philosophy in nineteenth-century Germany also enabled a new perspective on ancient Greek philosophy that often crossed the uncertain boundary between the historiography of philosophy and classical scholarship.[65] Prominent examples of this trend are Carl Prantl's and Friedrich Ueberweg's studies on the historical development of logical thought.[66]

Even in the 1860s, the reception of ancient Greek philosophy was still very much embedded in the legacy of Hegelian idealism, which was often the premise of highly influential works concerned with the history of ancient Greek philosophy that were also widely

---

[63] See Hegel, *Vorlesungen über die Geschichte der Philosophie*; Friedrich Schleiermacher, *Geschichte der Philosophie*, ed. August Heinrich Ritter (Berlin: Reimer, 1839); August Heinrich Ritter, *Geschichte der Philosophie* (Hamburg: Perthes, 1829–53).
[64] Friedrich Jaeger, "Geschichtsphilosophie, Hermeneutik und Kontingenz in der Geschichte des Historismus," in Wolfgang Küttler, Jörn Rüsen, and Ernst Schulin (eds.), *Geschichtsdiskurs, III: Die Epoche der Historisierung* (Frankfurt/M.: Fischer Taschenbuch Verlag, 1997), pp. 45–66: 55–61.
[65] See Scholtz, *Ethik und Hermeneutik*, pp. 286–313.
[66] See Carl Prantl, *Geschichte der Logik im Abendlande* (Leipzig: Hirzel, 1855–70), and Friedrich Ueberweg, *System der Logik und Geschichte der logischen Lehren* (Bonn: Marcus, 1857).

read by classical scholars, such as those by Eduard Zeller and Christian August Brandis.[67] Nietzsche was quite perceptive with regard to this particular development, although he did not feel exactly comfortable either with its Hegelian background, or with its popular appeal. Especially during the 1870s, he repeatedly insisted that historicizing philosophical thought denigrated the latter's critical potential:

> Who, for example, can clear the history of the Greek philosophers of the soporific miasma spread over it by the learned, though not particularly scientific and unfortunately all too tedious, labours of Ritter, Brandis and Zeller? I for one prefer reading Diogenes Laertius to Zeller, because the former at least breathes the spirit of the philosophers of antiquity, while the latter breathes neither that nor any other spirit. (*UM* III: 8)

But although it might be tempting to take such statements literally, Nietzsche did in fact learn a great deal from the historians of philosophy.

Nietzsche's own relationship to academic philosophy was, without doubt, rather ambivalent. To him it seemed that philosophy at German universities had lost its edge as soon as it became part of precisely those political foundation myths that he had encountered in Bonn and Leipzig. The close alliance between philosophy and the modern state had fateful consequences, as he pointed out in a note from May 1868 with the title "On Academic Philosophy." Immediately below the title, he intended to list the "usefulness of academic philosophy," but did not find anything positive to say: "mainly disastrous," was his laconic conclusion. Since higher education remained under the control and influence of the state authorities, German universities reflected the political interests and religious values of the state. As a consequence, Nietzsche suggested, German universities were generally unable to appoint philosophers who contradicted these interests and values; the philosophers themselves fell victim to the political fashions of the day, as could be seen with regard to the "Hegelians and

---

[67] Prominent examples are Eduard Zeller, *Die Philosophie der Griechen in ihrer geschichtlichen Entwicklung*, 2nd edn. (Tübingen: Fues, 1856–68); Christian August Brandis, *Geschichte der Entwickelungen der griechischen Philosophie und ihrer Nachwirkungen im römischen Reiche* (Berlin: Reimer, 1862–64); Friedrich Ueberweg, *Grundriss der Geschichte der Philosophie* (Berlin: Mittler, 1862–66).

their fall from grace." By aligning itself too closely with political power philosophy tends to lose its critical potential, while "true philosophy is being ignored and silenced" (*KGW* I/4, 62 [58]).

To some extent, Nietzsche's view of the political situation philosophy found itself in around the middle of the nineteenth century was correct. Hegelian philosophy, at least until the 1840s, was indeed very much connected to the Prussian state, and professorships in philosophy and other fields were integrated into a civil service structure dependent on the good will of state authorities. But by the late 1860s, German philosophy had lost some of its direct political influence, since it no longer lent itself easily to any specific political program. With the notable exception of the Prussian historians and those who worked in the so-called "sciences of the state" (*Staatswissenschaften*), most German professors between the 1860s and the 1890s had little interest in general political questions, unless they had an effect on the university research system. Furthermore, the political attitude of German academics was not necessarily illiberal. Some of the most influential and outspoken critics of Bismarck and, since 1871, of Imperial Germany, ranging from radical left-liberals to moderate liberals, belonged to the professorial elite.[68]

Nietzsche's prime example, "die Hegelei," might serve as a prominent reminder of the complex situation of those academic philosophers and scholars who took an active interest in the role of the state. During the 1820s, Hegel himself had already come under attack from both Prussian liberals and conservatives. Friedrich Carl von Savigny, the founder of the historical school of law, regarded Hegel's emphasis on the link between law and the universality of reason particularly irritating, while Hegel himself rejected the historical school of law.[69] Still influenced by the philosophical ideals of the later Enlightenment, Hegel's vision, though emphasizing the historical role of the Prussian state, did not sit easily with Savigny's practical demands for legal change that

---

[68] See Thomas Nipperdey, *Deutsche Geschichte, 1866–1918* (Munich: C. H. Beck, 1990–92), vol. I, pp. 576 and 590–5.
[69] For Hegel's criticism of the "historical school of law," see his *Elements of the Philosophy of Right*, ed. Allen W. Wood, trans. H. B. Nisbet (Cambridge: Cambridge University Press, 1991), §§ 3, 211–12 and 258. For Savigny's rejection of any philosophical foundation of law, see *Of the Vocation of Our Age for Legislation and Jurisprudence*, trans. Abraham Hayward (London: Littlewood & Co., 1831), p. 65.

were oriented toward nation-building.⁷⁰ After Hegel's death, Karl Ernst Schubarth again discarded the former's thought as too liberal and anti-Prussian, while Rudolf Haym in contrast criticized that Hegel's philosophy was a direct expression of Prussia's political interests.⁷¹ But by the time Karl Rosenkranz had finally idealized Hegel as the "philosopher of the German nation," shortly before the creation of a unified German Empire in 1871, most academic philosophers in Germany had already turned away from Hegel.⁷²

Nevertheless, despite Nietzsche's remarks of 1868 about the disastrous state of German philosophy, the latter was not at all in bad shape, at least from an institutional point of view. From the late 1860s onward, and culminating in the 1870s, a surge of new professorial appointments was directly connected to the rising interest in Kant. This development mirrored the rapid growth, by about 159 percent, of faculty positions at German universities in the second half of the nineteenth century, which resulted from enormous financial investment in higher education and research.⁷³ But in a central passage of his essay *David Strauss der Bekenner und Schriftsteller* (1873) Nietzsche continued his attack on the state of academic philosophy, focusing in particular on the renewed interest in the history of philosophy:

> It was these same self-contented people [i.e.: the contemporary scholars] who, with the same end in view of guaranteeing their own peace, took charge of history and sought to transform every science which might be expected to disturb their complacency into a historical discipline, especially so in the case of philosophy and classical philology. (*UM* I: 2)

For Nietzsche, it seems, the relentless historicization he discovered in academic philosophy and the humanities at large prevented real philosophical enthusiasm, whatever the financial investments.

---

⁷⁰ See Toews, *Becoming Historical*, pp. 283–92, and James Q. Whitman, *The Legacy of Roman Law in the German Romantic Era: Historical Vision and Legal Change* (Princeton, N.J.: Princeton University Press, 1994), pp. 105–12.

⁷¹ See Karl Ernst Schubarth, *Ueber die Unvereinbarkeit der Hegelschen Staatslehre mit dem obersten Lebens- und Entwicklungs-Princip des preußischen Staates* (Breslau: Aderholz, 1839), and Rudolf Haym, *Hegel und seine Zeit: Vorlesungen über Entstehung und Entwicklung, Wesen und Werth der Hegel'schen Philosophie* (Berlin: Gärtner, 1857), p. 359.

⁷² See Karl Rosenkranz, *Hegel als deutscher Nationalphilosoph* (Berlin: Duncker & Humblot, 1870).

⁷³ See Köhnke, *Entstehung und Aufstieg des Neukantianismus*, pp. 308–9, and Nipperdey, *Deutsche Geschichte, 1866–1918*, vol. I, 569–70.

But he also realized more than others that the status of philosophy as a critical discourse had become uncertain against the backdrop of the increasing influence of the natural sciences and political historiography on the intellectual culture of nineteenth-century Germany: "science" and "history," he pointed out in the autumn of 1873, exerted a detrimental effect on the courage "to live philosophically [*eine Philosophie zu leben*]" (*KGW* III/4, 29 [197]).

It is not surprising that Nietzsche should have contemplated an academic career in philosophy. He made his move between December 1870 and January 1871, already one year after he had been appointed to his professorship in Basel. Basel's academic culture was, however, neither willing nor ready to support such a move. The first chair in philosophy properly speaking was held from 1854 by Karl Steffensen, a relatively conservative figure who came to Basel from the University of Kiel and whose main interest was in the philosophy of religion.[74] After much internal deliberation, and with financial help from outside the university, the city's council for education finally decided in 1866 to establish a second professorship in philosophy. This post was taken up by the young Wilhelm Dilthey, a student of the neo-Kantian philosophers Kuno Fischer and Friedrich Adolf Trendelenburg. In contrast to Steffensen's more traditional stance, Dilthey's neo-Kantian background allowed him to bridge the widening gap between philosophy and the natural sciences. But Basel could not really provide the kind of prestige and financial support offered by German universities and after only two semesters Dilthey accepted a position at the University of Kiel in northern Germany. In 1868, Gustav Teichmüller, an expert on Aristotle and conceptual history, arrived as Dilthey's designated successor. Unlike Dilthey, Teichmüller was already fairly well established, and his work often crossed the boundaries between ancient philosophy and classical philology. Nietzsche himself was aware of Teichmüller's studies on Aristotle and, much later, Teichmüller's chief work *Die wirkliche und die scheinbare Welt* (1882) – a metaphysical treatise that was directed against the dominant neo-Kantian movement – had a profound impact on what is often called Nietzsche's "doctrine of

---

[74] See Peter Hirschfeld, "Karl Steffensen, 1816–1888: Ein Flensburger als Philosoph an der Universität Basel," *Basler Zeitschrift für Geschichte und Altertumskunde* 76 (1976), 19–75.

perspectivism."[75] Nevertheless, their direct personal contact in Basel was fairly limited; they knew of each other, without sharing much common ground.

Like Dilthey, Teichmüller soon tired of the provincial philosophical scene in Basel and its lack of opportunities and in 1870 he accepted the chair in philosophy at the University of Dorpat, now Tartu in Estonia.[76] Teichmüller's departure, and perhaps Nietzsche's wrongly assuming that Switzerland's seeming intellectual liberalism provided an ideal environment for ground-breaking philosophical research (after all, Lange had just started his professorship in Zurich), seem to have persuaded Nietzsche to apply for Teichmüller's position. In December 1870, Nietzsche mentioned the latter's move to Dorpat in letters addressed to his mother and sister back in Naumburg and to his former teacher Ritschl in Leipzig (*KGB* II/1, pp. 164 and 174), who was in any case quite bewildered about the philosophical interests of his former pupil. Finally, in January 1871, after a short visit to Richard Wagner in Tribschen, Nietzsche wrote to Wilhelm Vischer-Bilfinger, who had been responsible for his appointment as a philologist. Informing his older colleague that his main interests were now of a philosophical nature, he applied for Teichmüller's post and suggested his friend Erwin Rohde, then in Kiel, as his successor. Nietzsche's application was duly rejected.[77]

Despite his failure to establish himself as an academic philosopher, a profession he subsequently held in much disregard, Nietzsche continued to include philosophical topics in his philological lectures and writings. Above all, he began to realize that historical disciplines such as classical scholarship could have cultural relevance only if they were able to deliver a critique of contemporary cultural trends. For Nietzsche, this meant that they needed to be grounded in philosophical education. This

---

[75] See Gustav Teichmüller, *Aristotelische Forschungen* (Halle: Barthel, 1867–73), and *Die wirkliche und die scheinbare Welt: Neue Grundlegung der Metaphysik* (Breslau: Koebner, 1882). On Teichmüller, see now Heiner Schwenke, *Zurück zur Wirklichkeit: Bewusstsein und Erkenntnis bei Gustav Teichmüller* (Basel: Schwabe, 2006).

[76] Teichmüller was not the last philosopher to leave Basel relatively quickly. His student Rudolf Eucken, one of the main representatives of so-called *Lebensphilosophie*, arrived in 1872 and left Basel for Jena in 1874. His successor Max Heinze, primarily a historian of philosophy, took up his professorship in 1874 but left for Königsberg already in 1875.

[77] See Nietzsche's correspondence with Wilhelm Vischer-Bilfinger and Erwin Rohde: *KGB* II/1, pp. 175–8, 183, 189, 192–3. On this curious episode, see also Janz, *Friedrich Nietzsche*, vol. I, pp. 398–409.

becomes especially evident in his lectures on "Encyclopaedie der klassischen Philologie," which he gave in the summer of 1871 and which he seems to have repeated two years later in the winter semester of 1873/74.[78]

Generally speaking, encyclopedic lectures were a common feature of higher education in nineteenth-century Germany. August Heinrich Ritter's *Encyklopädie der philosophischen Wissenschaften* (1862–64) and Johann Gustav Droysen's Berlin lectures on the theory of history (1857–83), to name two prominent examples, shaped the educational canon in philosophy and historical studies for years to come.[79] In the field of classical scholarship, Friedrich August Wolf's lectures at the University of Halle, posthumously published as *Vorlesungen über die Alterthumswissenschaft* (1831–39), set the stage for the way in which the principles of classical scholarship were to be taught throughout the nineteenth century, but August Boeckh's lectures at the University of Berlin proved to be even more influential in the long run: providing classical scholarship with a thorough theoretical foundation, Boeckh was able to deliver his lectures over the years in front of literally thousands of students flocking to Berlin in order to become a part of what was then Germany's most exciting intellectual scene, among them two young Swiss scholars – Johann Jakob Bachofen and Jacob Burckhardt. Boeckh's lectures are indeed an interesting example of the way classical scholars sought to balance the relationship between philology and philosophy. At first sight, Boeckh clearly distinguished philology from philosophy inasmuch as the latter was supposed to be concerned with the "theory of knowledge," while the former was meant to focus on the "history of knowledge" within different cultural contexts.[80] But far from seeking to replace philosophy with a historical discipline, he stressed that both essentially dealt with the same problem, human knowledge

---

[78] Nietzsche might have had access to a transcript of Friedrich Ritschl's respective lectures, which the latter delivered in Breslau and Bonn between 1835 and 1843. On Ritschl's lectures, see Otto Ribbeck, *Friedrich Wilhelm Ritschl: Ein Beitrag zur Geschichte der Philologie* (Leipzig: Teubner, 1879–81), vol. 1, pp. 327–39.

[79] See August Heinrich Ritter, *Encyklopädie der philosophischen Wissenschaften* (Göttingen: Dieterich, 1862–64). Droysen only published a short summary of his work as *Grundriss der Historik* (Jena: Frommann, 1858). The complete lectures were published only decades after his death in 1884: *Historik: Vorlesungen über Enzyklopädie und Methodologie der Geschichte*, ed. Rudolf Hübner (Munich: Oldenburg, 1937).

[80] See Boeckh, *Encyklopädie*, p. 18.

(*Erkenntnis*); they differed only with regard to their respective approach. The "historiography of knowledge," comprising all forms and manifestations of human culture, could only proceed along philological lines, or so Boeckh believed.[81]

By the time Nietzsche began to compose his own encyclopedic lectures, however, theoretical reflection among philologists was in sharp decline. Nietzsche's own teacher Friedrich Ritschl was, to say the least, rather skeptical about the value of philosophy for safeguarding the foundation of philology. Above all, he regarded philology as a practical historical discipline detached from any theoretical issues.[82] Of course, after reading Kant, Schopenhauer and Lange, Nietzsche could not agree with his teacher's assessment. The lectures "Encyclopaedie der klassischen Philologie" often lament precisely the lack of philosophical education among philologists and historical scholars:[83] classical scholarship cannot be limited to a disinterested study of Greek and Roman antiquity but must also take into account the relationship between antiquity and modernity (*KGW* II/3, p. 437).[84] For Nietzsche, however, such historical orientation was primarily a philosophical problem.

In his attempt to formulate the relationship between philology and philosophy Nietzsche seems to follow Boeckh's earlier distinction between a historical and a theoretical perspective on human endeavors. When Nietzsche discusses, for instance, the meaning of *philologia* in Greek and Roman antiquity, he clearly differentiates between philosophical thought and philological practice: while the former should be regarded as a reflective operation necessarily based on knowledge from experience, philology should be seen as based on knowledge from texts (*KGW* II/3, pp. 342–3). What is at stake here is that fundamental tension between philosophy and philology, which can be traced back to Seneca's *Epistulae morales*, especially to letter CVIII where Seneca writes to Lucilius about the value of philosophical education

---

[81] See ibid., p. 10.
[82] See Ritschl, "Zur Methode des philologischen Studiums," pp. 25 and 32.
[83] For somewhat different accounts of Nietzsche's lectures, see Porter, *Nietzsche and the Philology of the Future*, pp. 167–224, and Benne, *Nietzsche und die historisch-kritische Philologie*, pp. 68–88.
[84] Along similar lines, see Gottfried Bernhardy, *Grundlinien zur Encyklopädie der Philologie* (Halle: Anton, 1832), pp. 47–8, which Nietzsche borrowed from the university library in Basel between April 1871 and April 1872.

(*KGW* II/3, p. 343).⁸⁵ Here, Seneca remarks that learning to argue philosophically is not a fanciful spare time occupation, but indeed a life-long and valuable undertaking.⁸⁶ Seneca himself, however, informs Lucilius that he gave up his concern with philosophical thought and instead turned to the realm of the spoken and written word (*itaque quae philosophia fuit, facta philologia est*).⁸⁷ For Nietzsche, however, it seemed only natural to reverse Seneca's distinction. In his inaugural lecture, "Homer und die klassische Philologie" (1869), written in a hotel room in Heidelberg en route to Basel, he concluded that philosophy superseded philology (*philosophia facta est quae philologia fuit*), and this was to determine the direction of his scholarship for years to come (*KGW* II/1, p. 268). Nevertheless, the extravagant intellectualism of nineteenth-century Basel was not really based on philosophy. Unlike Hegel and Schleiermacher in Berlin, Basel did not have any philosophical "master thinker." Most prominently, Jacob Burckhardt explicitly warned not to mix the study of history with philosophical speculation.⁸⁸

Nietzsche's emphasis on philosophical education was not only triggered by the lack of theoretical reflection he encountered among classical philologists. There were also political issues at stake. Nietzsche began to formulate the need for philosophical education against the background of an emerging modern German nation state after the Franco-Prussian War of 1870/71. This nation state could only be successful if it was organized along technocratic lines that stood in sharp contrast to neo-humanist ideals of organic wholeness: higher education was not supposed to serve the interests of the individual, as suggested by Humboldt's vision of *Bildung*, but rather the interests of the state. In the modern nation state, neo-humanist ideals fell victim to processes of modernization that were also reflected in those far-reaching administrative changes that took place in the realm of higher education. New financial investments in higher education, coupled with actual demand for academics in both the public and private sectors, led to an explosion of enrollment numbers: while students of theology declined rapidly, students of law, medicine, and the

---

[85] See already *KGW* I/5, 75 [3]. [86] See Seneca, *Epistulae morales*, CVIII. 4.
[87] Ibid., CVIII. 23. [88] See Burckhardt, *Weltgeschichtliche Betrachtungen*, p. 83.

teaching professions increased at unprecedented rates.[89] One of the causes of this development was the bureaucratization of public life, which required a substantial number of qualified officials, whose amount doubled between 1852 and 1871. Throughout the 1870s, the number of law students in Prussia alone virtually doubled. Clearly, within the context of the technocratic nation state neo-humanism was on its way out. The latter was still able to provide an imaginary educational ideal that could easily be integrated into the political foundation myths of the German Empire, but in practical terms it was of little relevance. It is precisely against the background of these developments that we have to understand Nietzsche's demand for a philosophical education as a counterweight to the technocratic demands of the modern nation state.

THE "GERMAN SPIRIT" AND THE FRANCO-PRUSSIAN WAR

Between January 16 and March 23, 1872, Nietzsche delivered five public lectures with the title "Ueber die Zukunft unserer Bildungsanstalten."[90] At first sight, these lectures seem to reflect a nostalgic vision for a lost educational ideal, an anti-modern desire to return to the Humboldtian neo-humanism of the early 1800s, itself rooted in Friedrich Schiller's earlier idea of an "aesthetic education of man."[91] In fact, Nietzsche's lectures are a far more complex document that mirrors the contradictions and tensions within the German cultural self-conception of the time.

Nietzsche himself will have been quite pleased about the way in which these lectures were advertised in the winter semester of 1871/72. The flyer on which they were announced at the University of Basel and in the city's public museum on the Augustinergasse suggested that they were part of the museum's program of public lectures, which also included Jacob Burckhardt's "Über Glück und Unglück in der Weltgeschichte" and "Die Griechen und ihr Mythos" as well as a lecture by the newly arrived Franz

---

[89] See Nipperdey, *Deutsche Geschichte, 1866–1918*, vol. I, pp. 568–86.
[90] The precise dates of these lectures are January 16, February 6 and 27, March 5 and 23, 1872. On some of Nietzsche's likely sources, see Jörg Schneider, "Nietzsches Basler Vorträge *Ueber die Zukunft unserer Bildungsanstalten* im Lichte seiner Lektüre pädagogischer Literatur," *Nietzsche-Studien* 21 (1992), 308–25.
[91] See Friedrich Schiller, *On the Aesthetic Education of Man, in a Series of Letters*, ed. and trans. Elizabeth M. Wilkinson and L. A. Willoughby (Oxford: Clarendon Press, 1967).

Overbeck on an unspecified topic (*GSA* 71/366). Such public lectures took place regularly in the city museum, which as an institution expressed the way in which the intellectual values of Basel's patrician liberal-conservative elite were linked to the economic backbone of civic life. Funded publicly, the magnificent neo-classical building in the Augustinergasse, which balanced symbolic references to antiquity with a functional architectural order, provided an ideal place where art, academic education, and civic community were able to intersect.[92]

Right from its opening in November 1849, the city museum's meeting rooms were intended for a program of public lectures, which often sought to bridge the gap between the specialized work taking place at the university and the more traditional educational interests of the patrician elite – after all, this was "their" university and "their" museum. These public lectures were not intended to be based on research accessible only to those already familiar with a particular discipline, but they were meant to enhance public life and *Bildung*. This becomes particularly obvious once we look at the other lectures announced for the winter of 1871/72.[93] They were dealing with the military campaigns of Italian city-states in the sixteenth century, the culture of travel in the Roman Empire, the political constitution of ancient Athens, and the agricultural history of economically useful plants. Basel's elite will have appreciated this program: a little military and legal history, some travel and some advanced gardening, rounded off by the fortunes and misfortunes of world-history.

Viewed against this background, Nietzsche, intent on presenting a more ambitious program, must have miscalculated his situation when he assumed that these public lectures would provide him with an ideal forum to outline his ideas for philosophical education and to turn himself into a public intellectual like his older colleague Burckhardt, whose lectures attracted an audience far beyond the usual student population. Nietzsche's lectures

---

[92] On the history of Basel's city museum, see Gossman, *Basel in the Age of Burckhardt*, p. 80. Although unique to Basel, the public funding structure of the city museum reflected a wider trend: the Städel-Museum in Frankfurt am Main (1817), the Wallraff Collections in Cologne (1824), and the Kunsthallen in Hamburg (1869) represent a similar intersection of art, higher education, and civic life. As such, it is of no surprise that these German cities, like Basel, had a dominant patrician cultural elite with liberal-conservative leanings.

[93] See *GSA* 71/366.

seem to have been quite successful. The philosopher Rudolf Eucken, who had just arrived in Basel as Gustav Teichmüller's successor, spoke of the enthusiastic reception of Nietzsche's lectures by the educated and mainly patrician audience, and a short review in the local newspaper, *Schweizer Grenzpost und Tagblatt der Stadt Basel*, published shortly after the first lecture on January 23, praised the "beautiful form" of Nietzsche's presentation and his "well-chosen words."[94] Although he was still an unfamiliar name in Basel, his audience seems to have followed his ideas with much interest, but Nietzsche himself, to put it mildly, was not pleased about the newspaper's "stupid account" that "misunderstood everything" he wanted to say (*KGB* II/1, p. 278).

That Nietzsche's audience might have misunderstood his ideas by identifying them with an anti-modern return to neo-humanist ideals will not have been the fault of Basel's patricians alone. The argument of his lectures is ambiguous and inconclusive – he might have known what he wanted to say, but not how to say it. In a semi-autobiographical manner, and in the style of a prolonged dialogue between several students and a self-proclaimed "philosopher," he mainly criticized what he believed to be the disastrous status quo of an increasingly specialized education system that lacked philosophical spirit (*KGW* III/2, p. 165). Nietzsche's problem is, practically speaking, that he does not really provide any viable alternative. Along Humboldtian lines, he merely seems to suggest that education needs to be understood as *Bildung* in the sense of an aesthetic and philosophical self-cultivation, thus reiterating the ideological program of the nineteenth-century *Bildungsbürgertum*, which never really had been put into practice, not even in the early 1800s.[95] For Nietzsche, then, education was endangered by the need for professional specialization and practical application, and in front of the Basel patricians he complained bitterly "that the exploitation of the scholar nowadays aspired to in the

---

[94] See Rudolf Eucken, "Meine persönlichen Erinnerungen an Nietzsche," in Sander L. Gilman (ed.), *Begegnungen mit Nietzsche* (Bonn: Bouvier, 1981), pp. 160–2: 160–1, and F. D., "Akademische Vorlesung von Hrn. Prof. Nietzsche über die Zukunft unserer Bildungsanstalten," *Schweizer Grenzpost und Tagblatt der Stadt Basel*, no. 30 (January 23, 1872).

[95] See Ulrich Muhlack, "Bildung zwischen Neuhumanismus und Historismus," in Werner Conze, Jürgen Kocka, Reinhart Koselleck, and M. Rainer Lepsius (eds.), *Bildungsbürgertum im 19. Jahrhundert* (Stuttgart: Klett-Cotta, 1985–92), vol. II, pp. 80–105.

service of science renders the *education* [*Bildung*] of the scholar increasingly haphazard" (*KGW* III/2, p. 161). Practical training and comprehensive education could not be reconciled, since they were fundamentally different in their orientation (*KGW* III/2, pp. 174–5 and 207).

Although Nietzsche was not able to provide any real alternative, his assessment of the state of science and scholarship in nineteenth-century Germany was correct. Generally speaking, German scholarship and science were primarily oriented toward research, and most German professors had little interest in teaching, let alone training. The altered political demands on the education system after 1871 triggered a fundamental shift that was to culminate, in the final decades of the nineteenth century, in what Theodor Mommsen and Adolf von Harnack, both writing from the perspective of the center of power in Berlin, termed "Großwissenschaft," or "Großbetrieb der Wissenschaft."[96] Imperial Germany provided a relatively stable political climate and administrative environment and, together with the rapid industrialization of the Rhineland and other regions, this also prepared the ground for grand-scale research projects. At times, such projects grew out of the traditional academies and institutes. More often, however, the technocratic demands of the modern nation state, in particular the increasing links between political administration, industrial production, and the natural sciences, required new institutions, such as the Physikalisch-Technische Reichsanstalt in Braunschweig and the Kaiser-Wilhelm-Gesellschaft in Berlin.[97]

The material success of German higher education after 1871 was, however, far less straightforward and its intellectual outlook far less monolithic than commonly believed. Heinrich von Sybel argued that secondary and higher education in the new German Empire needed to move away from the empty promises of neohumanist *Bildung* toward a more technically and practically oriented program of education in order to fulfill the economic

---

[96] See Adolf von Harnack, "Vom Grossbetrieb der Wissenschaft," *Preußische Jahrbücher* 119 (1905), 193–201, and Theodor Mommsen, "Antwort auf Harnack, 3. Juli 1890," in *Reden und Aufsätze* (Berlin: Weidmann, 1905), pp. 209–10.
[97] See Pierangelo Schiera, *Laboratorium der bürgerlichen Welt: Deutsche Wissenschaft im 19. Jahrhundert* (Frankfurt/M.: Suhrkamp, 1992), pp. 211–56, and Timothy Lenoir, *Politik im Tempel der Wissenschaft: Forschung und Machtausübung im deutschen Kaiserreich* (Frankfurt/M.: Campus, 1992).

demands of a unified German state. But it did not take long before, for instance, Johann Gustav Droysen and Heinrich von Treitschke, both supporting a German nation state under Prussian leadership, began to view the specialization of research, at least in the humanities, with much suspicion.[98] By 1882, when Prussia's most powerful civil servant, Friedrich Althoff, inaugurated a radical administrative modernization of the German education system, the sudden expansion of German universities led the Prussian Minister for Cultural Affairs, Gustav von Goßler, to lament the overproduction of academic specialists that were unlikely to find an adequate professional position.[99] But it is interesting to see that, even after 1871, when political and economic modernization placed new demands upon the practicalities of higher education, the neo-humanist ideal of *Bildung* was still part of bourgeois political culture. Although it lacked any practical dimension, it could be employed to safeguard a numinous form of national identity, since it became linked to notions of "culture" and "civilization."[100] The reasons why these initially cosmopolitan neo-humanist ideals could easily turn into their opposite had much to do with the social constitution of the so-called *Bildungsbürgertum*, that is, those whose social and professional standing was derived from their academic education. Nietzsche, whose public lectures on the future of educational institutions sought to target this very specific group, seems to have overestimated its actual importance. By the time he had left Bonn for Leipzig in 1865 only about 0.5 percent of his age group were enrolled at German

---

[98] See Heinrich von Sybel, *Die deutschen Universitäten, ihre Leistungen und Bedürfnisse* (Bonn: Max Cohen & Sohn, 1874); Johann Gustav Droysen, *Briefwechsel*, ed. Rudolf Hübner (Stuttgart: Deutsche Verlagsanstalt, 1929), vol. II, pp. 941–2; Heinrich von Treitschke, *Briefe*, ed. Max Cornelius (Leipzig: Hirzel, 1912–20), vol. III/2, pp. 585–6.

[99] See McClelland, *State, Society and University in Germany*, pp. 258–79; Jarausch, *Students, Society, and Politics in Imperial Germany*, pp. 23–77; Bernhard vom Brocke, "Hochschul- und Wissenschaftspolitik in Preußen und im deutschen Kaiserreich, 1882–1907: Das 'System Althoff'," in Peter Baumgart (ed.), *Bildungspolitik in Preußen zur Zeit des Kaiserreichs* (Stuttgart: Klett-Cotta, 1980), pp. 9–118.

[100] See Jörg Fisch, "Zivilisation, Kultur," in Brunner, Conze, and Koselleck (eds.), *Geschichtliche Grundbegriffe*, vol. VII, pp. 679–774. On the problematic intertwining of "education," "culture," and "civilization" in the political imagination of nineteenth-century Germany, see Georg Bollenbeck, *Bildung und Kultur: Glanz und Elend eines deutschen Deutungsmusters* (Frankfurt/M.: Insel, 1994), pp. 61–96 and 126–225, and Manfred Landfester, *Humanismus und Gesellschaft im 19. Jahrhundert: Untersuchungen zur politischen und gesellschaftlichen Bedeutung der humanistischen Bildung in Deutschland* (Darmstadt: Wissenschaftliche Buchgesellschaft, 1988), pp. 119–64.

universities, and by 1870, shortly before the Franco-Prussian War, the *Bildungsbürgertum*, for instance, in Prussia was below 1 percent of the population.[101] Nietzsche's ideal audience almost did not exist.

In any case, the actual political power of this social group was limited and thus contrasted sharply with its claims to represent civil society as a whole. As a consequence, Humboldt's ideals of *Bildung*, themselves originally rooted in the cosmopolitanism of the late Enlightenment, could easily be emptied of their liberal connotations. By the 1860s, and throughout the 1870s, once liberal ideas had also failed politically, *Bildung* had become part of German nationalism. Based on the idea of a Protestant heritage of German history, and on Prussia's German vocation, the problem of education was thus to fuel the ideological struggles of Bismarck's *Kulturkampf*. After the Franco-Prussian War liberal intellectuals and academics found themselves in a difficult situation, which in the long run destroyed the post-revolutionary program of constitutional reform.[102] Intent on polarizing relations between Prussian Protestantism and the Catholic minority, which constituted only about a third of the German population, Bismarck's policies were able to push most liberals, such as Sybel, into an increasingly nationalist direction, while others, like Treitschke, were in any case keen supporters of the Prussian cause.

For Bismarck and his followers, the *Kulturkampf* was a struggle for control over the educational and administrative institutions that would ultimately safeguard the historical and social identity of a German Empire tracing its legitimacy back to the German Reformation.[103] Already on November 1, 1871, Bismarck had demanded state supervision of primary and secondary education in order to reduce the regional influence of the Catholic Church. In 1871 a *Reichsgesetz* also prohibited the German clergy from discussing, even mentioning, politics in public, and in a pamphlet from 1872, the Swiss-born liberal Johann Caspar Bluntschli, a pupil

---

[101] See Wehler, *Deutsche Gesellschaftsgeschichte*, III, p. 127, and Jürgen Kocka, "Bildungsbürgertum: Gesellschaftliche Formation oder Historikerkonstrukt?" in Conze, Kocka, Koselleck, and Lepsius (eds.), *Bildungsbürgertum im 19. Jahrhundert* (Stuttgart: Klett-Cotta, 1985–92), vol. IV, pp. 9–20: 17–18.

[102] On the intellectual outlook of German liberalism and its lack of political pragmatism, see Thomas Nipperdey, *Deutsche Geschichte, 1800–1866: Bürgerwelt und starker Staat* (Munich: C. H. Beck, 1983), pp. 186–300.

[103] See Walser Smith, *German Nationalism and Religious Conflict*, pp. 19–49.

of Savigny and a professor of law at the University of Heidelberg, outlined the superiority of the modern state over the political tradition of the (Catholic) Church: sovereignty could exist in the state only as an organic unity, while any other institution or person was subordinated to the sovereignty of the state.[104] Bismarck himself repeated his ideas in a speech at the Prussian Chamber of Deputies on March 10, 1873, when he justified his politics against the Catholic Church as a defense of the modern German state.[105]

Under the influence of Richard Wagner's political aestheticism, and still adhering to the national sentiments he experienced during the Austro-Prussian War in Leipzig, Nietzsche himself was initially willing to accept the convergence of neo-humanist education and nationalism as part of a specifically German cultural ideal. One of the more questionable passages of Nietzsche's book on tragedy clearly points in this direction:

> We hold the pure and vigorous core of the German character in such esteem that we dare to expect that it will eventually reject those foreign elements which have been forcibly grafted on to it, and we consider it possible that the German spirit will take stock of itself once again. (*BT* p. 111)

A first step toward the crystallization, as it were, of the "German spirit," Nietzsche suggested, was taken by Luther's Reformation, which had already figured prominently in Hegel's earlier attempt to trace the "unfolding of consciousness" back to the inward "freedom" of Reformation thought, having liberated itself from Papal authority.[106] Despite his obvious aversion to Hegel and Hegelianism, Nietzsche presents a similar Protestant genealogy of German culture in his "Ueber die Zukunft unserer Bildungsanstalten," when his fictitious philosopher proclaims:

> We abide even more firmly ... by the German spirit, which revealed itself in the German Reformation and in German music and which, in the

---

[104] See Johann Caspar Bluntschli, *Rom und die Deutschen* (Berlin: Lüderitz, 1872). For Bluntschli's theory of the state, see *Allgemeines Statsrecht* [sic], 5th edn., rev. (Stuttgart: Cotta, 1876).

[105] See Bismarck, *Ausgewählte Werke*, vol. V, pp. 112–13 and 302–9.

[106] See Georg Wilhelm Friedrich Hegel, *Vorlesungen über die Philosophie der Geschichte*, in *Werke*, ed. Eva Moldenhauer and Karl Markus Michel (Frankfurt/M.: Suhrkamp, 1969–71), vol. XII, pp. 497–8. H. B. Nisbet's translation omits this passage and only provides a short summary. See Hegel, *Lectures on the Philosophy of History*, in *Political Writings*, ed. Laurence Dickey and H. B. Nisbet (Cambridge: Cambridge University Press, 1999), pp. 202 and 309, note 20.

formidable courage and austerity of German philosophy and in the newly tested loyalty of the German soldier, has proven the very power, disaffected by all illusion, that also makes us expect victory over the fashionable pseudo-culture of the "present." (*KGW* III/2, p. 186)

For a Swiss audience in 1872, such a remark would have sounded peculiar at least, but it is unlikely that this really was what Nietzsche had in mind. By the time he delivered his public lectures, his political convictions vis-à-vis Germany had undergone a decisive change that had been triggered by his experience of the Franco-Prussian War. On the eve of the war, he had warned in a letter to his friend Erwin Rohde that this conflict was bound to destroy "our threadbare culture" (*KGB* II/1, p. 130), but several weeks later he seems to have changed his mind. Following the call to arms, he asked Wilhelm Vischer-Bilfinger for a "holiday" from his academic duties in order to join in his "fatherland's" war efforts (*KGB* II/1, pp. 133–4).

We can only speculate why Nietzsche saw it necessary to enter into a war he could have avoided because of his residence in Switzerland; some of his friends, like Paul Deussen, were clearly bewildered.[107] It is likely that enthusiasm among the Wagner family for the looming war had contributed to his decision. After all, since May 1869 Nietzsche regularly visited Wagner and his entourage in Tribschen close to Lucerne. Echoing Ernst Moritz Arndt's inflammatory rhetoric against Napoleon, Wagner's future wife Cosima von Bülow was busy persuading Nietzsche of "the German vocation of Prussia," speaking of the "French arrogance," which it was "worthy to hate" (*KGB* II/2, p. 239). Writing about Nietzsche in her diaries, she notes: "I … try as hard as I can to arouse his enthusiasm for Prussia's right to represent Germany." Fantasizing about "how hateful the French nation appears," she even begins to compare what turned out to be one of the bloodiest wars on the European continent in the nineteenth century to a symphonic finale: "war is, so to speak, a dance performed with the most dreadful of powers, like a Beethoven finale in which he unleashes all the demons in a magnificent dance." Nietzsche, however, seems to have had other plans, and Cosima complained on July 18 that, instead of facing the French, "Prof. Nietzsche" had

---

[107] See Paul Deussen, *Erinnerungen an Friedrich Nietzsche*, 3rd edn. (Leipzig: F. A. Brockhaus, 1901), pp. 77–8.

fled "both the French and the Germans," hiking to Axenstein close to Lake Lucerne to avoid making a decision.[108] Indeed, writing from his hotel to Sophie Ritschl, the wife of his former teacher, Nietzsche expressed his concerns about the destructive effects of nationalist wars on cultural tradition (*KGB* II/1, p. 133).

Of course, Cosima's remarks are indicative of Wagner's own anti-French sentiment, often coupled with an anti-Semitic attitude, which had developed during the 1860s, when his essays "Was ist deutsch?" (1865) and "Deutsche Kunst und Politik" (1867) began to outline an increasingly foggy nationalist ideology, speaking of the historical mission of the German race – "the resurrection of the German Folk" against the materialism and utilitarianism that supposedly ruled France and Britain – and lamenting the "invasion of the German nature by an utterly alien element," the "Jews."[109] In January 1871, after the fall of the Second Empire, Wagner composed a poem *An das deutsche Heer vor Paris*, followed by a *Kaiser-Marsch* after the German victory. Nietzsche, who read Wagner's nationalist essay, and who showed much fondness for the *Kaiser-Marsch* throughout his life, was bound to adopt Wagner's view of the events that unfolded in Western France.[110] Indeed, at Tribschen – as much impressed by the alpine scenery seen across Lake Lucerne as by Cosima's talk of "Professor Nietzsche" – the young Nietzsche, still politically naïve, seems to have fallen into Wagner's trap. As soon as the news of the German victory in the battle at Woerth in the Alsace on August 6, 1870, had reached Switzerland, Ida Overbeck, the wife of Nietzsche's friend and colleague, noted that Nietzsche's mood became more "patriotic."[111]

Apart from the nationalist sentiments he encountered among Wagner and his entourage, Nietzsche's decision to enlist as a volunteer also seems to have had a more complex background. This becomes obvious when we glance at the short essay "Der

---

[108] Cosima Wagner, *Diaries, Volume I: 1869–77*, ed. Martin Gregor-Dellin and Dietrich Mack, trans. Geoffrey Skelton (New York: Harcourt Brace Jovanovich, 1978), pp. 245–6.
[109] Richard Wagner, "German Art and German Policy," and "What is German?" both in *Prose Works*, trans. William Ashton Ellis, vol. IV (New York: Broude Brothers, 1966), pp. 40, 54, 107, and 158.
[110] See *KGB* II/1, pp. 36, 105, 254 and 290; *KGB* II/3, pp. 154 and 156; *KGB* III/3, pp. 135.
[111] See Ida Overbeck's account in Carl A. Bernoulli, *Franz Overbeck und Friedrich Nietzsche: Eine Freundschaft* (Jena: Diederichs, 1908), vol. I, p. 235.

griechische Staat," which was based on a draft he had written in the first weeks of 1871, months after he had returned from the Franco-Prussian War (*KGW* III/3, 10 [1]). Emphasizing the "military profession" and the "military genius" as the foundation of the "state," albeit against the background of Plato's *Republic*, Nietzsche inadvertently continued an idea that had emerged several decades earlier in the context of German Romantic political thought and its reaction to the Napoleonic Wars (*TGS* pp. 184–5): the idealization of war as a creative "world-principle," which was able to awaken and channel cultural life in the service of a numinous "German spirit," underlies, for instance, the political ideals of Ernst Moritz Arndt during the so-called "Wars of Liberation." Political consensus and peace, Nietzsche suggested himself, appear to stifle what he believed to be an aesthetic state of exception exemplified only by art and conflict (*TGS* pp. 182–4).[112] This enthusiasm for war as a creative principle was furthermore fueled by his fascination with Heraclitus' notion of conflict and opposition as the origin of "becoming," which Nietzsche was going to discuss in more detail in his unpublished essay "Die Philosophie im tragischen Zeitalter der Griechen" of 1872/73.[113] The irony of these highly abstract speculations was, of course, that Nietzsche's actual experience of the Franco-Prussian War, once he was in close proximity to the frontline, was of a different kind.

Considering that the Franco-Prussian War was one of the most violent military conflicts of the nineteenth century, Nietzsche's own experience was untypical: he enrolled late, did not face any combat, and by the time he had reached the frontline, the war was virtually over, at least as far as the Imperial French army was concerned. After Bismarck had successfully stimulated nationalist sentiments among the German population, and once he had maneuvered the French government into declaring war on July 19, 1870, even though the Prussian King Wilhelm I seems to have felt uncomfortable with his chancellor's diplomacy, the French army, still assembling for a push into Germany, was surprised to

---

[112] Martin A. Ruehl, "*Politeia* 1871: Young Nietzsche and the Greek State," in Bishop (ed.), *Nietzsche and Antiquity*, pp. 79–97, and Barbara von Reibnitz, "Nietzsches *Griechischer Staat* und das Deutsche Kaiserreich," *Der altsprachliche Unterricht* 30/3 (1987), 76–89, both pointed to the historical context of Nietzsche's essay on the Greek state.

[113] Nietzsche's source is Diogenes Laertius, *Lives of Eminent Philosophers*, IX. 8.

find the far less professional German troops launching a fierce offensive into the Alsace and Lorraine. Nietzsche was still observing the events from Basel when the French Field Marshal MacMahon lost one of the early decisive battles, on August 6 close to Woerth in the Alsace, which opened the road to Paris after a particularly bloody encounter during which 20,000 soldiers were killed in only a few hours.[114] By the time Nietzsche had finally entered military service and received his initial medical training at Erlangen in Bavaria, the frontline had already moved elsewhere: by mid-August, combat centered on the area around Metz which itself was under siege from August 18.[115]

Nietzsche was dispatched to Alsace only on August 25, joining troops through Hagenau, Nancy, Pont-à-Mousson and Ars-sur-Moselle (*KGB* II/1, pp. 140–1), not even close to Sedan, where Napoleon III had to surrender to the German troops. Ordered to escort a group of wounded soldiers back to Karlsruhe, he fell ill with diphtheria and had to recuperate in Erlangen before he was able to return to Basel. His direct experience of the Franco-Prussian War lasted exactly one week, from August 25 to September 3, working in field hospitals in relative safety behind German lines. This obviously left him enough time, for instance, to visit the cathedral in Luneville, the park, and the local cafés (*KGW* III/3, 4 [5]). Many years later, however, in *Ecce Homo*, written in 1888–89, he will stylize his war experience as precisely that moment – "under the thunder of the battle at Woerth" and "during the cold September nights" outside the fortress of Metz – in which he conceived of *Die Geburt der Tragödie* (*EH* V:1).

On the one hand, such remarks are in many ways misleading. Nietzsche only read about the battle at Woerth in Swiss newspapers, and by the time the battle for Metz reached its decisive phase, he was already on the way home.[116] On the other hand,

---

[114] On the battle of Woerth, see Geoffrey Wawro, *The Franco-Prussian War: The German Conquest of France in 1870–1871* (Cambridge: Cambridge University Press, 2003), pp. 121–37.

[115] See ibid., pp. 240–53.

[116] Much later, and writing against the backdrop of her own questionable reactionary agenda, Nietzsche's sister Elisabeth was to glorify her brother's short excursion to the frontline and claim that he in fact desired nothing more than the life of a proper soldier involved in combat operations. Elisabeth Förster-Nietzsche, *Das Leben Friedrich Nietzsche's*, vol. II/1 (Leipzig: C. A. Naumann, 1897), pp. 31–4.

Nietzsche was indeed at Woerth on August 28, when he was ordered to locate the grave of a senior Bavarian officer and when he must have realized the true horrors of modern armed conflict. In a letter home, refreshingly free from any patriotic enthusiasm, he described the scenery as "that terribly devastated battlefield, covered by many sad reminders and smelling strongly of corpses" (*KGB* II/1, p. 137).

Nietzsche's experience at Woerth seems to have contributed to his changing political convictions, although it took him several months to express his first reservations toward the prevailing political imagination in Germany. Immediately after his return to Basel, but before the proclamation of the German Empire at Versailles, he still spoke of his pride in what he perceived to be the victory of German culture (*KGB* II/1, p. 145). But soon after, he grew suspicious of the political developments within Bismarck's Germany, which could already be felt during the 1860s.[117] In his first "Untimely Meditation," *David Strauss der Bekenner und Schrifsteller*, he finally detected the fateful irony on which the new German nation state, including its historical identity and cultural ideals, was founded:

Public opinion in Germany seems almost to forbid discussion of the terrible [*schlimmen*] and perilous consequences of a war, and especially of one that has ended victoriously: there is thus all the more ready an ear for those writers who know no weightier authority than this public opinion and who therefore vie with one another in lauding a war and in seeking out the mighty influence it has exerted on morality, culture and art. ... Of all the terrible consequences [*schlimmen Folgen*], however, which have followed the recent war with France perhaps the worst is a widespread, indeed universal, error: the error, committed by public opinion and by all who express their opinions publicly, that German culture too was victorious in that struggle and must therefore now be loaded with garlands appropriate to such an extraordinary achievement. This delusion is in the highest degree destructive: not because it is a delusion – for there exist very salutary and productive errors – but because

---

[117] Nietzsche's "Mahnruf an die Deutschen" (1873), which heralds Wagner as the embodiment of the German spirit, might easily be misunderstood as an example of Nietzsche's inflammatory illiberal and nationalist agenda. It is, however, a well-calculated public relations exercise. Tapping into the nationalist sentiments of the time, it was supposed to be distributed among German booksellers in order to raise money for Richard Wagner's overblown concert complex at Bayreuth. Fortunately, the pamphlet never reached publication, since even Wagner's advisers found it too harsh.

it is capable of turning our victory into a defeat: *into the defeat, if not the extirpation, of the German spirit for the benefit of the "German Reich."* (*UM* I: 1)[118]

This unusual opposition between "German spirit" and "Imperial Germany," which runs counter to the prevailing German public imagination after 1871, represents in many ways the opposition between neo-humanist ideals and technocratic modernity that Nietzsche had already presented in his public lectures on the future of educational institutions. Seen from this perspective, it would thus be shortsighted to construe Nietzsche's repeated talk of the "German spirit," in his public lectures, as an expression of nationalist sentiment, or as a Protestant foundation myth for German superiority. Rather, the "extirpation of the German spirit for the benefit of the 'German Reich' " was the defeat of neo-humanism, and in a relatively bizarre note from 1872/73 he listed what he regarded as the "mishaps" of German culture: Hegel, Heine, the glorification of war, and the "political fever" of the "national" (*KGW* III/4, 19 [272]).

But Nietzsche's argument that military victory can entail cultural defeat responds not only to the specific historical and political predicament of the nineteenth century. Rather, Nietzsche continues a specific tradition of Enlightenment cosmopolitanism, which attaches a positive value to cultural pluralism.[119] One crucial implication of the latter is that political communities do not derive their external as well as internal values from a military expansion of political, economic and territorial influence. As Herder noted in his discussion of patriotism during the 1790s: "A fatherland's glory can hardly in our time any longer be that savage *spirit of conquest* that stormed through the history of Rome and the barbarians, indeed of several proud monarchies, like an evil demon."[120] The cosmopolitanism Herder had in mind was

---

[118] R. J. Hollingdale translates Nietzsche's expression *schlimme Folgen* as "evil consequences," which is suggestive of an absolutist moral perspective. The German word for "evil" is, however, *böse*, and it is not by accident that Nietzsche avoids this expression: as shown by his emphasis on the effect of the Franco-Prussian War on German "morality," by the mid-1870s Nietzsche has already become rather suspicious about the foundations of moral sentiments and their connection to political life.

[119] See Pauline Kleingeld, "Six Varieties of Cosmopolitanism in Late Eighteenth-Century Germany," *Journal of the History of Ideas* 60 (1999), 505–24: 515–18.

[120] Herder, *Letters for the Advancement of Humanity*, in *Philosophical Writings*, p. 377.

marked by both a "sense of community" and the principle of "not letting oneself be organized by others."[121] Nietzsche's own appeal to the "German spirit" – as opposed to a "German Reich," which by its very definition seeks to replace cultural pluralism with an imperialist project – needs to be read in precisely this way, that is, as the expression of a very specific kind of cosmopolitanism, which will become more prominent in Nietzsche's idea of Europe during the 1880s.

The loss of neo-humanist ideals in favor of an imperial *Kulturstaat*, which Nietzsche lamented in his public lectures in Basel, was not only a problem of intellectual orientation. There were, he believed, direct political and social consequences, such as the rise of the German student corporations, the *Burschenschaften*, ranging from mere drinking societies to highly politicized groups with a clear nationalist agenda. Especially in the larger university cities, such as Berlin, Leipzig, Bonn and Munich, where 40 percent of German students lived, these corporations marked much of student life and compensated for the lack of ethical guidance within the research-oriented university system.[122] Together with his friend Paul Deussen, who was to become a historian of Indian philosophy as well as the editor of Schopenhauer's writings, Nietzsche himself had enrolled in one of these student corporations, the Franconia, in late October 1864 while he was a student in Bonn. One of the reasons for this move might simply have been that Nietzsche, who had grown up in rural Germany, was slightly overwhelmed by the urban environment of the Rhineland. Deussen even remarked that they were both swept into the Franconia by the sheer enthusiasm they encountered and by the presence of other former pupils of the Pforta boarding school.[123] Nietzsche also did not miss the fact that the Franconia student corporation had prominent alumni, such as the historian Heinrich von Treitschke (*KGB* 1/2, p. 15). Either way, barely ten months later, toward the end of August 1865, Nietzsche began to realize that his involvement in the student corporation was clearly a "faux pas"

---

[121] Ibid. Given the possible tensions between political self-determination and the kind of cultural pluralism outlined by Kleingeld, Peter Hallberg, "The Nature of Collective Individuals: J. G. Herder's Concept of Community," *History of European Ideas* 25 (2999), 291–304: 293, has hinted at an ambivalence in Herder's political orientation.
[122] See Jarausch, *Students, Society, and Politics in Imperial Germany*, pp. 90–134.
[123] See Deussen, *Erinnerungen an Friedrich Nietzsche*, p. 21.

and prevented him from devoting himself completely to his academic subjects (*KGB* I/2, p. 79).

A central aspect of restoration politics in the German states in the aftermath of the Vienna Congress was the attempt to control cultural life through censorship and by limiting academic freedom of speech. For those German students and professors who harbored national-liberal ideas this proved to be a difficult situation. The German student corporations, which were rooted in the "Wars of Liberation" and regarded themselves as national organizations defending, as their motto read, "Honor, Freedom, Fatherland," soon found themselves in conflict with a political system they sought to revolutionize from a fervent nationalist angle. In 1817, several hundred representatives of the student corporations assembled on the Wartburg, Luther's former haunt, celebrating three hundred years of German Reformation and the 1813 battle at Leipzig against the Napoleonic armies. But they also demanded the unification of the German states, which was a direct attack on the restoration politics promoted by most German rulers. In his periodical *Literarisches Wochenblatt*, August von Kotzebue, who supported Prince Metternich's authoritarian policies, harshly criticized this national-liberalism and ridiculed the student corporations for their peculiar mixture of revolutionary ideals, Christian sentiments, constitutional demands, and nationalist rhetoric. It was, however, precisely this mixture that was to turn the political ideas of the student corporations into a hotbed for revolutionary political extremism. In 1819, only two years after the congregation on the Wartburg, Carl Ludwig Sand, a student from Jena and a member of the local student corporation, traveled to the city of Mannheim and assassinated Kotzebue, stabbing him to death.[124] As a response, the Carlsbad Decrees of 1819 prohibited the student corporations and introduced general censorship across all German states until the late 1840s, seeking to suppress any nationalist sentiments for a unification of the German states.

Looking back at these events, Nietzsche emphasized in his lectures "Ueber die Zukunft unserer Bildungsanstalten" that

---

[124] See George S. Williamson, "What Killed August von Kotzebue? The Temptations of Virtue and the Political Theology of German Nationalism," *Journal of Modern History* 72 (2000), 890–943.

the "assassination of Kotzebue" was an act of "shortsighted enthusiasm," triggered by the lack of political orientation in a post-Napoleonic Germany that had betrayed neo-humanist ideals. He thus characterized the emergence of the student corporations as a political and social force in nineteenth-century Germany as an ill-fated attempt to compensate for the lack of intellectual leadership (*KGW* III/2, pp. 240 and 242). In contrast, Nietzsche introduced the idea of a public intellectual as a *Führer*, although it remains unclear whether he conceived the latter in terms of a "leader" or in terms of a "guide" (*KGW* III/2, pp. 242–4). While such terms ring both hollow and questionable after the catastrophic political experiences of the twentieth century, Nietzsche's choice of words merely seeks to tap into the political imagination of a time when such terms were common coinage not necessarily connected to militarism or totalitarianism.

But how does Nietzsche conceive of the role this public intellectual was supposed to play? His tentative answer was a return to the critical potential of a philosophical education that did not take reality at face value. After all, as he had already pointed out in his earlier lectures on classical philology, science and thinking had to begin with "wonder," or with what he termed "philosophical astonishment" (*KGW* III/2, p. 233). With this idea, Nietzsche aligns himself with Plato and Aristotle, who both regard "wonder" (*thauma, thaumazein*) as the origin of thought and learning.[125] As such, he seeks to emphasize the value of an ancient Greek concept, and thus of antiquity in general, for a critical reflection on the modern condition. While, for instance, Hegel criticized the assumption that "wonder" should be the origin of philosophical thought – pointing out that such wonder remains wholly subjective and that philosophy can only begin with cognition and reason – Nietzsche is acutely aware of the double meaning of *thaumazein*, especially in Aristotle: it refers to "wonder" not only in terms of "admiration," or "astonishment," but also in terms of "being perplexed."[126] Being "perplexed" in the face of an

---

[125] See Plato, *Theaetetus*, 155d, and Aristotle, *Rhetoric*, 1371a31–b5.
[126] See Georg Wilhelm Friedrich Hegel, *Philosophy of Nature: Part Two of the "Encyclopaedia of the Philosophical Sciences"* (1830), trans. A. V. Miller (Oxford: Clarendon Press, 1970), p. 3; *Philosophy of Mind: Part Three of the "Encyclopaedia of the Philosophical Sciences"* (1830), trans. William Wallace and A. V. Miller (Oxford: Clarendon Press, 1970), p. 200 (§ 449); *Aesthetics: Lectures on Fine Art*, trans. T. M. Knox (Oxford: Clarendon Press, 1975), vol. I, p. 315.

unknown situation, or while encountering a difficult problem, represents for Aristotle the beginning of critical and analytical thought, and this is also the reason why Schopenhauer, in the first volume of *Die Welt als Wille und Vorstellung* argues that philosophical thought cannot be deduced from any firm principles: "*Philosophy* has the peculiarity of presupposing absolutely nothing as known; everything to it is equally strange and a problem; not only the relations of phenomena, but also those phenomena themselves, and indeed the principle of sufficient reason itself, to which the other sciences are content to refer everything."[127] That philosophy always has to consider that which we regard as given as worthy of critical reflection is, for Schopenhauer, the main principle of philosophical thought.

As a keen reader of Schopenhauer, Nietzsche will not have missed the significance of this definition: perplexity as the source of the critical mind – this idea lies very much at the core of Nietzsche's understanding of the value of philosophical education. Right at the beginning of his course on "Die vorplatonischen Philosophen," which he delivered in the summer of 1872, only a few months after his lectures "Ueber die Zukunft unserer Bildungsanstalten," he remarked:

The intellect not only has to be surreptitiously delighted about itself, it also must have been completely liberated and celebrate Saturnalia. The liberated intellect contemplates the objects: and now, for the first time, the *ordinary* appears to be *remarkable, as a problem*. This is the true sign of the philosophical drive: the astonishment [*Verwunderung*] about that which lies before the eyes of everyone. (*KGW* II/4, p. 215)

Wonder and perplexity have to be regarded as the origin of philosophy and, ultimately, they lead to a growing problematization of both the intellectual and political foundations of modernity. But if neither the ideological commonplaces of mid-nineteenth-century Germany, nor the legacy of German idealism offered any serious perspective from which to examine the conditions of culture, perhaps history would provide a way out.

---

[127] Schopenhauer, *The World as Will and Representation*, vol. 1, 81. See also Aristotle, *Metaphysics*, 982b.

CHAPTER 3

The crisis of historical culture

It is one thing to argue that Nietzsche's historical thought should be regarded as a reaction to his intellectual environment and to the fundamental changes taking place in the second half of the nineteenth century. It is quite another to suggest that he in fact adopts a position that could be labeled as "historicist" and reacts to the crisis of historical culture that becomes manifest in nineteenth-century Germany. Nietzsche's many reflections on the use and abuse of history, from his four "Untimely Meditations" (1873–76) and *Menschliches, Allzumenschliches* (1878–80) to his later works, such as *Jenseits von Gut und Böse* (1886) and *Zur Genealogie der Moral* (1887), do not seem to have much in common with what is often regarded as nineteenth-century historicism. Many commentators have indeed suggested that Nietzsche should be seen as one of the staunchest critics of contemporary historical discourse and philosophy of history.[1] The question remains, however, whether it is really possible to detach Nietzsche's historical thought from the intellectual crisis historicism reflects on the path to modernity. The neo-humanist tradition he encountered as a student in Bonn and Leipzig was in any case closely related to historicism. Likewise, the problems Nietzsche faced in the late 1860s in his notes on the historical method were in many ways the problems of historicism itself, while his discussion of Kant and teleology is also deeply connected to the intellectual outlook of German historicism. Finally, the historical vision Nietzsche encountered in the work of Burckhardt emerged in relation to historicism. It is doubtful that Nietzsche simply transcended,

---

[1] See, for instance, Hubert Cancik, *Nietzsches Antike: Vorlesung* (Stuttgart: J. B. Metzler, 1995), pp. 88–92, and Karl Löwith, *From Hegel to Nietzsche: The Revolution in Nineteenth-Century Thought*, 2nd edn. (New York: Columbia University Press, 1991), pp. 175–200.

or ignored, the fundamental problems that arose in this wider context.[2] In his second "Untimely Meditation," *Vom Nutzen und Nachtheil der Historie für das Leben* (1874), Nietzsche encounters the crisis of contemporary historical culture in more detail. This forces him to come to terms with what Georg Simmel, at the end of the nineteenth century, was to call "the problems of the philosophy of history" and Ernst Troeltsch, writing at the beginning of the twentieth century, "the crisis of historicism."[3] Nietzsche's developing views about the value of historical knowledge for cultural orientation are thus bound to reflect the philosophical debates that, beginning in the later eighteenth century, led up to the crisis of historicism.

THE CRISIS OF HISTORICISM

It is intriguing that even today there is no clear definition of "historicism." The emergence of historicism is, nevertheless, often traced back to the late eighteenth century. Influenced by the wider secularizing effects of the European Enlightenment and, in Germany, by the rise of the historical school at the relatively new University of Göttingen, a slow transformation of historical thought began to take place that sought to establish new explanatory models and methods for historical understanding. While the theological underpinning of historiography had already become questionable in the later Renaissance, it was in the context of the Enlightenment that the study of history began to follow more openly a logic of secularization. This widened those factors which were seen as influencing history, from the life of particular rulers, or the history of particular cities and states, to geography, climate, customs, values, etc. By the late sixteenth century, historical discourse was generally divided either into "divine history" (*historia divina*), "natural history" (*historia naturalis*) and "political history" (*historia civilis*), or into "sacred and ecclesiastical history" (*historia sacra et ecclesiastica*) and "secular and political history" (*historia*

---

[2] Heinz-Dieter Kittsteiner, "Erinnern – Vergessen – Orientieren: Nietzsches Begriff des 'umhüllenden Wahns' als geschichtsphilosophische Kategorie," in Dieter Borchmeyer (ed.), *"Vom Nutzen und Nachteil der Historie für das Leben"* (Frankfurt/M: Suhrkamp, 1996), pp. 48–75: 52–3, even remarked that Nietzsche completed what Hegel had begun, namely the transformation of "reason" into "history."

[3] See Simmel, *Die Probleme der Geschichtsphilosophie*; Troeltsch, *Der Historismus und seine Probleme*; Karl Heussi, *Die Krisis des Historismus* (Tübingen: J. C. B. Mohr, 1932).

profana et politica). The distinction between ecclesiastical and political historiography that began to emerge in this context, of course, reflected the growing tensions between religious and political authority, and by the later eighteenth century "secular history" had overtaken "sacred history."

Once the study and writing of history had lost its theological underpinning, it was bound to turn toward philosophy for theoretical guidance, since philosophy itself displaced theology within the order of knowledge as the leading discipline.[4] Within the context of the European Enlightenment, historical knowledge increasingly provided secularized models for the interpretation of cultural processes along the lines of "reason," "humanity," and "emancipation," which widened the orientation of historical discourse toward new theoretical models and anthropological perspectives – a trend of which the historical school at the University of Göttingen became a prime example.[5] Publications like the *Allgemeine Historische Bibliothek* (1767–71) and the *Historisches Journal* (1772–81), both edited by the Göttingen historian Johann Christoph Gatterer, stood at the very center of German intellectual culture during this time. Indeed, the shift toward historical explanation represents a fundamental change that continued to shape the intellectual world throughout the nineteenth century. Once this shift had taken place, nothing was to be the way it had been before.[6]

It would be wrong to assume that the understanding of history within the eighteenth century was of a monolithic nature. Unilinear conceptions of historical development, often marked by a certain optimism about the future of "humanity," were in obvious competition with relativist models that emphasized the contingent nature of historical events. In France, Voltaire rejected any theological notion of history that was guided by "universal providence," but his own attempt at ordering history along the lines of a "principle of universal reason," though open toward the future,

---

[4] See Arno Seifert, "Von der heiligen zur philosophischen Geschichte: Die Rationalisierung der universalhistorischen Erkenntnis im Zeitalter der Aufklärung," *Archiv für Kulturgeschichte* 68 (1986), 81–117.
[5] See Peter Hanns Reill, *The German Enlightenment and the Rise of Historicism* (Berkeley, Calif.: University of California Press, 1975), pp. 127–89, and Georg G. Iggers, "The University of Göttingen 1760–1800 and the Transformation of Historical Scholarship," *Storia della Storiografia* 2 (1982), 11–37.
[6] See Foucault, *The Order of Things*, pp. 219–21.

still assumed a clear progression of events that was also reflected by German philosophers such as Lessing, Kant, and Fichte.[7] In contrast to Voltaire, and resisting the optimism of the early Enlightenment, Johann Gottfried Herder sought to underline the autonomy of different historical epochs, arguing that every historical period "has the *center* of its happiness *in itself*," while the Göttingen historian August Ludwig von Schlözer pointed out that the enormous complexity of historical processes could only be dealt with chronologically.[8]

The differences between Voltaire and Herder highlight the fact that, in the second half of the eighteenth century, historical thought was fundamentally characterized by a tension between an understanding of historical development as a goal-directed and, thus, teleological process on the one hand, and a concept of history that emphasized the contingency of events on the other. Herder's criticism, in his anonymously published *Auch eine Philosophie der Geschichte zur Bildung der Menschheit* (1774), of the assumption that history represents a goal-directed progress toward a universal improvement of humanity at large is particularly poignant:

> Those who have so far undertaken to unfold the *progress of the centuries* for the most part have in the process the pet idea: progress to *more virtue* and *happiness of individual human beings*. People have then for this purpose *exaggerated* or *made up* facts, *understated* or *supressed* contrary facts, *hidden* whole sides, *taken words* for [deeds], *enlightenment* for *happiness*, more and subtler *ideas* for *virtue* – and in this way people have made up novels "about the *universally progressing improvement of the world*" – novels that no one believes, at least not the pupil of *history* and the *human heart*. [9]

In contrast to such imaginary visions of cultural and political progress, Herder himself argued for the contingency of historical developments that make up any given cultural setting, emphasizing,

---

[7] See Voltaire, *La Philosophie de l'histoire* (1756), in *Œuvres Complètes*, ed. Theodore Besterman, William H. Barber *et al.* (Oxford: Voltaire Foundation / Geneva: Institut et Musée Voltaire, 1968–), vol. LIX, p. 114.

[8] See Herder, *This Too a Philosophy of History for the Formation of Humanity*, in *Philosophical Writings*, p. 299, and August Ludwig von Schlözer, *Vorstellung seiner Universalhistorie* (1771/72), ed. Horst-Walter Blanke (Hagen: Rottmann, 1990). See also Johann Christoph Gatterer, *Abriß der Universalhistorie in ihrem ganzen Umfange*, 2nd edn. (Göttingen: Vandenhoeck, 1773).

[9] Herder, *This Too a Philosophy of History for the Formation of Humanity*, in *Philosophical Writings*, p. 298.

for instance, that the *"progressive formation of a nation* is never anything but a *work of fate* – the result of a thousand *cooperating causes* of the *whole element in which they live*, so to speak."¹⁰

Herder's attack on any philosophical speculation that attributed to history the purpose of a simple progression toward reason and morality was clearly directed against Voltaire and "the philosophers of Paris," whose writings exhibited "the delusion that they form toute l'Europe and tout l'univers."¹¹ But even a decade later it posed uncomfortable questions for Kant, whose political thought in many ways rested on the assumption of a teleological "universal history of the world in accordance with a plan of nature," and for Gotthold Ephraim Lessing, who conceived of enlightenment as an educational process with a clear *"goal"* and *"purpose."*¹² Nevertheless, despite such claims about the status of history, historical knowledge itself threatened to remain knowledge of contingent facts, while philosophical knowledge was supposed to provide knowledge based on causes.¹³

But once the study of history had turned toward philosophy for theoretical orientation during the second half of the eighteenth century, not only did the traditional notion of history as the teacher of life and policy (*historia magistra vitae*) begin to lose its grip on the way in which historians dealt with the past, but it was possible to conceive of the course of history in the singular.¹⁴ Once history was seen in terms of a unified development, precisely those teleological models of explanation were able to gain ground, which stressed the goal-directed unfolding of reason, freedom, and consciousness within human history. Nietzsche encountered

---

[10] Ibid., p. 320.   [11] Ibid., pp. 321–2.

[12] Kant, "Idea for a Universal History with a Cosmopolitan Purpose," in *Political Writings*, p. 51, and Gotthold Ephraim Lessing, "The Education of the Human Race," in *Philosophical and Theological Writings*, ed. and trans. H. B. Nisbet (Cambridge: Cambridge University Press, 2005), pp. 217–40: 237 (§ 82).

[13] For the standard eighteenth-century distinction between *cognitio historica* and *cognitio philosophica*, which is based on Aristotle, *Poetics*, 1451b5–8, see, for instance, Friedrich Christian Baumeister, *Philosophia definitiva hoc est definitiones philosophicae ex systemate celeb. Wolfii: In vnvm collectae svccinctis observationibvs emplisque*, 7th edn. (Wittenberg: Ahlfeld, 1746), p. 1, and Kant, *Critique of Pure Reason* trans. Werner S. Pluhar, intro. Stephen Engstrom (Indianapolis, Ind.: Hackett, 2002), p. 693 (B 864), who differentiated between *cognitio ex datis* (history) and *cognitio ex principiis* (philosophy).

[14] See Reinhart Koselleck, "Historia Magistra Vitae: The Dissolution of the Topos into the Perspective of a Modernized Historical Process," in *Futures Past: On the Semantics of Historical Time*, trans. Keith Tribe (Cambridge, Mass.: MIT Press, 1985), pp. 21–38.

these models in the philosophy lectures of Carl Schaarschmidt in 1865 as well as in his discussion of Kant in 1868. But such models of historical development also provided the underpinning for the Prussian historians' emphasis on the formation of the nation state.

The changes that the study of history underwent in the course of the eighteenth century were often influenced by neighboring disciplines, especially by the relatively new field of philological scholarship and textual criticism. The first "philological seminary" (*seminarium philologiam*) in Germany, founded in 1738 by Johann Matthias Gesner at the University of Göttingen, still served the education of theologians, rather than historians. But when Christian Gottlob Heyne arrived in Göttingen in 1763 as Gesner's successor, he slowly disengaged philological criticism from theology, and in 1787 Friedrich August Wolf finally founded the *seminarium philologicum* at the University of Halle, which transformed philological scholarship into an academic discipline in its own right and with its own institutional infrastructure. By the beginning of the nineteenth century, when Barthold Georg Niebuhr began to lecture on Roman history at the University of Berlin in 1810–12, it was clear that historical and philological criticism were two sides of the same coin.[15]

Both historical and philological criticism, however, faced the same problem vis-à-vis the teleological conceptions of history that dominated German idealism. The philosophical notion of a linear, or dialectical, unfolding of reason, freedom and consciousness contrasted sharply with the critical and specialized study of source material, which had begun to highlight the contingent nature of historical events. But even though professional historians in Germany were often suspicious of philosophical speculation, the way they subscribed, for instance, to the notion of *Bildung* made them follow, often implicitly, teleological explanations. Wilhelm von Humboldt's 1821 lecture at the Berlin Academy, "Ueber die Aufgabe des Geschichtsschreibers," is as good an example for this as Leopold von Ranke's lectures "Ueber die

---

[15] On the institutional and theoretical development of philological scholarship in late eighteenth-century Germany, see Robert S. Leventhal, "The Emergence of Philological Discourse in Germany, 1700–1810," *Isis* 77 (1986), 243–60, and Anthony Grafton, "Polyhistor into Philolog: Notes on the Transformation of German Classical Scholarship, 1780–1850," *History of Universities* 3 (1983), 159–92.

Epochen der neueren Geschichte" (1854).[16] But while Humboldt clearly saw himself as continuing the secularizing efforts of the Enlightenment, Ranke at times seemed to reverse this project when he pointed out with regard to the practice of the historian "that all our endeavors spring from a higher, from a religious source."[17]

As soon as the study of history turned into a *Wissenschaft* within the context of the reform of the German university system in the first decades of the nineteenth century, such teleological models began to show their limitations. Again, Niebuhr might serve as a prominent example. While on a diplomatic mission to the Vatican in 1821, he remarked in a letter to the Prussian minister Heinrich Ludwig Nicolovius: "Seen with all clarity and detail, the study of history is useful at least for one thing: so that one understands how unaware the greatest and highest minds of our human race are that the eye through which they see has taken its form by chance."[18] More than fifty years later, Nietzsche returned to this passage in his second "Untimely Meditation," *Vom Nutzen und Nachtheil der Historie für das Leben,* fully aware that Niebuhr's suspicions had now become a central problem for the relationship between political imagination and historical culture in the nineteenth century (*UM* II: 1).

The problem both Niebuhr and Nietzsche, albeit from different perspectives, had to come to terms with can perhaps best be summarized as follows: at the very heart of nineteenth-century historicism stood a peculiar tension between contingency and teleology, between the historicity of individual facts and events, on the one hand, and the speculative explanatory models of German idealism, on the other. In emphasizing the historicity, and therefore contingency, of individual facts, historicism moved perilously close to relativism, while the attempt to order historical processes according to principles of causation which themselves had to be located outside history (e.g. consciousness, freedom, reason)

---

[16] See Humboldt, "Über die Aufgabe des Geschichtsschreibers," in *Werke*, vol. I, p. 587, and Ranke, "Über die Epochen der neueren Geschichte," in *Aus Werk und Nachlaß*, vol. II, p. 60.

[17] Ranke, *Idee der Universalhistorie*, in *Aus Werk und Nachlaß*, vol. IV, p. 77. For a fuller discussion of Ranke's orientation, see Toews, *Becoming Historical*, pp. 393–404.

[18] Barthold Georg Niebuhr to Heinrich Ludwig Nicolovius (September 15, 1821), in *Lebensnachrichten, aus Briefen desselben und aus Erinnerungen einiger seiner nächsten Freunde* (Hamburg: Friedrich Perthes, 1838–39), vol. II, p. 480 (no. 448).

generated quasi-theological trends that stood in sharp contrast to the daily work of professional historians. As soon as the study of history established itself as a *Wissenschaft*, its professional ethos often responded to theoretical uncertainties with a quasi-religious attitude.[19]

With the rise of scientific models of specialization at German universities, and with the parallel emergence of hermeneutics as a foundation for the humanities in the aftermath of Schleiermacher's lectures at the University of Berlin between 1805 and 1833, the historical profession realized the need to reassess its own theoretical framework and methods.[20] The most prominent example for this trend are Johann Gustav Droysen's lectures on *Historik*, delivered between 1857 and 1883 in Berlin. Droysen, who was also one of the teachers of Jacob Burckhardt, stressed that the work of the historian should be understood as a rule-governed practice that was to follow transparent interpretive methods, drawing a clear line between historiography and literature, which mirrored that between fact and fiction.[21] The study of history, together with the presentation of its results, was no longer seen as a purely rhetorical enterprise; its success was linked to sound hermeneutical strategies, or at least it was supposed to be. But since hermeneutics was far more than a specific scholarly strategy, this also meant that historical understanding could not be limited to the historical profession. Rather, it was to be regarded as the foundation, which enabled modern civil society to come to clear judgments about its cultural values and conditions.[22] This is, however, exactly where the crisis of historicism begins.

Many philosophers and intellectual historians would argue that Nietzsche's writings do not really belong to the context of the much-debated crisis of historicism, even though they might agree that he anticipated some of the latter's central problems. The question, then, seems to be the following: should the crisis of

---

[19] See Wolfgang Hardtwig, "Geschichtsreligion – Wissenschaft als Arbeit – Objektivität: Der Historismus in neuer Sicht," *Historische Zeitschrift* 252 (1991), 1–32.
[20] Schleiermacher's lectures were never intended for publication and only appeared after his death: *Hermeneutik und Kritik, mit besonderer Beziehung auf das Neue Testament*, ed. Friedrich Lücke (Berlin: Reimer, 1838).
[21] See Johann Gustav Droysen, *Historik: Textausgabe*, ed. Peter Leyh (Stuttgart-Bad Cannstatt: Fromann-Holzboog, 1977), pp. 217–83.
[22] See ibid., p. 5.

historicism be limited to that period when it is acknowledged by philosophers and historians alike that there is a crisis in the first place, that is, to the period between the 1890s and 1920s?[23] Often linked to the rise of political illiberalism within Germany's university education system, the crisis of historicism would thus fall into the final decades of Imperial Germany.[24] But the political crisis within German higher education itself had much deeper roots and was related to the cultural politics of the 1830s and 1840s, which fed into the formation of a modern German nation state.[25] The crisis of historicism was therefore triggered to a considerable extent by the modernization of the public sphere in Western and Central Europe during the early 1800s, which Jacob Burckhardt, for instance, sees very clearly as a watershed in modern European history.[26] This also implies, however, that the crisis-mentality that began to emerge in this context appears predominantly, not in the work of those historians that belonged to the mainstream of the German historiographical tradition, such as Ranke, Treitschke and Sybel, but at the margins, in the writings of Georg Gottfried Gervinus and Jacob Burckhardt or of political economists such as Wilhelm Roscher and Karl Knies.[27] At the same time, the decline of German idealism began to introduce a growing awareness of the contingency of historical processes, which questioned the internal logic of teleological speculations. Within this context, Nietzsche is of crucial importance – even though he still tends to be read as arguing for an aestheticization of historical knowledge.[28] Seen from this perspective, the crisis of historicism is preceded by a crisis of historical and political culture after the failed German revolutions of 1848/49, and it is precisely this crisis that becomes manifest in Nietzsche's second "Untimely Meditation." Once again, Nietzsche proves to be a particularly timely philosopher in that he is able to see the signs of a crisis

---

[23] See Bambach, *Heidegger, Dilthey, and the Crisis of Historicism*, pp. 33–55, and Iggers, *The German Conception of History*, pp. 124–228.
[24] See Fritz K. Ringer, *The Decline of the German Mandarins: The German Academic Community, 1890–1933* (Cambridge, Mass.: Harvard University Press, 1969), pp. 340–8.
[25] See Toews, *Becoming Historical*, pp. 19–65.
[26] See Jaeger, *Bürgerliche Modernisierungskrise*, pp. 140–6.
[27] See Friedrich Jaeger and Jörn Rüsen, *Geschichte des Historismus: Eine Einführung* (Munich: C. H. Beck, 1992), pp. 121–34.
[28] See Wittkau, *Historismus*, pp. 45–60.

of historical culture before most of his peers become aware of this crisis.[29]

Furthermore, it is safe to say that the crisis of historicism runs parallel to a rise of heightened theoretical reflection among professional historians. This development becomes particularly obvious during the first decades of the nineteenth century in the many lecture courses devoted to the "theory of history" (*Historik*) at the leading universities in Berlin, Bonn, Heidelberg, Jena, and Leipzig. To some extent, this trend was simply part of normal scholarly practice: at a time when the study of history was marked by increasing specialization, such theoretical reflections sought to determine the function of historical studies as a specific research program – even though it seems that most students, at least initially, were not exactly keen on such abstract courses.[30] It is, however, the students' reluctance to take such courses seriously that indicates a more complex situation: theoretical reflection on the status of knowledge within a particular discipline tends to destabilize whatever is regarded as normal scholarly, or scientific, practice. The study of history is no exception to this. The awareness that the experiential horizon of human societies was shaped by contingent historical processes, and that reason and consciousness were themselves embedded in such processes, ultimately endangered the concept of a teleological progression of humanity – although, for instance, Droysen still underlined the idea of "freedom" as one of the main driving forces behind historical events.[31]

Considering the complex intellectual configurations of what is generally seen as German historicism, it will be necessary to distinguish between different kinds of historicism.[32] First,

---

[29] Nietzsche continues to be timely today because the theoretical and practical problems he dealt with have returned to contemporary debate: the difference between "German historicism" and the so-called "new philosophy of history" is, at least on theoretical grounds, smaller than generally assumed. See F. R. Ankersmit, "Historicism: An Attempt at Synthesis," *History and Theory* 34 (1995), 143–61, and Ignacio Olábarri, "'New' New History: A *longue durée* Structure," *History and Theory* 34 (1995), 1–29.

[30] See Blanke, Fleischer, and Rüsen, "Theory of History in Historical Lectures," 346–54.

[31] See Droysen, *Historik*, p. 368. Such claims show the continued relevance of Hegel for Droysen. See Jaeger, *Bürgerliche Modernisierungskrise*, pp. 61–5.

[32] See Herbert Schnädelbach, *Geschichtsphilosophie nach Hegel: Die Probleme des Historismus* (Freiburg/Br.: Alber, 1974), pp. 20–30, and Gunter Scholtz, *Zwischen Wissenschaftsanspruch und Orientierungsbedürfnis: Zu Grundlage und Wandel der Geisteswissenschaften* (Frankfurt/M.: Suhrkamp, 1991), pp. 131–4.

historicism can be understood as a form of positivist historical study that accepts the objectivity of facts and sources. Historicism, then, would be at the very center of *Geschichtswissenschaft* in nineteenth-century Germany, representing a highly specialized and professional kind of historical studies. Second, historicism can be seen as a form of historical study that emphasizes the individuality and contingency of historical epochs and events. Third, historicism could simply be conceived as historicizing virtually every aspect of cultural life. Although these are clearly different kinds of historicism, what they have in common is an undeniable tension between, on the one hand, the effort to establish some kind of order that is able to explain the relevance of the past, and on the other, the need to accept the contingency of individual historical events, or processes, that subvert any such order.[33]

That Nietzsche's own historical thought should develop against the background of these intellectual configurations is far from surprising. If there is anything substantial he wishes to say about contemporary historical culture, then he is simply unable to avoid these issues. He is, in other words, unable to avoid the politics of history in nineteenth-century Germany, even though this has rarely been seen as a central aspect of his thought. In the following thick, contextual reading of *Vom Nutzen und Nachtheil der Historie für das Leben*, I will argue that this essay is crucial for understanding Nietzsche's work during the 1870s: this essay highlights his profound interest in the link between historical culture and the political imagination in nineteenth-century Germany. At the end of the 1870s, in *Menschliches, Allzumenschliches*, the first volume of which was published in 1878, shortly before he left his academic position in Basel, Nietzsche finally demanded that philosophy should regain an awareness for the intricacies of history: "But everything has become: there are *no eternal facts*. Just as there are no absolute truths. Consequently what is needed from now on is *historical philosophizing*, and with it the virtue of modesty" (*HA* 1: 2). The value of historical knowledge as a foundation for the critique of modernity increasingly takes center stage in Nietzsche's work. The second

---

[33] See Jaeger, "Geschichtsphilosophie, Hermeneutik, und Kontingenz in der Geschichte des Historimus," in Wolfgang Küttler, Jörn Rüser, and Ernst Schulin (eds.), *Geschichtschskurs, III: Die Epoche der Historisierung* (Frankfurt/M.: Fischer Taschenbuch Verlag, 1997), p. 46.

"Untimely Meditation" is therefore a crucial step into the direction of his later genealogical project as he formulated it, for instance, in *Zur Genealogie der Moral* thirteen years later.

WHAT IS ORIENTATION IN HISTORY?

Written between spring and winter 1873, Nietzsche's second "Untimely Meditation" has often been described as a more or less direct attack on German historicism.[34] Some commentators even pointed out that Nietzsche wished to present his readers with a powerful counter-image to the perceived historical relativism of his age by demanding, along metaphysical lines, a new "wholeness" and "beauty" with regard to our understanding of history, thus turning history into art, "life" into "literature."[35] This is in many ways a well-established narrative, which often concludes by declaring that Nietzsche believed science and history to be life-rejecting, in contrast to art which he supposedly regarded as life-affirming.[36] There are good reasons to assume that this is not the whole story. If he really believed science and scholarship to be life-rejecting, it is rather bizarre for him to continue throughout his life to read a considerable amount of material that, strictly speaking, falls into the categories of science and scholarship. More worryingly, though, to argue that Nietzsche seeks to replace philosophical argument and historical knowledge with aesthetic experience rests on the implicit assumption that Nietzsche's writings as a whole can be read against the background of his early *Die Geburt der Tragödie*.

To be sure, Nietzsche's historical perspective in his book on tragedy does privilege the aesthetic, often following an idiosyncratic reading of Friedrich Schiller's and Arthur Schopenhauer's theories of art. The idea that reality can be "justified" only as an "aesthetic phenomenon," coupled with the demand to "*look at*

---

[34] On the textual constitution and the development of Nietzsche's argument, see Jörg Salaquarda, "Studien zur zweiten Unzeitgemäßen Betrachtung," *Nietzsche-Studien* 13 (1984), 1–45.

[35] See Nehamas, *Nietzsche*, pp. 194–9, and Peter Berkowitz, *Nietzsche: The Ethics of an Immoralist* (Cambridge, Mass.: Harvard University Press, 1995), pp. 28 and 37–8.

[36] The assumption that Nietzsche erected a radical and absolute opposition between "history" and "life" continues to characterize the reception of the second "Untimely Meditation" among German historians. See, for instance, Wittkau, *Historismus*, pp. 49 and 53.

science through the prism of the artist," also influenced the peculiar historical perspective of Nietzsche's first book: his longing for a non-conceptual access to a primordial reality and the will through music in many ways rests on the desire to overcome the alienation of modernity by a return to a presumably lost unity between "man" and "nature" (*BT* pp. 5, 18 and 49–52). On the one hand, Nietzsche clearly continues a theme that already took center stage in Schiller's *Über die ästhetische Erziehung des Menschen* (1795) and it is necessary to point out that the book on tragedy clearly seeks to revitalize central tenets of Weimar classicism.[37] On the other hand, the aestheticization of reality, including historical reality, along the lines of the famous opposition between the Apolline and the Dionysiac tends to replace history with myth, and Nietzsche himself constructs a fateful convergence between a lost pre-Socratic unity and the hope for a return to this unity in contemporary German culture, especially the *Gesamtkunstwerk* of Richard Wagner.[38] Postulating the "Dionysiac ground of the German spirit," he dreams of a "supreme, artistic, primal joy in the womb of the Primordial Unity," which is supposed to culminate in a "*rebirth of the German myth*" (*BT* 94, 105 and 109). Historical knowledge, in other words, is relegated into the background by a new emphasis on foundation myths.

What is often ignored is that Nietzsche himself was well aware of the political overtones of his early aestheticism and shortly after the publication of *Die Geburt der Tragödie* began to renounce Wagner and the ideological program implicit in his first book. He remarked in the preface to the second edition of 1886 that his book on tragedy was, above all, the "*impossible* book" of an adolescent enthusiast, which underestimated the political consequences of replacing historical knowledge with a cultural foundation myth (*BT* p. 5):

And that I should have begun to invent stories about the "German character," on the basis of the latest German music, as if it were to

---

[37] See Schiller, *On the Aesthetic Education of Man*, pp. 79–115, 171–81 and 205–19, and "On Naïve and Sentimental Poetry," in H. B. Nisbet (ed.), *German Aesthetic and Literary Criticism: Winckelmann, Lessing, Hamann, Herder, Schiller, Goethe* (Cambridge: Cambridge University Press, 1985), pp. 180–232. See also Paul Bishop and R. H. Stephenson, *Friedrich Nietzsche and Weimar Classicism* (Rochester, N.Y.: Camden House, 2005), pp. 24–62. On Nietzsche's reception of Schiller, see in particular Nicholas Martin, *Nietzsche and Schiller: Untimely Aesthetics* (Oxford: Clarendon Press, 1996), pp. 29–44.
[38] For a more positive account of this, see Megill, *Prophets of Extremity*, pp. 71–5.

discover or re-discover itself – and this at a time when the German spirit, which had recently shown the will to rule Europe and the strength to lead Europe, had *abdicated*, finally and definitively, and, using the pompous pretext of founding an empire, was in a process of transition to mediocrity, democracy, and "modern ideas." Since then I have indeed learned to think hopelessly and unsparingly enough about this "German character, ..." (*BT* p. 10)

While Nietzsche was far from being a liberal thinker, he realized in 1886 that the metaphysical aesthetics of his book on tragedy had played into the hands of the numinous nationalist sentiments of the 1870s. His self-critical preface of 1886 is in many ways a warning that aestheticism, much like Wagner's music, is "a narcotic which both intoxicates and *befogs* the mind" (*BT* p. 10). Already in 1874, Nietzsche himself had not wished to follow down this route. But his second "Untimely Meditation" is also far removed from the writings of many of his philosophical predecessors that are indeed marked by notions of wholeness, such as Kant's "Idee zu einer allgemeinen Geschichte in weltbürgerlicher Absicht" (1784), Schiller's "Was heißt und zu welchem Ende studiert man Universalgeschichte?" (1789), or Hegel's lectures on the philosophy of history during the 1820s. Although Nietzsche regarded the seeming disintegration of cultural experience in modernity as a fundamental problem, by 1874 he was both unwilling and unable to subscribe to some kind of numinous unity between "man" and "nature," or to the assumption of a unifying teleological development that supposedly structured the course of historical events (*UM* II: 1 and 8). His encounter with Kant in 1868 had taught him some lessons. As a consequence he also thought the Hegelian position simply absurd, for it implied "that for Hegel the climax and terminus of the world-process coincided with his own existence in Berlin" (*UM* II: 8).

Nietzsche's account of Hegel is debatable, and there are many indications that he underestimated the theoretical outlook of Hegel's lectures on the philosophy of history. But his critical stance toward a simplification of complex historical processes according to speculative philosophical models was not without reason. It developed against the background of precisely the tensions that were characteristic of nineteenth-century historicism. As such, it would be wrong to assume that Nietzsche merely sought to point out the paralyzing, or life-denying, cultural effects of too much historical study. Certainly, one of the earliest reviews of his first three "Untimely Meditations," published in 1875 in the London journal *Westminster Review*, had praised his stance against the "useless prolixity and multifarious pedantry" of the historical profession, but this was not the main point of Nietzsche's project.[39] Rather, he wishes to examine the cultural and thus political value of history, without falling into the trap of philosophical and ideological absolutes. The politics of history is, thus, at the very center of the second "Untimely Meditation."

The starting point of Nietzsche's reflections is the "*malady of history*" (*UM* II: 10), which he sees as spreading through nineteenth-century Germany. This malady, he believes, mainly resulted from the inflationary knowledge about the past, and inflated public interest in the past. A broad obsession with the minute details of previous epochs and cultures, he claims, could be detected among both professional historians and the educated bourgeoisie:

> Historical knowledge streams in unceasingly from inexhaustible wells, the strange and incoherent forces its way forward, memory opens all its gates and yet is not open wide enough, nature travails in an effort to receive, arrange and honour these strange guests, but they themselves are in conflict with one another and it seems necessary to constrain and control them if one is not oneself to perish in their conflict. (*UM* II: 4)

For Nietzsche, then, the inflation of historical knowledge had a profound effect on historical culture as a whole. His main problem was not with the "hordes of scholars and researchers" that attend to the minute details of the past, but it was with the effects of their work on the public imagination, on "popular opinions [*Popularmeinungen*]" (*UM* II: 6). The crisis of historical culture that is often attributed to the intellectual culture of nineteenth-century Germany began to emerge only once the study of history left its disciplinary boundaries within the university and the academies behind, seeking to provide a much wider kind of political orientation.

[39] This was, however, the only positive remark in this review, which otherwise found harsh words for Nietzsche's "contempt for human virtues," and which portrayed him as one of the "successive builders of ontological card-castles" that dominate the "barren and bewildering metaphysics of Germany" with its "tremulous edifices" and "destructive" attitude to life. See the anonymous review essay "Contemporary Literature: Theology and Philosophy," *Westminster Review*, new series 47 (January–April 1875), 484–506: 501–3.

It is against this background that Nietzsche began to realize that the precarious state of contemporary historical culture was occasioned by the problem of what to do with historical knowledge. In other words, what was the political purpose and value of historical knowledge for modernity? On the one hand, Nietzsche stipulated, the inflation of historical material led to a continuous repetition and revision of the grand narratives of cultural history. Readers were confronted with an enormous amount of more or less interesting historical information about the customs of past civilizations, about their arts, philosophical opinions, political ideas and scientific achievements (*UM* II: 4), without really being able to process this information in a sensible manner and to relate this wealth of information to their own political conditions. On the other hand, the rapidly growing interest in history was able to fuel the public imagination. Political and cultural identity itself became increasingly dependent on the way it was connected to the past. This is perhaps particularly true with regard to the new German Empire as a modern nation state that was still busy defining what it meant to be a "nation."

To be sure, Nietzsche himself avoided going into any details and he also refrained from citing any prominent examples. But he really did not need to. No observer of the contemporary cultural setting in nineteenth-century Germany would have missed the intersection of political imagination and historical consciousness. The rise of political historiography in the Prussian School clearly illustrates the way in which attempts to bridge the gap between past and present were related to the establishment of a specific political identity. The construction of historical points of reference – e.g. Alexander the Great, the Roman Republic, the German Reformation, the French Revolution – as anticipating contemporary political ideals sought to order the present through complex historical analogies. Regardless as to whether these attempts were of a more liberal nature, as in the case of Theodor Mommsen and Johann Gustav Droysen, or of a conservative orientation, as in the case of Heinrich von Treitschke, political historiography was linked to a national project of collective identity.[40] Although it seems at first sight that

---

[40] See Georg G. Iggers, "Nationalism and Historiography, 1789–1996: The German Example in Historical Perspective," in Stefan Berger, Mark Donovan, and Kevin Passmore (eds.), *Writing National Histories: Western Europe since 1800* (London: Routledge, 1999), pp. 15–29, and Berger, *The Search for Normality*, pp. 21–55.

this national project mainly developed among the intellectual elite at German universities, it increasingly filtered into the public imagination at precisely the moment Nietzsche worked on his second "Untimely Meditation." While there was little popular support for a unified German nation state before 1870 (the smaller German states had in any case much to lose, since such a nation state would be dominated by Prussia), the realities of the Franco-Prussian War and the formation of a German Empire changed this situation almost overnight, leaving little room for federal structures and regional identities.[41] As a result of these changes, best-selling epic accounts of the perceived "German" past – from the historical novels of Gustav Freytag to the historiographical accounts of Ranke and Gervinius – began to shape the public imagination in an almost unprecedented way.[42]

The success of such publications is a clear indication for what Nietzsche perceived to be the "historical malady" of his time. But the link between nation and historical consciousness becomes even more apparent in a directly visible area: monuments (e.g. *Porta Westphalica, Hermannsdenkmal, Walhalla,* Bismarck statues), ritualized festivities (e.g. *Sedanstag, Schillerfeier*), and public imagery (e.g. *Befreiungskriege*) inaugurated the historical foundation myths for an imagined community, which sought to stabilize the political legitimacy of a German nation.[43] Politically sovereign and socially exclusive, the nineteenth-century European nation state invariably relied on complex historical strategies to ground its fragile contemporary identity in the past. The nation is always a

---

[41] See John Breuilly, "The National Idea in Modern German History," in Mary Fulbrook and John Breuilly (eds.), *German History since 1800* (London: Arnold, 1997), pp. 556–84. On the relationship between the German regions and the idea of a unified nation state, see Abigail Green, *Fatherlands: State-Building and Nationhood in Nineteenth-Century Germany* (Cambridge: Cambridge University Press, 2001), pp. 97–147.

[42] See Charlotte Woodford, "'Mit Gott für König und Vaterland': Contrasting Models of Patriotism in the Historical Novels of Theodor Fontane and Gustav Freytag," in Christian J. Emden and David Midgley (eds.), *German Literature, History and the Nation* (Oxford: Peter Lang, 2004), pp. 253–76.

[43] See Rolf Parr, *"Zwei Seelen wohnen, ach! in meiner Brust:" Strukturen und Funktionen der Mythisierung Bismarcks, 1860–1918* (Munich: Wilhelm Fink, 1992); Fritz Schellack, "Sedan- und Kaisergeburtstagsfeste," in Dieter Düding, Peter Friedemann, and Paul Münch (eds.), *Öffentliche Festkultur: Politische Feste in Deutschland von der Aufklärung bis zum ersten Weltkrieg* (Reinbeck: Rowolth, 1988), pp. 278–97; Thomas Nipperdey, "Nationalidee und Nationaldenkmal in Deutschland im 19. Jahrhundert," in *Gesellschaft, Kultur, Theorie: Gesammelte Aufsätze zur neueren Geschichte* (Göttingen: Vandenhoeck & Ruprecht, 1976), pp. 133–73.

historical community, which is only stabilized once historical points of reference move into the public realm, that is, once they become materially manifest in monuments, rituals and celebrations. Only as such a visibly historical community can the nation turn the many into one.[44] As such, the nation is marked by an awareness of the *longue durée* of its own formation, which establishes a historical continuity that allows the presumed past to be related to both present and future. It is this continuity that provides the backdrop for the symbolic construction of what has been termed an *ethnie*, that is, "a named human population with myths of common ancestry, shared historical memories and one or more common elements of culture, including an association with a homeland, and some degree of solidarity, at least among the élites."[45] These attributes accurately outline the political dimension of historical consciousness that Nietzsche, in his second "Untimely Meditation," deals with.

Once the presumed national past becomes visibly manifest in the public realm, it begins to resemble the fragmented displays of non-European cultures that had an effect on the public imagination from the 1870s onward, when Imperial Germany sought to fashion itself as a belated colonial power: the "artists" of the historical profession, Nietzsche points out, were indeed busy "preparing a world exhibition," and any critical observer, facing a "cosmopolitan carnival of gods, arts and customs," was reduced to a "strolling spectator" (*UM* II: 5).[46] But far from embracing such cultural heterogeneity, the obsession with historical foundation myths, together with the devout scholarly study of the past, gave way to an almost religious understanding of history as the unified unfolding of the nation state as a kind of moral community (*UM* II: 8). Reacting to this situation, Nietzsche emphatically sought to transform Kant's original question: "What is orientation in

---

[44] See Rudy Koshar, *From Monuments to Traces: Artifacts of German Memory, 1870–1990* (Berkeley, Calif.: University of California Press, 2000), pp. 29–52.

[45] Anthony D. Smith, *Myths and Memories of the Nation* (Oxford: Oxford University Press, 1999), p. 13.

[46] A particularly prominent example of this is the so-called "Rue des Nations" at the 1878 world exhibition in Paris: a series of architectural façades represents different historical and national building styles, thus contributing to the general disorientation experienced by the average visitor of the world exhibitions. See M. Christine Boyer, *The City of Collective Memory: Its Historical Imagery and Architectural Entertainments* (Cambridge, Mass.: MIT Press, 1994), pp. 259–63.

thinking?", which stood at the center of the latter's critical project, into another question that sought to account for the decisive changes in nineteenth-century intellectual culture: "What is orientation in history?" To some extent, then, Nietzsche seems to anticipate what Wilhelm Dilthey, at the beginning of the twentieth century, was to call the "critique of historical reason."[47] For Nietzsche, however, such a critique ultimately had to take a political direction.

At first sight, Nietzsche's question about historical orientation might not really stand in sharp contrast to the general direction the historical disciplines in Germany took after the Franco-Prussian War. Responding to the changed political circumstances, German historians increasingly conceived of themselves as providing political and cultural orientation for the educated reading public.[48] Much of this orientation was inscribed into the faultlines of liberalism, nationalism and, to a lesser extent, socialism. The "*malady of history*," Nietzsche observed in his essay *Vom Nutzen und Nachtheil der Historie für das Leben*, was marked not only by an excess of the historical, but also by a politicization of the past. Most prominent, and also many less prominent, German historians did not restrict themselves to the institutional boundaries of the university. As members of parliament, political columnists, and public speakers they sought to affect both actual policy decisions and the popular imagination of the past. Himself a well-informed observer of this situation, Nietzsche will not have missed these developments. But viewed from the deep-seated anti-modernism of Basel's intellectual culture, these developments will have confirmed to him that a different kind of historical orientation was necessary. For Nietzsche, orientation in history could be achieved only through a critique, not a reaffirmation, of contemporary historical culture and its foundation myths.

Germany was not an exception in the context of nineteenth-century European nationalism. The Prussian historians' idea of a "special path" with regard to the formation of the German nation state does not really correspond to the political realities, since the

---

[47] Wilhelm Dilthey, *Der Aufbau der geschichtlichen Welt in den Geisteswissenschaften*, in *Gesammelte Schriften*, vol. VII (Leipzig: Teubner, 1927), pp. 191–2.
[48] See Gangolf Hübinger, "Geschichte als leitende Orientierungswissenschaft im 19. Jahrhundert," *Berichte zur Wissenschaftsgeschichte* 11 (1988), 149–58.

logic of historical foundation myths is strikingly similar throughout most of Western and Central Europe. Nietzsche's own assessment of the politics of history thus cannot be limited to Germany, even though he was, of course, most familiar with the developments that took place in the intellectual field and political culture of 1870s Germany and that linked the outlook of the new German nation state to the modern European experience of crisis. These developments included a far-reaching reform of higher education, the rise of scientific materialism, the political failure of a cosmopolitan liberalism, and the polarization of religious conflict. On the one hand, this crisis mentality had much to do with the decline of Hegelianism and the economic modernization of the bourgeoisie.[49] On the other, the origins of this crisis mentality can be backdated to the second half of the eighteenth century.[50] Either way, this crisis mentality had become a central intellectual commonplace by the 1870s. Through the writings and lectures of his colleague Jacob Burckhardt, Nietzsche was himself well versed in the logic and rhetoric of crisis. Less blinded by the promises of progress than many of his contemporaries, Burckhardt saw the roots of "the great crisis of modern culture" in the eighteenth century, while the crisis itself seemed to accelerate after 1815, that is, when the Vienna Congress failed to provide a liberal political order within post-revolutionary Europe.[51] The perceived acceleration of historical processes within a situation of crisis becomes manifest, for instance, in the dissolution of traditional forms of political authority within the modern nation state. But as Burckhardt perceptively pointed out, the long-term effects of such crises tend to go unnoticed.[52] Nietzsche could not agree more. For Burckhardt, the crisis of modern culture was above all of a political nature, which threatened to culminate, sooner or later, in

---

[49] See Bambach, *Heidegger, Dilthey, and the Crisis of Historicism*, pp. 21–30 and 37–55, and Jaeger, *Bürgerliche Modernisierungskrise*, pp. 15 and 146–50.

[50] See Reinhart Koselleck, *Critique and Crisis: Enlightenment and the Pathogenesis of Modern Society* (Oxford: Berg, 1988), pp. 98 and 117, and Jürgen Habermas, *The Structural Transformation of the Public Sphere*, trans. Thomas Burger and Frederick Lawrence (Cambridge, Mass.: MIT Press, 1989), pp. 28, 88 and 94.

[51] Burckhardt, *Weltgeschichtliche Betrachtungen*, p. 132.

[52] See ibid., pp. 134–5, 159, 168, 181, and 188–9. Burckhardt's interest in crises is indebted to his witnessing the political changes and unrest in Basel, Germany and Italy during the 1840s. See John R. Hinde, "The Development of Jacob Burckhardt's Early Political Thought," *Journal of the History of Ideas* 53 (1992), 425–36: 428.

disastrous "world wars [*Völkerkriege*]."⁵³ Along similar lines, and looking back at the previous decade, Nietzsche remarked in his notebooks of June–July 1879: "I became anxious facing the uncertainty of the modern cultural horizon" (*KGW* IV/3, 40 [9]).

The uncertainty that was generated by the gradual displacement of cultural authority in nineteenth-century Germany was indeed one of the central themes of the essay *Schopenhauer als Erzieher* (1875). Here Nietzsche diagnosed the "symptoms" of a supposedly rootless culture marked by a feeling of haste, which not only threatened old certainties, but also seemed to destroy any hope for the future: "We live in the age of atoms, of atomistic chaos" (*UM* III: 4). In view of this dissolution of reality, the political and cultural order of the modern nation state could only be seen as deficient:

> For a century we have been preparing for absolutely fundamental convulsions; and if there have recently been attempts to oppose this deepest of modern inclinations, to collapse or to explode, with the constitutive power of the so-called nation state, the latter too will for a long time serve only to augment the universal insecurity and atmosphere of menace. (*UM* III: 4)

The political uncertainties of the nineteenth century, Nietzsche believed, were the after-effects of a much more fundamental disorientation. Four years after his essay on history, he pointedly remarked in *Menschliches, Allzumenschliches*: "Our age gives the impression of being an interim state; the old ways of thinking, the old cultures are still partly with us, the new not yet secure and habitual and thus lacking in decisiveness and consistency" (*HA* I: 248). This seemingly passing remark indicates that Nietzsche was very much aware that his historical thought developed in an age of transition within the political trajectories of modern European thought.⁵⁴ The latter was not caused by any singular political or intellectual event. Rather, it was the result of complex interactions that finally triggered an almost imperceptible but far-reaching transformation within the intellectual field, an acceleration of

---

⁵³ Burckhardt, *Weltgeschichtliche Betrachtungen*, p. 191.
⁵⁴ On the dynamics of such "transitions," see still Hans Blumenberg, "Epochenschwelle und Rezeption," *Philosophische Rundschau* 6 (1958), 94–120, and Foucault, *The Archaeology of Knowledge*, pp. 166–77.

history that culminated in an irreversible change in the symbolic order of culture: "Moreover, we *cannot* return to the old," as Nietzsche remarked, pointing to the need to examine the cultural and political orientation of his time (*HA* I: 248).

Crises are, of course, always based on uncertainty, even though sooner or later any crisis will come to an end. It is precisely because of this paradox that crises always entail the "question of the historical future."[55] Regardless as to whether the crisis at hand is real or imagined, the sheer experience of crisis is always linked to historical experience, that is, to the experience of crisis as a specific historical event. Nietzsche is no exception to this, even though his own reflections on this crisis, often following Burckhardt's lead, bear the signs of the crisis itself. As a result he is not the cool and distanced observer that Burckhardt is. But in *Vom Nutzen und Nachtheil der Historie für das Leben* Nietzsche began to realize that cultural and political authority were rooted in specific forms of historical imagination.

THE POLITICAL MOBILIZATION OF MYTH

Tracy B. Strong has rightly pointed out that, for Nietzsche, "the process of history is, if nothing else, at least the manner in which our past affects our present."[56] But instead of approaching this problem from a psychological perspective, Nietzsche's remarks in fact deal with the political relationship between past and present. At first sight, this might be counterintuitive. At the beginning of his second "Untimely Meditation" Nietzsche immediately links historical knowledge to the memory of individuals (*UM* II: 1). But his conclusion that too much historical knowledge is as destructive for cultures as too much memory would be for individuals is merely an analogy, since the remainder of the essay focuses on the role of history for societies and cultures rather than for single individuals. What he seeks to investigate is the political function of historical culture. In order to do so, he formulates the precarious relationship between past and present along the lines of three famous and much-debated models, which he termed

---

[55] Koselleck, *Critique and Crisis*, p. 127.
[56] Tracy B. Strong, *Friedrich Nietzsche and the Politics of Transfiguration*, enlarged edn. (Berkeley, Calif.: University of California Press, 1988), p. 31.

"monumental," "antiquarian," and "critical."[57] Each of these models describes a certain mode of formulating the relationship between past and present, but each of them is also fundamentally flawed.

Focusing on the grandeur of specific historical events, a "monumental" understanding of the past seeks to authorize a distinct master narrative of historical progression, culminating in a foundation myth for the present:

> That the great moments in the struggle of the human individual constitute a chain, that this chain unites mankind across millennia like a range of human mountain peaks, that the summit of such a long-ago moment shall be for me still living, bright and great – that is the fundamental idea of the faith in humanity which finds expression in the demand for a *monumental* history. ... Of what use, then, is the monumentalistic conception of the past, engagement with the classic and rare of earlier times, to the man of the present? He learns from it that the greatness that once existed was in any event once *possible* and may thus be possible again; he goes his way with more cheerful step, for the doubt which assailed him in weaker moments, whether he was not perhaps desiring the impossible, has now been banished. (*UM* II: 2)

Monumental conceptions of the past, Nietzsche argues, serve as a means against cultural resignation in the present in that they are able to contrast this present with an idealized version of past events, thereby suggestively implying either a possible return to a lost grandeur, or the continued presence of this grandeur as an ordering force within the present.

Needless to say, such a "monumental" model comes in many different guises, the "faith in humanity" that was promised by Enlightenment philosophy being only one particular example. During the 1870s, the political relevance of such a monumental understanding of history is indeed difficult to ignore and comes to the fore in the complex political symbolism and rituals that marked the newly unified Germany. The years 1870/71 must have been on Nietzsche's mind as that historical moment which created

---

[57] Nietzsche is certainly not the first author to opt for a tripartite paradigm of historical knowledge. In the eighteenth century, Johann Martin Chladenius, *Nova philosophia definitiva* (Leipzig: Lanckisch, 1750), p. 73, noted that the *ars historica* has to be regarded as that science which directs the intellect *in cognoscendis rebus singularibus, in cognoscendis rebus absentibus*, and *in cognoscendis rebus antiquis*. From a completely different perspective, Hegel, *Lectures on the Philosophy of World History*, pp. 11–24, divided the discourse of history into "original," "reflective," and "philosophical history."

not only the political entity of an "Empire" but also the imagined community and *ethnie* of a German "nation."

The political imagination of the German Empire was inextricably linked to monumental historical foundation myths, which often stood in considerable contrast to the actual modernization of Germany along technocratic lines.[58] Within this context, the German victory over the French army on the battlefield at Sedan was not merely presented as a military success. Rather, it was construed as a victory of German culture, civilization and historical destiny. From high-brow rectorial addresses at German universities to ceremonial speeches on the Emperor's birthday, "1870/71" was immediately embedded in a web of references – Luther, German idealism, the "Wars of Liberation," Protestant Prussia, *Reich*, Rhine, Bismarck, etc. – that reflected the supposed superiority of the German *Kulturstaat*.[59] This truly monumental narrative became a lasting structuring force within the public imagination, safeguarded not only by best-selling chronicles of the war years, but even more successfully by the popular poetry, songs and plays that were performed during the annual Sedan-celebrations. Certainly, most of these literary texts were of rather limited aesthetic value, but they did reactivate the pathos connected to the wars against Napoleon between 1809 and 1813, which now seemed to extend into the 1870s.[60] The historical foundation myths already present in a wide range of public monuments – such as the statue of Ernst Moritz Arndt on the Alter Zoll in Bonn which was unveiled in front of Nietzsche and his fellow students – were, however, part of an even more monumental historical narrative of German identity, which Nietzsche had encountered together with his friend Erwin Rohde on a summer trip to the Bavarian forest on August 18, 1867: the "temple" of Walhalla (*BAW* III, pp. 280–90 and 423–37).

---

[58] On the complexity of the German political imagination during the 1870s, see Wolfgang Hardtwig, "Bürgertum, Staatssymbolik und Staatsbewußtsein im Deutschen Kaiserreich, 1871–1914," *Geschichte und Gesellschaft* 16 (1990), 269–95.

[59] Jarausch, *Students, Society, and Politics in Imperial Germany*, pp. 160–1 and 201, discusses this with regard to rectorial addresses by Carl Bruns, *Deutschlands Sieg über Frankreich: Rede am 15. October 1870 in der Aula der Friedrich-Wilhelms-Universität zu Berlin gehalten beim Antritt des Rectorats* (Berlin: Vogt, 1870), and Emil DuBois-Reymond, *Über den deutschen Krieg: Rede am 3. August 1870 in der Aula der Königlichen Friedrich-Wilhelms-Universität zu Berlin gehalten* (Berlin: Hirschwald, 1870), as well as with regard to the imaginary genealogy from Luther to Bismarck.

[60] See Becker, *Bilder von Krieg und Nation*, pp. 70–2 and 292–376.

Located on a hillside near Regensburg with spectacular vistas over the valley of the Danube below, Walhalla was originally conceived by the Bavarian Crown Prince Ludwig I as a "Pantheon for the Germanic People" containing busts of Erasmus of Rotterdam, Martin Luther, Albrecht Dürer, Frederick the Great, Friedrich Schiller, and others. Projected soon after the Vienna Congress, it was intended to create a sacral space for the "German nation" that still only existed as an imaginary point of reference but that had outlasted both the Napoleonic occupation and the particularism of the German states. The architect Leo von Klenze – who had already built the massive Glyptothek (1816–30) and the Alte Pinakothek (1825–36) in Munich, and who was responsible for much of the neo-classicist architecture in the center of the Bavarian capital – transformed this somewhat vague idea between 1828 and 1842 into a temple site of enormous proportions. Ramps built into the hillside led up to the columns of a main building that was clearly modeled on the Parthenon in Athens and thus served as a symbolic site where different foundation myths were able to merge into a single monumental narrative about political identity: instead of the Parthenon's frieze of mythological scenes, the front façade of Walhalla, while still adhering to a Doric style, is dominated by a towering tympanum, which depicts the victory of the Germanic tribes over the Roman armies in the Teutoburg Forest.[61]

Much like Heinrich von Kleist's play *Die Hermannsschlacht* (1808), which presented the battle in the Teutoburg Forest as a Germanic foundation myth, the symbolism of Walhalla backdated the Wars of Liberation, together with an imagined German identity, into a numinous and distant past. On the one hand, it thus represented the new political theology of the nation and what has been called the "sacralization" of the national past – something Nietzsche, much later in 1887/88, was to call the "nihilistic religion" of "barbarians" (*KGW*VIII/2, 11 [370]).[62] On

---

[61] Leo von Klenze's program can be found in *Die Walhalla in artistischer und technischer Beziehung* (Munich: Literarisch-artistische Anstalt, 1842). Originally to be called *Pantheon der Deutschen*, since it was to contain busts of prominent German-speaking individuals, it was the Swiss-born historian Johannes von Müller, who suggested the name "Walhalla" in order to underline the Nordic element over the architectural allusions to the classical Greek order.

[62] See Aleida Assmann, *Arbeit am nationalen Gedächtnis: Eine kurze Geschichte der nationalen Bildungsidee* (Frankfurt/M.: Campus 1993), pp. 47–9.

the other hand, it also unfolded, as it were, the "nation" into a monumental historical narrative that was repeated at other symbolic sites all over Germany. Geographical territory was increasingly transformed into a landscape of monuments and spatial order sought to mirror the political structures of the presumed national past.[63] Small wonder, then, that the students Nietzsche and Rohde ended their holidays on their way back from the Bavarian forests in the summer of 1867 with an excursion to Luther's Wartburg.

The ideological mobilization of the German public in the name of the nation after 1870/71 – especially the new middle classes that were able to prosper in the early years of the modernized Empire – turned historical culture into an aesthetic commodity that only allowed for a monumental appreciation of the past. But once the establishment of German historiography, in particular the Prussian historians, had introduced the nation as the main reference point for the study of history, even those historians that had located themselves in a more liberal tradition, such as Heinrich von Sybel and Theodor Mommsen, were not immune to such monumental narratives.[64] In the second half of the nineteenth century, even historiography had a tendency toward what Nietzsche described as monumental, although it presented these narratives in a more sophisticated manner. While Leopold von Ranke's *Preussische Geschichte* (1847–48) and Heinrich von Treitschke's *Deutsche Geschichte im neunzehnten Jahrhundert* (1879–94) openly sketched out a national program dominated by Prussia, liberally inclined historians presented a more complex tableau of historical reference points.[65] In Johann Gustav Droysen's bestselling *Geschichte des Hellenismus* (1833–43), which could be found on the bookshelves of virtually every educated German middle-class household, and which sought to contribute, in Droysen's own

---

[63] See Reinhard Alings, *Monument und Nation – das Bild vom Nationalstaat im Denkmal: Zum Verhältnis von Nation und Staat im deutschen Kaiserreich 1871–1918* (Berlin: Walter de Gruyter, 1996), and Jörg Traeger, *Der Weg nach Walhalla: Denkmallandschaft und Bildungsreise im 19. Jahrhundert* (Regensburg: Bernhard Bosse, 1987).

[64] See, for instance, Sybel's remarks in "Ueber den Stand der neueren deutschen Geschichtsschreibung," in *Kleine Schriften* (Munich: Cotta, 1869), vol. 1, pp. 349 and 353.

[65] See Leopold von Ranke, *Neun Bücher Preussischer Geschichte* (Berlin: Veit und Comp., 1847–48), and Heinrich von Treitschke, *Deutsche Geschichte im neunzehnten Jahrhundert* (Leipzig: Hirzel, 1879–94).

words, to a *"truly historical view* of the present," the Macedonia of Alexander the Great often bore the characteristics of an ideal Prussia.[66] Likewise, Theodor Mommsen's *Römische Geschichte* (1854–56), which had been heavily criticized by Bachofen and Burckhardt, can be read as legitimizing historically the connection between democratic representation and monarchy, as it was often suggested by the national-liberal political program.[67] Mommsen's scholarship, in particular his account of ancient Rome, Nietzsche suggested, often had a tendency to follow the party-political fashion of the day – even Cicero was presented in the guise of a modern "journalist" (*KGW* III/3, 8 [113] and *KGW* III/4, 19 [196], 29 [51] and [184]).[68] It is in this sense that the dangers of interpreting the past through the lens of contemporary political interests became obvious. But the politics of a monumental view of the past could also become manifest on the level of that grand-scale scholarly practice that Mommsen directed himself and supported over many years: the *Monumenta Germaniae Historica*, one of the major achievements of German historical study in the nineteenth century, which had been outlined in 1819 by the Prussian politician Karl von Stein, who was revered by Ernst Moritz Arndt and who, in turn, supported Arndt's often spiteful propaganda against France.

Seen against this background, Nietzsche's conception of a "monumental" historical narrative, though often alluding to the pitfalls of German idealism, really should be understood as describing the way in which German historical culture in the period between the 1830s and 1870s was often, albeit not exclusively, centered on foundation myths of national identity. Once we take Nietzsche's own intellectual environment into account, there can be little doubt that, unlike in *Die Geburt der Tragödie*, he no longer really strives for some kind of mythical re-enchantment of the present in the name of a metaphysical aestheticism. In fact, he is rather apprehensive about the resemblance between a "monumental history" and a "mythical fiction" that "deceives through analogies" and "seductive similarities" (*UM* II: 2).

---

[66] Johann Gustav Droysen, *Geschichte des Hellenismus*, ed. Erich Bayer (Tübingen: Wissenschaftliche Buchgemeinschaft, 1952–53), vol. III, pp. xx–xxi.
[67] See, for instance, Mommsen's remarks on Caesar in *Römische Geschichte*, vol. III, p. 476.
[68] See ibid., vol. III, pp. 619–20.

"THE SOUL OF THE ANTIQUARIAN"

Monumental narratives about the past are, however, only one dimension of contemporary historical culture; their direct opposite are "antiquarian" models, which do not rest on an idealization of specific events, on foundation myths, but on a pious attention to the minute details of the past:

> By tending with care that which has existed from of old, he [i.e.: the antiquarian historian] wants to preserve for those who shall come into existence after him the conditions under which he himself came into existence .... The trivial, circumscribed, decaying and obsolete acquire their own dignity and inviolability through the fact that the preserving and revering soul of the antiquarian man has emigrated into them and there made its home. ... to detect traces almost extinguished, to read the past quickly and correctly no matter how intricate its palimpsest may be – these are his talents and virtues. (*UM* II: 3)

Antiquarian conceptions of the past are ultimately related to the demand to accurately reconstruct and retain the past for the present, focusing on minute details and seemingly peripheral elements. The attempt to inaugurate a political foundation myth is here replaced by the paradigms of preservation and conservation – not only seeking to secure a tangible past, but also emphasizing an understanding of cultural heritage that is based on notions of authenticity and uniqueness.

Nietzsche's repeated talk of "reading," "traces," and "palimpsests" clearly situates the antiquarian model within the context of philological scholarship. What he seems to have in mind is particularly the painstaking work of textual criticism, which he had already encountered as a student in Bonn and Leipzig.[69] As a professional philologist Nietzsche was well aware that the practice of emendation and recension that lies at the heart of textual criticism did not only provide a successful interpretive tool. It was also very much dependent on the practice of preservation that, during the nineteenth century, became manifest in the enormous efforts to collect and collate copious amounts of manuscripts, fragments, and inscriptions. To transform antiquity into a historical phenomenon that

---

[69] See Emden, "Learning How to Read," 101–5 and 107–8, and Benne, *Nietzsche und die historisch-kritische Philologie*, pp. 20–68.

could be studied relied on an authentic archive of source material that would occupy literally hundreds of philological scholars all over Europe.

The first major German project in this sense was the *Corpus Inscriptionum Graecarum* (1825–77) under the direction of August Boeckh, which ironically made it clear to the representatives of textual criticism, such as Gottfried Hermann, that their efforts were soon to become an ancillary discourse, a *Hilfswissenschaft*.[70] For Boeckh, this archive was merely a starting point for the historicization of ancient Greek culture as a whole. Small wonder, then, that the ensuing quarrel between Boeckh and Hermann quickly turned into a scholarly battle between *Wort-* and *Sachphilologie*, the effects of which could still be felt in the second half of the nineteenth century.[71]

The *Corpus Inscriptionum Graecarum* was in many ways responsible for the way in which the study of Greek and Roman culture began to shift its focus of attention from literary documents to public inscriptions. By the middle of the nineteenth century, epigraphy had widened the notion of textual criticism and established itself as one of the leading models for the study of ancient cultural history. This prepared the ground for even more ambitious projects. Nietzsche himself encountered one of these projects in the work of his teacher Ritschl, the *Priscae latinitatis monumenta epigraphica* (1862–64), which he held in high esteem and recommended to his students as a milestone of philological scholarship. What Nietzsche does not tend to mention, however, is that Ritschl's collection was itself part of a much wider project, the *Corpus Inscriptionum Latinarum*, founded in 1853 by Theodor Mommsen, who had conceived the idea of a truly colossal collection of Roman inscriptions during his stay in Italy in the 1840s.[72] Nietzsche himself was in no

---

[70] *Corpus Inscriptionum Graecarum*, ed. August Boeckh (Berlin: Reimer, 1825–77), and Gottfried Hermann, *Über Herrn Professor Böckhs Behandlung der griechischen Inschriften* (Leipzig: Fleischer, 1826).

[71] On the history of the *Corpus Inscriptionum Graecarum* and the quarrel between Boeckh and Hermann, see Most, "One Hundred Years of Fractiousness," 353–7, and Ernst Vogt, "Der Methodenstreit zwischen Hermann und Boeckh und seine Bedeutung für die Geschichte der Philologie," in Hellmut Flashar, Karlfried Gründer, and Axel Horstmann (eds.), *Philologie und Hermeneutik im 19. Jahrhundert* (Göttingen: Vandenhoeck & Ruprecht, 1979), pp. 103–21.

[72] On Mommsen's research in Italy and the beginning of the *Corpus Inscriptionum Latinarum*, see Stefan Rebenich, *Theodor Mommsen: Eine Biographie* (Munich: C. H. Beck, 2002), pp. 43–52, and Theodor Mommsen, "Über Plan und Ausführung eines *Corpus*

position to ignore the *Corpus Inscriptionum Latinarum*, for instance, in his lectures on Latin grammar of 1869/70, but he clearly emphasized Ritschl's contribution over all others (*KGW* II/2, pp. 199 and 268, and *KGW* II/3, p. 389). As a consequence of his adolescent adoration for Ritschl, Nietzsche's own course "Einleitung in die lateinische Epigraphik," delivered in 1871/72 at the University of Basel, was built around Ritschl's ideas, which he described as the most important epigraphic research that had ever been published (*KGW* II/4, p. 194).[73]

Despite this personal connection, Nietzsche's complete disregard for Mommsen's efforts, and his irrational aversion to the latter's scholarship, will have had much to do with his own intellectual environment in Basel. Both Bachofen and Burckhardt regarded Mommsen not only as a personal enemy, but also as representing everything that had gone wrong with "Prussian" learning. Mommsen, on the other hand, completely ignored Nietzsche, although he must have been familiar with the scandal caused by the publication of *Die Geburt der Tragödie* and the pamphlets by Ulrich von Wilamowitz-Moellendorff and Erwin Rohde. In any case, the young Wilamowitz, who had started this quarrel with a vicious *ad hominem* attack on Nietzsche's scholarly integrity, was a frequent guest at Mommsen's house from 1873 onward. In September 1878, he even married Mommsen's oldest daughter, Marie. It is quite ironic that, among the members of Ulrich von Wilamowitz-Moellendorff's Prussian *Junker* family, his marriage to Marie Mommsen caused much consternation: the liaison between a member of the Prussian aristocracy and the independent-minded daughter of a liberal bourgeois family, despite Mommsen's standing, was not tolerated easily. Mommsen, on the other hand, had much praise for his new son-in-law's scholarly efforts, but was far from happy with his political convictions, which were often too close to Heinrich von Treitschke's predilections for *Machtpolitik* as well as his anti-Semitic and anti-French sentiments. Behind Mommsen's back, Wilamowitz occasionally even sought to thwart

---

Inscriptionum Latinarum," in *Tagebuch der französisch-italienischen Reise 1844–1845, mit einem Anhang: Mommsens Denkschrift über das "Corpus Inscriptionum Latinarum" 1847*, ed. Gerold Walser and Brigitte Walser (Berne: Lang, 1976), pp. 223–52.

[73] Indeed, the origins of Nietzsche's course can be traced back to Ritschl's lectures and seminars at the University of Leipzig. See *GSA* 49/84, pp. 3–8, and *GSA* 54/89.

Mommsen's grand-scale projects at the Prussian Academy.[74] Thus, although the relationship between the liberal Mommsen and the conservative Wilamowitz was not without conflict, for Nietzsche both embodied a kind of "Prussianism" that stood in sharp opposition to the intellectual culture of Basel. When Nietzsche heard in 1880, for instance, that some of Mommsen's manuscripts and notes had been destroyed in a fire, he first showed empathy about this terrible loss, only to remind himself almost immediately that he did not like Mommsen anyway (*KGB* III/1, p. 29).

While Mommsen was able to enlist much support for the *Corpus Inscriptionum Latinarum* during the early stages of his project among the members of the German Archaeological Institute in Rome, the Prussian Academy in Berlin was understandably worried about both the financial cost and the logistical feasibility of such an undertaking. But once Mommsen had been elected into the Academy in 1858, and once he had taken over as the Academy's secretary in 1874, the very year in which Nietzsche published his second "Untimely Meditation," the *Corpus Inscriptionum Latinarum* became the first example of what was to be known as Prussian "Großwissenschaft," or "grand-scale scholarship."[75] The antiquarian model of preserving and reconstituting the past, which Nietzsche had described in his essay on history, had already become a reality. Following the principles of authenticity and totality, which Nietzsche attributes to the antiquarian model, the *Corpus Inscriptionum Latinarum* was supposed to bring order into the archives of the past, paying much attention to the minute details of hitherto neglected public monuments. Nothing, or so it seems, should be overlooked and everything, even from the most remote regions of the Roman Empire, was to be conserved for posterity in the manner of pious and devout scholarship.[76]

The critical framework of the *Corpus Inscriptionum Latinarum* was new, but its ideal goal – representing the totality of Roman life in the form of authentic source material – can be traced back to the Renaissance. The sixteenth-century Italian scholar Ulisse

---

[74] On this precarious relationship, see Jürgen Malitz, "Theodor Mommsen und Wilamowitz," in William M. Calder III, Hellmut Flashar, and Theodor Lindken (eds.), *Wilamowitz nach 50 Jahren* (Darmstadt: Wissenschaftliche Buchgesellschaft, 1985), pp. 31–55.
[75] See Adolf von Harnack, *Geschichte der Königlich Preussischen Akademie der Wissenschaften* (Berlin: Reichsdruckerei, 1900), vol. 1/2, pp. 900–13.
[76] On Mommsen's general principles, see Rebenich, *Theodor Mommsen*, pp. 121–7.

Aldrovandi, for instance, sought to compile a complete inventory of the antique statues that had survived in Rome, and heavy tomes on the *antichità italiane*, often bearing titles like *Roma Illustrata*, established a direct link between the visual archive of archaeology and the discursive strategies of historical study. In contrast to the much-cited assumption that such antiquarianism disappeared in the course of the eighteenth century under the influence of a more analytical study of ancient culture – connected in Germany to the names of Winckelmann, Heyne and Wolf – it is necessary to point out that the antiquarian model itself continued to shape modern scholarship deep into the nineteenth century.[77] Bernard de Montfaucon's *L'Antiquité expliquée et représentée en figures* (1710–24) and the *Receuil d'Antiquités* (1752–67) of the Comte de Caylus are colossal catalogues of ancient monuments, describing them in word and image, while Wolf, in his lectures at the University of Halle, wholeheartedly stressed that the task of classical scholarship was to register and record antiquity in its entirety.[78]

Nietzsche himself was well informed about the intellectual trends and historical imagination of the Renaissance through Georg Voigt's *Die Wiederkehr des classischen Alterthums* (1859) and Jacob Burckhardt's *Die Cultur der Renaissance in Italien* (1860). In fact, he attended some of Voigt's lectures at the University of Leipzig in 1866, while Burckhardt's work on the Renaissance was an inspiration for him throughout the 1870s. As a result, he also turned to the archaeological excavations in early modern Rome, which he discussed in his course "Encyclopaedie der klassischen Philologie" (*KGW* II/3, p. 349).[79] But the reactivation of antiquarian models – the preservation and cataloguing of surviving monuments – was also very much at the center of contemporary

---

[77] On the relevance of antiquarian models, see Thomas DaCosta Kaufmann, "Antiquarianism, the History of Objects, and the History of Art before Winckelmann," *Journal of the History of Ideas* 62 (2001), 523–41.

[78] Friedrich August Wolf, *Darstellung der Alterthumswissenschaft, nebst einer Auswahl seiner kleinen Schriften und literarischen Zugaben zu dessen Vorlesungen über die Alterthumswissenschaft: Als Supplementband zu dessen Vorlesungen*, ed. Samuel Friedrich Wilhelm Hoffmann (Leipzig: Lehnhold, 1833), p. 41.

[79] Compare Burckhardt, *Die Cultur der Renaissance in Italien*, pp. 141–9. In contrast to Burckhardt's work, Georg Voigt, *Die Wiederbelebung des classischen Alterthums, oder das erste Jahrhundert des Humanismus* (Berlin: Reimer, 1859), focuses more on the textual tradition of humanist thought and is less interested in the material factors that underlie Burckhardt's account.

archaeological discourse. It is surprising to note that, during the first decades of the nineteenth century, that is, in the immediate aftermath of Winckelmann and Heyne, few archaeologists found it necessary to question the theoretical framework of their enterprise. Indeed, deep into the nineteenth century, German archaeological thought was largely influenced by Winckelmann's classicism and the ideology of neo-humanism. Only by the mid-1830s did German archaeologists begin to ponder the theoretical principles of their work more seriously, when Konrad Levezow delivered a programmatic lecture at the Prussian Academy in Berlin on November 21, 1833, and Ludwig Preller began to publish a series of articles on the hermeneutical principles of archaeological work.[80] Nevertheless, before the middle of the nineteenth century, very few German archaeologists had been to Greece. The political situation in the Aegean – the Greek War of Independence as well as the strategic interests of Russia, Britain, and the Ottoman Empire – often prevented long-term scholarly engagements. As a result, much of Otto Jahn's work, for instance, was based on artifacts in German museums, such as the collection of vases in the Pinakothek in Munich, and Karl Otfried Müller's seminal *Handbuch der Archäologie der Kunst* (1830) was based on little first-hand experience in terms of fieldwork.[81] Müller himself finally reached Greece in 1839, only to die of a sunstroke a year later.[82]

In the final decades of the nineteenth century, however, there was a fundamental change, and Mommsen's philological "Großwissenschaft" at the Prussian Academy was finally mirrored by the archaeological projects of the time. To be sure, large-scale excavations in Greece and Asia Minor – by Ernst Curtius at Olympia, Heinrich Schliemann at Mycenae, and Alexander Conze at Pergamon – began in earnest only during the late 1870s.[83] But the erudite work of German and European scholars in Rome throughout the nineteenth century followed the empirical

---

[80] See Jakob Andreas Konrad Levezow, "Ueber archäologische Kritik und Hermeneutik," *Abhandlungen der Königlichen Akademie der Wissenschaften: Historischphilologische Klasse* (1833), pp. 225–48, and Ludwig Preller, "Über die wissenschaftliche Behandlung der Archäologie," in *Ausgewählte Aufsätze aus dem Gebiet der classischen Alter-thumswissenschaft*, ed. Reinhold Köhler (Berlin: Weidmann, 1864), pp. 384–425.
[81] See Karl Otfried Müller, *Handbuch der Archäologie der Kunst* (Breslau: Max, 1830).
[82] See Eduard Müller, "Biographische Erinnerungen," in Karl Otfried Müller, *Kleine deutsche Schriften*, ed. Eduard Müller (Breslau: Max, 1847–47), vol. I, pp. lxvii–lxviii.
[83] See Marchand, *Down from Olympus*, pp. 75–103 and 118–24.

perspective of antiquarianism, seeking the tangible reconstruction of an authentic past without really questioning the cultural value of their efforts. The institutional framework for these efforts was provided by the German Institut für Altertumskunde in Rome, which was founded in 1829 and was later transformed into the much more powerful Deutsches Archäologisches Institut. The results of these efforts could be visited in the museums of Berlin and Munich, which underwent a rapid modernization during the 1870s and now regarded their antiquarian task – collecting and representing European antiquity in its totality – as a feasible enterprise.[84]

As successful as such antiquarian efforts were in practice, they were also accompanied by considerable problems and limitations that were difficult to ignore, at least as far Nietzsche was concerned. Even though the antiquarian historian ideally seeks to preserve the past for the present, any link between past and present is severed: the preservation of the past as authentic distances it from the present, so that the past cannot retain any value for the present. In an ironic turn, antiquarian models tend to undermine precisely what they seek to achieve: historical understanding. Toward the end of the eighteenth century, the Göttingen historian Arnold Ludwig Heeren had already warned that the "micrological" obsessions he detected among some of his colleagues constituted a "threat to scholarship," which would be reduced to a mere "ancillary science."[85] Only a few years later, Friedrich Ast – a philosopher at the soon to be defunct University of Landshut close to Munich, whose work on hermeneutics rivaled that of Schleiermacher – pointed out even more directly that "antiquarian scholarship" was unable to provide a serious interpretive approach to history.[86] But while both Heeren and Ast sought to avoid the pitfalls of antiquarianism by presenting historical processes as an unfolding of "consciousness" (*Geist*), Nietzsche's previous encounter with German idealism prevented him from adopting such a point of view. Instead, he introduced a third model of historical understanding that was supposed

---

[84] See Adolf Michaelis, *Geschichte des Deutschen Archäologischen Instituts 1829–1879: Festschrift zum 21. April 1879* (Berlin: Asher & Co., 1879).

[85] Arnold Hermann Ludwig Heeren, *Geschichte des Studiums der classischen Litteraturen seit dem Wiederaufleben der Wissenschaften; mit einer Einleitung, welche die Geschichte der Werke der Classiker im Mittelalter enthält* (Göttingen: Rosenbusch, 1797–1801), vol. I, p. 6.

[86] Friedrich Ast, *Grundriss der Philologie* (Landshut: Krüll, 1808), p. 2.

to compensate for the limitations of both the monumental and antiquarian views of the past: historical understanding as "critique."

THE IMPOSSIBLE CRITICAL HISTORIAN

Nietzsche's critical model of historical understanding is perhaps the most controversial aspect of *Vom Nutzen und Nachtheil der Historie für das Leben*. How is a view of the past, which is ultimately bound to reject the past, able to provide orientation in history? Perhaps such a model is truly impossible, but for Nietzsche it will prove to be the first tentative step toward a genealogy of modern culture. Historians and philosophers adopting such a critical view of history, Nietzsche believes, are interested neither in fashioning grand narratives about the past, nor in preserving the past for the present. Rather, the critical historian regards history above all as a chain of failures, misdemeanors and errors, which continue to shape the cultural conditions within the present, but which need to be eradicated and overcome:

> If he is to live, man must possess and from time to time employ the strength to break up and dissolve a part of the past: he does this by bringing it before the tribunal, scrupulously examining it and finally condemning it; every past, however, is worthy to be condemned – for that is the nature of human things: human violence and weakness have always played a mighty role in them. (*UM* II: 3)

Although this conception of history seems quite radical in that it seeks to reject the past, or at least specific aspects of the past, most importantly it allows Nietzsche to emphasize that this past is less homogeneous than monumental and antiquarian narratives might make us believe. Nietzsche, in other words, begins to be interested in the long-term political effects of the way in which the past tends to haunt the present.

What at first sight is clearly a rather gloomy view should better be understood as a more realistic understanding of history. Of course, Nietzsche's realism is not without precedent. Already at the beginning of the Enlightenment, Pierre Bayle found it necessary to remind his readers that history was above all marked by crime and immorality, and Hegel complained that we generally fail to learn from history.[87] For Hegel, however, such crimes and disasters – the terror of the French Revolution, for instance – contributed to the dialectical unfolding of freedom and consciousness through the "*cunning of reason*" that limited the detrimental effects of the "passions."[88] Nietzsche was of course unable to accept Hegel's optimism. His earlier encounter with the legacy of German idealism prevented him from translating human crime, violence, and weakness into a positive historical force.

While a monumental view of the past always culminates in a questionable foundation myth for the present that relies on a homogeneous and enchanted image of the past, the critical model stresses the heterogeneity and contingency of historical events that resist their idealization. While an antiquarian view of the past is centered on notions of authenticity and preservation that separate the past from the present, the critical model seeks to account for the long-term effects of contingent historical events. For Nietzsche, then, historical orientation could consist neither in a justification of the present, nor in a disinterested account of the past.

That the problem of historical orientation is Nietzsche's main concern becomes more obvious when we consider the way in which he formulates the effects of the past on present cultural conditions:

For since we are the outcome of earlier generations, we are also the outcome of their aberrations, passions and errors, and indeed of their crimes; it is not possible wholly to free oneself from this chain. If we condemn these aberrations and regard ourselves as free of them, this does not alter the fact that we originate in them. (*UM* II: 3)

In other words, if it really should be the case that contemporary political and cultural conditions are in any way shaped by the past, we need to accept that the present is, above all, haunted by the errors, illusions and even crimes of previous epochs. Although this might not be particularly surprising, it has profound implications for Nietzsche's historical vision and will continue to shape the general political perspective of his later genealogical project. As

---

[87] See Pierre Bayle, *Dictionnaire historique et critique*, in *Œuvres diverses* (The Hague: Husson, 1727–31), vol. IV, p. 740, and Hegel, *Lectures on the Philosophy of World History*, p. 21.
[88] See Hegel, *Lectures on the Philosophy of World History*, p. 89.

Nietzsche points out on more than one occasion, taken to its extreme such a critical examination of the past would lead to an ahistorical point of view, which would dissolve the relevance of historical knowledge altogether and present us with a disenchanting "settling of accounts" (*UM* II: 1). Radical historical critique is perhaps only possible at the end of history, but even the nineteenth century has survived any proclamations of such an end, Hegelian or otherwise.

It is interesting to note that Nietzsche, highlighting the inherently problematic nature of such a historical critique, introduces the term "world-tribunal [*Weltgericht*]" (*UM* II: 8), which is a direct reference to both Hegel's 1817 lectures at the University of Heidelberg and Friedrich Schiller's poem *Resignation*, composed in 1784. Surfacing in the second half of the eighteenth century, the idea that a philosophical view of history would amount to a "world-tribunal" is, of course, a secular version of theodicy. For Leibniz, writing at the beginning of the eighteenth century, theodicy as a metaphysical model vindicated the existence of evil as part of divine justice.[89] But once the Enlightenment, after the catastrophic earthquake of Lisbon in 1755, began to question the logic of this model, God, as an external authority, was slowly taken out of the metaphysical equation. In contrast to the idea of a balance provided by divine justice, human individuals thus had to carry responsibility for their own moral actions, as Kant vividly reminded his readers on more than one occasion.[90] This implied, however, that humanity as a whole had to be the judge of its own historical situation; always the result of preceding generations, humanity itself had to account for its past.[91] It is precisely in this sense that Schiller's remark "world-history is the world-tribunal [*die Weltgeschichte ist das Weltgericht*]" exemplifies the inevitable logic of the Enlightenment, and more than thirty years

---

[89] See Leibniz, *Essais de théodicée sur la bonté de Dieu, la liberté de l'homme et l'origine du mal*, in *Philosophische Schriften*, vol. VI, pp. 114–16.

[90] See, for instance, Kant, "An Answer to the Question: What is Enlightenment?" in *Political Writings*, pp. 54–60: 54. Thirty years earlier Kant was, however, more willing to accept the peculiar logic of Leibniz's theodicy. See *Principiorum primorum cognitionis metaphysicae nova dilucidatio*, in *Werkausgabe*, vol. I, pp. 467–8.

[91] On this model, see Odo Marquard, "Indicted and Unburdened Man in Eighteenth-Century Philosophy," in *Farewell to Matters of Principle: Philosophical Studies*, trans. Robert M. Wallace, Susan Bernstein, and James I. Porter (Oxford: Oxford University Press, 1989), pp. 38–63.

later Hegel was still able to reassert that the consciousness of a specific people (*Volksgeist*) was ultimately subject to such a world-tribunal.[92]

Although Nietzsche should have found this view attractive, the absoluteness of Schiller's and Hegel's "world-tribunal" proved difficult to accept. The notions of human responsibility and judgment, which Schiller and Hegel projected into the course of history, carried theological overtones that were hard to miss. At the same time, the transformation of history into a legal or forensic process can be seen as one of the actual origins of the crisis of modernity: projecting the moral law into history led to a disguised theological conception of the historical that concealed the fundamental uncertainty of history and, thus, of the political.[93] The moralization of history culminated in a moralization of the political that Nietzsche was unable to accept.

The close relationship between religious tropes and the political, and the idea of a "world-tribunal" itself, remained prominent throughout much of the nineteenth century, especially in the Protestant thought of the German Empire. Despite the rapid secularization of the public sphere the image of a world-tribunal emerged in this context as a utopian promise able to match the revolutionary gestures entertained among socialist thinkers.[94] Nietzsche's interest in this problem in 1874 is therefore not as untimely as might be assumed. At crucial moments of social crisis in Imperial Germany the rhetoric of Protestantism continued to cast the presumed end of the world in terms of a grand-scale legal tribunal, while the perceived acceleration of historical time that was often regarded as one of the main symptoms of crisis was part of both religious and political consciousness.

But it was already in Hegel that the historical unfolding of reason and freedom toward a world-tribunal began to repeat the

---

[92] See Friedrich Schiller, "Resignation: Eine Phantasie," in *Werke: Nationalausgabe*, vol. 1, ed. Julius Petersen and Friedrich Beißner (Weimar: Böhlau, 1943), p. 168 (line 95), and Hegel, *Heidelberger Enzyklopädie*, in *Werke*, vol. XII, p. 559. See also Hegel, *Philosophy of Mind*, p. 277 (§ 548), which incorrectly translates the German *Weltgericht* as "judgment of the world."

[93] See Koselleck, *Critique and Crisis*, pp. 9–10 and 127–86.

[94] As Lucian Hölscher, *Weltgericht oder Revolution: Protestantische und sozialistische Zukunftsvorstellungen im deutschen Kaiserreich* (Stuttgart: Klett-Cotta, 1989), p. 25, pointed out, the difference between a theological and a political fixation of the future is minimal.

model of theodicy. Only a few years after his seemingly passing remarks at the University of Heidelberg in 1817, he was to be more open in highlighting the continued relevance of theodicy within a secular world. The "cunning of reason," which governed history, turned out to be a theodicy in disguise: "world history," he noted in the final paragraph of his lectures on the philosophy of history, amounted to a "justification of God in history."[95] Hegel's "cunning of reason" compensates for the loss of God as an external authority, which was the result of Leibniz's and Kant's views on the problem of theodicy. Leibniz's God, as it were, had become part of the historical process itself, which therefore began to hold an even stronger utopian promise.[96] Hegel's position is far from isolated, since its inherently eschatological promise was mirrored by much wider social and political hopes during the nineteenth century: what has been called the "unfolding of collective imaginations of the future" became particularly intense around 1830.[97] Hegel might have been successful in dissolving Christian eschatology into the philosophy of history, but an eschatological understanding of time continued to shape the intellectual outlook of German Protestantism in the second half of the nineteenth century.[98]

For Nietzsche, such ideas can only be seen as presumptuous, as an attempt to adopt an objective view on historical processes that was bound to fail from the very beginning, but that nevertheless remained at the heart of the modern cultural condition. Any justification of God within history would also justify, as a metaphysical principle, the belief in political progress, ultimately vindicating not only the existence of evil, but – in an ironic turn – also the existence of the modern nation state. For Nietzsche, affirming the Hegelian idea of a historical "world process [*Weltprozess*]" meant accepting, without question, "any form of power," regardless as to whether the latter was represented by "the government," "public opinion," or the sheer "majority of numbers" within

---

[95] Hegel, *Lectures on the Philosophy of History*, in *Political Writings*, p. 224.
[96] See Odo Marquard, "Kompensation – Überlegungen zu einer Verlaufsfigur geschichtlicher Prozesse," in *Aesthetica und Anaesthetica: Philosophische Überlegungen* (Paderborn: Schöningh, 1989), pp. 64–81: 76.
[97] Lucian Hölscher, *Die Entdeckung der Zukunft* (Frankfurt/M.: Fischer Taschenbuch Verlag, 1999), p. 85.
[98] See Hölscher, *Weltgericht oder Revolution*, pp. 61, 74–6 and 135–40.

society (*UM* II: 8). As bizarre as this conclusion might sound, it is not entirely inaccurate. Hegel himself noted in his lectures on the philosophy of right: "The state in and for itself is the ethical whole ... The state consists in the march of God in the world."[99] Seen from the vanguard of Nietzsche's radical historical critique, the philosophy of history had turned the myth of God into the myth of the modern state.

It is important to realize at this moment that the very notion of the state itself had undergone a crucial transition in German political theory after the French Revolution. German and European theories of the state throughout the seventeenth and eighteenth centuries often saw the latter in terms of a machine as, for instance, in Thomas Hobbes's description of the institutions of the "commonwealth" as essentially mechanical parts and in Johann Heinrich Gottlob von Justi's treaty on good governance.[100] Early modern German state theory, *Kameralwissenschaft*, which sought to provide the necessary training for administrative governance, conceived of the parts of the state as a complex mechanical arrangement in the service of social discipline.[101] But by the early nineteenth century – driven by the need to define a German nation vis-à-vis French imperial ambitions and influenced by Romanticism – the state was understood to be a unified organization and an organic community.[102] The internal structures, institutions and social hierarchies of this community, as they were formulated most famously in the state theory of Adam Müller, were the product of a goal-directed historical process.[103] Even though Hegel himself was not entirely in agreement with this

---

[99] Hegel, *Elements of the Philosophy of Right*, p. 279 (§ 258).
[100] See Thomas Hobbes, *Leviathan, with Selected Variants from the Latin Edition of 1668*, ed. Edwin Curley (Indianapolis, Ind.: Hackett, 1994), pp. 146–59 (chs. xxii–xxiii), and Johann Heinrich Gottlob von Justi, *Der Grundriß einer guten Regierung in 5 Büchern verfasset* (Frankfurt/M.: Garbe, 1759). On the context of these metaphors and models, see Barbara Stollberg-Rilinger, *Der Staat als Maschine: Zur politischen Metaphorik des absoluten Fürstenstaates* (Berlin: Duncker & Humblot, 1986).
[101] For a concise English overview of the German tradition of *Kameralwissenschaft* from the Peace of Westphalia in 1648 to the early nineteenth century, see Lindenfeld, *The Practical Imagination*, pp. 11–45.
[102] See Ernst-Wolfgang Böckenförde, "Organ, Organismus, Organisation, politischer Körper (VII–IX)," in Brunner, Conze, and Koselleck (eds.), *Geschichtliche Grundbegriffe* (Stuttgart: Klett-Cotta, 1972–97), vol. IV, pp. 561–622: 561.
[103] See, for instance, Adam Heinrich Müller, *Die Elemente der Staatskunst: Sechsunddreißig Vorlesungen* (Berlin: Haude & Spener, 1968), pp. 27, 32–3 and 56.

more conservative position, his own account clearly presented the state as a living being:

> The state is the actuality of the ethical Idea – the ethical spirit as substantial will, *manifest* and clear to itself, which thinks and knows itself and implements what it knows in so far as it knows it. ... The political constitution is ... the organization of the state and the process of its organic life *with reference to itself*, in which it differentiates its moments within itself and develops them to *established existence* [*zum Bestehen*].[104]

For Hegel, the organic unity of the state was more than merely an ethical whole. His emphasis on the state's organic life was clearly linked to a historical understanding of the state as the product of a teleological development. For Nietzsche, this was the foundation for the principal idea that he ascribed to Hegel's political and historical thought, namely that of the state as an outcome of a self-determined *Weltprozess* which by and larged escaped human intervention. Writing more than forty years after Hegel's death, Nietzsche assumed that the modern nation state, above all Imperial Germany, was built on precisely such a mythical narrative.

Nietzsche was neither willing nor able to embrace the idea of a *Weltgericht* that would have stood at the end of such a *Weltprozess*. To be sure, in his second "Untimely Meditation" he increasingly regarded historical critique as a legal process, praising a form of historical understanding that seeks to judge the past. But at the same time, he was fully aware that judging the past would really require an objective point of view, a complete knowledge, as it were, of all the facts pertaining to a specific historical event as a legal case. A truly critical view of the past along the lines he seems to have had in mind is therefore an impossible undertaking. On the one hand, it seems to threaten, even to destroy, the very foundations of the present: "Historical justice, even when it is genuine and practised with the purest of intentions, is therefore a dreadful virtue because it always undermines the living thing and brings it down: its judgment is always annihilating" (*UM* II: 7). On the other hand, such a critical examination would also need to turn against itself:

> ... for the origin of historical culture – its quite radical conflict with the spirit of the "new age," and "modern awareness" – this origin *must* itself

[104] Hegel, *Elements of the Philosophy of Right*, pp. 275 (§ 257) and 304 (§ 271).

be known historically, history *must* itself resolve the problem of history, knowledge *must* turn its sting against itself – this threefold *must* is the imperative of the "new age," supposing this age really does contain anything new, powerful, original and promising more life. (*UM* II: 8)

Examining the very foundations of the present cultural mentalities, a critical view of the past would have to regard itself as being rooted in the same foundations: we are invited to judge the past, but in doing so we will have to judge ourselves and thus the way in which we judge the past. Historical orientation, then, is a constant process of revision and re-examination that continued to inform Nietzsche's project even after the "Untimely Meditations." If history, in other words, was supposed to be of any cultural relevance, and if historical knowledge was supposed to have any political value, it could not be sufficient to merely re-enact the past. Or, as Nietzsche himself remarked in his essay on Schopenhauer: "If occupation with the history of past or foreign nations is of any value, it is of most value to the philosopher who wants to arrive at a just verdict on the whole fate of man" (*UM* III: 3). Somewhat overestimating his own position during the mid-1870s, Nietzsche obviously wished to be precisely such a philosopher.

One of the reasons why philosophers and historians alike rightly view Nietzsche's second "Untimely Meditation" with some suspicion is that his argument is not wholly convincing. In a letter written in March 1874, even Erwin Rohde, who then was still one of Nietzsche's closest friends and allies, carped at the lack of logical coherence and complained about the exuberant metaphors of Nietzsche's prose (*KGB* II/4, p. 421). Completed in only a few months, while Nietzsche was forced to focus much of his attention on his teaching duties at the University of Basel and the local Pädagogium, his second "Untimely Meditation" indeed leaves the impression of a transitional work. But as a work of transition, it is his first step toward a more substantial historical critique, which he still found difficult to formulate. In his later writings, once the genealogical project was in full swing, Nietzsche came to realize more fully the value and power of historical critique: "*Historical refutation as the definitive refutation.* – In former times, one sought to prove that there is no God – today one indicates how the belief that there is a God could *arise* and how this belief acquired its weight and importance" (*D* 95). This passage from *Morgenröthe*, published in

1881, highlights that the themes he addressed in 1874 constituted a decisive turning point in his evolving views on the political dimension of history. They were the beginning of a much more ambitious reflection on the political conditions of modernity. Indeed, shortly after the publication of *Vom Nutzen und Nachtheil der Historie für das Leben*, Nietzsche began to outline a series of plans widening his "Untimely Meditations" in order to cover such diverse topics as "the philologist," "Wagner," "journalism," "religion," "the state," "education," "socialism," "nature," "art," and "liberation" (*KGW* IV/1, 1 [3] and [4]). Although he did not complete these ambitious plans, he returned to many of these themes during the 1880s.

Already a quick glance at his notebooks from early 1875 clearly shows that Nietzsche saw it necessary to address the cultural conditions of modernity from an increasingly historical perspective: "In order to explain the current conditions of culture one will have to look backward," which would lead to "the insight that we are the multiplication of many pasts" (*KGW* IV/1, 3 [67] and [69]). Nietzsche himself was very much aware of the heterogeneous nature of modernity, which rendered it possible to question traditional cultural and political authorities on the one hand, but provided no real alternatives on the other. In the end, the blending of "railway-lines, the telegraph, the steam engine, the stock market" promised "images" of innovation and modernity, which, however, merely followed the logic "of the moment, of opinions and of fashions [*des Moments, der Meinungen und der Moden*]" (*UM* I: 11 and III: 6).

Passages such as these, which are easily misunderstood as the usual *fin de siècle* cultural pessimism, in fact pose a more serious question to European modernity: mass democracies are invariably consumer societies, in which political culture is closely related to the consumption of goods, from newspaper articles to the luxury items exhibited at the new department stores.[105] Only those who

---

[105] At first sight, this might be more relevant to the situation in France and Britain, but retail consumption also undergoes dramatic changes in nineteenth-century Germany. See Uwe Spiekermann, "Display Windows and Window Displays in German Cities of the Nineteenth Century: Towards the History of a Commercial Breakthrough," in Clemens Wischermann and Elliot Shore (eds.), *Advertising and the European City: Historical Perspectives* (Aldershot: Ashgate, 2000), pp. 139–71, and David Hamlin, "Romanticism, Spectacle, and a Critique of Weimar Capitalism," *Central European History* 38 (2005), 250–68.

consume, and thus partake in the opinions and fashions of the day, participate in political culture, while those who are economically excluded from consumption have limited options for direct political participation. At the same time, political culture itself exhibits a tendency toward the symbolic, toward images and representations: the mass democracies of European modernity are inevitably societies of the spectacle, in which the circulation of values is bound up with the circulation of things.[106] Playing on the similarity between the German words *Mode* and *Moderne*, Nietzsche hints at modernity's inability to examine either its own cultural conditions or its historical roots. His stance against the promises of modernity is above all a call to investigate modernity itself.

This does not mean that Nietzsche wished to reject modernity altogether. Rather, he reminds us that we have not yet quite understood the "*premises of the machine-age*," as he noted much later in the second volume of *Menschliches, Allzumenschliches* (*HA* II: ii.278). By the mid-1870s, he was well aware that a return to art and aesthetics, as specific modes of philosophizing, would be unable to deliver any insight into the political and cultural conditions of modernity. This also allowed him to address the relationship between "science" and "life" in a way that was decidedly critical of precisely that kind of aestheticism which is often attributed to his reflections in *Vom Nutzen und Nachtheil der Historie für das Leben*: "People who do not have any *scientific* culture babble when they talk about serious and difficult things, and they do so with arrogance. ... Since knowledge about truths exists in general, and since it grants pleasure, we wish to hold its flag up high, albeit without a pathetic grimace" (*KGW* IV/2, 23 [17]). Nietzsche, it seems, has realized the actual value of scientific culture, without succumbing to positivism or materialism as a way out of the contemporary crisis of historical culture. Rather, science – that is, *Wissenschaft* as a coherent and value-neutral practice of examination that subscribes to a relentless realism – enables us to see beyond the pathos of the beliefs, opinions, and cultural commonplaces that characterize the moral communities of modernity (*KGW* IV/2, 23 [76]).

[106] See Guy Debord, *La Société du spectacle* (Paris: Gallimard, 1992), pp. 39–40 (§ 41), and Arjun Appadurai, "Introduction: Commodities and the Politics of Value", in Appadurai (ed.), *The Social Life of Things: Commodities in Cultural Perspective* (Cambridge: Cambridge University Press, 1986), pp. 3–63.

Nietzsche's emphasis on the critical value of science during the mid-1870s was a decisive step forward.[107] In contrast to many of his contemporaries – historians and philosophers alike – he was well aware, or at least willing to accept, that cultural orientation cannot be reached by falling back on unquestioned authorities: "The best we can do is to confront our inherited and hereditary nature with our knowledge, and through a new, stern discipline combat our inborn heritage and implant in ourselves a new habit, a new instinct, a second nature, so that our first nature withers away" (*UM* II: 3). Two years after the publication of his second "Untimely Meditation," he remarked that "philosophers" and "artists" have a tendency "to read badly," to "underestimate the difficulty to really understand what someone has said" (*KGW* IV/2, 23 [22]). Nietzsche, then, should be read neither as a metaphysician, nor as an artistic philosopher, even though his language and style often force us to do so. Indeed, lamenting the growing distance between philosophy and science, and complaining about philosophy's "lack of historical sense," he begins to demand in *Menschliches, Allzumenschliches* a "historical philosophizing" in order to understand the very "conditions of culture" (*HA* I: 2, 7 and 25), that is, the ways in which what we regard as our cultural environment is produced over long periods in time. Philosophical critique, if it wishes to address these conditions of culture, always implies a form of historical critique – as such, philosophical critique is also always a political enterprise.

---

[107] This has also been argued by Lanfranconi, *Nietzsches historische Philosophie*, pp. 74–85, 137–45, and 158–61.

CHAPTER 4

Political lessons from cultural anthropology

It is difficult to ignore that Nietzsche's growing interest in the conditions of European modernity stands very much at the center of his so-called "mature" philosophy. Of course, epistemological and metaphysical questions shape much of his thought throughout the 1880s, as they did during the 1870s. But Nietzsche's genealogy begins to gain momentum as a philosophical project that lays bare the fragile intellectual foundations of those cultural values – religious, ethical, and otherwise – that are seen as the grounding of modern society. In a certain sense, then, genealogy is a critical discourse about the political conditions of modernity that seeks to turn into practice what Nietzsche, in his second "Untimely Meditation," had described as a critical model of historical study. By the late 1870s, while he was working on the first volume of *Menschliches, Allzumenschliches* (1878), a form of historical critique began to take shape that was even more far-reaching than Nietzsche himself initially had envisioned. In this context, he had to come to terms with three general problems.[1] First of all, the increasing secularization of European society and culture did not at all destroy or undermine the authority of Christian values, as can be seen with regard to the foundations of morality and the nation state as a moral community. Second, while science was able to introduce new powerful explanatory models, it was not really able to show up the illusory status of traditional moral and political values. In contrast, the practitioners of the sciences largely subscribed to traditional values and institutions. But there is also a third and more serious question that Nietzsche needs to address: how do we actually come to such values and institutions in the first place?

---

[1] See David Owen, "Nietzsche, Re-evaluation and the Turn to Genealogy," *European Journal of Philosophy* 11 (2003), 249–72: 252–3.

Genealogy thus begins to emerge as an attempt to overcome the crisis of historical and political culture by examining how this culture had emerged in the first place. The genealogical project of the 1880s and Nietzsche's earlier historical thought are inextricably linked. The project of a genealogy of European modernity does not begin with *Morgenröthe*, published in 1881, and its promise of a revaluation of all values, as is often claimed. Rather, it starts out with Nietzsche's increasing awareness of the symbolic order of culture during the 1870s.[2] The strength of his genealogical project consists in the fact that he is able to focus on the complexity of the formation of political mentalities. It is in this respect necessary to situate the beginnings of Nietzsche's genealogy within a complex network of intellectual influences that include some of the most prominent human sciences of the nineteenth century: cultural anthropology and the study of language. This increasingly anthropological orientation of Nietzsche's thought has consequences for his understanding of the political, especially as far as the relationship between state and religion in nineteenth-century Germany was concerned.

THE VIEW FROM OUTSIDE

It requires little attention to realize that at the center of Nietzsche's genealogy lies what, in a different context, he described as a profound "critical and historical mistrust" (*BGE* 209). Such skepticism, however, also needs a specific historical and cultural perspective that distances the skeptic from his own environment: "if the concern with the history of past or foreign peoples should have any value," it is also necessary for the philosopher "to overcome the present" and to "measure the difference of his own time against others" (*UM* III: 3). While this seems to be in many ways the foundation of historical understanding, Nietzsche quickly begins to turn this insight into a political demand: historical philosophy needs to distance itself from the "political events" of the day (*UM* III: 3). To put it more sharply, the critical power of historical understanding consists in turning away from the political

---

[2] Looking at Nietzsche from the perspective of Marx and Georg Lukács, Warren, *Nietzsche and Political Thought*, pp. 61–6 and 103, has described this interest in the symbolic order of culture as an "ideology critique."

configurations of the present. But this does not mean that he wished to ignore the present. Rather, by distancing himself from the present, he believed, the political and intellectual configurations of the latter will become more readily understandable. The view from outside, as it were, lies at the heart of Nietzsche's historical critique of modernity.

In order to gain a new perspective on the contemporary state of European culture Nietzsche even toyed with the idea of a longer trip to Tunisia in 1881:

> Please ask my old friend Gersdorff whether he would feel like joining me for a sojourn in Tunis for one or two years. Climate excellent, not too hot – voyage from Livorno via Cagliari very short, life there cheap. I want to live for a while among Muslims, especially at the place where their belief is strongest at the moment: this will sharpen my judgment and vision for all things European. (*KGB* III/1, p. 68)[3]

This letter to Heinrich Köselitz, written on March 13, 1881, in Genoa, clearly shows that the trip to Tunis was intended to be more than just a change of scenery. Subject to the expansionist tensions between France and the Ottoman Empire, Tunisia itself represents a highly symbolic location that exemplifies precisely those political concerns the professional historians of the German Empire, most notably Heinrich von Treitschke in his *Preußische Jahrbücher*, increasingly saw as connecting the study of the past to the strategic interests of Germany. Although Tunisia itself stood hardly at the center, for instance, of Treitschke's historical vision, it is interesting to see that, by the mid-1870s, his political perspective had widened substantially from Prussia's German vocation to the diplomatic and colonial interests of Imperial Germany.[4] Like this shift in Treitschke's geographical perspective, Nietzsche's interest in Tunisia – as short-lived as the latter undoubtedly remained – in many ways reflected the growing enthusiasm for colonial policy among the German public. While such colonial

---

[3] See Stephan Günzel, "Nietzsche's Geophilosophy," *Journal of Nietzsche Studies* 25 (2003), 78–91: 84–5.

[4] Compare, for instance, the "Prussian" direction of Treitschke's earlier essays collected in *Historische und politische Aufsätze, vornehmlich zur neuesten deutsche Geschichte* (Leipzig: Hirzel, 1865), with his articles "Deutschland und die orientalische Frage," *Preußische Jahrbücher* 38 (1876), 664–75, and "Die ersten Versuche deutscher Kolonialpolitik," *Preußische Jahrbücher* 54 (1884), 555–66. Once the "German question" was solved by the outcome of the Franco-Prussian War of 1870/71, Imperial Germany was able to pursue more global political ambitions.

ambitions were only a secondary concern for Bismarck, whose foreign policy mainly focused on Germany's strategic location in relation to Russia, France, and Britain, growing economic difficulties in the late 1870s and early 1880s had fueled the idea among bankers, industrialists and the wider public that colonial expansion would serve internal economic stabilization and thus prevent social conflict. The formation of the Deutscher Kolonialverein in 1882 was a direct result of these developments, and in 1884–85, in the context of the Berlin West Africa Conference, Bismarck himself played with the idea of a greater German political engagement outside Europe, even though French and British competition made the success of such adventures unlikely.[5] Nietzsche's own remarks about Tunisia indeed mirror these developments, and it is also in this respect that his dream of traveling to Tunisia reflects back on the identity of the German nation state within the political geography of Europe.

Tunisia, however, was a special case. Although it had been able to inaugurate, in 1861, the first political constitution in the Arab world, only a few years later the new state was bankrupt, and the Congress of Berlin in the summer of 1878, which sought to stabilize the precarious balance of power between the European nation states, opened the way for French intervention. By 1881, Tunisia was a French protectorate. Occupied by French troops and under French administration, Tunisia seems to have represented for Nietzsche a kind of liminal cultural space that was both within and outside Europe – an ideal place, in other words, to observe the intellectual and political upheavals of European culture without completely having to leave Europe behind. In other words, he sought to reverse the ethnographic perspective on the non-European "other" by conceiving of Europe itself as the "other." While concerns for his health, together with a desire for less provincial and more spectacular sceneries, were the main reason for Nietzsche's travels to the South of France and to Italy, a voyage to Tunisia, which is about 500 miles from Livorno across the Mediterranean, would have been a more political move. Nietzsche certainly did not lack the necessary financial funds for

---

[5] See Konrad Canis, *Bismarcks Außenpolitik, 1870 bis 1890: Aufstieg und Gefährdung* (Paderborn: Schöningh, 2004), pp. 209–29, and Martti Koskenniemi, *The Gentle Civilizer of Nations: The Rise and Fall of International Law, 1870–1960* (Cambridge: Cambridge University Press, 2002), pp. 123–7.

such a voyage. But given the French military intervention in Tunisia, he had to accept one month after his initial letter to Heinrich Köselitz that such a trip might prove to be too dangerous (*KGB* III/1, p. 83).

Although this trip never materialized, the view from outside that Tunisia seems to have promised entailed an ambitious cultural perspective. Furthermore, Nietzsche became increasingly interested in contemporary ethnographic studies and popular anthropological literature. In July 1881, his friend Overbeck sent Friedrich von Hellwald's *Die Erde und ihre Völker* (1877–78) from the university library in Basel to the Swiss village of Sils Maria, where Nietzsche whiled away the summer (*KGB* III/1, pp. 101 and 110).[6] Five years later, Nietzsche also discovered Friedrich Ratzel's *Anthropo-Geographie* (1882) in a bookstore in Munich (*KGB* III/3, p. 204).[7] Although Nietzsche did not have much that was positive to say about Hellwald, and although he barely mentioned Ratzel, his interest in these authors is a clear indication of a widening cultural perspective that also filtered through into his philosophical criticism. This becomes particularly obvious in the fifth volume of *Die fröhliche Wissenschaft* when Nietzsche demanded more openly an anthropological perspective on European modernity that could only be achieved by adopting a position of detachment:

> In order to see our European morality for once as it looks from a distance, and to measure it up against other past or future moralities, one has to proceed like a wanderer who wants to know how high the towers in a town are: he *leaves* the town. ... One must have liberated oneself from many things that oppress, inhibit, hold down, and make heavy precisely us Europeans today. (*GS* 380)

This, we shall see, is in many ways one of the most important foundations of the genealogical project: the quasi-anthropological investigation of European political mentalities.

Viewed against the disciplinary configurations of anthropological thought in the late nineteenth century, Nietzsche's anthropological turn should not be surprising. His reception of anthropological thought gained momentum in the second half of the 1870s,

---

[6] See Friedrich von Hellwald, *Die Erde und ihre Völker: Ein geographisches Hausbuch* (Stuttgart: Spemann, 1877–78).
[7] See Friedrich Ratzel, *Anthropo-Geographie: Grundzüge der Anwendung der Erdkunde auf die Geschichte* (Stuttgart: Engelhorn, 1882).

while he was working on his "Untimely Meditations" and his final philological lecture series, "Geschichte der griechischen Litteratur" (1874-75) and "Der Gottesdienst der Griechen" (1875-78). Already aware of some of the central themes of contemporary anthropology through his work in classical philology, but also through his encounters with Johann Jakob Bachofen and Jacob Burckhardt, Nietzsche began to concern himself with an aspect of the human sciences that seemed to bridge the gap between the traditional humanities, on the one hand, and the natural sciences, on the other.[8]

Without doubt, the institutional career of anthropology in Germany, dating back to the late eighteenth century, is remarkable. After Johann Polycarp Müller had delivered the first lecture on "anthropology" properly speaking at the University of Leipzig in 1719, anthropological thought quickly became one of the central concerns of Enlightenment philosophy in both France and Germany. Once Ernst Platner had published his ground-breaking *Neue Anthropologie für Ärzte und Weltweise* (1791), the study of cultural history could not ignore the more fundamental question of what it means to be human, even though this question could be addressed from different directions as can be shown with regard to the tense relationship between Kant and his former pupil Johann Gottfried Herder.[9] Although Herder's understanding of anthropology was more historical in orientation, thus providing a better model for taking into account the heterogeneity of cultural experience, Kant's definition of anthropology as the "doctrine of knowledge of the human being, systematically formulated," continued to set the standard deep into the nineteenth century.[10] But one of the main effects of nineteenth-century intellectual and scientific culture was that the notion of "human being" itself underwent decisive changes mainly due to the growing influence of biological thought. Nietzsche thus turned Kant's definition into

---

[8] Orsucci, *Orient – Okzident*, pp. 8–52 and 58–140, has traced in much detail the influence of contemporary anthropological research in Nietzsche's writings. The assumption that Nietzsche employed anthropological ideas in order to re-mythologize modernity, as it can be found in Williamson, *The Longing for Myth in Germany*, pp. 258–66, and Pfotenhauer, *Die Kunst als Physiologie*, pp. 15–56, is simply wrong.
[9] See John H. Zammito, *Kant, Herder, and the Birth of Anthropology* (Chicago: University of Chicago Press, 2002), pp. 137–54 and 347–8.
[10] See Immanuel Kant, *Anthropology from a Pragmatic Point of View*, ed. and trans. Robert B. Louden, intro. Manfred Kuehn (Cambridge: Cambridge University Press, 2006), p. 3.

a skeptical question: "How can man know himself?" (*UM* III: 1). This was not an isolated remark. By mid-1885, Nietzsche still toyed with the idea of a book, or longer essay, entitled "*The Problem of the 'Human Individual'* [*Das Problem 'Mensch'*]" (*KGW* VII/3, 34 [240]). Only a few years later, the opening sentence of *Zur Genealogie der Moral* highlights that this indeed remained a central concern: "We are unknown to ourselves, we knowers, we ourselves, to ourselves, and there is a good reason for this" (*GM* preface, 1). Needless to say, we might not be entirely comfortable with what we might find out.

Despite its enormous intellectual success German anthropology remained without an institutional home until the middle of the nineteenth century. But the close link between historical linguistics, itself still part of a much wider philological discourse, and psychology, a relatively new discipline which had separated itself from philosophy at the beginning of the nineteenth century, slowly began to establish anthropology in Germany as a discipline that was based on comparative methods. Against this background, the close relationship between classical scholarship and anthropological thought, which becomes manifest not only in Nietzsche's writings, but constituted an important intellectual trend throughout nineteenth-century Europe, was centered on the study of language and culture.[11] In 1860, the *Zeitschrift für Völkerpsychologie und Sprachwissenschaft* established itself as one of the leading journals in the field, and in 1861 German anthropologists held their first conference in Göttingen. The work of Moritz Lazarus on "ethno-psychology," continued by Wilhelm Wundt, was of particular prominence in this context, while Heymann Steinthal – together with Lazarus, editor of the *Zeitschrift für Völkerpsychologie und Sprachwissenschaft* – sought to continue Wilhelm von Humboldt's ideas on the close relationship between language and culture within this new theoretical framework.[12]

---

[11] See James Whitman, "From Philology to Anthropology in Mid-Nineteenth-Century Germany," in George W. Stocking, Jr. (ed.), *Functionalism Historicized: Essays on British Social Anthropology* (Madison, Wisc.: University of Wisconsin Press, 1984), pp. 214–29.

[12] See Moritz Lazarus, "Über den Begriff und die Möglichkeit einer Völkerpsychologie" and "Einige synthetische Gedanken zur Völkerpsychologie," both in *Grundzüge der Völkerpsychologie und Kulturwissenschaft*, ed. Klaus Christian Köhnke (Hamburg: Felix Meiner, 2003), pp. 3–25 and 131–238, respectively, and Wilhelm Wundt, "Ueber Ziele und Wege der Völkerpsychologie," *Philosophische Studien* 4 (1888), 1–27.

Steinthal's anthropological perspective clearly sought to transgress traditional disciplinary boundaries. In 1863 he reminded the annual conference of classical philologists, which was meeting in the German town of Meißen, that philological, historical, and psychological approaches to the study of human culture did not necessarily exclude each other.[13] At this time, Steinthal had already left philology behind, however, in favor of linguistics and psychology, proposing complex systems of comparative classification.[14] The taxonomy of language was increasingly seen as mapping the symbolic order of culture, but Steinthal, who is now perhaps unjustly overshadowed by the towering figure of Wilhelm Wundt, did not leave eighteenth-century ideas behind. The questions posed by Kant, Herder and others remained at the heart of much nineteenth-century German anthropology.

LESSONS FROM ANTHROPOLOGY

Nietzsche was clearly aware of contemporary debates in anthropology. In preparation for his lectures on Latin grammar at the University of Basel in the winter semester of 1869/70, he turned to two seminal publications that neatly summarized the contemporary state of knowledge: Theodor Benfey's overview *Geschichte der Sprachwissenschaft und orientalischen Philologie in Deutschland* (1869), published by the Historical Commission of the Royal Bavarian Academy of Science, and the German translation of Friedrich Max Müller's *Lectures on the Science of Language* (1862–64), first delivered at the Royal Institute of Great Britain.[15] For both Benfey and Müller, the complex relationship between language and culture was at the very center of the human sciences. Schooled as a classical philologist, and familiar with the central questions in the philosophy of language through Gustav Gerber's *Die Sprache als Kunst* (1871–73), it

---

[13] See Heymann Steinthal, *Philologie, Geschichte und Psychologie in ihren gegenseitigen Beziehungen: Ein Vortrag gehalten in der Versammlung der Philologen zu Meissen 1863 in erweiterter Überarbeitung* (Berlin: Dümmler, 1864).

[14] See Heymann Steinthal, *Die Classification der Sprachen dargestellt als die Entwicklung der Sprachidee* (Berlin: Dümmler, 1850), and *Grammatik, Logik und Psychologie: Ihre Principien und ihr Verhältniss zu einander* (Berlin: Dümmler, 1855).

[15] See Theodor Benfey, *Geschichte der Sprachwissenschaft und der orientalischen Philologie in Deutschland seit dem Anfange des 19. Jahrhunderts mit einem Rückblick auf frühere Zeiten* (Munich: Cotta, 1869), and Friedrich Max Müller, *Vorlesungen über die Wissenschaft der Sprache*, trans. Carl Böttger (Leipzig: Mayer, 1863–66).

was only natural for Nietzsche's interests to follow a similar route.[16] Indeed, the first lesson he drew from contemporary anthropological thought was the need to examine cultural mentalities through language. In fact, the study of language allowed Nietzsche a more successful access to the, as it were, natural history of cultural mentalities and, therefore, the political conditions of modern culture.

Already with regard to his lectures on Latin grammar, delivered at the University of Basel in the winter of 1869, it is obvious that a reflection on the relationship among language, knowledge, and culture lies at the heart of his historical vision. Nietzsche's introductory course is preceded by two general sections that are concerned with more theoretical topics, such as the debates about the origin of language and the general perspective of contemporary comparative linguistics. Within this context, he presented his students with a longer passage from Friedrich Wilhelm Joseph Schelling, which he found in Eduard von Hartmann's *Philosophie des Unbewussten* (1869): "without language we would be unable to conceive not only of a philosophical consciousness [*philosophisches Bewußtseyn*] but of human consciousness [*menschliches Bewußtseyn*] in general" (*KGW* II/2, p. 188).[17] Nietzsche's emphasis is very much on the idea that the development of human consciousness, and ultimately of human culture, cannot be separated from the development of language.

Nietzsche's reflections on this issue are supported by his reception of contemporary trends in the new linguistic sciences as he was able to find them in Benfey's seminal overview: the work of Friedrich Schlegel, Franz Bopp, Jacob Grimm, and Wilhelm von Humboldt, he noted, forces us to consider the relationship between different languages and to adopt a more historical perspective that ideally should be able to trace back the development of linguistic forms (*KGW* II/2, pp. 189 and 191). Different cultures speak and write differently, so that language reflects the historical as well as cultural development of a particular society or historical period – a general lesson Nietzsche seems to have

---

[16] Nietzsche mainly focuses on the first volume: Gustav Gerber, *Die Sprache als Kunst*, vol. 1 (Bromberg: Mittler, 1871). For a contextual assessment of Nietzsche's early reflections on language, see Emden, *Nietzsche on Language, Consciousness, and the Body*, pp. 9–60.

[17] Friedrich Wilhelm Joseph Schelling, *Einleitung in die Philosophie der Mythologie*, in *Sämmtliche Werke*, ed. Karl Friedrich August Schelling (Stuttgart: Cotta, 1856–61), vol. XI, p. 52. The quote can be found in Hartmann, *Philosophie des Unbewussten*, p. 227.

learned especially from Humboldt. Although there are only a very limited number of references to Humboldt in Nietzsche's writings, and although his knowledge of Humboldt's achievements in the field of comparative linguistics comes mainly through the work of Benfey, Nietzsche does indeed turn to Humboldt's extremely influential study *Ueber die Verschiedenheit des menschlichen Sprachbaues und ihren Einfluss auf die geistige Entwickelung des Menschengeschlechts* (1830–35).[18] For Humboldt, language needed to be regarded as embedded within a social and cultural context that ultimately reflected the cultural identity and consciousness of a particular epoch.[19] This made Nietzsche assume, much like Humboldt, that different linguistic frameworks provide different world-views: "the difference in character between peoples [*Charakterverschiedenheit der Völker*]" is predominantly a result of their "linguistic difference" (*KGW* II/2, p. 192). The history of cultural mentalities needed to be seen as running parallel to the history of language.

Of course, Nietzsche's emphasis on the interdependence of language and culture was not an isolated development in nineteenth-century classical scholarship. Friedrich August Wolf's programmatic lectures at the University of Halle already devoted much space to contemporary linguistic thought.[20] Following Wolf, and often adhering to the general direction of Humboldt's reflections on language and culture, German classical scholarship in the nineteenth century thus understood "philology" not predominantly as the study of ancient languages and linguistic documents, but as often focused on wider cultural and political developments.[21] The mentality of the ancient Greeks was not only mirrored in their linguistic documents – from lyric poetry and drama to philosophical dialogues and political treatises – but the Greek language itself needed to be regarded as the highest

---

[18] Benfey, *Geschichte der Sprachwissenschaft*, pp. 357–92 and 427–556, is also responsible for Nietzsche's knowledge of Bopp, Schlegel, and other nineteenth-century linguists.

[19] See Wilhelm von Humboldt, *The Diversity of Human Language Structure and Its Influence on the Mental Development of Mankind*, in *On Language*, trans. Peter Hearth, intro. Hans Aarsleff (Cambridge: Cambridge University Press, 1988), pp. 37–45.

[20] See Wolf's *Darstellung der Alterthumswissenschaft*, pp. 49–56, and *Vorlesungen über die Alterthumswissenschaft*, vol. 1, pp. 47–72.

[21] See, for instance, Boeckh, *Encyklopädie*, pp. 763–72; Gottfried Bernhardy, *Grundriss der Griechischen Litteratur mit einem vergleichenden Ueberblick der Römischen*, new edn. (Halle: Anton, 1861–72), vol. 1, pp. 20–37; Karl Otfried Müller, *Geschichte der griechischen Literatur bis auf das Zeitalter Alexanders*, ed. Eduard Müller (Breslau: Max & Co., 1841), vol. 1, pp. 4–17.

concentration of the Greek "mind."[22] As a result, Nietzsche was able to remark in one of his early notebooks that "the fixed point around which the Greek people crystallize themselves is their language" (*KGW* III/4, 19 [278]).

Nietzsche's interest in the relationship between linguistic development and cultural processes renders obvious his awareness of contemporary anthropological practice. Consider, for example, his description of this relationship within the oral cultures of Central Africa and elsewhere. Noting that the "prodigious process" of language development does not reach an end, he continued:

> among the wild and raw tribal societies of Siberia, Africa and Siam, two or three generations are sufficient to completely change their dialects. Missionaries in Central Africa have attempted to note down the language of primitive tribes and collected all expressions. Returning after ten years they found this dictionary obsolete and useless. (*KGW* II/4, p. 441)

The difficulties a truly ethnographic study of language and culture encounters are of staggering complexity.

Nietzsche's interest in contemporary anthropological thought was very much a product of his intellectual environment. In fact, the development of his interests in this area mirrors the rapid institutionalization of anthropology in the nineteenth century. In Germany this was achieved, on the one hand, through a series of academic journals founded in quick succession, such as the *Archiv für Anthropologie* (1866) and the *Zeitschrift für Ethnologie* (1869), and on the other, through a growing network of scholars from a variety of backgrounds that in 1870 formed the Deutsche Gesellschaft für Anthropologie, Ethnologie und Urgeschichte.[23] In 1869, at the Versammlung Deutscher Ärzte und Naturforscher in the Austrian city of Innsbruck, which was opened by Hermann von Helmholtz with a nationalist keynote address linking the success of German science to the idea of the German nation, the liberal physician Rudolf Virchow directed the first section on anthropology and ethnology.[24] This was a particularly important development, since the Gesellschaft Deutscher Naturforscher und

---

[22] See August Gräfenhan, *Geschichte der klassischen Philologie im Alterthum* (Bonn: König, 1843–50), vol. I, pp. 27 and 31.

[23] As Orsucci, *Orient – Okzident*, pp. 36–8, observed, Nietzsche was very much aware of the rapid development of anthropological thought in Germany.

[24] See Hermann von Helmholtz, "Ueber das Ziel und die Fortschritte der Naturwissenschaft: Eröffnungsrede für die Naturforscherversammlung zu Innsbruck, 1869," in *Vorträge und*

Ärzte, which organized these meetings every year in a different German or Austrian city, was a national forum that transported science into the public realm. The sheer size of these annual conferences should not be underestimated and renders obvious their direct influence on the establishment of scientific paradigms and institutional organization in Germany: in 1869, when Virchow directed the first section on anthropology, 979 scientists attended – by 1913, at the annual meeting in Vienna, that number had increased to 5,180.[25]

Considering the institutional formation of German anthropology, it is difficult to overlook that some of the most prominent natural scientists, including Helmholtz's competitor Emil DuBois-Reymond, took an active role in the promotion of anthropological thought. In the relatively short period between the 1870s and 1880s, the capital of Imperial Germany, Berlin, became the focal point for ethnographic and anthropological research. During the 1870s, Adolf Bastian – a former student of Virchow and probably the most important geographer of the time, who was also rather critical of Germany's colonial desires – began to offer the first proper academic seminars on "ethnology" at the University of Berlin. Of course, for Bastian, anthropology needed to be regarded as a "science of culture" that was to follow clear nomothetical models of explanation, which stood in some contrast to the historicism that marked the contemporary humanities. This understanding of anthropology operated, however, with a relatively fluid notion of "culture" that was dependent on the interaction between individual psychological experiences and material circumstances, and that was furthermore subject to fundamental historical transitions. Such transitions, Bastian argued, could be observed with regard to so-called "elementary ideas," which he believed to structure cultural processes on a mostly unconscious level: "Throughout the entire world, throughout all of the five continents, we can find the same homogeneous layer of identical elementary ideas ... underneath slight modifications on the surface (local variations,

---

Reden, 4th edn. (Braunschweig: Vieweg, 1896), vol. I, pp. 367–98: 397–8, and Smith, *Politics and the Sciences of Culture*, pp. 100–1.

[25] See Andreas W. Daum, *Wissenschaftspopularisierung im 19. Jahrhundert: Bürgerliche Kultur, naturwissenschaftliche Bildung und die deutsche Öffentlichkeit, 1848–1914* (Munich: Oldenbourg, 1998), pp. 119–37.

etc.)."²⁶ The "social body of the zoopolitical individual" is shaped by these elementary ideas, which remain present, for instance, in modern folklore.²⁷ Although Bastian remains notoriously vague about the nature of such elementary ideas, it became increasingly obvious to him that the latter could not be restricted to so-called primitive and archaic societies, but they might also serve as an explanatory model within a history of modern social mentalities and as such they would also be of direct political relevance.²⁸ Nietzsche's own genealogical project will develop along similar lines.

German anthropological thought did not develop in splendid intellectual isolation. Although there are fundamental differences between British and German anthropology – in the sense that the former was more evolutionary and the latter more historicist in orientation – the second half of the nineteenth century is marked by a close interaction between them. The first volume of Theodor Waitz's *Anthropologie der Naturvölker* (1859–77) was soon translated into English on behalf of the Anthropological Society of London and began to wield a considerable influence on the work of British anthropologists such as Edward Burnett Tylor and John Lubbock, whose own work on "primitive cultures" during the 1860s and 1870s was quickly translated into German and fed back into the anthropological debates in Berlin and elsewhere.²⁹

At the same time, nineteenth-century anthropological thought in general should not at all be reduced – neither in the British, nor in the German context – to the racial doctrines of nineteenth-century physical anthropology, which represented a specific discourse within contemporary anthropology.³⁰ Although writings such as Gobineau's infamous *Essai sur l'inégalité des races* (1853–55)

---

[26] Adolf Bastian, *Die Völkerkunde und der Völkerverkehr unter seiner Rückwirkung auf die Volksgeschichte: Ein Beitrag zur Volks- und Menschenkunde* (Berlin: Weidmann, 1900), pp. 12–13. See also Bastian's *Controversen in der Ethnologie: I, Die geographischen Provinzen in ihren culturges-chichtlichen Berührungspunkten* (Berlin: Weidmann, 1893), pp. 53–74.

[27] Bastian, *Die Völkerkunde und der Völkerverkehr*, pp. 12 and 14.

[28] See Adolf Bastian, *Wie das Volk denkt: Ein Beitrag zur Beantwortung socialer Fragen auf Grundlage ethnischer Elementargedanken in der Lehre vom Menschen* (Berlin: Felber, 1892).

[29] See Theodor Waitz, *Introduction to Anthropology*, edited with numerous additions by the author, from the first volume of "Anthropologie der Natur-völker," ed. and trans. J. Frederick Collingwood (London: Longman, Green, Longman, and Roberts, 1863).

[30] See, for instance, Rudolf Virchow's rejection of racial classification as a tool for the study of cultural difference, "Rassenbildung und Erblichkeit," in *Festschrift für Adolf Bastian zu seinem 70. Geburtstage: 26. Juni 1896, gewidmet von seinen Freunden und Vereherrn* (Berlin: Reimer, 1896), pp. 1–43.

have exerted a lasting influence on the political imagination of nineteenth-century Europe, some of the most prominent German anthropologists – notably Bastian and Virchow – had little patience for the idea that racial classification, especially on biological grounds, could serve as a particularly useful tool for the study of culture. While racist interpretations of culture were undoubtedly a prominent factor within the anthropological and archaeological thought of the nineteenth century, they gained momentum as a quasi-scientific "fact" only toward the very end of the century.[31] The racist doctrines of nineteenth-century anthropology and archaeology started out as unsophisticated prejudices that could easily be refuted, but by the end of the century they had become intellectualized to such an extent that even liberal-minded anthropologists and archaeologists began to subscribe to them.

Against this background, Nietzsche is, once again, a difficult case. Certainly, references to the racial doctrines that permeate nineteenth-century intellectual history can be found, with little difficulty, throughout his writings. As a child of his time it is not surprising that Nietzsche should often employ cultural tropes that, seen from our own perspective, are more than uncomfortable. Indeed, the racial tropes, including the metaphors of cultural and physical "degeneration," that he presented in many of his writings paint a highly ambivalent picture.[32] It is shortsighted, however, to reduce Nietzsche's own interests in contemporary anthropological thought to the racial doctrines of his time. Of course, most European anthropologists subscribed to the view that European civilization was superior to what they regarded as "primitive cultures," and the colonial interests of the later nineteenth century supported this belief. In a certain sense, however, anthropological thought also undermined these visions of cultural dominance, since modern culture was itself still influenced by the residues of archaic mythical thought. For Nietzsche this proved to be an attractive idea that was to guide his genealogical investigation of the symbolic order of European modernity.

---

[31] On the stages of this development, see Bruce G. Trigger, *A History of Archaeological Thought* (Cambridge: Cambridge University Press, 1989), pp. 111–14 and 163–7.

[32] See Hubert Cancik, "'Mongols, Semites and Pure-Bred Greeks:' Nietzsche's Handling of the Racial Doctrines of his Time," in Jacob Golomb (ed.), *Nietzsche and Jewish Culture* (London: Routledge, 1997), pp. 55–75. For a more rigorous analysis, see Moore, *Nietzsche, Biology, and Metaphor*, pp. 115–92.

The cultural anthropology presented in the writings of John Lubbock and Edward Burnett Tylor did indeed provide part of the intellectual framework within which, for instance, Nietzsche's views on the emergence of religion operate. Already familiar with much contemporary German anthropology, and triggered by a keen interest in evolutionary theories, Nietzsche purchased the German translation of John Lubbock's *The Origin of Civilization* (1870) in July 1875 and, around the same time, borrowed Tylor's *Primitive Culture* (1871–73) from the university library in Basel.[33] This direction of Nietzsche's thought is furthermore supported by his preparations for the lecture course "Der Gottesdienst der Griechen," which refers to a substantial amount of anthropological literature that he borrowed from Basel's university library in the second half of 1875. This included some of the most important comparative studies of Greek, Roman, and Germanic mythology, which operated at the intersection of anthropology and archaeology and which began to break new ground in the second half of the nineteenth century.[34] To name only a few examples: Heinrich Nissen's *Das Templum* (1869) sought to reinterpret the architectural order of ancient temples and their mythological function as a spatial representation of the symbolic order of culture, while in his *Der deutsche Volksaberglaube der Gegenwart*, first published in 1860, the Protestant theologian Adolf Wuttke, who was teaching at the University of Halle, presented one of the most detailed accounts of superstition and its continued influence on popular belief in modern times.[35] While Wuttke thus provided much food for thought with regard to the survival of mythological ideas in an increasingly secularized society, Nietzsche was also fully aware of the empirical foundations for such anthropological

---

[33] See John Lubbock, *Die Entstehung der Civilisation und der Urzustand des Menschengeschlechtes, erläutert durch das innere und äußere Leben der Wilden*, trans. A. Passow (Jena: Costenable, 1875), and Edward Burnett Tylor, *Die Anfänge der Cultur: Untersuchungen über die Entwicklung der Mythologie, Philosophie, Religion, Kunst und Sitte*, trans. Johann Wilhelm Spengel and Friedrich Poske (Leipzig: Winter, 1873). Lubbock's influence has been discussed by David S. Thatcher, "Nietzsche's Debt to Lubbock," *Journal of the History of Ideas* 44 (1983), 293–309, and Orsucci, *Orient – Okzident*, pp. 33–5.

[34] See, for instance, Karl Müllenhoff, *Deutsche Altertumskunde*, vol. 1 (Berlin: Weidmann, 1870), and Carl Bötticher, *Der Baumkultus der Hellenen, nach den gottesdienstlichen Gebräuchen und den überlieferten Bildwerken dargestellt* (Berlin: Weidmann, 1856).

[35] See Heinrich Nissen, *Das Templum: Antiquarische Untersuchungen, mit astronomischen Hülfstafeln von B. Thiele* (Berlin: Weidmann, 1869), and Adolf Wuttke, *Der deutsche Volksaberglaube der Gegenwart*, 2nd edn., rev. (Berlin: Wiegand & Grieben, 1869).

research. By the middle of the nineteenth century, and not completely free from political overtones, the empirical collection of data relating to Germanic customs and folklore had gained enormous prominence. Nietzsche encountered this approach in Wilhelm Mannhardt's study *Der Baumkultus der Germanen und ihrer Nachbarstämme* (1875): focusing on agrarian myths and religious cults, Mannhardt's work was based not only on a collection of primary sources, but also on questionnaires, which Mannhardt, at the time a librarian in Gdansk, distributed across Germany in order to gain first-hand information, for instance, on ancient harvest rituals.[36]

But Nietzsche was also aware of recent developments in Britain. While holidaying in Rosenlauibad in Switzerland in 1877, he met the London-based philosopher George Croom Robertson, editor of the newly founded journal *Mind*. Nietzsche praised the latter's attempt to reconcile philosophy and the life sciences by persuading Charles Darwin, Herbert Spencer and Edward Burnett Tylor to contribute to his journal. The fact that Nietzsche mentioned Robertson in three different letters to Paul Rée, Malwida von Meysenburg, and his sister Elisabeth suggests that the encounter with Robertson must have been quite stimulating – if only for Nietzsche (*KGB* II/5, pp. 266, 268 and 270). It is quite ironic that Robertson himself spent his time in Rosenlauibad translating an article by Wilhelm Wundt on "Philosophy in Germany," which was to appear several months later in the second volume of *Mind*. In this article Nietzsche's philosophy was portrayed as a bizarre combination of Schopenhauerian pessimism and religious mysticism on the verge of plain nonsense and therefore, Wundt argued, it was in many ways representative of the lack of sophistication among non-academic philosophers in Germany.[37]

As a consequence of Wundt's article, the philosophical establishment in Britain began to view Nietzsche with much suspicion. Nietzsche himself was, however, far more appreciative of recent trends in British philosophy that, as can be observed in the first volumes of *Mind*, were marked by the attempt to bridge the gap between philosophy and the sciences. It is clear that some of this

---

[36] See Wilhelm Mannhardt, *Wald- und Feldkulte, I: Der Baumkultus der Germanen und ihrer Nachbarstämme. Mythologische Untersuchungen* (Berlin: Borntraeger, 1875).
[37] See Wilhelm Wundt, "Philosophy in Germany," *Mind* 2 (1877), 493–518: 509.

reading furthered his own interest in anthropological thought throughout the 1880s. We can be quite certain that, judging from his personal library and his correspondence, his reading in this field was not limited to Lubbock and Tylor. He never shied away from plundering any text for ideas that might come in handy later on, and many of his notebooks are filled with obscure references that are often difficult to decipher.[38] But the comparative methods that lie at the heart of much nineteenth-century anthropology, linguistics and psychology turn out to be a prominent feature of Nietzsche's own genealogical approach, which he increasingly described as the "collection of an enormous amount of empirical material relating to human knowledge" (*KGW* IV/1, 8 [4]). From this point of view, the nineteenth century – the age of train journeys, telegraphic communication, eyewitness journalism, public museums, and historical scholarship – seemed the ideal intellectual environment for such an undertaking: "The advantage of our culture is the *capacity to compare* [*Vergleichung*]. We gather the most diverse products of earlier cultures and measure them; to do *this* well, this is our task" (*KGW* IV/2, 23 [85]). While discovering the prehistory of modern "humanity," or "civilization," is perhaps the central intellectual trope of nineteenth-century anthropology, Nietzsche was about to argue that the mentalities and natural conditions of this prehistory are still shaping the political realities of modern society.[39]

METAPHOR, MYTH, AND CULTURAL REALITY

The relationship between language and thought is certainly one of the most persistent themes of Nietzsche's intellectual career. It is virtually impossible to ignore the way in which this theme has influenced the general direction of his philosophical enterprise.

---

[38] Among the anthropological literature Nietzsche consults during the 1880s, we can find Otto Caspari, *Die Urgeschichte der Menschheit, mit Rücksicht auf die natürliche Entwicklung des frühesten Geisteslebens* (Leipzig: Brockhaus, 1873); Julius Lippert, *Die Religionen der europäischen Culturvölker, der Litauer, Slaven, Germanen, Griechen und Römer, in ihrer geschichtlichen Entwicklung* (Berlin: Hofmann, 1881); Albert Hermann Post, *Bausteine für eine allgemeine Rechtswissenschaft auf vergleichend-ethnologischer Basis* (Oldenburg: Schulze, 1880–81).

[39] For a short overview of "prehistory" as a specific model within the study of culture in nineteenth-century Europe, see Trigger, *A History of Archaeological Thought*, pp. 87–101, 114–18, and 150–63.

His somewhat hyperbolic suggestion, first expressed in the notes for "Darstellung der antiken Rhetorik," that all language is, in one way or another, of a rhetorical nature (*KGW* II/4, p. 426) certainly leads him to seemingly subversive epistemological conclusions, which come to the fore in his essay "Ueber Wahrheit und Lüge im aussermoralischen Sinne" and his notebooks from the early 1870s.[40] In its most radical sense, Nietzsche here opts for the idea that language is unable to provide any privileged access to Kantian things-in-themselves, and as such it also cannot be regarded as directly corresponding to reality. Rather, language needs to be seen as mediating between, on the one hand, pre-linguistic processes of perception and mentalization that are to be located in the body, and on the other, the cognitive processes with which we seek to order and accommodate our environment, regardless of whether we deal with our cultural or natural surroundings. Nietzsche's vision of language, then, focuses on the interface between body and world, human physiology and culture, thus aiming at " 'naturalizing' our humanity," as he put it in *Die fröhliche Wissenschaft*, by rethinking the relationship between language, consciousness and the body along anthropological lines (*GS* 109).[41] Nietzsche was thus not only bound to attack what he perceived to be the metaphysical fiction of "truth," but he also began to emphasize that conceptual knowledge of whatever kind rested on metaphors whose meanings had become fixed over time (*TL* pp. 144–50 and *KGW* III/3, 8 [41]): "*no proper knowledge without metaphor*," he noted laconically in 1872/73 (*KGW* III/4, 19 [228]).[42]

This is not the place to delve into the epistemological implications of Nietzsche's reflections on the relationship between language and thinking. A more detailed assessment of Nietzsche's position would show that his ideas are less radical than commonly believed.[43] But for the present context, it is sufficient to realize that

---

[40] On the rhetorical impetus of Nietzsche's philosophical thought, see Angèle Kremer-Marietti, *Nietzsche et la rhétorique* (Paris: P.U.F., 1992), and, historically more accurate, the contributions in Josef Kopperschmidt and Helmut Schanze (eds.), *Nietzsche oder "Die Sprache ist Rhetorik"* (Munich: Wilhelm Fink, 1994).
[41] See Richard Schacht, *Nietzsche* (London: Routledge, 1983), pp. 268–79.
[42] On the fundamental importance of metaphor for Nietzsche's philosophy, see Sarah Kofman, *Nietzsche and Metaphor*, trans. Duncan Large (Stanford, Calif.: Stanford University Press, 1993), and Emden, *Nietzsche on Language, Consciousness, and the Body*, pp. 61–87.
[43] See, for instance, the concise discussion of these problems in Maudemarie Clark, *Nietzsche on Truth and Philosophy* (Cambridge: Cambridge University Press, 1990).

the congruence between language and consciousness continued to be a decisive factor within his later philosophical writings, when he once again pointed out that the development of consciousness and thinking rests on the anthropological necessity to communicate through signs and to order the stream of perceptions through lasting images (*GS* 354). It is precisely this view that informs his repeated claim, throughout the 1880s, that cultural institutions, such as morality, should be interpreted as the result of a kind of sign-language (*KGW* VII/1, 7 [47], [125] and *KGW* VIII/1, 2 [165]). It is certainly questionable whether Nietzsche's suggestions are always defensible from a more comprehensive philosophical perspective. But any approach to Nietzsche's intellectual project that seeks to exclude the problem of language remains unpersuasive, for it underestimates the lasting significance of seemingly passing remarks, such as the claim that the "drive to form metaphors" needs to be seen as a "fundamental human drive" (*TL* p. 150).

Nietzsche's reflections on language are also marked by a decisive shift. In the context of his early writings and notes on the epistemological status of language between 1870 and 1874, he often highlights the deficient nature of language. That language did not correspond to reality, and that the latter could not be adequately represented through language but only indirectly through a complex set of tropes, leads him to a radical skepticism about knowledge as a whole: "Most people sense occasionally that their lives drift in a net of illusions. But few recognize how far these illusions extend," he writes in his notebooks of 1870/71 (*KGW* III/3, 5 [33]).[44] The assumption that knowledge is illusory simply because human individuals lack a privileged access to things-in-themselves certainly remains an impossible philosophical position. Even Nietzsche, as subversive as he might often sound, was forced to correct this view; his initial skepticism began to give way to a more positive account:

A comparison of the different languages makes it obvious that, where words are concerned, what matters is never truth, never the adequate expression: otherwise there would not be so many languages. The "thing-in-itself" . . . is impossible for even the sculptor of language [*Sprachbildner*] to grasp, and indeed not at all desirable. (*TL* p. 144)

[44] See also *KGW* III/3, 5 [35] and *KGW* III/4, 19 [179].

That things-in-themselves might not at all be desirable as a fixed point of reference for the organization of knowledge indicates that Nietzsche slowly began to realize that the cultural power of language does not rest on any privileged access to reality. In fact, whether or not such a privileged access was possible turned out to be of little relevance. Five years after the essay on truth and lying, he remarked in the first volume of *Menschliches, Allzumenschliches* that it was precisely our illusions about reality that shaped cultural and political institutions inasmuch as these illusions and their representation in language have grown over time into a complex web of beliefs, which generates cultural reality in the first place:

> That which we now call the world is the outcome of a host of errors and fantasies which have gradually arisen and grown entwined with one another in the course of the overall evolution of organic beings [*organische Wesen*], and are now inherited by us as the accumulated treasure of the past – as treasure: for the *value* of our being human [*unseres Menschenthums*] depends upon it. (*HA* 1: 16)[45]

Nietzsche's main emphasis is not really on the illusory status of knowledge, or culture for that matter, but rather on the slow historical development of initially arbitrary, albeit useful, beliefs into a complex set of cultural mentalities that we regard as a fixed and universally valid cultural reality.

Leaving aside, if only for the moment, the organicist metaphors of the above passage, that Nietzsche should indeed turn to such a historical perspective has much to do with his philological background. One of the most important discussions in nineteenth-century linguistics was concerned with historical semantics, that is, the diachronic study of minute shifts of meaning within language that are represented by morphological and phonological alterations of linguistic roots and, occasionally, complete words. The debates concerning the reconstruction of an Indo-European proto-language began already in the 1830s with the work of August Friedrich Pott and culminated during the 1860s in the seminal

---

[45] R. J. Hollingdale translates the German *organische Wesen* as "the organic being," which is incorrect since the German is in the plural. Further-more, his translation of *Menschenthum* as "humanity" is misleading, since the German expression for "humanity" is *Menschheit*. Nietzsche refers to that which makes us human, not to that which makes us into a single humanity. Finally, Hollingdale overlooks that the term "value" is emphasized in the original.

studies of August Schleicher.[46] In November 1869, Nietzsche read at least parts of Schleicher's mighty *Compendium der vergleichenden Grammatik der indogermanischen Sprachen* (1861–62), within which he could find the idea of an archaic proto-language that split up into different linguistic families, languages, and dialects. For Nietzsche, however, the importance of Schleicher's account was not so much based on the scholarly details – the theory of language descent and sound laws – but on the fact that Schleicher's approach was retrospective.[47] This was of crucial importance, for reading the history of language backward seemed to allow for an approach to the symbolic order of culture as it was represented, for instance, in the institutions of ancient societies, such as law. To give a particularly prominent example: one of Pott's and Schleicher's contemporaries, the philologist Jacob Grimm, who had initially been a student of Hegel's rival Friedrich Carl von Savigny at the University of Berlin, and who was thus deeply influenced by the historical school of law, sought to reconstruct the emergence of legal thought through the development of its symbolic representations in language.[48]

Within this context the study of etymology was of crucial importance. As a classical scholar by both education and profession, Nietzsche was certainly well aware of the state of contemporary etymological research. In a standard textbook on Greek etymology written by one of his own professors in Leipzig, Georg Curtius's *Grundzüge der griechischen Etymologie* (1858–62), he was able to find a particularly compelling idea: within language, the semantic framework of words and expressions is continuously shifting, for the members of any linguistic community will always

---

[46] August Friedrich Pott, *Etymologische Forschungen auf dem Gebiete der Indo-Germanischen Sprachen mit besonderem Bezug auf die Lautumwandlung im Sanskrit, Griechischen, Lateinischen, Litauischen und Gothischen* (Lemgo: Meyer, 1833–36), and August Schleicher, *Compendium der vergleichenden Grammatik der indogermanischen Sprachen: Kurzer Abriss einer Laut- und Formenlehre der indogermanischen Ursprache, des Altindischen, Alteranischen, Altgriechischen, Altitalischen, Altkeltischen, Altslawischen, Litauischen und Altdeutschen*, 2nd edn. (Weimar: Böhlau, 1866).

[47] See Simone Roggenbuck, "Die genealogische Idee in der vergleichenden Sprachwissenschaft des 19. Jahrhunderts: Stufen, Stammbäume, Wellen," in: Sigrid Weigel, Ohad Parnes, Ulrike Vedder, and Stefan Willer (eds.), *Generation: Zur Genealogie des Konzepts – Konzepte von Genealogie* (Munich: Wilhelm Fink, 2005), pp. 289–314: 294–311.

[48] See Jacob Grimm, *Deutsche Rechtsalterthümer* (Göttingen: Dieterich, 1828), and "Von der Poesie im Recht," *Zeitschrift für geschichtliche Rechtswissenschaft* 2 (1815/16), 25–99. For a fuller account of Grimm's approach, see Toews, *Becoming Historical*, pp. 318–71.

speculate more or less successfully about the various etymological origins of their expressions (*KGW* III/3, 3 [83]).⁴⁹ The emerging web of possible meanings, and the almost imperceptible shifts of meaning, seem endless, especially because the popular etymologies that feed into the public imagination are largely arbitrary. Nietzsche came to accept that a truly "scientific" etymology should ideally be able to provide the starting point for this "history of concepts [*Geschichte des Begriffs*]" (*KGW* II/3, p. 395).

Nietzsche's interest in the historical study of language as a springboard into the history of thinking clearly stands in a tradition that reaches back into the eighteenth century. Giambattista Vico, for instance, explicitly insisted that etymology rendered it possible to find not only the meaning of words and concepts, but also the meaning of the cultural institutions, ideas, myths, and rites within which these words were used. On this account, etymological research on a philosophical level unearthed something like a cultural history of thought.⁵⁰ Similar ideas circulated within the discussions triggered by two prize-questions from the Berlin Academy of the Sciences in 1759 and 1769 on the relationship between language and thought, and on the origin of language.⁵¹ One entry in these illustrious competitions, Johann Georg Sulzer's *Anmerkungen über den gegenseitigen Einfluß der Vernunft in die Sprache und der Sprache in die Vernunft* (1767), is particularly interesting in that Sulzer wholeheartedly emphasized that the history of reason ran parallel to the history of language: the history of language represented a genealogy of our conceptual knowledge. Nothing would be more useful to a philosopher, he pointed out, than a truly comprehensive history of language, which could serve as an ideal starting point for an investigation into the history of thinking.⁵²

---

⁴⁹ Nietzsche's knowledge about the history and theory of etymological research is mainly influenced by Georg Curtius, *Grundzüge der griechischen Etymologie*, 3rd edn. (Leipzig: Teubner, 1869), pp. 4–31.

⁵⁰ See Giambattista Vico, *The New Science*, trans. Thomas Goddard Bergin and Max Harold Fisch (Ithaca, N.Y.: Cornell University Press, 1968), § 354 and § 151–2. Vico's own position was influenced by a source Nietzsche himself was closely familiar with: Varro, *De lingua latina*, VII.109.

⁵¹ See Harnack, *Geschichte der Königlich Preußischen Akademie zu Berlin*, vol. II, p. 306–7.

⁵² See Johann Georg Sulzer, *Anmerkungen über den gegenseitigen Einfluß der Vernunft in die Sprache und der Sprache in die Vernunft*, in *Vermischte philosophische Schriften: Aus den Jahrbüchern der Akademie der Wissenschaften zu Berlin gesammelt* (Leipzig: Weidmann & Reich, 1773–81), vol. I, pp. 175, 178–9 and 180.

It is questionable that Nietzsche had any detailed knowledge of the discussions taking place in the eighteenth century, but his own approach is indeed similar to those of Vico and Sulzer. One of the reasons for this similarity is the revival of etymological studies in the context of nineteenth-century linguistics, which itself developed in the wider framework of contemporary anthropological thought. In 1854, Jacob Grimm suggested that etymological research would able to shed light on the historical development of cultures, and Georg Curtius emphasized shortly afterward that the focus of etymological research should be the historical development of concepts and their continuously shifting meaning.[53] Insofar as etymology highlighted the fundamental metaphoricity of language, it was seen as a foundation for the history of cultural mentalities.

Nietzsche increasingly began to find in myth an example for the effects that the history of language had on the symbolic order of culture. In his "Encyclopaedie der klassischen Philologie," he discusses at some length the development of mythological names. While "the comparative study of myths has stated that the *names* of deities have originally been predicates," any named object also tends to have "a multitude of predicates," many of which "are in turn used for other objects." Nietzsche's examples, drawn from Sanskrit, highlight the complexity of the web of meaning that results from this arbitrary predication: "earth, river, sky, twilight, cow, and language" ultimately become closely related terms, which in turn generate an equally complex set of possible myths (*KGW* II/3, p. 410).

The intimate connection between figurative language and mythology has certainly been a much-debated subject that, in the nineteenth century, linked the study of myth closely to both linguistics and anthropology. In the eighteenth century, Christian Gottlob Heyne had already argued that it was possible to discover the intellectual world of antiquity in the poetic language of mythical narratives, and in the nineteenth century Friedrich Gottlieb Welcker pointed out that names, personifications,

---

[53] Jacob Grimm, "Über Etymologie und Sprachvergleichung," in *Kleinere Schriften* (Berlin: Dümmler, 1864–90), vol. I, pp. 299–326: 302, and Curtius, *Grundzüge der griechischen Etymologie*, pp. 89–92.

symbols, metaphors, and allegories were at the basis of ancient natural religions.[54] Likewise, Karl Otfried Müller and, much later, Hermann Usener stressed that the symbolic order of myth rests on metaphor, personification, and anthropomorphism.[55] At the beginning of the nineteenth century, Schelling had taken this idea one step further and remarked that, since the operations of language resembled those of myth, language itself had to be understood as a form of mythological discourse.[56] Similarly, Johann Jakob Bachofen sought to discover a deep affinity between mythological discourse, symbolic language, and philosophy, which in many respects reflected the roots of his ideas in German Romanticism: myth and philosophy were both interpretive practices based on quasi-metaphorical associations of mental images and poetic figures.[57]

For Nietzsche, this background seems to have led to the crucial idea that the construction of myth is directly dependent on the anthropological importance of language. Arguing that myth was a precursor to philosophical thought (*KGW* II/4, p. 219), Nietzsche thus began to present myth in his lectures "Der Gottesdienst der Griechen," from an anthropological perspective as based on complex analogies between human action, natural phenomena, and the assumption of divine predestination (*KGW* II/5, pp. 365–6). What was at stake was an interpretation of the world and of experience according to human actions (*KGW* II/4, p. 236): natural phenomena – thunder, drought, disease, fire, and death – were ascribed to the supersensible workings of respective deities. Within mythical thought, then, nature was the sum of voluntary but supersensible actions, while the fact that nature remained chaotic was compensated by the rhetorical construction of meaning (*KGW* II/5, p. 367).

[54] See Christian Gottlob Heyne, "Sermonis mythici seu symbolici interpretatio ad caussas et rationes ductasque inde regulas revocata," *Commentationes Societatis Regiae Scientiarum Gottingensis* 16 (1808), 285–323, and Friedrich Gottlieb Welcker, *Griechische Götterlehre* (Göttingen: Dieterich, 1857–63), vol. I, pp. 46–87.
[55] See Müller, *Prolegomena zu einer wissenschaftlichen Mythologie*, pp. 65–6; Hermann Usener, *Götternamen: Versuch einer Lehre von der religiösen Begriffsbildung* (Bonn: Cohen, 1896), pp. 3, 5, 217, 304, and 317–21; Friedrich Max Müller, "Über die Philosophie der Mythologie," in *Einleitung in die vergleichende Religionswissenschaft* (Strasbourg: Trübner, 1874), pp. 301–53: 316.
[56] See Schelling, *Einleitung in die Philosophie der Mythologie*, in *Sämmtliche Werke*, vol. XI, p. 52.
[57] See Bachofen, *Versuch über die Gräbersymbolik der Alten*, p. 46.

As a central factor for the formation of cultural mentalities in archaic societies, myth is based on an intuitive perception of similarities that increasingly synthesized different forms of experience and ultimately projected an assumed system of laws onto the experience of nature and culture (*KGW*II/5, pp. 365 and 368–9).[58] Cultural orientation and political authority, Nietzsche came to conclude, rests on the formation of myth, and in *Menschliches, Allzumenschliches* Nietzsche thus began to explain the origin of religion as coming from the need to create symbolic order:

> The whole of nature is in the conception of religious men a sum of actions by conscious and volitional beings, a tremendous complex of *arbitarinesses*. ... The meaning of the religious cult is to determine and constrain nature for the benefit of mankind, that is to say *to impress upon it a regularity and rule of law which it does not at first possess*. (*HA* I: 111)[59]

This function of religion could not really be restricted to prehistoric times; rather, it constituted an archaic undercurrent, or residue, in modernity. For many cultural anthropologists in the nineteenth century, such undercurrents were particularly visible in the realm of popular superstition, which neither the Christian Church nor the state authorities were ever able to control. Superstition remained a curious problem, whose origins were to be found in the surviving rituals and beliefs of ancient societies, and throughout nineteenth-century Germany it was a powerful cultural force beyond the tradition of folklore, often to be found even at the radical fringes of Protestantism.[60] But superstition also appeared in the guise of spiritualism, which was able to gain much ground in Victorian Britain, where it played into a popular imagination that was already influenced by the dazzling displays of current physical research on electricity. The marvelous phenomena of electricity and magnetism that were displayed in lecture halls and on public occasions might have served the popularization

---

[58] To some extent, this argument can be traced back to David Hume, *Enquiries Concerning Human Understanding and Concerning the Principles of Morals*, 6th edn., ed. L. A. Selby-Bigge and P. H. Nidditch (Oxford: Clarendon Press, 1997), pp. 47–55, and *A Treatise of Human Nature*, ed. L. A. Selby-Bigge, 2nd edn. (Oxford: Oxford University Press, 1978), pp. 96–7, 107–9, and 111–12.

[59] Compare the remarks in Lubbock, *Die Entstehung der Civilisation*, p. 239.

[60] See Nils Freytag, *Aberglauben im 19. Jahrhundert: Preußen und seine Rheinprovinz zwischen Tradition und Moderne (1815–1918)* (Berlin: Duncker & Humblot, 2003).

of the physical sciences in Victorian Britain, but also supported mythical assumptions about invisible action at a distance, communication with the dead, and wondrous healing practices.[61] As Tylor put it in *Primitive Culture*: "Sometimes old thought and practices will burst out afresh, to the amazement of a world that thought them long since dead or dying ... as has lately happened in so remarkable a way in the history of modern spiritualism, a subject full of instruction from the ethnographer's point of view."[62]

"SURVIVALS" – RELIGION AND THE NATION STATE

From the point of view of cultural anthropology it was, of course, possible to argue that the scientific study of religious and popular beliefs would not only shed much light on the history of religion, but in the long run also clarify that Christianity remained the only authentic and true religion. Friedrich Max Müller, for instance, who had initially come from Germany to England in order to study Sanskrit documents in the archives of the East India Company, but stayed on at Oxford as a Fellow of All Soul's College, noted: "The oldest formations of thought crop out everywhere, and if we dig but deep enough, we shall find that even the sandy desert in which we are asked to live, rests everywhere on the firm foundation of ... religious faith."[63] Despite the existence of popular mythical beliefs, then, Christianity remained the high point within the evolution of religious thought: "The Science of Religion may be the last of the sciences which man is destined to elaborate; but when it is elaborated, it will change the aspect of the world, and give new life to Christianity itself."[64] For Müller, there was a clear distinction between religion and the surviving elements of archaic thought.

Nietzsche occasionally recommended Müller's work of mythology to his own students (*KGW* II/3, p. 410), only to completely

---

[61] See Iwan Rhys Morus, *Frankenstein's Children: Electricity, Exhibition, and Experiment in Nineteenth-Century London* (Princeton, N.J.: Princeton University Press, 1998), pp. 43–97, and Richard Noakes, "'Instruments to Lay Hold of Spirits:' Technologising the Bodies of Victorian Spiritualism," in Iwan Rhys Morus (ed.), *Bodies/Machines* (Oxford: Berg, 2002), pp. 125–63.
[62] Edward Burnett Tylor, *Primitive Culture: Researches into the Development of Mythology, Philosophy, Religion, Art, and Custom* (London: John Murray, 1871–73), vol. I, p. 15.
[63] Friedrich Max Müller, *Chips from a German Workshop, Volume I: Essays on the Science of Religion* (London: Longmans, Green, and Co., 1867), pp. xix–xx.
[64] Ibid., p. xxxii.

reject the latter's "science of religion" in his notebooks (*KGW* III/ 3, 5 [49] and [71]). For Nietzsche, Müller's approach was too much rooted in the Judeo-Christian tradition itself, which precluded any view from outside: Müller prevented himself from seeing Christianity as a sophisticated form of superstition, while Nietzsche – not least through his friendship with Franz Overbeck – could see Christianity only as a set of highly complex "mythopoetic forces [*mythenbildende Kräfte*]" that could be discovered in religion and philosophy alike (*KGW* III/4, 19 [62]).

In contrast to Müller, Tylor was more critical of his own cultural environment and sought to replace the notion of "superstition" with that of "survival." While the former had clearly negative connotations, Tylor's notions of survivals was more neutral: survivals were ideas, which originated in the past, but continued to exist in the present, even though their original meaning had been lost.[65] It became immediately clear that such survivals could not be limited to so-called "primitive" societies. Rather, Tylor came to recognize the "primitive" outlook of modernity itself: "some phenomena of our present civilisation," he noted, are "traceable survivals from more primitive states of culture," and once we accepted that the current "civilisation" was intimately connected to "past times," cultural anthropology would do well to focus on "the study of survival."[66] In *Primitive Culture*, he delivered a more detailed account of the relevance of such survivals for the perspective of the anthropologist:

> These are processes, customs, opinions, and so forth, which have been carried on by force of habit into a new state of society different from that in which they had their original home, and they thus remain as proofs and examples of an older condition of culture out of which a newer has been evolved. ... The serious business of ancient societies may be seen to sink into the sport of later generations, and its serious belief to linger on in nursery folk-lore, while superseded habits of old-world life may be modified into new-world forms still powerful for good and evil. ... Progress, degradation, survival, revival, modification, are all modes of

---

[65] See Edward Burnett Tylor, "On Traces of the Early Mental Condition of Man," *Proceedings of the Royal Institution of Great Britain* 5 (1866–69), 83–93: 91. For a fuller account of Tylor's notion, see Hans G. Kippenberg, "Survivals: Conceiving of Religious History in an Age of Development," in Arie L. Molendijk and Peter Pels (eds.), *Religion in the Making: The Emergence of the Sciences of Religion* (Leiden: Brill, 1998), pp. 297–312.

[66] Edward Burnett Tylor, "On the Survival of Savage Thought in Modern Civilisation," *Proceedings of the Royal Institution of Great Britain* 5 (1866–69), 522–35: 523 and 533.

the connexion that binds together the complex network of civilization. It needs but a glance into the trivial details of our own daily life to set us thinking how far we are really its originators, and how far but the transmitters and modifiers of the result of long past ages.[67]

Tylor was well aware of the way in which older cultural mentalities continue to shape the cultural conditions of modernity, even though his own discussion focused mainly on what he described as "primitive" expressions of culture, such as folklore and myth.[68]

When Nietzsche consulted Tylor's work in 1875, he immediately seized upon the latter's ideas, introducing the English term "survival" in *Menschliches, Allzumenschliches* and his notebooks (*HA* I: 64; *KGW* IV/1, 5 [155]; *KGW* IV/2, 24 [2]). Traces of mythical thought, he suggested, were particularly obvious in the way in which we continue to speak about nature, attributing to the latter a particular "will" to develop as, for instance, in the case of teleological models of organic evolution: "Mythology creeps even into the most sophisticated thinkers when they speak of *nature*. ... Will, nature are residues [*Überbleibsel*] of the old belief in deities," he remarked in his notebooks, and in *Menschliches, Allzumenschliches* he described our understanding of nature as resulting from the "remnants of allegorical and mystical interpretations" (*KGW* IV/2, 23 [18] and *HA* I: 8).

Nietzsche's emphasis on the representation of nature already highlights that, like Tylor, he had little interest in restricting "survivals" to the residues of archaic religious ideas. The after-life of archaic thought under the thin veil of modern religion (*HA* I: 111) indicated a much wider phenomenon: "survivals," "residues [*Überbleibsel*]", and "remnants [*Überreste*]" were at the very foundation of the symbolic order of political culture. Modern nation states, such as Imperial Germany, might require a rationalization of their political structures, especially on an administrative level. But as far as the actual foundations of the modern state as a nation were concerned, the deep structures of the political imagination continued to be marked by the importance of religious mentalities. Religious mentalities in the service of public policy were able to mobilize large sectors of society, for instance, in cases of conflict. For Nietzsche, the political function of what Tylor had

---

[67] Tylor, *Primitive Culture*, vol. I, pp. 15–16.   [68] See ibid., vol. I, pp. 63–144.

described as survivals became particularly obvious with regard to the formulation of strategic political interest along confessional lines that had themselves little to do with the actual interests at stake:

> The statesman excites public passions so as to profit from the counter-passions thereby aroused. To take an example: any German statesman knows well that the Catholic Church will never form an alliance with Russia, but would indeed rather form one even with the Turks; he likewise knows that an alliance between France and Russia would spell nothing but danger for Germany. If, therefore, he is able to make of France the hearth and home of the Catholic Church he will have abolished this danger for a long time to come. Consequently he has an interest in exhibiting hatred towards the Catholics and, through hostile acts of all kinds, transforming those who acknowledge the authority of the Pope into a passionate political power which, hostile to German policy, will naturally ally itself with France as the opponent of Germany: his goal is just as necessarily the Catholicization of France as Mirabeau's was its decatholicization. (*HA* I: 453)

Making France, as it were, more Catholic than it is, then, will help the formulation of public policy vis-à-vis Russia, precisely because it undermines any chances for a workable strategic alliance between France and Russia. More importantly, though, without the help of confessional polarization, achieving the isolation of Russia would prove to be more difficult. Nietzsche's example is not at all far-fetched. Preventing even the possibility of a military alliance between France and Russia was a central concern of Bismarck's foreign policy from 1878 onward, that is, the year Nietzsche published the first volume of *Menschliches, Allzumenschliches*. Only in June 1887, was Bismarck able to achieve a relative easing of these strategic tensions by concluding the so-called "Reinsurance Treaty" (*Rückversicherungsvertrag*), which forced Russia to adopt a neutral position in the event of a French attack on Germany.[69]

Despite the fact that the strategic alliances in the final decades of Imperial Germany worked out differently, especially in the run-up to 1914, Nietzsche successfully highlights the importance of religion within the public policy of the nation state: because of its appeal to emotional investment, religion, coupled with the myths

---

[69] See Nipperdey, *Deutsche Geschichte, 1866–1918*, vol. II, pp. 455–60.

of the nation, allows for the translation of policy interests into the wider public imagination, while the latter is at the same time able to influence the formulation of policy interests. Nietzsche thus came to understand that any political theory which fails to take the irrational dimension of the political into account – e.g. models of deliberative democracy aiming at rational consensus – also fails to properly recognize how political power is articulated.[70]

Against this background, Nietzsche begins to examine in more detail the social function of religion as a political institution within the state, that is, as a way of both mobilizing and controlling political participation for strategic means. Religion, thus, serves a specific function within the evolution of the modern state that, in an ironic turn, ultimately secularizes the state. At least this is what Nietzsche, somewhat optimistically, hoped for in 1878. The following passage thus needs to be read against the background of the imaginary convergence of Protestantism and the German nation state:

> As long as the state, or, more clearly, the government knows itself appointed as guardian for the benefit of the masses not yet of age, and on their behalf considers the question whether religion is to be preserved or abolished, it is very highly probable that it will always decide for the preservation of religion. For religion quietens the heart of the individual in times of loss, deprivation, fear, distrust, in those instances, that is to say, in which the government feels unable to do anything towards alleviating the psychical sufferings of the private person: even in the case of universal, unavoidable and in the immediate prospect inevitable evils (famines, financial crises, wars), indeed, religion guarantees a calm, patient, trusting disposition among the masses. Wherever the chance or inevitable shortcomings of the state government or the perilous consequences of dynastic interests force themselves upon the attention of the knowledgeable man and put him into a refractory mood, the unknowledgeable will think they see the hand of God and patiently submit to instructions from *above* (in which concept divine and human government are usually fused): thus internal civil peace and continuity of development is ensured. (*HA* I: 472)

The submission to unknown forces from "*above*" establishes an imaginary identity between divine and human government – and since there is no divine government, human government can take its place as a sacred power.

---

[70] On this problem, see Chantal Mouffe, *On the Political* (London: Routledge, 2005), pp. 6 and 24–34.

For Nietzsche, the modern state emerges as a variant of the absolutist state, not as a departure from the political theology of sovereignty that marked early modern European absolutism. It is as such that his critique of the imaginary correspondence between human and divine government continues a political demand of the French Enlightenment, especially Voltaire: "It is an insult to reason and to the law to say these words: *civil and ecclesiastical government.* You must say *civil government and ecclesiastical regulations*; none of these *regulations* must be made by anything other than the civil authorities."[71] If there is any justification for religion as a political institution within the modern state, it needs to be governed by secular institutions. But Nietzsche goes further in denying religion any political *raison d'être*. The reason for this is that religion as a political institution always entails a political theology that reverses the hierarchy between civil and ecclesiastical government Voltaire had hoped for. More than forty years before Carl Schmitt grounded political sovereignty in theological concepts, when he famously noted that the sovereign is "he who decides on the exception," Nietzsche was already outlining the danger of such assertions to the modern state.[72] By showing that Jean Bodin's early modern definition of sovereignty as "absolute and perpetual power" lives on in the modern state, he highlighted that the *raison d'état* continued to rest on the fusion of divine and human government – to the detriment of those who do not happen to influence power.[73] It is precisely the appeal to the realm of religion that renders the sovereignty of the state both unlimited and indivisible, which is the reason why Nietzsche remarks that "absolute tutelary government and the careful preservation of religion necessarily go together" (*HA* I: 472).

The social function of religion as an archaic survival in the realm of the political consists in safeguarding the unity of the state. But this is also the moment when, in the very same paragraph from *Menschliches, Allzumenschliches,* Nietzsche suddenly begins to argue that the fusion between divine and human government can be

[71] Voltaire, "Republican Ideas, by a Member of a Public Body," in *Political Writings*, trans. and ed. David Williams (Cambridge: Cambridge University Press, 1994), pp. 195–211: 198.
[72] Carl Schmitt, *Political Theology: Four Chapters on the Theory of Sovereignty*, trans. George Schwab, foreword Tracy B. Strong (Chicago: University of Chicago Press, 2005), p. 5.
[73] Jean Bodin, *On Sovereignty: Four Chapters from "The Six Books of the Commonwealth,"* ed. and trans. Julian H. Franklin (Cambridge: Cambridge University Press, 1992), p. 1.

broken. In a way that is reminiscent of the opening page of Immanuel Kant's 1784 article "Answer to the Question: What is Enlightenment?", he notes that the emergence of a "different conception of government" in "*democratic* states" invariably changes the relationship between religion and the state: replacing "tutelary government" with the notion of a "popular will" is a crucial step toward the secularization of the state, even though such a notion of "popular will" always tends to remain vague (*HA* I: 472).

Nietzsche's appeal to the popular will (*Volkswille*) is, of course, a reference to Jean-Jacques Rousseau's "general will" (*volonté générale*) in *Du contrat social* (1762).[74] For Rousseau, the sovereignty of the state is "nothing but the exercise of the general will" and, much like Nietzsche, he notes that absolutist states are governed by a false social contract, whose "goal is not public felicity" but rather the concentration of power.[75] Thus, for Rousseau the false social contract that needs to be corrected through representative government is based on an unequal balance of power: the argument for the general will is an argument against inequality, that is, "it substitutes a moral and legitimate equality for whatever physical inequality nature may have placed between men."[76] For Nietzsche, however, the disadvantaged are not necessarily those who are blocked from political participation because of an unequal distribution of power, but rather those who are "unknowledgeable." It is their lack of education that makes them fall victim to the false social contract and that prevents them from recognizing that their acceptance of the political status quo is rooted in the effect of religious mentalities. Nietzsche's emphasis on the educational aspect is thus closer to Kant's criticism of the "self-incurred immaturity" that hinders the development of "the public use of one's own reason" than to Rousseau.[77] For both Rousseau and Nietzsche, however, the general will serves as a counterweight to "tutelary government." This should not mean, however, that Nietzsche and Rousseau are generally in agreement; they might both deal with the internal logic of political order, but come to

---

[74] See Keith Ansell-Pearson, *Nietzsche contra Rousseau: A Study of Nietzsche's Moral and Political Thought* (Cambridge: Cambridge University Press, 1996), pp. 78–101.
[75] See Jean-Jacques Rousseau, *Of the Social Contract*, in *The Social Contract and Other Later Political Writings*, ed. and trans. Victor Gourevitch (Cambridge: Cambridge University Press, 1997), pp. 57 (II.1) and 95 (III.6).
[76] See ibid., p. 56 (I.9).
[77] Kant, "What is Enlightenment?", in *Political Writings*, pp. 54–5.

rather different conclusions. Rousseau's call for political change in the eighteenth century is in many ways an expression of the revolutionary spirit of the Enlightenment, while Nietzsche, much like Kant in 1784 before the French Revolution, remains unconvinced with regard to the value of revolutionary ideas.[78] For Nietzsche, Rousseau's revolutionary spirit would always entail a far-reaching moralization of the political along the lines of absolute value distinctions.[79]

Given the direction of Nietzsche's argument in the above paragraph from *Menschliches, Allzumenschliches*, it is necessary to note a fundamental difference between the Enlightenment notion of a *volonté générale*, which had first been introduced by Montesquieu's *De l'esprit des lois* (1748), and Nietzsche's historical perspective. While Rousseau's and Kant's arguments are directed against the early modern absolutist state, Nietzsche's reference to "absolute tutelary government" does not necessarily refer to this tradition. What he has in mind is the attempt to ground the modern German nation state in a Protestant tradition that marked much of nineteenth-century political culture. Even though German Protestantism was far from homogeneous and characterized by conflicting regional traditions that often corresponded to the territorial interests of the German states and their rulers before 1871, it increasingly came to provide a complex historical legitimation for both Prussia's German vocation and the subsequent public perception of Imperial Germany as a *Kulturstaat*.[80] As a political foundation myth that stretched from Luther's Reformation – itself one of the pivotal turning points in Hegel's lectures on the philosophy of history[81] – to the victory of the German army over Napoleon III on the battlefield at Sedan in 1870, German Protestantism remained an integral part of the Prussian-led *Reich*, which Bismarck was able to exploit during the so-called *Kulturkampf* against Catholicism during the early 1870s. While Bismarck's policies failed, the divide between Protestantism and Catholicism, together with the

---

[78] See ibid., p. 55.
[79] For a more detailed reading of Nietzsche's criticism of Rousseau's revolutionary spirit, see Marti, "*Der grosse Pöbel- und Sklavenaufstand*," pp. 26–43.
[80] See Friedrich Wilhelm Graf, "Protestantische Theologie in der Gesellschaft des Kaiserreichs," in: Graf (ed.), *Profile des neuzeitlichen Protestantismus* (Gütersloh: Mohn, 1990–93), vol. II/1, pp. 12–117.
[81] See, for instance, Hegel, *Lectures on the Philosophy of History*, in *Political Writings*, pp. 198–207.

uneasy relationship between liberalism and Protestantism, was a conflict over political authority in the new German nation state that continued until the early twentieth century.[82]

By the mid-1870s it indeed seemed that Hegel's passing remark about the state as consisting "in the march of God in the world" had been realized in the realm of the political.[83] But why, then, is Nietzsche optimistic that the imaginary correspondence between divine and human government, between religion and the state, is about to be undermined? The reason for his optimism has little to do with representative government, but rather with the fact that the relationship between Protestantism and the secular state in the second half of the nineteenth century was less straightforward than commonly assumed. Closely linked to German idealism, Protestant thought, first of all, invited its own secularization. The way in which, for instance, philosophers like Hegel and Schelling – ridiculed by Heinrich Heine – regarded Christianity and speculative philosophy as virtually identical, ultimately suggested that Christianity could be dissolved into philosophy.[84] The effects of this could partly be felt in the early publications of the Young Hegelians, like Bruno Bauer and Ludwig Feuerbach, who fully realized that philosophical critique had won out over religion and that, by implication, the link between religion and the state needed to be dissolved.[85]

There was, however, also a second trend that might have played into Nietzsche's optimism. Although Protestantism remained a cultural authority in Imperial Germany, actual religious practice was in decline. In Prussia alone, church attendance among the Protestant population decreased from c. 54 percent in 1862 to 44 percent in 1880 and 1881. By 1895, it had dropped to 39 percent. In the duchy of Saxony-Altenburg – sandwiched between Prussia

---

[82] See Gangolf Hübinger, *Kulturprotestantismus und Politik: Zum Verhältnis von Liberalismus und Protestantismus im wilhelminischen Deutschland* (Tübingen: J.C.B. Mohr, 1994), pp. 37–49 and 233–50.

[83] Hegel, *Elements of the Philosophy of Right*, p. 279 (§ 258).

[84] See Georg Wilhelm Friedrich Hegel, *Lectures on the Philosophy of Religion*, ed. P. C. Hodgson, trans. R. F. Brown, P. C. Hodgson, J. M. Stewart, and H. S. Harris (Berkeley, Calif.: University of California Press, 1984–87), vol. III, pp. 160–2, 245–7, and 345–7, and Schelling, *Einleitung in die Philosophie der Mythologie*, in *Sämmtliche Werke*, vol. XI, p. 255. For Heinrich Heine's critique, see his *Religion and Philosophy in Germany: A Fragment*, trans. John Snodgrass, foreword Dennis J. Schmitt (Albany: SUNY Press, 1986), pp. 146–58.

[85] See Bruno Bauer, *Kritik der Geschichte der Offenbarung* (Berlin: Dümmler, 1838), and Ludwig Feuerbach, *Das Wesen des Christentums*, 3rd edn., ed. Heinrich Schmidt (Leipzig: Kröner, 1848).

and Saxony and located just south of Schulpforta and Naumburg, where Nietzsche had spent his youth – 76 percent of the Protestant population attended church services regularly in 1862. By 1895 the number had decreased to 45 percent. In fact, this is a trend that can be observed across Germany.[86] Although there were obvious regional variations, the most rapid decline in church attendance occurred among precisely that part of the population that was both sufficiently educated to understand the intricacies of the political foundation myths and profited most from the political stability of the German nation state: merchants, industrialists, higher-ranking civil servants, bankers, university professors, and teachers. In contrast, for members of lower socio-economic classes, including the rural population, church attendance remained a central part of social life.[87] This was that part of the population that suffered most from, as Nietzsche put it, "the chance or inevitable shortcomings of the state government or the perilous consequences of dynastic interests" (*HA* I: 472). Threatened by the growing integration of the German economy into an international trade system as well as by the concentration of financial power, this was also that part of the population which was most likely to compensate the threats of modernity by accepting the state as a sacred entity and political action as governed by the divine – "the masses not yet of age," who see in "famines, financial crises, wars" inevitably "the hand of God" and whose life was thus governed by those archaic survivals and remnants that Nietzsche found in Tylor's work in cultural anthropology (*HA* I: 472). Social modernization in Imperial Germany did not automatically entail a broad secularization of society. It rather seems to be the case that religiosity within the nation state became more differentiated according to the economic and political interests of a diverse range of social groups.[88]

---

[86] See Hölscher, *Weltgericht oder Revolution*, p. 143. For more detailed statistics, see Lucian Hölscher (ed., with Tillmann Bendikowski, Claudia Enders, and Markus Hoppe), *Datenatlas zur religiösen Geographie im protestantischen Deutschland: Von der Mitte des 19. Jahrhunderts bis zum Zweiten Weltkrieg* (Berlin: Walter de Gruyter, 2001).
[87] See Lucian Hölscher, "Bürgerliche Religiösität im protestantischen Deutschland des 19. Jahrhunderts," in Wolfgang Schieder (ed.), *Religion und Gesellschaft im 19. Jahrhundert* (Stuttgart: Klett-Cotta, 1993), pp. 191–215: 201.
[88] See Olaf Blaschke, "Das 19. Jahrhundert: Ein zweites konfessionelles Zeitalter?" *Geschichte und Gesellschaft* 26 (2000), 38–75, and Christoph Ribbart, *Religiöse Erregung: Protestantische Schwärmer im Kaiserreich* (Frankfurt/M.: Campus, 1996).

Surprisingly, the obvious importance of the intertwining of religion and the nation state in Imperial Germany does not prevent Nietzsche from repeating the political hopes already expressed by Voltaire, Rousseau and Kant: the modern state can become a secular political institution. As soon as religion retreats into the realm of the private and is handed over "to the conscience and customs of every individual," the link between religion and the state is severed. At the same time, "the mood of those still moved by religion" becomes increasingly "*hostile to the state*," for human government cannot be revered anymore "as something half or wholly sacred" (*HA* I: 472). But since the power and influence of religion is practically limited within the state, Nietzsche concludes that the nation state is secularized to such an extent that "the foundations of the state too are undermined" (*HA* I: 472). While this at first sight seems to suggest that Nietzsche wished to do away with the body politic as a whole, his remarks are in fact merely directed against the modern nation state, which represented to him the sacralization of political power and was therefore marked by mythical conjectures:

> The belief in a divine order in the realm of politics, in a sacred mystery in the existence of the state, is of religious origin: if religion disappears the state will unavoidably lose its ancient Isis veil and cease to excite reverence. Viewed from close to, the sovereignty of the people serves then to banish the last remnant of magic and superstition from this realm of feeling; modern democracy is the historical form of the *decay of the state*. (*HA* I: 472)

The sacralization of political power that Nietzsche refers to in the first sentence of the above paragraph is indeed an intriguingly timely topic in the nineteenth century. Hegel clearly noted in his lectures on the philosophy of religion, which he delivered in Berlin between 1821 and 1830, that "religion and the foundation of the state are one and the same thing – they are *identical in and for themselves.*"[89] Given the location where he gave these lectures, this led him to the unsurprising conclusion that the identity between religion and state becomes particularly manifest in Protestant nations: the unity of the state and the possibility of political freedom

---

[89] Hegel, "The Relationship of Religion to the State," in *Political Writings*, pp. 225–33: 225.

that is expressed in the constitutional grounding of Protestant states requires that religion and the state are not separated.[90]

While Hegel is far from endorsing early modern European absolutism, the identity of state and religion is rooted in the idea of the absolutist ruler's divinity, as for instance in the *caractère sacré* of the medieval kings.[91] The structural difference between Catholic and Protestant political theologies is indeed minimal. It is, however, remarkable that the secularizing effects of the Enlightenment did not fundamentally change the notion of political authority as sacred and divine – as can easily be seen with regard to the imagery of the French Revolution.[92] The social and political rise of nationalism in nineteenth-century Germany is no exception to this. In the period between the Wars of Liberation and the Franco-Prussian War the collective identity of seemingly secular interest groups often linked images of war, divine destiny, and the demand for national unity. After the Franco-Prussian War, once the social modernization of the German nation state was well under way, Imperial Germany sought to fashion itself through a sacralization of political history, which established grand narratives of a divine national destiny from Luther's Reformation to the defeat of France.[93] It is precisely against this complex background that Nietzsche finds the belief in a "sacred mystery in the existence of the state" troublesome: it remains based on a mythical conjecture that prevents political realism. But from a historical perspective he also hopes that a decline in the willingness to accept mythical conjectures will further the secularization of the body politic. While accepting the relevance of the state as an "organizing power," as he remarks in the same paragraph (*HA* I: 472), and while he sees that the demise of the state would be a threatening development, Nietzsche is convinced in 1878 that the modern nation state is a

---

[90] See ibid., pp. 227 and 230.
[91] See Franz-Reiner Erkens, "Sakral legitimierte Herrschaft im Wechsel der Zeiten und Räume: Versuch eines Überblicks," in Erkens (ed.), *Die Sakralität von Herrschaft: Herrschaftslegitimierung im Wechsel der Zeiten und Räume* (Berlin: Akademie Verlag, 2002), pp. 7–32: 12–17.
[92] See Mona Ozouf, *La fête revolutionnaire, 1789–1799* (Paris: Gallimard, 1976), pp. 332–3.
[93] See Dietmar Klenke, "Nationalkriegerisches Gemeinschaftsideal als politische Religion: Zum Vereinsnationalismus der Sänger, Schützen und Turner am Vorabend der Einigungkriege," *Historische Zeitschrift* 260 (1995), 395–448, and Peter Walkenhorst, "Nationalismus als 'politische Religion'? Zur religiösen Dimension nationalistischer Ideologie im Kaiserreich," in Olaf Blaschke and Frank-Michael Kuhlemann (eds.), *Religion im Kaiserreich: Milieus, Mentalitäten, Krisen* (Gütersloh: Kaiser, 1996), pp. 503–31.

historical construct that will run its course and finally disappear. When he describes modern democracy as "the historical form of the *decay of the state*," he thus refers to the way in which democracy as an inherently secular institution undermines the sacralization of the political that lies at the core of the modern nation state.

Even though Nietzsche is occasionally portrayed as an essentially unpolitical and even antipolitical thinker, who was detached from the social and political demands of modernity and who preferred the solitude of a heightened individualism, his complex relationship to the state has not gone unnoticed.[94] While there is indeed little actual evidence for his presumed antipolitical attitudes, his views of the state continue to be a matter of debate. Did Nietzsche seek to replace the modern state with a new community of sovereign individuals and free spirits able to overcome the technocracy of bureaucratic institutions? Did he view the state simply as a predominantly destructive political institution?[95] Nietzsche's presumed rejection of the "state" as such, that is, as the modern political institution par excellence, is mainly based on a striking passage from *Also sprach Zarathustra* (1883–85), whose polemicism cannot really be seen as the high point of his political thought: criticizing the presumed identity of "the state" and "the people," he argues that the state is merely a secularized version of an illusory divine order, while the philosopher of the future can only exist beyond the realm of the state (*Z* 1: 11). But as such, his rejection of the state is directed against a very specific understanding of the state as embodying and expressing a numinous general will that always eludes precise articulation.

Nietzsche, then, is critical of the idea of a popular will as the foundation for the modern democratic state. But again, his actual position is far from clear at this point. It seems that after 1875/76 he in fact regarded the modern democratic state as a step toward

---

[94] Peter Bergmann, *Nietzsche – the last Antipolitical German* (Bloomington, Ind.: Indiana University Press, 1987), goes even so far as to suggest that Nietzsche had little interest in politics and that his views of political life are predominantly based on his aestheticism. A similarly antipolitical account can be found in Leslie Paul Thiele, *Friedrich Nietzsche and the Politics of the Soul: A Study of Heroic Individualism* (Princeton, N. J.: Princeton University Press, 1990), which presents a solitary Nietzsche detached from wider social and political concerns, and Tamsin Shaw, *Nietzsche's Political Skepticism* (Princeton, N.J.: Princeton University Press, 2007), pp. 26–9.

[95] See Appel, *Nietzsche contra Democracy*, p. 141, and Lester H. Hunt, "Politics and Anti-Politics: Nietzsche's View of the State," *History of Philosophy Quarterly* 2 (1985), 453–68.

emancipation from traditional political authorities, but that at the beginning of the 1880s, that is, after *Menschliches, Allzumenschliches*, he began to lose interest in democracy as a viable political alternative.[96] Perhaps Nietzsche's rejection of the modern state is not so much directed against the state as a juridical institution, but rather against the state as a site of democratic compromise among intellectually mediocre political parties and interest groups.[97] Such a compromise would have to be based on an understanding of the popular will as being formed through rational consensus and as representing a relatively clearly defined common good, which tends to disguise the fact that the political as well as the actual practice of politics are marked by neither consensus nor rationality. At best, the political becomes manifest as an agonistic negotiation of interests – at worst, it is constituted by the antagonism of hegemonial claims for power.[98] By the mid-1870s, then, it must have seemed to Nietzsche that the predominant effect of nineteenth-century mass democracy, at least in Germany, was not better informed and wider political participation, but a dangerous leveling of the playing field that left no room for dissent and critique: greater political participation could be achieved only at the cost of critical knowledge, which was precisely the reason why the citizens of the modern nation state continued to fall into the trap of political myths that prevented real participation.

Nietzsche himself provides a "model" for governance that stands in sharp contrast to the political participation of inexpert and directly elected officials: "the election of a lawgiving body" can only take place among "men of knowledge," which culminates in his demand to replace the political culture of mass democracy with an expert culture of independent individuals: "'More respect for the man of knowledge! And down with all parties!'" (*HA* II: i.318). But Nietzsche was also aware that this is a distant hope, for in the next paragraph he immediately returns to the present and laments the "*lack of rationality*" that he finds in German intellectual culture (*HA* II: i.319). Assuming, then, that Nietzsche is not generally opposed to the modern state as a political institution, does he favor an authoritarian state with clear totalitarian

---

[96] See Marti, *"Der grosse Pöbel- und Sklavenaufstand"*, pp. 189–205, especially 190–1 and 199.
[97] See Ottmann, *Philosophie und Politik bei Nietzsche*, pp. 124–9.
[98] See Mouffe, *On the Political*, pp. 10–21.

tendencies?[99] Such a conclusion would underplay Nietzsche's insistence in the second volume of *Menschliches, Allzumenschliches* that the "lawgiving body" of the state needs to be elected and that the members of the latter give their independent "vote" (*HA* II: i.318).

This is not to be taken lightly, for Nietzsche's criticism of the state is informed by the situation in Germany at that moment when Bismarck was able to use a failed assassination attempt on the Emperor Wilhelm I – carried out by the journeyman Max Hödel in Berlin on May 11, 1878, without any real political motives – as a justification for limiting constitutionally guaranteed civil rights. The so-called "Socialist Law" of October 21, 1878, was directed only partly against socialist opposition groups and essentially undermined any democratic political participation and expression.[100] Nietzsche's remarks on these events are as polemical as they are concise:

> The socialist movements are now more welcome than fear-inspiring, to the dynastic governments, because through them the latter can get into their hands *the right and weapons* for taking the exceptional measures with which they are able to strike at the figures that really fill them with terror, the democrats and anti-dynasts. – For all that such governments publicly hate they now have a secret inclination and affinity: they are obliged to veil their soul. (*HA* II: i.316).

Given this direct criticism of the exceptional measures within Bismarck's Imperial Germany as an authoritarian state it is indeed unlikely that Nietzsche should have hoped for an authoritarian turn of the political. His criticism was directed against the late nineteenth-century German nation state, an entity with parliamentary institutions, but authoritarian rule – an entity with democratic structures that could be bypassed if the political elite felt it necessary to do so. Nietzsche, then, is not quite as radical as it might seem but shares, for instance, Max Weber's assessment of the political situation in Germany toward the end of the First World War:

> There are only two choices: either the mass of citizens is left without freedom or rights in a bureaucratic, "authoritarian state" which has only

[99] See Dombowsky, *Nietzsche's Machiavellian Politics*, pp. 105–13.
[100] See Nipperdey, *Deutsche Geschichte, 1866–1819*, vol. II, pp. 395–403, and "Gesetz gegen die gemeingefährlichen Bestrebungen der Sozialdemokratie vom 21. Oktober 1878," in *Das deutsche Kaiserreich, 1871–1914: Ein historisches Lesebuch*, ed. Gerhard Ritter, 5th edn. (Göttingen: Vandenhoeck & Ruprecht, 1992), pp. 232–5.

the appearance of parliamentary rule, and in which the citizens are "administered" like a herd of cattle; or the citizens are integrated into the state by making them its *co-rulers*.[101]

For Weber, only the latter option was of any value, because rolling back democratic institutions in Germany would have fatal consequences for the state as a whole: "the energies of the masses would then be engaged in a struggle *against* a state in which they are mere objects and in which they have no share."[102] Nietzsche's reflections go into a similar direction: he does not reject modern political institutions as such, but merely the institution that he knew best: the modern German nation state. The danger of democracy, then, is not political participation as such. It is what Weber, again at the end of the First World War, described as the danger of a disorderly democracy: "In Germany we have *demagogy and the influence of the rabble without democracy*, or rather, *because we lack an orderly democracy*."[103]

But the German nation state was not an isolated case. It represented to Nietzsche the dilemmas and problems of European modernity as a whole: the latter was shaped only partly by a technical and scientific rationality and remained in many ways infused with mythical conjectures that became particularly manifest in the realm of the political. These residues of mythical thought, of course, had a long historical development and thus highlighted the way in which the political culture of modernity as a whole was haunted by its past. The claims of modern political and moral communities ultimately rested on the survival of specific customs and conjectures whose origins were increasingly forgotten, so that these customs could be, as it were, naturalized, in turn generating seemingly universal and fixed distinctions between "good" and "evil":

To be moral, to act in accordance with custom, to be ethical means to practice obedience towards a law or tradition established from of old. Whether one subjects oneself with effort or gladly and willingly makes no difference, it is enough that one does it. He is called "good" who does

---

[101] Max Weber, "Suffrage and Democracy in Germany," in *Political Writings*, ed. Peter Lassman and Ronald Speirs (Cambridge: Cambridge University Press, 1994), pp. 80–129: 129.
[102] Ibid.
[103] Weber, *Parliament and Government in Germany under a New Political Order*, in: *Political Writings*, pp. 130–271: 220.

whatever is customary as if by nature, as a result of long inheritance, that is to say easily and gladly, and this is so whatever is customary may be ... To be evil is "not to act in accordance with custom," to practise things not sanctioned by custom, to resist tradition, however rational or stupid that tradition may be ... How the tradition has *arisen* is here a matter of indifference, and has in any event nothing to do with good and evil or with any kind of immanent categorical imperative; it is above all directed at the preservation of a *community* [*Gemeinde*], a people ... Every tradition now grows more venerable the farther away its origin lies and the more this origin is forgotten; the respect paid to it increases from generation to generation, the tradition at last becomes holy and evokes awe and reverence. (*HA* I: 96)[104]

In view of the crucial importance of traditions for the preservation of moral and political communities, and taking into account that such tradtions essentially naturalize moral and political values for a society, Nietzsche increasingly focuses on the need to unravel the historical evolution of such moral and political communities:

Direct self-observation is not nearly sufficient for us to know ourselves: we require history, for the past continues to flow within us in a hundred waves; we ourselves are, indeed, nothing but that which at every moment we experience of this continued flowing. It may even be said that here too, when we desire to descend into the river of what seems to be our own most intimate and personal being, there applies the dictum of Heraclitus: we cannot step into the same river twice. – This is, to be sure, a piece of wisdom that has gradually grown stale, but it has nonetheless remained as true and valid as it ever was: just as has this other piece of wisdom, that to understand history we have to go in quest of the living remnants of historical epochs – we have to *travel*, as the father of history, Herodotus, travelled, to other nations – for these are only earlier *stages of culture* grown firm upon which we can *take a stand* – to the so-called savage and semi-savage peoples, and especially to where man has taken off the garb of Europe or has not yet put it on. But there exists a *subtler* art and object of travel which does not always require us to move from place to place or to traverse thousands of miles. The last three centuries very probably still continue to live on, in all their cultural colours and cultural refractions, *close beside us*: they want only to be *discovered*. In many families, indeed in individual men, the strata still lie neatly and clearly one on top of the other: elsewhere there are dislocations and faults which make understanding more difficult. (*HA* II: i.223)

[104] The term *Gemeinde* not only refers to an abstract "community" or an administrative "municipality," but also to a religious community in the sense of "congregation" and "parish." Nietzsche here points to the structural equivalence of religious, moral and political communities.

Traveling into the past, then, was as much an exercise in anthropological self-reflection as the ethnographic study of seemingly exotic cultures. Both would allow for a view from the outside, which Nietzsche himself cultivated while pondering the future of European culture from the periphery in Sorrento or Sils Maria, avoiding the political force centers of Berlin and Paris.

But the aphorism quoted above also develops a critical perspective on the value of history. At the end, Nietzsche hopes that such "self-education could, in the freest and most far-sighted spirits, one day become universal determination with regard to all future humanity." But, given the historical perspective of Nietzsche's aphorism, this utopian gesture comes with a caveat: the future of humanity will be as fragile and frail as we are today, that is, "humanity," if such a concept makes any sense at all, will continue to be riddled with the traces of whatever it believes to have overcome. There was little indication of a progression from *mythos* to *logos* that could be unearthed in the course of history: "We look back on a considerable length of human history; what will a humanity be like that looks back on us from an equal distance, that finds us still completely submerged in the residues [*Überbleibsel*] of earlier cultures?" (*KGW* IV/1, 5 [164]). Even the presumed rationality of secular modernity will, in the long run, be viewed as riddled with the traces of mythical thought.[105]

POLITICAL REALISM AND THE "FREE SPIRIT"

Nietzsche's uneasy relationship to political ideals is difficult to overlook.[106] His conception of the political is perhaps best understood as an exercise in political realism: given the state of European political culture and social order toward the end of the nineteenth century, his emphasis on the inescapable logic of political power in the modern nation state merely notes the obvious, namely that – despite liberal and social democratic proclamations to the

---

[105] See also Hans Blumenberg, *Work on Myth*, trans. Robert M. Wallace (Cambridge, Mass.: MIT Press, 1985), p. 629.
[106] For a prominent example see, Nietzsche's polemical opposition between the so-called "Laws of Manu," the Sanskrit compendium of sacred laws, and the moral ideals of the Judeo-Christian tradition (*TI* VII: 3–4 and A 56–7). See Thomas Brobjer, "The Absence of Political Ideals in Nietzsche's Writings: The Case of the Laws of Manu and the Associated Caste-Society," *Nietzsche-Studien* 27 (1998), 300–18. For an interpretation of the very same passages that come to the opposite conclusion, see Dombowsky, *Nietzsche's Machiavellian Politics*, pp. 42–3, and Conway, *Nietzsche and the Political*, pp. 34–9.

contrary – the political always entails a complex set of uncomfortable hierarchies. In fact, Nietzsche's understanding of political power anticipates very clearly Max Weber's famous definition of the state in his 1919 lecture in Munich, "Politik als Beruf":

> Just like the political associations which preceded it historically, the state is a relationship of *rule* [*Herrschaft*] by human beings over human beings, and one that rests on the legitimate use of violence (that is, violence that is held to be legitimate). For the state to remain in existence, those who are ruled must *submit* to the authority claimed by whoever rules at any given time.[107]

Despite his own preference for an "ethic of responsibility [*Verantwortungsethik*]," Weber outlines in this passage the fundamental insight that also marks Nietzsche's political realism.[108] Political ideals are rather questionable, since they rarely correspond to the realities of the political. Weber is quite correct in noting, much like Michel Foucault, that the question of authority, domination and hierarchy not only pertains to the modern state, but that it is generally part of any social organization: "Without exception every sphere of social action is profoundly influenced by structures of domination."[109]

Although this might be a tempting conclusion, Nietzsche does not adopt a strong program of political realism which claims that ethical judgments can be acceptable only if they are guided by considerations of advantage. In its most radical form, such a strong program would lead to the conclusion that ethical judgments play no role in political life. In contrast, Nietzsche seems to advocate a much weaker program that merely concedes ethical judgments to distort practical political reasoning if such judgments are the only

---

[107] Weber, "The Profession and Vocation of Politics," in *Political Writings*, pp. 309–64: 311.
[108] Ibid., p. 359. On Weber's *Verantwortungsethik*, see Wolfgang Schluchter, "Conviction and Responsibility: Max Weber on Ethics," in *Paradoxes of Modernity: Culture and Conduct in the Theory of Max Weber*, trans. Neil Solomon (Stanford, Calif.: Stanford University Press, 1996), pp. 48–101. That Weber's understanding of power and *Herrschaft* remained in many ways influenced by his reading of Nietzsche has not gone unnoticed. See Mark Warren, "Max Weber's Nietzschean Conception of Power," *History of the Human Sciences* 5/3 (1992), 19–37.
[109] Max Weber, *Economy and Society: An Outline of Interpretive Sociology*, ed. Guenther Roth and Claus Wittich (Berkeley, Calif.: University of California Press, 1978), vol. II, p. 941. See also Michel Foucault, "Nietzsche, Genealogy, History," in John Richardson and Brian Leiter (eds.), *Nietzsche* (Oxford: Oxford University Press, 2001), pp. 341–59: 349.

guiding principle of human agency. This would not preclude an ethical outcome of political action, but suggest that such an outcome is more likely in the long run if ethical judgments are relegated to the background and do not disguise that the political is inextricably linked to the assertion of power.

Throughout his writings after 1871 Nietzsche was often vehemently critical of daily politics and political thought, attacking not only liberals and socialists, but also the conservative nationalism that much later, at the beginning of the twentieth century, would seek to accommodate his ideas. In *Menschliches, Allzumenschliches*, for instance, he noted with regard to socialism, and by implication with regard to the rise of social democracy, that the inherent danger of the political consists in depersonalizing political interests and conflicts, transforming them into absolute value distinctions, which cannot seriously be questioned (*HA* I: 454).[110] Remarks such as these are, of course, uncomfortable from our own point of view. But he is nevertheless able to shed light on the tense relationship between political rationality and public demands that accompanies most Western democracies:

> The demagogic character and the intention to appeal to the masses is at present common to all political parties: on account of this intention they are all compelled to transform their principles into great *al fresco* stupidities and thus to paint them on the wall. This is no longer alterable, indeed it would be pointless to raise so much as a finger against it; for in this domain there apply the words of Voltaire: *quand la populace se mêle de raisonner, tout est perdu.* (*HA* I: 438)[111]

Nietzsche clearly wishes to take Voltaire's remark in a letter from 1766 seriously, underlining the ambivalent nature of modern mass democracy. But this does not only imply a growing distance from the contemporary liberalism of, say, John Stuart Mill and Auguste Comte. More importantly it implies a relentless political realism with regard to the affairs of the state, which is grounded in a historical perspective: "Our social order will slowly melt away, as all previous orders have done, as soon as the suns of novel opinions shine out over mankind with a new heat" (*HA* I: 443). Social and political order is historically contingent and does not rest on a

---

[110] For a fuller and historically contextual account of Nietzsche's critique of socialism, see Marti, "*Der grosse Pöbel- und Sklavenaufstand*", pp. 150–2 and 162–3.
[111] See Voltaire to Etienne Noël Damilaville (April 1, 1766), in *Œuvres Complètes*, vol. CXIV, p. 155.

teleological process toward a political ideal. But in the very same paragraph Nietzsche also seeks to distance himself from interpreting the historical contingency of the present as a sign for the possibility of a new political order that is qualitatively better than the present. The latter would consist in a "*desire*" for the present to be overturned, which is only possible if there is the hope that political ideals themselves can materialize in the future: "and one may reasonably harbour hope only if one credits oneself and one's kind with more power in head and heart than is possessed by the representatives of what at present exists. Usually, therefore, this hope will be a piece of *presumption* and an *overvaluation*" (*HA* I: 443).

Nietzsche's political realism, then, leads to an uncomfortable and idiosyncratic position. Unable to accept the political culture of the nation state, he is also unable to accept liberalism or socialism as a reasonable alternative. Rather, in a Machiavellian turn, he views the egalitarian political ideals of both liberalism and socialism not as centered on the question of "*justice*," but on that of "*power*" (*HA* I: 446): to put it more sharply, behind the political ideal of justice stands the desire for power. Seen from this perspective, it really seems to be the case that the liberal and socialist traditions of the nineteenth century – united in their common concern with the absoluteness of rights and the universality of justice – exhibit an internal inconsistency that Nietzsche's political realism is able to exploit:

> Noble (if not particularly judicious) representatives of the ruling class can by all means vow: let us treat men as equals, concede to them equal rights. To this extent a socialist mode of thought resting on *justice* is possible; but, as aforesaid, only within the ruling class, which in this case *practises* justice with sacrifices and self-denials. To *demand* equality of rights, on the other hand, as the socialists of the subject caste do, is never an emanation of justice but of desire [*Begehrlichkeit*]. – If one holds up bleeding chunks of meat to an animal and takes them away again until it finally roars: do you think this roaring has anything to do with justice? (*HA* I: 451)[112]

The practice of equality and justice is possible only from a position of superiority, whereas the demand for equality from below remains

---

[112] R. J. Hollingdale translates the German *Begehrlichkeit* as "greed," which in German would be *Gier*. While Nietzsche's reference to animals seems to justify the latter, he merely makes an analogy. The central role of the term "desire" in previous paragraphs underlines the coherence of Nietzsche's terminology.

an attempt to reverse the political hierarchy by asserting new forms of domination. It is in this respect that Nietzsche, once again, shares much common ground with Max Weber, who pointed out the dangers of such political desire: "the *un*organised mass, the democracy of the street, is wholly irrational."[113] It inevitably culminates in a "purely emotional 'radicalism'" that has little, if any, grounding in the complexity of historically shaped political realities. For Nietzsche, this will be a central characteristic of moral communities; as such, it is the political subject of his genealogy.

Considering Nietzsche's direct political statements from the early 1870s to his more controversial metaphors of the "will to power" and the *Übermensch* through the *camera obscura* of twentieth-century political ideology, he clearly leaves the impression of unreservedly espousing aristocratic ideals of social hierarchy that sit uncomfortably with our own democratic institutions.[114] Representing a "higher type" of humanity, the *Übermensch* is an exemplary exception that stands in opposition to modern mass society and its egalitarian desires which Nietzsche regards as fueled by the long tradition and continuing influence of Christianity (*AC* 4 and 5). As such, the *Übermensch* is not any specific individual, or a specific ideal that could be realized in the future. Whether this automatically implies that Nietzsche's political vision is authoritarian par excellence is, however, doubtful. While his understanding of the political is rarely compatible with contemporary liberalism, it seems to be the case that the authoritarian dimension of Nietzsche's *Übermensch* is overstated. Perhaps it is sufficient to note that the *Übermensch* is, above all, a metaphorical construction that Nietzsche uses as a blatant counter-image to a system of moral values derived from Christianity, that is, moral values that blur the distinction between religion and political life.

In fact, given Nietzsche's pronouncements throughout the 1880s, it seems as though the much-quoted *Übermensch* is a variant of what he describes elsewhere, in *Die fröhliche Wissenschaft* and *Jenseits von Gut und Böse*, as the "free spirit," that is, the autonomous and

---

[113] Weber, *Parliament and Government in Germany*, in *Political Writings*, p. 231.
[114] See, for instance, Keith Ansell-Pearson, *An Introduction to Nietzsche as a Political Thinker: The Perfect Nihilist* (Cambridge: Cambridge University Press, 1994), p. 166, and Detwiler, *Nietzsche and the Politics of Aristocratic Radicalism*, pp. 47–54. In contrast, Conway, *Nietzsche and the Political*, pp. 20–7, noted that the *Übermensch* needs to be seen as the realization of Nietzsche's perfectionism.

sovereign individual, "the lover of knowledge," who sets out into the "'open sea'" (*GS* 343).[115] Nietzsche's reference to the infinity of the open sea is neither purely rhetorical nor accidental. Rather, it represents the almost impossible task that the "free spirit" has to face. This is a task that is always threatened by failure as in the case of the "aeronauts of the spirit" that, in 1881, he mentions in the final paragraph of *Morgenröthe*: the latter fly out "into the farthest distance" and "strive whither we have striven, and where everything is sea, sea, sea," but as such they are also faced with the impossible task of ever reaching their destination: "Will it perhaps be said of us one day that we too, *steering westward, hoped to reach India* – but that it was our fate to be wrecked against infinity?" (*D* 575).[116]

The vain hope to reach India by sailing westward, of course, is precisely that voyage that is connected to the name of Columbus, whom Nietzsche refers to on several occasions in *Morgenröthe* (*D*, 37 and 547).[117] Between mid-November 1880 and late April 1881, Nietzsche himself composed the final version of *Morgenröthe* in the Italian port of Genoa, Columbus's birthplace. Also, two weeks before Nietzsche arrives in Genoa, he sends a postcard to his friend Paul Rée, who had just returned from a visit to North America: "Perhaps, my dearest friend, you have already returned and saved yourself and your philosophical thought from the dangers of the sea and from Americanness [*Amerikanerthum*]" (*KGB* III/1, p. 44).

Needless to say, the figure of Columbus is a well-established philosophical trope as, for instance, in Abraham Cowley's ode *To Mr. Hobs* (1656), which describes Thomas Hobbes as that "great *Columbus* of the golden lands of new philosophies," who leaves behind the, as it were, narrow waters of the Baltic Sea and the Mediterranean in order to cross the "seas and skies" of the "vast ocean" on the way to "unknown regions."[118] Nietzsche's link

---

[115] See also *BGE* 44, 214, 227, and 228.
[116] This image is indebted to the final line of Giacomo Leopardi's poem *L'Infinito* (1819): "E il naufragar m'è dolce in questo mare." See *Selected Prose and Poetry*, ed. and trans. Iris Origo and John Heath-Stubbs (Oxford: Oxford University Press, 1966), p. 212. Nietzsche quotes directly from Leopardi in his notebooks from late 1880: "Infinity! Beautiful it is 'to be wrecked in this sea'" (*KGW* V/1, 6 [364]). For a similar image, see also *GS* 382.
[117] On the figure of Columbus as a metaphorical device in Nietzsche's writings, see Peter Gasser, "'Columbus Novus': Zum rhetorischen Impetus von Nietzsche's Philosophie," *Nietzsche-Studien* 24 (1995), 137–61.
[118] Abraham Cowley, *To Mr. Hobs*, in *Poems: "Miscellanies," "The Mistress," "Pindarique Odes," "Verses Written on Several Occasions*," ed. A. R. Waller (Cambridge: Cambridge University Press, 1905), pp. 188–92.

between the "free spirits" and the "open sea" thus continues a rhetorical commonplace of early modern and modern European thought: transgressing the limits of traditional learning in a dangerous attempt to widen knowledge.[119] On the frontispiece of the 1620 edition of Francis Bacon's *Novum Organum*, two ships that have crossed the imaginary boundary between the "fatal pillars of Hercules" – the Rock of Gibraltar and Mount Hacho in North Africa – are returning home, bringing new knowledge from a *terra incognita* to the "old" world.[120] Accompanied by the motto "Many shall pass through, and knowledge will be increased [*multi pertransibunt et augebitur scientia*]," the returning ships have clearly transgressed the bounderies of traditional learning, since the "pillars of Hercules" signify, for instance, in Plato's *Timaeus*, the end of the known world.[121] At the same time, it is important to realize that Bacon's actual emphasis in this emblematic image lies on the ships' return to their point of departure, which calls attention to the fact that the success of their voyage was only possible because of the navigational mastery over nature: curiosity and control over nature makes public what used to be unknown, arcane, and forbidden.[122]

While Nietzsche clearly shares this sense of overcoming danger by entering the unknown and forbidden, his reference to the "open sea" marks a voyage without return and is influenced by those notions of the infinite that have emerged in the context of German Romanticism.[123] It is within this context, especially in the work of Friedrich Schlegel, that we can find an immediate connection between freedom and infinity that also has political implications.

---

[119] See still Carlo Ginzburg, "High and Low: The Theme of Forbidden Knowledge in the Sixteenth and Seventeenth Centuries," *Past and Present* 73 (1976), 28–41.

[120] Francis Bacon, *The New Organon*, ed. Lisa Jardine and Michael Silverthorne (Cambridge: Cambridge University Press, 2000), p. 6. On the *terra incognita* as a philosophical metaphor, see Hans Blumenberg, *Paradigmen zu einer Metaphorologie*, 2nd edn. (Frankfurt/M.: Suhrkamp, 1999), pp. 77–90.

[121] Bacon, *The New Organon*, p. 78 (Bacon quotes here Daniel 12.4, which in the King James version of 1611 runs: "many shall runne to and fro, and knowledge shall bee increased"). See also Plato, *Timaeus*, 24d-25d.

[122] See Peter Harrison, "Curiosity, Forbidden Knowledge, and the Reformation of Natural Philosophy in Early Modern England," *Isis* 92 (2001), 265–90: 279–82. The translation of arcane learning into public knowledge is an important philosophical strategy in Bacon's work. See Stephen Gaukroger, *Francis Bacon and the Transformation of Early Modern Philosophy* (Cambridge: Cambridge University Press, 2001), pp. 6–10.

[123] On the motif of the "infinite voyage," see Manfred Frank, *Unendliche Fahrt: Ein Motiv und sein Text* (Frankfurt/M.: Suhrkamp, 1979).

Defining freedom in his aesthetic writings initially as a "system of infinite progression", Schlegel goes on to proclaim several years later: "civil freedom [*bürgerliche Freiheit*] is only an *idea*, which can be made actual only through an infinite progressive approximation."[124] Although Nietzsche clearly remains suspicious about those notions of political freedom that gained currency in the immediate aftermath of the French Revolution – the "ideas of 1789" – there can be little doubt that his "free spirit" and his repeated reference to the "open sea" have strong political implications. But in contrast to Schlegel's optimism about civil society, Nietzsche began to view the institutions of civil society in the nineteenth-century nation state as the exact opposite of freedom. Seven years after the final volume of *Menschliches, Allzumenschliches* was published and six years after *Morgenröthe*, he noted in the fifth book of *Die fröhliche Wissenschaft* that modern society, contrary to its own political proclamations and hopes (*GS* 356), remained under the authority of blind "faith":

> Faith is always most desired and most urgently needed where will is lacking; for will, as the affect of command, is the decisive mark of sovereignty and strength. That is, the less someone knows how to command, the more urgently does he desire someone who commands, who commands severely – a god, prince, the social order [*Stand*], father confessor, dogma, or party conscience. ... Once a human being arrives at the basic conviction that he *must* be commanded, he becomes "a believer"; conversely, one could conceive of a delight and power of self-determination, a *freedom* of the will, in which the spirit [*Geist*] takes leave of all faith and every wish for certainty, practised as it is in maintaining itself on light ropes and possibilities and dancing even beside abysses. Such a spirit would be the *free spirit* par excellence. (*GS* 347)[125]

Nietzsche's "free spirit," in other words, is precisely the opposite of what he regards as the nature of politics within the modern

---

[124] Schlegel, "Vom Wert des Studiums der Griechen und Römer," in *Kritische Friedrich-Schlegel-Ausgabe*, vol. I, p. 631, and "Essay on the Concept of Republicanism Occasioned by the Kantian Tract 'Perpetual Peace'," in *The Early Political Writings of the German Romantics*, ed. and trans. Frederick C. Beiser (Cambridge: Cambridge University Press, 1996), pp. 93–112: 97. In the German original, the term "idea" is in italics. See "Versuch über den Republikanismus: Veranlaßt durch die Kantische Schrift zum ewigen Frieden," in *Kritische Friedrich-Schlegel-Ausgabe*, vol. VII, p. 12.

[125] While Josefine Nauckhoff's translation of this passage is entirely correct, the German term *Stand* also refers to "class" and "social standing." Furthermore, Nietzsche's use of the term *Geist* in this passage should not be confused with a Hegelian notion of "spirit," but simply refers to "intellect."

nation state, that is, a situation that Max Weber, three decades later, saw as the inevitability of the "demagogue" in modern politics: "Democratisation and demagogy belong together. ... For it is not the politically passive 'mass' which gives birth to the leader; rather the political leader recruits his following and wins over the mass by 'demagogy'."[126] In contrast, Nietzsche's "free spirit," as an autonomous individual, is able to avoid the effects of demagogy and political fanaticism.

The free spirit that Nietzsche outlines in the passage quoted above in fact clearly resembles the "*sovereign individual*" that he presents in the second essay of *Zur Genealogie der Moral*. Given that the fifth book of *Die fröhliche Wissenschaft* was published in 1887, the same year Nietzsche finished *Zur Genealogie der Moral*, this resemblance is hardly surprising. Although the sovereign individual is presented as the ultimate outcome of the same long-term process of social evolution that gives rise to the moral absolutes of "good" and "evil," and to guilt as the most central moral sentiment (*GM* II: 20), the sovereign individual is able to reach beyond its own past, to gain an independence from this past much like the critical historian Nietzsche descibed in his second "Untimely Meditation" (*UM* II: 3). In other words, the sovereign individual, "having freed itself from the morality of custom," constitutes "an autonomous, supra-ethical individual," who has recognized both the weakness and the dangers of traditional moral absolutes (*GM* II: 2). From the perspective of this sovereign individual, positive ethical judgments cannot be based on custom, guilt or an eternal order of moral evaluations; rather, they have to be grounded in "the extraordinary privilege of *responsibility*," that is, in the choice to accept accountability (*GM* II: 2). Such a choice is neither dependent on supernatural forces, such as "God" and "the soul," nor determined by metaphysical abstractions, such as "reason" and "freedom." Like the free spirits, "who give themselves laws, who create themselves," as Nietzsche already noted in the first edition of *Die fröhliche Wissenschaft* from 1882, the sovereign individual has to make its own world (*GS* 335). Four years later, in *Jenseits von Gut und Böse*, he continued this line of thought, emphasizing the inevitably precarious situation within which such an

---

[126] Weber, *Parliament and Government in Germany*, in *Political Writings*, pp. 220 and 228.

individual finds itself: "The 'individual' is left standing there, forced to give himself laws, forced to rely on his own arts and wiles of self-preservation, self-enhancement, self-redemption" (*BGE* 262).

To be sure, it would be both easier and safer to follow a morality of custom. But, for Nietzsche, the sovereign individual and the free spirit have already understood that such a "morality of mediocrity" unconsciously disguises its true motives behind an appeal to moral humility. The latter "can never admit what it is and what it wants! It has to talk about moderation and dignity and duty and loving your neighbors, – it will have a hard time *hiding its irony!*" (*BGE* 262) This irony is the result of the very fact that the claim for humility is, in fact, a claim for power. By 1887, once the genealogical project was under way, the close relationship between moral communities and the importance of power as the ordering principle of the political led Nietzsche to a conclusion that anticipated a tradition of modern political thought that stretches from Max Weber to Michel Foucault: "Instead of 'sociology'," Nietzsche demanded in a crucial notebook entry, "a *theory of the forms of rule* [*Lehre von den Herrschaftsgebilden*]" (*KGW*VIII/2, 9 [8]). This is precisely the problem that was on Weber's mind when, in the chaotic months immediately after the First World War, he outlined the question of *Herrschaft*:

In our terms, then, "politics" would mean striving for a share of power or for influence on the distribution of power, whether it be between states or between the groups of people contained within a single state. ... For the state to remain in existence, those who are ruled must *submit* to the authority claimed by whoever rules at any given time. When do people do this, and why? What inner justifications and what external means support this rule?[127]

For Weber, of course, the answer to this question was three-fold: the legitimacy of rule could be based on custom, charisma, or legality.[128] Nietzsche, however, was to approach this problem from a more anthropological perspective that sought to take into account what Foucault descibed as "the mechanisms of power which have invested human bodies, acts and forms of behaviour."[129]

---

[127] Weber, "The Profession and Vocation of Politics," in *Political Writings*, p. 311.
[128] See ibid., pp. 311–12.
[129] Michel Foucault, "Body/Power," in *Power/Knowledge: Selected Interviews and Other Writings, 1972–1977*, ed. Colin Gordon (New York: Pantheon, 1981), pp. 55–62: 61.

Leaving aside the seemingly peculiar perspective of Nietzsche's discussion of power and the political, if only for a moment, we are at least able to see more clearly that Nietzsche's "free spirit" and *Übermensch* are, above all, characterized by an unrelenting political realism that is aware of the nature of power. The *Übermensch* emerges as that exemplary individual who is able to perceive "reality *as it is*" (*EH* XIV: 5) in the same way as Niccolò Machiavelli and Cesare Borgia realized that there is relatively little space for Christian virtue ethics in the realm of the political.[130] Nietzsche himself recommends replacing Christian "virtue" with the Renaissance concept of *virtù* (*AC* 2). This is, of course, a barely hidden reference to Machiavelli, who uses *virtù* not in the sense of "virtue," as opposed to "vice," but in the sense of "skill," "energy," and "determination."[131] *Virtù* is the intellectual capacity that allows Machiavelli's prince, much like Nietzsche's sovereign individual and free spirit, to counterbalance the possibly detrimental effects of chance, or *fortuna*: *virtù*, in other words, allows the sovereign individual to live with the kind of uncertainty that would otherwise overwhelm the ability of ordinary individuals to act.[132]

Indeed, there is much to be learnt from Machiavelli, and Nietzsche's occasional references to the latter often highlight the close relationship between philosophical thought and the realm of politics, which is a central factor of a specific tradition of Renaissance humanism: the philosopher's active observation of political life is necessarily marked by moral and political skepticism.[133] Nietzsche himself shares this skepticism toward political ideals, which is perhaps best outlined by Machiavelli: "But because I want to write what will be useful to anyone who understands, it seems to me better to concentrate on what really happens

---

[130] Detwiler, *Nietzsche and the Politics of Aristocratic Radicalism*, pp. 51–4, has a more detailed account of Nietzsche's image of Cesare Borgia, while Ottmann, *Philosophie und Politik bei Nietzsche*, pp. 281–92, provides a balanced and contextual account of Nietzsche's reception of Machiavelli.

[131] See Niccolò Machiavelli, *The Prince*, ed. Quentin Skinner and Russell Price (Cambridge: Cambridge University Press, 1988), p. 30, where Price translates Machiavelli's expression *virtù di animo e di corpo* as "energy of mind and body."

[132] See ibid., pp. 84–7, and Bonnie Honig, *Political Theory and the Displacement of Politics* (Ithaca, N.Y.: Cornell University Press, 1993), pp. 66–9.

[133] See Richard Tuck, *Philosophy and Government, 1572–1651* (Cambridge: Cambridge University Press, 1993), pp. 31–64, and, with particular reference to Machiavelli, J. G. A. Pocock, *The Machiavellian Moment: Florentine Political Thought and the Atlantic Republican Tradition* (Princeton, N.J.: Princeton University Press, 1975), pp. 156–218.

rather than on theories or speculations. For many have imagined republics and principalities that have never been seen or known to exist."[134]

Although it might seem that the lessons in political realism that Machiavelli and other political thinkers of Renaissance humanism have drawn were defeated by the eighteenth century's discovery of "humanity" and universal moral norms, at least Herder noted the continued relevance of such realism: in ignoring the normative claims of "right and wrong, vice and virtue" such realism "measures out the result of given forces": "Does it not occupy itself with the most tangled, important problem that our species faces? [That is,] *human forces in relation to their effects and consequences.*" At the same time, however, Herder also views Machiavelli with "horror" and notes that "history's highest *interest*, its *value* rests on this human sensibility, the *rule of right and wrong.*"[135] Nietzsche begins to wonder, however, whether such rules of right and wrong are really quite as intuitive as Herder believed them to be. Despite his awareness of the fact that the "misuse of Christianity has caused countless evil in the world," Herder necessarily remained committed to a Christian understanding of virtue that is based on both sensibility and faith.[136] Nietzsche himself is unable to take this route, precisely because he increasingly comes to believe, as we are going to see in more detail in the following chapter, that moral communities based on faith move perilously close to fanaticism:

> For fanaticism is the only "strength of the will" that even the weak and insecure can be brought to attain, as a type of hypnosis of the entire sensual-intellectual system to the benefit of the excessive nourishment (hypertrophy) of a single point of view and feeling which is now dominant – the Christian calls it his "faith." (*GS* 347)

Faith, in other words, remains a one-dimensional intellectual predisposition, which runs counter to the openness of the "free spirit." Against this background, we are thus safe in assuming that Nietzsche's *Übermensch* and "free spirit" are not images of authoritarianism; rather, they represent an individual able to face the intellectual illusions and cultural crises of any given time, while

---

[134] Machiavelli, *The Prince*, p. 54.
[135] Herder, *Letters for the Advancement of Humanity*, in *Philosophical Writings*, p. 411.
[136] Ibid., p. 424.

accepting that political life is always marked by a struggle for domination and, thus, by an order of rank.[137]

Such an individual would have to subscribe to the virtue of political realism, the virtue of *Redlichkeit*, as Nietzsche notes in *Jenseits von Gut und Böse*:

> Genuine honesty [*Redlichkeit*], assuming that this is our virtue and we cannot get rid of it, we free spirits – well then, we will want to work on it with all the love and malice at our disposal, and not get tired of "perfecting" ourselves in *our* virtue, the only one we have left: .... And if our genuine honesty nevertheless gets tired one day and sighs and stretches its limbs and finds us too harsh and would rather things were better, easier, gentler, like an agreeable vice: we will stay *harsh*, we, who are the last of the Stoics! (*BGE* 227)

Given this relentless emphasis on honesty as a virtue, it is perhaps safe to say that Nietzsche's views are more illiberal than many postmodern commentators care to admit, but less illiberal than his critics are prepared to assume.

It is against the background of this relentless, and ultimately cruel, political realism that a specific understanding of political life lies at the heart of Nietzsche's writings during the 1880s: the realm of political life and social action is mainly characterized by the acquisition of power. From this perspective it is also clear why Nietzsche is highly skeptical with regard to translating those political ideals into actions that do not account for the reality of power, such as populist notions of liberty and equality. Once the latter are translated into social action – expressing, for instance, a presumed general will through elections – they cannot escape the logic of power and *Herrschaft*. It is, however, only through genealogy as a strategy of historical critique that Nietzsche is able to reach this position and because he grounds genealogy in a philosophical naturalism that seeks to bridge the gap between nature and normativity.

---

[137] See Daniel W. Conway, "Overcoming the *Übermensch*: Nietzsche's Revaluation of Values," *Journal of the British Society for Phenomenology* 20 (1989), 211–24.

CHAPTER 5

Genealogy, naturalism, and the political

There are two sides to Nietzsche's genealogy as it is formulated in *Jenseits von Gut und Böse* and *Zur Genealogie der Moral*. On a philosophical level, genealogy clearly seeks to challenge the validity of moral norms insofar as these norms are based on supposedly universal claims regarding human agency. Genealogy, then, is a critique of what has been termed "morality in the pejorative sense."[1] When Nietzsche makes his seemingly most outrageous claim – that genealogy seeks to achieve a "revaluation of all values" (*TI* preface and VI: 2; *EH* XI: 1) – he does not wish to reject all values. Rather, he wishes to address whether values have any value in the first place, that is, whether they are grounded in human nature or whether they are made by us and subsequently internalized to such an extent that we believe them to be grounded in human nature. This is clearly an ambitious undertaking, but the philosophical critique of moral norms is only one dimension of genealogy: morality in the pejorative sense does not exist outside the realm of the political, but makes direct political claims. The second dimension of genealogy is its political orientation. As a strategy to question the validity of moral absolutes, genealogy also questions their translation into political action: moral norms always create moral communities, and if such moral communities strive for internal homogeneity – regardless as to whether they are committed to rational liberalism or more authoritarian ways of life – they require absolutes that allow them to exclude that which is seen as threatening such homogeneity. To be sure, there are different kinds of moral communities, some more open than others. But as far as the dominant moral

---

[1] See Brian Leiter, "Morality in the Pejorative Sense: On the Logic of Nietzsche's Critique of Morality," *British Journal for the History of Philosophy* 3 (1995), 113–45.

community of the nineteenth century, the "nation," is concerned, it is difficult to overlook that the latter requires precisely those moral and political absolutes that are the subject of genealogy. Indeed, the political relevance of genealogy consists in exploring the historical formation of moral communities, thereby rendering obvious that their political legitimacy does not rest on absolute normative claims but on norms that have been made absolute.

In the present chapter I will not attempt a philosophical interpretation of Nietzsche's genealogy in the narrow sense of the term. What I am interested in, rather, is the way in which the philosophical claims of genealogy, including its naturalist perspective, mark the center of Nietzsche's political thought and, as such, respond to the political culture of modernity. This distinction is important for mainly two reasons. First, the genealogical project clearly constitutes Nietzsche's most lasting contribution to modern political thought. Second, even though genealogy continues to raise important philosophical questions today, it does not emerge in a historical vacuum but reacts to the political configurations of modernity just before 1900. But before it is possible to address these configurations in more detail, it will be necessary to outline Nietzsche's path to genealogy during the 1880s.

THE PATH TO GENEALOGY

Most of the writings Nietzsche was able to complete during the 1880s, with the notable exceptions of *Also sprach Zarathustra* (1883–85) and *Ecce Homo* (1888–89), are often marked by an increasingly historical perspective, which seems to confirm that his earlier reflections on the value of historical knowledge have far-reaching consequences for the general outlook of his later philosophy. Although genealogy itself represents an inherently historical strategy right from the beginning, it is interesting to see that the historical perspective of his later writings has triggered only limited interest. In fact, genealogy is often seen in opposition to history. But Nietzsche's education and professional practice in the historical discipline of classical scholarship still continued to shape many of the philosophical models and arguments he put forth in his later writings. Although genealogy often employs metaphors rooted in contemporary biological thought, such as the "physiology of morality" (*KGW* VII/2, 27 [14] and [37]), the genealogical method itself is also presented as a specific kind of reading, of tracing variants, and of interpreting signs. Given that textual criticism and evolutionary biology are marked by very similar historiographical models of inference and explanation, it should not be surprising that Nietzsche's argument easily moved between these seemingly different fields.[2] In his preface to the second edition of *Morgenröthe* from 1887, for example, Nietzsche openly emphasizes the critical value of philological interpretation as a means of slow and analytical reading:

> It is not for nothing that I have been a philologist, perhaps I am a philologist still, that is to say, a teacher of slow reading: ... For philology is that venerable craft which demands of its votaries one thing above all: to go aside, to take time, to become still, to become slow – it is a goldsmith's craft and connoisseurship of the *word* which has nothing but delicate, cautious work to do and achieves nothing if it does not achieve it *lento*. (*D* preface, 5)[3]

Genealogy, then, derives much inspiration from philology and the historical method as Nietzsche encountered them in his early work during the 1860s and early 1870s. But genealogy is not a philology, or hermeneutics, of culture, since it has strong naturalist commitments that, as we shall see, are rooted in evolutionary thought.[4] As a critical mode of thought, genealogy is thus able to bridge the artificial gap between the human and the natural sciences, drawing on practices that are common to the historical disciplines of the nineteenth century, including philology and

---

[2] See Aviezer Tucker, *Our Knowledge of the Past: A Philosophy of Historiography* (Cambridge: Cambridge University Press, 2004), pp. 85–91.

[3] R.J. Hollingdale translated Nietzsche's expression *Goldschmiedekunst* as "a goldsmith's art," which bears aestheticist overtones that are not justified by Nietzsche's subject, i.e. philology, which he generally understands as a "practice" or "craft." Likewise, when Nietzsche describes philology as a *Kunst* in the above passage, it would be better translated as "craft" instead of "art," since the nineteenth-century German *Kunst* also refers to "ability." In fact, in his early notebooks from spring 1869, he describes "philology" as an *ars critica*, which refers to the "skill" of philological criticism (*KGW*1/5, 75 [3]). Benne, *Nietzsche und die historisch-kritische Philologie*, pp. 96–150, has reconstructed the philological dimension of Nietzsche's later genealogical project in much detail, albeit without paying attention to the philosophical questions Nietzsche raises.

[4] Hermeneutic interpretations tend to relegate this naturalist dimension into the background. In this respect, the following account differs fundamentally from Eric Blondel, *Nietzsche – The Body and Culture: Philosophy as Philological Genealogy*, trans. Seán Hand (Stanford, Calif.: Stanford University Press, 1991), pp. 88–133, and Alan D. Schrift, "Between Perspectivism and Philology: Genealogy as Hermeneutic," *Nietzsche-Studien* 16 (1987), 91–111.

evolutionary biology. Seen from this perspective, it deals with the emergence of central cultural mentalities and with the way in which such mentalities have changed over long periods in time. In *Jenseits von Gut und Böse*, for instance, Nietzsche suggested that traditional metaphysical notions – e.g. self, causality, truth, objectivity, substance, force, and things-in-themselves – result from an undue generalization of linguistic and psychological conditions (*BGE* 3–4, 17 and 20). Without wishing to go into the detail of these more epistemological claims, I would argue that, for Nietzsche, the unconscious afterlife of these concepts has a profound influence on the way in which modern culture sees itself, and it would be particularly worthwhile to trace the evolution of central psychological commonplaces, such as moral sentiments, conscience, and guilt.

To some extent, Nietzsche's genealogical enterprise resembles and even refines Kant's project of a critical philosophy, although they come to radically different conclusions.[5] While Kant focused on the limits of reason with regard to our knowledge about the physical world, Nietzsche examined the limits of reason with regard to the historical evolution of cultural values. But although Kant's philosophy continued to be of crucial importance for Nietzsche's later epistemological reflections, we need to be cautious. Kant's critique of reason seeks to establish a methodologically firm ground for philosophical thought and is largely concerned with the formal conditions of reason, which includes the formal conditions of ethical judgment as they are laid out in the categorical imperative.[6] In this respect, Kant aimed at a homogeneous systematization of knowledge, whereas Nietzsche's historical philosophy sought to account for the heterogeneity of knowledge and the contingency of human experience: "The total character of the world ... is for all eternity chaos, not in the sense of a lack of necessity but of a lack of order, organization, form, beauty, wisdom, and whatever else our aesthetic anthropomorphisms are called" (*GS* 109). Nietzsche, it seems, would rather relinquish the unity of reason than accept its illusions.

---

[5] See Gilles Deleuze, *Nietzsche and Philosophy*, trans. Hugh Tomlinson (New York: Columbia University Press, 1983), pp. 89–94, and Strong, *Friedrich Nietzsche and the Politics of Transfiguration*, p. 36.

[6] See Kant, *Critique of Pure Reason*, pp. 111–14 (B xviii–xxiv), and *Critique of Practical Reason*, ed. and trans. Mary Gregor, intro. Andrews Reath (Cambridge: Cambridge University Press, 1997), pp. 17, 20, and 26–9.

But despite his skeptical attitude to philosophical grand narratives, it might still be possible to argue that Nietzsche's genealogy of European thought describes a historical and intellectual development from a mythical/theological world-view to a metaphysical one, which is then replaced in the course of the nineteenth century by a scientific world-view. Nietzsche himself, it seems, wished to enrich this scientific world-view with the congruence of art and life, thus overcoming the life-denying impulse of religion, metaphysics, and science.[7] Genealogy, however, operates on a different level: it seeks to understand first of all *that* cultural values have evolved, and secondly *how* they have evolved.[8] Seen against the background of Nietzsche's earlier work in the 1870s, which often emphasized the historical contingency of human experience, this precludes any homogeneous, or linear, historical process. Consequently, Nietzsche's genealogy also fundamentally differs from traditional notions of genealogy that, for instance, trace historical ancestors in order to establish political legitimacy or a collective cultural memory.[9] In his *Theogony*, for instance, Hesiod describes the origins and relationships of the ancient Greek deities, and at least since the early Renaissance genealogy has been regarded as a historical discipline that aims at the reconstruction of actual as well as imagined ancestry in order to legitimate political power.[10] *Genealogeín* is to speak about origins, *genealogía* is the tracing of descent, which in the course of the nineteenth century gained a new dimension given the rise of evolutionary models in the human and natural sciences.[11] For Nietzsche, however, the tracing of descent does not necessarily lead to origins – it breaks off without reaching the source.

Nietzsche is clearly aware that he cannot escape the logic of his own political and intellectual environment. That genealogy is

---

[7] See, for instance, Cox, *Nietzsche*, pp. 19–27 and 63–8.
[8] See Ruth Abbey, *Nietzsche's Middle Period* (Oxford: Oxford University Press, 2000), p. 4.
[9] See Jan Assmann, *Das kulturelle Gedächtnis: Schrift, Erinnerung und politische Identität in frühen Hochkulturen* (Munich: C. H. Beck, 1992), p. 50.
[10] See Kilian Heck, "Das Fundament der Machtbehauptung: Die Ahnentafel als genealogische Grundstruktur der Neuzeit," in: Sigrid Weigel (ed.), *Genealogie und Genetik: Schnittstellen zwischen Biologie und Kulturgeschichte* (Berlin: Akademie Verlag, 2002), pp. 45–56.
[11] See Peter J. Bowler, *The Mendelian Revolution: The Emergence of Hereditarian Concepts in Modern Science and Society* (Baltimore, Md.: Johns Hopkins University Press, 1989), pp. 6–8.

possible in the first place is a result of the fact that the political and intellectual conditions of the nineteenth century themselves begin to highlight the fragile foundations of modernity. It is in this respect that Nietzsche's genealogy unfolds as an internal critique that allows the observer to retrace the way in which the symbolic order of the political is dependent on the close functional relationship between metaphor and myth. Both are, as it were, two sides of the same coin. Metaphors, concepts, symbols and their underlying, often unconscious rhetorical strategies allow us to organize both our cultural and natural environment according to a highly efficient process of "abbreviation" that furnishes the background to the symbolic order of culture:

> The significance of language for the evolution of culture lies in this, that mankind set up in language a separate world beside the other world, a place it took to be so firmly set that, standing upon it, it could lift the rest of the world off its hinges and make itself master of it. To the extent that man has for long ages believed in the concepts and names of things as in *aeternae veritates* he has appropriated to himself that pride by which he raised himself above the animal: they really thought that in language he possessed knowledge of the world. ... A great deal later – only now – it dawns on mankind [*Menschen*] that in their belief in language they have propagated a tremendous error. Happily, it is too late for the evolution of reason, which depends on this belief, to be again put back. (*HA* I: 11)[12]

On the one hand, we are unable to live outside language; on the other, language continually seduces us into believing that our cultural experience is less contingent than it seems and that there are certain truths, including political truths, that hold water in all possible worlds.

The dilemma outlined in the above passage from *Menschliches, Allzumenschliches*, permeates virtually every aspect of Nietzsche's thought on language and culture. The epistemological merits of Nietzsche's position, to be sure, might be debatable. But we cannot ignore that his emphasis on the link between knowledge and metaphor seeks to come to terms with his growing realization that the order of culture, including the order of the political world and of morality, is not based on a privileged access to reality.

---

[12] Translation slightly modified. R. J. Hollingdale rendered *Menschen* as "men," which is more gender-specific than Nietzsche's own expression.

While the conditions of culture, such as a specific understanding of moral values, undoubtedly have factual consequences, they are nevertheless rooted in highly symbolic configurations. As a consequence, Nietzsche reformulates the above passage from 1878 in his notebooks from 1884/85 in the following way:

> with this invented and fixed world of concepts and numbers, man gains the means to take possession of an enormous amount of facts as if they were signs and to inscribe them into his memory. His superiority consists in this apparatus of signs [*Zeichen-Apparat*], especially since it removes him as far away as possible from individual facts [*Einzel-Thatsachen*]. The reduction of experience to *signs*, and the increasingly large amount of things that can be conceived as such: this is his *highest power*. Intellect as the ability to master an enormous amount of facts through signs. (*KGW* VII/3, 34 [131])

The "superiority" of human individuals, Nietzsche suggests, consists in the very fact that they are able to replace the world of facts with a world of signs which are useful but can have fatal consequences.

Nietzsche's remark entails an inherently political dimension. Political absolutism – as it is focused on a specific understanding of "nation," "race," "religion," or "morality" – is a highly symbolic discourse that always implies the negation, at times annihilation, of that which does not correspond to a particular set of values. The consequences of political absolutism are real: people kill, and are killed, in the name of nations, religions, and other moral communities. But political absolutes only gain momentum because they generate a set of values that are widely accepted as a self-evident truth and whose history has been forgotten. Indeed, those who live within the framework of such absolutes are unable to provide a coherent history of this very framework.[13] Thus, if genealogy should be a serious model for the examination of moral and political values it has to investigate how the dynamic relationship between language and knowledge has influenced the formation of these values over time. Evoking the empirical principles of anthropological field studies, Nietzsche describes this method in *Jenseits von Gut und Böse* as: "collecting material,

---

[13] See Daniel W. Conway, "Genealogy and Critical Method," in Richard Schacht (ed.), *Nietzsche, Genealogy, Morality: Essays on Nietzsche's Genealogy of Morality* (Berkeley, Calif.: University of California Press, 1994), pp. 318–33: 328.

formulating concepts, and putting into order the tremendous realm of tender value feelings and value distinctions that live, grow, reproduce, and are destroyed, – and, perhaps, attempting to illustrate the recurring and more frequent shapes of this living crystallization, – all of which would be a preparation for a *typology of morals*" (*BGE* 186).

Such a historical strategy is particularly necessary since, as Nietzsche points out in *Zur Genealogie der Moral*, the moral values and ethical designations that determine human agency are the result of a conceptual history, which we conveniently tend to forget. One of Nietzsche's most prominent examples is the intricate development of the Latin term *bonus* and the German *gut*:

> I think I can interpret the Latin *bonus* as "the warrior:" providing I am correct in tracing *bonus* back to an older *duonus* (compare *bellum*= *duellum*= *duen-lum*, which seems to me to contain that *duonus*). Therefore *bonus* as a man of war, of division (*duo*), as warrior: one can see what made up a man's "goodness" in ancient Rome. Take our German "*gut*": does it not mean "the godlike man," the man "of godlike race?" And is it not identical with the popular (originally noble) name of the Goths? (*GM* I: 5)[14]

As abstruse as this free-wheeling argument may be – the German etymology is simply wrong, the Latin only partly correct – Nietzsche wishes his readers to realize that words and concepts should not be taken for granted: it might be the case that a particular term within the order of our moral ideas might originally refer to its exact opposite. If the meaning of moral concepts is more complex than generally assumed, a kind of forensic practice seems to be an adequate means of examining the fragile foundations of our ethical world: "*What signposts does linguistics, especially the study of etymology, give to the history of the evolution of moral concepts*" (*GM* I: 17).

The reason why we, nevertheless, believe in the existence of permanent and non-historical knowledge about human nature is the fact that we simply, and necessarily, tend to overlook that much of our conceptual knowledge is based on central metaphors which have turned, over relatively long periods in time, into widely

---

[14] Although it seems unlikely that Nietzsche had any detailed knowledge of Hugo Grotius, the source of this passage seems to be Hugo Grotius, *De jure belli ac pacis libri tres* / *The Rights of War and Peace*, trans. Francis W. Kelsey (Oxford: Clarendon Press, 1925), I.i.2.

accepted beliefs. Nietzsche introduces this point in a decisive aphorism of *Morgenröthe*:

Words lie in our way! – Wherever primitive mankind set up a word, they believed they had made a discovery. How different the truth is! – they had touched on a problem, and by supposing they had *solved* it they had created a hindrance to its solution. – Now with every piece of knowledge one has to stumble over dead, petrified words, and one will sooner break a leg than a word. (*D* 47)

That words, and therefore language, stand in our way is a somewhat strange statement for Nietzsche, who believes that it is precisely words and language that lie at the core of our understanding of the world. But what stands in our way is not language in general; it is words which are taken as something else, that is, which are taken as embodying a non-historical truth. It is precisely these truths that lie at the core of moral communities and that are the subject of genealogy.

A NATURAL HISTORY OF MORAL COMMUNITIES

In the first two essays of *Zur Genealogie der Moral*, Nietzsche delivers a particularly pertinent example for the shifts and leaps the order of culture undergoes over time, including their consequences for the moral and political framework of human agency. Nietzsche, of course, is not the first to attempt a history of morality. The latter has already been a distinct genre of early modern European political thought, explaining the contemporary state of, say, natural law theory as the outcome of a progressive development from antiquity to the seventeenth century.[15] The perspective of such "histories of morality" also continued to influence the way in which eighteenth-century philosophers, such as Voltaire and Kant, conceived of the historical unfolding of reason, although Kant himself was not willing to endorse the voluntarist ethics that was often part of such histories of morality.[16] Critical philosophy and the universal nature of the moral law, thus, always stood in some tension to the historicity of Enlightenment as a process of

---

[15] See T.J. Hochstrasser, *Natural Law Theories in the Early Enlightenment* (Cambridge: Cambridge University Press, 2000), pp. 1–39.
[16] See ibid., pp. 187–219.

education, mirroring to some extent the seemingly unbridgeable gap between universal norms and contingent facts. For Nietzsche, however, normativity has a history, and in *Zur Genealogie der Moral*, he seeks to unravel precisely this history.

Focusing on the distinction between "good" and "bad," he argues in the first essay that a value-neutral notion of "bad" – in the sense of being "inferior" without the burden of blame – has been transformed into the notion of "evil" (*GM* I: 11). While premoral societies, in Nietzsche's account, are based on a hierarchy between "good," in the sense of "virtuous"/"noble," and "bad," in the sense of "inferior"/"common," modern societies have reversed this order by attributing social status to a specific order of moral sentiments.[17] By doing so, Nietzsche argues, "common" individuals ("slaves," in his colorful words) begin to feel hatred toward the "nobility," thus creating the *ressentiment* he locates at the center of the Judeo-Christian tradition, triggering the "slave revolt of morality" (*GM* I: 10 and 7): "evil" becomes that which does not adhere to the order of the "slaves'" moral sentiments merely by its very existence and which therefore is seen as the "other" of any given moral community.

A system of moral values, then, emerges on the side of the "slaves," or "commoners," in opposition to the freedom of the "nobles." Influenced by the French religious scholar and orientalist Ernest Renan – who had lost his professorship at the Collège de France in 1864 during the Second Empire because of his criticism of the Catholic Church, only to be reinstated by the Third Republic in 1870 – Nietzsche's account of this revaluation clearly links moral and religious order.[18] Morality, it seems, cannot exist outside the political absolutism of religion: the very idea of religious tolerance is a contradiction in terms. This does not mean that Nietzsche simply wishes to abandon the possibility of ethical

---

[17] Consider, for instance, the distinction in Roman law between *honestiores* ("more honorable men") and *humiliores* ("more humble men"). See *Fontes Iuris Romani Antejustiani*, ed. S. Riccobono, J. Baviera, C. Ferrini, J. Furlani, and V. Arangio-Ruiz, corr. edn. (Florence: Barbèra, 1941–43), vol. III, p. 405.

[18] In Renan's highly controversial "biography" of Jesus, first published in 1863, and ultimately responsible for his dismissal from the Collège de France, he presented a similar reversal of values that lies at the core of Christianity: "poor" equals "soft, humble, pious," while "rich" is linked to "impious, violent, evil." See Ernest Renan, *La Vie de Jésus*, 18th edn. (Paris: Lévy, 1883), pp. 180–2. See also *KGW* VIII/2, 11 [405] and 11 [407]. Nietzsche is, however, also critical of Renan's support for Christianity. See *TI* XI: 2; A 17 and 29; *KGW* VII/3, 35 [43].

judgments. Rather, he introduces what is perhaps best understood as a distinction between moral values and ethical judgment. Ethics can do without an absolutist understanding of values.

The moral notion of "evil," however, does not refer to an individual's actions, but rather to this individual's existence as primordially sinful.[19] As Nietzsche noted in the early 1880s, this is also the reason why moral and political communities, once an existential distinction between "good" and "evil" has become the central value claim of a sizable majority, easily sacrifice the individual for a presumed greater common good that, in reality, is a construct of custom:

> The origin of custom lies in two ideas: "the community [*Gemeinde*] is worth more than the individual" and "an enduring advantage is to be preferred to a transient one"; from which it follows that the enduring advantage of the community is to take unconditional precedence over the advantage of the individual, especially over his momentary wellbeing, but also over his enduring advantage and even over his survival. Even if the individual suffers from an arrangement which benefits the whole, even if he languishes under it, perishes by it – the custom must be maintained, the sacrifice offered up. (*HA* II.i: 89)

Moral righteousness and physical violence are closely linked and the politics of the greater common good entails a necessarily lopsided power relationship: of course, the willingness to sacrifice the individual invariably "*originates* ... only in those who are *not* the sacrifice" (*HA* II.i: 89). A Christian ethics of selflessness, which, for Nietzsche, remains in the background of modern liberalism but also socialism and nationalism, emerges as an inherently self-contradictory and dangerous position: "The 'neighbour' praises selflessness because *it brings him advantages*," not because such selflessness is the realization of a greater common good (*GS* 21).

Nietzsche's argument against traditional notions of selflessness indeed resembles the argument Bernard Williams brought against "external reasons" of human agency. According to the so-called "external reason thesis" it would be possible, for instance, to have a reason for acting selflessly even if our selfless actions do not serve our motivations. Any such reason, in other words, must be external to us and, thus, disconnected from our motivations.

---

[19] As Brian Leiter, *Nietzsche on Morality* (London: Routledge, 2002), pp. 235–42, argued, conscience has thus become moralized through religion, the latter increasingly providing the foundation for moral values.

In reality, however, it is virtually impossible to show that reasons for acting in one way or another are not connected to motivations. Our actions, in other words, have internal reasons.[20] Of course, this does not necessarily imply that we in fact have rational insight into our motivations, although this can be the case; but it nevertheless requires a deliberative process, which has to take into account those aspects of our motivations that might not be rational, our desires, inclinations and interests.[21] In the course of such a deliberative process we might even find motivations and reasons for acting in a particular way that we have not been aware of.[22] It is important to note, however, that for both Nietzsche and Williams the primacy of internal reasons dilutes any strict and absolute distinctions between good and evil.[23]

Moral notions of evil, then, always tend to disguise the practical self-interest of those who seek to establish absolute moral commitments. But they can only be successful in sacrificing dissenting individuals and minorities if the notion of evil they operate with refers to the very existence of individuals and social groups. In contrast, ethical notions of wrongdoing are limited to human agency and generally preclude statements about human existence as such. This is also the reason why Nietzsche, in his notebooks from early 1883, can claim: "Actions are *not evil as such,* but insofar as etc." (*KGW* VII/1, 7 [69]). Human beings as such cannot be judged from an ethical point of view, but merely the complex web of consequences that their actions might generate. Even the possible biological innateness and evolutionary formation of moral concepts does not imply that the existence of absolute moral beliefs and categories, such as evil, can be justified.

It is in this respect that Nietzsche seeks to distance himself from the dominant tradition of moral philosophy that stretches from Plato, Augustine and Aquinas to Kant and modern liberalism. At the center of this tradition stands the primacy of the good, either in historical terms, as in the case of Christian theology, or in an epistemological sense, as in the case of Kant. It is indeed

---

[20] See Bernard Williams, "Internal and External Reasons," in *Moral Luck* (Cambridge: Cambridge University Press, 1981), pp. 101–13.
[21] See ibid., p. 110. [22] See ibid., pp. 104–5.
[23] There is, however, also a fundamental difference. While Nietzsche would argue that Kant's categorical imperative would fall into the category of "external reasons," Williams endorses the latter more readily as an "internal reason." See ibid., p. 106. For Kant himself, of course, the moral law is "in us."

remarkable that the possible innateness of evil and the primacy of the good are crucial components of such a sophisticated moral philosophy as Kant's. Although he notes that both good and evil are innate and that both are therefore the "grand antecedent to every use of freedom given in experience," he also stresses that they cannot possibly coexist: it would simply be contradictory to assume that human individuals and their actions, as far as they are governed by the maxims of a universal moral law, oscillate between good and evil.[24] Given the universal nature of the moral law grounded in pure reason, the "original predisposition" of any individual is "a predisposition to the good" and thus subordinates freedom to the moral law.[25] Conversely, evil violates the moral law and has thus to be understood as a natural propensity to subordinate the moral law under the "free power of choice."[26]

Nietzsche understood the inherent problems of such a position: "There are absolutely no moral phenomena, only a moral interpretation of the phenomena" (*BGE* 108). Furthermore, Kant's arguments implied that evil was simply whatever resisted the universal claims of reason, that is, whatever remained arbitrary and unintelligible.[27] This is precisely Hegel's conclusion when he defines evil as a contradiction to the universal: evil is "that which of necessity ought *not to be*" and, furthermore, "ought to be cancelled [*aufgehoben*]."[28] Indeed, the way in which both Kant and Hegel situate the morally evil within the individual and in opposition to the universal can be seen as a prominent example for the moralization of political thought in German Idealism.[29] Such a moralization could have unintended consequences. On the one hand, it betrays an anxiety about the grey world of human actions. On the other, it is a rather small step from the definition of evil

---

[24] Kant, *Religion within the Boundaries of Mere Reason*, in *Religion and Rational Theology*, pp. 71 and 73.
[25] Ibid., p. 88. See also ibid., pp. 74–6.
[26] Ibid., p. 83. For a fuller discussion of Kant's notion of evil, see Richard J. Bernstein, *Radical Evil: A Philosophical Interrogation* (Cambridge: Polity Press, 2002), pp. 11–44.
[27] That evil is above all a problem of intelligibility is the central argument of Susan Neiman, *Evil in Modern Thought: An Alternative History of Philosophy* (Princeton, N.J.: Princeton University Press, 2002). But her conclusion that, therefore, the history of modern philosophy should be understood as focused on theodicy seems far-fetched and betrays a longing for moral authenticity that seems problematic from a Nietzschean perspective.
[28] Hegel, *Elements of the Philosophy of Right*, pp. 167 (§ 139) and 169 (§ 139, Addition H).
[29] See Heinz D. Kittsteiner, *Die Entstehung des modernen Gewissens* (Frankfurt/M.: Insel, 1991), pp. 226–83.

as the unintelligible "other" to the exclusion of the political "other" in the name of a specific moral majority. It is precisely in this respect that, for Nietzsche, the notion of evil represents the authoritarian streak of modern morality.

Nietzsche's own position is closer to Spinoza, who also sought to de-escalate the absolutism of moral claims at a time when moral communities, in the confessional struggles of the seventeenth century, sought to restrict political culture: "As to that which concerns good and bad [*bonum et malum*], these also indicate nothing positive in things considered in themselves and are simply ways of thinking, i.e. notions which we form from the fact that we compare things with one another."[30] There are good reasons why Spinoza's Latin term *malum* is generally translated as "bad" instead of "evil": if that which is *malum* simply hinders us from reaching excellence and understanding, it always depends on the specific contexts of human agency.[31] In contrast, the logic of moral evil is marked by a stunning simplicity that makes the career of this concept, and its continued persistence in the realm of the political, all the more remarkable: definitions of evil tend to be either banal or sentimental, while theological explanations remain riddled with precisely the kind of moral absolutism that feeds the notion of evil in the first place. Most definitions of evil start out from the primacy of the good, without being able to provide any serious justification for this primacy. Even seemingly realist accounts of evil that define the latter simply in terms of an undeserved harm, and that accept the inevitability of such harm, tend to succumb to the epistemological primacy of the "good life."[32]

Referring to the legal scholar Rudolf von Jhering, Nietzsche points out that seemingly universal and objective moral standards mainly have the function of "*securing the conditions of life within society through coercion*" (*KGW* VII/1, 7 [69]).[33] Seen from this

---

[30] Baruch de Spinoza, *Ethics*, ed. and trans. G. H. R. Parkinson (Oxford: Oxford University Press, 2000), p. 227 (Part IV, preface).
[31] See ibid., pp. 227 (Part IV, Preface) and 244 (Part IV, Proposition 27).
[32] See, for instance, John Kekes, *Facing Evil* (Princeton, N.J.: Princeton University Press, 1990), pp. 11–30.
[33] Nietzsche refers here to Rudolf von Jhering, *Der Zweck im Recht* (Leipzig: Breitkopf & Härtel, 1877–83), where the latter argued for a conception of law as safeguarding the interests of society. For Jhering, the interests of individuals are always subordinated to the interests of society, which separates his utilitarian perspective from that of British utilitarians and the Anglo-American tradition of law as protecting the interests of the individual.

perspective, moral norms can only be valuable if they actually perform this function. But they also undergo dramatic changes, as Nietzsche was able to see in the work of another prominent contemporary legal scholar, Albert Hermann Post:

> But the actions that make a delinquent penitentiary [*bussfällig*] or punishable differ between all peoples and between each stage of their respective evolution. In general, we can postulate that *what seems to be punishable in a concrete ethnic setting is that which threatens the existence of order within this setting*. ... As a consequence, there is no action that is criminal as such, and there is also no action that could not be punishable under certain circumstances. [34]

Describing a particular action, or a particular individual, as "evil" and thus as guilty and punishable, is always dependent on the specific political context. "Evil," then, is applied to that which seems to threaten the symbolic order of culture.

The enormous success of the Inquisition in early modern Europe – together with its construction of "witches" and "demonic acts" that in subtle forms stretches deep into the second half of the eighteenth century – is a particularly prominent example of the fact that the definition of evil is a factor in the constitution of political power and a means of social control.[35] The conceptual openness of "evil" renders it easy to label that which remains outside one's own political order as inherently evil. It is precisely in this respect that "evil" is, strictly speaking, not an ethical but a political category that is etymologically related to overstepping the boundary, or limit, of whatever is deemed as the standard of any given set of values. The "preservation of a *community*" clearly emerges as the central task of morality, which seeks to exclude "those things that seem to threaten the survival of the community" (*HA* I: 96 and *BGE* 201). This community is not based, however, on what it proclaims to be its guiding principles – e.g. selflessness, pity, equality, tolerance – but fear and suspicion: "How much or how little danger there is to the community ... this is now the moral perspective: and fear is once again the mother of

---

[34] Post, *Bausteine für eine allgemeine Rechtswissenschaft*, vol. I, p. 224.
[35] See Wolfert von Rahden, "Orte des Bösen: Aufstieg und Fall des dämonologischen Dispositivs," in Alexander Schuller and Wolfert von Rahden (eds.), *Die andere Kraft: Orte des Bösen* (Berlin: Akademie Verlag, 1993), pp. 26–54, and Martin Pohl, *Aufklärung und Aberglaube: Die deutsche Frühaufklärung im Spiegel ihrer Aberglaubenskritik* (Tübingen: Niemeyer, 1992), pp. 248–9.

morality. ... Everything that raises the individual over the herd and frightens the neighbour will henceforth be called *evil*" (*BGE* 201). As such, "evil" always implies the vilification of that which is perceived as the "other."[36]

As hypothetical as Nietzsche's account might seem at first sight, the implications of his view sketched out above are clearly a pressing concern for modern culture. The secularizing trends of modernity – the "disenchantment" of the world, as Max Weber called it – were surprisingly unable to replace notions of "evil," but rather transferred the latter from the realm of theological explanation to the realm of the political. This "re-enchantment" of the political takes place with regard to central conceptual commonplaces that are not necessarily linked to religion, although they bear religious overtones, such as "the nation." The absolutism of moral values centered on the seemingly primary distinction between "good" and "evil" is easily translated into the realm of the political, where it begins to outline complex symbolic relationships between the nation and an imagined "other" that is often perceived as a threat to the existence of the nation and, by implication, the state as a homogeneous moral community.

Nietzsche is, of course, aware that religion was on the defensive within European modernity, even though it continued to wield considerable institutional and political influence. In the final decades of the nineteenth century, it is difficult to overlook that "God is dead," as Nietzsche puts it in a notoriously famous passage of *Die fröhliche Wissenschaft* (*GS* 343). But the destruction of religion is also an ambivalent development. While he undoubtedly greets the death of God with much enthusiasm, he also describes this development in terms of a terrifying "destruction" of "European morality" (*GS* 343): "our whole European culture," he continued this thought sometime in early 1888, is characterized by a "tension that grows from decade to decade" and that is bound to culminate in "catastrophe" (*KGW* VIII/2, 11 [411]).[37]

While the postulated death of God has undoubtedly serious political consequences, it is problematic to assume that, for Nietzsche, the logical conclusion is an essentially authoritarian

---

[36] See Deleuze, *Nietzsche and Philosophy*, p. 119.
[37] The "death of God" as representing the disintegration of traditional political authorities is one of the long-term effects of the French Revolution as a specific historical event. See Marti, *"Der grosse Pöbel- und Sklavenaufstand"*, pp. 58–87.

position.³⁸ Nietzsche himself, however, does not subscribe to nihilism. Rather, he regards the latter merely as an inevitable intellectual development with deep historical roots that needs to be both studied in much detail and, ultimately, overcome.³⁹ In fact, his diagnosis is, at least in the first instance, value neutral; much like genealogy as a whole it does not opt for a specific political alternative, but rather seeks to describe what Nietzsche regards as a factual development. This should not be taken to mean, however, that he was unaware of the possible political consequences that his diagnosis entailed. On the one hand, the "*advent of nihilism*," which he presumes will unfold over the "next two centuries," leads to an unprecedented freedom that he greets with enthusiasm (*KGW* VIII/2, 11 [411]; *GM* III: 27; GS 343): nihilism opens up the possibility of recognizing that the world, in terms of nature, truly is transhuman and that human beings, including their moral values and other normative claims, are not a special case.⁴⁰ On the other hand, the advent of nihilism is also the logical result of an absolutist understanding of moral and cultural values: by translating absolutist moral values into the realm of the political, the prevalent order of culture destroys itself, even though Nietzsche himself does not explicitly outline any of the political consequences that are bound to follow.⁴¹

It is clear that genealogy entails a historical critique of the political. In this respect, Nietzsche also provides a rather intriguing discussion of morality that exceeds the psychological theories of many of his contemporaries. As the first few paragraphs already make clear, the historical perspective of *Zur Genealogie der Moral* is, above all, directed against that interpretation of moral development, which moves along evolutionary lines in order to postulate that the morally "good" is inevitably a result of social utility (*GM* I: 1–4). The evolution of moral values as part of a process of civilization – as it is represented in the tradition of Jeremy Bentham,

---

³⁸ See, however, Detwiler, *Nietzsche and the Politics of Aristocratic Radicalism*, pp. 83–97.
³⁹ See Reginster, *The Affirmation of Life*, pp. 21–53.
⁴⁰ See Daniel Conway, "Revisiting the Will to Power: Active Nihilism and the Project of Transhuman Philosophy," in Keith Ansell Pearson and Diane Morgan (eds.), *Nihilism Now! Monsters of Energy* (London: Macmillan, 2000), pp. 117–41: 118–23.
⁴¹ Nevertheless, in *Die fröhliche Wissenschaft*, "patriotism [*Vaterländerei*]" emerges as a particularly fatal political consequence: both French "chauvinisme" and obsessions with "Germanness," which resemble the hypnotic "fanaticism" of religion, are clearly "symptoms" of political developments that are just around the corner (*GS* 347).

Herbert Spencer, and John Stuart Mill, occasionally also Auguste Comte – is bound to culminate in bizarre consequences, at least as far Nietzsche was concerned. If, as Mill suggests, "happiness is ... the only thing desirable, as an end, all other things being only desirable as means to that end," he essentially argues, as Nietzsche believes, that maximizing pleasure is necessarily morally good and contributes to social welfare.[42]

If taken literally, the utilitarian model will always lead, however, to trade-offs with regard to social welfare. Consider, for instance, the problem of slavery. Any utilitarian argument against slavery would have to seriously consider the happiness and pleasure of slave owners. On this account, slavery could only be wrong because the happiness and pleasure of the slave owners do not sufficiently make up for the suffering that is clearly experienced by the slaves. Nothing wrong, then, with slavery as such. But the real utilitarian might even have to go one step further: as long as slavery makes economic sense by contributing substantially – for instance, through the production of inexpensive consumer goods – to the happiness and pleasure of a majority, it is perfectly acceptable. The reason for this peculiar consequence of utilitarianism is that the latter "ultimately treats people as lacking any distinctness, but as receptacles in which welfare is to be maximised with the greatest possible efficiency," thus disconnecting moral decisions from moral feelings.[43]

But the economic point of view that comes to the fore in utilitarian arguments also highlights the close link between mass democracy and consumption, both converging in the greater common good: happiness and pleasure might thus not be grounded in actual political participation, or action, but rather in the equal chance for consumption, which would outweigh other concerns normally attributed to the greater common good. Seen from this perspective, utilitarian arguments against social inequality and disenfranchisement would only make sense if such inequality and disenfranchisement are economically disadvantageous to a majority. Of course, Nietzsche is not the only one unable to accept such

---

[42] J. S. Mill, *Utilitarianism*, in *Collected Works*, ed. John M. Robson (London: Routledge, 1963–91), vol. X, p. 234.
[43] N. E. Simmonds, *Central Issues in Jurisprudence: Justice, Law and Right* (London: Sweet & Maxwell, 1992), p. 40, and Williams, "Utilitarianism and Moral Self-Indulgence," in *Moral Luck*, pp. 40–53: 52.

implications, but it is important to note that utilitarian arguments are not compatible with the sovereign individual that, after all, is supposed to adhere to an ethic of responsibility.

Nietzsche clearly believed that neither the utilitarianism of British philosophers, nor the altruism suggested by Comte in France were able to provide a truly critical view of the moral world.[44] Their emphasis on empathy as the pleasurable foundation of the greater social good reminds him precisely of the kind of morality he wishes to examine: the technocratic rationality inspired by the feats of modern science, which Nietzsche sees at the heart of both British utilitarianism and French positivism, continues the idea of a communal Christian morality that prevents an understanding of the actual formation of moral values within the symbolic order of culture.[45] While accepting that especially the "English psychologists" have been able to raise awareness of the very fact that morality evolves, and thus has a specific history in the first place (*GM* I: 1), Nietzsche is doubtful that the seeming liberalism of modern mass democracy, at least as far as Imperial Germany and Victorian Britain were concerned, should be seen as the pinnacle of moral development.

Nietzsche's rejection of a moral theory inspired by scientific positivism is also directed against the influence of Henry Thomas Buckle's popular *History of Civilization in England* (1857–61). The three essays of *Zur Genealogie der Moral* were published in November 1887; in May and June of the same year Nietzsche spent much time in the library of Chur in Switzerland, reading, among other things, a German translation of Buckle's work (*KGB* III/5, p. 79).[46] The latter's idea that at the core of civilization we can detect a law of progress that includes a perfection of morality in modern liberal society was bound to make Nietzsche suspicious: democracy and liberalism could not seriously be grounded in

---

[44] See also *D* 132 and *BGE* 228.
[45] Nietzsche's view of Comte is mainly based on J. S. Mill, "August Comte und der Positivismus," in *Gesammelte Werke*, ed. Theodor Gomperz (Leipzig: Fues, 1869–75), vol. IX, pp. 89–141. Of course, the way in which Nietzsche thus brings together Comte and British utilitarianism is not exactly unproblematic: Mill himself in fact believed that Comte is too "intoxicated" by morality as the end of human existence. See Mill, "Auguste Comte and Positivism," in *Collected Works*, vol. X, pp. 261–368: 336.
[46] Most likely, Nietzsche read the following translation: Henry Thomas Buckle, *Geschichte der Civilisation in England*, trans. Arnold Ruge (Leipzig: Winter, 1860–61). Another translation by Immanuel Heinrich Ritter appeared in 1870 but was less widely read.

a natural evolution of humanity (*GM* I: 4).[47] What Nietzsche rejected in the philosophical framework of authors such as Comte, Mill, and Buckle was not liberalism as such, but rather the underlying grand narrative of social progress, which was clothed in scientific terms but actually represented a political theology in disguise. As far as Buckle was concerned, Nietzsche was not the only one to voice skepticism. Although unconcerned with possible political implications, Johann Gustav Droysen, for instance, came to similar conclusions, arguing that Buckle's scientific positivism and his desire to project law-like developments into history ultimately underestimated the openness of historical processes.[48]

Either way, the ideas of solidarity and empathy that were promised by contemporary liberal notions of cultural progress stood in stark contrast to the reality of those processes that Nietzsche regarded as responsible for the formation of moral communities: moral values and sentiments are not based on the greater social good, but on the violence of resentment triggered by the "slave revolt" he described in the first essay of *Zur Genealogie der Moral*. This reversal of the order of culture, as he argues in the second essay, did not come overnight. It was based on the creation of "guilt" and "bad conscience."[49] In fact, guilt emerges as the most important factor for the formation of moral communities.

SOVEREIGN INDIVIDUALS AND THE ETHIC OF RESPONSIBILITY

Generally speaking, guilt is triggered as a specific moral sentiment when we fail to fulfill a particular obligation, either regretting or feeling inadequate to do so.[50] Nietzsche himself regards this

---

[47] The central importance of Buckle becomes more obvious if we consider that, in a letter from May 20, 1887, Nietzsche describes Buckle as "one of my strongest antagonists" (*KGB* III/5, p. 79).

[48] See Johann Gustav Droysen, "Die Erhebung der Geschichte zur Wissenschaft," *Historische Zeitschrift* 9 (1863), 1–22.

[49] For a detailed analytical assessment of the second essay of *Zur Genealogie der Moral*, see Simon May, *Nietzsche's Ethics and his War on "Morality"* (Oxford: Clarendon Press, 1999), pp. 55–77, and Leiter, *Nietzsche on Morality*, pp. 223–44. See also Mathias Risse, "The Second Treatise in *On the Genealogy of Morality*: Nietzsche on the Origin of the Bad Conscience," *European Journal of Philosophy* 9 (2001), 55–81: 63–7, and Christopher Janaway, *Beyond Selflessness: Reading Nietzsche's Genealogy* (Oxford: Oxford University Press, 2007), pp. 124–42.

[50] See May, *Nietzsche's Ethics*, p. 57.

particular moral feeling as a fairly late development in the evolution of moral sentiments, suggesting that our common understanding of guilt is actually based on the purely economic, and therefore value-neutral, relationship between debt and credit. He is drawing here on the importance of economic relationships within the realm of the political, which he had encountered during the 1860s in the lectures of Heinrich von Sybel in Bonn and Wilhelm Roscher in Leipzig. But even during the 1870s, he continued to read authors on political economy such as Henry Charles Carey, who did not approve of the British economists' emphasis on laissez-faire capitalism.[51] The idea that the principle of balance within culture is of an economic origin, which Nietzsche stressed during the late 1870s (*HA* II: ii.22 and *KGW* IV/3, 41 [23]) and which he seems to have derived from Carey, is still present in the debtor–creditor relationship he discusses in *Zur Genealogie der Moral*.

Since any society is based on economic exchange that needs to be regulated, and since not all debt automatically leads to the moral sentiment of guilt, the debtor–creditor relationship precedes the development of moral conscience in the narrow sense of the term (*GM* II: 4 and 8). The shift from the value-neutral concept of debt to the value-laden concept of guilt only occurs within a legal context, that is, when the debtor–creditor relationship becomes regulated through the notion of liability: not being able to fulfill obligations thus means causing a debt, which can only be compensated through penalizing the debtor. Nietzsche therefore argues that the material debt that occurred can be compensated by the more or less violent corporal punishment of the debtor (*GM* II: 5).[52] The psychological result of such punishment is crucial, for the debtor will invariably experience some sort of pain, while the creditor will experience power and superiority. The established hierarchy mirrors the reversal between "good" and "bad," which Nietzsche discussed in the first essay. On the side of

---

[51] See Henry Charles Carey, *Lehrbuch der Volkswirthschaft und Socialwissenschaft*, trans. Karl Adler, 2nd, corr. edn. (Vienna: Braumüller, 1870).

[52] The relationship between debt and legal order is a central theme of Josef Kohler's short anthropological study of law, *Das Recht als Kulturerscheinung: Einleitung in die vergleichende Rechtswissenschaft* (Würzburg: Stahel, 1885), which Nietzsche read in much detail, especially the passages on the "law of obligations [*Schuldrecht*]." On Kohler, see Bernhard Grossfeld and Ingo Theusinger, "Josef Kohler: Brückenbauer zwischen Jurisprudenz und Rechtsethnologie," *Rabels Zeitschrift für ausländisches und internationales Privatrecht* 64 (2000), 698–714.

the debtor, then, material debt will be related to the wholly negative feeling of having a "bad conscience," which – since it is based on economic exchange – leads to an experience of unworthiness and to the acceptance of the social hierarchy and its framework of absolute moral sentiments. The important point is, however, that the logic of economic exchange is transferred to the realm of psychological experience, which in turn is transferred to society at large and generates a complex system of virtues and values regulating social interaction (*GM* II: 8). It is for this reason that, as far as Nietzsche is concerned, "bad conscience" possesses a political dimension that is closely related to that of "evil."

Social control is, of course, a central task of moral conscience. As his discussion of religion in *Jenseits von Gut und Böse* shows, the genealogical perspective allows Nietzsche to formulate a realist account of this task. First of all, religion "binds the ruler together with the ruled," that is, it provides a political identity, ultimately "handing the conscience of the ruled over to the ruler." The conscience of the ruled, in other words, is under the administrative control of a power that is external to this conscience. Second, religion thus serves "as a means of securing calm in the face of the turmoil and tribulations of the *cruder* forms of government, and purity in the face of the *necessary* dirt of politics," preventing a more critical understanding of political power among the ruled that could eventually put the given order into doubt. Finally, religion also gives "the common people ... an invaluable sense of contentment with this situation" (*BGE* 61). In all three cases, the freedom and autonomy of the individual are curtailed not through actual, violent coercion, but by a more imperceptible form of coercion that Foucault has aptly described in terms of a "disciplinary power" that becomes increasingly complex in the course of the nineteenth century.[53] As long as they are grounded in an absolute distinction between "good" and "evil," guilt and conscience directly contribute to these disciplinary strategies of social control.

While it still seems possible for Nietzsche to assume that some moral sentiments – for instance, sympathy – are part of what it means to be human, the complexity of the emerging network

---

[53] See Michel Foucault, *"Society Must be Defended": Lectures at the Collège de France, 1975–1976*, ed. François Ewald, Alessandro Fontana, and Mauro Bertaini, trans. David Macey (New York: Picador, 2003), pp. 35–40.

of valuations, starting out from the notion of guilt, seems to be more dependent on the cultural and historical context. Although Nietzsche himself does not go down this route, it would also be possible to argue that, under different cultural conditions, guilt might be replaced by shame. Since the actualization of guilt is dependent on external penalties and punishments, while shame seems to be more self-regulative, the former could be seen as a more cruel moral sentiment.[54] This might be the reason why Nietzsche occasionally seeks to replace a guilt-based morality with an ethic of "duty" and responsibility (*BGE* 226). Far from being willing to reject ethical life out of hand, his emphasis on duty can be seen as providing a link between ethical decisions and freedom: the "*sovereign individual*," which he presents as the noble opposite of those that follow a guilt-based morality, has a "right to make promises," without being coerced into a symbolic debt that can never really be paid off (*GM* II: 2).

Given the importance of the right to make promises for the sovereign individual, it might be possible to describe Nietzsche's position as an "ethics of virtue."[55] We need to be cautious, however, with regard to this term. Even though he emphasizes in *Jenseits von Gut und Böse* that the "free spirits" will have "virtues," he is also careful to point out that "virtue [*Tugend*]" as a central concept of traditional "moral philosophy" is characterized by a certain "*tediousness*" (*BGE* 214 and 228). With this remark, Nietzsche on the one hand refers to the tradition of German idealism, especially Kant and Hegel, who both saw "virtue," in the sense of *Tugend*, as coextensive with morality in terms of a *Sittlichkeit* that was grounded in the formal principles of reason:

To behold virtue in her proper form is nothing other than to present morality stripped of any admixture of the sensible and of any spurious adornments of reward or self-love. By means of the least effort of his reason everyone can easily become aware of how much virtue then eclipses everything else that appears charming to the inclinations, provided his reason is not altogether spoiled for abstraction.[56]

[54] See Annette C. Baier, "Moralism and Cruelty: Reflections on Hume and Kant," in *Moral Prejudices: Essays on Ethics* (Cambridge, Mass.: Harvard University Press, 1994), pp. 268–93.
[55] See Lester H. Hunt, *Nietzsche and the Origin of Virtue* (London: Routledge, 1991), pp. 70–88 and 160–78.
[56] Immanuel Kant, *Groundwork of the Metaphysics of Morals*, trans. and ed. Mary J. Gregor, introd. Christine M. Korsgaard (Cambridge: Cambridge University Press, 1998), p. 35. See also Hegel, *Vorlesungen über die Philosophie der Geschichte*, in *Werke*, vol. XII, p. 307–8.

On the other hand, he also sought to distance himself from contemporary moral philosophy, especially Mill's utilitarianism, which defined the "multiplication of happiness" as the proper "object of virtue."[57] Despite the fact that virtue has different foundations in both idealism and utilitarianism, it is remarkable that Kant himself regarded virtue as the "dignity to be happy [*die Würdigkeit glücklich zu sein*]."[58]

But while Nietzsche's account differs radically from that of utilitarianism, he nevertheless continues aspects of Kant's and Hegel's views. Kant's link between virtue and duty is mirrored in Nietzsche's own interest in duty as a characteristic of the sovereign individual, even though Kant's discussion is based on the principles of pure reason and assumes that such duty constitutes an absolute and unchangeable conviction.[59] Likewise, when Hegel notes in one of his early writings that ethical thought requires a "natural description [*Naturbeschreibung*] of the virtues," this is precisely what Nietzsche seeks to achieve in his genealogy.[60] At the same time, however, Nietzsche comes to radically different conclusions, for the project of naturalizing morality (*BGE* 230) leads him to accept that there can only be two kinds of virtue: responsibility and honesty, neither of which can necessarily be derived from the greater social good. This is also the reason why he demands a realistic assessment of the usefulness of virtues and why he warns against transforming them into an absolute point of reference for the judgment of human agency:

> Our genuine honesty, we free spirits, – let us make sure that it does not become our vanity, our pomp and finery, our limitation, our stupidity! Every virtue tends towards stupidity, every stupidity towards virtue; "stupid to the point of holiness" they say in Russia, – let us make sure we do not end up becoming saints or tedious bores out of genuine honesty! (*BGE* 227)

---

[57] Mill, *Utilitarianism*, in *Collected Works*, vol. X, p. 219.
[58] Kant, *Kritik der praktischen Vernunft*, in *Werkausgabe*, vol. VII, p. 238 (A 198). Both Mary Gregor and Werner Pluhar translate this passage as "the worthiness to be happy." See Kant, *Critique of Practical Reason*, ed. and trans. Gregor, introd. Andrews Reath, p. 92, and Immanuel Kant, *Critique of Practical Reason*, trans. Werner S. Pluhar, introd. Stephen Engstrom (Indianapolis, Ind.: Hackett, 2002), p. 141.
[59] See Immanuel Kant, *The Metaphysics of Morals*, trans. and ed. Mary Gregor, introd. Roger J. Sullivan (Cambridge: Cambridge University Press, 1996), pp. 156–9.
[60] Hegel, "On the Scientific Ways of Treating Natural Law, on its Place in Practical Philosophy, and its Relation to the Positive Sciences of Right," in *Political Writings*, p. 161.

Instead of attributing to Nietzsche an ethics of virtue it might thus be more reasonable to speak of an ethic of responsibility as it also surfaces in *Zur Genealogie der Moral* (*GM* II: 2). This would help us in avoiding a more metaphysical interpretation of his political thought.[61]

As opposed to an ethics of virtue or power, an ethic of responsibility does not constitute a fully developed system of ethical commitments and normative claims. Any ethical system properly speaking, that is, an "ethics" would always be organized according to a conviction in Max Weber's sense: it would be based on the intention to achieve a specific ultimate end, without necessarily having to take into account the possible consequences and side-effects of those human actions that are seen as following from this intention. In contrast, the singular "ethic of responsibility" states that the ethical commitments to which the sovereign individual subscribes remain context-dependent and open to change: such ethical commitments are contingent upon the situation within which they take place and can only be made if the sovereign individual is able to know and, ultimately, to accept the foreseeable consequences of its actions, while acknowledging that there might be consequences, even detrimental consequences, that cannot be anticipated.[62] In short, Nietzsche's ethic of responsibility seeks to address that, in virtually every case, the world of ethical action is simply grey. His hopes for the sovereign individual, then, are quite pragmatic.

Nietzsche's emphasis on "the right to make promises" makes it apparent that the autonomous individual he has in mind does not operate outside society; the autonomous individual is not solitary, but inherently social.[63] Some commentators have nevertheless pointed out that Nietzsche's sovereign individual runs counter to the theoretical framework of modern liberalism in that he seems to adopt a moral perfectionism that essentially contradicts a liberal theory of justice as it was formulated, for instance, by John Rawls. It

---

[61] Such metaphysical interpretations are often based on a literal reading of *Also sprach Zarathustra* that culminates, for instance, in the claim that the sovereign individual faces "the world-historical task of directing the future as a whole." See Richard J. White, *Nietzsche and the Problem of Sovereignty* (Urbana, Ill.: University of Illinois Press, 1997), pp. 124–49: especially 149.

[62] See Weber, "The Profession and Vocation of Politics," in *Political Writings*, pp. 359–60.

[63] This is also noted by Appel, *Nietzsche contra Democracy*, pp. 81–102, whose reading, however, is based on *Also sprach Zarathustra*.

does not seem possible to integrate Nietzsche's sovereign individual into an "egalitarian conception of justice" that needs to be based on the principles of equality and fairness.[64] Most importantly, the actions of the sovereign individual would not need to conform to these principles as the bottom line as long as the sovereignty of the individual would be intact. As a consequence, Rawls himself has taken issue with Nietzsche's perfectionism.[65] At the same time, it is, however, remarkable that Rawls's discussion of the principle of fairness in relation to promises clearly stresses the need for the individual which makes such promises to be autonomous.[66]

Given that Rawls situates his arguments within an essentially Kantian tradition, it is not surprising that he should regard Nietzsche's much-discussed perfectionism as both misguided and dangerous: "The requirements of perfection override the strong claims of liberty" and, furthermore, serve as a "counterpoise to egalitarian ideas."[67] Nietzsche's sovereign individual, as it is outlined in *Zur Genealogie der Moral*, constitutes a threat to the normative claims of morality. At the same time, it should be noted, however, that Rawls's understanding of Nietzsche's perfectionism does not accurately represent the latter's actual position. In Rawls's account, perfectionism requires an underlying teleological principle, namely the duty to aspire to a specific ideal, "to develop human persons of a certain style" and "to advance the pursuit of knowledge and the cultivation of the arts."[68] Perfectionism, in other words, entails a striving for something that we are not, something that is external to the individual. In contrast, it is necessary to point out that Nietzsche's understanding of "human excellence" actually means "being (generically) the same and yet so much more excellent."[69] Thus, if Nietzsche really holds a position that could be described as perfectionist, it does not consist in a duty to

---

[64] John Rawls, *A Theory of Justice* (Oxford: Oxford University Press, 1972), p. 100.
[65] See ibid., pp. 25 and 325. On Nietzsche's perfectionism and Rawls's reaction, see also Conway, *Nietzsche and the Political*, pp. 52–6.
[66] See Rawls, *A Theory of Justice*, pp. 344–8, especially 345. On the question of promises, see also Stanley Cavell, *Conditions Handsome and Unhandsome: The Constitution of Emersonian Perfectionism* (Chicago: University of Chicago Press, 1990), pp. 113–15, and Annette Baier, "Promises Promises Promises," in *Postures of the Mind: Essays on Minds and Morals* (Minneapolis: University of Minnesota Press, 1985), pp. 174–206.
[67] Rawls, *A Theory of Justice*, pp. 325–6.   [68] Ibid., p. 328.
[69] James Conant, "Nietzsche's Perfectionism: A Reading of *Schopenhauer as Educator*," in Richard Schacht (ed.), *Nietzsche's Postmoralism: Essays on Nietzsche's Prelude to Philosophy's Future* (Cambridge: Cambridge University Press, 2000), pp. 181–257: 196.

develop others, but in the individual's duty to cultivate itself: the self-cultivation of the sovereign individual is a "*precondition*" for its capacity to respond to others and, thus, to develop an ethic of responsibility.[70]

To some extent, such self-cultivation is a residue of Nietzsche's earlier neo-humanist interests as they came to the fore in his public lectures in Basel, "Ueber die Zukunft unserer Bildungsanstalten," and in the third "Untimely Meditation," *Schopenhauer als Erzieher* (*UM* III: 5–6). But this should not be taken to mean that his arguments from the later 1880s can be reduced to a neo-humanist position that is based on a "Greek conception of moral beauty" as an educational program of human excellence.[71] We have seen that Nietzsche himself is rather skeptical about the reach of such an educational program, whose failure he also witnessed in practice during the late 1860s and early 1870s. Instead, I would argue that, in his writings of the 1880s, Nietzsche's notion of human excellence, as uncomfortable as this might be, is marked by a certain political realism: the human excellence of the sovereign individual is grounded in the assumption that some individuals are inevitably more autonomous, and more sovereign, than others.

It is in this respect that Nietzsche's understanding of autonomy differs from Kant's notion of an "autonomy of the will" as the basis for ethical judgments.[72] For Nietzsche, autonomy is not universal and *a priori*, but it is made, or established, by the reflexive action of an individual within a given situation. This also implies that this notion of autonomy is less limited than the autonomy of the will as it is formulated in Kant's *Grundlegung zur Metaphysik der Sitten* (1785) and *Kritik der praktischen Vernunft* (1788). The latter remains restricted by the coercive universality of the moral law: "the moral law commands compliance from everyone and indeed the most exact compliance."[73] To put it more sharply: for Kant, the moral framework of human decisions always stays the same, while Nietzsche allows for this framework to change. The reason for this fundamental difference between Nietzsche and Kant is of an

---

[70] See ibid., p. 220. [71] See, however, ibid., pp. 220 and 225.
[72] Kant, *Groundwork of the Metaphysics of Morals*, p. 47. See also *Critique of Practical Reason*, ed. Gregor, pp. 30, 38–9, and 74.
[73] Kant, *Critique of Practical Reason*, ed. Gregor, p. 33. See also Kant, "Idea for a Universal History," in *Political Writings*, pp. 45–6.

essentially political nature. While the necessity to obey the law, together with the coercive application of the law, constitutes for Kant the precondition of any civil society, Nietzsche would conclude that such a civil society represents precisely the kind of moral community that he attacked so vividly in *Zur Genealogie der Moral*, that is, a moral community whose values cannot be questioned. Given his own observations of political life in the nineteenth-century nation state throughout the 1870s and 1880s – especially Imperial Germany as an authoritarian nation state – Nietzsche has to conclude that there are indeed situations in which the trust that human beings put in others, and the promises they make to others, can and should be questioned. The sovereign individual would need to question any moral community, for instance, that exploits the trust that individuals place in its institutions, including the law.

Although it seems only apt to emphasize trust as the central point of reference for moral action, trust itself is more ambivalent than commonly assumed, since not everything that is the outcome of situations of trust, such as the exploitation of others, should really be accepted.[74] Indeed, the exploitation of others, especially in modern mass democracies, tends to be more efficient in a context of trust than if it is based on violent coercion. Precisely because the sovereign individual is able to recognize this, it can adopt a notion of trust that excludes moral absolutes: mutual trust can be acceptable and ethically justified only if each party is critically aware, and not only assumes to be aware, of the other's reasons for trusting and for continuing to rely on mutual trust.[75] But since such knowledge tends to be quite rare, especially in the realm of the political, the sovereign individual has always to consider the possible consequences of trust. This is the reason why Nietzsche demands of the sovereign individual to be "curious to a fault," even "to the point of cruelty," in the sense of a "genuine honesty" (*BGE* 44 and 227).

Against the background of what we have said so far, it is not surprising that Nietzsche not only should be skeptical about the possibilities of modern philosophical liberalism, but also should

---

[74] See Baier, "Trust and Antitrust," in *Moral Prejudices*, pp. 95–129: 95. For Kant, in contrast, such a position is almost impossible to hold, since he does not even allow for the possibility of lying out of moral duty. See Kant, "Über ein vermeintliches Recht aus Menschenliebe zu lügen," in *Werkausgabe*, vol. VIII, pp. 637–43.

[75] See Baier, "Trust and Antitrust," p. 128.

seek to distance himself from the contemporary liberal ideas of nineteenth-century political life. Indeed, from the perspective of the genealogical enterprise it must have seemed to him, for instance, that the evolutionary theories of social progress that permeated contemporary liberalism, on the one hand, and the political foundation myths of nationalism and religious identity, on the other, were really two sides of the same coin. They were both suggestive of a grand narrative of civilization which culminated in what he regarded as a hollow herd morality, subsuming all historical periods, peoples and human individuals under one specific "goal" as an "ascetic ideal" that precludes all other possible perspectives (*GM* III: 23). That, for Nietzsche, liberalism and nationalism follow the same structural logic – even though they are fundamentally different on the surface – might also be the reason why the political implications of genealogy continue to be uncomfortable for philosophical liberalism. Both German nationalism and nineteenth-century British liberalism share what Nietzsche perceives to be the "*morality of herd animals*," which comes to the fore in the "political and social institutions" of what he terms "the *democratic* movement." The latter consists in a set of absolute value claims that seem to represent "morality itself" and that are based on the assumption that "nothing else is moral" (*BGE* 202).

There is, however, a further complication with regard to Nietzsche's attack on the herd morality of the modern democratic nation state. His use of the term "democratic" is more complex than it might seem at first sight. The democratic movement that he detects in the nineteenth-century nation state is not necessarily a liberal one in the modern sense of the term and, more generally, mass democracies do not need to follow liberal ideals. One example might suffice. In the February 1887 elections to the German Reichstag – one year after the publication of *Jenseits von Gut und Böse* and only a few months before the publication of *Zur Genealogie der Moral* in November of 1887 – 68.6 percent of the votes went to parties that are best described as "value conservative" and "nationalist," while left-liberal and social democratic parties attracted only 24.2 percent of the vote.[76] The central

---

[76] The exact figures for value conservative parties in the 1887 elections are: National-Liberals (22.3 percent), Conservatives (25 percent), Catholic Zentrum (20.1 percent),

theme of these elections was the enlargement of the standing army by 10 percent in order to safeguard Germany's strategic position between France and Russia. Since Bismarck's first proposal to this effect had not been ratified by parliament in November 1886, he persuaded the Emperor, Wilhelm I, to dissolve the Reichstag, stopping just short of a *coup d'état*. Bismarck was well aware that a conservative and national-liberal majority as the almost certain outcome of new elections would authorize new military spending and at the same time protect his position vis-à-vis both the Emperor and the social democratic opposition. Although the resulting coalition between conservatives and national-liberals proved to be an unstable political configuration in the long run, one month after the elections, in March 1887, Bismarck's military budget was ratified by the Reichstag.[77] Leaving aside Bismarck's abuse of executive power in the name of national security, the elections also had another, unintended result: the anti-Semitic Deutsche Reformpartei achieved its first seat in parliament. From Nietzsche's perspective, mass democracy obviously fails to provide the autonomy that is the foundation for the "free spirit," instead fostering cultural and political conformity, together with the exclusion of minorities, in the service of national interests.[78]

Moral communities that are centered on absolute value distinctions, then, express what Fredrick Appel perceptively called the "moral imperialism of the herd."[79] The latter consists, on the one hand, in the relentless demand that there can only be one form of morality, which excludes any incompatible moral claims as deficient and deviant. The demand for such permanent and universal moral values expresses a hegemonic tendency. On the other hand, such moral imperialism can only be successful if its

---

anti-Semitic party (0.2 percent). By comparison, left-wing and left-liberal parties are still relatively small: Social Democrats (10.1 percent) and Left-Liberals (14.1 percent). While the votes for the Left-Liberals will continue to decline until 1912, the Social Democrats begin to gain ground from the 1890s onward. In the last elections of the German Reichstag in 1912, they are able to gain 34.8 percent of the vote, while the influence of more value conservative parties declined sharply. In the period between 1893 and 1912, anti-Semitic parties hover around 3 percent. See the data in Gerd Hohorst, Jürgen Kocka, and Gerhard A. Ritter (eds.), *Sozialgeschichtliches Arbeitsbuch: Materialien zur Statistik des Kaiserreichs 1870–1914* (Munich: C. H. Beck, 1975), pp. 173–6.

[77] See Nipperdey, *Deutsche Geschichte, 1866–1918*, vol. II, pp. 416–18.
[78] For a more detailed analysis of Nietzsche's criticism of such conformity, see David Owen, "Equality, Democracy, and Self-Respect: Reflections on Nietzsche's Agonal Perfectionism," *Journal of Nietzsche Studies* 24 (2002), 113–31: 119–25.
[79] See Appel, *Nietzsche contra Democracy*, pp. 43–6.

values emphasize the mediocre, which for Nietzsche becomes particularly apparent with regard to a British utilitarianism "in Bentham's footsteps" (*BGE* 228). As can be expected, Nietzsche's sovereign and autonomous individual stands in sharp contrast to this understanding of morality and would be a "thinker," who "treats morality as something questionable, question-mark-able, in short, as a problem" (*BGE* 228). Nietzsche's conclusion with regard to contemporary liberal moral philosophy is, however, not only "that the requirement that there be a single morality for everyone is harmful precisely to the higher men." His rejection of moral imperialism also includes a much-quoted remark that is often employed to highlight his presumed reactionary political views: "there is an *order of rank* between people, and between moralities as well" (*BGE* 228). This remark, I would argue, does not represent a specific political program, but it is the result of Nietzsche's relentless political realism: in contrast to the belief that "the happiness of the majority" and "general welfare" can really be attained universally, he notes that any moral community necessarily generates social hierarchies and that any given moral community will always assume its own morality to be superior to that of other moral communities.

In order to better understand Nietzsche's position, it is useful to compare it to Max Weber's distinction, in his 1919 lecture "Politik als Beruf," between an "ethic of conviction" and an "ethic of responsibility." Although Weber himself notes that both must be present in anyone who wishes to become a politician properly speaking, his own preference is clearly on the side of an ethic of responsibility.[80] After all, any ethic of conviction needs to operate with absolute and, thus, unjustified moral value claims that cannot take into account the consequences political action might have:[81]

We have to understand that ethically oriented activity can follow two fundamentally different, irreconcilably opposed maxims. It can follow the "ethic of principled conviction" [*Gesinnung*] or the "ethic of responsibility." It is not that the ethic of conviction is identical with irresponsibility, nor that the ethic of responsibility means the absence of principled conviction – there is of course no question of that. But there is a profound opposition between acting by the maxim of the ethic of conviction (putting it in religious terms: "The Christian does what is

---

[80] See Weber, "The Profession and Vocation of Politics," in *Political Writings*, p. 368.
[81] See ibid., p. 359: "'Consequences' ... are no *concern* of absolutist ethics."

right and places the outcome in God's hands"), and acting by the maxim of the ethic of responsibility, which means that one must answer for the (foreseeable) *consequences* of one's actions. [82]

Taking into account the consequences of human actions, of course, stands at the center also of Nietzsche's ethic of responsibility, since the sovereign individual's right to make promises entails an understanding of the consequences such promises can have, so that keeping to the promises themselves constitutes a responsibility. Furthermore, as Weber points out, such an ethic of responsibility always means that we cannot "presuppose goodness and perfection in human beings."[83] Nietzsche's ethic of responsibility, in other words, continues the political realism we could already observe in the context of his discussion of the modern state during the late 1870s.

THE TASK OF GENEALOGY

Regardless of the political conclusions that might be derived from Nietzsche's criticism of morality, the interpretive strategy he employs both in *Jenseits von Gut und Böse* and in the first two essays of *Zur Genealogie der Moral* presents genealogy as an internal critique that seeks to retrace the norms, values, and mental commonplaces that shape cultural processes at large. The genealogical project is primarily not interested in the actual origin of morality and moral communities; it merely seeks to examine the way in which they have undergone significant changes and how these changes affect the self-conception of moral communities. The history of these transformations does not lead the genealogist back to a metaphysical origin, such as "God," "reason," or "the soul." Rather, the genealogist focuses on a dense network of traces and symptoms that, taken as a whole, constitute the "descent" of the values that govern any given community.[84] The source of these values remains necessarily diffuse – not because of an intrinsic limitation of genealogy, but because a unifying origin for the determination of values is simply lacking. Not surprisingly, at the beginning of the first essay of *Zur Genealogie der Moral*, Nietzsche is already replacing the notion of *Ursprung* (origin) with that of *Entstehungsherd*, which is perhaps

---

[82] Ibid., pp. 359–60.   [83] Ibid., p. 360.
[84] See Foucault, "Nietzsche, Genealogy, History," pp. 342–3 and 345–7.

best translated as "site of emergence" (*GM* I: 2).[85] Indeed, the emergence of any given set of values is of greater importance in the long run than any speculation about its possible origin. In an antireductionist and anti-essentialist stance, Nietzsche seeks to dissolve the supposedly fixed identities we attribute to those moral and political values that we hold dear, pointing out their historical contingency and discontinuity, that is, the minute shifts of meaning and practice that determine the values with which we surround ourselves.[86]

This also separates Nietzsche's genealogical project of the 1880s from the psychological reflections his close friend Paul Rée presented in *Der Ursprung der moralischen Empfindungen* (1877). For Rée, moral sentiments do have a very specific origin that does not constitute a historical problem, but a psychological one: the need to mediate between an "egoistic drive" and a "non-egoistic," that is, ultimately altruistic drive:

Every person combines two drives within himself, namely, the egoistic drive and the non-egoistic drive.

Through the egoistic drive he strives for his own welfare, above all his own preservation, the satisfaction of his sexual instinct, and the satisfaction of his vanity. ... On account of the non-egoistic drive, a man makes the welfare of others the final end of his actions, whether he seeks their welfare for their own sake or refrains from harming them for their own sake. ... The fact that the egoistic actions just described are not only possible but occur all the time clearly indicates that the non-egoistic instinct is weak.[87]

Since both drives exist at the same time, even though the egoistic drive proves to be much stronger because of its biological background, Rée is now faced with the peculiar question of the origin of moral conscience. How is it possible, in other words, that the egoistic drive has thoroughly negative connotations, while the non-egoistic drive is transformed into something more praiseworthy despite its initial weakness? For Rée, this change is based on

---

[85] Carol Diethe translates *Entstehungsherd* as "breeding ground," which is certainly correct. In the medical sense, a *Herd* is the "seat" or "focus" of a disease, but also the site of any biological activity that makes something emerge.

[86] See Foucault, "Nietzsche, Genealogy, History," p. 357.

[87] Paul Rée, *The Origin of Moral Sensations*, in *Basic Writings*, ed. and trans. Robin Small (Urbana, Ill.: University of Illinois Press, 2003), p. 89. On this issue, see also Robin Small, *Nietzsche and Rée: A Star Friendship* (Oxford: Clarendon Press, 2005), pp. 82–7, and Janaway, *Beyond Selflessness*, pp. 74–89.

the social conditioning that already takes place in childhood and that makes the individual accept certain "distinctions" between moral and immoral actions:

> Once this distinction has been made, however, once someone has become accustomed to connecting the idea of praiseworthiness with a particular mode of action and the idea of blameworthiness with its contrary, it will easily seem to him as if he had not become accustomed to making these connections but had been making them from birth.[88]

Ignoring the origin of moral conscience in social conditioning transforms moral judgments into a natural kind and it makes morality as a whole appear as a seemingly universal set of normative standards. The origin of morality, then, is for Rée rooted in a predominantly psychological development. In contrast, Nietzsche turns this problem into a historical one that asks how such moral sentiments have evolved not only psychologically, but above all culturally. Raymond Geuss has thus described genealogy as a "historical dissolution of self-evident identities" that "does not automatically imply the rejection of what is subjected to genealogical analysis." Genealogy, then, can be defined as a "summon to develop an empirically informed kind of theoretical imagination under the conditions of perceived danger."[89] This danger would be, for instance, the radical consequences of certain moral values as soon as they are translated into the realm of the political. Nevertheless, Geuss's emphasis is here on "theoretical imagination" rather than "empirical" and "historical," and along very similar lines Bernard Williams pointed out that genealogy should be regarded as a "fact-defective" explanation: in contrast to showing, for instance, how a particular moral sentiment has come about in reality, Nietzsche seeks to outline why and how such a moral sentiment, say "guilt," was in principle able to become a central cultural category. Devoid of detailed historical source material, genealogy would thus describe the possibility of specific historical formations.[90]

As strictly speaking a counterfactual narrative, genealogy would merely be a variation of what Kant, in his essay "Mutmaßlicher

---

[88] Rée, *The Origin of Moral Sensations*, p. 100–1.
[89] Raymond Geuss, "Genealogy as Critique," *European Journal of Philosophy* 10 (2002), 209–15: 212–13.
[90] See Bernard Williams, *Truth and Truthfulness: An Essay in Genealogy* (Princeton, N.J.: Princeton University Press, 2002), pp. 31 and 37.

Anfang der Menschengeschichte" (1786), described as "*conjectural history.*" For Kant, the latter is helpful in particular if the philosopher seeks to clarify the origins of that which is claimed to be universal, such as "the first development of freedom from its origins as a predisposition in human nature."[91] Such conjectural history, however, already presumes what it sets out to prove, and Kant inevitably comes to the conclusion that "the course of human history as a whole ... develops gradually from the worse to the better."[92] Conjectural history seems a philosophical strategy through which, in principle, any conclusion could be supported. It is unlikely that this is what Nietzsche had in mind.

Although we should take the philosophical import of Nietzsche's genealogy very seriously, since it does indeed allow us to question the moral authenticity on which we claim our actions are based, even in a liberal society, we also need to pay attention to the fact that genealogy is far from "fact-defective" – at least Nietzsche did not believe that it was "fact-defective." The main indication for this is one of his most important sources: Albert Hermann Post's *Bausteine für eine allgemeine Rechtswissenschaft auf vergleichend-ethnologischer Basis*, published in two volumes in 1880–81. The latter has not been entirely overlooked but has received only limited attention in the English-speaking world.[93]

That Nietzsche should indeed turn to Post, ordering a copy of the latter's work from his own publisher Ernst Schmeitzner in Leipzig (*KGB* III/1, p. 94), is interesting in itself. Much like Johann Jakob Bachofen, Post was a legal scholar and practicing judge, whose interest in the theory of law was both historical and anthropological in orientation. Like Bachofen in Basel, Post

---

[91] Kant, "Conjectures on the Beginning of Human History," in *Political Writings*, pp. 221–34: 221.
[92] Ibid., p. 234.
[93] For first assessments, see Martin Stingelin's "Konkordanz zu Friedrich Nietzsches Exzerpten aus Albert Hermann Post, *Bausteine für eine allgemeine Rechtswissenschaft auf vergleichend-ethnologischer Basis* Oldenburg 1880/81 (2 Bde.), im Nachlaß vom Frühjahr-Sommer und Sommer 1883," *Nietzsche-Studien* 20 (1991), 400–32, and David S. Thatcher, "*Zur Genealogie der Moral*: Some Textual Annotations," *Nietzsche-Studien* 18 (1989), 587–99. While the Cambridge edition of *On the Genealogy of Morality* makes no mention of Post, Maudemarie Clark and Alan Swenson have referenced the latter's influence on a series of specific passages. See Friedrich Nietzsche, *On the Genealogy of Morality*, trans. and ed. Maudemarie Clark and Alan Swenson (Indianapolis, Ind.: Hackett, 1998), pp. 141–3, 145–6 and 154–5. At the same time, it needs to be emphasized that Post's influence on Nietzsche should not be restricted to specific passages.

was also politically active in his own relatively provincial urban environment, the Hanseatic city of Bremen in Northern Germany, where he was a member of the Senate. But while Bachofen's ideas were rooted in German Romanticism, Post, born in 1839, mainly shared Nietzsche's intellectual background. Only five years older than Nietzsche, he was initially influenced by Kant and Schopenhauer and fascinated by the tense relationship between German Protestantism and the rising influence of the natural sciences, especially evolutionary biology, on intellectual debate in Germany.[94] But Post was also an enormously productive legal scholar. By the mid-1860s, when Nietzsche was still a student at the University of Leipzig, he had already published substantial works on family and marital law and had drafted a system of private law for the city of Bremen, which was heavily influenced by contemporary discussions in political economy.[95] During the 1870s – again mirroring recent intellectual trends, such as the rise of anthropology – Post began to turn to an ethnographic account of legal practices and institutions: if the order of law, as was widely believed among contemporary anthropologists, shaped the order of culture as a whole, then a historical approach to the study of law could deliver a "scientific" model of explanation only if it was able to integrate indigenous legal practices into a universal theory of legal evolution. For Post, then, society was defined through the evolution of law and its symbolic practices. The focus of his scholarly endeavors became a "general science of law [*allgemeine Rechtswissenschaft*]" on anthropological grounds.[96]

---

[94] See, for instance, Albert Hermann Post's short treatise *Kirchenglaube und Wissenschaft: Ein Beitrag zur Klärung der religiösen Streitfragen der Gegenwart für gebildete Leser* (Bremen: Gesenius, 1868).

[95] See Albert Hermann Post, *Die Elemente des gemeinen deutschen und hansestadtbremischen Privatrechts auf Grundlage der modernen Volkswirtschaft* (Bremen: Gesenius, 1866).

[96] See Albert Hermann Post, *Die Grundlagen des Rechts und die Grundzüge seiner Entwickelungsgeschichte: Leitgedanken für den Aufbau einer allgemeinen Rechtswissenschaft auf sociologischer Basis* (Oldenburg: Schulze, 1884). For a detailed assessment of Post's work within the context of nineteenth-century law and scientific culture, see Rainer Maria Kiesow, *Das Naturgesetz des Rechts* (Frankfurt/M.: Suhrkamp, 1997). The international orientation of nineteenth-century anthropology and social science also meant that Post's impact on legal thought went far beyond the German context. In a long article on contemporary German philosophy, the French sociologist Émile Durkheim, for instance, singled out Post's contributions to the study of law. See "La science positive de la morale en Allemagne," *Revue philosophique* 24 (1887), 33–58, 113–42, and 275–84: 281–4. Post himself published a short English introduction to his theory as "Ethnological Jurisprudence," *The Monist* 2 (1891/92), 31–40.

Drawing on the anthropologist John Lubbock and the Victorian legal scholar Henry Sumner Maine, Post argued that the family and its blood relationships need to be viewed as the actual origin of legal relationships:

> The legal person [*Rechtssubjekt*], the individual human being as a bearer of rights and duties, which seems so self-evident to us today, has by no means always existed, but from a comparative-ethnological point of view it is the product of a long and complicated evolution. ... In the most primitive ethno-morphological communities [*ethnisch-morphologischen Verbänden*], which are based on blood relations, there are no individual rights and no individual duties. There is neither an individual crime, nor an individual guilt, neither individual property, nor individual marriage, nor fatherhood. Rather, the community, the lineage or the tribe as a whole is the only legal entity [*Rechtssubjekt*]. [97]

It was these early family relationships, Post believed, that were slowly transformed into the formation of state-like structures, growing over time into larger political associations, such as the modern European nation states of the nineteenth century.[98] Most interestingly, this evolution shifts notions of responsibility, duty, obligation, and culpability from groups to individuals, which – in Nietzsche's reading – is supported by the effect of corporeal punishments, which Post described in much detail from cutting off various body parts to disembowelment and other forms of capital punishment: "A specific kind of killing [*Tödtung*] through stoning has been reported from Fuertaventura and Lancerote. The executioner [*Nachrichter*] placed the head of the condemned on a flat boulder by the sea and hit it with another rock so hard that the brain spurted out."[99]

---

[97] Post, *Bausteine für eine allgemeine Rechtswissenschaft*, vol. 1, pp. 73–4. This account seems to be indebted to Henry Sumner Maine, *Ancient Law: Its Connection with the Early History of Society, and its Relation to Modern Ideas* (London: John Murray, 1861), pp. 173–4.

[98] Compare the account in Henry Sumner Maine, *Lectures on the Early History of Institutions* (London: John Murray, 1875), p. 30. Post's own concrete example for this development is derived from John Mitchell Kemble, *The Saxons in England: A History of the English Commonwealth till the Period of the Norman Conquest* (London: Longman, 1849), vol. 1, p. 70. During the early middle ages England is characterized by a network of localized communities that are slowly transformed in subsequent centuries into a monarchy as a specific political association.

[99] Post, *Bausteine für eine allgemeine Rechtswissenschaft*, vol. 1, p. 191. See also ibid., vol. 1, pp. 188–215, where Post discusses an amazing range of different forms of corporeal and capital punishment. Many of these examples are derived from Grimm, *Deutsche Rechtsalterthümer*, pp. 695–709.

The dismemberment and mutilation of the human body does indeed constitute an integral part of the history of law as a cultural institution, which would be incomplete without studying the history of punishments.[100] Presenting a wide range of documentary evidence, itself the result of the fieldwork carried out by nineteenth-century ethnologists, Post thus provided Nietzsche not only with a dense tableau of gruesome examples, but also with a wider historical narrative that was far from counterfactual or fact-defective. Post's anthropological and legal examples especially enrich Nietzsche's understanding of punishment, the importance of which he had encountered several years earlier in Rée's writings.[101] Above all, Post's historical anthropology of legal institutions – emphasizing throughout that what we regard as individual moral rights and duties are a very late development in the evolution of law – renders it obvious that Nietzsche himself conceived of genealogy as a less theoretical project than generally assumed.

Given this background, it does indeed make much sense to describe genealogy as a strategy that seeks to trace, and ultimately judge, the development of moral values on which the order of culture is based: genealogy consists in "disentangling," as Geuss noted, "the separate strands of meaning that have come together in a (contingent) unity in the present."[102] But genealogy also poses the uncomfortable question as to whether philosophy, without paying attention to history, has any value. One of the main tasks of genealogy is, thus, to show that whatever seems eternal, universal and without history – including the psychological make-up of our moral beliefs – has in fact a rather specific history in that it has been the subject of an ongoing transformation over time.

Nevertheless, the historical dimension of genealogy is not altogether unproblematic. While accepting the historical perspective of

---

[100] See Wolfgang Schild, "Der gequälte und entehrte Leib," in Klaus Schreiner and Norbert Schnitzler (eds.), *Gepeinigt, begehrt, vergessen: Symbolik und Sozialbezug des Körpers im späten Mittelalter und in der frühen Neuzeit* (Munich: Wilhelm Fink, 1992), pp. 149–68, and "Verstümmelung des menschlichen Körpers," in Richard van Dülmen (ed.), *Erfindung des Menschen: Schöpfungsträume und Körperbilder, 1500–2000* (Vienna: Böhlau, 1998), pp. 261–81.

[101] See Rée, *The Origin of Moral Sensations*, in *Basic Writings*, pp. 113–24.

[102] Raymond Geuss, "Nietzsche and Genealogy," in John Richardson and Brian Leiter (eds.), *Nietzsche* (Oxford: Oxford University Press, 2001), pp. 322–40: 333. Along similar lines, Blondel, *Nietzsche*, p. 76, has suggested that genealogy seeks to investigate the "production of culture."

Nietzsche's project, Geuss, for instance, has pointed out that the evolution of moral values does not really affect their current use, thus separating philosophy and history: "A form of valuation has the value it has ... and its origin or history is a separate issue."[103] Geuss is certainly correct in realizing that Nietzsche's genealogy does not wish to establish a "pedigree" of values that leads us back to a specific origin, for this would certainly constitute a genetic fallacy.[104] But his interpretation presents genealogy as an exclusively philosophical project that does not really require any historical perspective properly speaking.

Geuss's interpretation is mainly based on a decisive passage from *Zur Genealogie der Moral*. Debating the social, or cultural, "purpose" of "punishment," Nietzsche reaches the following conclusion:

> there is no more important proposition for all kinds of historical research than that which we arrive at only with great effort but which we really *should* reach, – namely that the origin of the emergence of a thing and its ultimate usefulness, its practical application and incorporation into a system of ends, are *toto coelo* separate; that anything in existence, having somehow come about, is continually interpreted anew, requisitioned anew, transformed and redirected to a new purpose by a power superior to it. (*GM* II: 12)

Nietzsche clearly seeks to avoid the problem of a genetic fallacy by noting that the "use" of anything is different from its "history," that its "use" in the present needs to be separated from its "uses" in the past. But his emphasis in the above passage is not at all on current usage. As the last sentence makes clear, he is particularly interested in the process of transformation itself. The way in which cultural institutions – e.g. legal punishment and everything that is involved in it, from a specific law in response to which punishment takes place to the act of punishing itself – are applied within a "system of ends" (e.g. social welfare) is indeed separate from the origin of the cultural institution in question. It would be futile to look at the cultural origin of punishment in order to deduce the value of its current application – for instance, in the modern state with very specific regulations of due process, proportionality, etc.

---

[103] Geuss, "Nietzsche and Genealogy," in Richardson and Leiter (eds.), *Nietzsche*, pp. 338–9.
[104] Ibid., p. 325. Ottmann, *Philosophie und Politik bei Nietzsche*, p. 178, has already highlighted the problem of a genetic fallacy in Nietzsche's genealogy.

In fact, he continues, the purpose that is currently ascribed to a specific value or institution will tell us little about its history:

> No matter how perfectly you have understood the *usefulness* of any physiological organ (or legal institution, social custom, political usage, art form or religious rite) you have not yet thereby grasped how it emerged: uncomfortable and unpleasant as this may sound to more elderly ears, – for people down the ages have believed that the obvious purpose of a thing, its utility, form and shape are its reason for existence, the eye is made to see, the hand to grasp. (*GM* II: 12)

The purpose of punishment within the modern state might thus be completely different from its original purpose. But the very fact that the purpose of cultural institutions undergoes significant changes highlights that any current purpose that is ascribed to a cultural institution is not the only purpose possible and thus does not rest on some kind of eternal truth.

Indeed, the history of cultural institutions highlights their inherent instability and that they need to be looked at critically. In other words, and to put it more sharply, knowledge about the history and transformation of cultural institutions and their underlying set of values prevents absolutist political claims – at least as long as one carefully avoids the trap of a genetic fallacy that confuses origins and conclusions. This is the general lesson to be drawn from Nietzsche's genealogical strategy. His insistence is on more history, not less – thus his lament that much contemporary thought lacks a "historical instinct" and a "will to knowledge about the past" (*GM* II: 4). As a consequence, he is already beginning to argue in *Die fröhliche Wissenschaft* that the certainty of knowledge does not rest on either "truth" or "logic," but it is the result of the ways in which specific valuations have been handed down historically. But, for Nietzsche, the historicity of political institutions and moral norms cannot be restricted to social life in the narrow sense of the term. Such historicity necessarily includes the biological. Epistemic and moral claims can become normative and, seemingly, timeless, only if they are embodied: "the *strength* of knowledge lies not in its degree of truth, but in its age, its incorporation [*Einverleibtheit*], its character as a condition of life" (*GS* 110).[105]

---

[105] Josefine Nauckhoff translates Nietzsche's term *Einverleibtheit* as "embeddedness," while Nietzsche himself seems to allude quite directly to the way in which knowledge has become appropriated on an organic level.

"TO TRANSLATE HUMANITY BACK INTO NATURE"

At the beginning of this chapter I have argued that there are two sides to genealogy: one that is philosophical and one that is political in orientation. Given the way in which Nietzsche focuses on the physical or physiological embodiment of moral values over a long period of time, we are safe in assuming that his historical perspective is grounded in philosophical claims that are best described as naturalism. Such a naturalist account of morality indeed forces us to address the empirical value and possibility of moral norms.[106] Although this easily invites misunderstanding, since it brings Nietzsche dangerously close to a reductionist position that he simply does not hold, there is much to be said for a naturalist account of genealogy.[107] Such an account is rooted in the assumption that human beings, including the ethical norms they subscribe to, are not a special case vis-à-vis the rest of nature, even though it might seem that the normative dimension of ethical judgments separates the latter from the natural world.[108] But if living within an ethical framework simply implies that we voluntarily, as a kind of "second nature," observe certain norms – that is, without external institutional surveillance and direct threats of physical punishment, but also without the hope for external rewards – it makes sense to relate the psychology of ethical judgments back to something beyond our ideational and cultural world; it is inevitable to assume, in other words, that the psychology of moral judgment cannot be examined in any serious way without taking into account natural drives and instincts.[109]

---

[106] See Leiter, *Nietzsche on Morality*, pp. 6–7, 136–59 and 182–4. Leiter's strong naturalist account has recently been criticized by Christopher Janaway, "Naturalism and Genealogy," in Keith Ansell-Pearson (ed.), *A Companion to Nietzsche* (Oxford: Blackwell, 2006), pp. 337–52.

[107] On the epistemological implications of such a naturalism, which I only refer to in passing, see Cox, *Nietzsche*, pp. 69–106.

[108] In contrast, Richard Schacht, "Nietzschean Normativity," in Schacht (ed.), *Nietzsche's Postmoralism: Essays on Nietzsche's Prelude to Philosophy's Future* (Cambridge: Cambridge University Press, 2001), pp. 149–80: 160–3 and 175–6, argues that Nietzsche's naturalism still assumes humans to be a special case, even though normativity is not an exclusively human phenomenon.

[109] See Williams, *Truth and Truthfulness*, pp. 22–7, and Williams, "Naturalism and Genealogy," in Edward Harcourt (ed.), *Morality, Reflection, and Ideology* (Oxford: Oxford University Press, 2000), pp. 148–61: 153. In sharp contrast to Randall Havas, *Nietzsche's Genealogy: Nihilism and the Will to Knowledge* (Ithaca, N.Y.: Cornell University Press, 1995), pp. 193–211, this also implies that it is simply not possible to give a non-naturalist account of the formation of moral norms in *Zur Genealogie der Moral*.

If Nietzsche really holds this view, however, he cannot defer to nature without a proper concept of the latter; he has to take seriously the explanatory claims of the natural sciences. Is genealogy, then, a scientific enterprise?

A cursory glance at Nietzsche's published writings and notebooks from the 1880s seems to reveal that he cannot possibly hold this position. In *Jenseits von Gut und Böse*, for instance, he not only thinks John Locke's empiricism absurd, but he delivers a sustained attack on that tradition of British thought, from Francis Bacon and Thomas Hobbes to David Hume, which is generally portrayed as preparing the ground for modern philosophical naturalism and which is also credited with establishing irreducible links between philosophical thinking and scientific method (*BGE* 20 and 252). Likewise, at the very beginning of *Zur Genealogie der Moral*, Nietzsche rejects those "English psychologists" (*GM* I: 1) who extrapolate the inevitable progress of morality toward an altruistic civil society from Darwin's theory of natural selection, as in the case of Herbert Spencer's *Data of Ethics* (1879).[110] Given his criticism of this tradition, within which he also situates his former friend and ally Paul Rée, Nietzsche should not be able to adopt a position that could be labelled as naturalist. But as usual, the issue is more complicated, for he does indeed endorse what I shall describe as a weak program of naturalism.

Although this is not the place for a properly detailed investigation into the problem of philosophical naturalism, it is necessary to distinguish between different kinds of naturalism.[111] First a substantive naturalism would have to claim that human experience in its entirety, including qualia and ethical norms, can only be explained successfully if reduced to physical functions and if such explanations are based on empirical study. Any substantive naturalism, then, amounts to a physicalist, or materialist, perspective on both the natural world and cognition.[112] While few philosophers might hold this position, it seeks to close the traditional gap

---

[110] See Herbert Spencer, *The Data of Ethics* (London: Williams and Norgate, 1879), pp. 201–18. Nietzsche owned the first German edition, *Die Thatsachen der Ethik*, trans. B. Vetter (Stuttgart: Schweizerbart, 1879).

[111] On the historical emergence of philosophical naturalism, see Gary C. Hatfield, *The Natural and the Normative: Theories of Spatial Perception from Kant to Helmholtz* (Cambridge, Mass.: MIT Press, 1990).

[112] John McDowell, *Mind and World*, with a new introduction (Cambridge, Mass.: Harvard University Press, 1996), p. 73, describes this as "bald naturalism."

between facts and values, between the natural and normative, by reducing values to facts.¹¹³ Substantive naturalism is inherently reductionist, and critics of naturalism often argue that such reductionism looms large in the background of all forms of naturalism. In contrast, a methodological version of naturalism makes only limited substantive claims and mainly holds that methods of explanation can be reasonable, and by implication successful, only if they correspond, or at least develop in analogy, to those methods that have been shown to be successful in the natural sciences. While substantive naturalism makes sense only within the framework of a methodological naturalism, the latter does not by itself entail any substantive claims, but is limited to epistemological issues and, thus, refrains from naturalizing ethical judgments or political arguments.¹¹⁴

Most interestingly, a third variant, which has been introduced by Joseph Rouse and which for want of a better term I shall call "practical naturalism," is able to avoid reductionist arguments by shifting the attention from scientific methods and the representation of nature to practices, that is, to the way in which we engange and interact with the natural world.¹¹⁵ Assuming that human beings are natural beings, any normative claims about reality that such beings make, and any norms that govern these claims themselves, are necessarily embedded in the material interaction with reality, since it is through the latter that normative claims ultimately acquire and sustain some kind of binding force. Human experience and agency, then, would need to be characterized as an interaction between that which we regard as natural and that which we believe to be social.¹¹⁶ Moreover, whatever we regard as nature is not fixed in the sense that it does not entail

---

¹¹³ Although this might not be immediately obvious, I would argue that Peter Railton's "moral realism" falls into this category. See his "Moral Realism" and "Facts and Values," both in *Facts, Values, and Norms: Essays Toward a Morality of Consequence* (Cambridge: Cambridge University Press, 2003), pp. 3–42 and 43–68.

¹¹⁴ See W. V. O. Quine, "Epistemology Naturalized," in *Ontological Relativity and Other Essays* (New York: Columbia University Press, 1969), pp. 69–90. For a sophisticated attack on strong versions of epistemological naturalism, see Michael Friedman, "Philosophical Naturalism," *Proceedings and Addresses of the American Philosophical Association* 71/2 (1997), 7–21.

¹¹⁵ See Joseph Rouse, *How Scientific Practices Matter: Reclaiming Philosophical Naturalism* (Chicago: University of Chicago Press, 2002), pp. 309–10.

¹¹⁶ See ibid., pp. 184–233.

a determinate concept of what nature is, but what we describe as nature is continuously reshaped by our interactions with the natural world.[117] In this respect, practical naturalism differs fundamentally from substantive naturalism, which has to start out from a predetermined concept of nature, but it also differs from methodological naturalism, which seems to assume that there are normative standards for scientific method and explanation that are located outside scientific practices.[118] Most relevant to Nietzsche, practical naturalism contends that cognition and normativity are always embedded in the material world, so that the traditional opposition between mind and matter is undercut.[119] The latter are merely two sides of the same coin in the same way in which Ludwig Wittgenstein noted: "Commanding, questioning, recounting, chatting are as much part of our natural history as walking, eating, drinking, playing."[120]

Leaving aside a more detailed discussion of these varieties of naturalism, Nietzsche, at least during the 1880s, holds a strong version of what I have described as practical naturalism and a weak version of methodological naturalism: social reality – including the inevitably historical formation of moral values, ethical judgments and political beliefs – is embedded in the natural world, and any critical examination of such a historically emerged social world has to proceed in analogy to scientific practices, albeit not necessarily methods.[121] The reason for the emphasis on practice has much to do with the practice of science itself: we might appeal to normative methods to explain the success of a particular scientific enterprise, whereas its success is in fact depending on practices that might not easily be represented in terms of normative methods. For Nietzsche, this implies above all that, much

[117] See ibid., p. 360.
[118] See, for instance, Alexander Rosenberg, "Normative Naturalism and the Role of Philosophy," *Philosophy of Science* 57 (1990), 34–43, who argues that epistemological claims are able to set normative standards for scientific method.
[119] See also John Haugeland, "Mind Embodied and Embedded," in *Having Thought: Essays in the Metaphysics of Mind* (Cambridge, Mass.: Harvard University Press, 1998), pp. 207–37.
[120] Ludwig Wittgenstein, *Philosophical Investigations*, trans. G.E.M. Anscombe (Oxford: Blackwell, 1967), p. 12 (§25).
[121] On the distinction between "weak" and "strong," or "hard" and "soft," versions of naturalism, see Hatfield, *The Natural and the Normative*, pp. 261–70. For a detailed critique of "hard" epistemological naturalism see Hilary Putnam, "Why Reason Can't be Naturalized," in *Realism and Reason: Philosophical Papers*, 3 (Cambridge: Cambridge University Press, 1983), pp. 229–47.

like Edmund Husserl at the beginning of the twentieth century, and responding to essentially the same scientific culture, he is bound to reject any form of naturalism that seeks to make substantive and reductionist claims. But unlike Husserl in his famous essay "Philosophie als strenge Wissenschaft" (1911), he does believe that naturalism is a valuable philosophical program.[122]

Seen against this background, it becomes clearer why Nietzsche, for instance, in *Jenseits von Gut und Böse*, ridicules those contemporary psychologists who seek to reduce the concept of the "soul" entirely to that of the "brain" as "clumsy naturalists" (*BGE* 12).[123] Responding to a central shift in nineteenth-century psychology and physiology, Nietzsche does not wish to return to antiquated philosophical concepts with little epistemic value. Rather, he warns that substantive versions of naturalism rest on metaphysical conjectures in disguise. The claims of what he polemically describes as "materialistic natural scientists" are based on "faith" and, similar to the popularized version of Darwinism, are "entangled with the Spinozistic dogma" *deus sive natura* (*GS* 373 and 349).[124] The latter merely replaces "God" with "nature" and, for Nietzsche, unwittingly contributes to the continued survival of religious and metaphysical residues in modern science (*KGW* VII/3, 36 [15] and *KGW* VIII/1, 2 [131]). This survival is ultimately also responsible for the presence of Christian ideals in philosophical systems that purport to be based entirely on the mathematical certainty of the "rational method," such as Comte's positivism, which insists on an eschatological notion of human progress and seeks to extrapolate a Christian virtue ethics from contemporary scientific method.[125] In contrast, Nietzsche seeks to advance what he believes to be a proper "naturalism in morality" (*TI* V: 4), that is,

---

[122] See Edmund Husserl, "Philosophy as Rigorous Science," in *Phenomenology and the Crisis of Philosophy*, trans. and ed. Quentin Lauer (New York: Harper & Row, 1965), pp. 69–147: 80–2. Husserl's essay, which was first published in *Logos* 1 (1910/11), 289–341, radicalised his earlier criticism of "psychologism" in his *Logical Investigations*, trans. J. N. Findlay, intro. and ed. Dermot Moran (London: Routledge, 2001), vol. I, pp. 40–55 and 101–22. On Husserl's attack on naturalism, see Dermot Moran, *Introduction to Phenomenology* (London: Routledge, 2000), pp. 142–6.

[123] On the shifts in psychology and physiology that Nietzsche responds to, see Michael Hagner, *Homo cerebralis: Der Wandel vom Seelenorgan zum Gehirn* (Berlin: Berlin Verlag, 1997).

[124] Spinoza, *Ethics*, pp. 226 (Part IV, Preface) and 231 (Part IV, Proposition 4).

[125] See the striking passages in Comte, *Auguste Comte and Positivism: The Essential Writings*, ed. Gertrud Lenzer (Chicago: University of Chicago Press, 1975), pp. 109, 279–97, 299, and 381–9.

a naturalism which accepts that human beings are merely rational animals, while also holding that rationality itself "operates freely in its own sphere" limited simply by the biological make-up of what makes us human.[126]

Throughout his intellectual career, Nietzsche's understanding of scientific practices and methods varied considerably, drawing on a dazzling array of disciplines that represented the scientific expert culture in nineteenth-century Germany, such as chemistry, physics, physiology and biology.[127] It goes without saying that this reading influenced his developing naturalism, which had initially been triggered by his reception of Friedrich Albert Lange's *Geschichte des Materialismus* (1866), Johann Carl Friedrich Zöllner's collection of essays *Über die Natur der Cometen* (1872), and a range of contemporary scientists who advocated a materialist turn in the study of human agency and experience.[128] Although Nietzsche's reading lists are occasionally selective and his conclusions not entirely unproblematic, no serious investigation into his understanding of the task of philosophy is able to ignore these scientific interests that run parallel to his equally strong interest in the nature of the political. Indeed, he even asked his publisher, Constantin Georg Naumann, to forward copies of *Zur Genealogie der Moral* to the scientific establishment in Berlin and Leipzig, including to Herman von Helmholtz, Emil DuBois-Reymond, and Wilhelm Wundt (*KGB* III/5, p. 188).[129]

The orientation of any philosophical naturalism, and Nietzsche's is no exception here, is obviously contingent on which scientific discipline, at any given moment, provides the dominant paradigm for understanding the natural world in terms of "normal science."[130] The latter always has a tendency to cross from clearly defined

---

[126] John McDowell, "Two Sorts of Naturalism," in *Mind, Value, and Reality* (Cambridge, Mass.: Harvard University Press, 1998), pp. 167–97: 85 and 115.

[127] See Thomas H. Brobjer, "Nietzsche's Reading and Knowledge of Natural Science," in Brobjer and Moore (eds.), *Nietzsche and Science*, pp. 21–50.

[128] In the late 1860s, Nietzsche consulted Jacob Moleschott, *Der Kreislauf des Lebens: Physiologische Antworten auf Liebig's Chemische Briefe*, 2nd edn. (Mainz: Philipp von Zabern, 1855), and Wilhelm Wundt, *Vorlesungen über die Menschen- und Thierseele* (Leipzig: Voss, 1863).

[129] Complimentary copies of *Zur Genealogie der Moral* also went to, among others, Jacob Burckhardt, Erwin Rohde, Franz Overbeck, Hippolyte Taine, Carl Schaarschmidt, and Ernst Mach.

[130] See Thomas S. Kuhn, *The Structure of Scientific Revolutions*, 3rd edn. (Chicago: University of Chicago Press, 1996), pp. 24–34.

expert cultures into the wider public and, within Nietzsche's own intellectual environment, this has been particularly the case with regard to the biological sciences, broadly speaking.[131] Increasingly drawing on evolutionary biology from Charles Darwin to Wilhelm Roux and beyond, Nietzsche, since the late 1870s, slowly begins to undercut well-established distinctions between the natural world and the world of human values, without, however, reducing the one to the other.[132] This becomes particularly obvious in his attempts to rethink traditional epistemological questions along the lines of the body: "behind all logic ... stand valuations or, stated more clearly, physiological requirements for the preservation of a particular type of life" (*BGE* 3). In much the same way as human consciousness does not stand in opposition to inevitably unconscious drives and instincts, the values and valuations that we see as governing human experience are inevitably embodied (*GS* 354 and *KGW* v/2, 11 [164]). As such, they are part of our evolutionary history, and Nietzsche remarks in his notebooks of late 1885 and early 1886: "*Valuations are innate* [*angeboren*], despite Locke!, inherited [*angeerbt*]" (*KGW* VIII/1, 1 [21]).

Nevertheless, Nietzsche would agree that these valuations develop most fully, and hence have the most lasting political consequences, in a context of social interaction. From the perspective of the genealogical enterprise, then, values, together with the social practices they generate, have evolved in both a historical and a biological way.[133] Any form of what we regard as social selection, which, in the first instance, leads to specific customs

---

[131] For a concise discussion of German biological thought during the 1870s and 1880s, see Nyhart, *Biology Takes Form*, pp. 168–305.
[132] Most influential among Nietzsche's sources, apart from Darwin, are Alfred Espinas, *Die thierischen Gesellschaften: Eine vergleichend-psychologische Untersuchung*, ed. W. Schlosser (Braunschweig: Vieweg, 1879); Georg Heinrich Schneider, *Der thierische Wille: Systematische Darstellung und Erklärung der thierischen Triebe und deren Entstehung, Entwickelung und Verbreitung im Thierreiche als Grundlage zu einer vergleichenden Willenslehre* (Leipzig: Abel, 1880); Wilhelm Roux, *Der Kampf der Theile im Organismus: Ein Beitrag zur Vervollständigung der mechanischen Zweckmässigkeitslehre* (Leipzig: Engelmann, 1881); William H. Rolph, *Biologische Probleme, zugleich als Versuch zur Entwicklung einer rationellen Ethik*, 2nd edn., enlarged (Leipzig: Engelmann, 1884); Carl von Nägeli, *Mechanisch-physiologische Abstammungslehre* (Munich: Oldenbourg, 1884). For a detailed study of Nietzsche's reception of contemporary biological thought, see Moore, *Nietzsche, Biology and Metaphor*, pp. 21–84.
[133] Rouse, *How Scientific Practices Matter*, pp. 3–4 and 302–3, describes this intersection of historical and biological development as the "Nietzschean commitment" of philosophical naturalism.

and, in the long run, to a set of seemingly universally valid moral norms, is always embedded in evolutionary processes of natural selection.[134] From the perspective of Nietzsche's practical naturalism, there is no real difference between social and natural selection. But this should not be taken to mean that his position is, after all, reductionist. Rather, he simply holds that natural selection plays a role in what we tend to assume to be merely social selection, while our social practices themselves have an impact, at least in the long run, on further natural selection. It is precisely in this sense that natural and social selection interact, and normativity emerges first of all through this interaction.[135]

Indeed, Nietzsche discusses this interaction in *Zur Genealogie der Moral*, when he focuses on the correlation between the physical effects of corporeal punishment and the emergence of a psychology of moral conscience. The formation of the latter "in man's pre-history" is based on a "*technique of mnemonics*" that mobilizes the physical organization of the body in order to produce normative forms of seemingly voluntary social control:

> "A thing must be burnt in so that it stays in the memory: only something which continues *to hurt* stays in the memory" – that is a proposition from the oldest (and unfortunately the longest-lived) psychology on earth. ... When man decided he had to make a memory for himself, it never happened without blood, torments and sacrifices: the most horrifying sacrifices and forfeits (the sacrifice of the first born belongs here), the most disgusting mutilations (for example, castration), the cruellest rituals of all religious cults (and all religions are, at their most fundamental, systems of cruelty) – all this has its origin in that particular instinct which discovered that pain was the most powerful aid to mnemonics. ... With the aid of such images and procedures, man was eventually able to retain five or six "I-don't-want-to's" in his memory, in connection with which a *promise* had been made, in order to enjoy the advantages of society – and there you are! With the aid of this sort of memory, people finally came to "reason"! (*GM* I: 3)

Social control, which is ultimately necessary for any form of political organization, can be successful only if the physical inscriptions of violence at its source have been physiologically

---

[134] See Richardson, *Nietzsche's New Darwinism*, pp. 70–94.
[135] In this respect, it seems too reductive to assume – as Christof Kalb, *Desintegration: Studien zu Friedrich Nietzsches Leib- und Sprachphilosophie* (Frankfurt/M.: Suhrkamp, 2000), pp. 235–4, does – that cultural commitments and social norms are merely a strategy to negate, and to detach ourselves from, natural drives.

internalized to such an extent that they are forgotten, while at the same time being passed on from one generation to the next as a form of organic memory and social habitus.

Nietzsche's somewhat radical idea that psychological states, such as those that make up what we regard as moral conscience, can be inherited through an interaction between social and natural selection does not come entirely unprepared. In a lecture at the Viennese Academy of Science in 1870, the physiologist Ewald Hering – most famous for his theory of color perception – suggested that the material organization of the brain contained the physiological inscriptions of past events in the form of so-called "engrams" – a theory that could easily be linked up with contemporary discussions about the inheritance of psychological characteristics.[136] Although highly speculative because of its lack of experimental verification, the possibility of organic memory had a considerable impact on both psychological thought and the wider public imagination in the final decades of the nineteenth century.[137] Nietzsche himself had consulted Francis Galton's *Inquiries into the Human Faculty and Its Development* (1883) while in Nice in early 1884 and he was aware of Hering's lecture through Zöllner's oddly titled *Über die Natur der Cometen* (1872) already long before the genealogical project began to take shape.[138] Furthermore, Wilhelm Wundt's 1877 article on "Philosophy in Germany," which appeared in the British journal *Mind* and with whose translator, George Croom Robertson, Nietzsche had several stimulating conversations while holidaying in the same year in Switzerland (*KGB* II/5, pp. 266, 268 and 270), situates Hering and Zöllner in the same context of scientific materialism.[139] Wundt, in

---

[136] See Ewald Hering, *Über das Gedächtnis als eine allgemeine Form der organisierten Materie: Vortrag gehalten in der feierlichen Sitzung der Kaiserlichen Akademie der Wissenschaften in Wien am 30.5.1870* (Vienna: Staatsdruckerei, 1876).

[137] See, for instance, Théodule Ribot, *L'Hérédité: Étude psychologique sur ses phénomènes, ses lois, ses causes, ses conséquences* (Paris: Librairie Philosophique de Ladrange, 1873). For the broad reception of such theories, see Laura Otis, *Organic Memory: History and the Body in the Late Nineteenth and Early Twentieth Centuries* (Lincoln: University of Nebraska Press, 1994).

[138] See Francis Galton, *Inquiries into the Human Faculty and Its Development* (London: Macmillan, 1883), and Zöllner, *Über die Natur der Cometen*, pp. xv–xvi. On Nietzsche's reception of the debate about organic memory, see Emden, *Nietzsche on Language, Consciousness, and the Body*, pp. 145–52.

[139] See Wundt, "Philosophy in Germany," 502–3.

1877 still the experimental psychologist, might have had little positive to say about either and was particularly skeptical about the way in which some of his colleagues in the empirical sciences occasionally left experimental verification behind. But it is important to realize that the debates about organic memory and evolutionary biology took place within the same intellectual field.

Against this background, it should not be surprising that, despite his criticism of the "English psychologists," Nietzsche did indeed agree with Darwin's assumption, expressed most fully in *The Descent of Man* (1871), that even moral conscience could be inherited. But while Darwin mainly reiterated earlier conjectures by Herbert Spencer that especially "virtuous tendencies" were inherited so that, at least in principle, the "standard of morality" was able to "rise higher and higher," Nietzsche was more skeptical:[140]

> These historians of morality (particularly, the Englishmen) do not amount to much: usually they themselves unsuspectingly stand under the command of a particular morality and, without knowing it, serve as its shield-bearers and followers, for example, by sharing that popular superstition of Christian Europe which people keep repeating so naively to this day, that what is characteristic of morality is selflessness, self-denial, self-sacrifice, or sympathy [*Mitgefühl*] and compassion [*Mitleiden*]. (*GS* 345)

Any attempt to extrapolate from evolutionary descriptions of the natural world a given set of moral claims unduly moralizes the natural world (*BGE* 13). In contrast, Nietzsche polemically regards the outcome of the interaction between social and natural selection as a story of illusions "which were passed on by inheritance further and further" precisely because they are life-preserving and useful (*GS* 110). The empirical value, then, of having moral norms lies in their usefulness. But whatever proves to be useful does not necessarily need to be correct. More importantly, though, assuming whatever is useful to be true in a metaphysical sense ultimately precludes the possibility of an honest skepticism, which, among other things, would need to question the given order of values

---

[140] Charles Darwin, *The Descent of Man* (London: John Murray, 1871), vol. I, pp. 102–3. In this passage, Darwin is well aware that he is speculating without empirical evidence and refers back to remarks by Herbert Spencer that were reprinted in Alexander Bain, *Mental and Moral Science: A Compendium to Psychology and Ethics* (London: Longmans & Co., 1868), p. 722.

(*GS* 111). The illusion of a fixed and universal order of the given, supported by metaphysical commonplaces and religious figures of thought, prevents individuals from realizing that social life does not inevitably need to aspire to a greater common good, but that social life is marked by a striving for power (*BGE* 199) – any aspirations to a greater common good can be realized only through what Nietzsche terms the "will to power" and are, thus, secondary. Instead of merely pointing to self-preservation, including the self-preservation of any given community, as the guiding principle of evolutionary processes, as it can be found in Spencer's more substantive naturalism, Nietzsche's claims are based on the assumption that an "*expansion of power*" governs both the natural and social worlds. Not surprisingly, he equates the "will to power" with the "will to life" (*GS* 349).

Of course, these reflections in *Die fröhliche Wissenschaft* and *Jenseits von Gut und Böse* suggest that Nietzsche, who had initially rejected teleological models of natural and human history after his reading of Kant in the late 1860s, reintroduces teleological arguments in his later writings. Does this mean, then, that genealogy is a metaphysical enterprise in disguise?[141] If genealogy wishes to provide any critical insight into the historical formation of the political, it is necessary to reconcile Nietzsche's outspoken attacks on teleology with his implicit reliance on teleological arguments, as in the case of his understanding of evolution as the growth and expansion of power.[142] Given Nietzsche's weak naturalist claims, however, genealogy does not require a strong teleological commitment, which would entail that historical processes follow an inevitable path of development toward a specific goal – even though Kant and Hegel at least to some extent suggest that this is the case. Surprisingly, Nietzsche, at least in the 1880s, learns a different lesson from German Idealism: as long as teleology remains a merely regulative idea, as in the case of Kant, and merely implies that things in the natural and social worlds "develop *out of each other*," as in the case of Hegel, teleological arguments are not

---

[141] Given Nietzsche's notion of power, Poellner, *Nietzsche and Metaphysics*, pp. 162–73, argued that he has to subscribe to metaphysical tenets that run counter to his self-proclaimed anti-teleological and anti-essentialist stance. See in contrast, Abel, *Nietzsche*, pp. 120–5.

[142] See Richardson, *Nietzsche's New Darwinism*, pp. 26–35.

altogether unreasonable (*GS* 357).[143] In other words, Nietzsche rejects teleology as describing a qualitative progress toward a presumably higher state of perfection, but he does accept teleology as describing the common temporality of the natural and social worlds: whatever organic drives and social practices can be found in the present, including those drives and practices that make up our moral framework, they have formed over time and are themselves the diffuse site of emergence, or *Entstehungsherd*, of future drives and practices.

Clearly, Nietzsche's position is not "Darwinian" in the popularized sense of the term, but it links a Darwinian evolutionary argument to earlier theories of organic development as they can be found, for instance, around 1800 in the work of Johann Friedrich Blumenbach and Jean Baptiste Lamarck and as they continue to influence biological thought at German universities in the nineteenth century. Indeed, in *Die fröhliche Wissenschaft* he even claims that Darwinism, standing in for evolutionary models in general, was only possible because of the philosophical and scientific configurations around 1800, such as Romantic *Naturphilosophie* (*GS* 357).[144] This claim is neither unreasonable nor surprising: Nietzsche's conception of life and the will to power shares many characteristics with Schelling's notion of life as it is presented in the latter's early writings on *Naturphilosophie*. Life is here defined as "a certain *form* of being, *a composite that is made up of different causes affecting each other*" and that is marked by a "*free play of forces*" that link the natural and intellectual worlds.[145] What Nietzsche and

---

[143] See Kant, *Critique of Judgment*, p. 280, and Hegel, *Enzyklopädie der philosophischen Wissenschaften im Grundrisse*, in *Werke*, vol. IX, pp. 502–16 (§ 368, Zusatz). An English translation of the latter, based on a different manuscript, can be found in Hegel's *Philosophy of Nature: Part Two of the "Encyclopedia of the Philosophical Sciences"* (1830), trans. A. V. Miller, foreword J. N. Findlay (Oxford: Clarendon Press, 1970), pp. 417–28 (§ 370, Zusatz).

[144] Although it is doubtful that Nietzsche was aware of this, German Romantic *Naturphilosophie* had infiltrated British biological thought in the first half of the nineteenth century and provided part of the theoretical framework within which Darwin began to propose his theory of evolution. See Richards, *The Romantic Conception of Life*, pp. 522–33.

[145] Schelling, *Von der Weltseele, eine Hypothese der höheren Physik zur Erklärung des allgemeinen Organismus*, in *Sämmtliche Werke*, vol. II, p. 566. On the epistemological problems generated by Schelling's notion of "life," see Frederick C. Beiser, *German Idealism: The Struggle against Subjectivism, 1781–1801* (Cambridge, Mass.: Harvard University Press, 2002), pp. 538–44. A source for Nietzsche's knowledge of Schelling is Albert Schwegler, *Geschichte der Philosophie im Umriß: Ein Leitfaden zur Übersicht* (Stuttgart: Verlag der Franckh'schen Buchhandlung, 1848), pp. 183–6.

Schelling have in common is an attempt to think life beyond a substantive and reductionist naturalism, on the one hand, and the dualism of mind and matter, on the other.

If Nietzsche's genealogical enterprise entails a weak naturalism, it also entails a weak teleology as it can be found in Schelling. Nature and the intellectual world ultimately converge in their common organization: nature does not represent the ideational world and vice versa but it merely renders the latter possible, which is the reason why Schelling is able to conclude in his early writings that "nature" should be understood as "Mind made visible" and our intellectual world as "invisible Nature."[146] It is also in this sense that they are part of the same historical, or temporal, process of "becoming" – an evolutionary process that for Schelling cannot reach any conclusion.[147] In the same way as Schelling distances himself here from Kant's stronger notion of teleology, Nietzsche, many years later, also argues for a weak teleology. The latter already comes to the fore in the late 1870s when – only partly referring back to Heraclitus – he points out that whatever "we humans call life and experience" is above all that which "has gradually *become*, is indeed still fully in the course of becoming" (*HA* I: 16).

At first sight it is clearly surprising that Nietzsche's notion of becoming should be seen as teleological. Viewed against the background of his continuous criticism of Kant and Hegel from the late 1860s to the late 1880s, teleological arguments, in one way or another, tend to predict large-scale historical developments as a goal-directed process, while the notion of becoming entails an unpredictability and openness toward the future. Given the political context of German Idealism, Kant and Hegel clearly favor civil society and the constitutional state as the concrete outcome of a teleological history, even though their

---

[146] See Friedrich Wilhelm Joseph von Schelling, *Ideas for a Philosophy of Nature as Introduction to the Study of this Science*, trans. Errol E. Harris and Peter Hearth, intro. Robert Stern (Cambridge: Cambridge University Press, 1988), pp. 41–2.

[147] See Friedrich Wilhelm Joseph Schelling, *First Outline of a System of the Philosophy of Nature*, trans. Keith R. Peterson (Albany, N.Y.: SUNY Press, 2004), p. 16. On Schelling's evolutionary framework and its debt to contemporary biological thought, see Richards, *The Romantic Conception of Life*, pp. 294–306, and Dietrich von Engelhardt, "Die organische Natur und die Lebenswissenschaften in Schellings Naturphilosophie," in Reinhard Heckmann, Hermann Krings, and Rudolf W. Meyer (eds.), *Natur und Subjektivität: Zur Auseinandersetzung mit der Naturphilosophie des jungen Schelling* (Stuttgart-Bad Cannstatt: Frommann-Holzboog, 1985), pp. 39–57.

respective accounts of modern political institutions are somewhat different.[148] Writing at the end of the long nineteenth century, Nietzsche realized, however, that modern civil society has a strong tendency to undermine itself through its very own ideals of moral authenticity, that is, the ideals that both Kant and Hegel saw as a necessary foundation of civil society. As a result, teleological arguments seem questionable from the perspective of Nietzsche's political realism.

Nevertheless, despite his distance from strong teleological arguments, Nietzsche's notion of becoming still retains a weak teleological structure, which comes particularly to the fore in his account of the natural history of moral communities: in the evolution of such moral communities, the usefulness of any given value cannot be the reason for its existence, but the existence of a value predetermines that a specific set of new values can emerge – a certain regime of truth, as Foucault would say – while other values are excluded from this development. For Nietzsche, then, the notion of becoming, as a weak teleological argument, seeks to describe processes of natural and social emergence. It is important to realize, however, that such processes can only be examined retrospectively, which is the reason why genealogy is an inherently historical strategy.[149] Although genealogy clearly highlights the contingency and radical changes that our moral norms undergo over a longer period in time, the way in which such changes are embodied and have become a kind of second nature nevertheless suggests a weak teleology, which is grounded in the assumption that moral norms, as they come to govern social life, are not universal and timeless but rather part of a continuing process of emergence.

The wholehearted emphasis on temporality and historicity, which continues to inform Nietzsche's genealogy throughout the 1880s, finally also seeks to close the gap between the natural sciences and historical disciplines that had repeatedly been opened in the final decades of the nineteenth century by neo-Kantian

---

[148] See Kant, "Idea for a Universal History" and his criticism of Moses Mendelssohn's skeptical view of human progress in *On the Common Saying: "This May be True in Theory, but it does not Apply in Practice"*, both in *Political Writings*, pp. 45–53 and 87–92, respectively. See also Hegel, *Elements of the Philosophy of Right*, pp. 372–80 (§§ 341–60) and *Lectures on the Philosophy of World History*, pp. 27–43.

[149] See Williams, "Naturalism and Genealogy," pp. 154–7.

philosophers like Eduard Zeller and Wilhelm Windelband.[150] What Nietzsche, at the beginning of *Menschliches, Allzumenschliches*, terms "the steady and laborious process of science," which itself cannot be detached from the historical and social world, "will one day celebrate its greatest triumph in a *history of the emergence of thinking* [*Entstehungsgeschichte des Denkens*]" (*HA* I: 16).[151] The possible conclusion of such an enterprise clearly anticipates the direction of his later genealogical project. The basic framework of the genealogical enterprise is already in place in the above passage from 1878, but Nietzsche furthermore argues that such a properly historical philosophizing "can no longer be separated from natural science" (*HA* I: 1). The attempt "to *naturalize* humanity," as he writes in *Die fröhliche Wissenschaft*, can be successful only if it results in a conception of the natural world that is "completely de-deified" (*GS* 109), which is to say: a conception of nature that, first, includes what we regard as the social world and, secondly, does not attribute a moral perspective to natural processes. For Nietzsche, then, the world in which we are forced to live is not becoming morally better, or more "evil" – it is just becoming.

Nietzsche's weak philosophical naturalism, together with his attempt to bridge the gap between scientific and historical forms of understanding, has to operate with a concept of science that excludes any pathos of conviction and thus mirrors his political realism:

In science, convictions have no right to citizenship, as one says with good reason: only when they decide to step down to the modesty of a hypothesis, a tentative experimental standpoint, a regulative fiction, may

---

[150] See Eduard Zeller, *Ueber Bedeutung und Aufgabe der Erkenntniss-Theorie: Ein akademischer Vortrag* (Heidelberg: Groos, 1862), and Wilhelm Windelband, *Geschichte und Naturwissenschaft: Rede zum Antritt des Rectorats der Kaiser-Wilhelm-Universität Strassburg, geh. am 1. Mai 1894* (Strasbourg: Heitz, 1894). On this gap between the natural sciences and the historical disciplines, see Irmline Veit-Brause, "Scientists and the Politics of Academic Disciplines in Late 19th-Century Germany: Emil DuBois-Reymond and the Controversy over the Role of the Cultural Sciences," *History of the Human Sciences* 14/4 (2001), 31–56, and Otto Gerhard Oexle, "Naturwissenschaft und Geschichtswissenschaft: Momente einer Problemgeschichte," in Oexle (ed.), *Naturwissenschaft, Geisteswissenschaft, Kulturwissenschaft: Einheit, Gegensatz, Komplemetarität?* 2nd edn. (Göttingen: Wallstein, 2000), pp. 99–151.

[151] R. J. Hollingdale renders the German expression *Entstehungsgeschichte des Denkens* as "a history of the genesis of thought." The English term "genesis" is more suggestive of origins, however, than the German *Entstehung*, which refers to the process of coming into existence.

they be granted admission and even a certain value in the realm of knowledge. (*GS* 344)

Although Nietzsche here seems to contradict himself, for he has just presented a conviction, even his own claims remain tentative: the "faith" that is necessary to put into science needs to be held in check by a constant "mistrust" (*GS* 344).[152] The political realism of the "free spirit," that is, the latter's relentless and cruel honesty, has to extend into the realm of science. An ethic of responsibility, in other words, needs to exist in both political life and science – even genealogy would have to be subjected to such honesty. Nietzsche, who in *Die fröhliche Wissenschaft* occasionally still uses quotation marks when he speaks about "'naturalizing' our humanity" (*GS* 109), therefore drops these quotation marks only a few years later in *Jenseits von Gut und Böse*:

> To translate humanity back into nature; to gain control of the many vain and fanciful interpretations and incidental meanings that have been scribbled and drawn over that eternal basic text of *homo natura* so far; to make sure that, from now on, the human being will stand before the human being, just as he already stands before the *rest* of nature today, hardened by the discipline of science, ... (*BGE* 230)

On the one hand, this naturalism is clearly the outcome of Nietzsche's epistemological concerns. On the other hand, it is also a result of the way in which Nietzsche, throughout his writings from the late 1860s onwards, seeks to link philosophical claims about social and political reality to scientific claims about the empirical world, especially claims made by the contemporary life sciences.

The philosophical dimension of genealogy, then, is a cautiously naturalist account of the formation of moral values. But what is the consequence of this account with regard to the political orientation of genealogy? Naturalizing human agency and the ethical world would, of course, ultimately contribute to what Nietzsche describes as the "self-overcoming" of an artificial Judeo-Christian Europe (*GS* 357 and *GM* III: 27). But there is more at stake for Nietzsche than merely a criticism of religious culture. In the end, genealogy has to ask what the result of such a self-overcoming and revaluation of

---

[152] See, in contrast, Havas, *Nietzsche's Genealogy*, pp. 166–9. That Nietzsche's naturalism is marked by inconsistencies and, at least, ambiguities has recently been stressed by Maudemarie Clark and David Dudrick, "The Naturalism of *Beyond Good and Evil*," in Ansell-Pearson (ed.), *A Companion to Nietzsche*, pp. 148–67.

values might look like. Nietzsche hints at this in a crucial passage of *Die fröhliche Wissenschaft*, when he describes what we might regard as the political effect of his naturalism. The latter forces us "to *become who we are*," that is, "human beings ... who give themselves laws, who create themselves" by being critically aware of the complex historicity of our normative commitments, socially and biologically speaking (*GS* 335). Only on this basis is genealogy able to cultivate "citizens who stand to themselves as sovereign individuals."[153] But how does this relate to the political realities of the later nineteenth century?

---

[153] Owen, "Equality, Democracy, and Self-Respect," 126.

CHAPTER 6

The idea of Europe and the limits of genealogy

There can be little doubt that, from the perspective of Nietzsche's genealogy, appeals to moral and political authenticity in the name of humanity seem questionable. Given the absolutism of those moral communities that purport to represent "humanity," the latter might turn out to be an overrated, perhaps even fatal concept in that it precludes a more realist account of political life. It is precisely in dealing with this question that Nietzsche begins to outline what I am going to call his "idea of Europe" as a possible alternative to the political culture of moral communities. Needless to say, Europe is like any other form of political identity "a construction, an elaborate palimpsest of stories, images, resonances, collective memories, invented and carefully nurtured traditions." But what makes Europe such an attractive alternative to Nietzsche is its unusual status as "something larger than the family, the tribe, the community, or the nation yet smaller and more culturally specific than 'humanity'."[1] Europe, in other words, suggests that an ethical community can exist which is both more open than the nation state and less vague than humanity. This is also Nietzsche's assumption.[2]

But Nietzsche's turn toward Europe also comes at a price. What is left for philosophy, as he noted in *Die fröhliche Wissenschaft*, is the unbearable freedom of the "open sea" (*GS* 343). His idea of

---

[1] Anthony Pagden, "Europe: Conceptualizing a Continent," in Pagden (ed.), *The Idea of Europe: From Antiquity to the European Union* (Cambridge: Cambridge University Press, 2002), pp. 33–54: 33 and 53. See also J. G. A. Pocock, "Deconstructing Europe," *History of European Ideas* 18 (1994), 329–46.
[2] See Stefan Elbe, *Europe: A Nietzschean Perspective* (London: Routledge, 2003), pp. 45 and 52; Nicholas Martin, "'We Good Europeans': Nietzsche's New Europe in *Beyond Good and Evil*," *History of European Ideas* 20 (1995), 141–4; Graham Parkes, "Wanderers in the Shadow of Nihilism: Nietzsche's Good Europeans," *History of European Ideas* 16 (1993), 585–90.

Europe remains ambivalent and, given the nature of genealogy, it might turn out to be an impossible idea, at least from Nietzsche's perspective. If anything, Europe remains a regulative ideal.[3] Toward the end of *Zur Genealogie der Moral* he notes: "These things will be addressed by me more fully and seriously in another connection (with the title 'On the History of European Nihilism'; for which I refer you to a work I am writing, *The Will to Power. Attempt at a Revaluation of all Values*)" (*GM* III: 27).[4] Because he never completed this text, his account of Europe also remains fragmented. Between 1887 and 1888, the "European problem" (*BGE* 251) features prominently on several occasions throughout his notebooks and he even points out that "the economic unification of Europe comes with necessity," that is, as an inevitable historical development that will cut across the direct interests of the nation states (*KGW* VIII/2, 11 [235]). But since concrete evidence of Nietzsche's political vision for Europe is relatively thin, we should hesitate to speculate that this political vision would have been an essentially liberal one in the modern sense of the term. While there is much to be said for Nietzsche's anti-essentialism and his emphasis on epistemological pluralism, his proclamations about "a new caste to rule Europe," at least at first sight, seem unacceptable from our own point of view (*BGE* 251). This necessary ambivalence of Nietzsche's idea of Europe also hints at the fact that there are limits to genealogy, especially as far as the practice of politics is concerned.

"THE CREATION OF THE EUROPEAN INDIVIDUAL"

The status of Nietzsche's political thought might be somewhat unclear, as is his position within the political context at the end of the nineteenth century, but it makes little sense to read Nietzsche as an inherently proto-fascist thinker, as some intellectual historians and political philosophers continue to do.[5] Nevertheless,

---

[3] As such a simply regulative idea, Nietzsche's image of Europe is not the megalomaniacal utopian alternative to the German nation state that Ottmann, *Philosophie und Politik bei Nietzsche*, pp. 240–5, describes.
[4] The main title "The Will to Power" is strongly emphasized in the original.
[5] See, for example, the comments in Wolin, *The Seduction of Unreason*, pp. 54–8; Schutte, *Beyond Nihilism*, pp. 161–88; Detwiler, *Nietzsche and the Politics of Aristocratic Radicalism*, pp. 193–6. For a rigorous account of the abuse of Nietzsche by National Socialist

any political interpretation of Nietzsche's writings faces a peculiar difficulty: while he accepts the need for an ethic of responsibility, it is indeed puzzling that an evidently political thinker like Nietzsche refrained from formulating a political philosophy properly speaking.[6] But the lack of a coherently articulated political philosophy does not at all disqualify Nietzsche as a political thinker. Rather, what makes his view of the political difficult is that he does not develop this view in contrast to any specific and well-defined political position – as Kant, Hegel and Marx do – and that he remains suspicious of political ideals:

> But have you ever asked yourselves properly how costly the setting up of *every* ideal on earth has been? How much reality always had to be vilified and misunderstood in the process, how many lies had to be sanctified ...?
> If a shrine [*Heiligthum*] is to be set up, a *shrine has to be destroyed*: that is the law – show me an example where this does not apply! (*GM* II: 24)

In contrast to an ethic of conviction that endorses the hegemonial dimension inherent in any political ideal, Nietzsche clearly seeks to attain a perspective from which to overcome the contradictory claims that he sees as structuring political culture in the second half of the nineteenth century, such as liberalism, nationalism, and socialism.

But does this mean that Nietzsche wishes to argue for an autonomy of the political? This might be a tempting conclusion, which would move his position close to a tradition of modern political thought that is perhaps best represented by Carl Schmitt and his legacy, for instance, in the work of Leo Strauss. Schmitt's political thought, at least throughout the 1920s and 1930s, rests on the "inherently objective nature and autonomy of the political," which is existentially detached from society, law, religion, and the economy.[7] At the other end of the political spectrum, Hannah Arendt also pointed to the autonomy of the political as that space within which "freedom" is able to articulate

---

intellectuals, see Manfred Riedel, *Nietzsche in Weimar* (Leipzig: Reclam, 1997), pp. 86–148.

[6] See Martha Nussbaum, "Is Nietzsche a Political Thinker?" *International Journal of Philosophical Studies* 5 (1997), 1–13.

[7] Carl Schmitt, *The Concept of the Political*, trans. George Schwab, foreword Tracy B. Strong (Chicago: University of Chicago Press, 1996), p. 27. Schmitt's argument for the autonomy of the political also influences Leo Strauss, *Natural Right and History* (Chicago: University of Chicago Press, 1953), pp. 35–80.

itself in an idealized "public realm" based on the Greek *polis*.[8] Equating, at least to some extent, freedom and the political, both emerge as necessary preconditions for political practice. But looking back at Nietzsche's political reflections throughout the 1870s and 1880s, it should be obvious that, for Nietzsche, the political cannot be understood on the basis of such an autonomy. The political is always marked by history and, as such, it cannot be separated from those aspects of human experience that over time have contributed to its formation, such as the psychology of guilt and conscience, the economic basis of legal relationships, and the social practices that reflect ethical commitments. In short, the idea of an autonomy of the political remains rooted in the presumed existence of political absolutes – such as nation, state, law, humanity, natural right – that Nietzsche is unwilling to share. Viewed against the background of the naturalist claims of Nietzsche's genealogy, both Schmitt's notion of the political and Arendt's notion of freedom are purely ideational and cannot account for the material and empirical conditions of the political. As a consequence, they also have to ignore the historicity of the political that stands at the center of Nietzsche's genealogy.

Nietzsche's repeated emphasis on the dangers of moralizing the political, one of the practical insights of genealogy, is based on the structural equivalence of moral and political absolutes. This becomes particularly obvious in his discussion of nationalism, which continues to be a prominent concern throughout the final years of his intellectual career. It is against this background that the idea of Europe begins to gain currency in his writings. In repeated attacks on the glorification of "Germanness" as describing a racial and moral community, he argued, for instance, that "those who preach hatred against the French" tend to forget that their own intellectual roots, including their symbolism of freedom and liberation, are primarily French (*HA* II: ii.216). In fact, it is the anti-French sentiments of the "Wars of Liberation" that "have provoked the catastrophe of nationalist madness [*das Unglück des Nationalitäten-Wahnsinns*]" on a European scale (*KGW* VII/2, 25 [115]). Nietzsche's prime examples for this trend are August Heinrich Hoffmann von Fallersleben's *Lied der Deutschen*,

---

[8] Hannah Arendt, "What Is Freedom?" in *Between Past and Future: Eight Exercises in Political Thought* (New York: Penguin, 1993), pp. 143–71: 149.

written in 1841, which had its roots in the national-liberal outlook and revolutionary agenda of the early student corporations in Göttingen and Jena, as well as Johann Gottlieb Fichte's *Reden an die deutsche Nation*, delivered at the Prussian Academy in 1807, while Berlin was occupied by the Napoleonic army.[9] Indeed, both in *Ecce Homo* and *Zur Genealogie der Moral* he unravels Hoffmann von Fallersleben's highly ambiguous stanza "Deutschland, Deutschland über alles," which refers to both the unification of the German states as well as to Germany's position within the European arena, as a mythical construction: connected to racial and moral absolutes this Germanness is bound to culminate in delusion (*EH* XIV: 2 and *GM* III: 26) – like any other nationalist trope.

To be sure, Nietzsche's critique of nationalism is not restricted to nineteenth-century Germany. The hypnotic effects of nationalism can also be observed in France, where they befog the "democratic bourgeoisie": "In fact, it is a coarsened and stultified France that thrashes around in the foreground these days, – it recently celebrated a real orgy of bad taste combined with self-admiration at Victor Hugo's funeral" (*BGE* 254). Hugo's funeral on June 1, 1885, was indeed a spectacle of extraordinary proportions: in a grand ceremony reminiscent of both the revolutionary festivals of the eighteenth century and the funerary rites for absolutist baroque rulers, Hugo's corpse was laid out on a *castrum doloris* in the middle of the Arc de Triomphe. Nation and art came together in a performance that transformed Hugo into a *lieu de mémoire* for the French nation as a whole.[10]

For Nietzsche, the emergence of such nationalist tropes is directly linked to the politics of history. By turning themselves into the handmaidens of Bismarck's nation state and the Protestant Church, German historians, for instance, have established what amounted to an Imperial historiography that continued the anti-French and anti-European foundation myths of the Wars of Liberation, underestimating that such presumed Germanness remained an eclectic historical construct from the very start (*EH* XIV: 2 and *BGE* 244). But despite his scathing criticism of Prussia's

---

[9] For Nietzsche's remarks on Hoffmann von Fallersleben, see *GS* 357 and *TI* VIII: 1. For his remarks on Fichte, see *KGW* VIII/1, 1 [196].

[10] See Avner Ben-Amos, "Les funérailles de Victor Hugo," in Pierre Nora (ed.), *Les lieux de mémoire* (Paris: Gallimard, 1984–92), vol. I, pp. 473–521.

German vocation in his writings and correspondence, Nietzsche did rarely engage directly with the Prussian school of historiography and its political vision, which by the 1880s had culminated in Heinrich von Treitschke's turn to a nationalist-conservative image of German history and his enthusiasm for *Machtpolitik* in the name of a German nation state dominated by Prussia.[11]

One of the very few direct attacks Nietzsche made on Treitschke's political ideas can be found in *Ecce Homo*, when he relates with barely hidden amusement that Bruno Bauer – a former student of Hegel and one-time friend of David Friedrich Strauß, who had lost his teaching position in Protestant theology at the University of Bonn in 1842 because of his increasingly atheist and politically radical views – recommended in one of his writings that Treitschke should read Nietzsche's "Untimely Meditations" in order to gain some orientation about political culture (*EH* VI: 2).[12] The irony of this remark should not be overlooked. While Nietzsche himself had little positive to say about Bauer, they did in fact share some common ground. Indeed, Nietzsche and Bauer, who had the same publisher at the beginning of the 1880s, both rejected nineteenth-century German liberalism and socialism as signs of political degeneration, and they both argued that Christianity was merely a sophisticated form of myth with detrimental political effects for modern society. But Bauer's conclusion that Christianity played an important role on the path toward political revolution differed fundamentally from Nietzsche's view that Christianity had always been a disastrous cult of mythical superstition.[13]

Like Nietzsche, Bauer also came to view the rise of European nationalisms, especially Prussia's German vocation, with some suspicion. He was particularly harsh about the transformation of liberalism into nationalism, which he could witness in the writings and public announcements by Treitschke and Heinrich

---

[11] See Andreas Biefang, "Der Streit um Treitschkes *Deutsche Geschichte* 1882/83: Zur Spaltung des Nationalliberalismus und der Etablierung eines national-konservativen Geschichtsbildes," *Historische Zeitschrift* 262 (1996), 391–422, and Karl H. Metz, "The Politics of Conflict: Heinrich von Treitschke and the Idea of *Realpolitik*," *History of Political Thought* 3 (1982), 269–84.
[12] Nietzsche refers here to Bruno Bauer, *Zur Orientierung über die Bismarck'sche Ära* (Chemnitz: Schmeitzner, 1880), pp. 287–8.
[13] For the most detailed assessment of Bauer's critique of religious consciousness available in English, see Douglas Moggach, *The Philosophy and Politics of Bruno Bauer* (Cambridge: Cambridge University Press, 2003), pp. 59–79.

von Sybel.[14] But unlike Nietzsche, who regarded the popular overvaluation of the German intellectual tradition from Luther to Hegel as a dangerous illusion (*TI* VIII: 1–4) and who diagnosed a "palpable *desolation* of the German spirit" (*GM* III: 26), Bauer continued to glorify a numinous "German spirit" that he saw as being threatened from the East.[15] As such, Bauer shared central aspects of Treitschke's political outlook, who himself regarded Russian expansion as the main threat to European stability and the ambitions of Imperial Germany. Furthermore, long before Treitschke's own anti-Semitic remarks during the 1880s, Bauer began to present the so-called "Jewish question" as a problem for the self-conception of any future German nation state. In his pamphlet *Die Judenfrage* (1843), which triggered a harsh response by Karl Marx that appeared in the *Deutsch-Französische Jahrbücher* of 1844, Bauer highlighted that the religious and political status of the Jewish population called into question the confessional allegiance of the Prussian state.[16] While Bauer's position seemed initially liberal in that he advocated disposing of the privileges of the Protestant elite, which had allowed them to dominate the civil institutions of the state, he argued fervently against the political emancipation of the Jewish population. The latter, he noted, should not claim any rights based on a particular cultural or religious identity.[17] Pointing to the confessional basis of the modern German nation state, he prepared some of the ground for the link between anti-Semitism and nationalism that can be found in Treitschke's later essay "Unsere Aussichten" (1879).[18] But in marked contrast to Treitschke, Bauer shared Nietzsche's unease with regard to the imperial vision of nationalism that was a central aspect of Bismarck's public policy. For Bauer, Bismarck's policies – the attempt to organize all cultural and economic interests in the service of the modern nation state – created a dangerous situation,

---

[14] See Bauer, *Zur Orientierung über die Bismarck'sche Ära*, pp. 50–9, 69–80, and 278–88.
[15] See Bruno Bauer, *Russland und das Germanenthum* (Charlottenburg: Bauer, 1853).
[16] See Bruno Bauer, *Die Judenfrage* (Braunschweig: Otto, 1843), and Karl Marx, "Zur Judenfrage," in Karl Marx and Friedrich Engels, *Werke*, vol. 1 (Berlin: Dietz, 1976), pp. 347–77. On the context of this debate, see also Rose, *Revolutionary Antisemitism in Germany*, pp. 61–9, 263–78 and 296–305.
[17] See Bruno Bauer, "Die Fähigkeit der heutigen Juden und Christen, frei zu werden," in Georg Herwegh (ed.), *Einundzwanzig Bogen aus der Schweiz* (Zurich: Verlag des Literarischen Comptoirs, 1843), pp. 56–71.
[18] See Heinrich von Treitschke, "Unsere Aussichten," *Preußische Jahrbücher* 44 (1879), 559–76.

which sooner or later was bound to trigger a world war that would obliterate the imaginary Germanic tradition he cherished.[19]

The complex irony of Nietzsche's relationship to Bauer and his views of Treitschke, that are the background to his inconspicuous remark in *Ecce Homo*, underline his detailed understanding of contemporary political culture. But his criticism of nationalist historiography, which he regarded as the handmaiden of the modern German nation state, had deeper roots. By the mid-1870s, Nietzsche had aligned himself strategically with Jacob Burckhardt's historical vision, whose anti-modern stance provided him with much inspiration against "overrating the state, the national" (*KGW* III/4, 32 [72]). As a consequence, he soon began to characterize his own age as being marked by "a disappearance of the national and the creation of the European individual [*des europäischen Menschen*]*,*" which stood in clear opposition to much German historical thought in the nineteenth century (*KGW* IV/2, 19 [75]). Once again, such remarks were not only directed against German nationalism. The kind of philosophical skepticism that Nietzsche, for instance, detected in seventeenth- and eighteenth-century French thought, "the last political noblesse in Europe," was also a powerful counter-image to the egalitarian ideologies of liberal social thought in Britain (*GM* I: 16 and *BGE* 253). Seen from this vantage point, political culture at the end of the nineteenth century was, for Nietzsche, a truly European problem.

Nietzsche's hope for a European political culture is closely linked to his diagnosis of European nihilism in *Die fröhliche Wissenschaft*. While this is not the place to attempt a broad overview of the uses of nihilism before Nietzsche, it is important to note that, by the late nineteenth century, the meaning of nihilism had undergone a crucial transformation that played into Nietzsche's discussion.[20] Nihilism is not a perennial philosophical problem, of course, but emerges as a problem first of all in the context of early modern rationalism. Throughout the late eighteenth and early nineteenth centuries, nihilism mainly referred to the perceived

---

[19] See Moggach, *The Philosophy and Politics of Bruno Bauer*, pp. 185–7.
[20] For historical overviews, see Manfred Riedel, "Nihilismus," in Otto Brunner, Werner Conze, and Reinhart Koselleck (eds.), *Geschichtliche Grundbegriffe* (Stuttgart: Klett-Cotta, 1972–97), vol. IV, pp. 371–411, and Wolfgang Müller-Lauter, "Nihilismus," in: *Historisches Wörterbuch der Philosophie*, ed. Joachim Ritter, Karlfried Gründer, and Gottfried Gabriel (Basel: Schwabe & Co., 1971–), vol. IV, cols. 846–54.

philosophical dangers of atheism and the decline of religion as a cultural authority.[21] As such, nihilism was often seen as corresponding to a philosophical skepticism that originated in the aftermath of Descartes and Spinoza, but that made even Kant's critical philosophy liable to accusations of nihilism.[22] In the second half of the nineteenth century, however, the originally philosophical notion of nihilism turned into a wider cultural trope, which was supported by the rise of materialism and a positivist understanding of science. Nietzsche, of course, was fully aware of this shift. The philosophical realization that "God is dead," he claimed, finally begins to filter through into the public sphere, "starting to cast its first shadow over Europe." The consequences of this development, nihilism, might not yet be entirely understood, but to the philosophically educated and historically minded observer it was clear that "our entire European morality" was about to "collapse" (*GS* 343), leaving behind a transhuman world.

While noting that Judeo-Christian morality was still needed as a comfortable and convenient illusion, the slow disintegration of religion as a cultural authority highlighted that the claims of the Judeo-Christian tradition, which continued to inform such divergent political positions as nationalism, liberalism and socialism, stood on thin ground (*GS* 346–7 and 352). In contrast to the demands for moral authenticity and a rigid order of the political that could be based on such authenticity, Nietzsche began to favor the image of a "homeless" and "wandering" European, who would be able to face the uncertainties that the decline of religion and metaphysics were about to leave behind (*GS* 377 and 380).

One could ask, of course, whether Nietzsche's preference for intellectual homelessness reflected his own situation as a, legally speaking, stateless person. After his official emigration from Saxony to Switzerland on April 17, 1869, he merely received a residence permit in Basel on June 16, 1869. Even the Swiss passport he carried

---

[21] See Hans-Jürgen Gawoll, *Nihilismus und Metaphysik: Entwicklungsgeschichtliche Untersuchung vom deutschen Idealismus bis zu Heidegger* (Stuttgart: Frommann-Holzboog, 1989), pp. 140–9.

[22] See ibid., pp. 22–114. A similar historical trajectory, reaching from Descartes to Fichte, has been outlined by Michael Allen Gillespie, *Nihilism before Nietzsche* (Chicago: University of Chicago Press, 1995), pp. 1–100. But while Gillespie suggests that Nietzsche essentially misunderstood the history of nihilism before the later nineteenth century, Gawoll (pp. 150–232) shows in much detail that Nietzsche's remarks are the necessary consequence of this intellectual tradition.

with him from September 1876 to 1889, and which was originally valid only for one year, did not claim Swiss citizenship or that he was a citizen of the canton Basel.[23] While Nietzsche's "wandering years" between 1879 and 1889 have often been romanticized, the legal status of his person does indeed fit nicely with his self-presentation as that socially unattached intellectual which Karl Mannheim described so aptly in the late 1920s: "attuned to the dynamically conflicting forces" of their time, such intellectuals were able to choose their political affiliations and social interests without losing a fundamental "distrust" of their cultural and intellectual environment.[24]

Nietzsche's status as an unattached intellectual – representing the condition of the modern intellectual par excellence – is not limited to his social life. Rather, it is closely linked to the psychological outlook of the "free spirit," that is, the autonomous and sovereign individual that is able to move beyond the "single point of view" of any particular philosophical canon, religious belief system, or party political program (*GS* 347). Grounded in a particular aspect of Nietzsche's epistemology, perspectivism, the "free spirit" has to accept that any interpretations about the world, and judgments made about whatever is seen as reality, are principally "perspectival estimations [*perspektivische Schätzungen*]," as he writes in his notebooks during the mid-1880s (*KGW* VIII/1, 2 [108]). Without wishing to enter upon a detailed analytical assessment of Nietzsche's epistemology, such perspectivism does not automatically entail epistemological, or ethical, relativism.[25] On the contrary, in order for perspectivism to hold water, some perspectives need to be shown to be more valid, accurate and justifiable than others. Only in this respect is Nietzsche able to note in *Jenseits von Gut und Böse* that "perspectival thought" is a "precondition of life" (*BGE*, preface).[26] The "free spirit" has to accept that any

---

[23] Some instructive remarks on Nietzsche's legal status as a "stateless person" can be found in Eduard His, "Friedrich Nietzsches Heimatlosigkeit," *Basler Zeitschrift für Geschichte und Altertumskunde* 40 (1941), 159–86: 164–73.

[24] Karl Mannheim, *Ideology and Utopia: An Introduction to the Sociology of Knowledge*, trans. Louis Wirth and Edward Shils (London: Routledge & Kegan Paul, 1936), pp. 157–8. Mannheim himself might not have had Nietzsche in mind when he wrote these passages, even though he regarded Nietzsche's genealogy clearly as a precursor to his own attempt at a sociology of knowledge. See ibid., pp. 20, 25 and 310.

[25] See Cox, *Nietzsche*, pp. 113–18 and 139–68.

[26] Some of Nietzsche's central epistemological claims about perspectivism are indebted to Teichmüller, *Die wirkliche und die scheinbare Welt*, pp. 17, 183–7, 223–4, 268–76, 315–19,

interpretation of the world remains of an experimental character; interpretations, in other words, are *Versuche* (*KGW* VII/3, 35 [36]).

Already in *Die fröhliche Wissenschaft* Nietzsche translates such seemingly radical epistemological claims into the psychology of the "free spirit," arguing in favor of "brief habits" over the lasting claims of normative convictions: "I love brief habits and consider them invaluable means for getting to know *many* things and states down to the bottom of their sweetnesses and bitternesses." Such brief habits, he notes, can be followed with passionate single-mindedness, but they are sooner or later replaced by new habits, intellectual occupations and "ways of life" (*GS* 295).[27] Clearly, this also has political consequences: Nietzsche's future European would need to be "able to stand contradiction," that is, be able to understand that which is not itself, and have the "*ability to* contradict," that is, the ability to challenge normative claims (*GS* 297).[28]

It is here that we encounter once again the sovereign individual, whose ethic of responsibility contradicts the ethic of conviction that underlies traditional moral communities and the normative claims of the moral law. The sovereign individual has to pose what Christine M. Korsgaard has termed the "normative question," namely: "what *justifies* the claims that morality makes on us"?[29] Nietzsche, of course, would reformulate this question: what justifies the claims that *we* attribute to what *we* regard as our normative ethical commitments? Korsgaard certainly does not wish to do away with the normativity of morality, but her answer to the above question is strikingly similar to Nietzsche's ethic of responsibility: "the source of the normativity of moral claims must be found in the agent's own will, in particular in the fact that the laws of

---

and 332–3. Robin Small, *Nietzsche in Context* (Aldershot: Ashgate, 2001), pp. 41–58, has examined Teichmüller's influence in more detail.

[27] See also *GS* 307.

[28] Drawing on Michel Foucault, "What is Enlightenment?" in Paul Rabinow (ed.), *The Foucault Reader* (New York: Pantheon, 1984), pp. 32–50, James Tully has described this as the true "Enlightenment critical attitude," which consists in "both respecting and challenging the prevailing forms of thought and action in the present." See Tully, "The Kantian Idea of Europe: Critical and Cosmopolitan Perspectives," in Pagden (ed.), *The Idea of Europe*, pp. 331–58: 358. A similar argument is developed in the close link between "critical freedom" and the "aspiration of belonging" as the basis of cultural recognition. See James Tully, *Strange Multiplicity: Constitutionalism in an Age of Diversity* (Cambridge: Cambridge University Press, 1995), pp. 198–209, especially 202.

[29] Christine M. Korsgaard, *The Sources of Normativity* (Cambridge: Cambridge University Press, 1996), p. 10.

morality are the laws of the agent's own will and that its claims are the ones she is prepared to make on herself."[30] On the one hand, this argument is based on Kant's categorical imperative, which Nietzsche himself viewed with much suspicion.[31] On the other hand, an implication is that ethical obligations are rooted in an autonomy that Nietzsche clearly subscribes to, even though he regards such autonomy as embedded in, and thus limited by, our biological make-up and history. This naturalist framework separates Nietzsche's political thought from the way in which Kant seeks to limit human autonomy in political life: it can be overruled by a "supreme authority," essentially the *raison d'état*, which itself should not be questioned.[32]

Although Nietzsche might ultimately misread Kant, or at least misunderstand the latter's intention, his criticism of the categorical imperative is not entirely unsubstantiated:

> What? You admire the categorical imperative in you? This "firmness" of your so-called moral judgement? The absoluteness of the feeling, "here everyone must judge as I do?" Rather admire your *selfishness* here! ... For it is selfish to consider one's own judgement as a universal law, and this selfishness is blind, petty, and simple because it shows that you haven't yet discovered yourself or created yourself an ideal of your very own – for this could never be some else's, let alone everyone's, everyone's! (*GS* 335)[33]

The selfishness of the universal claims made by the categorical imperative consists in the hidden hegemonial interest of whoever makes such claims in practice, that is, whoever seeks to establish himself as the only point of reference against which human action can be judged. Leaving aside the question whether Nietzsche here really makes sense of Kant, this passage from 1882 highlights that the absolutist stance of the categorical imperative in fact continues an understanding of normativity that already characterized what Nietzsche described as the Judeo-Christian tradition.

---

[30] Ibid., p. 19. [31] See ibid., pp. 90–130.
[32] See, for instance, Kant, *The Metaphysics of Morals*, pp. 129–30.
[33] Nietzsche refers here to the famous end of Kant's second Critique. See *Critique of Practical Reason*, ed. Gregor, p. 133: "Two things fill the mind with ever new and increasing admiration and reverence, the more often and more steadily one reflects on them: *the starry heavens above me and the moral law within me.*"

The kind of autonomy that Nietzsche envisions as the basis of normative ethical claims thus stands in contrast to what he regards as the nihilism of moral communities: at least, we must value our own values, habits, interests and inclinations, but we must also accept that our normative claims might undergo change, that normativity does not imply the absolutism of moral communities. It is by valuing our own values, however, that we also have the responsibility to value that which is not us – a position that Nietzsche only attributes to the "free spirits" and which represents the precise opposite to what he describes as a "slave morality" based on *ressentiment*.[34] The "man of *ressentiment*," as Nietzsche notes in *Zur Genealogie der Moral*, "has conceived of the 'evil enemy,' '*the evil one*' as the basic idea to which he now thinks up a copy and counterpart, the 'good one' – himself" (*GM* I: 10). In contrast, the autonomous individual – the future European that he hopes for – is able to develop ethical claims on the basis of his own autonomy:

> To be unable to take his enemies, his misfortunes and even his *misdeeds* seriously for long – that is the sign of strong, rounded natures with a superabundance of a power which is flexible, formative, healing and can make one forget ... A man [*Mensch*] like this shakes from him, with one shrug, many worms which would have burrowed another human being; here and here alone is it possible, assuming that this is possible at all on earth – truly to "*love* your neighbour." How much respect a noble human being has for his enemies! (*GM* I: 10).[35]

The double-bind of autonomy and responsibility that Nietzsche in this passage ascribes to the sovereign individual is the same double-bind that also characterizes his "free spirits" and his future European. Against this background, we can assume that Nietzsche's idea of Europe is the concrete political realization of this double-bind of autonomy and responsibility.

---

[34] Surprisingly, this position is not entirely incompatible with Jürgen Habermas, "Discourse Ethics: Notes on a Program of Philosophical Justification," in *Moral Consciousness and Communicative Action*, trans. Christian Lenhardt and Shierry Weber Nicholson, intro. Thomas McCarthy (Cambridge, Mass.: MIT Press, 1990), pp. 43–115. After all, for Habermas, the negotiation of interests and values can take place only once the values and interests of other people are at least recognized as such.

[35] Carol Diethe translates Nietzsche's neutral expression *Mensch* as "man," but in order to avoid any unintended connotations I have opted for "human being." There is no indication, at least not in this passage, that Nietzsche meant anything but a "human individual."

BEYOND THE MODERN NATION STATE

Nietzsche's European vision does not sit easily with the political culture of the nation state, and some commentators have described his later reflections on Europe as a truly transnational project.[36] After all, in *Menschliches, Allzumenschliches* he had already pointed to the detrimental effects of a Europe of nation states; each one of these nation states would conceive itself as a moral community that perceived other nation states as culturally and morally inferior and as harboring an "evil disposition":

> No government nowadays admits that it maintains an army so as to satisfy occasional thirsts for conquest; the army is supposed to be for defence. That morality which sanctions self-protection is called upon to be its advocate. But that means to reserve morality to oneself and to accuse one's neighbour of immorality, since he has to be thought of as ready for aggression and conquest if our own state is obliged to take thought of means of self-defence; moreover, when our neighbour denies any thirst for aggression just as heatedly as our state does, and protests that he too maintains an army only for reasons of legitimate self-defence, our declaration of why we require an army declares our neighbour a hypocrite and cunning criminal who would be only too happy to *pounce upon* a harmless and unprepared victim and subdue him without a struggle. This is how all states now confront one another: they presuppose an evil disposition in their neighbour and a benevolent disposition in themselves. (*HA* II: ii.284)

For Nietzsche, then, the nineteenth-century Europe of nation states rests on a combination between moral absolutism and fear, that is, a psychology of mutually assured destruction, which even modern liberalism was unable to escape: "As is well known, our liberal representatives of the people lack the time to reflect on the nature of man: otherwise they would know that they labour in vain when they work for a 'gradual reduction of the military burden'" (*HA* II: ii.284).

It is in this respect that Nietzsche shares much common ground with Herder, who, in the later eighteenth century, developed a European cosmopolitan vision that was ultimately based on the close link between community and self-determination.[37] For

---

[36] See, for instance, James P. Watson, "Nietzsche's 'Transnational' Thinking," *History of European Ideas* 15 (1992), 133–40.
[37] See Herder, *Letters for the Advancement of Humanity*, in *Philosophical Writings*, p. 377.

Herder, this was grounded, however, in the somewhat unrealistic assumption that the process of enlightenment itself would render obvious the irrationality of struggling militarily over national, dynastic and religious interests: "So let me believe, my friend, that the mad, raging system of conquest is not the basic constitution of Europe, or at least need not be so, and also will not be so for ever."[38] Although Herder continues to be seen by some as endorsing an early form of nationalism in that he underlines the need for political self-determination, he in fact attempts to link cultural pluralism and political self-determination in order to overcome, or at least counterbalance, the dynastic interests of the absolutist states.

Because of the common ground Nietzsche shares with Herder, his idea of Europe also differs fundamentally from the political vision of German idealism, in particular Kant, Fichte, and Hegel. Writing between the French Revolution and the Napoleonic Wars, Kant clearly saw a restricted cosmopolitanism as a European project, within which the moral law as it was formulated in the *Kritik der praktischen Vernunft* (1788) could be translated from the individual to entire nation states. Responding to the peace treaty that Prussia and France signed in Basel on April 5, 1795 and that made Prussia cede the left bank of the Rhine to France, Kant argued in his short treatise *Zum ewigen Frieden* (1795): "Each nation, for the sake of its own security, can and ought to demand of the others that they should enter along with it into a constitution, similar to the civil one, within which the rights of each could be secured. This would mean establishing a *federation of peoples*."[39] The unity of Europe, then, would be a federal unity; not the "amalgamation" that Nietzsche predicted (*HA* I: 475). Either way, the reality on the ground was rather different: since the peace treaty of Basel contributed to the growing partition of Europe, it prevented war between France and Prussia only for eleven years. But despite the failure of his hope for a new European order, Kant's political vision is clearly driven by pragmatic historical considerations, which become obvious in a striking passage from the *Metaphysik der Sitten*, published in the tumultuous year of 1797, when France and Austria signed their peace treaty at Campo Formio:[40]

[38] Herder, *Letters Concerning the Progress of Humanity*, in *Philosophical Writings*, p. 365.
[39] Kant, *Perpetual Peace: A Philosophical Sketch*, in *Political Writings*, p. 102.
[40] Like the peace treaty signed between Prussia and France in Basel, the treaty of Campo Formio was a result of power politics and contributed to the French hegemony in

Such a *union* [*Verein*] of several *states* to preserve peace can be called a *permanent congress of states*, which each neighboring state is at liberty to join. Something of this kind took place (at least as regards the formalities of the right of nations for the sake of keeping the peace) in the first half of the present century, in the assembly of the States General at The Hague. The ministers of most of the courts of Europe and even of the smallest republics lodged with it their complaints about attacks being made on one of them by another. In this way they thought of the whole of Europe as a single federated state [*föderierten Staat*] which they accepted as arbiter, so to speak, in their public disputes. [41]

While Kant is fully aware that such a congress has vanished from the practice of international relations in the late eighteenth century due to the rise of French power politics and expansionism, he clearly saw such a congress as the necessary practical outcome of a cosmopolitan philosophy of history: the political reference point of the teleological process that unfolded reason in history was undoubtedly a "civil commonwealth."[42] Needless to say, Kant would not have greeted the results of the Vienna Congress of 1814–15 with much enthusiasm.

Only a few years after Kant's cosmopolitan hopes, the political situation had changed dramatically, which forced German philosophers like Fichte and Hegel to reassess the reality of the eighteenth-century idea of Europe. Fichte published his popular lectures *Die Grundzüge des gegenwärtigen Zeitalters* in 1806, the year in which Napoleon, after decisive victories at Jena and Auerstedt, entered Berlin. Napoleon's occupation of Prussia, his swift move into Poland, together with the weak position of Austria, ended the quasi-federal traditions of both the Holy Roman Empire and the German Enlightenment. As a consequence of these developments, Fichte began to emphasize an image of Europe that was

---

Europe that was to unfold in the following decade. See T. C. W. Blanning, *The French Revolutionary Wars, 1787–1820* (London: Arnold, 1996), pp. 174–9.

[41] Kant, *The Metaphysics of Morals*, pp. 119–20. Translation slightly modified in accordance with H. B. Nisbet's earlier translation of *The Metaphysics of Morals*, in *Political Writings*, p. 171. Gregor renders Kant's *Verein* as "association" and *föderativ* as "confederated." When Kant speaks of a *Verein*, however, his emphasis is more on a political unity of states than would be suggested by the term "association." Also, while a "confederation" of states simply refers to a league or alliance of states around a common purpose, a "federation" of states refers to a political unity of states, whose members merely retain control over their internal affairs.

[42] Kant, "Idea for a Universal History," in *Political Writings*, p. 48. See Pauline Kleingeld, "Approaching Perpetual Peace: Kant's Defence of a League of States and his Ideal of a World Federation," *European Journal of Philosophy* 12 (2004), 304–25: 311–18.

no longer based on federal ideas; instead he noted that only a "Christian Europe" could be a "true fatherland" and thus able to transcend the political uncertainties of the present.[43] In contrast to the religious imagination of Novalis's *Die Christenheit oder Europa* (1799), which promoted a return to an essentially feudal Europe, Fichte's ideas were to some extent still based on cosmopolitan ideals.[44] But despite his emphasis on a common religiously grounded identity for Europe, the latter could not exist without the nation state.[45] Continuing a program he outlined in more detail in his *Der geschlossene Handelsstaat* (1800), he noted in his *Reden an die deutsche Nation* (1808) that only the economic and, by implication, cultural autarchy of the nation state, especially Germany, could be the "salvation of Europe."[46] This primacy of the nation state also remained a crucial factor within Hegel's political thought. Within the European context, only the autonomous state could provide the right conditions for the realization of freedom. Europe's future as a political entity rested since the late Renaissance on a balance of power that could be achieved only through diplomacy between independent states.[47] In his assessment of the consequences of the French Revolution and the Napoleonic occupation of much of Central Europe, Hegel developed the European arena as a political culture marked by the competing interests of nation states, even though the latter "form a family with respect to the universal principle of their legislation, customs, and culture [*Bildung*]."[48]

Leaving aside the question as to whether there really was any serious alternative given the political configurations of the Atlantic world, the nineteenth century is clearly characterized by the strategic interests and colonial ambitions of the major European

---

[43] Fichte, *Die Grundzüge des gegenwärtigen Zeitalters*, in *Werke*, vol. II, pp. 278 and 285–6.
[44] See Novalis, *Christianity or Europe: A Fragment*, in *Early Political Writings of the German Romantics*, pp. 59–79.
[45] See Fichte, *Die Grundzüge des gegenwärtigen Zeitalters*, in *Werke*, vol. II, p. 286.
[46] Fichte, *Reden an die deutsche Nation*, in *Werke*, vol. II, p. 754. See also Fichte, *Der geschlossene Handelsstaat: Ein philosophischer Entwurf als Anhang zur Rechtslehre und Probe einer künftig zu liefernden Politik*, in *Sämmtliche Werke*, ed. Immanuel Hermann von Fichte (Berlin: Veit & Co., 1845–46), vol. III, pp. 387–513: 475–513.
[47] See Hegel, *Vorlesungen über die Philosophie der Geschichte*, in *Werke*, vol. X, p. 418. There is no English translation of this passage.
[48] Hegel, *Elements of the Philosophy of Right*, p. 371 (§ 339), and *Lectures on the Philosophy of History*, in *Political Writings*, pp. 219–23.

nation states. At the end of the nineteenth century, Nietzsche seeks to come to terms with the negative consequences of this situation for a European political culture that had to overcome the absolute claims of traditional moral and political communities:

Indeed, at hearing the news that "the old god is dead," we philosophers and "free spirits" feel illuminated by a new dawn; our heart overflows with gratitude, amazement, forebodings, expectation – finally the horizon seems clear again, even if not bright; finally our ships may set out again, set out to face any danger; every daring of the lover of knowledge is allowed again; the sea, *our* sea, lies open again; maybe there has never been such an "open sea." (*GS* 343)

In this passage, Nietzsche not only speaks about the possibilities of philosophy and science after nihilism, but he also speaks about the state of political culture. This becomes clearer only a few years later in *Jenseits von Gut und Böse*:

Whatever term is used these days to try to mark what is distinctive about the European, whether it is "civilization" or "humanization" or "progress" (or whether, without implying praise or censure, it is simply labeled Europe's *democratic* movement); behind all the moral and political foregrounds that are indicated by formulas like these, an immense *physiological* process is taking place and constantly gaining ground – the process of increasing similarity between Europeans, their growing detachment from the conditions under which climate- or class-bound races originate, their increasing independence from that *determinate* milieu where for centuries the same demands would be inscribed on the soul and the body – and so the slow approach of an essentially supranational [*übernationalen*] and nomadic type of person who, physiologically speaking, is typified by a maximal degree of the art and force of adaptation. (*BGE* 242)

The ideal European of the future, for Nietzsche, would be the intellectual nomad, the socially unattached intellectual who was to stand at the center of Karl Mannheim's studies in the sociology of knowledge during the 1920s. The predominant "peculiarity" of such intellectuals consisted in the fact that they did not fit any given political position, "because they could adapt themselves to any viewpoint and because they and they alone were in a position to choose their affiliation."[49]

---

[49] Mannheim, *Ideology and Utopia*, p. 158.

Like Nietzsche, and taking his cue from Max Weber, Mannheim clearly hoped that the dangers of relativism would be compensated by an "ethics of responsibility."[50] But there is a further connection that brings Nietzsche's arguments into the twentieth century. Although he denies that there is an autonomy of the political, he does indeed come close, for instance, to Hannah Arendt's notion of "freedom": the latter can only exist as long as individuals act, but the close link between freedom and action, which Arendt, much like Nietzsche, links back to Machiavelli's concept of *virtù*, implies that any action has consequences beyond our control. The freedom of political action, then, generates the "unforeseeable" and "unpredictable," thus bringing something new into existence, or at least daring to do so.[51] It is this daring, together with his insistence on action, that separates Nietzsche from the tradition of German Idealism. For Kant, the autonomy of pure practical reason was inherently limited since it was an autonomy governed by laws, which themselves were construed as universal, while Hegel's emphasis on consciousness led him to the conclusion that freedom should predominantly be seen as the "will to be free."[52] In contrast, and anticipating Foucault, Nietzsche regards the freedom of the "open sea" as a possibility of going beyond the limits of both the supposedly universal laws of reason and our own historical conditions.[53]

The unstable and daring identity of Nietzsche's future "European" does not necessarily imply that Europe is a useless point of reference for political culture. Political cultures are in any event neither monolithic nor static, but they are fundamentally open to change and outside influences.[54] Of course, even in Nietzsche's supra-national Europe, "social imaginaries" – that is, "the ways in which people imagine their social existence" and "how they fit together" – would certainly generate a "common understanding that makes possible common practices and a widely shared sense of legitimacy."[55] But these practices, as Nietzsche knows, do not need to rely on the nineteenth-century nation

---

[50] Ibid., p. 190.   [51] Arendt, "What Is Freedom?", pp. 153 and 170.
[52] See Kant, *Critique of Practical Reason*, ed. Gregor, pp. 43–9, and Hegel, *Lectures on the Philosophy of World History*, in *Political Writings*, p. 211.
[53] See Foucault, "What is Enlightenment?", p. 50.
[54] See Tully, *Strange Multiplicity*, pp. 11–15.
[55] Charles Taylor, "Modern Social Imaginaries," *Public Culture* 14 (2002), 91–124: 106.

state. Indeed, in the spring of 1888 he gives two examples of such a European social imaginary: Napoleon's vision of Europe as a "political unity" and Goethe's imagination of a "European culture" that realized precisely those ideals of neo-humanism which failed in Germany throughout most of the nineteenth century (*KGW* VIII/3, 15 [68]).

Indeed, Goethe's vision of "world literature [*Weltliteratur*]," as he formulated it in the years before his death in 1832, was characterized by the conviction that, after the Napoleonic Wars and the precarious reorganization of Europe, the European nations would recognize their co-dependence and would thus be able to enter into a "free trade of ideas [*freier geistiger Handelsverkehr*]."[56] As unrealistic as this must have seemed from the German perspective after 1871, Goethe's "European culture" was not intended to level differences, but rather sought to transform such differences into a "feeling of neighborly relations."[57] The latter was furthermore grounded in a broad historical consciousness that went beyond the European arena: in his collection of poems *Westöstlicher Divan* (1819/27), he made it quite clear that those who were "unable to account for three-thousand years [*Wer nicht von dreitausend Jahren / Sich weiß Rechenschaft zu geben*]" would have to remain "inexperienced" and merely live "from day to day."[58]

Nietzsche's reference to Napoleon's transformation of Europe as the political equivalent to Goethe's cultural vision, however, proves to be more problematic. At least until the disastrous invasion of Russia in 1811/12, the latter's foreign policy was not guided by a notion of Europe that transcended the traditional nation state, but rather constituted a European extension of French power.[59] It was this imperial dimension that ultimately undermined the European reach of Napoleon's foreign policy.[60] French imperialism certainly brought administrative innovations and

---

[56] Goethe, "Einleitung zu Th. Carlyle, *Leben Schillers* (1830)," in *Werke*, vol. XII, p. 364. The reorganization of Europe after the Vienna Congress proved to be more complex than Goethe imagined. See Paul W. Schroeder, "Did the Vienna Settlement Rest on a Balance of Power?" *American Historical Review* 97 (1993), 683–706.
[57] Goethe, "Einleitung zu Th. Carlyle, *Leben Schillers* (1830)," in *Werke*, vol. XII, p. 364.
[58] Goethe, *Westöstlicher Divan*, in *Werke*, vol. II, p. 49.
[59] See Geoffrey Ellis, "The Nature of Napoleonic Imperialism," in Philip Dwyer (ed.), *Napoleon and Europe* (London: Longman, 2001), pp. 97–117.
[60] See Paul W. Schroeder, *The Transformation of European Politics, 1763–1848* (Oxford: Oxford University Press, 1994), pp. 388–431.

economic advantages, for instance, in the German Rhineland, which had traditionally close trade relations with France. But reform often went hand in hand with economic exploitation, so that the Napeoleonic modernization of Europe remains a highly ambivalent development.[61] Although Napoleonic foreign policy on a European level proved to be a failure, it showed at least that the project of an integrated Europe was not quite as far-fetched as it had seemed in previous centuries.[62]

Nevertheless, in exile on St. Helena, Napoleon did begin to express a desire for European integration, but his remarks throughout the so-called *Mémorial de Sainte-Hélène*, compiled by the Count de las Cases and published in 1823, need to be treated with some caution in that they represent a retrospective justification of his earlier foreign policy goals. It is in this respect that the image of Napoleon as an alternative to the dynastic rulers of the European nation states, which immediately gained currency through the writings of Heinrich Heine, Stendhal and others, remains a mythological construction *après coup*.[63] Nietzsche's own image of Napoleon, in contrast to his consistent admiration of Goethe, is highly ambivalent, often alternating between ridicule, criticism and reverence.[64] But in *Jenseits von Gut und Böse*, the figure of Napoleon emerges after all as a concrete manifestation of the sovereign individual, which is able to transcend what Nietzsche regards as the herd morality of nineteenth-century Europe. Although there have always been "herds of people," such as "racial groups, communities, tribes, folk, states, churches," which seem innately obedient if "compared to the relatively few who command," even those nineteenth-century Europeans who have the necessary authority to command claim merely to obey higher institutions, such as "their ancestors, constitution, justice system, laws, and God himself." The perfect moral and political community, that is, the contemporary nation state, seems to be governed by the illusion of

---

[61] See Alexander Grab, *Napoleon and the Transformation of Europe* (New York: Palgrave Macmillan, 2003), pp. 19–33.

[62] See Biancamaria Fontana, "The Napoleonic Empire and the Europe of Nations," in Pagden (ed.), *The Idea of Europe*, pp. 116–28: 123–4.

[63] See Paul Michael Lützeler, *Die Schriftsteller und Europa: Von der Romantik bis zur Gegenwart*, 2nd edn. (Baden-Baden: Nomos, 1998), pp. 99–102.

[64] See, for instance, the remarks in *HA* 1: 164 and 472; *GS* 23 and 282; *BGE* 209, 245 and 256. A fuller discussion can be found in Marti, *"Der grosse Pöbel- und Sklavenaufstand,"* pp. 236–48.

an equality in obedience. In contrast, "Napoleon's appearance" as a sovereign individual "who can issue unconditional commands" renders it obvious to Nietzsche that the "intolerable pressure" of such moral and political communities can be overcome: "the history of Napoleon's impact is practically the history of the higher happiness attained by this whole century in its most worthwhile people and moments" (*BGE* 199).

Viewed in the light of his remarks about Napoleon, Nietzsche's seemingly more uncomfortable claims about democracy and political power become understandable as an exercise in historically informed political realism: "What I'm trying to say is: the democratization of Europe is at the same time an involuntary exercise in the breeding of *tyrants* – understanding that word in every sense, including the most intellectual [*im geistigsten*]" (*BGE* 242).[65] In the same way as the French Revolution, despite its promises of popular sovereignty, made the rise of Napoleon possible, the modern parliamentary mass democracies of the later nineteenth century, despite their promises of equal political participation, could not really avoid the problem of rule, that is, of *Macht* and *Herrschaft*. Nevertheless, it is often argued that, in remarks like these, the political goal of genealogy emerges as the promotion of an essentially authoritarian concept of the political; the "breeding of tyrants" out of a highly industrialized mass democracy seems one of the preconditions for a new elitist political order that Nietzsche had in mind.[66] In contrast, I should like to suggest that when he speaks of a "tyrant," what he has in mind is not necessarily a "despot," but he merely points to the inevitability of rule that even mass democracies cannot avoid. It is in this respect that Nietzsche's "tyrant" shares much common ground with Machiavelli's "ruler" or "prince": since the reality of political life is not to be found in the way "one should live," and since "what ought to be done" is rarely in accord with "what is generally done," any "ruler who wishes to maintain his power must be prepared to act immorally when this becomes necessary."[67] Machiavelli,

---

[65] Judith Norman translates the German *im geistigsten Sinne* as "in the most spiritual sense." The German *geistig* is, of course, notoriously difficult to render in English, but in Nietzsche's context the term "spiritual" seems too metaphysical. There is no indication that Nietzsche did not simply refer to intellectual ability. See also *BGE* 203.
[66] See, for instance, Detwiler, *Nietzsche and the Politics of Aristocratic Radicalism*, pp. 117–43.
[67] Machiavelli, *The Prince*, pp. 54–5.

though, did not wish the ruler to act without any ethical considerations; given the central importance of political order for Machiavelli, it would have simply been counterproductive for him to argue that ethical considerations need to be entirely ignored, since the political can be realized successfully only in a *res publica*.[68] Rather, he sought to acknowledge that the nature of the political does not correspond to Christian virtue ethics.[69] Nietzsche's use of the term "tyrant" should be understood in precisely this way, that is, as contributing to the disenchantment of the political. But within the political culture of Imperial Germany in the late 1880s, there was little room for such realism and, as a consequence, for the idea of Europe.

POLITICAL REALITIES IN IMPERIAL GERMANY

The nomadic intellectualism of Nietzsche's idea of Europe was inspired by a cultural tradition that during the 1880s was publicly seen as endangering the unity of the German nation state: Judaism. Although many of his remarks on Jewish culture, in particular when they are connected to racial tropes, are often uncomfortable and seem to hint at an anti-Semitic dimension of Nietzsche's thought, it is necessary to realize that his respective ideas are more complex than such shorthand conclusions suggest. His striking interest in Judaism – as opposed to the Judeo-Christian tradition, which he ultimately saw as responsible for the dangerous alliance between religion and the political – is related to an endorsement of cultural difference that seeks to oppose demands for political homogeneity. Consequently, his own position cannot seriously be labeled as proto-fascist or anti-Semitic. Considering, for instance, central passages in *Morgenröthe*, it becomes clear that – once he had broken with Richard Wagner's outright anti-Semitism, which remains an embarrassing problem for many Wagner enthusiasts – Nietzsche began to view Judaism as an alternative cultural heritage to the Judeo-Christian tradition (*D* 205).[70] From his perspective,

---

[68] See Maurizio Viroli, *From Politics to Reason of State: The Acquisition and Transformation of the Language of Politics, 1250–1600* (Cambridge: Cambridge University Press, 1992), pp. 126–77.
[69] See Machiavelli, *The Prince*, p. 62.
[70] This is not the place to discuss Nietzsche's views of Judaism in detail. A thorough discussion can be found in Menahem Brinker, "Nietzsche and the Jews," in Jacob Golomb and Robert S. Wistrich (eds.), *Nietzsche, Godfather of Fascism? On the Uses and*

it seemed to anticipate a possible Europeanness in a post-national world.

Nietzsche's criticism of anti-Semitism had clearly philosophical reasons. These are to be found in his rejection of the "envy and hatred" that he saw as pervading the culture of the modern nation state and in his opposition to the "herd instinct" within a society rooted in absolute moral and political claims (*GS* 116).[71] By 1876, Nietzsche had also established a close friendship with Paul Rée, who had a complex relationship with his own Jewish background and who exerted some influence on Nietzsche's criticism of the blatantly anti-Semitic attitudes of the clan around Richard Wagner.[72] Embarrassed that even his publisher, Ernst Schmeitzner, was involved in anti-Semitic agitation, Nietzsche clearly felt the need to address the rise of anti-Semitism within Germany's intellectual culture on a personal level. But apart from personal and philosophical issues, his position also entails a wider political perspective, for the rise of European nationalisms in the nineteenth century is intimately connected to the rise of anti-Semitism, which can be observed, albeit not exclusively, in the context of late nineteenth-century Imperial Germany.

As a keen observer of contemporary political debates, Nietzsche was fully aware of the quarrel surrounding Heinrich von Treitschke's article "Unsere Aussichten," published in November 1879 in the *Preußische Jahrbücher*, which generated an astounding array of replies, repudiations and endorsements alike, in both the public press and academic circles.[73] While parts of this article are concerned with the strategic situation of Germany among the European nation states, Treitschke weaves together central themes of a particular kind of German nationalism against the backdrop of

---

Abuses of a Philosophy (Princeton, N.J.: Princeton University Press, 2002), pp. 107–27, and Michael F. Duffy and Willard Mittelman, "Nietzsche's Attitudes Towards the Jews," *Journal of the History of Ideas* 49 (1988), 301–17.

[71] On these philosophical reasons, see Yirmiyahu Yovel, "Nietzsche and the Jews: The Structure of an Ambivalence," in Jacob Golomb (ed.), *Nietzsche and Jewish Culture* (London: Routledge, 1997), pp. 117–34: 122–4.

[72] Small, *Nietzsche and Rée*, pp. 48–55, has discussed this issue with admirable clarity. On Nietzsche's distance from Wagner's anti-Semitism, which is coupled with his rejection of Wagner's nationalism, see Ottmann, *Philosophie und Politik bei Nietzsche*, pp. 101–5.

[73] More than 120 contributions surrounding the so-called "Berliner Antisemitismusstreit" are now collected in Karsten Krieger (ed.), *Der "Berliner Antisemitismusstreit" 1879–1881: Eine Kontroverse um die Zugehörigkeit der deutschen Juden zur Nation* (Munich: K. G. Saur, 2003).

the growing influence of anti-Semitism as an open political force in Imperial Germany: threatened by the "dangers from the East," he claimed, as well as by the destabilizing internal influence of Jewish culture, Germany's imperial ambitions were at the cross-roads.[74]

That an initially national-liberal historian like Treitschke was able to develop such an argument has, of course, much to do with the specific political outlook of nineteenth-century German liberalism. First, in contrast to British varieties of liberalism that were often linked to utilitarian ethical ideals or economic concerns, German liberalism had a tendency to regard itself as defending national unity against outside influences. Second, the social foundations of liberalism among the German middle class, whose economic and political interests liberalism seemed to represent, were fragile, to say the least.[75] As such, it was not too surprising that in nineteenth-century Germany, the concept of the "nation" underwent significant changes. Initially directed against the authoritarian and absolutist rule of the German kings and princes in the late eighteenth and early nineteenth centuries, the discourse of national identity increasingly moved away from emancipatory ideals of self-determination. By the second half of the nineteenth century, national identity was based on strategies of exclusion that sought to safeguard the nation as an imagined moral community, marginalizing social and ethnic groups that were, in one way or another, seen as undermining national interests: Socialists, Catholics, Jews, the Slavic population in East Prussia, and other minorities.

Toward the end of Bismarck's unsuccessful *Kulturkampf*, which sought to limit the perceived negative influence of Catholicism on German unity, the Catholic population was publicly replaced by both Socialists and the Jewish community as the "other" of the German nation state. As a consequence, Treitschke's own political views became increasingly radicalized.[76] More directly than many of his contemporaries, he linked up the imperial vocation of the German nation state, led by Prussia, to the politics of anti-Semitism

---

[74] See Treitschke, "Unsere Aussichten," 567 and 572–6.
[75] See Wolfgang J. Mommsen, *Imperial Germany, 1867–1918: Politics, Culture, and Society in an Authoritarian State*, trans. Richard Deveson (London: Arnold, 1995), p. 61.
[76] See Ulrich Langer, *Heinrich von Treitschke: Politische Biographie eines deutschen Nationalisten* (Düsseldorf: Droste, 1998), p. 388.

and to the exclusion of a perceived "other" from political legitimacy.[77] Treitschke's remarks in the article "Unsere Aussichten" fell on fertile ground in an environment marked by the convergence of Protestantism and nationalism. Since the 1860s, the journalist Wilhelm Marr had successfully polemicized against Germany's Jewish communities and anti-Semitic sentiments increasingly influenced public opinion during the economic depression between 1873 and 1875. Between 1878 and 1880 these attacks became increasingly virulent: Marr himself published his *Der Sieg des Judenthums über das Germanenthum* (1879) and founded the periodical *Antisemitische Hefte*, while Adolf Stoecker, second court chaplain to the Emperor and a member of the Reichstag for the conservative party, delivered a series of widely influential anti-Semitic speeches.[78] Indeed, Stoecker's role as both a politician and a *Hofprediger* (court chaplain) exemplifies the way in which the affinities between Protestantism and nationalism transformed anti-Semitic sentiments into a distinct political program.[79] From the 1881-elections onward, the anti-Semitic Deutschsoziale Reformpartei was able to gain seats in the German Reichstag, and by the late 1880s anti-Semitism had established itself as a political program across most Western and Central European states, including Germany, Austria, France, and Russia.[80] While the link between Protestantism and nationalism was undoubtedly important for the developments in Imperial Germany, the rise of political anti-Semitism in the European nation states crossed confessional boundaries, as can be seen with regard to the program

---

[77] Treitschke's intellectualized endorsement of popular anti-Semitism also made the latter broadly acceptable among philosophical and political thinkers in Imperial Germany. See Georg Geismann, "Der Berliner Antisemitismusstreit und die Abdankung der rechtlich-praktischen Vernunft," *Kant-Studien* 83 (1993), 369–80.

[78] See Wilhelm Marr, *Der Sieg des Judenthums über das Germanenthum vom nicht-confessionellen Standpunkt aus betrachtet* (Bern: Costenoble, 1879), and Adolf Stoecker, *Das moderne Judentum in Deutschland, besonders in Berlin: Zwei Reden in der christlich-sozialen Arbeiterpartei* (Leipzig: Wiegandt & Grieben, 1880). On Marr, see Rose, *Revolutionary Antisemitism in Germany*, pp. 279–95.

[79] See Martin Greschat, "Protestantischer Antisemitismus in Wilhelminischer Zeit: Das Beispiel des Hofpredigers Adolf Stoecker," in Günter Brakelmann and Martin Rosowski (eds.), *Antisemitismus: Von religiöser Judenfeindschaft zur Rassenideologie* (Göttingen: Vandenhoeck & Ruprecht, 1989), pp. 27–51, and Peter Pulzer, *The Rise of Political Anti-Semitism in Germany and Austria*, rev. edn. (Cambridge, Mass.: Harvard University Press, 1988), pp. 83–97.

[80] See Thomas Nipperdey and Reinhard Rürup, "Antisemitismus," in Brunner, Conze, and Koselleck (eds.), *Geschichtliche Grundbegriffe*, vol. I, pp. 129–53.

of the Christlichsoziale Partei in Austria during the 1890s and the "Dreyfus Affair" in France (1894–99).

Public intellectuals such as Stoecker and Treitschke contributed considerably to the success of anti-Semitism, which increasingly also gained much ground among German university students and their organizations.[81] Nietzsche, who referred on several occasions to Stoecker as one of the "anti-Semitic speculators" and as "that scoundrel of a court chaplain [*die Hofprediger-Canaille*]," was clearly aware of these developments (*KGW* VIII/2, 10 [54] and 11 [235]).[82] Seen from the perspective of genealogy, the link between Protestantism and nationalism illustrated that the nineteenth-century nation state was a moral community of political absolutes, which always entailed the exclusion of a perceived "other." Holidaying in Marienbad, he remarked in August 1880: "Today everyone celebrates the birthday of the Emperor, but amongst all those black and yellow flags I can only think of something terrible, such as the birthday of the plague" (*KGB* III/1, p. 35).

Nietzsche's stance against contemporary nationalism – rooted in the historical perspective that genealogy opened up on the political – is also marked by a certain limitation. He failed to realize that nationalism was not the only political force in an Imperial Germany whose political imagination continued to be marked to a considerable extent by much older federal ideas as a specific cultural trope.[83] His image of contemporary Europe – characterized by a profound "paralysis of the will," by being "weary of humanity," and by a "morality of pity" that was "the most sinister symptom of ... European culture" (*BGE* 208, *GM* I: 12, and *GM* preface: 5)[84] – thus shared some aspects of Treitschke's assessment.[85] Focusing on the tensions between the strategic interests of Britain, Russia, France, Germany, and Austria, the latter stipulated a

---

[81] See Norbert Kampe, *Studenten und "Judenfrage" im Deutschen Kaiserreich: Die Entstehung einer akademischen Trägerschicht des Antisemitismus* (Göttingen: Vandenhoeck & Ruprecht, 1988), pp. 152–84.
[82] See also *KGW* VIII/2, 10 [81] and 11 [245] as well as *KGW* VIII/3, 14 [45].
[83] See Maiken Umbach, "History and Federalism in the Age of Nation-State Formation," in Umbach (ed.), *German Federalism: Past, Present, Future* (Basingstoke: Palgrave, 2002), pp. 42–69: 63.
[84] Carol Diethe's translation of *GM* preface: 5, runs: "the most uncanny symptom of ... European culture." While "uncanny" is a literal translation of the German *unheimlich*, Nietzsche's use of the term implies something darker, which is the reason why I have used the English expression "sinister" to render Nietzsche's German.
[85] See, along similar lines, Burckhardt, *Weltgeschichtliche Betrachtungen*, p. 191.

"feeling of uncertainty" that questioned the actual "value of our humanity and enlightenment." For Treitschke, the "European questions" were mainly the problem of the strategic options that the "occidental world" was about to face.[86] In contrast to Nietzsche, he saw the alternative to this uncertainty in a "stricter notion of the state" and an "invigorated national sentiment" that was supposed to help Germany to situate itself ahead of Britain's and Russia's expansionist policies.[87] Leaving aside Treitschke's anti-Semitic rhetoric and his striving for *Machtpolitik*, he recognizes the strategic problems that began to shape world politics during the 1890s, in particular the disintegration of a precarious political equilibrium which resulted in the power politics that contributed to the outbreak of the First World War.[88] As long as imperialist expansion was limited to regions outside Europe, it did not seriously affect the political equilibrium that emerged after the Vienna Congress. But by 1890, the attention had shifted from political and economic expansion to a struggle among the major European powers for the central position within the European arena. In this context, German foreign policy was of crucial importance, since Germany's efforts to compete internationally with Britain, America and Russia were doomed to fail from the very beginning.[89] Of course, Treitschke was far from willing to contemplate the possibility of such failure and its consequences.

Postulating that "we Europeans" have inevitably entered upon a "new warlike age," Nietzsche himself did not see this development in wholly negative terms: the disintegration of the political equilibrium across Europe might indeed constitute a "favorable" development, for it would accelerate and intensify the kind of cultural "skepticism" that allowed for the rigorous questioning of traditional forms of knowledge and political identities: "This skepticism despises and nevertheless appropriates; it undermines

---

[86] Treitschke, "Unsere Aussichten," 567 and 570–1.
[87] Ibid., 576.
[88] Paul W. Schroeder, "The Nineteenth-Century System: Balance of Power or Political Equilibrium?" in *Systems, Stability, and Statecraft: Essays on the International History of Modern Europe*, ed. David Wetzler, Robert Jervis, and Jack S. Levy (New York: Palgrave Macmillan, 2004), pp. 223–41, has traced this disintegration in contemporary diplomatic documents.
[89] See Paul W. Schroeder, "International Politics, Peace, and War, 1815–1914," in T. C. W. Blanning (ed.), *The Nineteenth Century: Europe, 1789–1914* (Oxford: Oxford University Press, 2000), pp. 158–209: 191.

and takes possession; it does not believe but does not die out on this account; it gives the spirit a dangerous freedom, but is severe on the heart" (*BGE* 209). What Nietzsche seems to have in mind is an aristocratic intellectualism able to survive without the need for political ideals. Apart from Goethe and Napoleon, the Prussian King Frederick the Great was for Nietzsche an embodiment of this skepticism that was supposed to provide a new intellectual setting for Europe.

In all seriousness, Frederick the Great is hardly a likely candidate for the idea of Europe that Nietzsche seems to have had in mind. But Frederick the Great and Nietzsche both shared an orientation toward the French cultural tradition, and the first volume of *Menschliches, Allzumenschliches* bears a dedication to the memory of Voltaire, who had been a confidant of Frederick the Great at Sanssouci, the latter's court in Potsdam on the outskirts of Berlin. Indeed, the image of Voltaire at Sanssouci stands in sharp contrast to Adolf Stoecker's radical political agitation and Heinrich von Treitschke's desire for power politics, which were both focused on Berlin itself. Thus, the French philosophical interests Nietzsche praises in Frederick the Great are a barely hidden reference to himself, since he explicitly noted – for instance, in *Ecce Homo*, which he described as an "anti-German" book – that he was always bound to return to French thinkers (*EH* III: 3 and *KGB* III/5, p. 509).

For Nietzsche, Frederick the Great was a powerful counter-image to the German chancellor Otto von Bismarck and the Hohenzollern monarchy.[90] The "era of Bismarck," Nietzsche claimed, was an "era of German stupidity [*Verdummung*]" (*KGW* VIII/1, 2 [198]). Indeed, his occasional diatribes against Bismarck during the 1880s are often piercing and at times even amusing, for instance, when he noted that the "Europe of Herrn von Bismarck," locked in a feverish arms race, "represented the image of a hedgehog in heroic mood" (*KGB* II/5, p. 249).[91] But

[90] In 1878, Nietzsche sent a copy of the second edition of *Die Geburt der Tragödie* to the German chancellor, and Bismarck himself, it seems, at least browsed through *Menschliches, Allzumenschliches*. Nietzsche's publisher Ernst Schmeitzner in Chemnitz seems to have forwarded a letter written by Bismarck to Nietzsche who was holidaying in the Swiss Alps. It is unfortunate that this letter seems to have been lost. See *KGB* II/5, p. 345 and *KGB* II/6, p. 955.
[91] That Nietzsche was himself in a rather gloomy mood about the European arms race during the late 1880s, becomes obvious in a letter from Easter 1888 to his sister

Nietzsche's repeated criticism of Bismarck's policies does not imply that he wished for a more democratic civil society; erecting the Prussia of Frederick the Great as a counter-image to Bismarck's technocratic nation state does not exactly promise liberal convictions. It is necessary to realize, however, that Frederick the Great was not the only counter-image that Nietzsche deployed against the political culture of Imperial Germany. Surprisingly, he speaks very highly of the Emperor Friedrich III, who ruled only for three months in 1888 before his untimely death (*EH* x: 1). When Nietzsche, already mentally unstable, drafted a "declaration of war" against the Hohenzollern monarchy in December 1888, he explicitly excluded Friedrich III who had died in June of that year (*KGW* VIII/3, 25 [13]).

Nietzsche never discussed the reasons for his admiration of Friedrich III in any detail, but there is some common ground. Born in 1831, Friedrich III was educated as a young boy by the eminent classical scholar and archaeologist Ernst Curtius, who – supported by Friedrich's mother, Augusta of Saxony-Weimar-Eisenach – introduced him to the ideals of the neo-humanist tradition.[92] Despite obvious social differences, Nietzsche shared this educational background at Schulpforta. Moreover, between 1849 and 1852, then Crown Prince Friedrich Wilhelm enrolled at the University of Bonn, where Nietzsche was a student in 1864–5. Studying law, politics and history, the Crown Prince was able to meet many members of the national-liberal establishment, including Ernst Moritz Arndt. Nietzsche himself had visited Arndt's grave upon his arrival in Bonn and attended the unveiling of a monument for Arndt on the Alter Zoll overlooking the Rhine.

Friedrich III's relationship to Bismarck was undoubtedly tense. As a military officer during the Austro-Prussian and Franco-Prussian Wars, he supported Bismarck's plans for a German nation state under Prussian leadership.[93] In 1878 he represented his father,

---

Elisabeth (*KGB* III/3, p. 281), who was still in Paraguay, living in the bizarre colony *Nueva Germania* that was founded by her anti-Semitic husband, whom Nietzsche regarded with much disdain.

[92] See Yvonne Wagner, "Prinzen, Mütter und Erzieher: Zum Bildungsverhalten des preußisch-deutschen Hofes im 'bürgerlichen Zeitalter'," *Archiv für Kulturgeschichte* 80 (1998), 351–73: 353–60.

[93] See Patricia Kollander, "Constitutionalism or *Staatsstreich*? Bismarck, Crown Prince Frederick William, Crown Princess Victoria and the Succession Crisis of 1880–85," *European Review of History* 8 (2001), 187–201: 188–9.

Wilhelm I, who had been injured in an assassination attempt, and signed Bismarck's anti-Socialist policies into law, thus contributing to the latter's attempts at undermining the social democratic movement. The years 1878 and 1879 – precisely the moment when Nietzsche published the first volume of *Menschliches, Allzumenschliches* and the rise of anti-Semitism as a political program began to gain public attention – marked a conservative and nationalist turn in German politics, which neutralized not only the socialist but also the liberal opposition to Bismarck.[94] This was also the moment, however, when the Crown Prince began to distance himself from Bismarck both privately and publicly. But while opposing Bismarck's efforts to circumvent constitutional arrangements, and contemplating the possibility of ruling without Bismarck, he also did not wish to adopt the more radical liberal ideas of his wife, Crown Princess Victoria, who saw the British parliamentary system as the future for the political structure of Germany. He thus shared to some extent Nietzsche's own idiosyncratic political views, which favored neither authoritarian rule nor liberal democracy. When the Emperor died on June 15, 1888, Nietzsche noted in his correspondence of the same day: "The death of the Emperor has moved me deeply: in the end he was a small gleam of *free* thoughts, the last hope for Germany" (*KGB* III/5, pp. 383–4). Nietzsche's emphasis on the word "free" has little to do with the liberalism of modern mass democracies; rather, as in the case of Frederick the Great, he seems to have discovered in Friedrich III an example for the kind of "free spirit," which he saw as a necessary ingredient of cultural and political life and which stood in sharp contrast to the "cursed storm of German fanaticism [*Deutschthümelei*]" that dominated political culture in Imperial Germany (*KGB* III/5, p. 359). Whether Nietzsche's judgment in these matters is always apt, is an entirely different question.

MODERNITY AND THE LIMITS OF GENEALOGY

But what, then, are we to make of Nietzsche's political thought? Considering his observations on the problem of European political culture, it is indeed difficult to assume that he conceived of

---

[94] See Nipperdey, *Deutsche Geschichte, 1866–1918*, vol. II, pp. 382–408.

a liberal and democratic alternative to the developments he saw unfolding during the 1880s. His actual alternative, the idea of Europe, remains in many ways an intellectually elitist project that, despite unearthing the detrimental effects of political absolutes, does not always pay attention to the actual foundations of civil society. This intellectual elitism should not be confused, however, with a radical political program. As Nietzsche notes in a letter to Franz Overbeck in March 1887:

> Here is a curious fact of which I am increasingly being made aware. I have a certain "influence" – subterraneously, of course. Among all radical parties (socialists, nihilists, anarchists, anti-Semites, orthodox Christians, and Wagnerians) I enjoy a peculiar and almost mysterious reputation. ... The anti-Semites have fallen for Zarathustra, "the divine man"; there is a special anti-Semitic interpretation of it, which really has made me laugh. (*KGB* III/5, p. 47).

Nietzsche clearly found the appropriation of his ideas by radical political interest groups somewhat bewildering, if not outright bizarre. On the other hand, he does in fact embrace Georg Brandes's characterization of his ideas as a form of "aristocratic radicalism." In November 1887, the latter began a correspondence with Nietzsche, which lasted until January 1889, the same year in which Brandes published what was to become one of the most influential texts for the early reception of Nietzsche's philosophy.[95] In his first letter to Brandes, whom he addressed as a "*good European* and cultural missionary" (*KGB* III/5, p. 205), Nietzsche remarks on December 2, 1887:

> The expression "aristocratic radicalism," which you use, is very apt. This is, if you pardon my saying so, the most intelligent word I have thus far read about myself. How far this intellectual attitude [*Denkweise*] has already guided me in my thoughts, how far it will lead me still – I am almost afraid to imagine this. But there are paths, which do not permit one to return; and thus I go forward, because I *must*. (*KGB* III/5, p. 206).

---

[95] See Georg Brandes, "Aristokratischer Radicalismus: Eine Abhandlung über Friedrich Nietzsche," *Deutsche Rundschau* 16/7 (1890), 52–89. The original Danish publication of Brandes's essay in 1889 had a more limited effect than the subsequent German translation. In 1888 Brandes delivered a series of lectures on Nietzsche at the University of Copenhagen and during the early 1880s, while residing in Berlin, he was also in contact with some of Nietzsche's friends, most notably Paul Rée. See also Georg Brandes, "*Vorlesungen über Friedrich Nietzsche*" (*1888*) *und "Aristokratischer Radikalismus"* (*1889/90*), ed. Per Dahl and Gert Posselt (Basel: Schwabe & Co., 2006).

Nietzsche, it seems, is not entirely unaware of the fact that the implications of his intellectual elitism and political realism can be dangerous – at least, there could be consequences that he has not yet taken into account.

Given the tension between Nietzsche's praise for Brandes's expression and his criticism of radical political interests, it is necessary to understand "aristocratic radicalism" not so much as representing a specific party-political, or ideological, program, but rather as another expression for what Nietzsche himself termed the free spirits. In *Die fröhliche Wissenschaft*, it is the task of these free spirits to connect a *vis contemplativa* and a *vis creativa*: the critical observation of the present can be justified only if the free spirits also "really and continually *make* something that is not yet there." As such, they do not simply break with the past, or distance themselves from the present, but rather seek to make a contribution to "the whole perpetually growing world of valuations, colours, weights, perspectives, scales, affirmations, and negations." Of course, and this is where Brandes's characterization of Nietzsche's "aristocratic radicalism" needs to be situated, the free spirits cannot escape the logic of power and the social hierarchies that run through even the most liberal and democratic society: the contribution that the free spirits make to the world of values, acknowledging that these values cannot be universal and eternally fixed, is "constantly internalized, drilled, translated into flesh and reality, indeed, into the commonplace, by the so-called practical human beings" (*GS* 301). Nietzsche clearly sees the task of the free spirits as an inherently political one. As such, the free spirits should not be misunderstood as representing an aesthetic kind of individualism with little patience for the social and political worlds; they are not detached from the latter, but always embedded in them.

Perhaps it is possible to say that Nietzsche's free spirits and sovereign individual seek to extend into modernity the principles of Kant's notion of Enlightenment, albeit without subscribing to the latter's moral law and the universality of reason. Indeed, Nietzsche's free spirits closely resemble those "few" who, "by cultivating their own minds, have succeeded in freeing themselves from immaturity." Once this is achieved, Kant continues, these "guardians ... will disseminate the spirit of rational respect for personal value and for the duty of all men to think for themselves."⁹⁶ Of course, even Kant is aware that simply having the duty to think for oneself does not necessarily make the public really think for itself: Enlightenment remains an "unfinished project," albeit not entirely in the sense of Jürgen Habermas's expression.⁹⁷ Like Kant, Nietzsche argues that liberating oneself from what seems to be a given order of the present, that is, from the "many things that oppress, inhibit, hold down, and make heavy precisely us Europeans today" constitutes a first step toward freedom. But such an overcoming of one's own time, as he is careful to point out, always leads back to one's own time and, necessarily, to a new understanding of the present (*GS* 380).

The nation state as the central moral community of nineteenth-century modernity is a case in point, for the illusion of identity politics at the heart of the nation state ignores that the latter is about to dissolve into something else:

> Thanks to the pathological manner in which nationalist nonsense has alienated and continues to alienate the people of Europe from each other; thanks as well to the short-sighted and swift-handed politicians who have risen to the top with the help of this nonsense, and have no idea of the extent to which the politics of dissolution that they practice can only be *entr'acte* politics, – thanks to all this and to some signs that are strictly unmentionable today, the most unambiguous signs declaring that *Europe wants to be one* are either overlooked or willfully and mendaciously reinterpreted. (*BGE* 256)

Nietzsche's idea of Europe, of course, remains vague, and it does so for good reasons. As he notes toward the end of *Zur Genealogie der Moral*, the self-overcoming of the Judeo-Christian tradition of morality "by the will to truth's becoming-conscious-of-itself" was bound to be "that great drama in a hundred acts reserved for Europe in the next two centuries, the most terrible, most dubious drama but perhaps also the most rich in hope" (*GM* III: 27). Nietzsche's political realism, then, is not entirely devoid of a certain optimism.⁹⁸

---

⁹⁶ Kant, "What is Enlightenment?," in *Political Writings*, p. 55.
⁹⁷ See Jürgen Habermas, "Modernity: An Unfinished Project," in Maurizio Passerin d'Entrèves and Seyla Benhabib (eds.), *Habermas and the Unfinished Project of Modernity: Critical Essays on "The Philosophical Discourse of Modernity"* (Cambridge, Mass.: MIT Press, 1997), pp. 38–57.
⁹⁸ See Risse, "The Second Treatise," 70–1.

Despite the traces of a radical Enlightenment that can be found in Nietzsche's political thought, he also seeks to distance himself clearly from those contemporaries who regard themselves as representing the true heritage of the Enlightenment. In *Jenseits von Gute und Böse*, for instance, he thus seeks to separate the "*very free spirits, these philosophers of the future*" from the widespread use of freedom and liberty as party political concepts:

> In all the countries of Europe, and in America as well, there is now something that abuses this name: a very narrow, restricted, chained-up type of spirit whose inclinations are pretty much the opposite of our own intentions and instincts ... Their two most well-sung songs and doctrines are called: "equal rights" and "sympathy for all that suffers" – and they view suffering itself as something that needs to be *abolished*. ... We are something different from "*libres-penseurs*," "*liberi pensatori*," "*Freidenker*" and whatever else all these sturdy advocates of "modern ideas" like to call themselves. (*BGE* 44)

What clearly reads like a broad attack on the formation of democratic institutions and liberal civil society is in fact directed against a rather specific set of political illusions, such as the promises of popular sovereignty, the hope that broad political participation is able to overcome social inequalities, and the appeal to an intrinsic integrity of moral communities. As such, the "free spirits" and "philosophers of the future" are, "curious to a fault, researchers to the point of cruelty," pointing out the fragile foundations and inherent dangers of such political illusions (*BGE* 44).

Clearly, Nietzsche's political vision seems to have much in common with Edmund Burke, while sharing little ground with, say, Marx or modern liberalism.[99] Likewise, his political thought can also be "associated with conservative or aristocratic liberalism (Alexis de Tocqueville, Jacob Burckhardt and Hippolyte Taine) and its critique of the results of the Enlightenment and the French Revolution."[100] It is indeed safe to say that Nietzsche shared Tocqueville's skepticism with regard to what he called the "tyranny of the majority" and that he would have agreed with Burke's warning that wider political participation does not inevitably equalize social differences.[101] Along these lines, Nietzsche's

---

[99] See Warren, *Nietzsche and Political Thought*, p. 211.
[100] Dombowsky, *Nietzsche's Machiavellian Politics*, p. 3.
[101] See Alexis de Tocqueville, *Democracy in America*, trans. and ed. Harvey C. Mansfield and Delba Winthrop (Chicago: University of Chicago Press, 2000), pp. 235–49, and

critique of mass democracy does not reject democracy in general, but rather highlights the dangers of ignoring the limits of liberalism when we project too much hope into our political ideals. These limits, he reminds us, need to be part of the discussion.

Indeed, Nietzsche also shares this awareness of the limits of liberalism with Max Weber, who highlighted that even in the most well-meaning civil society the reality of the political remains characterized by the desire for power and domination.[102] Extending Nietzsche's arguments further into the twentieth century will lead us to Michel Foucault's archaeology of knowledge and power, highlighting the way in which the seemingly self-evident realities that surround us are shaped by networks of power relationships.[103] The realism with which Weber and Foucault seek to approach the problem of the political also highlights another tradition within which we have to situate Nietzsche's understanding of the political: as a historically grounded critique of the illusions that make up modern political communities, his genealogical project also prepares much of the ground for Walter Benjamin's investigations into modernity's social imaginary, or "dream world," and Karl Mannheim's sociology of knowledge as an attempt to examine the "social origin" of specific ways of thinking – an approach that, more recently, has been continued in Pierre Bourdieu's work on social practices.[104]

What the complex constellations of political thought that surround Nietzsche's genealogy, and that follow from it, have in common, then, is a disenchantment of the given, a distrust in the self-evidence and uncontested legitimacy of whatever we regard as "our" political world. This legitimacy is clearly contested in Nietzsche's own time; the historical, political and intellectual developments that he observes in European thought in the aftermath of the Enlightenment are finally seen as a crisis even

---

Edmund Burke, *Reflections on the Revolution in France*, ed. L. G. Mitchell (Oxford: Oxford University Press, 1993), p. 49.

[102] See, for instance, Weber, *Parliament and Government in Germany*, in *Political Writings*, pp. 167 and 169.

[103] See Foucault, "Truth and Power," in *Power/Knowledge*, pp. 109–33: 122 and 133, and "*Society Must Be Defended*", pp. 239–50.

[104] See Walter Benjamin, *The Arcades Project*, trans. Howard Eiland and Kevin McLaughlin (Cambridge, Mass.: Harvard University Press, 2002), pp. 388–415; Mannheim, *Ideology and Utopia*, pp. 2–3; Pierre Bourdieu, *The Logic of Practice*, trans. Richard Nice (Cambridge: Polity Press, 1990).

by those who do not entirely share his conclusions, such as Georg Simmel, Edmund Husserl, and Ernst Cassirer, to name but a few.

Nevertheless, liberally inclined readings have sought to interpret Nietzsche's political views as the very essence of democratic politics, arguing that his emphasis on "conflict," his notion of the "will to power," and even his "moral perfectionism" represent a radically democratic project.[105] Such a reading faces serious difficulties, however, once we take Nietzsche's own historical context seriously; it is not sufficient to ignore these difficulties by turning Nietzsche into a timeless philosopher, seeking to extract from the central themes of his writings a sympathetic view compatible with our own liberal inclinations.[106] To argue that the "multiplicity" of possible interpretations that Nietzsche's writings invite remains his "true political legacy" underestimates Nietzsche's complex position within the intellectual field and political culture of modernity.[107]

If there is anything such as Nietzsche's political legacy, then it lies in his genealogy, the historical dimension of the modern intellectual world it opens up, and in his attempt to "naturalize our humanity." As such, it consists in introducing uncomfortable questions that remind us of the profound difficulty of properly grounding our own democratic and liberal values. Genealogy shows that moral and political communities are fragile constructions.

There is, however, also another point to be made. For the overall direction of Nietzsche's attempt to overcome the historical and political crisis of modernity, genealogy is both a gain and a loss. It allows Nietzsche to adopt a more realist perspective, but it prevents him from outlining in more detail a valuable alternative, since the latter is always undermined by the critical potential of genealogy.[108] Whatever alternative genealogy might lead to, it is always limited by genealogy itself. In other words, genealogy renders it possible to recognize the illusions that govern our actions

---

[105] See, for instance, Alan D. Schrift, "Nietzsche for Democracy?" *Nietzsche-Studien* 29 (2000), 220–33; Dana R. Villa, "Democratizing the Agon: Nietzsche, Arendt, and the Agonistic Tendency in Recent Political Theory," in Alan D. Schrift (ed.), *Why Nietzsche Still? Reflections on Drama, Culture, and Politics* (Berkeley, Calif.: University of California Press, 2000), pp. 224–46; Warren, *Nietzsche and Political Thought*, pp. 221 and 247.
[106] See Appel, *Nietzsche contra Democracy*, pp. 159–64.
[107] Conway, *Nietzsche and the Political*, p. 120.
[108] See also Williams, "Naturalism and Genealogy," p. 160.

as illusions and it even enables us to understand the historical trajectory of these illusions, but it does not provide us with an escape from these illusions. This is, perhaps, the somewhat tragic dimension of the free spirits that Nietzsche advocates throughout the 1880s: recognizing the illusion does not prevent catastrophe. If Nietzsche had lived long enough to witness the disintegration of European society on the eve of the First World War, and to see the war itself, even if only from a distance, he might have glimpsed how thin the layer of moral communities really is and how deeply connected political righteousness and violence really are. Needless to say, we still continue to live with the illusions that were the subject of Nietzsche's genealogy and we will do well to take his political thought seriously.

Bibliography

FRIEDRICH NIETZSCHE: PUBLICATIONS, NOTEBOOKS, CORRESPONDENCE

The Anti-Christ, in *"Twilight of the Idols" and "The Anti-Christ,"* trans. R.J. Hollingdale (Harmondsworth: Penguin, 1968), pp. 113–87.

Werke und Briefe: Historisch-Kritische Gesamtausgabe, ed. Hans Joachim Mette (Munich: C. H. Beck, 1933–40).

Beyond Good and Evil, trans. Judith Norman, ed. Rolf-Peter Horstmann and Judith Norman (Cambridge: Cambridge University Press, 2002).

The Birth of Tragedy, in *The Birth of Tragedy and Other Writings*, trans. Ronald Speirs, ed. Raymond Geuss and Ronald Speirs (Cambridge: Cambridge University Press, 1999), pp. 1–116.

Daybreak: Thoughts on the Prejudices of Morality, trans. R.J. Hollingdale, ed. Maudemarie Clark and Brian Leiter (Cambridge: Cambridge University Press, 1997).

Ecce Homo, trans. Walter Kaufmann (New York: Vintage Books, 1989).

On the Genealogy of Morality, trans. Carol Diethe, ed. Keith Ansell-Pearson (Cambridge: Cambridge University Press, 1994).

On the Genealogy of Morality, trans. and ed. Maudemarie Clark and Alan Swenson (Indianapolis, Ind.: Hackett, 1998).

The Gay Science, trans. Josefine Nauckhoff, ed. Bernard Williams (Cambridge: Cambridge University Press, 2001).

Human, All Too Human, trans. R.J. Hollingdale, intro. Richard Schacht (Cambridge: Cambridge University Press, 1996).

Briefwechsel: Kritische Gesamtausgabe, ed. Giorgio Colli and Mazzino Montinari (Berlin: Walter de Gruyter, 1975–).

Werke: Kritische Gesamtausgabe, founded by Giorgio Colli and Mazzino Montinari, ed. Volker Gerhardt, Norbert Miller, Wolfgang Müller-Lauter, and Karl Pestalozzi (Berlin: Walter de Gruyter, 1967–).

The Greek State in *On the Genealogy of Morality*, trans. Carol Diethe, ed. Keith Ansell-Pearson (Cambridge: Cambridge University Press, 1994), pp. 176–86.

Twilight of the Idols, in *"Twilight of the Idols" and "The Anti-Christ,"* trans. R.J. Hollingdale (Harmondsworth: Penguin, 1968), pp. 19–122.

On Truth and Lying in a Non-Moral Sense, in *The Birth of Tragedy and Other Writings,* trans. Ronald Speirs, ed. Raymond Geuss and Ronald Speirs (Cambridge: Cambridge University Press, 1999), pp. 139–53.
Untimely Meditations, trans. R.J. Hollingdale, ed. Daniel Breazeale (Cambridge: Cambridge University Press, 1997).
Thus Spoke Zarathustra: A Book for Everyone and Nobody, trans. and ed. Graham Parkes (Oxford: Oxford University Press, 2005).

UNPUBLISHED MATERIAL, GOETHE- UND
SCHILLER-ARCHIV, WEIMAR, GERMANY

GSA 41/76: Nietzsche-Archiv, lecture notes, "Karl Schaarschmidt: Allgemeine Geschichte der Philosophie (Bonn, summer semester 1865)".
GSA 49/84: Nietzsche-Archiv, lecture notes, "Friedrich Ritschl: Die römische Epigraphik als Hülfsmittel zum Studium der lateinischen Grammatik" (Leipzig, winter semester 1865/66) and "Wilhelm Roscher: Grundlagen der praktischen Politik als Einleitung in die gesamte Staats- und Rechtswissenschaft" (Leipzig, winter semester 1865/66).
GSA 54/89: Nietzsche-Archiv, lecture notes, "Friedrich Ritschl: Historische Grammatik der lateinischen Sprache nebst Einleitung in die römische Epigraphik" (Leipzig, summer semester 1867).
GSA 71/366: Nietzsche-Archiv, announcement of the "Oeffentlichen akademischen Vorlesungen" (Basel, winter semester 1871/72).

OTHER PRIMARY SOURCES

Anon., "Contemporary Literature: Theology and Philosophy," *Westminster Review,* new series 47 (January–April 1875), 484–506.
Arendt, Hannah, "What Is Freedom?" in *Between Past and Future: Eight Exercises in Political Thought* (New York: Penguin, 1993), pp. 143–71.
Arndt, Ernst Moritz, *Werke: Auswahl in zwölf Teilen,* ed. August Leffson and Wilhelm Steffens (Berlin: Bong & Co., 1912).
Ast, Friedrich, *Grundlinien der Grammatik, Hermeneutik und Kritik* (Landshut: Thomann, 1808).
Ast, Friedrich, *Grundriss der Philologie* (Landshut: Krüll, 1808).
Bachofen, Johann Jakob, *Das Mutterrecht: Eine Untersuchung über die Gynaikokratie der alten Welt nach ihrer religiösen und rechtlichen Natur* (Stuttgart: Krais & Hoffmann, 1861).
Versuch über die Gräbersymbolik der Alten (Basel: Bachmaier, 1859).
Bacon, Francis, *The New Organon,* ed. Lisa Jardine and Michael Silverthorne (Cambridge: Cambridge University Press, 2000).

Bahnsen, Julius, *Zur Philosophie der Geschichte: Eine kritische Besprechung des Hegel-Hartmann'schen Evolutionismus aus Schopenhauer'schen Principien* (Berlin: Duncker, 1872).
Bain, Alexander, *Mental and Moral Science: A Compendium to Psychology and Ethics* (London: Longmans & Co., 1868).
Bastian, Adolf, *Die Völkerkunde und der Völkerverkehr unter seiner Rückwirkung auf die Volksgeschichte: Ein Beitrag zur Volks- und Menschenkunde* (Berlin: Weidmann, 1900).
Controversen in der Ethnologie: I, Die geographischen Provinzen in ihren culturgeschichtlichen Berührungspunkten (Berlin: Weidmann, 1893).
Wie das Volk denkt: Ein Beitrag zur Beantwortung socialer Fragen auf Grundlage ethnischer Elementargedanken in der Lehre vom Menschen (Berlin: Felber, 1892).
Bauer, Bruno, *Zur Orientierung über die Bismarck'sche Ära* (Chemnitz: Schmeitzner, 1880).
Russland und das Germanenthum (Charlottenburg: Bauer, 1853).
Die Judenfrage (Braunschweig: Otto, 1843).
Kritik der Geschichte der Offenbarung (Berlin: Dümmler, 1838).
"Die Fähigkeit der heutigen Juden und Christen, frei zu werden," in Georg Herwegh (ed.), *Einundzwanzig Bogen aus der Schweiz* (Zurich: Verlag des Literarischen Comptoirs, 1843), pp. 56–71.
Baumeister, Friedrich Christian, *Philosophia definitiva hoc est definitiones philosophicae ex systemate celeb. Wolfii: In vnvm collectae svccinctis observationibvs exemplisqve*, 7th edn. (Wittenberg: Ahlfeld, 1746).
Baur, Ferdinand Christian, *Ausgewählte Werke in Einzelausgaben*, ed. Klaus Scholder (Stuttgart-Bad Cannstatt: Frommann, 1963–70).
Die Tübinger Schule und ihre Stellung zur Gegenwart, 2nd edn., enlarged (Tübingen: Fues, 1860).
Die Epochen der kirchlichen Geschichtsschreibung (Tübingen: Fues, 1852).
"Die Einleitung in das Neue Testament als theologische Wissenschaft: Ihr Begriff und ihre Aufgabe, ihr Entwicklungsgang und ihr innerer Organismus," *Theologische Jahrbücher* 9 (1850), 463–566, and 10 (1851), 70–94 and 291–329.
Bayle, Pierre, *Œuvres diverses* (The Hague: Husson, 1727–31).
Benfey, Theodor, *Geschichte der Sprachwissenschaft und der orientalischen Philologie in Deutschland seit dem Anfange des 19. Jahrhunderts mit einem Rückblick auf frühere Zeiten* (Munich: Cotta, 1869).
Benjamin, Walter, *The Arcades Project*, trans. Howard Eiland and Kevin McLaughlin (Cambridge, Mass.: Harvard University Press, 2002).
Bernays, Jakob, *Grundzüge der verlorenen Abhandlung des Aristoteles über Wirkung der Tragödie* (Breslau: Trewendt, 1857).
Bernhardy, Gottfried, *Grundriss der Griechischen Litteratur mit einem vergleichenden Ueberblick der Römischen*, new edn. (Halle: Anton, 1861–72).
Grundlinien zur Encyklopädie der Philologie (Halle: Anton, 1832).

Bismarck, Otto von, *Ausgewählte Werke*, ed. Gustav Adolf Rein, Wilhelm Schüßler, Eberhard Scheler, Alfred Milatz, and Rudolf Buchner (Darmstadt: Wissenschaftliche Buchgesellschaft, 1962–83).
Blumenbach, Johann Friedrich, *Über den Bildungstrieb und das Zeugungsgeschäfte* (Göttingen: Dieterich, 1781).
Bluntschli, Johann Caspar, *Allgemeines Statsrecht* [sic], 5th edn., rev. (Stuttgart: Cotta, 1876).
Rom und die Deutschen (Berlin: Lüderitz, 1872).
Bodin, Jean, *On Sovereignty: Four Chapters from "The Six Books of the Commonwealth,"* ed. and trans. Julian H. Franklin (Cambridge: Cambridge University Press, 1992).
Boeckh, August, *Encyklopädie und Methodologie der philologischen Wissenschaften*, ed. Ernst Bratuschek, 2nd edn. (Leipzig: Teubner, 1886).
Bötticher, Carl, *Der Baumkultus der Hellenen, nach den gottesdienstlichen Gebräuchen und den überlieferten Bildwerken dargestellt* (Berlin: Weidmann, 1856).
Brandes, Georg, *"Vorlesungen über Friedrich Nietzsche" (1888) und "Aristokratischer Radikalismus" (1889/90)*, ed. Per Dahl and Gert Posselt (Basel: Schwabe & Co., 2006).
"Aristokratischer Radicalismus: Eine Abhandlung über Friedrich Nietzsche," *Deutsche Rundschau* 16/7 (1890), 52–89.
Brandis, Christian August, *Geschichte der Entwickelungen der griechischen Philosophie und ihrer Nachwirkungen im römischen Reiche* (Berlin: Reimer, 1862–64).
Bruns, Carl, *Deutschlands Sieg über Frankreich: Rede am 15. October 1870 in der Aula der Friedrich-Wilhelms-Universität zu Berlin gehalten beim Antritt des Rectorats* (Berlin: Vogt, 1870).
Buckle, Henry Thomas, *Geschichte der Civilisation in England*, trans. Arnold Ruge (Leipzig: Winter, 1860–61).
Burckhardt, Jacob, *Weltgeschichtliche Betrachtungen*, ed. Rudolf Marx (Stuttgart: Kröner, 1978).
Gesamtausgabe, ed. Emil Dürr et al. (Stuttgart: Deutsche Verlagsanstalt, 1930–34).
Die Cultur der Renaissance in Italien, 2nd edn. (Leipzig: Seemann, 1869).
Burke, Edmund, *Reflections on the Revolution in France*, ed. L. G. Mitchell (Oxford: Oxford University Press, 1993).
Carey, Henry Charles, *Lehrbuch der Volkswirthschaft und Socialwissenschaft*, trans. Karl Adler, 2nd, corr. edn. (Vienna: Braumüller, 1870).
Caspari, Otto, *Die Urgeschichte der Menschheit, mit Rücksicht auf die natürliche Entwicklung des frühesten Geisteslebens* (Leipzig: Brockhaus, 1873).
Chladenius, Johann Martin, *Nova philosophia definitiva* (Leipzig: Lanckisch, 1750).
Comte, Auguste, *Auguste Comte and Positivism: The Essential Writings*, ed. Gertrud Lenzer (Chicago: University of Chicago Press, 1975).

Corpus Inscriptionum Graecarum, ed. August Boeckh (Berlin: Reimer, 1825–77).
Cowley, Abraham, *To Mr. Hobs*, in *Poems: "Miscellanies," "The Mistress," "Pindarique Odes," "Verses Written on Several Occasions,"* ed. A. R. Waller (Cambridge: Cambridge University Press, 1905), pp. 188–92.
Curtius, Georg, *Kleine Schriften*, ed. Ernst Windisch (Leipzig: Hirzel, 1886).
Grundzüge der griechischen Etymologie, 3rd edn. (Leipzig: Teubner, 1869).
D., F., "Akademische Vorlesung von Hrn. Prof. Nietzsche über die Zukunft unserer Bildungsanstalten," *Schweizer Grenzpost und Tagblatt der Stadt Basel*, no. 30 (January 23, 1872).
Darwin, Charles, *The Descent of Man* (London: John Murray, 1871).
Das deutsche Kaiserreich, 1871–1914: Ein historisches Lesebuch, ed. Gerhard Ritter, 5th edn. (Göttingen: Vandenhoeck & Ruprecht, 1992).
Deussen, Paul, *Erinnerungen an Friedrich Nietzsche*, 3rd edn. (Leipzig: F. A. Brockhaus, 1901).
Dilthey, Wilhelm, *Der Aufbau der geschichtlichen Welt in den Geisteswissenschaften*, in *Gesammelte Schriften*, vol. VII (Leipzig: Teubner, 1927).
Droysen, Johann Gustav, *Historik: Textausgabe*, ed. Peter Leyh (Stuttgart-Bad Cannstatt: Frommann-Holzboog, 1977).
Geschichte des Hellenismus, ed. Erich Bayer (Tübingen: Wissenschaftliche Buchgemeinschaft, 1952–53).
Historik: Vorlesungen über Enzyklopädie und Methodologie der Geschichte, ed. Rudolf Hübner (Munich: Oldenburg, 1937).
Briefwechsel, ed. Rudolf Hübner (Stuttgart: Deutsche Verlagsanstalt, 1929).
"Die Erhebung der Geschichte zur Wissenschaft," *Historische Zeitschrift* 9 (1863), 1–22.
Grundriss der Historik (Jena: Frommann, 1858).
DuBois-Reymond, Emil, *Über den deutschen Krieg: Rede am 3. August 1870 in der Aula der Königlichen Friedrich-Wilhelms-Universität zu Berlin gehalten* (Berlin: Hirschwald, 1870).
Durkheim, Émil, "La science positive de la morale en Allemagne," *Revue philosophique* 24 (1887), 33–58, 113–42, and 275–84.
Espinas, Alfred, *Die thierischen Gesellschaften: Eine vergleichend-psychologische Untersuchung*, ed. W. Schlosser (Braunschweig: Vieweg, 1879).
Eucken, Rudolf, "Meine persönlichen Erinnerungen an Nietzsche," in Sander L. Gilman (ed.), *Begegnungen mit Nietzsche* (Bonn: Bouvier, 1981), pp. 160–2.
Fechner, Gustav Theodor, *Elemente der Psychophysik* (Leipzig: Breitkopf & Härtel, 1860).
Feuerbach, Ludwig, *Das Wesen des Christentums*, 3rd edn., ed. Heinrich Schmidt (Leipzig: Kröner, 1848).
Fichte, Johann Gottlieb, *Werke*, ed. Peter Lothar Oesterreich and Wilhelm G. Jacobs (Frankfurt/M.: Deutscher Klassiker Verlag, 1997).

Sämmtliche Werke, ed. Immanuel Hermann von Fichte (Berlin: Veit & Co., 1845–46).
Fischer, Kuno, *Immanuel Kant: Entwicklungsgeschichte und System der kritischen Philosophie* (Mannheim: Bassermann, 1860).
Fontes Iuris Romani Antejustiani, ed. S. Riccobono, J. Baviera, C. Ferrini, J. Furlani, and V. Arangio-Ruiz, corr. edn. (Florence: Barbèra, 1941–43).
Förster-Nietzsche, Elisabeth, *Das Leben Friedrich Nietzsche's*, vol. II/1 (Leipzig: C. A. Naumann, 1897).
Galton, Francis, *Inquiries into the Human Faculty and its Development* (London: Macmillan, 1883).
Gatterer, Johann Christoph, *Abriß der Universalhistorie in ihrem ganzen Umfange*, 2nd edn. (Göttingen: Vandenhoeck, 1773).
Gerber, Gustav, *Die Sprache als Kunst*, vol. 1 (Bromberg: Mittler, 1871).
Gerlach, Franz Dorotheus, and Johann Jakob Bachofen, *Geschichte der Römer* (Basel: Bahnmaier, 1851).
Goethe, Johann Wolfgang von, *Werke: Hamburger Ausgabe*, ed. Erich Trunz, 16th, rev. edn. (Munich: C. H. Beck, 1996).
Gräfenhan, August, *Geschichte der klassischen Philologie im Alterthum* (Bonn: König, 1843–50).
Grimm, Jacob, "Über Etymologie und Sprachvergleichung," in *Kleinere Schriften*, vol. 1 (Berlin: Dümmler, 1864–90), pp. 299–326.
Deutsche Rechtsalterthümer (Göttingen: Dieterich, 1828).
"Von der Poesie im Recht," *Zeitschrift für geschichtliche Rechtswissenschaft* 2 (1815/16), 25–99.
Grotius, Hugo, *De jure belli ac pacis libri tres/The Rights of War and Peace*, trans. Francis W. Kelsey (Oxford: Clarendon Press, 1925).
Harnack, Adolf von, "Vom Grossbetrieb der Wissenschaft," *Preußische Jahrbücher* 119 (1905), 193–201.
Geschichte der Königlich Preussischen Akademie der Wissenschaften (Berlin: Reichsdruckerei, 1900).
Hartmann, Eduard von, *Die Philosophie des Unbewussten* (Berlin: Duncker, 1869).
Haym, Rudolf, *Hegel und seine Zeit: Vorlesungen über Entstehung und Entwicklung, Wesen und Werth der Hegel'schen Philosophie* (Berlin: Gärtner, 1857).
Heeren, Arnold Hermann Ludwig, *Geschichte des Studiums der classischen Litteraturen seit dem Wiederaufleben der Wissenschaften; mit einer Einleitung, welche die Geschichte der Werke der Classiker im Mittelalter enthält* (Göttingen: Rosenbusch, 1797–1801).
Hegel, Georg Wilhelm Friedrich, *Political Writings*, ed. Laurence Dickey and H. B. Nisbet (Cambridge: Cambridge University Press, 1999).
Elements of the Philosophy of Right, ed. Allen W. Wood, trans. H. B. Nisbet (Cambridge: Cambridge University Press, 1991).

Lectures on the Philosophy of Religion, ed. P. C. Hodgson, trans. R. F. Brown, P. C. Hodgson, J. M. Stewart, and H. S. Harris (Berkeley, Calif.: University of California Press, 1984–87).
Lectures on the Philosophy of World History: Introduction, Reason in History, trans. H. B. Nisbet, introd. Duncan Forbes (Cambridge: Cambridge University Press, 1975).
Aesthetics: Lectures on Fine Art, trans. T. M. Knox (Oxford: Clarendon Press, 1975).
Philosophy of Nature: Part Two of the "Encyclopaedia of the Philosophical Sciences" (1830), trans. A. V. Miller (Oxford: Clarendon Press, 1970).
Philosophy of Mind: Part Three of the "Encyclopaedia of the Philosophical Sciences" (1830), trans. William Wallace and A. V. Miller (Oxford: Clarendon Press, 1970).
Werke, ed. Eva Moldenhauer and Karl Markus Michel (Frankfurt/M.: Suhrkamp, 1969–71).
Vorlesungen über die Geschichte der Philosophie, ed. Karl Ludwig Michelet (Berlin: Duncker & Humblot, 1833–36).
Heine, Heinrich, *Religion and Philosophy in Germany: A Fragment*, trans. John Snodgrass, foreword Dennis J. Schmitt (Albany: SUNY Press, 1986).
Hellwald, Friedrich von, *Die Erde und ihre Völker: Ein geographisches Hausbuch* (Stuttgart: Spemann, 1877–78).
Culturgeschichte in ihrer natürlichen Entwicklung bis zur Gegenwart (Augsburg: Lampart, 1875).
Helmholtz, Hermann von, "Ueber das Ziel und die Fortschritte der Naturwissenschaft: Eröffnungsrede für die Naturforscherversammlung zu Innsbruck, 1869," in *Vorträge und Reden*, 4th edn. (Braunschweig: Vieweg, 1896), vol. 1, pp. 367–98.
Ueber die Wechselwirkung der Naturkräfte und die darauf bezüglichen neuesten Fortschritte der Physik: Populär-wissenschaftlicher Vortrag (Königsberg: Gräfe & Unzer, 1854).
Herbst, Wilhelm, *Das classische Alterthum in der Gegenwart: Eine geschichtliche Betrachtung* (Leipzig: Teubner, 1852).
Herder, Johann Gottfried, *Philosophical Writings*, ed. and trans. Michael N. Forster (Cambridge: Cambridge University Press, 2002).
Werke in zehn Bänden, ed. Martin Bollacher, Jürgen Brummack, Ulrich Gaier, Gunter E. Grimm, Hans Dietrich Irmscher, Rudolf Smend, and Johannes Wallmann (Frankfurt/M.: Deutscher Klassiker Verlag, 1985–2000).
Hering, Ewald, *Über das Gedächtnis als eine allgemeine Form der organisierten Materie: Vortrag gehalten in der feierlichen Sitzung der Kaiserlichen Akademie der Wissenschaften in Wien am 30.5.1870* (Vienna: Staatsdruckerei, 1876).
Hermann, Gottfried, *Über Herrn Professor Böckhs Behandlung der griechischen Inschriften* (Leipzig: Fleischer, 1826).

Heussi, Karl, *Die Krisis des Historismus* (Tübingen: J. C. B. Mohr, 1932).
Heyne, Christian Gottlob, "Sermonis mythici seu symbolici interpretatio ad causas et rationes ductasque inde regulas revocata," *Commentationes Societatis Regiae Scientiarum Gottingensis* 16 (1808), 285–323.
Hobbes, Thomas, *Leviathan, with Selected Variants from the Latin Edition of 1668*, ed. Edwin Curley (Indianapolis, Ind.: Hackett, 1994).
Humboldt, Wilhelm von, *On Language*, trans. Peter Hearth, intro. Hans Aarsleff (Cambridge: Cambridge University Press, 1988).
  Werke, ed. Andreas Flitner and Klaus Giel (Darmstadt: Wissenschaftliche Buchgesellschaft, 1960–81).
Hume, David, *Enquiries Concerning Human Understanding and Concerning the Principles of Morals*, 6th edn, ed. L. A. Selby-Bigge and P. H. Nidditch (Oxford: Clarendon Press, 1997).
  A Treatise of Human Nature, ed. L. A. Selby-Bigge, 2nd edn. (Oxford: Oxford University Press, 1978).
Husserl, Edmund, *Logical Investigations*, trans. J. N. Findlay, intro. and ed. Dermot Moran (London: Routledge, 2001).
  "Philosophy as Rigorous Science," in *Phenomenology and the Crisis of Philosophy*, trans. and ed. Quentin Lauer (New York: Harper & Row, 1965), pp. 69–147.
Jahn, Otto, *Griechische Bilderchroniken, bearbeitet von Otto Jahn*, ed. Adolf Michaelis (Bonn: Marcus, 1873).
  Aus der Alterthumswissenschaft: Populäre Aufsätze (Bonn: Marcus, 1868).
  Archäologische Beiträge (Berlin: Reimer, 1847).
  Archäologische Aufsätze (Greifswald: Koch, 1845).
  "Über den Aberglauben des bösen Blicks bei den Alten," *Königlich-Sächsische Gesellschaft der Wissenschaften, philologisch-historische Klasse: Berichte über die Verhandlungen* 7 (1855), 28–110.
Jhering, Rudolf von, *Der Zweck im Recht* (Leipzig: Breitkopf & Härtel, 1877–83).
Justi, Johann Heinrich Gottlob von, *Der Grundriß einer guten Regierung in 5 Büchern verfasset* (Frankfurt/M.: Garbe, 1759).
Kant, Immanuel, *Anthropology from a Pragmatic Point of View*, ed. and trans. Robert B. Louden, intro. Manfred Kuehn (Cambridge: Cambridge University Press, 2006).
  Critique of Practical Reason, trans. Werner S. Pluhar, intro. Stephen Engstrom (Indianapolis, Ind.: Hackett, 2002).
  Critique of Pure Reason, ed. and trans. Paul Guyer and Allen W. Wood (Cambridge: Cambridge University Press, 1998).
  Groundwork of the Metaphysics of Morals, trans. and ed. Mary J. Gregor, introd. Christine M. Korsgaard (Cambridge: Cambridge University Press, 1998).
  Critique of Practical Reason, ed. and trans. Mary Gregor, introd. Andrews Reath (Cambridge: Cambridge University Press, 1997).

The Metaphysics of Morals, trans. and ed. Mary Gregor, introd. Roger J. Sullivan (Cambridge: Cambridge University Press, 1996).
Religion and Rational Theology, trans. and ed. Allen W. Wood and George di Giovanni (Cambridge: Cambridge University Press, 1996).
Political Writings, ed. Hans Reiss, trans. H. B. Nisbet, 2nd edn., enlarged (Cambridge: Cambridge University Press, 1991).
Werkausgabe, ed. Wilhelm Weischedel, 11th edn. (Frankfurt/M.: Suhrkamp, 1990).
Critique of Judgment, trans. Werner S. Pluhar (Indianapolis, Ind.: Hackett, 1987).
Kemble, John Mitchell, *The Saxons in England: A History of the English Commonwealth till the Period of the Norman Conquest* (London: Longman, 1849).
Klemm, Gustav, *Allgemeine Cultur-Geschichte der Menschheit, nach den besten Quellen bearbeitet mit xylographischen Abbildungen der verschiedenen Nationalphysiognomien, Geräthe, Waffen, Trachten, Kunstproducte u. s. w. versehen* (Leipzig: Teubner, 1843–51).
Klenze, Leo von, *Die Walhalla in artistischer und technischer Beziehung* (Munich: Literarisch-artistische Anstalt, 1842).
Kohler, Josef, *Das Recht als Kulturerscheinung: Einleitung in die vergleichende Rechtswissenschaft* (Würzburg: Stahel, 1885).
Krafft, Wilhem Ludwig, *Die Anfänge der christlichen Kirche bei den germanischen Völkern* (Berlin: Hertz, 1854).
Die Topographie Jerusalem's, mit Inschriften, Ansichten, Plänen und Karten (Bonn: König, 1846).
Krieger, Karsten (ed.), *Der "Berliner Antisemitismusstreit" 1879–1881: Eine Kontroverse um die Zugehörigkeit der deutschen Juden zur Nation* (Munich: K. G. Saur, 2003).
Kugler, Franz, *Handbuch der Kunstgeschichte* (Stuttgart: Ebner & Seubert, 1842).
Lange, Friedrich Albert, *Geschichte des Materialismus und Kritik seiner Bedeutung in der Gegenwart* (Iserlohn: Baedeker, 1866).
Lazarus, Moritz, *Grundzüge der Völkerpsychologie und Kulturwissenschaft*, ed. Klaus Christian Köhnke (Hamburg: Felix Meiner, 2003).
Leibniz, Gottfried Wilhelm, *Philosophische Schriften*, ed. C. I. Gerhardt (Berlin: Weidmann, 1875–90).
Mathematische Schriften, ed. C. I. Gerhardt (Berlin: Asher, 1848–63).
Leopardi, Giacomo, *Selected Prose and Poetry*, ed. and trans. Iris Origo and John Heath-Stubbs (Oxford: Oxford University Press, 1966).
Lessing, Gotthold Ephraim, *Philosophical and Theological Writings*, ed. and trans. H. B. Nisbet (Cambridge: Cambridge University Press, 2005).
Levezow, Jakob Andras Konrad, "Ueber archäologische Kritik und Hermeneutik," *Abhandlungen der Königlichen Akademie der Wissenschaften: Historisch-philologische Klasse* (1833), pp. 225–48.

Lippert, Julius, *Die Religionen der europäischen Culturvölker, der Litauer, Slaven, Germanen, Griechen und Römer, in ihrer geschichtlichen Entwicklung* (Berlin: Hofmann, 1881).
List, Friedrich, *Schriften, Reden, Briefe*, ed. Erwin von Beckrath, Karl Goeser, Friedrich Lenz, William Notz, Edgar Salin, and Artur Sommer (Berlin: Hobbing, 1927–35).
Lotze, Rudolph Hermann, *Medicinische Psychologie oder Physiologie der Seele* (Leipzig: Weidmann, 1852).
Lubbock, John, *Die Entstehung der Civilisation und der Urzustand des Menschengeschlechtes, erläutert durch das innere und äußere Leben der Wilden*, trans. A. Passow (Jena: Costenoble, 1875).
Machiavelli, Niccolò, *The Prince*, ed. Quentin Skinner and Russell Price (Cambridge: Cambridge University Press, 1988).
Mähly, Jacob, "Erinnerungen an Friedrich Nietzsche," *Die Gegenwart* 58 (1900), 246–50.
Maine, Henry Sumner, *Lectures on the Early History of Institutions* (London: John Murray, 1875).
  Ancient Law: Its Connection with the Early History of Society, and its Relation to Modern Ideas (London: John Murray, 1861).
Mannhardt, Wilhelm, *Wald- und Feldkulte, I: Der Baumkultus der Germanen und ihrer Nachbarstämme. Mythologische Untersuchungen* (Berlin: Borntraeger, 1875).
Mannheim, Karl, *Ideology and Utopia: An Introduction to the Sociology of Knowledge*, trans. Louis Wirth and Edward Shils (London: Routledge & Kegan Paul, 1936).
Marr, Wilhelm, *Der Sieg des Judenthums über das Germanenthum vom nichtconfessionellen Standpunkt aus betrachtet* (Bern: Costenoble, 1879).
Marx, Karl, "Zur Judenfrage," in Karl Marx and Friedrich Engels, *Werke*, vol. 1 (Berlin: Dietz, 1976), pp. 347–77.
Michaelis, Adolf, *Geschichte des Deutschen Archäologischen Instituts 1829–1879: Festschrift zum 21. April 1879* (Berlin: Asher & Co., 1879).
Mill, J. S., *Collected Works*, ed. John M. Robson (London: Routledge, 1963–91).
  "August Comte und der Positivismus," in *Gesammelte Werke*, ed. Theodor Gomperz, vol. IX (Leipzig: Fues, 1869–75), pp. 89–141.
Moleschott, Jacob, *Der Kreislauf des Lebens: Physiologische Antworten auf Liebig's Chemische Briefe*, 2nd edn. (Mainz: Philipp von Zabern, 1855).
Mommsen, Theodor, *Tagebuch der französisch-italienischen Reise 1844–1845, mit einem Anhang: Mommsens Denkschrift über das "Corpus Inscriptionum Latinarum" 1847*, ed. Gerold Walser and Brigitte Walser (Berne: Lang, 1976).
  Reden und Aufsätze (Berlin: Weidmann, 1905).
  Römische Geschichte (Berlin: Weidmann, 1854–56).

Review of Franz Dorotheus Gerlach and Johann Jakob Bachofen, *Geschichte der Römer* (Basel: Bahnmaier, 1851), in *Literarisches Centralblatt für Deutschland,* 7 (November 16, 1850), cols. 138–9.

Müllenhoff, Karl, *Deutsche Altertumskunde,* vol. 1 (Berlin: Weidmann, 1870).

Müller, Adam Heinrich, *Die Elemente der Staatskunst: Sechsunddreißig Vorlesungen* (Berlin: Haude & Spener, 1968).

Müller, Eduard, "Biographische Erinnerungen," in Karl Otfried Müller, *Kleine deutsche Schriften,* ed. Eduard Müller, vol. 1 (Breslau: Max, 1847–47), pp. lxvii–lxviii.

Müller, Friedrich Max, "Über die Philosophie der Mythologie," in *Einleitung in die vergleichende Religionswissenschaft* (Strasbourg: Trübner, 1874), pp. 301–53.

Chips from a German Workshop, Volume I: Essays on the Science of Religion (London: Longmans, Green, and Co.,1867).

Vorlesungen über die Wissenschaft der Sprache, trans. Carl Böttger (Leipzig: Mayer, 1863–66).

Müller, Johannes, *Handbuch der Physiologie des Menschen für Vorlesungen* (Koblenz: Hölscher, 1833–40).

Müller, Karl Otfried, *Kleine deutsche Schriften,* ed. Eduard Müller (Breslau: Max, 1847–47).

Geschichte der griechischen Literatur bis auf das Zeitalter Alexanders, ed. Eduard Müller (Breslau: Max & Co., 1841).

Aeschylos, "Eumeniden": Griechisch und deutsch, mit erläuternden Abhandlungen über die äussere Darstellung, und über den Inhalt und die Composition dieser Tragödie (Göttingen: Dieterich, 1833).

Handbuch der Archäologie der Kunst (Breslau: Max, 1830).

Prolegomena zu einer wissenschaftlichen Mythologie (Göttingen: Vandenhoeck & Ruprecht, 1825).

Nägeli, Carl von, *Mechanisch-physiologische Abstammungslehre* (Munich: Oldenbourg, 1884).

Niebuhr, Barthold Georg, *Lebensnachrichten, aus Briefen desselben und aus Erinnerungen einiger seiner nächsten Freunde* (Hamburg: Friedrich Perthes, 1838–39).

Nissen, Heinrich, *Das Templum: Antiquarische Untersuchungen, mit astronomischen Hülfstafeln von B. Thiele* (Berlin: Weidmann, 1869).

Novalis, *Christianity or Europe: A Fragment,* in *The Early Political Writings of the German Romantics,* ed. and trans. Frederick C. Beiser (Cambridge: Cambridge University Press, 1996), pp. 59–79.

Oken, Lorenz, *Lehrbuch der Naturphilosophie* (Jena: Frommann, 1809–11)

Overbeck, Franz, and Heinrich Köselitz, *Briefwechsel,* ed. David Marc Hoffmann, Niklas Peter, and Theo Salfinger (Berlin: Walter de Gruyter, 1998).

Overbeck, Franz, *Werke und Nachlaß,* ed. Ekkehard W. Stegemann, Niklaus Peter, and Marianne Stauffacher-Schaub (Stuttgart: J. B. Metzler, 1994–).

"Erinnerungen an Friedrich Nietzsche," *Neue Rundschau* 17 (1906), 209–31 and 320–30.
"Über die Anfänge der patristischen Litteratur," *Historische Zeitschrift* 48 (1882), 417–72.
Platner, Ernst, *Neue Anthropologie für Ärzte und Weltweise: Mit besonderer Rücksicht auf Physiologie, Pathologie, Moralphilosophie und Aesthetik* (Leipzig: n.p., 1791).
Post, Albert Hermann, "Ethnological Jurisprudence," *The Monist* 2 (1891/92), 31–40.
Die Grundlagen des Rechts und die Grundzüge seiner Entwickelungsgeschichte: Leitgedanken für den Aufbau einer allgemeinen Rechtswissenschaft auf sociologischer Basis (Oldenburg: Schulze, 1884).
Bausteine für eine allgemeine Rechtswissenschaft auf vergleichend-ethnologischer Basis (Oldenburg: Schulze, 1880–81).
Kirchenglaube und Wissenschaft: Ein Beitrag zur Klärung der religiösen Streitfragen der Gegenwart für gebildete Leser (Bremen: Gesenius, 1868).
Die Elemente des gemeinen deutschen und hansestadtbremischen Privatrechts auf Grundlage der modernen Volkswirtschaft (Bremen: Gesenius, 1866).
Pott, August Friedrich, *Etymologische Forschungen auf dem Gebiete der Indo-Germanischen Sprachen mit besonderem Bezug auf die Lautumwandlung im Sanskrit, Griechischen, Lateinischen, Litauischen und Gothischen* (Lemgo: Meyer, 1833–36).
Prantl, Carl, *Geschichte der Logik im Abendlande* (Leipzig: Hirzel, 1855–70).
Preller, Ludwig, "Über die wissenschaftliche Behandlung der Archäologie," in *Ausgewählte Aufsätze aus dem Gebiet der classischen Alterthumswissenschaft*, ed. Reinhold Köhler (Berlin: Weidmann, 1864), pp. 384–425.
Ranke, Leopold von, *Aus Werk und Nachlaß*, ed. Walther Peter Fuchs and Theodor Schieder (Munich: Oldenbourg, 1964–75).
Weltgeschichte (Leipzig: Duncker & Humblot, 1881–88).
Deutsche Geschichte im Zeitalter der Reformation (Leipzig: Duncker & Humblot, 1839–43).
Neun Bücher Preussischer Geschichte (Berlin: Veit und Comp., 1847–48).
Ratzel, Friedrich, *Anthropo-Geographie: Grundzüge der Anwendung der Erdkunde auf die Geschichte* (Stuttgart: Engelhorn, 1882).
Rée, Paul, *Basic Writings*, ed. and trans. Robin Small (Urbana, Ill.: University of Illinois Press, 2003).
Reil, Johann Christian, "Von der Lebenskraft," *Archiv für die Physiologie* 1/1 (1796), 66–7.
Renan, Ernest, *La Vie de Jésus*, 18th edn. (Paris: Lévy, 1883).
Ribot, Théodule, *L'Hérédité: Étude psychologique sur ses phénomènes, ses lois, ses causes, ses conséquences* (Paris: Librairie Philosophique de Ladrange, 1873).
Ritschl, Albrecht, "Ueber geschichtliche Methode in der Erforschung des Urchristenthums," *Jahrbücher für Deutsche Theologie* 6 (1861), 429–59.

Ritschl, Friedrich, *Opuscula philologica* (Leipzig: Teubner, 1866–79).
Neue Plautinische Exkurse: Sprachgeschichtliche Untersuchungen (Leipzig: Teubner, 1869).
Priscae Latinitatis monumenta epigraphica, ad archetyporum fidem exemplis lithographis repraesentata (Berlin: Reimer, 1862–64).
De Oro et Orione commentatio: Specimen historiae criticae grammaticorum Graecorum (Breslau: Schulze, 1834).
Ritter, August Heinrich, *Encyklopädie der philosophischen Wissenschaften* (Göttingen: Dieterich, 1862–64).
Geschichte der Philosophie (Hamburg: Perthes, 1829–53).
Rolph, William H., *Biologische Probleme, zugleich als Versuch zur Entwicklung einer rationellen Ethik*, 2nd edn., enlarged (Leipzig: Engelmann, 1884).
Roscher, Wilhelm, *Grundlagen der Nationalökonomie* (Stuttgart: Cotta, 1854).
Grundriss zu Vorlesungen über die Staatswirthschaft nach geschichtlicher Methode (Göttingen: Dieterich, 1843).
Rosenkranz, Karl, *Hegel als deutscher Nationalphilosoph* (Berlin: Duncker & Humblot, 1870).
Geschichte der Kant'schen Philosophie (Leipzig: Voss, 1840).
Rousseau, Jean-Jacques, *The Social Contract and Other Later Political Writings*, ed. and trans. Victor Gourevitch (Cambridge: Cambridge University Press, 1997).
Roux, Wilhelm, *Der Kampf der Theile im Organismus: Ein Beitrag zur Vervollständigung der mechanischen Zweckmässigkeitslehre* (Leipzig: Engelmann, 1881).
Savigny, Friedrich Carl von, *Of the Vocation of our Age for Legislation and Jurisprudence*, trans. Abraham Hayward (London: Littlewood & Co., 1831).
Schaarschmidt, Karl, "Vom rechten und vom falschen Kriticismus," *Philosophische Monatshefte* 14 (1878), 1–12.
Der Entwicklungsgang der neueren Speculation als Einleitung in die Geschichte der Philosophie (Bonn: Marcus, 1857).
Schelling, Friedrich Wilhelm Joseph, *First Outline of a System of the Philosophy of Nature*, trans. Keith R. Peterson (Albany, N.Y.: SUNY Press, 2004).
Ideas for a Philosophy of Nature as Introduction to the Study of this Science, trans. Errol E. Harris and Peter Hearth, intro. Robert Stern (Cambridge: Cambridge University Press, 1988).
Sämmtliche Werke, ed. Karl Friedrich August Schelling (Stuttgart: Cotta, 1856–61).
Schiller, Friedrich, "On Naïve and Sentimental Poetry," in H. B. Nisbet (ed.), *German Aesthetic and Literary Criticism: Winckelmann, Lessing, Hamann, Herder, Schiller, Goethe* (Cambridge: Cambridge University Press, 1985), pp. 180–232.
On the Aesthetic Education of Man, in a Series of Letters, ed. and trans. Elizabeth M. Wilkinson and L. A. Willoughby (Oxford: Clarendon Press, 1967).

Werke: Nationalausgabe, ed. Julius Petersen and Friedrich Beißner (Weimar: Böhlau, 1940–).

Schlegel, Friedrich, "Essay on the Concept of Republicanism Occasioned by the Kantian Tract 'Perpetual Peace'," in *The Early Political Writings of the German Romantics*, ed. and trans. Frederick C. Beiser (Cambridge: Cambridge University Press, 1996), pp. 93–112.

Kritische Friedrich-Schlegel-Ausgabe, ed. Ernst Behler, Jean-Jacques Anstett, and Hans Eichner (Paderborn: Schöningh, 1958–).

Schleicher, August, *Compendium der vergleichenden Grammatik der indogermanischen Sprachen: Kurzer Abriss einer Laut- und Formenlehre der indogermanischen Ursprache, des Altindischen, Alteranischen, Altgriechischen, Altitalischen, Altkeltischen, Altslawischen, Litauischen und Altdeutschen*, 2nd edn. (Weimar: Böhlau, 1866).

Schleiermacher, Friedrich Daniel Ernst, *Geschichte der Philosophie*, ed. August Heinrich Ritter (Berlin: Reimer, 1839).

Hermeneutik und Kritik, mit besonderer Beziehung auf das Neue Testament, ed. Friedrich Lücke (Berlin: Reimer, 1838).

Schlözer, August Ludwig von, *Vorstellung seiner Universalhistorie* (1771/72), ed. Horst-Walter Blanke (Hagen: Rottmann, 1990).

Schmitt, Carl, *Political Theology: Four Chapters on the Theory of Sovereignty*, trans. George Schwab, foreword Tracy B. Strong (Chicago: University of Chicago Press, 2005).

The Concept of the Political, trans. George Schwab, foreword Tracy B. Strong (Chicago: University of Chicago Press, 1996).

Schneider, Georg Heinrich, *Der thierische Wille: Systematische Darstellung und Erklärung der thierischen Triebe und deren Entstehung, Entwickelung und Verbreitung im Thierreiche als Grundlage zu einer vergleichenden Willenslehre* (Leipzig: Abel, 1880).

Schopenhauer, Arthur, *The World as Will and Representation*, trans. E. F. J. Payne (New York: Dover, 1966).

Schubarth, Karl Ernst, *Ueber die Unvereinbarkeit der Hegelschen Staatslehre mit dem obersten Lebens- und Entwicklungs-Princip des preußischen Staates* (Breslau: Aderholz, 1839).

Schwegler, Albert, *Geschichte der Philosophie im Umriß: Ein Leitfaden zur Übersicht* (Stuttgart: Verlag der Franckh'schen Buchhandlung, 1848).

Simmel, Georg, *Die Probleme der Geschichtsphilosophie: Eine erkenntniskritische Studie* (Leipzig: Duncker & Humblot, 1892).

Spencer, Herbert, *Die Thatsachen der Ethik*, trans. B. Vetter (Stuttgart: Schweizerbart, 1879).

The Data of Ethics (London: Williams and Norgate, 1879).

Spinoza, Baruch de, *Ethics*, ed. and trans. G. H. R. Parkinson (Oxford: Oxford University Press, 2000).

Springer, Anton Heinrich, *Handbuch der Kunstgeschichte: Zum Gebrauche für Künstler und Studierende und als Führer auf der Reise* (Stuttgart: Rieger, 1855).

Steinthal, Heymann, *Philologie, Geschichte und Psychologie in ihren gegenseitigen Beziehungen: Ein Vortrag gehalten in der Versammlung der Philologen zu Meissen 1863 in erweiterter Überarbeitung* (Berlin: Dümmler, 1864).
Grammatik, Logik und Psychologie: Ihre Principien und ihr Verhältniss zu einander (Berlin: Dümmler, 1855).
Die Classification der Sprachen dargestellt als die Entwicklung der Sprachidee (Berlin: Dümmler, 1850).
Stoecker, Adolf, *Das moderne Judentum in Deutschland, besonders in Berlin: Zwei Reden in der christlich-sozialen Arbeiterpartei* (Leipzig: Wiegandt & Grieben, 1880).
Strauss, Leo, *Natural Right and History* (Chicago: University of Chicago Press, 1953).
Sulzer, Johann Georg, *Vermischte philosophische Schriften: Aus den Jahrbüchern der Akademie der Wissenschaften zu Berlin gesammelt* (Leipzig: Weidmann & Reich, 1773–81).
Sybel, Heinrich von, *Die deutschen Universitäten, ihre Leistungen und Bedürfnisse* (Bonn: Max Cohen & Sohn, 1874).
Kleine Schriften (Munich: Cotta, 1869).
Geschichte der Revolutionszeit (Düsseldorf: Buddeus, 1853–68).
Die Deutsche Nation und das Kaiserreich: Eine historisch-politische Abhandlung, 2nd edn. (Düsseldorf: J. Buddeus, 1862).
"Über den Stand der neueren deutschen Geschichtsschreibung," *Preußische Jahrbücher* 1 (1858), 349–64.
Teichmüller, Gustav, *Die wirkliche und die scheinbare Welt: Neue Grundlegung der Metaphysik* (Breslau: Koebner, 1882).
Aristotelische Forschungen (Halle: Barthel, 1867–73).
Tocqueville, Alexis de, *Democracy in America*, trans. and ed. Harvey C. Mansfield and Delba Winthrop (Chicago: University of Chicago Press, 2000).
Treitschke, Heinrich von, *Briefe*, ed. Max Cornelius (Leipzig: Hirzel, 1912–20).
Deutsche Geschichte im neunzehnten Jahrhundert (Leipzig: Hirzel, 1879–94).
"Die ersten Versuche deutscher Kolonialpolitik," *Preußische Jahrbücher* 54 (1884), 555–66.
"Unsere Aussichten," *Preußische Jahrbücher* 44 (1879), 559–76.
"Deutschland und die orientalische Frage," *Preußische Jahrbücher* 38 (1876), 664–75.
Historische und politische Aufsätze, vornehmlich zur neuesten deutsche Geschichte (Leipzig: Hirzel, 1865).
Troeltsch, Ernst, *Der Historismus und seine Probleme: I, Das logische Problem der Geschichtsphilosophie* (Tübingen: J. C. B. Mohr, 1922).
Tylor, Edward Burnett, *Die Anfänge der Cultur: Untersuchungen über die Entwicklung der Mythologie, Philosophie, Religion, Kunst und Sitte*, trans. Johann Wilhelm Spengel and Friedrich Poske (Leipzig: Winter, 1873).

Primitive Culture: Researches into the Development of Mythology, Philosophy, Religion, Art, and Custom (London: John Murray, 1871–73).

"On Traces of the Early Mental Condition of Man," *Proceedings of the Royal Institution of Great Britain* 5 (1866–69), 83–93.

"On the Survival of Savage Thought in Modern Civilisation," *Proceedings of the Royal Institution of Great Britain* 5 (1866–69), 522–35.

Ueberweg, Friedrich, *Grundriss der Geschichte der Philosophie* (Berlin: Mittler, 1862–66).

System der Logik und Geschichte der logischen Lehren (Bonn: Marcus, 1857).

Usener, Hermann, *Götternamen: Versuch einer Lehre von der religiösen Begriffsbildung* (Bonn: Cohen, 1896).

Vico, Giambattista, *The New Science*, trans. Thomas Goddard Bergin and Max Harold Fisch (Ithaca, N.Y.: Cornell University Press, 1968).

Virchow, Rudolf, "Rassenbildung und Erblichkeit," in *Festschrift für Adolf Bastian zu seinem 70. Geburtstage: 26. Juni 1896, gewidmet von seinen Freunden und Verehrern* (Berlin: Reimer, 1896), pp. 1–43.

Voigt, Georg, *Die Wiederbelebung des classischen Alterthums, oder das erste Jahrhundert des Humanismus* (Berlin: Reimer, 1859).

Voltaire, *Political Writings*, trans. and ed. David Williams (Cambridge: Cambridge University Press, 1994).

Œuvres Complètes, ed. Theodore Besterman, William H. Barber *et al.* (Oxford: Voltaire Foundation; Geneva: Institut et Musée Voltaire, 1968–).

Wagner, Cosima, *Diaries, Volume I: 1869–1877*, ed. Martin Gregor-Dellin and Dietrich Mack, trans. Geoffrey Skelton (New York: Harcourt Brace Jovanovich, 1978).

Wagner, Richard, *Prose Works*, trans. William Ashton Ellis, vol. IV (New York: Broude Brothers, 1966).

Waitz, Theodor, *Introduction to Anthropology, edited with numerous additions by the author, from the first volume of "Anthropologie der Naturvölker,"* ed. and trans. J. Frederick Collingwood (London: Longman, Green, Longman, and Roberts, 1863).

Weber, Max, *Political Writings*, ed. Peter Lassman and Ronald Speirs (Cambridge: Cambridge University Press, 1994).

Economy and Society: An Outline of Interpretive Sociology, ed. Guenther Roth and Claus Wittich (Berkeley, Calif.: University of California Press, 1978).

Welcker, Friedrich Gottlieb, *Griechische Götterlehre* (Göttingen: Dieterich, 1857–63).

Wilamowitz-Moellendorff, Ulrich von, *Reden aus der Kriegszeit* (Berlin: Weidmann, 1915).

Griechisches Lesebuch (Berlin: Weidmann, 1902).

"Der griechische Unterricht auf den Gymnasien," in *Verhandlungen über Fragen der höheren Unterrichts, Berlin 6. bis 8. Juni 1900, nebst einem Anhange von Gutachten herausgegeben im Auftrage des Ministers der geistlichen, Unterrichts- und Medicinal-Angelegenheiten* (Halle: Verlag der Buchhandlung des Waisenhauses, 1901), pp. 205–17.

Zukunftsphilologie! Zweites stück: eine erwiderung auf die rettungsversuche für Fr. Nietzches "geburt der tragödie" (1873), in Karlfried Gründer, *Der Streit um Nietzsches "Geburt der Tragödie:" Die Schriften von E. Rohde, R. Wagner, U.v. Wilamowitz-Moellendorff* (Hildesheim: Olms, 1966), pp. 115–35.

Windelband, Wilhelm, *Die Philosophie im deutschen Geistesleben des 19. Jahrhunderts*, 2nd edn. (Tübingen: J. C. B. Mohr, 1909).

Geschichte und Naturwissenschaft: Rede zum Antritt des Rectorats der Kaiser-Wilhelm-Universität Strassburg, geh. am 1. Mai 1894 (Strasbourg: Heitz, 1894).

Wittgenstein, Ludwig, *Philosophical Investigations*, trans. G. E. M. Anscombe (Oxford: Blackwell, 1967).

Wolf, Friedrich August, *Vorlesungen über die Alterthumswissenschaft*, ed. Johann Daniel Gürtler (Leipzig: Lehnhold, 1831–39).

Darstellung der Alterthumswissenschaft, nebst einer Auswahl seiner kleinen Schriften und literarischen Zugaben zu dessen Vorlesungen über die Alterthumswissenschaft: Als Supplementband zu dessen Vorlesungen, ed. Samuel Friedrich Wilhelm Hoffmann (Leipzig: Lehnhold, 1833).

Wundt, Wilhelm, "Ueber Ziele und Wege der Völkerpsychologie," *Philosophische Studien* 4 (1888), 1–27.

"Philosophy in Germany," *Mind* 2 (1877), 493–518.

Vorlesungen über die Menschen- und Thierseele (Leipzig: Voss, 1863).

Wuttke, Adolf, *Der deutsche Volksaberglaube der Gegenwart*, 2nd edn., rev. (Berlin: Wiegand & Grieben, 1869).

Zeller, Eduard, *Die Philosophie der Griechen in ihrer geschichtlichen Entwicklung*, 2nd edn. (Tübingen: Fues, 1856–68).

Ueber Bedeutung und Aufgabe der Erkenntniss-Theorie: Ein akademischer Vortrag (Heidelberg: Groos, 1862).

Zöllner, Johann Carl Friedrich, *Über die Natur der Cometen: Beiträge zur Geschichte und Theorie der Erkenntniss*, 2nd edn. (Leipzig: Engelmann, 1872).

SECONDARY LITERATURE

Abbey, Ruth, *Nietzsche's Middle Period* (Oxford: Oxford University Press, 2000).

Abel, Günter, "Logik und Ästhetik," *Nietzsche-Studien* 16 (1987), 112–48.

Nietzsche: Die Dynamik der Willen zur Macht und die ewige Wiederkehr (Berlin: Walter de Gruyter, 1984).

Alings, Reinhard, *Monument und Nation – das Bild vom Nationalstaat im Denkmal: Zur Verhältnis von Nation und Staat im deutschen Kaiserreich* (Berlin: Walter de Gruyter, 1996).

Anderson, Benedict, *Imagined Communities: Reflections on the Origin and Spread of Nationalism* (London: Verso, 1983).
Ankersmit, F. R., "Historicism: An Attempt at Synthesis," *History and Theory* 34 (1995), 143–61.
Ansell-Pearson, Keith, *Nietzsche contra Rousseau: A Study of Nietzsche's Moral and Political Thought* (Cambridge: Cambridge University Press, 1996).
  An Introduction to Nietzsche as a Political Thinker: The Perfect Nihilist (Cambridge: Cambridge University Press, 1994).
Appadurai, Arjun, "Introduction: Commodities and the Politics of Value," in Appadurai (ed.), *The Social Life of Things: Commodities in Cultural Perspective* (Cambridge: Cambridge University Press, 1986), pp. 3–63.
Appel, Fredrick, *Nietzsche contra Democracy* (Ithaca, N. Y.: Cornell University Press, 1999).
Arndt, Martin, "Die Basler Syntroglodyten Overbeck und Nietzsche: Eine Freundschaft im Dissens," *Zeitschrift für Religions- und Geistesgeschichte* 53/3 (2001), 193–226.
Assmann, Aleida, *Arbeit am nationalen Gedächtnis: Eine kurze Geschichte der nationalen Bildungsidee* (Frankfurt/M.: Campus 1993).
Assmann, Jan, *Das kulturelle Gedächtnis: Schrift, Erinnerung und politische Identität in frühen Hochkulturen* (Munich: C. H. Beck, 1992).
Ausmus, Harry J., "Schopenhauer's View of History: A Note," *History and Theory* 15 (1976), 141–5.
Baier, Annette C., *Moral Prejudices: Essays on Ethics* (Cambridge, Mass.: Harvard University Press, 1994).
  Postures of the Mind: Essays on Minds and Morals (Minneapolis: University of Minnesota Press, 1985).
Bambach, Charles R., *Heidegger, Dilthey, and the Crisis of Historicism* (Ithaca, N. Y.: Cornell University Press, 1995).
Barbera, Sandro, "Eine Quelle der frühen Schopenhauer-Kritik Nietzsches: Rudolf Hayms Aufsatz *Arthur Schopenhauer*," *Nietzsche-Studien* 24 (1995), 124–36.
  "Ein Sinn und unzählige Hieroglyphen: Einige Motive von Nietzsches Auseinandersetzung mit Schopenhauer in der Basler Zeit," in Tilman Borsche, Federico Gerratana, and Aldo Venturelli (eds.), *"Centauren-Geburten": Wissenschaft, Kunst und Philosophie beim jungen Nietzsche* (Berlin: Walter de Gruyter, 1994), pp. 217–33.
Bauer, Martin, "Zur Genealogie von Nietzsches Kraftbegriff: Nietzsches Auseinandersetzung mit J. G. Vogt," *Nietzsche Studien* 13 (1984), 211–27.
Becker, Frank, *Bilder von Krieg und Nation: Die Einigungskriege in der bürgerlichen Öffentlichkeit Deutschlands, 1864–1913* (Munich: Oldenbourg, 2001).

Beiser, Frederick C., *German Idealism: The Struggle against Subjectivism, 1781–1801* (Cambridge, Mass.: Harvard University Press, 2002).
 Enlightenment, Revolution, and Romanticism: The Genesis of Modern German Political Thought, 1790–1800 (Cambridge, Mass.: Harvard University Press, 1992).
Ben-Amos, Avner, "Les funérailles de Victor Hugo", in Pierre Nora (ed.), *Les lieux de mémoire*, vol. 1 (Paris: Gallimard, 1984–92), pp. 473–521.
Benne, Christian, *Nietzsche und die historisch-kritische Philologie* (Berlin: Walter de Gruyter, 2005).
Berger, Stefan, *The Search for Normality: National Identity and Historical Consciousness in Germany since 1800* (Oxford: Berghahn, 1997).
 "Prussia in History and Historiography from the Eighteenth to the Nineteenth Century," in Philip G. Dwyer (ed.), *The Rise of Prussia, 1700–1830* (Harlow: Longman, 2000), pp. 27–44.
Bergmann, Peter, *Nietzsche – the last Antipolitical German* (Bloomington, Ind.: Indiana University Press, 1987).
Berkowitz, Peter, *Nietzsche: The Ethics of an Immoralist* (Cambridge, Mass.: Harvard University Press, 1995).
Bernoulli, Carl A., *Franz Overbeck und Friedrich Nietzsche: Eine Freundschaft* (Jena: Diederichs, 1908).
Bernstein, Richard J., *Radical Evil: A Philosophical Interrogation* (Cambridge: Polity Press, 2002).
Bezold, Friedrich von, *Geschichte der Rheinischen Friedrich-Wilhelms-Universität von der Gründung bis zum Jahre 1870* (Bonn: Marcus & Weber, 1920).
Biefang, Andreas, "Der Streit um Treitschkes *Deutsche Geschichte* 1882/83: Zur Spaltung des Nationalliberalismus und der Etablierung eines national-konservativen Geschichtsbildes," *Historische Zeitschrift* 262 (1996), 391–422.
Bishop, Paul, and R. H. Stephenson, *Friedrich Nietzsche and Weimar Classicism* (Rochester, N.Y.: Camden House, 2005).
Blanke, Horst Walter, Dirk Fleischer, and Jörn Rüsen, "Theory of History in Historical Lectures: The German Tradition of *Historik*, 1750–1900," *History and Theory* 23 (1984), 331–56.
Blanning, T. C. W., *The French Revolutionary Wars, 1787–1820* (London: Arnold, 1996).
Blaschke, Olaf, "Das 19. Jahrhundert: Ein zweites konfessionelles Zeitalter?" *Geschichte und Gesellschaft* 26 (2000), 38–75.
Blondel, Eric, *Nietzsche – The Body and Culture: Philosophy as Philological Genealogy*, trans. Seán Hand (Stanford, Calif.: Stanford University Press, 1991).
Blumenberg, Hans, *Paradigmen zu einer Metaphorologie*, 2nd edn. (Frankfurt/M.: Suhrkamp, 1999).
 Work on Myth, trans. Robert M. Wallace (Cambridge, Mass.: MIT Press, 1985).

"Epochenschwelle und Rezeption," *Philosophische Rundschau* 6 (1958), 94–120.
Böckenförde, Ernst-Wolfgang, "Organ, Organismus, Organisation, politischer Körper (VII-IX)," in Otto Brunner, Werner Conze, and Reinhart Koselleck (eds.), *Geschichtliche Grundbegriffe: Historisches Lexikon zur politischen Sprache in Deutschland* (Stuttgart: Klett-Cotta, 1972–97), vol. IV, pp. 561–622.
Bollenbeck, Georg, *Bildung und Kultur: Glanz und Elend eines deutschen Deutungsmusters* (Frankfurt/M.: Insel, 1994).
Bollinger, Andrea, and Franziska Trenkle, *Nietzsche in Basel* (Basel: Schwabe & Co., 2000).
Bonjour, Edgar, *Die Universität Basel von den Anfängen bis zur Gegenwart, 1460–1960* (Basel: Helbing & Lichtenhahn, 1971).
Borschmeyer, Dieter (ed.), *"Vom Nutzen und Nachteil der Historie für das Leben": Nietzsche und die Erinnerung in der Moderne* (Frankfurt/M.: Suhrkamp, 1996).
Bornmann, Fritz, "Anekdota Nietzscheana aus dem philologischen Nachlaß der Basler Jahre (1869–1878)," in Tilman Borsche, Federico Gerratana, and Aldo Venturelli (eds.), *"Centauren-Geburten": Wissenschaft, Kunst und Philosophie beim jungen Nietzsche* (Berlin: Walter de Gruyter, 1994), pp. 67–80.
Bourdieu, Pierre, *The Logic of Practice*, trans. Richard Nice (Cambridge: Polity Press, 1990).
Bowler, Peter J., *The Mendelian Revolution: The Emergence of Hereditarian Concepts in Modern Science and Society* (Baltimore, Md.: Johns Hopkins University Press, 1989).
Boyer, M. Christine, *The City of Collective Memory: Its Historical Imagery and Architectural Entertainments* (Cambridge, Mass.: MIT Press, 1994).
Boyle, Nicholas, *Goethe – The Poet and the Age, I: The Poetry of Desire (1749–1790)* (Oxford: Oxford University Press, 1991).
Breuilly, John, "The National Idea in Modern German History," in Mary Fulbrook and John Breuilly (eds.), *German History since 1800* (London: Arnold, 1997), pp. 556–84.
Brinker, Menahem, "Nietzsche and the Jews," in Jacob Golomb and Robert S. Wistrich (eds.), *Nietzsche, Godfather of Fascism? On the Uses and Abuses of a Philosophy* (Princeton, N.J.: Princeton University Press, 2002), pp. 107–27.
Brobjer, Thomas H., "Nietzsche's Relation to Historical Methods and Nineteenth-Century German Historiography," *History and Theory* 46 (2007), 155–79.
  "Sources of and Influences on Nietzsche's *Birth of Tragedy*," *Nietzsche-Studien* 34 (2005), 278–99.
  "Nietzsche's View of the Value of Historical Studies and Methods," *Journal of the History of Ideas* 65 (2004), 301–22.

"Nietzsche's Reading and Knowledge of Natural Science," in Thomas H. Brobjer and Gregory Moore (eds.), *Nietzsche and Science* (Aldershot: Ashgate, 2004), pp. 21–50.

"The Absence of Political Ideals in Nietzsche's Writings: The Case of the Laws of Manu and the Associated Caste-Society," *Nietzsche-Studien* 27 (1998), 300–18.

Brocke, Bernhard vom, "'Von des attischen Reiches Herrlichkeit' oder die 'Modernisierung' der Antike im Zeitalter des Nationalstaats," *Historische Zeitschrift* 243 (1986), 101–36.

"Hochschul- und Wissenschaftspolitik in Preußen und im deutschen Kaiserreich, 1882–1907: Das 'System Althoff'," in Peter Baumgart (ed.), *Bildungspolitik in Preußen zur Zeit des Kaiserreichs* (Stuttgart: Klett-Cotta, 1980), pp. 9–118.

Butler, Eliza M., *The Tyranny of Greece over Germany* (Cambridge: Cambridge University Press, 1935).

Calder III, William M., "The Wilamowitz-Nietzsche Struggle: New Documents and a Reappraisal," *Nietzsche-Studien* 12 (1983), 214–54.

Cancik, Hubert, *Nietzsches Antike: Vorlesung* (Stuttgart: J. B. Metzler, 1995).

"Otto Jahns Vorlesung *Grundzüge der Archäologie* (Bonn, Sommer 1865) in den Mitschriften von Eduard Hiller und Friedrich Nietzsche," in Hubert Cancik and Hildegard Cancik-Lindemaier, *Philolog und Kultfigur: Friedrich Nietzsche und seine Antike in Deutschland* (Stuttgart: J. B. Metzler, 1999), pp. 3–33.

"'Mongols, Semites and Pure-Bred Greeks': Nietzsche's Handling of the Racial Doctrines of his Time," in Jacob Golomb (ed.), *Nietzsche and Jewish Culture* (London: Routledge, 1997), pp. 55–75.

"'Philologie als Beruf': Zu Formengeschichte, Thema und Tradition der unvollendeten vierten Unzeitgemäßen Friedrich Nietzsches," in Tilman Borsche, Federico Gerratana, and Aldo Venturelli (eds.), *"Centauren-Geburten": Wissenschaft, Kunst und Philosophie beim jungen Nietzsche* (Berlin: Walter de Gruyter, 1994), pp. 81–96.

Canis, Konrad, *Bismarcks Außenpolitik, 1870 bis 1890: Aufstieg und Gefährdung* (Paderborn: Schöningh, 2004).

Cavell, Stanley, *Conditions Handsome and Unhandsome: The Constitution of Emersonian Perfectionism* (Chicago: University of Chicago Press, 1990).

Chickering, Roger, "Das Leipziger 'Positivisten-Kränzchen' um die Jahrhundertwende," in Gangolf Hübinger, Rüdiger vom Bruch, and Friedrich Wilhelm Graf (eds.), *Kultur und Kulturwissenschaften um 1900, II: Idealismus und Positivismus* (Stuttgart: Steiner, 1997), pp. 227–45.

Clark, Maudemarie, *Nietzsche on Truth and Philosophy* (Cambridge: Cambridge University Press, 1990).

Clark, Maudemarie, and David Dudrick, "The Naturalism of *Beyond Good and Evil*," in Keith Ansell-Pearson (ed.), *A Companion to Nietzsche* (Oxford: Blackwell, 2006), pp. 148–67.
Conant, James, "Nietzsche's Perfectionism: A Reading of *Schopenhauer as Educator*," in Richard Schacht (ed.), *Nietzsche's Postmoralism: Essays on Nietzsche's Prelude to Philosophy's Future* (Cambridge: Cambridge University Press, 2000), pp. 181–257.
Conway, Daniel W., *Nietzsche and the Political* (London: Routledge, 1997).
"Revisiting the Will to Power: Active Nihilism and the Project of Transhuman Philosophy," in Keith Ansell Pearson and Diane Morgan (eds.), *Nihilism Now! Monsters of Energy* (London: Macmillan, 2000), pp. 117–41.
"Genealogy and Critical Method," in Richard Schacht (ed.), *Nietzsche, Genealogy, Morality: Essays on Nietzsche's Genealogy of Morality* (Berkeley, Calif.: University of California Press, 1994), pp. 318–33.
"Overcoming the *Übermensch*: Nietzsche's Revaluation of Values," *Journal of the British Society for Phenomenology* 20 (1989), 211–24.
Cox, Christoph, *Nietzsche: Naturalism and Interpretation* (Berkeley, Calif.: University of California Press, 1999).
Daum, Andreas W., *Wissenschaftspopularisierung im 19. Jahrhundert: Bürgerliche Kultur, naturwissenschaftliche Bildung und die deutsche Öffentlichkeit, 1848–1914* (Munich: Oldenbourg, 1998).
Debord, Guy, *La Société du spectacle* (Paris: Gallimard, 1992).
Deleuze, Gilles, *Nietzsche and Philosophy*, trans. Hugh Tomlinson (New York: Columbia University Press, 1983).
Detwiler, Bruce, *Nietzsche and the Politics of Aristocratic Radicalism* (Chicago: University of Chicago Press, 1990).
Doering-Manteuffel, Anselm, "Eine politische Nationalgeschichte für die Berliner Republik: Überlegungen zu Heinrich August Winklers *Der lange Weg nach Westen*," *Geschichte und Gesellschaft* 27 (2001), 446–62.
Dombowsky, Don, *Nietzsche's Machiavellian Politics* (New York: Palgrave Macmillan, 2004).
Dreitzel, Horst, "Die Entwicklung der Historie zur Wissenschaft," *Zeitschrift für historische Forschung* 8 (1981), 257–84.
Duffy, Michael F., and Willard Mittelman, "Nietzsche's Attitudes towards the Jews," *Journal of the History of Ideas* 49 (1988), 301–17.
Ehrhardt, Wolfgang, *Das Akademische Kunstmuseum der Universität Bonn unter der Direktion von Friedrich Gottlieb Welcker und Otto Jahn* (Opladen: Westdeutscher Verlag, 1982).
Elbe, Stefan, *Europe: A Nietzschean Perspective* (London: Routledge, 2003).
Ellis, Geoffrey, "The Nature of Napoleonic Imperialism," in Philip Dwyer (ed.), *Napoleon and Europe* (London: Longman, 2001), pp. 97–117.

Emden, Christian J., *Nietzsche on Language, Consciousness, and the Body* (Urbana, Ill.: University of Illinois Press, 2005).
"Learning How to Read: Nietzsche in Leipzig," *Oxford German Studies* 35 (2006), 97–110.
"History, Memory, and the Invention of Antiquity: Notes on the 'Classical Tradition'," in Christian J. Emden and David Midgley (eds.), *Cultural Memory and Historical Consciousness in the German-Speaking World since 1500* (Oxford: Peter Lang, 2004), pp. 39–67.
"Metaphor, Perception, and Consciousness: Nietzsche on Rhetoric and Neurophysiology," in Gregory Moore and Thomas H. Brobjer (eds.), *Nietzsche and Science* (Aldershot: Ashgate, 2004), pp. 91–110.
"The Invention of Antiquity: Nietzsche on Classicism, Classicality, and the Classical Tradition," in Paul Bishop (ed.), *Nietzsche and Antiquity: His Reaction and Response to the Classical Tradition* (Rochester N.Y.: Camden House, 2004), pp. 372–90.
"Sprache, Musik und Rhythmus: Nietzsche über die Ursprünge von Literatur, 1869–1879," *Zeitschrift für deutsche Philologie* 121 (2002), 208–30.
Engelhardt, Dietrich von, "Die organische Natur und die Lebenswissenschaften in Schellings Naturphilosophie," in Reinhard Heckmann, Hermann Krings, and Rudolf W. Meyer (eds.), *Natur und Subjektivität: Zur Auseinandersetzung mit der Naturphilosophie des jungen Schelling* (Stuttgart–Bad Cannstatt: Frommann-Holzboog, 1985), pp. 39–57.
Erkens, Franz-Reiner, "Sakral legitimierte Herrschaft im Wechsel der Zeiten und Räume: Versuch eines Überblicks," in Erkens (ed.), *Die Sakralität von Herrschaft: Herrschaftslegitimierung im Wechsel der Zeiten und Räume* (Berlin: Akademie Verlag, 2002), pp. 7–32.
Faulenbach, Bernd, *Ideologie des deutschen Weges: Die deutsche Geschichte in der Historiographie zwischen Kaiserreich und Nationalsozialismus* (Munich: C. H. Beck, 1980).
Figl, Johann, "Nietzsches frühe Begegnung mit dem Denken Indiens: Auf der Grundlage seiner unveröffentlichten Kollegnachschrift aus Philosophiegeschichte," *Nietzsche-Studien* 18 (1989), 455–71.
Fisch, Jörg, "Zivilisation, Kultur," in Otto Brunner, Werner Conze, and Reinhart Koselleck (eds.), *Geschichtliche Grundbegriffe: Historisches Lexikon zur politischen Sprache in Deutschland* (Stuttgart: Klett-Cotta, 1972–97), vol. xvii, pp. 679–774.
Fontana, Biancamaria, "The Napoleonic Empire and the Europe of Nations," in Anthony Pagden (ed.), *The Idea of Europe: From Antiquity to the European Union* (Cambridge: Cambridge University Press, 2002), pp. 116–28.
Foucault, Michel, *"Society Must be Defended": Lectures at the Collège de France, 1975–1976*, ed. François Ewald, Alessandro Fontana, and Mauro Bertaini, trans. David Macey (New York: Picador, 2003).

The Archaeology of Knowledge, trans. A. M. Sheridan Smith (New York: Pantheon, 1982).
Power/Knowledge: Selected Interviews and Other Writings, 1972–1977, ed. Colin Gordon (New York: Pantheon, 1981).
The Order of Things: An Archaeology of the Human Sciences (New York: Vintage, 1971).
"Nietzsche, Genealogy, History," in John Richardson and Brian Leiter (eds.), *Nietzsche* (Oxford: Oxford University Press, 2001), pp. 341–59.
"What is Enlightenment?" in Paul Rabinow (ed.), *The Foucault Reader* (New York: Pantheon, 1984), pp. 32–50.
Frank, Manfred, *Unendliche Fahrt: Ein Motiv und sein Text* (Frankfurt/M.: Suhrkamp, 1979).
Freytag, Nils, *Aberglauben im 19. Jahrhundert: Preußen und seine Rheinprovinz zwischen Tradition und Moderne (1815–1918)* (Berlin: Duncker & Humblot, 2003).
Friedman, Michael, "Philosophical Naturalism," *Proceedings and Addresses of the American Philosophical Association* 71/2 (1997), 7–21.
Fritzsche, Peter, *Stranded in the Present: Modern Time and the Melancholy of History* (Cambridge, Mass.: Harvard University Press, 2004).
Fuhrmann, Manfred, "Die Querelle des Anciens et des Modernes, der Nationalismus und die deutsche Klassik," in *Brechungen: Wirkungsgeschichtliche Studien zur antik-europäischen Bildungstradition* (Stuttgart: Klett-Cotta, 1982), pp. 129–49.
Galison, Peter, "Multiple Constraints, Simultaneous Solutions," *PSA: Proceedings of the Biennial Meeting of the Philosophy of Science Association,* vol. II (Chicago: University of Chicago Press, 1988), pp. 157–63.
Garber, Daniel, "Leibniz: Physics and Philosophy," in Nicholas Jolley (ed.), *The Cambridge Companion to Leibniz* (Cambridge: Cambridge University Press, 1995), pp. 270–352.
Gasser, Peter, "'Columbus Novus': Zum rhetorischen Impetus von Nietzsche's Philosophie," *Nietzsche-Studien* 24 (1995), 137–61.
Gaukroger, Stephen, *Francis Bacon and the Transformation of Early Modern Philosophy* (Cambridge: Cambridge University Press, 2001).
Gawoll, Hans-Jürgen, *Nihilismus und Metaphysik: Entwicklungsgeschichtliche Untersuchung vom deutschen Idealismus bis zu Heidegger* (Stuttgart: Frommann-Holzboog, 1989).
Geismann, Georg, "Der Berliner Antisemitismusstreit und die Abdankung der rechtlich-praktischen Vernunft," *Kant-Studien* 83 (1993), 369–80.
Gerratana, Federico, "Der Wahn jenseits des Menschen: Zur frühen E. v. Hartmann-Rezeption Friedrich Nietzsches (1869–1874)," *Nietzsche-Studien* 17 (1988), 391–433.
Gethmann-Siefert, Annemarie, "Das Klassische ist das Utopische: Überlegungen zu einer Kulturphilosophie der Kunst," in Rudolf

Bockholdt (ed.), *Über das Klassische* (Frankfurt/M.: Suhrkamp, 1987), pp. 47–76.
Geuss, Raymond, "Genealogy as Critique," *European Journal of Philosophy* 10 (2002), 209–15.
"Nietzsche and Genealogy," John Richardson and Brian Leiter (eds.), *Nietzsche* (Oxford: Oxford University Press, 2001), pp. 322–40.
Geyer, Michael, and Konrad H. Jarausch, *Shattered Past: Reconstructing German Histories* (Princeton, N.J.: Princeton University Press, 2002).
Geyer, Michael, "Historical Fictions of Autonomy and the Europeanisation of National History," *Central European History* 22 (1989), 316–42.
Gillespie, Michael Allen, *Nihilism before Nietzsche* (Chicago: University of Chicago Press, 1995).
Ginzburg, Carlo, "High and Low: The Theme of Forbidden Knowledge in the Sixteenth and Seventeenth Centuries," *Past and Present* 73 (1976), 28–41.
Gossman, Lionel, *Basel in the Age of Burckhardt: A Study in Unseasonable Ideas* (Chicago: University of Chicago Press, 2000).
"Orpheus Philologus:" Bachofen versus Mommsen on the Study of Antiquity (Philadelphia: Transactions of the American Philosophical Society, 1983).
Gottfried, Paul, "Arthur Schopenhauer as a Critic of History," *Journal of the History of Ideas* 36 (1975), 331–8.
Grab, Alexander, *Napoleon and the Transformation of Europe* (New York: Palgrave Macmillan, 2003).
Graf, Friedrich Wilhelm, "Protestantische Theologie in der Gesellschaft des Kaiserreichs," in Graf (ed.), *Profile des neuzeitlichen Protestantismus*, vol. II/1 (Gütersloh: Mohn, 1990–93), pp. 12–117.
Grafton, Anthony, "Polyhistor into Philolog: Notes on the Transformation of German Classical Scholarship, 1780–1850," *History of Universities* 3 (1983), 159–92.
Green, Abigail, *Fatherlands: State-Building and Nationhood in Nineteenth-Century Germany* (Cambridge: Cambridge University Press, 2001).
Greschat, Martin, "Protestantischer Antisemitismus in Wilhelminischer Zeit: Das Beispiel des Hofpredigers Adolf Stoecker," in Günter Brakelmann and Martin Rosowski (eds.), *Antisemitismus: Von religiöser Judenfeindschaft zur Rassenideologie* (Göttingen: Vandenhoeck & Ruprecht, 1989), pp. 27–51.
Grossfeld, Bernhard, and Ingo Theusinger, "Josef Kohler: Brückenbauer zwischen Jurisprudenz und Rechtsethnologie," *Rabels Zeitschrift für ausländisches und internationales Privatrecht* 64 (2000), 698–714.
Günther, Horst, *"Der Geist ist ein Wühler": Über Jacob Burckhardt* (Frankfurt/M.: Fischer Taschenbuch Verlag, 1997).
Günzel, Stephan, "Nietzsche's Geophilosophy," *Journal of Nietzsche Studies* 25 (2003), 78–91.

Gutzwiller, Hans, "Friedrich Nietzsches Lehrtätigkeit am Basler Pädagogium," *Basler Zeitschrift für Geschichte und Altertumskunde* 50 (1951), 148–224.
Habermas, Jürgen, "Modernity: An Unfinished Project," in Maurizio Passerin d'Entrèves and Seyla Benhabib (eds.), *Habermas and the Unfinished Project of Modernity: Critical Essays on "The Philosophical Discourse of Modernity"* (Cambridge, Mass.: MIT Press, 1997), pp. 38–57.
"Discourse Ethics: Notes on a Program of Philosophical Justification," in *Moral Consciousness and Communicative Action*, trans. Christian Lenhardt and Shierry Weber Nicholson, intro. Thomas McCarthy (Cambridge, Mass.: MIT Press, 1990), pp. 43–116.
The Structural Transformation of the Public Sphere, trans. Thomas Burger and Frederick Lawrence (Cambridge, Mass.: MIT Press, 1989).
Hagner, Michael, *Homo cerebralis: Der Wandel vom Seelenorgan zum Gehirn* (Berlin: Berlin Verlag, 1997).
Hallberg, Peter, "The Nature of Collective Individuals: J. G. Herder's Concept of Community," *History of European Ideas* 25 (1999), 291–304.
Hamlin, David, "Romanticism, Spectacle, and a Critique of Weimar Capitalism," *Central European History* 38 (2005), 250–68.
Hardtwig, Wolfgang, "Geschichtsreligion – Wissenschaft als Arbeit – Objektivität: Der Historismus in neuer Sicht," *Historische Zeitschrift* 252 (1991), 1–32.
"Bürgertum, Staatssymbolik und Staatsbewußtsein im Deutschen Kaiserreich, 1871–1914," *Geschichte und Gesellschaft* 16 (1990), 269–95.
Harris, Horton, *The Tübingen School: A Historical and Theological Investigation into the School of F. C. Baur* (Oxford: Clarendon Press, 1975).
Harrison, Peter, "Curiosity, Forbidden Knowledge, and the Reformation of Natural Philosophy in Early Modern England," *Isis* 92 (2001), 265–90.
Hatfield, Gary C., *The Natural and the Normative: Theories of Spatial Perception from Kant to Helmholtz* (Cambridge, Mass.: MIT Press, 1990).
Haugeland, John, "Mind Embodied and Embedded," in *Having Thought: Essays in the Metaphysics of Mind* (Cambridge, Mass.: Harvard University Press, 1998), pp. 207–37.
Havas, Randall, *Nietzsche's Genealogy: Nihilism and the Will to Knowledge* (Ithaca, N.Y.: Cornell University Press, 1995).
Heck, Kilian, "Das Fundament der Machtbehauptung: Die Ahnentafel als genealogische Grundstruktur der Neuzeit," in Sigrid Weigel (ed.), *Genealogie und Genetik: Schnittstellen zwischen Biologie und Kulturgeschichte* (Berlin: Akademie Verlag, 2002), pp. 45–56.
Heidegger, Martin, *Nietzsche* (Pfullingen: Neske, 1961).

Heidelberger, Michael, *Die innere Seite der Natur: Gustav Theodor Fechners wissenschaftlich-philosophische Weltauffassung* (Frankfurt/M.: Klostermann, 1993).
Hentschke, Ada, and Ulrich Muhlack, *Einführung in die Geschichte der Klassischen Philologie* (Darmstadt: Wissenschaftliche Buchgesellschaft, 1972).
Herter, Hans, "Aus der Geschichte der klassischen Philologie in Bonn," in *Kleine Schriften*, ed. Ernst Vogt (Munich: Wilhelm Fink, 1975), pp. 648–64.
Hill, R. Kevin, *Nietzsche's Critiques: The Kantian Foundations of His Thought* (Oxford: Clarendon Press, 2003).
Hinde, John R., "The Development of Jacob Burckhardt's Early Political Thought," *Journal of the History of Ideas* 53 (1992), 425–36.
Hirschfeld, Peter, "Karl Steffensen, 1816–1888: Ein Flensburger als Philosoph an der Universität Basel," *Basler Zeitschrift für Geschichte und Altertumskunde* 76 (1976), 19–75.
His, Eduard, "Friedrich Nietzsches Heimatlosigkeit," *Basler Zeitschrift für Geschichte und Altertumskunde* 40 (1941), 159–86.
Hochstrasser, T.J., *Natural Law Theories in the Early Enlightenment* (Cambridge: Cambridge University Press, 2000).
Hohorst, Gerd, Jürgen Kocka, and Gerhard A. Ritter (eds.), *Sozialgeschichtliches Arbeitsbuch: Materialien zur Statistik des Kaiserreichs 1870–1914* (Munich: C. H. Beck, 1975).
Hollingdale, R.J., *Nietzsche* (London: Routledge & Kegan Paul, 1973).
Hölscher, Lucian (ed., with Tillmann Bendikowski, Claudia Enders, and Markus Hoppe), *Datenatlas zur religiösen Geographie im protestantischen Deutschland: Von der Mitte des 19. Jahrhunderts bis zum Zweiten Weltkrieg* (Berlin: Walter de Gruyter, 2001).
Hölscher, Lucian, *Die Entdeckung der Zukunft* (Frankfurt/M.: Fischer Taschenbuch Verlag, 1999).
Weltgericht oder Revolution: Protestantische und sozialistische Zukunftsvorstellungen im deutschen Kaiserreich (Stuttgart: Klett-Cotta, 1989).
"Bürgerliche Religiösität im protestantischen Deutschland des 19. Jahrhunderts," in Wolfgang Schieder (ed.), *Religion und Gesellschaft im 19. Jahrhundert* (Stuttgart: Klett-Cotta, 1993), pp. 191–215.
Honig, Bonnie, *Political Theory and the Displacement of Politics* (Ithaca, N.Y.: Cornell University Press, 1993).
Horstmann, Axel, *Antike Theoria und moderne Wissenschaft: August Boeckhs Konzeption der Philologie* (Frankfurt/M.: Campus, 1992).
"Die 'Klassische Philologie' zwischen Humanismus und Historismus: Friedrich August Wolf und die Begründung der modernen Altertumswissenschaft," *Berichte zur Wissenschaftsgeschichte* 1 (1978), 51–78.

Howard, Thomas Albert, *W. M. L. de Wette, Jacob Burckhardt, and the Theological Origins of Nineteenth-Century Historical Consciousness* (New York: Cambridge University Press, 2000).
Hübinger, Gangolf, *Kulturprotestantismus und Politik: Zum Verhältnis von Liberalismus und Protestantismus im wilhelminischen Deutschland* (Tübingen: J. C. B. Mohr, 1994).
"Geschichte als leitende Orientierungswissenschaft im 19. Jahrhundert," *Berichte zur Wissenschaftsgeschichte* 11 (1988), 149–58.
Hübinger, Paul Egon, "Heinrich von Sybel und der Bonner Philologenkrieg," *Historisches Jahrbuch* 83 (1964), 162–216.
Hunt, Lester H., *Nietzsche and the Origin of Virtue* (London: Routledge, 1991).
"Politics and Anti-Politics: Nietzsche's View of the State," *History of Philosophy Quarterly* 2 (1985), 453–68.
Hunter, Ian, *Rival Enlightenments: Civil and Metaphysical Philosophy in Early Modern Germany* (Cambridge: Cambridge University Press, 2001).
Iggers, Georg G., *The German Conception of History: The National Tradition of Historical Thought from Herder to the Present*, 2nd, rev. edn. (Middletown, Conn.: Wesleyan University Press, 1983).
"Nationalism and Historiography, 1789–1996: The German Example in Historical Perspective," in Stefan Berger, Mark Donovan, and Kevin Passmore (eds.), *Writing National Histories: Western Europe since 1800* (London: Routledge, 1999), pp. 15–29.
"The University of Göttingen 1760–1800 and the Transformation of Historical Scholarship," *Storia della Storiografia* 2 (1982), 11–37.
Jaeger, Friedrich, and Jörn Rüsen, *Geschichte des Historismus: Eine Einführung* (Munich: C. H. Beck, 1992).
Jaeger, Friedrich, *Bürgerliche Modernisierungskrise und historische Sinnbildung: Kulturgeschichte bei Droysen, Burckhardt und Max Weber* (Göttingen: Vandenhoeck & Ruprecht, 1994).
"Geschichtsphilosophie, Hermeneutik und Kontingenz in der Geschichte des Historismus," in Wolfgang Küttler, Jörn Rüsen, and Ernst Schulin (eds.), *Geschichtsdiskurs, III: Die Epoche der Historisierung* (Frankfurt/M.: Fischer Taschenbuch Verlag, 1997), pp. 45–66.
Janaway, Christopher, *Beyond Selflessness: Reading Nietzsche's Genealogy* (Oxford: Oxford University Press, 2007).
(ed.), *Willing and Nothingness: Schopenhauer as Nietzsche's Educator* (Oxford: Clarendon Press, 1998).
Self and World in Schopenhauer's Philosophy (Oxford: Clarendon Press, 1989).
"Naturalism and Genealogy," in Keith Ansell-Pearson (ed.), *A Companion to Nietzsche* (Oxford: Blackwell, 2006), pp. 337–52.

Janz, Curt Paul, *Friedrich Nietzsche: Eine Biographie* (Munich: Hanser, 1978–79).
"Die Berufung Franz Overbecks an die Universität Basel 1870," *Basler Zeitschrift für Geschichte und Altertumskunde* 92 (1982), 139–65.
Jarausch, Konrad H., *Students, Society, and Politics in Imperial Germany: The Rise of Academic Illiberalism* (Princeton, N.J.: Princeton University Press, 1982).
Kalb, Christof, *Desintegration: Studien zu Friedrich Nietzsches Leib- und Sprachphilosophie* (Frankfurt/M.: Suhrkamp, 2000).
Kampe, Norbert, *Studenten und "Judenfrage" im Deutschen Kaiserreich: Die Entstehung einer akademischen Trägerschicht des Antisemitismus* (Göttingen: Vandenhoeck & Ruprecht, 1988).
Kaufmann, Thomas DaCosta, "Antiquarianism, the History of Objects, and the History of Art before Winckelmann," *Journal of the History of Ideas* 62 (2001), 523–41.
Kekes, John, *Facing Evil* (Princeton, N.J.: Princeton University Press, 1990).
Kiesow, Rainer Maria, *Das Naturgesetz des Rechts* (Frankfurt/M.: Suhrkamp, 1997).
Kippenberg, Hans G., "Survivals: Conceiving of Religious History in an Age of Development," in Arie L. Molendijk and Peter Pels (eds.), *Religion in the Making: The Emergence of the Sciences of Religion* (Leiden: Brill, 1998), pp. 297–312.
Kittsteiner, Heinz-Dieter, *Die Entstehung des modernen Gewissens* (Frankfurt/M.: Insel, 1991).
"Erinnern – Vergessen – Orientieren: Nietzsches Begriff des 'umhüllenden Wahns' als geschichtsphilosophische Kategorie," in Dieter Borchmeyer (ed.), *"Vom Nutzen und Nachteil der Historie für das Leben": Nietzsche und die Erinnerung in der Moderne* (Frankfurt/M.: Suhrkamp, 1996), pp. 48–75.
Kleingeld, Pauline, "Approaching Perpetual Peace: Kant's Defence of a League of States and his Ideal of a World Federation," *European Journal of Philosophy* 12 (2004), 304–25.
"Six Varieties of Cosmopolitanism in Late Eighteenth-Century Germany," *Journal of the History of Ideas* 60 (1999), 505–24.
Klenke, Dietmar, "Nationalkriegerisches Gemeinschaftsideal als politische Religion: Zum Vereinsnationalismus der Sänger, Schützen und Turner am Vorabend der Einigungskriege," *Historische Zeitschrift* 260 (1995), 395–448.
Kocka, Jürgen, "Bildungsbürgertum: Gesellschaftliche Formation oder Historikerkonstrukt?" in Werner Conze, Jürgen Kocka, Reinhart Koselleck, and M. Rainer Lepsius (eds.), *Bildungsbürgertum im 19. Jahrhundert*, vol. IV (Stuttgart: Klett-Cotta, 1985–92), pp. 9–20.

Kofman, Sarah, *Nietzsche and Metaphor*, trans. Duncan Large (Stanford, Calif.: Stanford University Press, 1993).
Köhnke, Klaus Christian, *Entstehung und Aufstieg des Neukantianismus: Die deutsche Universitätsphilosophie zwischen Idealismus und Positivismus* (Frankfurt/M.: Suhrkamp, 1986).
Kollander, Patricia, "Constitutionalism or *Staatsstreich*? Bismarck, Crown Prince Frederick William, Crown Princess Victoria and the Succession Crisis of 1880–85," *European Review of History* 8 (2001), 187–201.
Kopperschmidt, Josef, and Helmut Schanze (eds.), *Nietzsche oder "Die Sprache ist Rhetorik"* (Munich: Wilhelm Fink, 1994).
Korsgaard, Christine M., *The Sources of Normativity* (Cambridge: Cambridge University Press, 1996).
Koselleck, Reinhart, *Critique and Crisis: Enlightenment and the Pathogenesis of Modern Society* (Oxford: Berg, 1988).
"Historia Magistra Vitae: The Dissolution of the Topos into the Perspective of a Modernized Historical Process," in *Futures Past: On the Semantics of Historical Time*, trans. Keith Tribe (Cambridge, Mass.: MIT Press, 1985), pp. 21–38.
Koshar, Rudy, *From Monuments to Traces: Artifacts of German Memory, 1870–1990* (Berkeley, Calif.: University of California Press, 2000).
Koskenniemi, Martti, *The Gentle Civilizer of Nations: The Rise and Fall of International Law, 1870–1960* (Cambridge: Cambridge University Press, 2002).
Kremer-Marietti, Angèle, *Nietzsche et la rhétorique* (Paris: P. U. F., 1992).
Kuehn, Manfred, *Kant: A Biography* (Cambridge: Cambridge University Press, 2001).
Kuhn, Thomas S., *The Structure of Scientific Revolutions*, 3rd edn. (Chicago: University of Chicago Press, 1996).
Landfester, Manfred, *Humanismus und Gesellschaft im 19. Jahrhundert: Untersuchungen zur politischen und gesellschaftlichen Bedeutung der humanistischen Bildung in Deutschland* (Darmstadt: Wissenschaftliche Buchgesellschaft, 1988).
Lanfranconi, Aldo, *Nietzsches historische Philosophie* (Stuttgart: Frommann-Holzboog, 2000).
Langer, Ulrich, *Heinrich von Treitschke: Politische Biographie eines deutschen Nationalisten* (Düsseldorf: Droste, 1998).
LaVopa, Anthony J., "Specialists against Specialization: Hellenism as Professional Ideology in German Classical Studies," in Geoffrey Cocks and Konrad H. Jarausch (eds.), *German Professions, 1800–1950* (New York: Oxford University Press, 1990), pp. 27–45.
Leiter, Brian, *Nietzsche on Morality* (London: Routledge, 2002).
"Morality in the Pejorative Sense: On the Logic of Nietzsche's Critique of Morality," *British Journal for the History of Philosophy* 3 (1995), 113–45.

"Nietzsche and Aestheticism," *Journal of the History of Philosophy* 20 (1992), 275–90.

Lenoir, Timothy, *Politik im Tempel der Wissenschaft: Forschung und Machtausübung im deutschen Kaiserreich* (Frankfurt/M.: Campus, 1992).

The Strategy of Life: Teleology and Mechanics in Nineteenth-Century German Biology (Dordrecht: Reidel, 1982).

Leventhal, Robert S., "The Emergence of Philological Discourse in Germany, 1700–1810," *Isis* 77 (1986), 243–60.

Liebel, Helen P., "Philosophical Idealism in the *Historische Zeitschrift*, 1859–1914," *History and Theory* 3 (1964), 316–30.

Lindenfeld, David F., *The Practical Imagination: The German Sciences of the State in the Nineteenth Century* (Chicago: University of Chicago Press, 1997).

Löwith, Karl, *From Hegel to Nietzsche: The Revolution in Nineteenth-Century Thought*, 2nd edn. (New York: Columbia University Press, 1991).

Lützeler, Paul Michael, *Die Schriftsteller und Europa: Von der Romantik bis zur Gegenwart*, 2nd edn. (Baden-Baden: Nomos, 1998).

McClelland, Charles E., *State, Society, and University in Germany, 1700–1914* (Cambridge: Cambridge University Press, 1980).

McDowell, John, "Two Sorts of Naturalism," in *Mind, Value, and Reality* (Cambridge, Mass.: Harvard University Press, 1998), pp. 167–97.

Mind and World, with a new introduction (Cambridge, Mass.: Harvard University Press, 1996).

Makkreel, Rudolf A., *Interpretation and Imagination in Kant: The Hermeneutical Import of the "Critique of Judgment"* (Chicago: Chicago University Press, 1990).

Malitz, Jürger, "Theodor Mommsen und Wilamowitz," in William M. Calder III, Hellmut Flashar, and Theodor Lindken (eds.), *Wilamowitz nach 50 Jahren* (Darmstadt: Wissenschaftliche Buchgesellschaft, 1985), pp. 31–55.

Mansfeld, Jaap, "The Wilamowitz-Nietzsche Struggle: Another New Document and Some Further Comments," *Nietzsche-Studien* 15 (1986), 43–58.

Marchand, Suzanne L., *Down from Olympus: Archaeology and Philhellenism in Germany, 1750–1970* (Princeton, N.J.: Princeton University Press, 1996).

Marquard, Odo, "Indicted and Unburdened Man in Eighteenth-Century Philosophy," in *Farewell to Matters of Principle: Philosophical Studies*, trans. Robert M. Wallace, Susan Bernstein, and James I. Porter (Oxford: Oxford University Press, 1989), pp. 38–63.

"Kompensation – Überlegungen zu einer Verlaufsfigur geschichtlicher Prozesse," in *Aesthetica und Anaesthetica: Philosophische Überlegungen* (Paderborn: Schöningh, 1989), pp. 64–81.

Marti, Urs, *"Der grosse Pöbel- und Sklavenaufstand": Nietzsches Auseinandersetzung mit Revolution und Demokratie* (Stuttgart: J. B. Metzler, 1993).

Martin, Nicholas, *Nietzsche and Schiller: Untimely Aesthetics* (Oxford: Clarendon Press, 1996).
"'We Good Europeans': Nietzsche's New Europe in *Beyond Good and Evil*," *History of European Ideas* 20 (1995), 141–4.
May, Simon, *Nietzsche's Ethics and his War on "Morality"* (Oxford: Clarendon Press, 1999).
Megill, Allan, *Prophets of Extremity: Nietzsche, Heidegger, Foucault, Derrida* (Berkeley, Calif.: University of California Press, 1985).
"Why was There a Crisis of Historicism," *History and Theory* 36 (1997), 416–29.
Meister, Richard, "Nietzsches Lehrtätigkeit in Basel 1869–1879," *Anzeiger der Österreichischen Akademie der Wissenschaften: Phil.-Hist. Klasse* 85 (1948), 103–21.
Metz, Karl H., "The Politics of Conflict: Heinrich von Treitschke and the Idea of *Realpolitik*," *History of Political Thought* 3 (1982), 269–84.
Moggach, Douglas, *The Philosophy and Politics of Bruno Bauer* (Cambridge: Cambridge University Press, 2003).
Mommsen, Wolfgang J., *Imperial Germany, 1867–1918: Politics, Culture, and Society in an Authoritarian State*, trans. Richard Deveson (London: Arnold, 1995).
Moore, Gregory, *Nietzsche, Biology, and Metaphor* (Cambridge: Cambridge University Press, 2002).
Moran, Dermot, *Introduction to Phenomenology* (London: Routledge, 2000).
Morus, Iwan Rhys, *Frankenstein's Children: Electricity, Exhibition, and Experiment in Nineteenth-Century London* (Princeton N.J.: Princeton University Press, 1998).
Most, Glenn W., "One Hundred Years of Fractiousness: Disciplining Polemics in Nineteenth-Century German Classical Scholarship," *Transactions of the American Philological Association* 127 (1997), 349–61.
Mouffe, Chantal, *On the Political* (London: Routledge, 2005).
Muhlack, Ulrich, "Bildung zwischen Neuhumanismus und Historismus," in Werner Conze, Jürgen Kocka, Reinhart Koselleck, and M. Rainer Lepsius (eds.), *Bildungsbürgertum im 19. Jahrhundert*, vol. II (Stuttgart: Klett-Cotta, 1985–92), pp. 80–105.
Müller-Lauter, Wolfgang, *Nietzsche: His Philosophy of Contradictions and the Contradictions of his Philosophy*, trans. David J. Parent (Urbana, Ill.: University of Illinois Press, 1999).
"Nihilismus," in: Joachim Ritter, Karlfried Gründer, and Gottfried Gabriel (eds.), *Historisches Wörterbuch der Philosophie*, (Basel: Schwabe & Co., 1971–), vol. IV, cols. 846–54.
Nehamas, Alexander, *Nietzsche: Life as Literature* (Cambridge, Mass.: Harvard University Press, 1985).
Neiman, Susan, *Evil in Modern Thought: An Alternative History of Philosophy* (Princeton, N.J.: Princeton University Press, 2002).

Nipperdey, Thomas, *Deutsche Geschichte, 1866–1918* (Munich: C. H. Beck, 1990–92).
Deutsche Geschichte, 1800–1866: Bürgerwelt und starker Staat (Munich: C. H. Beck, 1983).
"Nationalidee und Nationaldenkmal in Deutschland im 19. Jahrhundert," in *Gesellschaft, Kultur, Theorie: Gesammelte Aufsätze zur neueren Geschichte* (Göttingen: Vandenhoeck & Ruprecht, 1976), pp. 133–73.
Nipperdey, Thomas, and Reinhard Rürup, "Antisemitismus," in Otto Brunner, Werner Conze, and Reinhart Koselleck (eds.), *Geschichtliche Grundbegriffe: Historisches Lexikon zur politischen Sprache in Deutschland* (Stuttgart: Klett-Cotta, 1972–97) vol. I, pp. 129–53.
Nisbet H. B., "Naturgeschichte und Humangeschichte bei Goethe, Herder und Kant," in Peter Matussek (ed.), *Goethe und die Verzeitlichung der Natur* (Munich: C. H. Beck, 1998), pp. 15–43.
Noakes, Richard, "'Instruments to Lay Hold of Spirits': Technologising the Bodies of Victorian Spiritualism," in Iwan Rhys Morus (ed.), *Bodies/Machines* (Oxford: Berg, 2002), pp. 125–63.
Nussbaum, Martha, "Is Nietzsche a Political Thinker?" *International Journal of Philosophical Studies* 5 (1997), 1–13.
Nyhart, Lynn K., *Biology Takes Form: Animal Morphology and the German Universities, 1800–1900* (Chicago: University of Chicago Press, 1995).
Oexle, Otto Gerhard, "Naturwissenschaft und Geschichtswissenschaft: Momente einer Problemgeschichte," in Oexle (ed.), *Naturwissenschaft, Geisteswissenschaft, Kulturwissenschaft: Einheit, Gegensatz, Komplementarität?* 2nd edn. (Göttingen: Wallstein, 2000), pp. 99–151.
"Von Nietzsche zu Max Weber: Wertproblem und Objektivitätsforderung der Wissenschaft im Zeichen des Historismus," in *Geschichtswissenschaft im Zeichen des Historismus: Studien zu Problemgeschichten der Moderne* (Göttingen: Vandenhoeck & Ruprecht, 1996), pp. 73–94.
Olábarri, Ignacio, "'New' New History: A longue durée Structure," *History and Theory* 34 (1995), 1–29.
Orsucci, Andrea, *Orient – Okzident: Nietzsches Versuch einer Loslösung vom europäischen Weltbild* (Berlin: Walter de Gruyter, 1996).
Otis, Laura, *Organic Memory: History and the Body in the Late Nineteenth and Early Twentieth Centuries* (Lincoln: University of Nebraska Press, 1994).
Ottmann, Henning, *Philosophie und Politik bei Nietzsche* (Berlin: Walter de Gruyter, 1987).
Owen, David, "Nietzsche, Re-evaluation and the Turn to Genealogy," *European Journal of Philosophy* 11 (2003), 249–72.
"Equality, Democracy, and Self-Respect: Reflections on Nietzsche's Agonal Perfectionism," *Journal of Nietzsche Studies* 24 (2002), 113–31.
Ozouf, Mona, *La fête revolutionnaire, 1789–1799* (Paris: Gallimard, 1976).

Pagden, Anthony, "Europe: Conceptualizing a Continent," in Pagden (ed.), *The Idea of Europe: From Antiquity to the European Union* (Cambridge: Cambridge University Press, 2002), pp. 33–54.
Parkes, Graham, "Wanderers in the Shadow of Nihilism: Nietzsche's Good Europeans," *History of European Ideas* 16 (1993), 585–90.
Parr, Rolf, *"Zwei Seelen wohnen, ach! in meiner Brust:" Strukturen und Funktionen der Mythisierung Bismarcks, 1860–1918* (Munich: Wilhelm Fink, 1992).
Peter, Niklaus, *Im Schatten der Modernität: Franz Overbecks Weg zur "Christlichkeit unserer heutigen Theologie"* (Stuttgart: J. B. Metzler, 1992).
Pfotenhauer, Helmut, *Die Kunst als Physiologie: Nietzsches ästhetische Theorie und literarische Produktion* (Stuttgart: J. B. Metzler, 1985).
Pinkard, Terry, *German Philosophy, 1760–1860: The Legacy of Idealism* (Cambridge: Cambridge University Press, 2002).
Pocock, J. G. A., *The Machiavellian Moment: Florentine Political Thought and the Atlantic Republican Tradition* (Princeton, N. J.: Princeton University Press, 1975).
"Deconstructing Europe," *History of European Ideas* 18 (1994), 329–46.
Poellner, Peter, *Nietzsche and Metaphysics* (Oxford: Oxford University Press, 1995).
Pohl, Martin, *Aufklärung und Aberglaube: Die deutsche Frühaufklärung im Spiegel ihrer Aberglaubenskritik* (Tübingen: Niemeyer, 1992).
Porter, James I., *Nietzsche and the Philology of the Future* (Stanford, Calif.: Stanford University Press, 2000).
The Invention of Dionysus: An Essay on the Birth of Tragedy (Stanford, Calif.: Stanford University Press, 2000).
Pulzer, Peter, *The Rise of Political Anti-Semitism in Germany and Austria*, rev. edn. (Cambridge, Mass.: Harvard University Press, 1988).
Putnam, Hilary, "Why Reason Can't be Naturalized," in *Realism and Reason: Philosophical Papers*, 3 (Cambridge: Cambridge University Press, 1983), pp. 229–47.
Quine W. V. O., "Epistemology Naturalized," in *Ontological Relativity and Other Essays* (New York: Columbia University Press, 1969), pp. 69–90.
Rahden, Wolfert von, "Orte des Bösen: Aufstieg und Fall des dämonologischen Dispositivs," in Alexander Schuller and Wolfert von Rahden (eds.), *Die andere Kraft: Orte des Bösen* (Berlin: Akademie Verlag, 1993), pp. 26–54.
Railton, Peter, *Facts, Values, and Norms: Essays Toward a Morality of Consequence* (Cambridge: Cambridge University Press, 2003).
Randa, Hermann, *Nietzsche, Overbeck und Basel* (Berne: Haupt, 1937).
Rawls, John, *A Theory of Justice* (Oxford: Oxford University Press, 1972).
Rebenich, Stefan, *Theodor Mommsen: Eine Biographie* (Munich: C. H. Beck, 2002).

Reginster, Bernard, *The Affirmation of Life: Nietzsche on Overcoming Nihilism* (Cambridge, Mass.: Harvard University Press, 2006).
Reibnitz, Barbara von, *Ein Kommentar zu Friedrich Nietzsche, "Die Geburt der Tragödie aus dem Geiste der Musik" (Kap. 1–12)* (Stuttgart: J. B. Metzler, 1992).
"Otto Jahn bei Friedrich Nietzsche: Der 'Grenzbotenheld' als Wagner-Kritiker," in William Calder III, Hubert Cancik, and Bernhard Kystler (eds.), *Otto Jahn (1813–1869): Ein Geisteswissenschaftler zwischen Klassizismus und Historismus* (Stuttgart: Steiner, 1991), pp. 204–33.
"Nietzsches *Griechischer Staat* und das Deutsche Kaiserreich," *Der altsprachliche Unterricht* 30/3 (1987), 76–89.
Reill, Peter Hanns, *The German Enlightenment and the Rise of Historicism* (Berkeley, Calif.: University of California Press, 1975).
Ribbart, Christoph, *Religiöse Erregung: Protestantische Schwärmer im Kaiserreich* (Frankfurt/M.: Campus, 1996).
Ribbeck, Otto, *Friedrich Wilhelm Ritschl: Ein Beitrag zur Geschichte der Philologie* (Leipzig: Teubner, 1879–81).
Richards, Robert J., *The Romantic Conception of Life: Science and Philosophy in the Age of Goethe* (Chicago: University of Chicago Press, 2002).
Richardson, John, *Nietzsche's New Darwinism* (Oxford: Oxford University Press, 2004).
Riedel, Manfred, *Nietzsche in Weimar* (Leipzig: Reclam, 1997).
"Ein Seitenstück zur *Geburt der Tragödie*: Nietzsches Abkehr von Schopenhauer und Wagner und seine Wende zur Philosophie," *Nietzsche-Studien* 24 (1995), 45–61.
"Nihilismus," in Otto Brunner, Werner Conze, and Reinhart Koselleck (eds.), *Geschichtliche Grundbegriffe: Historisches Lexikon zur politischen Sprache in Deutschland* (Stuttgart: Klett-Cotta, 1972–97), vol. IV, pp. 371–411.
Ringer, Fritz K., *The Decline of the German Mandarins: The German Academic Community, 1890–1933* (Cambridge, Mass.: Harvard University Press, 1969).
Risse, Mathias, "'The Second Treatise' in *On the Genealogy of Morality*: Nietzsche on the Origin of the Bad Conscience," *European Journal of Philosophy* 9 (2001), 55–81.
Roberts, David D., *Nothing But History: Reconstruction and Extremity after Metaphysics* (Berkeley, Calif.: University of California Press, 1995).
Roggenbuck, Simone, "Die genealogische Idee in der vergleichenden Sprachwissenschaft des 19. Jahrhunderts: Stufen, Stammbäume, Wellen," in: Sigrid Weigel, Ohad Parnes, Ulrike Vedder, and Stefan Willer (eds.), *Generation: Zur Genealogie des Konzepts – Konzepte von Genealogie* (Munich: Wilhelm Fink, 2005), pp. 289–314.
Rose, Paul Lawrence, *Revolutionary Antisemitism in Germany from Kant to Wagner* (Princeton, N. J.: Princeton University Press, 1990).

Rosenberg, Alexander, "Normative Naturalism and the Role of Philosophy," *Philosophy of Science* 57 (1990), 34–43.
Rouse, Joseph, *How Scientific Practices Matter: Reclaiming Philosophical Naturalism* (Chicago: University of Chicago Press, 2002).
"Beyond Epistemic Sovereignty," in Peter Galison and David J. Strump (eds.), *The Disunity of Science: Boundaries, Contexts, and Power* (Stanford, Calif.: Stanford University Press, 1996), pp. 398–416.
Rowe, Michael, *From Reich to State: The Rhineland in the Revolutionary Age, 1780–1830* (Cambridge: Cambridge University Press, 2003).
Ruehl, Martin A., "*Politeia* 1871: Young Nietzsche and the Greek State," in Paul Bishop (ed.), *Nietzsche and Antiquity: His Reaction and Response to the Classical Tradition* (Rochester, N.Y.: Camden House, 2004), pp. 79–97.
"Basel and Nietzsche," *Nietzsche-Studien* 30 (2001), 499–503.
Salaquarda, Jörg, "Studien zur zweiten Unzeitgemäßen Betrachtung," *Nietzsche-Studien* 13 (1984), 1–45.
Sallis, John, *Crossings: Nietzsche and the Space of Tragedy* (Chicago: University of Chicago Press, 1991).
Sarasin, Philipp, *Stadt der Bürger: Struktureller Wandel und bürgerliche Lebenswelt, Basel 1870–1900* (Basel: Helbing & Lichtenhahn, 1996).
Schacht, Richard, *Nietzsche* (London: Routledge, 1983).
"Nietzschean Normativity," in Schacht (ed.), *Nietzsche's Postmoralism: Essays on Nietzsche's Prelude to Philosophy's Future* (Cambridge: Cambridge University Press, 2001), pp. 149–80.
Schellack, Fritz, "Sedan- und Kaisergeburtstagsfeste," in Dieter Düding, Peter Friedemann, and Paul Münch (eds.), *Öffentliche Festkultur: Politische Feste in Deutschland von der Aufklärung bis zum ersten Weltkrieg* (Reinbeck: Rowolth, 1988), pp. 278–97.
Schieder, Theodor, "Die deutsche Geschichtswissenschaft im Spiegel der *Historischen Zeitschrift*," *Historische Zeitschrift* 189 (1959), 1–104.
Schiera, Pierangelo, *Laboratorium der bürgerlichen Welt: Deutsche Wissenschaft im 19. Jahrhundert* (Frankfurt/M.: Suhrkamp, 1992).
Schild, Wolfgang, "Verstümmelung des menschlichen Körpers," in Richard van Dülmen (ed.), *Erfindung des Menschen: Schöpfungsträume und Körperbilder, 1500–2000* (Vienna: Böhlau, 1998), pp. 261–81.
"Der gequälte und entehrte Leib," in Klaus Schreiner and Norbert Schnitzler (eds.), *Gepeinigt, begehrt, vergessen: Symbolik und Sozialbezug des Körpers im späten Mittelalter und in der frühen Neuzeit* (Munich: Wilhelm Fink, 1992), pp. 149–68.
Schlesier, Renate, *Kulte, Mythen und Gelehrte: Anthropologie der Antike seit 1800* (Frankfurt/M.: Fischer Taschenbuch Verlag, 1994).
Schluchter, Wolfgang, "Conviction and Responsibility: Max Weber on Ethics," in *Paradoxes of Modernity: Culture and Conduct in the Theory of Max Weber*, trans. Neil Solomon (Stanford, Calif.: Stanford University Press, 1996), pp. 48–101.

Schnädelbach, Herbert, *Philosophy in Germany, 1831–1933*, trans. Eric Matthews (Cambridge: Cambridge University Press, 1984).
Geschichtsphilosophie nach Hegel: Die Probleme des Historismus (Freiburg/Br.: Alber, 1974).
Schneider, Jörg, "Nietzsches Basler Vorträge *Ueber die Zukunft unserer Bildungsanstalten* im Lichte seiner Lektüre pädagogischer Literatur," *Nietzsche-Studien* 21 (1992), 308–25.
Schneider, Ulrich Johannes, *Philosophie und Universität: Die Historisierung der Vernunft im 19. Jahrhundert* (Hamburg: Meiner, 1999).
Scholtz, Gunter, *Ethik und Hermeneutik: Schleiermacher's Grundlegung der Geisteswissenschaften* (Frankfurt/M.: Suhrkamp, 1995).
Zwischen Wissenschaftsanspruch und Orientierungsbedürfnis: Zu Grundlage und Wandel der Geisteswissenschaften (Frankfurt/M.: Suhrkamp, 1991).
Schorske, Carl E., "History as Vocation in Burckhardt's Basel," in *Thinking with History: Explorations in the Passage to Modernity* (Princeton, N.J.: Princeton University Press, 1998), pp. 56–70.
Schrift, Alan D., "Nietzsche for Democracy?" *Nietzsche-Studien* 29 (2000), 220–33.
"Between Perspectivism and Philology: Genealogy as Hermeneutic," *Nietzsche-Studien* 16 (1987), 91–111.
Schroeder, Paul W., "The Nineteenth-Century System: Balance of Power or Political Equilibrium?" in David Wetzler, Robert Jervis, and Jack S. Levy (eds.), *Systems, Stability, and Statecraft: Essays on the International History of Modern Europe* (New York: Palgrave Macmillan, 2004), pp. 223–41.
"International Politics, Peace, and War, 1815–1914," in T. C. W. Blanning (ed.), *The Nineteenth Century: Europe, 1789–1914* (Oxford: Oxford University Press, 2000), pp. 158–209.
The Transformation of European Politics, 1763–1848 (Oxford: Oxford University Press, 1994).
"Did the Vienna Settlement Rest on a Balance of Power?" *American Historical Review* 97 (1993), 683–706.
Schutte, Ofelia, *Beyond Nihilism: Nietzsche without Masks* (Chicago: Chicago University Press, 1985).
"The Place of History in Nietzsche's Thought," in Bernard P. Dauenhauer (ed.), *At the Nexus of Philosophy and History* (Athens, Ga.: University of Georgia Press, 1987), pp. 97–115.
Schwenke, Heiner, *Zurück zur Wirklichkeit: Bewusstsein und Erkenntnis bei Gustav Teichmüller* (Basel: Schwabe, 2006).
Seier, Hellmut, "Sybels Vorlesung über Politik und die Kontinuität des 'staatsbildenden' Liberalismus," *Historische Zeitschrift* 187 (1959), 90–112.
Seifert, Arno, "Von der heiligen zur philosophischen Geschichte: Die Rationalisierung der universalhistorischen Erkenntnis im

Zeitalter der Aufklärung," *Archiv für Kulturgeschichte* 68 (1986), 81–117.
Shaw, Tamsin, *Nietzsche's Political Skepticism* (Princeton, N.J.: Princeton University Press, 2007)
"Nietzsche and the Self-Destruction of Secular Religions," *History of European Ideas* 32 (2006), 80–98.
Silk, M. S., and J. P. Stern, *Nietzsche on Tragedy* (Cambridge: Cambridge University Press, 1981).
Simmonds, N. E., *Central Issues in Jurisprudence: Justice, Law and Right* (London: Sweet & Maxwell, 1992).
Skinner, Quentin, *Visions of Politics, Volume 1: Regarding Method* (Cambridge: Cambridge University Press, 2002).
Liberty before Liberalism (Cambridge: Cambridge University Press, 1997).
Small, Robin, *Nietzsche and Rée: A Star Friendship* (Oxford: Clarendon Press, 2005).
Nietzsche in Context (Aldershot: Ashgate, 2001).
Smith, Anthony D., *Myths and Memories of the Nation* (Oxford: Oxford University Press, 1999).
Smith, Helmut Walser, *German Nationalism and Religious Conflict: Culture, Ideology, Politics, 1870–1914* (Princeton, N.J.: Princeton University Press, 1995).
Smith, Woodruff D., *Politics and the Sciences of Culture in Germany, 1840–1920* (New York: Oxford University Press, 1991).
Sommer, Andreas Urs, *Der Geist der Historie und das Ende des Christentums: Zur "Waffengenossenschaft" von Friedrich Nietzsche und Franz Overbeck, mit einem Anhang unpublizierter Texte aus Overbecks "Kirchenlexicon"* (Berlin: Akademie Verlag, 1997).
Spiekermann, Uwe, "Display Windows and Window Displays in German Cities of the Nineteenth Century: Towards the History of a Commercial Breakthrough," in Clemens Wischermann and Elliot Shore (eds.), *Advertising and the European City: Historical Perspectives* (Aldershot: Ashgate, 2000), pp. 139–71.
Stack, George J., "Kant, Lange, and Nietzsche: Critique of Knowledge," in Keith Ansell-Pearson (ed.), *Nietzsche and Modern German Thought* (London: Routledge, 1991), pp. 30–58.
Lange and Nietzsche (Berlin: Walter de Gruyter, 1983).
Stingelin, Martin, "Konkordanz zu Friedrich Nietzsches Exzerpten aus Albert Hermann Post, *Bausteine für eine allgemeine Rechtswissenschaft auf vergleichend-ethnologischer Basis*, Oldenburg 1880/81 (2 Bde.), im Nachlaß vom Frühjahr-Sommer und Sommer 1883," *Nietzsche-Studien* 20 (1991), 400–32.
Stollberg-Rilinger, Barbara, *Der Staat als Maschine: Zur politischen Metaphorik des absoluten Fürstenstaates* (Berlin: Duncker & Humblot, 1986).

Strong, Tracy B., *Friedrich Nietzsche and the Politics of Transfiguration*, enlarged edn. (Berkeley, Calif.: University of California Press, 1988).
Taylor, Charles, *Hegel* (Cambridge: Cambridge University Press, 1975).
"Modern Social Imaginaries," *Public Culture* 14 (2002), 91–124.
Thatcher, David S., "*Zur Genealogie der Moral*: Some Textual Annotations," *Nietzsche-Studien* 18 (1989), 587–99.
"Nietzsche's Debt to Lubbock," *Journal of the History of Ideas* 44 (1983), 293–309.
Thiele, Leslie Paul, *Friedrich Nietzsche and the Politics of the Soul: A Study of Heroic Individualism* (Princeton, N.J.: Princeton University Press, 1990).
Toews, John E., *Becoming Historical: Cultural Reformation and Public Memory in Early Nineteenth-Century Germany* (Cambridge: Cambridge University Press, 2004).
Traeger, Jörg, *Der Weg nach Walhalla: Denkmallandschaft und Bildungsreise im 19. Jahrhundert* (Regensburg: Bernhard Bosse, 1987).
Tribe, Keith, *Strategies of Economic Order: German Economic Discourse, 1750–1950* (Cambridge: Cambridge University Press, 1995).
Trigger, Bruce G., *A History of Archaeological Thought* (Cambridge: Cambridge University Press, 1989).
Tuck, Richard, *Philosophy and Government, 1572–1651* (Cambridge: Cambridge University Press, 1993).
Tucker, Aviezer, *Our Knowledge of the Past: A Philosophy of Historiography* (Cambridge: Cambridge University Press, 2004).
Tully, James, *Strange Multiplicity: Constitutionalism in an Age of Diversity* (Cambridge: Cambridge University Press, 1995).
"The Kantian Idea of Europe: Critical and Cosmopolitan Perspectives," in Anthony Pagden (ed.), *The Idea of Europe: From Antiquity to the European Union* (Cambridge: Cambridge University Press, 2002), pp. 331–58.
"The Pen is a Mighty Sword: Quentin Skinner's Analysis of Politics," in Tully (ed.), *Meaning and Context: Quentin Skinner and His Critics* (Princeton, N.J.: Princeton University Press, 1989), pp. 7–25.
Umbach, Maiken, "History and Federalism in the Age of Nation-State Formation," in Umbach (ed.), *German Federalism: Past, Present, Future* (Basingstoke: Palgrave, 2002), pp. 42–69.
Veit-Brause, Irmline, "Scientists and the Politics of Academic Disciplines in Late 19th-Century Germany: Emil DuBois-Reymond and the Controversy over the Role of the Cultural Sciences," *History of the Human Sciences* 14/4 (2001), 31–56.
Vick, Brian, "Greek Origins and Organic Metaphors: Ideals of Cultural Autonomy in Neo-Humanist Germany from Winckelmann to Curtius," *Journal of the History of Ideas*, 63 (2002), 483–500.
Vierhaus, Rudolf, "Bildung," in Otto Brunner, Werner Conze, and Reinhart Koselleck (eds.), *Geschichtliche Grundbegriffe: Historisches*

Lexikon zur politischen Sprache in Deutschland (Stuttgart: Klett-Cotta, 1972–97), vol. I, pp. 508–51.

Villa, Dana R., "Democratizing the Agon: Nietzsche, Arendt, and the Agonistic Tendency in Recent Political Theory," in Alan D. Schrift (ed.), *Why Nietzsche Still? Reflections on Drama, Culture, and Politics* (Berkeley, Calif.: University of California Press, 2000), pp. 224–46.

Viroli, Maurizio, *From Politics to Reason of State: The Acquisition and Transformation of the Language of Politics, 1250–1600* (Cambridge: Cambridge University Press, 1992).

Vogt, Ernst, "Der Methodenstreit zwischen Hermann und Boeckh und seine Bedeutung für die Geschichte der Philologie," in Hellmut Flashar, Karlfried Gründer, and Axel Horstmann (eds.), *Philologie und Hermeneutik im 19. Jahrhundert* (Göttingen: Vandenhoeck & Ruprecht, 1979), pp. 103–21.

Voßkamp, Wilhelm, "Klassik als Epoche," in Reinhardt Herzog and Reinhardt Koselleck (eds.), *Epochenschwelle und Epochenbewußtsein* (Munich: Wilhelm Fink, 1987), pp. 493–514.

Wagner, Yvonne, "Prinzen, Mütter und Erzieher: Zum Bildungsverhalten des preußisch-deutschen Hofes im 'bürgerlichen Zeitalter'," *Archiv für Kulturgeschichte* 80 (1998), 351–73.

Walkenhorst, Peter, "Nationalismus als 'politische Religion'? Zur religiösen Dimension nationalistischer Ideologie im Kaiserreich," in Olaf Blaschke and Frank-Michael Kuhlemann (eds.), *Religion im Kaiserreich: Milieus, Mentalitäten, Krisen* (Gütersloh: Kaiser, 1996), pp. 503–31.

Warren, Mark, *Nietzsche and Political Thought* (Cambridge, Mass.: MIT Press, 1988).

"Max Weber's Nietzschean Conception of Power," *History of the Human Sciences* 5/3 (1992), 19–37.

Watson, James P., "Nietzsche's 'Transnational' Thinking," *History of European Ideas* 15 (1992), 133–40.

Wawro, Geoffrey, *The Franco-Prussian War: The German Conquest of France in 1870–1871* (Cambridge: Cambridge University Press, 2003).

Wehler, Hans-Ulrich, *Deutsche Gesellschaftsgeschichte, III: Von der "Deutschen Doppelrevolution" bis zum Beginn des Ersten Weltkrieges, 1849–1914* (Munich: C. H. Beck, 1995).

Deutsche Gesellschaftsgeschichte, I: Vom Feudalismus des "alten Reiches" bis zur "defensiven Modernisierung" der Reformära, 1700–1815 (Munich: C. H. Beck, 1987).

White, Richard J., *Nietzsche and the Problem of Sovereignty* (Urbana, Ill.: University of Illinois Press, 1997).

Whitman, James, *The Legacy of Roman Law in the German Romantic Era: Historical Vision and Legal Change* (Princeton, N.J.: Princeton University Press, 1994).

"Nietzsche in the Magisterial Tradition of German Classical Philology," *Journal of the History of Ideas* 47 (1986), 453–68.

"From Philology to Anthropology in Mid-Nineteenth-Century Germany", in George W. Stocking, Jr. (ed.), *Functionalism Historicized: Essays on British Social Anthropology* (Madison, Wisc.: University of Wisconsin Press, 1984), pp. 214–29.

Willey, Thomas E., *Back to Kant: The Revival of Kantianism in German Social and Historical Thought, 1860–1914* (Detroit, Mich.: Wayne State University Press, 1978).

Williams, Bernard, *Truth and Truthfulness: An Essay in Genealogy* (Princeton, N.J.: Princeton University Press, 2002).

Moral Luck (Cambridge: Cambridge University Press, 1981).

"Naturalism and Genealogy," in Edward Harcourt (ed.), *Morality, Reflection, and Ideology* (Oxford: Oxford University Press, 2000), pp. 148–61.

Williamson, George S., *The Longing for Myth in Germany: Religion and Aesthetic Culture from Romanticism to Nietzsche* (Chicago: University of Chicago Press, 2004).

"What Killed August von Kotzebue? The Temptations of Virtue and the Political Theology of German Nationalism," *Journal of Modern History* 72 (2000), 890–943.

Winkler, August Heinrich, *Der lange Weg nach Westen* (Munich: C. H. Beck, 2000).

Wittkau, Annette, *Historismus: Zur Geschichte des Begriffs und des Problems*, 2nd edn., corr. (Göttingen: Vandenhoeck & Ruprecht, 1994).

Wolin, Richard, *The Seduction of Unreason: The Intellectual Romance with Fascism from Nietzsche to Postmodernism* (Princeton, N.J.: Princeton University Press, 2004).

Woodford, Charlotte, " 'Mit Gott für König und Vaterland': Contrasting Models of Patriotism in the Historical Novels of Theodor Fontane and Gustav Freytag," in Christian J. Emden and David Midgley (eds.), *German Literature, History and the Nation* (Oxford: Peter Lang, 2004), pp. 253–76.

Woolf, Stuart, *Napoleon's Integration of Europe* (London: Routledge, 1991).

Wülfing, Wulf, Karin Bruns, and Rolf Parr, *Historische Mythologie der Deutschen, 1798–1918* (Munich: Wilhelm Fink, 1991).

Young, Julian, *Nietzsche's Philosophy of Art* (Cambridge: Cambridge University Press, 1992).

Yovel, Yirmiyahu, *Kant and the Philosophy of History* (Princeton, N.J.: Princeton University Press, 1980).

"Nietzsche and the Jews: The Structure of an Ambivalence," in Jacob Golomb (ed.), *Nietzsche and Jewish Culture* (London: Routledge, 1997), pp. 117–34.

Zammito, John H., *Kant, Herder, and the Birth of Anthropology* (Chicago: University of Chicago Press, 2002).

Zelle, Carsten, "Der Abgang des Herakles: Beobachtungen zur mythologischen Figurenkonstellation in Hinsicht auf Friedrich Nietzsche und Ulrich von Wilamowitz-Moellendorff," *Nietzsche-Studien* 23 (1994), 200–25.

Ziolkowski, Theodore, *Clio, the Romantic Muse: Historicizing the Faculties in Germany* (Ithaca, N.Y.: Cornell University Press, 2004).

Index

abbreviation 234
absolutism 204, 205, 206, 210, 235, 310
  of moral values 244
Aegean 161
aesthetics 95–6
  aestheticism 4, 55, 140–2, 155, 172
  aestheticization of historical knowledge 137
  education 112
  individualism 318
Africa 184
Aldrovandi, Ulisse 159
Alexander the Great 84, 144, 155
Allgemeine Historische Bibliothek 131
Alsace 122–3
Althoff, Friedrich 116
America 320
Americanness 221
animism 95
Anthropological Society of London 186
anthropological turn in Nietzsche's work 178, 186
Anthropologie, Ethnologie und Urgeschichte, Deutsche Gesellschaft für 184
anthropology 83, 90, 95, 96, 131, 174–216, 235
  and archaeological thought 187
  comparative methods in 180
  cultural 10–11, 174–216
  in the Enlightenment 179
  evolutionary orientation 186
  in Germany: historicist orientation 186; institutional development 179–81, 184–7
  physical 186
  racial doctrines in 186–7
anthropomorphism 76
antichità italiane 160
anti-essentialism 261, 287

antiquarianism 164
  and archaeology 160
  authenticity as goal 159
  in eighteenth century 160
  empirical perspective of 161
  relationship to philology 156–7
  during Renaissance 159–60
  as self-defeating 162
antiquity, concept of 29
anti-reductionism 261
Antisemitische Hefte 311
anti-Semitism 13, 158, 308–12, 317
  as European phenomenon 311
  and German nationalism 309
  political 311, 316
  and Protestantism 311
  rise of 309–12, 316
Appel, Fredrick 2, 258
Aquinas, Thomas of 240
Arc de Triomphe 290
archaeology 83, 160
  discourse in nineteenth century 161
Archiv für Anthropologie 184
Arendt, Hannah 288–9, 304
  on freedom 304
aristocratic
  intellectualism 314
  liberalism 320
  radicalism 317–18; *see also* Brandes, Georg
Aristotle 48, 107, 127
  on origin of philosophy 127, 128
  Poetics 48
army 299
Arndt, Ernst Moritz 31–3, 36, 119, 121, 152, 155, 315
  Geist der Zeit 31
Ars-sur-Moselle 122
artists 173
ascetic ideal 257

Ast, Friedrich 162
atheism 294
Atlantic world 302
Auerstedt, battle of 301
Augusta of Saxony-Weimar-Eisenach 315
Augustine 240
Austria 29–30
  Habsburg Empire 37, 39, 41
Austro-Prussian War 5, 7, 36–42, 118, 315
authenticity 156
authoritarianism 212, 213, 220, 242, 244, 307, 310
authority 217
autonomous individual 77, 224, 253, 259, 295; *see also* sovereign individual
autonomy 255–6, 288–9, 297–8

Bachofen, Johann Jakob 8, 81, 82–5, 91, 92, 109, 155, 158, 179, 197, 263–4
  anthropological conception of cultural history 84
  Geschichte der Römer 83–4
  Das Mutterrecht 84
  Versuch über die Gräbersymbolik der Alten 84
Bachofen, Luise 85
Bacon, Francis 222, 270
  Novum Organum 222
bad, as opposed to good 238; *see also* evil
Bahnsen, Julius 48–9
  Zur Philosophie der Geschichte 49
Basel 40, 79–128, 139, 158, 255, 263, 294
  accumulation of wealth in 81
  Augustinergasse in 112–13
  civic life in 80
  intellectual culture in 80–2, 147, 159
  neo-humanism in 80, 81
  Pädagogium 81, 82, 83, 170
  peace treaty of Basel (1795) 300
  Protestantism in 81
  public museum of 112–13
  university library 178, 188
  University of 8–9, 61, 79–80, 80–2, 158, 170, 181, 182
Bastian, Adolf 185–6, 187
  "elementary ideas" 185
Bauer, Bruno 207, 291–3
  Die Judenfrage 292
Baumgartner, Adolf 88
Baur, Ferdinand Christian 50–2, 91, 92, 95
  Die Epochen der kirchlichen Geschichtsschreibung 52
  Hegelian outlook of 52
  Lehrbuch der christlichen Dogmengeschichte 51
  skepticism about historical knowledge 52
Bayle, Pierre 163
"becoming" 281–2, 283
Begriffsgeschichte 16
Benfey, Theodor 181, 182, 183
  Geschichte der Sprachwissenschaft und orientalischen Philologie in Deutschland 181
Benjamin, Walter 14, 321
Bentham, Jeremy 245, 259
Berlin 19, 34, 80, 81, 83, 84, 86, 109, 111, 125, 185, 186, 209–14, 216, 274, 290, 301, 314
  museums of antiquity in 162
  University of 19, 82, 91, 92, 134, 136, 138, 185, 194
  Berlin West Africa Conference 177
Bernays, Jacob 24, 101
Bildung 19, 24, 27, 29–30, 36, 37, 40–1, 81, 111, 113, 114–15, 115–17, 134; *see also* neo-humanism
Bildungsbürgertum 114, 116–17
Bildungstrieb 74
biology 65, 74, 231, 264, 274, 275–81
  historicity of 268
Bismarck, Otto von 7, 22, 32, 33, 37, 41, 56, 84, 93, 105, 117–18, 121, 123, 152, 177, 206, 213, 258, 290, 292, 310, 314–16
  anti-Socialist policies 316
  coup d'état 258
  foreign policy 202
  Kulturkampf 206, 310
  military budget 258
  Socialist Law 213
  statues of 145
Blumenbach, Johann Friedrich 74, 280
  on *Bildungstrieb* 74
Bluntschli, Johann Caspar 117
Boccaccio, Giovanni 87
Boeckh, August 17, 19, 26, 82, 85, 109–10
  Corpus Inscriptionum Graecarum 157
  Encyklopädie und Methodologie der philologischen Wissenschaften 19, 109–10
  quarrel with Gottfried Hermann 157
  on relationship between philology and philosophy 102
Bohemia 38

Index

Bonn 20, 30, 34, 54, 56, 77, 79, 81, 85, 99, 100, 104, 116, 125, 129, 152, 156, 249
  "Arndt-Fest" 33
  Akademisches Kunstmuseum 25, 26
  Alter Zoll 31, 152, 315
  University of 6, 19, 21–36, 53, 101, 138, 291, 315
Bonner Philologenkrieg 34–6
Bopp, Franz 182
Borgia, Cesare 226
Bourdieu, Pierre 321
brain v. soul 273
brain, material organization of 277
Brandes, Georg 317–18
  aristocratic radicalism 317–18
Brandis, Christian August 104
Bremen 264
Buckle, Henry Thomas 247–8
  History of Civilization in England 247
Bülow, Cosima von 119–20
Burckhardt, Jacob 8, 75, 81, 82, 85–90, 91, 92, 109, 111, 113, 129, 136, 137, 155, 158, 160, 179, 293, 320
  on crises 87, 148–9
  Die Cultur der Renaissance in Italien 86–7, 160
  "Die Griechen und ihr Mythos" 112
  Griechische Culturgeschichte 88–9
  rejection of Hegel 89
  rejection of teleology 89
  relationship to cultural sciences 89–90
  on state, religion and culture 86–7
  "Über Glück und Unglück in der Weltgeschichte" 112
  "Über das Studium der Geschichte" 87
  on world wars 149
Burke, Edmund 320

Campo Formio, peace treaty of 300
capitalism, *laissez-faire* principle of 249
caractère sacré 210
Carey, Henry Charles 249
Carlsbad Decrees 23, 30, 126
Cassirer, Ernst 322
categorical imperative 232, 297
  selfishness of 297
Catholicism 206–7, 310
  Catholic Church 202, 238
  Catholics 310
  Catholicization 202
  Catholic minority in Prussia 117–18
causality 71
  in history 135
  as metaphysical concept 232
Caylus, Anne Claude Philippe de Pestels de Lévis de Tubières-Grimoard, Comte de 160
  Receuil d'Antiquités égyptiennes, étrusques, grecques, gauloises 160
chemistry 274
Christian
  Church 70, 198
  dogma 52
  theology 240
  virtue ethics 226, 239, 273, 308
Christianity 199–200, 220, 291
  misuse of 227
  and speculative philosophy 207
Christlichsoziale Partei (Austria) 312
Chur, library of 247
church attendance in Imperial Germany 208
Cicero 155
Ciceronian canon 87
citizenship 295
civil
  commonwealth 301
  society 11, 72, 73, 136, 223, 256, 281–2, 317, 320, 321
classical ideal 31
classical scholarship 6–7, 10–11, 17–21, 42–6
  anthropological turn in 97
  as historical discipline 97, 102
  as humanist discipline 24
  Nietzsche's early views of 45–6
  political dimension of 38
  self-conception of 18
classical tradition 27–9, 99
  political dimension of 29–30, 99–100
classicism 18, 161; German (*deutsche Klassik*) 30, 37, 141
code civil 32
coercion 242, 250
  and law 256
  see also violence
cognition 270
Collège de France 238
Cologne 33
colonialism 185
  in Imperial Germany 176–7
Columbus, Christopher 221
commonwealth 168
community 299
  concept of 239
  preservation of 243–4
  see also moral communities
comparative method 190
  in cultural anthropology 180
compassion 278

Index

Comte, Auguste 218, 246, 247, 248, 273
Congress of Berlin 177
conscience 232, 289
  bad conscience 248, 250–1
  and language 191–2
  see also moral conscience
consciousness, in history 133, 134, 135, 164
consensus 203, 212
consequences 253, 259–60
consumer society 171
contingency 62, 67, 75, 103, 135, 139, 164, 219, 238, 261, 266
  of human experience 232, 233
  of moral norms 282
  of social and political order 218
  and teleology 103, 135
conviction 252, 253, 259
  in science 283–4
  see also ethic of conviction
Conway, Daniel 1
Conze, Alexander 161
Corpus Inscriptionum Graecarum 157
Corpus Inscriptionum Latinarum 157, 158, 159
cosmopolitanism 8, 117, 124–5, 299–302
  as European project 300
  failure of cosmopolitan liberalism 148
Cowley, Abraham 221
  To Mr. Hobs 221
crisis 6, 321
  experience of in Europe 148–50
  of modernity 166, 322
critical historian 163–73
cruelty 256, 276
cultural
  heritage 156
  history 179
  mentalities 183
  pluralism 124, 300
  sciences: Burckhardt's relationship to 89–90; difference of history to philosophy 89; illiberal 89
culture
  and language 181–4, 234
  political dimension of 89
  symbolic order of 234, 247
Curtius, Ernst 161, 315
Curtius, Georg 24, 194, 196
  Grundzüge der griechischen Etymologie 194
custom 225, 239, 268

Dante Alighieri 87
Danube 153
Darwin, Charles 65, 189, 270, 275, 278
  The Descent of Man 278
  on inheritance of moral conscience 278
  The Origin of Species 65
"Darwinian" 280
Darwinism 273
debt, relationship to guilt 249–50
debtor–creditor relationship 249–50
degeneration 187
democracy 11, 209, 211–14, 218, 247, 257–8, 303, 320
  consensus in 203
  deliberative 203
  expert culture in 212
  in Imperial Germany 247
  mass 212, 246, 247, 256, 258, 307, 321
  and political power 307–8
  social 218, 316
  in Victorian Britain 247
democratic bourgeoisie 290
Democritus 45, 54
Descartes, René 73, 294
Detwiler, Bruce 2
deus sive natura 273; see also Spinoza
Deussen, Paul 119, 125
Deutscher Kolonialverein 177
Deutsch-Französische Jahrbücher 292
Deutschsoziale Reformpartei 311
De Wette, Wilhelm M. L. 91–2, 95
  Lehrbuch der christlichen Dogmatik 92
  Lehrbuch der christlichen Sittenlehre 92
Dilthey, Wilhelm 107–8, 147
  critique of historical reason 147
Diogenes Laertius 104
disenchantment 244, 308, 321
  through historical knowledge 165
dogmatism, metaphysical 59
Dombowsky, Don 2
domination 217, 220, 228; see also rule
Dorpat (Tartu) 108
Dreyfus Affair 312
Droysen, Johann Gustav 18, 31, 41, 83, 84, 85, 109, 116, 138, 144, 154, 248
  Geschichte des Hellenismus 154–5
  lectures on *Historik* 109, 136
dualism 281
DuBois-Reymond, Emil 185, 274
Dürer, Albrecht 153
duty 251, 265

East India Company 199
economy 288
  society based on economic exchange 249–50

economic consumption 246; relationships 249
education
  higher, in Germany 115–17
  and German nation state 111–12
  philosophical 102–12, 113, 128
  see also neo-humanism
egalitarianism 220, 254, 293
elitism 307, 317, 318
emancipation 78, 86, 131
embodiment 269
  see also incorporation
embryology 65
emergence 267–8, 282, 283
  natural 282
  site of (*Entstehungsherd*) 260, 280
  social 282
Empire 152
encyclopedic lectures at German universities 109
Enlightenment (*Aufklärung*) 4, 6, 8, 31, 41, 73, 103, 117, 124, 130, 131, 132, 135, 151, 163, 204, 210, 301, 318–19, 320, 321
  and anthropology 179
  historicity of 237
  radical 320
Entstehungsherd; see emergence, site of
Entwicklungsmechanik 65
epigraphy 157
epistemic claims 268
epistemology 284, 295–6
  and the body 275
equality 205, 219–20, 243
Erasmus of Rotterdam 153
Erlangen 122
eschatology 71, 167
  relationship to philosophy of history 167
ethic
  of conviction 259–60, 288, 296
  of responsibility 217, 247, 248–60, 284, 288, 296–8
ethical judgment 12, 224, 232, 238–9, 255
  historical formation of 272
  naturalist account of 271
  normative dimension of 269
  in political life 217–18
  psychology of 269
ethical commitments 289
ethical obligations 297
ethics 239
  Christian 239
  of duty 251
  of virtue 253

  as *Sittlichkeit* 251
  as *Tugend* 251
  voluntarism in 237
ethnie 146, 152
ethno-psychology 180
etymology 194–6, 236
  as history of thought 195
Eucken, Rudolf 114
Europe 72–3, 89, 142, 148, 215–16, 287, 319, 320
  as alternative to traditional moral communities 286
  civilization of 187
  cosmopolitanism in 300
  culture of 176–8
  democratization of 307
  economic unification of 287
  as ethical community 286
  Europeanness 309
  Europeans 14
  as federated state 301
  idea of 125, 285, 286, 317
  integration of 306
  morality of 178, 294
  of nation states 299–300
  as the "other" 177
  partition of 300
  political culture of 303
  political equilibrium in 313
  Protestant 72
  as regulative ideal 287
  secularization of society, 174
  supra-national 304
  as transnational project 299–300
European modernity
  anthropological perspective on 178
  conditions of 174–5
  symbolic order of 187
evil 214–15, 238–44, 250, 298
  conceptual openness of 243
  innateness of 241
  moral notions of 240–4
  as political category 243, 244
  realist accounts of 242
  unintelligibility of 241–2
  vindication of existence of 165, 167
"evil disposition" 299
evolution 66, 67, 231–2, 275, 278
  of moral communities 282
  and power 279
excellence 254–5; see also perfectionism
expansionism 313
experimental disciplines 57
expert culture 212
"external reason thesis" 239–40

faith 223, 227
  in science 284
fanaticism 224, 227
fear 243, 299
Fechner, Gustav Theodor 60–1, 62
  psycho-physics 60
federalism in Germany 312
Feuerbach, Ludwig 207
Fichte, Johann Gottlieb 20, 32, 70, 75, 132, 290, 300
  on Europe 301–2
  Der geschlossene Handelsstaat 302
  Die Grundzüge des gegenwärtigen Zeitalters 70, 301
  on the nation state 302
  Reden an die deutsche Nation 32, 290, 302
  "world plan" in 135
fin de siècle 171
First World War 202, 213, 214, 225, 313, 323
Fischer, Kuno 107
force (*Kraft*) 73–5
  as metaphysical concept 231–2
Förster-Nietzsche, Elisabeth 189
Foucault, Michel 2, 15, 16, 217, 225, 250, 304, 321
  archaeology of knowledge (*archéologie du savoir*) 16, 321
  on "disciplinary power" 250
  regime of truth 282
foundation myths 9, 40, 101, 112, 124, 141, 146, 147, 151, 152, 153, 156, 164, 208, 257, 290
Franco-Prussian War 5, 6, 9, 32, 39, 40, 70, 87, 93, 101, 111, 112, 117, 119–24, 145, 147, 210, 315
  war chronicles 152
Frederick the Great (King of Prussia) 153, 314–15, 316
free spirit, the 211, 216–28, 251, 258, 284, 295–8, 303, 316, 318, 320
  "brief habits" of 296
  psychology of 296
freedom 76, 77, 223, 224, 241, 288, 289, 319
  and ethical decisions 251
  in history 133, 134, 135, 138, 164, 166
  "open sea" 221–3, 286, 303–4
  and the political 289
  symbolism of 289
  of the will 223
  "will to be free" 304
French Revolution 30, 50, 144, 164, 168, 206, 210, 223, 300, 302, 320

Freytag, Gustav 145
Friedrich III (German Emperor), 315–16
Friedrich Wilhelm III (King of Prussia) 91
Friedrich Wilhelm IV (King of Prussia) 33

Galison, Peter 14
Galton, Francis 277
  Inquiries into the Human Faculty and Its Development 277
Gatterer, Johann Christoph 131
Geistesgeschichte 16
genealogein 233
genealogía 233
genealogy 7, 11–14, 60, 77, 90, 164, 174–5, 190, 220, 229–85, 286, 289, 307, 312, 321
  development of 230–7
  and discontinuity 261
  and *Entstehungsherd* 260
  as fact-defective 262–3
  genetic fallacy in 267–8
  as historical critique of the political 245
  historical dimension of 266
  as historical strategy 230, 282
  as internal critique of modernity 234
  and language 234–7
  limits of 286, 316–23
  and naturalism 281
  naturalist account of 269
  naturalist commitments of 230, 231
  as Nietzsche's political legacy 322
  and origin 260–2
  philosophical dimension of 269, 284
  political dimension of 229, 230, 266
  practical consequences of 12–13
  practical insights of 289
  as realist critique of the political 11
  realist perspective of 322
  relationship to classical scholarship/philology 230, 231–2
  relationship to philosophy and history 267–8
  Renaissance concept of 233
  and the sciences 282–4
  as scientific enterprise 270
  task of 260–8
  teleological commitment of 279
  traditional notions of 233
generation 65
Genoa 176, 221
Gerber, Gustav 181
  Die Sprache als Kunst 181
Gerlach, Franz Dorotheus 83
  Geschichte der Römer 83–4

German Archaeological Institute
  (Deutsches Archäologisches Institut,
  Rome) 159, 162
German
  character 141–2
  Confederation 37
  Customs Union 17
  Empire, proclamation of 123–4
  idealism 8, 10, 18, 22, 68, 70, 71, 72, 83,
    102, 103, 128, 134, 135, 137, 152,
    155, 162, 164, 207, 241, 279, 281,
    300, 304
  Imperial Eagle 94
  Nation: political legitimacy of 145;
    visualization of 153
  nation state: confessional basis of 292;
    formation of 147; identity of 177;
    see also Germany
  Reich 124, 125
  spirit" 118, 121, 124, 125, 142, 292
  states, unification of 37, 38–9, 126
Germanness 289–90
  as a historical construct 290
Germany
  federalism in 312
  higher education reform in 148
  as mythical construct 290
  as unified nation state 145
  see also Imperial Germany
Gersdorff, Carl von 35, 38, 39, 41, 59, 63,
  87, 93, 176
Gervinius, Georg Gottfried 62, 137, 145
Gesamtkunstwerk 141
Gesellschaft Deutscher Naturforscher und
  Ärzte 184–5
Gesher, Johann Matthias 134
Geuss, Raymond 262
Gobineau, Joseph Arthur, Comte de 186
  Essai sur l'inégalité des races 186
God 165, 168, 170, 260, 273
  death of 244, 294, 303
  "hand of" 203, 208
Goethe, Johann Wolfgang von 36–7, 38,
  305, 306, 314
  Westöstlicher Divan 305
  on "world literature" 305
good 245
  bonus 236
  greater common good 239, 246–7, 248,
    279
  gut 236
  as opposed to "bad" 238
  in opposition to "evil" 214–15
  primacy of 240–1, 242
Goßler, Gustav von 116

Göttingen 34, 82, 130, 131, 132, 134,
  290
  University of 51, 62, 82, 92, 131, 134;
    historical school at 130
governance 168, 212
government 203, 250, 299
  civil 204
  divine 203–4, 207, 208
  ecclesiastical 204
  human 203–4, 207
  representative 207
  "tutelary" 204–5, 206
Greek War of Independence 161
Greifswald, University of 25
Grimm, Jacob 182, 194, 196
"Großbetrieb der Wissenschaft" 115
"Großwissenschaft" 115, 159, 161
guilt 232, 248–51, 262, 289
  and debt 249–50
  debtor–creditor relationship 249–50

Habermas, Jürgen 319
habitus 277
Hagenau 122
Halle, University of 18, 51, 109, 134, 160,
  183, 188
Hamburg 79, 81
happiness 246, 252, 259; see also pleasure
Harnack, Adolf von 91, 115
Hartmann, Eduard von 48–9, 182
  Philosophie des Unbewussten 48, 182
Haym, Rudolf 42, 106
  "Arthur Schopenhauer" 49
Heeren, Arnold Hermann Ludwig 44, 62,
  162
  Geschichte des Studiums der classischen
    Litteraturen seit dem Wiederaufleben der
    Wissenschaften 44
Hegel, Georg Wilhelm Friedrich 10, 23,
  46, 47, 48, 52, 53, 71, 72, 75, 76, 82,
  87, 103, 111, 118, 124, 142, 165–8,
  194, 206, 207, 209, 210, 241, 251–2,
  279–80, 281–2, 288, 291, 292, 300,
  301, 302, 304
  "cunning of reason" 164, 167
  on God and history, 167–8
  Grundlinien der Philosophie des Rechts 168
  on historical contingency 72
  on origin of philosophy 127
  perfectibility as principle of historical
    development 72
  primacy of the nation state 302
  "reflective historiography" 46
  on the state 168–9, 207
  on the state and God 168

Index

on unintelligibility of evil 241–2
Vorlesungen über die Geschichte der Philosophie 23
Vorlesungen über die Philosophie der Geschichte 72, 142, 206
Vorlesungen über die Philosophie der Religion 209
"will to be free" 304
on world history 167
Hegelei 105–6
Hegelian 62, 85, 103, 104
Hegelians 104–5
see also Young Hegelians
Hegelianism 48, 148
Heidelberg 111
University of 93, 118, 138, 165, 167
Heine, Heinrich 124, 207, 306
Hellenism 84
Hellenic ideal 100
Hellwald, Friedrich von 89, 178
Culturgeschichte in ihrer natürlichen Entwicklung 89
Die Erde und ihre Völker 178
Helmholtz, Hermann von 60, 75, 184, 185, 274
Über die Erhaltung der Kraft 75
Heraclitus 121, 215, 281
"herd instinct" 309
Herder, Johann Gottfried 68, 72–3, 74, 77, 91, 124–5, 132, 179, 181, 227, 299–300
Auch eine Philosophie der Geschichte zur Bildung der Menschheit 132
Briefe zur Beförderung der Humanität 73
on community 299
on cosmopolitanism 299–302
criticism of Voltaire 133
cultural pluralism in 300
on cultural self-determination 299–300
on "European collective spirit" 72
on history 132–3
Ideen zur Philosophie der Geschichte der Menschheit 68
on patriotism 124
on progress 132
on world history 72, 73
Hering, Ewald 277
"engrams" 277
Hermann, Gottfried 17, 157
quarrel with August Boeckh 157
Hermannsdenkmal 145
hermeneutics 136
biblical 51
Herodotus 49
Herrschaft 307; see also rule

Hesiod 233
Theogony 233
Heyne, Christian Gottlob 26, 82, 134, 160, 161, 196
hierarchy, political and social 217
Hirzel, Carl
Grundzüge zu einer Geschichte der classischen Philologie 44
historical school of law 83, 105, 194
historicism 45–6, 71, 75, 96, 129–39
crisis of 6, 9–10, 18, 130–40
different kinds of 138–9
in nineteenth century 135–40
in Protestant theology 91
rise of 103
historicity 135, 282
and biology 268
historicization of reason 102
historiography
affinity to mythology 84
Imperial 290
nationalist 293
political 144
relationship to philology 134–5
Historisches Journal 131
Historische Zeitschrift 21
history
acceleration of 149
antiquarian conception of 151, 156–62, 163
of concepts 195
"conjectural" 263
critical conception of 151, 163–73
of cultural institutions 268
evolutionary 275
as forensic/legal process 165–7
historia civilis 130
historia divina 130
historia magistra vitae 133
historia naturalis 130
historia profana et politica 130
historia sacra at ecclesiastica 130
laws of 52, 64–78
lectures on theory of (*Historik*) 138
long-term political effects of 163, 164
"malady of" 143–5, 147
monumental conception of 150–5, 156, 163, 164
moralization of 166
natural 272
of philosophy 106; as discipline at German universities 103
and reason 301
teleological conceptions of 134, 279–82

history (cont.)
  value of 216
  as *Wissenschaft* 135, 136
historical
  consciousness 10
  convergence with nature 71–2
  critique 165, 169–70
  culture 143; crisis of 129–30, 143, 175; in Germany 155; origin of 169; political function of 150
  development: relativist models of 131; unilinear conceptions of 131
  disciplines, relationship to natural sciences 282
  identity 7
  instinct 268
  knowledge 7, 49–53, 59, 61, 64, 143–4, 230; aestheticization of 137; and aesthetic experience 140; *cognitio historica* 50; excess of 150; political dimension of 9; political value of 170; relevance of 165
  method 7
  "philosophizing" 139, 173, 175, 283
  orientation 146–7, 164, 170
  relativism 135
  thought, transformation in eighteenth century 130–4
  time, acceleration of 166
  understanding 53, 136, 169, 175–6
Hobbes, Thomas 168, 221, 270
Hödel, Max 213
Hoffmann von Fallersleben, August Heinrich 289–90
  Lied der Deutschen 289
Hohenzollern monarchy 314, 315
Hollingdale, R. J. 43
Holy Roman Empire 301
honesty (*Redlichkeit*) 228, 252–3, 256, 284
Hugo, Victor 290
  funeral of 290
human agency 240, 241, 242, 252, 253, 271, 274
  naturalist account of 284
human experience 271
humanism, Renaissance 226–7
  universities 87
humanity 28, 72, 131, 151, 191, 216, 227, 248, 286, 289
  naturalist account of 269–85, 290, 322
Humboldt, Wilhelm von) 18–19, 23, 24, 28, 29–30, 36, 40–1, 75, 81, 111, 112, 114, 117, 134–5, 180, 182–3
  "Betrachtungen über die Weltgeschichte" 71

on teleology 71–2
"Über die Aufgabe des Geschichtsschreibers" 71, 134
Ueber die Verschiedenheit des menschliches Sprachbaues und ihren Einfluss auf die geistige Entwickelung des Menschengeschlechts 183
see also neo-humanism
Hume, David 270
Husserl, Edmund 273, 322
"Philosophie als strenge Wissenschaft" 273

idealism 103
  post-Kantian 54
  see also German idealism
identity politics 319
"imagined communities" 40
Imperial Germany 4, 13, 79, 105, 115, 117, 124, 137, 185, 201, 209, 210, 285, 292, 308–16
  as authoritarian nation state 256
  as built on a mythical narrative 169
  as colonial power 146, 176
  economic depression in 311
  foreign policy 313
  formation of 6, 8, 106, 145
  as *Kulturstaat* 206
  modernization of 208, 210
  as modern nation state 144
  political imagination in 152–5
  Protestantism in 207
  social crisis in 166
  see also Reich; German Reich; German Empire
Imperial Rome 86
imperialism 313
incorporation (*Einverleibtheit*) 268; see also embodiment
individual
  European 287–98
  nomadic 303
  supra-national 303
  see also autonomous individual; sovereign individual
Indo-European proto-language 193
inequality 205
inheritance 275
  of moral conscience 278
  of psychological characteristics 277–8
Innsbruck 184
Inquisition, the 243
Institut für Altertumskunde (Rome) 162

Index

intellectual history 15–16
"Cambridge School" of 16
interpretation 296

Jahn, Otto 20, 23, 24–7, 28, 33, 34–6, 99, 101–2, 161
  "Die Bedeutung und Stellung der Alterthumsstudien in Deutschland" 26, 28, 101–2
  on classical scholarship 26–7
  "Über den Aberglauben des bösen Blicks bei den Alten" 26
Jena 91, 126, 290
  battle of 301
  University of 92, 138
Jews 310
  community 310–11
  culture 310
  population, political emancipation in Germany 292
"Jewish question" 292
Jhering, Rudolf von 242
Judaism 308–9
Judeo-Christian tradition 14, 200, 238, 284, 294, 297, 308–9, 319
Justi, Johann Heinrich Gottlob von 168
justice 219–20
  egalitarian concept of 254
  as fairness 254
  theory of 253–4

Kaiser-Wilhelm-Gesellschaft (Berlin) 115
Kameralwissenschaft 168
Kant, Immanuel 8, 11–14, 23, 44, 52, 53, 54, 56, 57, 58, 63, 64–5, 67, 70, 71, 72, 73, 76, 106, 110, 132, 134, 142, 146, 165, 167, 179–80, 181, 205–6, 209, 237–8, 240–2, 251–2, 255, 262–3, 264, 279–80, 281–2, 288, 294, 297, 300–1, 318–19
  analogy of experience 66
  autonomy of pure practical reason 304
  autonomy of the will 255–6
  "Beantwortung der Frage: Was ist Aufklärung?" 205
  categorical imperative 232, 297
  causation 68
  "civil commonwealth" 301
  "conjectural history" 263
  constitution 300
  critical philosophy 232, 237
  definition of anthropology 179
  on democracy 205
  on Europe 301
  on "evil" 241
  "federation of peoples" 300–1
  on freedom 241
  Grundlegung zur Metaphysik der Sitten 255
  "Idee zu einer allgemeinen Geschichte in weltbürgerlicher Absicht" 68, 142
  Kritik der praktischen Vernunft 255, 300
  Kritik der Urteilskraft 64, 69
  on law 256
  Metaphysik der Sitten 300
  on moral law 241, 255, 318
  "Mutmaßlicher Anfang der Menschengeschichte" 262
  notion of Enlightenment 318–19
  "permanent congress of states" 301
  on primacy of the good 240–1
  public use of reason 205
  pure reason 241
  Die Religion innerhalb der Grenzen der bloßen Vernunft 69–70
  on teleology 65–6, 129, 281; and history 68–70
  things-in-themselves 191
  "transcendental aesthetic" 58; "analytic" 58
  unintelligibility of evil 241–2
  universality of reason 318
  on virtue (*Tugend*) 251
  Zum ewigen Frieden 300
Karlsruhe 122
Kelterborn, Louis 88
Kiel 108
  University of 107
Kiessling, Adolf 81
Kleist, Heinrich von 153
  Die Hermannsschlacht 153
Klemm, Gustav 89
  Allgemeine Cultur-Geschichte der Menschheit 89
Klenze, Leo von 153
Klopstock, Friedrich Gottlieb 20
Knies, Karl 137
knowledge
  conceptual 191, 234–5, 236; history of 195
  heterogeneity of 232
  and language 235
  and metaphor 234
  see also epistemology; history
Königgrätz 38
Korsgaard, Christine M. 296–7
Köselitz, Heinrich 13, 88, 176, 178
Kotzebue, August von 91–2, 126–7
Krafft, Wilhelm Ludwig 21, 52

Kugler, Franz 85
  Handbuch der Kunstgeschichte 85
Kulturkampf 93, 117–18, 125, 206, 310

Lamarck, Jean Baptiste 65, 280
  Philosophie zoologique 65
Landshut, University of 162
Lange, Friedrich Albert 8, 44, 54, 56–60,
    63, 64, 65, 66–7, 75, 108, 110, 274
  Die Arbeiterfrage 57
  on biological organization 58
  on causality 67
  *Geschichte des Materialismus und Kritik
    seiner Bedeutung in der Gegenwart* 54, 56,
    57, 60, 66, 274
  influence on formation of
    neo-Kantianism 57
  and the natural sciences 57–60
language 194
  cultural power of 193
  and cultural reality 181–4, 193, 234
  deficient nature of 192
  etymology 194–6
  and genealogy 234–7
  as interface between body and world 191
  and knowledge 235
  and legal thought 194
  and mythology 197–8
  Nietzsche's views of 192–3
  relationship to thinking and
    consciousness 190–7
  study of 175
  and symbolic order of culture 196
Las Cases, Emmanuel, Comte de 306
  Mémorial de Sainte-Hélène 306
law 256, 288, 289
  as cultural institution 266
  ethnographic account of 264
  evolution of 264, 266
  "general science of law" (*allgemeine
    Rechtswissenschaft*) 264
  historical school of law 83, 105, 194
  history of 266
  legal thought 194
  natural law 82
  natural right 289
  Roman law 82
  symbolic practices of 264
Lazarus, Moritz 180
legal
  institution 268; historical anthropology
    of 266
  person (*Rechtssubjekt*) 265
  relationships: economic basis of 289;
    origin of 265

Leibniz, Gottfried Wilhelm 73, 165, 167
Leipzig 19, 20, 25, 34, 35, 40, 54, 77, 79,
    80, 81, 99, 104, 108, 116, 118, 125,
    129, 138, 156, 194, 249, 263, 274
  battle of 126
  University of 6, 17, 19, 36, 44, 60–4, 92,
    160, 179, 264
Lessing, Gotthold Ephraim 70, 132, 133
  Die Erziehung des Menschengeschlechts 70
Levezow, Konrad 161
liberal society 263
liberalism 1–2, 4, 30, 77, 117, 147, 219,
    220, 231, 239, 240, 247–8, 253–4,
    256–7, 288, 293, 294, 299, 320
  aristocratic 320
  foundations among German middle
    class 310
  in Germany 291, 310
  limits of 321
  national orientation in Germany 41
  relationship to Protestantism in
    Germany 207
  transformation into nationalism 291
  see also national liberalism
lieu de mémoire 290
life 65, 172, 275, 280–1
  "will to life" 279
life sciences 64, 65, 66, 71, 284
linguistics 180, 193–6
  historical semantics 193
Lisbon earthquake 165
List, Friedrich 17
Literarisches Wochenblatt 92, 126
living force 66, 73–4; *see also* vitalism
Livorno 176, 177
Locke, John 270, 275
Lorraine 122
Lubbock, John 186, 188, 190, 265
  The Origin of Civilization 188
Lucerne 119
  Lake Lucerne 120
Ludwig I (Bavarian Crown Prince) 153
Luneville 122
Luther, Martin 118, 126, 152, 153, 154,
    206, 210, 292

Macedonia 84, 155
Machiavelli, Niccolò 2, 226–7, 304
  on *fortuna* 226
  on *res publica* 308
  on rule 307–8
  on *virtù* 226, 304
Machiavellian 219
machine-age 172
Macht 307

Index

Machtpolitik 40, 158, 291, 313
Mac-Mahon, Marie Edme Patrice Maurice, Comte de 122
Maine, Henry Sumner 265
Mannhardt, Wilhelm 189
   Der Baumkultus der Germanen und ihrer Nachbarstämme 189
Mannheim 126
Mannheim, Karl 14, 295, 303–4, 321
   on "ethics of responsibility" 304
   on sociology of knowledge 321
Marburg School of neo-Kantianism 56
Marburg, University of 57
Marienbad 312
Marr, Wilhelm 311
   Der Sieg des Judenthums über das Germanenthum 311
Marti, Urs 3
Marx, Karl 288, 292, 320
mass society 220
materialism 53–4, 61, 64, 270, 274, 294
   limits of 60
   scientific 61, 148, 277
Maximilian II (King of Bavaria) 86
Mecklenburg 38
Megill, Allen 4
Meißen 181
memory 276–8
   organic 277–8
   "technique of mnemonics" 276
Mendelssohn, Moses 70
   Jerusalem oder über religiöse Macht und Judenthum 70
metaphor 61, 190, 191, 192, 197, 234–5
   and knowledge 234
   metaphoricity 196
   and myth 234
metaphysics 59, 233
Metternich, Prince Klemens Wenzel of 126
Metz 122
Meysenburg, Malwida von 189
militarism 127
Mill, John Stuart 218, 246, 248, 252
Mind 189, 277
modernity 171–2, 244
   conditions of 174–5
   crisis of 166, 322
   European 11, 214
   foundations of 234
   heterogeneous nature of 171
   historical critique of 176
   political demands of 211
   political foundations of 128
   prehistory of 190
   and secularization 216, 244
Mommsen, Marie 158
Mommsen, Theodor 18, 41, 83–4, 115, 144, 154, 155, 157, 158–9
   on Cicero 155
   on civic Rome 84, 155
   Corpus Inscriptionum Latinarum 157, 158, 159
   on *Großwissenschaft* 161
   Monumenta Germaniae Historica 155
   Römische Geschichte 83, 155
Montfaucon, Bernard de 160
   L'Antiquité expliquée et représentée en figures 160
Monumenta Germaniae Historica 155
monuments 145, 146, 154
monumentulum amicitiae 93
moral
   absolutes 289, 299, 309
   action 256
   authenticity 263, 282, 294
   beauty 255
   claims 268
   communities 172, 174, 214, 215, 220, 227, 229–30, 235, 238, 239, 244, 248, 256, 286, 296–8, 299, 303, 306, 320, 323; absolutism of 298; evolution of 282; importance of power for 282, 225; natural history of 237–48; nihilism of 298; self-conception of 260
   conscience 277; origin of 261–2; psychology of 276
   feeling 246
   "herd" 257
   humility 225
   imperialism 258–9
   judgment 297
   law 166, 241, 255, 296–8, 318; universal nature of 237–8
   norms 269; philosophical critique of 229; as second nature 282
   righteousness, connection to violence 239
   sentiments 232, 238, 249, 250, 251
   values: absolutism of 244; embodiment of 269; evolution of 245; historical formation of 272; naturalist account of 284
morality
   Christian 247
   concepts of: biological innateness of 240; evolutionary formation of 240
   as cultural institution 192
   "histories of" 237
   history of 237
   laws of 296

morality (cont.)
  of mediocrity 225
  naturalist account of 252, 269
  normative claims of 254
  in pejorative sense 229
  physiology of 230
  as second nature 269
  slave revolt of 238
  task of 243
  see also ethics
morphology 65, 71
Müller, Adam 168
Müller, Friedrich Max 181, 199–200
  Lectures on the Science of Language 181
  on "science of religion" 199–200
Müller, Johann Polycarp 179
Müller, Johannes 65
  Handbuch der Physiologie des Menschen 65
Müller, Karl Otfried 82, 83, 101, 161, 197
  Handbuch der Archäologie der Kunst 161
  Prolegomena zu einer wissenschaftlichen Mythologie 82
Munich 125, 153, 161, 178, 217
  Alte Pinakothek 153, 161
  Glyptothek 153
  museums of antiquity 162
Mushacke, Hermann 19
Muslims 176
Mycenae 161
myth 4, 11, 149–50, 190, 216
  and cultural orientation 198
  and metaphor 234
  and philosophy 197
  and political authority 198
  political mobilization of 150–5
  see also foundation myths
mythology 196–8
  affinity to historiography 84
  Germanic 188
  and language 197–8
mythological names 196

Nancy 122
Napoleon Bonaparte 9, 31, 119, 152, 301–2, 305, 314
  abdication of 30
  foreign policy 305
  invasion of Russia 305–6
  occupation of German states 33, 153, 302
  transformation of Europe 305–7
Napoleonic army 290
Napoleonic Wars 6, 7, 28, 30, 50, 121, 300, 305
Napoleon III 122, 206

narratio rei gestae 50
nation 289
  concept of 144, 145–6, 152, 310
  as historical community 146
  as moral community 230, 289
  moralization of the 244
  as racial community 289
  see also nation state
national liberalism 30–1, 33, 39, 126, 155, 310
national security 258
nationalism 6, 80, 93, 117, 125, 142, 147, 218, 239, 257–8, 288, 289–93, 294, 312, 319
  and anti-Semitism in Germany 309
  in Europe 147, 291
  as European phenomenon 309
  and German Protestantism 311–12
  in Germany 11, 31–3
  relationship to neo-humanism 118
  rise of 210
nation state 167, 265, 291, 292, 310, 319
  and education 111–12
  European 86, 145
  as moral community 146, 310, 312, 319
  national identity 310
  political identity of 11
  political power in 216–18
  primacy in German thought 302
  and religion 201–3, 202–11
  sacralization of national past 153
  strategies of exclusion 310
natural drives 269
natural history 272
naturalism 11–12, 214, 228, 269–85, 289, 297
  different kinds of 270–2
  and metaphysics 273
  methodological 271, 272; weak program of 272
  "naturalizing humanity" 191, 269–85
  normative claims of 271
  practical 271–2, 276; strong program of 272
  and reductionism 281
  and scientific practice 271
  substantive 270–1, 272, 273, 279, 281
  and teleology 281
  weak program of 270, 279, 281, 283
natural sciences 59–60, 174, 264
  moralization of 76
  relationship to historical disciplines 282
natural selection 276, 277, 278; *see also* social selection
nature 269, 271

control over 222
deus sive natura 273
laws of 76
moralization of nature 278
and normativity 228
as related to history 71–2, 75–6
representation of 271
temporalization of 71–2
Naturphilosophie 280
Naumann, Constantin Georg 274
Naumburg 108, 208
neo-humanism 6, 7, 8, 19, 24, 27, 29–30, 33–4, 40–1, 64, 77, 99, 111–12, 114, 115–17, 125, 127, 129, 161, 255, 305, 315
  in Basel 80, 81
  as ideological trope 99
  and moral beauty 255
  relationship to nationalism 118
neo-Kantianism 23, 54, 56–7, 59, 107, 282
  Marburg School of 56
New Testament 94
Nicolovius, Heinrich Ludwig 135
Niebuhr, Barthold Georg 83, 134, 135
  lectures on Roman history 134
Nietzsche (writings)
  Also sprach Zarathustra 211, 230
  "Darstellung der antiken Rhetorik" 191
  David Strauss der Bekenner und Schriftsteller 76, 88, 106, 123
  Ecce Homo 24, 55, 122, 230, 290, 291, 293, 314
  "Einleitung in die lateinische Epigraphik" 158
  "Encyclopaedie der klassischen Philologie" 9, 97, 109, 110–11, 160, 196
  Die fröhliche Wissenschaft 10, 11, 77, 178, 191, 217, 223, 224, 244, 268, 279, 280, 283, 284, 285, 286, 293, 296, 318
  Die Geburt der Tragödie aus dem Geiste der Musik 8, 25, 54, 85, 93, 95, 98–9, 100–1, 122, 140–2, 155, 158
  "Geschichte der griechischen Litteratur" 179
  "Der griechische Staat" 120–1
  "Der Gottesdienst der Griechen" 97, 179, 188, 197–8
  "Homer und die klassische Philologie" 90, 94, 111
  Jenseits von Gut und Böse 10, 11, 13–14, 31, 129, 217, 224–5, 228, 229, 232, 235–6, 250, 251, 257, 260, 270, 273, 279, 284, 295, 303, 306–7, 320
  lectures and seminars in Basel 96–8

Menschliches, Allzumenschliches 5, 11, 53, 129, 139, 149–50, 172, 174, 193, 198, 201, 202, 204, 212–16, 218–19, 223, 234, 283, 299, 314, 316
Morgenröthe 170, 175, 221, 223, 231, 237, 308
notebooks 50–3, 55, 65, 67, 235, 240, 295
"Die Philosophie im tragischen Zeitalter der Griechen" 97, 121
Schopenhauer als Erzieher 149, 170, 255
"Sokrates und die griechische Tragödie" 93
"De Theognide Megarensi" 21
"Ueber Wahrheit und Lüge im aussermoralischen Sinne" 61, 97, 191
"Ueber die Zukunft unserer Bildungsanstalten" 9, 36, 112–15, 118, 126–7, 128, 255
Vom Nutzen und Nachtheil der Historie für das Leben 3, 9, 10, 36, 48, 49, 94, 130, 135, 137, 139, 140, 142, 143–5, 147, 150–1, 156–68, 169–73, 174, 224
"Vorlesungen über lateinische Grammatik" 158, 181–3
"Die vorplatonischen Philosophen" 128
"Wir Philologen" 29, 97, 99
"Zur Geschichte der Theognideischen Spruchsammlung" 21
Zur Genealogie der Moral 10, 11, 13–14, 129, 140, 180, 224, 229, 236, 237, 238, 245, 249–50, 253, 254, 256, 257, 260–1, 267–8, 270, 274, 276–7, 287, 290, 298, 319
nihilism 245, 303
  European 287, 293–4
Nissen, Heinrich 188
  Das Templum 188
nobility 238
nomadic intellectualism 308
normativity 271, 276, 285, 296
  historicity of 238
  of moral commitments 296–8
  of moral norms 269; *see also* morality
  of morality 254
  and nature 228
normative methods in science 272
"normative question" 296
Novalis (Friedrich von Hardenberg) 302
  Die Christenheit oder Europa 302

Oken, Lorenz 65
  Lehrbuch der Naturphilosophie 65
Olympia 161

"open sea" 221–3, 286, 303–4; *see also* freedom
organic development, theories of 280–1
origin (*Ursprung*) 260–2, 267–8
  of moral communities/morality 260–2
Ottmann, Henning 3, 4
Ottoman Empire 176
Overbeck, Franz 88, 91–5, 112, 178, 200, 317
  on Christian dogma 95
  on Christianity 94, 95
  friendship with Nietzsche 94–5
  "Über Entstehung und Recht einer rein historischen Betrachtung der Neutestamentlichen Schriften der Theologie" 94
  Ueber die Christlichkeit unserer heutigen Theologie 94
Overbeck, Ida (née Rothpletz) 93, 120
Oxford 82, 199

Paris 122, 133, 216
Parthenon 153
perfectionism 253–5
  moral 322
  teleological principle of 254
  see also excellence
Pergamon 161
perplexity, as the origin of philosophy 128; *see also* philosophical astonishment; wonder
perspectivism 108, 295–6
  estimations 295
pessimism 54, 77
Petrarch, Francesco 87
Pforta boarding school (*Schulpforta*) 20–1, 22, 125, 208, 315
philhellenism 26, 99
philology
  as form of cultural history 183
  relationship to historiography 134–5; to philosophy 102, 109–12
  as "science" (*Wissenschaft*), 44
Philosophische Monatshefte 23
philosophy
  academic 103–7
  astonishment, as origin of 127–8; *see also* wonder; perplexity
  critique as political enterprise 173
  education 9, 102–12, 113, 128
  eschatology 167
  of history 72, 103, 168; cosmopolitan 301; difference to cultural sciences 89; relationship to
  lack of historical sense in 173

and myth 197
  relationship to philology 102, 109–12
  relationship to politics 226
  relationship to the state in nineteenth-century Germany 104–6
  value of 266
physicalism 76, 270
physics 60, 274
Physikalisch-Technische Reichsanstalt (Braunschweig) 115
physiology 60, 61, 64, 71, 273, 274
Pillars of Hercules 222
Platner, Ernst 179
  Neue Anthropologie für Ärzte und Weltweise 179
Plato 14, 121, 127, 222, 240
  Republic 121
  Timaeus 222
pleasure 246; *see also* happiness
pluralism
  cultural 124, 300
  epistemological 287
polis 289
political, the 1, 13, 166, 175, 207, 212, 214, 220, 229–85, 294, 321
  autonomy of 288–9, 304
  disenchantment of 308
  empirical conditions of 289
  historical dimension of 289; formation of 279
  historicity of 289
  irrational dimension of 203
  moralization of 166, 289
  symbolic order of 234
political realism 13, 163, 216–28, 250, 255, 282, 283, 284, 286, 307–8, 318, 319
  historical perspective of 218–19
  strong program of 217
  weak program of 217–18
politics, political
  absolutes 289
  authority and myth 198
  communities 214, 215, 239, 303, 306
  culture 171–2, 214, 293; crisis of 13, 175; in Europe 216
  economoy (*Nationalökonomie*) 62–3, 264
  historiography 144
  ideals 217, 314, 321
  mentalities, formation of 175
  participation 212, 214, 246, 307, 320
  parties (Imperial Germany): democratic 257; Deutsche Reformpartei 258; nationalist 257; national-liberal 258

power: in the modern nation state
  216–18; sacralization of in the modern
  state 209–11; *see also* power; rule
 practice of 212, 287
 relationship to philosophy 226
 symbolism in Imperial Germany 151
 theology 11, 204, 210, 248
 thought, moralization of 241
Pont-à-Mousson 122
popular will 205–6
Porta Westphalica 145
positivism 57, 58, 248, 273, 294
Post, Albert Hermann 243, 263–6
 on anthropology 264–6
 *Bausteine für eine allgemeine
  Rechtswissenschaft auf vergleichend-
  ethnologischer Basis* 263
 ethnographic account of law 264
post-Kantian thought 71
Potsdam 314
Pott, August Friedrich 193–4
power 42, 219, 279
 acquisition of 228
 balance of 302
 and democracy 307–8
 disciplinary power 250
 distribution of 225–6
 as evolutionary principle 279
 expansion of 279
 as *Herrschaft* 42
 as *Macht* 42
 and morality 225
 logic of 318
 political 212, 233, 243, 249
 "will to power" 2, 220, 279, 280, 287, 322
 see also rule; domination
practical political reasoning 217
practice 304
 of politics 212, 287, 289
 scientific 272
 social 275–6, 289, 321
Prantl, Carl 103
predestination 77
prehistory 190, 276
Preller, Ludwig 161
Preußische Jahrbücher 49, 92, 93, 176, 309
"primitive cultures" 186, 187, 200
progress 132, 303
 eschatological notion of 273
 human 273
 idea of 52
 social 248
promise, promising 251, 253–5, 276

Protestant Church 70, 290
Protestant theology 50–1, 91–2, 291
 relationship to historicism 91
 "Tübingen School" 50–1, 92
Protestantism 72, 117, 118, 124, 166, 167, 198, 203, 206–8, 264, 292
 and anti-Semitism 311
 German 10
 and nationalism 93, 311–12
 relationship to liberalism 207
 relationship to secular state 207
proto-fascism 287, 308
Prussia 7, 10, 31, 33, 34, 35, 37–40, 41, 70, 80, 81, 84, 86, 91, 93, 105–6, 116–17, 145, 154, 155, 207, 310
 confessional allegiance to the state in 292
 East Prussia 310
 expansionism of 39
 German vocation of 117, 119, 176, 206, 290–1
 as Protestant 117, 152
Prussianism 159
Prussian Academy of Sciences (Berlin) 71, 134, 159, 161, 195, 290
Prussian Chamber of Deputies 84, 118
Prussian school of historiography 22, 85, 134, 144, 147, 154–5, 291, 93
psychology 61, 180, 273, 276
 experimental psychology 60
public sphere, modernization in Germany 137
punishment 249–51, 265–6, 269, 276
 origin of 267
 purpose of 267–8
 and the state 268

raison d'état 204, 297
rank, order of 228
Ranke, Leopold von 18, 20, 21, 85, 86, 92, 134–5, 137, 145, 154
 Deutsche Geschichte im Zeitalter der Reformation 86
 "Ueber die Epochen der neueren Geschichte" 86, 134
 Preussische Geschichte 86, 154
 Weltgeschichte 86
rationality, technocratic 247
Ratzel, Friedrich 178
 Anthropo-Geographie 178
Rawls, John 253–5
reason 131, 224, 251, 260, 276
 in history 133, 134, 135, 164, 166
 limits of 232
 public use of 205

reason (cont.)
  pure reason 252
  universal laws of 304
  universality of 131, 241, 318
reductionism 271, 273, 276
Rée, Paul 189, 221, 261–2, 270, 309
  origin of moral conscience 261–2
  Der Ursprung der moralischen Empfindungen 261
Reformation 117, 118–19, 126, 144, 153, 206, 210
Reginster, Bernard 2
regulative fiction 283
Reich 124, 152, 206
Reichstag 84, 258, 311
  1887 elections 257–8
Reil, Johann Christian 74
Reinsurance Treaty (*Rückversicherungsvertrag*) 202
relativism
  epistemological 295
  ethical 295
  historical 135
religion 233, 288
  conflict 148
  as cultural authority 294
  decline of 294
  decline of practice in Imperial Germany, 207–8
  function of 198, 203–11
  identity 257
  and nation state 201–3, 202–11
  and the political 308
  political absolutism of 238
  as political institution in modern state 203
  relationship to state 175
  and rule 250
  social function of 204–11
  as system of cruelty 276
  tolerance as contradiction in terms 238
Renaissance 86, 87, 130, 160, 302
  archaeological excavations in Rome 160
Renan, Ernest 238
responsibility (*see also* ethic of responsibility) 165, 166, 224, 238, 252–3, 265, 298
ressentiment 248
"revaluation of all values" 175, 229, 284
revolution 166
  revolutions of 1848/49, 137
Rheinisches Museum für Philologie 21
Rhineland 33, 34, 125, 306
  industrialization of 115
Rickert, Heinrich 9, 59

righteousness, as linked to violence 323
"right to make promises" 251, 253–5
Ritschl, Albrecht 51, 91
Ritschl, Friedrich 23–4, 25, 27, 28, 44, 51, 63, 79, 108, 110, 157–8
  epigraphic research of 24
  "Zur Methode des philologischen Studiums" 43
  "Ueber die neueste Entwickelung der Philologie" 28, 42–3
  Otto Jahn: initial support for 25; quarrel with 34–6
  Priscae Latinitatis monumenta epigraphica 24, 157
  views of classical scholarship 40, 42–3
Ritschl, Sophie 120
Ritter, August Heinrich 103, 104, 109
  Encyklopädie der philosophischen Wissenschaften 109
Robertson, George Croom 189, 277
Rohde, Erwin 24, 45, 79, 93, 94, 100, 108, 119, 152, 154, 158, 170
Roman law 82
Romanticism 7, 30, 82, 168, 197, 222, 264
  philosophy of nature in 280
  political thought in 121
Rome 84, 87
  archaeology in 161–2
  Empire 86, 159
  Republic 144
  Roma Illustrata 160
Roscher, Wilhelm 17, 137, 249, 62
  on cultural history 62
  on laws of economic development 62
  on legal history 62
  lectures on "Grundlagen der praktischen Politik als Einleitung in die gesamte Staats- und Rechtswissenschaft" 63
  on stages of economic development 62–3
Roscher, Wilhelm Heinrich 63
Rosenkranz, Karl 106
Rosenlauibad 189
Rouse, Joseph 15, 271
Rousseau, Jean-Jacques 205–6, 209
  Du contrat social 205
  general will (*volonté générale*) 205–6
Roux, Wilhelm 275
Royal Bavarian Academy of Science 181
Royal Institute of Great Britain 181
rule (*Herrschaft*) 217, 225, 228, 250, 307–8
  legitimacy of 225
  parliamentary 214
  and religion 250
Russia 202

Sachphilologie v. *Wortphilologie* 157
sacralization of national past 153
sacrifice 239, 240, 276
Sadová 38, 41
Sand, Carl Ludwig 91, 126
Sanskrit 199
Sanssouci 314
Savigny, Friedrich Carl von 82, 83, 105–6, 118, 194
Saxony 25, 37, 38, 81, 208, 294
Saxony-Altenburg 207
Schaarschmidt, Karl 22–3, 53, 72, 134
Schelling, Friedrich Wilhelm Joseph 10, 52, 182, 197, 207, 280–1
  on nature and the intellectual world 281
Schiller, Friedrich 29, 101, 112, 141, 142, 153, 165–6
  on "aesthetic education" 112
  Resignation 165
  theory of art 140
  Über die ästhetische Erziehung des Menschen in einer Reihe von Briefen 141
  "Was heißt und zu welchem Ende studiert man Universalgeschichte?" 142
  on world history as world-tribunal 165
Schillerfeiern 145
Schlegel, August Wilhelm 25
Schlegel, Friedrich 20, 28, 30, 182, 222–3
  civil freedom 217
  on freedom and infinity 222
Schleicher, August 194
  Compendium der vergleichenden Grammatik der indogermanischen Sprachen 194
Schleiermacher, Friedrich Daniel Ernst 52, 91, 95, 103, 111, 136, 162
  lectures on *Hermeneutik* 136
  Über die Religion 91
Schliemann, Heinrich 161
Schlözer, August Ludwig von 132
Schmeitzner, Ernst 263, 309
Schmitt, Carl 204, 288, 289
Schopenhauer, Arthur 8, 22, 23, 44, 46–8, 52, 53, 54–6, 61, 63, 64, 87, 101, 110, 125, 264
  concept of "will" 54, 55
  metaphysics 55, 56
  on origin of philosophy 128
  Parerga und Paralipomena 54
  pessimism 189
  theory of art 140
  Die Welt als Wille und Vorstellung 47–8, 49, 54, 55, 128
Schubarth, Karl Ernst 106

Schutte, Ofelia 2
Schwegler, Albert 23, 72
  Geschichte der Philosophie im Umriß 23, 72
Schweizer Grenzpost und Tagblatt der Stadt Basel 114
science 172, 174, 233
  critical value of 173
  distance from philosophy in nineteenth century 173
  method 271, 272
  "normal" 274
  practice 274
sciences of the state (*Staatswissenschaften*) 105; *see also* state; *Kameralwissenschaft*
Second Empire 238
secularization 131, 166, 174, 203, 205, 207, 208, 210
  and historical studies 130
Sedan 122, 152
  battle of 206
Sedanstag 145, 152
selflessness 239–40, 243
self-overcoming 284–5
Seneca 110–11
Shakespeare 101
shame 251
Siam 184
Siberia 184
Sils Maria 178, 216
Simmel, Georg 9, 14, 130, 322
"site of emergence" (*Entstehungsherd*) 261
skepticism 313–14
Skinner, Quentin 15, 16
slavery, 246
  slaves 238; morality 298; revolt 238, 248
  owners 246
social
  contract 205; *see also* Rousseau
  control 243, 250, 276–7
  imaginary 304–5, 321
  selection 275–6, 277, 278; *see also* natural selection
  utility 245
  welfare 246–8, 267
  world as historically emerged 272
socialism 77, 147, 166, 213, 219, 238, 239, 288, 291, 294
socialists 310
"Socialist Law" 213
sociology 225
  of knowledge 303, 321
Socrates 101
Sonderweg (special path) of German history 5, 147
Sorrento 216

soul 260
  soul v. brain 273
sovereign individual 211, 217, 224–5, 247, 248–60, 285, 295–8, 306–7, 318
  ethical commitments of 253
sovereignty 204, 209
  popular sovereignty 307, 320
Spencer, Herbert 189, 245, 270, 279
  Data of Ethics 270
  on inheritance of moral conscience 278
Spinoza, Baruch de 242, 273, 294
  on bad/evil 242
spiritualism 198–9
  and electricity 198
  and physical sciences 199
Springer, Anton Heinrich 21, 85
St. Helena 233
state 204, 209, 217, 289
  authoritarian 213
  constitutional 281
  decay of 209, 211
  democratic 211–14
  democratic compromise in 212
  hostility to the 209
  as juridical institution 212
  as *Kulturstaat* 125, 152
  as myth 168
  as organic community 168–9
  Prussian 105
  as sacred entity 208, 210–14
  as secular institution 209
  relationship to philosophy in nineteenth-century Germany 104–6
  relationship to religion 175
  sacralization of political power in the 209–11
  theories of 168–9
  see also nation state
Steffensen, Karl 107
Stein, Karl von 155
Steinthal, Heymann 180–1
Stendhal (Henri Beyle) 306
Stoecker, Adolf 311–12, 314
Strauß, David Friedrich 291
Strauss, Leo 288
Strong, Tracy B. 150
student corporations (*Burschenschaften*) 125–6
  Christian sentiments among 126
  Franconia (Bonn) 125–6
  motto of ("Honor, Freedom, Fatherland") 126
  nationalist rhetoric among 126
  revolutionary agenda and ideals of 126, 290

Sulzer, Johann Georg 195–6
  Anmerkungen über den gegenseitigen Einfluß der Vernunft in die Sprache und der Sprache in die Vernunft 195
superstition 95, 198–9, 200, 209, 291
"survival" 200–2, 214
suspicion 243
Sybel, Heinrich von 18, 21–2, 27, 31, 33, 34, 38, 49, 57, 115, 117, 137, 154, 249, 291
  Geschichte der Revolutionszeit 22
  lectures on politics (University of Bonn) 63
  liberal-conservative constitutionalism of 31
sympathy 250, 278
system of ends 267

Taine, Hippolyte 320
Tartu (Dorpat) 108
Teichmüller, Gustav 107–8, 114
  Die wirkliche und die scheinbare Welt 107
teleology 8, 54, 64–78, 279–82
  Burckhardt's rejection of 89
  and contingency 103, 135
  and history 134
  in Kant 65–6, 129
  and naturalism 281
  and perfectionism 254
  strong notion of 282
  weak notion of 281, 282
temporality 282
Teutoburg Forest 153
textual criticism 51, 156, 231
theodicy 165–7; *see also* evil
theology, "scientific" 95
things-in-themselves 56, 58, 191, 192–3, 232
Third Republic 238
Thucydides 49, 62
Thuringia 38
Tocqueville, Alexis de 320
tolerance 243
totalitarianism 127, 212
Treitschke, Heinrich von 18, 31, 39, 41, 49, 92–4, 116, 117, 125, 137, 144, 154, 158, 176, 291–3, 309–13, 314
  anti-French sentiments of 158
  anti-Semitism of 158, 292, 313
  Deutsche Geschichte im neunzehnten Jahrhundert 92, 93, 154
  on *Machtpolitik* 158, 291, 313
  and nationalism 292
  "Unsere Aussichten" 292, 309, 311

Die Zukunft der norddeutschen Mittelstaaten 39
Trendelenburg, Friedrich Adolf 107
Tribschen 108, 119–20
Troeltsch, Ernst 9, 130
trust 256
truth 191, 235, 237, 268
　aeternae veritates 234
　as metaphysical concept 232
　regime of 282
Tübingen School of Protestant theology 50–1, 92; *see also* Protestant theology
Tunis 176
Tunisia 176–8
Tylor, Edward Burnett 11, 186, 188, 189, 190, 199, 200–2, 208
　Primitive Culture 188, 199, 200–1
　"survivals" 200–2, 214
"tyranny of the majority" 320

Übermensch 220–1, 226, 227
Ueberweg, Friedrich 103
Usener, Hermann 24, 79, 197
utilitarianism 246–7, 252, 259

valuation 251, 275–6
values 174, 229, 298, 318
　cultural 174
　descent of 260
　and facts 271
　moral 76, 174
　naturalized account of 215
　order of 278
　political 174
　"revaluation of all values" 175, 229, 284
Vatican 135
Versailles 123
Versammlung Deutscher Ärzte und Naturforscher 184
Vico, Giambattista 195–6
Victoria (Crown Princess) 316
Vienna 35, 185
Vienna Congress 30, 32, 37, 126, 148, 153, 301, 313
violence 163, 164, 217, 248, 249–51
　connection to morality 239
　mutilation of human body 266
　physical inscriptions of 276
　and righteousness 323
　see also coercion; punishment
Virchow, Rudolf 184–5, 187
virtù 226, 304; *see also* Machiavelli
virtue 226, 251–3
　Christian notion of 227
　ethics of virtue 251, 253
Vischer-Bilfinger, Wilhelm 79–80, 108, 119
vitalism 66, 71, 74
　vis viva 73–4
　vital forces 65
　see also living force
Voigt, Georg 160
　Die Wiederkehr des classischen Alterthums 160
volonté générale 205–6; *see also* Rousseau
Voltaire (François-Marie Aronet) 77, 204, 209, 218, 237, 314
　on civil government 204
　on ecclesiastical government 204
　Herder's criticism of 133
　on history 131, 132

Wagner, Richard 25, 94, 101, 108, 119–20, 141, 142, 171
　anti-French sentiments of 120
　An das deutsche Heer vor Paris 120
　"Deutsche Kunst und Politik" 120
　Kaiser-Marsch 120
　political aestheticism in 118
　Wagner, anti-Semitism of 120, 308–9
　"Was ist deutsch?" 120
Waitz, Theodor 186
　Anthropologie der Naturvölker 186
Walhalla 145, 152–4
war, glorification of 124
Warren, Mark 2
"Wars of Liberation" 9, 30, 121, 126, 152, 153, 210, 289, 290
Wartburg 126, 154
Weber, Ernst Heinrich 60–1, 62
Weber, Max 14, 59, 213–14, 217, 220, 224, 225, 244, 253, 259–60, 304, 321
　on charisma 225
　on conviction 253
　on the demagogue 224
　on democracy 220
　on democratization 224
　on "disenchantment" 244
　on distribution of political power 225–6
　on domination 321
　on "ethic of conviction" 259–60
　on "ethic of responsibility" 217, 259–60
　on legality 225
　on legitimacy of rule 225
　"Politik als Beruf" 217, 259
　on power 321
　on rule (*Herrschaft*) 217
　on the state 217
　on violence 217

Weber, Wilhelm 75
  Elektrodynamische Maassbestimmungen 75
Weimar 38, 91, 141
Welcker, Friedrich Gottlieb 25, 85, 196
welfare 246, 259, 261; *see also* social welfare
Weltgericht, *see* world-tribunal
Weltprozess, *see* world process
Westminster Review 143
Wilamowitz-Moellendorff, Ulrich von 20, 98–9, 99–100, 158–9
Wilhelm I (King of Prussia and German Emperor) 33, 121, 213, 258, 316
"will to life" 279
"will to power" 2, 220, 279, 280, 287, 322; *see also* power
Williams, Bernard 239–40, 262
  "external reason thesis" 239–40
Williamson, George S. 4
Winckelmann, Johann Joachim 18, 26, 27, 29, 30, 160, 161
  aesthetic paradigms of 26–7
  celebrations 27
Windelband, Wilhelm 9, 56, 59, 283
Windisch, Ernst 63
witches 243
Wittgenstein, Ludwig 272
Woerth (Alsace), battle of 122–3
Wolf, Friedrich August 17–18, 26, 109, 134, 160

Vorlesungen über die Alterthumswissenschaft 19, 109, 183
Wolin, Richard 2
wonder, as the origin of philosophy 127–8; *see also* perplexity; philosophical astonishment
world exhibitions 146
world history 90, 113, 165
world process (*Weltprozess*) 167, 169
world-tribunal (*Weltgericht*) 165–7, 169
Wortphilologie v. *Sachphilologie* 157
Wundt, Wilhelm 60, 180–1, 189, 274, 277
  "Philosophy in Germany" 189, 277
Württemberg 91
Wuttke, Adolf 188–9
  Der deutsche Volksaberglaube in der Gegenwart 188

Young Hegelians 207

Zeitschrift für Ethnologie 184
Zeitschrift für Völkerpsychologie und Sprachwissenschaft 180
Zeller, Eduard 104, 283
Zöllner, Johann Carl Friedrich 60–1, 274, 277
  Über die Natur der Cometen 61, 274, 277
Zurich 56, 108

Lightning Source UK Ltd.
Milton Keynes UK
UKHW010258311020
372549UK00001B/38